Mock Joya's
THINGS JAPANESE

by

MOCK JOYA

The Japan Times, Ltd.

ISBN4-7890-0281-0 C0501

First edition: November 1958
New edition: September 1985

Published by The Japan Times, Ltd.
5-4, Shibaura 4-chome, Minato-ku, Tokyo 108, Japan

Printed in Japan

PREFACE

Up to some fifty or sixty years ago, the general public of foreign countries did not know about Japan and the Japanese, some even being ignorant of the existence of such a country. But with the news of the Russo-Japanese War, 1904-5, they became suddenly interested in the little country of the Orient that was fighting the great European power.

As I went to the United States two years after the War, when the American public was just beginning to know something about Japan, I met everywhere many persons desiring to have more information about my country. Gradually I was asked, even in my student days, to tell friends and others about Japan and the Japanese, and then when I became a reporter of *The World*, New York, I wrote articles on the history, customs and problems of the Japanese, besides covering regular assignments.

As I found that most Americans did not know about Japan, and as I was also unfamiliar with the thought and habits of the American people, I realized that it was necessary for us to know each other's historical backgrounds, traditions and customs in order to come to mutual understanding and respect. While I did my best to know American traditions, folklore and customs, I came to find joy in explaining things Japanese to Americans.

Thus my task of writing and talking on Japanese folklore and customs began almost fifty years ago. Coming back to Japan after World War II, I started to write such articles for *The Japan Times*. All these years I have kept up this work of writing on our ways of thought and customs for the said journal and other publications, and speaking before the gatherings of foreign residents and visitors, and also for the NHK overseas broadcasting.

In this volume I collected those I believe to be worthy of being presented to foreign readers out of my past articles and talks. The items in "Quaint Customs and Manners of Japan" Vol. 1-4; "Milestones in Life"; "Japan; the Life and Legends"; and Japanese Customs and Manners" are mostly included in the present book, revised or rearranged with additional materials.

Many of Japanese thoughts and customs may appear strange to other peoples, but they have their backgrounds and meanings to us. It is my hope that their explanations may help foreign peoples understand our ways and sentiments.

In publishing this volume, I wish to express my thanks to the many foreign and Japanese friends as well as unknown readers who kindly encouraged and helped me by giving their valuable suggestions and criticism.

Mock Joya

Kamakura, October 1958

PUBLISHER'S NOTE

The past few years have seen a sort of boom in the publication of books about Japan and the Japanese people. In these books, probing the secrets of Japan's economic success, the characteristics of Japanese-style management, the distinguishing features of Japan's social structure and the essence of the Japanese mentality, attempts have been made to penetrate to the heart of Japan by studying and analyzing the land and its people from various angles.

Although Mock Joya's Things Japanese might appear to be yet another book introducing Japan to foreigners, it is basically different from other such books on the market. As a glance at the table of contents will show, it gives a complete picture of the background to Japanese life and culture, covering a vast range of subjects from customs and manners, popular beliefs and religious rites, tales and legends to natural phenomena and fauna and flora. In this book can be found the "roots" of Japanese culture which is being forgotten and lost in modern Japanese society.

The first edition was published in 1958 by Tokyo New Service, Ltd. and was followed by several revised editions. For the past 15 years or so, however, it has been out of print. In order to make this valuable work available to the public once more, The Japan Times obtained the permission of the late Mock Joya's daughter, Mrs. Kazuko Kaihori, and Tokyo News Service, Ltd. to bring out a new edition partially revised by The Japan Times.

Toshio Tojo

August 1985

CONTENTS

Chapter 1   Apparel and Utensils

Chapter 2 Cures and Medicines

Chapter 3 Dwelling Houses and Other Buildings

Chapter 4 Fetes and Festivals

Chapter 5 Fish, Birds and Animals

Chapter 6 Folk Tales

Chapter 7   Food, 'Sake' and Tobacco

Chapter 8   Living Habits

Chapter 9   Marriage, Funerals and Memorials

Chapter 10   Natural Phenomena

Chapter 11   Plants and Flowers

Chapter 12   Popular Beliefs and Traditions

xv

Chapter 13   Recreation and Entertainment

Chapter 14 Religious Rites

Chapter 15   Social Customs

Chapter 1
Apparel and Utensils

BEKKO-ZAIKU

BEKKO-ZAIKU or tortoise-shell work is one of the handicrafts of Japan that developed in the earliest period, and reached its highest stage of perfection in Edo days. It is used in many articles kept at the Shoso-in, Nara, which was erected to preserve the art works of the Nara period (710-794) and many of earlier days.

The tortoise-shell used in these works come from the *taimai*, a kind of turtle that is found around Okinawa, Taiwan and the Ogasawara Islands. The scales are light yellow with black spots.

When the scale is heated it becomes soft, and then the thin upper layer is peeled off. This thin layer which is almost transparent is used for making various artistic and valuable things. By pressing, it can be made to take various shapes.

For many centuries *bekko* was largely used to make decorative goods, such as boxes, trays and other household goods. But the popular use of *bekko* seems to have developed in Tokugawa days in the 17th century when women's way of hair dressing changed.

Combs and *kogai* (hair fasteners) came to be made of *bekko*. *Kogai* which was at first only a simple long stick became elaborate. There were *kogai* of silver, gold, ivory and other materials, but *bekko kogai* was the most expensive, as it had elaborate ornamental pieces at both ends, made to represent flowers, butterflies and other shapes. It is recorded that once Lord Echizen arrested a woman who displayed a very costly *bekko kogai* on her hair for being too recklessly extravagant.

Bekko kogai were handed down as family heirlooms. Because it was very expensive, imitation *bekko* of bones, tusks and other materials appeared. Some imitations were so well made that they could not be told from the real *bekko*.

BELLS

THE RINGING of *furin* or wind-bells makes us feel cool and refreshed, not only because of the breeze that makes it ring, but also due to its clear, penetrating tone. The people love to have *furin* in the house during the summer days, as they find its clear ringing a real comfort in fighting the heat. In olden days there were *furin-ya* or wind-bell vendors and stalls specializing in the sale of all kinds of wind-bells.

Bells play various roles in the country; there are numerous varieties, ranging from tiny ones as small as peas to huge temple bells.

Generally speaking, bells are divided into two kinds. Small bells are called *suzu*, meaning cool and refreshing because of their clear ringing. On the other hand, big bells are called *kane*. *Suzu* and *kane* are of different shapes. *Suzu* generally come in small round

1

shapes, hollow with tiny metal balls inside. When a *suzu* is shaken or moved about, it rings. *Kane* is in the so-called bell shape, and sounded by striking upon it. *Suzu* has been always connected with Shinto and shrines, while *kane* is related to Buddhist temples and rites.

Furin or wind-bell is a type that comes between *suzu* and *kane*. Being in the bell-shape, its general outline is like *kane*, but it has a striker suspended underneath, to which is attached an oblong cardboard for catching the breeze. It is generally made of metal, as bells are, but recently there have also appeared *furin* made of glass. Though in tone glass *furin* may be just as pleasant, it is not so picturesque.

Used in various different ways, *suzu* or small bells may be said to be very closely interwoven in the life of the people. It was first used in shrines, but is now also used extensively in general households. Little children, both boys and girls, often have tiny *suzu* attached to their sashes for ornamental purposes, and they love to have the bells ringing as they move about. *Geta* or wooden clogs of little girls sometimes have tiny bells attached underneath, which give out tinkling sounds as they walk. Pets, such as dogs and cats, have *suzu* attached to their necks, to show where they are. Japanese women, particularly those of the old-fashioned type, love to attach *suzu* to their scissors and other articles. Such *suzu* are generally made of copper alloys, but sometimes of silver or gold alloys. They are also very elaborately made, with inlaid or curved designs.

Big bells or *kane* are found at temples, and in olden days there were many famous bell casters. The technique of making good bells is very difficult, and, though there are thousands of bells throughout the country, there are only a few that give a musical and pleasant sound.

Of the large bells in the country, the one at the Chion-in Temple, Kyoto, which is 18 feet high, and another at the Todaiji Temple at Nara, which is 15 feet high, are especially famous. The largest one in the country was the one at Shitennoji, Osaka, which was 26 feet high, and cast in 1902 but unfortunately this bell was not properly cast, and did not give any sound at all. Those were temple bells that used to announce the time to the people by their hourly or bihourly ringing. There are still many temples in the country that give the hourly or noon bell ringing. Many of those temple bells were scrapped for the last war, but fortunately there still remain many famous old ones.

BIZEN WARE

BIZEN-YAKI is a unique type of ceramic ware produced in Japan. It is produced at Inbe, Okayama Prefecture, which is said to be the oldest ceramic-producing district of the country.

Bizen-yaki is unique because this kind of porcelain has no glaze or color, but is nevertheless lustrous and beautiful. Another distinction is its hardness. A *Bizen* ware rings like metal when struck.

Bizen-yaki was originally called *Inbe-yaki*, and at first dishes and bowls used for shrine services were produced. *Inbe* meant persons making utensils for shrine ceremonies.

At the beginning, Inbe produced only wares for ceremonial use and jars for storing seeds. Then gradually porcelain for household use came to be made.

It was the rising popularity of *Chanoyu* or tea ceremony that made Inbe ware famous, as it was highly valued by all tea masters. Tea bowls made there became so famous that Toyotomi Hideyoshi (16th century) encouraged the production with various favors. Then during the Tokugawa era, Lord Ikeda of the province gave his protection to the kiln.

The method used there has remained unchanged since olden days. Bottles, jars, bowls and other articles molded in clay are placed in the kiln and fired continuously for 10 days with pine wood. No glaze is applied, but the fire and ash produce a ware of reddish brown, bluish brown or brown with bluish spots.

Bizen ware is so hard that often chains of rings of clay are made which are so strong that they are used in hanging up heavy flower vases.

Bizen ware has no designs or artificial colors, and in that respect it is unique. The texture and natural color are so rich that they do not require any artificial touch to make them perfect works of art.

BROOM CHARM

HOKI OR BROOMS are the most indispensable household item in Japan, as Japanese rooms have to be swept clean every morning, and often many more times. *Osoji* or house sweeping is a task that Japanese housewives must perform daily. Thus many different kinds made of straw, bamboo and other fibers are used.

For gardens there are bamboo rakes and brooms made of bamboo branches or *hoki-gusa*, a kind of goosefoot that grows about three feet high with many branches and cultivated particularly to make *hoki*.

Room brooms are made of softer fibers, mostly straw, particularly of millet. The daily use of brooms also created the habit of putting them to other purposes than to cleaning.

When a visitor is unwelcome or overstays his welcome, a broom is rested against the wall with the handle on the floor, unknown to him. It is believed it has the power to drive him away quickly. In many places, it is thought to bring bad luck if one steps on or walks over a broom.

If one shoulders a broom, there will be rainfall soon, it is believed in the Nagano district.

The most widely believed tradition is that the *kami* of *hoki* is also the *kami* of childbirth. When a broom is passed gently over a mother with child, she will have an easy delivery, it is said. In many households, when an expectant mother is in the lying-in room, a broom is set up in a corner of the room to insure an easy delivery.

The traditional Takasago figures of an aged couple who are regarded as symbols of long life and happiness, carry a broom and a rake. The broom is the symbol of easy child delivery and family happiness.

Thus the *hoki* is also regarded as a divine deity protecting family happiness. Therefore, it must be handled with respect, never stepped on or handled roughly.

CHARCOAL

THE world's greatest and best producer of many kinds of charcoal is Japan. This is because Japanese households still use charcoal for cooking and heating, despite the increasing use of oil, coal and electricity for such purposes.

Though charcoal was produced quite early in the country, it is only since about 300 years ago that it came to be generally used for domestic purposes. It was first made in this country to melt ores and metals. Thus charcoal making developed at metal mines. There are many tales of charcoal makers in

3

remote mountains becoming rich and powerful.

Up to the 14th century, charcoal was quite a luxury even in the aristocratic households of Kyoto. Those who used it handled it with their fingers, for tongs were not known.

But gradually it replaced wood and revolutionized the domestic customs of the people.

In the ensuing 300 years, the technique of making charcoal rapidly developed. At first wood was just piled up and fired, and then at the proper moment, earth or water was poured over it to put the fire out. In the northern mountains, charcoal was made in holes dug in the snow. Later holes were dug in the ground. With the use of kilns, the quality was improved and standardized.

As charcoal is made in the mountains far from villages, charcoal makers came to form special groups and established their own living and social customs. Even today many of them live in mountain huts where no women are allowed to come.

Many districts have a tradition that the method of making charcoals in earth holes was taught by Kobo-daishi, a famous Buddhist priest of the 10th century.

The most commonly used kind is made of *kunugi* or other kinds of oak. In the Tokyo area this variety is called *Sakura-zumi*, but it is not made of *sakura* (cherry) wood, being named after Sakura, Chiba Prefecture, where a very good charcoal of this type is produced. In Osaka, it is known as *Ikeda-zumi*, after the Ikeda district where it is made.

There are hard and soft charcoals. The soft kind gives greater heat than the hard, but burns out quicker. Hard charcoal continues to burn for a long time, without much change in its temperature. Thus for cooking the hard kind is generally used. But blacksmiths use soft charcoal, mostly *matsu-zumi*, or pine charcoal, to get the high temperature required for heating iron.

Bincho is famous as the hardest charcoal. It was first made by Bingoya Choemon of Kii (present Wakayama Prefecture) in the Genroku era (1688-1704) and came to be called *Bincho* after his name. It is made of slender branches of *kashi*, a kind of oak, and looks whitish. Thus it has been often called "white charcoal." It is very hard and rings like metal when struck.

Other types are *maru* (whole) charcoal, and *wari* (split) charcoal. The first is made of whole wood, the latter of split wood. Generally speaking, split charcoal is cheap and does not burn long. Good charcoal is made of whole wood.

For *chanoyu* and other uses, charcoal is made of very slender branches. It looks beautiful and often is used together with larger pieces.

CHAWAN AND OWAN

THE JAPANESE use *chawan* or porcelain bowls for rice and *owan* or lacquered wooden bowls for soup. This custom is comparatively new. In ancient days foods were placed on leaves or in earthenware, and the old habit is still preserved at shrines.

The people used plain, crudely made wooden plates and bowls generally for holding and serving foods. *Owan* or *wan* originally meant any kind of bowl made of whatever materials, but as bowls used at tables were all wooden, the term has been used generally for wooden bowls.

With the wide use of lacquering that was introduced from Korea, almost all household wooden utensils came to be lacquered. So bowls were also lacquered. Mostly vermilion or black lacquers were used, vermilion bowls being regarded more aristocratic than the black ones.

Chawan or porcelain bowls are said to have been introduced in the Muromachi period (1392-1573), but at first they were used for drinking tea only.

It was in the early Edo period or the beginning of the 17th century that porcelain bowls first appeared on Japanese tables. They were first used by the merchant class of Edo for eating rice, and became rapidly popular. Aristocrats and rural folks were slow in adopting *chawan* for their rice. In rural districts it was believed that if one ate rice out of a procelain bowl daily, he would never attain any success. But the new fad of using porcelain bowls for rice became gradually widespread. It was, however, reserved for only daily meals, and for formal dinners and guests *chawan* were never used.

The Japanese drink many kinds of tea, and thus have different types of teacups and bowls. They become quite attached to these *chawan* or tea-bowls. Many persons treasure and use the same cups or bowls for years, and would not feel happy unless their tea is served in their favorite *chawan*. Of course some of these *chawan* are masterpieces of ceramic art, but besides their artistic value, personal attachment develops out of long use.

Western peoples also have fine teacups, but they have no personal sentiment about them. This difference in their attitude towards teacups comes from their different ways of holding them. Westerners take up their teacups by the saucer or handle. The Japanese hold their *chawan* in the palms of their hands.

The *chawan* for drinking whisked powdered tea at a tea ceremony, and that for *bancha*, the common tea usually drunk at home, are generally large and thick. If they were thin, they would be too hot to be held in the palms. So they are made especially thick and heavy.

As the tea drinker holds the *chawan* nestled snugly in the palm of his hands, he feels the warmth gradually radiating from it and enjoys the touch of the smooth glaze that covers the bowl. So the shape and glaze must be just right to give the hands the desired pleasant feeling. These points are just as, or more important, than the color and design of the decoration.

Each *chawan* has a different charm for the tea drinker. There are *chawan* for the summer season and others for cold winter days. Women sometimes are offered small special *chawan*.

For drinking green tea, small, thin cups are used because it is never brewed as hot as the whisked powdered tea or *bancha*.

CHOCHIN

CHOCHIN or Japanese paper lanterns were first used for religious services to replace torches which were burned at all-night rites in earlier days.

It is recorded that a *chochin* was first used at the service of Hotei-in Temple held on January 30, 1086. But it was actually about four centuries later that *chochin* came to be popularly used with the development of candles made from pine resin.

In the Tensho era (1573-92) they were greatly improved and made so they could be folded up when not in use. The paper is pasted over thin bamboo hoops which are placed one above the other with a narrow space between.

In the 17th century, or the beginning of the Tokugawa regime, *chochin* became one of the most important household articles. Not only did many different types appear, but they also came to be used by all classes of people at night, becoming a utensil of general use and not restricted solely to religious services as before. Under the feudalistic social system, the Tokugawa authorities set various rules for their use. The types used by *samurai*, firemen and commoners were definitely fixed.

With their increasing popularity, *chochin* were made more beautiful and decorated with designs. All households, *samurai* and commoner, put their family crests or marks on their *chochin*, so that they could be identified in the dark.

They were used also indoors in summer, more for decorative purposes than for obtaining light.

In the early Meiji period, *Gifu chochin* (Gifu lanterns) made of very thick paper, and beautifully painted with flowers and other designs, were made. *Gifu chochin* are now the representative indoor *chochin*.

Besides those used at temples and shrines, *chochin* now commonly used are *Gifu chochin* in summer, and round red *chochin* carried in processions or displayed during festivals.

CLOISONNE

SHIPPO or cloisonné is one of the famous Japanese arts, but it is only since the Meiji era that the *shippo*-making technique was developed as to produce such intricate and beautiful pieces. *Shippo* means seven gems, signifying the varied gemlike luster and colors produced.

On a metal base the design is formed by thin wires, and the spaces between the lines are filled with enamel of different colors. Then the whole thing is baked at a high temperature. It is painstaking, delicate work.

It is recorded that as early as in the reign of Emperor Shomu (724-748) *shippo* pieces were brought from China where the cloisonné-making art had been highly developed during the Tang dynasty (618-907).

But it was in the Muromachi period (1392-1573), that the Japanese began to fully appreciate the beauty of *shippo*. Following the popular interest in cloisonné, Hirata Hikoshiro of Kyoto studied the technique from a Korean artisan, in the Keicho era (1596-1615). He was encouraged by the Tokugawa authorities.

As Japanese artisans became able to produce good cloisonné, *shippo* was used in decorating various articles such as the handles of the sliding doors of Katsura Palace, Kyoto, and also for decorating various parts of the Toshogu Shrine at Nikko.

But real development of the art was due to the efforts of Kaji Tsunekichi who, in the Tenpo era (1830-1844), made the first scientific study of *shippo* by breaking up Chinese cloisonné. Through his efforts many secrets of the Chinese art hitherto unknown to Japanese artisans were found.

It was the export of *shippo* objects that suddenly increased in the early Meiji years that brought about signal progress in the *shippo*-making technique. In the fourth year of Meiji, 1871, *shippo* plants were opened at Tokyo, Yokohama and Nagoya. Demand and competition rapidly improved the quality.

COMB

KUSHI or combs were not used at first in Japan to comb or adorn the hair. They were originally used as a mark of sacredness. Thus they did not come in the common shape of combs, but were long sticks of bamboo tied together. Being a token of sacredness, combs were used to designate married women.

It was with the later introduction of Chinese combs that they gradually came to be used as hair ornaments and to dress the hair. Thus they are comparatively new.

Many customs originating from the ancient idea that combs are a sign of sacredness still remain.

The act of throwing away a wife's comb is still regarded as an omen of the separation of a married couple. Old-fashioned folks still refuse a comb as a gift, or will not pick up a comb found on a street, as such acts will bring evil fortune.

In Okinawa it is believed that if a woman leaves her comb on the veranda at night, an evil spirit will take it and bring her some misfortune.

Once, a girl who was planting rice in a paddyfield was swallowed by a big snake, but her comb caught in the throat of the snake and caused its death. So a shrine was erected for the comb which saved the girl, according to an old story.

The use of combs as hair ornaments really became popular at the beginning of the Tokugawa era or about 300 years ago. Elaborate combs made of selected wood, tortoise-shell, ivory and gold appeared. Many of them were beautifully decorated with lacquer or inlaid work and came to be handed down as family treasures.

COSMETICS

BEFORE the introduction of soap and other modern cosmetics, Japanese women had their own way of beautifying themselves. First, in washing their faces they used *nukabukuro* or little cotton bags containing rice-bran. The bag was moistened and applied to the face and hands, or all over the body when taking a bath.

The moistened bran gives off a whitish juice which is believed to be good for the skin. This old-fashioned *nukabukuro* is still used by many women.

Women shaved their faces as they wanted to keep them perfectly smooth. Even today Japanese women shave as they cannot bear to have even a little bit of down on their faces.

Oshiroi or Japanese face-whitener contained lead carbonate, cadmia, clay, diatom earth and other substances. They came in liquid, powder and cake forms. They gave a very white coating to the face, but its manufacture is now prohibited because of the lead content that makes its application harmful to health. Formerly, many actors, *geisha* and others were poisoned by the constant heavy use of the lead-containing *oshiroi.*

Lip rouge used by Japanese women was made from the petals of a red flower called *benibana* (Carthamus tinctorius) or rouge blossom, and gave a very bright red color to the lips. The flower petals are crushed to obtain the rouge. One feature of this rouge is that when it is applied heavily it takes on a greenish gold tint. It is harmless and has also been used in dyeing many foodstuffs.

In washing hair, Japanese women used *funori* or a kind of seaweed, Gloiopeltis furcata var coliformia. The hair is washed with *funori*, and then rinsed with warm water. Many still prefer it to soaps and shampoos.

DYES

IN THE OLD days, Japanese women dyed the hemp yarns and fabrics for their clothing with leaves, flowers and roots. Such dyes produced beautiful shades of various colors that cannot be duplicated with modern chemical dyes.

7

But most of these natural dyes have disappeared as the primitive methods of production and dyeing take much time, and products are limited and expensive.

The Education Ministry recently decided to protect and preserve the old methods of producing *murasaki* (purple) and *akane* (madder red) dyes, still used in Akita Prefecture. These dyes have been produced in the Akita and Iwate districts for more than a thousand years. Hemp and cotton fabrics dyed with them were formerly highly valued, and particularly in Edo days they were eagerly sought by the ladies of the upper class.

Bunjiro Kuriyama, 68, of Hanawamachi, Akita Prefecture, is said to be one of the very few who still knows how to make such ancient dyes in the orthodox way. The entire process of making such dyes and dyeing fabrics and yarns will be scientifically studied and filmed by the Education Ministry.

Murasaki is a perennial plant, found wild all over the country, that bears white blossoms in summer. The root of this plant is used for making purple dye.

Akane is a perennial vine that has fat reddish roots. It is named *akane* (red root) because of the color of its roots, which make madder red dye.

The roots are pounded into pulp and then boiled in water with wood ash. Yarn and fabrics are then dipped in the dyes. They have to be dyed several times to make the colors fast. After dyeing, the yarns and fabrics are hung from the ceiling six to twelve months to settle the colors. It takes four years or more to complete the entire process of dyeing by such ancient methods.

EMBROIDERY

IT WAS Buddhism which encouraged the development of the Japanese art of embroidery. Japanese women must have embroidered from early times, but nothing is known of the early embroidery. But it can be said that real artistic progress came after the introduction of Buddhism.

It is recorded that, in 605, Empress Regnant Suiko ordered the making of an embroidered picture of Buddha. This was the first picture of Buddha in embroidery, and was of course made by court ladies at the Empress' command. Then, when Prince Shotoku died in 621, the Princess made court ladies embroider two *Mandalas* or pictures of Buddha, for the salvation of the Prince's soul. Fragments of the two *Mandalas* are still preserved.

The two events made the embroidery of Buddhist pictures very popular among noble ladies. Embroidery is a work that requires delicate technique and patience, but the ladies of the court and others embroidered Buddhist pictures as a religious duty.

The common use of embroidery came in the Tenpyo era, 729-749, when it came to be applied for decorating *obi*, bags, footwear and household goods.

The real Japanese art of embroidery, however, developed in the Tokugawa period during the 17th and 18th centuries, when women's costumes and habits became elegant and luxurious with the stabilization and advance of the national life. Not only women came to wear costumes and *obi* which were gorgeously decorated with rich embroidery, but also *Noh* and *Kabuki* plays gave an opportunity to show richly embroidered costumes to the best advantage. Gold and silver threads and gems were used in much of such embroidery work.

FANS

FOR THE Japanese, fans are not merely for fanning on hot summer days, but they are quite indispensable in ceremonial, social and daily activities throughout the year. Almost all races have had their fans since very early days, but nowhere else in the world have fans become such articles of necessity and utility as in Japan.

There are two kinds of fans. *Uchiwa* (flat fans) and *ohgi* or *sensu* (folding fans).

The *ohgi* or folding fan has been used by the Japanese since very early days. At first it was not used for fanning oneself on hot days. In the early period it was held in one's hand or placed in front as one prayed or spoke to *kami* (God). By about the seventh century or Nara period, however, the custom of using fans at ceremonies and formal occasions was firmly established.

This original use of *ohgi* is still practiced, though in a modified way, at ceremonies and by *Noh* drama reciters who hold their fans while reciting and place them in front of themselves when they are not reciting.

The early *ohgi* was made of thin pieces of *hinoki* or Japanese cypress wood, bound together by silk cords. Then came fans made of paper and silk stretched over a frame of ribs. Fan ribs are generally of bamboo, wood, ivory, steel or copper. There are slender round ribs and flat ribs. Ribs have increased in number to 19 or 20, but old ones had only five or seven.

Sensu or folding fans are often sent as gifts in summer, but it is not simply because they are handy things to have on hot days. Fans are a symbol of respect and goodwill, and thus as early as the Heian period, 794-1192, it was customary for the Emperor to give fans to his officials and others as the summer season commenced.

But it was not only in summer that fans were used as a gift to convey goodwill. On New Year's Day and other happy occasions, the Emperor also gave fans. The Emperor also presented fans as a mark of respect to many shrines. This custom was formerly widely followed even by the common people who took fans to their shrines on important visits.

Particularly when any member of the family, friend or relative was to start on a long journey, it was customary to present him with a fan, as a prayer for safe travel and a mark of goodwill. Murasaki-shikibu mentions in her *Genji-monogatari*, written in the early 11th century, that when Genji-no-kimi went on a trip to Iyo province, Lady Yugao and Lady Utsusemi presented him with fans to wish him a pleasant and safe journey.

Also fans became a necessary article to carry when one formally received a caller or met others, to show that they were meeting with goodwill.

Up to the end of the Tokugawa period, when a pupil first visited the house of his teacher, he presented fans as a sign of respect.

Yuino (betrothal present) is still not complete without a pair of fans, and for many other happy ceremonies, fans have to be carried by participating persons.

Thus fans, which originally were used to fan a breeze in summer, came to possess significance in the life of the people, and this symbolic sense is still preserved in the custom of sending them as a seasonal gift in summer.

Ohgi were, of course, used by aristocrats at first. They came to be commonly used and beautifully and expensively decorated. When Emperor Higashiyama (1687-1709) went to Saga

9

and held a boating excursion on the Oi River, one of the ladies dropped her fan into the river. The open fan floated down the river making a pretty picture. Other ladies followed her example and threw their fans. There were many beautiful ones carried away by the stream and all were highly pleased. This was the start of *ohgi-nagashi* (fan-floating) as an aristocratic pleasure to be followed by many.

In the An-ei era (1772-81) a game called *tosenkyo* (fan throwing) became popular. A small target in the shape of the gingko leaf was set upon a small stand. A player threw an open fan at a target from a distance of several feet. It became popular among women of the upper class. Soon the play was abused for gambling or other purposes, and the Shogunate authorities prohibited it.

It was revived in the Meiji era and played by women and children, but it is very seldom played now.

The *uchiwa* or flat fans are utilized in many ways. The most common use to which an *uchiwa* is applied is as bellows. When housewives or maids kindle a fire for cooking, they take up an *uchiwa* to accelerate the burning of the wood. Then again, this type of fan is also used for carrying things, taking the place of a tray.

In the hot summer season, the Japanese almost invariably carry folding-fans. They fan themselves on trains, on tram-cars, in their offices, or even while walking. It is regarded as the first item in etiquette to offer an *uchiwa* to a visitor during the hot season. In theaters, cinema houses or any large gathering of crowds, fans will be seen constantly waving all over.

The wide and particularly ceremonial use of fans has developed the art of fan-making. Fans are really art objects. The most luxurious folding-fans are made of specially made paper or silk, polished

bamboo, or ivory, and then decorated with paintings or designs in gold or lacquer. Fans painted by famous artists are highly valued.

Uchiwa or flat fans are generally more simple and are for practical use. But there are also some elaborate ones, made of rich paper, silk, or brocades, and painted by noted artists. Cheap *uchiwa* are used for advertising purposes. This utilization of fans started in Japan as early as the Tokugawa period. Fans advertising various merchandise are freely distributed by merchants.

Shibu-uchiwa is the cheapest but strongest kind. This type is made on a strong frame and the paper is given a coating of *shibu* or persimmon tannin juice to make it water-resistant and durable. Thus, it is often called *Kaki-uchiwa* or persimmon *uchiwa*. *Shibu-uchiwa* is only used in the kitchen to fan a wood or charcoal fire.

Being always used in the kitchen, it has been regarded as a utensil of the lowest rank that should never be brought to any other room. Since the late Tokugawa days *shibu-uchiwa* has come to be regarded as a symbol of poverty. *Binbo-gami*, god of poverty, is represented as a frail old man holding a *shibu-uchiwa* in his hand.

In the old days there were *mizu-uchiwa* or water fans. These were either made of woven leaves or were lacquered. They were dipped in water before use so that the breeze they would create would be cool.

Many temples and shrines of the country issue charms for salvation, protection or good health. While most such charms are in the form of tablets, there are also some made in unique shapes.

The Toshodaiji Temple, at Gojo, Nara, one of the most famous and oldest Buddhist temples of the country, issues an attractive charm in the form of a fan. It is a little *uchiwa* with a stem, the whole length being 26 cm. The fan is not the usual round shape but in a flattened heart shape, and the stick that runs through it has a bright, ornamental bow tied at each end. Some Sanskrit writings are on the face of the fan.

This *hosen* (treasure fan) of the Toshodaiji is valued by Buddhists as it is believed it will protect the bearer from thunderstorms, sickness and fire. If a wife has it, she will have an easy childbirth. When it is planted in a field, a good crop is assured, as it will drive away insects and diseases.

Regarding its origin, it is told that Ganjin-wajo, a great Chinese Buddhist priest who came to Japan in 753, established the Toshodaiji Temple. Later he became blind, but taught many Japanese priests. Sitting in meditation in the summer, mosquitoes covered him. Seeing this, his disciples brought *uchiwa* or round fans and fanned away the insects.

But Ganjin-wajo made them stop their fanning and said that it was his duty and training to serve and help others with what he could give. Thus after his death, his disciples offered *uchiwa* or round fans at the memorial service annually held for him.

The temple began to issue fan charms to visitors. But being in the shape of a fan, and charmingly made, it has been regarded more as a religious toy than a charm. The Toshodaiji fan has a great attraction for children and women.

FORMAL DRESS

IT WAS during the reign of Empress Regnant Suiko in the seventh century that rules regulating the formal dress of Imperial Family members and nobles were first laid down. The Emperor, Empress, Imperial members and court officials still wear such court costumes on occasions of court rites and functions, though the designs have changed from the ancient styles.

A long robe with wide, long sleeves and hats made up the formal dress for men. Women wore the *junihitoe* (12 layers) and dressed their hair in a special style. Costumes for court nobles and officials were much simpler. In feudal days, high military leaders were given court ranks, and so they wore court dress appropriate to their rank on formal occasions.

In Edo days, *kamishimo* (literally upper-lower) became the commonly used formal wear not only for *samurai* but also for many commoners. *Kamishimo* is so called because it is divided into two parts — the upper sleeveless coat and the lower skirt.

When the Meiji government was established, discussions were held as to what sort of formal dress the country should adopt. In 1871, a conference was held in the presence of the Emperor to decide whether the existing court dress or Western dress would be adopted for formal functions.

Thus, for the Emperor a sort of military uniform, which is still displayed at the Meiji Shrine Museum, was designed. But soon this fell into disuse as the Emperor came to wear the uniform of *daigensui* (commander-in-chief of the Army and Navy) in public. The Empress and other ladies of the court also dressed in Western fashion for formal occasions. Nobles and high-ranking officials were also designated styles in conformity with their rank and titles.

For the common people, the swallow-tailed coat became the formal wear, following European custom. Even newspapermen had to wear the swallow-tails and toppers to attend the opening of the Diet or other formal functions.

This formal wear for nobles and officials and the swallow-tail for others are no longer used. But in recent years the morning coat has become popular among men as evidenced by the large number of grooms wearing it at their wedding services. In recent years the Empress and other female members of the Imperial Family often appear in public in Japanese kimono.

FUDE AND SUMI

FOR WRITING and painting, the Japanese people still use *fude* (writing brush) and *sumi* (ink cakes), although pencils and fountain pens have come into wide use. Both *fude* and *sumi* have not changed much in the past 15 or more centuries.

More than 200 kinds of hair are used in making *fude*. Weasels, sheep, horses, badgers, squirrels, dogs, deer, muskrats and other animals supply the hair for *fude*. The best kinds for making high-grade *fude* are still imported from Szechuan province of China.

Fude is said to have been invented in China in the second or third century. There are many kinds of *fude*, differing in size and type of hair. One *fude* tip is made of several layers of different kinds of hair to meet different needs. The hair is first washed and steamed or rubbed in ashes to remove oily substances. Then they are classified by length and stiffness. *Fude* tips are then inserted into the hollow of a piece of bamboo.

Sumi or cake ink is also of Chinese origin, but in Japan it was first made by a Korean priest in 610 during the reign of Empress Regnant Suiko. Japanese calligraphers and painters still value good Chinese *sumi*, and say that Japanese makers are not up to their requirements.

The making of *sumi* is tedious work. It is made of soot and glue. Formerly soot was obtained by burning sesame oil or rape-seed oil in lamps. In *sumi*-making plants, there are rows of tiny oil-burning lamps on shelves. Soot is collected on a covering placed over each lamp. The collected soot is mixed with glue and perfumes and cast in molds.

Sumi is believed to improve in quality with age, and thus old *sumi* is highly treasured.

Proper *suzuri-ishi* or ink-stones are necessary to make ink. When the stone used for making *suzuri* is too soft or coarse in texture, good writing ink cannot be produced. Too hard or too smooth stones are equally unsuitable.

With water in the well of the ink-stone, the ink-cake is rubbed over the surface of the stone until the water attains the desired blackness and thickness for writing.

FUROSHIKI

THE *FUROSHIKI* of Japan is unique and world-famous. Of course, in all countries big handkerchiefs have been used sometimes in wrapping up and carrying things, but never have any other people learned to use anything like it. *Furoshiki* is one thing without which the people of Japan cannot live even a single day.

Furoshiki is the handiest thing for wrapping up and carrying any conceivable thing. It, of course, comes in all sizes, from about one foot square to 10 times that size. It is convenient because, when not in use, it can be folded up and put into a pocket or handbag. A square piece of any fabric will make one *furoshiki*. But special fabrics of silk or cotton are designed, woven and dyed to make good ones. Many wealthy or noble families have their family *furoshiki* specially made with their traditional crests and in family colors.

Furoshiki is believed to have been used by the people since the days of the Muromachi period or 14th century. The present users mostly do not know that *furoshiki* originated in the bathroom, although its very name means 'bathroom spread.'

When Ashikaga Yoshimitsu built the so-called Muromachi Palace in Kyoto in the 14th century, there was a big bathroom so that attending feudal lords and high officials could take their bath in the palace. Next to the bathroom which had a big tub, a large room where those lords and officials could undress was constructed. The floor of the second room was of bare boards, and as the bathers came to the dressing room from the bathroom, their feet left wet marks on the floor. So to keep their clothing safe from direct contact with the wet floor, and also to make it possible to identify their clothes easily, they each brought a piece of square cloth, which they spread on the floor. Upon this spread they placed their clothing and other things, and turned the four corners over the center so as to keep everything together. This cloth came to be known as *furoshiki* or bathroom spread.

Soon afterwards, it is said, the *furoshiki* came to be used in carrying clothing to and from the bathroom whenever an official wanted to change his clothes after the bathing. The convenience of the *furoshiki* soon popularized it and it was adopted by all classes of the people.

So *furoshiki* is used every day by the people for carrying anything, from office workers' lunches and school children's textbooks to vegetables, potatoes or even bulky bedding or furniture.

FUTON

THE WORD *futon* (Japanese bedding)
came from the Chinese pronunciation of the Sung dynasty (10th to 11th century). The term was brought back by Japanese Buddhist priests who studied in China, but it did not mean bedding.

At first it meant the round seats *Zen* priests used to sit on when they sat in meditation. The *futon* was enlarged later, mostly to an oblong shape to be used as cushions or seats when they wanted to sit down comfortably.

But when this Chinese term was introduced, the Japanese had no proper name for their bedding and as they were improved, gradually came to be called *futon*.

In the early days, the people did not have much bedding to speak of. It is recorded that they slept on piles of beaten straw or sacks woven of straw. This habit of sleeping on beaten straw is still kept up in many northern districts.

Some authorities say that the Japanese cultivated rice not only as food, but also to obtain materials for their sleeping accommodations.

The oldest term that can be found for bedding is *yobusuma* (night dress). This was *fusuma* (dress) which was made larger to make the sleeper more comfortable. This *yobusuma* or original *futon* developed to become the present *futon*.

Japanese bedding generally consists of one or more oblong *futon* stuffed thick with cotton to be used as the mattress, and large *kimono*-like coverings, or flat, square or oblong *futon* to cover up the body.

GETA

THE JAPANESE have used *geta* or wooden clogs since earliest times. It is notable that *geta* have not changed much during these many centuries, and are still worn by the people as their ancestors did.

The only change seen is that, in ancient days, *geta* were made of hard and heavy wood, but since about the 17th century, they have come to be made of lighter and softer wood with *kiri* or paulownia wood the most common since the Tokugawa period.

It may be also mentioned that *geta* became shorter in height. In the Tokugawa days, tall *geta* were called *yama-geta* (mountain *geta)* or *dochu-geta* (travel *geta*), as such were used mostly when traveling long distances or over mountain roads. It was said that tall *geta* were more suitable for such walks.

As everything became luxurious in the Tokugawa days, *geta* also showed luxurious trends. During the Bunka-Bunsei era (1804-1830) *geta* with little drawers to hold scent bags or tiny bells appeared. Such *geta* were used by fashionable women. Many women also discarded their *geta* after a few days, as they liked to always wear new *geta*.

Hanao, or thong for men's *geta*, were mainly made of kid or horse leather in Edo days, while women's thongs were of silk or velvet. It was at the beginning of the Meiji era that thongs of other materials, colors and designs appeared.

A notable change has occurred in recent years, particularly after the recent war. *Geta* for women have become larger, proving that Japanese women have become bigger in stature.

Geta are often used as presents to friends in sick-bed in the hope that the patients will soon be able to wear them. But again, some people believe that if *geta* are given to a lover, the donor will lose the love of the other, as affection will walk away.

HACHIMAKI

YOUNG MEN and children who carry *mikoshi* or portable tabernacles on their shoulders and parade through the town on the local shrine festival day wear *hachimaki* or sweat-bands of white or red cotton cloth. It is an indispensable part of their costume. *Hachimaki* is a symbol of action or great physical exertion. The wide use of Western caps and hats has greatly reduced its popularity, but it is still used by farmers and outdoor workers, or when special importance is attached to any physical labor.

Hachimaki is usually a cotton band, white or red, worn around the head. When it is tied in the front it is called *muko-hachimaki* or forward band, and *ushiro-hachimaki* or backward band when tied at the back. But commonly it is believed that the band tied in the front makes the wearer strong and aggressive. Sometimes the band is twisted before it is put on the head, and then it is called *neji-hachimaki* or twisted band.

It was *bushi* or warriors who first started to wear the band. They wore *eboshi*, a cap that had no visor. It came in various shapes, but was very insecure on the head. In order to keep it in place, a band of white cotton was tied around its lower edge. Commoners, wearing no *eboshi*, simply adopted the band. Thus originated the *hachimaki*.

Once adopting it, farmers and other outdoor workers found it indispensable in their work. Then during the Edo days, firemen invariably wore it when they went to fight a fire. Those Edokko who loved to watch roaring fires also came to wear it whenever they ran out to see the fires. When gangsters of Edo got in a fight, they first drew out of their bosom *tenugui* or Japanese towels and tied them around the head as *hachimaki*, so that they would be prepared for the utmost exertion of strength.

Hachimaki is losing its original significance, but on the occasion of community festivals, the old custom of wearing *hachimaki* is still observed all over the country.

HANAGAMI

HANDKERCHIEFS were introduced to Japan only in the early Meiji days. The people have always used paper for blowing their nose or wiping their hands and mouth. The use of paper in this way is quite old. As it is recorded that the Chinese were already using paper in this way in the sixth century, the custom must have come to Japan about the same time.

It has become etiquette for the Japanese to carry neatly folded *hanagami* (tissue paper) in one's bosom or sleeve. The wide use of handkerchiefs has not changed this habit. The Japanese must carry paper even though they also have handkerchiefs. Women usually have packets of *hanagami* in their handbags.

The *hanagami* used by Toyotomi Hideyoshi, the 16th-century administrator, is still preserved at the Myoho-in Temple, Kyoto. It is interesting to note that at the Vatican Museum there is displayed *hanagami* carried by Hasekura Rokuemon, who was sent to see the Pope by Lord Date Masamune in 1615. The paper carried by the envoy must have greatly interested the Romans and is still preserved there.

Hanagami is originally meant for toilet purposes, but it also has many other uses. It often takes the place of little dishes for placing sweets.

At *chanoyu* or tea ceremony, everyone carries his or her paper on which to put cakes or with which to wipe the cup. But for *chanoyu* a much better quality paper than ordinary *hanagami*, cut to the proper size, is used.

With the habit of carrying *hanagami*, *hanagami-ire* or folders, for the convenience of carrying and keeping *hanagami* clean, were made. But soon *hanagami-ire* came to be used not only for holding paper, but also to keep money and other little objects in. *Hanagami-ire* is thus the forerunner of Japanese pocketbooks or money folders.

HAPPI

HAPPI is regarded by foreigners as a symbol of Japan as characteristic as *geisha* and *sakura*. Foreigners first gave the coolies' coat this name, but as silk *happi* especially made for export appeared, it was given the new name of *happi* coat.

The term *happi* came from the Chinese word *'fapei'* which meant not a coat but a chair cover. The introduction of Buddhism to Japan also brought various temple furniture, among which were chairs. Even today at many temples there are massive chairs brightly lacquered for priests. A cloth cover placed over such a chair was called *fapei* which became *happi* in Japan.

When the Shogun Tokugawa established the capital in Edo, a system of *hikeshi* or fire fighters was organized, and at first feudal lords were ordered to form fire brigades. *Samurai* in charge of fire fighting were dressed in leather coats, but lower servicemen who formed the fire brigades wore white cotton or hemp coats, with marks of their lords printed on the back. This coat came to be known as *happi*, probably because it looked like the Buddhist chair cover.

Later fire-fighting units were also established by local civilians and all fire fighters came to wear similar coats, but black in color, with their respective marks. Gradually the *happi* came to be used in wider circles. Carpenters, plasterers and other outdoor workmen adopted it for use.

Thus it became a workman's coat.

In the Meiji Era, when the *jinrikisha* was invented, the *happi* came to be worn by *rikisha* pullers. As business companies were formed, the lower employees were also similarly dressed. It is the *rikisha* men's *happi* that really made it famous among foreign visitors. Many wealthy families made *happi* with their family crests and distributed them among workmen who were generally employed by them.

Noh dramas have a costume called *happi*, but it is quite different from the common kind. In *Noh*, an actor wearing a *happi* signifies that he is dressed in armor.

It is generally at the year-end or New Year that the families distribute their *happi*. Whenever workers come to these families to work, they wear the *happi* given by them. On occasions of family celebrations or funerals, it is the pride of a family to have many workers come wearing their *happi*.

The custom of giving out *happi* at the year-end and New Year is still followed among wealthy merchants, though it is now much restricted.

The short coat named *hanten* is said to have appeared after the Tenpo reform carried out in 1841 by Lord Mizuno Tadakuni, when among other things the wearing of luxurious *haori* (outer coat) by the common people was prohibited. To take the place of the *haori*, a simplified coat came to be worn and was named *hanten*.

Hanten was also commonly called *shirushi-banten* (marked coat) as it bore the crest, mark or design of patrons, master workers or contractors who provided their workers with *hanten*.

HASHI

THERE are many kind of *hashi* or chopsticks. Those for eating meals are one, whereas kitchens have another kind for cooking purposes, and for picking up cakes and sweets there is a different kind. Wood is the principal material, but ivory, bones, tusks, bamboo and various metals are also used. Wood and bamboo *hashi* are often painted or even decorated with designs.

In feudal days, there were gold and silver *hashi* used by aristocrats, but such are no longer used, as they are not convenient for daily use. It was formerly believed that silver chopsticks would become tarnished if there was any poison in the food.

Among chopsticks used daily at meals, those of ivory are most highly valued, as they turn to a mellow amber color with use. Each member of the household has his or her chopsticks always placed in a *hashi* box.

On formal occasions, however, plain wood *hashi*, mostly of willow or cryptomeria wood, are used. Of such, *yanagibashi* or willow-wood *hashi* is used on such formal occasions as New Year's Day. *Rikyubashi*, named after the famous tea master, is much used in Japanese restaurants, and is thick at the middle, tapering at both ends.

Sugi-bashi or cryptomeria wood *hashi* is the most common. A new type of this kind called *waribashi* is a new introduction. It comes as one piece of wood which can be easily pulled apart to make two pieces, as there is a groove made along its length. This is sanitary and convenient. Once used, it is discarded. This kind is now largely used at restaurants.

Hashi is said to have been originally a single slender piece of wood or bamboo, which was bent to pick up things. Then later it was replaced by two sticks. So *waribashi* means a return to the original form with improvements.

It is regarded as unlucky to hand food with chopsticks to another's chopsticks. Also it is considered bad to use a pair of sticks made of different materials.

Hibashi is another kind of chopsticks which are used for picking up charcoal in a *hibachi* or fire-box.

Hashi used for eating food had also a significance of being sacred. It is still customary for a pair of chopsticks to be placed upright in the bowl of rice offered to a dead person, or placed at a memorial service for the dead. The chopsticks thus placed mark the sacredness of the offered rice, and also are a sign to prevent the coming of evil spirits to disturb the peace of the dead.

HATA AND NOBORI

AS ORNAMENTS at ceremonies and festivals, and also as military emblems, *hata* or banners have been used since early days. These banners are long and narrow. The top narrow end is attached to a stick or bar, and is tied by cords to a pole, so that the *hata* will freely hang down. Such long banners, mostly of brocade, are still used at Court ceremonies, and old-style processions at shrine festivals.

But there is another type of banner called *nobori*, which is always used at shrine festivals. *Nobori* is distinctly different from *hata*. It has *chi* or loops made of cloth along one side of its length at regular intervals. The pole is passed through these loops so that the banner is held flat.

Nobori did not appear until the 15th century. It was Hatakeyama Masanaga, a famous general of the Muromachi period, who first made this kind of banner in 1456, and called it *chitsuke-hata* or banner with loops, it is said. Since

then *nobori* have come to be widely used as battlefield emblems and also at ceremonies and festivals.

On the *nobori* of shrine festivals the name of the shrine or such inscriptions as *Tenka Taihei* (Peace in the Country) or other happy expressions are often written.

On *hata* used at Court, too, pictures and words have been written since as early as the sixth century.

Nobori at shrine festivals are regarded as sacred, and sometimes even as holy symbols of the deity. It has been thought an act of disrespect to either mishandle or mistreat them.

There was once a very interesting incident, illustrating the feelings involved with *nobori*. In 1928, some villagers of Ibaraki Prefecture pulled down a *nobori* displayed at a festival in a neighboring district. Those who were celebrating the festival became infuriated and brought a suit against the evil-doers. The case was brought to the Supreme Court, and finally the offenders were punished.

HEAD COVERINGS

IN ANCIENT days the Japanese generally wore some kind of hat or cap when they went outdoors. Those worn by the common people were very crude, but aristocratic and wealthy men wore elaborate hats, *eboshi* (ceremonial hats), and others. Women wore big round and flat hats, or carried thin silk cloths over their heads.

Farmers and outdoor workers also wore hats generally woven of bamboo sheaths or straw. Warriors wore helmets of steel, while low-grade retainers had head coverings of leather or other material.

This hat wearing habit came to be gradually discarded as *samurai* hair fashion changed with the continued years of peace. In the Tokugawa days, all *samurai* wore big hair knots, making it very difficult to wear hats over them. So they stopped wearing hats except for during military drills and such occasions.

At the same time, women's hairstyles became more elaborate and they too gave up wearing hats. The habit was kept up only by monks, travellers on foot, outdoor workers and a few others.

With the Meiji Restoration, the *samurai* class was abolished and the *chon-mage* hair knot was ordered cut off. With the short haircuts, hat wearing suddenly revived. This time, however, it was Western-style hats and caps which were eagerly adopted by the Japanese males in both cities and rural regions, even though they were dressed in *kimono*.

During the recent war years, all males were obliged to wear *sento-bo* or combat caps. But when the war ended, they found it hard to buy hats and caps, as the supply was very short and prices were high. Thus the number of men going bare-headed greatly increased. Even today, very few young men wear hats, although hats are becoming popular with young women who wear Western dress.

HEMP CLOTH

PURITY and obedience are the basic qualifications of Japanese women, and they are symbolized by *asa* or hemp fiber. In the old days *asa* fiber constituted an important part of marriage gifts, besides being used as a symbol of purity at shrines and festivals.

Originally the Japanese people dressed in costumes made of hemp cloth. Not only for clothes, but also for making bedding, matting and netting, hemp was used. Even when cotton and silk fabrics were later introduced from Korea and China, hemp goods were always used on formal or religious occasions.

At first hemp cloth was in natural color or undyed, and when colored fabrics appeared, the white or undyed hemp cloth or fiber came to be regarded as a symbol of purity. Bundles of natural *asa* fibers are offered to shrines or presented as gifts on the occasion of marriages or other happy celebrations.

In the ceremony of purification conducted at shrines by Shinto priests, the *gohei* is used for driving away evil spirits and impurities. The *gohei* is a strand of undyed hemp fiber attached to the end of a short stick. The priest waves the *gohei* over the heads of persons or things to be purified. Evil or impure spirits do not come where purity reigns, according to Shinto tradition, and so the waving of the *gohei* sends away all evils and brings purity.

As a symbol of woman's virtue, *asa* or hemp also means obedience. Hemp fiber can be dyed in desired color. Thus it came to be regarded as the symbol of obedience. The first duty of Japanese women, it was believed in the old days, was to obey her husband's wishes. The use of hemp fiber in wedding ceremonies and presents expresses the hope that the bride will be faithful and obedient to her husband, and will follow the customs of her new family. In the old days, wives were divorced for not conforming to the established customs of the family into which she entered upon marriage. Wives must be willing to be "dyed any color their husbands may choose," an old saying went.

HIDARI-MAE

WHEN foreign ladies wear *kimono*, they often wear it with the left side under the right, in the same way they button their coats. Japanese friends sometimes laugh at this wrong way of donning *kimono*, but more often they feel alarmed, as *hidari-mae* or wearing *kimono* with the right side over the left is considered unlucky.

Only the dead are dressed in *hidari-mae* fashion, according to popular custom. Since *hidari-mae* is considered unlucky, the term is also used to indicate ebbing fortunes or persons facing bankruptcy.

Originally, however, the Japanese people wore their costumes, with the right side over the left. But in the Nara period or seventh century, court costumes were designed after the Chinese fashion. These costumes were worn with the right fold under the left, as it was the fashion to follow the Chinese way.

Thus in wearing *kimono* there developed quite a confusion, some following the original way, and others adopting the new Chinese fashion.

Emperor Gensho (715-724) who made various administrative reforms, unifying the system of measures and adopting a new local government system, therefore issued the so-called Yoro Regulations, which among other things, declared that all the people must wear their *kimono* with the left fold over the right.

Thus by Imperial order, the people were made to wear their clothes as prescribed by law.

Since then *hidari-mae* has come to be regarded as the wrong way and gradually avoided as a sign of unlucky fortune or even death.

With the introduction of Western dresses for women, the former antipathy to *hidari-mae* has greatly disappeared in cities, but in rural districts where older folks are still dressed in Japanese *kimono*, *hidari-mae* is still taboo.

HOKI

HOKI or house brooms are sacred as they sweep out evils, it has been traditionally believed, and from this idea there developed many customs which are still followed by old-fashioned persons.

The custom of placing a *hoki* upside down when a visiting guest has overstayed his welcome is very common all over the country. To step on or over a broom on the floor is believed to invite a curse or punishment.

In the Nagano district, the people have been told not to shoulder a broom, because such an act will bring rainfall. In many districts a *hoki* is set up at the festival for *yama-no-kami* or mountain god.

The early *hoki* was only a bundle of straw tied to a stick, but many kinds developed. House brooms are different from garden brooms and the traditional belief of regarding *hoki* as sacred concerns only those used indoors.

Hoki has also been used as a charm for a safe and easy child delivery in many parts of the country. It is placed upside down at the foot of the mother-to-be in prayer for successful childbirth, as it sweeps away all evil spirits and sickness.

In Kumamoto, Yamaguchi, Nagano and other regions, it was customary in former days to set up a broom in the delivery room, and offer it a bottle of *sake* or rice wine. After a safe child delivery, the broom was taken to the local shrine and tied to a tree in the compound where it was left for three days.

It is also commonly believed that when a dead body rises or moves, a broom is the only thing that will make it keep still. This belief came from China. There was once in China a portrait

19

painter named Liu, and one day he was asked to paint the face of a neighbor who had died. While he was sketching the dead man's face, the body suddenly rose. It was said that a dead body would chase a living man, and so he was afraid to run. Soon, however, the dead man's son returned and put his dead father again on the bed by the use of a broom.

HOSHO PAPER

HOSHO is one of the finest kinds of Japanese paper. It is dazzling white, thick and very soft. It is still used extensively in writing formal or ceremonial notes, or wrapping up importand gifts. No other country produces such paper.

Hosho came to be so named because this kind of paper was used by officials in writing important orders since as early as the Ashikaga period (16th century). Such documents were called *hosho* (sacred documents), and so the paper itself came to be known by the same name. The whiteness of the paper brings out the blackness of the ink. As the paper is very soft, it has to be handled with much care or else it will be soon soiled.

Hosho paper is made of the fiber of the *kozo* or paper mulberry. To the carefully bleached fiber are added finely ground rice powder, and a glue made from the bark of the *norinoki*. The paper is made carefully by hand, and special attention is given to eliminate the smallest piece of dirt or foreign matter from the mixture, to make it pure white.

As it requires much more care in making *hosho* than other kinds of paper, it is naturally quite expensive. But it has always been used in official circles, and also by commoners for ceremonial use.

Formerly the province of Echizen was most famous for this paper, but now the Kiniyasu and Yoshii districts of Ehime Prefecture are the great producing centers. Almost 6 million pounds, of *hosho* paper, or about 90 percent of the national output, are annually produced in this area.

HYOTAN

HYOTAN or bottle gourd is one of many kinds of gourds raised in the country. The ripe gourd is dried and the seeds inside are taken out to make it a hollow vessel. It was formerly used widely for holding *sake* or other liquids. The *hyotan* comes in different shapes, but most of them are narrow in the middle and wasp-waisted, with the bottom part much larger than the upper. But good-shaped *hyotan* are rare and thus highly valued.

Hyotan is also regarded as a good luck charm. It was used often as a design for family crests and also on war banners in the old days. It also appears on fabrics and art objects. Small *hyotan* made of wood were attached to the sash worn by children as a charm against accidents and sickness. Sometimes little *hyotan* were dressed in *kimono*, with human faces painted on the top part.

The idea of regarding *hyotan* as a lucky charm is believed to have developed from the ancient belief that *kamisama* or invisible divine spirits lived in the hollow of big trees, gourds, boats, boxes or other small spaces.

Hyotan that stand upright are regarded as the best, but such are few. It is said that though one plant may have many gourds only the one that grows on the main central vine stands upright.

Once a rich man in Kyoto had three sons, and before he died he gave each one a gourd. After his death each son insisted that he was the one to inherit the family fortune, producing the gourd given by the father as proof of his right. The case was taken to Itakura Katsushige, *shoshidai* or governor of Kyoto. Hearing their case, the lord asked them to produce the gourds. As the three gourds were placed before the lord, only the one produced by the youngest son stood upright, and so he was judged the rightful heir to the family wealth.

The *hyotan* has been deeply woven into the people's life, and there are many common *hyotan* expressions. 'Hyotan-kara koma' (a horse from a *hyotan*) means an unexpected result. 'Hyotan-ni tsurigane' (hyotan and a hanging bell) means a wide difference or contradiction, referring to the fact that though both the *hyotan* and a big temple bell may hang down, they are vastly different. 'Hyotan namazu' (hyotan and a catfish) means slippery or noncommital as a *hyotan* cannot hold a slippery catfish.

INDIGO BLUE

THE JAPANESE people still love *kimono* made of cotton fabrics dyed with *ai* or vegetable indigo dye. But cotton cloth made of *ai*-dyed yarns is becoming rare, as cheaper chemical dyes are now more commonly used. But the traditional belief in the durability and unfading nature of *ai*-dyed cloths is still very strong.

Ai is a perennial plant of the pea family. Formerly it was very extensively cultivated since early days, having been brought originally from China. The process of making the dye and dyeing with it is primitive and complicated, making it costly now.

Ai leaves are gathered in summer, just before the blossoms appear. The picked leaves are piled up and watered, and in about 45 days they ferment. The fermented leaves are pounded and kneaded into balls of a convenient size. They are then placed in an earthenware vat which is buried in the ground up to its rim. It is filled with water, after which soda ash, lime and barley bran are also added. The proportion of these ingredients differs according to the quality of the *ai* leaves, and a proper mixture can be made only by persons of experience.

Vats are placed in rows under the eaves. Between the vats small holes are dug into which sawdust is put and set on fire. Thus, the vats are kept at a temperature of about 30 degrees day and night for 10 days, at the end of which the dye is ready.

To dye yarn or cloth, they are immersed in the vat for three minutes. then the material being dyed comes out an iron-rust color. But when they are hung out on poles, the air oxidizes the dye, changing the color to indigo blue. This process must be repeated 10 to 20 times to get a deep indigo color.

Chemical dyes usually weaken the fabric, but natural *ai* dye makes them more durable, and the color never fades. Thus, farmers and other outdoor workers prefer *ai*-dyed *kimono* to other kinds.

INDIGO PAPER

KONSHI or *kongami* is a strong paper dyed in indigo, and has been particularly used in writing Buddhist sutras in gold paint. It is still produced in a very small quantity by some Kyoto paper makers.

It is fine for sutra copying because it is strong and durable, and thus can be preserved for a long period. Sutras copied on *konshi* during the Heian period (794-1192) are still preserved at Chusonji at Hiraizumi, Jingoji at Kyoto, and other temples.

The famous Goju-no-to or five-storied pagoda at Yanaka in Tokyo was destroyed by fire in 1957, and from under the foundation was unearthed a strong container of bones and a Buddhist sutra written in gold paint. This sutra was on *konshi* which showed no deterioration after having been buried underground for 168 years.

Konshi is *ganpi* paper made of *ganpi* tree fiber. The *ganpi* produced in Shiga Prefecture is still used for making *konshi* today.

The best quality of *ganpi* paper is selected and then placed in an *'ai'* or indigo dye vat. The dyeing process is repeated seven to eight times in order to give the paper a deep blue color. When it is properly dyed, it is put in water for a whole day and night. The water must be changed several times during the washing process, so that the paper will be entirely free of the lye contained in the indigo dye. The quality of the finished paper depends on thorough washing, as any lye left on the paper will lesson its durability.

The washed paper is then dried and beaten with a wooden mallet to give it a smooth flat surface and a fine sheen.

The same process is still followed in making *konshi* today, but as the demand for this special kind of paper is now very limited, it is of an inferior quality compared with the old *konshi.*

JEWELRY

ANCIENT Japanese women had very few jewels, according to the general interpretation of the term. They never wore rings on their fingers until the Meiji era when the ring-wearing habit was introduced from the West. This lack of jewelry was due to their costumes and living modes. Women wearing rings are still comparatively very few. Only those dressed in Western style wear necklaces, bracelets and brooches.

Japanese women of the old days had only *kanzashi* (ornamental hair-pins) and *kushi* (combs) as ornaments. To these hair ornaments they gave just as much thought and money as in selecting their dress.

There were two distinct kinds of both *kanzashi* and *kushi*. One was for daily wear, and thus was not very expensive, although most artistically and exquisitely made. The kind worn for ceremonial or social occasions was more important and elaborate. While those for daily use showed much variation in design and workmanship according to the fashion of the age, the formal or ceremonial pieces changed only slightly, and thus were handed down from mothers to daughters as family treasures.

These hair ornaments were mostly made of tortoise shell, silver and gold, with carved or inlaid designs, or with delicate ornaments in lacquer. Common combs were made of wood, while *kanzashi* for daily use were of silk, wood or other materials.

Though these elaborate hair ornaments of Edo days are no longer used today, they are still treasured as specimens of the most artistic craftmanship.

Kushi or hair combs were at first regarded as a sign to mark the presence of a sacred spirit, or a charm against evil. The comb was very important to women as it was a sign of being married, and also a charm to protect their honor and virtue. Thus combs figure in many tales in which the love or life of women is involved. As combs came to be elaborately and beautifully made, they were valued as family treasures.

Since wearing a comb in her hair at first indicated that a woman was married, the simple act of throwing it away meant her intentions to have the marriage canceled. It was taboo to pick up a comb found on the street, as it was believed that it had the power of possession over its holder and might bring evil fortune.

Not only did people avoid picking up a lost comb, but it was also thought that if one threw away her comb she was courting the curse of evil spirits as she was no longer protected by the sacred spirit.

Obidome, a kind of buckle or clasp on the band used for tying *obi* or the Japanese broad sash, came later, and is still the only ornament Japanese women have for their *kimono*. In the old days only woven cords or cloth bands were used in tying up the *obi*. At first *obidome* were made of silver, gold or other metals with delicately executed designs in carved or inlaid work. Master artists produced excellent pieces. But of late *obidome* decorated with diamonds and other gems have appeared. Lacquered wood carvings or little porcelain pieces with artistic designs are modern additions to *obidome*. However, old-fashioned people still prefer *obidome* that are not showy but possess quiet refinement.

JINDAI-SUGI

SUGI (cryptomeria) or Japanese cedar is one of Japan's native trees that is seen all over the country towering to a height of 20 meters or more. Thus it has been widely used since ancient days as building material and for making various utensils.

Japan is a volcanic land and eruptions have taken place at many districts since the prehistoric period. The hot lava pouring out of volcanoes covered large forests of *sugi* and other trees. Buried under the lava and ashes for many centuries, the trees underwent a process of carbonization.

When the semicarbonized *sugi* is mined after long burial, it is found to be of a hard texture, beautiful with a bluish black color. This buried *sugi* is called *jindai-sugi* (prehistoric *sugi*) and is valuable wood used for decorative purposes in houses and also to make various objects. *Jindai-sugi* has been used particularly in making boxes, book cases and ceiling boards for fine rooms.

It has been found in the Izu Peninsula, Hakone, the Tanba district of Kyoto and Fukui Prefecture so far. As it is becoming rare, its value has risen.

There is another kind of buried wood called *umoregi* or fossil wood which is more highly carbonized than *jindai-sugi*. *Sugi* and other trees have turned into *umoregi*. It is between the *jindai-sugi* and lignite in the degree of carbonization. Dark brown in color, it clearly shows the wood grain.

Umoregi is used to make various small articles. Sendai in the northeastern part of the country is famous for articles made with this material which is found in the district of the Natori and Hirose rivers of Miyagi Prefecture. But the supply is also becoming very small.

The term *'umoregi'* is also commonly used, meaning to live in obscurity.

JINRIKISHA

JINRIKISHA or *rikisha* have been just as symbolic of Japan as *geisha* and *Fujiyama*. But those seen today are sorry remnants of what *jinrikisha* were years ago.

The name *jinrikisha* (man-power cart) first appeared in 1870, but it stood originally for a two-wheeled wooden cart with an overhead awning placed on a bamboo frame. This new invention caused quite a sensation in Tokyo, and was eagerly used by the people. Three years later, Taisuke Akiba first started the business of manufacturing *jinrikisha* in quantity. Soon its construction was improved, and the bamboo awning frame was replaced by a steel frame one. In 1879 the wooden wheels were made narrower and came to have solid rubber tires.

It is recorded that in 1883, 13 years after it first appeared, they numbered 168,000. The export of *jinrikisha* started as early as 1875, with them going to China, India, Korea, Singapore and the South Sea Islands.

Its popularity served to improve its construction, and it came to be beautifully lacquered with brass or nickel-plated metal parts. Wealthy families made their own private *jinrikisha* with family crests. People in a hurry had their *rikisha* pulled and pushed by two or three men. At railway stations and busy street corners, there were *jinrikisha* stands where pullers waited for their turns day and night. There were two-seater *jinrikisha* for carrying couples.

The height of its popularity came in the period between 1910-20 when pneumatic tires came into fashion. *Jinrikisha* pullers required long training, but made good money. Many boasted of their ability to run 50 to 60 miles a day.

With the introduction of motor cars, *jinrikishas* naturally began to disappear. After the surrender, however, they were revived due to the scarcity of taxis and also as they attracted Occupation personnel. There are about 500 in Tokyo today, but all are in poor condition.

KAKASHI

KAKASHI, scare-crows, are generally made in the form of a farmer wearing a wide round hat and a *mino* or reed rain-coat, to scare away birds and animals from farms. They are often seen carrying a bow and arrow. In many districts farmers love to make *kakashi* as realistic as possible, but on the other hand, crude ones not resembling human forms are often seen.

Though *kakashi* are now generally made in the form of a human being, the name originated from *kagase* (let smell). In the old days, old rags, meat or fish bones were put on sticks and burnt to scare away birds and animals with the evil smell. This old way of burning things around farms is still used in many places. The term *kakashi*, as now used, means anything that is used to drive away birds and animals from farms.

Wooden boards with several bamboo sticks hanging on them are placed on farms on slender poles. When the wind blows, the board sways and produces a loud clattering sound that drives away birds. Of late, empty cans and old metal pieces are used in place of the wooden boards with bamboo sticks.

Colored streamers or bright shining things are tied on ropes or poles, and as they reflect the sun and glitter they help to frighten the birds away.

Around a farm, *shimenawa* or narrow straw ropes with cut white paper are placed. *Shimenawa*, as it is used at shrines, is a mark of purity and sacredness. It is placed on farms as a prayer for a good harvest. Sacred places will not be visited by evil spirits and diseases, and it is commonly believed that farms marked with *shimenawa* will not be molested by animals, birds or insects.

KAMADO

KAMADO, mud or stone ovens, are still largely used in rural districts for cooking. In cities, gas and electricity are quite widely used for cooking and heating. But most Japanese houses still use charcoal for cooking meals and warming the rooms.

Though charcoal is much used, its use is comparatively new in ordinary households. Charcoal has been made since very early days, but was used only by blacksmiths, sword-makers and cast-iron goods producers.

In ancient days, wood was burned in the *irori*, Japanese open fire-places for cooking. *Irori* wood fire served as the only source of light at night and also warmed the house in winter. In those days, it was the duty of the housewife to look after the fire.

Then the *kamado* was develped for cooking purposes. At first it was made outside the house, or in a little hut built for that purpose. Meals were cooked over the *kamado* in kettles or pans. But in the Tokugawa period, it became smaller and greatly improved, as the supply of wood became short due to the felling of forest trees and opening up of new farms.

In recent years, the *kamado* has undergone even more improvement. Many have chimneys now to keep smoke out of the house, as in most cases the *kamado* is built in the kitchen.

It was toward the end of the Muromachi period or early in the 16th century that charcoal became a household fuel in aristocratic and *samurai* families. All through the Tokugawa period, the *kamado* was used for cooking, and charcoal for heating the rooms among the better classes. Only in the Meiji period did the use of charcoal become general in common households for cooking and heating.

KAMIKO

THE FACT that the ancient Japanese wore *kamiko* or clothes made of paper is one proof that the people were successful in producing very good and strong paper even in those early days. Though later *kamiko* came to be worn only by those of the poor class, at first it was worn by all the people, nobles as well as commoners. There is a record that Toyotomi Hideyoshi, military ruler of the country in the 16th century, was fond of wearing *kamiko*. Even in later periods when silk dress became common among the upper class, *kamiko* was worn as a home dress or to relax in. Some wore *kamiko* as an undergarment because of its soft texture and warmth.

Kamiko is a contraction of *kami-koromo* or paper dress. The making of *kamiko* is not so simple as it might sound. At first pieces of very strong paper are selected. They are pasted together to form the usual shape of woven cloth. The paper is then made stronger and water-proof by applying to it a starch made of devil's tongue, or the astringent juice of *kaki* or persimmon. When it is treated with the persimmon juice it becomes brown in color. Thus there are two kinds of *kamiko*, the brown and the white. The paper thus prepared is then thoroughly rubbed by hand, so that it will become soft as silk. It is then cut and sewed together to form a *kimono*.

Kamiko feels soft and very comfortable when it is worn next to the skin, because of its soft texture, and then in winter, it is very warm. As home wear, *kamiko* probably has no equal. The only shortcoming it has is that it is not strong enough for rough wear as silk or cotton is and then it soils easily, but cannot be washed.

The popularity of *kamiko* made various local districts famous for the good *kamiko* they produced. Particularly Shirakawa in the northeast, Abekawa of Suruga province, and Osaka were famous for the excellent *kamiko* they produced and sold to all parts of the country.

KASA

KASA IS OFTEN a confusing Japanese term, particularly to foreigners, as it may mean a farmer's sedge hat, a lady's parasol, an umbrella, a lamp shade, a lady's veil, a beach parasol, a hood, a mushroom top, a bowl lid, a writing-brush cover and many other things.

Kasa comes from *kazasu* which means to hold aloft. Thus the word first meant anything to be held up to protect oneself from rain or sun or from being seen by others.

The oldest type of *kasa* was woven of rush leaves. It was round and flat, with a raised portion in the center for the head. Such *kasa* is mentioned as early as the eighth century. Thus at the beginning the *kasa* was a head covering, which came to be made of different materials and in various shapes.

Women of the upper class who did not show their face to the public used head coverings which sometimes came down to the knee. At many shrine festivals, dancers still wear *kasa* with veiling attached around the rim. These are remnants of ancient ladies' *kasa*.

Higasa or parasols were first used in Japan by nobles and high priests in the Heian period (794-1192), but the men did not carry the *higasa* themselves. When such nobles or high priests went outdoors, their attendants walked behind them holding the parasols over their heads. Thus the early *higasa* were very large, four or five feet across and had long poles as handles.

At the beginning of the Tokugawa period or the 17th century, scholars and physicians followed the habit of the nobility of using sun shades but as they were not of such high social rank, they carried small parasols themselves.

The original big *higasa* with long poles are still used on the occasion of various festivals in which old costumes and equipment are shown in sacred processions.

In the late 18th century, when the common people adopted luxurious habits with the comfort and peace of life under Tokugawa rule, women came to use parasols on summer days to shade themselves from the hot sun. As women began to carry *higasa*, naturally they became smaller in size and brighter in color.

Deep straw hats worn by priests and others, covering their entire face and having slits to enable the wearers to see, also developed from the type of *kasa* protecting the wearers from public view.

Of course, *higasa* for both men and women had bamboo ribs and were covered with strong Japanese paper.

Western umbrellas, which came to be popularly used in the Meiji era were often used by men as sun shades in summer because of their lightness. In rural districts old men are still seen using Western umbrellas as sun shades in summer.

While the Japanese style *amagasa* (umbrella) has now been replaced by modern umbrellas, there are both Japanese and Western style *higasa*. The Japanese type has bamboo ribs and is covered with paper or silk, while the Western *higasa* has steel ribs and is covered with various different materials.

In ancient days, all men, regardless of their position or occupation wore hats. *Eboshi*, a little pointed hat that was lacquered black, was usually tied on their heads. But sometimes, those who did not possess a proper *eboshi* or were too lazy to wear them, used to tie on their foreheads a piece of black paper cut in a triangle so that it looked as if they were wearing *eboshi*. From this developed the old custom of tying a triangular piece of white paper on a dead person's forehead.

Of course, later, only nobles or those with court rank wore *eboshi* and commoners wore only sedge or other kinds of *kasa.*

KI-HACHIJO

KI-HACHIJO, the herb-dyed and handwoven silk fabric produced on Hachijo Island, 259 miles south of Tokyo, still commands a very high price because of its special beauty and texture. The silk is dyed yellow, black and brown, but the yellow color produced by the dye from a reedlike grass called *kariyasu* is particularly beautiful, and so the fabric is called *Ki-hachijo* or yellow silk of Hachijo.

The fabric was highly appreciated from very early times and as far back as the 13th century, strong rivalry arose among military lords to gain control of the island to monopolize its supply. As *Ki-hachijo* was the most important product of the island, it came to be offered to the ruling lord in payment of land tax. The system of receiving *Ki-hachijo* for tax payment was followed by the Tokugawa *bakufu* and even by the Meiji government until 1909.

Ki-hachijo received in lieu of tax payments was brought to the mainland and sold to women of the upper and military classes, but soon its popularity extended to the women of the common class. Thus besides the tax payment *Ki-hachijo*, which was recorded to have reached 630 pieces (one piece was about 10 meters long) in 1722, there naturally came also many private shipments.

The scarcity and high cost of *Ki-hachijo* encouraged the production of imitation *Ki-hachijo*. Even today good *Ki-hachijo* made in Hachijo is limited and very expensive, and more imitation pieces are sold.

While *Ki-hachijo* made the island famous, Hachijo is also known for the many criminals banished there for punishment. Banishment was second only to the death sentence in severity in Tokugawa days. It is recorded that Ukita Hideie and 12 of his family members were exiled to Hachijo in 1606 as the first exiles to the island. Since then for 265 years until the fourth year of Meiji or 1871, 1,865 persons were banished to Hachijo.

KIMONO MATERIALS

COTTON and silk fabrics are the principal materials for making Japanese *kimono*. Quite a variety of thin woolen goods are also used, but these woolen fabrics are quite new, having been made since the development of the woolen weaving industry in the Meiji era.

However, both cotton and silk, too, are comparatively new things in Japan.

Silk is said to have been introduced to the country in the third century, but the progress of the silk industry was slow and production never sufficient to clothe the majority of the people. Silk was only used to make wearing apparel for the aristocrats and the rich. The first import item in the early Tokugawa foreign trade through Nagasaki was silk yarns and fabrics from China.

Cotton came to be produced in Japan only about 300 years ago. Of course cotton seeds were said to have been brought into Japan about a thousand years ago, but cotton cultivation did not develop speedily.

Before the large production of cotton and silk fabrics, the people used *asa* or hemp cloth to make their clothes. But among fabrics generally called *asa* in the old days, they included fibers obtained from the barks of various other plants. Particularly the barks of wisteria and similar trees were largely used to make threads to be woven into fabrics for *kimono*.

Today the common people wear silk *kimono* for going out, but for daily wear, they have cotton *kimono*. Good hemp *kimono* worn in summer are very expensive, and are not for the common people now.

KINUTA

IN THE old days it was the duty of women in rural districts to weave fabrics to make clothes for the entire family. Such home-made material as well as those purchased were coarse and stiff. So they had to be beaten soft before being sewn up into clothes. For this purpose *kinuta*, a wooden pin, looking somewhat like western rolling pins, was used.

The cloth was wound around a round piece of wood or folded and placed on a flat wooden board or stone. Then it was beaten with a *kinuta*.

The women used to do the beating particularly in the evening and the sound could be heard in all houses in rural villages.

As they worked the women thought of the happiness or misery of their life, recalled their dead parents or longed for the early return of their husbands away on a journey.

The *kinuta* came to be mentioned in poems and literary writings as the symbol of peaceful country life, or women's unexpressed sentiment. In *hokku*, the 17-syllable poem, *kinuta* is regarded as a topic for the autumn season. In many such poems, it symbolizes solitude, quietness or even sadness.

There is also a *Noh* drama called *Kinuta*. In this play, a wife in Kyushu longs for her husband who has gone to the capital and has not returned for a long time. Beating her *kinuta* every evening, she prays and hopes for his early return. But finally, she dies of sorrow.

When her husband returns after her death, he holds an elaborate memorial rite for her. Her spirit appears and tells him how she pined for his return.

KOMON FABRICS

THE MOST delicate fabric dyeing process used in Japan is that of *komon* (small design). This type of dyeing is quite old, and in early Tokugawa days, it was mainly used for fabrics used to make *kamishimo*, the formal sleeveless coat and trousers for *samurai*. Later, because of its beauty, this kind of dyeing came to be applied to silk goods for women's wear. *Komon* goods are still produced, though the production is now greatly limited.

For this dyeing, a stencil has to be first made. As *komon* designs are made of fine lines, straight or curved, and small dots mostly, the cutting of the stencil is a very delicate process. The stencil board is made by pasting together more than 20 sheets of fine paper. Designs are cut out with sharp knives.

The stencil board is about one foot wide and a foot and a half long. In order to make a continuous design on the fabric, the lines and dots at one end of the stencil have to fit exactly with those at the other end. When the weather becomes especially dry or wet, the board stretches or contracts. Thus much care is required to keep the stencil in good condition.

The stencil board is placed flat on the stretched fabric, and a paste made of rice is applied to fill all the cuts. Then the stencil is moved over the cloth, until all the fabric has been stencilled. When the paste is dry, the fabric is dyed. The paste is washed off when the dyeing is finished.

Thus the open cuts in the stencil remain white, and the rest of the fabric dyed in the color selected.

Komon fabrics with small designs do not look beautiful when viewed from a distance, but close observation will reveal the delicate beauty of the fine lines and dots.

KOROMOGAE

THE FOUR seasons of the year clearly marked the life and habits of the people in old days. Though much of this practice is now gone, its effects are still seen in the daily life of the modern people.

For instance, as the summer season commenced on May 6, regularly on May 5 the people used to change their spring dress to summer clothing. Thus *koromogae* or dress change was an important annual event in the life of the people. As there are four seasons, *koromogae* was observed four times a year with a definite   I for each change. It is this traditional habit that created the habit of the people to possess so many varieties of clothing.

The seasonal change of dress was strictly observed by the Imperial Court since very early days, under fixed rules. The Tokugawa Bakufu authorities followed the example of the Court and also adopted a set of clothing regulations.

Thus *koromogae* or dress changing days originated. That is to say, the people wore *katabira* or summer unlined dress from May 5; *awase* or lined dress from September 1; *wataire* or cotton-stuffed dress from September 9, and again *awase* from April 1, the next year.

In this way, *katabira* or summer clothes were worn four months in one year, *awase* or lined dress for one month in April and nine days in September, and *wataire* or cotton-stuffed clothes seven months in winter.

Although the system of *koromogaye* was most strictly observed during the Tokugawa days, the seasonal change of clothing is no longer followed now. But the people still wear different kinds of clothing in the four seasons of the year. Only they do not change their dress so strictly on fixed dates. This habit has greatly increased the varieties of clothing the people possess. Then again the former strict system of formal dress to be worn on official or ceremonial occasions has caused the people to possess different clothes for homewear and for going out. Furthermore, social and ceremonial occasions demand special kinds of dress, the formal dressing etiquette being still observed to some extent. Again, in modern times almost all people possess some western clothes.

Kimono constitute the most valuable and important family property. Particularly, it is the eager wish of housewives to possess as many kinds and varieties of *kimono* for not only themselves, but also for all the members of the family.

Various characteristics of the people as well as many phases of Japanese culture are thus reflected in the shapes, designs and colors of the clothes, as well as in the traditional customs and beliefs with respect to clothing.

KUROMOJI

TOOTHPICKS are sometimes called *kuromoji* because the best kind is made of kuromoji, a plant of the camphor tree species. Common varieties are made of willow or other cheap wood. *Kuromoji* toothpicks are handmade and come in a distinctive shape, generally larger than the common kind. They are the best toothpicks in the world.

Kuromoji is a little plant that grows to about five or six feet tall with a dark green bark. The wood is beautifully white and the bark has a very pleasant smell. The bark was used in the old days as medicine, and a tea made by brewing the bark was taken for curing beriberi or applied to the skin for curing boils and cuts.

Kuromoji-abura or oil is obtained by steaming small branches and leaves of *kuromoji*. The yellowish oil is insoluble in water and used in making perfumes, soaps or hair oils. The Izu district is famous for this unique oil.

But in the old days *kuromoji* was a very valuable tree that possessed much significance and many uses. It was also thought to possess power against evil and poisons. In many districts it was believed that *kuromoji* wood would neutralize the poison of *fugu* or globe fish.

Bear hunters of Yamagata, Echigo, Akita and Aomori used *kuromoji* branches in their rites for bears. When they killed bears, they held a rite of thanks to the mountain god. They took out the entrails of their kill and put them on skewers made of *kuromoji* branches. Then they broiled the entrails over a fire and placed them on the ground by sticking the *kuromoji* spits into the earth.

In many mountain regions, hunters and woodsmen ate their *bento* or lunch with chopsticks made of *kuromoji* wood, as they believed that they would live long if they followed this custom. *Kuromoji* chopsticks were also used in many mountain districts as gifts to others, as an expression of goodwill and prayer for happiness.

Kuromoji toothpicks originally came to be used because of the people's belief in their power dispel evil and neutral poisons, and also because they had a very pleasant flavor. However, the original significance is now almost entirely forgotten.

In making toothpicks of *kuromoji* wood, the most important point is that each toothpick must have the bark on one side. Thus most of the white wood is wasted and they become naturally expensive.

Toothpicks are called *ko-yoji* or *tsuma-yoji*, meaning small *yoji*, to differentiate them from *yoji* (tooth brushes).

Old-fashioned men and women carry *yoji-ire* or toothpick holders which are often made of old brocade or rich leather. Ivory, gold or silver toothpicks were made in the old days for the rich, but they were never popular as they are not practical.

KUSUDAMA

WHEN NEW restaurants or *pachinko* halls are opened many wreaths of artificial flowers and several *kusudama*, or bright balls of blossoms with long tassels of many colors, are displayed at the entrance. This use of *kusudama* is quite recent. Formerly it was used only on such festive occasions as the New Year, Dolls' Festival or May 5 Boy's Festival.

Kusudama (medicine ball) is believed to have originated in the Heian period (794-1192). At first fragrant woods and herbs were placed in a small cloth bag, which was decorated with the blossoms of *shobu* or iris and other flowers. Long silk threads of five different colors were attached to it. This was hung in the house on May 5 to dispel evil spirits and disease.

The Emperor invited nobles and officials to Butokuden Palace on this day and gave each a *kusudama* and drinks of *sake*. The guests wore the *kusudama* they received from the Emperor, and thus decorated they drank *sake*. It was a ceremony to insure the happiness and good health of all.

This ancient custom of giving *kusudama* continued until the beginning of the 17th century. It was discontinued by Emperor Gomizunoo (1611-1629).

Since that time, *kusudama* has lost all its connection with Court functions. It came to be used as an ornament in the households of the common people, or as a plaything for children. Thus, the original meaning of *kusudama* to ward off evil and sickness with the fragrant medicines and woods became forgotten.

KYARA

KYARA or aloes wood (Aguilaria agallocha) is the most valuable of fragrant woods that are burned as incense. It is worth more than its weight in gold. Its name came from the Indian word, *Kala-agura*.

This fragrant wood is said to have been first brought from China in 593 in the reign of Empress Regnant Suiko. The *ko-boku* or incense wood was so rare that only the Imperial Court and high nobles were able to enjoy them. It was something the common people only heard and dreamed of, but could not actually smell or see. So the term *kyara* came to be used as a synonym for anything particularly gorgeous, expensive or rare.

The fragrant wood was presented by the rulers of Korea and China to the Imperial Court, and early traders brought them from India and other southern regions. Even powerful military lords could not obtain the best of them, however eagerly they tried.

It is recorded that Oda Nobunaga, the great military ruler, wanted to have a piece of the famous incense wood kept in the Shoso-in, Nara, but unable to gain it in a normal way, took some soldiers on March 23, 1574, to the Shosoin, and threatening the guards, entered the building by force and cut two small pieces of the famous incense wood named *Ranshatai*.

The same wood which came to Japan in the reign of Emperor Shomu (724-749), of which Nobunaga sawed off small pieces, is still in the Shosoin, after 12 centuries. If a tiny piece of it could be brought out, it would command a price that would be hard to calculate.

KYOKUSHI

JAPAN has always produced very good paper and has developed many uses for it. Most Japanese paper, which is highly valued all over the world, has been made for many centuries. But there is one kind of Japanese paper which became world famous and which was first made in the Meiji era.

It is called *kyokushi* (bureau paper) because it was first made by the Government Printing Bureau in 1879. As it is heavy, strong and durable, it is often called Japanese parchment.

When this delicately yellow paper came to be known abroad orders for it came from many European countries where it was used in place of parchment for writing or printing important documents or making de luxe editions of books. It may be remembered that it was used for writing the text of the Versailles Treaty that ended World War I.

With the growing demand, many private paper mills began its production. It is handmade and production is painstaking and expensive. Only the *mitsumata* fiber is used which must be carefully prepared and freed of all foreign matter. Every sheet must also be carefully dried by hand.

Because of the big demand and the

31

high cost of genuine *kyokushi*, there has appeared a cheaper kind which is made with some mixture of wood pulp.

However, nothing can beat the real *kyokushi* for its strong quality to withstand rubbing, its smoothness of surface, its non-shrinking quality and elasticity.

LANTERNS

WHENEVER the people of Japan are in a joyous or festive mood, they like to display *chochin* or carrying lanterns. As the annual festival of the village shrine comes, the first thing the villagers do is to hang up *chochin* at their doors or gates and light them at night. For many public celebrations, *chochin-gyoretsu* or lantern processions are held. In cities *chochin* are no longer used to guide one on dark nights, but in rural districts they are still used very widely. Then on summer evenings, beautifully decorated *chochin* are hung in the house or garden. The people think that the soft light of *chochin* makes them feel cool, and is better than bright electric lights.

The name *chochin* came from the Chinese term for the hanging lantern. *Toro* or fixed lanterns were placed in Buddhist temples at first, and it seems that since about the beginning of the 17th century in the Tokugawa period that *chochin* or carrying lanterns appeared. With the development of convenient types to be easily carried around, they came to be very extensively used.

Generally speaking, *chochin* are made by covering with paper a form made of fine bamboo sticks, with a firm bottom to hold the candle. It is the type that is made to fold up that has popularized its use.

There are lanterns for rooms and others for the garden. Mostly they are beautifully decorated with designs painted in soft colors. Gorgeous rich colors would make lanterns out of place in Japanese houses.

Rural folks still have their family lanterns marked with their crests. The mark on the *chochin* makes it very convenient for identifying the person carrying it on dark nights.

Many temples boast huge *chochin* measuring sometimes more than ten feet in diameter that are presented by worshipers.

Hozuki-chochin or the red-berry lantern is the kind most commonly used. It is round, small and red-colored. This was at first made as a toy or plaything for children. But its bright red color appealed to the people, and it is used in lantern processions and at festivals. *Takahari* or high-poled lantern is one that was formerly placed at gates and house-doors. The *samurai* had a special kind which they used while riding horses. *Umanori-chochin* or horse-riding lantern has a long and fixable handle, with which it is held in the rider's *obi* sash, so as to have both hands free. *Odawara-chochin*, named after the town of Odawara, is cylindrical and made to fold up when not in use. Because of its convenience, this type has been very widely used by the common people.

Gifu-chochin that originated in Gifu city is a modern addition. It is a type made in a delicate oval shape, with designs of flowers, birds or insects painted on the thin paper covering. It is now popularly used in summer for decorative purposes.

Of all types of lanterns, *mawari-doro* or revolving lantern is the most interesting. It is so contstructed as to show a picture as it moves around. Generally it comes in a round shape like a drum. The frame is made of two sections, the inner and the outer. The outer frame is covered with thin

Japanese paper which is either white or has designs in faint colors. The inner frame is suspended from the outer frame, to revolve easily. It has no bottom, and is covered with a sheet of white paper on which a series of pictures are painted in black, or forms cut out of black paper are pasted. The top side of the inner frame is covered with strips of paper cut and arranged in the fashion of windmill blades. The heat rising from the burning wick set in a shallow dish of oil at the center of the bottom of the outer frame, sets the inner frame in motion.

Many persons love to construct their own *mawari-doro* as their ancestors used to do every summer. It is not difficult to make, even for little children.

LIGHTERS

MANY persons may be surprised to learn that as early as the middle of the Tokugawa era or 200 to 250 years ago, feudal lords and other smokers of Japan used mechanical lighters to light their tiny smoking pipes. Furthermore, the most astonishing point is that old Japanese lighters were constructed practically on the same principle and technique as modern American and European lighters. Japanese lighters were also more artistically and exquisitely made than their modern counterparts.

There are not many specimens remaining, but one now in the collection of Tamotsu Murayama of Tokyo is representative of the lighters used in the middle Tokugawa period, and proves that old Japanese lighters are indeed works of art.

The outer case of the lighter is of a lovely shape that resembles a football but with ends not so pointed. The shape is such that it nestles in one's palm. It is about one inch long and half an inch

wide. The whole thing is beaten into shape out of a steel plate. There is a small ring in the center of the ball through which a cord may be passed to attach the lighter to one's belt, and around this ring is a design similar to a chrysanthemum flower executed in brass.

The upper half opens on hinges when a button on the side is pushed. Then one lifts up an arm that holds at its end a piece of flint. When another button on the side is pushed, the arm snaps back and strikes an extending arm of steel. The spark thus caused ignites the *hokuchi* or tinder placed in a small bowl. The lighted tinder lights the pipe. The structure is thus quite similar to the modern type of lighters.

The lighter in Mr. Murayama's collection shows wear of long use, but it still works perfectly. On the bottom side are delicately inlaid several *ume* or Japanese apricot blossoms in two colors, white and pink. It is executed not merely as a utensil, but also as a work of art.

Ancient Japanese carried these lighters when they went on journeys, picnics or hunting tours. At home they had *tabakobon* or a special box of charcoal fire for pipe lighting.

MASKS

THE JAPANESE have highly developed the art of making masks. Among art treasures of the country there are many exquisite and artistic examples. Masks are associated with religious rites, and also with dramatic performances and music. They are indispensable in *Gagaku*, the ancient music and dance introduced in the ninth century and still preserved in the original form. They are also required in *Noh* plays that were perfected in the 14th century, and also used at shrine festival performances.

The oldest masks preserved in the country are those of *Gigaku* brought from Korea in the seventh century. Masks are of two types: large masks that cover the whole head, and small masks that are placed in front of the face. *Gigaku* masks are of the large type, while others are the small face type.

Masks are used to make the wearers represent the spirit and character manifested in the music or dance. Accordingly masks made for such dramatic and musical performances were perfected artistically. Experts who produced fine masks were highly respected, and are still counted among the great artists.

Masks have also been used for other purposes, too. In praying for rain, the mask of *Ryu-o* or dragon king, who is believed to control rain, is used in many districts. At Iwate and other districts, the people used masks of *Kamado-sama* or god of the cooking stove in prayer for always having sufficient food.

In the Tokugawa days, when travel barriers were erected at different places to restrict public travel, two fierce looking masks called *Ikatsu-men* or scaring masks used to be hung at the guard office and persons questioned were forced to look up at the threatening masks so that they would tell no lies.

Children also love to wear masks in play, but such toy masks only appeared in Edo days. At first they were sold at shrines as charms for good luck, but soon became popularized as children's toys.

MATOI

FIRE-FIGHTING companies with modern equipment are organized all over the country, but there are still old-fashioned fire-fighters who wear the old costumes and follow ancient traditions. At the New Year fire brigade review and other occasions they display their acrobatic feats on top of tall bamboo ladders, each company marching after its *matoi* or standard.

The firemen's *matoi* bears the company's mark on its top, and has heavy flapping tassel-like streamers more than a meter long. The *matoi*-holder twists the handle around as he heads the procession, swaying the streamers.

The *matoi*, however, was originally used by fighting men, and it was first called *umajirushi* or horse emblem. Takeda Shingen, noted fighting lord of the 16th century, is said to have first used the *umajirushi* to mark his battle headquarters. Thus the *umajirushi* or *matoi* became a military standard to mark the position of an army leader's headquarters. Toyotomi Hideyoshi and Tokugawa Ieyasu also had their own *matoi* as their standard or emblem.

In 1719 Ooka Echizen-no-kami, governor of Edo, ordered the organization of 48 companies of fire-fighters in Edo in view of the frequent big fires that consumed many houses and killed many persons. They were civilian fire-fighters, as feudal lords had their own fire-fighting equipment.

To differentiate those 48 companies, each came to have a standard made after the *umajirushi* of warring days. Thus the firemen's *matoi* became not only their symbol but also stood for their honor and courage. In the old days, whenever a fire started, the fire company went to the spot and hoisted its *matoi* on the roof of the house where they determined to stop the spread of the fire. Many firemen perished together with their *matoi*, not willing to retreat from their battle line.

The spirit and tradition of the brave civilian fire-fighter of Edo are still retained in the *matoi* which is held in respect by the fire-fighters of Tokyo and many other big cities.

MAYUDAMA

IT IS generally on January 15 that farmers make *mayudama* (cocoon jewels) and place them at the door or in their rooms in prayer for a big cocoon crop during the year.

To make *mayudama*, little pieces of *mochi* are put on slender branches of *yanagi* (willow) or other trees. The *mochi* pieces look like small pretty flowers blossoming on the branches, but they really represent cocoons, though they do not look very much like them. In some places *mayudama* are made on other dates.

In Saitama and other districts, they make very large *mayudama*, the branches standing more than ten feet high. Generally, however, they are three to four feet high.

In Akita, 12 straws are bound together, and little pieces of *mochi* are attached to them, to represent cocoons formed on straw beds.

Mayudama were first made for the protection and safety of cocoons, and at the same time, in the hopes of getting a bountiful cocoon crop during the year.

Little pieces of colored paper are also cut in various shapes and hung on the branches. Often gift paper cut to look like old coins are tied to the branches. Images of various deities, too, are sometimes placed on the branches.

It is these decorated kinds of *mayudama* which are often seen even in city households, where the original meaning of *mayudama* has been forgotten and they are offered merely for good luck and happiness.

MERIYASU

MERIYASU is now a common term meaning any kind of knitted goods. This word is believed to have originated either from meias (Portuguese) or medias (Spanish). It was first used at Nagasaki which was the only foreign trade port during the Tokugawa days. *Meriyasu* is said to have been introduced to Edo in the Enpo era (1673-81).

At first *meriyasu* stood only for knitted socks, but it came to mean any knitted goods as it does today.

Adopting the name *meriyasu*, the Japanese picked up three Chinese characters to write out the name. They are *baku-dai-sho* or no-big-small. *Meriyasu* stretches out, and thus becomes small or big. Of course it is ridiculous to read *baku-dai-sho* as *meriyasu*, but it is generally done so even today. Lately the word has been written out in *kana*, but the Chinese characters are still seen quite often.

There is also a certain kind of song called *meriyasu*. These songs originated in the Tokugawa days, and were sung to the accompaniment of *shamisen* music. It is not clearly known how they came to be so named. Some explain that the songs could be sung short or stretched out long, as with the knitted goods. This explanation, though supported by many, is absurd. On the other hand, others say that the name *meriyasu* in this case means that the songs should be sung softly and sentimentally.

There is another strange expression, used by many Japanese in reference to wearing apparel.

It is the word *kotton* or cotton and seems to have originated in early Meiji days. But it means woolen goods. This came from the fact that fine woolen goods made by William Cotton in

England were imported then. So the people came to call good woolens 'cotton.' This is still used by some who cannot give up old habits.

MIRRORS

SINCE mythological days, Japanese have regarded mirrors as the symbol of the soul or conscience, which must be kept clear and unclouded as mirrors should be to function properly. This idea has made the people give tender care to their mirrors which they have always held in respect. What one respects must be perfect, and so, even in remote early days, wonderful mirrors in silver, iron, bronze and nickel, that not only gave clear reflection of images, but were wrought in artistic perfection were produced.

The mirror is the first of the three Imperial treasures, symbols of the Imperial Throne. Once it was thought that the possession of the Mirror, the Jewel, and the Sword made one the rightful ruler of the country. The Mirror signifies wisdom, the Jewel, technique, and the Sword, strength, it is said. Many Japanese shrines have mirrors as the symbols of their deities. Upon looking at the shrine mirror, it is said, one can see clearly his own thought in his reflected image. One who has an evil thought will be afraid to look into a mirror.

Mirrors are always associated with women everywhere. To the Japanese woman, they also stand for womanly virtue. Mirrors form the most important item among the articles a bride takes to her new home. In the old days, the family mirror was handed down from mother to daughter.

Concerning mirrors, there is a touching story. Once in the town of Matsuyama lived a widowed peddler with his daughter. Being a peddler, he had to go away on trips, leaving his daughter at home alone. Naturally the girl felt very lonesome while her father was away. The father was very sorry, and one day when he was starting on a journey, produced a box in which the mirror used by his wife had been stored since her death. Without opening the box, he told the daughter that whenever she felt lonesome while he was away, she should open the box and look inside, and then she would not be lonely as her mother would be there.

After her father left the house, she opened the box with impatience, and in the mirror inside she saw a beautiful young woman. How beautiful was her mother she thought, and smiled. Then the mother in the box smiled back at her. Since then she never felt lonesome even when her father was away.

MOKUGYO

MOKUGYO (wooden fish) is a wooden drum used at Buddhist temples which was introduced to the country in the middle of the 17th century from China, where it was used at temples to announce the hours. The hollowed fish-shaped wooden drum gives off a deep sonorous sound when beaten with a padded stick. Coming to Japan it was first used to announce meal time at *Zen* temples.

But the shape of the *mokugyo* changed in China, becoming round like a pouch in the Ming dynasty (14th-17th centuries), decorated with a dragon with two heads, and came to be used for sutra chanting.

This type of *mokugyo* is now generally seen and used in the country. It is made of camphor wood and requires expert hands to make. Some *mokugyo* are very large, reaching almost a meter across in width and have to be made out of a single piece of seasoned camphor wood.

It is said in China *mokugyo* was first used to cure Buddhist disciples of idleness, because the fish keeps its eyes always open and observes everything day and night. But the following story is also told as to its origin.

One Indian disciple failed to observe the teaching of Buddha and for punishment was turned into a fish upon his death. A big tree grew out of the fish and as the rough sea tossed the tree, the fish suffered much pain. It attributed its suffering to the failure of Buddha to teach him properly while he was a disciple.

Once when Buddha went on a boat, the fish wanted to harm him in revenge, saying that because of his bad teaching so much suffering was brought upon him. But Buddha answered that it was because the disciple had neglected his teaching that he was punished.

Realizing that he was wrong, the fish asked Buddha to save him from his suffering by making something for the Buddhist service out of the tree growing on its back. Then the fish died.

So Buddha cut the wood into the shape of a fish and used it to announce meal time to save all beastly persons.

MONPE AND KAPPOGI

MONPE, or baggy trousers for women, have become popular throughout the country since the war. Through the air-raid days, and the postwar period of *kaidashi* (going to the country to buy rice) and crowded trains, women have worn them. This kind of work trousers has been used from the olden days in various rural and particularly mountain regions. Each district has a different style and name for it, such as *fungomi*, *tattsuke monpe* and karusan, but now *monpe* seems to have become their national name. It was the war that in-

troduced them to the women of the cities and towns. Early work pants for women were mostly of leather and skins, and later made of strong hemp cloth until those of cotton became common.

Another work costume for Japanese women is the *kappogi* or cooking apron. While *monpe* were introduced from rural districts to urban areas, *kappogi* developed in cities and later was introduced to farming villages. *Kappogi* first appeared about 40 years ago, probably developing from aprons. It is a white gown-like apparel with baggy sleeves drawn tight just below the elbow. It covers only the front and side of the wearer and comes down to the knees. As its name implies, it is for wearing in the kitchen while engaged in cooking and dish washing. It was invented to protect the *kimono* from being soiled. So it is a new kind of work clothes. Originally it was worn only in the kitchen. But gradually, lazy women have made it a habit to keep it on, even after finishing cooking, or even to go shopping. This tendency of going out of the house in *kappogi* produced more elaborate ones decorated with lace and embroidery. But it should only be worn in the kitchen.

MUGIWARA-ZAIKU

AS BARLEY is harvested, rural children love to make various articles with fresh *mugiwara* or barley straw as they have few or no toys to play with. Of course, what they make by weaving *mugiwara* are generally tiny baskets, dolls or mats and such, which are crude and simple. But the weaving of such articles gives them much pleasure and also training that becomes valuable when they grow up.

In cities, too, children enjoy making things with barley straw, and *mugiwara* dyed in colors are sold in toy shops. With colored straw, they can make delightful designs. Many kindergartens use *mugiwara* weaving as one of the handicrafts for little children.

The making of toys and other things with barley straw started very early. During the Tokugawa Period a highly artistic technique of making various ornamental articles or household goods with *mugiwara* developed. Particularly the village of Omori, now included in Tokyo Metropolis, was famous for its *mugiwara* products, which were eagerly purchased by the people.

At the same time, the art of pasting flattened and colored straw cut in various shapes on wooden boxes and other articles appeared.

Then in the Meiji era, barley straw braids for making ladies' hats and baskets became important export items.

For these articles, it is always barley straw that is used. Wheat straw is never used, as the latter is too stiff and unsuitable for turning it into delicate shapes.

While rice straw is widely used for making ropes, mats and other articles that are indispensable to the people's life, barley straw is utilized for making toys and ornamental goods. Thus the two kinds of straw have their respectively different fields of utility, and both are sources of much income to farmers.

NAGAMOCHI

NAGAMOCHI (long chest) is now seen only as an ancient relic in old families or among museum collections, but up to the early Meiji era, it was an important household necessity. It is a big long box, about a meter high, a meter wide, and two meters long, with shallow hinged covers. *Nagamochi* originally meant anything long so that containers to hold long objects came to be so named.

At first the Japanese people placed their clothing and valuables in hemp bags. The term *o-fukuro* (bag keeper) is still used for mothers because they were in charge of the clothes and other treasures of the family. Then bamboo baskets came to be used for that purpose.

Nagamochi appeared first in the 11th or 12th century, as *Azuma-kagami* mentions its existence in 1186. At first it might have been of woven bamboos, as a *kago-nagamochi* (basket *nagamochi*) is mentioned in old records.

Generally, *nagamochi* was made of paulownia wood because of its lightness and moisture-resisting quality, and also of white fir wood. As *nagamochi* becomes quite heavy when fully loaded, those with small wheels underneath appeared to facilitate moving it.

As they became a commonly used container for preserving clothing and other articles, those used by the wealthy and aristrocratic became elaborate and artistic. Many were beautifully lacquered with family crests in gold, strengthened with ornamental metal pieces along the edges. It was the pride of parents to have many *nagamochi* holding clothes and valuables for a daughter to take to her new home on marriage.

Tansu or chest of drawers, which later came to be more commonly used than the big *nagamochi*, appeared only 300 years ago. It is also made of paulownia wood and comes in sections. Generally two or three sections are piled on top of each other. One section is about a meter high and half a meter deep.

At first the *tansu* was also of basket work and used for storing books. Gradually it developed and came to be used to hold clothing exclusively. As *nagamochi* disappeared in the Meiji era, it was replaced by the *tansu*.

NENNEKO

THE JAPANESE baby is still tied to the back of its big sister or mother. In warm weather, it is tied to the back with a soft cotton band, but in the colder season, it is covered with *nenneko* or a big loose padded coatlike wrapper. For daily use, plain cotton ones, often much soiled, are used, but when the baby is taken on a visit, silk *nenneko* with bright designs is used.

In most households it is the elder sister's task to look after the baby, and she goes around with her little charge tied on her back. Sometimes, a girl is employed as *komori* (baby nurse) to carry the baby.

Of course, there are many different styles of *nenneko* according to districts, not only in the fabrics used but also in the shape.

In some Kanto and northeastern regions the custom of the mother or some other woman carrying the baby in the bosom of her own dress is still seen. Particularly in the Nagasaki district, mothers carry their babies in their bosoms whenever they go out of the house. Sometimes naked babies are held close to the skin of the mothers.

This custom of keeping babies close to the mothers' bodies is said to have come from the belief that the baby's soul is unsettled and feels uneasy, and thus is always trying to escape. So it must be kept close to the mother's body.

All Japanese babies seem to be very comfortably tied to their mother's back. Long used to the habit, the mothers too are able to do all their housework and even field labor with their babies tied on their backs.

NINGYO-FUDE

THE DISTRICT of Arima in Hyogo Prefecture, is famous for production of *fude* or writing brushes. Because good bamboo for making *fude* is grown there, the industry has prospered from very early days. In feudal days, men selling *Arima-fude* traveled all over the country. They also taught the art of *fude* making to other people. Writing brushes are still beautifully made in the region. The bamboo is first boiled, washed in water, bleached in sulphur and then polished.

Ningyo-fude or doll-brushes were formerly a special product of Arima and were highly appreciated by people all over the country. But unfortunately it is no longer made, as it requires skill and delicate work. Only some old families still keep them as old relics.

Ningyo-fude were gaily decorated with silk threads of different colors, and when one held it upright in a writing position, a tiny doll appeared from its top end. When it was laid down sideways, the doll disappeared. This interesting and pretty *fude* came to be treasured as an ornamental plaything.

As to its origin, it is said that the consort of Emperor Jomei (593-641) had no child, but after visiting Arima she gave birth to a boy, who was named Prince Arima. A *fude*-maker of Arima named Isuke called his brush *ningyo-fude* to celebrate the birth of Prince Arima.

But there is another story. A certain young prince did not like studying calligraphy and his teacher had a hard time making him try his brush. He contrived a novel *fude* which produced a little doll when held upright to write. This amused the little prince. To see the doll come out, he held his *fude* and wrote many characters.

OBI CUSTOMS

OBI IS THE symbol of Japanese women, and also the most decorative part of their costume. At first all tied their loose *kimono* with cords made of hemp threads. Then in the Nara period in the eighth century, court officials used leather bands when they adopted new dress fashioned after the Chinese style. Then commoners and women began to wear wider *obi* of woven cloth.

A woman's *obi* became different from men's in about the 15th century — wider and ornamental in color and design.

At first the ancient people tied their girdle cords as well as the *obi* in front. Children first started to tie theirs behind and older folks imitated the children's way.

But the ancient way of tying *obi* in front is still kept up in some rural districts. In some places, on the wedding day, the bride ties her *obi* in front. In Saga and other places, when a husband dies, the widow ties her *obi* in front for three days. Thus the name of *'goke-obi'* (widow's *obi*) is still used.

In many regions when girls reach their third year, an *obi* is presented by relatives to celebrate the happy occasion. The seven-five-three celebration held for children in autumn also started from this idea of regarding *obi*-wearing as a mark of their growth.

As *yuino* or betrothal present, an *obi* is still sent by the groom's family to the bride's parents. There was also an old habit of a man who received an *obi* from a woman keeping it in a box and letting no other person see it.

As the *obi* is valued, it was said that if one made clothing out of it she would die soon. When a wife died, her *obi* was torn in pieces and placed in her coffin in some regions.

In many localities, on festival days, little girls go to the shrine, shouldering the rich *obi* of their families. Then, in some villages the wife of the headman carried offerings to the shrine on the festival day, displaying her best *obi* on her shoulder.

PAPER

JAPANESE paper is unique, and its soft but strong quality has won it world fame. The paper industry of Japan is 13 centuries old, and it is remarkable that the original hand-making process is still used.

There are many kinds of Japanese paper, from thick parchment-like ones to almost transparent thin sheets. A great deal is exported.

The oldest paper made in Japan is known as hemp paper, as it was made of hemp fiber. The Buddhist sutra printed in 727 was on this type of paper, and at the Shosoin, Nara, where many treasures of the Nara era (710-794) are preserved, more than 1,000 sheets of hemp paper are kept.

The art of paper making is said to have been introduced to Japan by a Korean priest in 610. But even in those early days, the Japanese people never used hemp rags to make paper. They used the vegetable fibers of the hemp directly. Thus from the very beginning, Japanese paper came to possess its own distinct characteristics.

Soon the bark fiber of *kozo* or paper mulberry came to be recognized as a better material than hemp fiber for making good paper. *Kozo* paper is smoother and easier to write on than the old hemp paper. Thus Shotoku-taishi (573-621) encouraged the cultivation of paper mulberry in view of the increasing demand for paper for printing Buddhist sutras.

When the Meiji government started

to print paper money, the supply of *kozo* paper was not sufficient to meet the demand, and the Government Printing Office started to use paper made of *mitsumata* fiber. Since then all bank notes of Japan are of *mitsumata* paper.

There are also various other kinds of Japanese paper made from different vegetable fibers. They are mostly handmade. *Kozo* and *mitsumata* however are the principal materials used.

The most widely known kinds of Japanese paper are *hosho, ganpi, kyokushi, tengujo, nishinouchi,* and *minogami.* They all have their own special characteristics. Their uses, too, are different.

The material for paper-making is pulp made from *kozo* (paper mulberry), *ganpi* (Miktroemia gampi), and *mitsumata* (Edgewortha crythantha). Straw or rags are never used. The bark of these trees is immersed in water and wood ash. Then it is placed in a running stream for two days and nights. The bark thus cleaned is beaten by wooden mallets until it becomes pulp. To the pulp is added the proper quantity of water and a starch made from tree roots and bark.

Then the paper-making screen frame is put into a tub of the pulp solution by hand. The frame is moved up and down and in all directions. The sheets thus made are piled up, and when dry, each sheet is peeled off.

Japanese paper is strong because the fibers used are long, and furthermore all fibers are interwoven and locked together firmly in the process of tossing the screening frame in all directions in the tub. The primitive method still used after 13 centuries is scientifically approved.

Districts where paper is produced are Kochi, Ehime, Gifu, Tottori and Saitama, where the necessary trees are cultivated, and where good running streams are found.

PEARLS

SHINJU or pearls are now used as ornaments. The gem of the sea was regarded in old Japan as sacred and used as offerings to *kami* or gods.

The Japanese people must have known about pearls since very early days as they ate shellfish and must have found pearls in the shells they opened. But it is not clearly known since when *shinju* came to be used as offering to *kami.*

In the *Nihon-shoki* (Ancient Record) a tale about *shinju* is mentioned. In 423 Emperor Ingyo went to Awaji Island in the Inland Sea to hunt. On the mountains he saw many deer, monkeys and boars. But as the party went up, they could find no trace of the animals.

The emperor could not understand why the game had disappeared and asked a diviner to find out. The diviner said that the *kami* of the mountain was angry, and he must be pacified by an offering of a pearl from the sea.

So fishermen were gathered and sent into the sea to find a pearl. But the sea was deep and none could reach the bottom. A fisherman named Osashi appeared and jumped into the water, tying a long rope around his waist. He reached the bottom and found a large abalone shell that contained a magnificent pearl. He tugged at his rope to be pulled up, but he died before he reached the surface. It was found that the bottom was 60 fathoms deep.

The pearl brought up by Osashi was presented to the *kami* of the mountain by the emperor. The *kami's* anger calmed down and soon many deer and boars appeared. The imperial hunting party bagged many animals.

There are many other tales in which pearls are used as offerings to divine deities. Pearls seem to have been also used as ornaments since very early days.

Pearl oysters (Pinctada Martensi) that produce the best kind of pearls are called *Akoya-gai* in Japan, after Akoya Bay, Shizuoka Prefecture, where the best of the shell-fish is abundantly found.

Pearls are found in oysters, abalones and other kinds of shell-fish, and it is natural to expect that early Japanese inhabitants must have found pearls in some of the shells they opened for eating. But in early days they were used only in a very limited way. They were pulverized for use as medicine although it is not known for what illness pearls were believed to be good.

Since ancient days, many people all over the world have believed that pearls breathe and that they will die and disintegrate if kept long in closed boxes. Pearls contain moisture or oil, and when they are kept dry too long, they will lose their luster and their value is reduced. Thus many believe that pearls have to be constantly handled and kept close to the human skin to enable them to 'breathe' or obtain moisture.

In Japan where the air is humid there is practically no danger of pearls becoming dry. But this belief that contact with the human skin will keep pearls in good condition has now been disproved. Human sweat contains acid which is harmful to pearls. So pearl lovers are advised to wipe them with a dry soft cloth or wash them in water. No harm is done to pearls by immersing them in plain or soapy water.

PILLOWS

THE ANCIENT Japanese used bundles of straw or wooden blocks as pillows. Often in families with many children or apprentices, the young people slept with their heads on a long log, and the father or employer would strike one end of it with a hammer to wake them up in the morning, it is recorded.

As wood block pillows generally in use were heavy, a new type called *hako-makura* or box pillow was invented. Oblong wooden boxes, about five or six inches high, two inches wide and eight inches long, becoming smaller at the top, were made for women. For comfort a small pad stuffed with beaten straw, cotton or beans was attached on top. Those for men were not so high.

The *hako-makura* was improved in appearance to become delicate and beautiful in shape and make, and decorated with lacquer and designs. Some had little drawers for keeping various toilet articles or medicines. The pillows were made quite high purposely because they were placed outside the *futon* or Japanese mattress stuffed with beaten straw or cotton.

This type of *makura* was used becaue the people, both male and female, dressed their hair elaborately in olden times and they did not wish to spoil the coiffure while sleeping. They rested their neck on the *hako-makura* while their head would be free.

Children who did not dress their hair as well as adults had *kukuri-makura*, bag-like pillows, made by stuffing well-beaten straw, beans or buckwheat hulls.

Hako-makura was used by many men up to the beginning of the Meiji era when the custom of knotting their hair was abolished. But women kept using them all through the Meiji period, as they still did their hair up in the old way. *Hako-makura* is still used by a few old women who keep up the ancient hair fashion. Soft, flat pillows are now commonly used by all.

Porcelain pillows introduced from

China are still used by many, particularly in summer, because they are cooling.

POCKET WARMERS

MANY Japanese love their *kairo* or pocket warmers during the cold winter months. Generally it comes in a handy small metal box which can be easily put into the bosom or back of Japanese dress, or the pocket of a Western style suit. It radiates comfortable warmth, and keeps warm without refilling for many hours. There are larger types which are used to warm beds the whole night long.

It is an ingenious invention of Japan, first making its appearance in the Genroku era (1688-1703) of the Tokugawa days. It is not known who invented it. The secret of *kairo* lies in the *kairobai*, the special charcoal that burns inside the box. This comes in a small cylindrical paper-covered form, about three inches long. *Kairobai* is made by baking the calyx of eggplants into charcoal and pulverizing it. This powdered charcoal burns very well and very slowly when only a little supply of air is given. The *kairo* container has several tiny holes, but even if the box is wrapped up in thick flannel or other kinds of cloth, it never goes out.

The greatest feature of *kairo* is that it is always comfortably warm, never getting too hot. It can even be kept on one's stomach or back, directly over the underwear the whole day. Even today many folks in the country cannot go without their *kairo* in winter despite many other means of warming themselves.

Other kinds of *kairo* that use gasoline or other chemicals have appeared in recent years, but the new kinds have never become as popular as the old-fashioned one, because all of them soon become too hot and uncomfortable, or give out an unpleasant odor.

RICE STRAW

THE JAPANESE people have learned since early days the value of *wara* or rice-plant stalks left after threshing as material for making things for their daily use. No other rice-growing people have used *wara* so extensively and efficiently as the Japanese.

The Japanese people and particularly those of farming villages cannot live a single day without the use of many things made of the straw. The making of things with rice straw has been the night-work of farmers and their households. Of course, some straw products have recently been made by machinery, but still farming people love to make them at home during long winter evenings.

First in importance is the making of the straw rope which is invariably used in tying up farm products. In packing and shipping various goods, the rope is absolutely necessary. *Mushiro* or straw matting comes next. They are made generally in a size of three by six feet, but vary in thickness. Farmers use *mushiro* for spreading cereals and other things out to dry. The mats are also widely used in wrapping up boxes and other things for shipment. The base of *tatami* or floor mats is made of straw, packed hard to a thickness of about two and a half inches. *Zori* and *waraji* or Japanese sandals made of straw are worn by the rural people. The snow-shoes of Japan are of straw, and very warm and comfortable. *Noren* or straw screens are also made, but they are gradually going out of fashion.

A peculiar custom of sleeping in straw is still popular among the rural people of the cold northern regions. The straw is first beaten well to make it soft. The bedroom which has only a bare wooden floor is filled with the beaten straw to a depth of two to three feet and when the time to sleep comes, the people take off their day clothes and, naked, bury themselves in the straw. It is said that under the straw covering they are warm and comfortable. On sunny days, the straw is taken out of the room, and aired in the sun, so that it will be dry. Many of the people prefer the primitive covering of loose straw to ordinary *futon* thickly padded with cotton.

SANDALS

ZORI or sandals are most characteristic of Japanese footwear. There are many kinds, from crude ones woven of straw or bamboo sheath to elaborate kinds made of felt, leather and brocade silk. Wealthy ladies have many pairs to match the colors and designs of *kimono*.

Zori developed from *ashinaka* (half sole) that was widely used by all kinds of people since about 800 years ago. *Ashinaka* is a sort of small straw *zori*, enough to cover the front half of the foot, leaving the heel unprotected. Generals, officials and all classes, men and women, wore it, as shown in old paintings. The statue of Saigo Takamori, the early Meiji leader, at Ueno Park shows him wearing them, as it was still commonly used in his native place of Kagoshima.

This strange footwear surprised early Chinese and Portuguese visitors, many of whom wrote about them. It is said that such accounts of *ashinaka* gave foreigners the impression that the Japanese people had no heels.

As full-length *zori* and *geta* developed in the Tokugawa era, however, *ashinaka* went out of fashion in big towns, but has been used in rural districts until today. But now it is only used in wading into shallow rivers or climbing steep, slippery mountain lanes. Thus it is used not as footwear to protect their feet, but as a spike to prevent slipping.

Waraji, straw sandal with a heel guard and laces for trying, that also developed from *ashinaka*, was formerly widely used in foot traveling, and is now seen only in farming areas. Both *ashinaka* and *waraji* are being fast replaced by *jikatabi* or rubber-soled *tabi*, that was introduced some 50 years ago. *Tabi* was originally of leather and worn outdoors only, and the indoor *tabi* appeared in the Tokugawa period. *Jikatabi* may be called the revival of the original *tabi*.

SUKIIRE-GAMI

JAPAN produces many kinds of handmade paper famed for its beauty, toughness and durability. One of the most unique and highly decorative is *sukiire-gami* which has beautiful leaves, blossoms, insects and other foreign matter inserted in the process of its manufacture.

Though encased between layers of paper fibers, the shapes and colors of the inserts are plainly visible and the colors do not change for many years.

The manufacture of such decorative paper started very early. It is recorded that Emperor Godaigo (14th century) while at the Yoshino Palace ordered paper with bright ivy leaves inserted in its fibers. Since then many poets have used *tanjaku*, the oblong paper for writing poems, made of *sukiire-gami*.

In the Tokugawa era, many feudal lords used to hold elaborate *Noh* drama parties, and often the invitation cards or entrance tickets were made of *sukiire-gami*. The paper embedded with colored leaves, pine needles, *sakura* blossoms, apricot flowers and such came to be very widely used by aristocrats and men of letters during the Bunka-Bunsei era, that is the early 19th century.

However, sheets of paper inserted with butterflies and other insects are of recent origin. The Nawa Museum of Entomology at Gifu first manufactured these. Not only butterflies found in Japan, but also those of other countries are used.

Nagano Prefecture produces fine paper with inserted colorful leaves and blossoms.

SUMI-NAGASHI

SUMI-NAGASHI (India-ink flow) is an old but neglected art. In recent years, however, it has been revived and is being applied in new ways.

This is the art of transferring to paper designs formed by liquid *sumi* spread over the surface of water in a basin. Weird and charming designs are printed on white paper when it is placed over the water.

It is not clear when this art originated but it is known that in the 12th century it had already attained a high degree of development. The earliest known specimens are preserved at the Nishi-Honganji Temple, Kyoto.

It is a volume of poems by 36 poets, believed to have been written in about 1110, or more than 850 years ago. The poems are written on sheets of paper having *sumi-nagashi* designs.

The method of making *sumi-nagashi* is simple. First an ink stick is rubbed on ink stone with a little water. Sometimes pine resin is added to the prepared ink. The tip of a *fude* or writing brush that has absorbed the ink is dipped into water in a flat basin and the ink spreads in a circle in the water. As the brush is pulled out, a slender bamboo or wooden stick like chopsticks is passed through

one's hair to make it slightly oily.

The tip of this stick is passed slowly through the ink blot on the water and the ink spreads out, due to the effect of the oil on the stick. As the artist moves the stick through the basin water, fantastic designs develop.

Black ink is mostly used, but often various colors are also added to make the design more complicated and beautiful. When a desired design appears, a sheet of white paper is placed flat on the water surface, and the design is transferred to the paper. The value of *sumi-nagashi* lies in the fact that every time the design changes, and there are no two alike.

In place of paper, a piece of cotton or silk fabric may be used. *Sumi-nagashi* paper, silk or cotton are used for various decorative purposes.

While this art of *sumi-nagashi* has almost been forgotten by the people for many centuries, the family of Hiroba in Fukui Prefecture has kept it up. Jizaemon Hiroba, the present head of the family, was recently honored as a National Cultural Asset.

SUMINAWA

SUMINAWA (ink thread) is a unique and indispensable tool of Japanese carpenters. This device is used to draw straight lines on logs and boards. It has been used in Japan since very early days, as it is mentioned in the *Manyoshu.* It is also recorded that it was in use in the reign of Emperor Yuryaku in the fifth century. But this ancient tool is still used by all Japanese carpenters, masons and others.

Suminawa is made of wood, and although ready-made ones are for sale, many carpenters like to make their own. It has a shallow bowl in the center for holding cotton soaked in *sumi* or ink. At one end is a thin spool around which a long, thin but strong thread is wound. The end of the thread goes through a hole to the ink bowl, and then out at the other end, through another hole. To the end coming out of the second hole is attached a strong and sharp pin.

To draw a straight line on a board, for instance, the pin is firmly pushed in at the point where the line is to start, and then the thread is pulled out to another spot where the line is to end. The thread is stretched tight, and then it is picked up with the fingers and lifted a few inches, preferably near the center of its length. It is then released suddenly to snap back, resulting in a clear straight line drawn the whole length. The advantage of using this method is that, even on a slightly uneven surface, the line can be clearly made.

The thread can be made as long as desired or as long as the spool can hold. A straight line can be drawn twenty or thirty feet or longer on timber or board.

With *suminawa* is also used a pen made of bamboo. The writing part is a flat bamboo, about one-third of an inch wide, and is very thin, coming to a knife-like edge. This blade-like edge is split minutely crossways. These cuts hold ink, and by drawing the blade length-wise, a line or figures can be drawn. Carpenters use this for putting marks on boards.

SWORDS

JAPANESE swords are world-famous because of their superior quality. Long years of internal fighting developed the art of sword-making in Japan. Good swords must cut through steel armor and helmets. So sword-smiths did their best to produce the needed swords.

It was particularly in the 12th and 13th centuries that great sword-smiths produced masterpieces. They became more than weapons, considered as art masterpieces and family treasures. Yet the fame of Japanese swords is not traditional or sentimental. It is scientifically proved that there is no equal in the world.

There are good reasons why Japanese swords are so superior, according to Kosuke Iwasaki, a great authority on Japanese swords. The first is that Japanese swords are made of *tamahagane* or steel refined from sand-iron which is almost pure. Then in refining charcoal is used. Another point is that the refining is done at a low temperature. These three points have served to produce steel which is almost absolutely pure. Sand-iron produced in the province of Izumo is regarded the best.

Master sword-smiths developed their secret techniques to produce with *tamahagane* so obtained, good swords that do not bend or break, however roughly used, and are sharp and strong enough to cut through anything.

Some Japanese wood sculptors use only tools made of *tama-hagane*, finding them superior to any other kind. Iwasaki also says that safety razor blades made of *tama-hagane* cut better and last longer than any foreign make. So he predicts wider use for *tamahagane* in the future.

TABI

THE JAPANESE custom of wearing *tabi* or socks indoors is comparatively modern. For many centuries the people were required to be barefooted when they wore formal attire. It was taboo by common etiquette to wear *tabi* in the presence of others. It is recorded that in the Imperial Court of the Muromachi period in the 16th century, *tabi* were absolutely prohibited. It was also forbidden in the Tokugawa Shogun's palace. Only those of extremely advanced age or those who were sick could wear *tabi* in the Imperial Court or in the Edo Castle of the Tokugawa Shogun, with special permission.

The history of *tabi* is very old. At first, used only for outdoor wear, they were made of leather. The shape was the same as the present *tabi* but made deeper to cover the ankle. They were always taken off as one entered a house. Gradually, however, they came to be used indoors too. Of course the indoor *tabi* were never used outdoors. Then, as the indoor *tabi* appeared, the outdoor *tabi* lost their popularity.

It was in the Tokugawa period that *tabi* made of cotton fabric were introduced. Tradition has it that it was due to the scarcity of leather that cotton and silk were used to make *tabi*. Throughout the Tokugawa days, although the indoor use of *tabi* became very common, it was still the rule of etiquette to be barefooted. In the Meiji period, this rule was generally discarded, kept up only by *geishas* to the beginning of the 20th century. *Geisha* girls were then still proud of their strict manner of going barefoot to the parties they were invited to.

Now it has become customary to wear *tabi* on formal occasions. Usually men wear black *tabi*, and women white. But on ceremonial occasions men have come to wear white *tabi* too. *Tabi* of other colors are worn only at home.

The size of the *tabi* is measured in *mon*, an ancient copper coin valued at one-tenth of one sen, laying coins in a line to measure the *tabi* length.

TAKE-NO-KAWA

THE TENDER bamboo sprout, as it emerges from the soil in spring, is protected by a layer of leaf-like sheaths called *take-no-kawa*. As the sprout

grows, the sheaths attached to each joint fall off, one by one, as it does not need protection any more. The sheaths of some species of bamboo are as large as a foot wide and two feet long. They are thin but very strong.

Take-no-kawa is utilized in Japan in many ways. The widest use is for wrapping up meats, fish and other foodstuffs. Particularly for meat shops, *take-no-kawa* is indispensable in wrapping up sliced meat. it is also used in packing *musubi* or rice-balls when they are taken for lunch.

As its fiber is very strong, *take-no-kawa* is torn into narrow strips and woven into *zori* or sandals which are worn in rural districts. On long winter evenings, farmers and particularly womenfolk weave these *zori* for their families, and sometimes market them. *Take-no-kawa* strips are used in tying up many different things.

Big flat hats woven of *take-no-kawa* strips are widely used by farmers and other outdoor workers in summer. They are light and strong, withstanding the sun and rain.

A round flat pad covered with *take-no-kawa* is still used in rubbing down paper on woodcut blocks in the process of printing *ukiyoe* and other woodcut pictures.

Take-no-kawa has also come to be used for various decorative purposes. Lamp shades and other household goods made of *take-no-kawa* have rustic charm.

TANZEN AND DOTERA

TANZEN or *dotera* is informal *kimono* that is worn indoors only. It seems to have been first made early in the Tokugawa era, and from the very beginning it was called 'informal wear for the commoner.' It is worn over *yukata* or plain cotton *kimono* after taking a bath in cool or cold weather, or for sleeping.

However, at hot spring resorts, it has recently become almost a common habit for all visitors, men and women, to take walks or go out shopping in these informal *kimono* supplied by the hotels. There is no denying it is very pleasant, after taking a bath, to wear only *yukata* and throw a *tanzen* over it if the weather gets cool.

This informal *kimono* is generally thickly padded with open sleeves, made somewhat larger than ordinary *kimono* for comfort. It has one distinct feature in that the neck is faced with black cloth.

It is generally called *dotera* in Kansai districts, but is known as *tanzen* in Kanto. The following story is related concerning the origin of the word *tanzen*.

In the Kan-ei era (1624-1644), a public bathhouse was opened in front of the residence of Lord Matsudaira of Tango, in Kanda, Edo. This bathhouse came to be known as *Tanzen* (in front of Tan), meaning that it was just across the street from the residence of Tango-no-kami.

At the time many public bathhouses had a second-floor rest area where the bathers sat down and had tea while resting after their bath. Some of such houses had women to attend on the patrons, and thus became quite gay places.

At the *Tanzen* bathhouse, visitors wore these comfortable *kimono* after the bath. As the *Tanzen* bathhouse was particularly famous, the dress came to be called *tanzen*. This bathhouse, however, was soon closed by the authorities because it became too gay.

TASUKI

TASUKI or sashes used by housewives and maids in tucking up their sleeves allow them the free motion of arms and also keeps the sleeves from getting soiled. They are of indispensable convenience for women who still wear *kimono* at home, particularly in doing household work. The narrow sashes or cords are passed over the shoulders and under the armpits to form a cross at the back, tying up the sleeves away from the wrists and close to the body.

Tasuki have been used since the earliest period, but originally not by housewives. At first they were used to keep offerings to *kami* or shrines pure and clean. In ancient days, the people wore tunics with narrow and close-fitting sleeves and there were no flapping long and wide sleeves. But in performing the sacred duty of presenting offerings to *kami*, the priests or officials tied up their sleeves with *tasuki* so that the sleeve cuffs should not touch the offerings. They were never used on any other occasion or for any other purpose.

In the early Tokugawa days when the common people commenced to wear *kimono* with wide and long sleeves in their daily life, the ancient *tasuki* were adopted for convenience in household tasks. Women in doing kitchen work or sweeping the rooms wore them so that they could work more efficiently and also keep their sleeves from being soiled. Men too, used them in their indoor or outdoor work.

Thus *tasuki* have become a symbol of manual labor. No one is permitted to receive guests or make calls wearing *tasuki*. When a maid is called by her mistress, she must take off her *tasuki* before making her appearance. Today men seldom use *tasuki* because they have special clothes for manual work, so it is now mostly the women who use *tasuki* which are still quite indispensable to them.

TATARA STEEL

THE MYTHOLOGICAL legend of Susano-no-mikoto, brother of Amaterasu-omikami killing Yamata-no-orochi or a giant eight-headed snake to save the people from its destruction, and finding in its tail a sword named Murakumo, is well known. He presented the sword to Amaterasu-omikami.

But in the mountains of Izumo where this is believed to have taken place, the first iron and steel industry of the country developed. In the region of Torigami, Izumo, there remains the legend of early iron making by the so-called Tatara process. In that district a few old men who have learned the traditional steel-making method are still found.

Tatara steel was not only the first steel made in the country, but is of a very fine quality. It is made of iron sand that is found abundantly in those mountains. Ancient iron makers concentrated the iron sand in water troughs, and fired it in a crudely made mud furnace with charcoal. Slugs thus obtained were crushed by water mills and then refined in a primitive charcoal kiln, fanned by tall bellows.

Tatara originally referred to the bellows, and then the word was used to indicate the hut in which the bellows and kiln were housed.

It was with Tatara steel that later people made not only household utensils, but also swords and armor. Famous Japanese swords owe to Tatara steel their excellent quality.

Iron sand found in the mountains in Izumo is still famous, and is mined even nowadays to produce a fine quality pig iron for producing special steels.

TENUGUI

TENUGUI or Japanese towels are not only used in bathing and washing or wiping the face and hands, but also in covering the head against the sun or rain.

Tenugui is said to have been introduced in the eighth century from China where it was used at official rites.

In the Heian period in the ninth century, its use became general, but it was used only at various rites and services as in placing offerings, cleaning utensils for Buddhist services, for receiving the hair cut off at the service performed on entering Buddhist life, and also as offerings to temples and priests.

Tenugui for these purposes made of white cloth, mostly hemp, were from three to 13 feet in length.

It was in the Kamakura period (12th to 14th century) that tenugui came to be adopted for wider and practical uses. It was used as a head covering, or bound around the head when one was engaged in any strenuous physical labor to stop the sweat from streaming down. It was also used to bind the hands of captured enemies or criminals to prevent their escape. It also came to be generally used in bathing. Thus its length naturally became short.

At the same time, the original ceremonial use of the tenugui was also popularized. It came to be widely used for gifts to persons going on journeys, or as presents to be taken on making visits, or as otoshidama (New Year presents). As its use widened, many families dyed their family crests on their tenugui which were given to others as offerings or presents. Thus tenugui in colored design appeared. They became beautiful and were used by persons attending outdoor affairs such as cherry blossom parties.

In the Edo period, *tenugui* was very popularly used as presents or gifts on all occasions. Because of this habit, the people today often give western-style towels instead of *tenugui.*

Originally, however, they were much longer, reaching five or six feet in length, while the ones in present use are three feet long. In the old days they were mostly used to cover the head, particularly by women.

At first they were used by the common people only, but since the middle of the Tokugawa period or the beginning of the 18th century, they came to be used by the *samurai* class also, as their use became manifold. Originally *tenugui* were made of cotton cloth, either white, unbleached or in plain colors such as blue or pink. In the middle of the Tokugawa period they came to have two or three bands of colors as designs or with each half in a different color. Then *tenugui* with simple designs of flowers and birds were introduced.

In the latter Tokugawa period, with the influence of *Kabuki* dramas, there appeared silk *tenugui*, which were of course ornamental and had elaborate designs. Then the practice of printing shop names on *tenugui* developed, and since then they have been much used for advertising purposes.

The designing of *tenugui* is very difficult as the design must show well whether they be spread out or folded. In the first part of the Meiji era, *tenugui* makers formed a society to study their design, and many artistic or delicate *tenugui* designs were produced. However, those well-designed *tenugui* are now no longer seen, and today their advertising value seems to be given more consideration than their artistic appearance.

TRUNKS

TSUZURA is the original Japanese trunk to keep and carry clothing and other things. At first, *tsuzura* was woven of strips of vines and leather. Later it became lighter as bamboo and wood were used. When the basic basket work is completed, the whole thing is covered with thick Japanese paper, and then heavily lacquered, mostly in reddish brown. It came in an oblong shape with a cover that was almost as deep as the body.

It was in the Kamakura period, or about 700 years ago, that *tsuzura*-making greatly developed due to its having become a popular household necessity. During the Tokugawa period, *tsuzura* was indispensable in transporting the clothing and other articles of feudal lords and their retainers who had to travel to Edo from their territories every other year. Brides also brought their clothes and belongings in *tsuzura.*

The early *tsuzura* were big, but gradually they became smaller for convenience in transporting. Generally it was three to four feet long, one to one and a half feet wide, and about a foot deep. There were much larger ones too. Recent makes are much smaller.

Even with the introduction of Western bags and trunks, the *tsuzura* is still used by certain groups of people. Of course old families still have ancient *tsuzura* as they last a long time. It is still indispensable for theatrical people who have to travel often with their costumes.

In the Kansai or Osaka district, many merchants still use *tsuzura* in carrying their merchandise.

Kori is quite similar to *tsuzura* in shape, but is made much simpler with strips of bamboo, vines or other materials. *Kori* is generally not painted or lacquered.

URUSHI

THE *URUSHI* or lacquer tree is found all over the country. One is often poisoned when one unknowingly touches it while walking through wooded regions. The plant also existed in China, and long before the Christian era, the Chinese had lacquered wares, it is said. In Japan the *urushi* dates back only to the time of Emperor Keiko (71-130). Yet it is Japan that developed the art of lacquering, and thus japan is used as a term for lacquer.

When Yamato-takeruno-mikoto was dispatched by Emperor Keiko to subjugate hostile tribes in the mountains of Yamato, his forces had to advance through dense forests cutting down trees that obstructed their way. One of his men broke a branch and there appeared a sticky and milky juice. This juice came to be applied on wooden and other wares. The value of *urushi* was immediately appreciated and *urushibe* or lacquer workers appeared.

Soon plain turned wooden bowls used for holding food came to be covered with lacquer. In the Nara period of the seventh century, the art of lacquer work developed highly. With the mixture of oil and pigments, various colors were produced and not only tableware but also boxes, ornaments and other things came to be beautifully lacquered. Such artistic lacquer products of the period are still preserved at the Horyu-ji and Shoso-in.

At the same time, Chinese lacquerware was also introduced and served to improve the Japanese technique. In the Tokugawa period, beginning in the 17th century, lacquerware came to be popularly used. Many districts started producing their particular types of lac-querware. The lacquer industry became so important that the Tokugawa shogunate set up an *urushi-bugyo* or lacquer administrator.

Lacquer has the excellent qualities of beautiful luster, resistance to moisture and acid, and producing a hard surface. *Urushi* juice is milky white when obtained by making cuts on the tree, but becomes black as it is stirred and hardened in moisture at a certain temperature. Thus in the old days, lacquer juice was treated in a bath tub.

The female *urushi* trees bear little berries from which a wax which was also very widely used was formerly obtained.

VEILED WOMEN

MEN AND women wear *tenugui* or Japanese towels over their heads when they work outdoors to protect themselves from the sun and insects. In many northeastern districts women wear larger square pieces of cotton cloths, something like a *furoshiki* or wrapping cloth, over their heads, folding them into a triangular shape. In some places long white cotton pieces are used for the same purpose.

But in Akita, Yamagata and other places the strange custom of women veiling their faces completely with only narrow openings for the eyes still remains. Long pieces of white cotton fabrics are used and skillfully wrapped to leave only narrow slits for the eyes.

The veil is called *hankotanna* (face band). Of course the veiling is to protect their faces from the sun and insect bites, but this story is told as to its origin.

The local lord was fond of beautiful women, and whenever he saw a beautiful girl on a street or farm, he would call her and keep her in his mansion. All the women became afraid to be noticed by him and began to veil their faces so that they would not attract his attention.

Whatever its origin, it is notable that the habit is followed only in these regions, and is not known in most parts of the country.

But the custom of brides covering and hiding their faces is still seen in many districts. In Aomori, the bride wears a *katsugi* or veil dress over her head. A *katsugi* is a veil made of a very thin fabric and worn loosely over the head and shoulders so that the face is invisible. She takes it off only when she enters the groom's house.

In Okinawa, too, the bride wears a thin hemp veil over her head at the wedding ceremony. Also at funerals women wear white cotton cloths over the head to hide their faces.

WOOD VARIETIES

WOOD being the most abundantly and easily obtainable material for the Japanese people, they have used it to build their houses and make various implements and tools. From long experience in using wood, they have learned the different qualities of various kinds of wood and found the most suitable kind for particular purposes.

For houses, they have found that *hinoki* (cypress) and *sugi* (cryptomeria) are the most beautiful, durable and strong. Thus even today these woods are used for the better kind of wooden structures.

For *tansu* (chest of drawers) and boxes, *kiri* (paulownia) wood is used, because *kiri* wood protects the goods in such containers from moisture, and also has a beautiful grain. For chopsticks *sugi* and *yanagi* (willow) wood are used, because both kinds are soft and flexible.

For carving *han* (seals) and *hangi*

(wood blocks for printing), *tsuge* (box-tree) is used because of its fine texture. *Tsuge* is also used in making the pieces for *shogi* or Japanese chess. Also *ume* or apricot and *sakura* (cherry) woods have been largely used for making woodblocks and seals.

For making the joints for *kasa* (paper umbrella), *egonoki* (snowbell) wood is used, as it is hard and does not wear out. *Katsura* (Judas-tree) wood has been used to make the boards for drying hand-made paper, because it can be made smooth and will not show the grain even after long use. *Kurumi* (walnut) wood is used to make the moving parts of *hata* or old weaving looms, as it does not crack or split.

For making *goban* or the board for playing the game of '*go*,' the *kaya* or *toreya* wood is always used. As the *goban* must be thick, some big piece of wood is needed. *Kaya* grows big, so this wood lends itself particularly well for this purpose. In playing the game, *ishi* or stones are placed by the players alternately on the board. The *kaya* wood gives a pleasant sound when the stones are placed upon it. As they are laid down with some force, the board wood yields slightly but soon regains its levelness. *Go* players do not feel happy unless they play on *kaya* wood boards.

YATATE

YATATE or Japanese pocket writing set is no longer used for practical purposes. Sometimes it is found in curio shops, and excellent pieces are in the hands of collectors. But it is an ingenious product that may be called the forerunner of modern fountain pens. The Japanese gave up its use only when foreign pens and pencils were introduced.

Yatate consists of a small round and flat bowl in which is put some cotton soaked in writing ink, and a hollow stem in which is kept a writing brush. The stem is stuck in one's belt to carry it conveniently wherever one goes. In the old days, it was used by all merchants and travellers.

Yatate is generally made of bamboo, wood, brass, iron or silver. Those used by wealthy persons were works of art with elaborate designs and decorations, and such are treasured by collectors.

The name, *yatate*, is misleading as it means an arrow bag. The bow and arrow were the principal weapons of ancient fighting men, and they carried arrow bags whenever they went on military campaigns. But they also carried various other things in their arrow bags, such as writing paper, writing brushes, *suzuri* (inkwells) and others.

It was because of this habit that, when a pocket set of writing brush and ink was made, it came to be called *yatate*. It is not known when *yatate* first originated, but it became widely popular in the Tokugawa era that commenced in the early 17th century. Up to the early Meiji days, *yatate* was an indispensable article for almost all classes of people.

YUKATA

YUKATA makes Japanese women look very charming and lovely, it is said, and many *ukiyoe* artists loved to paint women dressed in this kind of *kimono*. *Yukata* is the cool summer *kimono* made of cotton, with decorative designs dyed in all shades of indigo blue. For young girls, a touch of red is often added to brighten the designs of their *yukata*. *Yukata* is simple and cool, but yet chic and picturesque in strong contrast to heavy and gorgeous winter or formal dress. It is informal everyday wear in hot summer months.

Yukata came from *yukatabira* (bathing *katabira*) to distinguish it from *katabira* or linen dress for ordinary summer wear. Originally *yukatabira*, as its name indicates, was worn after taking a bath, for drying up the body. Thus it took the role of bath towels at first. They used to put on one *yukata* upon coming out of the bath tub, and changed it for another until the body was thoroughly dried. Thus it was also called *minugui* or bodywiper. Later, *yukata* come to be used as dress instead of as a bath-towel. But its connection with bathing was not entirely severed, and *yukata* became the proper wear after taking a bath.

On hot summer days, it was formerly customary for the people to water the garden in the late afternoon to bring a cool breeze, and take a hot bath to wash off the day's sweat. Then dressing in *yukata* they sat down to a cool dinner. After the dinner, they sat on benches in the garden to enjoy the cool evening breeze, or went out to visit street stalls. Thus *yukata* was, then, to be worn after a day's toil, for enjoying the cool evening in comfort and leisure.

The comfortableness of this dress, however, rapidly popularized it, and soon it became the common wear in summer at all hours and on all occasions.

The chief characteristic of *yukata* lies in its washableness, as it has to be washed properly every day. Then to make the wearer feel cool in it, it is decorated with bright designs in indigo. The designs for men's *yukata* are generally in sober tones compared with those for women and childen. *Yukata* used to be very cheap, but the rich women prided on the exceptional designs of their *yukata* and also the wide variety they possessed. To keep up the beauty and picturesqueness of *yukata*, it is absolutely necessary that it must be cleanly washed and starched.

There is nothing more deplorable than a dirty and soiled *yukata*.

Most of the shrine festivals of Japan come in summer. For the festival of the community shrine, all the residents used to make special *yukata* of a uniform design and wear them on the occasion. Each community rivaled others in designing more attractive *yukata* than neighboring districts had at their festivals. Men, women and children wear *soroe-yukata* or uniform *yukata* on the festival day. Dressed in the bright *yukata*, all danced merrily in the compounds of their shrine. Others who did not dance, paraded through the town or village, dressed in the *yukata*, and shopped at little stalls that offered various novelties. *Soroe-yukata* was thus quite a local feature in which particularly women and children showed much joy.

Japanese hotels supply guests with *yukata*. If they go out wearing them, anyone can tell where they are staying by the designs of their *yukata*.

54

Chapter 2
Cures and Medicines

ANMA

ANMA or Japanese massage is different from Western massage. It is not intended to cure any disease, but is given to make one enjoy rest and impart a feeling of relief. It is very popular among men and women of all ages. *Anma* relieves the tension of muscles and makes one forget fatigue and worry. It becomes a habit and many people have to have it almost daily. At hot springs and other resorts *anma* is particularly in demand.

Anma was originally introduced from China and the Taiho Law of 701 mentions *anma* experts. But the Japanese technique of *anma* is said to have been established by Akashi Kanichi in 1320. *Anma* however soon lost its popularity, and it was only in the Tokugawa era that it was revived. During that period many schools appeared with different techniques. High-ranking *anma* were honored by the Court and government and enjoyed public respect.

In the Tokugawa era, the profession of *anma* was protected by the state, as only the blind could be engaged in this work. This was one of the social measures to protect and help them. In those days blind boys and also sometimes blind girls were apprenticed to experts.

The training was formerly very hard. Today anybody can become an *anma*, but must pass a state examination to obtain a license to operate. Thus they must study something about the physical structure of the human body, sanitation and have some medical knowledge.

Most *anma* are still blind people. Formerly they used to blow a small flute as they went about, and the people used to call them in as they heard the sounds. However, except in some rural districts, this *anma* flute is no longer heard.

COLD CURES

VARIOUS cold cures have been used by the people since very early days. Some of them may be primitive and crude, but they have been found quite effective as proved by their continued use for many generations. The basic principle of most such cures is to sweat out the cold. The simplest and most common way to cure a cold is to take a very hot and long bath and then immediately go to bed with heavy coverings. It makes the patient sweat profusely and cure his cold. A sufficient dose of hot *sake* and good sleep are always prescribed for those who are fond of alcohol.

Then with the hot bath, various steaming hot drinks are taken. Such hot drinks, medicinal or otherwise, also have good effects in sweating out the cold. The most common among such hot drinks are *shoga-yu* or hot ginger drink,

55

which is made by pouring hot water over grated ginger, *mikan-yu* or hot orange drink, made by adding hot water to orange juice, and *oroshi-yu* or grated radish drink made with grated Japanese radish and hot water. Various medicinal herbs are steamed in hot water and taken as a cold cure.

Then, there is observed in many rural districts a peculiar cure of eating roasted oranges. The ordinary mandarin orange is put on fire, and roasted until its outer skin is burned almost entirely black. The cold sufferer is made to eat it, the charred skin and all. With roasting, the orange has a bitter taste, and is believed to be good in curing colds.

Tamago-zake or hot *sake* with egg is popular among many people as a cold cure. About a pint of *sake* is put in a pan and heated until steaming, and then the yolk of one egg is put in it, and thoroughly beaten. It makes a good eggnog and becomes an excellent cure for colds. As the alcoholic percentage is reduced by heating, the drink can be taken even by those who are not fond of alcoholic drinks.

Then, there was formerly a very interesting and pleasant way of curing colds, and its disappearance is being regretted by many. To make the bath cure more effective, many public bathhouses used to sell their own particular cold-cure drinks which were to be taken while bathing. Furthermore, there was a popular custom of ordering *udon* (hot wheat noodle soup) or *soba* (buckwheat noodles in hot soup) from neighboring noodle houses and eating it while comfortably bathing in the hot tub. Up to the middle of the Meiji era, this custom was very popular in various cities and towns. Enjoying the warmth of the hot tub, one can leisurely eat a steaming bowl of *udon* or *soba*. The noodles taste particularly good, as the eater is in a pleasant turn of mind brought about by the warm bath. It cures the cold, but at the same time, it is liable to create a habit. Whether one has a cold or not, whenever he goes to the bathhouse, he is tempted to order a bowl of *udon*. Yet, this was believed to be a very good way for curing one's cold in the old days, and its disappearance is regretted by many.

DOKUKESHI

AS THE weather becomes warm, on the streets of Tokyo and many other cities and towns will be seen groups of women dressed in neat cotton *kimono*, carrying on their shoulders small packs wrapped un in black *furoshiki*, and shouting "*dokukeshi, dokukeshi.*"

They are peddlers of *dokukeshi* (poison neutralizer), a patent medicine said to be good for curing food poisoning and stomach troubles. These women come from the village of Kakuta and neighboring places in Echigo province on the Japan Sea.

The women are of all ages from about 17 and up and they go about in groups. As soon as the weather becomes comfortably warm, they start on their peddling trips, and return home after about three months' travel. The original *dokukeshi*, a yellowish pill, is said to have been first made by a Buddhist temple. The peddling of the medicine throughout the country started in Tokugawa days.

The earnings of those peddlers were formerly said to have been more than what the males of the village made in an entire year.

After the end of the war, about 2,500 women of the district have been peddling *dokukeshi* every year, making total sales of more than ¥300,000,000 a year.

The coming of *dokukeshi* peddlers is welcomed by city dwellers to whom it is a sign of warm weather, and a warning against food poisoning in summer.

FURIDASHI

FURIDASHI (steeped in hot water) is now used as a term to indicate liquid medicines made by boiling herbs in hot water. Ancient Chinese medical science that was introduced to Japan used various herbs as medicines. *Furidashi* consisted mostly of medicines used before the introduction of Western medical science.

But this type of medicine is still very popular among the people, particularly women, and there are more than 500 firms exclusively engaged in selling *furidashi* medicines. Some of these makers are more than 300 years old, and still enjoy good business.

Most of the *furidashi* now being sold are said to be good for improving blood circulation, regulating urination, and keeping the body warm. The medicines come as chopped-up bark and roots, which are steeped in hot water. The liquid thus infused is taken for its medical essence.

Commonly used bark and herbs for making *furidashi* are *okera*, roots of Atractyllis lyrata (a kind of chrysanthemum), *keihi*, peelings of Cinamonium casais (a kind of orange), *tohi*, peelings of Pericapium Auranti (a kind of orange), *bukuryo*, Paephyma hollen (a mushroom), and *shokyo*, roots of Rhizoma Zinniberis (ginger). Sometimes *ninjin* or ginseng is used, but this is very rare as this medical root is very expensive.

GAMA

GAMA, a big toad belonging to the kind called bufo, is found all over Japan, and grows often to more than one foot from its nose to the other end. It is eerie and grotesque in appearance. It has glaring eyes and warts all over the back. It moves slowly and in a dignified manner.

Popularly it is believed that the *gama* exhales a poisonous breath that harms other animals and humans, and possesses magical power. In fact, facing danger or an enemy, the *gama* produces a whitish poisonous liquid from pores on its back.

Regarded as an animal with magical power, the *gama* figures in many traditional tales and folklore. Particularly there is a story regarding a hermit named *Gama-sennin*, who is generally pictured standing on a huge *gama*. It is said that *Gama-sennin* performs various magic with the help of the *gama*.

Gama-no-abura, or *gama*-oil, is still popular among rural people as a medicine to cure skin diseases, cuts, burns and many other things. At village festivals and summer evening stalls there still appear *gama-abura* men who, displaying huge specimens of *gama*, tell the miraculous virtues of *gama* oil. They always have a good many purchasers everywhere.

Gama oil is made by placing a *gama* in an earthenware pot, and roasting it over a fire. As the *gama* is heated, thick oil oozes out of its body. The oil is collected and made into a paste. It is generally sold packed in *hamaguri* (clam) shells.

However, genuine *gama* oil is becoming rare now, and what is sold as *gama-no-abura* is mostly an artificial mixture that contains no oil squeezed out of the *gama*.

GINSENG

CHOSEN-NINJIN or Korean ginseng is still believed by many Japanese as a miracle medicine that cures all kinds of illness and prolongs life. The sweet and aromatic root of the plant is used as medicine.

Ginseng was first introduced to Japan from Korea, but as its demand increased it came to be cultivated in this country as early as the beginning of the 18th century. The import and sale of ginseng was such a profitable and important business that the Tokugawa government established *Ninjin-za*, an official ginseng shop at Surugacho, Nihonbashi, Edo.

In Tokugawa days, physicians prescribed ginseng when all other medicines and treatments failed, but it was very expensive and beyond the reach of the common people. There were many tales of daughters selling themselves into prostitution to buy ginseng for their sick parents. A story goes that a man who recovered from serious illness after taking ginseng had so much difficulty in paying back the debt incurred to buy the wonder medicine that he finally committed suicide to save himself from further trouble.

There are two kinds of ginseng used as medicine, white ginseng made by just drying, and brown ginseng made by drying after steaming. It is either sliced and chewed, or brewed like tea and drunk.

Modern science says ginseng has no miraculous curing power, but admits that it serves to relieve fatigue, improve digestion and stimulate metabolic function.

Kaesong, Korea, where the cease-fire talks were held, has long been famous for producing the highest grade of ginseng.

HARI-RYOJI

TO THE uninitiated, *hari-ryoji* or acupuncture may sound as though it is a very painful treatment, particularly when it is explained to them that needles, one to three inches long, are pushed into the flesh at various parts of the body. But, in reality it does not give any pain at all, and not a drop of blood is to be seen in the entire process.

Hari-ryoji is a popular treatment that is applied to cure all sorts of mental and physical disorders. It was first introduced from China, but in as early as the 25th year of Emperor Kinmei or 562, it became very popular. It is proved by ancient documents that it made rapid development after coming to Japan, and as it is today, it can well be called a Japanese treatment.

The theory of the treatment lies in that the needles thrust into the body at proper places will directly or indirectly stimulate the nerves and muscles and thus effect the normal functioning of all internal organs. Particularly, it is believed that the treatment is good for curing nervous breakdown, spasm, paralysis, blood congestion and inflammation. There are 660 spots all over the human body that control the nerves and muscles according to the theory of *hari-ryoji*. It is at such spots that the needles are pushed into the flesh for stimulating the function of the afflicted nerves and muscles.

The needles used in this treatment are of silver, gold or platinum, and are classified into 10 grades by their lengths and thickness. They are generally 1.2 to 3 inches long, and their thickness ranges from 0.15 to 0.45 mm.

Acupuncturists are divided into several schools all of which have developed in Japan, and the most famous are the Sugiyama, Irie, Misono and Nishimura schools. They use different kinds of needles, and have different ways of applying the needles to the body, but on the whole their treatment has no substantial difference at all.

The most common method of pushing the needles into the flesh is to place first a slender metal tube over the very spot where the needle is to be thrust, and then the needle is placed inside the tube and pushed into the flesh by the thumb. Then again, the metal tube is not used, and the needle is just thrust into the flesh by the fingers. The third method is to tap the needle into the flesh with a small hammer.

Though it may sound unbelievable, the treatment causes no pain at all, and gives instant relief in many cases. However, it is also said that the treatment is liable to become a habit. But as no medicine is used, even though one becomes an addict of the treatment and could not feel happy unless he is given it every other day or so, there is no ill effect at all.

Formerly *hari-i* or acupuncturists were specializing in the treatment alone, being proud of their technique and position. Recently the treatment is mostly given by *anma* or masseurs who have passed government examination and possess licenses to give the treatment to the public.

HOME CURES

HERBS and other home medicines used by the Japanese for curing sickness and improving health are numerous. Many of them are results of long experimenting for generations and are scientifically proven to be effective. Yet others are mere superstitions. Still there are many people who prefer old-fashioned home cures to modern scientific medicines.

Home cures, effective or otherwise, differ according to districts. Here are some of them which may be of interest to many people, although their effectiveness is not guaranteed.

To cure a sore throat, eat roasted orange seeds.

To prevent seasickness, put a pinch of sulphur on the navel.

If a woman wishes to make her first child-birth safe and easy, drink the juice obtained by boiling chrysanthemum flowers.

When one has a toothache, put on the tooth the ash from burning pine needles.

To cure leprosy, drink the juice made from boiling *gingko* nuts.

If one has dreadful dreams nightly, eat only yams.

The best cure for a carbuncle is to apply a butterfly squashed in sesame oil.

When poisoned by fresh lacquer or poisonous plants, wash the spot with the juice made by boiling a crab.

The high temperature accompanying smallpox or measles can be quickly lowered by taking the juice made by boiling the core of willow wood.

The juice made by boiling the root of the peony tree is good for curing diarrhea.

For a person who becomes short of breath when walking rapidly, the juice obtained by boiling chickweed with salt is recommended.

To cure the after-effects of heavy drinking, take the juice made by boiling cloves, while hot.

Fat men or those with beri-beri should drink the juice made by boiling together dried cuttle-fish and licorice.

Pain in the muscles or bones can be cured by drinking the juice made by boiling the root of wisteria.

The juice made by boiling the cast-off shell of a cicada will cure a running ear.

To remove freckles, brew leaves and blossoms of pear, add some honey and apply the juice to the face.

For curing a dog bite, put on black sugar.

For burns, apply the white of an egg or *shoyu* (Japanese soy sauce).

To soften rough skin, put some *sake* in the bath water.

To prevent hair from becoming white, drink the juice made by brewing the stalks of the chrysanthemum plant.

When an insect stings you, get a leaf of morning-glory, and crush it to obtain its juice. Apply the juice to the spot.

When a dog or cat scratches your hand, roast a chestnut, crush it into pulp and apply to the spot.

To prevent chilblain, apply to hands and feet the tannic acid obtained from persimmons.

To cure heat rash, rub a thin slice of cucumber on the skin or brew peach leaves and apply the juice.

For stomach-ache, burn *take-no-kawa* or bamboo sheath, and take the ash with hot water.

Diabetics are advised to take for their meals *sekihan* (rice cooked with red beans) with roasted sesame and salt, and also to eat plenty of seaweed.

To cure measles, eat *kinkan* (kumquat) cooked in sugar, or take the ash made by roasting fish bones.

KUKO TEA

A KIND of tea brewed with the leaves of the *kuko* or box-horn is still drunk by many Japanese as a medicine that gives health and long life.

The *kuko* is found in most parts of the country, it being very often planted by garden gates and fences, as the vines that grow about three meters creep over them beautifully and bear little purple flowers in spring. The young leaves were used as vegetables in the old days.

The medicinal value of the plant is believed to have been taught by the Chinese who regarded it as a sacred plant. It is recorded that the first emperor of the Ch'in dynasty (third century B.C.) of China ordered a search for the medicinal plant of *kuko* which was said to prevent aging and death. In Japan, too, there is a record that one named Takeda lived to the ripe age of 120 during the reign of Emperor Buntoku in the ninth century, because he drank *kuko* tea daily.

Because of the traditional belief that the leaves, seeds and roots of the *kuko* contain a medicine that prevents sickness and prolongs life, the custom of drinking *kuko* tea developed since very early days.

Though the habit had gradually been forgotten by modern city dwellers, due to the recent revival of popular faith in old herb medicines, *kuko* tea has come to be imbibed by many persons again.

Scientists recognize the presence of many valuable chemicals in the plant, but are wary about its claim of being health-sustaining and death-defying.

But *kuko* tea drinkers have faith in their daily drink and their number is increasing.

KUMA-NO-I

AMONG old-fashioned family medicines of Japan, one that is still very popular is *kuma-no-i* (bear's gall). It is believed to be particularly good in curing stomachaches. Rural children are often forced to take it against their loud protest, whenever they have stomach troubles, because it is very bitter and hard to swallow.

In the old days, the gall was considered the most valuable part of a bear. Of course bear meat was eaten and the fur was used as a floor spread, but it was for the gall that bears were hunted.

Bears have become scarce recently, but whenever a bear is caught the first thing the hunters do is to open the bear's body and remove the gall.

Kuma-no-i is dried and sliced, and almost every rural household keeps a few slices wrapped up in paper, ready to be used in any emergency when its members have stomachaches. The faith of the people in *kuma-no-i* is not all superstition. It has properties that help digestion, and its practical effectiveness has kept up its popularity.

Bear gall is now scarce. Many imitations which are galls of other animals or are worthless fakes have appeared. To the people *kuma-no-i* stands for anything bitter. In many modern patent medicines, *kuma-no-i* is often used. This is particularly true in the case of stomach medicines for children.

KUROYAKI

THROUGHOUT the country there are shops which are called *kuroyaki-ya*, specializing in the sales of various kinds of *kuroyaki* or charred plants and animals which are believed to possess medicinal efficacy. The belief in the curative power of such medicines may be superstitious, but the very existence and apparent prosperity of those shops endorse the still widespread belief in the value of such *kuroyaki*. Many of such *kuroyaki-ya* have been doing profitable business for a century or more.

This custom is based on the belief that various plants and animals when carbonized by roasting possess properties to give vitality and cure diseases. It is said to have been started by some Japanese physicians who studied the medical science of China as well as plants and animals for utilizing them for medicinal purposes.

The general practice of selling *kuroyaki* is reported to have originated in the era of Kansei, 1789-1801, and as it soon became very popular, shops specializing in their sales were opened in many big cities and towns. Modern science and even most of the younger generation of the country laugh at *kuroyaki*, but it cannot be denied that those numerous *kuroyaki-ya* still enjoy sufficient business to maintain themselves if not making good profit.

Various *kuroyaki* are believed to cure diseases, and each shop has specialities of its own. Of course as *kuroyaki* medicines come in powder, ashes or shapeless masses, it can never be told of what materials they are made. The buyer goes to the shops, in whose *kuroyaki* he has confidence.

Mention must be made here of some varieties of *kuroyaki* which are generally sold and believed to be effective in curing special diseases.

The *kuroyaki* of the legs of *tsuru* or cranes is good for curing whooping cough. Moles, crows and herons, when charred black, will cure hysterics and dizziness. The *kuroyaki* made of apples will cure beri-beri. The charred snake or copper pheasant is good for tuberculosis patients, and also improves the health of those of weak constitution. Asthma can be cured by taking the *kuroyaki* of sparrows or pigeons. Those who suffer from poor eyesight will benefit by taking the *kuroyaki* of lamprey eels. Monkey's brain, or the head of chickens or kites, will cure syphilis.

The *kuroyaki* of *imori* or newt (water lizard) is particularly very famous. It is believed that when a married couple takes the charred lizard, they will live happily together. Because of this original belief, it came to be known as a 'love medicine.' Tradition has it that when a man is in love with a girl, he should spread some *kuroyaki* of *imori* over her, or make her take it with her meal or drink unknowingly, and then she will come to love him.

Nobody needs to believe in the efficacy of those *kuroyaki*, but there is no harm in trying them.

LEECH CURE

HIRU or leeches were formerly used for medical purposes. Live leeches were sold at medicine and other shops up to the Meiji era, even in cities. Some old-fashioned rural folk still insist on the effectiveness of a *hiru* cure, and use *hiru* caught in the neighborhood.

There are many kinds of leeches. In Japan there are the *mizu-hiru* (water leech), *uma-hiru* (horse leech), *yama-hiru* (mountain leech), *umi-hiru* (sea leech) and others. It is, however, the *mizu-hiru* which has been used for curing various illnesses.

This leech is about 5 to 19 cm long, and has a sucking disc at each end. The mouth is inside the front sucker. The body is formed of rings and the leech walks by moving the hind part up to the front and then extending the fore portion forward as spanworms do.

It is the blood-sucking nature of the leech that has been utilized in curing diseases. The so-called *hiru* cure was first mentioned in the seventh century and believed to have been introduced from China. Soon in the eighth century it gained many followers, and then in the Heian period or the ninth to 12th centuries, it became widely popular.

In the old days, people believed that bad blood was the cause of various kinds of sickness, which could be cured by drawing out the bad blood. Thus when one had a boil or a swelling, a *hiru* was placed over the spot to suck out the bad blood. The leech is a greedy blood sucker and goes on drawing blood until it is removed.

When persons complained of stiffness of the neck or shoulder, leeches were placed at such places and made to draw blood, as the stiffness was believed to be caused by the accumulation of bad blood.

Though it is no longer possible to buy live leeches in the cities, in rural areas where they can be easily obtained, the old blood-sucking cure is followed by many.

MEDICINAL TEAS

THERE are many drinks made of herbs which are called *cha* (tea), though they have no tea in them. They are so named simply because they are drunk daily as tea substitutes and have medicinal value. Quite a large number of people are in the habit of taking such *cha* daily.

Sekikoku-cha is brewed from an orchid which is also raised for its blossoms. Just before its flowers come out, the plant is dried in the shade, and then brewed to make the drink. This *cha* is held to be good for increasing vitality.

Habu-cha is the most popular herb tea. The juice of the leaves of this plant, Cassia Occidentalis, is used for curing insect bites. The seeds of the plant are roasted and brewed. This *cha* is good for regulating digestive organs.

Kekka-cha is made from the roots of *Kanokogusa*. The roots are put in a cup and hot water poured over them. It is sure to cure insomnia.

Mame-cha or *hama-cha* is brewed from the stems and leaves of *Kawaragetsumei*. The stems and leaves are gathered together and dried. The drink brewed from them is good for kidney trouble and weak stomachs.

Ama-cha, or sweet tea, which is drunk on April 8 to celebrate the birthday of Buddha, is also commonly used by many persons. The leaves of Hydrangea Hortensis are slightly dried and rubbed by hand. Then they are completely dried. This tea has a very sweet taste. Formerly it was used as a sweetening material before sugar was introduced. *Ama-cha* is good for curing diabetes.

MEDICINE PEDDLERS

MEDICINE peddlers from Toyama have been known all over the country for more than 300 years. Rural dwellers particularly wait eagerly for their annual visits so that they can replenish their supplies of various kinds of medicines. This unique system of peddling trade developed under the encouragement and protection of the feudal Lord of Toyama.

During the Genna era (1615-1624), there was a famous physician named Mosu Jokan at Katayama, Bizen province, who produced a medicine called *Hangontan*. It soon became famous all over the country as a popular medicine. Particularly the Lord of Toyama became a great addict of this medicine. So he arranged with Mosu Jokan to have the medicine made by Matsuiya Genbaemon of Toyama for distribution.

Thus started the famous *Hangontan* of Toyama. To encourage the sales of the medicine, the feudal clan established the *Hangontan* Office and superintended the manufacture and sales of the medicine.

The sales method adopted was to send out peddlers throughout the country. The unique feature of the system is that the sales are not made in cash, but a box or bag containing the medicine is left free at each household. A year later the peddler comes around again and collects money for the amount of medicine consumed in the past year, leaving a fresh box or bag. This novel system has been operating for more than 300 years.

The coming of the Toyama medicine peddler is an annual event in small rural villages. Later, not only *Hangontan*, but also other medicines as well as various novelties and goods of daily necessity were brought by the peddlers.

Under the original system the peddler had the exclusive right to cover a certain district, and in many cases the peddler employed many subordinates to go around all households within his territory. This territorial right was so valuable that it was often sold or pledged as security for loans. This fact proves how profitable the business was. Various local clans also levied on the medicine peddler certain taxes or payments for permitting them to sell their medicines within their territories.

At first the country was divided into 21 districts, and the holders of the sales rights in them formed a union.

Today the system has changed, and the Toyama medicine peddling operation is now under a stock company. The company no longer specializes in *Hangontan*, but makes various modern patent medicines. But the peddlers still visit all the districts throughout the country once a year as usual, leaving boxes or bags of medicines to be paid for a year later. These Toyama medicines are popular even among the residents of big cities.

NIRA CURE

NIRA is a kind of leek with a stronger smell than onion. It has been used by the Japanese as a medicine and is believed to warm up the body. Particularly when one's stomach is out of order, *nira-zosui* or rice gruel with chopped up *nira* is eaten. In rural districts where it grows wild, it is much used not only as a medicine but also as a vegetable.

It is said that not only humans take *nira* as medicine, but also many fish and birds eat it. When carp and other river fish or sparrows swallow some foreign materials by mistake, particularly small pieces of iron, it is said they eat *nira* to remove them from their body.

Once a villager of Tanba province shot an arrow at a heron. He succeeded in hitting the bird, but it flew away wounded, so a story goes. Next evening he found that someone was stealing the *nira* he had planted on his farm. Determined to catch the thief, he went out to the farm at night and waited for the thief, hiding himself behind a tree. In his hand he held his bow and arrow ready.

Soon he heard a rustling noise in a patch of his *nira* field. He shot an arrow, and when he went over to the spot, he found a heron dead with his arrow in its body. He carried the bird home and to his surprise he found that besides the arrow that had killed the bird, there was an arrow wound in its body which was packed with bits of *nira*.

He knew then that it was the same heron he had shot at before. The bird with the arrow head in its body tried to remove it by stealing his *nira* and putting it into the wound that still held the arrow head.

O-KYU

THE MOST effective scolding that would make even the most naughty Japanese children instantly behave has been the parents' shout of *o-kyuo suyeruyo* (will put a moxa on you). The mention of *o-kyu* makes children tremble with fear, because whether they have the experience of its application or not, they all know how painful it is. So *o-kyu* has often been used as a means of punishing children for mischievous conduct or disobedience.

O-kyu is a treatment made by putting a tiny pinch of moxa on any part of the body and setting it on fire. But originally it was for curing illness and not for punishing children. The name moxa which is now universally used comes from *mogusa,* the Japanese name for the soft wool made by drying and rubbing the leaves of *yomogi* (mugwort).

O-kyu is said to have come from China, but it is in Japan that this practice has really developed. That is why the Japanese name of *mogusa* is internationally used in the changed form of moxa. Traditionally it is said that the Buddhist priest Kukai, who is more commonly known as Kobo-Daishi, developed the technique of moxa-cauterization in the ninth century.

The principle of *o-kyu* is established on the theory of regulating or improving the blood circulation and nervous system by irritation and stimulation. All illness and physical defects cause poor blood circulation and irregular functioning of the nervous system. *O-kyu* is said to cure illness or improve health by irritating or stimulating blood circulation and the nervous system, which are not functioning properly, by the application of heat. It is said to be particularly effective in curing rheumatism, neuralgia, fatigue and digestive organ illness. Under the theory of *o-kyu* there are 657 vital spots over the entire human body. To some of those spots *o-kyu* is applied. Most common spots are along the spine or just under the knees. There are professionals who mark the spots on the patient's body, where *o-kyu* is to be applied for curing his illness.

On those spots *mogusa* or moxa is placed, and lit with a burning *senko* or incense stick. As *mogusa* burns, the patient feels a cutting pain. The burning moxa leaves a burn mark on the skin. At one spot moxa is generally put three times or more. Theoretically speaking, a tiny pinch of moxa is just as effective as a big one, but many persons prefer to have big ones, thinking that the bigger the size of moxa placed, the more effective it is though also more painful.

In feudal days, many young men boasted of their courage to stand big moxa burns, and competed to see who could stand the biggest. Sometimes a mountain of moxa, two or three inches in diameter and height, was applied on the leg or arm to test the courage of the boastful young men.

The usual application of moxa leaves a mark on the skin, but of late various new ways adopted leave no mark. A thick layer of strong paper, a slice of green ginger or other material is put under the moxa so that no burn will be left on the skin.

RABIES

HOW EARLY Japan had rabies, is not known. Rabid dogs might have been just regarded as mad dogs. It seems to be around 1898 that hydrophobia was recognized by the people as a dreadful disease for dogs and other animals. Particularly after the Russo-Japanese war, 1904-05, the people came to feel great alarm over the large number of dogs becoming rabid and biting humans. It was then believed that the disease was brought over from Manchuria and Siberia.

But according to various documents, hydrophobia was known to Japan much earlier, though it was not called by that name. Shigenari Motoyoshi, a member of the Chiba prefectural assembly, found a document written about 150 years ago by Negishi Morinobu, in which a magic cure for the bite of mad dogs is mentioned.

The cure mentioned is very interesting and may be worthy of study. It prescribes first of all pouring water constantly on the bite made by a mad dog. Then it recommends the eating of raw soya beans. It says that one who has been bitten by a rabid dog does not find the raw beans distasteful. When the beans begin to taste raw, the eating can be stopped.

There might be something in this cure, because soya beans contain more than 20 kinds of amino acid, including alginin and also lecithin. Moreover, the linolic acid found in soya beans has the function of reviving one from fatigue. All these ingredients found in soya beans might really counteract the rabies poison. There may be something in this remedy to guide scientists in the study for the cure and prevention of rabies, as has often been found true with many primitive cures.

SMALLPOX

RED FLAGS are today danger signals or used by labor and Communist demonstrators. But in ancient days, pieces of red cloth were charms against smallpox.

Smallpox is said to have come to Japan in the seventh century soon after the arrival of Buddhism. It claimed many victims, but as there was then no cure for the illness, many died or were left pock-marked. The people had no way but to appeal to their guardian *kami* for protection.

They thought there was a *Hoso-gami* or god of smallpox, and offered prayers and food to it for protection from the disease.

Though no explanation can be given, they began to believe that the red color protected them from the disease. Thus the patient was given a red cap and red *tabi* (Japanese socks). Their *futon* or bedding was also covered with red cotton fabric. Thus surrounded by things bright red in color, they thought the patients would recover.

Furthermore, friends and relatives gathered and feasted on *sekihan* or red beans and rice. The red rice was offered to the local and family shrines. In making their prayer to the shrine, they also used *gohei* (sacred staff) decorated with strips of red paper, instead of the white paper usually used.

In some districts they made straw dolls, and put them at a cross roads together with *sekihan* balls and *waraji* or straw sandals, to enable *Hoso-gami* to make its journey home comfortably. Small coins were often added to pay for his trip expenses.

Vaccination was introduced into Japan in the Tenpo era (1830-44), and the *Bakufu*, realizing its value, opened a Vaccination Bureau in the Kaei era (1848-54) at Kanda, Edo. The modern law of compulsory vaccination was issued by the Meiji government in October 1874.

Chapter 3
Dwelling Houses and Other Buildings

BAD LUCK HOUSES

JAPANESE people still attribute bad luck or sickness to faulty construction of their houses, in violation of the rules of *kaso* or house features. When gates, window, kitchens, toilets or wells are not placed in the proper location, they still believe that bad luck is bound to come. The most important part in *kaso* is the northeast direction from the center of the house, where no windows, gate, or toilet should be placed. House builders are still very sensitive about the northeast.

Many people believe one should not move to a new house northeast of the old one. If he must, he has to move first to a temporary place in another direction, and make a second move to the intended house from there.

This belief came from China where it was believed that in the northeast were the stone houses of devils. The rules of *kaso*, however, were originally made at Loyang, China, in full consideration of the topographical, climatic and other natural conditions of the city. So the original rules, however excellent for Loyang, do not apply to towns and villages of Japan, which are very different in those respects.

The tradition of the northeast direction has been very seriously considered in construction. When Kyoto Palace was built, a big temple was erected on top of Mt. Hiei on the northeastern outskirts of the capital to check the entrance of devils from that direction. When it was decided to move the capital from Kyoto to Tokyo (then Edo) after the Meiji Restoration, many opposed the step as Tokyo lies northeast of Kyoto, but the young leaders of the Restoration were brave enough to make the change despite the superstition. But Kaneiji Temple was erected by Tokugawa authorities at Ueno to halt the invasion of the devils from the northeast.

In 1930, somebody in the Tokyo Metropolitan Office found that the mayor's office was in the northeast corner of the Municipal Building, and the Municipal Council passed a resolution to move the mayor's office to some luckier corner. But somehow it was never carried out.

BIGGEST TORII

OF all *torii* in Japan, the one at Itsukushima Shrine, Miyajima, in the Inland Sea, is probably the most famous, because it is the biggest in the country and stands in the sea.

The shrine itself is one of the oldest, having been erected in the reign of Empress Regnant Suiko (592-628). It is dedicated to Ichikishima, Tagori and Tagitsu, three daughters of Susano-o-no-Mikoto.

The shrine structure was rebuilt many times in the past. Its novel and particular architectural features are the long, wide corridors that extend into the sea. Visitors from the main island, as they approach Miyajima on boats, see the great *torii* in the sea with the background of the shrine structure and its corridors set against the green hills behind.

The great *torii*, said to have been first erected by Taira-no-Kiyomori about eight centuries ago, has been rebuilt eight times in the past.

As it stands today, it measures 53 feet high with a 77-foot crossbar. The huge pillars measure 33 feet around at the bottom. The *torii* is made of a huge camphor tree. The present *torii* was erected in 1875, and the lower portions of the high pillars were replaced in 1951 with new camphor wood.

CHA-NO-MA

IN JAPANESE homes, the *zashiki* or guest's room is the finest and most important room. It is to this room that guests are asked to come in, and it is also there that formal family functions are held. It is never for daily use. Being so important, the best available wood and fixtures are selected for its construction, and valuable paintings and ornaments are displayed in this room.

But for daily home life, the *cha-no-ma* (literally tea room) is very important though not so elaborately made as the *zashiki*. In small houses, generally the *cha-no-ma* is located between the kitchen and the *zashiki*. It is in this room that the family gathers, for meals or for evening talks. It is also the wife's room where her friends and neighbors, paying a short visit, are always invited.

The room may have come to be called *cha-no-ma* because tea is served such visitors there, and also family members gather there for their tea. In the room, therefore, there must be a *hibachi* or charcoal brazier which is very often

made of exquisite woods and carefully polished. In many old-fashioned families, a kettle is always kept steaming over the fire in the *hibachi*, so that tea can be readily made if a visitor comes.

Serving a cup of tea is the first act of social etiquette in Japanese homes. Thus the room where the tea is served becomes very important. However, the real significance of the *cha-no-ma* lies in the fact that the whole family gathers there for meals or evening chats. Thus the *cha-no-ma*, but in old-fashioned mosphere of home life, and the term is very often used in that sense.

Of course, apartment houses or residences in modern style do not have the *cha-no-ma*, but in old-fashioned homes and particularly in the rural districts, the *cha-no-ma* still retains an important significance in the family and social life of the people.

In the cold region of the country, the room where the *irori* or Japanese fireplace is built, performs the role of the *cha-no-ma* as the whole family gathers, eats, receives visitors, and sometimes even sleeps around it.

DOMA

DOMA or earth floor is an important part of the rural Japanese house. The unfloored portion is generally at the front or back of the house. But in some districts the *doma* runs the whole length of the house, running from front to back. In the rural house, the *doma* is the place where grain, straw and other farm products are handled, and where the cooking also is done.

The unfloored portion of the house is also called *niwa*. This name came to be extended to mean also the yard in front of the house where farm products are sunned on fine days. Gradually, however, the word *niwa* came to be used to indicate gardens. But in rural districts, *niwa* still means the unfloored parts of the house.

The *doma* is not only the workroom of a farming family, but also its kitchen. Many farming households have very large *doma* where stone mortars are kept, a well is placed, and space is set aside for crops and foodstuffs, as well as cooking stoves, and kitchen utensils. Sometimes, next to the kitchen *doma*, there is a board-floored room, where the family has their meals.

The earth floor is beaten hard by constant pounding by many people for several years. Sometimes the floor has little lumps all over, giving it a wavy surface. In many parts of the country, this kind of *doma* floor is regarded as a sign of good luck and happiness. The people make much of such *doma* floors, as the wavy surface cannot be made purposely, but happens naturally.

In some old cities, like Kyoto for instance, there are still many houses that have a long *doma* on one side of the house. In most such city houses, there are three or four rooms in a row, each room opening on to the *doma*. The limited frontage of city building lots made it necessary to have this long *doma* on one side, so that the kitchen in the rear could be easily reached.

FINE WOODWORK

IN BUILDING wooden houses, the Japanese have, through their long experience, found beauty in the texture and grains of various kinds of wood. As they came to appreciate the beauty of natural wood, they have tried to use it to the best advantage. They have selected only such woods that possessed outstanding characteristics and beauty for the construction of their houses. For each part of the house, a different kind of wood is used. The wood for pillars differs from those used for making the ceiling. It is because of this selection that a good Japanese house is very expensive to build.

As the wood is cut and squared, the best side is used for the surface. This love of the texture and grains of wood has made Japanese carpenters very skilled planers. Only by planing the wood smoothly and perfectly flat can its beauty be brought out. It is recorded that one master carpenter planed two boards so precisely that when the two boards were put together, they could not be separated.

Also in making furniture and utensils, the wood is left in its natural state to show its beauty. There are unpainted *tansu* or chests, tables, trays and boxes which are beautiful and artistic because of the texture and grains of the wood. The best kind of *geta* (clogs) is not the lacquered and decorated ones, but plain ones of soft close-grained *kiri* wood.

To keep the wooden parts of a house clean and beautiful requires constant and painstaking care. All of the woodwork must be dusted, wiped clean and polished every day. With such care, the woodwork mellows with age, retaining its natural grains and texture.

In humid Japan, wood, paper and soft walls absorb moisture and keep the rooms dry, while painted woods and walls drip with moisture. This scientific fact is apt to be ignored by many foreigners.

GARDENS

JAPANESE gardens are unique, and in them are revealed the artistic sentiment of the people. Thus, in the art of garden designing, the people have long shown exceptional talents and artistic touches.

There are, however, several different types of Japanese gardens. The oldest and most aristocratic is the type called the boating garden, perfected in the Heian period, 794-1192. This is a large garden, with a pond in which are several islands. There are rocks and trees around the pond. In olden days, aristocrats went out on boats and held music or drinking parties on the boats in the pond.

The pond garden started in the early Edo period or the 17th century. There is a pond, but not for boating. Around the pond are laid winding paths, and the people go walking through the garden to enjoy its beauty. In the garden are generally teahouses, shrines, bridges, trees and flowering plants.

Then there are smaller gardens with ponds, but their beauty is viewed from the house. In this type, there are waterfalls and rocks to represent natural mountain scenes.

The so-called flat garden has grounds covered with mosses or with sand, swept level and clean. The garden is dotted with rocks and trees.

The tea garden that developed with the tea ceremony is a miniature presentation of nature. It is laid for the purpose of making those going to the teahouse forget the busy and noisy world, and thus compose themselves to enjoy tea. In a small space there are rocks, trees, a water basin and lanterns.

The temple garden has rocks and trees, but no water. The ground is covered with beautiful sands.

The so-called happy garden has symbols of happiness. Symbols of cranes and turtles, which are said to live long, made in stone or clipped trees are placed. Then pines, Japanese apricot and bamboo, the three plants of happiness, are generally used.

The dry garden is the most symbolic of Japanese gardens. There is no water, but waterfalls are represented by slabs of stone and streams by white sands.

Trees are planted to form the background.

Miniature gardens present famous natural scenes in miniature in the garden.

GEGYO

ORIGINAL Japanese architecture, as preserved in shrine buildings, is unique and symmetrically beautiful. One feature of early Japanese architecture is that in shape and construction shrine buildings and common dwellings were the same, while in other countries architecturally the places of worship and houses of the people were always distinctly different.

Of course, Japanese dwellings and other structures have greatly changed since those early days while shrines have kept their original form.

One of the unique characteristics of shrine buildings is the *gegyo* (hanging fish), an ornamental piece placed on the upper portion of the gable on both sides.

It is made of wood or metal with floral or other designs carved out. The Gold Pavilion of Horyuji Temple, Nara, built in 607 has the oldest existing specimen of *gegyo* decoration. It is made of copper with an arabesque design.

This ornamental piece came to be called *gegyo* because at first it was in the shape of a fish, and placed on the roof as a charm against fire, so it is commonly said.

It appears that *gegyo* was at first used on shrine buildings and then on other structures including dwellings. But it is interesting to note that this decoration has also been used on Buddhist temples, palaces and great mansions of the people.

Thus, it is still seen on shrines, temples, castles and houses of great families in rural districts. But it is evident that *gegyo* of later periods and particularly of private dwellings are much smaller and simpler in design than ancient specimens.

Yet, it still remains as a symbol of original Japanese architecture.

GOJU-NO-TO

MANY temples in Japan have beautiful *goju-no-to*, or five-storied towers. Five roofs of graceful curves make the towers architectural beauties. This type of tower originated in India, where it was erected for preserving the ashes of Buddha. But later it became one of the buildings of a temple. One at Horyu-ji Temple, Nara, erected in the seventh century, is probably the most famous *goju-no-to* in the country.

These towers are marvels of wooden construction, built without any nails or bolts. Some are more than a hundred and fifty feet high, but have withstood storms and earthquakes for many centuries. Though they are beautiful, they are not erected merely as architectural ornaments for temples.

The five stories stand for earth, water, fire, wind and sky, counted from the lowest upward, which are called *godai*, or Five Greats in Buddhism. They are the elements in the universe from which are produced all things under the sun. Thus the towers symbolize the universe and everything existing in it.

These five elements are also expressed in stone towers. Five stones of different shapes, representing the *godai* elements, are piled up. These stone towers are not very large, being mostly from three to ten feet high. The stone for earth, which is placed at the base, is square, the next for water is round, the third for fire is triangular, the fourth for wind is a semicircle, and the top for

sky is a ball.

Tombstones for aristocrats and great personages were formerly made in the shape of this *godai* tower. It signifies that when the human dies, he returns to the five elements of which the body was made.

The Buddhist belief in *godai*, or five elements of the universe, is expressed in these five-storied towers, as well as in the ancient stone tombs.

HINOKI-BUTAI

AS JAPANESE houses are built of wood, it is necessary to select strong and durable lumber for their construction. As the wood is used in its natural unpainted condition, the texture, color and grain of the wood has become important to make the house beautiful.

Of various kinds of lumber used for house construction, the *hinoki* or Japanese cypress has been considered the best since earliest days.

Better kinds of houses as well as stages for *Noh* and *Kabuki* plays came to be built of this wood. Even today *hinoki* is valued as the best lumber for good Japanese houses.

Thus there developed the commonly used term 'hinoki-butai' (*hinoki* stage), literally meaning *hinoki* board-covered stage. But the term came to be used to indicate a first-class stage.

After the great fire of Meireki that destroyed the major portion of Edo in 1657, there were three principal *Kabuki* theaters in the capital — the Nakamuraza at Sakae-machi, the Ichimuraza at Fukiya-cho, and the Moritaza at Kobiki-cho. These three theaters were then called the three Edo theaters.

They ranked as the highest *Kabuki* theaters of the country and when the term *hinoki-butai* was used, it referred to those three and to no other theaters in the country.

71

Therefore to appear on the stage of those three best theaters was the greatest ambition of all actors at the time. Thus *hinoki-butai* came to mean the greatest opportunity for success or a place to show one's ability.

Gradually this theatrical term has come to be used in other fields, too. The rostrum of the Diet building is the *hinoki-butai* for politicians, and the lecture room at the university is a young professor's *hinoki-butai*.

HOUSES IN SUMMER

THE JAPANESE house looks different, probably better, when summer comes. As anyone can feel when summer comes, it is really made for warm weather and not for a cold climate. First of all, most of the outer *shoji* or paper screen doors are removed to permit a better flow of cool air. This makes the rooms open and bright, while in the winter season they look small and dark. Then in better houses, the paper sliding doors are replaced by summer doors, made of a split bamboo or reed screen put in the frames. Air goes through the screen, thereby making the rooms cool.

More commonly *sudare* or hanging blinds made also of split bamboo or reeds are hung where the *shoji* used to be in winter. Some of the expensive *sudare* have borders of rich silk brocade and decorative tassels. *Sudare* and the above-mentioned screen doors cool the rooms, while privacy is maintained.

Old-fashioned people spread a matting of split bamboo or rattan on the *tatami*, as it is cool to the touch and very comfortable in the hot weather. There are also special *zabuton* or cushions for summer use.

The picture in the *tokonoma* or alcove and many household utensils are changed with the season.

Another thing that makes its ap-

pearance in summer is *furin* or windbells. It is a tiny bell to which is attached an oblong piece of stiff paper. The slightest breeze makes it tinkle pleasantly. The cool sound, the people believe, makes them forget the heat.

Gifu-chochin or large lanterns covered with thin paper and decorated with paintings also come out in summer. Bright electric lights are hot, and so many people light candles in the *Gifu-chochin* instead, to enjoy the cool evening in the mellow light.

IRORI AND KOTATSU

IRORI or hearth was the heating system used in ancient days in all classes of dwellings in Japan. Nobles had their *irori*, and later the houses of all *samurai* had the *irori-no-ma* or the hearth room. Then, in farmers' houses *irori* has always been one of the most important parts. Yet with the changes in the architecture of houses, and particularly with the development of town life, *irori* disappeared from the houses of town residents. It is now left only in houses in rural districts, in which it still plays a very important role.

Irori is made by making a square hole, six to ten feet square, in the center of a room. The hole is bordered with stone or wooden boards, and filled with wood ash. Over this ash is burned wood. In winter the room with *irori* becomes the center of the household, where the entire family lives and sleeps. Over the fire in the *irori* is always kept a big kettle suspended from an overhanging beam, and thus there is always hot water ready for making tea. Various things are also cooked there. However, as the kitchen proper is built elsewhere for ordinary cooking, the *irori* is used only for auxiliary cooking. On cold evenings, children love to place sweet potatoes in the hot ash of the *irori*, and eat them when properly baked, or warm their *mochi* over the fire. They eat their meals around the fire, where they also receive callers. Sometimes they sleep in *futon* spread around the *irori*. So the *irori* room becomes the living room, the dining room, and the drawing room for the whole family in the winter season.

Guests are invited to sit by it and there are places designated for the master of the house, his wife and other members of the family. The family eats around it and also does their various household tasks there.

There are many customs connected with the *irori*. All are told not to put, even by accident, their feet on the *irori* edge board. This is just as bad as hitting one's father on the head with his foot. No one is allowed to unnecessarily disturb or play with the ashes in the *irori*. If one puts his foot into them, it will cause birds to kill all the rice plants in the nursery bed, it is said. They are warned against dropping water, nails or other impure things into the ashes, as such acts will surely bring misfortune to the family.

A large kettle is suspended over the hearth by a *jizai-kagi* or adjustable hanger made of wood or metal. The hook is so arranged that it can be lowered or raised.

This hook is also very much respected, and should not be unnecessarily moved. If one plays with it, he will become poor, or meet with rough going when he travels by ship.

In some districts, whenever something is lost or misplaced in the house, a strip of paper is tied to the hook. Then the missing object will be soon discovered, it is still believed.

To the people of the cold regions, the *irori* is not only a necessity but also a place to be regarded as sacred. So they take good care of their *irori*, in which it

is even believed by some that the *hino-kami* or god of fire lives.

The heat from the *irori* keeps the entire house fairly warm and dry. The room where the *irori* is made has no ceiling, this being for ventilating the smoke. The smoke goes out from the narrow space along the eaves of the straw or reed-thatched roof. It is the smoke from the *irori* that keeps the roof from being damaged by moisture or insects, which otherwise would make their nests in the straw or reeds. There are many houses with straw or reed roofs that have given up the use of *irori*, and in such cases the roof decays very quickly because of moisture and insects.

Irori is still widely used in farming houses, but in towns and cities, it has almost entirely disappeared. *Kotatsu* has replaced *irori* in urban houses. *Kotatsu* is believed to have developed from *irori*, the main difference being, however, that *kotatsu* is generally made smaller than *irori*.

Moreover, charcoal or *tadon* (balls of dust charcoal), is used in *kotatsu*, which gives out no smoke. Over the *kotatsu* is placed a wooden frame, which is covered with a *futon* or heavy padded covering. The people sit around the *kotatsu* with the *futon* covering their legs. Sometimes it is made so that the people can sit down as they do on chairs, so that they can be more comfortable. This is, however, a modern type of *kotatsu*. As charcoal or *tadon* is used, no smoke rises from it. Thus it is now preferred to *irori*. There is also a movable type of *kotatsu*, which is just a wooden box with the covering frame, with the charcoal fire inside, and may thus be taken to any place. But the movable type is not as warm as the one set in the floor.

The term *kotatsu* is said to have come from China, as it was introduced first by Buddhist priests who went there some 600 years ago. *Kotatsu* might have come from China originally, but in its general construction, it seems more proper to regard it as an improved type of *irori*.

NAGAYA

NAGAYA (long house) now means poorly constructed tenement houses. Originally, however, it meant any house which was narrow and long. But in the *Uji Tales*, compiled in the early part of the 13th century, *nagaya* means small tenement houses, made by dividing long narrow structures into small sections.

Thus the word came to stand for small dwellings, generally used by the poorer people. The standard size was *'kushaku-niken'* (2.7 m by 3.6 m) and under one long roof there were often as many as six or 10 sections. Such *nagaya* are still seen in many quarters.

In the Tokugawa days, many of the *samurai* or warrior class lived in these long houses but of course they were much better constructed.

All feudal lords had Edo residences, many of which were great mansions. Within the compound lived all the retainers and their families. Those of higher ranks had separate houses but those of the lower ranks or bachelors lived in *nagaya*.

These *nagaya* were generally constructed around the lord's residence. Most of them were two-storied structures, and each house had a window on the outward side. To enter it all had to pass through the gate of the residence.

When merchants or peddlers came and shouted their wares outside the *nagaya*, the dwellers inside put their heads out of the windows to look at the wares and bargain for them. When anyone wanted to buy vegetables, fish, other foods or wares, he would lower a bamboo basket tied to a rope out of the window to the man below, placing money in it. The peddler would put the desired thing in the basket, taking the money, and the buyer would then draw the basket up.

Such a method of purchase was not really permitted. They all had to go out of the house and the gate if they wanted to buy anything from the peddlers, but buying out of the window was common practice according to many existing stories.

NOREN

MANY shops of the country still have *noren* or curtains over their entrances. It generally bears the name and trademark of the shop in white on cotton cloth dyed in black, brown or gray.

It was first brought by Buddhist priests from China where it is called *nuanlien*, and introduced to temples to be used as a blind or curtain. Shops, which formerly had straw mats or curtains at the door to keep away wind and sun, gradually adopted the newly introduced cloth curtain.

As each shop marked its name and trademark on its *noren*, it became its symbol, and also came to stand for its reputation or standing.

When a shop apprentice ended his long service and became an expert in the trade, he was formally allowed to start his own business with permission to use the *noren* of his employer-master. This was called *noren-wake* or 'dividing the *noren*.' This privilege was not given unless the apprentice was found able to keep up the tradition and reputation of his master's shop. Among merchant circles, this was regarded as a great honor.

Noren has also come to stand not only for the shop and its wares, but also for its credit or good-will. When a shop is sold, the buyer has to pay for its *noren*, besides paying for the building, equipment and stocks of goods. *Noren* in this case is the same as good-will.

There is another type of *noren*, called *nawa-noren* or straw-rope *noren*. This is used only by low-class drinking places, and has even become almost a general term for such establishments.

ONIGAWARA

AT THE edges of the Japanese tiled roof are large decorative tiles, which are called *onigawara* or demon tiles. They are so called because such big tiles are mostly like the grotesque mask of a demon made in relief. Of course, all end tiles, with or without the demon mask, are called *onigawara*. Such *onigawara* are now regarded only as ornamental pieces to strengthen the ridge line of the roof.

But it is not for ornamental purposes that *onigawara* first came to be placed there. At first there were placed at the roof edges the *oni-ita* or demon board of wood on which the mask of a demon was placed. The wooden board was sometimes covered with copper plates to make it weatherproof. A large ornamental tile with the demon's mask replaced the ancient wooden boards.

The demon on *onigawara* represents *Kahaku*, a river deity. The original idea was to prevent the house from being destroyed by fire by placing the mask of the river deity. So the *onigawara* was primarily a charm for fire prevention.

Some *onigawara* have, therefore, the Chinese character for water engraved, instead of the mask of the demon. Again the shape of a turtle is also seen on *onigawara*, as a charm against fire.

Thus *onigawara* was primarily a charm although the fact is forgotten by modern folks, who regard it only as an ornamental piece.

It is interesting to note that gargoyles found on the roofs of many ancient European buildings look somewhat similar to the *onigawara* of Japan, but they are intended to keep the roof-water off the sides of the building, and are not a charm to prevent fire.

On thatched roofs in the country, *shobu* or a kind of iris, which blossoms beautifully in May, are sometimes planted. They are planted not to decorate the roof, but to prevent fire. It has been also believed that *shobu* charms away devils and sickness.

REED–THATCHED ROOF

KAYA-YANE (reed-thatched roof), *mino* (reed-leaf raincoat), and *suge-gasa* (sedge hat) have been the most picturesque symbols of the farming community of Japan. They may be all very crude and primitive in materials and construction, but because they have many good points, they are still preferred to modern substitutes by the people of farming villages.

Kaya-yane or roof thatched with *kaya* or reed (miscanthus) leaves is as old as the country. It has recently disappeared from cities, simply because of its prohibition by law on account of it being easily inflammable. If there were no such law, the reed roof would have remained popular even in crowded cities. In rural farming villages, most of the old or big houses are still reed-thatched. Many people regret the disappearance of this massive reed roof, as it is not only picturesque but makes the house very comfortable.

The *kaya-yane* is laid very thick, particularly in cases of temple buildings or big houses, sometimes reaching more than three or four feet deep. The thick reed roof keeps the house cool in summer and warm in winter. Then, it lasts as long as the house itself stands if proper care is given every three or five years. There are many *kaya-yane* which are more than 100 years old.

Yet to keep the roof in good condition and make it last long, it is necessary to have *irori* or the old-fashioned open hearth in the house. The smoke rising from the *irori* will keep the reed leaves in the roof dry and drive away insects. When the reed leaves become damp or insects make their nests in the layers, the roof decays quickly. In some *kaya*-roofed houses the old-fashioned *irori* is given up, and in such cases the roof and houses decay very quickly. So the old open *irori* must always come with *kaya-yane*.

In many different districts of the country there is a custom of planting *shobu* (a kind of iris) on the ridge of the reed roof, in the belief that the plant will keep sickness from the house. As the layers of reeds are very thick, the planting of the flowering iris does not ruin it at all.

Mino or reed-leaf raincoats are not yet surpassed by any modern raincoat for practical use by outdoor workers. The long leaves used in making them are from *chigaya* (a special kind of reed narrower and longer than other kinds). The leaves are put together ingeniously so that they form loose layers one above the other, covering the entire body. Sometimes a *mino* is made in two sections, one to be tied at the neck, and the other at the waist, the upper one lapping over the lower. It is made like a cape and has no sleeves. However heavy the rain might be, *mino* will keep the wearer dry, while also allowing free motion of the wearer's legs and arms.

Suge-gasa or sedge hats always go with *mino*. These are large round hats, in the shape of overturned shallow bowls. They are light and large to keep the sun and rain off of the wearer's face

and neck. In ancient days, *suge-gasa* were worn by all people, from the nobles down to the lowest workers. But later, they came to be used only by farmers and other outdoor workers.

Rice-planting comes just in the season of *tsuyu* or rainy season. Thus, over the vast paddy fields, there are always seen farmers wearing *mino* and *suge-gasa* planting rice in the rain.

ROCKS IN GARDENS

FROM very early days the people of Japan have found beauty or something to admire in natural rocks. The same tendency is also found among the Chinese. The love and admiration of rocks seem to be a characteristic of Oriental peoples. It is recorded that in the reign of Empress Regnant Suiko (592-628) the Chinese Emperor presented a piece of rock to the Japanese Empress. To Western people it might be inconceivable how a piece of rock was selected as a gift from one emperor to another. Yet to Orientals, a fine rock of exceptional beauty is the most valuable gift that one may receive.

In the Japanese garden, rocks form the center of its design, and no garden is complete without rocks. The rock garden of the Ryoanji Temple, Kyoto, laid in 1473, is one of the most famous gardens of the country. It has 15 rocks, laid in groups of seven, five and three, and the rest of the garden is covered with white sand. There is not a single tree nor an inch of lawn. Still it is called one of the finest gardens in the world.

Rocks are a symbol of nature, and in them the people see all the beauty and grandeur of nature. The people's love of rocks is presented in various ways. The art of *bonseki* (tray garden) or landscapes made in miniature on trays with natural rocks of various shapes and sand have developed since the seventh century. It has become an art to make beautiful and delicate miniature gardens on trays with nothing but small rocks and sands.

There is also a custom of placing a natural rock of special beauty or shape as an ornament in a room. Furthermore, some people place a rock in a shallow basin filled with water, and daily pour water upon it for many years until they see mosses grow on it.

To find good rocks is the first step to lay out a good Japanese garden. Garden lovers go to extreme expense and trouble in their search for fine rocks. They are brought from distant mountains, and when they are too big they are cut into small pieces and assembled together again upon reaching the garden.

Many garden rocks are buried deep in the ground. Those garden rocks are never cut. If one is too big for the selected spot in the garden, it is buried half into the ground. It is believed that deep 'rooted' rocks show more strength and weight than the smaller ones that are just placed on the ground. All garden rocks must always remain in their natural condition, and should not, under any circumstances, be cut or polished. All the beauty of rocks lies in their naturalness.

SHACHIHOKO

ON THE roofs of many ancient palace buildings, castles, towers and gates of feudal architecture, there stand dolphin-like monsters in bronze or tile, with their tails raised high above their heads. The figures represent *shachihoko*, and they are ornamental, of course, but originally they were placed on roof ridges to protect such buildings from the menace of fire.

In general appearance, a *shachihoko* is like a fish, covered entirely with large black or gray scales. Its head is like that of a dragon of the common conception. Both its fins spread out like two huge wings. In place of its back fin, it has huge sharp thorn-like projections growing from the back of the head to the tail. It has a spouting hole on the top of its head like a whale, and it is said to be so powerful as to be able to kill a big whale instantly.

It is not known how this strange sea monster came to be the protector of buildings from fire. Probably its grotesque appearance and particularly the spouting hole that might send out water to quench any fire may have given rise to this common belief.

Usually there is always a pair of *shachihoko* placed on one roof, one at each end of the ridge. One of the pair is believed to be the male and the other the female. It is traditionally said that at first the two figures faced inward, but later they came to face outward. Yet there is no proof to this story.

Shachihoko are always found standing upside down. They place their heads on the roof, and supporting their weight on their wing-like fins, they raise their bodies in the air with the tails gracefully curving. Being thus high over the heads, the bodies placed at each end of the roof ridge, they form quite dignified ornaments for buildings.

Shachihoko are never presented in any other position but in the form of standing on their heads. There are no pictures showing *shachihoko* lying down flat, or swimming in the ocean. Though believed to be sea monsters, they are always shown high on the roof.

Thus, *shachihoko* came to be used as a synonym for 'standing upside down on the head.' Also the term '*shachiko-baru*' (to be stiffly dignified) comes from the name of this grotesque roof ornament.

SHIKII

SHIKII or doorsill stands for the house entrance and often for the house itself. When a member of the family leaves the house in anger or disagreement with other members, he will say *'Nidoto shikii-o mataganai'* (I will never again step over the doorsill), because to rejoin the family he must step over the doorsill to enter the house.

When one owes money to a friend or relative, has acted unkindly, or failed to fulfill an obligation to him, he naturally feels reluctant to visit the house. In such cases, he would say, 'I cannot make myself visit the house, because the doorsill is high.' *'Shikii-ga takai'* (doorsill is high) is a term used to express the awkwardness or self-consciousness one feels in visiting the house of a person to whom he has not acted properly and feels ashamed.

A visitor must step over the sill to be welcomed by the family. One who is not welcome is not allowed to step over it. Thus it is discourteous to speak across the *shikii.* 'Shikii-goshi' (over the *shikii*) is to be avoided.

Beggars or peddlers who are unwelcome are never permitted to step over the sill.

As a 'high doorsill' stands for the dignity or honor of the house, inversely when the fortunes of a family has declined, the expression *'shikii-ga hikukunatta'* (the doorsill has fallen lower) is often used in some districts. But this term more often means that it has become easier to visit the house as the circumstances that made it difficult to call on the family have been removed or the visitor has determined to make a visit despite his shameful past attitude.

Thus in the daily life of the people, the *shikii* of the house has quite an important meaning.

SHRINE ARCHITECTURE

THE ARCHITECTURE of Shinto shrines is representative of the oldest architecture in Japan, and it is only in the construction of Shinto shrine buildings that the type and form of ancient buildings in Japan are now preserved.

The shrine architecture, having been used only in the construction of Shinto shrines, has naturally become a symbolic feature of Shinto. Japanese houses underwent considerable changes because of the outside influence and changes in the people's customs and culture, but Shinto shrines remained the same for 20 centuries.

There are various different types of shrine architecture at present, but the fundamental features are retained in all types.

The type of architecture used at the Izumo Taisha is the oldest form of Shinto architecture, generally known as the *Taisha* type. The main features of this type are that the building is square with a large pillar in the center, and the stairway leading to it is not made at the center, but in the right half of the front. The entire building, of course, is of unpainted natural wood, and the roof is thatched with wood chips, and on the top of the roof are placed several cross bars called *chigi.* This type of architecture is said to retain the features of the prehistoric buildings of the country.

The second in historical order is the type called *Otori*, and its representative shrine is the Otori Shrine, Yamato province. This building is also square, but has no central pillar, and the stairway is made at the center of the front side. In other respects, however, this type resembles the *Taisha* type.

The third type, called the *Sumiyoshi*

type, has an oblong building, but the narrow side is the front, and the interior is divided into two parts, the rear part being sacred.

The *Shinmei* type, which is very common, has an oblong building, but the long side is the front. This type of architecture is seen in a great number of shrines.

In the *Kasuga* type, the width of the stairway stretches over the entire front length of the building.

In those earlier types of shrines, there was only one building, but in the *Hiyoshi* type that developed later, two buildings came to be joined together, the rear building being the sacred part, and the front building the worshipping place.

From this type there developed a style possessing separate sacred and worshipping buildings. Sometimes the two buildings are connected by a corridor, but they are also often made quite independent of each other.

As time went on, shrine buildings became elaborate in structure, but in ancient great shrines, the original style has been preserved and retained.

STONE LANTERNS

ISHI-DORO or stone lanterns are found in temple and shrine grounds and also in many parks and private gardens. They are today mostly ornamental, and are very rarely lighted.

Ishi-doro developed from crude torches and bonfires which were lighted at shrines and temples. They were offerings to Buddha or deities, but also for giving light at services and rites which were at first held always at night. But such lanterns gradually came to be used in private houses and placed at roadsides to guide the people at night.

It was the development of temple architecture that improved stone lan-

terns. The oldest existing *ishi-doro* is at the Tomaji Temple, Yamato, which was erected in 682.

Through the Heian (794-1192), Kamakura (1192-1336) and Muromachi (1392-1573) periods, stone lanterns became elaborate and artistic. Then in the Momoyama (1573-1615) and Edo (1615-1867) periods, stone lanterns underwent notable changes. Tea masters adapted temple lanterns for their tiny gardens. Thus those tea garden lanterns were made smaller and simpler than temple lanterns, and soon became popular in all large gardens.

Thus, there were produced many different types of *ishi-doro* which are said to number more than 200. Differences are seen in their shapes and workmanship.

All lanterns, however, consist of the foundation stone, which is sometimes buried deep into the ground, the round pillar which is often decorated with carvings, the shelf upon the pillar, the light box, and the roof on top, which has an ornamental ball at the center.

The foundation and the roof come in a triangle, square, oblong, diamond, hexagon or octagon shape. Those of the hexagon shape are most numerous, followed by square ones.

Stone lanterns are mostly of granite, but other kinds of stone are often used in making them. Bronze lanterns are generally for temples and shrines.

Besides the general shape, there are many minor features that differ according to the styles.

Many old families are proud of their lanterns in their gardens, because such are considered as a sign of wealth. In fact *ishi-doro* are very expensive, beyond the reach of common people. Yet there are still expert *ishi-doro* makers who always have many orders to fill.

SUDARE

SUDARE, which may be called Japanese hanging screens or blinds, make Japanese houses beautiful and cool in summer. *Sudare* are made of polished split bamboo or reeds, and used in place of *shoji* or paper-covered sliding doors and other partitions to enable a better flow of breeze.

Though their origin is unknown, they have been used since very early days. As they are mentioned in *Kagero Nikki* which tells of life in the 10th century, they must have been used in the houses of the aristocrats from very early times. But their common use seems to have become popular only about two and a half centuries ago. One record says that *sudare* were first sold in Edo at the shop of Yamamoto Zenbei at Ryogoku in the Shotoku era (1711-1716).

Sudare used at the Imperial Court and shrines are generally called *misu* or sacred *sudare*. *Misu* differ from common *sudare* in having all sides covered with brocade borders and decorated with bright red silk tasels. There are also metal hooks attached to adjust the length of the *misu* whenever necessary.

But the purpose of the *misu* used at palaces and shrines is not for ventilation in summer, but to prevent those outside from obtaining a clear view of the inside. They are primarily for maintaining the sacredness or dignity of such structures. Consequently, *misu* and *sudare* differ fundamentally in their significance. Of late, however, *misu*-type *sudare* have come to be used in ordinary houses in summer, as they look artistic with the brocade borders and tassels.

Misu are often called *ao-sudare* or green *sudare*, because they are made of fresh bamboo and retain its green color.

TATAMI

THE MANNER in which the people of Japan sit on the *tatami* or mats is unique. They squat squarely on their toes and heels. There are many other people who sit with legs crossed in front, but no other people squat down as the Japanese do.

Originally the people did not sit down in such a manner, and this custom developed in the long period in which Japanese architecture and living modes underwent gradual changes.

At first Japanese dwellings were simple wooden huts, and some were only semi-caves. The floor of those early houses was of bare wooden boards. During this period they used crude stools to sit on, or sat cross-legged as Indians do. Furthermore, men and women alike were dressed in a two-piece suit consisting of a simple upper tunic and loose, baggy trousers.

Then, in the latter part of the sixth century, the houses of noblemen began to grow elaborate with the introduction of Chinese architecture. Tiled roofs covered palaces, temples and other massive edifices, but the common people still lived in simple thatched huts. But one development in this period was the use of a low dais covered with *tatami* as a bed. At first such raised platforms were used by nobles only, but in the seventh century they became popular in the houses of all classes. This type of dais was only for sleeping and thus covered only a small corner of a room. They had posts for hanging curtains and nets, resembling the old-fashioned bedsteads of Europe.

Toward the end of the Heian period or 11th century, *tatami* became more generally used, and in many houses they were used as seats for honored guests. It was also about this time that *shoji* or sliding doors were put in houses.

In the Kamakura period or 13th century, *tatami* were placed all around the room, leaving only the central portion bare. Sitting on the raised *tatami*, they crossed their feet on the bare floor. Soon, *tatami* came to cover the entire floor, and the old dais or bedstead disappeared. Thus the Japanese came to sleep on matted floors since the 13th or 14th century.

The adoption of the matted floor radically changed the indoor customs of the people. While formerly they used tables and stools for eating their meals, the new fashion of eating from a low tray placed individually before each person was introduced. It was in this manner that squatting as it is still done now developed.

The *tatami*-covered floor and the habit of squatting rapidly changed the household habits of the people, particularly after the Kamakura period. First, women's dress changed from the old two-piece suit to a one-piece affair, as this gave them more comfort and ease in the squatting posture. Men had to dress in the manner prescribed by law when in an official capacity or when making calls of etiquette. But gradually they adopted a one-piece suit with long loose sleeves for comfort at home.

The life on *tatami* regulated their daily habits. Interior arrangements and decorations changed, because everything in the room is to be seen from the sitting position. Various household utensils, such as *hibachi* (fire box), *futon* to sleep in, low individual eating trays, *tabi* (Japanese socks), and many other such household goods, originated because of *tatami*.

Tatami are now made of a thick straw body, about three inches thick, three feet wide and six feet long, which is covered with a fine matting woven of rush. The size differs slightly according to district. A new *tatami* is pleasant and beautiful, giving a delightful smell. There is a saying that *tatami* and wives are best when new.

TEA ROOMS

MANY foreigners visiting a *chashitsu* (tea room) where *cha-no-yu* or the so-called tea ceremony is held, complain of the smallness of the room and suggest that if the room were bigger and brighter, it would be more pleasant and comfortable.

It should, however, be borne in mind that the room is purposely made small. It is generally about nine feet square, and sometimes much smaller, but into that space are crowded five or more guests besides the host and his tea-making utensils. There is no room to move about, and so persons not used to *chashitsu* feel cramped.

But the tea room is made small to make all within it feel intimate and harmonious. Sitting down with sleeves brushing fellow guests on both sides, they can understand the others' expressions and better catch the fine tones of their speech. It is this intimacy that is aimed at in holding the tea party.

Also the smallness of the room makes them pay closer attention to the room, decorations, pictures, flowers and utensils, for the selection and arrangement of which the host has given much care. The soft music of the water boiling in the kettle and the whisking of the tea in the bowl can be clearly heard by all.

The aim of the tea ceremony, to bring people harmoniously together, face to face, with no artificial barriers, and in modesty, is thus attained better in a small room. If it were held in a larger and brighter room, all the delicacy so intended would be lost.

For this reason *chashitsu* is made

small and plain, to make those entering the room feel intimate and learn the beauty and harmony of nature.

TORII

TORII is the symbol of shrines. Where there is a *torii* there is a shrine, and some shrines have many *torii* which form long tunnels leading to them.

Torii originated from the ancient custom of offering live cocks to shrines. The Sun Goddess established the empire according to the old tradition, and early shrines erected in the country were dedicated to her. On the other hand, cocks were always associated with the sunrise. So it was regarded proper to offer cocks that stand for the sun.

At first a live cock was placed on a bird perch erected in front of the shrine. The perch was made of three wooden sticks, one placed horizontally for the bird to perch on, supported by two upright sticks placed at both ends. The perch was made permanent and birds were brought and placed thereon. Naturally the perch became the symbol of the shrine, though it retained the original name of *torii* (bird perch). As it stood for the shrine, it also became a sign to indicate a place of sanctity. Therefore, *torii* were erected not only at the front of the shrine, but also at its back and sides. Later, however, it became customary to have them only in front of shrines.

Torii were originally made of wood, but stone and bronze came to be used later. Of late, concrete *torii* have appeared. They come in all sizes, some attaining considerable height. There are many different types of *torii* now.

Some shrines in the country have a great many *torii.* The Inari Shrine at Fushimi, near Kyoto, for instance, is famous for its long row of red *torii.*

Hundreds of *torii* are presented by worshipers. Some make their prayers to the shrine for health or success, and when their prayers are answered, they erect new *torii* to express their thanks. Of course, there are many other worshipers who present *torii*, with no connection to their wish or prayer.

Inari shrines are regarded as guardians of farm crops, and thus are most common and numerous in the country. To Inari shrines, farmers and others present red *torii* in prayer for a good harvest.

The original type of *torii* had straight round posts and bars, of natural unpainted wood. Even today this type is called the *Shinmei* (shrine) type. This type is most widely used, although in some cases they are not of unpainted wood, but of metal or stone.

Then there appeared elaborate types of *torii*, with curved bars of square wood. There are also some which have sideposts besides the two main posts. All these artistic types of *torii* are of later development. Among such kinds of *torii*, there are the *Kasuga*, *Kashima*, *Sanno* and other types.

There is also another type *torii* which is often seen. It has something like sidedoors at the base of the two posts, quite similar to Chinese temple gates.

There are such different types of *torii*, but they are all the gates to Shinto shrines, and indicate the presence of such shrines.

YUKIGUNI

MANY districts facing the northern Japan Sea are called *yukiguni* (snow country), because for almost three months these places are covered with ten to fifteen or more feet of snow.

Houses in those areas are built strong enough to withstand the heavy weight of snow on the roof, but still the people have to shovel snow off the roof almost daily, to keep the houses from collapsing. Thus all around the houses there are piles of snow as high as or even higher than the roof-top. To go to the next house, a tunnel has to be dug through the snow hill that has risen between the two houses.

Shops and houses on the town streets have wide eaves, extending five to ten feet outward to keep the walk along the street clear of snow. Thus a tunnel-like walk is made for the convenience of the people. To reach the other side of the street, tunnels have to be made at proper intervals.

Children love the snow and are outdoors all the time, sliding on its hardened surface. They also love to dig caves and tunnels in snow mountains which are formed around and over their houses and towns. They play within the snow caves which are quite comfortable and warm.

The people wear deep snow-shoes made of straw, and pull goods on crudely made sleighs. But as no farm or outdoor work is possible, grown-ups spend the whole day indoors, sitting around the huge *kotatsu*. Their winter life centers around the *kotatsu*, or Japanese fireplace. It is a square hole, generally three to six feet square, cut in the floor and filled with straw ash. A charcoal fire burns in the center, and a wooden frame over a foot high, is fitted into the place over the cut in the floor. Over the frame is placed a heavy quilted covering.

The whole family as well as visitors sit around the *kotatsu* with hands and knees under the covering, talking or taking tea and meals on the *kotatsu* frame. The long winter evening thus becomes very pleasant for them. Some people even sleep with their feet stretched under the covering of the *kotatsu*, so they can be warm through the night.

Since very old days snow has been stored up in winter in those regions for use in summer and used to be presented to the Tokugawa shogun every summer.

Echigo on the Japan Sea is particularly famous for its *yukigura* or snow storehouse. A huge hole three meters deep and about 40 meters square is dug on a hill top. The snow is packed into this hole over which a roof is made of straw matting and then covered with cut *kaya* or miscanthus to a thickness of almost one meter. Thus the snow inside is not affected by the outside temperature.

When summer comes, the packed snow is sawed into convenient sizes and shipped out.

The people also use *kanjiki* or snow shoes when they have to go out. The snow shoes are made of bamboo frames, about half a meter long. The novel feature is that a strong rope is tied to the front end of the shoe and the wearer holds the rope in each hand. As he takes a step he pulls up the rope to make moving the foot easier.

ZASHIKI

ZASHIKI in the Japanese-style dwelling, which is only used for guests and often called the guest room, is an outstanding feature of Japanese architecture. Modern apartment houses have no *zashiki*, but good Japanese houses are judged by it.

It is the best room in the whole house built with the best obtainable materials and its features are the *tokonoma* (alcove) and the side shelf. Containers with flowers of the season, and *kakemono* or wall hangings or paintings or calligraphy are placed there.

Old dwellings were divided into an unfloored part and a floored section. The floored section had no covering and the people used *enza*, individual round seats made of straw, to sit on. The section where such round seats were used came to be called *zashiki*, meaning literally seat spread.

It is only since the Muromachi period or the 15th century that the entire room came to be covered with *tatami* or floor mats. Then when houses underwent a radical change with the introduction of Zen-style buildings, a special room to entertain guests came to be set aside. The old name of *zashiki* came to be used for such rooms.

In feudal days in the households of the merchant class, who only had small houses in congested areas, the *zashiki* was made on the second floor, while the family lived below. Occasionally it was built in the *dozo* or thick-walled storehouse that big merchants always had. All this was due to the original idea that the *zashiki* must be separate from the living section used by the family.

The tradition of the *zashiki* is still kept up in most of Japanese-style houses.

Chapter 4
Fetes and Festivals

BABY'S FETES

IN THE olden days there were four ceremonies held immediately after the birth of a baby. The evening of the birth, the evening of the third day, the evening of the fifth day and the evening of the seventh day were all occasions on which to fete the arrival of the child. The first three have practically disappeared, and only the *oshichiya* (seventh evening) ceremony remains. However, some remote rural villages often observe the *san-ya* (third evening) festival.

Oshichiya is the first important day for the baby, for it is introduced to all the relatives and friends of the family. Some of them may have seen it before, but not until the seventh evening is it officially and properly introduced. This fete is very significant, because the baby has had no name until that evening, so it is in fact its christening day and its introduction to society.

Actually the name of the baby is often decided upon before its birth and it is called by name in most cases during the first six days, but traditionally the christening takes place on the evening of the seventh day.

Commonly the father names the baby, but the mother often insists upon naming the child as she wishes, if it is a girl. To avoid any disagreement between the parents, a *nazuke-oya* (christening parent) is often selected to choose the name.

On this seventh-evening fete, the mother does not appear. The baby is shown to all the visitors, dressed in its best costume and solemnly held up by the nurse or the grandmother, and then the name it will bear is announced by the father. When the actual feasting begins the baby is taken away.

This occasion is naturally a joyous one, and everything pertaining to it signifies joy and pleasure.

Sekihan (red rice) is the main dish served at the feast. Rice cooked with *azuki* (red beans) is always used on happy occasions, and *tai* (sea bream) is the fish that adorns the table. The fish must be prepared for serving whole, as any fish without a head is unlucky. Various dishes made from fish, meat and vegetables follow. *Sake* (rice-wine) is offered everyone, for all must be merry and happy for the sake of the new-born child.

A small amount of the *sekihan*, or in some districts *mochi* (rice-cake), is distributed among neighbors and friends. It is sent to the friends and neighbors with the hope that they also will rejoice at the birth of the baby and pray for a long happy life for it.

BIRTHDAY CELEBRATIONS

CELEBRATION of a birthday is universal, but the Japanese *tanjobi* (birthday) celebration differs from that of other countries. All over the world 'birthday parties' are held to celebrate the anniversary of a birth, but probably no other people place such importance upon the birthday celebration as the Japanese.

The *tanjobi* is more than a birthday anniversary. On that day the people rejoice because of the good year just passed and hope for many happy and prosperous future years. Again they offer their gratitude to the gods for the care and attention given them in the past. At foreign birthday celebrations, the parents receive little consideration, for the party is solely in honor of the one whose anniversary is being celebrated. At *tanjobi* celebrations, however, gratitude to one's parents for their loving care, and joy that they are still alive are emphasized. The celebrations are held only while the parents are alive, and, when the fathers and mothers have died, they cease, since those who were the cause of the celebrations are no more.

Since more meaning is attached to the *tanjobi* while the parents are alive, the celebration is more elaborate in the case of babies and children. The first *tanjobi* of a baby is made a great occasion. Feasting and festivity in all families, however poor, is the rule of the day. Toys and other presents are given to the baby by friends of the family, but the custom of giving birthday presents is not as common in Japan as it is in other countries. Feasting is the more important feature of the occasion.

On each succeeding birthday, the child is taught to have love for its parents and to feel gratitude for their care.

BON FESTIVAL

URABON-E, more commonly called *Bon,* is a corruption of the Sanskrit 'Ullambana.' This is a service held by the relatives of the dead who wish to express their gratitude to the departed. At first this festival was held for parents and grandparents, but gradually it came to be celebrated for other dead as well. *Urabon-e* comes on the fifteenth day of the seventh month, according to the lunar calendar.

There is a very interesting story about the origin of this service. Once there was a man in India who wished to see what life his dead parents were leading. He saw in his vision his mother suffering from hunger, not having been able to get anything to eat after her death. So he prepared a generous bowl of food for her. But as she approached the bowl it filled with fire and she could not take it. In disappointment, the dutiful son asked the help of a famous Buddhist priest, who said that the sins his mother committed in her earthly life had brought the present punishment upon her, and that she could be saved only by the mercy of Buddha. Therefore he called several priests and held a mass for his mother. This mass was held on the fifteenth day of the seventh month, and it saved his mother from the agony of hunger. It is said that from this story the *Urabon-e* service originated.

Thus Ullambana was started, and introduced to Japan in the third year of Empress Regnant Saimyo, or 657. It came to be observed as an annual Court event since the fifth year of Tenpyo or 733. Though at first it was observed by the Court and noblemen alone, it soon became popular among all classes of the people as the Buddhist faith' spread. Ullambana was corrupted to *Urabon-e* in Japan, and then commonly it came to be called just *Obon.*

After its introduction into Japan, the *Bon* festival changed greatly in character and became not only a religious service, but also an occasion for joy. The Japanese people commonly believe that on this day the spirits of the dead return to the homes where they used to live in their earthly life.

To guide the spirits on their return, lighted lanterns are hung in every house where such services are held. These lanterns are often very beautiful and elaborate, although they are always made of white paper.

As the service originated from the old Indian story of a mother's hunger after death, various foods, especially vegetables, are placed for the dead to satisfy their hunger with. Such vegetables are not used afterwards, since they have been partaken of by the spirits. So these vegetables are floated down rivers or tossed into the sea.

Obon used to be quite an important social event, and for attending the family *Obon* service, such persons engaged in work away from their native places invariably returned home. To factory and shop apprentices or household maids, *Obon* and January 15 were the only two holidays in the whole year in the Tokugawa period, when they were permitted to return home to their parents.

Eager to properly guide the spirits of their ancestors on the day, it is customary to light lanterns at all houses. Some such lanterns were formerly very elaborate, especially made for the occasion. The most important feature of the service is the offering of food. To the ancestors are offered rice, vegetables, fruits, cakes, sweets and flowers. There are prepared special foods to be served to invited guests and friends. It is the spirit of giving food to fellow people that underlies this religious service. It is a religious day, but also quite a joyful social occasion.

Nagasaki, Kyushu, is famous for its *Obon* rite, which is more colorful than services held in other regions. On the evening of July 14, the people take in hand *Obon* lanterns at their doors and then proceed to the family grave. Tables are set up for offerings and lanterns are lit. Thus the whole cemetery turns into a mass of lighted lanterns. Children set off fireworks and crackers.

In the old days people held feasting parties at the cemetery, but this custom is not widely observed now.

On the following evening *seiryo-bune* or spirit boats are floated. The preparation of the boats is begun weeks before the day. The frame of a boat is made, with sticks and bamboo, and then covered with straw and matting making it quite water-tight. On the evening of the 15th, food and other offerings are put in the boat and lanterns are hung. The boat has sails made of paper or cotton cloth.

When ready, the boat is carried by the whole family to the seashore and floated to the sea. This closes the festival of *Obon*. But on July 16, a feast is held with chicken or lobster and other good things being served. During the festival, the people do not take any animal food, but when the rite for the ancestors is over, they eat meat to mark the return to normal life.

Bon-odori is another feature of *Obon*. It is a community dance held in all rural districts on some evening around July 15. It is a holiday for all the people, the young and old, male and female, who gather and dance in temple or shrine compounds, often until the next morning. Dances and songs differ according to districts, and symbolize their respective traditions.

Toro-nagashi or lantern-floating is the picturesque ending to the *Obon* service. To guide the ancestral spirits back to the other world, little floats are lighted with candles and floated down rivers or on the sea. Hundreds and thousands of such lighted floats are set off at one place, and the people eagerly watch them float down the river or be carried by the wind far away from the shore. Lafcadio Hearn was once so fascinated by the *Toro-nagashi* at Yaizu that he took off his clothing and swam after the numerous lighted floats that were carried away by the tide from the shore.

BOY'S FESTIVAL

TANGO-NO-SEKKU, Boy's Festival on May 5, is an occasion to express thanks for the healthy growth of boys and pray so as to make them safe from sickness and evil influence.

It has become since Tokugawa days one of the most important annual events of Japanese families with boys. But it originated in an ancient rural custom. May is just the time when insects begin to appear to harm plants. So since very early days, farmers tried to drive them away by frightening them with bright banners and grotesque figures, placed around their farms in the early part of May every year.

Later, these figures came to be made better, particularly to represent warriors famed for their fighting power. As the warrior-dolls were made artistically, they were gradually displayed indoors, not to scare away insects, but to teach young boys manliness and keep them from evil.

In such a manner, the present Boys' Festival developed. Warrior-dolls, miniature arms—swords, war helmets, bows and arrows—and banners were displayed formerly to impress upon boys the spirit and accomplishments of *samurai*.

The *Tango* festival was observed from very early days, and *shobu* (myrtle flag) was always used on that occasion. In the early days of the 17th century, it

was customary for young boys to play with *shobu* plants on the *Tango* days. They made thick bundles of *shobu* plants, and with them struck the ground and enjoyed the loud noise thus made. It is said that the louder the noise, the more satisfied they were. This was one form of play they enjoyed on the *Tango* festival.

The Tokugawa authorities greatly encouraged the observance of the *Tango* festival as a means for stimulating a martial spirit. Not only were the ancient customs and play of the festival preserved, but also new features were introduced. Following the encouragement given by the *Bakufu* authorities, the *samurai* families came to hold elaborate festivals. The common people who envied the privilege of the upper classes followed their example. But as class distinctions were very strict then, merchants and farmers could not observe the festival so elaborately.

The outstanding feature of the festival today is the carp streamer, *koi-nobori*. Huge paper or cloth carp are displayed atop tall poles in the garden. The carp which can easily swim up rapid streams that stop other fish stands for courage and power to attain high aims. In many districts, little boys are made to crawl through the paper carp, from the mouth to the tail, for good luck. Kite flying is also a feature of the May 5 festival in many localities.

The *koi-nobori* or carp streamer came into use for the first time in the An-ei era (1772-1781), as the people found that the indoor display of paper dolls and such was not sufficient to glorify the festival. This custom of hoisting huge paper or cloth carp streamers, or red and white common streamers was rapidly popularized throughout the country. Paper or cloth carp sometimes are 30 feet or more in length, while there are tiny ones of only a few inches which are placed indoors.

In many districts of the country, kite flying was also engaged in on the *Tango* festival. Huge kites sometimes as big as thirty by fifty feet were used. The boys enjoyed kite-fighting. A boy let his kite or kite-line entangle another boy's and made it fall.

Also *Kashiwa-mochi*, or sweet rice cakes wrapped up in oak leaves, are distributed among neighbors and friends. The boys are given *shobu-yu* or bath with myrtle-flag leaves. The leaves are believed to have the power to expel sickness and evil spirits. On house-roofs and eaves *shobu* leaves are placed on the day. Some straw-thatched roofs of farmers still have myrtle-flags planted in them to keep the families free from evil influence.

CHANGE OF LUCK

AT THE Tenjin Shrine of Kameido, a suburb of Tokyo, is observed on January 25 one of the most unique customs of the country. It is called *Usogae (uso* exchange).

When one visits the Tenjin Shrine he finds little wooden birds, crudely carved and painted. These birds might be taken for almost any kind of little birds, but they are intended to be *uso* (Oriental bullfinch; Pyrrhula greiventris). They are made in all sizes, and larger ones naturally cost more than smaller birds.

Visitors to the shrine purchase these wooden *uso*, and then take them to the office of the shrine, where they are exchanged for similar wooden *uso*. It is believed that when their *uso* are exchanged with those offered by the shrine office, they bring good luck.

Uso also means 'falsehood,' and they believe that by exchanging those *uso*

birds, they exchange 'falsehood' for 'truth.'

At the Kameido Tenjin Shrine, this custom of exchanging *uso* has been observed since 1820, and therefore it is more than 100 years old. But in feudal days, *Usogae* was observed in quite a different way. At that time, *uso* birds were offered by the shrine, and visitors exchanged them with those held by other people. That is to say, they first went to the shrine, and received the wooden *uso* from the shrine. Then they started to walk around in the shrine compound, holding their *uso* in their sleeves. As people passed one another, they quickly exchanged their *uso* with those in other people's sleeves. But this custom was soon prohibited by the Tokugawa authorities, because it gave opportunities to pickpockets to pilfer various valuables from others. It was since then that the habit of exchanging *uso* at the shrine office was started.

It is the Tenjin Shrine at Dazaifu, Chikuzen, that really started this custom of *Usogae*. But there it is always observed on the evening of January 7. The Kameido Tenjin copied the custom observed at the Dazaifu Tenjin. At Dazaifu, it was believed that among numerous *uso* birds given away by the Tenjin Shrine there was one made of pure gold, and the one who received it would be favored with extreme good fortune during the year. There, however, developed various robberies and crimes on the occasion of *Usogae* because it was held at night.

All those wishing to have good luck, or to exchange 'falsehood' for 'truth,' should visit the Kameido Tenjin on January 25, and exchange their wooden *uso* with those given by the shrine. The Tenjin Shrine is near the Yanagi-shima tram car stop, Honjo.

EBISUKO

MANY stores, particularly dry-goods shops, hold *Ebisuko* special sales from the first part of October, although formerly *Ebisuko* was held on October 20. *Ebisu* is the guardian deity of shopkeepers and *Ebisuko* was held on October 20 or January 20 to pray for good business. In honor of the deity, goods came to be offered at reduced prices on those days.

While *Ebisuko* sales are still held by many stores, the former custom of holding a special service for *Ebisu* is kept up only by old-fashioned merchants. Offerings were made to *Ebisu* and all shops held big merry parties, inviting friends and patrons. There was a custom of holding sham auction sales of all articles in the room where the feast was held, each guest making big imaginary bids. By having such fun the shop-owners thought that their business would prosper.

The special sales were at first only a secondary affair to enliven the business and please patrons of the shops. Dry-goods stores offered remnants at sacrifice prices.

Present storekeepers may not be so zealous in worshiping *Ebisu* and holding big parties in his honor but they do not overlook the opportunity of sales and attracting the public to their shops. *Ebisu* is one of the seven gods of good fortune and in painting and sculpture is represented as a genial person, holding a big *tai* (sea bream), fish of good luck, and a fishing pole. It is not known clearly why *Ebisu* came to be regarded as the deity bringing prosperity and good business, but since about the eighth century he has been worshiped by the people as the deity of good fortune.

Merchants, therefore, have paintings or carvings of *Ebisu* in their stores and make offerings and prayers to them. *Ebisu* is particularly remembered by storekeepers when they hold *Ebisuko* in October as a chance to pep up business.

EIGHTY-EIGHTH YEAR FETE

YONE-NO-IWAI (rice celebration) became popular because the character standing for *yone* (rice) can also be read as 'eighty-eight.' When the three numerals standing for 'eight, ten, eight' are conventionalized into a design, they form the character *yone*, or rice.

Yone-no-iwai, or the 88th celebration, is a modern one, introduced much later than the original *Nenga* (age fetes).

Rice as the principal food of the people has always been regarded as sacred. From the very beginning of history, *yone* or *kome*, as it is called, was respected by the people, for it was their food, their life, their happiness, and also stood for purity.

So the 88th year is celebrated as a happy and joyous occasion, because it is the age of *yone*. Besides its figurative relation to rice, this year is especially popular because the Japanese people have always loved double numbers. They celebrate the third day of the third month, the fifth day of the fifth month, the ninth day of the ninth month, and, especially, the 77th and the 88th birthdays.

At this celebration all the children, grandchildren and greatgrandchildren gather together, for it is a matter of family pride for so large a gathering of blood relations to meet in honor of their *toshiyori* (old man).

FESTIVAL FLOATS

IT IS the great pride of any local community to possess many richly decorated *dashi* or festival floats, because the magnitude and beauty of a shrine festival are decided by the number and richness of floats. Many of those festival floats are hundreds of years old, and are admired as wonderful works of art.

Generally a *dashi* has a huge image of some historical or legendary person, or real or imaginary animals on it. Again, sometimes, a miniature mountain decorated with plants and blossoms adorns it. Constructed on wheels, the *dashi* is drawn by men or oxen in the festival procession. Drum beaters and flute players, who supply music throughout the procession, generally ride along on most of the big *dashi*.

The procession of *dashi* at the Gion festival in Kyoto is probably the most picturesque of all festivals in the country, because of the many magnificent old *dashi*, which represent the highest developed arts of doll making, weaving, dyeing, embroidering, metal working, carving and lacquering.

Dashi is an ornament to a festival, which makes it beautiful, gay and joyful. But in the beginning it had a significant, religious meaning. It originated from *Shimeshi-no-yama* (marking mountain) which was used in ancient days at the Imperial Palace on the occasion of *Daijo-e* or harvest rites. On this occasion of the Shinto rites of presenting the newly harvested rice to the heavenly *kami* or gods, two temporary shrines, *Yuki* and *Suki*, were erected. In front of each of these shrines was placed *Shimeshi-no-yama*.

This consisted of a miniature mountain made of earth, on which was planted a pine or some other sacred tree, decorated with a miniature sun and moon, and banners. Images of fairies were also sometimes placed on the tree. Its height is said to have been as tall as 25 feet, but smaller ones were more common.

The *Shimeshi-no-yama* was placed as a mark to show the heavenly *kami* where to land. The marking was necessary because the *kami* had to be guided so that he would not step on any unholy spot.

Later this custom came to be adopted by shrines in calling down the heavenly *kami*. Gradually, however, the *Shimeshi-no-yama* became ornamental with its decorative feature appealing more strongly to the people than its original religious meaning. In time shrines came to possess many *dashi* that were made after the original *Shimeshi-no-yama*.

FIRE RITE

HITAKI-MATSURI (fire-burning festival) of Shimonomiya Shrine at Aso, Kyushu, is unique, and also one of the longest festival rites as it continues for 58 days, from August 19 to October 16.

On the first day of the festival, the sacred palanquin of the shrine goes to *Hitaki-den*, the fire-burning building. *'Hitaki-otome'* or fire-burning maiden is selected by turn from young girls, 12 to 13 years old, from the surrounding three villages. It is this maiden who undertakes the burning of the fire.

This maiden, accompanied by her mother, lives in a small hut beside the fire-burning building and must attend the task of feeding wood to the fire, day and night for 58 days. She is helped by her mother who must also prepare food for the maiden. At night the mother attends to the fire in her place.

On October 16 the fire-burning ends, and the palanquin returns to the shrine. Then the closing ceremony of the festival is held, and sacred music and dances are offered at the shrine all night. The maiden dances bare-foot amid the bonfires.

This strange rite is based on an ancient tradition. Once Takei-watatsu-no-mikoto, mighty god of Aso mountain went hunting with Kihachi, a young attendant. Playfully the god shot his arrow in various directions and ordered Kihachi to retrieve it. As he was made to run after the arrow 99 times, Kihachi lost his temper, and finally kicked the arrow toward the god.

Angered at the insolent act of Kihachi, the god chased him. Kihachi ran as fast as he could, but was finally shot by the god's arrow. The soul of Kihachi went to the heavens and became a star, but he could not forget his hatred of the god. To avenge the wrong done him, Kihachi shed frosts down on the Amo valley at the height of the summer season.

But his revengeful act caused suffering to the villagers whose crops were spoiled by the unseasonal frost. They thought of appeasing Kihachi's soul and making him stop the summer frost. Thinking that Kihachi must be cold in the heavens, they started to burn a fire to warm him.

The tradition is kept up by the *Hitaki-matsuri* which is still faithfully observed by the villagers.

FORTIETH-YEAR CELEBRATION

THE CUSTOM of observing *Nenga* (year celebration) originally came from China. But as early as the Nara period (710-784), it was adopted by the Japanese public as well as by the Imperial Family. *Nengas* were held to celebrate the attainment of the 40th, 50th, 60th, 70th, 80th and 90th years. But during the Ashikaga period (1392-1573) the years were changed and the 61st, 77th and 88th years came to be celebrated. Today the two systems are mixed, and the different series are celebrated according to different districts.

The first *Nenga* comes when a person attains his 40th year of age. The Japanese believed a man to be on the threshold of old age when he turned 40, which is commonly called *shoro* (beginning of old age).

The Chinese had contrary ideas, however. Confucius (551-479 B.C.) said that 'at 40 one is no longer misled.' Men are perplexed and led astray in their youth, and not until they are 40 do they have the judgment and wisdom to govern their conduct wisely. At 40 a man is supposed to be fully developed and to have reached the age of sound judgment and reasoning. According to this Chinese idea, men are not fully grown until they reach the age of 40.

The reason why men of 40 were regarded as old men in Japan was probably because in feudal times they sometimes held full responsibility at the age of seven, and always at 15.

So the attainment of the 40th year is celebrated as an important milestone in a man's life. And if he really has acquired good judgment at that age, it is indeed an occasion worth celebrating. The celebration generally consists of elaborate feasting. Friends and relatives are invited to partake in the feast.

In the cities of today this custom is gradually dying out, for the modern busy world no longer considers a man old at 40. But in rural districts where the people still marry young, and where the duty of every male consists solely of succeeding to the tasks of his father, 40 is regarded as quite old. Marrying young, such rural people usually have grown-up daughters and sons at 40, which fact alone would make them feel quite old.

FUTOMANI FETE

A UNIQUE rite of foretelling the year's

agricultural crop by the ancient divination method of roasting a deer bone is annually held at the Mitake Shrine, located on top of Mt. Mitake in the Chichibu-Tama National Park, Tokyo. It is held on January 3 and is called *Futomani-matsuri*. A special platform is erected for the service and products of land and sea are offered to the shrine. First a fire is made by rubbing a stick made of *shuzakura*, a kind of cherry tree, against a wheel made of *hinoki* or Japanese cypress wood. It is a tedious task, and takes more than 10 minutes to make it spark.

When the fire is made, a metal grill is placed over it. Then a shoulder bone of the deer is put upon the grill. In about 20 minutes the bone begins to show cracks.

The bone is then carefully studied and the fortune is told by the size, number and shape of the cracks. When the reading of the cracks is completed, it is noted on a long piece of paper, on which are printed the names of all crops: rice, millet, wheat, barley, buckwheat, soybeans, red beans, carrots, burdock, sweet potato, onion, eggplant, cucumber, tea, mulberry, tobacco, silk cocoon, hemp and others.

Each item is given a number, ranging from one to 10. The number 10 denotes a 100 percent crop, so accordingly the larger the number, the better the crop.

As neighboring farmers have depended on this divination for their plantings during the year, the results of the *Futomani* fete divination are publicly circulated on January 15.

The divination by reading cracks on animal bones was the earliest method of fortune telling, but with the introduction of the Chinese method of prophecy, the ancient method was almost forgotten. The *Futomani* fete of the Mitake Shrine is a rare and interesting old rite that is still preserved.

HATSU-UMA

HATSU-UMA (first horse day), after *risshun* (beginning of spring) according to the old calendar, falls on February 10. It is commonly regarded as the day for the festival of Inari Shrine, generally marked with a red *torii* and fox statues. As Inari is the guardian deity of farmers, the festival is very extensively observed in rural districts as a community holiday.

But originally the festival was observed on *hatsu-uma* for a good harvest and known as *haru-matsuri* or spring festival. The *hatsu-uma* festival is usually held on the first horse day in February, but in some districts it is held in November or April.

The *hatsu-uma* festival is held in various different ways and many strange customs have developed. Feasting is generally the main feature, and in some districts *dango* or rice-dumplings are specially made. In some villages the people do not drink tea on that day. Horses are often gaily decorated and led to the shrines on mountain tops as a rite for a good harvest.

In Nagano Prefecture, where sericulture is extensively done, *hatsu-uma* is a festival for the god of silkworms. In other districts farmers who had calves born to their cattle in the past year offer *sake* drinks to all the neighbors to celebrate their good luck.

Since Inari is the farmers' guardian, they also hold a festival at Inari shrines. To the villagers, and particularly to children, *hatsu-uma* of Inari-san is one of the greatest annual events.

The shrines are decorated with long banners, and children gather to beat drums and participate in the rites. All the villagers visit their local Inari-san, and at many large ones booths are erected to sell novelties and foodstuffs. Theatrical entertainments and other shows are given, often by the villagers themselves.

Many old families have family Inari shrines in their compound, and such families also hold a *hatsu-uma* festival for their deities.

HINA-ICHI

HINA-ICHI or doll fairs are opened at many places in February, to display and sell dolls for *Hina-matsuri* on March 3. Of course, *hina-ichi* today are not as picturesque as they used to be due mainly to special displays of dolls and other utensils for the doll's festival held at big department stores. However, it is still an annual event, particularly in Tokyo.

Hina-ichi started in Edo in the Kyoho era (1716-1736). Particularly after the second year of Kansei, 1790, it developed into a big annual event in Edo life. Those held at Jukkendana (Nihonbashi), Owaricho (Ginza), Kojimachi, Komagome, Nakacho (Ueno), and other places were occasions for a grand gathering of Edo people. *Hina-ichi* became so popular then that the people went there not only to buy dolls, but also to enjoy the display and take part in the busy atmosphere.

To hold the doll fairs, the officials of such districts applied to the authorities for a permit, setting the days and places, and also promising to make fair deals. But in those days, dolls were not sold at tagged prices, and buyers bargained to beat down the price. This custom is still retained in some cases, although today prices are generally fixed.

Jukkendana in Edo where the *hina-ichi* started was in fact a famous locality for seasonal fairs. Besides the *hina-ichi* in February, another fair for the May 5 Boy's Festival as well as of toys and decorations for New Year's were also held.

Until a few years after the end of the recent war, temporary stalls used to be opened at Ginza and other busy streets of Tokyo for the display and sale of *hina* dolls, and of the May 5 dolls.

HINA-MATSURI

THE MAIN dolls displayed for *hina-matsuri*, dolls' festival, which now takes place on March 3, are in pairs, representing a man and a woman. This feature has not changed even with the introduction of various modern dolls.

Nearly 1,000 years ago, there was a custom of children playing with two beautiful little dolls, made to symbolize a man and a woman. This play was called *hina-asobi* or doll play.

It was about 300 years ago in the Tokugawa period that the present picturesque *hina-matsuri* developed. There are mainly four types of dolls for the festival—paper dolls, wooden dolls, clay dolls, and dressed dolls. Paper *hina* are probably the oldest, as they came from the ancient custom of making paper images and throwing them away to expel evil spirits. As the paper *hina* are made in a standing form, they are also called *tachi-bina*, Standing dolls. Clay dolls were first made in rural areas. Both clay and wooden dolls, gaily colored, are still very much used.

Hina-matsuri, or the dolls' festival of March 3, has become meaningless since it came to be observed by the solar calendar, or about one month earlier. Originally it was a simple seasonal event, particularly for farmers and their families, and took place just when the warm, pleasant spring season began, and the farmers had some leisure time to enjoy the occasion. The adoption of the solar system set the date about one month ahead, and so it is now held when the weather is still cold and the farmers have no time to spare.

In ancient days, on March 3 by the lunar calendar, all the people, men, women and children, made crude dolls of paper, and in making them they transferred their ill-fortune or sickness to the dolls. Then gathering these dolls, they went to a nearby brook or river, and cast them, bearing all their evils, into the water. It was thus an occasion for a family outing. This was the original *hina-matsuri*, but all these features are now lost as it is held one month earlier.

The custom of displaying elaborately dressed costly dolls at *hina-matsuri* began in the Tokugawa period, when *dairi-bina* or Court dolls came to be somehow mixed up with the ancient *hina-matsuri*. Dairi-bina were elaborately made and richly costumed to represent the life and customs of the Imperial Court. These dolls were kept by families which could afford them, and there was no fixed day for their display.

The present *hina-matsuri* is a mixture of the original *hina-matsuri* and the *dairi-bina*, but without the seasonal significance important in the old days.

The regular set of *hina* dolls, today, consists of 15 dolls, two *dairi-bina*, three *kanjo* (ladies-in-waiting), five musicians, two retainers, and three guards. They are displayed on the shelves in the order mentioned. The principal male figure is placed to the right of the female doll, with bowls and plates for food below.

Many modern *hina* have appeared representing actors, actresses, baseball players and others. But they must always come in pairs—a man and a woman.

Hina-matsuri used to be one of the very few occasions when little Japanese girls had their own parties. It is customary for them to invite their small friends to these parties at which they partake of the sweets and food offered to the dolls. Sometimes they cook and prepare the food and cakes to be offered to the dolls. They drink *shirozake*, a sweet mild rice wine, on the occasion.

Old country families still treasure their family *hina-matsuri* dolls and doll furniture which are preserved for centuries. Brides sometimes take their own dolls to their new homes.

Formerly *hina* dolls were brought out only on March 2 and put away on March 4, although today they are displayed for many days or even weeks. So girls lamented the storing away of the dolls after two days' display. This regret is remembered in many local songs.

'*Ohina-sama   rainen-mo   gozare.*
Sangatsu sakura hanami-sa gozare.'
('*Ohina-sama*, come again next year. Come to see the cherry blossoms of March' still sing girls in Chiba.)

HORSE FESTIVAL

NOMA-OI (wild horse chase) of Soma, Fukushima Prefecture, is one of the most interesting outdoor spectacles. It is held at the festival of Myoken Shrine of the town of Hara. Formerly the shrine was the guardian deity of Lord Soma. At first the lord used to drill his mounted *samurai* every year on the plains of Hibariga-oka near the shrine by making them chase wild horses.

Since the Meiji era this old military drill of mounted warriors has been changed into an outdoor spectacle, though the old name of *Noma-oi* is still retained. It is performed by men dressed in ancient armor on July 12 on Hibariga-oka.

As the mounted men gather, fireworks are set off to release a flag. As the flag comes down, all the armored riders rush toward it. When a rider catches the flag with his whip, he gallops to the viewing stand. As he announces his name, he is given a wooden tablet of the shrine which he puts on his back. Again he rushes to get another flag. A new flag is shot up from another spot, as soon as the first one is caught. Thus sometimes, one rider succeeds in getting several flags.

When the flag-catching event ends, all the riders who got flags proudly parade through the town, carrying their tablets on their backs. On the following evening, the townsfolk celebrate the successful riders by burning bonfires.

A rite is also held to select a white horse to be presented to the shrine. Formerly a white horse had to be found from among wild horses. But today armored riders go up to an enclosure where are kept several wild horses among which is placed a white horse and enter the enclosure to catch the desired horse. In this is retained some features of the ancient wild horse chase.

In the old days there was a banquet after the *Noma-oi* which was brightened by singing and dancing. There is no such banquet now, but the song and dance are still preserved by the local people.

KAKASHI MATSURI

KAKASHI MATSURI (scare-crow festival) is held in many farming districts on October 10. It is a rite to express gratitude to scare-crows that guarded the crops all through summer, braving rain and storm. All *kakashi* are collected from the farm, and placed in an honor post in the garden of a farmer's house. To them are offered *mochi* and other foodstuffs. At the same time, all those who helped during the past season are invited to a feast. In

this way, Japanese farmers show their appreciation of the part played by their scare-crows. Farming tools are also gathered and thanked for their help.

Kakashi or *kagashi* originally meant to smell. In ancient days, animal hair and hides, rags soaked in oil, and many other things were burned on farms to drive out wild animals. The term came to be used for anything used to protect farm crops. Thus the figure of a farmer dressed in rain hat and straw coat, for scaring away birds and animals came to be also called *kakashi*. Of course, the *kakashi* is now greatly modernized. Some wear trousers and felt hats.

The *kakashi* figure is also said to stand for Yamano-kami, god of the mountain, who comes to the farm in January and in autumn to drive out evil spirits and also teach farmers how to raise their crops. Coming to the gate of a farmer's house, Yamano-kami used to 'henpai' or dance by stamping his feet on the ground and also sang songs. He danced the 'henpai' also on the narrow paths through the rice fields.

Farming villages still hold local dramatic shows in autumn. The main feature of such shows is the *Sanbaso*, a stamping dance, developed from the *henpai* of Yamano-kami to remove evil spirits. Other plays on the program are only supplementary.

Even today in the modern *Kabuki* theater *Sanbaso* is given, particularly when a new theater building is opened. In the old days, every day's performance started with this dance. It is also a purification dance.

KUMA MATSURI

KUMA-MATSURI or bear festival is a sacred rite of the Ainus, and because of its quaint features, it has even come to be regarded as a show attraction. However, it is often criticized as being cruel as a bear is killed at the rite.

But to the Ainu the bear festival has a significant, religious meaning. Their god comes to them, clothed in the skin of the bear. They believe when the god in the bear wishes to return to the land of its parents it comes to be caught and killed. So when Ainu hunters go bear-hunting and return empty-handed, their neighbors and friends laugh at them, as they have failed because of their loss of the god's confidence.

Bears and deer were formerly hunted by Ainus in considerable numbers but the bear was always the principal game. When a hunter brought home a bear, it was a great occasion for the whole village, as not only were they glad to have the bear meat and fur, but they also believed that the bear caught the hunter's arrow by its own wish to return to the land of his parents.

When a cub was caught, it was raised with the tenderest care by the women-folk who gave their own breasts to the little bear, as they believed that god had entrusted the cub to them to raise it. If they cared for the cub, the whole village would be free from all evils, they thought. So the cub was welcomed as the coming of a god into the house or village.

When the cub grew up, it was killed so that it could return to the land of its parents. The women who raised it for years cried as though they were losing their own babies.

At the rite, various offerings were presented to the bear, to be taken back to the parents' land to convey to the god how tenderly the people cared for it while it was with them. They believed that on hearing the bear's report the god would be pleased and be kind to the people all the time.

So the bear-killing rite is not a cruel or barbaric act to the Ainus.

MATSURI

JAPAN is a country of festivals. Not only do the people observe numerous festivals every year, but also they have intense interest in them and delight in spending much time and money for their observation.

There are two kinds of *matsuri* or festival. The first is the solemn and sacred *matsuri* which is held in wor-shiping *kami*, and the other is the *matsuri* of *Ujigami* or local shrines. It is said that *matsuri* originated in offering various things, singing and dancing, when Amaterasu-omi-kami had hidden in the Ama-no-iwato. *Matsuri* originally meant worship or service, and it is held in that sense by the Imperial Court and also at the occasions of the festivals of great shrines.

Matsuri was thus at first a service to *kami*, and sacred music and dancing were offered, after ceremonial Shinto services. But as similar *matsuri* came to be held for *Ujigami* or local shrines, it came to possess more popular features.

All important rites of the Imperial Court and many shrine festivals are held at night. The *Dai-jo-e*, the most important rite held after enthroning a new Emperor, takes place at night. So do many rites held personally by the Emperor in the sanctuaries of the Imperial Palace. Local shrines also have formal nocturnal rites for the annual or periodical festivals, many of them continuing until daybreak.

This custom of holding important rites at night came from the ancient idea that a new day started after the evening meal.

Torches and lanterns are used to illuminate the rites at the Palace and shrines. The solemnity of such occasions is greatly enhanced by the quiet and dark atmosphere in which they are held. The light shed by torches and lanterns, furthermore, adds mystic or romantic touches.

In ancient days, those privileged to attend such night rites remained at the places of service until daybreak. This was commonly called *okomori*, which is still observed by many ardent followers of ancient rites. *Otsuya* (night watch) for the dead is still widely observed. This also developed from the original all-night rite.

At shrines, though formal festival celebrations are mostly held at night, the festive part is held both at night and in the daytime. It was for convenience's sake that processions and entertainments came to be held in the daytime, as children particularly wished to join in.

Every district in the country has its *Ujigami* or local guardian deity, and each shrine has a festival day every year. On the occasion of such *matsuri* which is sometimes called *sato-matsuri* or village festival, the Shinto service is of course held to worship the shrine, but the *Ujiko* of the shrine have one day of merry-making. In preparing for the *matsuri*, they spend many days and much money. Formerly it was even customary that the people of the district, men and women and children, would make new clothes to wear on the occasion. The entire village or district is decorated with lanterns, and floral ornaments. On the day of the festival the people visit the shrine in gay costumes, and the shrine compounds are packed with small shops and shows.

Among the important features of *matsuri* are gay processions in costumes. *Dashi* or huge statues of historic personages on wheels are drawn through the streets, with music and singing. Many families hold merry parties at home, and during the *matsuri* which sometimes lasts two or three days, the entire business of the district is suspended, and the people devote themselves to amusement and enjoyment. *Matsuri* is a great occasion for recreation in rural districts.

Many villages and towns vie with one another to hold better and merrier *matsuri*. This kind of *matsuri* differs much from the solemn and sacred *matsuri*, but it has been deeply interwoven with the daily life of the common people of the country.

MIYA-MAIRI

MIYA-MAIRI is the first real festival in a baby's life, because with its deeper religious significance it means more than mere feasting and feting.

Miya-mairi means 'to visit shrines,' and on the occasion of its observance the baby is taken to the shrine of the local deity, *Ujigami*, guardian and protector of the people of the district.

The day for this ceremony differs according to the sex of the baby. If the child is a boy, *miya-mairi* is held on his 32nd day, and if a girl it takes place on her 33rd day. But often this is reversed and the girl's *miya-mairi* may come before the boy's. In some districts it is held on the 30th and the 31st day.

The baby is dressed in its best *kimono*, and is usually carried on the back, or in the arms of its nurse or grandmother, or its mother. In cities motor-cars are now put into service. But such modern conveniences detract greatly from the beauty and romance of the custom. The party usually consists of several relatives and friends, who form a procession to the shrine. Each member of the procession carries one of the baby's beautiful bright *kimono* on his back, and the group makes a colorful and picturesque scene.

Arriving at the shrine, the priest performs the ceremony of purifying and blessing the baby. In his impressive formal dress, he then leads the way into the altar room, recites the sacred ritual, and waves the *gohei* (sacred staff with cut paper) over the baby's head to drive away evil and bring upon it the blessing and love of the *kami*.

Thus, the baby is freed of any evil it may have brought with it from the other world, and enters this life clean, pure and noble.

When the ceremony at the shrine is ended, the baby is taken to visit its relatives and friends. However, this custom of making a round of visits after the *miya-mairi* is quite recent. It is said that the Shogun Ietsuna (1641-1680), when an infant, was carried to the residence of Lord Ii on his way home from his *miya-mairi*. Thus originated the custom of making visits to relatives and friends.

When the *miya-mairi* party visits the homes of friends, bags of *ame* (wheat gluten) are given the hosts and their families as presents from the new baby. In the olden days, to supplement the mother's milk the baby was fed on *ame*, and because of that, *ame* has come to mean food for the baby, so to give *ame* as a present means the willingness of the baby to share its food with its friends.

In return for the *ame*, the friends present the baby with *inu-hariko* (papier-mache dogs), symbolizing the hope that he will grow as fast and be as healthy as puppies.

Then the procession starts homeward, carrying the baby's clothes and long strings of *inu-hariko*, in all sizes. At home, feasting begins and all visitors are cordially welcomed.

O-HIGAN

O-HIGAN, or equinox week both in spring and autumn, is the time when the Japanese people make special visits to their family cemeteries to pay respect to their ancestors. Having been so long followed by the people, this Buddhist service has also created many customs that make it a big social event.

Higan, meaning other shore, comes from the Buddhist term *paramita* which expresses the idea that Buddha guides the people from the shore of carnal life to the other shore of Nirvana or enlightenment. But the Japanese have adopted the idea in their ancestor worship, and the *higan* rite has been followed by the people, regardless of their religious faith.

It is said that the Imperial Court held the first *higan-e* or *higan* rite in 1043. Ever since, the day has been observed by all the people to worship the family dead. Thus *higan* is a Japanese rite, and even though it originated in a Buddhist idea, no other Buddhist people hold such a service.

The custom of making the equinox week a special religious one is said to have been started by Prince Shotoku in the seventh century. During the seven days of the equinox week, all families hold religious rites for the dead, or visit temples to have prayers said for their ancestors, and then visit family cemeteries.

The Meiji government made the equinox day a national holiday, in view of its religious significance to the people. The Emperor himself offers prayers for the Imperial ancestors on that day.

The visit to the family cemetery is a happy event, and in some districts, the people have quite a merry time taking food and *sake* there. Usually they sweep the ground, offer incense and flowers, and say prayers to their ancestors.

The custom of offering food to the dead during the week developed a general custom of giving such specially prepared food to friends and neighbors. Of course no meat is used in *higan* food.

The most common *higan* food is *ohagi* or soft rice-ball covered with sweetened bean-paste. *Sushi* or vinegared rice with vegetables is also made in many households to offer to the ancestors and also to neighbors.

PRENATAL CEREMONY

THE FIRST festival to be celebrated for a baby is the *iwata-obi*. This is held before the baby's birth to mark the beginning of his existence.

It is believed that four months before birth a baby receives its *tamashii* (spirit), and after that time its existence is recognized. So his 'coming to life' is welcomed with joy. In olden times the *iwata-obi* was held two months before the baby's birth, but today it is usually held four months before its appearance in the world.

Iwata-obi is the name of a piece of unbleached white silk, eight feet long, which is wound around the mother's body. It is the common belief that the silk will protect the baby and insure it a healthy and happy life. Formerly only white silk was used, but later white, red or yellow cotton was sometimes substituted. Red, according to the Japanese, stands for happiness and joy, white for purity, and yellow is supposed to have the power to dispel evil.

The modern Japanese believe merely that the *iwata-obi* keeps the mother's body warm and holds the baby in a normal position. Flannel is often used for the *iwata-obi* today instead of silk or cotton, and sometimes woolen yarn is chosen for it, as it is capable of expansion and contraction.

Presenting this cloth to the expectant mother was made a ceremony in the olden days. The husband handed the cloth with his left hand to his wife, who received it with her right. Then the wife's mother solemnly wound the cloth around her, underneath the outer garment.

By this festival the unborn child is recognized as a living entity, possessing a human spirit. After the actual winding of the cloth, the family, relatives and friends gather to offer felicitations to the wife, and an elaborate feast follows. In the case of the first child in the family, the festival has a special significance since the Japanese have always thought a great deal of the continuation of the family line.

The day selected for this occasion is invariably the day of the *inu* (dog), one of the signs of the lunar calendar, as the Japanese believe this will insure the mother's health.

With this ceremony and the following feast the baby is welcomed into the family circle, and the relatives and friends pray for the joy and health of the child to be born.

RARE AGE CELEBRATION

TU FU, a famous Chinese poet of the eighth century, wrote: 'Since ancient times, the age of 70 has always been rare in human life,' and because of that, in China the 70th year began to be called the 70th year *koki*, using two Following this usage, the Japanese called the 70th year *koki*, using two Chinese characters meaning 'ancient' and 'rare' and pronouncing them in the Japanese way. So *koki* conveys the idea expressed by Tu Fu that men of his day seldom lived to be 70 years old.

The Chinese regarded 50 years as the ordinary limit of human life, so 70 was considered a good old age rarely attained on earth. And because of the popularity of the famous poet among the Chinese and Japanese, they have always attached special importance to this celebration.

Koki-no-iwai, or the 70th year celebration, is one of the most important fetes in Japanese life for those who live long enough to enjoy it, so the sons, daughters and grandchildren hold a gala celebration in honor of one who attains it.

In any family, the observance of *koki-no-iwai* is not only important, but a great honor. The people are very proud of the fact that a member of their family has lived to the age of 70. Reverence for old age is very strong among the people, so they look forward to the joy and honor of such a family celebration. But it was Tu Fu, the poet, who really started the custom, and those who live to enjoy this celebration should thank him for it.

SECOND-CHILDHOOD FETE

LONG ago, the 60th birthday was commonly celebrated, but since *Honke-gaeri* (completion of the sexagenary cycle), that is, the 61st birthday, became popular, the rites for the 60th year have gradually been forgotten.

Honke-gaeri is a great celebration, not only because the person has lived to be 61, but because according to the Chinese the 61st year marks the completion of the sexagenary cycle that began in the year of his birth. *Honke-gaeri*, therefore, has a deeper meaning than merely suggesting that one has enjoyed a long life.

All the earlier *Nenga* or year celebrations are given by the person himself and to these he or she invites friends and neighbors to share the happiness. But the *Honke-gaeri* celebration is given by the sons and daughters to honor their father or mother. On this occasion the celebrant is said to become a baby again. So in olden days he wore a

red *kimono*, red cap, and red *tabi* (socks) to signify his new youth.

Thus dressed in red, the old man takes the seat of honor. His children, grandchildren, relatives and friends gather to wish him a new life and further happiness. Presents are brought by friends and acquaintances, and in wealthy families the *Honke-gaeri* celebration is made very luxurious and elaborate. A good-sized fortune is sometimes spent on this occasion.

In China and Japan it was believed that the length of human life was only 50 years and that those living to more than that age were especially favored with more than their share of time.

So throughout the country, this celebration of the 61st year is still observed, for the people have a great respect for old age.

SEIMON-BARAI

YEAR-END bargain sales are given the strange name of *Seimon-Barai* or pledge cancellation in Kyoto and Osaka. This name has an interesting history.

In feudal days, there was a shrine called Kanja-dono at Kyogoku, Kyoto, dedicated to a deity who had the power to permit the cancellation of pledges and promises. In those days, the women of licensed quarters were reputed for being ready to make pledges of love or promises of marriage. But they felt ashamed of making these false pledges, and so they visited this shrine on a certain day in autumn every year, and prayed for release from promises and pledges they had made in the past year, and asked for pardon. This annual visit to the shrine was called *Seimon-Barai* or pledge cancellation.

This custom was taken up by drygoods merchants of Kyoto and Osaka as a means of boosting their year-end sales. They thought that they also might have cheated their patrons or did things for which their conscience made them ashamed. So they started to follow the custom of the gay ladies, calling the year-end sales of remnant dress goods *Seimon-Barai.*

At first *Seimon-Barai* sales were held by dress-goods merchants only. But soon the custom spread to other merchandise. Of course, modern merchants, even in Kyoto and Osaka, have forgotten the original meaning of *Seimon-Barai,* which are nevertheless held annually merely as an occasion for special sales to attract buyers.

SETSUBUN

FUKU-WA-UCHI ONI-WA-SOTO (In with good luck, out with the demon) is loudly heard in all households throughout the country on the evening of *setsubun* (change of season) which falls in the first part of February. In shouting those words, the heads of households scatter roasted beans, to drive out the demon and all evil fortune. *Setsubun* is a time-honored festivity that is popularly observed by the people for insuring good luck for the year.

Setsubun, as its name indicates, marks the end of the winter season under the old calendar, and the season of spring begins on the following day, which is called *risshun* (birth of spring). So ordinarily it has no relation with the calendar year, but due to the popular idea that a new year begins with spring, *setsubun* gradually came to possess the same significance to the people as New Year's Eve. It is from this conception that the occasion came to be observed for wishing a good and happy new year.

With this observance of *setsubun* it may be said that the people of Japan have three New Year's Eves — one under the solar calendar, another under the lunar calendar, and *setsubun.* The New Year's Eve under the lunar calendar is not observed now, although in rural districts New Year's is still widely observed according to the lunar calendar. The *setsubun* is more popular and more widely observed than the New Year's Eve under the solar calendar. It is also more picturesque and interesting with the *mame-maki* or bean-throwing custom.

This *setsubun* is also called *mame-maki* (bean throwing), *oni-yarai* (devil chasing) and *tsuina* (evil dispersing). It is said to have developed from the old custom held on New Year's Eve, in which men dressed as devils were chased out to bring in a happy New Year.

The custom of *oniyarai* is at least more than 1,000 years old, as it is mentioned in *Tosa Nikki.* At first it was a Court function, and later adopted by the common people. In the old days, *daizu* or soya beans were put in a wooden cereal measure and offered to Toshitoku-jin, a deity who is believed to have taught the people rice cultivation. Then they loudly called out, '*Oni-wa-soto fuku-wa-uchi*' (out with the devils, in with good luck) as it is still done today.

It was during the Tokugawa regime that *setsubun* particularly developed into a very elaborate and picturesque custom. Since olden days each household has held quite a merry party on the occasion. Moreover big temples hold public *setsubun* festivities on a considerably extensive scale. To draw the public to such festivities, they select *toshi-otoko* (the year's man) for throwing roasted beans for expelling the demon and inviting good luck for all present. For this honored duty, generally persons of reputation or local popularity are selected. Noted actors, wrestlers and other such public figures are given the honor. It is thought that appointment as *toshi-otoko* will ensure the person's good fortune during the year. Of late, actresses and other women are sometimes selected for throwing beans at such temple affairs. Over the heads of the crowds of people gathered at such temples, the *toshi-otoko* scatter roasted beans with the merry shout of *fuku-wa-uchi, oni-wa-soto*. It is considered lucky to catch those thrown beans.

In all households, it is customary not only to throw beans at the demon, but also to eat them. Each person has to eat as many beans as his or her age totals, and then one more. The extra bean stands for the New Year. The eating of the beans insures their good health and brings good fortune.

Then again, those beans, as many as one's age and one more, are wrapped up in paper, and placed at some crossroad at night. If other persons step on those beans, all evils that accompanied the person during the past year will be driven off, it is believed.

On *setsubun* many rites are still observed to dispel evil spirits and prevent calamities. First, as the most common feature of the day, a dried sardine head and a small branch of *hiiragi* (holly tree) are placed at the house entrance. The evil smell of the dried fish head is believed to drive away devils, and the thorny leaves of the *hiiragi* will stop any evil insect from entering the house.

In many districts, tree branches are burned in the yard, as the crackling noise of the fire will drive away snakes and insects. The important feature of throwing roasted beans to drive away evils and devils and invite good luck is said to have originated in cities, and later followed in rural districts.

SEVENTY-SEVENTH YEAR CELEBRATION

THE SEVENTY-SEVENTH year cel-

ebration is called *ki-no-iwai* or *ki-no-ji-no-iwai* (celebration of the word 'joy'). This name requires an explanation, since there is more in the name than the celebration itself.

The Chinese character meaning 'joy' is pronounced *ki* in Japanese. When this character is written in script, it looks as though it consists of three distinct letters standing for 'seven, ten, seven.' Because of this particular coincidence, the 77th year came to be called the age of *ki* (joy).

At first no importance was attached to the 77th birthday. Seven is a lucky number, and so is a double seven, but when *Nenga* (year celebration) became popular, the people did not give any special thought to the 77th year of life. Celebrations were held on the 70th birthday and on the 80th, but none in the 77th year.

But the strange resemblance between the script character for *ki* and those for 'seven, ten, seven' was noticed, and someone named the 77th year the year of *ki* or joy. It is not known with whom the idea originated, but as the Japanese people have always been naturally superstitious about Chinese characters and their meanings, the notion immediately caught the popular fancy. Soon the custom of celebrating the 77th birthday spread all over Japan, and that year came to be called 'the age of joy.'

No one objects to a 'joyous year,' and to live until that age is indeed fortunate, so this birthday has become one of the most important *Nenga* in a person's life.

It may sound absurd to foreigners to connect 77 with 'joy' simply because the two have a similar appearance when written in script. But to the Japanese mind this similarity has a great significance, even a sacred message.

So the 77th birthday is considered a

very joyous and important occasion not only because of the long life of the celebrant, but also because of the felicitous significance of the year.

SHICHI-GO-SAN

SHICHI-GO-SAN (seven-five-three) that is observed on November 15 is the most picturesque national event in the autumn season. It is the day when boys and girls who are seven, five or three years old are dressed in their finest clothes and taken by their parents to local shrines. It is a custom that has been popular in the country since the Tokugawa days, and is founded on the traditional belief that local guardian deities protect and look after the health and growth of children.

On November 15, the children of seven, five or three years of age are taken to the shrines of *Ujigami* or *Ubusuna*, their guardian deities, to thank them for their healthy growth and good health in the past years and also to pray for the deities' further protection to insure their development to sound manhood or womanhood.

All Japanese have their *Ubusuna* or guardian deities. Newborn babies are taken to the shrines of the local deities on the 30th day after birth in the case of girls, and on the 31st day after birth in the case of boys. Thus presented to the local *kami*, the babies become formally the *ujiko* or the proteges of the tutelary deities who will ever look after their welfare. It is to those *Ujigami* or patron deities that they are taken on November 15 to express thanks and to pray for further protection.

Although at present all children of seven, five or three years are taken to the shrines on November 15, formerly only boys of three and five years, and girls of three and seven years were taken. When they are three years old,

both boys and girls are taken to the shrines, because it is believed that at the age of three, they pass their babyhood, and thus mark a new period in their life. When boys of the *samurai* class reached the age of five, they were formally introduced to their feudal lords. On that occasion the boys wore for the first time their formal *hakama* or skirts. There was also held the ceremony for their first *hakama* wearing. Thus the age of five was a very important one for ancient Japanese boys, and the *Shichi-go-san* festival for boys of five years was particularly significant. But there was observed no festival for girls of five years. The girls had their big festival when they were seven years old, as at that age they wore for the first time the stiff formal *obi*. Up to that age they wore just a loose cloth around their waist. This marked the growth of baby girls to the first stage of womanhood. Formerly boys of seven years did not have *Shichi-go-san*.

Japanese parents being ever so indulgent in thinking of the pleasure of their children, rival in dressing their children of seven, five or three years, in the finest possible dress and take them to the local shrines. Then they hold big parties for the children, inviting relatives and neighbors. Presents are given the children by the relatives and friends of their parents.

Around the shrines to which the children are taken on the day there are sold *ame* (sweet wheat gluten) wrapped up in long white bags, richly decorated. *Ame* was formerly regarded as food for babies, and when mothers did not have milk, often babies were fed on *ame*. Many bags of *ame* are purchased by the parents when they take their children to the shrines, and given them as well as to friends and neighbors. It is traditionally believed that *ame* distributed on this day will bring good luck to the children.

TABE-ZOME

EATING is one of the most important occupations of humanity. So when Japanese baby is 120 days old, *tabe-zome* or 'eating for the first time' is celebrated. Of course, at this tender age, a baby cannot eat solids, but on the day of *tabe-zome*, it is fed with tiny morsels of food. This ceremony is like a prayer that the child will grow rapidly, and never lack for food during its life.

The ceremonial features of this rite have been lost in recent years, but in old households they are still observed though in a simple and unpretentious way. As on other occasions of family rejoicing, relatives and close friends are invited to share in the happy festivity.

A set of table utensils, including bowls for rice and soup, a little table, dishes and chopsticks are prepared especially for the baby. If the baby is a boy, every utensil is black, inside and out, and the tiny table and miniature bowls are of black lacquer. But if they baby is a girl, all the utensils are red inside and black outside. The table top is red and the sides are black. It is not known exactly how or when this custom governing the different colors for the different sexes originated.

In the Kansai (western) district and many provinces, *kanagashira* (the gurnard fish) is served on behalf of the baby on this occasion. He does not eat it, but the fish is put on his table. When that particular fish is out of season, a dried or preserved one is used. In some rural fishmongers' shops a few preserved fish of this kind are always kept in stock and rented out as required when the *tabe-zome* festival is held by their patrons.

On the table where the guests are served, *kanagashira* usually does not appear; in its place there is *tai* (sea bream). *Sekihan* (red rice) is the main dish for the friends at the banquet.

When everything is ready, the mother, or sometimes the grandmother of the baby, takes it on her knee and sits in front of the tiny table. As the guests seat themselves, the mother thanks them all for the kind interest shown the baby, and, taking up the little chopsticks, picks up a grain of rice and puts it into the baby's mouth. So the baby has eaten some solid food, and has taken a firm hold upon life. This ends the ceremony and the baby is carried away to another room.

Tabe-zome also is significant because it is the first time the mother attends such a party after the birth of the baby.

TANABATA FESTIVAL

THE *TANABATA* festival of July 7 was formerly quite an important national event, but its traditional popularity has much waned of late. Old folks still remember the joy they had at each *Tanabata* festival in their childhood. In the Tokugawa period there were observed *Go-Sekku* or five big festivals, which came on January 1, March 3, May 5, July 7 and September 9. Thus *Tanabata* of July 7 was one of the five big annual events.

The observance of the festival tells of women's life in Japan. *Tanabata* originated in the ancient traditional belief that the Star Weaver which is separated by *Ama-no-gawa* (Heavenly River) or Milky Way from her lover, the Altair, all the year round, meet once a year on the evening of July 7. Also it tells that Japanese women worshiped the Weaver as weaving was one of their most important household tasks in early days. Thus it is primarily a girls' festival. But since it became a national event in the seventh year of Tenpyo Shoho or 755, it has been most elaborately observed by all the people through 10 long centuries.

The romantic belief that the Weaver and the Altair met only once a year appealed to the imagination or the sentiment of young girls. For the success of their own love they eagerly prayed at the festival. Also they prayed that the evening would be fair in weather, as they thought that, if it rained, the Milky Way would be flooded and the two stars would not be able to meet.

But the festival itself came to be observed as a general one to be enjoyed by all as an occasion for merry-making and feasting. Offerings are made to the two stars. Good meals and special sweets are prepared. In olden days, all families planted long bamboos in their gardens and women and children tied onto bamboo branches *tanzaku* or oblong sheets of paper for poem writing, on which they had written their own compositions on the festival or general subjects.

Then there used to be *Tanabata-odori* or folk dances by little girls. Beating drums, they danced in circles on the evening of the *Tanabata* festival.

Young girls firmly believed that if they observed the festival earnestly, they would gain skill in weaving and sewing. It was their greatest ambition to be good weavers and sewers. Women's life in Japan used to center on their clothing which had to all be made at home. In ancient times all families wove the cloth they needed for dressing all their members. That task was entirely done by women. Even later, when clothes came to be woven by professional weavers, there were no ready-made dresses available. Each family made the clothes for all its members. Thus women had to spend every evening sewing clothes. This side of the

women's life served greatly in popularizing the *Tanabata* which is observed for the Weaver.

Yet, all those traditional and picturesque customs of the *Tanabata* festival have mostly disappeared in recent days. The festival is observed at some kindergartens and primary schools, but rarely now do city dwellers celebrate the day as it was by their mothers and grandmothers. Modern Japanese girls are not so romantic as to believe in the story of the Weaver and the Altair, nor are they interested in the art of weaving and sewing. Yet in rural districts it is still observed, though most of the younger folks do not know what the significance of the festival is. Yet they enjoy the day, as with it comes something good to eat and their mothers are in good spirits.

TA-UCHI

TA-UCHI (rice-field work) or *ta-asobi* (rice-field play) is a New Year rite still observed by farmers and rural folks in many districts of the country. This old custom is observed to pray that the coming rice crop will be good. As the New Year is the time to pray for a good and happy year, this rite is important for farmers.

In many regions, villagers gather in the local shrine compounds on some morning between January 11 and 15. Marking a sacred lot in the shrine grounds, they solemnly go through the action of planting and harvesting rice. This make-believe rice cultivation is thought to insure good harvests in the coming autumn.

In other places, the rite is performed by individual households. It is done in the yard of each house, where a sacred lot is also marked off and the whole family joins in the act of planting, cultivating and harvesting rice.

In those mountain regions where snow covers the ground, the *ta-uchi* rite is performed in the snow. Pine needles are planted in the snow as rice-plants.

As it is also a very joyful occasion, the people mark it with feasting and singing.

Many farmers also make quite a ceremony of doing their first piece of work of the year. They go to the woods to gather the first bundle of kindling or do the first ploughing of the year. Many go out to the field just to stand there and pray for a good yield during the year.

To farmers, this aspect of New Year celebrations of performing *ta-uchi* rites and praying for good harvests is more important than the other side of mere merry-making.

THIRTEENTH YEAR FETE

THE NUMBER 13 is not unlucky in Japan. On the contrary, it is considered as a good, lucky number. For example, the age of 13 is considered lucky. In the olden days boys and girls were regarded as having attained manhood or womanhood then. To celebrate this occasion the fete of *Jusan-mairi* or the 'Thirteenth Year Ceremony' was held. Today, at the age of 13, boys and girls are considered mere children, but the fete of *Jusan-mairi* is just as popular as it ever was. The fete is not observed in many of the eastern districts, but is widely celebrated in Kyoto, Osaka and other western territories.

Jusan-mairi is held on March 13 of the lunar calendar. On this day, girls and boys are dressed in their finest clothes and go with their parents to a temple or a shrine to pray for fortune, wealth and wisdom.

The fete of *Jusan-mairi* is said to have originated in Kyoto, the ancient seat of the Imperial Court, which always observed this fete for its younger members. The Horinji Temple of Saga, Kyoto, has been the temple to which the children were and are taken on the occasion.

The fete was originally held at the temples of the Shingon sect of Buddhism, but it gradually became so popular that temples of other denominations and even shrines began to also celebrate the occasion.

One picturesque feature of this fete is the sale in temple compounds of 13 varieties of sweets for children. These are made in many different shapes and colors, and the purchase and presentation of these sweets to the children is an important part of the festivity. They are believed to bring good fortune to the ones who enjoy them. These small candies are made for this occasion alone.

This festival, now held on April 13, is in some localities more popular than the *Shichi-go-san* (seven-five-three) festival of November 15 that has recently become more and more elaborate throughout the country.

Particularly in Kyoto, gay processions to the Horinji Temple, Saga, of richly dressed children are held on the day. All parents take their 13-year-olds to the temple, and pray to *Koku-bosatsu* (Akasa-garbha) to get their children blessed.

Koku-bosatsu is the Buddhist deity of wisdom, generally presented in statues and paintings as sitting on the Lotus Throne, wearing the crown of Five Wisdoms on its head. In the left hand, it holds a lotus blossom of virtue and good fortune.

While the *Shichi-go-san* festival is held to pray for the healthy growth of children, *Jusan-mairi* is to pray they will become wise. Therefore, it is sometimes called *Chie-mairi* or worship for wisdom.

In the old days *Jusan-mairi* was far more popular than *Shichi-go-san* among the Kansai people, but of recent years *Shichi-go-san* has become almost a national celebration. However, old-fashioned parents of Kyoto and other localities still observe the 13th year festival.

Of course, the number 13 is never unlucky in Japan.

TOKANYA

TOKANYA (10th night rite) is a harvest rite held on October 10 in many Kanto districts and other localities. It is the occasion to thank *Tano-kami* or the god of rice fields, who returns to the mountain upon seeing the ripening of rice.

It is believed that *Tano-kami* comes down from the mountain in the spring to guard the growth of rice plants, and when harvesting time comes, returns to the mountain. *Kakashi* (scare-crows) represent *Tano-kami*, protecting the rice from evils and insects, it is believed.

On the day, scare-crows are brought to the farmer's yard, and all the farming implements are placed around them. *Kakashi* are often dressed in farmers' *mino* or straw raincoats. The scare-crows are offered *mochi* or rice cakes in thanks for their watchful protection of the rice plants all through the summer.

In the evening children make thick straw ropes or bundles and go around the house, beating the ground with the straw. This is a rite to chase moles from the rice fields and to pray for a good harvest next year. Often the straw is hung on the branches of fruit trees, as it is believed that the ropes placed on the trees on *tokanya* will make them bear more fruit next year.

It is also said that when *daikon* (Japanese radish) hear the noise of children beating the ground with the straw ropes, they grow big. In some districts the people do not eat *daikon* on this day, as they wish them to grow bigger.

Although the traditional date is October 10 by the lunar calendar, rites are usually now held about a month later, when the rice harvest is actually completed.

Chapter 5
Fish, Birds and Animals

AHO-DORI

AHO-DORI or a kind of albatross is a rare bird now facing extinction. The few remaining birds are seen only on Torishima (Bird Island) a small volcanic island located at the southern end of a chain of islands south of Izu Peninsula.

Torishima was formerly uninhabited, visited only by storm-driven fishing boats from time to time, but it was called a bird paradise, because there were numerous sea fowl and other birds living on the island. Thus up to about 50 years ago, the island was known for an innumerable number of *aho-dori* and other sea fowl.

In 1886, Hanuemon Tamaki started an enterprise to obtain bird feathers, and also bones and droppings accumulating there to make fertilizer. On the north shore of the island, he built a village and called it Tamaki-mura, taking many workers there.

But in August 1902, a volcanic eruption took place covering the whole island with lava, ashes and sand, and killed all the inhabitants numbering 120 living at Tamaki-mura. After the volcanic disaster, a few persons came to settle there, but unfortunately there was another big eruption in 1940. No human life was lost, however, as the eruption was predicted beforehand, and all escaped to safety.

But these two big eruptions changed the features of the island. Wooded or grass-covered mountain sides became bare, sulphuric steam rising from many points.

Thus the birds so numerously inhabiting the island almost suddenly disappeared. The number of *aho-dori* which was so large in Meiji days is now said to be only seven, according to the latest report, and it is feared that they might soon decrease. Thus in 1957 the bird came to be internationally protected.

It was in 1947 that a weather observatory was established on the island, and now 36 men stay there on a six-month shift.

BEARS AND BOARS

BEARS AND BOARS are the two greatest wild game of Japan and they have been hunted since ancient times.

Kuma, or bears, are hunted for their gall bladders, and not for their meat or skins, although those are also very valuable. It has been said that the bear's gall bladder is worth its weight in gold. Even today this is true, while the meat and skin do not bring so much money.

Kuma-no-i, made from bear's gall bladder, is a valuable medicine, and despite the appearance of new modern chemical medicines, it is widely used by the people. It can be purchased at all medicine shops throughout the country. It is particularly effective for curing stomachache.

Bears are hunted in early spring when the snowfall ends or during the winter hibernation period. Hunters take care not to shoot bears in the stomach, so that the gall bladders will not be injured.

Inoshishi, wild boars, do much damage to farms, and in many regions boars have to be killed to protect farms. Boar hunting is dangerous, as they are hard to kill and are liable to attack hunters. While boars are hunted by farmers for their own protection and by sportsmen for pleasure, the meat is valuable. During the winter season boar meat is in much demand, as it is believed that the meat warms the body. City butcher shops call boar meat *yama-kujira* or mountain whale. It is said that when meat eating was tabooed, the people gave this name to boar meat so that they could say they were not eating any meat.

Ancient warriors held boar hunts as a sport to train their men, and such hunts were done on a big scale with hundreds of men participating.

BECKONING CATS

ORNAMENTAL cats made of clay, porcelain, wood, bronze and other materials, with their front left paws raised to their left ears, are seen in many Japanese houses. They are called *maneki-neko*, beckoning cats, and are particularly to be seen in shops and restaurants. They are so named because of a popular tradition that when a cat passses its left paw over its left ear it is a sign that visitors will come. Thus *maneki-neko* is used as a charm to draw visitors or customers to shops and restaurants. Women and particularly *geisha* are fond of these cats.

There is an interesting story about the origin of this charm cat. Usugumo was one of the famous and accomplished women of Yoshiwara. One day her favorite cat was very nervous and followed her everywhere, pulling at her dress. Her friend who happened to be there tried to chase the cat away, but it clung to its mistress' dress. Angered, he drew his sword and killed it. But as its head was severed, it flew upward and caught a big snake that was on the ceiling beam and killed it. The cat was trying to warn Usugumo of the snake, but she did not understand.

Usugumo so mourned the death of her cat that even after holding an elaborate funeral service and erecting a tombstone for the faithful cat, she could not get over its death. One of her admirers, pitying her, had a master artist carve a cat out of imported aloes-wood. It was made in exact replica of her lost cat, and had its left paw raised to its ear. She fondled it daily and played with it, offering it meals. This carved cat became very famous, and became the first of the *maneki-neko*.

About the idea that cats bring good luck, there is the following tale.

There once stood an old temple that was almost a ruin at Setagaya, Edo. A priest by the name of Shudo lived there alone, with only a cat to cheer his poor and solitary life. To the cat he used to say almost daily, 'You are of no use. You are raised and fed here at the temple, but what have you done in return?'

One day, Ii Naotaka, Lord of Hikone, who was a great figure during the Tokugawa rule in the middle of the 17th century, happened to pass by the temple with several of his retainers on an outing through the Setagaya area. At the temple entrance, he saw a cat sitting by the road and beckoning with its paw.

Attracted by the strange act of the cat, the party entered the temple. Priest Shudo welcomed the distinguished visitors and offered them tea. As

Naotaka and his party were resting at the temple, there was a sudden heavy downpour with thunder. Naotaka exclaimed how lucky he was to have been invited into the temple by the cat and thus spared from the rain.

Naotaka often visited the temple after this, as he liked the priest. Seeing that the temple was in a sad condition, he offered to build a new one. Thus the temple prospered and, as many visitors began to come, the whole village was happy. Priest Shudo named the temple Gotokuji, after Naotaka's pen name.

The cat subsequently died, and a stone tablet was erected for it. As it was Ii Naotaka who said that the cat must be an incarnation of *Kannonbosatsu* as it brought such luck to the temple, the people came to call it the Good Luck Inviting Cat. Thus a hall was erected in the cat's honor in the compounds of the temple, and named the Good Luck Inviting Hall.

Believers in the story came to chip off little pieces of the cat stone and scattered them in front of their shops or houses, beliving that the stone bits would bring good fortune.

All through the Tokugawa days, the Gotokuji was very famous and many visitors came. The story of the cat is now remembered only by a few, but the temple still stands with its Good Luck Inviting Hall and the cat stone.

BIRD FORTUNE-TELLER

YAMAGARA, a little bird the size of the common sparrow, is a fortune-teller. Its keeper brings it to local festivals or amusement quarters to give the people an opportunity to have their fortunes told by the bird.

He sets up a little shrine on a stand, and puts the bird cage at the other end, about three feet away. When one wishes to have his fortune told, the keeper opens the cage gate. The *yamagara* is allowed to step out and hop toward the shrine. Coming to the shrine door, it rings a tiny bell by pulling at the bell string, and then goes up the steps. It enters the shrine through the door, and comes out, holding a folded paper in its bill. It hops back toward its cage, and the keeper takes the paper to hand it to the waiting person.

On the folded paper is written his fortune. The bird picks up one out of many folded papers, bearing different forecasts which are kept within the shrine.

Yamagara fortune-telling appears to have started about 150 years ago, in the Bunka-Bunsei era. The bird is extremely clever and can be trained to perform various tricks. At first it appeared as an entertainer trained to run up a ladder, and do other little tricks. Then someone thought of the fortune-telling stunt.

In training, the bird is given its feed in the same feed basket. When it becomes sufficiently tame, the basket is put outside the cage. When the cage is opened, it goes to the basket to get its grains. The basket is placed farther away each day. Thus it is trained to hop to the shrine. When it brings back the folded paper, the keeper gives it a seed or two to eat.

BULL-FIGHTS

JAPAN has its own bull-fights, but not the kind known in Spain or Mexico. Instead of a man fighting a bull, here the fight is between two bulls.

It is now only in Uwajima district of Iyo, Shikoku, that the bull-fight is preserved, but in early days it seems to have been held in many other parts of the country. Once it was quite popular in Echigo district facing the Japan Sea, but it is no longer known there.

In Iyo province of Shikoku, bullfighting is the most popular sport, and huge sums of money are paid for good fighters. When the championship match is held, the whole neighborhood makes it a holiday and throngs to view the fight with bets placed on the outcome.

When the two bulls are taken to the fighting arena, they charge at each other, and hooking their horns together, they push and twist. The fight lasts generally from 30 minutes to one hour but sometimes victory is claimed in only a few minutes. The fight ends when one bull shows its unwillingness to fight any more, or tries to run away from the opponent. That is to say, when one bull acknowledges that the other is stronger, the fight ends.

As to the origin of this bull-fight at Uwajima, it is interesting to hear what old residents of the district say. Farmers of Iyo province use many cattle in their farm-work, either in plowing or drawing carts. When there is not much work, the cattle are pastured on hills far away from their villages. Left free on the pasture to lead their own life, bulls in one group start to fight, and the strongest, so designated after many fights, becomes the boss of the group. Then other bulls and cows regard it as their leader. The leader protects the group from attacks by dogs and wolves. Order is kept by the boss bull.

But when a new bull is brought into the group, naturally a fight starts between it and the boss bull. This fight often becomes so fierce that many cattle are even killed or scattered away from the group. To prevent such damage, early farmers thought out a way of training the newcomer to recognize the authority of the boss bull. The new bull is put together with the boss bull in a small enclosure, and then the two fight to decide which is stronger.

From this custom developed seasonal or annual fighting matches to decide the champion bull of the entire district.

CARP TRADITION

KOINOBORI (carp streamers) are a symbol of the May 5 festival which is commonly called the Boy's Festival. They stand for manliness and advancement. It is since the Bunsei era or the beginning of the 19th century that they have been hoisted at the festival.

Carp are said to be able to swim up waterfalls, but scientists now disclaim any such feat. They say salmon are better and more rapid swimmers. But the carp is a hardy fish, living for a long time. Some are said to live for as many as 40 years. They are vigorous, and even if kept out of water, they stay alive for quite a time.

The traditions of carp came from China where they are regarded as the king of fresh-water fish. Thus they have been used as an offering on happy occasions.

When a son was born to Confucius, a friend brought him a huge carp to congratulate him on the event and also to hope for the healthy growth of the baby. Confucius was so happy with the gift of the carp that he named his son Li (carp), it is recorded.

In the Chinese tradition it says that a yellow carp which succeeds in going up the waterfall of the Huang Ho (Yellow River) turns into a dragon.

In many parts of Japan there are tales in which old carp living in ponds or rivers are regarded as the masters of such waters, and they are never molested. Various stories of such master carp helping people, taking human form or bringing evil upon those who disturb their quarters are told. Such big carp are regarded as holy in many districts.

The breeding of carp is said to have

developed in Japan in Edo days. Not only are carp sold as food, but also as pets to be admired for their beauty. Many temple and shrine ponds have beautiful carp. Many new types of beautiful carp have been bred. Those called *Nishiki-goi* or brocade carp have become very famous. Some have red and white spots on a white body, or have red, black and white markings. Such beautiful carp are not eaten.

CAT ISLANDS

THERE ARE several islands in Japan which are called *Neko-jima* or cat islands, because there are cats but no dogs. To bring a dog to such islands is taboo. Tashiro-jima on the northern Pacific coast, off Noto Peninsula, and Shikine-jima off the Izu islands are well-known for the dog taboo.

Shikine-jima was uninhabited up to the early Meiji years, and only the residents in the neighboring islands used to go there for cultivation or cutting trees and grasses. But strange to say there have always been cats on the island, and it was taboo to bring a dog to the islands. It was said that the *kami* of the island did not like to hear the barking of dogs.

At Tashiro-jima, the taking of dogs to the island was prohibited because cats, which are the enemies of dogs, lived there.

The taboo of dogs on such islands, some authorities explain, was due originally to the ancient habit of burying the dead on islands off the shore.

The belief that cats and dogs do not like each other seems to be quite old, as it is mentioned in *Makura-no-soshi* written by Seisho-nagon in the 10th century. Dogs are friends of man, but it has been said that cats are always independent and never obey a master's wish.

In *Kojiki*, the oldest records, when

cats grew mature, they entered high mountains, and never came out again, except to find mates.

In many regions there was a belief that when cats were taken into the house with a promise that they would be kept for a certain number of years, they went away when the time-limit expired. There is a story told in Izu that when a cat was promised to be kept three years, it started to leave the house at the end of that period. When the master followed it, it went into a deep valley, and entered a cave. There the cat was seen dancing with a fox. There is also a traditional belief that foxes took the form of cats in order to enter human houses.

CATS

IT IS TRADITIONALLY said that cats were first brought to Japan from Korea in the 10th century. The commonly accepted story says that the new kingdom of Kaoli or Koma that was established in Korea in the 10th century sent ships to Japan, and for protecting their provisions and cargo from mice, cats were carried on board those ships. The Japanese saw those cats on board the Korean ships for the first time, it is said. Some of those Korean cats were subsequently presented to the Imperial Court. Thus, from the very beginning, cats became the pets of the ladies of the Court.

But as it was stipulated by Court rules that any person not possessing a Court rank of the fifth grade or higher was not permitted to enter the inner circles of the Court, those cats were given the fifth grade in Court rank. Thus they became officially aristocrats, enjoying privileges that were denied even to human beings.

No other pets were allowed to be kept within the Court. Having come from Kaoli or Koma, they came to be called *Okoma-san* and were waited upon by duly appointed official attendants.

Cats as pets soon became popular among the women of all classes. But they remained aristocrats. They have always been waited upon and carefully looked after. While dogs and other pets are ordered to obey their master, men had to obey the wishes of cats.

Cats as pets in Japan are said to be more numerous than dogs. Yet on the other hand, there are many tales that make them out as animals of a mischievous or revengeful nature, often impersonating and killing people.

In Aso, Kyushu and Akita Prefecture, there were also *neko-yama* or cat mountains, where cats lived in great numbers, it was said. There are tales of men meeting sorry experiences as they accidentally came upon these cat mountains. The cats formed huge communities and lived like humans, so the stories say.

In many mountain regions, loggers were afraid of cats. If they met them on the way to the mountains, they used to return home, and rested until the next day. Fishermen of various districts were also afraid to mention the name of *neko* (cat), because the *funagami* (boat deity) did not like cats. So they avoided the word '*neko*' and used other terms to indicate the animal.

But in view of the large number of wild cats, the felines must have existed in the country all along. Japanese cats have very short tails. Many old-fashioned people do not like cats with long tails.

Neko-wa-mamono, a popular saying goes. It means that cats are witches. It is popularly believed that when cats become old, they become able to understand human speech, walk on their hind legs, and act like humans.

Because of this belief, cats of old age are seldom kept. Particularly, it is regarded unlucky to keep old tomcats when younger ones are born, although old tabby cats can be kept even when they have kittens or even grandkittens.

Mike-neko or tricolored cats are regarded lucky, and particularly tricolored tomcats are valued by fishermen as mascots.

Having become popular as aristocratic pets, cats gave the Japanese language many common expressions, such as: *neko-no-me* (cats' eyes) meaning fickleness; *neko-ze* (cats' back) meaning round-shoulderedness; *neko-baba* (cats' stealing) implying embezzlement; *neko-kaburi* (cats' feigning) denoting feigned innocence or hypocrisy; *neko-nade-goe* (tone of loving cats) meaning coaxing voice; *neko-no-hitai* (cats' forehead) signifying smallness in area; *neko-kawaigari* (like loving cats) means extreme fondness.

A *geisha* is often called *neko;* but it is because cats' hides are used in making *shamisen*, their musical instrument. But some say that it is because a *geisha* is also to be petted.

As to the traditional belief that cats understand human speech and sometimes act like humans, scientists explain that cats are one of the most intelligent species of animal, and thus are able to understand humans to a great extent. They have a very good memory, and that explains the belief that cats avenge any evil done to them.

It is also believed in Japan that old cats leave the house and disappear when they realize that their death is approaching, and thus they never show their dead bodies to humans.

When a sick person sleeps with a black cat, he will recover, it is believed in some districts. But there is a story in Shinano in which a cat did not leave a sick man's side, so the man decided to get rid of it as soon as he became well. When he recovered he put the cat in a *furoshiki* and went out, telling the household that he was going to throw it away. He never came back, nor did the cat.

Cats understand human words and even speak them, it is often believed. In Yamaguchi district, it was customary for peddlers of *gomame* or dried fish to come every spring. One day a person heard the call of *"gomame, gomame"* very softly outside. He opened the *shoji* screen and looked out. There was nobody but a cat basking in the sun. The cat being fond of *gomame* had called out as the peddlers did.

There is another story of a cat chasing a rat along an overhead beam in a room, but it slipped on the smooth surface and was heard to cry out, 'Shimatta' (confound it).

While a priest was sleeping at night, a cat at the bottom of his bedding rose and went out. Then he heard the cat outside saying, 'The priest is sick now and I cannot go out with you.' Next morning, remembering what he had overheard, the priest said to the cat, 'Don't mind me. Go wherever you want to go.' Thereupon the cat went out and never returned, an old story goes.

CATS AND DOGS

CATS AND DOGS are not friendly. There are several stories that tell how they came to be so hostile to each other. One such is the story of Koshiki Island.

There was once a kind-hearted boatman who loved animals. One day he saw children beating a snake, a dog and a cat. He rescued them from the hands of the mischievous youths and took them all home. The snake happened to be the Princess Ryugu (of Undersea Palace). In thanks for his kind act, the snake gave him a magic ring that would bring anything he wanted. Thus the boatman became rich.

A cow dealer of Osaka heard of the magic ring and succeeded in robbing it from the boatman, who consequently became poor. The dog and the cat, learning of the loss of the ring, set out to regain it. Reaching the house of the cow dealer, they found it concealed deep in a big jar. But as they could not reach it, the cat caught a mouse and made it bring up the ring.

They started to return home, the dog holding the ring in its mouth. But on a bridge over a river, the dog met another dog. As they commenced to snap at each other, the ring dropped into the river.

Thereupon the cat went to the river edge and, catching a crab, ordered it to gather all the crabs of the river and have them search for the lost ring. The magic ring was again found, and the dog proudly returned home with it.

The dog told the story to the boatman, saying that by his own efforts he had succeeded in regaining the ring. But the cat became angry at the boasting dog and told the part it played in finding the ring. The boatman then punished the dog for telling a falsehood, and ordered that the dog should always eat outdoors while the cat ate in the house.

Since then the dog and the cat were never on good terms. Even today dogs and cats are always fighting, cats eating in the house, and dogs eating outdoors.

CATTLE-HORSE

THERE IS a unique animal called *ushi-uma* or cattle-horse on Tanegashima Island in Kagoshima Prefecture.

Although it is called the cattle-horse, it is not a cross between a cow and horse. Despite its misleading name it is a horse, but its features resemble those of cattle. One seeing the animal for the first time will be unable to say whether it is a horse or a cow. He has to accept it as a horse, because scientists say so.

The striking feature of the *ushi-uma* that makes it so unlike any other kind of horse is that it has no mane. But what makes it look so funny and strange is its tail, which is totally different from that of ordinary horses. It is stubby without the long hair characteristic of horsetails. Without a mane and long tail-hairs, two distinct features of horses, it could never be accepted as a horse, if scientists had not already given a definite verdict.

Yet, even eminent scientists are unable to explain how or why this strange species of horse has appeared on the island of Tanegashima, and nowhere else. Because of its uniqueness, the government has ordered its protection and preservation.

Tanegashima is also famous for having the first Western firearms brought there. During the Tokugawa days, Western firearms were commonly called Tanegashima, because of their initial introduction to the island. The fame of Tanegashima is fading, but the island still has the distinction of having this unique animal.

CATTLE SACRIFICE

USHI OR CATTLE have been raised in the country since the earliest times to obtain milk, meat, horns and leather, and also for pulling plows and carriages. But, at the same time, it was thought that they possessed a divine spirit, and were often regarded as a deity or a messenger of *kami*. The idea of regarding cattle as a charm for rain or against evil and diseases is still believed in many rural districts.

At first cattle were sacrificed as offerings to *kami*, particularly at festivals. They were killed when prayers for rain were offered or when epidemics killed many persons. The sacrificing of *ushi* must have been so alarmingly frequent, causing many cattle to be killed, that an order was issued in 791 to prohibit farmers from killing them as sacrifices.

The order, however, did not diminish the power attributed to *ushi*, and as the actual killing was prohibited, the people came to offer cattle hides to shrines as prayers or at festivals. When a great epidemic threatened the capital of Kyoto, cattle hides were offered and they were also hoisted at street corners.

In many folk tales, the *ushi* appears as the incarnation of a sacred spirit. As cattle are meek and easy to handle, in the farming community it became the task of women to feed and handle them, while horses, which are more difficult to handle, were attended by men. Thus there are many tales of cattle and women.

The famous story concerning Zenkoji Temple in Nagano, tells how a cow led a bad woman to the temple and her salvation. She was hanging out a piece of cloth when a strange *ushi* came running and as it passed her, it carried away the cloth, twisted on its horns. She ran after the animal but lost it, and found herself in the compound of the temple.

The famous Gion Shrine of Kyoto has as its deity *Gozu-tenno* (cattle-headed heavenly king), who is believed to be an Indian deity. Also at Uzumasa, Kyoto, an *Ushi-matsuri* or cattle festival is held in which the people ride on cattle.

CHICKENS

CHICKENS are raised everywhere for meat and eggs. Cocks are, in many countries, trained for fighting. But the Japanese people have found something more in the value of chickens. Since the early days of their history, they have made pets of chickens, and named them *niwatori*, garden fowls.

The Japanese came to love the clear and loud crow of cocks and often called them *koeyoshi* or fine voice. This may sound strange to other peoples who may think that the cocks' crowing is not beautiful, but the Japanese species of domestic fowl crow more beautifully and clearly than the cocks of Western kinds.

They called cocks *totenko* after their crowing, and this name came to be written out in Chinese characters signifying the glowing sun of the eastern sky. It is regrettable that the ancient *totenko* is now seldom heard, as the Western species that give more meat and eggs have largely replaced them.

It is the Japanese people who succeeded in developing *niwatori* which are beautiful. By selection and cross-breeding, they produced cocks with long tails, which sometimes reach a length of more than 20 feet. This beautiful new species was particularly developed in Kochi Prefecture, Shikoku Island.

They are kept in cages with high perches so that their long tails will not be spoiled. Once a day they are taken out to the garden for a walk. Much care is necessary to keep the long tails beautiful and clean and also to give them proper feed.

Specimens of this long-tailed cock have been exhibited in foreign countries and received much admiration. But foreign breeders of chickens have not yet succeeded in producing such cocks as the Kochi people are proud of, though they have made wingless chickens because they cannot see in chickens anything valuable besides meat and eggs.

CHINKORO

CHIN or Japanese spaniels were once the most popular lap dogs in Japan, particularly in the Tokugawa and Meiji years. They were even exported in large numbers to foreign countries. But today there are only a few kept by dog fanciers, and many *chin* lovers have formed an organization to preserve this Japanese dog.

It is not clearly known how or when this small, lovable dog developed. Authorities, however, agree that the *chin* was a product of interbreeding various small dogs, not only of Japan but also those brought from China, Tibet, Annam and Europe.

At any rate, as early as the beginning of the Tokugawa era in the 17th century, the *chin* had already become a definite type and records show that the Japanese *chinkoro* were being exported to Europe in the middle of the 18th century.

In Edo there were many dog shops specializing in *chin*. As a household pet, it became most popular. It is a well-known fact that they were presented to Queen Victoria of England more than 60 years ago.

The word '*chin*' is commonly said to come from '*chi-nu*,' a contraction of '*chisai-inu*' (small dogs). On the other hand, Morihiro Higashikuni, president of the Chin Dog Preservation Society, presents the view that the term '*chin*' came from the Chinese expression '*chintso*,' meaning 'to sit up.' The people still say '*chin-chin*' when they want to make dogs sit up.

It is unfortunate that it has become difficult to find good *chin* dogs in the country. Good *chin* must now be imported from other countries.

CICADA

THE *SEMI* or cicada has been the symbol of hot summer days since very early times. As the people loved its singing, the *semi* has been the theme of poems included in the *Manyoshu* and *Kokinshu*, the earliest collections of poems in the country. Even today the *semi* is a popular topic for all poets.

There are many varieties of *semi*, and some begin to sing in the late spring, heralding the coming hot weather. Then, some appear in autumn. They can, however, be easily distinguished by their singing.

But it is when the summer reaches its peak in temperature, that *semi* become numerous and sing loudly. In many places their singing becomes so loud that by hearing their singing, one feels hotter. Then, on the other hand, when *semi* sing early at morning or late in the dusk, there is something cooling and solacing in their songs.

Particularly little boys rejoice when *semi* appear and sing. Armed with nets attached to long bamboo poles, they go out to catch *semi*. They are not difficult to catch, and some boys keep them in little bamboo cages. But captured *semi* do not live long.

Many children become engrossed in *semi-tori* (cicada catching) and are away from home the whole day, and mothers become worried. They even forget lunch.

Common varieties are given many different names according to locality. Depending upon the season when they appear, some are called *haru-semi* (spring cicada), *natsu-semi* (summer cicada), and *aki-semi* (autumn cicada). By their singing, some are called *tsuku-tsuku-boshi*, *kana-kana* and *min-min*. Then there are *kuma-zemi* (bear cicada) and *abura-zemi* (oil cicada), probably so named from their shape and color. *Higurashi* (sun-setting cicada) is so called because this kind sings most loudly at sunset.

Of course, those living in crowded city quarters do not like the loud cicada singing which irritates them on hot afternoons. But those in rural districts are fond of cicadas, and many welcome them as they feel the quietness when hearing nothing but cicada singing.

One of the famous *hokku* of Basho goes:

Shizukesa ya
Iwa ni shimiiru
Semi no koe.

It is difficult to translate *hokku*, but Ronald Dore skillfully reads it as follows:

Against profound silence
Even the rock is soaked by
The cicadas' noise.

CRABS

KANI OR CRABS appear in many legends of Japan, and even in mythological tales.

When Toyotama-hime-no-mikoto was about to give birth to a baby, a lying-in hut was erected by the seashore. As there were numerous little crabs on the shore, an attendant was detailed to the task of sweeping them away from the hut. He was called *kani-mori* or *kami-mori* meaning crab attendant.

Later when an office was opened in the Imperial Court to undertake construction work and maintenance, it was called *Kamon-ryo*, and house cleaning came to be known as *kani-harai* or crab sweeping. Thus from the mythological tale, *kani* came to stand for sweeping and cleaning.

Because of the tale, the *kani* has also come to be linked with babies. The first discharge of a newborn baby is still called *kani-baba*. In the old days among

118

aristocratic circles, the first garment given to a newborn baby was known as *kanitori-kosode* or *kanitori*, that is, crab-taking clothes.

In many parts of the country, stories are told in which crabs fight giant snakes. There are temples named *kanidera* or crab temples. There are also tales of crabs saving people's lives or performing some benevolent act.

There are many kinds of crabs: land crabs, sea crabs and fresh-water crabs. Many are edible and those caught in the northern seas are famous for their excellent meat.

Heike-gani or Heike-clan crab caught of the shallow waters of the western part of the Inland Sea have become famous because of a tale that came to be attached to them.

This species of crab has a human face marked in relief on its back. When the Heike or Taira clan was defeated by the Genji or Minamoto clan in a sea battle off Dan-no-ura in the Inland Sea, Heike soldiers who were killed turned into these crabs, so it is traditionally believed.

CROWS

OF ALL BIRDS of the country, *karasu* is the most despised, the most unpopular. By *karasu* people mean both the crow and raven, although in Chinese characters the difference is clearly made. *Karasu* is an evil omen, a bird that brings ill-fortune to the people. Almost all over the country, it is believed that when a crow crows over the roof of a house, it foretells a death in that household. They even go to the extreme of being frightfully afraid of hearing the crowing of *karasu* anywhere, especially in the dusk of evening. A specially loud crowing or a gathering of many crows is regarded as the sign of some disastrous or dreadful event.

But this evil *karasu*, however, is highly respected and honored when its rough outline is printed on a piece of paper. *Go-o* is a piece of white paper on which rough and grotesque forms of *karasu* are printed. It has long been used as a medium for finding thieves or evil-doers; it is also used in taking an oath or swearing to statements. When one wishes to swear that what he says is absolutely true, he takes this *go-o* paper, burns it, and swallows the ashes. It is believed that if the statement proves untrue, the *karasu* will become angry for sacrificing them without warrant, and will devour the liar.

Go-o of Kumano are specially valued and respected by the people, not only in the past days of superstition, but even today. Their use has not at all diminished among country people. When something valuable is lost or stolen, people nearby are all asked to swallow *go-o* to prove that they are blameless. The faith of the people in the power of *go-o* and the revenge of the *karasu* is so strong that many evil-doers have actually confessed their wrong by not being able to swallow the ashes of the white paper. Many are said to have vomited blood when the *go-o* ashes were swallowed.

To the shop of a paper dealer there came one day a *samurai* to make a purchase. But when he left the shop, there was found a large sum of money on a mat near where he sat. Soon the *samurai* came back and asked for the lost money, but the master of the shop insisted that no such money had been left behind. The *samurai* went away, but he returned again in a short while, carrying a live crow under his arm. To the shopkeeper he loudly shouted: "Watch what the future has in store for you!" and then drawing a short sword, he cut out the eyes of the crow, and threw the shrieking bird at the shopkeeper. Soon it was said that the *samurai* committed suicide, but from that time, the fortunes of the paper dealer declined. Finally he became blind, and had to beg at houses for his food. This story was related by Saikaku as the confession of a blind priest.

The evil bird, so widely despised and hated by the people, is again known to be the messenger of many *kami*. The *karasu* is the messenger of the Kumano Shrine, the Suwa Shrine of Shinano, and the Hiyoshi Shrine of Omi. The story that Emperor Jinmu, when he had lost his way in the mountains of Kumano, made a crow guide him on his way is well known to all.

Even the crowing of the *karasu*, which is so commonly regarded as an evil omen, is a good omen when heard at the hours of *u* (6 o'clock a.m.) and *uma* (noon). At *u* it means wealth, and at *uma* it foretells happiness and prosperity. In China, a three-legged crow is believed to be the symbol and spirit of the sun. The *karasu* loves the sun, and rises early in the morning and crows at the sun before other birds stir out of their nests.

In China and Japan, the *karasu* is considered as a model for filial children. They say that the *karasu* has the virtue of caring for its aged parents. When parent crows become old, losing many of their feathers, feeble in wings and legs, their children come and feed them. They are also very affectionate. It is the belief in Japan and China that *karasu* mates love one another dearly.

On a large tree in the garden of a soldier, according to an ancient tale of Japan, nested a *karasu* couple with their baby. The male *karasu* went far to gather food for his mate and child, but while he was away, another male crow came and persuaded the female of the nest to fly away with him. They left,

leaving the helpless baby crow in the nest. When the first male crow came back after his long journey, he found the nest deserted by his mate, and the baby on the verge of death. He tenderly folded his wings around the baby, and lamenting for his faithless mate, died from despair. The soldier, seeing the death of the disappointed male crow, became tired of his humdrum life and became a Buddhist monk.

There are many shrines in the country which issue *karasu-uchiwa* or fans with crows painted in black on their festival days. The neighborhood people obtain the black crow fans and place them over their house entrances to ensure their welfare and happiness.

Karasu or crows are regarded as evil omens. There is a traditional belief that a crow's cawing foretells death. But crows are also believed to be the messengers of various deities. In many districts, food is thrown to them in the mountains in worshiping *yama-no-kami* or mountain deity.

Formerly hunters and woodsmen regarded crows as the guardian of their mountains. Particularly at the beginning of the New Year when they went to the mountain for the first time in the year, they used to carry *mochi* or rice cakes with them and, calling the crows, they scattered them in prayer for a successful and happy year. Then, by the way the crows ate the *mochi*, they predicted their fortune for the year.

But at some shrines, food is offered to the *karasu*. This may come from the idea of appeasing them so as not to bring evil fortune.

On the other hand, there are many districts where *karasu* are regarded as bringers of good luck. Fishermen of Tanegashima Island who have a custom of casting their first nets of the year on January 3, hope that crows will appear on the day to ensure a good catch during the year. The sight of even one crow on the day delights all of the islanders.

In the Aomori district, as in many places, farmers hold a rite for *yama-no-kami* when the farm deity leaves for the mountain upon the conclusion of rice harvesting. The Aomori farmers hang *mochi* wrapped up in straw on the branches of trees around their houses, and loudly call to the *karasu* to come and eat it. The *karasu*, so greatly despised, become the messenger of *yama-no-kami* on the day, and the farmers offer *mochi* to please both the *kami* and the crows.

In some places, one's fortune is told by the *karasu*. Small rice dumplings are made, as many as the number of people in the family. Each dumpling is placed on tree branches around the house. By the way crows eat the dumplings, the fortune of the whole family and also the individuals is told.

Thus crows seem to possess both a good and evil side, but generally they are despised as evil birds.

CUCKOO TALES

IN MANY districts of Kyushu, there are still many legendary tales in which the *kakko* or cuckoo has one black and one white leg. In some tales, one leg is white, and the other featherless. At any rate the two legs are not the same.

As to the cause of the cuckoo having one leg different from the other, various stories are told according to district. In a story told in Buzen province at the northern end of Kyushu, an evil-minded mother-in-law was always mistreating her stepchild. One day while the father was away, she killed the child while he was taking off his backyard.

The father came home and called for the child while he was taking off his work trousers, but the child did not answer, and he realized that the child was not at home. He rushed out of the house to look for the child, with one leg still in his trousers and the other out. But he could not find the child, and the father soon died in despair. Thus his spirit turned into a cuckoo with one black leg and one white.

In another part of Kyushu the story is slightly different. The father lived alone with his child. But one day when he came home, he found that the child had mysteriously disappeared. He rushed out in such a hurry that he still had leggings on one leg. Though he searched far and wide, he could not find his child. Finally exhausted, he died and his spirit turned into a cuckoo.

In some parts of Buzen it is said the cuckoo has no feathers on one leg. The cuckoo was formerly a human, and while he was away from home, he learned that his father was seriously ill. He was in such a hurry to return to his father's bedside, that he started out with *waraji* (or straw sandal) on one foot, without waiting to put on the other. This experience in its former life gave the cuckoo one featherless leg.

DEIFIED CLAMS

THE O-E SHRINE at Oe-machi, Tottori Prefecture, is erected in honor of two deified shellfish, so says a legend that dates back to mythological days.

Okuninushi-no-mikoto, who later became the ruler of the district of Izumo and also commonly came to be worshiped as *Daikokusama*, god of harvest and happiness, was a kind-hearted and upright man. But his elder brother Yasogi was cruel and cross. There was a particular reason why Yasogi hated Okuninushi. For Yasogi wanted to marry Yakami-hime, a beautiful daughter of a neighboring ruler, but she chose Okuninushi and rejected Yasogi.

Yasogi, blind with envy and hatred, wished to do away with Okuninushi. One day he heated a big stone red-hot and then going to Okuninushi said that there was a brown boar in the grass. Okuninushi rushed out to catch the boar. As he grabbed what he thought was a boar, he was severely burned.

Seeing her son so badly burned, his mother thought that Okuninushi would die. In order to save him she went up to heaven and asked the aid of *Kanmusubi-no-kami*. Her earnest pleading was answered and the heavenly deity dispatched two female physicians, *Umuki-hime* and *kisagai-hime*, to treat Okuninushi's burn.

Umuki is a clam and *kisagai* is an ark shell, and the two physicians were the deities of those shellfish.

To cure the burn on Okuninushi's body, *Kisagai-hime* crushed a shell into powder and *Umuki-hime* obtained a medicinal liquid from a shell. They mixed the powder and liquid to make a paste and applied it to Okuninushi's burn. The treatment was so effective that instantly the severe burn was healed and Okuninushi was saved from death.

In reward for this service, the female physicians were enshrined at O-e, and came to be worshiped ever since by the local people as their guardians.

DOG SOLDIERS

IT IS RECORDED that dogs were first used for military purposes in Japan in the 14th century. Hata Tokiyoshi of the Nitta clan is said to be the first Japanese who trained dogs for military duties. Since then, many feudal lords and military leaders have kept trained dogs. Ota Dokan who built Edo Castle in 1457 was famous for keeping trained dogs and using them in action.

In those days dogs were used to carry secret messages. Particularly when a castle was besieged by enemies and had to ask for help, dogs with messages were sent through enemy lines to bring help.

But some dogs were also trained for reconnoitering. They were trained to observe conditions in the enemy camp and report on them.

Hata Tokiyoshi possessed a giant dog, named *Inu-shishi* or dog lion, who was skillful in reconnoitering. On battlefields, Inu-shishi appeared in light metal armor for protection against enemy arrows.

In February 1339, Hata, with only a small force in Takasu Castle, Echizen province, was surrounded by the overwhelming troops of Ashikaga, and faced immediate defeat. One dark night, Hata secretly came out of the castle with Inushishi. Patting his head, he said to the dog, "Don't forget to bark the signal. Now go and look."

Some time later a dog barked near the enemy camp. Then Hata said, "He barked once. That means the enemy has not gone to sleep yet. We have to wait until morning. Let us get some sleep."

As dawn came, Hata was awakened by Inu-shishi rubbing his body against him. He looked at the dog, and saw his tail wagging. He rose with joy, shouting "The dog wags his tail. The enemy is asleep. Let us attack them without a moment's loss."

So his troops charged against the surrounding enemy, and surprised them in their sleep. Thus it is recorded he was able to break through the lines of the enemy that surrounded his tiny castle.

DRAGONFLIES

THE *TONBO* (dragonflies) appear to have been almost worshiped by the Japanese people in olden days. Certainly it is true that it was considered a lucky insect. Since the time of Jinmu Tenno, the archipelago of Japan had been named after the dragonfly, because the formation of the islands of the country presents a rough outline of the insect. The *tonbo* was the symbol of many characteristics of the country, and formerly the land was called 'the land of the dragonfly.' Even in recent literature, *Tonbo* or *Seirei* is used as a synonym for Nippon.

At one time the *tonbo* was the symbol of the country, and it was thus respected. But apart from its being the symbol of the nation, due to its shape, there are found no characteristics of the insect that might command so much respect and worship. The dragonfly appears to be delicate and lovely, but in fact it is a fighting insect. With its strong jaws and teeth, it easily kills and eats up much larger and stronger-looking insects. The female of the species is particularly vicious and cruel.

It may be from this fighting quality of the insect that in former days the *tonbo* was much respected by warriors. Among *bushi* it was nicknamed *shogunmushi* (general-insect), or *kachi-mushi* (victory-insects). Knots of ropes and ribbons made in the style of the dragonfly were especially used by *bushi* families. A design of dragonflies adorned the undergarments of fighting men, in the belief that the wearer would be victorious and lucky. The habit of using dragonfly designs on things worn by fighting men was popular until the end of the Tokugawa regime when the *bushi* class was dissolved.

Even today, dragonfly designs are used on garments for boys, and things used by them. They are seldom seen on things for girls. This is a survival of the former custom. It is not clearly known why the dragonfly was considered as a lucky insect that would bring victory.

At any rate the belief seems to have originated in quite early days. It is stated that Emperor Yuryaku (fifth century) greatly praised the dragonfly because he had seen it destroying other insects. This may be the first record of the respect accorded to the dragonfly. From this story of Emperor Yuryaku, and the fact that the country was formerly named after the insect, people began to ascribe virtues to the *tonbo*, it appears. But why the *bushi* of the Tokugawa period paid so much respect to the insect and believed it almost the spirit of victory and used it in designs and charms worn by warriors going to the battlefront, is not clear. It is explained by some authorities that the respect given the insect as the symbol of the country had somehow been gradually extended, and it finally became the guardian spirit of the *bushi*.

The *tonbo* is a fighter, and probably the fact was well-known to the people of old, and they loved the way a dragonfly mercilessly attacked and devoured other insects. It is really cruelty, but they mistook it for bravery.

The belief has not entirely died out, and today many people believe that little boys wearing *tonbo* designs will be fortunate and lucky. To many people the *tonbo* stands for manliness and courage, if not for the spirit of Nippon.

ELEPHANTS

ELEPHANTS are the most popular animals with children visiting zoos in Japan as well as in many other countries. In the old days, some Japanese worshiped elephants.

It is recorded that the first elephant came to Japan in the 14th century. It must be remembered, however, that elephants inhabited the region now called Japan many thousands of years before human habitation as proved by elephant bones found buried underground. But as far as we are concerned, the first elephant was presented by the Chinese emperor to the third Ashikaga shogun, Yoshimitsu. It was welcomed with much ceremony as the people had never seen such an animal before.

Next we hear of an elephant in the Tokugawa period. It was in 1729 that an elephant was sent from Nagasaki to Kyoto. Of course, it walked all the way except across the Kyushu-Honshu channel. When it was shown to Emperor Nakamikado, His Majesty was so pleased that he conferred on the elephant the Court rank of the fifth grade. So the common people had to bow before it.

The honored animal was brought to Edo, where the people thronged to see the strange beast. Finding it so different from other animals, many thought it sacred. Also the fact that *Fugenbosatsu* (Visvabhadra), one of Buddha's disciples, is always presented sitting on the back of an elephant, boosted the idea of regarding the animal as sacred.

On the occasion of the festival of Sanno Shrine, one of the famous festivals of Edo, a special float was made in honor of the elephant, and the people paid their respects and made offerings to it, with a prayer for good fortune.

FIREFLIES

Hotaru koi
Atchi no mizu wa karai zo
Kotchi no mizu wa amai zo
Hotaru koi.
Come, fireflies,
The water on that side is
  bitter.
The water on this side is
  sweeter.
Come, fireflies.

THUS CHILDREN sing as they go

firefly hunting, carrying fans and bamboo branches. *Hotaru* or fireflies are found all over the country, and they can be easily caught with fans or even by hand. Children gather them as they appear in the dusk of evening over streams and ponds. They are kept in little cages covered with gauze. In cities, *hotaru* are sold in cages at street stalls.

There are many varieties of fireflies in the country, and some glow brighter than others. Numerous places are famous for them, and people form firefly viewing parties to visit such localities.

Hotaru-gassen or firefly battles are one of the most wonderful summer sights. Huge masses of fireflies come from different directions and mingle in confusion as they come together, making hillsides and streams bright with tiny yellowish lights. In most places it is traditionally said that these fireflies are the incarnated souls of the soldiers of the Minamoto and Taira families, who fought many centuries ago. Not satisfied with the battles they fought in their human form, they continue to fight even after they have been turned into fireflies.

The country is full of many romantic as well as tragic tales based on the belief that fireflies are the souls of dead people.

In the old days, many districts had a holiday when the people went to see fireflies. The best known of such customs is of Yamaguchi City, which was started about 600 years ago by Lord Ouchi and has been held annually. It is dedicated to the *hotaru*, and for one day, it is prohibited to catch them and those held in captivity have to be released.

Five famous districts where *Genji-botaru* are found in abundance are protected by law. They are Sawabe-mura, Miyagi Prefecture; Saito-mura (Kamata

River), Yamanashi Prefecture; Okazaki (Ikuta River), Aichi Prefecture; Moriyama (Lake Biwa), Shiga Prefecture; and the suburbs of Yamaguchi City. Around Tokyo the Minugawa River, near Omiya City, Saitama Prefecture, is famous for *Genji-botaru*.

In cities and towns, fireflies are sold in little cages at stores or by peddlers.

FISH FUNERAL

THE OWNER of a Japanese restaurant at Atami once became seriously ill, and physicians were called from Odawara and other neighboring towns, but learned doctors were unable to improve her condition. She became weaker and weaker. An old fisher-woman of Atami then suggested that the family should hold a funeral service for *konoshiro* (Konosirus punctatus) in order to save the life of the patient.

Konoshiro is a little fish about seven inches long and is a kind of sardine. In many parts of Japan there has been a superstitious belief that *konoshiro* will die in place of persons whose death is not desired. So the family and relatives of the Atami restaurant-owner gathered, and bringing in a *konoshiro*, dressed it in the miniature white funeral costume. A tiny coffin was made, and Buddhist priests were called to recite sacred sutras. Incense was burned, and candles were lit and all relatives and friends of the patient held a deathwatch. The coffin was taken to the temple yard and buried with due ceremony.

The patient did not know what was happening, and only wondered at why so many people had gathered at the house. But strangely, soon after the funeral her condition showned marked improvement, and she recovered although all physicians had given up hope of recovery.

The traditional belief in *konoshiro* is still very strong among certain classes of people, especially in fishing villages.

Once a young *geisha* became seriously ill, and her death was already declared to be a matter of days by her physicians. To save the life of the young *geisha*, a *konoshiro* funeral was held in the proper manner and setting. This saved her life, and she was ever thankful for *konoshiro*. Of course she did not dare eat any *konoshiro*, as it had saved her life. But one day, she unwittingly ate *konoshiro* at a party, after which she immediately fell ill. Upon investigation she learned that the fish she had eaten was *konoshiro*, and when she heard the name *konoshiro*, her face turned pale, and she hurriedly returned home. But just as she stepped inside her house, she fell dead.

Thus in many fishing villages, fishermen and their families will not eat *konoshiro*, and often when *konoshiro* are caught in a net or by line, they are set free. Many will catch *konoshiro*, but will not eat it.

FOXES

FOXES POSSESS the power to bewitch people, and do various mischief by transforming themselves into men, women and many other things, it is still believed by many people. All rural districts have such tales and traditions.

Modern city folk laugh at such stories, but many old men will narrate their own experiences of having been bewitched by foxes.

Here is one report published by the Iwate Nichinichi Shimbun, a newspaper in the northeastern district, on November 13, 1922:

There is a mineral spring in back of the village of Wainai, where Chukichi Ishidate, 67, was living as the caretaker. On the night of November 6, someone knocked at his door. The old man woke up and went to see who it was. As he opened the door, there stood six big men, all armed with shotguns. Raising the guns, they shouted "Give us ¥300. If you do not, we will kill you!"

Afraid for his life, he took out his purse which contained ¥35.68, all the money he had. Such a small amount would never do. As they came nearer, the old man dashed out of the door, shouting "Murder, murder!"

He ran to the village of Wainai, and told everybody about the attack by six men. The policeman, firemen and others followed him to his place. But there was no sign of the six. In the hut lay the old man's purse on the mat, the contents intact. But his tub of cooked rice was empty and fish and other foodstuffs were gone. Then they saw the footprints of foxes on the mats. They all laughed at Chukichi for having been bewitched by foxes and losing his stock of food.

Several days before, the old man had smoked out a fox from its cave by burning pine needles at the entrance. He had killed the fox and sold the fur at the village. The companions of the killed fox came to take revenge on Chukichi for the murder of their friend, the villagers said.

FOX LEGEND

THE PEOPLE of the Ayato district, Aichi Prefecture, still pay respect to the spirit of the fox because of an incident that happened there.

Korenao, son of Koretaka, the village head of Yorita, was one day walking along a country road. Suddenly a fox appeared as though chased by a hunter and hid behind him. He held the animal in his arms and petted it. Then, Yasouemon, a farmer, came running up and said that it was a fox he had been

hunting for some time and asked the young man to hand it over to him.

"It is no common fox. It has such beautiful fur, and furthermore it will soon bear young. If you ever kill it, you will receive severe punishment," Korenao said. Yasouemon understood, and so the fox was released.

Autumn came and the whole village was happy with its annual harvest festival. An official of the feudal lord, Matsumoto Sakon, came to inspect the crop and fix the amount of tax. A great welcome was given him with drink and music. The villagers sang and danced all night in a holiday spirit.

Next day, Matsumoto started to fix the amount of tax to be paid by each farmer. Korenao attended in place of his father. The official demanded that as a pledge for tax payment, O-nui, daughter of Yasouemon, and O-tama, her friend, whom he had seen at the party the day before, be handed over to him.

Korenao flatly rejected such a proposal. Becoming angry at being refused, the official drew his sword and threatened to kill the young man. Thereupon O-nui, O-tama and a number of others came forward to save Korenao. But the angry man's sword flashed right and left, and appeared to have killed O-nui, O-tama and the rest. In the meantime, Korenao managed to escape and as he looked back at the bodies of the girls who had apparently been killed, there was only the blood-covered remains of a fox.

The grateful fox had come to their aid and both of the girls were safe. O-nui and O-tama entered the Enmeiji Temple nearby and became nuns under Myoseini, the nun at the temple who taught the two girls sewing.

The spirit of the grateful fox still lives, the people believe.

FREEING FISH AND BIRDS

THE ACT of setting free fish and birds held in captivity is regarded as the noblest manifestation of charity. Often, therefore, decorated cages filled with pigeons are carried in a funeral procession, and at the end of the service, the birds are set free in prayer for the salvation of the deceased. On various other occasions of celebration and festivals, pigeons are also freed to wish benevolence to all. Charitable persons purchased fish or birds and gave them freedom.

In the old days, at shrines and temples, a service of *hojo-e* or freeing fish, birds and other animals was held annually. One held at the Iwashimizu Hachiman Shrine, Kyoto, in A.D. 720 is recorded to be the oldest. Since A.D. 863 it became an annual event held every autumn. But the annual service was discontinued with the Meiji Restoration. The Usa Hachiman Shrine of Oita Prefecture was also very famous for its *hojo-e* service.

At the *hojo-e* service, the people brought fish or birds which they had purchased and set them free. It is mentioned that at some places the people brought fish and made a procession to a river or the seaside nearby, where they held services and then put the fish back in the water to enjoy freedom.

The service was held not only as an act of charity, but it also contributed much to teaching the people, particularly children, that every living thing should be loved and not killed. In temples and shrines birds and also fish are kept, but they should not be molested and no one is allowed to catch them.

FURUHON MUSHI

OLD JAPANESE books or paintings on Japanese paper very often have tiny holes eaten out by insects, often ruining them to a lamentable extent. The insect that does this damage to Japanese paper is generally called *furuhon-mushi* or *shimi* (old book insect), or Gastrallus immarginatus Mueller that belongs to the family Arobiidae.

It is very small, measuring only about 3 mm when fully grown, and chestnut brown in color. But the full-grown insect does not harm books or paper. The culprit is its larvae. The full-grown female of the insect lays her eggs between the sheets of paper or within rolled-up paintings.

The eggs hatch into tiny, light yellowish larvae, measuring about 4 mm. The larvae have strong mouths and chew the paper, emitting saliva. *Furuhon-mushi* also invade the bamboo stems of *fude* or writing brushes and make holes in the bamboo.

After eating the paper, the larvae become full-grown insects and fly away. The female returns to the books to lay her eggs.

All books used to be printed on Japanese paper, so they were subject to damage by *furuhon-mushi*. Thus book collectors and lovers had a hard time protecting their valuable books and paintings from them.

As soon as the wet *tsuyu* season was over, they used to take out their books and paintings from their cases or storerooms, and spread them in the sun or in dry rooms. Each volume had to be opened to ascertain if any hole had been bored by the insect.

Doyo-boshi or summer drying of books and pictures was done not only during the summer season, but also in the dry autumn season.

Of course at present there are various effective chemicals to kill insects and preserve old books. Modern books are now printed on Western-type paper, which is not favored by the insect.

GOLDFISH

TO HEAR *"Kingyo, kingyo"* shouted by goldfish peddlers is a joy to the Japanese, as it heralds the coming of the warm and pleasant season. *Kingyo* is the pet of all classes of people and particularly of children.

Japanese goldfish have become world-famous, but it is not indigenous. It came first from China in the early part of the 17th century. Then, from the Netherlands, Ryukyus and Hawaii came new species. Japanese *kingyo* fanciers have succeeded in the past 300 years in producing such gorgeous species that they have won world fame.

The original Chinese variety was small with insignificant tails. The novel fish became a pet among aristocrats at once. As the fad of keeping goldfish spread to the common people, it was raised in large quantities. It was so popular that when other kinds were brought into the country, the Chinese species was called *wakin* (Japanese goldfish) to distinguish it from newcomers. But its popularity declined with the introduction of more gorgeous kinds. However, it is still produced, as it is easy to keep and can be sold cheaply.

The kind called *maruko* or fat and round species was brought by Dutch traders in the Hoei era (1704-1711), or about a hundred years after the Chinese variety. It is fat and round and has gorgeous colors. Its beauty won the heart of all fanciers. It has lumps on its head and its particular feature is the lack of back fins.

Then in the Kansei-Bunka period (1789-1818), Ryukyu goldfish were brought in. This kind has a small mouth and a large tail. Japanese fanciers soon crossbred the Dutch *maruko* with the Ryukyu species, and produced what is called *oranda-shishi-gashira* (Dutch lion-head), having a gorgeous head and wonderful tails that are divided into three or four parts. This variety sometimes grows to one and a half feet long in seven or eight years.

Last came a Hawaiian variety in about 1904-1905. This kind has bulging eyes and is multicolored. Because of the projecting eyes. it was named *demekin* (bulging eye) by Dr. Kakichi Mitsukuri.

The small *wakin* is not very fancy, but can be easily kept by anyone, if it is not fed too much. Overfeeding is what kills goldfish very often. *Kingyo* have to be kept in bowls or pots as large as circumstances permit, and fresh water must be added daily.

GROWING FISH

BORA (gray mullet) is a common fish with no particular beauty or excellence in taste, but the Japanese have long regarded it with respect. It is because they believe the fish stands for success and advancement. So the common habit of using this fish on occasions of special importance has developed. Particularly on boys' birthdays or upon their departure from home to embark on life, it has become customary to place this fish on the table. It represents the wish of fond mothers to bring good luck and success to their sons. The fish has had little significance for girls, because formerly it was only boys who were expected to advance and succeed.

Bora gained this significance because it is a 'growing fish.' All fish grow, of course, but *bora* has different names as it grows. It is called *ina* when it is young, and is given the name of *bora* when it matures. Furthermore, if it grows bigger, it is given another name, *todo*, meaning final. It is hoped by mothers that their boys will grow and advance as the fish grows through the three stages of *ina*, *bora* and *todo*.

Of course, there are other fish that have more than one name, but it is only the *bora* that is called the fish of success and advancement.

HATSU-GATSUO

HATSU-GATSUO or the first bonito of the season was formerly highly valued as a delicacy. It is said that in the Tokugawa days, many Edo residents even pawned their valuables in order to eat it.

Bonito live in warm and clear sea water. It approaches the shore of Japan from the south, riding on the Black Current in the May-June season. It has been eaten since very early days, but in the old days, the people did not eat fresh *katsuo*. They ate it after drying it. Thus *katsuobushi* or dried bonito, which is so widely used in seasoning foods, developed.

It is only since about the Kamakura period or some 700 years ago that fresh bonito came to be generally eaten. In Edo it was not eaten until about 300 years ago but it was prized so highly that when the first shipment reached Edo, the first fish was presented to the *shogun*. The fish was not sold until the first piece was offered to the Tokugawa family head.

It was in the first part of the 18th century that the fame of *katsuo* became so great that even the merchant and artisan classes wanted it. It was, however, so expensive that many of them could not buy it with ready cash, and had to borrow money or pawn their clothing.

Thus various stories came to be told about *hatsu-gatsuo* and commoners. Raw slices of bonito, since then, have come to be regarded as the most delicious *sashimi* to eat in season.

'*Meni-aoba, yama-hototogisu, hatsu-gatsuo*' (green foliage to the eye, cuckoos in the mountain and the first bonito of the season) runs an old popular poem, meaning that those three items are the things that make the season so pleasant.

Bonito has dark and light green stripes on its body when it is dead, but while alive these stripes are almost invisible.

Dried bonito is not only shaved and used for seasoning foods but also sent as a gift on festive occasions.

HORSE-CARTS

A MAN LEADING by a rope a horse that draws a cart is a familiar sight in Japan. Western visitors often wonder why he does not sit on the cart and drive the horse. Neither do the Japanese people know exactly how this custom was formed.

There seem to be various circumstances that developed this strange custom. Firstly, the horse was used in Japan as a pack animal, and thus it was quite natural for the owner to lead by a rope the horse carrying goods on its back. Then, horses were much used by military men, but they were not used for drawing carts.

In the old days there were *ushi-guruma* or ox-drawn carts. Elaborately decorated ox carts were used by Court nobles and particularly ladies as a means of transportation. Ox carts for carrying goods were popular all over the country and they were, of course, led by ropes by men.

But there were no horse-drawn carts.

Thus, it was the custom in the country at first to use horses only as riding or pack animals. Later the horse came to be attached to carts which were formerly drawn by men. But as no improvement was made in the form or construction of the cart, except for enlarging the shafts, there was no place for the man to sit and drive the horse. As he used to lead the pack-horse, he led the horse that drew the cart.

This may also be due to the fact that the Japanese people never learned the art of driving horses, though they mastered the technique of riding them. Then some say that Japanese horses were vicious and always had to be led even when attached to carts so that they would do no harm to people on the street.

It was only after the introduction of Western-type horse-carriages in the early Meiji days that the country saw for the first time men driving horse-drawn carriages. When Western-style horse-carriages were still novelties in the country, men used to run ahead of the horse to warn the people of the approach of the carriage.

HORSEFLIES

NOBODY PAYS any attention to *abu* or horseflies unless they are bothering him. But there is a certain kind of *abu* in Japan that has become world-famous.

It is the *onsen-abu* or hot-spring horsefly that is found at Iimori Hot Spring, Nasu in Tochigi Prefecture. It is a rare horsefly, having come to attract the attention of scientists all over the world, because it lives comfortably in hot water. The British Museum which received specimens from Tokyo University many years ago pronounced it the most unique kind of horsefly in the world.

Onsen-abu is no different from other horseflies in general appearance, but it has a special characteristic that is not seen in any other horsefly or insects. Its eggs hatch in hot water, and through its chrysalis stage, it survives under hot water. Even when it develops into a full-grown horsefly, it practically lives in hot water.

For an insect, love of hot-water bathing is unheard of. Visitors to the Iimori Hot Spring, where the water is 50 degrees centigrade or 122 degrees Fahrenheit, have always marvelled at the tiny insects enjoying dips in hot water. Nobody yet has found out why this insect has come to be so fond of hot-water bathing. It is only known that they must have just followed the customs of the Japanese people enjoying a very hot bath.

IBOTA WAX

IBOTA (Ligusttrum ibota) is an insignificant bush that grows to about two meters and has tiny white blossoms. But because it is liked by *ibota-no-mushi* (ibota insect), Ericerus pela, which boasts of no beauty, it has been closely linked with the life of the people.

The larvae of the *ibota* insect produce a fine waxy thread and form ball-like coverings for their protection on the branches of *ibota* trees. It was formerly believed that this waxy thread was good for removing warts. So *ibota* (wart remover) became the name of not only the insect, but also of the plant.

This waxy thread produced by the insect is gathered, boiled or heated and cleaned of foreign matter. Thus in this way a fine wax named *ibota-ro* or *ibota* wax is produced.

This *ibota* wax has been used by Japanese artisans for polishing furniture, cabinet work and other things.

It is also used to make sliding doors move smoothly and noiselessly.

Ibota plants are found growing wild in many mountain regions, and the gathering of *ibota* wax is still an important task of many mountain farmers. Aizu in the northeastern district is particularly famous for *ibota* wax. But as the plant is found almost everywhere, and even in some gardens, many gather the wax, and use it without refining for polishing their wooden utensils.

However, though the name still remains, it is no longer used for removing warts.

KIRIN

THE GIRAFFE is known in Japanese as *kirin*. This is misleading, however, as there is another animal named *kirin* that has been known to the people before they ever heard of a giraffe. It is not known how the giraffe came to be so called when it was first introduced to the people.

The original *kirin* was an imaginary animal of China which has been very highly respected by the Japanese as in China. The *kirin* is a benevolent animal that rarely makes an appearance, but when it does, it is a sign that a great sage is to appear soon to rule the country with wisdom and kindness.

It is from this belief that there developed a commonly used term 'kirin-ji' or *kirin* boy, to indicate a bright and promising youth.

As depicted in paintings and sculpture, the *kirin* is an animal resembling a deer but much larger. It has a cow's tail, and one horn in the middle of its head. Its hoofs are like those of a horse. The hair on its underside is yellow, but the body is covered with stripes of five bright colors. It is a strange but beautiful animal that eats neither fresh plants nor living animals.

Children who now gather around the giraffe in zoological gardens mostly do not know of the legendary *kirin*.

KURAGE

THE *KURAGE* (jellyfish) is found in many seas and rivers, but only the Japanese and Chinese eat it. Of course there are many varieties, but only the bluish and brown kinds are eaten. Some are poisonous, of which the red variety is known to be the most toxic.

There is a story that, at first, *kurage* was like any other kind of fish. But once it failed to perform a task given it by the Undersea Lord, and accordingly it was punished. Not only was it severely beaten, but its bones were also taken out. Thus it became a shapeless jelly-like thing that did not look like any fish.

The *kurage* is believed to have no eyes, and its movements are guided by little shrimps that live inside its body. Actually small shrimps or fish are sometimes found inside them.

Sea bathers are often poisoned by the *kurage*, and receive long scratches on their arms and legs when they come in contact with the poisonous variety. Their legs or feelers have poison lines, and when they touch any hostile object, the poison is injected into the enemy immediately. The poison is not deadly, but gives much pain. It is potent even after the *kurage* is dead.

It is interesting to note that *kurage* poison was the first chemical weapon used in war. It is recorded that in the Toyotomi-Tokugawa battle at Osaka in 1615, Sanada Yukimura used *kurage* poison as a chemical weapon.

He gathered many red *kurage* on the seashore of Kii. The *kurage* were dried and powdered. As the wind blew toward the enemy, he scattered the poisonous powder in the air. The wind-carried poison fell on enemy soldiers and caused great pain.

Thus, Sanada Yukimura may be said to be the first user in the world of a chemical weapon.

LADY BOAR

THE *INOSHISHI* (wild boar) is a dangerous animal, and not only men but many other animals of the forest are afraid of boars. In many parts of Japan there is a belief that snakes are afraid of wild boars, and that they disappear at the sight *inoshishi*. Even the mention of the name *inoshishi*, they believe, will chase away the most vicious snake. In olden days people uttered the name of *inoshishi* whenever they encountered snakes on mountains or lonely paths.

Akuma-dachi,
Waga tatsu michi ni yokotaeba
Yamatachi hime ni ari to tsugen.
(Red-spotted snakes, if you cross my path,
I will tell lady boars that you are here.)
Kono michi ni nishiki-madarano mushi araba
Yamatachi hime ni tsugete torasen.
(If brocade-spotted snakes are on this road,
I will tell lady boars to kill them.)

These two old poems prove that the people believed that the mere mention of boars would make snakes crawl away. The two are quite similar, but it is very strange that in both poems the *inoshishi* is made a lady. It is beyond the understanding of ordinary people why the vicious boar is called a lady, even in a poem.

In olden days there were reported to be many people who were skillful in catching snakes, or who could cure people bitten by poisonous snakes. One such man was named Izaemon, and the people of his district believed that when they entered the woods, they would never be bitten by snakes if they kept shouting "Izaemon, Izaemon." They believed that the name of this man who could counter the poison of a snake was known to every snake, and at the mere mention of his name all snakes would scatter.

There are also many charms to drive away snakes. Izaemon also had the power to chase them from a distance of 10 to 15 miles. It is said that the charm consisted of a paper on which was written one of the above-mentioned poems, which are said to have been written by him.

Wild boars are thus made charms to drive away snakes, because it is generally believed that boars are very fond of snakes and eat them whenever they are found. The people thus came to use the name of *inoshishi* in scattering snakes.

LIZARDS

IMORI, YAMORI, AND *TOKAGE* are three common types of lizards found in Japan. They are quite alike in shape, and only differ in their color and mode of living. Some of them are quite beautiful, but the people have always abhorred them, and are afraid even to touch them.

This dislike for these lizards has been caused by a superstitious belief that they are revengeful and are able to use supernatural evil spirits. There are related many tales in Japan which tell of various evils done by those lizards.

But it is rather pitiful that they have been so greatly disliked by the people, as they do no harm, and are not at all poisonous. The strong love that exists between the male and female of these lizards has been the cause of their misfortune. This strong love surprised the people, and many expressions of this attachment caused them to believe that evil spirits have possessed the lizards.

Once a farmer built a house, but after that his wife died, and his children also became ill. His neighbors circulated a rumor that some evil spirit might be living in his house. Consequently a search was made, and it was found that on a beam of the house, there was an *imori* fastened by a nail. The house had been built several years before, but the lizard was still alive. The farmer in building the house had nailed it without knowing of its presence. This discovery proved the theory of the evil spirit, and the people said that because the lizard was nailed there, it killed the farmer's wife and made the children sick. The strange fact that the lizard survived, nailed to the beam, was sufficient to make the people believe in the tale.

But when one of two mated lizards is nailed in such a way, it is always the habit of its companion to bring food to the impaled sufferer, and there is nothing strange in the above-mentioned case of a lizard living several years nailed to a beam.

Imori-no-kuroyaki (roasted and powdered lizard) is still considered a love potion. It is because the *imori* is very affectionate and will never leave its mate, that this belief has originated. An *imori* is caught alive and then burned by fire and made into a powder, which is then sold as a love potion. It is believed that when one sprinkles this powder on a girl he loves, his love will be requited. It is a superstitious belief, but yet we cannot deny its popularity, as stores specializing in this love potion prosper even today.

MONKEY FUR

THOSE WHO have read or seen the *Noh* play *Utsubozaru* (arrow-bag monkey) wonder why the *samurai* so persistently wanted to obtain the trained monkey from its owner and to kill it to get the fur to make a bag for his arrows, as the fur of monkeys is not particularly beautiful.

Rarely are there monkeys with very fine, silky fur but the trained monkey in the story must have been one of such rare ones. Unless one realizes this point, the play becomes meaningless.

As to how some monkeys have especially beautiful fur, various explanations are offered. Monkeys live in groups, and each group has its boss who is wise and powerful and rules over all the others. But sometimes a monkey becomes rebellious and runs away from the group.

Such rebels become lone monkeys who live by themselves in the mountains. Naturally they roam over a wide area and lead their own life. Sometimes when such lone monkeys manage to obtain sufficient good food, their fur becomes beautiful, it is believed.

The monkey in the *Noh* drama must have been such a monkey or its baby which had been caught and trained.

Group monkeys generally do not have good fur because it is always the boss monkey who eats the best food and the other monkeys eat only what is left for them. The food obtained by such group monkeys is generally limited and is not of much variety.

The lone monkey, if it is fortunate in food hunting, is able to eat as much as it desires, and by roaming through the mountains, it finds various kinds of good food. Yet even among lone monkeys, one with fine silky fur is quite rare.

Thus in ancient days, beautiful monkey fur was very highly valued. So when the *samurai* saw the monkey with the beautiful fur, he wanted to have it at any cost. However, seeing the affection the trainer had for his monkey, he had to change his orginal plan to kill the monkey for its fur.

MONKEYS

THE *SARU* (monkey) is regarded by many people as unlucky, as *saru* also means 'to go away.' Among those who especially hesitate to call a *saru* by its proper name are stock speculators, gamblers, restaurant owners and many shopkeepers. These people will never say *saru*, and when they must mention the animal they call it *ete*. The mere mention of *saru*, they believe, will cause their luck and patrons to go away. One should particularly avoid mentioning the animal by its common name on the occasion of a wedding ceremony, as it would cause the misfortune of the bride running away.

But this unlucky *saru* is also believed to possess the power to dispel evil spirits and shield one from the evil eye. Little toy *saru* made of cloth, wood or clay are given to children to save them from the evil eye. Among toys for Japanese children, those of *saru* predominated because of this belief. On the upper center of the back of the children's or babies' outer clothing, tiny *saru* made of cloth and stuffed with cotton are attached. In the talisman bag of children, a similar *saru* is often placed. These *saru* toys are attached to the babies' clothing or given to them as toys, in the belief that they will drive away evil spirits. And it is also said that such *saru* will carry away all sins and evils of the babies.

In a book describing the procession of a daughter of the Lord of Satsuma to Edo, it is said that among the many large oblong boxes containing clothing and utensils for the daughter, that were carried on long poles, there were several gaily decorated with white and red banners and tiny *saru* of cloth.

Regarding this belief of *saru* possessing the power to dispel evil spirits, we have to go back to the time of the landing of our ancestors on the islands of Japan. When the heavenly party came as far as the place called Ama-no-Yachimata, it was reported that there lived a great *kami* who was the lord of the surrounding country. He is described as being seven feet-tall, possessing a nose five feet-long. His eyes shone as a huge mirror, and his face was ruddy. His appearance was so fierce and his eyes were so penetrating that none of the thousands of heavenly persons could directly face the strange monster. His name was Saruta-hiko and he was really a huge monkey. His fierce eyes and terrible countenance were strong enough to dispel any evil spirit, not to mention the heavenly persons who met no enemy that they could not conquer. From this story *saru* became to be believed to possess the power to shield one from any evil eye.

But strange to say, while all the heavenly *kami* were helpless against Saruta-hiko, Uzume-no-mikoto, who is reputed to have been the most ugly of all female *kami*, subdued him and made him guide the Imperial party to Isuzugawa.

Of Saruta-hiko, it is said that, once while fishing by the seashore, his hand was caught firmly by a shellfish, and he almost drowned. Even today in the Kumano district many monkeys come to the shore, and while attempting to catch fish, are often caught by crabs or shellfish.

In former days at various country places, little shrines housing images of *saru* were found. Pregnant women went to these shrines, and after making their prayers, carried away these images. They place the images by their bedside, to ensure them sn easy and happy delivery. The *saru*, it is rumored, has no suffering during delivery, and worship of the images would give women ease and comfort at their time of trial. After a happy delivery the women make other images of the *saru* and offer them together with the ones they had borrowed from the shrines.

Huge monster monkeys were formerly worshiped as *kami* of the country, and in many parts they were even appeased by the offering of beautiful young girls, but the ancient records say that such practices were stopped by the acts of mighty warriors who bravely confronted such monsters and killed them.

The messenger of the Hiyoshi Shrine is a *saru*. This, however, is because of the monkey's strong love for sunshine. As soon as the sun sets in the evening, the *saru* becomes crestfallen and inactive, and nothing seems to arouse it during the dark hours of night. But the moment the sun rises, it becomes active and chatters away merrily. For this reason, it is chosen as the messenger of the Hiyoshi Shrine.

The *saru* is never friendly with the *karasu* (crow) and destroys every crow nest it finds. *Saru* is the messenger of the Hiyoshi Shrine, and *karasu* is the messenger of the Kumano Shrine. A strange fact is that these two shrines were never friendly.

MONSTER ABALONE

THE PACIFIC coast of Boshu, Chiba Prefecture, is famous for its heavy sea, *ama* or women divers, and *awabi* (abalone). The villagers on the coast are mostly fishermen, and while men go out fishing on boats, women dive into the sea to gather the *awabi* and other shellfish.

There is a story of a woman diver and a monster abalone. At the bottom of the sea, off a point called Iwawada, there lived an exceptionally big *awabi*, larger than the common umbrella. It was the lord of all abalones and of the sea. But this monster shellfish always stayed peacefully at the sea bottom and did not like any disturbance. If anything disturbed it, it became angry and caused big waves.

Fishermen and women divers worked only on fair days when the sea was calm, and rested when the sea was rough. There was a young diver who was in love with a young fisherman. They met whenever they were not working. Once, fair days continued and they had no chance to meet. So she wished for a stormy day.

Remembering the monster abalone, she swam out to the point where the sea lord lived and dropped a tiny pebble. Thus disturbed, the abalone became angry and caused high waves. The fishing boats did not go out and she was able to meet her young man.

She tried her trick again and succeeded. On the third occasion she became careless or too eager and threw down several stones into the sea.

Suddenly, without any warning, a fierce storm arose, causing towering waves with heavy rain and thunderclaps. The young man fishing in the offing tried to return to land, and the woman diving for abalones swam desperately for the shore.

They did not reach safety but before they were swallowed up by the angry waves, they managed to reach each other. Holding each other firmly, they disappeared.

MUKADE

MUKADE (hundred legs) or centipedes are a kind of poisonous insect found in Japan. There are many varieties, but most measure 10 to 15 mm, have 20 pairs of legs and their backs are dark brown while the underside is yellowish. They live in the soil or in rotten tree trunks. In summer, they sometimes come into the house and torture people with their sharp poison fangs. Sometimes they drop from the ceiling upon persons sleeping below. They seldom make an appearance in the daytime.

The bite of the insect is painful and sometimes lasts several hours. Thus the people are very much afraid of them, but the *mukade* has also been used as a medicine since very early days. When one is caught, it is put in a bottle of oil. In a few months, the oil becomes an excellent cure for cuts, wounds and burns. It is even said that when a finger is completely cut off by some accident, the application of the *mukade* oil will make the finger adhere to the stump again.

Thus many rural households still keep this oil ready for any emergency, firmly believing in its curative property. Small cuts and burns are actually cured by its application.

As the insect is poisonous and found in many parts, many tales have come to be told in which giant *mukade* torture humans. Thus it is not only feared by the people, but some have come to regard it as a symbol of the evil spirit.

However, the villagers of Osato in Saitama Prefecture worship it as the sacred messenger of their community deity of Sakagami Shrine. So the inhabitants respect it and will never kill it. Their reverence of the insect, furthermore, is manifested by their custom of presenting to the shrine *mukade-ema*, or wooden boards on which a picture of the *mukade* is painted.

MUSHI-OKURI

JUNE IS THE TIME when farmers hold rites for chasing away insects from their farms and villages. Many districts have fixed days to perform this ancient rite to protect their crops. Often June 8 is made the day for *mushi-kuyo* or insect rite.

Villages have their own methods of *mushi-okuri* or driving away insects. In some places they hold services at their Buddhist temples and pray insects will be driven away as is done in the Chiba district. In many regions, bundles of pine branches or other wood are set on fire and carried throughout the village. Feathers and heads of fish are burned at other places to chase out insects.

Long branches of bamboo are carried over the farms to the end of the village and there set on fire. Or crude dolls, made of straw are stuffed with food and carried in a procession throughout the village, to pray to the spirit of insects to leave the district.

There is also a widely believed tradition about Saito Sanemori, a great general of the Heike clan of the 12th century. It is said that in a battle Sanemori caught his foot on a rice root and fell. As he fell he was killed by the enemy. He blamed his downfall and defeat on the rice and determined to take revenge on the rice by turning into insects.

Following this tradition various rites are observed in many parts of the country to drive away Sanemori. The villagers gather at night, carrying burning bundles of straw fixed on long bamboo sticks, and walk all over the village shouting loudly, "Make way for the procession of Sanemori-sama." The processions often are made more effective by the beating of drums and blowing of *horagai* (conch trumpets).

These methods were very effective, as the smoke, smell and noise drove away insects.

NIPPON OKAMI

IN THE OLD DAYS *okami* or wolves were found all over Japan. They figured in many folk tales, but they are now entirely extinct in the country.

There were two types of wolves in the country at first, one coming from the northern Siberia area before the Japan Sea separated the Japanese islands from the continent, and which was large and thickly furred, and the southern kind that came from the Indonesian region and was smaller. But these two types became mixed.

Until the beginning of the 18th century, wolves inhabited mountain regions and never approached villages or farms. As they fed on deer, hares, foxes, badgers, snakes, birds, frogs and insects, they were regarded by farmers as their friends who destroyed the enemies of farm crops. Thus farmers never killed wolves, and furthermore, even hunters made it an unwritten law not to kill them.

Many mountain shrines made wolves the messengers of their deities and thus the rural people even came to worship *okami*.

But in 1732 hydrophobia developed among mountain wolves and spread even to domestic animals in villages. Thus an official order was issued to kill them. Again in 1742 and 1768 the same epidemic caused the death of many wolves, and to protect domestic animals strong measures were adopted to hunt and kill *okami* whenever possible.

Thus the number of wolves in the country rapidly decreased, but they became famous with the visit to Japan in 1823 of Dr. Philipp Franz von Siebold, a German physician who found the Japanese *okami* to be a unique type with small ears and short legs, and gave them the name of *Nippon okami*.

In 1878, a Japanese *okami* was taken to the London Zoological Garden as a rare specimen. But already by that time wolves had become scarce. A wolf purchased by an American named Andersen from a hunter of Ogawamura, Yoshino, Nara Prefecture, in January 1905 is said to have been the last seen in this country.

The northern-type wolf is believed to have totally disappeared almost 20 years before the southern type was exterminated.

OKOZE

OKOZE (Minous adamsi) is a small insignificant fish, but in Japanese legends it occupies a very important place, because it is especially favored by *yama-no-kami* (god of mountains). There are even instances when *okoze* was really worshiped as a holy thing. As it is the favorite of *yama-no-kami*, it is particularly worshiped or valued by hunters, woodsmen and fishermen.

In a village of Hyuga, it is still believed that *okoze* is divine. The hunters wrap up an *okoze* in white paper, and say to it: *"Okoze-dono*, if you will allow me to catch a boar shortly, I will unwrap you and let you see the sunlight."

They believe that *okoze* will then bring them luck, and enable them to catch boars. But strange to say, even when the hunter obtains the desired boar, the *okoze* is not shown the sunlight, being still wrapped in the paper. It is really a trick on the *okoze*, but hunters keep on doing it again and again, without doing their part of letting the *okoze* see the sunlight.

A similar belief is held by hunters of Kii, but they are even worse, and from the beginning they intend to trick *okoze*. Believing that *yama-no-kami* is fond of *okoze*, they carry an *okoze* in their bosom, wrapped in paper. They pray to *yama-no-kami* to give them boars, and if their wish is granted, they promise to show the *okoze*. But when boars are taken, only a bit of the head or tail of the fish is shown. They believe that *yama-no-kami*, seeing this small part of *okoze*, wishes to see its full form, and will give them further luck.

Once in the old days, lumber was cut on a certain mountain, but because of a lack of water in the river, it could not be floated down to town. The villagers offered a live *okoze* to *yama-no-kami* and prayed for a fuller river. The next morning the river was full, and lumber was carried down in rafts.

Fishermen also believe in the virtue of *okoze* and whenever they are in a storm or danger they pray to *yama-no-kami* for delivery, promising to offer *okoze* when they are saved. In many fishing villages of the country, dried *okoze* are seen nailed to the doors of the fishermen's houses. These are placed there not only for fishing luck, but also for the purpose of driving away evil spirits from the house.

In some districts it is believed that ordinarily *okoze* has no such virtues, but a special kind of *okoze*, which is larger and more beautiful than the ordinary kind, is the type to be offered to *yama-no-kami* for luck. Such fine *okoze* command very high prices, and many people buy them at any cost.

yama-no-kami is generally a wolf, and for a wolf to love *okoze* is indeed strange. *Okoze* is a delicious fish, and possibly wolves may like *okoze* more than other fish. But this fact is not yet proved.

But because it is loved so much by *yama-no-kami*, *okoze* has come to be so valued and appreciated by many people. For a small fish, it is indeed amazing how much it influences woodsmen, hunters and fishermen, as well as many other people who nail dried *okoze* to their doors.

PHEASANTS

KIJI or *kigisu* (Phasianus vericolor) is the most beautiful of the pheasant family, and is found only in Japan. Early Dutch visitors wrote about it, and Commodore Perry's report mentions it. It is much admired for its beauty and meat which the people have eaten since very early days. The bird is also woven into many folk tales. It was formerly abundantly found in mountain regions, and before the war it was seen even in the suburbs of Tokyo.

The bird is of greenish black color with a metallic luster, with red around its eyes and ears. The bill is pointed and dark blue. The coxcomb is red, and the tail is long and green. The hen, of course, is not so beautiful as the cock. It flies very fast, but not far.

Since ancient days, *kiji* has been associated with the people's life. Its name is mentioned in the oldest folklore, and its meat has been a table delicacy since the earliest days. At first the meat was broiled and eaten, but later, a soup made of *kiji* meat became very popular. Before the popularity of beef and pork, *kiji* meat was one of the most cherished meats in the people's diet.

The bird is reputed to possess very keen senses. It knows the coming of an earthquake beforehand, according to popular belief. When the *kiji* gives a shrill scream at night or suddenly makes an unexpected flight, it is an indication that an earthquake will come. Though science may laugh at it, this is still very strongly believed.

The *kiji* is associated in the minds of the Japanese with parental devotion to children. *Yakeno-no kigisu* (pheasants in a forest fire) is synonymous for parents. sacrificing themselves to save their children.

Former Prince Yoshimaro Yamashina, world-known ornithologist, kept pheasants among the numerous birds at his Tokyo residence. When Tokyo was bombed during the war, next morning he found the pheasant cock and hen charred black in the garden, protecting their chicks which were also dead.

It is said that when pheasants have eggs and are threatened by fire, the hen lies on its back and holds the eggs within its wings, and the cock pulls the hen by its tail to a place of safety.

POND SNAIL

ALTHOUGH TODAY *tanishi* (the pond-snail) has lost its superstitious hold upon the minds of the people and has become a common variety of snail, it had formerly a very strong influence upon the acts and beliefs of many people. In the rural districts children love to gather *tanishi* which are eaten in almost all farming districts. Paddy-fields and muddy little streamlets are where the little snails are found and caught. But in former days the people were afraid to catch any of them, because they were believed to possess a mighty power controlling the destiny of men and also regarded as the masters of rivers and ponds.

In some parts of the country *tanishi* is called *tanushi* (master of the pond), which may explain the common belief that *tanishi* is the master and lord of ponds and rivers. It has the power to punish any man or beast that may displease it by intruding upon the sacred domain of *tanishi*, the lord of rivers and ponds, as a sacred monster.

In the district of Aizu, there once stood the Wakamiya Hachiman Shrine,

and before the shrine were two large ponds which were commonly called by the people of the neighborhood 'ponds of *tanishi*.' If anyone caught the *tanishi* of the ponds, that night he would hear a voice in his sleep demanding to have the *tanishi* returned to the ponds. If they were not returned, the voice would come nightly until they were put back in the ponds. When a man was sick, he would take a *tanishi* out of the pond, and promise that if his illness passed, he would return to the pond two *tanishi*, but if he remained ill, the *tanishi* would never be returned. The Hachiman Shrine loved the *tanishi* in the ponds, and the people regarded them as the servants of the Hachiman Shrine.

In China, too, *tanishi* were regarded as sacred and as the spirit of rivers. One of the famous stories about *tanishi* in China goes thus: A man lived by a clear, beautiful rivulet, and in order to keep the water clean, he built bamboo fences so that trespassers would not spoil the stream. He loved the beautiful rushing rivulet. One day by the side of the river, he caught one white *tanishi*, and placed it in an earthenware jar. After that, every time he returned home after a short absence, he found that his kitchen was full of various foodstuffs, ready to eat. He was bewildered. One day he secretly watched, and found that out of the shell of the white *tanishi* in the jar, came a woman. He suddenly caught her and did not allow her to return to the shell. Thus threatened, she finally confessed that the spirit of the river knew of his love for the river and its clear water and appreciated his precautions in keeping clean, and knowing that he was living alone, the river-spirit sent her to take care of his house.

There are said to be many similar tales in China concerning *tanishi*.

One old Japanese book says that

there was once a Fudo temple in the district of Shinano, held in high esteem by the people. Those who suffered from eye diseases prayed at this Fudo temple, and they would be cured if they did not eat *tanishi*. Even if the *Fudo* was worshiped from a great distance, their prayers would be answered and eye diseases cured if worshipers did not catch *tanishi* or eat them. But one day a fire threatened the temple, and the priest carried away the Fudo statue, and to save it from the fire, threw it into a rice-field nearby. After the fire was put out, they came to take the statue out from the paddy-field, and it was seen that innumerable *tanishi* had covered the statue in order to save it from attack and destruction by fire.

Old medical books of the country often state that *tanishi* were good for eye diseases.

During the warring period of the country, it is recorded, the fortune of battles were often augured by watching the battles of *tanishi*. A servant of Lord Onodera of Yamakita was hurrying to the castle one winter morning. He saw that out of the great pond of the castle, there ran an ugly muddy mark on the snow as if a huge stone had been dragged. The mark climbed the high bank and over three stout fences, and finally ascended the veranda into the house. Entering, he found a huge ugly object, looking like a rock, measuring five feet in diameter. On close inspection it turned out to be a huge *tanishi*. It took seven men to drag it back to the pond. Shortly afterward, the lord lost his territory, castle and position.

PURPLE BUTTERFLY

ALL NATIONS have their national flowers, and some also have national birds. *Sakura* or flowering cherry is the national flower of Japan, though some

regard *kiku* or chrysanthemum as the symbolic blossom of the country. *Kiji* or Japanese pheasant is Japan's national bird, because of its beautiful feathers.

The Japan Society of Entomology has recently selected the *oomurasaki* (large purple) as the national butterfly of Japan. It is almost four inches from the tip of one wing to the other. Its bright purple wings have white and yellow marks, and red spots on the edge of the wings.

Many butterflies are beautiful, but no other kind approaches the *oomurasaki* in beauty. It is really the queen of Japanese butterflies and deserves the honor of being selected as the national butterfly.

It may also be mentioned that the late Dr. Tomitaro Makino, world-renowned botanist, pointed out the *fuki* (bog rhubarb) of Akita as the most outstanding of Japanese plants. The *fuki* of Akita stands seven feet high, and its leaf is about four feet across. Its stem is almost five inches around. This plant has a characteristic of growing bigger in colder rather than warmer regions.

Since early days in rural Akita districts, when the people are caught in the rain, they break off *fuki* leaves and use them as umbrellas. Such large *fuki* still grow in the district and cotton cloth with the impression of the large *fuki* leaf are sold as souvenirs of the region.

The large stem of the Akita *fuki* is eaten, but it does not taste as good as the smaller common variety which is widely used as a vegetable.

QUAKE MAKER

THE BELIEF that the great *namazu*, a kind of sheatfish that lives under the earth, causes earthquakes by shaking its tail, is very old. Nobody, however, can clearly explain how this traditional belief originated.

Namazu is an ugly-looking freshwater fish, generally growing to about a foot long, somewhat flat in shape, dark brown in color, scaleless and having a pair of long feelers on each side of its big mouth. The fish is edible and those caught in running waters taste quite good.

Its association with earthquakes is believed to have come from the fact that the fish is often found at the mud bottom of ponds. This fact might have given the people the idea that the fish lives underground.

When the fish shakes its feelers, a slight tremble of the earth occurs. But it has been traditionally believed that when it moves its strong tail, a great earthquake takes place, destroying houses and causing death to animals and humans.

East of the Kashima Shrine in Ibaraki Prefecture, there is a stone pillar driven into the earth. It is called *Kaname-ishi* or pivot stone. According to popular tradition, the stone is there to hold down the head of the great *namazu* so that it will not shake its body. The head of the fish lies just under that spot, it was believed. Furthermore, in the old days, the *Kaname-ishi* itself was tied securely to the ground with strong wisteria vines, so that the pivot stone holding down the fish would never be shaken out of place however hard the *namazu* might struggle for freedom.

Thus the old people believed the stone and vine ropes would keep the country safe from any major earthquake destruction.

RATS

RATS WERE formerly welcomed by the Japanese people, as they are symbols of good luck. In many districts, the people rejoiced when rats gnawed the New Year *kagami-mochi* or rice cakes, as it was a sign foretelling good harvests and prosperity during the year.

Particularly, when a rat ate some of the offerings presented to the *kamidana* or family shrine, the people felt happy as they thought the *kami* had accepted their offerings and eaten them.

Rats were also believed to be the messengers of *Daikoku*, the deity of good fortune and wealth. So the people never mistreated the *kami's* messengers.

Many stories are told of rats returning the kindness of people. Once a poor old man had only one small rice-ball for his meal, but he shared it with a rat. The rat was thankful and later invited the old man to *Jodo* or Paradise, and gave him a huge amount of gold and silver in return.

Another tale says that once an old farmer took some dumplings with him to his fields. While he was eating them, he dropped one into a hole in the ground. The old man wished to regain his lost dumpling, and entered the hole, chasing after the rolling dumpling. In the hole, he found many rats eating and dancing and having a gay party. He was welcomed and entertained by the rats. His neighbor heard of the old farmer's luck, and purposely entered the hole, but he was at once set upon by numerous rats and chased out.

There still remains a belief that rats will stay in a house while that family is prosperous and there is food to eat, but that when rats leave the house, it is a sign that the family luck is changing or the house will soon be destroyed by fire.

RIVER MASTER

IT IS STRANGE for the people of Japan, who are so fond of eating *unagi* (eel), to consider it sacred. Eels are slippery, and they stand for all things slippery, and for such a slippery thing to be regarded as sacred and holy is indeed strange. But the people of Japan, being so fond of eels, probably have come to regard it as a holy thing.

The Mishima Shrine of Izu has for its messenger an eel. It is not quite known why or on what basis the eel was selected among all other things to be the representative and messenger of so virtuous and benevolent a *kami*. It is not the only case in Japan, and it is said that in some places there are shrines dedicated to eels which are said to possess all the virtues of protecting and giving fortune to those who believe in them.

At a certain place in Kii, it is reported that there is enshrined an eel which has only one eye. There it is believed that when prayers are offered to this shrine, rain is certain to come, and in dry seasons pilgrims go to the shrine.

In many parts of the country it is also believed that great eels inhabit large lakes and ponds, commanding and ruling over all fish and plants of the lakes.

When Gamo Hideyuki attempted to throw poison into the Tadami River, in the 16th year of Keicho (1611) a huge eel appeared, taking the form of a monk, to stop his attempt. This eel was the *nushi* (master) of the river, and as it learned of the plan, it tried to save the lives of all fish in the river. Therefore, taking the form of a monk, it appeared before Gamo Hideyuki.

There is another story, similar to the above, in which the *iwana* (bulltrout) figures. In Shinano district many believe that the *iwana* turns into a monk. The purpose of *iwana* taking the form of a monk is to prevent people from fishing. Becoming a monk in form, it propagates the teaching of Buddha not to take the life of any living thing. In Shinano this legend is believed, and it is said that once an *iwana* became a monk and preached the evil of taking lives, and at a certain house it was treated to a meal. When it returned to the river, unfortunately, it was soon caught by a fisherman. When the *iwana* was cut open, there appeared dumplings which the *iwana* monk had eaten at the house.

There may be other fish that have tried to stop people from fishing, but in Japan eels and *iwana* are the only two which are credited with such attempts to save the lives of their fellow fish.

If fish were in the habit of erecting shrines, as the Japanese people are, it is certain that eels and *iwana* would be given the greatest shrines. While both fish are very much valued by the people, their efforts to stop fishing have had no effect upon the people, who still keep on catching them. The *iwana* is valued as one of the cleanest and purest of fish, and commands a high price. The love of the Japanese people for eels is well-known.

SACRED CRANES

THE *TSURU* or crane is the noblest bird, the Japanese traditionally believe. All cranes are stately in appearance, but *tancho* (Megalornis japonensia), one of the six varieties that annually migrate to Japan, is the most beautiful, with a white body, red crest and black-edged wings, standing four to five feet.

The *tsuru* is a symbol of long life, fidelity and monogamy. Being regarded as sacred, it is made into ornaments and pictures. Its meat was formerly much valued, but it does not taste good.

The bird comes to Kagoshima, Yamaguchi and a few other places from Siberia early every summer to lay eggs and raise its young. The people respect and never molest them, often giving them help. It is protected by law.

The people of the districts where the *tsuru* annually comes love it particularly. Parents tell their children to behave 'like the *tsuru*' because the bird is always well-mannered, never fighting over food and being ever faithful to its mate. The young always walk or fly behind the parents.

It often happens that a *tsuru* becomes sick or crippled and thus becomes unable to leave the country with the others. In such cases, its mate will remain with the disabled one. If neighboring people find such birds, they always give them food and protection, or else they would perish.

As it is sacred, palaces and gardens of feudal lords used to formerly have cranes for adornment and also to bring good fortune. When they could not afford to keep live cranes, they placed cranes made of iron in their gardens.

SALAMANDERS

JAPANESE salamanders have been shipped to various foreign zoological gardens in recent years. This lizard-like amphibious animal is found in Europe and America, but the Japanese species, Megalobatrachus japonicus, is world-famous as it is the most colossal of all, growing to four or five feet in length.

It is called *sansho-uo*, because its back is like the warted bark of the *sansho* (Xanthoxylum piperitum) tree. The salamander has black spots and warts on its back, while its underside is either yellow or reddish. It has four legs, the two in front having four toes each and the back ones five.

It lives in mountain streams, and there are many kinds in Japan of various sizes and colors. The Hakone mountains are famous for it, but the Hakone variety is rather small and has a reddish belly. Some people eat its meat, which is said to be quite tasty. In the old days many rural people used salamander meat as a medicine for weak infants. The salamander is known to make a sound like a baby crying.

Many strange tales are told about this queer-looking animal. It is said that when one is cut length-wise into two, each will soon grow into a whole. Then, it has the ability to squeeze itself out of the tiniest hole.

SALMON TAISUKE

TO THE Imaizumi River, Miyagi Prefecture, salmon come in late autumn and go upstream to lay eggs. The people catch them with nets but formerly there was a custom of cutting holes in the net to allow some salmon to escape.

This strange custom was based on a legend about a cattleman of Takekoma Village. He was originally of a *samurai* family but, after settling in Takekoma, he engaged in raising cattle. However, annually huge eagles came and carried off calves, and he suffered the loss of many.

As a desperate means of saving his animals, he hid himself within the hide of an ox and waited for the birds, intending to attack them when they grasped his hide.

A huge eagle came down and caught him in its claws and, lifting the whole weight, started to fly away. After a long day's flight the bird dropped the hide on a tree on an island in the middle of a big ocean. After the eagle disappeared, the cattleman managed to climb down the tree to the ground, but there was no means of leaving the island.

A mysterious old man suddenly appeared and saying that he was *Taisuke*, an incarnation of the salmon, proposed to carry the stranded man on his back safely to the Imaizumi River, to which his associates were in the habit of going on October 20 every year, as the people of the district were their friends.

Thus the stranded cattleman was safely brought home by Taisuke. In appreciation of *Taisuke*'s kindness, the cattleman went to the river every year on October 20, and cut holes in the salmon net so that some fish might escape.

The story of *Taisuke*, the incarnated salmon, became known and the salmon which saved the cattleman came to be called the *Taisuke* Salmon.

SHARKS

THE *SAME* (shark) is known as a man-eating fish, and is dreaded by swimmers and fishermen. In Japan, likewise, it is a menace to many fishermen as well as swimmers, but again in this country it has been considered as something more than a mere fish. Divine power had been ascribed to *same* from very early times, and it has also been regarded as a messenger of *kami*.

Probably the first mention of *same* in this sense in Japan is found in the record of the mythological age. It is mentioned that Hikohohodemi-no-kami was sent on the back of a *same*, and again that when Toyotama-hime became angry at her husband because he looked into her secret hut where she was giving birth to a baby, she turned into a *same*, some 40 feet long, in order to show her anger, and swam across the sea.

Much later, it is said that one day a woman's leg was bitten off by a *same* and carried away by the sea monster. Her father, distressed at the misfortune of his daughter, prayed to *kami* for revenge. Shortly afterwards, over a hundred sharks came chasing one particular shark. The father caught and killed the one surrounded by the others, and in its belly was found the lost leg of his daughter.

All through the ages the *same* has been held as a divine creature in Japan, and in some parts is still believed to be so, although it is a fact that the number of *same* frequenting the coasts of Japan has considerably diminished of late.

Isobe-Daimyojin of Ise is even now reverently worshiped by fishermen, and the messenger of Daimyojin is a shark. The sacred shark is said to be about 30 feet long. Fishermen worship and believe in the power of the shark to save them from drowning. If any of the fishermen who believes in Daimyojin is about to drown, it is said that the sacred shark will come from somewhere and bear the suffering man on its back to the shore. Believers in the shark always carry a strip of the bark of the sacred tree in the garden of Daimyojin. When ships are attacked by sharks, they will throw the sacred bark into the sea, and the sharks scatter instantly. All sharks know and fear the sacred *same* which will come to the rescue of believers. Every year on the day of the festival of the shrine, there appear several sharks on the shore nearby. If there is anyone injured or killed by shark during the year, these sharks will chase the guilty shark to the shore and chastise it for hours. When fishermen meet these sacred sharks on the sea, they make offerings to them and rejoice at the good luck they had in meeting the sharks. The sacred shark will swim a fixed course every day, and innumerable bonito fish follow the shark. Fishermen catch the bonito and secure much profit. It is said that the fish will dive under the boats of the most earnest believers in the powers of the shark and bring bonito to them. But they never approach boats manned by unbelievers. Fishermen also offer prayers to the shark to give them good catches. In making this prayer the fishermen always restrict the number of days on which they will fish. To believers the prayer comes true, and for a number of days, they will have easy and plentiful catches. But if they continue to fish after the time-limit has expired, the boats will sink. When the bottom of such a destroyed ship is examined, it is found that the boards are planed down to the thickness of paper. The pressure of the water had broken through the thin bottom. It is believed that sharks planed off the bottom boards of the unfaithful by brushing their backs against the bottom.

Believing that the *same* is the messenger of *kami*, many have come to worship the *same* itself for their protection and also blessings.

While believing in such powers of the *same*, it is very strange that the Japanese people eat *same* freely. Of course they do not dare eat the meat of the sacred *same*, but they eat any other. *Same* are daily brought to fish markets, and the demand for the meat is quite large. *Same*, of course, is not a very high-priced fish, but its meat is palatable.

SHIKA

SHIKA OR DEER were formerly found abundantly throughout the country. They played an important role in the life of the people. In ancient days fortunes were told by the cracks in the roasted shoulder bones of deer, and deer heads were offered to various shrines. Deer bones found in ancient shell mounds give evidence that much deer meat was eaten in the old days.

The Ainu ate not only venison but also clothed themselves in deer skin.

The deer has a habit of remaining in the mountains during the day and coming down to the plains and farms at night. Its greatest enemy is the boar which the people in the old days used in hunting deer. They made them chase the deer from the mountain, and as the deer were forced to enter valley streams, the hunters caught them. Thus there developed the term *mizu-shika* or water deer.

Unborn baby deer were formerly believed to have a certain medicinal value and were highly prized.

In many parts of the country, children used to enjoy a game called *shika-asobi* (deer play) in which one stoops and the other rides on his back. The latter spreads out his fingers and asks the boy on whom he is riding how many antlers the deer has. If the correct answer is given, they change positions.

In Iwate and Miyagi districts in the northwest, a *shika-odori* or deer dance is still held. The people wear deer heads over their own, carrying bamboo on their backs and beating drums that are fastened to their waists. Of course the deer head is not real, but is a wooden frame covered with hair and often with real antlers.

The term *shika* appears in ancient accounts but sometimes it does not mean deer. *Shika* meant not only deer, but also monkeys and other wild animals.

Today, deer are found only in certain districts. The people know only the sacred deer kept at Nara, Itsukushima and a few other places.

SHIKOKU FOXES

SHIKOKU, the smallest of the four main islands of Japan, has no fox legends, simply because there are no foxes, although many fox stories are told in other parts of the country. There is a tale as to how Shikoku became foxless.

One night the wife of Lord Kono of Shikoku went to the water-closet but she came out as two women, indistinguishable in feature and dress, equally beautiful and elegant. Not only did they look alike but they also talked and laughed exactly the same.

Seeing his two beautiful wives, Lord Kono became perplexed and angry. He ordered all his servants and retainers to find out which was his true wife, saying it was a devilish trick and that the false one must be destroyed. The two women were questioned, but they both said they were the lord's true wife.

So the two women were placed in separate rooms and closely watched. Several days later, one woman was found to act strangely when she was having her meal, and she was severely questioned and threatened. Then she loudly shouted to Lord Kono, "I am your master and you will be severely punished for your uncivil act." All were certain then that she was the false one, as the real wife would never speak in such a harsh tone, and more pressure was brought upon the false wife.

Finally she could not stand the sharp and pressing questions and turned into a fox. Lord Kono angrily ordered that the fox be instantly killed for causing such trouble and suffering to the whole family.

At that very moment, several thousand people, men and women, came to the gate and demanded to see the lord. When Lord Kono came out, they said that they were the foxes of Shikoku and the fox caught and ordered to be killed was their leader. Their leader had taken the shape of the lord's wife just for fun, they explained, and did not mean any real harm. Furthermore, they

threatened that if their leader was killed they would bring severe curses on the family. Listening to their pleading and threats, Lord Kono proposed that he would not kill the fox but demanded that all the foxes leave Shikoku forever.

Thus the matter was settled, and the foxes, numbering more than 5,000, left the island on many boats and went across the Inland Sea. Since then there have been no foxes in Shikoku.

SHOJOJI

THE *TANUKI* or badger that appears in many Japanese tales is generally said to be fond of producing drumlike music by beating its fat belly with its front paws. This belief is quite old as *tanuki* music is mentioned in ancient tales.

A hunter went to a mountain to catch a badger, an old story goes. A female *tanuki* in the form of a Buddhist nun appeared before him and preached to him against killing any living thing. Much affected by the preaching the hunter decided to go away, but then he realized that it must have been a trick played by a badger. So he raised his bow to shoot.

The nun, now turning into a badger, started to run away, beating its belly and making drum music.

For more than 100 years the *tanuki* of Shojoji has been famous. Particularly, a song composed by Ujo Noguchi has become one of the most popular among Japanese children. Roughly translated, it goes, 'All come to Shojoji's garden on a moonlit evening, and play the belly drum. Don't be outdone by the priest. Come out all.'

The story of the *tanuki* of Shojoji at Kisarazu is said to date back to the Bunsei era, 1818-1830. At that time the priest at the Shojoji Temple was one named Hoto who was very fond of music. He used to gather children and teach them songs.

One autumn evening when the full moon shone beautifully, he gathered many children in the temple garden and, forming a circle, they all danced and sang. In those days, the neighborhood of the temple was still wild and many *tanuki* and other animals lived there.

Hearing the singing of the children, many *tanuki* came out to watch. Soon they all began to beat on their bellies and joined in the merrymaking. Some beat so hard that they punctured their bellies and died. There still stands a tomb for the *tanuki* who died there.

SINGING FROGS

THE SINGING of the *kajika* is welcomed by the Japanese in summer. But *kajika*, the singer, is only a small frog. *Kajika* is sold by dealers of singing insects, and even sometimes by department stores. Many lovers of the singing frog raise them at home.

It is a tiny variety of frog and inhabits cold mountain streams. The male who sings is less than half an inch long and very slender, while the female is much larger. Its back is dark gray, but its underside is lighter or almost pinkish white. Its legs have black lines. It can be easily identified by small round suckers at the tip of its toes.

It is the male *kajika* that sings so beautifully. Those who are used to the unpleasant noise generally raised by common frogs can never realize that such clear and ringing music could come from one of them.

Kajika, said to be found in no other country, have been loved by Japanese for their singing since very early days. It has become a popular subject for short poems.

There are many kinds of frogs in the country. There are grotesque toads, to which are attributed evil spirits. *Ao-gaeru* or green frogs are also called *ama-gaeru* or rain frogs, and it is said that their singing will bring rain. In rural districts, *aka-gaeru* or red frogs are collected by children. Their legs are edible and said to be good for curing oversensitiveness of little children. Recently big edible frogs have been raised in many ponds. Their croaking is a nightmare to neighbors.

Kajika is the only kind that is loved by the people. It is petted because it is so small, and also sings beautifully.

SINGING INSECTS

THE *MUSHI-URI*, insect peddler, carrying tiny bamboo cages hanging from both ends of his shoulder pole, does not need to shout out his wares, for the chorus of the hundreds of singing insects he carries can be heard a block away.

The people think the singing of insects is the music of nature, and make special trips to the country to listen to them, or buy them in cages from insect men. Although the people's love of insect singing is expressed in the earliest literature, it is only about 250 years ago that the insect man selling caged insects made his first appearance.

Chuzo, who had a greengrocery shop in Edo, one day caught several *suzumushi* (Homoegryllus japonicus) and kept them at home. The singing of the insects at once attracted neighbors who expressed a wish to keep such insects, too. This gave Chuzo an idea. Closing up his shop, he went to collect and sell them. He also studied the proper way of feeding and breeding them. Soon, he had many imitators.

The music given by various kinds of insects just as the hot summer season is at its height has appealed always to the nature-loving sentiment of the Japanese people. In poems, pictures and daily habits, much has been made of those singing insects. The insect music is quite delightful, calms down the tired nerve, and at the same time tells the people that the delightful autumn is coming. Traditionally crickets sing to the people, *Kata-sase suso-sase samusa ga kuruzo* or "Sew your sleeves, sew your skirts, the cold weather is coming." Thus hearing them sing, Japanese housewives realize that they must get busy and start their sewing to prepare for the coming cold season.

The people's love of insect music developed many delightful habits. They made special trips to mountains and other places, famous for insect music, to enjoy listening to the autumn music of nature. Those singing insects are not found everywhere, but prosper only in regions where the condition is favorable for their life. Many hold "insect-listening parties" at their homes, inviting friends and giving them an opportunity to listen to insect music and enjoy the cool quietness of an autumn evening.

In cities, there comes insect peddlers who carry little bamboo cages filled with singing insects. On many streets there also appear insect selling stalls. The appearance of those stalls and peddlers adds a refreshing feature to the people's life in the hot season.

The tiny cages in which the insects are sold or kept are very beautiful and delicately made. They are artistically made of finely-sliced and polished bamboo, and are quite lovely articles in themselves.

Among the popular singing insects there are various kinds of cricket and grasshopper species, but the most common are *suzumushi, matsumushi, koorogi, kutsuwamushi, kantan, kanetataki,* and *kirigirisu.* Of those, the cricket species are better singers than grasshoppers, and particularly *matsu-*

mushi and *suzumushi* are regarded the most aristocratic singers.

Those singing insects are specially raised, and there are many great lovers of insect music who yearly raise their own insects for enjoying their singing in autumn. Wild insects sing just as good as raised insects, but do not live long when they are put in cages. It is on that account that for commercial purpose and private enjoyment, singing insects are raised. It is a very delicate task that requires very minute attention all the year around.

A common large flower-pot made of earthenware is filled with fine rich soil, mixed with some sand. Over this pot is built a fine mesh wire cage. Within this cage are kept the parent singing insects. In the late autumn they lay eggs in the soil of the pot. The parent insects subsequently die. In the spring, the eggs hatch and then young insects are to be very tenderly cared for, offering them proper food. When they grow, they are taken to separate cages. Out of those insects are selected those to become the parents of the next year's singers.

SPIDER TALES

SPIDERS FIGURE in many tales of the country, impersonating humans or doing various mischief.

Once there was a hooper who used to say that he would take a wife if he did not have to feed her. A woman came to him who said she never ate meals, and asked to be made his wife. So he gladly welcomed her to his house. She never ate at meals, but strangely his stock of rice and other foodstuffs began to disappear very rapidly.

One night he heard some noise in the kitchen and he went to investigate it secretly. There he saw his wife undoing her hair. When her hair was parted it revealed a big mouth, into which she fed bowls of rice and *miso* soup. Then he found that his wife was a spider.

A story told in Bizen or Okayama district says that while the husband was away, his wife entertained many other women at dinner. When he returned and looked inside, he found that his wife and all the women were spiders. So he ordered his wife to leave.

Thereupon the wife said that before she left she would prepare a bath for him. The bath was soon ready, and he got inside the tub. But she came and lifted the bathtub with her husband and hot water in it on her head. She walked easily with her burden to the mountain, but when she took time to rest at a temple, he ran away.

In another story while a man in Shikoku was taking a bath, a mountain woman came and carried the tub and man on her head to the mountain. When she passed under an overhanging branch of a tree, he grabbed the branch and pulled himself out of the tub. But while he was hanging on the tree branch, another woman came and said to the first one, "Unless you are more careful, you will never have a human for your husband. Humans are clever. Become a spider and get him, but watch out, and don't get hit on your left armpit."

That night, a huge spider entered his house. So he hit it on its left armpit and killed it.

TAI

TAI (SEA BREAM) is the best and noblest fish, the Japanese people believe, and on all festive occasions there must be *tai*. It has been highly valued since the earliest time, and it is also mentioned in many mythological tales.

There are three kinds of *tai—madai*,

chidai and *kidai*— but it is the kind called *madai* or true *tai* that is valued. Because it is so much respected, there are many traditional tales told about it.

In Chiba Prefecture, there is a bay called Tai-no-ura, which is famous for *tai*. Tradition has it that on February 16, 1222 when Priest Nichiren, founder of the Nichiren sect of Buddhism, was born at Kominato on the bay, lotus blossoms appeared on the sea, and numerous *tai* splashed about in the sea. Thus the fishermen of the bay regarded the *tai* as sacred and never caught them. Furthermore they gave food to the fish, and thus the bay became full of fine *tai*. Subsequently the bay came to be called *Tai-no-ura* or *Tai* Bay.

The sea off Saizaki, Hiroshima Prefecture, in the Inland Sea, is famous for floating *tai*. At the time of the spring tide, thousands of *tai* appear floating on the sea surface. It is now scientifically explained that by the rapid current the *tai* are suddenly carried from the depths to the shallow sea, and their air bladders are quickly inflated by the sudden change in sea pressure, thus they lay flat on the surface, gasping.

But it is traditionally said that when Empress Jingu was on her way to Korea on a ship in the year 200 and passed this spot, a seaman on board let a *sake* jug fall into the sea. The *tai* in the sea drank the *sake* and became drunk and floated helplessly on the surface.

Every spring, when the great tide comes, many *tai* are seen floating on the surface off Saizaki, and boats are out to catch the "drunken" fish.

TANUKI

BECAUSE it is a lovable animal, images of *tanuki* made in pottery, stone or metal are displayed in many shops, restaurants and private houses. Looking very comical as they stand on their hind legs, they are sometimes 10 feet high.

The *tanuki* is an animal peculiar to the Far east, inhabiting the region extending from eastern Siberia through Korea and Japan to north China. It is generally called in English racoon dog or badger, but it is different from either of them. Scientifically it is called Nycterentes virervinus Temminick. In general form, it resembles a fox though much smaller. Dark grey with a section of its belly white, it has a stubby tail covered with heavy fur. It has short legs and does not run well or far. It is active at night and sleeps in the daytime in a hole. Being clumsy in digging its own hole, it usually lives in a hole made by another animal.

From very old times, easily tamed, but very shy, the *tanuki* has been reared and petted by the people. Yet, traditionally it is believed to have powers of bewitching humans. There are numerous stories telling how *tanuki* took the forms of human beings and did mischief. But unlike the stories told about foxes, another animal famous for bewitching people, *tanuki* tricks bear no malice and there is always something comical about what it doe under disguise.

Typical is the famous story of *Bunbuku-chagama*, in which a *tanuki* turns himself into a tea-kettle and brings wealth to a Buddhist priest. Sometimes a *tanuki* image carries a *sake* bottle. This stands for the *tanuki* of *Bunbuku-chagama*, who went to buy *sake* for the priest.

In northeastern districts *tanuki* are still raised for their furs which are very valuable, and also for meat to make *tanuki-jiru* or *miso* soup with *tanuki* meat. Other farmers make them pets for children.

Tanuki has become a term to mean cunning or feigned action, because of its fondness to tease people by turning themselves into human beings or other objects. *Tanuki-ne* means feigned sleep, and *tanuki-jijii* a cunning old man.

Almost all districts have their local stories of *tanuki*, but particularly in the islands of Shikoku and Sado there are numerous tales. It is said that foxes do not live on such small islands, and only *tanuki* thrive. So those small islands are proud of the *tanuki* and their many comical stories.

THOUSAND WOLVES

THE STORY OF *senbiki-okami* or thousand wolves is told in many parts of the country, with different accounts of many wolves attacking solitary mountain travelers.

A hikyaku or professional carrier of messages in feudal days was once passing through the dense mountain region of Noneyama in Tosa province, so one story goes. There he saw a woman surrounded by a large pack of wolves. He helped the woman climb up a tall tree, but the wolves formed themselves into a ladder by one standing on the shoulder of another. She was again in danger of being caught by the wolves.

The *hikyaku* drew his sword and struck down several wolves to save her. The leader of the pack then shouted, "Now we must call the mother of the blacksmith of Sakihama." Soon there appeared a huge white-haired wolf which started to climb up the wolf-ladder.

Alarmed, the man struck the head of the wolf with his word, but it bounced off with a metallic sound. He saw then that the huge wolf was wearing an iron kettle on its head. With all his might, he gave a second blow on its head, and the wolf fell down deeply wounded. Seeing the white wolf wounded, all the wolves scattered.

He helped the woman down and went to Nonemura to finish his errand. On his way back, he went through the village of Sakihama and stopped before the blacksmith's shop. He heard the sound of someone groaning in pain. He asked what the trouble was, and was told that the old woman of the house had fallen on a rock and injured herself.

Hearing that, he rushed into the house and stabbed the old woman to death with his sword. He then told all the villagers what had happened on the previous day in the mountain. As they examined the body of the old woman, it was revealed that an aged wolf had killed the blacksmith's wife and taken her place.

Similar tales are also told in Yamanashi, Tottori, Niigata and other districts.

THUNDER BIRD

JAPANESE mountain climbers have always regarded it a very good omen to see a *raicho* (thunder bird) or Lagopus mutus on tree tops or high peaks. This bird is only rarely seen, so that all climbers hope to catch sight of it.

Though it is named after thunder, there is nothing about it to remind any one of rolling thunder. It is a small bird of tame appearance, a little larger than the common pigeon, and closely resembles a pheasant. It changes the color of its feathers in winter and summer, for self-protection. In summer months when it is sometimes seen by mountain climbers, its body is spotted with dark brown and black spots and only its wings and breast are pure white. But in winter it becomes entirely white.

It is only found in high mountains. Yarigatake, Ontake of Kiso, and Nori-

kuragatake are famous places for *raicho*. It is never seen in the lower plains of the country, but in the Kurile Islands it is found on flat plains.

Nobody has explained why it is called *raicho* or thunder bird. One story goes that the bird is so sacred that lightning will not hit trees and rocks that have been touched by the bird. Believing the tale, many mountain climbers camp under trees or rocks where *raicho* were seen perching, as they are certain of not being hit by lightning and thunder that are quite frequent in such high mountains.

Another commonplace explanation is that *raicho* is so named because it inhabits the high mountain regions where thunder originates.

TOADS

IN SUMMER evenings *gama*, or the toad, will come out from its hiding place and slowly make its way to gardens. It is ugly and there is something unpleasant in its shape and slow movement. Yet it seems so dignified, and does not pay any attention to things around it. It sits still and waits for the coming of mosquitoes, flies and other little insects. As an unfortunate fly nears it, it opens its huge mouth with a snap, and the fly is sucked into its throat.

In all ancient tales of magic and supernatural phenomenon in Japan there always appear the *gama*. It is somehow inseparable from the uncanny art of the magician. In old pictures men possessing supernatural powers are often shown standing upon the back of a huge *gama*. It was formerly believed to possess the power of hypnotizing men, insects, and animals, and its breath was thought to be poisonous. Many fantastic stories of former days tell of *gama* that blew fire and smoke from their mouths.

One of the special supernatural

powers that have been attributed to *gama* is that of disappearing entirely when no way of running away is visible. There is an old saying that one can keep *gama* in a bamboo basket, but he can never keep it in a wooden box.

Gama are extremely patient, and also have the power to contract their body into a small space. When one knows of this peculiarity of the *gama*, he may be able to understand why it has been regarded as possessing magic power. Put a *gama* in a wooden box, tightly closed, and make one small hole in it. Then next morning, the box will be empty, as in some mysterious way, the toad manages to squeeze its body into the hole and hop away. But when two small holes are made in the box, the next morning you will find the toad still there. Due to there being two openings by which it may escape the *gama* tries one, and finding it very small, goes to the other. And thus all night, it will try one hole and then the other in trying to escape, and before he succeeds morning comes, and it is still in the box.

The magical power of the *gama* is quite doubtful, and it is believed that such supernatural power has been attributed to it because of its strange ability of getting away through tiny openings and crevices.

The oil obtained from the body of *gama* is said to be a very good cure for cuts and wounds, and even today, there are many peddlers who sell *gama* oil.

TOKI

A ¥10 POSTAL STAMP with the design of a *toki*, a rare bird, has been issued in connection with the International Council for Bird Preservation Convention in Tokyo. *Toki*, often called the Japanese crested ibis, is now a bird found only in Japan, as its scientific name, Nipponia nippon, indicates.

It looks like a white heron but is a little larger. It has a long black hooked beak, the end of which is pink, and red feet. The bird is white but the underside of its wings and tail is pinkish. This pink color is called *tokiiro* or *toki* color.

It is a very cautious bird, living on small fish, frogs and such found in ricefields or ponds in mountain regions. It is very particular and has a peculiar habit of washing in clear water the fish it has caught before swallowing it.

This bird existed in great numbers in the old days up to the end of the Tokugawa era, but now only a few are seen on Sado Island in the Japan Sea, and in Ishikawa Prefecture, and its protection is urged by bird lovers.

Its beautiful feathers were the cause of its becoming so rare today. The feathers used to be much used for decorative purposes. The sacred sword at Ise Shrine is decorated with *toki* feathers. Aristocrats and feudal lords used a great deal of it for various decorative purposes.

The bird rapidly decreased in number early in the Meiji era. Today, according to authorities, there are said to be only nine *toki* in the whole country, five in Ishikawa Prefecture and four on Sado.

TURTLES

TURTLES stand for long life, and are always held in respect by the people of Japan. They are found almost everywhere along the coasts of Japan, but they are very seldom eaten. At some places hundreds of them come up on the shore in summer to lay eggs in the sand, but they are not molested, although the eggs are quite often gathered and sold. Huge turtles, measuring four or five feet, are not rare, and such are often caught in fishermen's nets. But when such turtles are netted, the fishermen rejoice, believing them to be signs of good luck. They are tenderly taken out of the nets, and placed on the sandy shore upside down so that they cannot run away. But they never think of killing such turtles. Instead, they bring large bottles of *sake* (Japanese rice-wine) and let the turtles drink their fill. It is commonly believed that turtles are fond of *sake*, and in fact they consume gallons of it, apparently with no ill effects. When the fishermen have given them *sake*, they free them and let them return to the depths of the sea. This custom is almost always observed by the fishermen of the country, and they all believe the finding of turtles in their nets to be a sign of good luck and also of a good fishing season.

In some parts of the country it is believed that when turtles are freed after being given *sake*, they will at first dive under the waves, but at a short distance from the shore, they will raise their heads above the water and bow to the people on the shore in thanks for the drink.

Further, in the district of Kii, there are many people who eat the meat of turtles, but strange to say, they do not kill them themselves, but entrust this task to certain families who have always engaged in killing turtles generation after generation. The people eat the meat of turtles killed by such professional turtle-killers, but they will never put their hands on them themselves.

In ancient times, it appears that the people worshiped *kame* (turtles) as *kami* or messengers of *kami*. There are many tales confirming this. Kashima Myojin is reported to have travelled over the sea on the back of a turtle named Hayagame. In an old book it is also written that when the annual festival is held at Yurajima, Awaji, turtles, big and small, gather near the shore. There

are also many tales in which the same turtles returned time and again to the same shore. The story of Urashima, Japanese Rip Van Winkle, travelling on a turtle, is one of the most popular tales of the country.

Urashima, a young boy of a fishing village, one day saved a turtle from the mischievous hands of little children and set it free. Some days after, while fishing, Urashima saw a turtle coming up, and after thanking him for his kind act in saving its life, it proposes to take him on its back to *Ryugu* (Paradise under the Sea). Urashima rides on the back of the turtle and visits *Ryugu*, where he is welcomed by the queen of *Ryugu*. Urashima lives many happy days with the queen, forgetting all about his parents and his village. But finally he remembers them and proposes to return. On parting, the queen gives him a little box, but asks him not to open it. Again riding on the back of the turtle, he returns to the shore of his village, but strangely the sights along the shore are different from what he used to see. He walks around, but the faces he sees are all strange. He inquires, but nobody seems to know him or his parents. Disappointed, he sits down on the beach, and opens the box, despite the advice of the queen not to open it. White smoke rises out of the box when its lid is removed. Instantly, Urashima becomes an aged man, more than a hundred years old, dressed in threadbare and old clothing. He learns that, although he believed he had spent only a few days in *Ryugu*, hundreds of years had passed away.

In the provinces of Kii and Awaji where turtles are found abundantly, they are considered as *kami* and duly respected. At a certain town of Awaji, a turtle used to come every year to lay eggs until a few years ago. This turtle was considered as *kami*, and the people of the town held an elaborate ceremony in worship of it. The turtle was about three feet in length, and it always came to the same spot during the summer and laid 144 eggs in 12 rows, and 12 eggs in each row. When the turtle was seen coming up on the shore, the people came out to watch respectfully, and even Shinto priests were called to witness the laying of the eggs. The place where the eggs were laid was marked off by *shimenawa* (straw rope to mark holy places), and no children were allowed to come near the spot. The Shinto priest came and prayed for the safe hatching of the eggs. It was believed that unless such precautions were taken, waves would suddenly rise in anger and destroy all those on the shore. For three months the eggs were thus carefully guarded, and when they hatched and the little turtles left with their mother, the people gathered and in very polite language offered their respects to them. Before leaving, the turtles were given plenty of *sake*.

The people in some districts carefully watch where turtles lay their eggs, and measure the distance from the water edge to where the eggs are laid. By the distance, they judge how high waves would come in autumn, and when the distance is very wide, they prepare for storms in autumn.

The Japanese say that when one has his finger snapped by a turtle, it would never let go until thunder roars. While none seems to have proved this fact, it is a very common belief of the people. In the United States and India there is a similar belief, it is said, but the truth of the belief is not yet ascertained.

UGUISU

UGUISU or bush warbler (Horormis cantans), a little greenish brown bird that is found wild all over the country, is the herald of spring, and also has been regarded as the most beautiful winged singer since very early days. Not only has its singing been extolled in poems, but it is also kept as a pet. Sometimes *uguisu* is erroneously called an English nightingale, but the bird is not related to nightingales, being more similar to one that is commonly known as bush warbler.

Of course the bird chirps all the time, but in the early spring when it calls its mate, it sings particularly long and beautifully. Being a wild bird, it is hard to keep in cages, but attracted by its singing, many bird lovers keep them at home to enjoy its songs.

Especially since the Tokugawa period, *uguisu* have become such a popular pet that the people learned to train them to sing better. Good singers naturally command high prices. Many feudal lords are said to have possessed many good singers which had special attendants to care for them. Such birds were kept in elaborate cages, many of them being made of polished bamboo, lacquered and decorated, with screens of fine ivory frames. Their care and training have thus developed to a fine technique.

Since those early days, *uguisu* lovers held occasional contests of their birds to determine the best in the country. Such contests are still held annually in many parts of the country.

The popularity of *uguisu* has much waned in recent years, but there are still quite a large number of *uguisu* lovers who are giving their utmost attention to train the birds to sing better than others.

The idea that the *uguisu* is the herald of spring has not died out, and when people hear *uguisu* singing, they know that the spring season has come. The peoples's love of *uguisu* is expressed in many different ways. Greenish brown color is called *uguisu-iro* or *uguisu* color. In spring there appears a Japanese cake named *uguisu-mochi*. It is made in a shape and color that suggest the bird. This cake is made and sold only in the early spring when the *uguisu* sings its spring song.

The keeping of *uguisu* is an expensive hobby, and also demands great care, but many are willing to take such pains to possess good singers.

UKAI

UKAI OR CORMORANT fishing in the Nagara River in Gifu, has become world famous, but it is also done in many other rivers. It is one of the most primitive methods of fishing adopted not only in Japan but also in many Asian countries. As it is mentioned in the *Kojiki*, the oldest Japanese record completed in the eighth century, the method must have been in use since the very beginning of the country.

The cormorant with its long neck and long hooked beak is a good fisher, as it is a good diver. It is also very greedy, and this characteristic has been utilized to catch fish for men. Wild birds are caught and trained to catch fish, and they quickly learn to obey the trainers as they are very bright.

In Japan, cormorants are generally used to catch *ayu*, a slender trout-like freshwater fish, but in China the birds are used to catch catfish or other large varieties.

Cormorant handlers became important as *ayu* which is regarded as the best freshwater fish was presented to local lords or the Court. The presentation to the court of *ayu* caught by cormorants is mentioned as having taken place as far back as 885. This custom was followed all through the Kamakura and later periods.

Thus cormorant fishing in many important rivers came to be protected by local lords as well as the Court, and cormorant trainers and handlers were officially recognized.

Cormorant fishing in the Nagara River became particularly famous as it came under the protection of the Imperial Court, and the cormorant handlers there were regarded as Court officials. Thus even today ancient Court customs are still retained by Nagara cormorant handlers.

In Japan, cormorants have rings on their necks so that they will not swallow the fish they have caught, and are thus forced to give up the fish stuck in their long necks. It is not known when this method was first adopted, but in China no such rings are used, probably because there the birds catch larger fish which they cannot swallow.

WITCH CATS

NEKO WA MAMONO (a cat is a witch) says a Japanese proverb, and cats are believed to do much mischief by bewitching people. Especially are old cats known to be really devilish in their tricks. If anyone kills a cat, it is believed that he will be cursed during seven lives. So the cat's bewitching power remains even after its death.

Thus the people are greatly afraid of old cats, but kittens are loved. It is only when cats are possessed of some evil spirit that they become witches and do all the harm to men and beasts. Such cats are generally believed to be of an enormous size.

A cat when possessed of the evil spirit will often take the form of a human being, especially that of a woman. Seldom does it take the form of a man, and all tales of evil cats circulated in the country are of those taking a feminine form. The cruel part of such tales is that when a cat takes the form of a woman, it usually first eats her up and then takes her place. Among the legends and tales of the country there are innumerable stories of cats eating women and taking their places, and other people not knowing the change until after great mischief and harm have been done. Also there are stories in which cats eat babies and children, but such are not impossible, there being cases of cats actually eating small babies.

The literature of the country is so full of tales of cats impersonating women that it is not necessary to relate them, but most of them are of the following type.

A man is living happily with his wife, but suddenly he and others realize that the wife has begun to act strangely. At first she is believed to be ill. Strange acts continue to puzzle all. Finally, one day, the husband opens a closet seldom used, and there he finds the bones of his wife scattered about. Then he knows that the woman who is acting as his wife is really a cat that has eaten up his wife and taken her place.

There are also many tales in which a devil cat devours many children.

But not all cats are witches and devils; there are cats which are almost worshiped. *Mike* (tricolored cats) are especially valued by many people. They believe *mike* will bring good luck to their families. Fishermen pay high prices for *mike*, believing that they bring them luck in fishing and also save them from shipwrecks. In fishing villages *mike* are treated royally and tenderly cared for by fishermen and their families.

In some districts of the country it is still believed that black cats cure spasms. Whenever one has such an attack, he gets hold of a black cat and places it on his stomach and it is believed that the attack will instantly sub-side. Also, in old days, it was believed that if a person, suffering from melancholia, would get a black cat in his house, he would be soon cured. Thus black cats are believed to possess virtues to cure various diseases. The native Japanese cats have very short tails; in fact they appear as if they have no tail at all. Many people do not like cats with long tails, or are even afraid of them, believing that it is those long-tailed cats that take human form and bewitch people.

In some places it is also believed that cats will betray thieves and when robbers enter and carry away things, the householder shouts loudly "If things are not returned the spirit of cats will torment you." They believe such a threat will make robbers return the spoils.

WOLVES

THE *OKAMI* (wolf) is a vicious animal that does harm to farms and domestic animals. Everywhere it is dreaded and held as an enemy of towns and villages. This vicious animal has long been considered as the spirit of various mountains of Japan. It was worshiped and its help was asked for the protection of farms and farming people.

Okami was formerly often written in Chinese characters implying great god, and it was regarded as the messenger of many *kami* that ruled and protected mountains. Okawa-Daimyojin of Tanba was said to use *okami* as its sacred messenger, and was commonly called Okami-Daimyojin. In the mountains in the neighborhood of the shrine, there were many wild *okami* present, but strangely they were never known to harm farms or molest people. When *okami* and other wild beasts happened to work damages to farms in other territories, a prayer was offered to Okawa-Daimyojin to loan its sacred *okami* for a certain number of days. It was said that Daimyojin immediately sent its *okami* to such territories and drove away all wild animals that did harm to farms and domestic animals.

It was also said of the Mitsumine Shrine of Chichibu, Musashi, that the *okami* killed wild animals whenever the people asked for protection of their farms. The charms of the shrine would keep anyone safe from attack by wild animals. This charm is a piece of paper with a rough sketch of *okami*, and is also reputed to prevent the occurrence of fire.

Many fishermen of the country still present *okoze* (Minous adamsi: a tiny fish) to *okami*, the spirit of the mountain, to blow them favorable winds. Regarding this superstitious belief, Mr. Kumagusu Minakata, the famous botanist, states that he once saw a screen of pictures in which a curious tale was related. *Okami*, the spirit of the mountain, fell in love with beautiful *Okoze*, and was about to marry her, but a monster octopus heard of it and became exceedingly jealous, and asking the aid of *ika* (cuttle-fish) and other fish, it formed an enormous army and attempted to carry away fair *Okoze* on her way to the wedding ceremony.

In the Kumano district it has been believed until quite recently that the *okami* was the chief of all animals, and when anyone was bitten by rats, he was fed with the cooked meat of *okami* and the wound was immediately cured. The sacred messenger of Tamaki Shrine of Yamto is *okami*. This shrine has been worshiped by the people because it was believed that many diseases were cured by its messenger. When any district was damaged by deer, wolves or other wild beasts, the people went to ask for the loan of the sacred *okami*. When the man making his request to the shrine returns, the sacred *okami* accompanies

him, and the footprints of the messenger always precedes the man, although the body of *okami* is never seen. Before the man and *okami* arrive at his house, all wild beasts scatter away. In front of this shrine stands a huge cryptomeria tree, and its bark is cut away and carried to one's farm in the belief that it will scare away wild beasts.

A story similar to that of the sacred *okami* of Tamaki Shrine is also recorded in an old book. It says:

There stands a little shrine in the mountains of Imazu, Bitchu, called Konoyama-Gongen. About 25 miles away from the shrine, and farther into the steep mountains, there is a little village called Shimo-Kamiyo-mura. Whenever harvest time arrives at the village, wild wolves come and devour the harvest, leaving not a single grain for the people who toiled and cultivated the farms. In order to prevent this destruction, they must go to the Gongen Shrine and ask for protection. When this prayer is offered, one *okami* follows the man and comes to the village to stop the coming of wild *okami*. The man never knows that he is accompanied by the sacred messenger, *okami*, but whenever he crosses a stream, he hears splashes and sees wet footmarks made on the dry stones by the invisible *okami*. But from the very night when the select-man returns to his village, wild beasts never molest the harvest and farms. The messenger-wolf sets about to kill wild animals that harm the people, and will not leave the village until every one of such beasts is killed and devoured.

Wild wolves still do harm to many farms in mountain districts, and they are feared by the people. But on the other hand, they worship many shrines and temples which are known to use *okami* as their sacred messenger.

Chapter 6
Folk Tales

ADACHI-HIME

A GREAT FAMILY named Miyagi lived at Adachi, now part of Tokyo, more than 500 years ago. The family was childless and prayers were offered to Kumano-Gongen in Wakayama for the deity's blessing for a boy or girl. Several years later a beautiful girl was born and named Adachi-hime. As she grew up she became the talk of all the neighborhood because of her beauty.

When she was 17 she was married to Saemon-no-jo Toshima, the son of another great family on the other side of the Iruma River. Saemon-no-jo was a fine young man, excelling in various manly accomplishments. He became the envy of the district for obtaining such a beautiful wife.

Everyone thought Adachi-hime was happily married but her life was really one of sadness. Her husband loved her but her mother-in-law found fault in everything she did. Saemon-no-jo felt pity for his wife and tried to comfort her, but his mother scolded him for being tender to his wife.

Adachi-hime could not stand her mother-in-law's daily nagging and thought of returning home to her parents, but she remembered that she was taught that once married, a wife had no other home to go back to.

Finally she resolved to die and secretly left the house at night. As she reached the Iruma River, her five maids followed her, saying that they would die with her if she intended to kill herself. They cried together for a long time, and then all jumped into the river together.

The villagers who envied her marriage learned for the first time how unhappy she was. Her father, who had prayed for a child to Kumano-gongen, appealed to the temple priest for help to console the soul of Adachi-hime. He was told to make Amida statues for the six maidens for the salvation of their souls.

So six Amida statues were made out of a single tree and placed in the six temples in the district. The village who felt sorry for Adachi-hime and her five maids visited the temples and prayed for them. Thus started the custom of making pilgrimages to the six temples which continued until quite recently.

Of the six temples where the Amida statues were placed, four were destroyed during the recent war. Now only the Keimeiji Temple at Numadamachi and Muryoji Temple at Nishigahara are left.

AGELESS WOMAN

THERE ARE many tales of persons who have lived long, and among them are also stories of women who have had a long life and married innumerable times.

Several young men of Chikuzen, Kyushu left on their ship, the Imari Maru on a trading cruise, carrying Imari porcelain ware. They stopped at many ports and when they reached Tsugaru, a northeastern port, one of them lost his way while going around the villages selling his ware.

As he was walking through a dense forest, he met a woman doing her washing by the stream. He asked to be allowed to spend that night in her house.

When he told her that he had come from Chikuzen, the woman uttered a cry of joy saying that she too had come from that district more than 600 years ago. Then she told her strange story.

She, so she said, was a sea diver when young but fell ill. A kindly person brought her a certain shellfish which she ate. She grew well and had never aged since. She married but her husband died. She married again and again, only to be bereft of her husband. Then as she saw her children, grandchildren and great grandchildren die, she felt sad.

So she left the village and went on a tour of temples all over the country. But she never aged and as she reached Tsugaru, she had married again and already had several children.

She told the young man that when he returned home, she wished he would go to the big pine tree called *Funa-domematsu* (boat tying pine) on the shore of Chikuzen, and see if the shrine she erected over the empty shell out of which she ate the miraculous shellfish was still there.

An old book that relates this story mentions that the young men left Chikuzen on their trading trip in 1782, and so she must first have been married at the beginning of the 11th century.

ANGELS' BATH

TENNYO are dressed in *hagoromo* or wing-robes, by which they fly. Coming down to the side of the sea or mountain lake, they take off their *hagoromo* and bathe. Various sections of the country have tales of such visits of angels.

The most famous of such tales is made into the famous *noh* play, *Hagoromo*. In this story, an angel comes down to Miho-no-Matsubara, the pine-covered promontory in Suruga Bay, and hangs her *hagoromo* on a pine tree while she goes to bathe in the sea. A young fisherman notices the robe by its strange fragrance. Attracted by its beauty, he takes the robe away.

When the angel comes out of the sea and finds her robe gone, she begs him to return it. Finally the young man asks the angel to show him the heavenly dance. When she dances, he returns the robe, and she is then able to fly back to her own land.

But in tales told in various other sections of the country, many *tennyo* are tricked into remaining in the country by young men hiding their robes, without which they cannot return home. Some of such *tennyo* marry the young men and bear children. They make good and beautiful wives in almost all cases. But some of them fly away as soon as they find their robes.

In a certain district there used to be a saying, according to old records, that *tennyo* wives should never be allowed to see their wing-robes until they had three children, because they would instantly fly away if they found their wings before they became the mother of three children. Many cases are told of *tennyo* wives, as soon as they found their robes again. This proved that these *tennyo* wives were never happy in this world.

ARMLESS MAIDEN

THERE ONCE lived a wife who hated her little stepdaughter. She told her husband that she would rather be divorced than live with the girl, an old story says.

So one day the father told the daughter to come with him to see the festival at the next village. But it was to a lonely mountain that he took her. There the father suddenly raised a hatchet and cut off both her arms and ran away. As she was struck, she fell and rolled down into the valley. She reached a stream below and there she washed her wounded shoulders with the clean water.

A fine-looking man happened to come along on a horse. Hearing her story, he took her to his house. His mother cared for her as though she were her own daughter.

The armless girl grew up beautiful and bright and the young man loved her. So they were married. But soon the husband had to go to Edo. While he was away a fine boy was born, and the aged mother sent a messenger to Edo to tell her son the great news.

On the way, the messenger went to a house for a drink of water, but it was the house where the armless girl was born. The messenger told the woman there he was carrying the message of an armless mother giving birth to a baby. Then the woman realized that it was her hated stepdaughter. So while the messenger was resting she stole the letter he was carrying and replaced it with a false one.

When the husband in Edo received the letter from home, he read that a baby ugly as the devil was born, while the original message told about the birth of a lovely boy. Yet he gave the messenger a reply asking his mother to take good care of the baby.

When the messenger stopped at the stepmother's on his way back, she again changed the reply to say that he did not want an ugly child nor an armless wife.

When the wife received the reply from Edo, she left the house with the baby tied on her back. But as she stopped to get a drink from a stream, the baby slipped and fell into the water. Surprised she stretched out her hands to save the child. Then she realized she had both arms again.

Soon after the husband returned from Edo and immediately set out to search for his wife and son. He found her with sound arms and with his fine son. Later the girl's father and stepmother were punished by the official for their cruel acts.

BANZABURO OF NIKKO

KAMI-SAMA is almighty, but there are many tales of mere humans helping and saving *kami* (god). The story of Banzaburo of Nikko is one of the most widely known of such stories. Banzaburo is still worshiped in many northeastern and north Kanto areas as *Yama-no-kami* or mountain *kami*.

Banzaburo was a famous hunter, whose skill was known to all in the surrounding regions. When Futara Gongen was at war with the *kami* of Mt. Akasaka, Gongen was in difficulty, but Banzaburo came to his help, thus defeating the *kami* of Mt. Akasaka. Gongen highly appreciated Banzaburo's part in the war, and gave him the sole right of hunting in all the neighboring mountains under his rule, and eating any animal he wished. Thus Banzaburo came to be worshiped by all hunters.

There is another version of the tale, in which not only Banzaburo, but also his brother Banji figures. Banji and Banzaburo were brother hunters and ruled the mountains of Nikko, but when Priest Jikaku opened a temple in the mountain in the Jokan era (859-877), the brothers listened to his preaching. Adopting the Buddhist faith, they gave up hunting, as Buddha prohibited the taking of any life. So the whole Nikko mountain area where the word of the brothers was law, became a paradise for all wild animals and birds, as no hunting was allowed there. Particularly wild boars felt very grateful and went to priest Jigaku to express their thanks. But to the boars the priest said that they should go to Banji and thank him.

At the annual festival of Futara Mountain, a *shishimai* or boar dance is still performed, but that dance has to be given first before the temple erected for Banji, and then at the temple for Priest Jigaku.

BEAR AND HORSE

THE HIGH PLATEAU on the border of Akita and Aomori Prefecture is famous for horse breeding and also for numerous bears that often killed many horses.

There once lived a farmer named Daihachi who boasted of his great physical strength. He used to say that if he ever met a bear, he would wrestle with it and kill it with his bare arms.

But Daihachi was poor, and had to think of selling his last horse he had kept for eight years. The horse trader took advantage of his position and offered a very low price. Daihachi was unwilling to sell his horse so cheap, but his son Rikizo told his father that he should sell it. Daihachi refused to sell it, however.

Next morning, the horse was not in its stable. For three days no sight of it was seen around the house. Disappointed in not finding the horse Daihachi went out to cut some grass in the mountain. There he saw his horse peacefully eating grass. He was happy again and kept on cutting grass. Then hearing a noise he looked up to see a huge bear standing before him. He rushed and grabbed the bear in his arms, but the bear was stronger than he thought. As they struggled they both rolled down on the ground.

Then his horse neighed sharply, and hearing the horse, the bear loosened his hold on Daihachi and rushed after the horse, a much better feed than Daihachi. The horse stood standing still, as if waiting for the on-rushing bear, and then Daihachi saw that as the bear rushed on, the horse jumped and ran toward the cliff above a high waterfall with the bear chasing it.

Daihachi followed them. At the top of the cliff, he saw the horse going around the cliff top toward the bottom of the valley. As Daihachi went below, he found his horse calmly standing by the bottom of the waterfall, watching the bear which was crushed to death on a rock.

Daihachi proudly returned home, leading his horse with the body of the bear on its back.

BEE MINISTER

KYOGOKU MUNESUKE, Prime Minister under Emperor Toba (12th century) kept many bees, and he was so fond of them that he gave each a name, according to an old story. His bees were so tame that when their names were called they flew immediately to his side. Whenever any of his officials did some wrong or displeased him, he would call one of his bees to sting that person.

Whenever he went to Court his bees followed his cart, flying about the cart windows. But he always ordered them to stay on the roof of the cart, and so they did. He was called by the people Bee Minister.

His fondness of bees, however, was criticized by many persons, who said that it was a foolish and wasteful hobby to be indulged in by a person of such a high position.

One day in May, a beehive fell from the roof of Toba Palace, and many bees were scattered in front of Emperor Toba. With the sudden flying of many bees, all the officials attending the emperor were so surprised that they ran away from their attack.

But Munesuke, who was also in attendance, calmly picked up a *biwa* (loquat), and peeling its outer skin, held the fruit in his hand. The bees at once swarmed to the fruit and stayed there. Munesuke handed the *biwa* with all the bees on it to an attendant to be taken away. Thus none was attacked.

The emperor highly appreciated Munesuke's ability in handling the bees, and since then nobody laughed at the prime minister's bees and his indulgence in caring for them.

BLACK CAT

THERE WERE once two sisters, and while the elder who had married a rich man led an easy and comfortable life, the younger who had married a woodsman had to carry a heavy load of kindling wood to town daily to sell them, according to an old story.

Often the young sister was not able to sell her load, and not wishing to carry the heavy burden back to her mountain hut, she threw the wood into the sea so that she could return home quickly. Such days came frequently, to her distress.

One day, as she threw her load into the water, a strange girl appeared out of the sea and asked her to come with her to *Ryugu* or the palace of the sea god. On the way, the sea girl told her that if the sea god expressed a wish to give her a parting gift, she should ask for a black cat.

The sea god thanked her for the kindling she occasionally sent down to the palace, and asked her what she wished as a gift. As advised, she mentioned a black cat. In granting her wish the sea god told her that the cat must be daily fed with a quantity of red beans.

Carrying the black cat home, she fed it with the instructed amount of red beans daily. The cat each day gave her the same quantity of gold. Thus the young sister became rich.

The elder sister learned of the good fortune of her younger sister and desiring to enjoy the same luck went to the house of the latter. She succeeded in borrowing the cat by force. She was impatient and gave the cat a double quantity of red beans. The cat, however, did not give any gold and soon died from overeating.

The young sister lamented the death of her cat and buried it in the garden. Soon the citrus tree that she planted over the cat's tomb bore beautiful fruit. She used the fruit as New Year's decoration in the belief they were related to the black cat that brought her so much wealth and happiness.

BOWLS TO LEND

IT HAS BEEN customary in Japan to hold drinking and feasting parties at home on all festive occasions, marriages, funerals, memorials, gatherings, or special days of importance, inviting relatives and neighbors. Thus most families have always kept bowls, plates, trays and other utensils for many persons, sometimes enough for 100 or more guests.

When a family does not have sufficient utensils, they must be borrowed from another. In many districts, thus, there developed a custom of having community sets of table utensils to be loaned to families not possessing them for such occasions.

In connection with this custom, the tale of *kashi-wan* (bowls to lend) is told in many regions in which required utensils are mysteriously supplied.

In the village of Ryukakuji, not far from Narita in Chiba Prefecture, there is a cave which is said to have loaned bowls and other utensils if notice was given a day ahead. But once a person failed to return them, and ever since the cave stopped lending while at the same time the whole village lost its prosperity, it is said.

At the Hachiman Shrine of Sekimoto in Ibaraki Prefecture, there is a cave by the stone steps, where once lived a strange person. When anybody needing table utensils told him how many bowls, dishes and trays he wanted on a certain day, the exact number of the desired ware was placed next day by the cave. Here too the lending stopped when someone failed to return the articles.

At the Chonenji Temple, near Takasaki City, Gunma Prefecture there is a well which is said to be bottomless and reach *Ryugu* (palace of the dragon king). If one wrote a letter mentioning the number of things he wanted to borrow and dropped it into the well, the dragon king placed the desired things by the well, it is said. Here too, one borrower broke a dish, and that angered the dragon king so much that no letter of request brought out any utensils any more.

Similar tales are told in many Kanto districts but it is to be noted that most of them are told in districts near a river, and it is the dragon king or river monsters who lend out bowls and dishes.

BRIDAL DRESS

THE ZENYOJI TEMPLE at Koiwa in Edogawa Ward, Tokyo, has a tale of a priest buying a bridal dress for a ghost. It is an old temple, recorded to have been established in 1527, but the incident that caused the story took place during the reign of the third Tokugawa shogun Iemitsu or about the middle of the 17th century, when Priest Kenyu was the head of the temple.

One day, a fisherman of Koiwa went out on his boat, but he had no lunch that day and caught no fish, the story says. When he was about to return home in disgust, he found the body of a young woman in the water. He took it to the Zenyoji Temple where Priest Kenyu held a service for her and buried her in the temple compound.

Then, nightly a woman ghost appeared on the huge pine tree of the temple, and it became the talk of the neighborhood. Priest Kenyu, wanting to investigate, went out to meet the ghost. When he saw the ghost on the pine tree, he asked her what she wanted.

She replied that her father was poor, and could not buy her bridal dress, even though her marriage was arranged, and because she could not have the proper costume to make her a bride, the marriage was canceled. Realizing that she could never marry because of poverty, she had killed herself by jumping into the water.

Hearing her story, the priest said, "I will buy you a bridal dress, so don't feel unhappy." Next day he went to Edo and purchased a bright wedding gown and placed it on the pine tree where the ghost appeared every night.

The bridal dress mysteriously disappeared from the pine branch and the ghost never appeared again. But in place of the beautiful costume, one sleeve of the plain dress the poor girl had worn when she was found floating on the water, was left behind.

The pine tree came to be called *Sode-*

ga-matsu or sleeve pine.

BROTHER MOUNTAINS

HIKODAKE GONGEN-YAMA at Shimomiya, Kumamoto Prefecture and Fudo-iwa at Gamo in the same prefecture, were brother mountains. Their mother treated Fudo-iwa with affection, but mistreated Gongen-yama because the latter was her stepson. Daily she fed Fudo-iwa with *azuki* or red beans, which was a luxury food, but gave Gongen only soya beans which were very cheap.

Her kindness to Fudo-iwa did harm to her favorite son, because *azuki* was not very nourishing and he became weak. On the other hand, Gongen grew big and strong, being raised on the nourishing soya beans.

But the two brothers were very fond of each other. One day they played tug-of-war, putting a long strong rope around their necks. As they pulled, Gongen won, being stronger of the two. When Gongen jerked the rope with all his strength, the rope severed the head of Fudo-iwa. The head rolled down to a village named Kubara.

There still stands a rock called *Kubi-iwa* (head rock), and the soil around it is of a reddish color, due to the red beans Fudo-iwa had been eating daily.

Between the two mountains was Yurugi-dake, or shaking mountain. During the tug-of-war between Gongen and Fudo-iwa the rope scraped the side of this mountain, shaking it as the two pulled hard. On the mountain side, there are still seen two deep scars made by the straining rope. It is also said that no tree or grass grows on the two scars.

BUDDHA'S GRACE

TO A LITTLE temple in the mountain of Tanba province, there once came a young priest to meditate and gain enlightenment. Winter came and snow covered the mountain, and so none came near the temple. Nor was the priest able to go down to the nearest village, miles away.

His food reserve was soon exhausted and he had nothing to eat. He could do nothing but remain in his bed, as his strength declined. Daily he waited for the time to die, only praying silently.

"I heard that a prayer once offered would be answered. I have been praying for years. I do not desire promotion in rank nor any wealth. What I want now badly is food," he prayed.

So praying he looked outside and saw some black object rolling to the temple entrance. It was a boar killed by a wolf. There was the food he had so eagerly wanted. He thought that Buddha had pity on him and brought the boar inside. But he was a priest and could not eat meat, the human instinct was strong, and he could not fight the urge of hunger. Finally he cut off a piece of the leg meat of the boar, cooked it and ate it. He did not repent that he had broken a Buddhist pledge not to eat meat.

The long winter passed and the heavy snow melted. Some villagers came up to the temple to inquire how the solitary priest had fared during the long snow-covered winter. But they found in a kettle many chips of wood and thought that the priest had been eating it as food.

But as they looked up, they saw that a big piece was cut off from the leg of the wooden Buddha statue in the temple. They asked the priest how he came to cook the wood cut off the statue.

The priest then realized that Buddha appeared as a boar so that he could satisfy his hunger. Offering thanks to Buddha, he prayed that if Buddha was so merciful, the statue might be restored to its former shape. His prayer was again answered and the statue was restored.

BULRUSH EARS

THE WHITE HARE of Inaba is a popular figure in a Japanese mythological tale, known even to little children. When the hare found itself unable to return from Okinoshima Island to the mainland, it met a *wani* (crocodile). The hare asked the crocodile how many crocodiles there were in the sea, and to prove their number, it made all of them come out to the sea surface. When the crocodiles had gathered to be counted, the hare stepped on their backs, and managed to reach the mainland. Upon reaching land, the hare told the crocodiles how it had tricked them to come up together so it could reach the mainland. Thereupon the crocodiles became angry, and catching the hare, stripped it of it fur exposing its raw flesh and made it suffer.

While it was suffering and weeping, the 80 deities came and out of mischief advised it to bathe in the sea water, dry itself in the sun and be exposed to the wind. However, Onamuchi-no-kami took pity on the hare and said, "Go quickly to the river and wash your body, spread out *kaba* or bulrush ears and roll on them, and then you will regain your fur."

The *kaba* grow in swampy places or in water, and in summer have brown-colored candle-shaped ears about 20 cm long. The ears are velvety to the touch. The hare was advised to cover up its raw body with the bulrush ears.

Primitive people had a very wide use for bulrush ears. They were the first material for clothing and bedding, and the hare was told to follow their example. Bulrush ears were also used as torches. They were soaked in oil and lighted.

The pollen of bulrushes was formerly used as a medicine for asthma and was known as *ho-o* or *kaba* yellow. The brown color is still commonly called *Kaba-iro* or bulrush color.

Broiled eels are called *kaba-yaki*. It is said that eels so prepared came to be given this name as they resemble bulrush ears in color and shape.

BUNBUKU CHAGAMA

THE STORY of *bunbuku chagama* or badger-kettle is one of the most popular folk tales. As generally told and sung, one day the priest of the Morinji Temple in Tatebayashi, Gunma Prefecture, put a kettle on the fire. As it became heated, a tail came out of it, and the kettle jumped off, taking the shape of a *tanuki*, or badger. Afraid to keep such an eerie kettle, the priest sold it to a ragman. At the ragman's house, the kettle walked to the man's bed and awakening him, announced that it could walk a tightrope, and persuaded the ragman to hold a tightrope show. The ragman became rich with the show of the tightrope-walking badger-kettle.

But the famous Morinji kettle made of solid iron is, contrary to the popular tale, still preserved. There is another version of this story. Priest Gesshu of Morinji temple held a large service in 1570, inviting a thousand people. But there was no kettle big enough to serve tea to all comers. While the priest was worried about this problem, Morizuru, a boy attendant, brought a big kettle from some unknown source. The kettle held enough hot water to serve more than a thousand cups of tea without any additional water. So everybody wondered.

It was Priest Tennan who later came to the temple and thought that something was wrong with the boy who brought the miracle kettle. Knowing that the priest suspected him, the boy ran away.

It was found that Morizuru was originally brought from Ikaho by the former Priest Shotsu in 1426, or 144 years previous to the occasion of the magic kettle incident. As it was said that he disappeared on February 28, 1587, he was at the temple 161 years.

Thus calculated, the people began to think that Morizuru was a badger in human form, and the kettle he brought must be sacred. So it was named *Bunbuku Chagama*, or happy kettle, and made a temple treasure. A special shrine was erected for Morizuru.

The kettle is still preserved. It is a very good kettle of the so-called Tenmyo type. It measures four feet around, and weighs about thirty pounds.

CHICKEN SONG

"I WISH TO BE the birds of Mankoji Temple. I wish to be the chickens," goes an old folk song sung in Aichi Prefecture. It expresses the envy for the comfortable life of the temple chickens. The song has a strange origin.

In 1573, Tokugawa Ieyasu was fighting the forces of the Takeda clan in that district. One day he had to retreat to Yamano-yoshida and stayed overnight at the Mankoji Temple. He issued an order that next morning at the first cock crow he would leave.

But that night, a cock crowed unexpectedly before midnight. At the crowing, all rose and left the temple as ordered. The Takeda forces who came to attack Ieyasu at daybreak found the enemy gone.

So Ieyasu was saved by the untimely crowing of the cock. In appreciation Ieyasu gave a tract of land to the temple to provide feed for its chickens, and also made the land tax-free. Later third Tokugawa shogun Iemitsu established a temple for Ieyasu at the Mankoji Temple.

Thus the chickens kept at the temple came to be well provided for and the temple itself became prosperous. On the other hand, the farmers in the neighborhood began to suffer from high taxation. At first the tax was one-half of the crop, but later it was increased to 60 percent of the harvest, farmers being allowed to keep only 40 percent.

The farmers gradually began to envy the temple with its tax-free land, and its chickens that had sufficient feed all the time. So they began to sing this song, expressing their wish that they might become the chickens of the temple.

Besides singing the song, they appealed to the authority to have the tax rate lowered. After many failures, they finally succeeded and had the tax lowered to the former rate of one-half the crop.

The ancient song which the people sang in hard times remains even today, sung by present residents who may have forgotten its origin.

CHILDREN'S FRIEND

CHILDREN of the cold northeastern regions love to ride on their crude home-made sleighs whenever the ground and hills are covered with snow. An interesting story is told in connection with the Kumano Shrine, Iwate Prefecture.

Some children who did not have a sleigh entered the shrine, and taking out the wooden statue enshrined there, they rode on it sliding down the snow-covered hill. With shouts and laughter they had a delightful time, but one old man of the neighborhood saw the children riding the shrine statue.

Angrily he shouted to the children to stop and chased them home. Then he picked up the snow-covered statue and brushing off the snow carried it back to the shrine.

But that night the old man had a very high fever and moaned and tossed in his bed. The neighbors took alarm and called a woman medium, as it was customary for the villagers to cure the sick through the service of a medium.

The medium came and in a trance she spoke the words of the Kumano statue.

"You have done an uninvited and unnecessary thing. Just when I was having a good time playing with the children, you suddenly came and chased them away. I do not like that. Unless you offer me a bottle of *sake* and red-bean rice, I will take your life."

Hearing this the neighbors hurried to take the *sake* and the red-bean rice to the shrine and prayed for forgiveness. Only then was the old man cured.

Since then the shrine has been worshiped as the friend and guardian of children.

CHRISTIAN MARTYRS

BRIGHT RED blossoms of *manjushage* (Lycoris radiata) bloom in early autumn in patches along country roads, on river banks and at other places. They mark the routes taken by early Christian missionaries in propagating the new faith, and the spots where Christian martyrs were buried, a popular story tells.

Manjushage are gorgeous with six flowers with long curling petals blossoming in a circle at the top of each stalk that is about one foot tall. They appear in clusters marking bright spots here and there on the green countryside. The flower is also called *higanbana* (equinox flower) because it blooms just about the time of the autumn equinox. It is also known by the name *keiketsuso* (chicken blood plant), because of its bright red color.

Shinin-bana (dead-man's flower) is another name for it. This is because it is often found in cemeteries, and also because the blossoms come out after the leaves have died. Winter and spring the plant has long green leaves, but in late summer the leaves wither and then the flower stalks rise from the bulb under the ground. Thus it is commonly said that the *manjushage* flower blooms after the plant is dead.

Though the blossom is gorgeously bright, the people never pick it because the plant is poisonous, its bulb containing the poison lycorine.

The name *manjushage* came from *manjusaka* meaning "flower of the heaven" in Sanskrit. Yet a traditional story says that the plant was first brought to the country by Portuguese Catholic missionaries.

Some of these early missionaries from Portugal who came in the 16th century brought the bulbs of the plant. As they went on tours of Christian propagation, they planted the bulbs by the roadside. They told their fellow missionaries and followers that the red blossoms of the plant would tell every autumn what routes they had taken in their journeys into the interior of the country. "Where the patches of the red blossom end, you will know, will be the place where we have died," they said. The persecution of Christians became severe and many missionaries were murdered or died of sickness in remote districts. Where they died are supposedly marked with patches of the red blossoms.

CRANE WIFE

THERE ARE many tales of fish, foxes, snakes, and birds repaying human kindness. Some turn into beautiful women and marry the men who saved them. One of the most widely told stories is about *tsuru-nyobo* or the crane wife.

One honest young man, while cutting grass on a hillside, saw a *tsuru* or crane unable to fly or walk, as an arrow had pierced its body. Taking pity on the bird, he drew out the arrow and released it.

A few nights later, a strange girl came to his door. As she stayed with him, she became his wife. The young man was poor, and as the New Year approached he could not make proper preparations for the annual celebration. His wife sat at her loom and wove a beautiful cloth. He took the fabric to the lord of the district. Very much pleased with the beautiful cloth, the lord paid well, and then ordered another piece of a similar fabric.

When he returned home with money and told his wife that the lord wanted another piece, she became very sad. She said she did not know if she could make another piece, but she would try. She made her husband promise that he would not enter the room where she would be weaving until the fabric was finished.

The young man was curious and peeped into her room. He found a lean crane that was almost featherless picking a few stray feathers to feed into the loom. As she saw her husband peering in, she said angrily, "You promised not to look. I am the crane you saved, and I came to serve you. I was not sure I had enough feathers left to weave another piece."

So saying, she quickly left the house. The husband went after her, but could not find her.

CURING TREE

IN THE compounds of the Sho-o-ji Temple, Kitamiyashiro-cho, Adachi-ku, Tokyo, near Arakawa Canal, stands a memorial tablet for Adachi-hime and a *bodaiju* (lime tree).

The tablet and *bodaiju* are worshiped by many diabetics as it is traditionally said that they have power to cure their illness.

Adachi-hime was a famous beauty in the Adachi district 12 centuries ago. She had many offers for marriage, but finally married a *samurai* named Toshima Saemon-no-jo. The marriage was a happy one, but Saemon-no-jo's mother was hard on her daughter-in-law. Adachi-hime waited on her mother-in-law with respect and kindness, but the old lady invariably found fault with everything she did. Finally the mother's attituide became so unbearable that Adachi-hime committed suicide, together with her five maids who sympathized with her, by jumping into the Arakawa River. The group suicide of the young girls was very widely reported throughout the city.

Adachi-hime's father, after the death of his daughter and her maids, lost all hopes in this material world, and started on a Buddhist pilgrimage, going to Kumano Gongen in Kii province. There he carved six statues of Buddha and gave them to the temples of six villages. He also erected a little hut and placed within it another Buddha statue he made. This hut became the Sho-oji Temple.

Near the hut, he buried his daughter's *juzu* or rosary made of lime tree wood. But from the buried rosary grew a lime tree. The people of the neighborhood came to worship the tree as it was miraculous that a tree should grow from a buried rosary. In some unaccounted way the traditon was started that a lime tree has power to cure diabetes.

DAFFODIL

THERE ARE many legends and tales about *suisen* (Sacred Daffodil). The

Chinese people who give so much importance to this flower have called it the Water Spirit, which stands for purity, nobility, and long life.

There is one interesting tale that relates the origin of this blossom that blooms so beautifully in winter.

Once there lived two sisters, both unusually beautiful. They were orphans, and lived only with each other. The elder, however, had suddenly died, and the younger sister was so deeply touched by the death of her elder sister that nothing gave joy to her. Daily she used to loiter around gardens and hills, and lamented the loss of her dear sister.

In one of such solitary walks through hills, one day she came upon a little pond. As she neared the edge of the water, she was surprised to find her dead sister looking sadly at her from the bottom of the pond. She was indeed alarmed to find that her elder sister was in such a lonely place. But the younger sister became happy because if she came to the pond, she could look at her dead sister. She daily visited the pond and fondly looked at the face of her sister which appeared amidst the leaves of stray weeds floating on the water.

Of course this girl did not realize that it was the reflection of her own face that she was looking at in the pond and which she believed to be that of her dead sister.

The spirit of the pond saw her coming to the pond daily, and taking pity upon her, decided to turn her dead sister into something beautiful so that she could always love and cherish it.

Next day, when the young sister came to the edge of the pond as usual, she saw for a moment the face of her dead sister, but suddenly the face disappeared and a tiny white, fragrant blossom appeared in its place.

Then she knew that her sister had become the flower that filled the air with a noble fragrance. Thus she was able thereafter to tenderly care for the blossom and love it every day.

The blossom rose out of the water, and it came to be called the Water Spirit or *suisen*.

DANCING TREE

THE AINU have a story about a dancing tree. Once there stood a giant old tree in the forest. It was always happy, and in joy waved its branches all day. Thus it was named the dancing tree.

A lumberman coming to the forest and seeing the giant tree, was impressed by its size. But saying "its inside might be rotten," he raised his huge axe to see if it was sound.

The spirit of the tree heard his remark and became angry at his insinuation. To punish him for such an insult, the tree hardened its bark, and when the man struck it with his axe, it made no dent but the blade of the axe was chipped off.

Some years later, a kind-hearted and civil man approached the tree and politely asked if he could cut it down to build a ship for trading. Asked in such a courteous manner, the spirit of the tree readily agreed to be cut down by him. So the tree was cut and carried to the port to be made into a ship.

When the ship was built and ready to start on its first voyage, the lumberman who insulted the tree many years ago came along and asked the ship owner to take him on board. His request was granted. Soon the ship was ready to sail. But immediately there arose a heavy storm and it became difficult for the ship to start on its voyage.

The ship owner thought that there must be some evil influence that was trying to stop the maiden voyage of his ship. Remembering that the new hand was a lumberman, the owner asked him if he had ever insulted the tree that was used in building the ship. The lumberman was already in awe of the tossing storm and confessed that he had.

The ship owner instantly demanded that he leave the ship. As soon as he did so, the angry sea calmed down and the ship was able to make her first voyage successfully. Later the ship owner became wealthy and led a happy life. On the other hand, the lumberman who was made to leave the ship remained poor and unhappy.

DEVIL'S FLUTE

HIROMASA, a great-grandson of Emperor Daigo (10th century) and a fine musician, went to the Suzaku Gate one night when the moon was clear and beautiful. There he played his flute, enhanced by the moon. Then another person appeared there and also played a flute. They never spoke, but played on. They met there and played several nights.

The unknown player played well, his flute giving forth a wonderful tone. Finally Hiromasa proposed to exchange their flutes. After that, whenever the moon was beautiful Hiromasa went to the same place to meet the other musician, but they never got their own flutes back, always playing the other's instrument.

When Hiromasa died, the emperor had the flute that he had borrowed from the strange Suzaku Gate player brought out, and made the Court musicians play it, but none was able to get any music out of it. Finally Jozo, a famous flute player was called, who was able to play it as well as Hiromasa.

The emperor then told Jozo that Hiromasa had got the flute near the Suzaku Gate, and asked him to go there at night and play it. One moonlit night

Jozo went to the famous gate and played the flute.

Thereupon, someone in the gate tower shouted in a loud voice, "It is really as fine a flute as I have always thought."

Thus it became known that the flute belonged to the devil who lived in the Suzaku Gate tower. The emperor treasured it as one of the Court treasures. It was said to have been a beautiful flute with designs of two leaves. It later came to be known as the "Two-leaf flute."

DEVIL'S MASK

KOKO-ZAKA (hill of devotion) in the province of Tango (Hyogo Prefecture) has a strange story regarding the origin of its name.

A daughter, much devoted to her mother, had to leave home to serve as a maid in a great rich family in another village. She took with her a wooden mask made after her mother, so that whenever she thought of her mother, she could look at her.

Working in the new household, she opened her sewing cabinet and looked at the mask she kept in its drawer in the early morning before her work commenced and at night just before going to bed.

The household soon learned her secret of looking at the mask. The master of the house, who was of a playful nature, thought of surprising the maid. He had a mask of a devil made, and substituted it for the mask in the maid's sewing cabinet.

That evening the maid opened her sewing box as usual, and to her great surprise, she saw the mask of a devil instead of the face of her beautiful smiling mother. She thought something dreadful must have happened to her mother, and immediately asked to be allowed to end her service to return home.

Carrying her sewing cabinet and a few pieces of clothing, she started for home, but on the road, she was caught by several highwaymen. Taken to their house, she was ordered to serve them *sake* and food. As they became quite drunk, she retreated to another room, and again opened her box. Just as she was holding the devil's mask in her hands, the drunken bandit chief called her.

So she put the mask on and went to their room. When they saw her they thought that she was a devil and fled out of the house. Finding herself alone she did not know what to do, but at that moment an old priest appeared at the door. Hearing her story, the priest told her to gather up all the valuables and money in the house and return to her mother.

After the maid left his house, her master realized that he had done wrong in surprising her in such a crude way, and apologized. She did not return to serve at the house, but maintained cordial relations with the family. Thus, the place where she was attacked by the highwaymen came to be called *Kokozaka*.

DIVINE PEACH

MANY ANIMALS are made *kami*, but it is very rare that any fruit is worshiped as such.

Okamizumi-no-Mikoto is one of such rare examples. This Mikoto is originally neither human nor divine, but it is merely a fruit. All over the country the blossoms of *momo* (peach) bloom beautifully, and the flowers are loved and admired by the people as one of the most delicate, beautiful, and feminine of our flowers. Okamizumi-no-Mikoto is only another name for this fruit of *momo*.

It is legendary, and there is an interesting story connected with this holy name for *momo*.

When Izanami-no-Mikoto went to "the Land of Eternal Night," her husband, Izanagi-no-Mikoto followed her. But his presence greatly angered Izanami-no-Mikoto who had him chased out of the land, sending out many people of the Eternal-Night Land. Hotly pursued by these people he ran as fast as he could. He was afraid to be caught by them, but there were so many of them chasing him that he could not shake them off. But by the roadside he saw a peach tree bearing much beautiful fruit. He shook the tree, and picking the fallen fruit he threw them at the chasing enemies. *Momo* flew one after another, and struck the enemies. It did not give them much pain, but as these people had never seen *momo* fruit they were surprised to see the fruit thrown at them, and fled.

Thus Izanagi-no-Mikoto succeeded in driving away the chasers from the Land of Eternal Night. So happy over his success, and thankful for the aid of the *momo* fruit, he gave it the honorable name of Okamizumi-no-Mikoto. Thus the peach came to be counted among the *kami* of the country.

DREAM HINTS

AMONG TALES told in many parts of the country there are quite a large number of stories in which persons become rich and prosperous by hints given them in dreams.

In the Nanbu district of the northeastern region there is a story about *Danburi-choja* (dragonfly millionaire). Once a poor but honest farmer was working on his farm, and as he rested a while in the midafternoon, he fell asleep from fatigue. A dragonfly came, and after touching the mouth of the sleeping farmer, flew to a mountain on the other side of the valley. It repeated this strange trip several times.

The farmer's wife saw the unusual flights of the dragonfly, and when she aroused him, he told her that he had had a strange dream. In the dream he had gone to the other side of the mountain, where he found clear running water. When he drank from it he found it was fine *sake* (wine).

The farmer and wife together went to the spot where he visited in his dream, and there they found a stream, the water of which was *sake*. Furthermore all the pebbles along the stream were of gold. They gathered the gold and sold the stream *sake*.

Another tale of a similar type concerns two travellers. Resting under the shadow of a big pine tree by the road, one of them fell asleep. A bee came out of his nostril and flew away, to return again and again. When he awoke, he told his companion that he had dreamed of visiting a place full of gold. They went to the place and became rich.

In Echigo they tell the story of Ninsuke who was guided in his dream by a bee to a pot of gold on Sado Island. In the Mt. Fuji region of Yamanashi a story goes that while one man was asleep a bee came out from his nostril and flew away, as another was watching the sleeper. As the sleeper woke up, he followed the route taken by the mysterious bee and found a pot of gold. The watcher secretly followed the sleeper, and saw him dig out the pot. When the second man examined the pot, he saw the words "Seven in all" written on the bottom of the pot. The two agreed that there must be six more pots. They dug together and found them.

DRINKING WIFE

TWO LUMBER cutters who went into the mountains and stayed overnight in a mountain hut had the same dream, a story told in the northeastern region says.

They dreamed that one of them had a baby boy born at his house, and the other a baby girl. *Yamano-kami* or mountain god told them that the girl was born with the luck of one *sho* of salt and one drinking cup, and the boy with the fortune of one *sho* of rice.

They were surprised to have had the same dream, but when they returned to the village next morning, they learned that a boy had been born at one house and a girl at the other, during the night.

The boy and girl grew up healthy and strong, and subsequently they married and prospered. But the wife was extravagant and used one *sho* of salt every day, and never stopped drinking *sake* out of her cup. Furthermore, she invited many friends to join in her drinking. The husband was timid and did not like to drink but his wife's daily drinking habit and extravagance became too much for him, and finally he divorced her.

She walked out of the house, without complaining, to the mountain. She became hungry and then she saw a patch of land planted with radishes. She pulled one out to eat and from the hole gushed out *sake*. Singing in joy, she drank it. Refreshed she walked on. Then seeing a light in the distance, she walked toward it, and found herself before a miner's hut. She entered the hut and stayed there that night with the miner. In the morning she saw that everything in the hut was gold and told the ignorant miner what a huge wealth he possessed. Together they took the gold to the village and became rich.

Many years passed, and the village to which the miner and the woman moved to enjoy their wealth grew into a town of much activity. One day the woman met an old wood-cutter accompanied by a younger man. They were her father and her former husband, apparently still poor.

EARTHWORM

THE *mimizu* or earthworm has white rings around its neck, and there is an old story telling how it came to have them.

In ancient days before the introduction of cotton, Japanese women made hemp yarn and wove them into cloth to make their dresses. To make fine yarn and weave thin cloth required skill and patience. Many who were untalented had to wear coarse dresses as they could not make any better.

There once lived a woman who was careless and impatient, and could only weave roughly. But her neighbor was a maker of fine hemp cloth, but she was slow in her work.

In those days a market was held periodically, and it was an occasion of joy for women to go there in their best clothes. It so happened that when market day approached the two women started to make their new dresses to wear to the market.

The first woman was able to make her dress quickly, but it was coarse and ill-made. The other, being slow, had only finished her skeins of very fine hemp yarn. When market day came, she had no dress to wear. The market had to be visited, and so she wound her skeins around her neck, and made her husband carry her in a big jar on his back, so that nobody could see she had no dress on.

Approaching the market place, she saw the first woman walking in her coarse but new dress. The sight angered her, and sticking out her head from the jar, she shouted "There goes a coarse weaver." Hearing this insult, the first woman said, "Even coarse, I wear a dress. Break the jar, and you will find a naked woman."

Thereupon the husband felt so ashamed of his wife that he let the jar fall to the ground. The jar broke, and there was a naked woman with only skeins of hemp around her neck. So ashamed was she that she buried herself in the ground to hide. She turned into an earthworm.

Thus the earthworm has white rings around its neck.

EEL TALE

KABAYAKI or broiled eels have become a popular dish with Edo residents since the Tenmei era (1781-1789). As the number of *unagi-ya* (eel restaurants) increased, there developed a belief among those engaged in the business that to kill many eels daily was an unmerciful act and one should not stay in such business long if he hoped for happiness and salvation after death.

Thus when they opened their shops, they usually made a pledge that in five or seven years they would give up the business.

To a *kabayaki-ya* at Teppozu, there came one night a messenger from its great patron, and as he found the door of the shop already closed, he knocked loudly on it, a story says. The knocking brought no one to the door, so the messenger shouted from outside that his master wanted *kabayaki* for his guests next day at noon.

"No more eels. No eels," a voice replied from the other side of the door. So the messenger went home, reporting that the *kabayaki-ya* was out of eels and suggested that the order be given to another shop.

Early the next morning the master himself went to the *kabayaki-ya* and angrily complained, saying that even though there were no eels last night, a new supply could be obtained in the morning and cooked in time for lunch.

The *kabayaki-ya* man was surprised as he knew nothing of the order nor the reply that there were no eels. He took the patron to the pool where the eels were kept. But among them he saw an especially big one with ears on its head.

He then realized that it must be this big eel that heard the messenger's order and cried out "no more eels" the night before in order to save the eels from being killed.

He suddenly was reminded of his killing many eels daily, and lamenting his act of destroying life, rushed out of the house and went to the Daimokudo Temple, at Omori. There he became a Buddhist monk to devote the rest of his life to offer prayers for the numerous eels he had killed.

ENDLESS TALES

SO-CALLED ENDLESS tales are still preserved in many rural districts. These stories were formerly loved by children who were interested to find out how and when they would end. The endless tales are tedious repetitions that could go on forever, if the narrator is able and the listeners are willing. Children often go to sleep as they listen to them.

In a year of famine, rats in Nagasaki could not find any food, and thought that if they went to Satsuma at the southern end of Kyushu they might find enough to eat. So all the rats boarded boats to migrate to Satsuma. But as the fleet came to Shiranui Sea, they saw another big fleet of boats coming toward them.

As the two fleets neared, the rats found that the other boats were full of rats from Satsuma, who were trying to find food somewhere else as there was none in Satsuma. So the rats in both fleets realized that their plans were hopeless.

In despair, one Nagasaki rat shouted out that it was hopeless and it would be better to die than be hungry forever, and then jumped into the sea. Seeing this, one Satsuma rat also preferred to die and jumped into the water. Another Nagasaki rat followed the example, and a Satsuma rat jumped into the sea each in turn, and thus the story is endless.

Most endless tales are quite similar. An acorn falls from its branch, slides down bamboo leaves, hits a stone wall, and bounces off to drop into the stream below. Another acorn drops from the branch, slides down bamboo leaves, hits a stone wall, and bounces into the water. Acorns keep on falling off the branches, and dropping into the stream.

While simple and meaningless, children love to hear such stories that keep their attention without end.

ENSHRINED FOX

IN THE DISTRICT of Ayato in the northern mountain region of Aichi Prefecture, a fox is enshrined and worshiped as the spirit of the forest.

Yorita Korenao was the son of the village head. One day, a fox chased by a hunter came toward him and hid itself behind his skirt. Then Yasouemon, the hunter, came up to him and asked that the fox be turned over to him, as he had been chasing it all day.

But Korenao refused, saying that the fox was not only a beautiful one, but also a female with a baby and that it should be allowed to go free. Realizing that Korenao was firm, Yasouemon left without getting his fox.

Soon afterward Matsumoto Sakon, an emissary from the Lord of Yoshida came to the village to arrange the amount of tax to be paid. As it happened to be the day of the village festival, the official was invited to enjoy the sights and to be feasted. Among the gathered crowd, Matsumoto noticed two beautiful young girls, Onui, the daughter of hunter Yasouemon, and her friend Otama.

Next day Matsumoto commenced his official task. Korenao represented the village in determining the tax amount. Then Matsumoto proposed taking Onui and Otama to Yoshida as security for the tax payment.

Korenao refused to listen to such a proposal whereupon Matsumoto become angry, and drawing his sword threatened Korenao. Onui, Otama and others present surrounded Korenao to protect him. But Matsumoto brandished his sword killing them and several other girls.

Then a loud noise was heard and white smoke rose to blind all. When the smoke cleared, there sat Korenao, Onui, Otama and the other girls who seemed to have been killed by Matsumoto. On the floor was the blood-covered body of the fox which was once saved by Korenao.

The fox at the sacrifice of its own life had saved the people. The villagers tenderly buried the fox and raised a shrine for it. Onui and Otama then became Buddhist nuns.

EVIL MELON

ONE DAY Fujiwara Michinaga, adviser to the emperor, was resting at home, as it was predicted that some evil might fall upon him on that day, so an old tale goes. Priest Kanshu, the diviner Seimei, physician Tadaaki, and Yoshiie, a warrior, were in attendance, ready to

give their services if required.

Kofukuji Temple sent a messenger to Michinaga's house with a basket of freshly-gathered melons. But considering the day, Michinaga asked the diviner whether to accept the gift or not. Seimei was ordered to give a decision. After divining, Seimei answered that one of the melons in the basket contained poisonous air. He proposed that incantations be said in order to reveal the poison air. So Priest Kanshu was ordered to chant and pray.

While he was praying the melon began to move slightly. Then Michinaga asked Tadaaki to remove the evil air from the melon. Holding the melon in his hands, he turned it around and put in two needles at two spots. The melon stopped moving. Yoshiie was then asked to cut open the melon. As he cut it with his sword, a small snake was found coiled within it, with Tadaaki's needles sticking in its eyes. It was also found that, as Yoshiie cut the melon, his sword had severed its head from its body.

This tale was widely circulated and the people gave great praise to the talents of the priest, diviner, physician and swordsman who attended Michinaga. The life of Michinaga was saved by the wise decisions and acts of those three men. At the same time, the story served to support the popular belief in evil days when all must be careful of their acts in order to avoid the predicted evil.

FALLEN KAMINARI

THUNDER is caused by *Kaminari-sama* (devil of thunder and lightning) who rides on a cloud and beats a thunderous roar on a row of drums on his back, it is traditionally said. The people dread him as the noise of thunder scares them, and lightning damages houses and kills people and animals.

There are many tales of *Kaminari-sama*. But in a *kyogen* (comic Noh drama) play, *Kaminari-sama* has a strange experience.

In the play, a physician started on a journey, and as he was passing through a vast waste field, the sky suddenly became dark. Heavy rain poured down with thunder claps and blinding lightning.

There was no shelter at hand, and trembling in fear he placed himself flat on the ground. Then he heard a loud voice asking, "Who are you, stooping down there?" He answered that he was a poor physician passing through the field. "Are you a physician?" the strange voice said. "I am *Kaminari* but I missed my step and falling down here, I hit my loin so hard I cannot move. If you are a physician, cure me at once and make me well."

The physician said that he only treated human patients, and had no experience with *Kaminari*, so he did not know what to do. But *Kaminari-sama* became angry and roared loudly that if the doctor refused to treat him, he would just seize the physician in his hands and kill him. So the doctor agreed to treat *Kaminari-sama*. Since there was no way to brew his medicine there, the doctor said he had to use a needle-cure.

Taking out a long sharp needle from his medicine box, he pierced it into the loin of *Kaminari*, who cried out in pain as the needle entered his body. Three times the doctor used the needle, and *Kaminari* regained his strength.

Kaminari proposed to give the physician one of his drums as a reward, but the physician refused it saying it was no use to him. He told *Kaminari* that if he wanted to thank him, he should promise to cause no damage by thunder bolts. for 3,000 years. *Kaminari* said that was too long, and they compromised on 800 years.

FIGHTING MOUNTAINS

MANY MOUNTAINS are said to be rivals and fought one another. One of the most famous battles fought by mountains is that between Nikko Mountain and Akagi Mountain. The *kami* of Nikko appeared as a huge snake, and fought the *kami* of Akagi who came as a giant centipede. Then a warrior named Sarumaru-dayu came to join the side of Nikko. He was a great archer and with his long-reaching arrows, managed to defeat the Akagi Mountain *kami*.

To celebrate this victory, each January 4th, the priest of Nikko used to climb to the top of the mountain to conduct a ceremony of sending an arrow in the direction of Akagi.

At Akagi a festival was held on the same day. The service was to draw out the arrow stuck in the door of the Akagi Myojin Shrine, and to offer *mochi* to the mountain *kami*.

The rivalry between Nikko and Akagi strongly influenced the people of both districts. Those who worshiped the Akagi Myojin never made a pilgrimage to Nikko, believing that if they did the Nikko Mountain would become angry and cause a storm to destroy them.

The district of Ushigome in Edo was mainly opened up by people who came from Akagi and erected the Akagi Shrine there. Of course, many Tokugawa retainers also lived in that area, but they could never visit Nikko as they were all *ujiko* or children of Akagi Shrine.

Nikko was the holy place for all Tokugawa men, since the tomb of the founder of the regime was there. Thus, when retainers living in Ushigome were sometimes ordered to go to Nikko on official business, they had to obtain permission from Akagi Shrine to be temporarily released from their association with the shrine, so that they could go to Nikko.

FISH MONUMENT

A MONUMENT was erected to a fish that poisoned many persons who killed and ate it, to appease its anger. This monument still stands at the Ryuhoji Temple at Kikuyabashi, Asakusa, Tokyo.

The story of the monument goes back to 1853, when a little river named Shinborigawa used to run behind the temple, although at present there is no sign of it.

One day a big carp was seen swimming in the river, and one named Tsunejiro jumped into the water to catch it. It was no easy matter to catch the big fish which measured almost a meter. The people gathered to admire the big carp as it was landed by Tsunejiro after a long fight, but they suggested that the fish should be placed in the pond of the temple. So it was put there.

Next day, the fish died in the pond, as a result of being severely beaten by Tsunejiro. The priest wished to bury the fish in the temple cemetery, but many said that it was pitiful to waste such a big, fine fish. So it was finally cut up and cooked in a big kettle.

Forty-seven persons gathered to eat it, it is said. They found it very good, but that night, all of those who ate the fish had a severe stomachache and suffered considerably. Next morning, Tsunejiro who originally caught the fish and five others died.

The neighbors then realized that those who died were killed by the curse of the carp which they ate. Forty-one people, in particular, who ate the fish

but managed to live repented and wished to do something to appease the spirit of the fish. So they erected a stone monument and carved the shape of a carp on its face in prayer for the salvation of the fish they ate.

The carp monument still stands, but the old tradition of the carp is forgotten. It is now generally worshiped as a charm for love, as "*koi*" (carp) also means "love."

FOX MESSENGERS

THE TALES of foxes playing various mischief by taking the form of humans and other objects are told all over the country. But there are also stories in which foxes have served the interest of the people, and for such meritorious conduct they have been enshrined and worshiped.

Among such foxes are those which were kept by feudal lords and trained to be messengers or letter-carriers. Fox messengers were said to have been able to travel several hundred miles in one day.

Iwai Daizen, resident governor under the Lord of Yonezawa once sent an important document to Edo by two carriers. But after dispatching the carriers, he realized that he had sent the draft of the letter instead of the formally written one. Edo was more than 200 kilometers away and there was no way to regain the draft. So he told his trained fox to go and overtake the carriers and change the draft with the formal letter.

The fox went and returned in one day, but it was so exhausted that it soon died. When the original carriers returned home many days later, it was learned that as they neared Edo they became sleepy and while they were dozing the fox reached them and exchanged the letters. So the carriers delivered the properly written letter instead of the draft with which they started, not knowing they were changed.

Often such fox messengers were killed by dogs or trapped by humans. There is a story that once the Lord of Matsumoto in Shinano sent a fox messenger to Kyushu.

The fox taking the form of a man stopped on the way at a rest house. But as he left without paying for his tea, the people became suspicious. To see if the letter-carrier was a man or a fox, they tempted him with a piece of *aburage* or fried *tofu*, which foxes are very fond of. When he grabbed at it they set upon him and killed him. When his body was examined there was a letter written by the Lord of Matsumoto.

FROG GROOM

FROGS FIGURE in many Japanese tales, in which they often act and speak as humans. One of such stories runs as follows:

An old childless couple prayed to *kami* for a child. Soon the old woman found that one of her knees began to swell up, though there was no pain. One day the old man slapped his wife's swollen knee with his hand playfully, whereupon a frog jumped out.

"I am the child sent by *kami*," it shouted. Though it was only a frog, the couple treated it with love as it was given them by *kami-sama*. One day the frog told the couple that he was going to look for a wife and asked them to make *mochi* or rice cakes to take on his trip. Carrying several pieces of *mochi* in a cloth bag, he started on his wife-finding trip.

He came to the home of a wealthy family in a village. He jumped into the house and landed on the *butsudan* or the family Buddhist altar.

When the head of the family came in to offer incense to his ancestors, the frog told him that he was the child of *kami* and wished to stay overnight. He handed the master his bag of *mochi*, saying that it contained his valuables and that if anything in the bag was lost, the family must give him in return the most valuable thing in their possession.

At night, the frog secretly approached the bag left in the master's care, and taking one piece of *mochi*, put it in the mouth of the youngest of the three daughters of the family, who were all fast asleep.

Next morning, the frog angrily shouted that one of his things in the bag was gone and demanded that the youngest daughter be given him. So the frog returned home to the old couple with his beautiful bride and asked that a wedding ceremony be held immediately. The old couple rejoiced at the return of the frog and invited all the villagers to the wedding.

They heated a bath and asked the bride to take her bath first. Then the frog took his bath, but as he jumped into the bathtub, he changed into a fine young man. So all ended happily for the old couple, the frog-man and his bride.

GAMBLER'S LUCK

ONCE THERE was a young *samurai* who had nothing else to boast of but his pious pilgrimages to Kiyomizu Temple. In fact, he had the rare record of making a thousand-day pilgrimage twice, without skipping a single day. Thus he was certain to receive the most favorable protection of Buddha and gain happiness and salvation.

This pious *samurai* was also very fond of gambling. In gambling he lost everything. His swords, clothing and all he owned were already offered as gambling stakes. Finally he offered to stake his two thousand-day pilgrimages to Kiyomizu Temple. All laughed at his offer, but one gambler finally came out to take up his strange bid. They played amidst the curious watching friends, and the *samurai* lost.

The winner wanted to make the transfer of the two thousand-day pilgrimages truly binding. He took the *samurai* to Kiyomizu Temple, and there in the presence of the temple priest he made the loser write a note surrendering his pilgrimages. Thus the transaction was completed.

From then on, the *samurai* lost all his luck. He became poorer and poorer, and finally be was arrested for some minor crime and put in jail.

On the other hand, the winner, with the protection of the two thousand-day pilgrimages, was successful at anything he put his hands on. Becoming wealthy, he married. Not only did he enjoy a very happy family life, but he also rose in influence and became an important local official.

The winning gambler's luck was entirely due, it is said, to the pilgrimages to Kiyomizu which he won from the unfortunate *samurai*.

GHOST SHIPS

THERE ARE still some old fishermen who like to tell their experiences of meeting ghost ships on the sea. There are various tales of *yurei-sen* or ghost ships, and while such stories are hard to believe, some strange phenomena might have caused such belief in them.

Ghost ships run against the wind and her lights are never reflected on the sea surface, it is believed in many parts. Sometimes fishermen hear voices on a ghost ship, but are never able to make out the shape of the ship.

A ghost ship, it has been said, will suddenly appear in front of a fishing boat, but if the boatmen stop their ship,

the ghost ship disappears. It charges fast toward a boat, and if the boatman steers to one side in order to avoid hitting the mystery ship, the phantom ship will change her course and keep on coming upon the boat.

As the ghost ship nears, a voice comes out of her demanding the loan of a water dipper. If the boat man lends a dipper, it will be used by the ghost ship's men to pour water into the boat.

In some places it is believed that if one throws cooked rice into the ghost ship, it will disappear.

There are many ways by which one may be able to distinguish ordinary ships from ghost ships, it is said.

When in doubt bake a fish or human hair on the boat; if it is a ghost ship then it will disappear. Or touch his own boat with an iron fire tong, and then, if it is a ghost ship, it will vanish. When one looks at a ghost ship through the narrow space between fingers, or two pieces of wood, it will become invisible.

Old fishermen were afraid to meet a ghost ship because they thought it was a sign of some bad luck. Some also believed that the spirits of shipwrecked crews appeared on a ghost ship, and the custom of throwing cooked rice developed from this belief.

GOLD BUDDHA

ONCE THERE lived a rich man who was an ardent Buddha worshiper, and it was his great pride that he possessed a beautiful gold Buddha statue which he worshiped daily. A young servant who was also an eager Buddhist worked at his house and he hoped that one day he would possess such a fine Buddha statue as his master's.

When the servant went to the mountain one day to gather wood, he found a piece of tree-root that was shaped like a Buddha statue. He carried it home, and placing it in his room offered it flowers and food. But seeing him worshiping the crude statue, his master and other servants laughed at him.

As the servant was honest and hardworking, the master hoped to keep him in his employ and thought up a plan to make him stay long. He proposed a wrestling match between his gold Buddha and the servant's statue, and said that if his gold Buddha lost the match he would give the servant all his wealth, but if the tree-root Buddha lost the servant would have to work for him all his life.

So the match was arranged. The servant rushed into his room and spoke to his Buddha that his master had proposed the unreasonable match and expressed his fear that he would lose. He would rather run away with his Buddha, he said. But the Buddha told him to have no fear.

So he took the statue to the room where the match was to take place. But he was sad because he knew he would lose. As the two statues were placed to wrestle, the master urged his gold Buddha to win, while the servant shouted to him to wrestle bravely.

But the gold statue began to weaken and finally fell down and lost. The tree-root statue was placed where the gold statue stood before and all gathered to worship it.

The beaten master had to leave his house, carrying his gold Buddha. He had to beg for food and lodging. He asked the statue why such ill-fortune came on him. The statue answered that its opponent might be a tree-root, but the servant sincerely worshiped it. The master had no faith in his statue and so his support had given it no strength.

GRATEFUL WASP

YOGO-DAYU who had his castle near the town of Miwa was defeated by his enemy, and had to leave his stronghold with only a handful of men, so an old story goes.

He hid himself in a cave in Hatsuse Mountain. Over the entrance of the cave, he saw a spider weaving its web. Then a wasp was caught in the web, and was struggling to free himself. Himself being chased by enemies, Yogo-dayu entertained a sense of compassion for the wasp and released it from the spider's snare.

In his dream that evening, the wasp appeared and thanked him for his kindness in freeing it. The wasp then said that it would teach him how to defeat the enemy. When Yogo-dayu said that it was impossible, the wasp said that it had a fine plan.

"Gather at least twenty or thirty men, and then I will do the rest," the wasp said. "In the mountain behind there are hundreds of my comrades in their nests. Build a temporary hut near the former site of your castle, and gather as many gourds, jars, and bottles as possible. Then see what I will do."

So Yogo-dayu did as he was advised by the wasp. In no time hundreds of big wasps came and hid themselves in the gourds, jars and bottles. The leader wasp came to Yogo-dayu and told him to send a message to his enemy, inviting them to come for a talk.

As the note was dispatched, about three hundred men on horses surrounded Yogo-dayu's hut. But as the enemy came charging, the wasps flew out from their hiding places and surrounded them. The enemy soldiers, though brave and skillful in the use of swords, did not know how to fight the attacking wasps. Soon they were in pain and ran away pell-mell, leaving behind many dead wasps.

Yogo-dayu and his men gathered the

bodies of the dead wasps, and burying them, erected a small shrine over the place.

Years later, a grandson of the enemy leader, who became a Buddhist priest, came to the spot and burned the shrine up, as it was erected by Yogo-dayu who had defeated his grandfather. But for this act he was chased out of his temple.

GROWING CHOPSTICKS

ALL OVER the country stories are told of chopsticks growing into big trees. There even stand up to this present day, so it is said, huge towering trees that grew up from chopsticks that were planted in the earth by some great persons centuries ago.

The oldest of this tradition may be one about the giant *sugi* or cryptomeria tree of Sugizaka, Shiga Prefecture, as it is said that, when Amaterasu-omikami, mythological founder of the nation, took her luncheon there, she planted her chopsticks into the ground.

When Prince Shotoku erected the Kudara Temple in the same province, he put his chopsticks into the ground, and prayed that if the temple would grow in influence, chopsticks would also prosper and blossom. The chopsticks grew into two giant trees and have blossomed beautifully.

When a poor Buddhist pilgrim reached the Kannon Temple in Okayama, his feet were sore, and he did not know if he could continue his journey. So he put his chopsticks into the ground and prayed for a safe trip. He was surprised when he passed the same spot several years later, to see two giant willow trees standing on the exact spot where he had left his chopsticks. Thus the name of *Futatsu-yanagi* (two willows) was given to the locality. Some 200 years ago the two willows were washed away by a flood and new trees were planted in their place, it is said.

This tradition of growing chopsticks is heard at many places, but authorities now say that the people never believed that chopsticks would grow into trees. They believed that the power of *kami* or Buddha would be able to do anything, however impossible. When some saints or influential persons visited their locality, the ignorant people thought that such miracles would happen. Thus their trust in the divine power, and their expectation of some miraculous act have given rise to this tradition of growing chopsticks, it is explained.

GUARDIAN SISTERS

IN OKINAWA, brothers have great respect for their sisters, who are considered their guardians. Sister respect has reached almost the degree of religious worship.

When a young man goes on a journey, he carries a lock of his sister's hair, or a *tenugui* (Japanese towel) given by her as a talisman to protect him during the trip. The talisman *tenugui* is usually white and made of palm fiber cloth or cotton.

A commonly sung Okinawa song runs:

"Onari-ga tesaji, maboru kandaimono, Hikimawachi tamaware, Yamato made-mo" (The sister's *tenugui* is my guardian deity, protect me even to the land of Nihon.)

Once a young man went out on a boat, but a storm arose and caused a big leak, a story says. He prayed to the *tenugui* given by his sister, and a *Takase* (shellfish) appeared, filing the gap in the ship bottom. So he managed to return safely. Ever since hats worn by the people to shade them from the sun have been made in the shape of *Takase* shells.

Young men so respect their sisters that at New Year's celebrations and other festivals, special festive foods are first offered to the sister.

In Okinawa, sisters are called *Onari*. But this term is also used in many districts of Japan proper. In many rural areas, the women who bring the midday lunch to the ricefield at rice-planting time are called *Onari*. In Hiroshima district, women's work in cooking is called *Onari*.

In many places, also, *Onari* is mentioned in rice-planting songs. Thus it is believed that women who served in the sacred religious rice-planting ritual were called by this name.

HATSUSHIMA LEGEND

HATSUSHIMA, a little island off Atami, Shizuoka, which is reached in one hour by motor boat from the popular hot spring resort, is famous for camellia blossoms and the sad love story of Ohatsu and Ukon. But the popularly told story of Ohatsu is a modern version of a much older legend that goes back to mythological days.

The female deity of the island and the male deity of Izusan on the mainland were in love. To meet her love the female deity used to go to the mainland every night on a raft, guided by the bonfire made by the male deity. One night, however, a storm arose, and extinguished the bonfire. The female deity struggled in the storm and darkness and finally perished. Her body was washed to the shore under Izusan mountain.

The male deity was later enshrined at Izusan Shrine. The female deity is still worshiped as the guardian deity of Hatsushima Island.

This was the original legend of Hatsushima, but it was made more romantic as time went on. According to the commonly told version, Ohatsu, a 17-year-old maiden of Hatsushima fell in love with Ukon, a young man of the mainland. Ohatsu promised to marry him after 100 visits to the mainland.

Nightly she set out in a big wooden tub which she used for bathing, and the young man burned a bonfire on the hill to guide her. But on the 99th night, another young man who was jealous of the love between Ohatsu and Ukon, extinguished the bonfire. Losing sight of the guiding light, Ohatsu could not reach the mainland, and died in the sea.

The young man who had patiently waited for the last of the 100 visits of Ohatsu after which they could be happily married was so sad when he found that Ohatsu had died that he entered the priesthood, determined to devote his life to the task of praying for the salvation of his lost love.

HOKO-SAN

HOKO-SAN (service maid) is a crude stubby papier-mache doll made in Kagawa Prefecture, Shikoku, representing a house-maid dressed in country dress. But it is not a doll for play. It is a charm worshiped by the people. When a child is sick, it is made to hold *Hoko-san* in its arms. Then the doll is thrown into the sea. It is believed that the doll will carry away the sickness and restore the child to health.

Once there was a country maid named Omaki, who was not beautiful but a good, tenderhearted girl. She entered the service of a *samurai* (warrior) household and was given the duty of looking after the young daughter of the family.

But the daughter became seriously ill, and physicians did everything possible for her, but it was announced that her sickness was incurable and contagious. Thinking in her little heart that if she caught the disease from the daughter, it might be possible to cure her, Omaki purposely became infected with the dreadful sickness.

As she had caught the disease now, Omaki was sent to an isolated island, as all feared that she might further spread the sickness. Left alone there, the faithful little maid died.

This traditional tale gave birth to the *Hoko-san* doll. Not only did it become famous as a folk doll of the district, but because of Omaki's eager desire to cure the sickness of her charge, the crude doll made after her became a charm for curing the sickness of children.

Kagawa Prefecture is famous for many papier-mache dolls. Besides the *Hoko-san* which is the most widely known novelty, there are also *yome-iri* dolls. *Yome-iri* (wedding) dolls are little dolls representing *tai* (sea bream), and other happy figures. It is customary in the district for a bride to take many of the dolls to the children of the family and relatives of the groom. The more dolls that are brought, the happier will be the marriage, it is believed.

HUNTER'S DOG

ONCE IN THE district of Nanbu in the northeastern region, there was a famous hunter named Sataroku, whose skill in hunting bears and boars was recognized by the lord of Nanbu. Thus he was given an official permit to hunt on any mountain of the country.

As it was Sataroku's habit to hunt bears in the early spring when they would come out of their winter holes, one spring day he set out with his dog Shiro (white) to look for them in the mountain. Seeing none, he went deeper into the mountain. Soon he found that he had entered the Sannohe district, which was beyond the ridge from the Nanbu area.

He realized then that he had forgot-

ten to bring with him the official permit allowing him to hunt anywhere, but he was already too far from home to go back for it. As he went along the mountain ridge, his dog barked and he saw a big blue boar. He aimed and shot his gun but the boar disappeared.

As he went up, he found blood marks on the snow, leading down to the valley beyond. The boar had gone down the valley, dead or wounded, he knew, and when he followed the blood, he found the dead boar at the bottom.

Then suddenly two hunters appeared and said that the boar had been killed by them. Sataroku and the two argued. Then the two said that if Sataroku was from Nanbu, he had no right to hunt on the ridge. Sataroku did not have his permit with him and was unable to prove his right. So he was taken as a poacher to the district office where he was immediately beheaded for his crime.

When he was arrested, his dog Shiro hurried home, and entering the house jumped up at the *kamidana* (family shrine) in which the permit was kept. As the dog repeatedly tried to jump up on the shrine, Sataroku's wife realized that the dog wanted to get at the permit. When she gave the paper to the dog, it rushed outside.

Shiro was too late, for his master was already killed. The dog remained there and kept on barking sadly for several days. So the spot where Sataroku was executed came to be known as *Inuboe-mori* or dog-barking forest.

IMOSE-JIMA

A MAN AND HIS WIFE of Tosa province, Shikoku, were so poor they had no farmland to cultivate, an old story goes. So they left their native village and went to another province, where by sheer effort they managed to cultivate a farm and obtain good crops. Gradually they came to possess a large stock of foodstuffs, as well as many household goods and implements.

So they decided to return home to their native place with all their valuable possessions. Hiring a boat, they loaded all their valuables on it to take home. They also wished to take home some good workers with them to help them cultivate their new farm. So the man and his wife went to find such help, leaving only a boy and a girl, both 10 years old, on the boat to keep watch on the goods.

The boat was tied to a stake by the seashore, but somehow the rope became untied and began to drift with the tide, before the two children knew what had happened. Alarmed, they shouted for help, but nobody came. They could only cry aloud in despair as the tide carried the boat southward. After many days of both fair weather and storms, the boat reached a little island.

The children found no inhabitants there. Fortunately there was a stock of food on the boat, which sustained them. They also realized that a bag of seed rice was among the most valuable of their possessions. So they planted the seeds, and cultivated the land as best they could.

The first crop was good, and so they lived together on the island with no other inhabitants. Many years passed and the children grew up. Finally they became man and wife.

Thus the island came to be known as *Imose-jima* or man-and-wife island as there were no others living there. This small island is believed to have existed south of Tosa province, Shikoku.

INOKASHIRA BENTEN

THE BENTEN SHRINE in the Inokashira Park of Tokyo has an interesting snake story. A wealthy family in the neighborhood named Suzuki had no children, and the husband and wife prayed to the Inokashira Benten for a child. Their prayers were soon answered, and the wife gave birth to a girl.

The child grew up into a beautiful girl. The parents had difficulty in selecting her husband, as there were so many proposals, but finally a decision was made, and the date of the wedding ceremony was set.

Just before the day of the wedding, the girl asked her parents' permission to visit Benten Shrine to express thanks for the divine protection it had always given her. The parents consented, telling a man in their employ to accompany her.

When she arrived at the shrine, she asked the man to leave her and go home. But as he had been instructed by her parents to look after her, he was reluctant to do so. As the girl insisted, he decided to obey her, but watched her without being seen.

As he watched, the girl jumped into the pond of the shrine and became a huge snake. Surprised, he ran home and told of what he had seen. The parents realized then that the girl had been sent by Benten-sama herself, as they wanted a child so much. But as she could not marry a mortal, she had left and returned to the Benten Shrine pond.

JAPANESE CINDERELLA

WHEN A fisherman dived into the sea for fish one day, he found at the bottom a Buddha statue. He carried it home and erected a little hut to house the statue. Buddha, appearing before him in a dream, thanked him for erecting the hut and asked him to tell what he desired most.

The fisherman had a little daughter,

but her beauty was marred by her thin and short hair. He was greatly worried over this, and so he asked Buddha to give her long, black and luxuriant hair.

Buddha kept his word, and soon the daughter's hair became long and thick. As she grew up, she became beautiful, with her wonderful hair reaching over 10 feet. Her long hair was the envy of all the girls of the neighborhood. Her father thought much of her tresses as they were a gift of Buddha. When any hair fell from her head, he picked it up and placed it on a branch of a garden tree, so that none would step upon the hair given by Buddha.

As the emperor was one day watching a sparrow making its nest on the eaves of the palace roof, he noticed a long hair trailing down from the nest. It was undoubtedly human hair which the bird must have brought to its nest. He wanted to see the owner of such wonderfully long hair. So he sent out a notice to find this girl.

It was not difficult to find her, as no other girl had hair 10 feet long. When she was brought before him, the emperor was so pleased with her beauty that she was made to live at the palace. As it was her long hair given by Buddha that had brought her the good luck, she asked the emperor to build a fine temple for the statue which her father had found in the sea. Her wish was granted, and a magnificent temple was constructed.

Thus it is traditionally said that the Dojoji Temple in Wakayama Prefecture, which later became famous because of the love story of a young girl, Kiyohime, and a Buddhist priest, Anchin, and dramatized into both *Noh* and *Kabuki* plays under the title of *Dojoji*, came to be erected.

JEALOUS BRIDGES

THERE are in Japanese tradition many bridges which are jealous of others which are either longer or more famous than themselves.

There was once the famous bridge in Kai or present Yamanashi Prefecture, named Kunitamo-no-ohashi. It was the longest bridge in the province, being almost 360 meters long and also a very old one. The bridge was the pride of the neighboring people.

But everyone walking over the bridge was warned not to speak of the Enkyo bridge or recite pieces from the *Noh* drama 'Nonomiya.'

The big bridge of Kunitamo was jealous of the fame enjoyed by the Enkyo bridge, also of the same province. The Enkyo bridge is not as long as the Kunitamo, being only about 100 feet in length. But it runs over a gorge more than 100 feet deep, and furthermore the bridge is very skillfully constructed with no support underneath. The gorge is also famous for its scenic beauty, and many still go there merely to see the beauty of the wooded mountains on both sides and the rushing gorge far below. Thus the Enkyo or Monkey Bridge became the most famous suspension bridge in the country.

The *Noh* drama 'Nonomiya' is a story sympathizing with a jealous woman. The bridge does not like any piece from the *Noh* sung on it, probably as it reminds it of its own jealousy.

Thus if anyone mentions the Enkyo, or recites a short piece from 'Nonomiya,' it has been traditionally believed that the bridge will become angry and cause some terrible misfortune to befall him.

JINDAIJI HORSE

JINDAIJI TEMPLE, which is located near Fuchu, Tokyo, is one of the oldest temples in the Kanto or Tokyo area. It was first erected in 733. Its main Buddha statue is famous, although the present temple building is of quite recent construction.

The temple's spacious wooded compounds attract many hikers and picnickers. Visitors eagerly purchase the Jindaiji straw horse as a souvenir. It is crudely made, about 10 cm high, and presents a horse firmly planting its legs and neighing. It comes in pairs, one horse having a red and white tape wound about its belly, and the other a patterned tape.

The straw horse is a modern product, but the origin is based on a poem included in the *Manyoshu*, the oldest collection of poems. The poem tells of a man who was suddenly called to the army, and hurriedly had to start for Kyushu in the south without time even to catch his pastured horse. The straw horse is made to represent the brown horse the man had to leave behind.

A number of years ago when it happened to be the year of the horse, a man called Asada Rikizo living near the temple thought of making straw horses after the sentiment expressed in the old poem. The horse gained popularity at once and has come to be highly appreciated by lovers and collectors of folk toys.

JINDAIJI TEMPLE

THERE IS A strange story about the origin of Jindaiji Temple in Chofu, a suburb of Tokyo. It goes back to the Nara period, more than 12 centuries ago, when the district was called Kashiwano.

There lived a rich village head named Ukon who was fond of hunting, but his wife was a woman of compassion and repeatedly asked her husband to stop killing animals and birds. Her daily words against killing innocent creatures finally made Ukon give up hunting.

The family became very happy and their daughter grew up to be a beautiful girl. One day a young man named Fukuman came to the village and fell in love with Ukon's daughter.

Learning of the love affair between his daughter and Fukuman, Ukon became angry, strongly opposing the marriage of the two. To keep his daughter from the young man, Ukon put her on a little boat and let it drift on a lake nearby.

Fukuman saw the boat going away from the shore to a distant island, and prayed that he might also be carried across the lake, promising to erect a great temple in appreciation, if his wish came true. Before his prayer ended, a huge turtle appeared in the lake. Riding on its back, he soon reached the island and was reunited with the girl.

This strange incident so impressed Ukon that the young man must be a gifted one that he allowed them to marry. Soon a boy was born to them and when he grew to be a young man, he became a Buddhist priest. He went to China to study and on his return erected a temple as his father had promised in his prayer. This is the Jindaiji Temple. He came to be known as Priest Manku.

Besides the temple there is a shrine called Kohaku Shrine on the very spot where Ukon's residence stood, dedicated to Ukon and his wife.

Many persons, however, say that this story was made up as a means to spread the Buddhist faith among the people in the Musashi area many centuries ago.

JO-FUKU

IT IS HISTORICALLY known that Hsu Fu was a high official under the first emperor of the Chin dynasty of China in the third century. But there is a widely circulated legend that he came to Japan on his emperor's order to obtain the elixir of life, or a medicine that would make a man perenially young and immortal.

It is said that he left China for Japan with several thousand soldiers and servants in many big ships. But on the way he encountered many storms and when he arrived, his party was cut down to less than half.

In the town of Shingu, Wakayama Prefecture, a shrine has been erected to him. There is also his tomb and those of seven of his men.

In Japan, Hsu Fu is called Jo-fuku. The shrine for Jo-fuku is of Chinese architecture. The people of the neighborhood say that the shrine is very old and has been rebuilt many times. His tomb stands not far from the shrine.

Jo-fuku is highly respected and locally his shrine and tomb are visited by the people. It is told that after he settled at Shingu, he taught techniques of navigation and the art of whaling to Japanese fishermen and others of the area.

Thus he died greatly respected and loved by all his neighbors. But nothing is told about the magic medicine he came so far to find. Some say that because he could not find it, he did not go back to China.

JUMYO-GAI

THE STORY of a woman living several hundred years, retaining her youth and beauty by eating a strange shellfish is told in many coastal districts. The magic shellfish is called *jumyo-gai* (long-life shellfish) or *mannen-gai* (10,000-year shellfish).

A boatman of Chikuzen, Kyushu, once entered the port of Tsugaru in the northeastern part of the country. When he landed he went inland where he met a beautiful woman about 30 years old. They began to talk, and when the boatman said that he came from Chikuzen, the woman's face brightened with joy. She told him that she was also from that district.

She told him much about Chikuzen, but many things she said were unintelligible to him. As he looked puzzled, she explained that she was speaking of matters that took place many hundreds of years before. She said she was 640 years old, and had outlived 24 husbands.

When she was young, she had become very ill and a kindly person brought her a strange shellfish to eat, she said. From then she had become stronger and younger. When her children and grandchildren had died, she left her native place and went to many different areas, marrying 24 times.

The shell out of which she had eaten the magic meat, she said, she had buried under the pine tree in Chikuzen to which Empress Jingu had tied her boat before she left the place. She asked the boatman to look for it when he returned to Chikuzen.

The boatman found the shell buried under the pine tree as the mysterious woman in Tsugaru had told him. He treasured it as the shell still had its magic power. When the sick were made to drink water out of the shell, they miraculously recovered and became stronger than before.

His shell became so famous in the community that in the ninth year of Kansei or 1797, he was called before the

Lord of Chikuzen to tell the story of the miraculous life-giving shell, so an old book says.

KAMI ROCKS

ON THE SHORE of Kushiro Bay, Hokkaido, there stand two rocks which are worshiped by the Ainu as the male and female *kami* (god) stones. The male stone stands near the sea and is round in shape, about two meters across, and stands a meter high. The female stone is about 35 meters inland, and is about a half meter across and a quarter meter high.

The following story is told about the stones:

Soon after the Earth was formed, the heavenly *kami* looked down on it and observed how the humans were living. The *kami* saw that the Ainu were almost naked and ate the crabs they caught. Saddened by such a condition of the Ainu, the *kami* took pity on them.

To teach them a better way of life, the heavenly *kami* sent down a male and a female *kami*. The male *kami* taught the Ainu how to catch fish with line and hook, and obtain animals with arrows while the female *kami* taught the Ainu women how to use fire, weave cloth and sew.

Thus the Ainu came to lead a much happier life. As their mission was finished, the male *kami* and the female *kami* decided to return to heaven. But the Ainu wanted them to remain.

The two *kami* could not reject their wishes. Desiring that even the future descendants of those Ainu should be allowed to enjoy the happiness they managed to give the people, they turned themselves into two stones.

It was their intention to be with the Ainu always, standing by the seashore and reminding them of their goodwill and hope for their happiness.

In 1909 when work for constructing Kushiro harbor was started, the Ainu *kami* rocks were marked to be destroyed. But as a workman put his chisel on the male rock, he suddenly moaned and fell down. He was carried to Kushiro Hospital, but died in three days. So the rocks have been left untouched.

KANNON'S GUIDE

A YOUNG *SAMURAI* who had no position, no money, no family and no friends prostrated himself before the Kannon Temple at Hase and asked Kannon to guide him as to what to do, an old story goes. As he sat there so long, the priest took pity on him and brought him some food. He ate but refused to leave the spot. Finally the priests had to carry him out bodily.

As he left the temple, he picked up a piece of straw by the road. A little way ahead, a horsefly flew around his head and annoyed him. So he caught the fly and tied it to the straw.

As he passed a richly decorated cart, a small boy looked out and wanted the *samurai's* horsefly on the straw. He willingly gave it to the boy. In thanks he was given three big oranges.

Then he met a group of persons standing on the road. On approaching them he saw that one woman of the party was sick and wanted water to drink. But as no house was near, there was no way to get water. So he offered his three oranges to her. In appreciation the woman gave him three rolls of white cloth.

Further on, he saw a horse down the road. The horse was dead and the owner was lamenting because it had been a good horse, and he could not take back even its hide. The *samurai* bought the dead horse with one roll of cloth, and then covered the horse's body with another. Suddenly the horse revived and stood up. With the horse he went to a farmhouse, and paid for his lodging and the horse's fodder with the last roll.

The owner of the house loved riding horses and wanted to go on a trip. He asked the *samurai* to let him go on a trip on his horse, and to take care of the house and farm while he was away. So the *samurai* settled down on the farm, and made a tenant cultivate it. The owner never came back, and the *samurai* became a wealthy, happy man.

KAWAGOE DAISHI

THE KITAIN TEMPLE, commonly called Kawagoe Daishi, at Kawagoe, Saitama Prefecture, is one of the oldest temples in Kanto. It was originally established in 830, and some parts of the structure built at the beginning of the 17th century are still preserved. The temple possesses many valuable art and religious relics.

The important position the temple held in the old days may be judged from the fact that when Tokugawa Ieyasu died in 1616 at Kunozan (Shizuoka Prefecture) his body rested at this temple for four days on its way to Nikko to be buried.

Many traditional tales, mostly related to snakes, dragons and storms, are told about this ancient temple. The region is famous for thunderstorms and strong winds, and it is likely such tales developed from this fact.

Once at midnight, an unknown woman called at the temple, one of the Kitain stories goes. When the priest saw her, she asked that the temple bell should not be rung for 100 days from that day. The woman was so serious and earnest in her request that the priest had to comply with it, in fear of some evil she might bring upon the temple.

Not understanding the purpose of her wish, the priest followed the woman when she left the temple, but she disappeared completely near a deep ditch at the south end of the temple.

True to his word, the priest did not sound the bell for 99 days. Then when the last day came, the priest had another mysterious woman visitor who asked him to ring the temple bell which had been silent so long.

The priest was in a perplexing situation. One day more and the promise to the first woman would be kept, but he could not refuse the earnest wish of the second woman. Finally he consented, whereupon the woman asked to have the temple bell sounded at once.

When the deep note of the bell sounded after the long silence, the woman suddenly turned into a dragon and disappeared. But the bell did not give out a deep, sonorous trailing sound as it did before. The priest finally found out that the first woman was a dragon that did not like the sound of the temple bell, and the second was another dragon that loved it.

KIKIMIMI

MANY COUNTRIES have stories of poor men becoming suddenly rich or meeting unexpected good fortune, because they were able to understand the words of birds and animals. Japan also has many such little tales, which are generally named *kikimimi* or hearing ear.

In many northeastern districts it is called *kikimimi-zukin* or hearing hood, which is believed to be made of red cloth. One wearing this hood over his head will be able to understand birds and animals.

It is said that a poor but pious man received one from Inari-san, a local deity. With its help he was able to hear from birds the cause of the sickness of the daughter of the village's richest family. He tells the girl's father what his daughter is suffering from, and thus she soon recovers. He is richly rewarded and becomes wealthy.

The story of Jido Maru whose mother is said to have been a fox is very well-known. When the boy put his ear to a treasure left by his mother, he heard a bird say, 'Jido Maru, go to the capital, and you will prosper. Go quickly.' So he went to the capital, and there he became famous as a fortune-teller, telling people's fortunes by listening to the bird in the treasure.

Kikimimi or listening ear is sometimes confused with the famous story of Urashima, the Japanese Rip Van Winkle.

While the queen of *Ryugu* or Undersea Paradise was swimming in the form of a *tai* (sea-bream), she was attacked by a bigger fish. A fisherman saved her. The queen took him to *Ryugu* to express her thanks. Then a maid to the queen told him that the queen would certainly offer to reward him, but that he should never ask for money or jewels. She advised him to ask for *kikimimi*. Receiving *kikimimi* and using it, he learned from a bird that the pebbles in a certain river were all gold. He went there and gathered the gold. Furthermore, he was told by another bird that the daughter of the local lord was made ill by a snake. He told the lord, and the girl recovered and he was rewarded with her hand in marriage.

In Gifu there is a story that a certain *sake*-brewer had a strange box, and when one put his ear to it, he heard the talk of the underground world. It is said that once an apprentice of the *sake*-brewer saved a turtle, and he was given this strange box that would help anyone to hear what was being said underground.

KINTARO

KINTARO is the idol of Japanese boys. He stands for health, strength, a good nature and loyalty. Mothers pray that their boys will grow up as strong and natural as Kintaro, to whom are attributed all qualities desirable in boys. Kintaro is nature's boy, unspoiled by evil associations.

Kintaro is one of the most common toys for boys, and is found among the dolls displayed at the boys' festival of May. Kintaro is represented in the doll as a boy of about 5 or 6 years old, robust and healthy. He is always naked and his skin is pink. The whole body is well-developed, and somewhat fat. He leads a bear on a rope, and carries a big hatchet over his shoulder.

Kintaro was a boy raised in the mountains of Ashigara by his mother, according to commonly accepted tradition. Living with the mountain woman, he had no other boys to play with. Bears and other wild animals were his daily playmates. Thus living a life of nature, he grew strong and healthy. He did not spend his days in play alone, but went into the forests and cut down huge trees with his hatchet to obtain kindling wood for his mother. He was obedient to her and did everything to help her.

So in the people's mind, Kintaro is always associated with bears and big hatchets. But particularly the unspoiled boyishness of Kintaro that developed from his solitary life with nature in densely forested mountains is the characteristic the people value most.

The story of Kintaro originated with Kintoki Sakata, one of the four famed fighting men in the service of Yorimitsu Minamoto, commonly called Raiko, one of the generals of the Court in the 10th century. Kintoki was particularly known for his physical strength and superb fighting ability. Later, people regarded him as a model fighting man. His boyhood name was Kintaro, and so the tradition of Kintaro developed. In old Japan, boys had boyhood names which they discarded upon attaining manhood and adopted adult names.

KINTARO SARDINES

IWASHI or sardines are abundantly caught in the seas around Japan, and have been the most popular fish eaten by the people, but in the old days, they were not eaten by the upper classes as *iwashi* were common and cheap.

It is recorded that Murasaki-shikibu (11th century), the famous authoress of *Genji-monogatari*, was very fond of *iwashi*, but whenever the smell of the *iwashi* being grilled was noticed in the house, her husband Nobukata scolded her severely for eating the lowly fish.

Iwashi caught in Amano-hashidate Bay, Kyoto, has been regarded the best-tasting and is commonly called *Kintaro iwashi*.

There is a tale about the origin of this *iwashi*. Fujiwara Yasumasa, lord of Tamba, was enjoying a boat picnic one summer day in the bay of Amano-hashidate. Accidentally he dropped into the sea his favorite treasure made in the shape of a golden cask. As he did not wish to lose his treasure, he called many fishermen out and made them search for it with nets. The nets brought up many sardines, but no gold treasure. The lord was very angry, but the fishermen told him that he must be satisfied because although he had lost the gold cask, a quantity of such excellent sardines had been caught.

They came to be called *Kintaru-iwashi* (gold-cask sardines) which later changed to *Kintaro-iwashi*. Because of the rich plankton in the bay, the

sardines at Amano-hashidate are of superior quality.

When the sardines are grilled, they give off a very strong smell. It was believed from early days that the heads of grilled sardines would drive away devils and evils with their strong smell. More than 1,000 years ago, sardine heads came to be placed at the gates of the Imperial Court as a charm against evils. This custom is still followed by many families in the New Year season.

KITCHEN GOD

ON THE WALL behind the *kamado* or cooking stove in many houses of Tohoku, the northeastern district of Japan, a crude wooden mask representing an ugly boy is placed as the guardian of the kitchen.

Once in that district there lived an old couple. One day the old man went to the mountain to gather kindling. He found a cave on the mountainside. As it was said that an open cave would invite some evil spirit to live in it, he decided to close the opening with his bundle of tree branches. As he put one bundle at the opening, it slid inside. So he placed another, but that also went in. He soon found that all the bundles he had gathered over three months had all gone into the cave.

Suddenly a beautiful woman came out and thanked him for the bundles he gave her. At her invitation, the old man entered the cave and found therein a great house with all his bundles of branches stacked high.

He was treated to a good meal, and as he was leaving, the woman brought an ugly child, and asked the old man to take him home. The child was really ugly, and at the old man's house he did nothing but put his finger on his navel all the time.

Annoyed at this habit, the old man

one day picked up a *hibashi* or fire tongs and hit sharply at the boy's navel. As he did so a gold nugget rolled out. He jabbed at his navel with a *hibashi* three times a day, and every time a nugget came out. He was then happy and began to live a comfortable life.

But the old woman was greedy, and when the old man was away, she pushed the *hibashi* repeatedly and forcefully at the child's navel. But no gold came out, and the boy died.

That night, the boy appeared in the old man's dream and said, 'Don't cry for me. Make a mask of my ugly face, and place it where everybody will see it, and then prosperity will come to you.'

So the old man carved out a likeness of the child's face, and placed the mask over the *kamado*. It continued to bring him good luck. Thus the custom of hanging the mask is followed in the district.

KOBO DAISHI

KUKAI, who is more commonly known as Kobo Daishi, was a great Buddhist priest who travelled extensively throughout the country for the salvation of the people until he died in 834 at the age of 61. He was so eagerly welcomed and respected everywhere that traditional tales are still told of his visits, including stories of miracles.

At innumerable spots throughout the country there are bamboo or other trees which have grown from the walking cane of Kobo Daishi. At some places, so it is told, a big forest has sprouted from a single cane.

He was so fond of travelling that he did not stop travelling even after his death, it is said. There is a statue of him at Koyasan Temple, Wakayama Prefecture, which was built by him, and every year on April 21 a ceremony is held of changing the garment covering the statue. When the old one is taken off, its lower edge is frayed and spotted with mud, showing that he went to distant rural villages during the year.

Many wells and springs are attributed to him. Particularly, whenever he visited districts where the supply of good water was short, he opened a well of good water by sticking his cane into the ground. Such springs or wells are named after him.

At the Shimizu Inari Shrine, Shimizu-cho, Yanaka, just behind Ueno Park, Tokyo, there used to be a small pond. This pond was made by Kobo Daishi when he saw an old woman carrying a bucket of water on her head from quite a distance and felt sorry for her. It was believed that the water of the pond cured diseases.

When Kobo Daishi visited Kanamari, Awa in Chiba Prefecture, an old woman gave him a bowl of rice gruel, but it tasted watery. She explained that she was too poor to buy salt. Kobo Daishi thrust his cane into the ground, and immediately a pond was formed filled with salt water.

KOBUTORI

THE STORY of *kobutori* (tumor snatching) is one of the oldest and most widely told folk tales of the country, with many variations according to district.

An old man who had a *kobu* or a big fleshy tumor on his right cheek, went hunting and came to a dense forest. A thunderstorm broke out, and trying to find shelter, he entered a cave he found on a mountainside. As he entered, he heard voices. He was afraid but went in, following the voices. He saw several devils sitting together and drinking, each taking turns in dancing. Stimulated by the atmosphere, the old man could not help stepping out and dancing, to the utter surprise of the devils.

'Who is he?' all shouted. But his dance charmed them all and they applauded him loudly. The devils then asked him to come again and dance for them. He willingly promised to do so. Then one devil proposed that he should be made to leave something behind so that he would come back again. They argued over what to make him leave. Finally one of them pointed to a big *kobu* on the man's face. Since it was a charm of good fortune, if they took the *kobu*, he would surely return. So they held him and removed the *kobu*.

When the old man returned home, the neighbors asked him how he came to lose his *kobu*. Another man who had a tumor on his left cheek heard the story, and wanted to go and get rid of it.

The second man went to the cave and was welcomed by the devils. But when he danced, he did so poorly and all the devils became angry. They stuck the *kobu* of the first man on his right cheek and told him not to come back again. Thus he returned with *kobu* on both cheeks.

KOGA SABURO

THE LEGENDARY tale of Koga Saburo, who is said to have travelled to many countries underground, was made into a *Kabuki* play written in 1704, and thus has become very famous.

Taro, Jiro and Saburo were three brothers, and Saburo, the youngest, married Kasuga-hime. The two elder brothers were very jealous of Saburo and his beautiful wife.

Once the three brothers, with Kasuga-hime, went on a seven-day hunting trip to Ibuki Mountain. When the hunt ended, Kasuga-hime disappeared. Saburo went to look for her all over the country, but could not find her.

He went to Tadeshina Mountain, and finding a deep cave there, he lowered himself in a big basket. At the bottom he saw a Buddhist temple, in which Kasuga-hime was reading a sutra. Together they left the cave, but Kasuga-hime found that she had left a mirror given her by her father in the cave, and Saburo went back to get it. Then Jiro appeared and cut the basket rope so that Saburo could not get out.

As Saburo could not get out of the cave, he travelled underground, visiting more than 70 different countries. Finally he wanted to go home and appeared out of the ground at Asamayama. Reaching Koga, his native place, he slept at the temple where his father was buried.

Next morning, some children came to the temple and shouted that there was a big snake. Saburo then realized that he had taken the form of a snake. Saburo had heard a priest say that if a man who wore clothes of an underground country was turned into a snake, he would regain his human form if he jumped into Sekisho Lake.

So Saburo jumped into the lake and came out as a human, and was welcomed by the priest who then led him to Mikasa Mountain to join Kasuga-hime.

Saburo is enshrined at Kamimiya of Suwa Shrine, Shinano, and Kasuga-hime at the Shimomiya of the same place.

Somewhat different tales of Koga Saburo are told in various other parts of the country.

KUNAU

FUKUJU-SO (Adonis amurensis) has bright little golden blossoms. Its buds are silver gray, the leaves are green, but its blossoms are bright gold. Its name in Japanese means 'wealth-long-life-plant.' Because of its golden blossoms and also its lucky name, the flower is much admired by the people who use it especially for decorating their homes for the New Year celebration.

The blossom prospers in cold climates, and is seldom found in warmer and southern parts of the country. It seems to have been primarily introduced from Hokkaido when the territory was still called Ezo-ga-shima. There still remains a romantic tale in Hokkaido about this golden blossom.

Once there lived in Ezo a beautiful goddess called Kunau. Her father betrothed her to the god of the earthmole. But she did not care for the groom-elect selected by her father. Her refusal to marry the god of the earthmole so angered her father that she was reduced to becoming a common wild blossom as punishment for disobeying her father.

Thus she turned into a blossom which came to be known as Kunau or Kunaunonnon.

By the Ainu people, *fukuju-so* is still called Kunau. The tale of the Goddess Kunau is related by Ainu parents to their little daughters as a lesson teaching them the duty of obeying their parents. But if they were sure of being transformed into such beautiful blossoms, Ainu maidens might oppose the command of their parents to marry and follow the example of Goddess Kunau.

LAKE TAZAWA TROUT

LAKE TAZAWA in Akita Prefecture is famous for *benimasu,* a kind of river trout. The following story is told about the origin of this fish.

There once lived a beautiful maiden named Tatsuko who was very proud of her beauty and offered eager prayers asking that she be allowed to keep her beauty forever. An answer came from the gods saying, 'Go to the north of the mountain, and when you find a clean spring, drink the water.'

Daily she went in search of the spring but she could not find it. Some time later, she one day went with several of her friends over the mountain. They reached a stream in which strange fish were swimming which they caught and ate.

Tatsuko then became very thirsty and drank the water of the stream. As she drank she noticed that down in the stream there was a bubbling spring. Then she realized that it must be the spring she was told to drink from. Eagerly she drank, but the more she drank the thirstier she felt.

So she kept on drinking, but gradually she felt strange changes occurring in her body. Suddenly her beautiful body turned into a dragon. Alarmed at the sudden change, her friends ran down to the village and told her mother what had happened. The mother hurried to the stream, and seeing her daughter turned into a huge hideous dragon, wept in despair.

The mother brought a pine torch to find her way in the dusk to reach her daughter, and threw it into the stream as she wept. The torch, as it hit the stream, turned into a fish. That, they say, is the origin of the river trout of Lake Tazawa.

MAGIC HOUSE

IN THE HANAMAKI district of Iwate Prefecture, there once lived a wealthy family named Miura, and a story is told about the rise of this family.

One day when the family was still poor, the wife went up the mountain in search of wild *fuki* (bog-rhubarb). As she could not find any, she went deeper into the densely wooded mountain. She lost her way, and then saw a great black gate. Within it stood a magnificent house, beautiful gardens and stables filled with cattle and horses. But she saw no one about.

Timidly she entered the house. There, in a big room, were arranged rows of fine lacquered trays with various bowls and dishes. At one corner a kettle was boiling over a brazier. But finding no one in the house, she became frightened and hurriedly left the house. She did not tell anyone of her experience, because she thought nobody would believe her.

Soon afterward, one morning as she came to the clear stream flowing in front of her house, she saw a beautiful red bowl floating down the stream toward her. She picked it up and taking it home, used it as a cereal measure, as any bowl picked up could not be used to eat from.

But strangely, after she began using the red bowl to measure out cereal from the cereal bin, the cereal in the box never diminished in volume. The bin was always full without adding to it. Thus fortune and happiness came to the Miura family.

In the district it is traditionally believed that there is a strange house in the mountain which is generally called the magic 'lost' house, because it is only seen by one who has lost his way in the mountain. Anyone finding the house is allowed to take home any utensil he sees in the house, as those things are there for him.

The Miura woman entered the house, but took nothing as she was not covetous. So the bowl floated down the stream by itself to be picked up by her, and thus to bring good luck to her, it is explained.

MAGIC RICE-BAG

YOTSUNE of Echizen province, who was a faithful believer in Bishamon (Vaisravana), god of treasure, did not have anything to eat and felt hungry. So he asked for Bishamon's help. A beautiful woman appeared at his door and produced an earthenware bowl filled with food and told him to eat it if he wanted to.

When she left, he took a mouthful of the food and immediately felt full. He did not eat anything more for three days, after which he ate a little from the bowl whenever he was hungry. But in a few months the bowl became empty and then he prayed again to Bishamon.

Again the woman came to his door, and said, 'I have brought you this order. Go to the high mountain beyond the valley in the north, and standing there, shout the magic word "Narita," and then there will appear a person. Give the order to him, and take what he brings.'

The order said, 'Give two *to* (one bushel) of rice.'

He went to the high mountain as instructed, and then shouted 'Narita.' Instantly there appeared before him a strange-looking, one-eyed being, with a horn on his forehead and dressed only in a red loincloth. When the order was shown, the devil-like one said that though it was for two *to* of rice, only one *to* would be given.

Yotsune received one *to* of rice in his bag and came home. The rice in the bag never diminished though he took out a portion daily. The lord of the district heard of Yotsune and the magic bag and asked for it, so Yotsune said that he would give the lord a hundred *koku* or a thousand *to*.

When the lord took a hundred *koku* of rice from the bag, the bag became empty and so it was returned to Yotsune. At his home he was able to take one *to* of rice from the bag whenever he wanted for all his life and became a rich man.

MARRIAGE SONG

TOSA, A FISHERMAN of Ishigaki Island who had a beautiful wife, one day went to fish for octopus at low tide. As he put his hand into a hole in a rock, somehow his hand was caught and he could not draw it out. The tide began to rise, and soon he would be submerged and drowned.

Just at that moment, Toku, a fellow fisherman, happened to come, and Tosa asked him to help him to draw his hand out of the hole. Toku replied that if Tosa made him a promise, he would save him. Tosa agreed, and asked what Toku wanted. 'Give me your beautiful wife,' Toku said. Better to live than die, Tosa thought, and consented.

So Tosa was saved. When the two reached Tosa's house, they told the wife what had happened and the promise that was made. Hearing them, the wife said that what was promised must be kept, and asked them to select a good day and make preparations for her marriage with Toku. She told Toku that he must wait until she was ready to marry him.

Several months later, the wife asked Toku to come, and after offering him *sake* and food, told him that it was wrong to marry another's wife, but that it was equally wrong to break a promise. Then she proposed that a song telling of her marriage with Toku be written and that all the islanders sing it. 'Then, all will know I have married Toku, and all will be well,' she said.

So the song was written. It told how Toku saved a man's life and gained a beautiful wife. The song became immediately popular, making Tosa, his wife and Toku all happy.

MASAKADO

THE KANDA MYOJIN has been one of the most popular shrines in Tokyo since Edo days. There are also many other Myojin shrines throughout the country. It is commonly said that the Myojin Shrine is dedicated to Taira-no-Masakado, the notorious 10th-century rebel against the Imperial Court, who was finally defeated and beheaded. Many tales make him a man of wild nature, full of adventure and romance. He had a great following while in power, and after his death he came to be worshiped.

One story told about him is that he married a *tennyo* or angel who came down to Lake Omoga, Shimosa, to bathe, and had three sons by her.

As a fighting man he made his name quite early. It is told that on the battlefield his enemies were always confused by finding seven Masakados — seven warriors looking exactly like him, wearing the same costume and riding the same horse — and thus they were easily defeated. Gradually he gained territories and followers, and in 936 he proclaimed himself the new emperor. But his fortune was shortlived, for he was soon defeated by the Imperial forces and beheaded. When he was buried seven tombs were built.

He had seven lives, it is believed. His seven lives were the incarnation of the seven stars of Ursa Major, which are under the rule of Myoko-Bosatsu or Sudarsana. It is explained by some that because of this belief, he came to be associated with Myojin Shrine.

In different places in Tokyo and Chiba Prefecture, his tombs are still to be seen. At some places seven tombs mark the place where he was buried. At Otemachi, Tokyo, where the former Finance Ministry building stood, there is a spot marked as the place where his head was buried. But no one knows where his body or seven bodies were actually buried.

MIHARU-GOMA

THE DISTRICT of Miharu, near Koriyama, Fukushima Prefecture, has been famous for the fine horses it produces. It also produces the *Miharu-goma* (Miharu horse), a crudely cut wooden horse, which is praised as one of the most notable folk toys of the country. This wooden horse is based on a traditional story almost 12 centuries old.

In 791, Sakanoue-no-Tamuramaro was commissioned by the Court to subjugate Ota Onimaru, a hostile rebel leader of Miharu. Before he left the capital Priest Enchin who founded Kyoto's Kiyomizu Temple presented Tamuramaro with 100 small wooden horses carved out of the remnant of the wood used for making five Buddha statues, to encourage his soldiers during the expedition.

Tamuramaro's forces had many hard battles. Men and horses became exhausted under the pressure of the strong enemy. When the men were much discouraged, suddenly there appeared 100 saddled horses before them. As they rode the fresh horses, their courage returned and they won a brilliant victory.

Some time later, a Miharu man made crude wooden horses after the traditional mystery horses of Tamuramaro, and gave them to his children and other village youngsters to play with. Strangely it was soon found that children playing with these horses became strong and healthy, even the weak ones rapidly gaining strength.

Thus the horses became famous and were regarded as a charm for children's health. The horses even gave childless mothers the desired children. They came to be called *kosodate-goma* or child-raising horse.

The crude horses thus became an object of worship and popular outside the district.

Miharu-goma comes in different sizes, but generally it is small, being about 3 cm high. The original *Miharu-goma* was black, and often called *Miharu kuro-goma* (black horse), but white *Miharu* horses are also made now.

MISCHIEVOUS OTTERS

TALES OF *kawauso* or a kind of otter playing various pranks on Edo residents are still remembered by the old folks. According to such tales, *kawauso* seem to have lived in many rivers and canals of Edo.

It looks like a badger, but has a flat tail and webbed feet. Its back is dark-brown in winter but reddish-brown in summer and its underside is gray. The fur is highly valued. It loves to catch fish and there are stories that in January many *kawauso* parade together, carrying stringed fish.

The *kawauso* comes out of the water on rainy evenings, it was said, and suddenly jumps onto the umbrella of a passing person, often scratching the face of the surprised walker.

According to one tale, a *samurai* was passing by the moat near Toranomon one wet evening. He saw a small boy walking in front of him, splashing in the muddy street without an umbrella. The boy's kimono was trailing in the mud, and so he shouted to the boy to pull it up. The boy went on, not heeding the advice. So the *samurai* reached out and hitched the boy's *kimono* up, and then he saw a shining tail under it.

He realized that the boy was a

kawauso playing a trick on him. So he seized and threw him into the moat. Next morning he went to the spot, but there was no sign of anyone having been drowned there.

A *Kabuki* actor named Ichikawa Chobisuke who was famous for his somersaulting ability one day was on his way to Honjo. Suddenly his umbrella became heavy and he could not walk on. Holding onto his umbrella, he did a somersault, landing on a *kawauso* and killing it.

MOMO

THERE ARE many tales and traditions about the *momo*, the Japanese peach tree. In most such stories the plant, fruits and leaves of *momo* possess some mysterious power to bring happiness to the people. This belief in the power of the *momo* is quite old, dating back to mythological ages.

Once Izanagi-no-mikoto was chased by 1,500 demons, so an ancient tale goes. He had no way of escaping from them. But when he reached Hirasaka, he saw a *momo* tree standing there. Quickly he plucked three peaches and threw them at the fast advancing demons. Hit by them, the demons stopped and then hurriedly scampered away, as they could not fight the power of the fruit.

Escaping the attack of the demons, Izanagi-no-mikoto thanked the *momo* tree for its help in saving him. Then he said, 'Just as you saved me now, help the people of the country whenever they are in trouble.' In appreciation of its help, he gave the *momo* tree the name of Ookantsumi-no-mikoto or great sacred fruit deity.

Since then, it is said that the peach plant has always looked after the happiness and good health of the people.

Momo-shu or wine made from *momo*

is believed to possess medicinal value. *Momo* leaves are still used to cure insect bites and heat rashes by rural folks. They are also put in the bath water in summer to keep the skin in good condition.

The tale of Momotaro or a boy born from a peach found by an old woman in a stream, is the most famous folk tale of the country, loved by all children even today.

MONKEY GROOM

THERE WAS once an old farmer who found it hard to cultivate his fields properly, as he was no longer able to work as hard as he had. Thus his fields were neglected. A long spell of dry weather parched his farm, and though he knew that water had to be brought to save the crops, he had not the strength to undertake such a strenuous task.

One day, standing by his fields, he said to himself aloud, 'The rice will soon be dried up. If there is a man who will water my fields, I will give one of my daughters to him.'

As he spoke, a monkey suddenly appeared and filled the fields with water, as though by magic. The old man was surprised and looked at the monkey.

'You said you would give a daughter to one who watered your field, and I want your daughter,' the monkey told him.

The farmer was an honest man so when he returned home, he told his three daughters what had happened.

The eldest daughter said she had no intention of marrying a monkey. The second daughter also refused to sacrifice herself for her father but the youngest daughter, when she was asked to speak her mind, agreed to marry the monkey.

So the monkey came to the farmer's house to take its bride home to the mountain. Before leaving the house with her monkey groom, the third daughter asked her father to give her a large earthenware jar to take with her.

The jar was given her as a wedding present. She made the monkey carry the heavy jar on its back, and the two started on their journey to the mountain. When they came to a steep precipice that led to a deep valley by the road, the bride stopped her groom, and pointing to a bright flower blooming on the edge of the cliff, asked the monkey to get the blossom for her. The monkey went over to the edge and stooped to get the flower, but in so doing it slipped and fell. As it fell down the precipice, it was caught in the jug it was carrying on its back, and died at the bottom of the valley.

MONKEY'S COIN

THERE WAS once an aged couple who made their living by selling cotton cloth woven by the wife. Daily the husband went out to peddle the cloth. One day when he was returning home from his daily trip, he saw on a lonely path a hunter aiming his gun at a female monkey in a tree. Pitying the monkey, the old man rushed toward the hunter to stop him from firing the gun. But just as he reached the hunter, the gun went off.

The shot did not hit the monkey but shattered the shoulder of the old man. Thereupon the hunter ran away. From the brush below, a child monkey came out and helped the mother monkey carry the wounded old man to their hut. Tenderly they cared for him and when he was able to return home, they gave him a coin that had magic power, in thanks for his kind act in saving the mother monkey's life.

The monkey's coin brought luck and wealth to the aged couple, but soon the story of the unexpected good fortune of the old man became known to an evil-minded neighbor who immediately schemed to steal the coin.

The old man discovered the loss of his lucky coin and that his good luck was deserting him. Determined to regain the charm, the wife ordered Tama, her pet cat, to search for the lost piece of money. But the cat was not willing to undertake the difficult task. He caught a mouse and demanded that it find the coin, threatening to eat it up if it failed to do so.

The mouse had to do as he was told and so it entered every house in the village to look for the lost coin. Finally it found it in a chest-of-drawers of the evil man. In order to get at the coin, the mouse cut a hole in the side of the chest with its sharp teeth, and managed to obtain the lost magic coin.

Proudly returning to the cat, the mouse handed the coin to the cat, who immediately took it to the old woman. She was so happy to regain it for her husband that she gave the cat a double portion of meat as a reward, an old story says.

MONKEY'S SUICIDE

IN THE VILLAGE of Shinozaki (now Edogawa Ward), Edo, in the Enpo era (1673-1681), lived a man and his wife, named Kihachi and Shino, an old Edo tale goes. They had no children, and obtained two monkeys, a mother and a baby, from their neighbor, Goemon, in exchange for some rice, as they wanted a pet.

One day Shino was doing her laundry, and had a tub of hot water nearby. When she was not looking, the baby monkey fell into the hot water. As it cried, the mother monkey came running and picked it up from the tub, and Kihachi and Shino tenderly cared for the badly burnt monkey. But it died, and Shino buried it behind the house.

After the baby monkey died, the mother cried in sadness, and did not eat any food. Thinking that the monkey was blaming her for the death of the baby, Shino told it that the little monkey was careless and fell into the hot water.

Then the mother monkey went to the kitchen and brought back a wooden cover for the tub, as though it wanted to say that if Shino had placed it on the tub, the baby would not have fallen in and died.

Seeing this, Shino cried, saying that the mother monkey was blaming her for the death of the baby, and she told the monkey that she was sorry for being so careless. But the monkey kept on crying and became weaker, as it did not eat.

The monkey's constant crying made Kihachi irritable, and he said to it loudly, 'Shino said she was sorry. So stop crying.'

Still crying, the mother monkey went out of the house, and at the spot where the baby was buried, dug it out with its fingers. Carrying the body in its arms, it went to a river and jumped in to die.

The story was told widely in the district as an example of a monkey's sorrow for the death of its baby.

MOTHER SNAKE

IN A VILLAGE on the slope of the Unzendake mountain in Hizen province, Kyushu, there once lived a young hunter who had a beautiful wife. She was really a snake, so the story goes. When a baby was born, she told him not to look into her room, but becoming curious, he peeped in. He saw a big snake coiled in the center of the room, holding a baby.

The wife, coming out of the room,

told her husband that she had to leave him as he had seen her in snake form. Then she pulled out her right eye and giving it to him, said, 'When the baby cries, let it lick the eyeball.' Then she left and went back to the mountain.

The hunter treasured the eyeball, letting the baby lick it whenever it was hungry. The eyeball became known to all the villagers, and all talked of its wonderful value. The lord of the district heard of it and took it away from the hunter.

The baby kept on crying and its hunger was not satisfied. So the hunter took the baby to the mountain lake, and sitting there both of them cried. Suddenly a big wave rose in the lake, and a one-eyed snake appeared. When the hunter told his story, the snake plucked out its left eye and gave it to him.

With the eyeball, the baby grew rapidly, but the lord heard of the second eyeball and again took it away from the hunter. Distressed, the hunter resolved to kill himself and the baby by jumping into the mountain lake. As the two approached the lake, the blind snake appeared. Hearing the story, the snake said that it would take revenge. It told him to go with the baby to a certain place where milk would be obtained.

When the two left, a big eruption took place, and the mountain crumbled down to fill farms and surrounding seas. That was the snake's revenge.

MOUNTAIN GIANTS

ALL OVER THE country, tales have been told of *yama-otoko* (mountain men) or giants who lived in the mountains and scared the people by suddenly appearing in villages. Often hunters going into the mountains met them unexpectedly. Big footprints measuring more than three feet long were sometimes found on the snow-covered ground. The *yama-otoko* is generally clad in a crude garment made of leaves.

In some northeastern districts the mountain giant is said to be about 15 feet tall. When he comes to a village, he is paid great respect by villagers who offer him food and drink, and it is said he often plays with the children.

In the Shirakura mountain region, people often saw huge footprints of a giant in the snow, and it was believed that those who saw them soon died. Echigo folks have a tale that the giant left his footprints on farms on either side of a river when he stepped over it.

In some places *yama-otoko* is said to be a woman.

A farmer of Johoji village, Rikuchu, entered a mountain and met a giant. He gave him some of the *mochi* or rice-cakes that he had brought for his lunch. The giant seemed to enjoy the *mochi*, and then asked the farmer if he had finished tilling his farm. As the farmer replied that he had not, the giant said, 'Bring three hoes and some *mochi* to your field at night and I will till it for you,' and he named a date.

The farmer did as he was told, and when he went out to his field the morning after the agreed night, he saw his farm thoroughly tilled and all the *mochi* gone.

Other districts also have tales of mountain giants asking for *mochi* of which they seem to be very fond.

It is not known, however, whether mountain giants really existed, or how so many tales have developed about them.

MT. FUJI MYTH

MANY MYTHS are told of Mt. Fuji, and one of the oldest is that the mountain rose in a single night. An old woodsman who subsequently became the Rip Van Winkle of Japan saw it actually rising out of the flat land of Suruga.

Just as he was about to retire, a loud noise rent his ears. He thought it was a big earthquake, and carrying his little children, he rushed out of his hut. He saw a great mountain rising where the land was flat, its peak wreathed in flames, and tongues of fire shooting out of it. The mountain was so grand that he named it Fuji (never die.)

One day a priest visited him and asked if he prayed regularly. He answered that with his family he was too busy to pray. The priest drew a picture of the horrors of hell, and his rebirth as a toad or a worm. At those words the woodsman trembled with fear. Then he went to extremes. He prayed day and night, refusing to do anything else. His wife stormed at him, and urged him to go out and get food and firewood for the family. He rose in anger and left the hut, saying that he would have nothing more to do with his wife and children.

He climbed Mt. Fuji that he loved, and a rabbit passed his way. As he followed the animal, he saw a crevice in the mountainside. He looked in and saw two women playing at a game of *go* (Japanese chess). He went in and watched the game, but the women took no notice of him. But one woman made a wrong move, whereupon he shouted, 'That's wrong.' Then as the women looked at him, they turned into foxes and ran away. He tried to follow, but his legs were stiff and he could barely move. Then he found that his whiskers had grown to his knees.

With pain, he came down, but found no house where his hut used to stand. He asked an old woman what had happened to his hut. The woman looked up and said, 'You must be mad. The woodsman has not been heard of for 300 years. He quarelled with his wife and went away.'

The woodsman lived several years more. It is said that his spirit haunts the mountain when the full moon shines.

NAMAZU TALE

THE *NAMAZU* (sheatfish) is a weird fish, darkbrown in color, flat, with long whiskers, and lives in the mud. In the old days it was believed that a giant *namazu* living under the land caused earthquakes by shaking its tail. The fish also appears in many local tales.

Once Priest Jokaku of the Izumo Temple, north of Kyoto, dreamed of his father, many years dead. In the dream his father told him that a big storm would come in two days. He said he had been turned into a *namazu* and was living in a tiny pool of water under the temple roof with other fish. When the storm blew down the temple, he would be thrown out and killed by mischievous children, the father said, and asked his son to help him by catching and throwing him into the Kamo River.

Jokaku did not believe the strange dream but told it to his wife. But on the afternoon two days after the night he had the dream, the predicted storm came and immediately the big temple was blown down. From the wreck several fish were thrown out. Jokaku rushed out of the crumbling temple to the garden and saw a big *namazu* in front of him.

The fish was big and tempting and the desire to catch it came to his mind. He managed to get hold of it with a big stick. He caught it and took it to his wife. He told her to cook it but his wife strongly advised him not to kill the *namazu*, refusing to touch it.

So Jokaku cooked it himself and started to eat it. But after a few mouthfuls, a bone stuck in his throat, and though he struggled to take it out,

his efforts failed. Thus he struggled and suffered pain, and finally died.

Everybody said that his death was punishment for not obeying his father's wish and killing the *namazu*. His wife and children, therefore, refrained from eating *namazu* all their lives, it is said.

OBASUTE-YAMA

THE STORY OF *obasute-yama*, mountains where aged parents are taken and left to die, is circulated in many parts of the country with local variations. The idea of carrying feeble old parents, particularly mothers, to remote mountain tops and leaving them there without shelter or food to die, sounds cruel. The widely told story may give a false impression that the ancient Japanese actually carried out such an inhuman practice.

Actually the real idea behind this traditional tale is quite the opposite. The story was started with the idea of teaching children the duty of being kind and considerate to their old parents. When one studies different *obasute-yama* tales, it will be found that the aged parents taken to mountain tops were always saved by some kind act of their children or others.

A son started to take his aged mother to the mountain, carrying her on his back as she was too feeble to walk, but as he went up the mountain he noticed that whenever they came by a tree, the mother broke off a little branch. Becoming curious, the son asked her why she was breaking the branches. She replied that by those broken branches he would find his way home after leaving her at the mountain top. Impressed by his mother's kind thoughts for him, the son turned round and brought her back. This is one of the most typical *obasute-yama* tales.

One old mother was left on the mountain to die, but the mountain god took pity on her as he knew she was a good woman. Giving her many valuable treasures, he made her return to the village. A greedy woman in the village heard the story of the fortunate woman, and thought of a plan to have similar luck. She asked a man to carry her to the mountain and leave her there. But the mountain god was not fooled by her, and scared her off with many tricks. So she had to run back to the village.

ONE-EYED ENMA

THE STATUE of one-eyed *Enma* (judge of hell) enshrined at the Genkakuji Temple, Hatsune-cho, Bunkyoku, Tokyo, is renowned for its power to cure eye disases and has many worshipers.

The temple was erected in 1624. Soon afterward an *Enma* statue was found in a nearby pond. It was fished out and placed in the temple. At first nobody paid any particular attention to the *Enma*, but suddenly it became famous throughout Edo, and many worshipers thronged to the temple. Ever since it has been called the *Enma* of Koishikawa, after the district.

The *Enma* became famous as it lost one eye. The following story is told about it.

An old woman was seen daily coming to worship the *Enma* and offering *konnyaku* (a jelly-like food). Her visits, were noticed by many persons because *konnyaku* was a strange offering to *Enma* or any other deity. So she was asked why she was offering this particular food to the *Enma*.

She explained that her eyes were becoming weak and all medicines had failed. So she had come to the *Enma* to pray for his help. One day as she was kneeling before the statue and praying fervently, she heard the *Enma* speak to her, 'I will gouge out one of my eyes and give it to you.'

Upon hearing these words, she woke up from her trance and looked up at the *Enma's* face. To her utter surprise, one of his eyes was gone, and blood was streaking down from the empty socket. She looked around and she could see everything clearly.

She had not dreamed the *Enma's* words and her prayer was heard. The *Enma*, pitying her, had sacrificed his eye for her.

In deep appreciation, she wanted to offer the *Enma* something she valued most. But she was poor and had nothing to give. She was very fond of *konnyaku*, and so she decided to give up eating this and offer it to the *Enma* for restoring her eyesight.

The one-eyed *Enma* of Koishikawa is still visited by those suffering from eye troubles.

ONE-EYED FISH

THERE ARE quite a number of stories about one-eyed fish, while some places have traditions of one-eyed snakes. Such tales are mostly connected with shrines or temples.

The Ioji Temple at Takaido in a Tokyo suburb was formerly visited by persons who had eye diseases. It was said that when one threw a freshwater fish into the pond of the temple, it soon became one-eyed. When any such one-eyed fish was found outside the pond, it always had to be returned to it.

Kamakura Gongoro was a great warrior of the Kamakura period, famed for his courage and dramatized in *Kabuki*. Once on a battlefield an arrow pierced his eye, but without withdrawing it, he kept on fighting. Now there are many ponds in the country which are reputed to be the place where he washed his injured eye. The fish in such ponds are all one-eyed, it is said. At some places it is believed that after his death Gongoro turned into a one-eyed fish.

The fish in the pond of Fukumura Valley in Awa province are all one-eyed. It is traditionally said that once a warrior, seeing a big snake on the rock in the pond, drew his bow. The arrow hit the snake's left eye. For this crime, the warrior was cursed by the snake. Not only did he soon die, but also his whole family became extinct from an unknown cause. The curse of the wounded snake did not end there. In anger the snake made all the fish in the pond one-eyed to impress upon the people of the area that snakes should never be molested.

OSAYO

IN THE PROVINCE of Echizen, white lilies are called *osayo*. While there are many stories and traditions about wild white lilies that grow abundantly in many parts of Japan, Echizen is the only district where such a romantic name is given to the blossom.

The story of Osayo originated in the days of Tokugawa Ieyasu, the founder of the Tokugawa rule, or about 300 years ago. Osayo was a beautiful girl, though born of poor parents. All the young men of the neighborhood were in love with her.

Just at that moment, a young artist of the Shijo school of Japanese painting came to a mountain nearby. Living in a humble hut, he daily sketched scenes around him. Osayo fell in love with him.

The young artist came to visit Osayo at her house when her parents were away. As a signal to let him know when her parents were away, she used to put a white lily blossom at her window. The white lily could be seen even on moonless dark nights, and she wisely selected it as her signal. Whenever the

young painter saw the white lily at her window, he was filled with joy and spent delightful hours with Osayo.

But suddenly the visits of the artist stopped. It was learned that one of the jealous young men of the village had killed him, knowing that the artist had monopolized the affection of Osayo.

When Osayo learned of the death of her lover, she spent days of lamenting, holding a white lily blossom to her breast.

It is on account of this story that the white lily came to be called Osayo in the province of Echizen. It is a beautiful name to be given to the white lily blossom that is so often connected with tales of women and their love affairs in Japan.

OTAE-ZAKURA

NEAR KATAHARA Station on the Mikawa railway line, Aichi Prefecture, there is an old castle ruin. A cherry tree called *Otae-zakura* stands there to mark the tomb of Otae, a girl who is still worshiped as the guardian deity of the old castle.

The story of Otae took place in the 16th century, when Matsudaira Ietada, lord of the castle, and a powerful ally of Tokugawa Ieyasu, was only 13 years old. At that time, the Matsudaira family was in discord with the Imagawa clan that advanced westward into Mikawa province from Suruga, in the hopes of rising against the Tokugawa powers.

The Imagawa clan dispatched a spy to the castle of Matsudaira at Katahara with the object of killing Ietada. Akegarasu Samanosuke, the spy, managed to enter the service of Matsudaira. As he was a master fencer, Samanosuke was assigned to teach fencing to the young master who was then called Matashichi.

Samanosuke watched for an opportunity to fulfill his mission. Otae, the nursemaid for Matashichi, however, was a clever woman, and she found out that Samanosuke was a spy who intended to kill her charge. So she closely watched the spy, and was always near Matashichi whenever he had his fencing lessons with Samanosuke.

One day, Samanosuke proposed to show the use of a real sword, instead of the usual bamboo stick for training. Otae realized then that he would try to kill her master, and was ready for any development.

Feigning to show the young master the use of a sword, Samanosuke raised his sword over Matashichi. Then Otae rushed forward and drawing a short sword from her bosom, she thrust it into Samanosuke's body.

Matashichi was saved, but Samanosuke's sword which was intended for the young lord fell on Otae, and she was instantly killed. As she had saved the life of her young master, Otae was enshrined as the guardian of the castle. The lord and all the people offered prayers for her.

OTOKO-ISHI

AT MEZURASHI PATH, marking the boundary of Ise and Yamato provinces, there stands a stone which is called *Otoko-ishi* or boy stone. When any woman in the district is about to give birth to a baby, she, her husband or her mother climbs to the path and throws a little stone at *Otoko-ishi*. If the stone is hit, it is a sign that a boy will be born. This custom, which is still observed, comes from an ancient tale.

The Kasuga Shrine of Nara and the Daijingu (Grand Shrine) of Ise came to dispute over the boundary line of their territories. They agreed that they would set out from their respective shrines, and the place where they met

would be the boundary.

Kasuga *kami* who rides on a deer, thought that as the Daijingu would come on his sacred horse, he would be beaten unless he started before the Daijingu did. So he started at midnight without waiting for dawn. He went far into the Daijingu's territory and met the other at Miyanomae-mura.

If that place was made the boundary, the Ise territory would become very small. So they arranged to make a bamboo-leaf boat and let it float on the water, and the place where the boat reached would be set as the boundary.

But the water was calm, there was no wind and the boat did not move. So the *Kami* of Ise threw a stone into the water to cause ripples and move the boat. The boat finally reached Funado, which was made the boundary.

The stone the Ise *kami* threw still stands, and is known as *Otoko-ishi*, possessing the power to give a male baby to any woman hitting it with a small stone.

PETRIFIED WOMEN

THERE ARE many legends which tell stories of women petrified into stone, but the most widely known is that of Matsura-Sayohime. Matsura-Sayohime was the wife of Otomo-no Sadehiko, a great warrior. In 562, Sadehiko went on an expedition to the peninsula of Korea with a large force. When he embarked on his boat for Korea, Sayohime stood on a hill-top by the sea and waved to her departing husband. As she stood on the rock, watching the ever-diminishing boat, she turned into a stone.

At Kobiko, Saga province in Kyushu, there now stands the Sayohime Shrine. The shrine is dedicated to the petrified Sayohime, and within the shrine building is preserved a stone about six feet high, which is said to be the petrified Sayohime. The stone represents Sayohime in her garment of *Katsugi*.

The story of Sayohime has become so popular that in Kyushu there are many places which bear her name, and the legend of her turning into stone is actually believed by the people of those districts.

At Iwakiyama, Aizu, there is a stone which is believed to be a petrified woman. When a girl named Ajuhime climbed a mountain, her old maid followed her, but knowing that after the girl's entrance into the mountain there would be no chance of again seeing her, the old maid lamented, and as she sat there and wept she turned into a stone.

While these legendary tales about women turned into stone are generally believed by the masses, it is explained that these tales actually originated from the worship of mountains and stones. That is to say, because the people so highly respected mountains and stones on mountains, they came to create such legendary tales about stones that they particularly worshiped.

PIOUS AND WORLDLY

THERE IS an old story about a pious priest and a worldly mountain hunter that still teaches us a lesson.

There once lived in the mountain of Atago-yama a Buddhist priest and his boy apprentice. They lived in a small hut, and the priest spent his days repeating sutras and never went outdoors, while the boy looked after him.

Also on the mountain was a hunter, strong but ignorant, who feared no man or beast. The hunter often passed by the priest's hut and came to know him. Sympathizing with the plain living the priest and boy had in the solitary hut,

he often brought fruit and other things to them.

Once when the hunter came to the hut, the priest told the mountain man how happy he was because his constant reading of sutras had finally brought him enlightenment and *Fugen-bosatsu* (Samantabhadra) had visited him several times at night. The priest invited the hunter to stay at the hut that evening, as surely the *Bosatsu* would make an appearance that night.

The hunter did not know who *Fugen-bosatsu* was or what his appearance meant, but attracted by the possibility of any strange sight he might see, he agreed to stay. As the evening advanced, suddenly the sky became light as though a full moon had risen. Then in the bright sky, there stood *Fugen-bosatsu* riding a white elephant.

The priest flattened himself on the mat to worship the figure and so did the boy. Rising, the priest asked the hunter whether he had seen the *Bosatsu* and worshiped him.

The hunter saw the *Bosatsu*, but he wondered why the sacred figure had revealed himself to him who knew nothing of the faith, could not read a sutra, and was not at all pious. The priest read sutras and the boy was also pious, and so the *Bosatsu* came to them, but why, he wondered, had the sacred being become visible to him, too.

He then thought that there must be something behind the *Bosatsu's* appearance. So he took up his bow and shot an arrow at the breast of the *Bosatsu.* Suddenly the bright light went out, and then a great noise was heard in the valley below.

Next morning, they all went down to the valley and found the body of a huge *tanuki* or badger with an arrow in its heart.

POISONOUS MUSHROOMS

AT THE KINPOZAN TEMPLE the oldest priest was elected as *betto* or the head priest in the old days. Once, the second priest of the temple who was learned and experienced hoped that the head priest would soon die so that he could be promoted to the rank of *betto*. But the old head priest was strong and healthy, and showed no sign of dying.

'The *betto* is more than 80 years old but he is healthy, and I may die before him as I am already 70,' the second priest said to himself. So he planned to poison the *betto* as he knew of no other way to attain the headship of the temple, though he felt it a terrible thing to do for a Buddhist priest.

Finally, he hit upon a scheme of making the *betto* eat *watari* or a poisonous mushroom. As the autumn mushroom season came, he went alone to the mountain to gather *watari*. Secretly he cooked the poisonous mushrooms. Then he went to the *betto*'s room and told him that a friend had brought him some good mushrooms and he wished the head priest to eat them with him. For himself, the second priest cooked non-poisonous mushrooms. They sat down and ate the mushrooms.

The second priest was dumbstruck, as the *betto* ate the mushrooms, knowing them to be poisonous *watari*. The fact was that the *betto* was fond of *watari*, and as he was used to eating them, he had become immune to their poison.

The second priest's plan failed, and the old priest lived a long time, keeping the rank of *betto*.

RAT'S TEETH

THE RAT has only two upper incisors or sharp front teeth, while most animals have four. A story tells how it came to have only two.

The rat and the badger were friends and neighbors living in the same fields. They went out together to find food, but hunting for food daily tired them. The rat suggested to the badger that they plant millet in the field, as then they would have food ready at hand. The badger readily agreed to the proposal, but when the time came to sow, the rat did not appear. So the badger had to do it alone.

Soon the millet grew and bore grain. The badger went out one day to harvest the crop, but to his surprise the field was bare of millet ears. Thinking that some birds might have eaten them, he asked the various birds in the field. They did not know anything about the millet, nor did they know who took the grain.

So he went of the hole of the rat to inform him of the sad incident. As the badger came to the entrance of the hole, he heard a little rat saying loudly how good the millet cake its father had made the night before was. The badger realized that it was the rat who had taken away all the millet crop, after leaving its cultivation entirely up to him.

In anger, he rushed into the hole and catching the rat in his strong paws, called him a low-down thief. The badger threatened to pull out all the rat's teeth so that it would never be able to eat any food.

But remembering that the rat had long been his friend, the badger did not have the heart to pull all its teeth out. He took out only two of the four upper incisors so that the rat would not be able to eat so much and so fast as he used to.

As punishment for this thieving rat, all rodents even now have only two sharp front teeth.

REVENGING HORSE

FUKUMATSU, a woodcutter, was a hard master, and not only his son, Fukutaro, but also his horse had to work from early morning to night, without a day of rest, an old tale goes. So both the son and horse were always tired and grew weak.

On January 3, one year, the weather was beautiful, and Fukumatsu sharply ordered his son Fukutaro who was warming himself at the fireside to start immediately for Kajikazawa where cut wood had been stored and bring it home. But the son replied, 'This is the third day of the New Year and nobody works. Let me and our horse rest a day.'

'There is no New Year for us. Get up and don't waste such a fine day,' the father shouted.

So Fukutaro hitched the horse to a sleigh, and wearing snowshoes started for Kajikazawa, miles up the river, following his father. When they reached the wood pile, it was covered with snow, and they had to remove the snow to get at it. But while they were working, a fierce blizzard came, and Fukutaro proposed to return without the wood, but his father said that they must finish loading the sleigh.

Finally the sleigh was fully loaded and they were ready to start on the trip home. But the horse stood motionless. It would not move even though strongly whipped. 'You lazy horse. After feeding you for five years, you don't obey me,' the father shouted. But the horse was actually frozen and could not move.

So the father and son started a fire under the horse. As the fire roared and the flame almost reached the animal's belly, the horse suddenly raised its hind legs and hit Fukumatsu, causing his death.

Hearing the story of the death of Fukumatsu, the villagers said that the horse had taken revenge for the long cruel treatment by Fukumatsu not only of itself, but also of his son. Furthermore, all agreed that everyone must rest at least during the New Year season.

RIVER-BOTTOM WEAVER

TALES OF THE sound of weaving looms being heard from the bottom of streams or ponds are told in many parts of the country. This type of legend is said to have developed from the ancient custom of weaving and sewing new clothes for the local *kami* for the annual festival.

At first the task of weaving and sewing the sacred costume was given to a virgin girl of the district. She was placed in a specially-made weaving hut by a clear stream.

Strangers who did not know of the existence of the weaving hut were surprised to hear unexpectedly the sound of a weaving loom by the river-side. They must have spread the story that there was someone weaving at the river bottom.

The pond called Hiyasha in Shiga Prefecture formerly did not have much water. It was said that, if a living human being was sacrificed to the pond, there would be abundant clear water. An old woman named Hiyashi who had raised the lord of the district, offered herself to be buried under the pond water. After she was buried, the pond never lacked water even in years of drought. Since then it has been said that if one walks by the pond one will hear the old woman weaving her loom.

There is a similar story told of the Onja pond of Kazusa. A young wife threw herself into the pond and died, because she did not get along well with her mother-in-law. The old woman particularly criticized her skill at weaving. Unable to stand the abuse, the young wife threw herself into the pond. Whenever rain falls, one can hear the sound of her weaving loom at the bottom of the pond.

SADO RICE

SADO IS A small island in the Japan Sea and was once famous as a rich gold-producing center. This island produces much good rice which not only is enough to meet the local needs but is also shipped out to the rest of Japan.

There is a story told of how rice growing began here.

A boy, Sansuke, was born in the province of Tosa, Shikoku. One day he went fishing in a boat with his stepfather but a sudden storm arose and the boat drifted for many days. Finally it reached the island of Sado. Sansuke was sent by his stepfather to go up the mountain to gather kindling. But when he returned to the shore with the wood, he saw that the boat with his stepfather was already putting off.

He shouted after it but it never came back. He climbed to the top of the mountain to watch the boat far out on the horizon. Then he wept and longed for home. His stepfather had always been hard on him, and now he was left behind, abandoned on the island.

He decided to die by jumping into the sea. As he gathered the sleeves of his scanty *kimono* he felt some small objects in the seam of the garment. He opened up the seam and there he found several grains of rice.

Looking at the grains, he realized that his mother, who had died when he was very small, had put the rice grains there as she sewed the kimono for him. It must have been his mother's prayer that if he should be abadoned by his

stepfather, he could sow the rice and make his living.

Upon learning the meaning of the grains, he took courage and resolved to plant the rice and live bravely. After planting and tenderly caring for them, he managed to harvest good rice in the autumn.

Thus rice cultivation started on Sado island, it is believed. At Matsugasaki, Sansuke's memory is enshrined and still worshiped by the islanders.

SAGISO

HIMONYA, a suburb of Tokyo, has a traditional tale about the *sagiso*, a little plant that has small white blossoms, for which the district has become famous.

Once, Lord Odaira of Dewa went hawking with a party of his retainers, and as they reached a marsh at Himonya he saw a *shirasagi* or white heron. He ordered Nuinosuke, one of his men, to shoot it with an arrow. Nuinosuke skillfully hit the bird with his arrow.

As the bird was brought to him, Lord Odaira saw that a *tanzaku* (a long piece of paper for writing poems) was attached to its leg. Looking at the *tanzaku*, his face turned pale because he recognized the hand of his daughter, and furthermore the poem written there was her death song. He knew then that his daughter married to the lord of Setagaya had committed suicide because of the troubled relations between the two families.

Soon afterward, Lord Odaira sent his troops to attack the Setagaya castle to settle the strained relations of the two families with arms.

Next spring, a plant grew from the spot where the blood of the heron had fallen when it was shot down by Nuinosuke. It grew tall and in early summer tiny white blossoms appeared.

The flower looked like a heron in flight, and it was named *sagiso* or heron plant. The plant multiplied and the little white flowers have made the district famous. They also keep alive in the memories of the residents the ancient tale of Lord Odaira's daughter's suicide and the shooting of the heron which was her pet that she had taken with her when she married.

SANSHODAYU

IT WAS FORMERLY said in Tsugaru district at the northern end of the main island of Honshu that if anyone from the province of Tango (now included in Kyoto) went there, the weather would become bad, that there would be high waves at sea, and no ships would be able to come in or leave. The belief in this tradition was so strong that when officials had to visit the Tsugaru region during the feudal days, they took care that no man from Tango province was among their party.

This tradition dates back to the era of Eiho (1081-1083). At that time Iwaki Masauji was the lord of Iwakiyama, Tsugaru, but while in Kyoto, he was punished and exiled to the west region, on false charges.

His daughter Anjuhime and son Zushi-o, together with their mother proceeded to the west to meet their father. On the way, at Echigo, they were caught by a bad man. The mother was sold to Sado island, while the two children were sold as servants to Sanshodayu, a wealthy family of Tango.

While in service there, Zushi-o escaped to a Buddhist temple. On the charge that she helped her young brother escape, Anjuhime was killed by Sanshodayu.

Later Zushi-o grew up and demanded justice. He managed to bring official punishment on Sanshodayu and the man who sold him, his sister and mother. Thus Zushi-o and Anjuhime became famous and are still enshrined at the Iwaki Gongen.

The people of Tsugaru thus came to hate Sanshodayu and all those from Tango province, who they thought would only bring bad fortune to them.

The story of Sanshodayu has been made into a *joruri* play. Mori Ogai, the famous writer of the Meiji era also wrote of the story of Sanshodayu.

SARU-JIZO

THE MONKEY appears in many ancient Japanese tales. Among various types of monkey stories, there is one which is commonly called *Saru-Jizo*, or Monkey-*Jizo*. Each version, of course, differs considerably according to the district, but the main theme is generally the same.

Once an old man went up a mountain to cut grass for animal feed. He took baked buckwheat cakes for his lunch and placed the package on a tree stump while he worked. Some monkeys saw the package of cakes and stole it. As they began to eat the cakes, sitting down in a circle, the old man sat down and watched them in silence.

Then the monkeys came to him, and said. 'Oh here is a *Jizosama*, but this is no place for him. Let us carry him across the river and put him in the shrine there to worship.'

So saying, they formed a sort of seat with their long arms, and placed the old man on it. They merrily carried him away, singing funny songs. The old man was almost ready to laugh, but he closed his eyes and sat solemnly. Soon they reached a shrine on the other side of the river. The old man was set down there, and soon other monkeys gathered and made offerings to him.

Finally, when all the monkeys were

gone the old man opened his eyes, gathered all the coins thrown around him, and started home. On his way back, he bought some new *kimono*.

A neighbor woman heard the story, and made her husband do the same thing to get rich. So this old man went to the mountain with buckwheat cakes as the first old man did. The monkeys came and carried him on their laced arms as expected. But the songs by the monkeys were so funny that the old man laughed and opened his eyes while he was in the middle of the river.

The monkeys were surprised and became angry, and loosened their arms upon which the old man sat. He fell into the river and was barely able to save himself. When he went home soaking wet, his wife had already burned all his clothes, expecting to see him in new *kimono*.

SEEING THE FUTURE

A LARGE TREE stood on the edge of a high precipice at Osarube, in northern Akita Prefecture, and at the end of its huge branches stretching out over the deep valley hung something that looked like a human body. Somehow the villagers said that it was Sakunojo who had disappeared many years before, having been carried away by *tengu*, a long-nosed goblin, and hung there. So it was said the strange body remained on the tree branch for many, many years.

But one day, the strange body on the tree suddenly disappeared, and Sakunojo, the farmer, returned home. But it had been 80 years since his disappearance. He told his grandchildren and greatgrandchildren the following story.

Eighty years before when he was only 40 years old, he went to the mountain to get kindling wood. A giant appeared and asked him if he wanted to see the past or the future. He replied that of the past he knew something and expressed his wish to see the future that would come only after his death.

'Then I will end your life now, and revive you in 80 years' time. And I will give you 30 years to live after your revival,' the giant said, and at once strangled Sakunojo to death.

When Sakunojo opened his eyes, the giant said that he was alive again and he could return home, expressing regret for having kept him hanging on the tree so long. As he walked home he saw that the mountains and villages were changed, but he recognized his house which was still standing.

The villagers did not believe his story. But his grandchildren and great-grandchildren said that they heard there was one named Sakunojo among their ancestors. The returned man knew all that had happened in the village and the surrounding neighborhood more than a hundred years before, so some believed him to be the Sakunojo who had disappeared for so long.

It was said that he was respected by all his neighbors and lived happily his extra 30 years, dying in the fifth year of Shotoku, 1715.

SHADOW ROBBER

THERE WAS once a retainer of a feudal lord who was known for his cowardice, but because of that reputation he used to pretend that he was strong and courageous, according to an old story.

One day he had to rise early in the morning because of his duties. His wife got up while it was still dark to prepare his breakfast. As she was working in the outdoor kitchen, she saw on the *shoji* or paper sliding door of the house the shadow of a large person with flowing hair, and thought that a robber had come to break into the house. She did not realize that the shadow was her own, cast by the waning moon on the *shoji*, and that she had not yet fixed her hair.

She ran inside and quickly woke up her husband. As she said that a robber was trying to break into the house, he took up his sword, boasting he would easily kill the thief. As he went out, he saw the shadow of a big man carrying a drawn sword and shaking with fear. Not knowing that it was his own shadow on the *shoji*, he ran to his wife, and said that the robber was a big man but a coward, trembling with fear. He was afraid to go and meet the robber and asked his wife to go and chase him away.

Reluctantly she went, but as she went out she collided with the *shoji* and fell down. She happened to fall on her husband, who then thought that the robber had caught him, and fainted with fear. Only when his wife shook him and told him that she had only broken the *shoji*, did he become conscious.

But the husband was angry and said that the robber had escaped because she failed to act quickly. She then laughed at him and called him a coward, and all the villagers laughed at him when they learned what had actually happened.

SHICHIBEI JIZO

AT OME, a suburb of Tokyo, there stands a small stone statue of *Jizo* or Ksitigarbha, barely two feet high, which is commonly called *Shichibei Jizo*. It is still worshiped by many, but its origin is unknown to most people.

There once lived a wealthy farmer named Shichibei who was famous for his ability to outwalk and outrun anybody. He was able to go after sunset a distance of almost 50 kilometers and be back by daybreak, it was said.

It was this speed-walking that led him to the habit of visiting distant houses and robbing them of money and valuables. As his robberies became frequent, the authorities tried to catch this mysterious evil-doer.

One day, hearing that Kanta, a neighboring woodcutter, who was poor and had many children was suspected of the crime and arrested, Shichibei went to a spot in the forest where he was hiding his spoils, to take out some money to give to Kanta's family, but he was nabbed by the officials. As he was led away, Shichibei asked that the money be given to Kanta's wife.

For his crime, Shichibei was executed. Nobody was willing to take over his land and house, as the people thought they were cursed. The land remained a waste, but in the Taisho era, it was donated to the county of Nishitama, and a county office erected there.

But in the construction of the office building, many carpenters met with accidents. All thought that something must be done to appease the spirit of Shichibei. So a small stone statue of *Jizo* was made and placed in the building. In 1923 the office was abolished and the statue was placed outside on the road.

This statue called *Shichibei Jizo* had many worshipers as the people believed that prayers offered to it would make them walk fast and long, would cure beri-beri, and also protect them from thefts. Even many stalls were opened on its festival day held every month.

SNAIL'S TALE

A POOR farmer's wife lamented that she did not have a child, and prayed to *Omizu-gamisama* (god of water) daily for a baby. She finally gave birth to a baby, but to their utter surprise the baby was only a *tanishi* or pond snail. But knowing that the baby was given them by the grace of *Omizu-gamisama*, the farmer and his wife tenderly put it in a lacquer bowl filled with water and sand and placed it on the *kamidana* (family shrine shelf).

Twenty years passed but the snail never grew larger. One day, when the husband was about to start out carrying the tax rice on a horse to the town, he said with regret that if he had a son, he would help with such a task. Then, a voice from the bowl on the *kamidana* said, 'I am tired of being in the bowl, I will get out and work. Put me on the horse, and I will take the rice bales to town.'

So the snail was put on the back of the horse that carried the rice bales. The snail shouted orders to the horse, and also sang songs on the way to town. Arriving at the house of the village head, the snail shouted that he had brought the tax rice. The people recognized the horse, but did not see its owner around. 'Help unload the bales as I cannot,' the snail said. All were surprised, but as they looked at the horse in astonishment, they noticed a small snail on its back.

When the bales were unloaded, the village head took the snail into the house and offered him a meal. It ate heartily while all watched with great interest. They put it on their palms and petted it. The village head became fond of the snail and said that he wanted to keep it in his house. 'Our families have been on good terms for generations, I will give you one of my daughters if you will stay with us,' he said. The snail replied that he would marry the elder daughter and then returned home on the horse.

So the marriage of the snail with the headman's daughter was arranged. Dressed in her finest costume, the daughter went to the farmer's house to marry the snail. One day the young bride went to visit the Yakushi Shrine on its festival, carrying her husband-snail in the fold of her *obi.* When she arrived at the shrine gate, the snail said to her that she had to leave him there as it could not enter the shrine. So she went alone and prayed to Yakushi-sama to make her snail-husband a man. When she returned to the gate, the snail could not be found, though she searched all around, even entering the muddy ricefields.

'My dear wife,' somebody said behind her, and when she turned around a fine-looking young man stood there. 'I am your husband,' he said. 'Look at me. I was in the shape of a snail because I was born by the grace of the water god, but your prayer to Yakushi has made me a man.'

SNAKE BONE

OF SNAKE stories, there are many about snake bones which were treasured and worshiped. There is one snake bone tale told in two neighboring places in Tokyo which are almost identical and related.

Once a farmer went to a little pond at Kitazawa, and there he saw a small snake. He raised his sickle and playfully threatened it. The snake became angry and as it raised its head in fury, it became big. Frantically the farmer waved his sickle and cut off its jaw bones.

Then the snake dived into the water and entered an underground channel that ran to the lake at Inokashira. There it died, and the water of the lake turned red, it was said.

The jaw bone cut off by the farmer was enshrined at the Hosenji Temple at Nakano.

A similar incident took place at Tatsumayama, where the Higashi-Nakano railway station now stands, situated between Nakano and Kashiwagi. Here, however, half of the snake's jaw was placed in the Enshoji Temple at Kashiwagi, and the other half at the Hosenji Temple of Nakano.

Thus the Hosenji Temple had jaw bones from the two incidents. But the two tales are independently told and believed to be true.

Formerly when farmers of Kashiwagi prayed for rain, they brought water from Lake Inokashira, and poured it over the snake jaw bone enshrined at the Enshoji Temple, and then carried the bone through the village.

The two stories originating at different places, had the common point that the snake returned to Lake Inokashira after having been attacked by the farmer and losing its jaw bone.

At both temples, the snake bone was worshiped by the villagers in the old days. The tales are still believed by the local people, though the bones themselves do not exist any more.

SNAKE SHRINE

KIZAEMON was a poor farmer of the village of Gochoda in Saga Prefecture. As he had no child he prayed with his wife to the deity of Momidake mountain for a child for 21 days. On the final day of their prayers, they heard a divine voice which said that they would never have a child of their own, and they would have to adopt as their child the first thing their feet touched on the way home from the prayer offering.

Happy with the message, they started for home, but the first thing that touched their feet was a tiny snake. They looked at the snake with surprise and astonishment, but they had to follow the divine voice, and took the snake home.

As they fed and cared for the snake, it grew rapidly, and in five years reached 15 feet in length. The snake understood human words, and followed them everywhere. But the villagers were afraid of the big snake that always came with Kizaemon or his wife and gradually they came to avoid the two.

Finally Kizaemon talked to the snake and asked it to leave the house, so that they could live in peace with their neighbors. The snake seemed to understand his meaning and shortly disappeared. But after that the two aged quickly and became much poorer.

Just about that time, the canal by which water was brought to the village from the Shioda River collapsed, and when it was repaired, it broke again. The village suffered from a shortage of water and was unable even to plant rice.

The village head consulted a diviner to find a remedy to this unhappy situation. The diviner said that the canal's collapse was caused by a big snake that used to be kept by someone of the village and it was the wish of the snake to make the villagers contribute things to the person who fed it, so that he could live comfortably.

Kizaemon was the only one in the village who had kept a snake and fed it. So the villagers decided to collect the water-canal rice and give it every year to Kizaemon. From then the canal never failed to supply water and crops became abundant. So the *Ide* (water canal) Shrine was erected for the snake, and annually the villagers make visits to it in appreciation for its service to the village.

SNAKES AND SWORDS

MANY SUPERSTITIOUS stories of snakes are told in various countries. Japan is no exception. Snakes are not only regarded as sacred and worshiped as such, but also stories of snakes committing various acts are found all over the country.

In many of these tales, the snakes turn into swords or swords become snakes. It is probably from the similarity of their shape that such tales have developed.

Once a *samurai* went to Sendai on business, but when the time came for him to leave, he did not possess a sufficient sum of money to pay the inn bill. So he left his sword as a pledge for the payment of the unpaid balance. But the morning after he returned home, he saw that his sword had come back, taking the form of a snake.

Another *samurai* went on a journey, carrying a famous sword which was a family treasure. On the top of a mountain pass he rested, placing the heavy sword on a stone nearby. When he started again he forgot his sword. Soon he realized it and hurriedly dispatched a servant to fetch it. As the servant approached the stone he saw a huge snake sitting on it, and hesitated from going near it. He returned and reported it to his master. The master himself went back again, and he saw the sword on the stone but no snake.

A young *samurai* lay in a drunken sleep by a riverbank. Village youngsters saw him and planned to play a trick on him. But they could not get near the drunken *samurai* as a red snake was lying upon the sleeping man. When the *samurai* woke up, the snake had turned back into his sword.

SNAKE'S GRATITUDE

ONCE A WOMAN who approached a stone bridge going into the capital, saw that a young girl walking ahead of her had dislocated one of the stone slabs that formed the bridge, and noticed a small spotted snake come out from underneath the slab, so an old tale goes. The snake followed the young girl who, not knowing of the snake, entered Unrinji Temple. The woman who saw the snake following the girl, became curious, and also went into the temple. In the temple building the snake was seen sitting beside the girl, and when she left the temple for home, the snake was again following at her heels.

Determined to watch the snake, the woman went to the house, and announcing that she had come from a country village, asked to be allowed to stay at the house for the night. She was welcomed into a room, where she saw the snake sitting by the girl, but nobody seemed to notice its presence. She could not tell the people of the house about the snake, as she was afraid of causing any trouble.

Next morning the girl said that she had a strange dream during the night. In her dream she saw a woman whose lower body was a snake standing by her. The woman said that because of her sad past she was changed into a snake and entombed under the stone slab of the bridge, unable to move. 'But yesterday you tilted the slab and freed me,' said the woman in the dream. 'Furthermore, you took me to the temple and made me listen to the sermon of mercy. I am now saved, and will be reincarnated as a human being. To show my gratitude I will pray that you will always be happy and prosperous.'

When she told of her strange dream the snake was no longer there. Then the woman who followed the snake to the house explained how she saw the snake come from the bridge and follow the girl.

It is said that the girl soon married a person of virtue, position and wealth, and was happy all her life due to the gratitude of the snake she accidentally saved.

SNOW MAID

IN ECHIGO, Akita and Fukushima districts where heavy snow covers the fields and mountains for four long winter months, an old legend of *yuki-musume* or the snow maid is told. Versions differ somewhat according to district, but everywhere it is believed that *yuki-musume* is an evil spirit that brings harm to the people.

In these districts, little children are told on winter evenings to go to bed early or else *yuki-musume* will come and get them. In their cold beds the children are in the grip of fear as they hear the soft footsteps of the snow maid walking in the deep snow.

The grotesque forms trees take as they are heavily covered with snow are the origin of *yuki-musume*. Old pictures of *yuki-musume* generally show her with a long smooth face, almost featureless, long hair over her shoulders and lower body tapering to a narrow point. Thus she appears as if she has only one leg. This one-legged shape seen in many kinds of ghosts is said to have developed from *yuki-musume*.

But traditionally, *yuki-musume* is the spirit of a woman who fell into a deep mountain valley when she was going along a snow-covered mountain pass at night and died.

The rural people believe that when one meets *yuki-musume* on a mountain road, she will ask him to hold her baby, but if he agrees and takes her baby, the child will become heavier until he is buried under the snow by the baby's weight.

In Aizu district, it is said that if one rejects the request of *yuki-musume* nothing happens to him, but if he complies he will get into trouble. In another region, it is said that if one turns his

back to her, he will be pushed into a deep valley. There are also tales of *yuki-musume* marrying young men, and one of such stories was translated by Lafcadio Hearn.

In Echigo province, when heavy snow covers the mountain, cries of babies and women are heard down in the bottom of snow-covered valleys. They are the cries of those who were lured to the bottom of the valley by *yuki-musume*.

SOZEN

THE HORSE BREEDERS of Tohoku, the northeastern district of Japan, still worship *Sozen* as the deity governing the birth and growth of horses. Particularly when they send their colts to the horse fair or when their horses foal, they do not forget to offer *sake* to *Sozen.*

Opinion varies as to the identity of this deity, but generally it is now believed that *Sozen* originally meant sacred white horse. As white horses are highly prized, all breeders naturally hoped that they would have gray colts that would become white with age.

White horses were regarded sacred. They were formerly presented to shrines as horses for the enshrined deities. Emperors rode on them. To have gray colts, therefore, used to be the foremost wish of all horse breeders, and this hope developed into the worship of *Sozen.* Thus, the northeastern horse breeders have their *Sozen-ko* or *Sozen* worshiping groups.

In some places, *Sozen* is also regarded as the guardian deity of silkworms. Probably the people thought that the deity who protected horses would also be good enough to look after the silkworms.

The *Myoken* (Sudrsti) or North Pole star is also worshiped as the guardian deity of horses. It is not known clearly how this Buddhist saint came to be worshiped by horse breeders and dealers.

Hunters formerly never shot their arrows or bullets northward, as *Myoken* reigned in the north. The deity was not only the guardian of horses but also of wild animals.

White horses are no longer held sacred but horse breeders and dealers still believe in the power of *Sozen* to bring them good horses, and thus make prayers and offerings to him.

SPARROW AND SWALLOW

IN SOME PARTS of Japan it is believed that the *suzume* (sparrow) and *tsubame* (swallow) were formerly sisters. Being sisters, of course, they looked alike. But like so many other sisters, they differed in nature, and because they were so different in their character, they came to look so distinctly different as they are today.

It is not explained how they looked when they were sisters, but they are today very different in appearance.

When they were still sisters and were playing together, the news that their parents were seriously ill reached them. The news surprised them both, and they decided to return home immediately and see their parents. But swallow was a vain, foppish bird, and before it started on its journey home to see its dying parents, it took its time in making its toilet and adjusting its feathers. Because it took so much time in making preparations for the journey, it lost much time, and when it reached home the parents were already dead. On the other hand, when the news reached sparrow, it was making its toilet, but without finishing, it flew away at once towards home and was able to see its parents before they died.

Now, because sparrow was so filial as to stop everything and fly away to its parents, it was blessed by heaven and always has sufficient food to eat. But as it stopped its toilet when the sad news came, it became ugly from that moment. So sparrow is now dark and ugly to look at, but it always has good things to eat.

On the other hand, swallow is now beautiful as it finished its toilet leisurely even when its parents were dying. But as it did not think of its parents at their dying moment and failed to reach them in time, it was punished by heaven and it has to travel all over the world for its food, and it even has to eat mud.

Thus it was from the time of the death of their parents that their appearance suddenly changed. Further, since they have changed in their forms and colors, they are not at all friendly. The nests made by swallows are often taken possession of by sparrows. Again, sparrows' nests are taken by swallows. They are not even on speaking terms with each other. They seldom meet, as the swallow has to travel so far and often to find its food and cannot stay in one place. But the sparrow is happy, with plenty of food nearby and does not need to travel far for its food, although it lost its beauty and color because of its thought for its dying parents.

So the swallow and sparrow were sisters formerly, but because they were so different in nature, they became so different in color and shape. Heaven gave them proper rewards for their good points, and punished them for their shortcomings.

This story is especially believed in the Kumano district where it is known to every child, but even in other places it is believed by older people though it might not be known to young folks.

STOLEN DREAM

THE JAPANESE are told to keep good dreams secret. When you have had a very pleasant dream that promises you unexpected good fortune, don't tell it to others. If you do, somebody may steal your happy dream and you will lose the good fortune it predicted.

Once, in a town in Bitchu (now Okayama Prefecture), the son of the town chief was visiting a woman dream interpreter, a story goes. There he saw a richly dressed young man, son of the provincial lord, attended by several servants, enter the house. He heard the lord's son telling about his dream and asking the woman interpreter its meaning. The woman told him that the dream was exceptionally good, and predicted that the dreamer would become a great official.

When the lord's son and his party left, the town youth went to the dream interpreter, and said "Give me that dream he had." He explained that she had known him all his life; but the lord would soon be transferred to another district, and his son was nothing to her. The young man urged her to give him the lucky dream.

Finally she consented and said that, if he could tell the dream in exactly the same words, she would give it to him. As he had listened to the lord's son describing his dream, the young man was able to repeat it word for word. Then, the woman interpreter told the young man that the dream predicted his rapid rise in official position and he would become a great statesman.

Thanking her, he returned home and applied himself diligently to his studies. Gradually he rose in official status, and was finally sent by the emperor to China. Thus he became a great man as the dream he stole had predicted.

On the other hand, the lord's son, the original dreamer, had no luck and never attained a notable post because his dream had been stolen.

STOPPING THE SUN

RICE PLANTING has always been a great event for the Japanese, and naturally there are many traditional tales about it. In many parts of the country there was a custom of finishing the rice planting in one day, and this inspired many tales.

The Kosan-ike in the San-in district was formerly the ricefield of the village leader. Every year he employed a large number of men and women to finish planting rice in his field in one day. But once it happened that when the sun began to set behind the western hill, a portion of his vast field had not yet been planted. The sun must be stopped from setting, the village leader thought, and he raised his golden fan and beckoned to the sun to stop.

The charm worked. The sun stopped and he was able to finish planting.

But the next year the same thing happened. He again raised his golden fan and asked the sun to stop. It might be that the repeated request angered the sun, or his power of wealth had waned. At any rate, the sun did not listen the second time. Instead, his vast field suddenly turned into a waste lake, no longer producing rice.

There was another in Yonabaru in Kumamoto, Kyushu, who held thousands of acres of ricefields, and on planting day, he used more than a thousand workers, cattle and horses. One May day when his fields were being planted the sun began to set, and so he raised his golden fan and pulled back the sun a little way so that the planting could be finished.

He succeeded, but soon he regretted

his act. He brought 3,000 caskets of oil to a hill near his fields, and set them on fire. Then he told other people that he had planted by the light given off by the burning oil. However, he could not escape punishment. Soon his big house and all his warehouses were destroyed by fire. The hill on which he had burned his oil was scorched black, and not even weeds have grown there since.

SUMIDAGAWA

SUMIDAGAWA is the main river passing through Tokyo. Many legends and tales have been told about this river since Edo days. The most famous of them is about a boy named Umewaka-maru and his mother.

The *Noh* play named *Sumidagawa* appeared in the middle of the Muromachi period or about the beginning of the 16th century. This story became the basis for numerous versions that appeared later. A story named *Sumidagawa* was written in 1656, and soon it became the scheme for the music of *joruri*. Then in 1770, the famous playwright Chikamatsu Monzaemon wrote his play *Sumidagawa* for *Kabuki*. The story has also been adapted for *nagauta*, *kiyomoto*, *tokiwazu* and other forms of music.

One day in March as told in the *Noh* version, a boy went to the bank of the river and fell moaning. He said he was Umewaka-maru, a son of a Kyoto nobleman, but one day when he was returning home he was carried away by an abductor and taken east. Becoming sick, he could not walk a step farther, so his abductor deserted him.

In pity the people cared for him, but he soon died. They buried him by the river where he was found and planted a willow tree there. A year later, on his death anniversary, the neighbors gathered at his grave and offered prayers for him.

Then a woman who came on a ferryboat and saw the gathering of the people on the shore, asked what they were doing. As she was told the sad story of the boy, she realized that the dead boy was her son. Maddened with grief, she joined the people and, ringing a bell, she loudly offered Buddhist prayers.

At that moment, from the tomb appeared the form of the young boy, and as he watched his mother's face, he mysteriously disappeared.

Sumidagawa is one of the first Japanese tales telling of the love of a mother for her child, and is still very popular as indicated by the frequent presentation of the story on the stage and in music.

TAKETORI MONOGATARI

TAKETORI-MONOGATARI (Tale of a Bamboo Cutter) is the oldest story in Japan. The author is unknown, but it is said to have been written in the ninth century. The story itself is much older, and references to it are made in *Manyoshu*.

The story has another unique feature. Tales of humans loving or marrying non-human or superhuman beings are common in all countries, but in *Taketori-Monogatari*, the bamboo cutter adopts and raises a non-human as his child. This type of story is rare.

An old man engaged in cutting bamboo one day comes upon a bamboo that glows with light. He cuts it and finds within a beautiful little girl three inches high. He takes her home and raises her as his child. In three months she grows into a woman so beautiful that she comes to be called *Kaguya-hime* (Brilliant Maiden).

Her beauty attracts many young men, but all fail to win her favor. Finally five young noblemen are left.

Kaguya-hime tells them she will marry the one who carries out her desire. Then she gives each an impossible task. The first one is asked to get a stone basin of Buddha from India, but he produces only a temple basin and fails. The second is told to get a gem branch from Horai (Island of Eternal Youth), but his imitation made of gold, silver and gems is found out. The third is to bring a fur coat that will not burn, but the coat he brings burns upon testing. The fourth is asked to bring a gem from the neck of a dragon, but his ship is wrecked in a storm. The fifth is given an order to bring a *koyasu-gai* (cowrie shell) of a swallow, and thinking that the bird has such a shell he climbs atop a roof, and falls to the ground and dies.

Finally, the emperor asks her to marry him. But when the emperor touches her hand, she vanishes, leaving a drug for eternal life. The emperor does not wish to live forever after losing her, and burns it up on top of Mt. Fuji.

TALKING TURTLE

SEVERAL VILLAGERS of Nakatsu-mura, near Ogaki, found a giant turtle in an old pond high on a mountain. They put the turtle in a bamboo basket and started toward Ogaki to sell it to a fish dealer.

As they passed another pond, a voice from the bottom of the pond said clearly, 'Where are you going?' Then the turtle in the basket they carried answered, 'Today I am going to Ogaki.' 'When are you coming back?' asked the voice from the pond, and the turtle replied, 'I shall not stay there long. I will be back tomorrow.'

Hearing the conversation between the turtle in the basket and someone in the pond not only surprised those carrying the basket, but also made them

afraid of the turtle. They thought the turtle they had caught must be the *nushi* or lord of the pond and possessed some mysterious power.

One of the villagers said that they should set the turtle free, but the others objected and explained that the turtle would not be killed even if it was sold, as it had clearly said that it would be back the next day.

So they decided to sell the turtle as originally planned, but they resolved to make some offerings to the temple from the money they gained, and then kill no more living things in their lifetime.

They proceeded to the town of Ogaki and sold the huge turtle to a fish-monger. Several days later, as they happened to be in the town, they stopped by at the fishmonger's. Seeing them, the fish dealer said that the turtle he had bought from them was a monster with terrible strength. He said the turtle had been placed in a strong cage which could not be cut open even with big knives, but by the next morning it had gotten away.

This tale is one of many told all over the country about fish, birds or animals that possessed the power of speech. Most of them gained this power because of their advanced age or by possessing supernatural powers.

TAMAMONOMAE

THE STORY of Tamamonomae, a fox-woman, has been made into *Noh* and *Kabuki* plays. Legends in which foxes impersonate humans are numerous, but the Tamamonomae tale is outstanding, because it begins in India, goes to China and ends in Japan.

A fox born in India attained a great age, and its fur turned to a golden color. Furthermore, its tail multiplied as it became older and finally it had nine tails. The nine-tailed fox turned into a beautiful woman and managed to marry an Indian prince. But her impersonation was found out by a physician who noticed that her pulse beat was not that of a human.

So she fled to China, where she became the wife of a Yin emperor, and influenced him in imposing an evil and cruel rule. But here again, her real self was discovered and she could not stay there.

At that time, Kibi-no-Makibi, a Japanese official sent to China in the eighth century, was waiting for a ship to take him home. She managed to be employed by Kibi as his maid and was taken to Japan with him. But as soon as the ship reached Japan, she disappeared and for 500 years nothing was known of her.

When it was learned that Prince Murakumo would soon become the emperor, the fox-woman made an appearance and attempted to enter the Court by some means. But her identity and plan were discovered by Abe-no-Seimei, and she fled to the wild plain of Nasu.

As it became known that a fox-woman with evil powers had gone to Nasu to hide, troops were dispatched to catch her. Locating her, 15,000 fighters surrounded the spot. The fox-woman realized that she could not escape capture even with her evil powers, and turned herself into a rock so she would not be caught.

Her anger and grudge against humans remained in the rock, and anybody who approached the rock was killed by its poison. So the rock came to be known as *Sesshoseki* or life-destroying rock, about which many other tales came to be told.

TAMA SNOW MAID

MANY TALES of *Yuki-onna* (Snow Maid) are told in regions deeply covered with snow in winter, but the Tama River district of Tokyo also has a snow maid story.

Minokichi, a young wood-cutter living by the Tama River, went one cold winter day with his aged uncle to bring down kindling from the mountain. As they reached the Tama ferry on their way home, a snowstorm arose. While they sat and waited in a hut for the ferryboat, they fell asleep. It was bitter cold, and when Minokichi woke up, he saw a strange white woman standing in the hut.

The woman went to the sleeping uncle and passed her hand over his mouth. Then coming toward Minokichi, she said that as he was young she would spare his life and commanded him not to tell anyone what had happened in the hut. Then she disappeared. The uncle was dead and Minokichi carried him home on his back.

One winter's day a year later, Minokichi again came to the ferry where he saw standing a young woman dressed for travel, carrying a broad hat. She asked him the way to Edo, so he told her that it was dark and for a woman to travel to Edo was difficult. He proposed to go a little way with her. She told him that she had come from the mountain on the other side of the river and was going to Edo to obtain work.

As it had begun to snow, Minokichi took her to his home. She did not leave the house the next morning. She stayed and married Minokichi. Ten years passed and they had three children.

One evening, as she was putting the three children to bed, Minokichi who was watching her suddenly said, "Just like her." "What do you mean?" she asked. "You look just like the woman I saw at the ferry hut 10 years ago," he replied.

"I am that woman. I have stayed here

because I love the children. I have been here 10 years but it is now time for me to return to the other side of the river. Good-bye," she said, and with that she mysteriously disappeared.

Even today, children of the district say that snow comes from the mountain on the other side of the Tama River.

TARO DIGGER

KANAZAWA, the greatest city in Hokuriku, on the Japan Sea, is famous for Kenroku Park, one of the three famous gardens of Japan, and also for various cultural relics and artistic products. It was Lord Maeda, one of the greatest and richest feudal lords in the Tokugawa era who built Kanazawa into such an important city.

It is said Kanazawa (gold marsh) was so named because gold dust was found there by Imohori Togoro (Togoro, the taro digger) whose tomb still stands at Fushimi Temple in the city. Recently, however, some say that it was one named Togashi Jiro who found gold there.

Togoro was a poor man who made his living by digging taro potatoes in the mountains, and had only a tiny hut, the legend says. One day to his humble home came a beautiful maiden named Wago, the daughter of Ukon Mannobu, a rich man in Hatsuse, Yamato province. She stayed on as Togoro's wife.

In digging the taro, Togoro threw out the earth in which were many gold nuggets, but he did not know they were valuable. Some he collected and took home. One day, seeing a duck on the ground, he threw the gold nuggets at the bird.

Then his wife told him that the nuggets he threw at the bird were gold and very precious. He replied that in the holes he dug for taro there were many

of them. So saying, he went to the mountains and returned with a bagful of gold nuggets, and washed them in a little stream.

That stream is now the Izumi-no-mizu in Kenroku Park, it is said. Because of Togoro finding gold, the place came to be called Kanazawa or gold marsh.

Similar stories of someone accidentally finding gold in the mountains, not knowing its value, are told all over the country.

THIEF THANKED

A FARMER named Kiuemon went one day to cut and gather grass. In the dense growth, his sharp sickle caught a giant snake, but when he noticed it, its head was already cut off, and he saw only its tail wiggling, so it is told in the Chichibu mountain region.

When he returned home, he told of the incident to his wife. It happened that a thief was hiding behind the bales of beans stored in the next room, and he heard Kiuemon's tale.

When the farmer and his wife went to bed, the thief came out shouldering a bale of beans, but suddenly he uttered a cry of fear and surprise. He saw some shining object jump out of the basket to carry grass and go into the water jar in the kitchen.

Then he remembered the farmer's story of killing a snake, and realized that the shining thing must be the snake head that had fallen into the basket which Kiuemon had carried home.

Also it occurred to the thief that the snake head had jumped from the basket to the water jar to poison the water and thus kill the farmer and his wife in revenge.

Realizing the seriousness of the situation, the thief rushed into the farmer's room, forgetting that he had come there to steal beans, and aroused him by shaking him roughly. Awakening suddenly, Kiuemon saw a strange man bending over him and asked what he was doing in the house. Then the thief told him that the head of the snake the farmer had killed during the day was in the water. It was the snake's aim to kill him, he explained.

Kiuemon felt so grateful to the thief for waking and saving him that in appreciation he gave him the bale of beans.

THOUSAND SANDALS

THE TALE of *tennyo* or angels coming down to bathe and losing their heavenly robes is told all over the country with different variations. The *tennyo* story told at Amami-Oshima, between Kagoshima and Ryukyu is unique.

Once there was an old man who lived with a black dog, One day he heard strange, sweet music which seemed to come from a lake nearby. He found an angel's robe hanging on a pine tree and took it home. The angel who was swimming in the lake discovered the loss of her robe, without which she could not return to heaven.

In search of it she went into the old man's house. Entering, she asked for some tobacco, and came to live with him. She bore him three children. One day when the second child was looking after the baby, he began to cry. The child told the baby that if it would stop crying he would open the millet storehouse and take out and give it the heavenly robe hidden there.

The angel happened to hear what the second child said and learned where her robe was hidden. Immediately she went to the millet storehouse and, taking out her robe, she rose to heaven with the second child.

Finding that the angel had returned

to heaven, the old man decided to go after her, wearing a thousand *zori* or sandals. He made sandal after sandal, but when he had made 999, he found that he could make no more. Then his dog offered itself to take the place of the last sandal.

So he rode on his 999 sandals and the black dog and managed to reach heaven. The old man met his angel again but he did not try to come down. Nor did the dog return to earth. The old man became the star that is seen first at dawn, and his dog became another that comes out after the old man's star.

The angel took the second child who revealed the hiding place of her robe with her but nothing is said about her two other children in this tale.

TREE'S VENGEANCE

THERE ONCE stood on the summit of Kakenoyama mountain, in the province of Awa, Shikoku, a giant *kusunoki* (camphor tree), a mighty monarch of the forest, which was regarded sacred by the villagers of the surrounding area. The people told the time of the day by its shadow and worshiped it as the guardian deity of the mountain and villages.

But an unexpected thing saddened the hearts of all the people. An order came from Lord Hachisuka of the province to the magistrate of the district that the sacred *kusunoki* must be cut down at once. Taiko Hideyoshi was planning an expedition to Korea (1592) and Lord Hachisuka was one of his chiefs upon whom fell the task of building a strong naval unit. The giant camphor was selected as the tree to provide timber for building a great war vessel.

The villagers had no right or power to stop the felling of the tree they had worshiped for generations. With sadness and fear they gathered around the tree as woodcutters brought by the magistrate started to wield their hatchets against the mighty trunk. As the first woodcutter struck his hatchet on the tree, it quivered and the tree shed some of its leaves. But only shallow cuts could be made by the strongest of woodcutters, and out of such cuts blood oozed.

The first day's work was slow, despite the loud urging of the magistrate. The next morning the tree showed no mark of the cuts made on the previous day. It was the same day after day. No progress was made in cutting down the tree. Finally the magistrate called a holy man from Tokushima, and made him pray before the sacred camphor. In a trance, he said that a woman and an unborn child must be sacrificed. Hearing this, the magistrate and all the villagers showed fear and despair.

Then O-yasu, the wife of the magistrate, appeared on the scene. Before anyone could understand what she intended to do, she put herself in a shallow cut on the trunk, which quickly closed after her. She and her unborn child were sacrificed, and in two days the tree was cut down.

In a few months the *Taian Maru,* a mightly war vessel, was constructed with timber obtained from the sacred tree, but it hit a rock in the Naruto Straits on its maiden voyage, and went down to the sea bottom without taking part in the expedition.

After the tree was cut down, O-yasu's body was taken out of the tree and buried by its stump. A shrine erected by the villagers for her still stands there and is worshiped by them.

TSUBAKI

TSUBAKI (Japanese camellia) is found all over Japan except in Hokkaido, but seems to grow best in warm districts. There are more than 200 kinds, but the wild variety that is found on many mountains and hills has single red petals.

Blossoms range in color from a light shade of red to white, or white with patches of red, and come in single or double petals. The shape of the leaf is also different in many cases. There are many famous spots for *tsubaki.*

In the feudal days, the people of the military class did not like this blossom, because in most varieties the head drops off whole and not petal by petal as in the case of most flowers. To the military men, the fallen *tsubaki* blossom symbolized the cutting of their heads, the most dreaded fate for them. Thus they regarded the *tsubaki* as unlucky.

But the common people have always loved the flower and *tsubaki* trees are planted in gardens and the branches used in flower arrangement.

It blossoms in winter or early spring and bears fruits in autumn which are gathered and pressed to obtain highly valued cooking and hair oil. *Tsubaki* oil is a profitable product of many districts.

The leaves are glossy and beautiful, and thus often used to decorate or wrap soft Japanese cakes. When tobacco was first introduced into the country, cut tobacco was rolled in *tsubaki* leaves in some districts. It is said that the leaves improved the taste. Deer are fond of the bark of these trees. The ash obtained by burning the leaves was formerly used as a dye.

There is a kind of *tsubaki* named *sazanka,* which flowers in autumn and bears fruit the following spring. This plant, with single-petal white blossoms, is also a popular garden tree.

The following tale is told about *Tsubaki-yama* (Camellia Mountain) at

Aomori Bay.

A young man who used to go to Aomori annually to carry timber to western ports on a small ship, fell in love with an Aomori woman. One year, when he was about to leave Aomori, the maiden asked him to bring back some *tsubaki* seeds on his next trip, as she had heard that western women used camellia oil on their hair and they had long glossy black hair. He promised to bring her some seeds.

But he did not come north for two years because of various reasons. When he returned in the third year with the promised camellia seeds, he found that he was too late. The girl had waited two years for him, but as he failed to make an appearance she thought that he did not love her. In despair, she had jumped into the sea and killed herself.

Learning of her death, the young man went to her tomb at the top of the hill overlooking the bay, and planted the camellia seeds around the spot where she was buried. These seeds grew into big trees and blossomed every year.

But it was said that, if anyone started to break a branch of the trees, a beautiful woman always appeared to stop him. So none touched the camellia trees. Later a shrine was erected in honor of the maiden, and it was named Tsubaki Myojin or Camellia Deity. Women worship at the shrine for good luck, particularly for success in love.

Once a person stole a branch of one of the camellia trees, but on his homeward trip the sea suddenly became rough and he had to throw the branch away to save himself from death, so a story goes.

TURTLE'S TRICK

A TURTLE'S WIFE was sick with stomach trouble and asked her husband to get a monkey's liver, as it was said to be the best remedy for her sickness. The turtle wanted to get the liver for his wife and went ashore. He waited for a monkey to appear and approaching one, calmly inquired if there was abundant food on the mountain. Food was scarce, the monkey replied.

Thereupon, the turtle told the monkey, 'Near our place is a vast forest full of good fruit. I will take you there if you wish.'

Believing the turtle's words, the monkey agreed to go with him. The turtle carried the monkey on his back and went into the sea. When they were far from the shore the turtle turned to the monkey and said, 'You don't know it, but my wife is sick, and so I brought you out here to get your liver.'

The monkey then knew that he had been tricked and became angry, but calmly he said, 'You are ignorant. Monkeys do not carry their livers in their bodies. They keep the livers on tree branches? If you wanted liver, why didn't you say so? I could just take down my liver and also many others from the trees and give them to you.'

The simple-minded turtle believed the monkey, and proposed to return to the shore, but he made the monkey promise again to give him his liver.

When they reached the shore the monkey jumped off the turtle's back and hurriedly climbed a tree. Looking down on the turtle, he shouted, 'You big fool, how could a liver be out of one's body?'

Only then did the turtle realize that the monkey had planned to trick him, but his anger made him shout at the monkey in the tree, 'Monkeys are certainly fools. You did not know there was no fruit at the bottom of the sea.'

TWO DIVINERS

MANY DIVINERS are said to have been able to know past events and predict the future. One old tale proving the remarkable ability of such diviners runs as follows.

To a solitary farmhouse in an almost uninhabited region where only a young woman lived, came a strange traveller. He asked for a night's lodging. As he sat down in the house, the woman asked him to return the sum of 1,000 *ryo* he owed her. Surprised at the strange demand, he asked for an explanation.

The woman said that her father had died 10 years before, and on his deathbed he told her that exactly 10 years after, there would come a traveller to the house, and she should ask him to return the thousand *ryo* he owed. Until that time, the father said, she should never leave or part with the house, however hard it might be to make her living. So the woman sold almost everything in the house, but remained there as commanded by her father.

The traveller meditated a while, and then asked the woman if her father had been interested in divinity. She answered that he was a great diviner.

Then the traveller smiled, and walking to a pillar in the room, tapped it with his knuckles. Hearing a hollow sound at one spot, he ordered the woman to cut open the pillar at that spot. Within the hollow a bag containing 1,000 *ryo* was found.

The woman was bewildered, but the traveller remarked that he was also a diviner, but her father was a greater one.

Her father, he explained, saw that 10 years after his death a diviner would come to the house. So he hid the money in the pillar, knowing that the visiting diviner would find it for the daughter.

So he had told the daughter not to leave the house for 10 years. Her father must have realized that if he had left her money, she would soon spend it. So he made her wait that long to get the money.

URIKO-HIME

THERE IS A story told in the Dewa region in the northeastern part of the country about *Uriko-hime* (Melon Maid) of Kurokawa village.

There lived a farmer named Magosaburo in Kurokawa, who one day saw a melon floating down the river. He picked it up and taking it home placed it on the shelf of the *kamidana* or family shrine. Suddenly some time later, he heard a baby crying. He looked all over the house and as his eyes reached the shelf, there he saw a baby girl born out of the melon.

He tenderly reared the baby who grew to be a beautiful girl. He named her *Uriko-hime* and loved to watch her all the time. He neglected his farm, as he was unhappy if he did not keep on looking at her. He carried her everywhere he went. As he could not do any work carrying her, he drew her picture and placed it in the field where he could see it while he worked.

One day, however, a strong wind came and carried the picture away. He could not find it anywhere. One day the lord of a nearby castle found something like a kite caught on the branches of a pine tree in his garden. When he had it taken down, it turned out to be the picture of a beautiful girl.

The lord had never seen such a beautiful girl, and thinking that the original of the painted maiden must exist somewhere, he sent his men through the neighborhood to find her. Magosaburo spent every day looking for the picture, and while he was away, the lord's men reached his house. Finding *Uriko-hime*, they carried her to the castle of their lord.

Magosaburo was in despair when he heard that she had been taken to the lord's castle. But when he went there to see her he was not allowed to enter. Remembering that she was fond of chestnuts, he went as a chestnut peddler and daily visited the castle.

Uriko-hime was very unhappy in the castle and spoke to no one. One day she heard the peddler's shout "Chestnuts, chestnuts," and she smiled. The lord saw her smile for the first time, and was struck by her beautiful smiling face. Wishing to see her smile again, he rushed out to the street and, catching the peddler, proposed exchanging clothes with him.

Dressed as the peddler and carrying the basket of chestnuts, the lord shouted, "Chestnuts, chestnuts" and looked at the maiden from the street, and she smiled. He was happy and kept on shouting "Chestnuts" on the street.

Magosaburo, dressed as the lord, entered the gate and met *Uriko-hime*. As night came, the gate was closed and when the lord dressed as the peddler sought to enter the castle, he was rejected. Magosaburo remained in the castle, happy with *Uriko-hime*.

USELESS NURSE

A LITTLE POND near Numazu, Shizuoka Prefecture, was commonly called *Uba-kainai* (useless nurse) in Edo days. A nurse carrying a little child on her back went near the pond one day, the story goes, and as the child saw his own reflection in the water, he struggled to get a better view and fell from the nurse's back into the pond and drowned. The nursemaid was so ashamed of her failure to look after her charge that she also jumped into the water.

The father of the child went to the side of the pond, and gazing at the water, lamented saying the nurse was *kainai* (useless). Then bubbles came up from the bottom of the pond as though the spirit of the nurse had responded to the master's remark.

Ever after, whenever anyone came to the pond and uttered the word *kainai*, bubbles rose from the bottom to the surface, it was said.

Similar tales are heard in many parts of the country. At the village of Rengeji in Echigo there was a well named *Obagaido* (old woman's well). When one stood at its side and shouted *"oba,"* bubbles rose from the bottom. But no other words would make the bubbles come up. It was said that once a maidservant accidentally dropped a child into the well and it died. In repentance, she also jumped into the well.

By the Otonashi River in the Bungo district, Kyushu, there was a well named *Nenbutsu-sui* (prayer water). Here bubbles rose whenever someone came to its side and called out *"Namu-amida-Butsu"* (Save us, Merciful Buddha), the Buddhist invocation.

At the village of Tomo-oka, southwest of Kyoto, there was a pond named *Nenbutsu-ike* (prayer pond). The pond had no water usually, but when one stood by its side and said *Nenbutsu* or the Buddhist prayer, water rose from the bottom.

UTSUBO-BUNE

THERE ARE many ancient tales told about *utsubo-bune* or dugout boats that drifted to the shores of Japan. They must have come from various regions, but mostly from China and the South Sea areas. Sometimes they were manned by people, men or women, but more often those on board were dead when they reached these shores.

At any rate, the coming of these drifting log boats was a great event to the ancient inhabitants. Not only were the persons and things on board such boats strange to them, but they attached various meanings to their coming and also to things that came in such boats.

One ancient record of the *utsubo-bune* that came to the shores of Hitachi says that the boat was shaped like a round incense box. It was 13 feet long with iron plates lining the bottom. The boat had a cover, and under it was a dead woman with red hair. There was also a jar of water, and the woman held a wooden box fast to her bosom. Many tales came to be told about the woman and her box.

Toyora of Hitachi also has a story that, in the reign of Emperor Kinmei in the seventh century, an *utsubo-bune* brought a daughter of the Chinese emperor, who left her country on account of hateful treatment by her foster mother. A story is also circulated that she brought silk cocoons to Japan.

A fisherman on his homeward voyage noticed an *utsubo-bune* drifting, and towed it to the shore. On the boat was a little girl about 12 years old. She said she was from China and the fisherman raised her. Growing into a beautiful woman, she married a nobleman's son. Her tomb still stands at a place called Funakoshi.

The persons and things that came on these drifting dugouts have often been enshrined and worshiped, because the ancient people thought there must be something divine in the boats and persons to brave the vast sea and frequent storms to reach their shores.

UZAEMON ZAKURA

MANY TALES are told about *sakura* blossoms. There is a cherry tree near Enshoji Temple, at Kashiwagi, Shinjuku, Tokyo, which is known as the *Uzaemon Zakura.*

In the ninth century, there was a Court official named Kashiwagi Uzaemon at Nara. He fell in love with a maiden named Sannomiya, but his love affair came to be talked about in the capital. He was greatly worried and took to drinking. Because of his conduct he was exiled to the province of Musashi and thus he settled in the locality which came to be named after him as Kashiwagi.

Soon he learned that Sannomiya had given birth to a boy. Wishing that his son would grow to be as bright as the *sakura* blossoms, he obtained a small cherry tree from Nara, and planted it in his garden. Daily he tended the tree as though it were his son, hoping for the boy's healthy growth.

Several years passed, and a messenger came from Nara, bringing his pardon. But Uzaemon was then very ill and could not return home. Realizing that he could never again set foot in Nara, he only expressed his wish that his boy would grow well and strong. With this prayer he died.

The villagers who knew Uzaemon's history, particularly of his love for his boy in Nara and his tender care of the *sakura* tree, resolved to take care of the tree, naming it *Uzaemon Zakura.* It is said that the boy grew up to be a fine man and always had the fragrance of *sakura.*

The cherry tree planted at Kashiwagi by Uzaemon of course died, but the villagers, who felt sorry for him, planted another tree there to perpetuate his eager wish for his boy. Thus *Uzaemon Zakura* still exists, blossoming beautifully every spring, as the tradition has been kept up by the villagers for generations.

WARAI BANASHI

MANY OLD *warai banashi* or funny stories are still loved by rural children. They are mostly very simple and foolish. Many are tall tales telling of unusual deeds or objects.

In one tale a hunter armed with a crooked gun shot at a group of badgers and killed all of them as the bullet kept going around in a circle. In another tale several hundred ducks were on the lake, but as the water froze during the night, their legs were frozen with the ice and they could not fly away. A farmer went out with a sickle and collected all the ducks by cutting their legs. He tied the ducks to his waist band but as they flapped their wings together, he was carried up. Finally he fell on top of a five-story tower.

One man in Fukushima, it is told, boasted that he once saw a big wooden tub, in which a thousand cattle could have their feet washed. Another man said that he saw a bamboo that reached heaven. The first one asked what such a tall bamboo could be used for, and the second replied that it would be used to bind the tub for a thousand cattle.

The well-known story of an angel losing her feather garment while bathing often ends as a *warai banashi*. While the angel was bathing in the lake, a farmer stole her feather garment and made her stay with him. But later she found where the man was hiding her robe and putting it on, she flew back to heaven. Then the farmer buried a thousand cattle in his field, and over the spot planted a melon seed. The melon plant grew rapidly and tall, finally reaching heaven. Using the melon vine as a ladder he climbed up to heaven, where he found his angel. He was happy with her and stayed in heaven.

Such *warai banashi* no longer interest city children, but in rural districts children are still heard telling such ancient funny tales.

WEAVER'S EARTHLY LOVER

TANABATA (star festival), one of the most ancient festivals, is still observed throughout the country on July 7 because of its beautiful and mystic tradition. The idea of having a festival for the Weaver or Star Vega came from China, and *tanabata* (originally meaning weaving looms or weaving maidens) is mentioned in the *Manyoshu* poems. At the Shosoin treasure repository in Nara, some utensils used for its observance in those early days are still kept.

Weaver and Altair, lovers separated by the Milky Way, meet once a year on July 7, it is said. Magpies carry the Star Vega on their wings to cross the heavenly river. If it rains, meeting becomes impossible, and so the people pray for fair weather.

Offerings of fresh vegetables and fruits are placed on a table set in the garden. In many districts one is even allowed to steal vegetables from other people's farms for *tanabata* offerings. Formerly, as part of the festival, strings of five colors, red, yellow, green, white and black, were tied to branches of a bamboo erected in the garden, but narrow strips of paper of five colors are now used.

Ancient people used to write on the leaves of the *kapi*, a kind of mulberry, with ink made by rubbing an ink stone in dew drops gathered from taro leaves. This act was believed to ensure one's advance in various skills. Today the people write words and poems on *tanzaku* or narrow strips of paper and hang them on bamboo branches.

Though *tanabata* is based on a Chinese tradition, many rites observed on the evening in various districts show its relation to farm work. Though city people pray that it will be fair, many rural folks still hope for rain. There are regions where farmers believe that rain, however little, will surely come during that evening. When it rains heavily and washes away the *tanabata tanzaku*, they feel quite happy.

In some districts, farmers still follow the custom of washing their cattle and horses on this evening. Children, too, have water poured over them. Farmers then wash their farming tools and clean their wells and nearby rivers. At Matsumoto in Nagano, children's clothing is hung from the house eaves. In other places straw dolls are made and floated on the rivers.

Thus, not only is *tanabata* regarded as a farm rite, but in certain parts it is observed as part of the rite for ancestral spirits held mainly in the middle of July. There is a tendency to make *tanabata* a community festival, though in the past it was mainly a family rite.

Kuo Han, a student, according to one story, was enjoying the cool evening breeze at his humble house on a summer day. Suddenly he noticed a rare perfume in the air, and when he looked up he saw a beautiful maiden attended by two maid-servants entering his house. She said she was the Weaver, and that with the permission of the Heavenly King, she had come to visit the human world.

Suddenly his little house turned into a magnificent palace, and the two maids attended eagerly to all household duties. The maiden left the house in the morning, but returned at night. One night Kuo said to her that Altair might become angry if she came to him every evening. Smiling, she replied, "Don't worry, he is on the other side of the Milky Way, which he cannot cross."

On July 7, the girl left the house, and did not return for five days. The stu-dent asked her why it took so long for her to come back. She replied that five days in the human world make only one day in heaven.

But the visit of the Weaver Maiden to the Earth became known to the Heavenly King, and she was immediately ordered not to visit the human world again.

So they had to part. On leaving, the Weaver Maiden gave Kuo a jeweled box as a remembrance of her. The student gave her an ornament by which she might be reminded of her visit to his house.

WEEPING BUDDHA

THERE ARE many tales in Japan in which Buddha statues weep in sorrow or cry in pain. Many Buddha statues cried in pain as they were carried away or damaged by robbers.

The following story is told about the *Yakushi* (Bhechad-jaguru) statue of the Kaizoji Temple, Kamakura. Every night the priests of the temple heard a sound like a baby crying in the wooded hill behind the temple. Priest Gen-o, who had founded the temple, decided to investigate the curious sound. As he entered the wood on the hill one night, he saw a small tombstone which was surrounded by a golden luminous light. He took off his *kesa* (surplice) and covered the tombstone with it. There-upon the crying stopped.

Next morning he took several men to dig out the tombstone. Under the stone they found a wooden statue of *Yakushi*, without arms or legs. Priest Gen-o had the statue repaired and placed in his temple. After that no more midnight crying was heard.

There is another story of a painted picture of *Fudo-myoo* (Acara) shedding tears of blood. Priest Chiko, famous in the 13th century, became ill, and his pupil Shoku who was then only 18 years old, proposed to sacrifice his life for the sake of his teacher. He prayed that he would become ill in place of Priest Chiko. He suffered great pain in his sickness, and as the pain became unbearable, he glared at the picture of Fudo which he daily worshiped, and asked the god of fire to take him speedily to the other world without further suffering.

Hearing his eager prayer, Fudo took upon himself Shoku's sickness. In his suffering his head was covered with fire and bloody tears fell from his eyes.

This painting of Fudo was later placed in Miidera Temple, at Otsu, Shiga Prefecture, and it was said that the marks of bloody tears remained on the painting.

WEEPING ROCK

THE TALE OF *yonaki-ishi* or night-weeping rock is known to all Japanese children. The story, said to have been started in the Nara period in the eighth century, is about a big rock at Naka-yama, near Nissaka village, Shizuoka Prefecture, which is still believed to weep at night.

Once there lived a woman at Nissaka who was about to give birth to a baby. As she was penniless, she went to Kanaya to borrow some money, the story goes. While she was still on the road, darkness fell. A highway robber appeared and attempted to kill her. In fear she hid behind a big rock nearby, but the robber stabbed her to death with a sword. The blade of his sword was chipped off as it struck the rock. The baby, however, was miraculously saved.

The priest of Kyuenji Temple, near the spot where the woman was killed, heard the baby crying. He went out and, bringing the baby to the temple,

fed it with *ame* (wheat gluten). The boy was named Otohachi and was apprenticed to a sword-maker at the age of eight.

One day a *samurai* came to the swordsmith's shop and asked to have his sword sharpened. The boy found that the sword had not only a chipped edge, but it smelled of his mother. Knowing that the *samurai* was the robber who had murdered his mother, Otohachi killed him and then committed suicide.

Since that time, so the legend goes, the Nakayama rock began to weep at night.

There are many different stones in various parts of the country which are said to have cried nightly. In the compounds of the Soneiji Temple, Kou-no-dai, Chiba, there still stands a flat stone about one foot wide and two feet long. During the days when Satomi Yoshiro had his castle at Kou-no-dai, the stone cried, and when Satomi beat it with his sword, the crying stopped. There is a scar left on the face of the stone, which is believed to have been made by Satomi's sword.

In Agatsuma-gun, Gunma Prefecture, there is also a *yonaki-ishi.* Once, a beggar woman with a baby rested under the stone, giving her breast to the baby. Suddenly the stone fell upon them and killed them instantly. From that day the stone cried nightly, until the villagers held a great memorial service for the unfortunate woman and her baby.

There are many other stones which cried for babies thrown away by their mothers. It is believed that mothers who threw away their babies placed them behind stones standing at crossroads, in the hope of their being found by some kind-hearted persons. But travellers who happened to hear babies' cries without seeing them, believed that the stones were crying. At night they could not see the babies, and hearing only their cries and thinking that no babies could possibly be there, thought that the stones had cried.

Whether or not this theory holds, there are numerous tales about night-crying stones with various different tales. But it is always women and babies who are behind such legends.

WHIRLWIND

IN THE Aichi-Mie district many tales are told of a sudden whirlwind that kills horses. The wind may be caused by the peculiar topographical condition of the area and locally it is called *daiba* or *giba*, meaning horse-killing wind.

A whirlwind suddenly arises and circling, it approaches a horse. Becoming bigger, it goes around the horse which then neighs and stamps in fear. Soon, however, the horse falls down and dies. The wind then stops suddenly and disappears. When a *samurai* riding a horse meets the horse-killing wind, he must draw his sword and wave it over his head. Then he and his horse will be safe, it has been said.

The legend of a little woman dressed in a scarlet costume and wearing a golden crown, and riding a tiny bright golden-colored horse is also told in connection with the horse-killing wind.

This mysterious woman rider and the beautiful toy-like horse suddenly appear on the road, as though they had floated down from heaven. When they approach a horse, it is taken by fear and neighs loudly, tossing its head. The mystery horse then comes near the horse, extending its tiny legs forward, finally touching the nose and ears of the horse with its legs.

Thereupon the mysterious woman disappears, but the horse dies after circling around three times.

Because of many tales of the horse-killing wind, horse drivers of the district came to follow the habit of wearing an outercoat called *mago-hanten.* Whenever they see the mystery wind coming, they take off the coat with which they cover the heads of their horses. By this method, the horse is saved from death by the wind, it has been believed.

In former days, horsemen of the district also put on their horses cloth girths with a special inscription to protect them from the mischief of the horse-killing wind.

WHITE CAMELLIAS

ECHIGO PROVINCE on the Sea of Japan has a story about the white camellias of Sado.

Two merchants of Echigo who peddled their wares from house to house went on a trip together. While they were resting at a roadside, the elder of the two fell asleep. As the younger one watched his sleeping companion, he saw a horsefly come out from his nostril and fly away toward Sado Island, but it soon returned to the nostril.

When the sleeping man awoke, he told his companion that he had seen a strange dream in which he saw the garden of a very rich man in Sado where white camellias were blooming. From the root of the camellia tree a horsefly came out and told him to dig there. When he did so, he unearthed a jar filled with gold coins.

Hearing the dream, the younger asked the older man to sell him his dream and succeeded in buying it. Soon they returned to their homes.

The younger man who bought the strange dream secretly proceeded to Sado Island where he managed to find the mansion of the richest man there. He asked to be employed at the house as a gardener and waited for the blossoming of white camellias. Spring came, but all the camellia flowers that came out were red and there was not a single white one. He waited another year. His patience was rewarded and a camellia tree was covered with white blossoms.

At night, he dug under the tree, and there he found a big jar full of gold coins, as the dream he had purchased predicted. He was, however, a careful man. He hid the jar and waited for six months. Then he asked the master of the house to let him go home. Returning to Echigo, he lived a rich and happy life.

YAOHIME

IT IS SAID to have been in Wakasa, now included in Fukui Prefecture, that the tradition of Yaohime or the 800-year-old virgin maid originated, but shrines dedicated to her are found not only in Wakasa but also in many other districts. The story of Yaohime, with slight variations according to district, is one of the most popular folk tales in the land.

The story as told in Wakasa says that in the days of Emperor Yuryaku in the fifth century, several men were invited to a feast by a strange who was not like themselves in dress, manner or speech. The strange host offered them various kinds of food, but they did not touch any because it looked very strange. Upon taking their leave, however, one of them carried away a small piece out of a bowl filled with food. Returning home, he wrapped the piece in paper and put it on a shelf.

His daughter, upon finding and opening it, took a tiny bite of the food. She found it tasted very sweet and ate it all. What the girl ate happened to be the meat of *ningyo* or mermaid. She became very beautiful and bright. From that day she never grew older, ever remaining 15 years old.

Traditionally it was said that when one eats the meat of *ningyo*, one will live a thousand years. But learning that the lord of Wakasa wanted to live a long life, she offered 200 years of her life to the lord. Thus she lived 800 years a virgin, retaining the beauty and freshness of a 15-year-old girl to the very end.

A shrine was erected in her honor when she died, and it has been visited by persons desiring a long life. As the story spread to other parts of the country, Yaohime shrines came to be built in many other districts.

There are many ancient records of *ningyo* or mermaids appearing in the sea around Japan. Most of the descriptions given in books or paintings said to have been sketched from actual mermaids make them out as beautiful young women, with breasts, head and arms like a human being but with a fish-like lower part. Sometimes, however, there are pictures of *ningyo* whose entire body is like a fish and only the head with short hair is human in form. In such pictures, *ningyo* do not look like women.

YAWNING WIFE

THERE WAS once a lord who was hot-tempered, and known for his hasty conduct. One day when the dinner continued long into the evening, the lord's wife who was serving her master became tired and yawned. The lord then became extremely angry and, putting her into a small boat, set it adrift on the sea.

The boat reached a small isolated island and she was saved by kind villagers. Soon she gave birth to a boy. When the boy became 12 years old he asked his mother why he had no father, when all his friends had one.

Sadly the mother told him how she was punished and exiled to the island for her careless yawning. Hearing her story, the boy decided to go to the mainland and see his father, although his mother strongly argued the uselessness of his attempt.

As the boy neared his father's castle, he saw beautiful camellias blossoming on the roadside. He broke off a branch and as he went to the castle gate carrying it in his hand, he loudly shouted, "Who wants golden camellias?"

The lord happened to hear the boy's shout, and knowing that a golden camellia was unusual, he ordered that the person be brought in.

When the servant brought the boy in, the camellia he carried was just an ordinary camellia. "What an impudent fellow you are. You have a camellia branch with ordinary blossoms, but shout that you have golden ones," he said angrily.

Then the boy calmly replied, "This is no ordinary camellia branch. If it is planted by a person who does not yawn, it will bear golden blossoms."

"You speak outrageously. There is nobody in the world who does not yawn," shouted the lord.

"That is so. But you exiled your dear wife for just yawning," the boy sharply retorted.

Then the lord realized the haste of his act that caused so much suffering to his wife and son, and hurriedly called her back to the castle.

YOMEKO

NEZUMI or house mice are called *yomeko* (brides) in many parts of the country.

There are various tales of how mice came to be called this. One told in the Iwate district in the northeastern region of the country goes as follows:

At a mountain temple there was once a young apprentice named Hanawaka, but his conduct displeased the temple priest, and he was ordered to leave. After wandering around, he came to the house of an old woman. She was a woman of evil reputation but helped the young man to obtain a position as a servant in the home of a wealthy family of the village.

He worked hard and was appreciated by his master whose three daughters noticed him particularly because of his skillful flute-playing. The master was so pleased with him that he proposed that the young man marry one of his daughters.

Unable to decide which of the three girls he should marry, Hanawaka consulted the old woman who had befriended him. She suggested three tests and advised him to marry the one who passed all of them. The first test was to weave a bundle of hemp into an *obi*, the second was to walk over silk floss with sandals without catching the silk, and the third was to break off a tree branch on which a sparrow was resting, without scaring off the bird.

The youngest daughter successfully carried out the three tasks and the young man married her. But the two elder sisters were so disappointed that they turned into mice. Their father took pity on them, and calling them *yomeko*, offered them food. Ever since the whole village came to call house mice *yomeko*.

Chapter 7
Food, 'Sake' and Tobacco

ASAKUSA-NORI

ASAKUSA-NORI or dried laver is one of the unique table delicacies of Japan and generally comes in square sheets, looking like thick carbon paper. Laver fronds are eaten by many other peoples of Europe and Asia, but nowhere else are they made into dried sheets.

Asakusa-nori is dark green, and when it is heated crisp it turns slightly purplish. It is eaten by itself with a little *shoyu*, put in soups or used as flavoring over many dishes. It is also used in wrapping up *sushi* or vinegared rice into a roll. It seems quite tasteless to those not used to it. But the people love its flavor and taste. Modern scientists say that it contains much vitamin A.

Asakusa-nori originated in Edo as the name implies. In the early 17th century the district of Asakusa was on the sea and good *amanori* (Poryphyra teneral) was found there. The drying and making it into sheets must have developed there in the early years of the Edo period.

Amanori has flat fronds about a quarter inch wide and is one to two feet long. It is found in Tokyo Bay, particularly along the shores of Omori, Haneda and Chiba. Its demand among Edo people developed the method of its cultivation.

Late in autumn, bamboos and trees with branches are set in rows in the shallow sea. The *amanori* attach themselves to the trees and grow. During the winter months, they are gathered. They are then cleaned and washed in sea-water and spread on screens in the same way Japanese papers are made. The screens with the thin layers of *nori* are dried in the sun. Of late, indoor artificial drying methods have been adopted.

In Edo days, *Asakusa-nori* was one of the famous products of the feudal capital, and was sent by Edo people to friends in other parts of the country. Even today the custom is still kept up by Tokyo residents. *Nori* is gathered in many other parts of the country, but that produced in Tokyo Bay, still called *Asakusa-nori* though Asakusa no longer produces *nori*, is considered the best.

Nori appears to have become a definite table delicacy in the late ninth century, and in the early days Izumo, Shima and Tosa were famous *nori*-producing areas.

There is another kind of *nori* commonly called *ao-nori* or green laver but this is quite a different kind from *amanori*. It is light green in color and is not made into sheets but simply dried and sold in small bundles. This *ao-nori* is also used in powdered form sprinkled over foodstuffs and in making various cakes.

All seaweeds are nourishing, containing much iodine and many kinds of vitamins. It is said that *ao-nori* is more nourishing than *amanori*.

AYU

AYU, A VARIETY of trout, is considered the best freshwater fish by Japanese epicureans. Many think it is only found in Japan, but the species is also seen in Korea, Taiwan and Southern China. It is often called *ko-gyo* (fragrant fish) because of its taste, and *nen-gyo* (year fish) as the fish generally lives only one year.

Young *ayu* hatched in the river in late autumn go down the stream to the sea, and come up-river the next spring to lay eggs there. While in the sea, the fish feed on plankton, but in the river they eat diatom and other sphagna found on the bottom of the stream. The taste and value of the fish depend on the kinds of river mosses they eat, as it is what they feed on that give them their particular taste.

But since early days, the *ayu* has also been regarded as a lucky fish. There was a practice of foretelling one's fortune by the result of *ayu* fishing. It is recorded that when Empress Jingu went to Matsura, in north Kyushu in 200 to prepare for an expedition to Korea, she went to the Tamashima River to fish for *ayu* and learn whether the plan would be successful or not. Standing on a rock in the stream, she cast her line and caught a good *ayu*. The happy prediction greatly pleased her.

Ever since it has become customary for the women of the district to go *ayu* fishing in the first part of April (lunar calendar) for fortune prediction.

Ugai or cormorant fishing is a method of catching *ayu* that has been practiced in the country for more than 12 centuries. Wild cormorants are caught and trained for the purpose. In the old days, cormorant fishing was under Court protection and cormorant handlers still wear ancient Court costume.

A new way of fishing for *ayu* is called *tomozuri* or decoy fishing. A live *ayu* is fastened to a line that has hooks, and as it is lowered into the stream other *ayu* approach the decoy fish and are caught by the hooks. This method utilizes the fish's instinct of protecting its domain. When the fish sees a strange fish within its area, it tries to chase the invader. The *ayu* in the river regard the decoy as an intruder and approaches it to scare it away, but then is caught.

AZUKI

THE JAPANESE people eat a great deal of beans and peas, from which they obtain protein. Of various beans and peas they use, *daizu* (soybeans) and *azuki* (red beans) are the most important. Soybeans are not only cooked and eaten but also used in making *tofu* (bean curd), *miso* (bean paste), *shoyu* (sauce), *natto* (fermented beans) and others.

In the quantity used, *azuki* falls far below *daizu*, but they are nonetheless very important in the life of the people.

They were at first included among medicinal materials. Many people still believe in its healing properties. All beans were formerly believed to possess the power to dispel evil and diseases.

Red beans are still eaten by many rural folks to cure various diseases. For beri-beri, *azuki* is believed to be the most effective medicine. It is also recommended for stomach and blood ailments.

Red beans are also cooked in rice on many occasions. On January 15 the custom of eating rice gruel with red beans is still widely followed. Old-fashioned people eat *sekihan* or rice with red beans on the 1st and 15th of every month. On various festive occasions the red-bean rice is regarded as a necessity.

The habit of eating red-bean rice periodically was formerly believed necessary to preserve one's health.

Most Japanese sweets contain *an* or sweetened bean paste made of red beans.

Of course the red color of the *azuki* is very attractive, and the red-colored rice bright and appetizing. This might have helped to make red-bean rice popular.

But fundamentally it is the people's belief in the curative property of *azuki* that has popularized its use and made it inseparable from their life.

BENTO AND KASHI

BENTO NOW stands for any kind of food packed in a box, but originally it meant the wooden food container. The term *bento* came to be popularly used from the time Oda Nobunaga moved his headquarters to the Azuchi Castle on Lake Biwa in 1576.

The Japanese ate only two meals a day at first. It was in the beginning of the 19th century that town dwellers came to eat three meals regularly. Of course, farmers and others who did strenuous physical labor ate many times a day, carrying their food wrapped up in bamboo sheaths or large leaves to their places of work. *Mochi* (rice cake), *dango* (dumplings) and such were carried to the fields to be eaten. These were called *kashi*, which originally meant fruit.

There was a custom among most people to eat or nibble *kashi* secretly. This custom is still seen among rural folks who insist on having their *bento* unobserved by others.

The *samurai* class was also in the habit of carrying *bento*, as it was not customary for them to eat at public eating-places, although they were allowed to buy and eat *mochi* and other *kashi* snacks.

When the people came to eat three times a day, what was eaten between meals came to be called *kashi*, which now stands for all kinds of sweets.

The custom of eating *bento* or *kashi* on a journey is still kept up by present-day travelers who eat often and much on trains and buses. The old two-meal habit is preserved by some Japanese-style inns, which provide only breakfast and dinner, and regard lunch as an extra serving.

Bento and *kashi* tell the history of Japanese eating habits. Their consumption does not diminish even with the increased number of restaurants and eating-places all over the country.

CATTLE

JAPANESE FARMERS used cattle for plowing in very early days. It is now proved that as early as 1,700 years ago cattle were used to plow the rice-fields. The people also ate beef and drank cow's milk.

Japan had a large number of cattle in those early days. It is recorded that many cattle horns were sent to China during the Tang period (618-907), and that in one year 7,800 horns were presented to the Tang emperor.

Cattle were also sacrificed for various *kami* or deities but in 791 an Imperial order was issued to prohibit this. Since then cattle hide has been offered at festivals. It also came to be used as a charm to drive away evil spirits.

The early Japanese not only drank cow's milk but also made *so*, a kind of cheese, which was largely used as medicine. *So* was made by boiling down milk to one-tenth of its quantity.

According to Engishiki, the Court rules completed in 927, the country was divided into 46 provinces. These provinces were divided into six groups, and each group presented *so* to the Court every sixth year. The quantity of *so* presented to the Court in six years was mentioned as 933 *sho* or about 3,545 pints.

So was used as medicine at the Court, and also by a large number of the people.

In the feudal ages, cattle-drawn carts were used by Court nobles while the people also used carts drawn by cattle to a very large extent. Horses were used for riding, but seldom to draw carts until a much later time.

Beef eating declined with the spread of Buddhism, and *so* also disappeared.

CHAMESHI

CHAMESHI (tea rice) is a fancy kind of cooked rice. Not only is it made at home, but also there are restaurants specializing in this. But *chameshi* as it is cooked and eaten today has no tea in it, and is only a modern imitation of the original.

It is said to have been thought up by Buddhist priests. It is recorded that in the Genroku era (1688-1704), it was first cooked at the Todaiji and Kofukuji temples of Nara. The priests used brewed tea in cooking rice, and added some salt, mixing beans and peas as well with the rice.

Chameshi today is cooked with *shoyu* and *mirin* (sweet wine). Since it has a brownish color, it looks like tea rice. Thus the modern *chameshi* tastes better, though it has no tea flavor.

Often vegetables, fish or meat, chopped small, are added to make it richer. *Chameshi* restaurants make such specialties, but the simple kind is also offered at many places. Individual cooking pots are used at many restaurants.

Cooked at home, it is a welcome variation to the daily meal.

The original *chameshi* may still be had in the Kyoto-Osaka area in a modified form. It is called *cha-gayu* or tea gruel. Tea leaves used once are placed in a cotton bag and the bag put in the pot cooking the morning gruel.

Many Kansai people are unhappy unless they have their tea gruel every morning.

CHAWAN-MUSHI

SOMETIMES *chawan-mushi* is regarded as a kind of soup, but it is quite different from ordinary soups, being somewhat similar to Western custards.

Chawan-mushi is not often found on the tables of the poor, because making it is complicated and takes time. But it is in no way a costly dish, although some restaurants make extremely luxurious *chawan-mushi* by using rare ingredients. It is a dish that is relished by all kinds of people, but it tastes better when taken with rice than with *sake*, although many people eat it with their *sake*.

To make *chawan-mushi*, first *katsuobushi* (dried bonito) is shaved into fine flakes, and a handful is put in water and boiled. Then the *katsuobushi* flakes are taken out of the water which is left to cool. When the *katsuobushi* soup thus obtained is cooled, it is poured into individual *chawan-mushi* bowls (china bowls with covers).

At the same time, eggs are beaten, and the beaten eggs and the soup are mixed in the same quantity in the bowls. To this mixture are added fish meats, chicken and various vegetables. Then the bowls are covered, and put in a large and deep pan. Water is poured into the pan, to cover the bowls only about half-way 'from their bottoms. Then the pan is put on the fire. The pan is covered, and the steam rising from the water in the pan will cook the *chawan-mushi* in the bowls.

When it is cooked, the bowls are taken out and served with the covers. Recently spoons are given with *chawan-mushi* in some places, but it should be eaten with chopsticks. The bowls are hot, but when they are slightly cooled they can be taken up in one's hands, and what cannot be picked up with chopsticks may be drunk from the bowls.

The taste of *chawan-mushi* differs according to the ingredients used. It can be made of almost all kinds of products. But generally those in season are used. Among the ingredients commonly put in *chawan-mushi* are sliced *kamaboko* (fish-meat sausage), broiled eels, boned small fish, chicken, *shiitake* (mushroom), *ginnan* (gingko nuts), *mitsuba* (honeywort), *seri* (marsh parsley), sliced bamboo and other vegetables.

As proper *chawan-mushi* not only must have these various different the ingredients, but also has to be put in separate special *chawan-mushi* bowls with a cover and steamed, it is not made at the homes of the poor. It is, therefore, regarded as a sort of luxurious dish.

Chawan-mushi is welcomed by foreign tourists and residents as it is agreeable to their tastes, although sometimes the act of eating it with chopsticks is difficult for them. However, it is not wrong to eat it with spoons, as is often done.

Chawan-mushi may be one of the few Japanese dishes that resemble Western dishes in taste.

CHAZUKE

CHAZUKE is a unique way the Japanese people sometimes eat rice. No other people are known to eat rice in this manner. Some Japanese are in the habit of finishing their meal with a bowl of *chazuke*.

Chazuke is generally made at home by pouring hot tea over a bowl of rice and eaten with some pickles. The people love the taste of the fragrant tea and rice together. It is also the quickest way to finish a bowl of rice as the rice is swallowed with the tea without chewing. Often *chazuke* is used as a term for the simplest kind of meal.

There is another more elaborate kind of *chazuke*. This is also eaten at home, but there are restaurants specializing in serving this kind of *chazuke*. *Chazuke* lovers go there to enjoy the finest kind of *chazuke*. Many such restaurants have their own special recipes.

Generally speaking, slices of *tai* or other fresh fish, small pieces of roasted *nori*, shavings of *katsuobushi* (dried bonito), various pickles and other things are placed on top of the rice in a bowl. Then fragrant boiling tea is poured over it, and the whole thing is eaten with chopsticks. Sometimes a cover is placed over the bowl for a few minutes to let the hot tea work into the rice, fish and other things.

Dried fish, roasted and shredded into fine pieces, is also used in place of raw fish.

Being hot, *chazuke* is welcomed on cold winter days. Many people love to eat it in summer too, and say that it is the best thing to eat when the appetite is dulled by the heat.

COOKING

JAPANESE COOKING is unique in the world because the natural environment of Japan is unique, and the characteristic nature of the people is also different from that of other peoples. Since primitive days, it has been natural for peoples to live on foodstuffs which are obtainable in their immediate environment. Japanese people have thus lived mainly on cereals, vegetables and fish. The country being surrounded by seas, they have developed as the greatest fish-eaters in the world. The wide variety of fish and shellfish that are found in the seas, rivers and lakes of the country has brought out almost unlimited varieties of fish dishes on the Japanese table.

Some of the original tribes which formed the Japanese race appear to have been meat-eaters, but the lack of animals on the islands and also the influence of Buddhism subsequently made the people refrain from eating meat. The estheticism that developed with the coming of Buddhism, and the development of the tea cult have also served to make Japanese cooking simple and plain.

The artistic temperament of the people, then, added decorative features to Japanese cooking. Besides these natural and artistic sides of Japanese cooking, it must also be remembered that one factor that makes Japanese dishes so different from those of other nations is that Japanese dishes are either taken with rice or with *sake*. They are never eaten independently. In judging the merits of dishes, the people say "This is good with rice, but not good with *sake*." This is because the people rate the merit and taste of a dish from its association with either rice or *sake*. One kind of dish, therefore, is good when taken with rice, while another is good with *sake*.

There are fundamental differences between dishes for *sake*-drinking and dishes for rice-eating.

As in case of all countries, Japanese foods have recently undergone considerable changes, due to the introduction of foreign dishes and habits. The people, and particularly city dwellers, at present enjoy Japanese, Occidental and Chinese cooking. Yet, to the majority of the people, there is nothing that suits them better than old-fashioned Japanese dishes.

Many Japanese dishes have recently become very popular even among foreign tourists and residents in the country. *Sukiyaki* and *tenpura*, for instance, are now world-famous and these dishes appeal to Western tastes as well as to the Japanese. But it is not necessary to say that both *sukiyaki* and *tenpura* are comparatively new to the country. Among original Japanese dishes also, there are many that can be enjoyed by foreigners, although up to the present they were not so widely known.

The cooking of Japanese dishes is very difficult, and there are many dishes that can be made only by experienced cooks.

DAIKON

DAIKON or Japanese radish is the most commonly eaten vegetable in Japan. There are many kinds and some round and some long, from tiny ones to *Sakurajima-daikon* produced in Sakurajima, Kagoshima, which comes in as large a size as three feet in circumference. It is daily eaten by all classes of people. *Daikon*, cut into strips or small pieces, fresh or dried, and cooked, constitutes a staple food item.

Daikon is good for aiding digestion as it contains much pepsin. *Daikon-oroshi* or grated raw radish is said to be particularly good in this respect.

Daikon has been made into *ko-no-mono*, or pickles, since early days. Pickled vegetables are eaten at meals and also with tea between meals. At first *daikon* used as *ko-no-mono* (fragrant thing) was raw and not pickled. When the New Year *toso* — a medicinal *sake* — was drunk at the Court, sliced raw *daikon* was served. It was to clean the mouth and remove any taste in the mouth, so that the drink could be fully appreciated.

Then as the pickling of vegetables developed for preserving them, *ko-no-mono* came to mean all pickled things. Some records say that at first *ko-no-mono* was pickled in *miso*, or bean paste.

At any rate, pickled vegetables soon became so popular that they have become daily necessities of the people, with *daikon* remaining the most popular.

Then *takuwan* appeared. The smell of *takuwan* has become quite representative of Japan. Priest Takuwan, a famous Buddhist who died in 1645, introduced this new type of pickled *daikon*. The *daikon* is dried in the sun a few days, and pickled in a tub with rice-bran and salt, with heavy stones as a weight placed on top. The tomb of Takuwan at Tokaiji Temple, Shinagawa, has a round natural stone on top, and such stones came to be known as *Takuwan-ishi* or *Takuwan* stone.

DEER MEAT

SHIKA OR DEER must have been abundantly found in the country in the old days and the meat eaten extensively by the people. They were particularly numerous in Hokkaido and easily caught.

There are still many spots in Hokkaido which are called *shika-otoshi* or deer pit. The Ainu, forming a wide circle, used to chase a large number of deer to the top of a high cliff, and as the animals fell into the valley below, they were killed. Dogs were used in the chase.

The people also formed an enclosure into which they chased the deer, and closing the entrance killed them. In some lake districts, deer were driven into the lake by entire villages — men, women and children. The men then went out in boats and killed the swimming deer with stout sticks.

In the Meiji era, the number of deer killed in Hokkaido increased with the introduction of hunting guns. In those years it is recorded that more than 60,000 deer skins were shipped out of Hokkaido annually.

With the abundant supply of deer meat, the government established in Sapporo a deer-meat canning plant in 1878. Thus Hokkaido was known as the greatest deer district of the country. But suddenly the number of deer decreased. One winter there was a very heavy snowfall on the Pacific side of the island, to where deer went to winter from the Japan Sea side where the snowfall was generally heavy. The snow killed so many deer that their number was suddenly cut in half.

The deer-meat canning plant had to be closed due to the shortage of deer meat, and in 1895, deer hunting was prohibited by law to preserve them.

However, as the agricultural development of Hokkaido progressed rapidly and deer came out to damage crops, the law was scrapped and five years afterward deer hunting was again permitted.

Wild deer have now become very few, and the old mass deer hunting has become just a tradition.

DRINKING CUPS

AT JAPANESE BANQUETS, it is customary to exchange *sakazuki* or *sake*-drinking cups. At a proper moment, the host goes to the honor guest to receive his *sakazuki*. At the host's request, the guest empties his cup and hands it to him. When the cup is filled and drunk by the host, it is returned to the guest who also drinks out of it. This exchange of *sakazuki* means the recognition of friendship among equals or conferment of honor on those of lower social or official ranks.

When there are many guests, the host has to go to each of them to receive his cup in succession. Cups are also exchanged at informal drinking parties among all present to signify that all are good pals.

This offering or exchanging of *sakazuki* is an old custom. Marriage is solemnized by exchanging *sakazuki* between the bride and the groom. Feudal lords used to give a cup of *sake* to their retainers in recognition of their special services of merit. But the *sakazuki* given by a lord to his retainer was not returned, as retainers were in no position to offer their masters a drink.

It is also from this custom that the system of granting Imperial cups developed. To honor men and women for their meritorious services to the state, the emperor gives gold, silver or lacquer *sakazuki* marked with the Imperial crest, according to the degree of merit. The awarding of Imperial cups is done without actually drinking *sake*.

Then, among gangsters, gamblers and travelling showmen, the idea that to receive *sakazuki* from another is to pledge oneself to a bond of service or fraternity is still very firmly held.

DRINKING CUSTOMS

THE JAPANESE people were not originally accustomed to drinking *sake* alone. *Sake* must always be taken in company with others. So *sake* drinking has always meant drinking parties.

This habit originated from the custom of offering *sake* to *kami* and sharing it with all the neighbors. *Sake* was at first made for *kami* and festivals, and each family brewed its own, storing it for festivals and other important occasions.

It was at first the woman's task to make *sake*, and women were always present at *sake* drinking parties.

At ancient drinking parties, *sake* was served in a big cup and each one drank out of the same cup.

For men to drink alone in feudal days was regarded as something shameful. If one was to drink, he had to share it with others. However, in those days there was a commonly used term, *ippai-zake*, meaning one bowl of *sake*. When a worker or helper finished his day's work, the master of the house invited him to the kitchen to have a bowl of *sake*. So invited, he sat in a corner of the kitchen to drink a bowl of *sake* brought by a servant. There he drank it alone.

That was the only occasion when one drank *sake* by himself. Therefore, one who drank alone was considered inferior to others accustomed to drinking in the company of guests and friends.

Even today, *sake* lovers like to have friends to drink with them. The passing or exchanging of drinking cups developed from the ancient custom of drinking from one big cup.

All Japanese *sake* drinking parties end in noisy disorder with everyone becoming fully intoxicated. The noisier and more riotous it is, the greater the success of the party.

Drinking parties originated in *sake* drinking at festivals for *kami*. Upon harvesting rice from the community shrine's rice-field, the people who grew the crop gathered and made *sake* with the new rice. Drinking the *sake* together, they all became merry and drunk. Even in the Imperial Court, drinking parties in the old days ended in a mess of drunken violence and revelry.

It is to be noted, however, that *sake* jars kept at home as well as *sake* drinking parties used to be controlled by the housewives. Some authorities even go so far so to say that through their control of *sake*, women held power over men in the old days.

Women and daughters took part in these drinking parties. It was their task to serve *sake* to all present. Their ability to urge all to drink more and to entertain them was highly valued. For the pleasure of the drinking guests, the women sang songs and danced.

Those fond of *sake* drinking still think that *sake* drinking is not complete without service and entertainment by young women.

The Japanese use tiny porcelain cups for drinking *sake*, their favorite rice wine. But these little cups called *shoku* or *choko* have been in use for only about 200 years.

At first shallow earthenware cups, as still used at Shinto shrine rites, were used for drinking *sake*. Then came lacquered wooden cups, some of which were made big enough to hold one *sho* or about half a gallon or more of the wine.

At a feudal drinking party, a set of three or five lacquered wooden *sakazuki* or drinking cups, the smallest one placed on the top and the biggest one at the bottom, were brought out. The person seated in the place of honor took up the top-most or smallest cup and drank out of it. Then the cup was presented to the next person, and the rest of the party in turn. When all drank out of the first cup, the second or larger cup was given to the first person. This process was repeated until all had enough. Those at the lower end had to wait a long time for their turn.

These sets of *sakazuki* are still used at wedding ceremonies and other formal occasions. At a wedding service, the bride drinks the first cup and passes it to the groom. Then the second

cup is taken by the groom, and given to the bride. The third and last cup is passed from the bride to the groom.

Small porcelain cups seem to have been introduced when the habit of heating *sake* became popular. Originally *sake* was drunk cold and is still taken cold at ceremonies. *Sake* of inferior quality was warmed up to improve its taste. This habit became popular and all grades of *sake* were heated. For drinking hot *sake*, small cups are convenient. With the use of individual small cups for drinking warm *sake*, drinking party habits also changed a great deal. The habit of offering one's cup to another may be said to be a remnant of the former way of passing around one cup to all present.

EEL-EATING DAY

THE PEOPLE eat eels on the day of *ushi* or ox in the *doyo* (dog day) season which starts on July 20 and lasts until August 6. It is the day when all *unagi* or eel shops do their record business of the year. Some years have ox days twice in the period of 18 days.

Eels are eaten on this day because it is commonly believed that broiled eels will give vitality in fighting the hot climate. As the custom was started in Edo, Tokyo people particularly do not feel comfortable unless they have eels on that day.

Eel eating has been enjoyed by the people since ancient days, and *kabayaki* or broiled eels are mentioned in records of the 14th century. The origin of the custom of eating eels on the ox day of the *doyo* season is not clear. But it is commonly said that it was Gennai Hiraga, an Edo *samurai* and writer, who started it. An eel-shop owner whom Hiraga knew, complained of poor business in the hot summer days, it is reported. So he wrote a sign reading

Ushi-no-hi (day of ox), and made the eel man put it at the shop entrance. The people thought that it must be the day to eat eels, and so the habit started, as Hiraga planned.

So it was first a purely Edo custom, but gradually it spread to other parts. If this story is true, the custom must be about 200 years old.

To make *kabayaki*, the eel is opened lengthwise, and after taking out the bone, it is cut into a convenient size. Each piece is then put on bamboo skewers, and broiled over a charcoal fire. After the first broiling it is steamed, and then put in a specially prepared *shoyu* and broiled again. During the second broiling, the piece is put in the pan of *shoyu* several times. In the Kansai district the eel is broiled without steaming.

The broiled eel is served as it is, or placed over a bowl of rice. The latter kind, named *unagi-donburi* (eel bowl), is very popular.

Science has now proved that the meat of *unagi* contains many vitamins, while all other fish have few vitamins in their meat, though their livers are full of vitamins. So eels are very nutritious.

In China, too, eels have always been considered as having curative powers, particularly for consumptives. An old tale told in China says that once there was a family with a beautiful young girl. But the girl had consumption and became weaker and weaker. As there was no hope for her recovery, the parents put her into a little coffin while she was still alive, and set it afloat in a nearby steam.

A young fisherman fishing below found the coffin. When he opened it up, he saw the girl inside who was still alive though very weak. He carried her home and tenderly cared for her. He fed her with eels he caught daily in the river. She grew well rapidly and became beautiful. When she regained her health, the fisherman married her.

FUGU

FUGU OR GLOBE-FISH is one of the most luxurious delicacies on the Japanese table. But many timid persons are afraid to eat it because they are afraid to die as the fish contains a poison — tetrotoxin — particularly in its ovaries and liver. When properly cleaned and cooked, it is quite safe. But many who prided themselves on being experts in preparing the fish have died.

Fugu eaters, however, enjoy the slight numbness that is caused by the poison. Furthermore, they say that the eggs and liver, that are said to contain the poison, taste best. So there is considerable risk in eating *fugu*.

From olden days numerous persons have died of *fugu* poisoning, and even now many victims are reported every year. Yet lovers of *fugu* cannot stop eating it, and seem to be willing to risk their lives for a taste of the meat. *Fugu* meat is beautifully white, and when it is sliced thin and arranged on a large Japanese dish with blue or red designs, the designs are clearly discernible through the meat.

There are various prescribed ways to counteract poisoning from *fugu*. One of the oldest ways is to drink indigo dye, while another one is to bury the patient in the earth up to his neck. Another so-called antidote is to take egg whites or a glassful of soapy water. But these treatments have seldom saved the poisoned persons.

There are many kinds of *fugu*, different in shape, size and color. *Fugu* eating particularly developed in Kyushu and Kansai where the best edible kind is found in abundance. In northern areas, *fugu* eating is not known.

The *fugu* has a strange habit. When it

is attacked by an enemy it inhales air into its stomach, and thus puffing itself into a ball-like shape, tries to scare away the enemy. Hence it came to be generally called globe-fish. Small *fugu* are caught and handled roughly to make them angry and puff up. Then in the enlarged shape, they are killed to make toy lanterns which are sold at country festivals and fairs.

GINNAN

GINNAN or nuts of the *icho* (gingko) becomes an added delicacy on the Japanese table in late autumn. It is cooked in many ways or used in soups. It is at times simply roasted and eaten. It has a gem-like green color and poignant taste.

Icho trees are peculiar to the Orient, and grow to a huge height of over a 100 feet. There are male and female trees, and only the female bears fruit. The nut is covered with yellowish, ill-smelling fleshy stuff, and within the hard white shell is the edible part covered with a thin film-like skin.

When the nuts fallen from the tree are gathered, they are placed in tubs of water to remove the fleshy outside. Then the white shells are washed and dried. The shell has to be cracked open with nutcrackers or little hammers. Then the inner nuts are roasted and the filmy skin can be easily removed.

The eating of *ginnan* is said to have been encouraged by Zen priests in the 12th century to obtain nourishment. *Ginnan*, in fact, is very rich in food value, containing vitamins B, B1, B6 and C, iron, calcium and sulphur.

Left unshelled, *ginnan* can be kept all the year around. They are sold at shops dealing in dried foodstuffs. But it is always in autumn when the fresh nuts come out that the people like to roast them over *hibachi* in the evening and eat them while hot.

Ginnan was formerly regarded as a medicine to cure and prevent coughs, and many still believe in this virtue of the nuts.

Icho leaves are fan-shaped and become beautifully yellow in autumn. Hence the leaves are used in many decorative designs. Many families have various designs of the *icho* leaf as their crests.

The Chinese call the *icho* tree 'duck's feet' because of the shape of its leaf. Even today in Japan, Chinese characters standing for 'duck's feet' are pronounced *icho*.

GOBO

GOBO OR *gonbo* (burdock), belonging to a genus of the aster family, is one of the Japanese vegetables which foreign visitors find novel. *Gobo* as sold at greengrocers' comes as a long black tapering root about 30 cm long.

This plant is found in many countries, but Japan is the first to cultivate it as a vegetable, since more than 1,000 years ago. It was Dr. Philip Franz von Siebold, a Dutch scientist, who came to Japan in 1823 who introduced this Japanese vegetable to Europe. When he returned home in 1829 he took *gobo* seeds and had them planted in the Netherlands. Since then Japanese *gobo* have been cultivated in France and Germany.

It seems that at first the *gobo* was more valued as medicine than as a vegetable. The dried roots were taken as an effective medicine to improve stomach conditions, and as a general health restorative. The seeds were also brewed to obtain medicine for skin diseases.

It is probably because of this health-giving function of the root that the plant came to be so widely cultivated and also used as a common vegetable.

It still constitutes one of the most commonly consumed vegetables in the country. There are many varieties produced in different localities. As a vegetable it is prepared in many different ways. In cooking *dojo* or loaches, slivered *gobo* is indispensable.

Slivered *gobo* is fried as *tenpura*, or sauteed in oil. The latter is commonly called *kinpira-gobo*. Sliced fine, it is put in *misoshiru* or bean paste soup. It is very often cooked with fish or meat. Boiled *gobo* is also mashed and treated with pounded sesame dressing. The commonest way to prepare *gobo* is to cook sliced pieces in *shoyu*, sometimes with sugar added.

As a plant, *gobo* is not at all novel, but the improved *gobo* as produced in Japan with the long and soft root is found nowhere else in the world.

GOHAN

GOHAN or boiled rice constitutes the main portion of the ordinary Japanese diet, and the amount of rice consumed daily by farmers, laborers and such is surprisingly large. It seems that many Japanese take their nourishment mostly from rice.

Rice was not originally produced in the country, and it was brought over by the early settlers from the south. Since very early days, rice formed the principal part of the people's diet. At first, however, rice was not polished, and the so-called unpolished rice was commonly eaten. It was in the long peaceful days of Tokugawa that the people sought luxury and *hakumai* or polished rice came to be generally eaten by the people.

In recent years, however, it has been found that the highly polished rice so relished by the people lacked vitamins and would cause beriberi. Thus the use of unpolished and semi-polished rice has been much encouraged of late. Of course, from the early days, the use of barley, millet or other cereals in mixture with rice has been common. Even today, most farming people eat a rice-barley mixture.

The way the people cook rice is also different from that used by many other peoples. As the people have for so long eaten rice as their main staple, their sense of taste in eating rice has been highly developed. Well-cooked *gohan* requires skill. It should not be too hard nor too soft, but just right. Rice is first washed thoroughly in water, changing the water several times, and then left in water for some hours before cooking. It is put in a heavy iron rice-boiling pot and cooked over a wood fire, charcoal, gas or an electric stove. According to the size of the kettle and the kind of fire, it takes from 30 minutes to one hour to cook. But it is said that rice tastes best when cooked over a wood fire.

When barley is mixed with rice, it has to be cooked first before cooking with rice, or else crushed barley has to be used. Generally 10 to 20 per cent of barley is mixed with rice, but in some extreme cases as much as 40 per cent is used.

Besides the plain white boiled rice, various special forms of rice are cooked. The most popular is *sekihan* (red rice), which is used on festive and other happy occasions. There are many families which make *sekihan* on the first day of every month. For *sekihan*, ordinary rice is not used. Instead, *mochigome* (rice for *mochi* making) or glutinous rice is used. The method of cooking is also different. Washed *mochigome* mixed with red beans is steamed, and not boiled.

But as the cooking of *sekihan* requires special steaming implements, at many common households ordinary rice mixed with red beans is cooked in the ordinary way to make a substitute for *sekihan.*

Then, there is what is commonly called *cha-meshi.* It is the common rice cooked with a little *shoyu*, tea and *mirin.* The color thus obtained is light brown. Then sometimes also *matsutake* (mushroom) or other vegetables are added in cooking this kind of rice. *Gomoku-meshi* is cooked by mixing various kinds of vegetables. Sometimes oysters, chicken and other meats are mixed with rice in a similar way.

Rice fried with meats and tomato sauce is something newly added to the menu of the Japanese people, but that is a foreign dish adopted for the people's diet.

Nigiri-meshi is a ball of rice made by pressing rice between the two palms, and is used as a lunch on picnics or trips. Generally *umeboshi*, pickled apricot, is placed in the center of the ball. *Nigiri-meshi* is made into various shapes, some round and some triangular. Salt, or salt and sesame, is sprinkled over the outside of the ball, but it is also often covered with *nori* (dried seaweed).

GOMAKASHI

GOMAKASHI is a common word used to mean deception, trickery or cheat. From it also developed a verb, *gomakasu*, which has such meanings as to cheat, embezzle, dodge, shirk, quibble, fake or to make excuses.

But this word is comparatively new and came from the name of a cheap kind of common cake, *gomakashi* or *gomagashi* (sesame seed cake).

It was about 150 years ago that there appeared in cheap sweet shops in the poorer quarters of Edo, small cakes which were sprinkled with sesame seeds. They looked attractive, but they did not taste as good as they looked. But among the poorer people of Edo, they sold well because of their low price.

Thus *gomakashi* became a name for any cheap but poor cake. Then gradually it was extended to mean anything that is not as good as it appears. In this manner *gomakashi* came to possess the meaning of deception, cheating or trickery. As it came to be widely used in this sense, it was also given a verb form, *gomakasu.*

Of course, there were cakes made with sesame seeds before this. They were called *goma-doran* or *goma-mochi.* Such cakes were popular in the Kansai and other districts in the 18th century, and might have existed even before that time. Though it is not known what kind of cakes they were, they must have been good cakes.

Goma or sesame seeds have long been used in cooking by the people, who have long regarded them as a highly nutritious food seasoning. The early sesame cakes must thus have originally been good rich cakes.

KABAYAKI

UNAGI (EEL) baked brown is called *kabayaki.* It is said that formerly *unagi* was opened, and skewers were inserted lengthwise, and then baked over a fire. The long brown piece resembled the ear of *gama* or bulrush, and thus came to be called *gamayaki* or *kabayaki.* Today, however, *kabayaki* is not made in such a long piece. The opened *unagi* is cut into small pieces, and skewers are put sideways into the small pieces. Thus, while the color is brown, the shape no longer resembles the ears of the bulrush. Yet it is still called *kabayaki.*

The people of Japan have been great eaters of *unagi*, and the common way to eat *unagi* is to make it into *kabayaki*. *Unagi* has been so popular that there have always existed restaurants that specialized in making *kabayaki*, and they are called *unagi-ya* or *kabayaki-ya*. In the latter part of the Tokugawa period, there developed a special custom of eating *unagi* on the *ushi-no-hi* (ox day) of the summer *doyo* season. It is not clearly known how this custom originated, but it is commonly said that, as people did not eat much *unagi* during the hot summer season, a certain *unagi-ya* started the story that *unagi* eaten on the *ushi-no-hi* would drive out evil spirits.

At any rate, on the *ushi-no-hi* of *doyo*, there is such a large demand for *unagi* that orders cannot be filled immediately, and the people have to order them hours ahead.

The cooking of *kabayaki* seems simple, but it requires experience. In making *kabayaki*, a live *unagi* has to be used, as dead *unagi* do not taste good. However, it is said that at some cheap restaurants dead *unagi* are used. A live *unagi* has to be first caught by hand, which is in itself a very difficult task, as an *unagi* is very slippery and unexperienced persons can never hold one. When caught, a nail is put through its head on a *mana-ita* or cutting board and then, with a sharp knife, its back is opened. The bone is taken out, and the eel is cut into convenient pieces. Skewers are put through sideways, two or three to each piece. Then, the pieces are put over a charcoal fire. After being sufficiently grilled, they are steamed to soften their meat. The final stage consists of again grilling the steamed pieces over a charcoal fire, after putting them in a specially prepared sauce, and even while being grilled the pieces are put into the sauce several times.

When *kabayaki* is served, they are eaten with the sauce. Good *unagi*, well cooked, melt in the mouth. It is very rich, and *kabayaki* is a luxury to many common people.

Then there is *unagi-donburi*. The *kabayaki* as cooked according to the above method is placed on rice, over which the sauce is then poured. It is generally put into a lacquered wooden box or a china bowl. Some people prefer *unagi-donburi* to ordinary *kabayaki*.

Due to the increased consumption of eels, the supply of eels grown naturally in rivers and lakes has become insufficient, and consequently there has recently developed a new industry of cultivating eels in small ponds. But because of the difference in foods, those eels raised artificially do not taste as good as the others naturally caught in rivers and lakes. The eels grown wild are therefore much more expensive than those artificially raised.

KAGEZEN

WHILE A member of the family is absent from home on a journey, every day his meal is prepared and his place properly set, as though he were really there to eat it. As the family sits down to a meal, the rice bowl of the absent one is filled, and so is his soup bowl. Other dishes of fish or vegetables are placed on the table for him. This meal offered to the person is called *kagezen* or shadow table. This is done in the hope that the absent one will not lack food wherever he might be. The custom is very old, and must have started in the early days when traveling within the country was full of hazards and hardship.

It is only in the old-fashioned families today that the *kagezen* is daily offered to the absent person at every meal, whether the person be the father, a son or anybody else. Other families which do not observe the custom strictly offer to the absent person a meal only on some special occasions, such as on New Year's Day, the birthday of the absent one, or the village shrine festival, when a special meal is prepared. On such occasions, the *kagezen* is placed in the hope that the absent person will enjoy the day as do those waiting for him at home.

In the old days, each person of the family had his or her own individual lacquered table, about one foot high and a foot square. *Ozen*, as this table is called, was placed before each at meal-time, and upon it were placed bowls and dishes of food, and chopsticks. The members of the family sat around the room with the head of the family and male members at the head and the wife and other women at the lower end. When any of them was absent from home, his or her *ozen* was placed at the usual place, with all the bowls and dishes of food on it.

At present, however, the individual *ozen* has mostly fallen into disuse except in some remote rural districts. A large table is now generally used, around which the family members sit at meals. Even in this case, the place for the absent one is often kept, and his or her meal is placed on the table. The custom reminds all that one of them is away and they must think of him.

KAMABOKO

KAMABOKO, which is often called fish sausage, is a Japanese table delicacy, indispensable on ceremonial occasions. The origin is quite old, as the name is mentioned in documents of the early 12th century.

It is made of white fish meat. Fish used for making *kamaboko* are generally sea bream, cod, shark, flatfish and others. Its taste and price differ according to the kinds of fish used.

White fish meat is ground into paste and seasoned with salt, sugar, sweet *sake* and starch. The paste is placed on a piece of wood, about two inches wide and six inches long, to form a semi-circular shape. Then it is steamed. Sometimes it is baked slightly after steaming, to give a burned brownish color. The outside is then given a coating of red dye.

It is sliced into thin pieces and eaten or put in clear soups.

In the early days, fish paste was wrapped around a piece of bamboo, and as its shape resembled the ear of the *kama* (bulrush), it came to be so named. It is no longer made in this ancient style. But the present-day *chikuwa* (bamboo ring), which is also made of white fish meat paste, resembles the original *kamaboko* in a way, but it has no bamboo stick.

Hanpen is another kind of white fish meat cake. It comes in about a two-inch-square form. The paste in this case is made a little softer than for *kamaboko*. A noted cook named Hanpen of Suruga (present Shizuoka) first started to make this kind of fish paste, after whom it was named.

On ceremonial tables, red and white *kamaboko* are used. Many localities are famous for their special types of *kamaboko*.

KASHI

THE JAPANESE are great eaters of *kashi* (sweets and cakes) and its variety is great. Not only are all children fond of it but when a visitor comes, tea and *kashi* must be offered. In visiting it has become etiquette to take a gift of *kashi*. Tea ceremony requires it. In general use, *kashi* often means anything taken between meals.

The term originally meant fruits or nuts. Its seems that in primitive days, fruits and nuts were eaten between meals.

Japanese cakes and sweets as known today were first made after Chinese sweets which were introduced in the Heian period (8-9th centuries). They were at first called *togashi* (or Chinese cakes). *Togashi* was made of rice, wheat or bean flour and fried in oil. Among them was *senbei* (cracker) made of wheat flour and fried. It was from this that rice flour *senbei* later developed. There was also *yokan* (sweet bean jelly) which was made of red bean flour and sweetened with the juice obtained from *kuzu* (arrowroot).

In the Kamakura period (14th century) Priest Lin Chingyin brought from China *manju* (buns filled with sweetened bean paste). *Senbei*, *yokan* and *manju* became the principal *kashi*, and with their introduction, fruits came to be called *mizugashi* or juicy *kashi*.

Sugar was introduced into Japan in the Muromachi period (16th century) and with sugar all kinds of *kashi* improved greatly in taste. At about the same time various Western cakes and sweets were brought in. Soon a great variety came to be made in Japan — *konpeito* (confits), *kasutera* (Spanish sponge cake), *karumera* (caramel) and others, and were eagerly eaten by those in the upper classes.

Since then Japanese *kashi* has rapidly improved in terms of taste and technique.

KATSUO-BUSHI

IN JAPANESE cooking, *katsuo-bushi* or dried bonito is essential, because not only does it serve to improve the taste of food, but it is also very nutritious. In making soups or cooking fish or vegetables, *katsuo-bushi* is always necessary.

To make *katsuo-bushi*, bonito is cut into four pieces lengthwise after removing the head and bones. It is then boiled and left in a room to dry. Every day it is taken out into the sun and dried. This drying process is generally completed in about one to three weeks, according to the weather, and then it becomes very hard. Thus dried, it can be kept for years. However, once or twice a year it has to be sunned and aired.

Every household has a *katsuo-bushi* shaver which consists of a planer on top of an oblong box. *Katsuo-bushi* is pushed over the blade of the planer, and shaved flakes fall into the box below. Besides being used in cooking, shaved *katsuo-bushi* is also eaten as it is with *shoyu*.

Katsuo-bushi has always been expensive, and poor families used it only on special occasions. In the old days, wealthy families kept a stock of *katsuo-bushi* for daily use and emergencies. It also was an important item as a field ration of ancient warriors.

Not all *katsuo-bushi*, however, is made of bonito. Cheaper kinds are made of tuna or mackerel. Shaved *katsuo-bushi* packed in bags or boxes have recently appeared, but generally they are not of a good grade.

Small dried fish are also used in place of *katsuo-bushi*. They are just as nutritious, but are not so good as dried bonito.

KAWARA-SENBEI

KAWARA-SENBEI is a sweet Japanese cracker made in the shape of a *kawara* or roof tile, which is still very popular among children. It comes in all sizes, some as large as a foot across. Many localities sell *kawara-senbei* made in the shape of the ancient roof tiles of their famous temples.

Senbei originally meant wheat dough fried in oil, but the cracker-like *senbei* is believed to have been first made almost 400 years ago. It is said that in the Azuchi-Momoyama period, 1573-1600, when sweets became scarce after the long warring period, Kobei, a pupil of the famous tea master Rikyu, first baked wheat dough sweetened with sugar into a flat cake. This soon won public favor.

Then an old woman living by the Minato River in Kobe started to bake the dough between two *kawara* or roof tiles. Ever since, Kobe has been famous for its *kawara-senbei.*

It soon came to be produced at many other localities. But it was in Edo that *kawara-senbei* made a notable development. To make it quickly to meet the increased demand, iron moulds were made. Two moulds are hinged together. The dough is poured into one mould and the other covers it. One side is baked over a charcoal fire. Then the moulds are turned over so that the other side will also be properly baked. Big moulds that made four pieces at the same time were also made.

To wheat dough and sugar, Edo makers sometimes added *miso*, a bean paste, roasted peas and other things. Many fancy kinds have been introduced.

But it is still the big *kawara-senbei,* looking like temple roof tiles, which are most popular even today.

KONNYAKU

KONNYAKU is known to foreigners perhaps only in its shredded form called *shirataki* (literally translated, white waterfall) in *sukiyaki* cooking. But it is a very widely used vegetable in Japan. Not only is it used extensively in family cooking, but it is also regarded as indispensable for *oden*, a popular dish particularly liked by *sake* drinkers.

Konnyaku is made from the root of the *konnyaku* plant (Amorphophallus konjac), which originally came from China. The *konnyaku* plant is cultivated in many mountain regions of the country. Particularly Fukushima and Gunma are known as producing centers. It is cultivated on land too poor to produce any other crop. The plant produces fat taro-like roots. The outer dark skin of the root is peeled off and sliced into thin pieces, then dried and pulverized. Powdered *konnyaku* is boiled in water with milk of lime. A hard jelly-like substance is obtained and made into convenient shapes.

Children of rural districts often play with *konnyaku* balls as they bounce like rubber balls.

It has been said since early days that one must eat *konnyaku* to keep one's internal organs clean. Thus the use of *konnyaku* has been kept up.

A piece of *konnyaku* is heated in boiling water, and then wrapped up in towels. Heated *konnyaku* is placed over one's stomach when one has a stomachache or used to warm cold feet. Heated *konnyaku* stays warm for several hours.

The demand for *konnyaku* has increased recently even beyond supply, as it is used for many industrial purposes. It is used in making medicinal capsules, cough medicine and other things.

Konnyaku starch is furthermore used to make artificial leather, toilet goods, gunpowder, a strong adhesive glue and also bacteria culture. Thus, the cultivation of *konnyaku* is quite profitable.

KORI-MIZU

ALTHOUGH icecream, ice-tea, ice-coffee, soda and other modern summer drinks have become widely popular in Japan, the people still cherish their old-fashioned *kori-mizu* when the hot season comes. Little clean *kori-mizu* or ice-shops, with white flags showing the character *kori* (ice), rows of glass bowls, and cool mat-covered benches, are familiar sights all over the country.

Kori-mizu means ice-water, but it is different from the American ice-water. A block of ice is put on a shaver or shaving machine, and the fine shavings are put into a glass bowl. To the ice is added syrup or fruit juices.

For cooling food and drinks in summer, the Japanese people used ice or stored snow from very early times. The first documented record informs us that, in the reign of Emperor Nintoku in the fourth century, *himuro* or ice storage houses were already in existence. Of course, in those early days the use of ice or packed snow was limited to aristocrats. In the Tokugawa days, feudal lords in northern districts annually presented to the shogun cartloads of ice for his summer use.

But it is really after the introduction of artificial ice in 1882, when a Dutchman operated the first ice-making plant at Yokohama, that ice came to be generally used in summer.

As old-fashioned summer drinks in this country, there have always been cold tea or *mugi-yu* or barley tea. *Mugi-yu* is made by brewing roasted barley and cooling it in bottles placed in deep wells, or in running streams. Powdered tea is also often put in ice-cold water and whisked, making a fragrant and refreshing drink.

MANJU

AT A JAPANESE dinner, guests are served green tea and Japanese sweets, just before starting to eat and drink. This custom of eating sweets at the very beginning of dinner was introduced from China in 1332 by the Chinese

Zen Priest Lin Chingyin, it is said.

Coming to Japan, he lived at Nara and made *mantou* or Chinese buns filled with chopped meats, marking it with the Chinese character for Lin in red powder.

Mantou means a bun eaten at the beginning of a meal, and Lin's *mantou* soon found favor with Japanese monks and officials, who also came to make similar buns and eat them at the beginning of a meal.

Mantou, called *manju* by the Japanese, became very popular. In the Ashikaga period, about 130 years after the first *mantou* was made, Shao-pan, fifth descendant of Priest Lin, opened a shop in Kyoto and started to sell Shioze *manju,* naming it after the family of the Japanese woman he married. This was a Japanese bun filled with *an* or sweetened bean paste.

A branch shop was opened at Tenmacho, Edo, and soon Shioze *manju* ranked among the famous sweets of Edo.

With its increasing popularity many new types of *manju* were made, many localities making such naming them after local history or traditions.

Manju is now mostly made of wheat flour, but is sometimes mixed with buckwheat. The shape and taste, particularly of the sweet paste filling, differ according to maker and locality.

MATSUTAKE

MANY Japanese welcome the autumn season particularly because it brings *matsutake* and other edible fungi. Among numerous mushrooms growing in the country, many are valued as table delicacies, but the most popular are *matsutake* (Armilaria *Matsutake),* *shiitake* (Cortinellus *Shiitake),* and *shimeji* (Tricholoma conglobatum).

Matsutake, however, is the king of all

edible mushrooms. It grows in red pine forests, and sometimes becomes quite large, the opened umbrella-shaped pileus measuring more than eight inches. But it tastes best when the pileus is half opened in a cap-like shape. In Kansai and other districts where it grows abundantly, *matsutake* gathering is an occasion for enjoyment. Carrying *sake*, rice, and cooking utensils, the people go to the red pine forests which are specially preserved for the growth of *matsutake*. They pick *matsutake*, cook them, and have a day's picnic. But in the Kanto area, *matsutake* is seldom found as red pines are rare.

Matsutake is eaten in many different ways. *Matsutake* in *sukiyaki* is very popular. *Dobin-mushi* or *matsutake* cooked in small earthen pots in specially prepared soup is particularly enjoyed. *Matsutake-meshi*, or rice cooked with *matsutake*, is a delight to all during the season.

Shiitake, though second to *matsutake* in epicureans' esteem, is more extensively used. It grows twice a year, in spring and autumn. Fresh *shiitake* is delightful, but dried *shiitake* is used all the year round to give various foods a better taste. To cultivate them, spawns are placed in shallow cuts made in the logs of chestnut, beech or pasana trees, and kept in the shade. The logs are watered from time to time, and the *shiitake* sprouts in spring and autumn.

MENRUI

MENRUI or noodles are the favorite of the people. The three main varieties are *soba*, *udon*, and *somen*. *Soba* is made of buckwheat flour, while both *udon* and *somen* are made of wheat flour.

Soba is said to have been introduced from China about 12 centuries ago, and as the cultivation of *soba* plants became popular in the country, the consumption of *soba* noodles increased. *Somen* is only another kind of *udon*, but its method of manufacture is slightly different from that of common *udon*. *Udon* is made by kneading wheat flour and cutting it into noodles, but in making *somen*, the kneaded wheat flour is made into very fine noodles, by putting *goma-abura* (sesame oil) on them. Thus *somen* tastes slightly oily, but is made into very fine noodles.

When *soba* was first introduced into the country, it was not eaten as noodles. The *soba* flour was kneaded and small pieces of the dough were put into a soup, or the flour was put into boiling water to make a hot *soba* paste. The latter is known as *soba-gaki*. The making of *soba* noodles developed much later.

The people of Japan are great eaters of noodles, and *soba* and *udon* are very popular as a light luncheon for office workers and others. There are various kinds of *soba* and *udon*.

In the case of *soba*, there are first *mori* and *kake*. *Mori* is the cold *soba*, and eaten with a specially prepared sauce. The *soba* flour is kneaded and made into a thick dough. It is cut into long strips and boiled in big pots. Taken out of the pots, the *soba* is cooled. *Mori* is a pile of such cold *soba*. This is preferred by *soba* eaters to other kinds, because it retains the original *soba* flavor. *Kake* is hot *soba*. The boiled *soba* is again cooked in a soup seasoned with *katsuo-bushi*, *shoyu*, salt and *mirin*. *Kake* is hot and thus preferred on cold winter days.

Then, there are *tenpura-soba*, *tamago-toji*, *tsukimi-soba*, and other kinds of *soba*. These are special *soba* made by putting various things in *kake*. *Tenpura-soba* has *tenpura* in *kake*, *tamago-toji* is a bowl of hot *soba* with beaten eggs, and *tsukimi-soba* has various vegetables and *kamaboko*.

Kamo-nanban has duck meat and vegetables in hot *soba*, but often poultry is used instead of duck meat although the name of *kamo-nanban* is used.

Udon is seldom eaten cold. It is mostly eaten as *kake* or other specially prepared *udon*. The *soba* in the above-mentioned different special dishes can be replaced by *udon*. Then, in winter there is *nabeyaki-udon*. It is cooked in shallow individual earthenware dishes with covers. In the hot *udon* are added various vegetables and other things. It is cooked very hot, and thus welcomed on cold winter nights.

Kama-age udon is another *udon* dish, popular in winter. *Udon* cooked hot is placed in a large wooden tub with a cover, together with the hot water in which it was cooked. Thus it stays hot for some time. The *udon* is eaten with a specially prepared sauce.

Somen is a small-sized *udon*, so to speak, but because of its special preparation process, its color is much whiter, and the noodle is much finer. *Somen* is eaten cold in summer, same as the cold *soba*. It is more often put into soups together with various vegetables, meats, or fish.

In cooking *soba* and *udon*, the most difficult part is the making of the soup or sauce. Generally *katsuo-bushi* is the main ingredient used in making the soup, but also *konbu* is sometimes used. *Shoyu*, *mirin* (sweet *sake*), and salt are of course added.

Grated *daikon* (white radish), sliced onions, and peppers are used in eating soba or *udon*.

MIKAN

MIKAN or Japanese mandarin oranges are now very famous. *Mikan* were first brought from China, and it is recorded that it was at Yatsushiro, Kumamoto Prefecture, that mandarin trees were first brought and planted during the reign of Emperor Suijin, or about 2,000 years ago. Whether the record is correct or not, we are not sure, but it seems that oranges were planted in Japan quite early.

Imported oranges gave the aristocrats of the country their first taste of this fruit. For long they were beyond the reach of the common people. A document written in 1420 relates that the lords and ladies of Muromachi Palace were very fond of *mikan*, but they were extremely difficult to obtain.

Thus at first the fruit was considered a rare luxury or as medicine. Orange juice and peels have been used since the first introduction of the fruit for curing various diseases. Dried orange peels were formerly sold at medicine shops. *Mikan* peel is still an important ingredient in so-called herb medicines.

Oranges were so valuable that the people did not waste even the skin, which they cooked with sugar to make a sweet paste. Many rural folks still preserve orange peels and make this paste at home.

In some districts it is believed that for curing one's cold an orange should be roasted in the *hibachi* or *kotatsu*, and when the skin is burned black, it should be removed and eaten whole while hot.

Mikan-shu or orange wine is also made by adding sugar and *mirin* (sweet *sake*) to orange juice. This is taken more as a medicine than as a drink. A sip of *mikan-shu* every evening will relieve fatigue and ensure health, it is still believed by many persons.

MISOSHIRU

MISOSHIRU or *miso* soup is one of the most important items in the diet of Japanese people. To the majority, a breakfast is not complete without it.

Miso was brought from China. Buddhist priests who did not eat meat welcomed *miso*, and popularized it among the people. *Shoyu* and *miso* were introduced from China and became most important in Japanese cooking.

Miso is made of soya beans, wheat or rice, and salt. These items are put in wooden tubs and caused to ferment. They then form a thick paste. There are different kinds of *miso* according to the different proportions of materials used, as well as the method of manufacture. Various districts are famous for their distinctive kinds of *miso*. Thus there are *Edo-miso*, *Sendai-miso*, or *Sanshu-miso*. Furthermore there are white kinds of *miso* which are called *shiro-miso* because of their color. *Shiro-miso* is generally sweeter in taste than the ordinary kind.

Miso is widely used in cooking, but it is also taken in its original form. There are several kinds of *miso* which are specially made for eating purposes and not for seasoning. Various vegetables, fish, meats, and other things are mixed with *miso* to make it more tasty. Among such kinds are *tekka-miso*, *tai-miso*, *yuzu-miso*, and others. *Tekka-miso* has various sliced vegetables in *miso*; *tai-miso* has flakes of *tai* (sea-bream); and *yuzu-miso* has the flavor of *yuzu* or citron.

These special kinds of *miso* are taken with rice. But this use is a special one, and the proper use of *miso* is for seasoning.

Misoshiru, the common breakfast food of the people, is made by making *miso* soup with various materials. Most commonly vegetables are put in *misoshiru*. Sliced *daikon* (white radish), *tofu*, *wakame* (seaweed), onions, and such vegetables are most commonly used. But fish are also sometimes used.

Probably the Japanese are the only people who take soup in the morning. But *misoshiru* is also eaten at other meals. Among farming and other country people, often *misoshiru* is taken three times a day, and forms their principal dish to be taken with rice. In many farming households, a big kettle of *misoshiru* is made in the morning, and it is warmed up again at luncheon and supper. This practice simplifies the work of the housewives in preparing meals.

Misoshiru is very nutritious, and with rice and *misoshiru* many Japanese are able to keep up their health. Particularly in Japan it is believed that *misoshiru* is good for heavy tobacco smokers, as it has the power of removing nicotine, it is said.

While common *misoshiru* is made of vegetables or *tofu*, that with fish is regarded a luxury. Especially *misoshiru* with *koi* (carp) meat is called *koi-koku* and is regarded as being extremely nutritious. Old-fashioned mothers take *koi-koku* when they have babies, as it is believed that the dish will increase their quantity of milk. For weak persons *koi-koku* is also highly recommended.

Misoshiru with meat is something new, but it is welcomed by many people. Sliced pork or beef is placed in *misoshiru*. *Satsuma-jiru* is another kind of *misoshiru* with meat and vegetables. This is somewhat similar to Western stews. Meats and all kinds of vegetables are cooked together in *miso* soup, and is made much thicker than ordinary *misoshiru*. Sometimes small dumplings are also put in *Satsuma-jiru*. This is believed to have originated in Satsuma in the early Meiji era, and consequently has been called *Satsuma-jiru*.

255

MOCHI

ONE THING the Japanese people can never go without in celebrating New Year's is *mochi* or rice-cake. To children, particularly, the making or purchase of *mochi* a few days before the year-end is an occasion of great joy. To be unable to buy a few *mochi* for children is regarded as the greatest trial of poverty at the year-end.

Mochi is shortened from *mochi-ii* (round rice). Steamed rice is beaten into a pasty state to make *mochi*. It seems to have been made into convenient flat round pieces from the very beginning. Thus derived its name of *mochi-ii*.

At first it was offered to *kami* and shrines, and then came to be eaten on various festive occasions. It was from the Heian period (794-1192) that it came to be specially eaten at New Year's.

Zoni or *mochi* in soup came to be eaten particularly on New Year's Day since about the Muromachi period (1392-1573). As *mochi* is used on all happy occasions, *zoni* is also eaten at wedding banquets and other festivals.

Kagami-mochi, or the New Year decoration of a round *mochi* placed on top of a large one, is a product of the Tokugawa period when artistic and decorative trends rapidly entered the peaceful life of the people.

Mochi is a symbol of happiness, and used at all festivals, the erection of new houses, and other felicitous occasions.

In the old days, *mochi-tsuki* was done in every household. Rural people made it themselves, but in cities *mochi-tsuki* men brought *usu* (mortars), pestles, big kettles and rice-steaming frames to each household. In the presence of the whole family they pounded *mochi* for them. The eating of the newly-made *mochi* was done with great ceremony.

Nowadays in cities, *mochi*-making is generally done by confectionery shops which take orders and deliver the *mochi*. Thus much of the joy of *mochi*-making has been lost. However, many city shops display *usu* and *kine* (pestles) for sale in December, proving that these *mochi*-making utensils are still in demand.

Even though city folk do not actually make it themselves, many prefer to see it made before their eyes, and so have *mochi*-pounders come to their houses.

Mochi has always been eaten on festive occasions, and in some places it is eaten as a daily food. On New Year's Day, it is presented to *kami* and one's ancestors. Originally the *mochi* presented to *kami* was divided up and given to each person to ensure his good health and fortune. Many people still believe that *mochi* gives strength to the body.

This rice-cake is made of *mochi-gome* or glutinous rice, but millet, arrowroot, bracken root, or horse-chestnuts are often mixed according to districts, to give a different taste or to increase the quantity of *mochi*.

MOCHI-TSUKI

THE LAST WEEK in December is *mochi-tsuki* (ricecake-pounding) time. It is eagerly looked forward to by all, particularly children. *Mochi* is indispensable in celebrating New Year's. And its making has always been a great affair in each household.

MYOGA

MYOGA (Zingiber Mioga) is a table delicacy of the Japanese people, but it has been said that when one eats *myoga*, he will become forgetful.

Myoga is a little plant that grows naturally in shaded mountain areas, but because of its popularity as a vegetable, it is cultivated by farmers. In late spring, flower buds, measuring about two inches in length, covered by many layers of tender sheaths, grow out from the ground around the plant. The blossom is quite large and of a light yellowish color. The buds are eaten by people who put them in soup or cook them with other vegetables.

Regarding the belief that *myoga* makes one forgetful, there is a popularly circulated story. A traveller came to a country inn one day. The innkeeper noticed that he had a heavy money belt. He consulted his wife on a scheme of giving the traveller a dish of *myoga* and making him forget the money belt.

Myoga was thus included in the dishes offered to the traveller. But the next morning, after the traveller left, the innkeeper realized that the traveller did not forget his money belt, but had forgotten to pay his bill.

The belief is said to be based on a Buddhist story. One of the disciples of Buddha was very forgetful and could not even remember his own name. So he was made to carry a placard suspended from his neck, on which his name was written, so that he could look at it each time he forgot. He was so forgetful that he could do no other work but sweep the garden. When this forgetful man died and was buried, little plants grew around his tomb. This was the *myoga*, which came to be the symbol of the forgetful man.

But some authorities doubt the Indian origin of this popular belief.

NUT EATERS

RICE HAS BEEN the main food of the people from the very beginnings of the country, but in mountain districts where rice paddyfields are difficult to make, the people also have eaten many kinds of millet to supplement the small supply of rice. In some such areas, the people have also eaten various nuts in large quantities.

Particularly in the mountain regions of Hida, Gifu, and Yamanashi, *kuri* (chestnuts) and *tochi-no-mi* (horse chestnuts) have been part of the daily diet.

For instance, at Tokuyama village in Gifu, the *tochi* forests were owned by the village, and horse chestnuts were gathered by the villagers in autumn and equally divided among them.

The gathered horse chestnuts are soaked in water overnight and then dried and stored, or the outer shell is removed and the nuts are pulverized. *Mochi* or noodles are made with this flour. The people of such districts must have *tochi mochi* for their New Year, or else they do not feel happy.

In mountain villages of Yamanashi Prefecture, chestnuts are boiled and mashed to make dumplings.

As *tochi* and *kuri* can be easily preserved, they are eaten all the year round. It is said that in many mountain villages one meal, at least, is nothing but nuts in various forms as noodles, *mochi*, or dumplings.

Although the food situation has changed in recent years and more rice than before is eaten, the people of those areas still cannot forget the taste of their nut *mochi* or dumplings, and like to eat them almost daily.

The practice of mixing millet with rice, which was formerly very popular in many rural areas, is still kept up in places where rice production is limited.

City families often cook chestnuts with rice, but such is regarded as a rare delicacy, particularly loved by children.

ODEN

AS THE WEATHER turns cooler, the *oden* stall becomes a popular eating place, particularly in cities. This unique food, so relished by the commoner, has a lengthy history, and underwent various changes in the past.

Oden first consisted of a piece of *tofu* (bean-curd) pierced on long bamboo skewers and baked with *miso*. Held by the projecting bamboos it was heated over the ashes or *irori* (Japanese open fireplace). When it became hot, it tasted extremely good. That was the original form of *oden*.

Since the Kan-ei period, 1624-1644, the delicacy became particularly popular even among townfolk, and was improved with the addition of various spices to the *miso*. Also *konnyaku*—devil's tongue paste—came to be treated in the same way.

The name *oden* came from *dengaku*, a form of ancient show. The *dengaku* players in the act called *Sagi* (heron) wore a skirt of white with a colored upper garment. The *tofu* with *miso* on bamboo skewers closely resembled the *dengaku* player acting the part of the heron.

This type of primitive *oden* is still enjoyed in rural districts. But the so-called *oden* stalls in cities serve a slightly different kind, often called *nikomi-oden* (cooked *oden*).

In a large pan pieces of *konnyaku*, *tofu*, *sato-imo* (taro), *kamaboko* (fish sausage), *ika* (cuttlefish), *tako* (octopus) and other things are cooked. The sauce in which they are cooked is seasoned with *shoyu*, *miso*, sugar, and *mirin* (sweet wine). The fish and vegetables are eaten hot, right out of the pan. *Sake* drinkers visit *oden* stalls to enjoy *oden* between sips of *sake*.

At home *oden* is made in the cold season, as eating *oden* out of the steaming pan warms one up.

ONE-SIDED FISH

WHEN A SHOGUN liked a fish that was placed on his table, he ate the meat on the upper-side and then asked for another fish, as he had liked it very much. But in the kitchen there was no more of the same fish. The shogun's wish, however, had to be satisfied. The attendant took away the plate and, turning over the fish, brought it back to the shogun. This story is often told to show that the shogun was ignorant and did not know there were two sides to a fish.

But it was and still is the habit of epicures to eat only one side of a fish. It is because the meat on the under-side never tastes as good as the upper-side.

On a Japanese table, a fish is served with its head to the left and the belly toward the eater. When a fisherman catches a *tai* (sea-bream) or any other good fish, he puts it down with the tail to the right and the belly toward him. This position is never changed as it goes through the hands of fish dealers and cooks. That is to say, the same side is always kept on top. The side that is kept upward all the time maintains freshness and tastes better than the under-side that touches baskets, boards, and plates.

Thus fishermen, fish dealers and cooks always handle good fish with much care, so that the same side is always kept upward. Of course, cheaper and smaller varieties of fish are not given such care, and they are handled in the most convenient and practical way.

Being great fish eaters, the Japanese people have developed a very keen sense and taste in eating fish. If anyone laughs at the story of the shogun for not turning over the fish and eating the other side, he does not know how to eat fish, being unable to tell the difference in taste between the upper-side and the under-side of a fish.

OSECHI

DURING the New Year season, and at least for the first three days, Japanese eat *osechi* or special New Year food.

The New Year is the greatest festival of the people, and it is observed throughout the entire country by people of all classes and occupations. Food is important at all festive occasions. But it is quite strange that *osechi* or New Year's food is not at all elaborate or luxurious. At other festivals or ceremonies better and richer foods are offered and eaten.

From the richest down to the poorest, the same kind of simple *osechi* is eaten. This is its great significance that may be termed democratic, to use a modern expression.

During the last few days of the passing year, all housewives and daughters busy themselves in preparing *osechi* which is generally some inexpensive fish and vegetables cooked at home. Radishes, carrots, spinach, and other vegetables are cooked. The fish and vegetables are cooked separately in soy sauce and sugar. To add color, *kamaboko* (fish sausages), colored red and white, are sliced. *Kazunoko* or herring roe soaked in soy sauce is often included.

These things simply cooked, are put in a *jubako* or square, flat, tiered receptacle made of porcelain or lacquerware. At every meal during the New Year these boxes are brought out and each takes whatever he or she wishes.

RED RICE

ON FESTIVALS, birthdays, and other happy occasions, the Japanese family eats *sekihan* or red rice. Many old-fashioned families still insist on eating red rice on the first and fifteenth days of every month for good luck. To the people in general, *sekihan* marks special occasions of happiness.

Sekihan is different from the ordinary rice eaten at daily meals. *Mochigome* or glutinous rice, a species different from *uruchi*, the rice in common use, is used. *Sekihan* is also steamed, whereas ordinary rice called *gohan* or *meshi* is boiled. *Azuki* or red beans cooked with the *sekihan* gives the rice its red coloring, the color of joy.

The custom of eating *sekihan* on happy occasions has a long historical background. In ancient days, the people steamed their rice and never boiled it. *Genji-Monogatari*, which tells of Court life of the 11th century, narrates that the people generally ate steamed rice, and also mentions the existence of rice gruel made by boiling, for sick or aged persons.

It is said to be around the 16th or 17th century that the eating of boiled rice became gradually common among women and persons with weak digestive organs. Boiled rice came to be called *hime-meshi* or lady's rice, while steamed rice was given the new name of *kowa-meshi* or hard rice. Whether the people in general became weaker in digestive strength or became fond of the softer rice, boiled rice became more popular than the harder steamed rice in the Tokugawa period.

Yet on all formal occasions or at formal meals, only *kowa-meshi* was served. Thus the custom of eating steamed rice has been kept up, and the custom of eating it on special occasions is still preserved.

Steamed hard rice is commonly recognized as having a richer taste than boiled non-glutinous rice. But most people prefer the common kind for their daily meals, because *sekihan* is too rich.

As to the question of whether the ancient Japanese had two kinds of rice, one for steaming and another for boiling, no clear reply can be given. The kind of rice the people formerly cultivated and ate must have been different from the present species which is the result of long experimentation and breeding. It is generally believed that the ancient rice was glutinous, though it might not be the same as the present *mochigome* variety.

RINGO

VERY GOOD apples are now produced in Japan, but apple cultivation here is only about half a century old. The native Japanese apples are little sour crab apples which were called *ryugo*. The name later changed to *ringo*.

It is believed that Western apples were first introduced to the country about 100 years ago. It is not known how *ringo* came to be planted in the country.

There is a story that several apple saplings were brought by Commodore Perry. They were planted in the Koishikawa garden of Lord Mito, which is now a botanical garden. This story, however, is not confirmed.

Another says that *ringo* were first brought from China in the Bunkyu era (1861-1864), and that the Lord of Fukui first planted them at his villa in Sugamo, Edo.

Whoever first brought Western apples to Japan, they soon found the soil and climate agreeable to them in Tohoku or the northestern region. It is in Aomori, Akita, and Hokkaido that apple cultivation has now been extensively developed.

A story is circulated as to how apples were first grown in Tohoku.

In the early Meiji days, a certain Tohoku man went to Tokyo, and ate a Western-style meal for the first time. Toward the end of the meal, he was served an apple, a fruit he had never seen before. Though much attracted by the beautiful and inviting fruit, he did not eat it. Instead, he took it home to Tohoku, and placed the whole fruit in his garden. The apple sprouted, and grew to bear fruit.

SAKANA

THE JAPANESE people are the greatest fish eaters in the world, and they probably eat more varieties of fish than any other people. *Sakana* or fish is the most important item in the diet of the people, and although *sakana* originally means fish, it is also used to indicate all things that are eaten with rice or *sake*. *Sake-no-sakana* means those things eaten with *sake*.

Japan is surrounded by seas, and also has many rivers and lakes. Fish is obtainable in any part of the country, and because of both the warm and cold currents running along the islands of the country, the variety of fish caught is extremely large. It is impossible to give the names of the hundreds of different kinds of fish eaten. Whale meat is also eaten. Besides ordinary fish of the sea and rivers, they eat even *tako* (octopus), *ika* (cuttlefish), *same* (shark), *fugu* (globefish), and many others which are never eaten by other people. There are all kinds of lobsters, shrimps, crabs, oysters, clams, and other kinds of shellfish.

The fish used for cooking are generally divided into three main groups. These are fresh, salted, and dried. Then, according to the methods of cooking, fish dishes are classified into *yaki-zakana* (baked fish), *ni-zakana* (cooked fish), and *sunomono* (vinegared fish).

In making *yaki-zakana*, in most cases salt is sprinkled over the fish before baking. Small fish are baked whole, but larger ones are cut into convenient slices. *Yaki-zakana* are eaten with *shoyu* or vinegar. *Oroshi,* grated white radish, or grated ginger is used with it.

Then, there are *tsukeyaki.* This dish is made by putting fish in *shoyu* before baking, and also applying more *shoyu* over them while baking. *Tukeyaki* are always made with sliced fish, and not with whole fish.

Sunomono is made by putting sliced fish in vinegar. *Tako* (octopus), *ika* (cuttlefish), and various shellfish are cut open and put in vinegar.

Ni-zakana, as the name explains, is made by cooking fish in *shoyu,* sugar, and perhaps *mirin* (sweet sake). This is the most common way of cooking fish, but *yaki-zakana* is preferred by *sake* drinkers. The real taste of fish is retained in *yaki-zakana,* while in *ni-zakana* it is greatly lost.

In winter, the people prefer to make soup with vegetables and fish, and eat it as it is being cooked over a charcoal *konro* or electric stove placed on the table. This dish is very popular in winter, as the hot soup warms the body. In the soup are cooked not only fish but also various kinds of vegetables and *tofu.*

Salted salmon and cod are very widely eaten. They are sliced and baked. Because of the cheapness of salted salmon and cod, they are called fish for the poor.

Many kinds of fish are dried, and they are welcomed in mountain districts where fresh fish are rare. Large fish are opened and then dried flat, but small fish are dried after merely taking out their entrails. Dried fish are eaten by baking them. Small fish and shrimps are cooked in *shoyu,* and such are called *tsukudani* and sold at stores. *Tsukudani* keep for a long time because of their salty taste. They are particularly popular for use in *bento* or boxed lunch.

The taste of *kamaboko* or fish sausage differs according to the kind of fish used. *Kamaboko* is eaten as it is, or put into soups or cooked with other things.

SAKE DRINKING

THE JAPANESE people are fond of drinking parties, probably because they developed from ancient community customs. Drinking parties were formerly called *saka-mori,* which is derived from the old term *moru.* In ancient days when the spirit and necessity of mutual help and dependence were very strong in small communities, men and women gathered periodically or on special occasions, and ate together, sharing the food they brought. Such meals held to strengthen the bonds of unity and create closer relations were called *moru* (to share).

The old meaning of *moru* still remains in some northeastern regions where relatives or those pledged for cooperation are called *morabi.*

Moru at first meant eating together, but as *sake* came to play an important part in collective eating, it came to be called *saka-mori.* At first the supply of *sake* was not very abundant, but as the rice drink came to be more readily produced, drinking became the main feature of such community parties.

Both men and women were present at such early community parties. When only men got together and drank, the parties were never called *saka-mori.* The idea remains intact in Kyushu where drinking parties attended by men and women are called *saka-mori,* but parties with men alone are never called by that name.

Even in the early days, there were strict rules and etiquette to be observed. The order of seating was definitely set, and a large drinking cup was passed around, even after the introduction of smaller individual cups.

Each community at first had its seasonal *saka-mori*, besides those on various special occasions. This ancient idea still seems to be preserved, as women must be present at drinking parties and whenever people wish to get together and drink they try to find some pretext or meaning for their gathering.

The prohibition movement that was started in Japan almost half a century ago failed to gain any results. It is a great mistake to try to stop *sake* drinking in Japan where marriages are consummated by drinking *sake*, and bottles of *sake* are daily offered to shrines and ancestors. Today, it is the government itself that is urging the people to drink more *sake* and beer so that tax revenues may increase.

Sake drinking being traditional, it is no disgrace in Japan to become fully drunk. On many occasions, persons who fail to become thoroughly drunk are regarded as unsociable. The state of complete intoxication may even be said to be social requirement. Particularly in rural districts, the host at any feast or celebration party expects all his guests to become fully drunk, and if any of them do not take sufficient drink, the host feels offended. Of course, in most cases the host himself becomes so drunk that he is unable to know how his guests enjoyed the party.

Drunkenness being regarded as what might be expected to happen naturally after drinking, what one does or says when drunk is never held against him. Petty misdeeds committed under the influence of alcohol are always excused. In this respect, however, women are not treated equally, and drunken women are not so easily excused as men

in the same state.

Some authorities say that it is because of this habit of excusing anything done in a state of drunkenness that the Japanese have not learned or trained themselves to behave when they are under the influence of alcohol. It is also said that the peculiar nature of Japanese *sake* makes many people easily drunk.

SAKE EATING

SAKE — Japanese wine brewed from rice — is the national drink, but also is called *hyakuyaku-no-cho* or the foremost of a hundred medicines. Yet before it came to be taken as a drink or as a medicine to ensure good health, *sake* was taken as food. In ancient days, *sake* was counted among common foods, and never regarded as a drink or luxury. Being a kind of food, *sake* was not drunk, but eaten at first. *Sake-o-kurau* (to eat *sake*) is an expression which is still used in the country, though at present it is considered vulgar. The reason why *sake* was at first considered a food is probably due to the fact that in those days it was very crudely brewed, and came in the form of a thick gruel.

Sake was also originally taken cold. This custom is still observed in Court and Shinto ceremonies, at which the *sake* offered to *kami* is partaken of by worshipers cold. The habit of warming *sake* is believed to have started in the eighth century or the beginning of the Heian period. It is not known how the custom originated. But it is recorded that at first *sake* was warmed only in the cool period from September 9 to March 2, and in the warmer or summer season it was always taken cold. This leads one to believe that at first *sake* was heated in order to help drinkers keep their bodies warm in the cold season.

However, gradually the custom of warming *sake* was extended to other seasons as well. But even then, *sake* of good quality was always taken cold, only the inferior kinds being heated. What is believed to have popularized warm *sake* is the fact that *sake* of inferior grades tastes better when heated to a certain temperature.

Most inferior grades of *sake* contain some fusel oil, but the bad taste from the oil evaporates when heated.

Common people, particularly merchants and farmers, came to warm their daily *sake* in the Tokugawa period, when nobles and others of the upper social classes still adhered to cold *sake*. Now cold *sake* is taken only occasionally at ceremonies, and all *sake* drinkers prefer the warmed drink.

The temperature to which *sake* should be warmed to taste best is said to be 50 degrees centigrade, or body warmth.

SASHIMI

SASHIMI or sliced raw fish may be called the most characteristic of Japanese dishes, as fish is not generally eaten raw by other peoples. It is said by some authorities that the Japanese custom of eating sliced raw fish was brought by the early settlers from the South Seas. It is not known whether this story is true or not, but among Japanese fishermen there is still found a habit of eating small live fish just as they are caught in their nets.

Almost all kinds of fish can be made into *sashimi*, but the most popular *sashimi* are made of *tai* (sea-bream), *koi* (carp), *maguro* (tuna), *katsuo* (bonito), and *hirame* (flatfish). But *same* (shark), *kujira* (whale), *ebi* (lobster) and various shellfish are also sometimes made into *sashimi*.

The *sashimi* of *tai* is regarded as the best, but so-called Edokko or Tokyo residents prefer *maguro sashimi* to *tai sashimi*. *Tai* has a plainer taste than *maguro* which is rich and fatty. Tokyo residents relish *maguro* because it is rich, but also because it is difficult to obtain good *tai* in the Tokyo area.

Sashimi looks easy to make, as the fish is simply sliced and nothing else is done. But there is a great difference in taste according to the skill of *sashimi* makers. When cut by inexperienced hands, *sashimi* loses all its good flavor and taste. To make good *sashimi*, of course, good and fresh fish have to be obtained, but then comes the skill of experienced cooks.

Sashimi is made into different shapes, and according to the shapes and manner of slicing they are given different names. *Hira-zukuri* or flat-slicing makes long and narrow slices, and this type is the most common one, and has the fish cut in thin slices. *Ichimonji-zukuri* or one-line cutting is generally used for making *sashimi* of *koi* or carp. *Sainome-zukuri* or cube-cutting cuts fish into small cubes and not in thin slices. *Kawa-zukuri* or skin-slicing is the method used in making *sashimi* without removing the skin of the fish. *Hegi-zukuri* is the method by which the fish meat is not cut by a knife, but is scraped off with a knife blade. These different methods of making *sashimi* are adopted for different fish, and naturally these different methods produce different tastes.

Arai is a type of *sashimi* used especially in the hot summer season. Sliced *tai* or *koi* is placed on a dish and then hot water is poured over them until their outside turns white and the slices curl up. In the case of *koi* or carp, this method is used not only in summer but also in other seasons of the year.

Sashimi has to be arranged on a *sashimi* dish, which is different from other dishes, in a very artistic and beautiful manner. The slices have to be so arranged as to stimulate the appetite of the diners. On the *sashimi* dish, there must be *tsuma* besides the slices. *Tsuma* not only adds color to the dish, but is also to be eaten. Things used as *sashimi-no-tsuma* differ according to season, but they are mostly leaves of *shiso* (Perilla nankinensis), sliced carrots, *udo* (Aralia cordata), *aonori* (green seaweeds), chrysanthemum blossoms, sliced cucumbers, sliced radishes, and such. Most of the *tsuma* are not cooked, but are in a raw fresh state. These *tsuma* not only add beautiful colors to the dish, but also serve to freshen the taste buds after taking each slice of *sashimi*. *Sashimi* without *tsuma* is regarded as vulgar.

Sashimi is eaten by dipping a slice into a small dish of *shoyu*. Epicureans and restaurants use especially prepared *shoyu* for *sashimi*, but common people often use the ordinary *shoyu*. Special *sashimi-shoyu* is made of *katsuo-bushi* (dried bonito) soup, *shoyu*, and *mirin* (sweet *sake*). Sometimes, *sashimi* is eaten with vinegar or a mixture of vinegar and *shoyu*.

Also, in the *sashimi-shoyu* is added the grated radish called *oroshi*, or grated *wasabi* (eutrema), or mustard. According to the kinds of fish used for making *sashimi*, the people use either *oroshi*, *wasabi*, or mustard.

Sashimi is liked by *sake* drinkers, and invariably at drinking parties *sashimi* is offered first. But at the same time, *sashimi* is also good with rice. Many persons eat their rice with *sashimi*. Some people place slices of *sashimi* over a hot bowl of rice, with *oroshi*, or *wasabi*, and *shoyu*, and then pour steaming hot tea over it. When the *sashimi* is *tai*, this is called *tai-chazuke*, and it is one of the special dishes preferred by many lovers of good food.

SATSUMA-IMO

THE SWEET POTATO first came to Japan about 350 years ago, after travelling all around the world via Europe and China from its land of origin in Central America. It is called *kansho*, but came to be known by many different names — *Satsuma-imo*, *Ryu-kyu-imo*, and *Kara-imo*, bespeaking the route of its introduction from China first to Ryukyu, and then to Satsuma in Kyushu.

Satsuma-imo came to be generally cultivated in the country about 200 years ago, entirely through the efforts of Aoki Kon-yo, scholar and student of Dutch culture. In the sweet potato he found a crop that could be raised in comparatively poor soil, which would be a welcome foodstuff whenever rice and wheat crops failed. He strongly urged the Tokugawa government authorities to encourage its cultivation. He approached farmers directly, and as he always talked of the sweet potato, he was nicknamed *Kansho-Sensei* or Professor Sweet Potato. He published a book on *Satsuma-imo* and how to grow it in 1735.

Kon-yo's foresight in encouraging the growing of *Satsuma-imo* was deeply appreciated by farmers and others as the crop saved them many times from famine. Farmers still pay respect to his memory. During the Pacific War, too, many people had nothing but boiled sweet potatoes to eat.

Satsuma-imo is cooked in many ways as a vegetable. Baked or boiled sweet potato is taken as a snack, particularly by children. In winter, little *yakiimo-ya* (roasted sweet potato shops) still flourish in cities, enjoying quite a thriving business.

SEAWEEDS

MANY KINDS of seaweeds grow abundantly in the sea around Japan, and the people have been using them from ancient days as food and for other purposes. Probably no other people make so much use of seaweeds, and some say that the Japanese owe much of their health to the habit of eating them.

Konbu (Laminaria japonica) is a large species, growing to more than one foot wide and ten feet in length. It is found in the sea off Hokkaido and the northeastern parts of the main island. *Konbu* is used at weddings, Shinto and other festivals as the symbol of prosperity and long life. The dried *konbu* is used for making Japanese soup stock and as a seasoning in cooking. Many people, particularly of the Kansai district, are fond of chewing sliced *konbu*, which is often called Japanese chewing gum. This kind of *konbu* is sold in convenient packages.

Among other edible seaweeds, the most popular are *wakame* (Undaria pinnatifia), *arame* (Eisenia bicyclis), and *hijiki* (Turbinaria fusiformis). All these are favorite seafoods of the people.

Amanori (Porphyrateneral) is dried and sold in thin, square sheets. Near seashores, tree branches are placed to gather *amanori*. In winter they are harvested and spread on straw screens to dry. This dried *nori* is one of the delicacies of the Japanese table.

Many seaweeds have industrial value. From *tengusa* (Gelidium amansii) is made isinglass, which is an important export item. From *funori* (Gloiopettis fureato var. coliformis) is obtained a certain glue which is used in various ways by the people. *Kajime* (Eckloma cava), gathered in great quantities, is burned to obtain kelp to manufacture iodine. The iodine manufacturing in-

SHIMOFURI BEEF

BEEF EATING has become popular in Japan only recently, since about 100 years ago, although beef was eaten by the people in ancient days. Buddhism prohibited meat eating, and it was the coming of foreigners in the late Tokugawa period that revived the habit. General beef eating is comparatively new, it may be said, but Japanese beef has now become famous.

The original Japanese cattle were small in stature, and formerly used for drawing carts or doing farm work. To improve them, foreign cattle were imported to produce better crossbreeds.

Here beef cattle are raised quite differently from the way used in other countries. Beef cattle are never raised in large pastures as is done in foreign countries. A few animals are kept by each farmer in a stall next to his living quarters, and tenderly looked after day and night with love and care as given to his own children.

Omi and Ise provinces are famous for good beef cattle, but these districts did not originally produce them. It is in Hyogo, Okayama, Tottori, Shimane, and other areas that the best calves are raised. Such good calves are brought to Omi or Ise for raising. It is said that the water and rice of these districts are particularly good for cattle raising.

The calves are fed the best fodder, rice, rice bran, beans and other nutritious foods. Then daily the calves are brushed and massaged. It is said that this massaging makes the meat tender and spreads the fat through the meat in slender net-like veins. This type of meat is called *shimofuri* (fallen frost) or pepper-and-salt, and is the best beef in the world.

By such kind treatment, proper

feeding and daily massage, the meat is made tender and tasty. So it is no accident that Japanese farmers produce excellent beef. Of course, not all Japanese beef is good, and only selected calves carefully raised in the proper environment produce the kind of beef that has now become famous.

SHINCHA

SHINCHA or new tea of the year is welcomed by tea drinkers, as the fresh green tea has a better and mellower taste than the old, and also gives a brighter color when brewed. Thus *shincha* is highly valued.

The first young leaves of the plant make the best tea and the second or third growth produces inferior grades. *Shincha* is of the first growth which gives it its inviting taste.

Young tea leaves contain catechu that turns into tannin, an astringent substance. Good varieties of tea are rolled fine and are dark green in color, while cheaper ones are coarsely rolled and brownish. The so-called *sencha* or green tea is not fermented, but black tea is fermented and Oolong tea semi-fermented. Thus green tea contains more vitamin C than other kinds.

Tea also contains carotene, glutamin and vitamin B2. Because of these chemical contents, tea was first used as a medicine, and its medicinal value is still appreciated.

Brewing green tea is quite an art, and tea loses its good points when improperly brewed. *Gyokuro*, the best grade of green tea, has to be brewed in hot water of 60 to 70 degrees for one to two minutes. The cups must be warmed to the same temperature. For *sencha* or common green tea, the water must be 75 to 85 degrees, and the brewing time must be one-half to one minute. *Bancha* or cheap tea must be brewed in 85 to

100 degree water for about one minute. Thus the cheaper the tea, the hotter must be the water. Also old tea must be brewed longer.

Powdered tea for *chanoyu* — tea ceremony — is made of the young leaves of aged tea plants, which are specially raised. Leaves from younger plants never make good powdered tea. The dried leaves are ground in stone mortars into a fine powder.

SHOYU

IN DESCRIBING the Japanese art of cooking and dishes, it is necessary to explain about *shoyu*, because it is the most essential seasoning in making Japanese dishes. It is often said that the smell and taste of *shoyu* characterize Japanese dishes.

Shoyu was brought over to Japan from China in the sixth century by Buddhist priests, it is generally believed, but at first the use of *shoyu* was limited to aristocratic circles which eagerly adopted Chinese customs. It was in the 14th century that the use and manufacture of *shoyu* became popular in the country.

The province of Kii, or the present Wakayama Prefecture, is where *shoyu* was first made in Japan. Today the city of Choshi, Chiba Prefecture, is famous for the production of excellent *shoyu*, but the ancestors of the Hamaguchi family, the *shoyu* makers of Choshi, migrated from Kii to Chiba in 1616, and settling there started the manufacture of *shoyu*. Although there might have been other districts where *shoyu* was produced in the early days, available records tell that *shoyu* was first manufactured in the province of Kii. Thus, it may be said that Wakayama Prefecture is the source of *shoyu* manufacture in this country.

Before the coming of *shoyu*, the people seasoned their dishes with only salt, and thus the introduction of *shoyu* naturally caused a radical change in the art of cooking in Japan. It may even be said that the Japanese style of cooking originated with the introduction of *shoyu* from China.

But coming to Japan, *shoyu* has undergone considerable changes, both in the method of manufacture and its taste. Today Japanese *shoyu* is quite different from Chinese *shoyu*, though the latter is the model for the former.

Shoyu is made of soya beans, barley, and salt. But there are different kinds of *shoyu* according to the method of manufacture and also materials used. It is a salty brown-colored liquid. The color, however, differs also according to kinds, some being lighter than others. There is a variety which is almost colorless.

Although *shoyu* is used in very small quantities in cooking Japanese dishes, the total amount consumed in the country reaches an enormous volume, because every family uses it three times a day or more. It is calculated that the quantity of *shoyu* used per capita in the country is about eight *sho* or nearly four gallons a year.

The taste of *shoyu* is found unpleasant by some foreigners when they first try it, but with use they generally find it pleasant. Today, much Japanese *shoyu* is exported to various foreign countries, to be used by cooks or for making various kinds of sauces.

But, it is no exaggeration to say that the taste and flavor of Japanese dishes are mostly produced by *shoyu*. Not only is *shoyu* used in cooking, but it is also used on pickles and other vegetables, as well as with *sashimi*, sliced raw fish. Where Western people use salt, the Japanese people use *shoyu*.

SMOKING PIPES

MANY HAVE wondered how the people of Japan have come to use smoking pipes with so small a bowl. They are probably the smallest bowls to be found anywhere. The bowl being so small, one pipeful is only good for two or three puffs, and then the bowl has to be refilled with tobacco. No authentic reply is yet given to this question. But it is considered most probable that in first adopting the habit of tobacco smoking as it was introduced by European traders in the 16th century, the Japanese found that the foreign tobacco used for pipe smoking was too strong for them. Thus ingeniously they contrived to make pipes with smaller bowls, and also to cut tobacco much finer than the Western tobacco, so that pipe smoking would be much milder. Of course, with finer cut tobacco, small bowls are better than big bowls.

Then, *kiseru* or pipes are sometimes made very long. Formerly there were ones almost three feet long, which were mostly used by women. The longer the pipe, the sweeter and cooler the smoke. But such long pipes were used only indoors.

In its construction, *kiseru* is divided into two types. One is made entirely of metal, while the other has a metal bowl and a mouthpiece with bamboo between them. Common *kiseru* are made of brass, but the better ones are of silver or gold with curved or inlaid designs. As it is the habit of the Japanese to give an artistic touch to everything they love, *kiseru* was also made very elaborately and artistically. The bamboo part of the pipe is called *rao*, a name which is said to have come from Laos, an area in Indochina where good pipe bamboo is produced.

Tobacco pouches were made of rich

silk or leather, mostly very richly decorated. Then *netsuke* for attaching the pouch to the *obi* or girdle were made of ivory, metal, lacquer, or other materials in exquisite artistic designs and work. All other articles connected with smoking became artistic objects, and even today they are highly valued. The offering of a pipe and tobacco to a visitor was formerly counted as one of the rules of social etiquette.

The cleaning of the Japanese pipe requires quite an art and technique, because of its slenderness and length. Formerly there were professional pipe cleaners who went around to clean pipes. They cleaned pipes or replaced the old bamboo stems. In the Meiji era a new invention was adopted for pipe cleaning. It was a small steam boiler with a tiny outlet. The pipe cleaner carried this on his wagon, and by attaching a pipe to the steam outlet and letting the steam blow out, the pipe was instantly cleaned thoroughly. A whistle put on the boiler told the people that the pipe cleaner was coming. Children used to gather and watch him clean pipes.

SNAKE EATERS

SNAKES are commonly eaten as a delicacy in many rural districts. All kinds of snakes are eaten, but *mamushi*, a poisonous snake, is regarded the best. Some persons are professionally engaged in catching and selling them. Generally, rural folks eat what snakes they happen to catch in fields and hills. There are always persons willing to offer good prices for live *mamushi*.

Snakes are skinned and broiled. The taste is somewhat similar to that of *unagi* or eels, but much richer. In some localities, snakes are cooked with rice. The meat, after the bones have been removed, is mixed well with the rice.

Snakes are said to be very nutritious, and particularly good for persons of weak health or those recovering from a long illness. The liver of live snakes, particularly of *mamushi*, taken raw, is valued as a tonic that gives instant benefit.

Mamushi-zake or *sake* in which *mamushi* has been kept for some time, is drunk by many as a stimulant. Other snakes are also used, but *mamushi-zake* is the most famous.

There are snake shops in cities and towns. They sell live and also pulverized snakes. Snake powder is taken as a medicine or stimulant. As the powder is tasteless, even those who would not eat broiled snake can take it.

Recently snake powder has come to be often used in cooking, as it is believed that its addition improves the taste of the food and makes it more nutritious. With the spread of this use of snake powder, enterprising merchants are selling it at department and other stores.

SOBA

SOBA OR BUCKWHEAT noodle is a distinctly Japanese food as no other people eat buckwheat flour in such a form. *Soba* is popular because it is rich in nourishment and cheap. Many office workers take *soba* for lunch. From the very beginning, *soba* has been regarded as good for health. An old saying goes, '*Soba* takes the rust off all internal organs.'

Scientists have endorsed this belief, as they have found that flour made of Japanese *soba* plants that have white blossoms is richer in vitamin B than that made of the buckwheat with pink blossoms found in other countries.

Soba is believed to have been introduced to the country more than 700 years ago, but its cultivation was suddenly increased in 1382, when continued dry weather caused a serious famine throughout the country and farmers were urged to plant *soba.* Large quantities of *soba* have been eaten by the people ever since.

But at first they did not make noodles. The dough was made into convenient shapes, and after boiling them, the people ate them with a sauce made of *shoyu* and sweet *sake*. This is called *soba-gaki* and is not only made at home but also offered at some *soba* shops even today.

Kiri-soba (cut soba) or noodles are believed to have first appeared 400 years ago. The noodles are eaten cold or in hot soup. Fish, meats, vegetables, and other ingredients are mixed in the soup.

While *soba-gaki* is made entirely of *soba* flour, *soba* noodles are made of wheat flour, eggs or *taro* mixed in the *soba* flour to make it easier to shape the noodles. It is said that about a 25 to 30 percent mixture of wheat flour is ideal.

Because the people believe in its medicinal power, they have been eating *soba* on many festive occasions, New Year's Eve, dolls' festival, memorial services, and harvest festivals. City dwellers love to eat *soba* between meals or late at night.

Soba produced in cold regions is said to be the best, and thus Shinano (Nagano Prefecture) is famous for it. Hokkaido is now the greatest center of buckwheat production.

SOUVENIR CAKES

IN AND AROUND the compounds of many famous shrines and temples special cakes or sweets are sold for visitors to take home as reminders of their visits.

Such shrine or temple cakes can be divided roughly into three kinds. The first kind originated as charms. Offerings made to the shrine or temple were distributed to visitors as charms. This kind is still regarded as sacred, even though it is now made for sale and has nothing to do with offerings.

The second kind has some historical or other connection with the shrine or temple concerned. The third are commercially produced souvenirs and have no special meaning except that they are sold at the temple or shrine.

The Shinmei Shrine in Shiba, Tokyo, sells a cake called *Daidai-mochi*. It was first sold at a shrine festival in 1618 to be purchased by visitors and presented to the shrine. Later it came to be sold not only on the festival day, but also on other days throughout the year.

At the Daibutsu or Great Buddha of Nara, *Daibutsu-mochi* is sold. The original shop selling the *mochi* is said to have been erected in 1586 with the timbers left over from the construction of the building housing the Great Buddha. During the construction of the huge structure, the workers were served *mochi* in the afternoon. So the same kind of *mochi* came to be made and sold to visitors.

The Gion Shrine of Kyoto has its *chigo-mochi* (mochi for the festival procession of children). Such cakes were formerly presented to the shrine on its festival day and then distributed among little children who took part in the festival procession. The tradition is still kept up by the sale of *chigo-mochi* at the shrine. It was first offered in 1808, it is said, later discontinued and then revived about 150 years ago.

SUGAR

THE JAPANESE people use much sugar in cooking, and the mixed taste of *shoyu* (Japanese sauce) and sugar is one of the outstanding features of Japanese dishes.

Almost everything is cooked in *shoyu* which not only improves the taste, but also adds nutritious value to the food, as it is made from soya beans, wheat, and salt. It is *shoyu* used in cooking that supplies the people with almost all salt required by their body.

Fish, meats, eggs, and vegetables are all cooked in *shoyu*. Rural folks use more *shoyu* than city residents, preferring their dishes very salty. This is because their outdoor work makes them perspire much, thus creating the need for more salt.

The use of sugar in cooking fish, meats, potatoes, and other kinds of vegetables may sound strange to most Western people, but the sugar-*shoyu* combination gives a very strong taste and a distinct flavor.

The reason for the addition of sugar in cooking is that rural people seldom eat cakes or other sweets, except on the few annual festivals. They are generally heavy eaters, taking four to five meals a day in the busy farming seasons. But they seldom take sweets after or between meals. So their requirement of sugar in the diet is taken care of by the use of sugar in cooking.

Furthermore, by experience they have found that foods cooked in sugar and *shoyu* can be preserved longer than those cooked only in *shoyu*.

SUIMONO

SUIMONO is a Japanese soup, but it generally stands for clear soup. The people must have liked soup from the very beginning, but it is not known what kinds of soup they had. However, the fact that they had liked soups in the early days, may be learned from the fact that in the Heian period (ninth century), Court officials and aristocrats used to hold parties named *Shiru-ko*. The

Shiru-ko was a very elaborate and luxurious affair, but to those present was offered only one kind of soup and nothing else. The cooks tried their best to produce the best kind of soup, as on the occasion nothing else was to be offered to the guests. Such a party offering only one kind of soup and nothing else is unheard of in other countries.

Soups were formerly called *atsumono* (hot thing), because they were the only hot dish taken. It is quite recently that other hot dishes have been introduced.

While soups of other nations are based mostly on meat, Japanese clear *suimono* are made with *konbu* (seaweeds) or *katsuo-bushi* (dried bonito). *Suimono* is one of the most difficult dishes to make, and to make *suimono* of good flavor and taste requires experience and skill. Japanese *suimono* must be clear, and any that is not perfectly clear is regarded as bad.

Many expert cooks have found their own special ways of making their famous *suimono*, but generally *konbu*, or *katsuo-bushi*, or both, are first put in boiling hot water, and then taken out after a few minutes. *Shoyu*, *mirin* (sweet *sake*) or salt is then added to make the *suimono*. Japanese *suimono* have various kinds of vegetables, poultry, fish, or other meats in them, but they are generally cooked separately, and put in the soup after it is ready. In this sense, *suimono* is very different from Western soups in which all ingredients are cooked together. In Japan, the *shiru* (liquid) is cooked separately and put in the soup bowls just before serving. Thus in *suimono*, those things are auxiliary.

Then the special feature of *suimono* is that everything placed in it is cut or made up artistically, so that when one takes off the cover of the *suimono-wan* (bowl) there will be presented to the eye a beautifully arranged picture of different hues. Color scheme is very important in *suimono*. Thus sometimes a small fish is cut open and then twisted into a knot when it is to be put in *suimono*. Vegetables, too, are cut into attractive shapes.

Poultry and other meats are also used in *suimono*, but they do not form the main part of the soup, being only additional ingredients. For the sake of appearance, such meats are often minced and made into small balls. In the feudal days, *tsuru-no-suimono* or soup with crane meat was regarded the most delicious and costly. It was not because of the taste of *tsuru* meat, but more because of its rarity.

As in other countries, *suimono* is taken at the commencement of a meal. But when *sake* is served at the meal, *suimono* is taken with *sake*, and when the time to eat rice comes, another soup is served. In such a case, generally it is not a *suimono* which is eaten with rice, but *miso-shiru* or a kind of thick soup. This habit also explains the Japanese custom of distinguishing things to be taken with *sake* and with rice.

SUKIYAKI

SUKIYAKI is a modern addition to the Japanese menu, and although it is only about 80 years old, it has become one of the most popular dishes of the people. Furthermore, *sukiyaki* has now become famous all over the world. *Sukiyaki* and *tenpura* are pointed out by foreign visitors as the two outstanding dishes of Japan.

There are a few controversies over the origin of the name, and the most commonly accepted theory is that formerly it was cooked on blades of plows, and therefore this way of cooking was called *sukiyaki* or plows roasting. However, there is no proof that this story is authentic.

Sukiyaki is the cooking of sliced beef, pork, chicken or duck over thick iron pans. Beef is the most common meat used for *sukiyaki*, but chicken and pork are equally good.

In making *sukiyaki*, the first requirement is a flat thick iron pan, as when the pan is thin, it is impossible to make good *sukiyaki*. During Imperial duck hunts, small individual thick iron pans are used in cooking the duck meat. This pan is oblong in shape and extremely thick, and its top is almost level, with only a slight depression to hold the meat. This pan reminds one of the shape of the Japanese plow, and there might be some relation between *sukiyaki* and plow *(suki)* as generally believed.

There are different ways of cooking *sukiyaki*. The method used in cooking duck meat at Imperial hunting parties may be the original one. Slices of duck meat are put into a mixture of *shoyu* and *mirin* (sweet *sake*), and then put on the heavy iron pan placed over a charcoal fire. When the pan becomes hot, the meat is almost instantly cooked, and it is turned over swiftly and eaten. It is extremely delicious. This method is believed to be the original way of cooking *sukiyaki*. The same method can be used in cooking the ordinary *sukiyaki* at home in the common *sukiyaki* pan with beef or pork.

Then, the next method is to melt the fat of meat or butter on the hot pan, and then cook the meat on the pan. The cooked slices of meat are eaten with *shoyu* or salt. This method is quite new, but yet it is liked by many persons. This method, however, enables the people to eat enormous quantities of meat, as the thin slices will just melt in their mouths.

The third method is the most common one. In the *sukiyaki* pan is first put

271

a specially prepared sauce made with *shoyu, mirin, konbu* or *katsuo-bushi*. Then sliced Japanese onions, *tofu, shirataki* (kneaded devil's tongue root), other vegetables, and sliced beef are added to be cooked. When they are cooked, the people sitting around eat from the pan. In autumn, *matsutake* and other mushrooms are also cooked together with meats. Beef, pork, duck, and other kinds of meat are cooked in the same manner.

The last-mentioned is the most popular way of cooking *sukiyaki*, but originally, perhaps, slices of meat were merely cooked on heated iron pans.

There is no other new dish that has become so popular throughout the country within such a short period. At present, *sukiyaki* is a national dish, and particularly preferred by foreigners to other dishes of the country.

SUSHI

SUSHI is a unique item on the list of Japanese foods. To make it, the best grade of rice is cooked, and while it is hot, vinegar, sugar, and salt are added. It is fanned to cool quickly. When the rice is cooled, vegetables or fish, chopped up and cooked, are mixed with it. This is the most common way to make *sushi*. It is eaten at meal-times and also between meals. For picnics and other outdoor events, it is regarded most convenient. Women are said to be particularly fond of it.

Originally, however, *sushi* meant pickled fish made by placing fish between layers of cooked rice. When the rice ferments and becomes sour, the fish becomes delicious in taste. This method of pickling fish is still followed in many local districts. *Funa-zushi* (pickled crucian carp) of Lake Biwa is very famous, for instance.

At first the fish thus pickled was eaten, but the fermented rice was thrown away. But that might have given the people the idea of adding vinegar to cooked rice. Rice made sour by adding vinegar came to be specially made and eaten by the people. Thus *sushi* as it is known today came into existence.

However is was in the Tokugawa period that *sushi* became particularly popular and the technique of making it developed. Edo and Osaka, eastern and western centers of Japanese culture, developed two distinctly different kinds of *sushi*. Up to that time, the *sushi* commonly eaten was what is now called *chirashi* (loose) or *gomoku* (mixed), or a kind that is made by merely mixing chopped-up and cooked vegetables in rice flavored with vinegar.

Osaka developed *oshi-zushi* (packed *sushi*) or *hako-zushi* (box *sushi*). This is made by putting the vinegared rice into a square wooden box, and after placing fish and vegetables on the rice, weight is applied to press the whole into a solid mass. Taken out of the box, the mass is cut into convenient small pieces. This has become so typical of Osaka that it is also called Osaka-*zushi*.

On the other hand, Edo developed *nigiri-zushi* or palm-packed *sushi*. The rice is taken up in the left hand, and with the help of the first two fingers of the right hand, it is molded into an oblong shape. Over this is placed a slice of raw fish or other delicacy. This *nigiri-zushi* represents Edo culture. It is recorded that, at the very beginning of the 19th century, one named Yohei started to make *nigiri-zushi*. Whoever its originator, it appears evident that the origin of *nigiri-zushi* is related to *Kabuki*. It was customary for *Kabuki* viewers to take meals while viewing plays, as the program continued from early dawn to dusk. For convenience, small rice-balls, just big enough to be consumed in one or two bites, were eaten by those theater-goers. These rice-ball were called *maku-no-uchi* (between curtains). This *maku-no-uchi* must have inspired the making of small and handy *sushi* pieces.

Nigiri-zushi is now popular all over the country. Besides these various kinds of *sushi* there is *mushi-zushi* or steamed *sushi*. This is preferred in the winter months.

Inari-zushi is a favorite of country folks. The prepared rice is stuffed into a bag of cooked *aburage* or fried *tofu*. In the rice are mixed cooked *renkon* or lotus roots and other vegetables. When stuffed, the bags are tied with cooked *kanpyo*.

SWEETS IN SEASON

THE JAPANESE are sensitive to seasonal changes, probably because of the climatic condition of the country and their attachment to nature. Since early days they have taken particular interest in eating fish and vegetables of the season. Thus they have come to have certain sweets which are eaten only in the proper seasons and never at other times.

Sweets peculiar to Japan are *mochi-gashi* or cakes with sweetened bean paste inside. *Mochi* in this case is different from rice cakes which are also called *mochi*.

In February, when the lunar calendar spring starts, there are *uguisu-mochi* or bush-warbler cake. This is made roughly in the shape of the bird and coated with green bean powder, to make it look like the *uguisu* which is loved for its song.

In March there is *kusa-mochi* or *mochi* made with ground leaves of mugwort. The leaves give the cake a greenish color. This cake is said to have been first made in the 15th century by

Zen priest Tsugen at Arima. Mugwort leaves have been used as a medicine since early days. *Kusa-mochi* is indispensable for the dolls' festival of March 3.

Then comes *sakura-mochi* wrapped up in the salted leaves of *sakura*. This was first made by a gatekeeper at the Chomeiji Temple, Mukojima, Edo, in 1717. *Sakura* leaves are preserved in salt and they give a fragrant flavor of *sakura* to the sweets inside. Though it first appeared in Edo, it is also made in many other parts of the country.

Kashiwa-mochi, or *mochi* wrapped up in oak leaves, is a sweet eaten on the occasion of the Boys' Festival, May 5. *Kashiwa* leaves stand for long life and family prosperity, as on the oak tree old leaves do not fall until new leaves come out. Thus oak leaves have been regarded as a lucky symbol.

In many rural districts the people make *kuri-mochi* or cake with chestnuts. Formerly October 9 was called chestnut day and rural folks cooked chestnuts in rice, and also made *kuri-mochi* to celebrate the day.

TAISHI-KO

CARPENTERS, masons, roof-tile layers, wall plasterers, floor-mat makers and others connected with house construction in Edo used to have a fraternal organization called Taishi-ko. Such organizations came to be also established by similar workers in many Kanto districts.

Originally it was said to be a religious organization, and the workers worshiped as their guardian deity Shotoku-taishi, the great Imperial prince who formulated the first constitution of the country, ordered the compilation of the nation's history, encouraged Buddhism and urged intercourse with China, in the seventh century.

But there are other views saying that Taishi-ko was named for Kobo-daishi, the great Buddhist priest of the 10th century. It is also explained that Taishi stood for a deity or holy man, and Taishi-ko may have been a fraternity worshiping some deity who later was forgotten.

With the sudden growth of Edo, there developed a lack of workers. Workers gathered for their Taishi-ko meetings and discussed the question of getting their wages raised. Thus the Taishi-ko was the first organization in Japan to fix workers' wages.

On the other hand, Edo had frequent big fires which necessitated constructing new houses and consequently the wages of such workers rose considerably. The Edo authorities were not blind to such a tendency, and in 1836, the *Bakufu* authorities issued a notice that as construction workers had been holding Taishi-ko meetings for raising their wages, such meetings should be stopped and wage increases be prohibited.

But such a step did not end the functioning of the Taisho-ko. The fraternity of workers served as the organ for fixing their wages and it became the forerunner of the modern labor union.

TAKO-NYUDO

THOUGH the *tako*, octopus, is an eerie animal, the people of Japan are fond of eating it. It is boiled, sliced and put in vinegar, or cooked with vegetables. There are many varieties, from tiny ones of about one inch long to giant monsters measuring several feet from the head to the tip of the legs. Many seaside districts have tales of giant *tako* attacking and overturning fishing boats, or coming ashore and damaging vegetable farms. But those up to about one foot are eaten generally.

The common kind lives on rocky sea bottoms, and to catch them, fishermen use *tako-tsubo* or earthenware pots about one and a half feet long and about eight inches across in the middle, with an opening at the top. With ropes they are lowered to the sea bottom. *Tako* find *tako-tsubo* comfortable places to sleep in. The next day, the fishermen raise the pots and extract them.

The *tako* looks comical as it walks on its eight arms. Thus, popular tales and pictures present *tako* as a grotesque figure with a pouting mouth, and *hachimaki* (cloth head-band) tied around its red head, dancing with a fan in one of its eight legs. From the dancing *tako* has developed the common term of *tako-nyudo* (octopus monster) used in referring comically to baldheaded persons. There is a *Noh* farce called *Tako* in which the ghost of a *tako* tells about its former life to a Buddhist priest.

The *tako* is carnivorous, feeding on small fish and shellfish after poisoning them. But it is commonly said, though untrue, that when it has nothing to eat, it consumes its own arms, which soon grow again. When a business firm has no profit, but pays a dividend on its shares out of its capital or other funds, the dividend is called *tako-haito* (octopus dividend).

TEA VARIETIES

THE JAPANESE drink various kinds of tea. Most varieties are green, but *kocha* or black tea is becoming quite popular among the urban people. Before the war, Oolong tea produced in Taiwan was also drunk to a certain extent.

Tea drinking was introduced by Priest Saicho in 805, but it was in the 13th century that it became general. The people have become so fond of drinking tea that they have to drink several cups every day.

Green tea is divided into *gyokuro*, *sencha* and *bancha*. Then there is *matcha* or *hikicha*, which is the powdered tea used in the so-called tea ceremony. These varieties are made by different processes of manufacture from different kinds of leaves.

Gyokuro is the finest of green tea. For its production, the best trees are required. To avoid direct sunlight when new buds appear, reed-screen coverings are placed over the plants. Then the tenderest buds are picked by hand. The leaves are steamed, then rolled by hand over a warm pan, and dried. *Gyokuro* is rolled into very dark green slender slivers. The brewing of *gyokuro* is delicate, as it requires being made in hot water of exactly the right temperature.

The best leaves of ordinary cultured tea plants make *sencha*, which is commonly used by tea lovers. Old etiquette says that only *gyokuro* or *sencha* can be offered to guests.

Leaves left after picking for *sencha*, and old leaves and slender stems make *bancha*, the most common kind of tea. In color, *bancha* is not green but resembles black tea. *Bancha* that has a great number of stems mixed with the leaves is generally called *kawa-yanagi*. *Bancha* is cheap and is the common people's drink.

For making powdered tea, old and good plants have to be chosen. Selected leaves are steamed but not rolled. When dried they are pulverized. There are two kinds of powdered tea, *koicha* (thick tea) and *usucha* (weak tea), but *usucha* is more popularly used.

TEA WATER

MANY TEA lovers of Edo or ancient Tokyo used to dispatch special messengers to Kyoto to obtain water for making tea. The messengers had to travel on special *kago* or palanquins, going day and night, to bring the ordered tea water. It was expensive and took many days. But it was worthwhile to go to such trouble and expense, if good water could be especially obtained, because water is the first consideration in making tea, and without it no good tea can be served.

Throughout the country there were many places famous for good water for tea making. Ochanomizu (tea water) is the canal between Kanda and Hongo in Tokyo, and as its name indicates, in Edo days the water there was found to be well suited for brewing tea. That might not be conceivable today, because there is now nothing but muddy, ill-smelling water there. But a hundred years ago, when Edo was not so crowded, there used to run good clear water which was particularly suitable for tea making.

There are said to be three kinds of water — the water from mountain streams, the water from wells, and rain water. To these there must also be added the modern city water. These four kinds of water differ in chemical content and taste. For making tea, it has been found by experience of many centuries and study that the water from mountain streams is the best for tea making. This even has scientific endorsement.

Tea is spoiled by water that contains iron, salt or many other chemicals. Other impurities also harm its taste. Generally speaking, well water is not good because it has various impurities. Yet distilled water, though it might be chemically pure, is not good for tea making. Thus rain water, which is very close to distilled water in quality, cannot be used for tea. Further, the water of the modern city water system is comparatively pure, but not good tea water because of chloride and other chemicals used as disinfectants. The water for tea must not have such chemicals, but yet it must contain a certain quantity of calcium to make the tea taste good.

It is the proper amount of calcium contained in the water that brings out the best in the taste of tea. It is only at a few rare places that such water can be found, and they naturally have become famous.

Then, the water that is good for tea also makes good *sake* (Japanese rice-wine). *Sake* depends solely on the kind of water used in its brewing. Above the Yoro waterfall near the city of Gifu there is an old spring that is famous as a source of good tea water. There developed the *sake* brewing industry. From the famous Yoro water there developed the traditional tale of water turning into *sake* when a poor boy carried it to his sick father who was fond of *sake*. Nada, near Kobe, is also famous for *sake* brewing because of its proper calcium content. Nada water is consequently also suited for tea.

Since olden days tea lovers have gone far to get proper water. With the introduction of the modern water supply system and the spoiling of many mountain streams, it has become more difficult to find good tea water. This accounts for the reason why old people are saying that good tea can no longer be enjoyed in cities and towns.

TENPURA

TENPURA is a well-known Japanese food that has been widely introduced to foreigners, but it is a comparatively new dish in this country. It is only since about 100 years ago that *tenpura* came to be popularly enjoyed by the people.

The Japanese fried vegetables in oil before, but they learned the new way of frying fish in oil from Christian missionaries who came to the country in the 16th century. This new way of frying fish seems to have first become popular in Kyoto, and gradually was introduced to the eastern district.

In 1616, Tokugawa Ieyasu, founder of the Tokugawa dynasty, was in retirement at Shizuoka. On April 17 he ate *tai* (sea-bream) cooked in the new way for the first time. As it tasted good, he ate a great deal. A few hours later he died. Thus *tenpura* killed him, it is said.

What we call *tenpura* was already known at that time, but it was not called by that name. It is said the word was used in the middle of the 18th century.

As to the origin of this name, nothing certain is known, but it is generally believed that the term came from the Portuguese or Spanish word meaning temple or templar, and that the word was first used in Edo.

In Edo, it was in about 1785 that little street stalls selling *tenpura* first appeared, although in Kyoto such stalls were seen almost 150 years before they were introduced to Edo people.

Tenpura came to be made and sold at regular shops or restaurants in Edo in about 1865 and rapidly became a favorite of the people.

Tenpura implies fried fish or vegetables. Generally sesame oil is used for making *tenpura*. But some of the famous *tenpura* restaurants at present use olive oil mixed with sesame oil. The best sesame oil — *goma-abura* — has to be used for making *tenpura*.

Lobster — *ebi* — is the most common fish used for *tenpura*, and good *ebi* is quite expensive. At one time, however, various cheap *tenpura* places used American prawns from the Gulf of Mexico, or Manchurian prawns from Dairen. It is, however, quite easy to distinguish good domestic *ebi* from imported cold-storage *ebi*, even after being fried.

Various different kinds of fish, cuttlefish, shellfish and vegetables are also used. *Tenpura* is made differently from Western fried fish. Before putting them into a boiling pan of oil, the fish or vegetables are covered with a thin dough of wheat flour and eggs. The making of this dough is very difficult, and the taste of *tenpura* much depends on the dough. Then, the temperature of the oil is important, as different ingredients have to be fried at different temperatures.

Tenpura must be eaten hot, and stale *tenpura* is not worth anything. Thus, commonly at *tenpura* restaurants, the people sit in front of the frying pot and eat the hot *tenpura* as they are served from the pan.

As one eats *tenpura* as it is served from the pan and waits for the next, it is surprising to realize how many fried fish one can eat. *Tenpura* is relished not only by the Japanese, but also by many foreigners. There is nothing like *tenpura* in the whole world.

There is also *tendon.* It is a big bowl of rice on which hot *tenpura* are placed and eaten with specially prepared sauce. Some people prefer *tendon* to *tenpura* and rice, as it has a different taste from ordinary *tenpura.*

Tenpura is eaten with a specially prepared sauce. The sauce is made with *shoyu, mirin, katsuo-bushi,* and other seasonings.

Grated *daikon* is commonly mixed with the sauce. But there are some people who eat *tenpura* with only salt. It is said that by eating them with only salt, more pieces can be eaten.

TOBACCO TRADITION

NOTHING became a universal habit so quickly as smoking. It was introduced into Japan in the middle of the 16th century by way of England and Europe, about 60 years after Christopher Columbus' discovery of America. Thus, while the Japanese were probably the last people to be introduced to this habit, in these 400 years the people formed habits and traditions of smoking unknown in other countries.

First of all, Japanese women took to smoking just as quickly as men, while in other countries, smoking by women is quite a recent fashion.

In many districts, tobacco leaves were regarded as something sacred. At the former Court of Ryukyu, when women from small islands came and offered their respects to the king, they were invariably given tobacco leaves to take home and keep as treasures.

At Yukizawa-mura, Akita, no one in the whole village smoked tobacco even when smoking became quite a common habit. It was believed that Raijin-sama, the local deity, did not like tobacco, and so none of the villagers smoked.

In Shinano, there is a strange story. There was a cave where a devil woman named Ogaru lived. The villagers offered a pinch of cut tobacco at the entrance of the cave, and it was said that the tobacco soon disappeared. Thus it was believed that the devil woman took the tobacco.

It also became a matter of etiquette to offer tobacco to visitors or friends. In the gay quarters, there was the custom of a hostess offering a lighted pipe to visitors. She filled her pipe and lighting it, puffed once or twice, and then offered the pipe to a visitor. This custom of offering a lighted pipe is believed to have developed from the ancient custom of sharing food and wine with others.

Japanese women took to smoking tobacco much earlier than their sisters in many other countries. Smoking, ever since it was introduced into the country more than 300 years ago, was almost equally done by men and women.

Of course, today American women,

for instance, are great smokers, but 30 or 40 years ago, American visitors to Japan were surprised to see so many Japanese women smoking pipes.

Women used smaller pipes than the men, but smoking was popular among high-ranking women as well as common wives. They were slow to give up pipe-smoking even when cigarettes became popular.

The Japanese developed various sentiments about tobacco and smoking. It is recorded that in many districts, pinches of tobacco were offered to *kami* every morning to pray for the welfare of the family.

On the other hand, when smoking became a common habit, there were many districts where smoking was taboo, because the people believed that their guardian deities did not like the smell of tobacco. Of course, such a taboo no longer exists today.

There are two types of *kiseru* or Japanese smoking pipes. One is the shorter kind, generally being about five or six inches long, and made entirely of iron, brass, silver or various alloys. The longer kind has a short metal mouthpiece and a small metal bowl for packing tobacco, connected by a bamboo tube. This kind often comes very long, to over three feet.

The term *kiseru* is said to have developed from a Spanish word for clay, of which early Western pipes were made. A proper thickness and quality of bamboo is necessary to make a good pipe, and in the old days, bamboo from Laos in Indochina were used for the best pipes. Thus the bamboo part of *kiseru* came to be commonly called *rao*.

Long pipes are troublesome to clean, and also the bamboo has to be changed from time to time. Thereupon a unique trade of going around changing *rao* and cleaning pipes developed. The pipe-cleaner is called *rao-ya*.

The *rao-ya* has now become quite rare, particularly in cities, but one still sees him going around Tokyo streets from time to time. He pulls a little cart, upon which he has a small steam boiler, and the constant whistling from his boiler announces his approach.

He cleans a *kiseru* by forcing steam through it. He also carries a stock of various kinds and lengths of *rao* or bamboo to replace old ones.

His cart is always surrounded by eagerly watching children, as the process of letting steam run through the pipe is fascinating. The children also enjoy watching the tiny whistling boiler.

In rural districts, where the habit of smoking tobacco by *kiseru* is still popular among older folks, the *rao-ya* is a necessity.

TOFU

TOFU IS ANOTHER introduction from China, but has been greatly improved in Japan. Today, Japanese are greater eaters of *tofu* than Chinese.

While the consumption of *tofu* in the country is great, it cannot be produced on any large scale because of its manufacturing process and also due to the fact that *tofu* cannot be kept long without spoiling. The *tofu* manufacturing method has not changed much since the early days, with the only exception being the use of electric motors in running grinding stones.

Soya beans are first put in water for about 10 to 24 hours according to season. The soaked beans are ground in stone grinders. The product is then filtered through cotton cloths. The residue remaining is used as pig or cattle feed as well as food. The liquid is then heated over a slow fire, together with a quantity of water. Then the heated liquid is poured into a small wooden tub with little holes all over its sides, lined with fine cotton cloth. A certain quantity of bittern is added, and then pressed. The bittern serves to solidify the liquid, while water is drained off through the holes in the sides of the tub. *Tofu* thus made is sliced into convenient sizes and sold.

Then there are *yaki-dofu* and *aburage*. For making *yaki-dofu*, *tofu* is made harder than the ordinary kind and the thin slices are held by bamboo skewers and put over a fire to be slightly baked. *Aburage* is made by frying slices of *tofu* in sesame oil. *Ganmodoki* is another kind of *aburage*, made by mixing finely cut vegetables with *tofu* before frying. *Koya-dofu* is frozen *tofu*. It is made by leaving small slices of *tofu* out in the open during winter nights, at Koyasan, Shinano, and other mountain districts.

Innumerable dishes are made with *tofu*. First, it is put in *misoshiru* or clear soup. Then also, *tofu* is eaten cold in summer. This is called *hiyayakko*, and is very popular. *Tofu* is sliced into small cubes, and then cooled in cracked ice. It is eaten with *shoyu* seasoned with various spices.

Tofu is cooked with various meats, fish, or vegetables. Also it is quite often cooked in *sukiyaki*. Or, in other words, *tofu* is used with almost everything that is cooked with *shoyu* and sugar.

Dengaku is a special *tofu* dish. Slices of *tofu* are put on bamboo skewers, and then baked over a charcoal fire. When they are properly baked, specially prepared *miso* is spread over the *tofu*. There are different kinds of *dengaku*, according to the kinds of *miso* used. Generally ordinary *miso* is ground smooth, and to it is added sugar to slightly sweeten it. To the *miso* thus prepared is added various spices. In spring, when young leaves come out, *kinome-dengaku* or young-leaf *dengaku* is very popular. The *miso* for this *dengaku* is made with fine slices of young leaves of *sansho* (Japanese pepper).

The *miso-shiru* with *tofu* is very popular, and is generally eaten with breakfast. *Tofu* in itself does not make a dish, except in the case of *hiyayakko*, and it is mostly used as a side ingredient to make various dishes.

TOKOROTEN

KANTEN (isinglass) or gelatin made from seaweed is an important export item of Japan, as it is extensively used in cooking, for making cakes, as starch for textiles or as a base for bacteria cultivation. *Tengusa* or agar-agar, a kind of seaweed that is found on the seabed, is mainly used to make *kanten*. It is gathered by fishermen and divers along the coasts of the country.

But the *kanten* itself is manufactured in the cold mountain regions, such as Nagano and Yamanashi. The *tengusa* is boiled in water, and when the strained liquid is cooled in oblong boxes, it becomes jelly-like. This jelly is called *tokoroten*.

The *tokoroten* is placed outdoors in the cold for several days to freeze. The frozen jelly is then dried in the sun, and finally becomes *kanten*.

It is recorded that Minoya Taroemon of Fushimi, near Kyoto, first made *kanten* in 1652. The famous Buddhist priest Ingen who erected the Manpukuji Temple at Obakusan in 1661 named it *kanten* (cold weather), as it is made in the cold winter weather.

The jelly-like *tokoroten* has been much eaten since Edo days during hot weather, as it can be easily cooled by placing it in cold water. It is still sold in rural districts as a cooling delicacy in summer. An oblong cake of *tokoroten* is put into a long narrow wooden box that has wire mesh at the bottom. When the jelly is pushed from the other end, it comes out in narrow shreds. The shreds are eaten with vinegar or sweet syrup.

Tokoroten was also formerly much used for printing purposes. Letters or pictures were drawn in indelible ink on paper and placed face down on the flat surface of the *tokoroten.* When the paper was lifted off, the writing remained on the *tokoroten* surface. By placing a sheet of paper upon the surface and rubbing it slightly, a clear impression was made on the paper. Quite a number of prints were obtained from one original.

TSUKEMONO

THERE ARE various kinds of *tsuke-mono* or pickles. Many lovers of *tsukemono* say that if they have good *tsukemono* they do not require anything else to eat with their rice. For farmers and many other people, *tsuke-mono* is the only thing they have at their meals. In many old-fashioned districts, a housewife's value is measured by her ability to make good *tsukemono,* as it is considered one of her most important duties.

Takuwan is the most common of all *tsukemono.* The most frugal meal is called 'rice and *takuwan,*' but at the same time, *takuwan* is placed on the tables of all classes of people, and even the richest and most aristocratic eat it almost daily. *Daikon* — large white Japanese radish — are pickled in bran and salt. Generally they are put in large wooden tubs, and each layer of *daikon* is covered with the mixture of bran and salt. When the tubs are full, heavy weights are put on the top. In a few months, *daikon* becomes *takuwan.* *Takuwan* has a peculiar smell which is sometimes said to be similar to that of cheese. The peculiar smell of *takuwan* is not agreeable to foreigners, until they are used to eating them.

Then there is *nuka-miso.* Various vegetables are pickled in a soft paste of bran in tubs. *Nuka-miso* is made quickly, and particularly in summer, things put in the tubs in the evening can be eaten the next morning. Among things put into *nuka-miso* are cucumbers, egg-plants, cabbages, *daikon,* and other green vegetables. Each household has its own *nuka-miso* tub, which has to be attended daily. It requires some experience to make good *nuka-miso.* But in winter, it is the most unpleasant task for housewives and maids to put their hands into the *nuka-miso* tubs, because the bran paste becomes icy cold.

Misozuke and *narazuke* are special kinds of *tsukemono.* Generally only cucumbers, eggplants, melons, and a few other things are made into *misozuke* or *narazuke.* *Misozuke* is made by putting those vegetables in tubs of *miso,* and *narazuke* by putting them into *sake-no-kasu* or residue left after making *sake.* Naturally *misozuke* has the flavor of *miso,* and *narazuke* that of *sake.* These two are the most artistocratic in the *tsukemono* family.

These different kinds of *tsukemono* are placed on the tables of the Japanese people at each meal, and the quantity of *tsukemono* consumed by the families of farmers and laborers is extremely large. Even at afternoon teas, *tsuke-mono* is offered with tea in many rural districts. *Tsukemono* means more to the Japanese than pickles do to Western people.

UMEBOSHI

UMEBOSHI or pickled *ume* (Japanese apricot) is indispensable to the diet of the people. It is very sour, but many still believe that one *umeboshi* a day will ensure their health. On New Year's Day, *umeboshi* is placed in the first morning tea for good health throughout the year. Even today many persons insist on having it daily at breakfast.

Rural families as well as many city households pickle their own *umeboshi*. Farmers plant *ume* trees around their house to obtain *ume* for pickling. The *ume* fruit is picked generally in June when they are fully grown, but still green and not yet ripe. Japanese *ume* is seldom eaten raw as it is not sweet like foreign kinds.

Green *ume* is washed and put into tubs with salt. Weights are put on the fruit in the tubs. After about 20 days, the fruit is taken out and spread on mats in the sun during the daytime. This drying is repeated several times. Finally leaves of *chiso* (Perilla nankinensis) are put into the tubs to add fragrance and color. *Umeboshi* thus made can be kept several years, and the older they become the more mellow they are in taste. Many families boast of *umeboshi* five or ten years old.

When pickled, the fruit becomes wrinkle; thus often wrinkled old faces are called *umeboshi*.

Umeboshi is put in *musubi* or rice-balls which are carried for lunch or on picnics, as it will keep the rice from spoiling.

Ume-shu or apricot spirit, made by putting green *ume* in *shochu* (distilled spirit of about 40 percent alcohol) with sugar, is a delightful drink. It is also made by many households when *ume* fruits are gathered.

Wakayama and other districts have extensive *ume* orchards for producing fruits for *umeboshi*. Odawara near Hakone is famous for *umeboshi* wrapped up in the leaves of *chiso*.

A cup of hot tea with *umeboshi* is good for curing a cold, it is widely believed.

WASABI

MOST JAPANESE do not enjoy their *sashimi* (raw fish) or cold *soba* (buckwheat noodles) if they do not have *wasabi* (Eutrema *wasabi*), or Japanese horseradish with it. Grated *wasabi* is added to the *shoyu* or sauce with which *sashimi* or *soba* is eaten. It is also indispensable in making *nigiri-zushi* — small kneaded balls of vinegared rice with slices of fish.

Wasabi has a strong pungent taste that often brings tears to the eyes of the eater. It is widely used because *wasabi* improves the taste of food. Moreover, it is believed *wasabi* has the power to prevent any possible food poisoning. The people also like the fresh green color of grated *wasabi*, as it adds a contrasting color to the slices of fish.

The *wasabi* plant grows in mountainous regions, and has heart-shaped leaves and small white blossoms. It is cultivated for its roots which come in an ugly, twisted shape, three or four inches long and as thick as a finger.

It grows where its roots are always covered by clear running water. Around Tokyo it is largely cultivated in the Amagi mountains of Izu and the Okutama district. *Wasabi* farms are very profitable.

The roots are also cut into small slices and then pickled in *sake-no-kasu* or draff left after brewing *sake*. *Wasabi*'s pungent taste mixed with the flavor of *sake* appeals to the people. Odawara on the main Tokaido railway line is famous for this product.

YASAI

IN THE ART of cooking *yasai* or vegetables, the Japanese are at their best. They have always eaten many and various kinds of vegetables since very early days, but the introduction of Buddhism which prohibits the eating of meat has greatly developed the art of cooking vegetables.

Shojin-ryori by Buddhist priests greatly developed as they became powerful in the country. Priests had improved the art of cooking, and developed such techniques as to produce excellent and the most varied tastes by using only vegetables. Even today, the cooking at various temples is so famous that epicureans go there to be permitted to taste their cooking.

In the varieties of vegetables eaten, the Japanese people surpass all other peoples. Besides the common vegetables such as radishes, carrots, potatoes (both Irish and sweet), cucumbers, eggplants, onions, and such, there are used in Japan bamboo, various kinds of mushrooms and others which are unknown to foreign peoples. Among mushrooms, there are *matsu-take*, *shiitake*, *shimeji*, and other varieties, which are relished by the people. Bamboo shoots are delicacies.

Although the people eat so many vegetables, they seldom eat them raw, but always cook them with *shoyu* and sugar, put them in vinegar, or pickle them.

Vegetables are also fried. *Shojin-age* is the name given to vegetables fried in perilla oil. In making this, vegetables are sliced into convenient sizes, and then covered with a thick wheat-flour dough, and then put in boiling perilla oil. It is, in other words, vegetable *tenpura.*

Shojin-age is very popular among country folks and particularly at various Buddhist functions *shojin-age* is offered. All kinds of vegetables can be made into *shojin-age*.

Although the people like to cook vegetables, they do not cook them too well, as too much cooking will spoil their taste. They prefer to keep vegetables fresh to retain their natural flavor and taste even after cooking.

Vegetables are cooked with *shoyu,* sugar, *mirin, katsuo-bushi,* and other seasonings. But they are also frequently cooked with meats or fish. Some of the most critical persons do not like to have vegetables cooked with sugar, because they believe that vegetables already contain sufficient sugar, and thus there are methods of cooking vegetables without sugar. Sometimes vegetables are cooked with salt alone, or merely boiled and eaten with salt.

YOKAN

YOKAN IS THE most representative Japanese sweet. Not only is it produced all over the country, but there are numerous varieties to meet the taste and purse of all classes of people, from the most critical to little children.

Yokan originally came from China where it was at first a table delicacy. Zen sect priests introduced it in their dishes. The first import of sugar in 754 brought a radical change in Japanese sweets, though at first sugar was solely used as a medicine or luxury item.

Yokan was greatly improved in the Muromachi period (1392-1573) with the progress of the tea ceremony. When *yokan* was first produced, it was the kind which is now called *mushi-yokan* (steamed *yokan*). Red beans are boiled and crushed, and with sugar and wheat flour the juice is made into a thick paste. The paste is put in molds and steamed.

In the Tokugawa period isinglass was first produced, and by using isinglass instead of wheat flour, *neri-yokan* or well-stirred and smooth *yokan* was first made in the Tensho era (1573-1592). This new variety instantly became extremely popular, as when it is well made, it keeps for years without spoiling.

There are various kinds of *yokan*, some being made of white or green peas instead of red beans. Some have designs in colors. In certain kinds designs are put inside so that they will show when cut into thick slices.

Yokan is relished by tea drinkers, who think that the taste of tea is enhanced by the sweetness of *yokan*. Many districts produce special *yokan*, which are sold as specialties of the place.

Mushi-yokan is still popular and tastes entirely different from *neri-yokan*. However, it can be kept for only a few days, and has to be eaten while fresh in order to appreciate its taste.

YONAKI-SOBA

BEING very fond of noodles, the Japanese have long liked to eat hot bowls of noodles on cold winter evenings. From this has developed *yonaki-soba* which became particularly popular from the beginning of the Tokugawa period or the 17th century.

Yonaki-soba (night-singing buckwheat noodles) means buckwheat noodles cooked in hot soup and sold at little movable stands which are opened on street corners on winter evenings. Sometimes these stands are moved to different locations during the night. To those who had to be out late on cold evenings after there were no more transportation facilities, *yonaki-soba* stands were oases of comfort and warmth. The stand is of simple make and can be carried on a shoulder pole, generally having an oil lantern and *furin*, a wind-bell.

In the Osaka and Kyoto districts it is called *yonaki-udon*, because the people there prefer *udon* (wheat noodles) to buckwheat noodles. *Yonaki-soba* was also called *yotaka-soba* (night-hawk noodles). It was so named because *yotaka* (street girls) patronized these stands, it is said. Another story goes that for the convenience of *takasho* (hawkers) the stand-keeper had a shelf, known as the hawk-shelf, made on the stand where a hot bowl could be placed at shoulder height so that the hawker could eat the noodles from the bowl with his right hand, while holding the hawk in his gloved left fist.

Shortly after the Russo-Japanese War (1904-1905) there appeared another type of hot noodles, with the increased popularity of Chinese food. The peddler of Chinese noodles announced his approach with weird music he produced with a Chinese trumpet, commonly called *charamela*, which is originally a Portuguese word. Of course *yonaki-soba* has changed in recent years, but still the hot bowls of noodles, either buckwheat, wheat, or Chinese, are in much demand on cold winter evenings.

Chapter 8
Living Habits

ANBA-SAMA

MATSURI or Japanese festivals are mainly held as shrine rites, expressions of prayer, or seasonal and local events of recreation. But there are also festivals having unique origins.

Fishermen on the Pacific coast, in Chiba, Ibaraki, Fukushima, Miyagi and Iwate, have a festival for a female deity who is commonly called Anba-sama. The Osugi-Daimyojin, a shrine at Aba in Hitachi province, is said to be the main shrine of Anba-sama.

The festival is held now when fishing is particularly poor, in prayer for a good catch. It was formerly also observed when epidemics of smallpox prevailed.

For the *matsuri*, fishermen bring out their nets and boats to a certain spot on the beach and pile them up. On top of the pile they place a small shrine for Anba-sama, who is generally believed to be the parent deity of Funadama-sama or the spirit of fishing boats.

As long as Anba-sama is kept on the pile of boats and nets on the beach, they cannot go out fishing. If they do, they will meet with disaster, it is said.

This festival originated from an act of sabotage by fishermen when their masters or boat owners forced them to overwork. By piling up boats and nets and placing Anba-sama on the pile, they expressed their refusal to work. So no fishing was done while the pile remained on the beach as a sign of sabotage. Thus it became a traditional method of Pacific coast fishermen in demanding rest from extorted labor, knowing that their masters or employers would not dare remove Anba-sama.

But the original meaning of the festival is now lost and it has become just a rite in prayer for a good catch.

BANZAI

BANZAI is the exclamation of joy or felicitation uttered by the Japanese on all happy occasions. It is shouted at big national events as well as on occasions of personal joy. Children say *'banzai'* when they are given something good to eat. People shout it loudly to mark the happy conclusion of meetings.

Banzai, meaning 10,000 years, was first introduced from China where the term was used as a salutation to the emperor. It is recorded that during the Taika era (645-654) when the culture and administrative system of the Tang dynasty of China were brought into the country, four banners with the inscription of *banzai* were erected in the garden of the Imperial Palace.

Also it is mentioned that when Emperor Yuryaku (456-479) returned from a hunting trip to Katsuragi Mountain, he was warmly greeted with shouts of *banzai*. Thus in those early days, it was a term of salutation to the emperor as it was in China. It was shouted in particular at the Emperor's coronation and other great events held at the Imperial Court, but never used by the common people.

The common use of *banzai* is quite recent. As a public expression of joy or happiness, it has a history of less than a hundred years.

On February 11, 1889, a great national celebration was held for the promulgation of the Constitution that opened the modern era for Japan. To honor the great event, a magnificent ceremony was held at Court with the attendance of the Emperor and the public held gay processions all over the country.

It was Dr. Shoichi Toyama of the Imperial University who proposed shouting *banzai* as a fit exclamation to express the public's joy on the occasion. Toyama lined up professors and students of the university before the Nijubashi of the palace, and all joined in shouting *banzai.*

Since then it has become a common shout to be uttered on all happy occasions, public or private.

BLACKENED TEETH

THE JAPANESE had very good teeth in the old days because they blackened them. The custom of blackening teeth is believed to have been observed since the earliest times. It died out almost entirely in the Nara period in the eighth century, but was soon revived.

In the 12th century, when the country was in a state of continued war between the Genji and Heike clans of warriors, only women blackened their teeth.

In the Tokugawa period that began in 1600, all men of the Imperial Court continued the habit, but other males gradually discontinued the custom. All girls started to blacken their teeth when they reached the age of 13, as a sign of attaining womanhood. It also became the symbol of married women. The old custom was followed by some married women even in the early years of the Meiji period.

The teeth blackening material used in the early days is not known, but it must have been similar to what was used in the Tokugawa period and early Meiji era when teeth were blackened by the application of iron and tannin acid. The usual method was first to prepare an iron solution by putting pieces of iron in *sake* or vinegar. A jar of this solution was always kept handy.

When the teeth were to be blackened, this jar or pot containing vinegar and iron was heated. When the brownish liquid was properly warmed up, a brush made by beating one end of a stick of willow wood into fiber was dipped into it. Then, to this brush wet with the iron solution were applied powdered gallnuts containing tannin acid. The brush was applied thoroughly to the teeth over their entire surface.

The operation had to be repeated almost every morning in order to keep the teeth in good color. This trouble appears at times to have made the custom unpopular among the lazy or lowest classes of people. Nevertheless, the daily blackening kept their teeth clean and sound.

COUNTING UNITS

THE JAPANESE always count things by units, never by numbers only.

Human beings are counted by the unit of *nin* (person). Thus three children are *sannin* (three persons of children). Shoes, socks, and *tabi* are counted as so many *soku* (foot). Paper, dishes, carpets, handkerchiefs, boards, and other thin and flat things are counted as *mai* (sheet); houses as *ken* (eave). One owns two *ken* of houses and not two houses. Matches, pencils, cigarettes, and other long and slender things are counted as *hon* (stick). *'Ippon kudasai'* (give me one stick), one says, when asking for a cigarette.

Mirrors and many other flat things are counted as *men* (face). Chopsticks are counted as *zen* (tray), as formerly individual trays for meals were used, and each *zen* or tray had chopsticks upon it. Dresses are referred to as *chaku* (wear). Books are counted as so many *satsu* (volume). One buys two volumes of books, and not two books. *Tatami* or floor mats are so many *jo* (bed), as at first *tatami* was used as a bed, not as a floor covering.

Wa (wing) is the unit for birds; *hiki* (piece) for animals and insects. Scissors, cooking knives, hoes, guns, and other long things are counted as *cho*, which stands for anything long. *Cho* was also used for *kago*, ancient palanquins, as they were carried on long poles.

Koto (Japanese harp) and *yumi* (bow) are counted as *hari* (strings). Chairs and tables are counted by the unit of *kyaku* (leg).

The 20th year is called *hatachi*, and the 20th day of the month *hatsuka* in spoken Japanese but these terms are now becoming obsolete, particularly among the young people. In the old days *'hata'* was used to mean the number 20, and *'chi'* meant piece, and so *hatachi* was used not only in referring to the 20th year of a man's age but also in counting 20 pieces. In the same way, the 20th day of the month was called *hatsuka*.

There are two ways of counting numbers in Japan. One way is to call the numbers from one to 10 *hitotsu, futatsu, mittsu, yottsu, itsutsu, muttsu, nanatsu, yattsu, kokonotsu,* and *toh.* The *'tsu'* at the end means a piece or pieces.

This appears to be the oldest way of counting, but another way, probably adopted after the Chinese system of the Han dynasty, also came to be used in the country. In this system the numbers from one to 10 are called *ichi, ni, san, shi, go, roku, shichi, hachi, ku,* and *ju.* This way of counting is now more widely used for numbers and days than the old way.

Young folk are often puzzled when the old counting terms are used. Young saleswomen very likely will not understand when they are asked to give *'tohako'* (10 boxes) of articles, as they would say *'juppako'* (10 boxes). Everywhere we hear children say *'ikko'* (one piece) where older persons would say *'hitotsu.'*

The new counting terms are simple and shorter but old folks say that they sound harsh, while the old way is softer and pleasanter to the ear.

With the rapid popularity of the new system, the old way may soon become only literary or considered fancy, not to be used in daily conversation.

GYPSIES

SANKA ARE, so to speak, the Japanese counterparts of gypsies. Though their origin is unknown, such groups of wandering people are found from Kyushu to the Kanto area. They differ, of course, according to districts, and are called by various names. *Misokuri, minahoshi,* and *pon* are some of the names by which these people are sometimes called.

The *sanka* have no fixed place of residence, moving from one place to another, according to the season or their needs. They build crude huts called *seburi* or tents, but they are neither vagabonds nor beggars. The men generally catch fish or wild animals, while the women make baskets and household utensils with bamboo, selling them to buy whatever simple things they might need.

It is particularly noteworthy that bamboo basket making is done by almost all *sanka* women throughout the country. Their wares are crude, but there are some interesting articles made by them.

Once or twice a year, those in one area hold a gathering to which quite a large number assemble. They drink, dance and sing, having quite an enjoyable time. It is also an occasion to trade what they have or need. They do not bother other people.

Though they change their residence from time to time, they do not purposely avoid other people with whom they trade and speak.

However, it is reported that the *sanka* are fast dying out. Their ways of living are also changing, coming nearer to those of other people. Some predict that the *sanka* may soon completely disappear.

HAKA-MAIRI

UNDER THE OLD family system or tradition, the first duty of the head of a family was to look after the tombs of his ancestors. If a son was unable to erect a proper grave for his father, it was regarded as an unpardonable shame.

Though the old family system has disappeared, the people are still in the habit of erecting fine tombstones for their parents and visiting them quite often. *Higan* or equinox week from September 20-26, is the period of *haka-mairi* or cemetery visiting as is also the spring equinox week.

The whole family visits the family cemetery some time during the week. First they sweep the compounds clean, and then offer flowers and *senko* (incense sticks). Another important rite is to pour water over and around the tombstone. Then all kneel and pray, often repeating Buddhist sutras.

The rite of pouring water is distinctly Buddhist. The water poured on the tomb is called salvation water, and it is believed that the water will aid the dead in attaining salvation. Thus this ceremony of pouring water is important in *haka-mairi.*

In ancient times, the grave was only an earth mound, and the water was poured all over the mound. As tombstones came to be erected to mark the burial grounds, it became customary to pour water over the stone. Generally shallow holes are made in the base stone of the tombstone to hold water.

Many people today have forgotten the meaning of pouring water and think that it is only a matter of custom. Old-fashioned people still think that water is necessary for the salvation of their ancestors, and oppose the modern habit of paving the cemetery ground with stones or concrete as such will not permit the water to reach the remains or bones buried underneath.

HAREBI

UNTIL THE Meiji era the Japanese had no Sundays as a day of rest, and even today Sundays are not observed by rural folks. But they had their own days of rest called *hare-no-hi* or *harebi* (bright or formal days).

Harebi stands for annual family or community events and festivals, marking seasonal farming events such as harvesting, planting, praying for rain or insect expulsion, and also important events in human life such as birthdays, annual celebrations, marriages, funerals, and journeys.

These *harebi* are sacred, and should be observed with a clean body and pure spirit. Thus they are different from ordinary days. No work should be done and no evil thought should enter one's mind on those days.

To differentiate *harebi* from ordinary days, special foods are prepared. Instead of the daily rice, they eat *mochi* (rice cakes) or noodles, or make *sekihan* (rice with red beans). Farming people do not eat much fish on ordinary days, and so they must have fish on *harebi*.

They do not wear working clothes, but dress themselves in better or formal costumes which are called *haregi* or apparel for *harebi*. Women taking part in *ta-ue* or rice planting still dress in fine, bright *kimono* as rice planting is one of the *hare* events.

The old custom of wearing head coverings with *haregi* is still seen among women of rural districts. Such head coverings are still regarded necessary on *harebi* or in meeting guests in many districts. Also on *harebi* they still wear better *geta* (clogs) or *zori* (sandals).

HEAD BASKETS

THE CUSTOM of women carrying various goods on their heads was formerly followed all over the country. But, somehow, it gradually disappeared from inland or mountain districts, and now it is seen only in districts near the seashore.

Ohara girls in the neighborhood of Kyoto are the only exception. They still carry vegetables and other things on their heads. This custom and their unique costume have made them quite famous.

It is, however, notable that this custom of carrying things on the head has always been followed by women, and never by men.

On many islands and in seaside areas, not only is it the duty of women to carry things, but they also must be able to carry very heavy weights on their heads. Big tubs of water, piles of kindling or even bales of rice are carried by women on their heads. Many of them are able to carry a load of more than 150 pounds and walk quite a distance over mountains in this manner.

There are different ways of carrying things on the head. On the Izu islands and in some other places, the women carry a long wooden or bamboo pole on their heads and the goods are hung from both ends of the pole.

In other places, big baskets are held on the head to carry the weight on both the head and the back. A wide band is attached to a big basket, and the band is passed over the woman's head. The basket rests on the shoulder, and thus the weight is divided between the head and shoulders.

Women carrying weights on their heads daily have good figures and walk gracefully. They learn to walk correctly, otherwise they will soon be fatigued. Up to the Meiji era, or about 50 years ago, there were peddlers of *ame* or toffee, whose coming was a joy to all children. He carried a big flat wooden tub on his head, and announced his coming by beating a drum. As children gathered around him, he sold toffee attached to small bamboo sticks, sometimes decorated with flags.

In rural districts there are still seen many persons who carry things on their heads for peddling.

HESOKURI

THE WIFE'S secret savings are generally referred to in the Kanto district as *hesokuri*, or literally navel hoarding. This strange name seems to have been used for comically expressing the packet of secret money she keeps in her bosom.

But such savings of housewives were formerly called *haribako-gin* (sewing box silver), as most of them kept their little savings in their sewing boxes among the needles and threads.

It seems that it was mostly in cities and towns that wives were in the habit of secretly keeping *hesokuri*. With this money they generally bought not only things for themselves but also for their children. For many husbands their wives' *hesokuri* sometimes happened to be very convenient.

In those feudal days rural wives were permitted to own land, property and money in their own names. These wives' properties were often called *watakushi* (private). In many districts wives were allowed to possess farm land and cattle as their *watakushi*.

In farming regions there was formerly a custom for wives to work at night and other spare moments to earn pocket money. They made straw sandals or wove cotton fabrics.

In many northeastern districts, wives were permitted to cultivate undeveloped lands, and they were free to use the proceeds from their labor on such lands as they wished. Thus, though such rural wives were very badly treated, they had some means of earning petty pocket money.

But those in towns had no means of earning any money and they had to save something out of the daily household expenses by hoarding it in their bosoms or sewing boxes.

HOT BATHS

THE HABIT of taking hot baths is an outstanding trait of the Japanese people. Particularly in taking extremely hot baths the people have no equals in the world. While almost all Japanese institutions have their origin or something similar in China, this hot bathing habit is unique. Some people attribute this custom to the people's sense of cleanliness. Actually it is not due to such sentimental reasons, as hot baths are not necessary to keep onself clean.

There is a far more fundamental reason for the hot baths of the Japanese people. It is from the vital necessity of protecting and preserving their health under the peculiar climatic condition of the country. The climate of Japan is very humid, and particularly during the *tsuyu* or rainy season, from the middle of June to the middle of July, and the summer season, the air is very humid, sometimes registering 80 or 90 percent humidity. During the continuing sunless and rainy days, everything is saturated with moisture. All food decays quickly, tobacco becomes moldy, shoes and leather goods are covered thick with mold, pages of books become damp, matches will not light. The dampness numbs the spirit of the people, dulls their digestive organs, and makes them feel depressed and irritable.

It is then that a jump into a very hot bath will 'take all dampness out of the system,' revive the spirit, stimulate the digestive organs, and make one feel happy again. The hot bath is what enables the people to keep their health during the rainy and summer seasons.

In the cold winter season too, the hot bath is indispensable to the Japanese people. The Japanese house, particularly of the traditional old architecture, is extremely cold in winter, with wide openings and no proper heating system. Thus in many parts of the country the temperature falls several degrees below freezing point for three to four months during winter. The hot bath helps to keep the people warm in winter. As the bath is extremely hot there is no fear of catching cold afterward. In fact, many Japanese take extremely hot baths and sweat in order to cure a cold.

Because of the vital necessity of hot baths, almost all households have their own bathtubs, but in cities and towns there are numerous public bath-houses for the convenience of those who have no private tubs. The public bath-house is also a social institution where neighbors enjoy friendly gossiping daily while bathing.

Many people are so fond of bathing that they do not feel right unless they have their bath daily, or even twice a day, upon rising in the morning and just before going to bed.

It is this fondness for hot baths that has popularized the hot-spring resorts of the country. Japan being volcanic, there are numerous mineral hot springs. To these places the people who have money and time flock to enjoy bathing in hot mineral baths. They go to these resorts for the specific purpose of enjoying hot baths, and therefore many of them jump into the baths as often as four or five times a day. Those mineral hot-spring baths have curative medicinal virtues efficacious for various diseases or wounds.

HOT-SPRING BATHING

BATHING in natural hot springs has been enjoyed by the Japanese since prehistoric days. They called hot-springs *kamiyu* (divine bath) as they believed hot-springs had the supernatural power to cure illness and invigorate their spirit. Tamatsukuri spring in Izumo province is the oldest on record.

In the early days, only those living in the immediate neighborhood enjoyed bathing in the hot springs, but gathering there they gossiped and had delightful parties, drinking and eating. In the Heian period (794-1192) hot-spring bathing became luxurious as nobles and wealthy persons began to come from distant areas. In the Kamakura period (1192-1333) hot-springs in the Kanto and northeastern districts were opened up, as the seat of administration moved from Kyoto to Kamakura.

The curative value of hot-spring bathing was very early believed in by the people. Science now supports the traditions of the miraculous power of hot springs in many cases. But many go there merely for carefree holiday enjoyment.

There are numerous varieties of hot springs in the country. Each type has its own curative power according to its chemical contents.

Plain hot-springs are most numerous and are good for warming the body, invigorating blood circulation and curing rheumatism and neuralgia. Yumoto and Tonosawa in Hakone and Kinugawa (Tochigi) belong to this type.

Carbonic acid springs are mostly cold and have to be heated for bathing. The water is sometimes taken internally because it is said to be good for stomach problems. Arima (Hyogo), Ayukawa (Wakayama) and Isobe (Gunma) are famous for this kind of water.

Alkali or bicarbonate of soda springs are good for burns, wounds and skin diseases. The best-known are Murota (Kumamoto) and Kazawa (Gunma).

Salt hot-springs are good for blood circulation and neuralgia. Arima (Hyogo), Wakura (Ishikawa), Atami, Yugawara and Miyanoshita (Hakone) are the best-known.

Sulphuric acid springs improve blood circulation and cure neuralgia. Kona (Shizuoka), Izusan (Shizuoka) and Yamashiro (Ishikawa) belong to this type.

Iron springs are good for women's diseases. Ikaho (Gunma) and Beppu (Oita) are famous.

Sulphur springs are good for skin

diseases and rheumatism. Ashinoyu (Hakone), Yumoto (Nikko) and Akakura (Niigata) are of this type.

Acid springs are peculiar to Japan. Strong acid and high temperature inflame the skin and cure rheumatism and venereal diseases. Kusatsu and Nasu-Yumoto (Tochigi) are in this category.

Alum springs are good for skin disease and women's sickness. Yuno-hanazawa (Hakone) and Myoban Onsen (Oita) are the best-known.

Radium springs cure skin diseases and rheumatism with radium emanation. Masutomi (Yamanashi), Ena (Gifu) and Ikeda (Shimane) are of this type.

HOUSEMAIDS

MANY OLDER housewives say that they can never have such good domestic help now as they did in the old days. They refer, of course, to the Meiji period when old feudal customs of the Tokugawa days were still largely followed.

In the Edo period, daughters of wealthy farmers or well-to-do merchants entered the domestic service of *samurai* families or great merchants to get proper training to be ready themselves for marriage. They not only received no pay but also had to provide themselves with the right clothes.

They generally remained in these families for three to four years. There were many *samurai* families which had a rule that no maids should remain after they reached the age of 25. In their service they were taught proper etiquette, cooking, sewing and other household duties. Furthermore, they had to learn flower arrangement, tea ceremony, calligraphy and music, as such were recognized as the necessary qualifications for all accomplished women.

Such maids were treated as family members, and even after they left service, they maintained close relations with the families of their masters.

Unless young girls were trained in such domestic service with good families, they did not have any chance of a good marriage.

The maids were permitted to visit their own families only on a few occasions. When they returned from such visits they had to bring *omiyage* or presents, not only to the families but also to all fellow servants.

There were many cases when daughters served in the same families and this was kept up for generations.

In the early Meiji years, this feudal system was still being kept up and good families never lacked faithful and efficient maids. Domestic service was regarded as a finishing school for young girls.

IDATEN

A GREAT RUNNER or a marathon runner is often called *Idaten,* a term which sometimes also means lightning speed. But actually *Idaten* is Veda, the guardian of Buddhism and temples.

Idaten is pictured as a great fighter, dressed in strong armor and carrying two swords. He is said to be very wise and leads a pure life, transcending all human desires. He is commissioned by Buddha to protect Buddhism and temples. Thus, all Buddhist temples came to have statues of *Idaten.* Often they were also placed in storehouses and kitchens of temples.

Though he was highly trusted by Buddha and was given so important a task as guarding Buddhism and temples, it is traditionally said that he had a bad habit of napping while on duty day and night.

Once the devil took advantage of his failing to stay awake on duty. While *Idaten* was napping, he broke into the temple where the holy ashes of Buddha were enshrined. Stealing the holy relics, the devil ran away. When *Idaten* woke up and discovered the loss, the devil was already a great distance away.

Realizing he had failed in his duty and becoming extremely angry at the devil that had outwitted and shamed him, *Idaten* immediately set out after the escaping devil, with firm determination to regain the lost relics.

Though he was greatly behind the running devil, *Idaten* went after the robber with such great speed that he managed to catch up with him and regain the holy ashes. Thus, he was able to maintain his honor and fulfill the trust placed in him by Buddha.

The speed with which he went after the devil was so remarkable that he was recognized as the fastest runner ever known. Even today his name stands for a great runner or lightning speed.

IKI-NINGYO

MANNEQUINS or display dolls are now extensively used in shops of Japan to show off *kimono* and dresses. They are known by the Western name of mannequins, and some people think they have been newly introduced from the West. But life-size dolls that looked like living persons appeared in Japan almost 200 years ago. They were known as *iki-ningyo* or live dolls.

It is recorded that one named Matsumoto Kisaburo opened a show at Osaka and displayed life-size dolls depicting foreigners in their costumes. He used the name of *iki-ningyo* for the first time.

Then in 1853, a Kyoto doll maker held a doll show at Ryogoku in Edo, old Tokyo. As the *iki-ningyo* show was so well received by the residents, the art of making such dolls rapidly developed,

and they became an Edo attraction.

The famous doll maker Yasumoto Kamehachi cannot be forgotten as he gave *iki-ningyo* artistic and dramatic touches. His doll show presented the best scenes from *Kabuki* plays that became the popular talk of Edo. In posture and expression, his dolls looked like *Kabuki* actors on stage. It was the same Yasumoto who first made *kiku-ningyo* or chrysanthemum dolls which are still shown in autumn.

The head of the *iki-ningyo* was first carved out of a wood block, but later various other materials came to be used to make the head, hands and other parts. Porcelain or papier-mâché heads appeared.

The popularity of *iki-ningyo* also produced novel dolls whose features were made of seeds, sea shells or basket work. The dolls made of basket work were particularly admired, as not only their faces but even their hands and fingers were woven.

At first *iki-ningyo* was made for display, but with its popularity it came to be owned by women of *samurai* and rich merchant families. Life-size *iki-ningyo* representing famous actors in their *Kabuki* roles were not only ordered by such women, but very often presented to them as gifts.

The old *iki-ningyo* has its individual personality and costumes while modern mannequins are only figures to be dressed up.

ISHI-BURO

IN MANY districts facing the Inland Sea, such as Yamaguchi, Hiroshima, Okayama, Ehime and Kagawa, an old strange type of bathtub, generally called *ishi-buro* or stone bathtub, is still to be seen. While many of them are no longer used, there are still some which are used by the local people even today.

Although no definite year of its first appearance is known, it is recorded that they were already in existence in the Kamakura period, or more than 700 years ago.

The *ishi-buro* is laid out in the open. An oblong bathtub is built of stone, generally a little over half a meter wide, about a meter deep and two meters long. Three of the outer sides are covered with mud, the opening being made on the narrow end. A roof is made so that rain water will not drip into the tub.

The method for heating the water in an *ishi-buro* is unique.

Dry tree branches and leaves are first placed in the tub and set on fire.

The burning branches heat the stone sides of the tub. When the stones are well heated the tub is cleaned of the ash and buckets of water are brought and poured on the heated stones. As the water hits the heated stones, dense steam forms, making a sufficient quantity of hot water in the tub.

When the bath is ready, a person enters the tub, warms and cleans himself or herself. When the first bather leaves the tub and refreshes himself with cool water followed by a brisk rub with towels, the second bather enters.

Where this type of bath is still used, generally several persons wait for their turn outside, gossiping together and sometimes enjoying some sweets and tea. But when there are many waiting to take a bath, the bathtub water must be renewed, and the process of burning branches and heating the stones is repeated to give the later bathers a sufficiently hot bath.

ITADAKIMASU

WHEN THE Japanese sit down to eat, whether it be for a meal or some cakes, they say *Itadaki-masu* before taking up chopsticks or the plate of cakes. This expression is generally used to express thanks for food, and may be regarded as somewhat similar to the grace Christians say at their meals. Children have been taught to thank *kami* (god) and parents for their food.

However, the origin of this strange expression is not clear. It may come from the word *itadaki*, meaning the top of the head, or the verb *itadaku*, meaning to wear on the head or to be crowned.

Somehow the term has come to mean to receive or to be given. Though there is no basis in fact, sometimes it is explained that this meaning came from a habit the people had when they received gifts or rewards. To receive a gift politely, one holds it in both his hands, and raises it high to the level of the eyes or higher and then bows. The appreciation of the gift is thus expressed by holding it high in the hands. This act is also called *itadaku*.

In ancient days it was the custom in aristocratic circles to touch the head of a child with a small *mochi* on New Year's Day to insure his happiness and prosperity, and this *mochi* was called *Itadaki-mochi.*

The verb *itadaku* is now often used to mean simply to eat.

When the meal or refreshment is finished, all say *gochisosama.* This means thanks for the food or treat. *Chiso* originally meant running about in haste or making great efforts. But it subsequently came to mean the energy and effort a host expends in preparing a feast for guests. So it became customary for the guests to express appreciation for the host's efforts in arranging the feast. Thus *Gochisosama* is still said after each meal or snack.

Children are taught by their mothers to say *Itadakimasu* and *Gochisosama.*

KAGO

THE EARLIEST vehicle in Japan was the *ushi-guruma* or ox carts which were used for ceremonial purposes mostly and not as a general means of conveyance. Mention is made of the *koshi* or palanquin in the *Nihon Shoki*, the ancient records. It was used only by the Emperor, Empress and members of the Imperial Family.

The *koshi* was somewhat like the shrine palanquins still used today at festivals and carried on the shoulders of several persons by means of long poles running under the covered enclosure in which the rider sat. The *koshi* was not for the common people, and the Tokugawa Government issued a special order that common people should not ride on them.

Only military men rode on horses although the animals were used to draw carts for carrying goods. The people led the horses drawing carts but never rode them.

It was in the Tokugawa period that a vehicle called *kago* appeared. It differed from the ancient *koshi*. An enclosure in which the rider sat, hung from a long, sturdy pole, was shouldered by carriers at either end. The earliest *kago* was very simple, consisting only of a plain seat suspended from the pole. It is said that at first the *kago* was used to carry prisoners.

As it came to be widely used, the *Bakufu* laid down strict rules. Its use was restricted to nobles, Tokugawa family heads, important feudal lords, high priests, official physicians and such. Distinction was also made as to types and colors to be used according to the rank and class of the riders, so that at one glance the public could tell the status of the occupants.

In 1675, the Tokugawa Shogunate permitted 300 *kago* in Edo for the use of the common people. They were commonly called *tsuji-kago* (street-corner *kago*) as they waited at street corners for their calls.

KANE AND KUJIRA

NOWHERE is the system of weights and measures so complicated and confusing as in Japan. It is caused primarily because of the adoption of various foreign systems in addition to what the country had originally. The recent adoption of the metric system has brought about further difficulty. For instance, the rice ration is fixed at 2.5 *go* for each person per day, but the rice people receive at the food distribution offices is measured in kilograms. The common people do not know how much 2.5 *go* of rice will weigh in kilograms. It is irrational in the first place to mix bulk measurement and weight in calculating one item. The weight of rice, of course, differs according to weather, its kind, and its moisture content.

For measuring length, *shaku* is the Japanese standard, but there are two kinds of *shaku—kane* and *kujira*. *Kujira* (whale) is so called because the rule was originally made of whalebone, while *kane* (metal) is so called because it was made of metal. The use of *kujira* is exclusively limited to dry goods and cloth, while all other things are measured in *kane jaku*.

Once there lived an enterprising dry goods man. In serving his patrons, he always gave an extra length of cloth after measuring the required length. Thus he gave about 10 percent more than his patrons paid for. This brought big business to his shop. Other dry goods men noticed it, and soon followed his example. Thus one *shaku* of dry goods came to be longer than the original *shaku*. It is thus how the special *kujira jaku* system developed, it is told.

The size of a Japanese room is calculated by the number of *tatami* or mats therein. However, the size of one *tatami* is not always equal throughout the country. There are three different sizes, commonly called Kyoto *tatami*, Nagoya *tatami* and Tokyo (or Edo) *tatami*. The Kyoto *tatami* is the largest, being 6.3 *shaku* long and 3.65 *shaku* wide; the Nagoya *tatami* comes next, 6 *shaku* long and 3 *shaku* wide; and the Tokyo *tatami* is the smallest, 5.8 *shaku* long and 2.9 *shaku* wide. In many matted rooms, the sizes differ considerably when the different *tatamis* are used. It is not known why the *tatami* size became smaller as it came eastward from Kyoto. One view says that it is an economic question. A house with Tokyo mats can be built at a considerably lower price than that of an equal number of Kyoto *tatami*. Another says that Edo men were smaller in stature than Kyoto men.

Shoes and *tabi* (socks) are measured in *mon*. The smallest coin used in feudal days was a round copper coin with a square hole in the center, and it was called *mon*. So *to-mon* or ten-*mon* means the length obtained by putting 10 coins together in a line.

Then, probably the most confusing weight unit is *kin* which came from the Chinese *chin*. One *kin's* actual weight differs according to commodity. Sometimes it equals 100 *monme*, but at other times, it means 120, 160 or even 180 *monme*. Hence, whenever anything is offered in *kin*, one must be sure to know how many *monme* it is.

Distance is measured in *ri* (36 *cho*), *cho* (60 *ken*), and *ken* (6 *shaku*). Even for the Japanese it is no easy task to translate at once 15 *ri* 47 *cho* and 2 *ken* into miles or kilometers. Then, miles, kilometers and yards are also used in measuring distance. Land is measured in *tsubo* or about 6 feet square, but farms are calculated in *cho-bu* (10 *tan*), *tan* (10 *se*), and *se* (30 *tsubo*). So one *cho-bu* is about 2.45 acres. Of late, the metric standard is being used in statistics and others.

Now, think of the poor children who have to learn all these complicated systems of weights and measures.

KASHIHON-YA

KASHIHON-YA or book-lending shops are seen all over the country catering to certain classes of the reading public. Most of the books loaned out at such places are light reading material and books for children. At many shops even magazines are loaned out. A notable feature is that there are books not sold at ordinary books shops but are specially published for lending purposes.

Thus the people who frequent *kashihon-ya* are different from general book-readers. In this sense, the *kashihon-ya* are somewhat different from circulation libraries of other countries.

The *kashihon-ya* is quite old, as they appeared almost as soon as books for general reading came to be published. The first book with illustrations published by the wood-block printing process is said to be *Ise Monogatari*, appearing in 1068. In the middle of the Edo period or toward the end of the 18th century many fiction and other books for light reading were printed.

Such books came to be eagerly read by the merchant and artisan classes of Edo. The works of Santo Kyoden (1761-1816) and Kyokutei Bakin (1767-1818) were particularly popular. But they were quite expensive and beyond the reach of the common people.

Thus the business of lending out books started. Some publishers came to issue only 200 or 300 copies of books especially for the *kashihon-ya*. In those early years the employees of such book shops used to visit their clients' houses, carrying many books wrapped up in huge *furoshiki*. They collected the finished books and fees and left new ones. They came regularly at intervals of three to 10 days.

The clients in the Edo days and even in the early Meiji years were mainly shop employees and women of the middle working class. It is recorded that *geisha* and women of gay quarters were particularly great readers of *kashihon-ya* books. Perhaps this trend might have been due to the fact that most of the books published were love stories.

KASHIMA CHARM

THE KASHIMA SHRINE of Hitachi province (now Ibaraki Prefecture) issues a charm for easy child delivery. It comes in the shape of *hara-obi* or belly-band for pregnant women, and is commonly called *Hitachi-obi*. It is traditionally said that the *hara-obi* used by Empress Jingo (10th century) is kept at the shrine. It is customary for pregnant women in Japan to wrap bands of cloth around their stomachs in the fifth month of pregnancy.

But the *Hitachi-obi* charm based on Empress Jingo's sash came to possess another meaning. The sashlike cloth came to be used to divine whether one's love was answered or not. A man or woman, who was in love, brought a long cloth on which he or she wrote his or her own name and the name of the other whose sentiment it was desired to learn. The shrine maiden knotted the cloth and offered it to the shrine. It was believed that the deity would give the answer. This was done in particular on the shrine festival day.

The *obi* divination and the charm for child delivery of Kashima Shrine is so widely known that there is even a *Noh* play called *Hitachi-obi*.

There also developed a simplified love divination at the shrine. Anyone in love writes on a narrow strip of paper his or her name, and also that of the one with whom the person is secretly in love. Then the paper is twisted into a string-like shape. With the twisted paper, one goes to the fence built on the east side of the shrine building. Using only two fingers of his left hand, he tries to tie the string onto the fence. If the attempt succeeds, his or her love will have a bright prospect, but if it fails, there will be no hope for the love. Anyone who has tried it soon discovers that it is no easy task to tie a piece of twisted paper to the fence with only two fingers of the left hand. Left-handed persons, though, may find it otherwise.

KATSURA

KATSURA or wigs have been used by Japanese women since about the ninth century. Today there is no other country where wigs are so much used as in Japan. *Katsura* or *kazura* originally meant flowers and tree branches used as hair ornaments. Then false hair used to form the long trailing hair adopted by the aristocratic women in the Heian period also came to be called *katsura*.

The art of making *katsura* made special progress in the Tokugawa period when women's hairstyles became elaborate and *Kabuki* dramas required wigs for actors who also took women's parts. The making of theatrical *katsura* became thus a specialized technique. The characters in each play required special wigs, and there are said to be still more than 1,500 different wigs for theatrical purposes.

Bald men came to wear wigs in the early Meiji days, but the popularity of wigs among women suddenly increased about 30 years ago when young Japanese women began to dress their hair in Western fashion. When they had to dress formally as at wedding ceremonies or at New Year's, they were unable to have their short fair fixed in the traditional Japanese style, and thus they used wigs on such occasions. *Geisha* wear wigs when they are properly dressed, as their hair is mostly cut short now.

But it was the *Kabuki* wig makers who developed the art of *katsura* making. At first a thin copper plate was used to form the base to fit the actor's head, and hair was planted one by one on it. Then the implanted hair was tied up and dressed into the required style.

Today instead of the copper plate, a frame made of light metal is used. A piece of *habutae* silk is stretched on the frame and the hair planted in the silk. Theatrical wig makers specialize in making *katsura* for the stage alone. As there are traditional fixed hairstyles for *Kabuki* roles, they require long training.

KIRIBI

IN THESE DAYS of matches and lighters, *hiuchi-ishi* (flint and steel) is still one of the indispensable household utensils in many Japanese families.

Of course, the flint and steel are no longer used for starting a fire, and so there is no need for having tinderboxes. But the ancient custom of purifying persons and things with *kiribi* (fire-striking) or sparks made by striking flint is still observed in old-fashioned families. Fire has the power of purifying everything, it has been believed from the oldest times.

Over the offering to be presented to *kamidana*, family shrines, the flint is struck so that the sparks will purify it,

as unclean things should never be dedicated to shrines. Again, whenever one is to start on a long or important journey, he is purified at the door by the sparks of the flint in prayer that his journey may end in success and he may be safeguarded.

Furthermore, there are still many old-fashioned families both in cities and villages, where wives follow the old habit of striking *hiuchi-ishi* as their husbands leave the house every morning for work. It is a prayer for their success and safety.

Whenever any article symbolizing especially good fortune arrives, flint sparks are struck over it, so as to safeguard the good luck.

Thus, *hiuchi-ishi* sets are still sold at shops of kitchenware dealers throughout the country.

KOMORI

BABIES ARE STILL tied to the back of a *komori*. The old *komori* system for looking after babies is still kept up in rural districts. *Komori* are young girls, generally from 12 to 16 who are hired to take care of babies.

Even in the old days, *komori* in cities were hired for board, clothing and wares. They were simply employees hired by families with babies. But in rural districts, *komori* and babies are very closely connected, and the intimate relation lasts their whole life.

In many districts, particularly in the Izu islands, the ancient *komori*-baby relation is still kept up. A *komori* is sometimes regarded as being only second in status to the babies' parents and brothers and sisters.

In rural areas, they have their three meals at the babies' houses and return home in the evening. At New Year's and *Obon* in summer, the babies' parents give presents to the families of the *komori*.

Komori sing *komori-uta* or lullabies. They have babies tied to their backs the whole day or play with them if they are a little older. Their songs serve two purposes, first to put the babies to sleep, and second to amuse them. Many *komori-uta* have developed into local folk songs.

In their songs the *komori* complain of their hard lot or tell of being homesick, particularly when they work far away from their own parents. Some songs are of love and future happiness.

The *komori-uta* also expresses hope that the babies will quickly fall asleep, promising them some reward for doing so, but again the babies are threatened with punishment if they keep on crying without going to sleep.

KOYOMI

IT IS NOT KNOWN whether the primitive Japanese had calendars or not. It is, however, believed that at first the Japanese year began in April, and the day of the full-moon was the first of the month. The January 15 rite in celebrating the New Year that is still observed is said to retain the original calendar idea.

In primitive days, people judged the seasons and time for planting seeds and other farm work by observing natural phenomena. The habit of farmers to put their hands into the soil to see if the time for sowing had come was followed up to quite recent times.

It was in 604 that the Chinese calendar system was adopted by the country. This was a lunar-solar calendar. When Chinese divination was introduced into Japan, the zodiac signs and the five elements were attached to the days and months, and through those signs the fortune of the day and month came to be told. Thus, the *koyomi* (calendar)

became not only a calendar but also a guide to the daily work and life of the people.

Yasui Shunkai, a great mathematician, made the first Japanese calendar after calculating the longitude and latitude at many points and observing 308 stars. His *koyomi* called Teikyo Koyomi was adopted in 1685.

It was Shunkai who established such important seasonal days as *Hachiju-hachiya* (88th evening) and *Nihyaku-toka* (210th day) which have ever since guided Japanese farmers. He fixed that the 88th evening from the lunar calendar *risshun* (start of spring) was the last day for frost, and seed planting could be done after that date without the fear of frost.

Then observing typhoons that visit the country every year and do much damage to crops, he learned that the 210th day (present September 1) was the time when typhoons most usually came and thus warned the people of the dreadful disaster.

Later, this *koyomi* was further revised by the Horeki (1754), Kansei (1798), and Tenpo (1843) calendars.

In 1873, the solar system was adopted by the Meiji Government. Thus, the old *koyomi* officially disappeared. But the general public, particularly the rural folk, still insist on obtaining old *koyomi* information, which has for so many generations guided their farm work and daily life.

At present the Standard Japanese Calendar is compiled by the Tokyo Astronomical Observatory and published by Tokyo University. But to meet popular demand, the old type of *koyomi* with modern data is issued by Ise Shrine. This *koyomi* is sold all over the country, giving not only such information as the sunrise, the moonrise and the tides, but also the days, months and seasons by the lunar system, old zodiac signs, elements, fortune, sowing time and other data.

KUKURI-ZARU

THE MONKEY has been regarded as a lucky symbol since olden days, and thus it appears in many customs and even in plays. In particular monkeys were regarded the guardian of children, and toys made in the form of monkeys were not only given to children to play with but also as a charm to protect them. Many toy monkeys are still produced in many districts. Though they are popular, they have, however, lost their hold on the people as a charm for children.

Stuffed toy monkeys called *kukuri-zaru* (fastened monkey) were carried about as a charm by little boys and girls up to the middle of the Meiji era when they were still dressed in *kimono*. It was tied with a string to the back of the child's *kimono* just between the shoulders.

Such cloth monkeys were also offered to shrines and temples, generally tied to bamboo branches, by the parents to pray for the happiness and healthy growth of their children. In Kii province (Wakayama) there was formerly a giant sacred camphor tree, and parents of newborn babies offered toy monkeys to the tree.

Monkey charms were made of different materials, and often tied to the sashes of little children. A jumping monkey, a toy in which a monkey jumps up on a bamboo stick, was very popular, not only to amuse the child but to guard him.

In place of the *kukuri-zaru*, often an oblong piece of red cloth about the size of a calling card, was sewn on to the back of children's *kimono*. It was said that when a child with this charm on his back fell down in the street, *kami* (god) protecting him would instantly come and pick him up by the red flap. Also it was thought the red cloth would scare away all evil spirits that might come to harm the child.

LOVE SUICIDE

A MAN AND WOMAN in love who cannot openly marry because of various reasons still commit *shinju* (faithful love) or love suicide. Such suicides seem to have become numerous since the Genroku era in the early 18th century, and praised as the culmination of faithful love. *Shinju* has become a popular theme for plays and fiction.

It was Lord Echizen, civil administrator of Edo, who laid down a law concerning *shinju*, in the Kyoho era (1716-35) as he believed that the custom was not good for public morals.

He thought that the name *shinju* (faithful love) was too good for such acts of suicide, and gave it a new name, 'aitaijini' or mutual death, in the new law. When there were no letters or other evidence left to show that it was a love suicide, the case was treated as an unnatural death, and no punishment was given.

When the man died and the woman lived, she was made a *hinin* or outcast. But if the man survived and the woman died, he was punished as the murderer of the woman.

In those days, class distinctions were very strict, and a son or daughter of a family could not love a servant or maid. When *shinju* was committed by people of different classes, the law was very strict. In case of a *shinju* between persons of the employer class and the employee class, if the survivor was of the employee class, the man or woman was made a *hinin*. But if the survivor was of the upper class, he or she was punished as a murderer.

The man or woman who was made a *hinin* had to live with the *hinin* group and be under the control of the *hinin* head. But it was also possible for a *hinin* to buy freedom by giving money to the *hinin* head. The relatives and friends of those who were sentenced to become *hinin* often paid money immediately to the *hinin* head so that the punished could return home free, without spending a day with the *hinin* group.

MAIGOFUDA

IN AIR RAIDS many children became separated from their parents, as their houses were burnt up and they had to run away to safety through burning streets. Though they managed to escape from death, many could not find their parents again, because they could not tell who they were or where they lived. If those city dwellers had kept up the ancient custom of *maigofuda*, such children might have been united again with their parents, brothers and sisters.

Maigofuda or lost-child plate is a small plate of wood or metal on which the name of the child and his or her address are written or engraved. This plate was attached to the sash of the child. This custom appears to have developed in the latter Edo days, when children were often lost in the crowds at busy shopping districts or on the occasion of festivals. It came to be very widely adopted during the Tokugawa days and the Meiji period. But probably since children came to be dressed in Western clothes, the custom seems to have gradually died out. At present it is seen only among very old-fashioned families.

At first *maigofuda* was used only for identification, but soon the people made it into a thing of beauty. The plate became elaborate, some being made of brass or silver, while commonly used wooden plates were lacquered. It is generally oval in shape, about one inch long. Shops specializing in making it appeared. Then the plate was often placed in gorgeous brocade or silk bags, in which were also placed sometimes various *omamori* or charms to protect the child from accidents or sickness.

In the old days, the *maigofuda* one used in his or her childhood was one of a few things that always brought back memories of one's childhood. Many mothers and grandmothers stored away the *maigofuda* which were used by their children and grandchildren as a memento of bygone days.

MARU SHIP

JAPANESE merchant ships are often called by foreigners *maru* ships, since the names of ships have this ending.

There are various different explanations as to why ships have this name ending.

The term *maru* means round or complete. The enclosure of feudal castles was called *maru*, because they are generally round in shape.

But *maru* was also used to indicate shops or merchants' establishments in the old days just as *ya* has been a common suffix of a shop name.

In the Kamakura period (1192-1333), big wholesale merchants were called *toimaru*, and the trade names of all big merchants bore the ending *maru*. Thus they were called *Musashiyamaru, Echigoyamaru* and so on.

Naturally when such merchants or wholesalers built and used ships to transport their goods, they named the ships after their trade names.

As one owner had many ships they all had the same *maru* name but to distinguish them were called such and such *maru* No. 1, No. 2 and so on. This custom is still retained in the names of many small fishing boats owned by one fisherman or company, as for instance, in the name *Horyu Maru* No. 3.

Some people confuse *maru* with *maro*, a suffix used in boys' names in the old days. Also swords, flutes and other highly treasured things were given names with the *maro* ending.

But *maro* had an entirely different origin from that of *maru* for ships. *Maro* meant intimacy or dearness. Thus parents added *maro* to their son's names to show their fondness. The same thing applied to inanimate objects to which the owners were greatly attached.

Maro was also used formerly as a first-person pronoun. Many nobles and such called themselves *maro*.

Later *maro* was corrupted into *maru* probably because of the similarity in sound and also because it was easier to write.

Some also say that ships were named *maru* because they were considered floating castles. However there seems to be no foundation to this.

MELON-SEED FACE

A BEAUTIFUL woman must first of all have an *urizane-gao* or melon-seed face, it was believed in Tokugawa days. It meant an oval face. But in much earlier days, the full round face was in favor, as proved by old pictures and sculptures. The change from the round face to the oval is greatly due to the change in female costumes and also in general living conditions. In ancient days, women were dressed in loose costumes and kept themselves mostly indoors. Then in the Tokugawa period *kimono* and *obi* became popular. This new dress for women decidedly regulated women's looks and manners.

The most important change brought about by the use of *kimono* and *obi* is the beauty found in the slender figure, because it best brings out the elegance and particularly the beautiful lines of *kimono* and *obi*. The plump fat figure never shows up well in *kimono*. To harmonize with the slender body, the face should not be round and full, but oval. Then hands and feet also have to be small and slender. Hence the woman with the oval face, narrow waist, small hips, and delicate hands and feet was regarded as beautiful.

Black hair and fair skin have ever been counted as features to make beautiful women. It was said 'A fair skin hides seven defects.' Yet it was the fine smooth texture of the skin that the people admired most. Rough skin was considered as vulgar.

The women of Tokugawa days attached much importance to their manner of walking, sitting down or carrying themselves. Utmost attention was given to always keeping the lines of *kimono* undisturbed, and they moved only the lower part of the legs below the knee so that the beautiful lines of *kimono* would not be disturbed. This made them point their toes slightly inward when walking.

The modernization of the country brought the round full face back to popularity, and the well-developed body is preferred to the slender figure. No girl now walks with her toes pointing inward.

MUSHIBOSHI

MUSHIBOSHI or *kimono*-airing is an important task for Japanese housewives. It was formerly held mostly in summer, but now it is done in autumn, as dry air is better for airing clothes than the humid summer climate.

This custom of airing every *kimono* in the household once a year is quite old. It originated from the Japanese habit of storing numerous *kimono* in *tansu* or chests of drawers and because of the high humidity of the country. All Japanese households have huge numbers of *kimono* as different kinds are required for ceremonial wear, for common use, for mourning and for social calls, and, furthermore, materials, styles and designs change with the seasons. It has been one of the joys of Japanese women to possess more *kimono* than their neighbors.

As the *kimono* are placed in *tansu*, they become mildewed and little insects damage them by laying eggs among their layers. Hence, selecting a bright dry day, all the clothing is pulled out of the *tansu*, and hung over ropes stretched across the rooms in all directions. The superfluous apparel is aired on poles in the garden. On *mushiboshi* days there is hardly any room in the house for one to stand or sit down.

While *kimono* are being aired, the housewives with the help of maids and daughters mend ripped seams or remove stains if necessary. It is another big job to store all the aired clothing back in *tansu*, as each item has to be properly folded and put in the proper place, or else it becomes almost impossible to find one when needed.

In big households with much clothing, it is impossible to finish *mushiboshi* in one day; consequently, for several days, the order of the household is completely disturbed by the fluttering *kimono* all over the rooms.

NIGHT HARVESTING

IN AOMORI and other northeastern districts the old term 'yotagari' (night harvesting) meaning pocket money of housewives is still remembered and even used sometimes.

In feudal days, housewives, particularly of the farming class, were not given any pocket money. To give them necessary cash to meet their personal needs and also to buy things for their children, they were given small plots to farm by their husbands.

But they could cultivate their farms only in their spare time, which was mostly at night by torch or moon light, Thus their harvesting came to be called night harvesting or *yotagari*. By selling their crops, they obtained money for their personal use. The planting of their farms was also called *yomaki* or night sowing.

In the Hokuriku territory on the Japan Sea and other areas, there was a similar custom called *homachi*. A farmer gave his children, except the eldest son, small pieces of land to cultivate for their own use. The eldest son was excluded because he was the one to succeed to the entire family farm. Such pieces of land were called *homachi* farms.

In many rural districts, there was also a custom of farmers allowing their farm hands to cultivate their own crops in their spare time to gain some cash for their use. Sometimes such farm hands paid rent for the lands they cultivated. Again such farm hands were permitted to make charcoal or do other work on holidays for their own benefit.

In most parts of the country, it was also customary for housewives and children to weave straw mats or make sandals at night. They were allowed to use the cash obtained by selling such products for their own use.

O-FUKURO

THE JAPANESE mother is given many different names, and one which is fondly given by her children is *o-fukuro* (honorable bag). It may sound odd to those who do not know its meaning, but it is one to honor and respect her. The name also proves how important was her position in the family even in ancient feudal days.

In the old days, it was customary for the Japanese to keep clothing and other household articles in bags of cotton, silk or hemp, for preservation and convenient storing. When such goods were taken out of the house, they were also carried in those bags. It was the housewife's duty to take care of numerous bags. That meant that she was in charge of all family goods and household affairs.

The old mother did not easily transfer this duty to the wife of her son until she knew for certain that the young woman was fully capable of conducting household affairs according to established tradition and social requirements of the family. For the young wife to be given this duty of looking after household bags was a great honor. Thus to show respect for the woman holding the important task, the mother came to be called *o-fukuro* by the members of the household and others.

This proves how important a position the housewife, particularly the mother, of old Japan held in the family as well as in the community. In public and outside affairs, women had no voice, but at home, most Japanese housewives and particularly mothers held the family purse and ruled all domestic affairs.

Later, as *furoshiki* or wrapping cloths became popular about 600 years ago, the old bags went out of use.

OKAGESAMADE

THE JAPANESE people used to believe that they owe their life, happiness and well-being to *shi-on* or the four benefactors. The four are heaven and earth, the ruler, parents and *shujo*

(all sentient beings). This idea is said to have developed from Buddhism.

No explanation is necessary for the first three benefactors, but the most significant is *shujo*, which includes all living things, animals, birds, fish and plants. The people recognized their obligation to nature, all natural phenomena and natural objects.

This belief in the four benefactors is expressed in the commonly used expression *'okagesamade'* (by the grace of benefactors), which is used in reply to inquiries about health or business. When asked how one is or how business is, the stock answer is *'okagesamade.'*

But people who use this expression daily do not generally realize its meaning, and even think it is strange or meaningless. *'Okagesamade'* means that one's health is good and his business is fair, due to the graces of the four benefactors.

Though the people use the term by habit, not knowing its significance, it is still a good and polite reply to daily inquiries.

The people were taught in the old days to remember the four benefactors and to appreciate their benevolence. In the past, Buddha often replaced heaven and earth, as the idea was originally introduced with Buddhism. And in the feudal days teachers were often included among the four. But the ruler, parents and *shujo* were never left out of the four.

The idea of the four benefactors has been revealed in the thought and customs of the people for generations. *'Okagesamade'* is still used in daily conversation.

OKINAWA WOMEN

THE WOMEN of the Okinawa islands used to tattoo their hands, but now only old women can show any tattoo marks.

In the old days, even 10-year-old girls used to have tiny marks on their hands. Many visitors to the islands 30 or 40 years ago wrote about the pretty little tattooed hands of the small girls.

The tattooing on the hands of Okinawa women is generally of very small and simple designs. Most common are stars, diamonds, arrows and such. The tattooing was done on the back of the hand, near the base of the fingers or at the wrist. Miyakojima women had them three or four inches above the wrist.

Tattoo marks, though simple, differed individually, and there were certain styles of design which were peculiar to the islands or districts. Thus, by tattoo designs, one was able to tell what islands or districts they came from.

For instance, in some cases the arrow design had only the arrow-head and shaft, but in others, feathers on the arrow were also shown. The way the mark was arranged or how they were placed on the back of the hand was another indication of different localities. Tattooing was prohibited in the early Meiji period, but there were still many parents who had their small daughters tattooed according to the old custom. It is these girls who are now old women who can show how Okinawa women used to tattoo their hands.

Okinawa is famous for a certain kind of cotton fabric with minutely woven designs. There is a story that formerly Okinawa women tattooed the same marks on their hands as the design on the fabrics they had woven. This may be true as many of the tattoo marks are similar to the designs on the fabrics.

PURIFYING SALT

WHEN AN unwelcome visitor finally leaves the house, the old-fashioned housewife will hurry to the kitchen and, taking a pinch of salt, scatter it all over the house entrance. Then she is certain that the ill omen that he brought will not harm the family. This is an age-old custom to undo what mischief or evil spirit the visitor might have brought, or to guard against the influence of the devil that came with him.

Salt is a symbol of purity. Purity stands for goodness, holiness and virtue. Anything bad, evil or wrong is regarded impure and likely to invite evil thought and effect. Purity conquers all impurity. Thus salt is used for purification.

Since very ancient times, salt has been used for driving out evil spirits and impurities. It is thought that devils and evil spirits are everywhere, and therefore to make it certain that a place is free of them, salt has to be scattered. In the *sumo* or wrestling match, the wrestlers pick up salt and scatter it over the sands in the wrestling circle. It is for driving out all evils so that the match will be fair and honorable. Then again, the throwing of salt by the wrestlers is their pledge that they will fight fairly.

Restaurants and many other shops place small piles of salt at their entrances every morning in prayer for good and prosperous business. The salt will invite good business. This custom is observed by those who engage in such business which depends on the patronage of good people. To the good and pure comes prosperity is the idea behind this custom.

Death is regarded to be evil, and anything connected with death or the dead person is impure and unhappy. Such impurity will bring misfortune and sickness. Hence, whenever one returns from attending a funeral or a visit to the dead, he is not allowed to enter the house until he is freely purified at the entrance with salt. All the evils that might have come with the funeral or the dead are driven away by the purity of the salt, and so he is allowed to enter the house. Otherwise the evil will enter the house and may cause misfortune or sickness to the whole family.

To purify hands and mouths with salt has been traditionally followed throughout the country. From this also developed a rural habit of cleaning teeth in the morning with salt and finger, in place of tooth-powder and tooth-brush.

SAYONARA

SAYONARA is a pretty expression that is loved by the Japanese people as well as by many foreigners, because of the sentiment it conveys and also because it is pleasant to the ear.

But *sayonara* is one of the strange Japanese expressions that particularly puzzle foreign students of the language. Dictionaries define *sayonara* as 'in that case,' 'if it is so,' or 'then.' In such a sense, the word *sayonara* by itself is meaningless. Yet the people who use the term never think it strange.

It has to be explained that the original expression used at taking leave was *'sayonara oitoma shimasu'* (then, I will take my leave). It means that as all talking or business has been finished, or it is time to leave, the visitor is departing. This expression was shortened in common use, and only the first part is now used, leaving out the main portion.

Sayonara is often further shortened to *'saraba,'* *'sainara'* or *'abayo.'* The first is no longer commonly used, the second is used in the Kansai district, and the third which is a corruption of the first is used by little children.

There is another term *'osaraba,'* which developed from *sayonara*, but means the discharge of servants or employees. This term is often used to mean the severance of relations in general.

SEVENTY-FIVE DAYS

IF YOU EAT something that you have not tasted before, your life will be prolonged by 75 days, according to an old Japanese belief. It is not known how this originated, but to eat anything new is a very pleasant experience, and as the people are generally epicureans, they have always taken joy in trying something novel.

It seems, therefore, that the saying started from their desire to find something new to eat. If a new food will give one an extra 75 days of life, it is worth the trouble and cost.

This belief, then, brought another saying. A stingy man might cheat himself of the extra 75 days because he will not spend money to taste something new, which is generally costly.

'Seventy-five days' has quite another meaning, according to the way the expression is used.

'Hito no uwasa mo shichiju-go nichi' (People's talk lasts only 75 days), goes the Japanese saying.

Of course, this is quite true as the public is forgetful, and rumors they hear and circulate will soon die. The saying is thus given as consolation to one who is unfortunately made the object of some evil rumor. But, at the same time, it also tells how sensitive the people are to what others think and say about them.

STORE NAMES

MOST JAPANESE stores have a *yago* or store name, which is different from the family names of the owners. The store name stands for the history of the shop, its reputation and business standing.

Store names developed from the old custom in rural districts of giving house names to resident families. These names had nothing to do with family names or lineage, being only a convenience in referring to the people of the community. Furthermore, in the old days, the common people either had no family names or everybody in one village often had the same surname.

Thus each family came to be called by a nickname or some term to distinguish it from another. A house in a high locality was called *Kamiya* (up house), and one on lower land *Shimoya* (low house). A house with a big tree was called *Oki* or big tree, and one under a hill, *Yamashita* (below the hill). Sometimes professions gave the house their names. A house without a name meant that the dweller was a newcomer to the community.

Stores, therefore, were always called by the house names of their owners. However, with the Meiji Restoration all families were given names and while the families were called by their new names, their stores were still known by their old house names.

When big cities developed, many came from other parts to open stores. Many of such merchants called their stores after their home districts. Thus there are still many stores having provincial names, such as *Shinanoya, Echigoya, Joshuya, Sagamiya* and others.

Big department stores, old shops and all other stores are mostly called by their *yago* or store names.

Of course, there are now many shops that have fancy names, different from the old house or store names.

SUMI-NAGASHI

SUMI-NAGASHI (ink flow) is an old technique to print designs on paper, silk or other fabrics by letting ink or color float on water. It is believed to have been highly developed in the 12th century, and is mentioned in the *Kokinshu,* a collection of poems compiled in 905.

Into a pan of water, the tip of a writing brush soaked in *sumi* or Chinese ink is slowly dipped and then the ink oozes out on the surface of the water, as it is oily in substance. A slender stick is then stuck into the water and slowly moved around in the pan. With the movement of the stick, the ink on the water surface spreads out in various directions, taking grotesque or fantastic shapes.

When the ink design on the water is found satisfactory, a sheet of paper or cloth is placed evenly on the water. It absorbs the ink design, and when the sheet is taken out and dried, it has become imbued with the ink design. As the slightest movement in the water changes the design, it is impossible to obtain two sheets with the same design.

The beauty or value of *sumi-nagashi* lies in the fact that each print is different.

At first only ink was used, but later different colors as well as gold paint came to be used to produce diversified designs.

Sumi-nagashi paper has been used mostly for writing poems. The Nishi-Honganji Temple at Kyoto possesses the oldest specimen preserved of a collection of poems written on such sheets, said to have been made in 1110.

Paper formerly used for making *sumi-nagashi* were *hosho* or *torinoko,* both heavy and strong Japanese paper. But also *habutae* silk and cotton fabrics came to be largely used.

For various decorative purposes and also for women's *obi* or wide sashes, silk and other fabrics with *sumi-nagashi* prints have come to be adopted.

TACHIMONO

THE CUSTOM of giving up something one is especially fond of when praying for recovery from illness or for the attainment of some wish, is still practiced by old-fashioned people. The abstention is generally from one to three years. They give up salt, *sake*, tea, fish, meat or other food. It is usually an individual pledge, but in some places, it is done as a community matter, and all villagers give up the same thing for a fixed period of time.

Furthermore, in making such pledges and sacrifices, many also make daily visits to their shrines or temples. *Nissan* or daily visits have been very common among religious persons whenever they make special prayers. Once the vow is taken to make *nissan*, they must visit the temple or shrine, rain or shine, every day during the decided period. The omission of a single day will nullify the whole plan.

The idea of giving up various foods and other things for praying to *kami* is said to have originated in the purification required for those performing Shinto rituals. In the old days, those undertaking Shinto rites had to confine themselves for certain days indoors, isolating themselves from the impure world, keeping their bodies clean and eating only pure and simple food.

A carpenter named Hassan of Edo had warts on his hand, and proposed to give up eating *tako* (octopus) of which he was very fond. He promised this in prayer to Tako Yakushi of Meguro which was reputed for its power to remove warts. It is said his prayer was soon answered and his warts disappeared.

Some months later, he was invited to a party by friends and on the table there was boiled *tako*. Because he was so fond of it, he forgot his pledge and eagerly ate it. One of his friends noticed it and said, 'You gave up eating *tako* to remove your warts, but now you are eating it. Why do you do this?'

'I know,' he replied, 'but you see I am fond of boiled *tako* and the pledge is very inconvenient. So I changed *tako* to spiders, because they both have eight legs, and now I do not eat *tako* but eat spiders.'

Some days later, Hassan saw warts reappearing on his hand. He did everything to remove them but failed. Furthermore, warts also were found on the hands of his children. Hassan was sorry that he broke the pledge, but it was too late, and he could not undo what he had done. Worried, he became sick and soon died.

So people still say that if you once make a pledge to not eat something, never touch the *tachimono* you decided to avoid.

TAKE-NI-SUZUME

TAKE-NI-SUZUME (bamboo and sparrow) is a popular literary expression, and also is a combination seen in paintings, sculptures and other artistic works. The combination is seen on the art objects of the Shoso-in, Nara, so it must have been quite popular since the Nara period (seventh century). The bamboo and sparrow design is also a family crest of many old families. It is said to have been first used by the Kanshoji family of Kyoto. Later such big feudal lords as Uesugi, Date, Yamaguchi and others adopted it.

The bamboo is seen everywhere in Japan and sparrows are numerous, nesting in bamboo forests. The bamboo is used for many purposes and thus bamboo forests are valuable. Many big bamboo forest are kept to produce *take-no-ko* or sprouts which are a delicacy of the people in spring.

Suzume, however, have always been regarded as the farmer's enemies as they eat rice and other crops, although they also destroy many insects that are harmful to crops.

At Asano, near Nagoya, there is a big bamboo forest. The site is believed to be the place where Asano Nagamasa, great fighter under Toyotomi Hideyoshi, had his residence. It is rumored that the bamboo was first brought to the site by Nagamasa from Korea when he joined Hideyoshi's expedition to Korea in 1592.

The bamboo in this forest is famous for its enormous size, the fine *take-no-ko* it annually produces and the huge number of sparrows that nest in the forest. The people of the neighborhood have complained of the big noise the sparrows make, disturbing their peaceful life, and eating up so much of their rice.

But they can do nothing to scare away the sparrows. Only when there are big storms are the sparrows knocked dead by the tossing of bamboos among which they nest. In the morning after each big storm, children bring home bags full of sparrows.

TATTOOING

THERE ARE two distinctly different types of tattooing in Japan, *irezumi* and *horimono*. But of late these two terms are confused. Particularly by some persons, *irezumi* is used to indicate all kinds of tattooing. Both originated in the Tokugawa era, but *irezumi* is older. *Irezumi* was originally used in punishing and marking criminals. Petty criminals who were sentenced to banishment from their district of residence or given the punishment of beating were also branded with three bands of tattooing each about one-third of an inch in width, on their right or left arms.

Horimono, the other type of tattooing, became popular during the era of Bunka or the beginning of the 19th century. This class of tattooing developed to a state of high artistic technique, surpassing almost all tattooing arts of other countries, past and present. It was particularly loved by many Edokko or commoners of Edo. Firemen, artisans, gamblers, *machiyakko* (chivalrous men about town) and others decorated their bodies with *horimono*.

The gorgeous and ornamental tattooing covering the whole black and front as well as arms and legs became so popular that even many young women had beautiful designs tattooed over their bodies. It was the pride of those people to show their tattoo-marks in public bath-houses.

Tattooing is very painful, as sharp needles are used to prick holes in the skin to insert black and various color pigments to paint the design. Delicate and complicated designs naturally took much longer to complete than simpler ones. The persons being tattooed had to suffer many months of daily pricking, but they all bore the pain bravely for the satisfaction of having beautiful or gorgeous designs on their bodies. The popularity of *horimono* developed many famous master artists.

Gorgeous blossoms of peony, cherry, chrysanthemum and other flowers, great pine trees, landscapes, dragons, birds, tigers and other fierce animals, dramatic and historical figures, beautiful women, religious figures and such are the most common designs of *horimono*. Black, blue and red are the usual colors used. Tattooing that covers a large area of the skin naturally affects its function and it is said that tattooed persons become very sensitive to cold weather.

Tattooing was prohibited at the beginning of Meiji, but there are still many men as well as women who boast of their beautiful *horimono*.

In the Tokugawa days and the early Meiji years there was a custom among some men and women of tattooing their respective names on their arms as a pledge of love. Tattooing cannot be removed, and so the names remain on their arms for life. This type of tattooing of names or simple designs on arms does not come under the category of *horimono*.

TUB-BATHING

GYOZUI or tub-bathing is one of the things that serve to make life in the hot season pleasant and comfortable. It is a sort of simplified bathing. Instead of a proper bathtub, only a large round washing tub is generally used. The tub is filled with warm water, and one sits in the tub to wash his body of sweat. People who are fond of bathing find in *gyozui* something quite different from the usual hot bath. The hot bath warms one, but *gyozui* only washes off the sweat or dirt and cools.

This *gyozui* is a source of delight and happiness to all the people in summer, particularly as it is taken outdoors. The washing tub is generally brought out to the garden for the *gyozui*, taken just when the evening air becomes cool. Office and factory workers look forward to their *gyozui* while sweating in crowded tramcars on their way home from work.

To children too, it is a source of much joy. They play with their toys, a water-pistol or something that floats in the tub. Often they are scolded by their mothers for playing too long in the tub, making others wait for their turn.

Gyozui, however, often causes quite an embarrassing situation for women, as the tub is placed outdoors. But Japanese women are quite prepared for such occasions. The people think nothing of seeing women taking their *gyozui* as they are used to the sight from childhood.

Gyozui means 'purifying water.' Originally the term was a religious one, meaning the purification of the body by water in austere exercises, or in ascetic penance. From ancient days, people have believed that water purifies them of sins as well as dirt. In Shinto and Buddhist austerities, there has been a custom of plunging into pools or standing under waterfalls, in order to purify one's body and soul. Later, this custom was somewhat simplified so that often by merely pouring water over the body, head or hands, people believe that they have been purified. It is from this simplified purification that the modern *gyozui* developed. Of course, it now has no religious significance.

UBUYU

A JAPANESE baby is given a bath as soon as it is born. The *ubuyu*, or birth-bath, is very important, and in ancient days there was a solemn rite for giving the baby its first bath, particularly in aristocratic circles.

While the baby was being given its first bath, Buddhist sutras or some other classical writings were read to give it guidance. Then bow strings were snapped by the side of the bathtub to drive away evil spirits.

Yet in those early days, the first bath was not given on the day of the baby's birth, but several days later. Nobles and wealthy parents put gems, gold and silver in the baby's *ubuyu* tub to ensure its prosperity. The head of a tiger, or a picture of one, was held over the bath. Its reflection in the water was thought to protect the baby from sickness and evil.

A dipper made of a coconut shell with a handle was used to put water into the bathtub.

Then, after the *ubuyu* came the rite of dressing the baby. This was also important as it signified the baby's fortune in having good clothes all its life.

Today the *ubuyu* is much simplified and the baby is bathed by the midwife as soon as it is born without much ceremony, but the bath is indispensable. When the delivery time approaches, the first thing the household does is to heat water in a big kettle to be ready to give the baby its *ubuyu*.

In some rural districts the custom of giving a bath to a dead body just before putting it in a casket is still observed. This was very widely followed in olden days.

Thus the life of a Japanese began and ended with a bath.

WIDOWS' SHOPS

THE POSITION of *goke* or widows was a very hard one in the old days, particularly in farming regions. Women undertook the task of rice planting, but the weeding in rice paddyfields in the hot summer and harvesting were too strenuous for women. When a farmer died leaving his wife a widow with small children, she could no longer work the farm and obtain a harvest.

Neighbors were often kind and allowed her to gather rice ears left on the field, but such gleanings would not feed her and the children. So the widow had to marry again, or work as a maid for another family. Some wove cloth for others or raised silk cocoons, but in rural districts to make one's living by

such work was very difficult.

Many widows therefore came to open little shops in the villages to sell cheap sweets to children. Such small shops in many districts were first opened by widows. Other types of shops operated by widows began to appear. They were called *niuri* or cook and sell. That is to say, cooked vegetables, beans or small fish were offered for sale. This business prospered in many cases because of the tendency to simplify the preparation of foods on special festive days, and also to relieve housewives of their kitchen work during the busy farmwork months.

The commercial activity of widows, furthermore, expanded as their shops began to sell *sake* or rice-wine. *Sake* was originally brewed by each household and then came to be made by rich families on a large scale. In many small communities, the people had to go far to buy *sake*, and thus the convenient little shop selling *sake* prospered.

Even today little shops are seen in farming villages, selling sweets, household utensils and some kinds of food. They have developed from widows' shops of the old days, and even today many of them are operated by widows.

WINTER TRAINING

DURING the *kan* or cold season lasting for 30 days, there are seen throughout the country men and women of various ages running barefooted in the evening to temples and shrines, dressed only in the thinnest cotton summer dress. They are making *kan-mairi* or cold-season worship. In the old days, many men went naked, except for a loincloth, to make their *kan-mairi*, but now the law requires them to wear at least a covering over most parts of their body.

Reaching their destinations, the worshipers offer their prayers for good luck and health. Some pour cold water over their heads and bodies while saying their prayers.

The visit to temples and shrines in the cold winter evenings, in the thinnest clothing, it is believed, will bring them good luck and make their prayers heard.

The *kan* season is also the time to undergo various training. *Kan-geiko* or cold-season training is still popular among students of *jujitsu*, fencing, singing, calligraphy and many other arts. During those cold days, they rise before dawn and get through their training. It is strenuous and hard, and so they believe the result will be great. Many young girls studying singing or Japanese music also have their *kan-geiko* in the early hours.

But sometimes the entire period of 30 days is too long for such training, and in many cases the *kan-geiko* is held for only two weeks of the coldest period, from January 21 (*taikan* or big cold) to February 4, when the spring season commences according to the lunar calendar.

WOMEN'S HOLIDAYS

IN FEUDAL DAYS, Japanese women had to serve their fathers, husbands, brothers and elders, and do heavy household and farm work, without being allowed to have enjoyment. Thus there developed a custom of women having a day or days for their amusement, when men had to serve them.

Such women's days came at rice planting in many districts because women had the main task in the planting rite. So on the day of rice planting, husbands and brothers shouldered the task of preparing food and serving it to the women.

In the Kawakami district of Fukui Prefecture, women formerly observed 'oshinmeiko' (sacred woman's rite) by gathering at a house selected by lots. All took offerings of food and placed them on the shelf erected for the sacred woman. All the village women stayed there the whole day, eating, talking, singing and laughing, while the men of the village remained quietly in the *naya* or outer house of each household, and were not allowed to show their faces outside.

At Shirakawa village in Gifu, there was formerly a custom of men undertaking the cooking during the first three days of the New Year, while women did no work and spent the days in idleness.

In some villages of Ishikawa Prefecture they held toward the end of December a rite for inviting *ta-no-kami* or farm god to the house. But the one who took charge of the rite was the eldest woman in the household, and all the men had to follow her orders.

In some places in Ryukyu the so-called *Shisugu* festival was held in June and August by the lunar calendar. During this festival all the men had to stay outdoors, while the women stayed inside, doing as they pleased.

YUBIKIRI

WHEN TWO children make up after a petty quarrel, each extends his right hand, with the little finger stretched out. They hook their little fingers together, and say 'Yubikiri' (finger-cutting). Then their quarrel is over and forgotten, and they have made a promise to be on good terms again.

It is not known how or when this *yubikiri* custom originated, but it is believed to have been based on the belief that when one breaks a promise made with *yubikiri* he will lose his little finger. *Yubikiri* is a pledge to keep a promise, and once the pledge is made, one has to observe it or else he will lose his little finger.

Yubikiri is commonly observed by little children, both boys and girls. But sometimes girls still observe the pledge even when they are almost grown-up. Of course, today no significance of its original meaning is attached to the pledge of *yubikiri.* Yet it is very widely observed among children as a practical method for making promises or pledges.

Pledges or promises were formerly made in various ways by the Japanese. Ancient people pledged by their *kami* or guardian deities, and said that they would be willingly punished by their *kami* if they failed to fulfill the pledges they made.

Yet such pledges of a religious or traditional nature existed more for form than for actual results. Thus they were quite meaningless in the actual life of the people. In feudal days, therefore, common people who laid more stress on actuality than on form thought out some effective ways of showing their sincerity in making pledges. Some such methods are very strange and may even be absurd. Yet to those who used them, even such methods were of extreme importance.

It is related that an Edo merchant lacked money to pay his debt, and he went to a money-lender. But he had no security to offer, and so he pledged to the money-lender that until he could pay back the loan, he would not use his right sleeve. So saying he took his right arm out of the sleeve, and left the money-lender with the needed money, but with one sleeve dangling loose off his shoulder. For days and months he went around, with his right arm bare and his right sleeve dangling loose. The people laughed at the sight, but if he put his arm through the loose sleeve, he would lose face. Strange was the pledge, but he kept it until he paid back the money.

There are many other stories telling strange ways of making promises. Praying for the recovery of her dear child from sickness, an old mother pledged to *kami* that she would go without eating salt for one year. She actually did so. Many persons pledged not to drink tea for a certain period, and the significance of this may be realized when it is remembered how the people are fond of drinking tea at all hours of the day. Yet such strange pledges were always strictly kept, because not only did they wish to keep their promises, but they also feared to lose face among their neighbors and friends.

Chapter 9
Marriage, Funerals and Memorials

BRIDE STEALING

THE CUSTOM of *yome-nusumi* (bride stealing) was followed in the old days throughout the country, although such cases were most numerous in Kyushu, occasional in the central and Kanto regions, and rare in the northeastern district.

Bride stealing took place when a girl and a young man were in love but the parents of the girl opposed their marriage, or when the parents could not openly approve although in their hearts they were willing to let their daughter have her wish, because of the sentiment of other families, or some economic or social consideration.

In such cases, the young man usually secured the cooperation of other youths of the community to carry out the act of stealing the girl. Everything was arranged beforehand, and at the proper time, the girl was stolen by her sweetheart and his friends and taken to his house.

In so doing, the fact of stealing the girl had to be loudly declared throughout the village, and the parents of the bride notified. In some districts, the girl, in leaving her house, loudly shouted 'I am going away,' to announce to the whole village her determination to marry the man she selected without her parents' consent.

When the girl was stolen, the wedding banquet was held by the young friends of the groom, who cooperated in stealing her, but the parents of the bride were never invited to this party.

Even though the process of stealing and marrying the girl was very simple in most cases, the marriage thus consummated was recognized as a proper and binding one.

Thus in the rural districts where feudalistic ideas and customs strongly prevailed in the old days, the girl had the right to select her life partner. Even her parents could not stop her marriage and community cooperation was often stronger than parental authority. At the same time, Kyushu girls seem to have been stronger-willed than their sisters in the northern districts.

BRIDE'S TRIAL

THE BRIDAL procession headed by the gorgeously dressed bride and followed by her parents and relatives carrying lighted lanterns in the evening to the house of the bridgroom is still seen in most rural districts, although the custom has almost disappeared in urban areas. It is a great occasion for the entire neighborhood, and nobody wants to miss it.

The coming of the bride is heralded by the arrival earlier in the day of her trousseau and household utensils. The whole village waits for her arrival and she is heartily welcomed to the neighborhood, but strangely the sentiment is expressed in a manner as to embarrass, torture or ridicule her.

The most common welcome given her is to throw mud, sand or water on the bride as she slowly approaches her new home. Of course she is in her formal bridal costume of rich silk and embroidery. There are also several districts where children slap the bride's hip with their hands or slender bamboo canes.

Some children build a barrier almost three feet high of sticks and tree branches across her path. She must step over it. But being fully dressed in many layers of heavy formal *kimono*, it becomes quite a task for her to step gracefully over the barrier while the whole village is watching her. In some places, the bride is greeted by vile shouts.

After she enters the house of the bridegroom, children often manage to approach the paper-screen window of her room. Making holes in the paper with wetted fingers, they peep in and watch her.

All these strange customs are said to be done to test her courage and patience. Others say that it is a lesson to teach the bride to become afraid of going through the same experience again — that is to have another wedding ceremony in her life. But the most sensible explanation is that all these things are done just for the fun of teasing her.

FORTY-NINTH DAY

IT IS COMMONLY believed that for the period of 49 days following a death, the spirit remains under the roof of the house where it had lived when alive. Hence on the 49 day, the family gathers again as it bids a final farewell to the earthly world.

The service held on this day is extremely important, and *Shijuku-nichi* (forty-ninth day service) is observed strictly by all families. This marks the end of the first period of mourning.

The *Shijuku-nichi* service is held either at home or at a Buddhist temple, before the tablet inscribed with the Buddhist name of the dead. Candles are lighted, incense is burned and the priests recite sutras. Sincere, long prayers are offered by members of the family, friends and relatives.

But this service is not one of sorrow; it is held with the joyful realization that the dead has gone to *Gokuraku*. The prayers and offerings made earlier are believed to have influenced the Ten Judges to give a favorable verdict to the departed. To ensure a felicitous future life for the dead, the members of the family and their friends have made sacrifices, abstaining from eating meat and fish, and foregoing their accustomed pleasures. Dressed in dark mourning clothes, they have prayed for the reincarnation of the spirit into a better and more beautiful life.

Because it is believed that the spirit does not leave the house until after *Shijuku-nichi*, none of the personal effects of the dead are touched. The *kimonos*, for instance, have been carefully cared for during the 49 days, since the spirit that used them in life is still in the house.

But when the *Shijuku-nichi* service is held, and the spirit of the dead has made its proper entrance into *Gokuraku*, an inventory of the personal effects left behind is made. These are distributed among the members of the family, friends, relatives, servants and acquaintances as *katami* (keepsakes). This distribution is a tedious though important affair, because no one who has been in close contact with the dead must be forgotten, and the selection of articles is made according to the degree of intimacy.

And so, at last with the *Shijuku-nichi* service the dead finally leaves the world, and his earthly friendships are terminated.

FUNERAL CEREMONY

FUNERAL CUSTOMS vary greatly according to different districts, but most funerals nowadays are conducted by Buddhist rites. The basic rules for a Buddhist funeral are given in an ancient sutra. It reads, 'Cleansed with hot water, dressed in cotton cloth, placed in a golden coffin, sprinkled with ointment, covered with aromatics, burned in a fire, bones collected and placed in a tower.'

According to these instructions the dead formerly were washed with hot water. The task was called *yukan* (hot water bathing), which was an important part of the funeral ceremony in the past. This practice has died out in the cities, but in some rural districts it is still observed. The dead are dressed in white cotton clothes, not only because the sutra says so, but because white is considered pure and clean.

Formerly, valuables and clothing were buried with the body, but this is no longer done. In the country, too, copper coins, or pieces of paper on which the outlines of coins were roughly painted, were placed in the coffin. The ancients believed that *Sanzu-no-kawa* (Sanzu River) divided this world from *Gokuraku* (Paradise), and so coins were required to pay for the ferry ride across the river. Since they also believed it was a lengthy journey to *Gokuraku*, straw sandals and a strong staff to lean on were placed in the coffin to aid the traveler.

Members of the family, friends and relatives gather to watch by the dead all through the night before the funeral, in a ceremony called *'otsuya'* (passing the night together). Today the *otsuya* is still an important part of the funeral rites. It is the last occasion on which the gathered group can be with the dead. Throughout the night Buddhist scriptures are recited by the priest, incense is burned and offerings are made. The visitors bring offerings for the dead, such as flowers, candies, sweets, incense and money, and are served food and drink. Meat and fish are seldom served.

The funeral procession used to leave the house at night, but today it leaves at any hour. The custom of cremation in Japan is as old as Buddhism, and most of the dead have been and are cremated.

The burial does not end the funeral services in Japan, for various other rites are held for many days after. The funeral is one of the most important functions in Japan, and all the relatives and friends who can, participate in the rites, as well as the neighbors.

HIDING BRIDE

ON KUDAKA ISLAND of Ryukyu, a little island of less than three miles in circumferece, there was observed until quite recently a strange custom of the bride running away from her groom on the day of their wedding ceremony. Most present wives of the island have had such an experience, though the custom is not generally followed now.

From the wedding party, the bride ran away and had to be in hiding so that she would not be found for four days, during which period the groom, with the help of his friends, had to search for the missing bride. Formerly the brides hid themselves for as long as 20 days. It is said that girls were pleased with the shortening of the hiding period. In the old days, brides who were easily found were ridiculed by others. One woman was reputed to have stayed away from her groom for 72 days.

The island is small, but its mountains are sacred, and men were not allowed to enter mountain regions. Some brides hid themselves in the mountains and secretly came down to the village for food.

When the bride was finally found, she was roughly treated by the groom and his friends. Then she had to cry loudly. Hearing her cries, the neighbors would gossip about her period of hiding, whether it was too short or too long. If she was caught in the daytime, she was confined to a room, with the groom's friends guarding outside. If she came at night, she was immediately taken by the groom to his room.

Of course, all this hiding and searching were done just to conform to the old custom, as a sort of marriage ritual. At any rate, it is said the bride and groom, as well as their friends and neighbors enjoyed the custom, as it gave them considerable fun and excitement. Some explain that the custom gave the young folks a better appreciation of their marriage, because one values something that has to be searched for than what can be obtained easily.

HUSBANDS ON TRIAL

A STRANGE marriage custom called *nenki-muko* or time-limit husbands is still followed in some rural districts, particularly in northeastern regions. Formerly it was observed in much wider areas.

Upon marriage, the husband goes to the house of his wife, and for a certain period he works for her family. Then when the agreed period ends, he leaves the house, taking his wife, and goes to his father's house or to his own to live. Sometimes wages are paid by the families of the wives of such husbands

on trial.

The system seems to have developed from the idea of making the husband of a daughter work for a certain period for her family so that his character and efficiency in farm work could be ascertained. Of late, however, the system is adopted mostly when the eldest son of a family is still too young to do farm work, so that his big sister's husband can help the family on the farm. This trial marriage is followed also when the parents of the girl are intending to make their daughter and her husband live in a separate house from their own, and so want an opportunity to get acquainted with her husband and learn for certain that he will take good care of her.

The period of this trial is generally three or five years. Thus such husbands have often been called *sannen-muko* (three-year husbands) or *gonen-muko* (five-year husbands).

While living as trial husbands, they are considered as adopted children of the family during the specified period, and must be obedient not only to their parents-in-law, but also to their brothers- and sisters-in-law.

INCENSE MONEY

WHEN ANYONE dies, it is customary for his relatives, friends, neighbors and even acquaintances to offer the family of the deceased *koden* or incense money. Of course, flowers, fruits, incense, cakes and other offerings are brought, but *koden* must also be given.

It is a sum of money wrapped up in a formal and fixed manner. As its name shows, it is meant to pay for incense to be burned for the dead. This custom developed from the spirit of mutual help in time of need. All friends and neighbors intend to contribute some money toward the heavy funeral expense to be borne by the unfortunate family.

It has also long been a custom of the Imperial Family to give a sum of money toward funeral expenses upon the death of any person who has given special service to the state.

As in the case of all other gifts, *okaeshi* or a return present has to be given for each *koden.* Things to be given as the return present for *koden* differ according to locality. In some rural districts, a special kind of *manju* or Japanese sweet cake is distributed.

In cities, generally, boxes or cans of green tea are used as the return present. The quality and quantity of tea are decided by the amount of the *koden. Furoshiki,* Japanese wrapping cloths, and other things are also used.

This custom of giving return presents for *koden* is not followed now by many city families. Some donate the *koden* money to charity or religious organizations, in prayer for the spirit of the deceased. A tendency to ignore the return present habit is notably seen among the intellectual. Of course, in case of an Imperial grant, there is no return present.

KAIMYO

WHEN A Japanese Buddhist dies, he is given *kaimyo* or a Buddhist name by the priest of the temple which looks after his family cemetery. His *kaimyo*, consisting of several Chinese characters and praising his virtue and works, is written on an *ihai* or memorial tablet and also engraved on his tombstone.

Kai originally meant 'sila' or the commandment given to one accepted as a disciple. The custom of giving *kaimyo* was first started by Zen temples in the early 14th century, and was soon followed by other sects.

Kaimyo soon came to be given to laymen upon their death. But it is only since the Tokugawa era that *kaimyo* has come to be engraved on tombstones. At first the people marked burial places with only bamboo fences or natural stones. The introduction of Buddhism brought the custom of erecting tombstones. At first they were ornamental piles of several stones for memorial purposes and were not necessarily placed at burial places.

Tall square tombstones now generally seen came into use during the Tokugawa era, when all tombs were marked with *kaimyo*, and not with the *zokumyo* or worldly names. Of course, today, tombs are more often marked with *zokumyo* than *kaimyo*.

Formerly, when a husband died, often the widow had her *kaimyo* also marked on the stone erected for her husband, in prayer that she would be buried in the same tomb when she died. But in this case, her name was marked in red as she was still living. When she died and was buried there, the red color was washed off.

KATAMI

WHEN A Japanese dies, his personal effects are divided and distributed among relatives and close friends as *katami* or keepsakes. This custom must be quite old, as the term is mentioned in many *Manyoshu* poems. It is still observed in almost all parts of the country. In the old days it must have been a system of dividing the property left by the deceased.

Usually personal effects, mostly clothing and daily handled articles such as books, watches, furniture, desk utensils, jewelry, ornaments, smoking pipes and walking sticks, which were regularly used and loved by the dead are distributed as *katami.*

Katami-wake or keepsake division

often becomes a very difficult and troublesome affair, as everyone wants to receive the most valuable mementos. Arguments often arise, but generally the division is decided by the closest kin in consultation with principal relatives.

Clothing is considered the most important *katami*, as it is believed that the spirit of the person who wore them still remains therein. Hence the best clothes are given to the children, brothers and sisters or close relatives of the dead. Many other valuable keepsakes go to these intimate relatives.

In the distribution of minor mementos to neighbors and friends, trouble often occurs, as it generally happens that there are not enough proper things to satisfy them all. But those who are ignored would feel resentment. Therefore, much care must be taken to divide properly the personal effects of the dead.

Katami-wake is one important family affair which must be attended to after the conclusion of the funeral service.

KIRISAGE

LONG BLACK hair was the pride of Japanese women until the Meiji period in the late 19th century. In ancient days women wore their long hair tied together and hanging down the back. At that time long, glossy black hair was an important requirement for a beautiful woman.

As the customs and living conditions changed radically in the Tokugawa era, women began to arrange their hair in ornamental ways. Hairstyles for little girls, ladies, young wives and old women became definitely established.

Elaborate coiffures were demanded not only by social rules and customs, but also desired by all women to make them beautiful and dignified — they stood for womanhood.

Then there developed a custom of widows cutting their hair short, to signify that their womanhood had ended and they had no desire to marry again, remaining faithful to the deceased husbands. The widow's short hair was called *kirisage* (cut and let down), as the short hair was let down behind and tied or held by clips.

An order issued by the Meiji Government in 1873 provided that 'a woman who cut her hair short without reason shall be fined 6.25 sen and up to 12.5 sen.' Thus women were prohibited from cutting their hair short.

Therefore, when a widow cut her hair short she had to report the fact to the local government office, and in due time, she received an official notice saying, 'The husband is dead, and his widow has cut her hair short. It cannot be said that she had no reason for making her hair short. Thus she will be allowed to do so.'

That is to say, widows could cut their hair short with official permission. This law, however, was abolished in 1880, making all women free to cut their hair if they wished. Otherwise modern women would be punished for bobbing their hair.

KUYO

KUYO OR *tsuizen-kuyo* is a Buddhist service for the repose and salvation of the dead. It is held not only for ancestors and members of the family who have died, but it is also observed popularly for fish, animals and various inanimate objects.

The custom of burying fish and animals, and setting up stone or wooden markers on the spot was followed by the people long before the introduction of Buddhism. This ancient habit must have been further encouraged by Buddhist principle. Today, though most of such *kuyo* services are held with Buddhist rites, there are many which show no Buddhist influence.

Kuyo is very commonly held for needles, fish, eels and dolls. These services differ according to districts, but the idea is to pray for the salvation of those things which were sacrificed for the livelihood or comfort of human beings.

All over the country at fishing villages *kuyo* rites for fish which have been caught and eaten are held. It is customary on such occasions to release some fish in the sea or a river. Eel-shop keepers also hold similar services annually for the salvation of the numerous eels they had prepared for human consumption.

The most picturesque is *hari-kuyo* for broken needles. This became popular in the Edo period. Sewing was the most important work for women. In the course of their work they broke many needles. Formerly, in Edo days, it was on February 8 that all girls brought their broken needles to convenient temples or shrines, and buried them with proper services. It became quite a social affair, with many beautifully dressed women gathering together. In the old days girls were told to keep all broken needles in little boxes to be buried at the annual service.

On February 8 they bring them out and hold a service of thanksgiving, at the same time praying to Goddess Awashima, guardian deity of women. Whenever convenient, they visit Awashima shrines, but generally they gather at nearby shrines or other places. There they bury the broken needles and thank them for their service to them.

The custom is fast dying out but many old-fashioned women like to observe the day, probably in memory of the old days when they had to sew dai-

ly. Despite the use of sewing machines, and the popularity of Western dress, sewing is still an important duty of women. Thus *hari-kuyo* does not die.

Little children also hold *kuyo* for dolls they have broken in the past year, and feel sorry for.

MARRIAGE GO-BETWEEN

NAKODO or marriage go-betweens are still regarded necessary in solemnizing marriages, but they now exist in name only, having in most cases nothing to do with the actual arrangement of a wedding. By some people, however, it is believed to be quite an honor to act as *nakodo*, and many persons boast of having been *nakodo* to 50 or 100 couples.

The custom of having *nakodo* often gives the wrong impression that in Japan marriages have been arranged by families and that girls in particular have no voice in selecting their mates. In the old days there were no *nakodo*. Young men and women freely selected their mates. Throughout the country there still remain various customs that prove that girls have always enjoyed the right of free choice. Formal wedding ceremonies are often held in many parts much later than the actual marriage, sometimes a year later.

In Shimane district there was a strange custom of girls running away. When a girl decides to marry her man, she stands at the door of her house, and with one foot inside and the other outside, she loudly shouts, 'I am running away.' She repeats it several times, but no one appears to stop her. So she steps out, and goes to the man waiting to take her to his house.

In many districts young men go to live in the households of their selected women, and only after the formal ceremony do the women live with the husbands' families.

At first marriages took place among people living in the same village or district. Only when marriages with persons living in distant districts became numerous did the system of *nakodo* develop. The girls of the *samurai* class, however, had no freedom in marriage. These girls were secluded and had no chance to meet young men. Their marriages were thus arranged by their parents. But the *samurai* class constituted only a very small portion of the entire population and their customs were due to their own special conditions. Yet this custom in the *samurai* class often made many think that common Japanese girls had no freedom in marriage.

A marriage brought about through the offer of a go-between who was a prominent person was believed to assure the future of the young couple. Thus, there developed a custom of selecting prominent persons as nominal or official *nakodo*, even though the marriage was actually arranged by some insignificant friend.

There is, however, a common expression, *nakodo-guchi* or *nakodo* talk. Eager to arrange a marriage, inconsiderate *nakodo* sometimes exaggerate the good points of the prospective bride and bridegroom and their families, hiding their shortcomings. Such marriages often end in failure.

When the families concerned find the proposal of a *nakodo* for a marriage between them desirable, a *miai* or meeting is arranged. The young man and the girl accompanied by their parents are to meet for the first time. Formerly a theater or picnic party was arranged for this purpose. Now more often they meet at a restaurant or teashop, or at the house of the *nakodo*.

Lately it has become customary for the two young people to make their decision after knowing each other more intimately. So the so-called *miai*-marriage is no longer made without considering the wishes of the young people.

MIBOJIN

A MOVEMENT has recently been started for abolishing the common custom of calling widows *mibojin*. This term is quite old, but came to be much abused since the Meiji years. Originally widows might call themselves *mibojin*, but it was unpardonable for others to give this name to any widow. The term really means 'a person who has not yet died.'

According to old Japanese ideas, man and wife are one and inseparable. In particular, it was the role of the wife to follow the fortune of her husband. When the husband died, she also died spiritually. She never thought of remarrying. She cut her hair short and withdrew from public activity. It was thus widows sometimes called themselves *mibojin* or persons who have not yet died from a sense of devotion to the deceased husband that would make them even think of killing themselves to follow their mates.

It was formerly a custom among devoted couples to be buried in the same graves when they died. When the husband died first, for instance, the tombstone erected over his grave bore the names of both the deceased husband and the still-living wife. However, the engraved name of the living widow was filled with red ink. When she died she was buried in the same tomb, and the red ink removed from her name on the stone.

Many war widows are finding it hard to remarry now while they are addressed by friends and others as *mibojin*. Moreover, the feudalistic idea against widows remarrying is still very strong among old-fashioned people. To enable young widows to marry if they wish, this movement for abolishing the name of *mibojin* has been started, in the hope of finally destroying the traditional ban on widows' marriage.

The common Japanese word for widows is *goke* which is much more preferable than the abused *mibojin*.

NENKI

THE HAPPINESS of the spirit of the dead in the afterworld, according to devout Buddhists, depends largely upon the prayers and offerings made by family and friends left behind in this world.

After *Shijuku-nichi*, the spirit of the dead finally leaves this world and enters a new life, reincarnated. The departed might appear as another man, or woman, an animal, a bird, or an insect. And in this new reincarnation the happiness of the new soul is believed to be in proportion to the frequency and earnestness of the prayers offered and the religious services performed by those who are left behind. If a relative is leading a miserable life in his new existence, he can be saved and helped to a better existence.

This shows why all Buddhists believe that the services after death are very important for the happiness of the departed. *Nenki* (years service) are numerous. *Ikkaiki* (first service) comes on the first anniversary of the death, and *Sankaiki* (third service) comes on the second. There is no 'second service' and the second anniversary is called 'third service.' This is because the Japanese way of counting years and ages is used, and all following services are also numbered according to the Japanese way of counting. The sixth anniversary is called *Shichikaiki* (seventh service), 12th anniversary *Jusankaiki* (13th service), and the 50th service is celebrated on the 49th anniversary.

After the 50th service, a service is held every 50th year. These services are special occasions, observed by all Buddhist families wishing for the happiness of the dead. Some devout people observe every anniversary after a death with some sort of religious service. Generally, however, only the above-mentioned *Nenki* are kept.

These *Nenki* are important occasions, and people who do not hold such services for their ancestors are considered unfilial and dishonorable. And since filial piety is one of the greatest virtues taught by the Buddhists, many Japanese outdo themselves by meticulous observance of all these services.

So even after death, a Japanese is feted and remembered by his descendants and friends for many years.

OKAKURE

OKAKURE (disappear or lost to sight) is a term often used in the case of a person's death. It comes from the traditional belief that the physical body dies but the soul lives on. So death means the separation of the soul from the body that has ceased to live. Buddhists believe that the soul of the deceased stays in the home for 49 days.

From this belief in immortality of the soul have come various customs. The first bowl of cooked rice is offered to the ancestors every morning. Whenever the family has special food, either made at home or given by others, it is not eaten before it is first offered to the spirits of the family ancestors.

When a marriage, or the graduation of a son from school, or another important event takes place, the matter is reported to the ancestors. The Emperor follows this custom, and reports all important state and Court affairs to the Grand Shrine of Ise where the spirit of the Imperial ancestor lives.

The country has many shrines dedicated to great historical persons. It is to give the souls of such persons fitting places to reside and where the people may pay their respects to them.

All are immortal, and when death comes, it only means the disappearance of the physical body, but the soul lives on. So one does not die but only disappears from the sight of others. The soul, though invisible to mortal eyes, watches with keen interest what is going on in the family or the whole material world.

OTSUYA

OTSUYA or all-night watch is a very important part of the Japanese funeral or memorial service. It is indeed more important in many respects than funeral rites performed at temples, shrines or churches.

When someone in the family dies, the following evening or a later evening is selected for holding *otsuya* when relatives and friends of the deceased and neighbors assemble and stay until the next morning, keeping watch by the remains of the dead.

It is a religious rite that has been observed since early days equally by all the people, whether their faith be Shinto, Buddhist or Christian. During the night the assembled people join in offering prayers, burning incense, or reciting Buddhist sutras, led by Buddhist priests who are always in attendance on the occasion. They have gathered in memory of the deceased, and so naturally they talk of his or her virtues, faults, mistakes, successes, habits and manners. It is an evening to visualize and remember the deceased.

Then, again, with the gathering of so many persons all through the night, it also becomes an occasion to eat and

drink. To enjoy pleasant feasting on the evening of *otsuya* is believed also to be a manifestation of respect to the dead. The more joyful and merrier the *otsuya* the more satisfied is the family of the deceased, as it is an indication of respect paid by friends and neighbors to his memory.

Not only is *otsuya* held immediately upon death, but it is also observed in later memorial services.

This custom of vigil first originated in offering all-night prayers at temples and shrines. Many people used to stay in the temple or shrine building, sitting there and offering their prayers. This custom is said to have become particularly popular during the Heian period, eighth to 12th centuries. At night, when the whole temple or shrine building became vacant and silence reigned, they thought it was the most suitable time to offer their prayers.

The all-night praying thus developed in shrines and temples gradually came to be observed at home. Also, as a means to pray for the salvation of the soul of the deceased and also to express their sorrow for the loss of the dear one, the people came to hold all-night prayers at home. Thus it is a very important part of the funeral or memorial service, and in small local communities it often becomes a community affair, just as a village marriage is.

SEVEN DEATHS

JAPANESE Buddhists believe that the dead do not go immediately to the other world. They think there is a neutral span — *Chuin* — between this life and the next, and that during this period the deceased is neither dead nor alive, but hovering between the two worlds.

It is said that during *Chuin* seven times is the dead one returned to life to die again. The seven deaths are supposed to come at intervals of seven days. A person dies; his family laments, holds the funeral service and buries or cremates the body. But his spirit lives on with his family. Then when the seventh day comes, he dies again. On the 14th day, he has his third death, and so on, until the seventh death, which comes on the 49th day. Each death is made the occasion for family worship.

The first death is lamented by the family and friends, because at that death the body disappears. But the second death also is important, and *Shonanuka* (first seventh day service) is the first elaborate religious service to take place after death. In old families and in the rural districts, *Shonanuka* is an occasion for all who knew the deceased to come and pray for his salvation, making offerings and burning incense and candles. Buddhist priests are called in and they recite sacred sutras while the family and friends join in prayer that the dead eventually may find his way to *Gokuraku* (Paradise). This service is significant, because of its bearing upon the fate of the spirit of the dead.

Only after his seventh death can the dead one leave this world entirely, and until then his spirit remains at home, between death and life. With every death he approaches nearer to his real end.

Because of this belief, the dead is treated as though not entirely gone from this life, although the body may be already buried or cremated. Every day food is placed on the altar. The spirit of the dead must eat, since it still lives a strenuous life. It is during this period of neutral negation that the Great Judge will decide on the sphere to which the dead shall be sent, whether it be to *Gokuraku* (Paradise) or to *Jigoku* (Hell).

In this period 10 judges appear, it is said, to examine one after the other the record containing the deeds, crimes and good works of the dead in this world. According to the result of this examination, the future fate of the dead will be decided. The period of neutral negation is, as it were, his court trial, and until the final verdict is given, his fate is not decided. It is believed that the size of the gathering of the mourning persons, the earnestness with which they pray and the worthy tales of the dead related by those present will influence the decision of the judges.

Since Buddhists believe in reincarnation, they think that the spirit never dies, but only takes a different form. And this is decided upon by the Great Judge according to the evidence presented at the examination by the 10 judges.

SHRINE WEDDING

IN JAPAN the wedding ceremony is usually held at the house of the groom's parents. In some districts, however, it has been customary to hold it at the residence of the bride's family.

The wedding rite is quite simple, and the marriage is solemnized by the rite of drinking cups of *sake* or rice wine by the bride and groom, with the attendance of only their parents and go-betweens who arranged the matrimonial agreement between the two families.

In the Japanese wedding or marriage, there was no religious feature from the very beginning.

But in old days, and even today in rural districts, the wedding ceremony is understood to possess a great deal of community significance. Thus to the banquet announcing the marriage, held immediately after the wedding rite, are invited not only the members and relatives of the two families, but also friends and neighbors. The banquet, therefore, often continues for several days.

Furthermore, in provincial communities, it is still customary for all friends and neighbors to assist in preparing and serving the wedding banquet.

Thus a marriage has been considered also as a community affair. But since the latter part of Meiji era, new wedding rites, to which religious significance has been given, were introduced.

The so-called shrine wedding first appeared in Tokyo in 1900. It was held at the Daijingu Shrine, the Tokyo branch of the Ise Shrine. It was then located across the street from the present entrance to the new building of the Imperial Hotel at Hibiya. The shrine later moved to Iida-machi, and then to the present site at Fujimicho, Chiyoda Ward.

The church wedding which was held by Japanese Christians in rapidly increasing numbers in the Meiji era seems to have caused the innovation of the wedding service with *Shinto* rites. Soon, shrine weddings gained popularity, and many shrines in big cities set up facilities for conducting the wedding service. Buddhist temples then also followed the example.

Later, so-called wedding halls, where the *Shinto* wedding rite is held, with facilities for wedding banquets and dressing rooms for brides, were established.

TSUNOKAKUSHI

THERE ARE many interesting customs in connection with Japanese marriage, particularly the wedding ceremony. The process of arranging marriage, the wedding ceremony and the costume of the bride are all governed by traditional old customs.

One of the most outstanding features is the *tsunokakushi* (horn-cover) worn by the bride around her head. It is a sort of a band made of red and white silk gauze. It is intended to warn the bride against jealousy, or keep her from becoming jealous.

Jealousy has been regarded as the worst and greatest of the shortcomings of women, and in old days girls were particularly taught to suppress the sentiment of jealousy. Jealous women had horns of jealousy on their heads, traditional tales said. *Tsuno-o-dasu* (to grow horns) is an expression which means 'to become jealous.' Jealous women are devils with horns, children were told.

Buddhism particularly preached the evil of jealousy. It was women believers of the Ikko sect of Buddhism who first wore *wataboshi* or floss silk caps when they paid visits to temples, in their eager wish to stop 'their horns of jealousy' from growing. This was the beginning of the custom of wearing something over the head for suppressing jealousy.

Of course, the so-called *wataboshi* or floss silk caps had been much in use in old days, and particularly they were worn by all women when they wore ceremonial costumes or when they went outdoors. But in such cases they were worn merely as head-coverings and nothing else.

The custom first created by the Ikko sect which had women wear *wataboshi* on their visit to temples, came later to be applied to brides on their wedding day. *Tsunokakushi* means 'to hide the horns,' but the wearing of *tsunokakushi* by the bride does not mean that she is hiding her horns of jealousy. It really signifies her eager wish to be free of jealousy, the worst evil attributed to Japanese womanhood.

Thus, *wataboshi* or floss silk caps became *tsunokakushi*, but because the floss silk cap is so inconvenient in wearing over the *takashimada*, the highly elaborate Japanese wedding coiffure, at the beginning of the Meiji era the old-fashioned *wataboshi* gave way to the modern silk-gauze band of red and white.

The Japanese wedding ceremony and the bridal costume have undergone many changes in recent years, but *tsunokakushi* is still worn by the Japanese bride at her wedding ceremony, as long as she is dressed in the Japanese fashion. It may be a sign that the Japanese bride is still eagerly wishing not to become a jealous wife.

The traditional belief of women being jealous is, of course, a product of feudal customs, and many authorities think ancient Japanese wives were really very jealous, and there were good grounds for their being so. If that be so, the *tsunokakushi* custom will quickly die out with the disappearance of the feudalistic social structure and customs.

TWO TOMBS

THE ANCIENT custom of burying the dead at one place and erecting a tomb somewhere else to worship the spirit of the dead can be still seen in many districts. Kyushu and the northern end of the northeast region are the only places where no trace of this custom is seen.

It may differ slightly according to districts, but where this custom is followed, the dead are buried in public cemeteries, but no tomb or any mark is erected. Such common cemeteries are generally on some elevated spot near the village border or by the sea or a river. Once the dead are buried there, no visit to the place is made.

But the tomb for the spirit of the dead is erected mostly in temple compounds or somewhere convenient and near to the respective homes.

Therefore the place where the body is buried is often called the body-tomb, and the tomb erected for the worship of the soul of the dead is called the worship tomb.

This custom of burying the body at one place and worshiping the spirit of the dead at another is believed to have developed from the original Japanese idea that the physical body is only a temporary house for the spirit. So in the burial of the dead body all that is required is to dispose of it.

But the spirit of the dead must be respected and worshiped. Thus a tomb to house the spirit is erected at a convenient place for offering prayers and holding memorial and other services.

Actually this old custom is no longer observed in most cases, but all over the country there still stand burial grounds and worship tombs erected by our forefathers for the spirit of the dead.

WEDDING CEREMONY

THE JAPANESE wedding ceremony is called *yomeiri*, or 'bringing the bride into the family of the bridegroom.' The ceremony always used to be held at night, but the practice of having it performed in the afternoon or even in the morning has become common in large cities. The ceremony has no religious significance in Japan, but of late, it is often held at Shinto shrines or before the tablets of the family ancestors.

The bride is brought to the house of the bridegroom by her parents and the 'go-between' couple who originally arranged the marriage. She wears the bridal costume and a stiff white band called *tsunokakushi* (horn-cover) on her head, because it is believed that all women have horns of jealousy, which must be hidden under the band at the wedding. However, the ornate bridal costume and the traditional method of hairdressing are not always used in the cities nowadays, for the Western costume has taken their place in many cases.

In the room where the ceremony is held, the bride is seated facing the bridegroom. Only the parents of the bride and the bridegroom, the 'go-between' couple, and little serving girls are present. When all is ready, a set of three *sake* (rice-wine) cups is brought before the bride. She takes the upper cup, and one of the girls fills it with *sake* in three pouring motions. She drinks this in three sips. Then the same cup is taken to the bridegroom, and filled. He drinks the *sake* in the same manner. The second cup is then offered first to the bridegroom and then to the bride. The bride drinks first from the last cup and then the bridegroom. Since the three cups are filled three times each, and the *sake* is drunk each time in three sips, the marriage ceremony is called *san-san-kudo* (three, three, nine times).

The *san-san-kudo* is the main feature of the Japanese wedding ceremony, and by this little rite the marriage is solemnized.

The wedding banquet to which the friends and relatives are invited is held immediately after the ceremony of *san-san-kudo*. The bride usually changes into another bridal costume when this part of the ceremony is held.

The ceremony of binding the two families together also consists of drinking *sake*. The members of the two families sit in rows, facing each other; the head of each family sitting at the head of each row, with his wife next to him. The bridal couple are last in line. First, the father of the young man takes a sip of *sake*. The same cup is handed to the bride, finally going to the mother of the bridegroom. The second cup starts with the father of the bride, goes to the bridegroom and ends with the mother of the bride. The last cup begins with the father of the bride, goes to the father of the bridegroom, the bride's mother, the groom's mother, the bride and the bridegroom. This ends the formal introduction of the members of the two families to each other.

Formerly there were no honeymoons in Japan. The custom of going on a trip after the marriage ceremony was introduced here very recently. What was observed in place of a honeymoon was *sato-gaeri* (returning to the bride's former home), and this custom is still generally followed throughout the country. Even when honeymoon trips are made, *sato-gaeri* is one of the first pleasant duties of the young married couple.

The day after the happy event is spent in feasting, according to the old custom, and, on the second day, the bride goes with her husband to the homes of his relatives and friends to be formally introduced, while guests also are invited to the house to meet the bride.

On the third day, *sato-gaeri* takes place, when the bride visits her own family. She is escorted by members of her husband's family to her former home. Formerly the husband did not accompany her on this visit, but went on the fourth day after the wedding, or the second day of the bride's *sato-gaeri*, but now they often make the trip together. He usually takes with him presents for all the members of her immediate family and in some cases also for other relatives in return for those which the bride brought to his relatives.

With the arrival of the husband, another ceremonial feast is given to introduce him to the relatives of the bride's family. He also is taken to the homes of relatives and friends. The husband spends a night with his wife's family, and the following morning they go home together. In the olden days, it was customary for the husband to give his wife a special *kimono* to wear on her *sato-gaeri* visit. All her other costumes are provided by her family, but the one she wears on her *sato-gaeri* visit is a present from her husband.

With the popularity of honeymoons, the custom of *sato-gaeri* is fast dying out. The fact that many brides now come from distant homes, too, has made it almost impossible for them to visit the home they have so recently left.

YOMEIRI-DOGU

YOMEIRI-DOGU or bride's trousseau does not mean only her clothing and personal items. It includes not only clothing for all seasons, but also bedding, furniture, kitchen utensils, tableware and everything else required for the new home. It is because of the elaborate *yomeiri-dogu* required for a daughter's wedding, that it is commonly said that any family with three daughters would go bankrupt.

Weddings have become much simpler recently, but old-fashioned families still make elaborate preparations for their daughters' marriage. In many districts, *yomeiri-dogu* is put on view for all neighbors, just before the wedding. The people talk about the quantity and quality of the *yomeiri-dogu.*

While the bride brings all these things, the groom does not make any preparation at all. Thus a poor young man finds himself surrounded by articles of luxury which he had never seen before the wedding day.

This custom of providing the bride with everything she might require for years has come from the ancient maternal family system. In ancient days, until the rise of the military class, the family line was kept up by the women. That is to say, the eldest daughter succeeded to the headship of the family, marrying a man from another family. No male of the family was the family successor.

Though this old custom has died, the idea that the needs of the bride must be taken care of by her own family and not by the groom's still remains. Hence the bride must bring everything she needs as well as things for the groom.

The old maternal family system is also left in a common custom among rural folks of having the married daughter return to her mother's house to give birth to her child. It is because the daughter's child must be born in her own house and not in her husband's.

YOME-TATAKI

THE CUSTOM of *yome-tataki* or bride-beating is still observed in many rural districts of the country. Although the custom differs slightly according to district, usually it is with wooden sticks or twisted straws that new brides are beaten on their backs. It is believed that brides who receive such a beating will be healthy and give birth to good children.

Of course, there are various evil features connected with this custom. At some places little children observe the custom of *yome-tataki* in order to obtain offerings of money and sweets from families having new brides. With the offer of money or other things, some brides are saved from the ordeal of being beaten. The origin of the custom, however, is to wish the new bride good health and many children.

In many districts, the *yome-tataki* is performed whenever a new bride comes to the district. Young people armed with sticks and other things enter the house of the bride and demand her appearance. Fearing to be beaten by them, the bride hides somewhere, and then the family gives the young people some money or sweets to ask them to beat only softly upon the bride. They consent and when the bride is taken out from her hiding place, she is beaten only for formality's sake.

But in other districts, this custom is observed during the New Year festival. It is commonly on the 15th of January that the *yome-tataki* is held. Children and others carrying sticks go to all houses where new brides came during the past year, and demand that the brides be shown so that they can beat upon their backs.

Bride-beaters always sing their peculiar songs when they go on with the bride-beating work. Moreover, the sticks vary according to district. Commonly they are stout sticks with their tips painted red. In some places, straws are twisted into hard sticks and used, but these straw sticks are just as hard as wooden sticks.

Generally speaking, brides are not beaten hard, but on exceptional occasions they are given quite a punishment by the young village people, if their grooms' families are hated for some reason.

In several rural districts of the country, the *yome-tataki* is one of the most important features of their New Year celebration, with the young people looking forward to the fun of becoming bride-beaters.

Bride-beating sticks are regarded with respect, as the people believe that those sticks have the virtue of giving health and many children to new brides.

YUINO

YUINO ORIGINALLY meant a promise or arrangement for marriage. But later it came to indicate the gifts exchanged between the families of a man and woman to confirm the agreement of their marriage.

In ancient days when men went to the houses of the women upon marriage, presents were given by the man's family to the parents of the woman. In Tokugawa days it was customary in upper classes for the man's family to send a gift as the sign of a promise to receive the bride into the family. Then on the day of the wedding, some presents were brought to all members of the groom's family.

Today, however, it is customary to exchange *yuino* as a confirmation of the marriage arrangement, but in some rural districts only the man's family send *yuino* and nothing is returned by the girl's family, as was done in ancient days.

Yuino traditionally consists of dry goods, *tai* (sea-bream), kegs of *sake*, *surume* (dried cuttle-fish), *konbu* (dried laver), hemp, floss silk and folding fans, which are all symbolic of long life or happiness.

But today these goods are not actually exchanged, and only a piece of fine paper with the names of these articles inscribed is presented. With this *mokuroku* or list of gifts, the man's family sends the girl's family a sum of money for clothes, and in return the girl's family gives a sum for the groom's *hakama* or ceremonial skirt. The amount to be returned by the girl's family is generally one-half of what is given by the man's family.

The *mokuroku*, the envelope of money and folding fans, are placed on a white wooden tray with legs. A messenger takes the gift to the other family. But for convenience' sake, generally the *nakodo* or go-between acts as the messenger to exchange the *yuino* between the two families on a lucky day.

Chapter 10
Natural Phenomena

BIRTH YEAR

THERE ARE 12 animals which stand for respective years in a fixed order. They are *ne* (rat), *ushi* (cow), *tora* (tiger), *u* (rabbit), *tatsu* (dragon), *mi* (snake), *uma* (horse), *hitsuji* (sheep), *saru* (monkey), *tori* (fowl), *inu* (dog), and *i* (boar).

But why are the animals limited to those 12? How is it that the cat or other animals are not included to symbolize years? It is traditionally told that when Shaka or Buddha died, the people and animals who followed his teaching were saddened and hurried to his death-bed. But of all the species of animals, only those 12 came. So they were honored by being selected to symbolize the characteristics of years. The cat did not believe in the teaching of Buddha and as it did not hurry to his death-bed, it is excluded from the 12.

Then, although the rat occupies the first position in the line of years, it gained that honor by a trick. It was really the cow that first hurried to Buddha's death-bed, it is told. But just as the cow started on the journey, the rat jumped on its back, and when the cow reached the destination, the rat jumped off its back and entered ahead. So the cow was deprived of the honor of being the first to reach Shaka's death-bed.

There being 12 animals, every 13th year has the same animal as its symbol. Then, the five elements of wood, fire, earth, metal and water are also given to the five succeeding years in the order given. As both the 12 animal symbols and the five elements are used together for symbolizing years, there is obtained a common multiple of 60. So every 61st year has the same animal and element symbols.

It is from this calculation that when a person reaches the 61st year the occasion is celebrated with much joy. It is called *kanreki* or return of the year, and the attainment of that age is regarded as a great event. It is commonly believed that on *kanreki* one will gain a new childhood or is reborn. Thus, on the occasion of celebrating the day, the old man or woman is the honored guest at a big banquet held by his or her children and grandchildren. The person is dressed in red-colored clothes and a red cap, as formerly it was customary to clothe newborn babies in red costumes. The *kanreki* festivity and its red costume are still widely observed in rural districts. In cities too, children and grandchildren take much joy in honoring their parents or grandparents on their *kanreki*. Being the reborn child, the *kanreki* person has to obey the orders of the younger members of the family, moralists used to teach.

The year of *ne* or *nezumi* (mouse) by the old Japanese calendar, is a year of abundant food and much activity. The mouse is the symbol of *Daikoku*, one of the *Shichifukujin* or the Seven Gods of Good Fortune, which is the god of wealth and the guardian of the kitchen.

Daikoku is always represented in painting and sculpture as a smiling, old man of benevolent appearance, standing on two bales of rice, holding a large cloth bag over his left shoulder, and carrying in his right hand a *kozuchi* or magic mallet. There is a mouse on the rice bales on which *Daikoku* stands. The rice bales stand for food, of course, the bag on *Daikoku's* shoulder holds all kinds of wealth, and the magic mallet in his hand will bring out anything one may desire.

The mouse is inseparable from *Daikoku* and is the symbol of wealth and particularly of abundant food that are promised by *Daikoku*, for wherever there is a mouse there is food.

Then, the mouse is also never idle, always busy finding and bringing in food. It does not carry food in one big bulk, but it makes many trips a day, taking a small bit at a time. It accumulates its big supply of food by constant labor. So the year of *nezumi* is a year of constant labor and activity, that will bring abundant food to all. No big gain at one speculative stroke is predicted for the year, and all have to work constantly, gaining a little at one time to have the abundance of food and other wealth.

The year of *ne* also stands for timidity and humbleness. That means that all should do their work patiently and be humble for whatever success they might gain during the year. The mouse is famous for rapidly multiplying, and so in this year expansion in every field of human activity is assured.

There is an old tradition that a house is safe as long as it has mice in it. It is believed that the mice know beforehand the coming of a flood or the occurrence of fire. If the house in which they live is to be destroyed by such calamities as fire or flood, they will disappear before the disaster. The presence of the mouse is therefore believed to be an assurance of the safety of the house and people.

If one is born in the year of *ushi* or cow, he will be steady and hardworking. Their mind and movements are often slow, but they will attain their objective with determination. Particularly *ushi* women will make good housewives.

Many old-fashioned married women hope that no girls will be born in the tiger year. This is a very unlucky year for girls to be born in. To boys, however, it is a very good year, as they will be aggressive and active. But girls born in this year are said to be headstrong and obstinate, a characteristic which is regarded unwomanlike. Furthermore, tiger-year girls will leave their husbands. The traditional tiger, under whose influence tiger-year girls are born, is able to run 1,000 miles and back in one night, it is said. So even when they marry they will soon come back.

Girls born in *tora* years had small chances of marriage, because superstitious families would not accept them as the wives of their sons.

But women who find marriage more difficult than *tora*-year girls, are those born in the year of the *hinoe-uma* or horse that emits fire. Women born in this year are believed to devour their husbands, and so none would marry them. Mothers used to tell their daughters born in this year that they should never expect marriage. The girls, too, accepted their fate, and determined to remain unmarried.

Yaoya O-Shichi, whose life was woven into many dramas and plays of the Edo period, was a *hinoe-uma* girl. Her father, a green-grocer, lost his house in the big Edo fire of 1681, and moved to a new house in front of the Enjoji Temple, Koishikawa. O-Shichi fell in love with Sahei, a temple boy. But under the watchful eyes of the temple priest, O-Shichi could not meet him as often as she wished. Instigated by an irresponsible person in the neighborhood, she set fire to the temple, hoping that when the temple was lost, it would be easier to meet Sahei. The fire destroyed the temple and many other houses. For the crime of incendiarism, she was sentenced to death by *hi-aburi*, that is, by being tied to a stake and burned to death.

O-Shichi was not only unlucky in love and marriage, but also had to die by fire, because she was born in the year of the fire-emitting horse.

It has been generally believed since Edo days that numerous fires will occur in the year of the *hinoe-uma*.

Persons born in the year of *u* or rabbit are meek and weak. They are good-natured, but easily led astray by others who are stronger-willed. They have a lovable personality, and will be liked by all. They will never become leaders, but they will be always happy, as they meekly accept their fate.

Those of *tatsu* or dragon year are entitled to the best fortune. They will advance to high positions and become wealthy. But they are apt to fall from their high positions unexpectedly. They have attained the highest level, from which they have no chance to advance higher, but may fall down.

The *mi* or snake year foretells an abundant life. Snakes are lucky, and will bring wealth. But at the same time, those of the snake year are crafty and vindictive. They cannot be trusted, though they may become rich and prosperous.

The snake is generally regarded as a symbol of jealousy and vindictiveness. Many tales have jealous women turning into snakes for vindictive purposes. But on the other hand, it is also popularly believed that snakes are a lucky sign, predicting monetary profit.

So the year of the snake is welcomed by many as a lucky time when they will be fortunate in acquiring a goodly amount of money. So in *mi-no-toshi*, and particularly on the day of the snake, those believing the tradition visit the shrines of Benten or Benzaiten (Sarasvati), as snakes are the messengers of the deity.

Benten is one of the seven gods of good luck. Benten originally stood for wisdom and prosperity, but commonly it is a feminine deity of music and beauty. As snakes are said to be her messengers, the people who believe in the charm of the snake for monetary benefit visit the shrines.

Particularly on the first day of the snake of any year, there is always a huge crowd visiting Benten. The first snake day of the snake year has a double charm.

The Zeniarai-Benten of Kamakura has been popular among the people of the entire Kanto area ever since Tokugawa days. A peculiar custom of washing money in the shrine pond is observed. The believers take their bank notes, bonds and securities to the shrine. After praying before the deity, they wash their money and bonds. They firmly believe that, when washed with the pond water their money will double. Because of this custom, the shrine has been called Zeniarai-Benten or coin-washing Benten.

Of course formerly only coins were washed, and so they were dumped into a pail of water drawn from the pond. As hard coins are now of small sums and the people use more paper money, water is merely sprinkled over the bundles. There are some eager persons who do not hesitate to dip their thick bundles of bank notes into the water, but then they have a hard time wiping

333

the wet notes dry.

The year of the horse is predicted to be active and progressive.

Horses are regarded sacred by the people. This comes from the tradition that when *kami* descend to earth from heaven, they come on horseback. Thus in many shrines sacred white horses are kept for their *kami*. Visitors feed the sacred horses and pray for their welfare. It is also said that the big ears of the horses will hear all prayers without fail.

When and where it is impossible to keep horses, stone or wooden images are kept in barns specially erected in the shrine compounds.

It is believed that those born in *uma* years love luxury and good appearance, have a chivalrous sentiment, enjoy public respect but lack steadiness. They will be blessed with good fortune if they try hard sincerely and gain the confidence of others.

The *hitsuji* or sheep is defenseless, and so persons born in this year often come to failure, not because of their own fault, but by the selfish will of others. The persons of this year, however, are tender and kind in nature, and loved by all associates. But they are too weak to fight through hardship and rivalry.

Saru or monkey-year men are clever, but lack constancy. They are qualified to become teachers, religious workers and artists. But they are not of a practical bent, being influenced by temperament and inconsistency. *Saru*-year persons will succeed if they pursue their work with determination.

Tori or fowl-year persons are fickle, and change their minds often. Thus they seldom succeed. But they are clever and fond of mechanical work. They are good-hearted, but they cannot stick to one endeavor very long. They are changeable in temperament and in-

clination.

Inu or dog-year men are faithful, but achieve little success unless they are well-guided by others. They need good men to guide and protect them. Their lovable nature, however, wins them friends. Dog-year men are advised to have strong-willed wives able to push them on to success.

Those born in the year of the boar are courageous and head-strong. Boars are said to be not able to turn aside once they have started on their rash run. So the persons of this year are reckless, and often come to grief.

They are active and progressive, but have the fault of doing rash things for which they regret later. They are advised to think before acting.

DAY'S FORTUNE

EVERY DAY has its fixed fortune. Thus there are lucky as well as unlucky days. This superstitious belief that originally came from China with the old lunar calendar still guides the daily life of many Japanese. There is a day which is believed to be good for holding wedding ceremonies. Then there is a day which is avoided by all for holding funerals. Old-fashioned people still consult the lunar calendar to decide on what day to go on a journey or open a new business. They believe that the day's fortune will decide the final result of business transactions or trips started.

Under what is called the *rokuyo* (six days) system, there are six different days coming in the order of *sensho*, *tomobiki*, *senpu*, *butsumetsu*, *taian* and *shakku*. January 1 is *sensho*, January 2 is *tomobiki*, January 3 is *senpu*, and so on. Then February starts with *tomobiki*, March with *senpu* and so on. It goes on for the first six months and the same order is repeated from

July to December. Thus the first day of July has the same fortune of the first day of January.

Of all these six days, *taian* is the luckiest day. It is invariably on this day that wedding ceremonies are commonly held. The marriage consummated on this lucky day is assured of success, happiness and prosperity. Then business transactions or anything else done on the day is promised success and prosperity. The day is particularly good for opening new shops or entering new occupations. Trips are successful if started on *taian* days.

Butsumetsu is the unlucky day for everything, and also *shakku* is a very unlucky day. Those two days are avoided as far as possible for doing anything new or important. Things done on those days are bound to end in failure and sadness. It is commonly believed that it is on these days that people are killed, things are stolen, or other unpleasant misfortunes happen.

Tomobiki is a semi-lucky day, but it is also believed that whatever happens or is done on the day is liable to happen again. Thus it is a good day for happy matters, but an evil day for unpleasant things.

Particularly to be avoided is holding funerals on *tomobiki* days, because it is believed that if a funeral is held on the day, there will be another funeral soon in the same family. Even such persons who do not give any thought to other days of the *rokuyo* become quite sensitive about *tomobiki* if unpleasant things happen on the day.

Sensho is the day when disputes or legal matters will result in success. It is also a good day to undertake urgent or important affairs. Journeys may also be started on this day with success and a happy ending.

Senpu is the opposite of *sensho*, and a very bad day for disputes and legal mat-

ters. All avoid making any dispute with others or starting anything important on this day.

Some may say that the superstitions about the old lunar calendar are dying, but if one notices how many wedding ceremonies are held on *taian* days, and how many of the Japanese are unwilling to hold funerals on *tomobiki* it will be clearly seen how strong is the hold of the superstitions on the people as yet. Particularly among rural folks the lunar calendar is still the guide for their daily life. Modern calendars do not give the old *rokuyo* days, but older people are always ready to tell the young generation what fortune the day has for them.

DOYO

DOYO IS A period for 18 or 19 days at the end of each of the four seasons. There are, therefore, four *doyo* in one year, but in the general use of the term, it always means the summer *doyo*, because of its predominating importance and as the three others are almost forgotten.

According to an ancient Chinese theory, the seasons were controlled by *gogyo* or the five elements of fire, wood, soil, metal and water. That is to say, fire controlled summer, wood spring, metal autumn and water winter. The last element — soil — controlled the 18 days at the end of each season. The days controlled by the soil were called *doyo*, the end of which marked the beginning of the next season.

The hour when *doyo* begins was meteorogically fixed. The four *doyo* started when the celestian longitude reached 27, 117, 207 and 297 degrees respectively. So there were good reasons for marking the season with *doyo*.

Doyo fixes the seasonal period and governs crops. Farmers set their activities by it. The *doyo* period is fixed by the position of the sun, and so it may be said to be scientifically based. That is to say, the spring *doyo* starts on April 17 when celestial longitude reaches 27 degrees. Then, the summer *doyo* commences on July 20, with the sun at 117 degrees; the autumn *doyo* on October 20, when the sun's position is 207 degrees; and the winter *doyo* on January 18, with the position of the sun at 297 degrees. The spring and autumn *doyo* have 18 days, but the summer and winter *doyo* have 19 days. After the end of each *doyo* the next season starts.

The summer *doyo*, or dog-days from July 20 to August 7, is most important, because the weather during the period will determine the rice crop. It is believed that the weather on *doyo-saburo* or third day of *doyo* will determine the size of the coming harvest.

To city dwellers, *ushi-no-hi* or cow's day during the summer *doyo* has become quite important. It is the day when the people, particularly Tokyo residents, eat their *unagi* or eels. The custom is said to have been started about 150 years ago by the citizens of Edo. As to its origin many different stories are told. But on the day, tons of eels are consumed in Tokyo alone. It is believed that the eating of eels on the cow's day in the *doyo* season will ensure one's health through the hot season. In some years, there are two *ushi-no-hi* during the period, and then eel merchants do double business.

In the summer *doyo* period, it has also been an old custom to bring out and air clothing. It is called *doyo-boshi*. Formerly it was quite an event, as all the clothing was taken out and hung over ropes stretched in all directions throughout the house, so that the dampness they accumulated during the *tsuyu* season would be aired out.

Rolling waves that beat the shores in summer are called *doyo-nami*, because they come just at that time. *Doyo-nami* are not high, but come at regular intervals. They are caused by a distant storm in the south of the country.

DRINKING CUPS

THE JAPANESE drink their *sake* from tiny porcelain cups, but this habit is less than 200 years old. In former days, the people used big lacquered wooden cups. Of course in those days, *sake* was taken cold and not warmed.

At early banquets, *sake* was served in a set of three or sometimes five *sakazuki* or drinking cups. The largest one was placed at the bottom with the smallest placed on the top. First the uppermost or smallest one was filled with *sake* and taken to the person at the head of the room. He sipped a mouthful or two, and the cup was passed to the next person. All drank from the same cup. Thus those at the end of the room had to wait long for their turn.

But soon there developed a custom of starting one cup from the head of the room, and another from the end, so that everyone did not have to wait long for their drinks. The three cups were passed around three times each. This ceremony was called *san-san-kudo* or three-three-nine times. But today this way of drinking is only observed at wedding ceremonies.

Small individual porcelain or lacquered cups appeared in the Tokugawa period. This was partly due to the new habit of warming up *sake*, but it might have been thought up by those who had to wait long when the same cup was passed around in order.

At first *sake* of poor quality was warmed up to improve its taste. *Sake* was also often warmed in the cold winter season. This habit, started by poor men, became popular among all classes of *sake* lovers, and also at any season of the year.

At Japanese formal parties it is still customary to exchange *sakazuki*. At a proper moment, the host goes to the honored guest to receive his *sakazuki*. At the host's request, the guest empties his cup and hands it to him. When the cup is filled and drunk by the host, it is returned to the guest who also drinks out of it. This exchange of *sakazuki* means the recognition of friendship among equals or conferment of honor on those of lower social or official ranks.

When there are many guests, the host has to go to each of them to receive his cup in succession. Cups are also exchanged at informal drinking parties among all present to signify that all are good pals.

This custom of offering or exchanging *sakazuki* is old. Feudal lords used to give a cup of *sake* to their retainers in recognition of their special services of merit. But the *sakazuki* given by a lord to his retainer was not returned, as retainers were in no position to offer their masters a drink.

It is also from this custom that the system of granting Imperial cups developed. To honor men and women for their meritorious service to the state, the Emperor gives gold, silver or lacquer *sakazuki* marked with the Imperial crest, according to the degree of merit. The awarding of Imperial cups is done without actually drinking *sake*.

Then, among gangsters, gamblers and traveling showmen, the idea that to receive *sakazuki* from another is to pledge oneself to a bond of service or fraternity is still very firmly held.

EARTHQUAKE FORECAST

JAPAN IS A land of earthquakes. The number of earth tremors felt in one year reaches many thousands and those felt by seismographs would run into tens of thousands. Most of them are slight tremors and do little damage, but once in a while a big quake causes a huge loss of human life and destruction of many houses. In the Kanto area earthquake on September 1, 1923, 105,000 lives were lost and 60,000 were injured, while nearly 3,000,000 houses were either smashed outright or destroyed by fire and tidal waves that followed, and 700,000 more houses were partially damaged.

Therefore, it is quite natural for the people to be in extreme fear of earthquakes. *'Jishin, kaminari, kaji, oyaji'* (earthquake, thunder, fire, father) runs an old saying, showing that earthquakes are the first of the four things the people fear most.

Fearing them and suffering from their destruction, since very ancient days the people watched and studied the effects of dreadful earthquakes, though not so scientifically. This study was made through many centuries, handed down from generation to generation. The long and careful observation of earthquakes developed a method of predicting weather by the hour when an earthquake happens. Modern scientists may laugh at this, yet there might be something in the conclusions reached after careful observations made for centuries of the hours of earthquakes and the weather conditions following their occurrences.

This custom of foretelling weather by the hours of an earthquake became popular in Tokugawa days, and is still observed by old folks, particularly in the rural districts. They have put this weather prediction method in the following words:

Nine brings sickness:
Five and seven, rain:
Four tells weather dry:
Six and eight, the coming wind.

In old days in Japan, the hour-reckoning method was different from that at present. The present-day two hours were figured as one hour, and the counting went backward. Thus the present ten o'clock was the hour of four; eight o'clock the hour of five; six o'clock the hour of six; four o'clock the hour of seven; two o'clock the hour of eight; and twelve o'clock the hour of nine. Thus, when the above saying is translated into present clock hours, it becomes:

Twelve o'clock, sickness:

Eight and four o'clock, rain:

Ten o'clock tells weather dry:

Six and two o'clock the coming wind.

If an earthquake happens at the hour of five, or eight o'clock, it is a prediction that the following day will have rain. When earthquakes predict changes in weather, such changes come within a day or two. But the earthquake at twelve o'clock foretells the spread of sickness, and its prediction may not come true immediately after the shock.

Modern people may not have faith in the above method of foretelling weather by earthquakes, but it may be worth noting.

ECLIPTIC LUCK

THE SUN RULES their fortune, it has always been thought by the Japanese. This belief has even developed to almost sun worship in the case of many persons. The beginning of the nation is told with the legend of the Sun Goddess. Lucky days come when the earth is in a good relation to the sun, it is believed. From this tradition has come the common expression *kodo-kichijitsu* or day of ecliptic luck. It is always on such lucky days that wedding ceremonies and other happy celebrations are held.

Not only does the sun rule man's for-tune, but it also controls the growth of farm crops. So farmers follow the signs of the sun in sowing and harvesting crops.

The four seasons of the year — spring, summer, autumn and winter — are ruled by the sun. Though the old calendar used in Japan was based on the moon, the four seasons have always been based on the sun. Hence months and seasons do not agree. For instance, the lunar New Year in 1948 started on February 10, but the spring season began five days earlier on February 5. It may thus be said that spring began in December of the previous year.

The Japanese season of spring begins on *risshun* (beginning of spring), February 5, when the celestial longitude or the angle of the sun's path to the equator reaches 315 degrees. Summer starts on *rikka* (beginning of summer), May 5, when the celestial longitude reaches 45 degrees, autumn commences on *risshu* (beginning of autumn), August 3, with the angle of the sun's path at 135 degrees, and winter on *ritto* (beginning of winter), November 7, with the celestial longitude at 225 degrees.

Farmers all over the country still follow tradition based on the sun's movement for their farming activities. All important dates for farming are calculated from *risshun* or the beginning of spring, and not from the beginning of the calendar year — lunar or solar.

Hachijuhachiya (88th evening) which is an important day for farmers, as it is commonly believed that frost is likely to form up to that date and spring sowing should be done after that day, is the 88th day after *risshun.* Then *nihyaku-toka* (210th day) and *nihyaku-hatsuka* (220th day) are the days when terrible typhoons are expected to visit Japan from southern regions to cause serious damage to farm crops. They are also calculated from *risshun* and fall on September 1 and 11, respectively.

FULL MOON FESTIVAL

THE FULL MOON of mid-autumn is believed to be the most beautiful, although each lunar month has one full moon. Thus a rite to worship and admire the moon is held on the day by all classes of people.

The autumn moon is particularly beautiful as the air becomes dry and the sky clear, after the humid summer season. The appreciation of the beauty of the moon is further enhanced by the popular worship of the moon as something divine.

Little children call the moon *nono-sama*, a term which is originally a baby word for Buddha. As soon as they notice the moon, babies are told to worship it. '*Nono-sama* is watching you,' the mother often says when the baby does not behave. This spirit of worshiping the moon naturally heightened the people's love of the moon, particularly the autumn full moon. All are quite disappointed if the moon is invisible on that evening due to bad weather.

From ancient days the people have formed parties to watch and admire the autumn moon. At home they erect little stands in the garden or veranda to place offerings to the moon. This consists of *dango* or rice-dumplings, fruits and vegetables of the season. Blossoming *susuki* (Miscanthus sinensis) which is always associated with the moon is placed in vases on the stand.

Sitting at a place where the moon can be conveniently viewed, they drink *sake* and partake of specially prepared food. They compose poems on the moon. Or, to get the best view of the moon, they go to the top of a hill or to the shore of the sea or a river.

In the old days, elaborate parties were held at Court and by great nobles to view the moon. No such great parties are held today, but all households, rich or poor, observe the traditional rite of worshiping the full moon of autumn.

The month of August is associated with the moon in many traditions of the people. In *hanagaruta* or flower playing cards, the symbol for August is the full moon. Rites as well as parties to view and appreciate the beauty of the August moon are held.

In the Shonai district of Yamagata Prefecture, a moon-watching rite called *Goriyaku-sama* (divine favor) is held on August 25. It is believed that on that evening the moon shows itself in a strange, unexpected shape by which the fortune of the year can be judged.

It is a special day for the people. They stop their work early, and after dinner, women and children dress in their best clothes. As night approaches, they gather in houses, from which all the *shoji* have been removed, situated near bridges or other places from where the moon can be viewed to advantage. Of course, if it rains that evening, the rite is canceled.

As the moon rises, the people watch it with hushed interest and follow its movement through the sky. They look to see if the crescent moon is pointing up, sideways or down. The moon changes its shape as it proceeds westward. Sometimes it takes the shape of a boat or a candle, they say.

The people foretell their fortune for the year, particularly of their rice crop, by the way the moon changes.

In Okinawa, the people go up to a high place on the evening of August 15 and look over the village bathed by moonlight. By what they see, they learn what house or houses in the village will have some unexpected turn of events during the year.

In many southern and western localities, *tsunahiki* or tug-of-war is held on the *jugoya* evening to foretell the harvest and fortune. The same rite is held in northeastern districts on January 15.

Kanai in Kagoshima is famous for its tug-of-war. The boys, 10 to 15, of each district participate in the game. A rope, from 100 to 200 yards long, and one to two feet thick is made, with a loop at each end. In the evening the rope is brought to a street corner where a strong stake is driven into the ground.

As the moon rises and the rope is stretched along the street with its center at the stake, the boys from one section hold one end and those from another the other end. The tug-of-war starts at the beating of a drum. As one group succeeds in pulling the rope and the loop at the other end nears the stake, the loop is put over it.

Then the fun commences. The boys whose rope has been looped over the stake, jump on the boys of the other end to make them lose their hold on the rope. Sometimes they manage to pull the rope and put the other loop on the stake. The struggle is repeated many times, until the rope breaks or purposely is cut to end the game with the approach of dawn.

The winning side will be favored with a good harvest and luck, while the losing side must wait until the next *jugoya* to have a better chance.

The game of *kagefumi* or shadow stepping was enjoyed by children during Edo and Meiji years. Going outdoors on a bright moonlit evening they tried to step on each other's shadow cast by the moon on the ground. Some became bold and tried to step on the shadow of a passing man or woman. To have one's shadow stepped on by others was considered to be unlucky.

GOOD WEATHER DOLL

TERU-TERU BOZU or sunshine doll is still made by many Japanese, particularly little boys and girls. Whenever rain continues day after day and they are kept indoors, or when some picnic or outing is scheduled, they make *teru-teru bozu* to pray for fair weather.

First they roll some paper into a small round ball, and wrap it up with another sheet to make the head of the doll. A sheet folded into a pointed triangle shape is attached to form the body. Sometimes eyes are painted on the head.

Teru-teru bozu thus made are hung from tree branches in the garden, and then the children chant *Teru-teru bozu, ashita tenki ni-nare (Teru-teru bozu,* bring fair weather tomorrow). They can then go to bed with the hope that the following day will be fine.

When *teru-teru bozu* answers the prayer of the children and brings fair weather, she is given a drink of *sake* in many districts. When she fails, she will be left dangling in the rain until she wilts and drops into the mud as punishment. Next time, it is hoped, she will answer the children's prayer.

This little custom is followed in the Kanto area more widely than in other districts, but it originated in Kyoto, where it seems to have first been started by the ladies of the aristocratic circles. *Teru-teru bozu* is mentioned in *Kagero-Nikki,* a diary written by a woman covering a period of 21 years in the 10th century. The custom evidently must have already been popular at that time.

It is also said that the custom came from China. In China, as early as in the Ming dynasty (14th-17th centuries), there was a custom of making a doll with a red or green paper costume, to pray for fair weather.

Both in China and Japan, *teru-teru bozu* is regarded as a female, but in Japan she is made entirely of white paper, while the Chinese gave her red or green dresses.

KUWABARA

WHENEVER a distant rolling of thunder is heard or a flash of lightning seen, many persons who are particularly afraid of thunderbolts utter loudly '*Kuwabara, kuwabara.*' By merely shouting '*kuwabara,*' one will be safe from lightning, it is widely believed.

The origin of *kuwabara* is not definitely known, but it has nothing to do with mulberry plants, though it means 'mulberry fields.' It seems, however, to have originated in the village of Kuwabara in the province of Izumi, which forms a part of the Present Osaka Prefecture. Many centuries ago, it is said, numerous thunderbolts played havoc throughout Izumi province and caused great casualties, but the village of Kuwabara alone remained miraculously unscathed. This strange fact made the villagers and neighboring people believe that there must be something about Kuwabara that scared away lightning. When the approaching thunderbolt hears the shout of '*Kuwabara,*' it will go away as it will not visit any place known by that name, it is commonly believed.

Then, there is another version which is an elaboration of the above story. Once a thunderbolt fell into a well in the village of Kuwabara by accident, but the villagers quickly put a strong cover over the well. So the thunderbolt could not get out of the well and return to the sky. Only when it promised that it would never again visit the village did the villagers consent to lift the cover and let the thunderbolt return home.

Since that time no lightning ever struck the village, the story goes.

In both stories, the thunderbolt has some reason to avoid the village of Kuwabara. The very name of the village will cause fear in the heart of the thunderbolt. So the people say '*Kuwabara*' whenever the rolling thunder approaches, believing that the mention of the village name will surely ensure their safety from thunderbolts.

As this belief is widely held by the people, *Kuwabara* came to possess a much wider significance. It is believed to keep one from any other danger, threat or misfortune. Thus when the people hear of unpleasant news, or misfortunes falling on others, they will say '*Kuwabara*' to ensure themselves against such calamities or evils.

LEAP MONTH

IN THE OLD lunar calendar, a month is the period from one full moon to another, or, to say precisely, 29 and a half days. Thus, for practical purposes, a month of 29 days and a month of 30 days come alternately. In 12 months, therefore, there are only 354 days, or 11 days less than in the solar calendar. In this manner, the lunar calendar season will gradually fall behind the actual season of nature, so that whenever it comes 29 or 30 days behind the season, an extra *uru-u* month or leap month is created, in order to catch up with the movement of the sun. Thus, the *uru-u* month comes about every third year, but may come at any time during the year. When it comes in February, for instance, it is believed that the winter season will be not only one month longer than usual but the cold will be very severe. Moreover, if the extra month comes in summer, it is predicted that the heat will be unbearable and the dog-days long. Thus the year with a leap month has 13 months in all. But in the lunar calendar there is no leap year of the solar calendar which gives February an extra day.

The lunar calendar has so long governed the life and activities of the people and particularly farmers, that the custom of fixing the time for sowing, harvesting, drying cereals, pickling *daikon* (radish) or many other farming activities by the seasons of the lunar calendar has not at all died out, although to use the old calendar is now prohibited. Formerly it had been customary to have the lunar calendar days also marked on the solar calendar, but this custom was prohibited some years ago. At present, therefore, for ordinary city or town dwellers it is impossible to know the lunar calendar days, but farmers who are strictly following the lunar seasons know without referring to any printed calendar the days and seasons of the lunar calendar. It is because they will be lost and become unable to obtain good farm harvests if they forget the lunar calendar even for one day. They believe that the lunar calendar fits the natural changes of seasons far better than the solar calendar.

LUNAR CALENDAR

THE OLD lunar calendar adopted in Japan since the reign of Emperor Kinmei (539-571) was replaced by the solar calendar in 1872 as one of the first steps to modernize the country. Thus the old calendar based on the movement of the moon is no longer officially recognized.

Yet the people, particularly those of rural districts, still go by the old calendar. Thus the sale of old lunar calendars becomes brisk at the beginning of every year.

This old-fashioned calendar, how-

ever, is different from what was issued in ancient years. It gives the days of the week, festivals, national holidays, and the hours of sunrise and sunset by the solar calendar, while it also gives many important seasonal features of the lunar calendar. Thus this calendar generally becomes a small volume of more than 100 pages.

Besides the solar calendar information, *koyomi* (calendar) tells the people what lies in store for them according to the zodiacal years of their births, and the good and bad directions during the year. Each day's fortune is also mentioned, so that the people may know what can be expected of the day. The 24 seasonal events of the lunar calendar are particularly important to farmers, whose farming activities have long been guided by the seasons.

Such festive events as *setsubun* (bean throwing day), *nyubai* (beginning of the rainy season), *higan* (equinoctial day), *obon* (feast of the souls), the 210th day, and others are mentioned in the new calendar, but they are taken from the old.

A *koyomi* also is a book of divination in most cases. Not only does each day have a different fortune, and one's fortune differs according to the year of birth, but it also tells how to tell one's fortune by physiognomy, palm lines or moles on the face. The *koyomi* is also a marriage guide, as it tells the affinity between men and women of various birth-year fortunes.

For those believing in old medicinal traditions, ancient herbs and medicinal treatments are mentioned. Even the interpretation of various dreams is given, so that one will know what his dream means.

NINE SUNS

ONCE DURING the reign of Emperor

Suijin in the first century, there appeared nine suns in the sky in a row. The people were alarmed at the strange sight and feared that some evil calamity would come, an old book relates.

An eminent astronomer was consulted, who said that the one at the northern end was the real sun, and all the others were crows taking the shape of the sun. So it was proposed to kill the evil crows, and a high tower was erected, while eight master archers were selected. Standing on the platform of the tower, the eight were ordered to shoot their arrows at the eight crow-suns. The crows were killed and the eight suns disappeared.

There are many other tales in which arrows have been shot at the sun. In Kumamoto it is told that once an earth mole found the sun too hot and thought of shooting an arrow at the sun in anger. But a toad learned of the mole's plan, and secretly told the sun what the mole was planning to do. The sun thought the mole impertinent, and to punish it, buried it under the ground. At the same time, the sun was thankful for the toad's act, and rewarded it by always keeping the river water warm while it was rearing its young.

In another story a man-eating mole thought that if there was no sun and it was always dark, it would be able to eat more men. So it planned to shoot the sun and kill it.

NONO-SAMA

JAPANESE children call the moon *nono-sama*. Originally it was Buddha or a prayer to Buddha that was called *nono-sama* in baby language. But by also calling the moon *nono-sama* the moon has become an object of worship to Japanese children. In old-fashioned families, the grandmother still teaches her little grandchildren to bow and pray to *nono-sama* whenever the bright moon rises.

Thus the idea of worshiping and praying to the moon has been planted in the minds of Japanese children for many centuries. The resemblance of the full moon to the halo of the Buddha statue, it is said, first created the habit of worshiping the moon and calling it *nono-sama*.

Along with this idea, children are also told that the moon is always watching them and would know what they were doing. 'Don't. The moon is watching and laughing at you,' says the mother, whenever little children misbehave.

The beauty and romance of the moon have been enhanced by the religious attitude that is created in the children's mind, and there also developed the custom of organizing special parties to view the moon. By seashores or on mountains where the moon can be viewed to the best advantage, moon-viewing parties are held.

The moon of love and romance has created a very strange expression in the Japanese language. *Gekka-hyojin* (man under the moon and on the ice) means a person who arranges a marriage. This strange term is based on traditional tales of China.

In the Tang period, Wei Ku one day saw a traveler resting by the road. The man was sitting down, leaning against his traveling bag, and reading a book by moonlight. He saw a red rope in the traveler's bag, and asked him what it was for. 'For tying people in marriage,' the traveler replied. So the man under the moon became a term to indicate one who arranges a marriage.

In the second tale, Ling Hu-tse, in the Chin period, once dreamed that he stood on ice frozen over a stream and talked with a person who was under the ice. He had the dream interpreted by a diviner. As he stood on the ice, he represented the positive, the diviner explained, and the man under the ice was the negative. As they talked, the positive and the negative were united, and the dream predicted that Ling was going to arrange a marriage.

Putting these two old Chinese stories together, the strange expression *gekkahyojin* (man under the moon and on the ice) was coined.

NO-THUNDER VILLAGE

OLD RESIDENTS of Kasai, Edogawa, Tokyo, still believe that no thunder comes to their district. Behind this tradition there are three related incidents.

When Kasai was only a small fishing village, an old Buddhist priest came to a poor fisherman's house one night and asked for lodging. Next morning the priest said that he had no money to pay for the kindness and left a wooden statue of *Fudo* (Acala) as a token of his appreciation. A few years later an epidemic visited the village. The villagers said that the disease was caused because the *Fudo* statue was neglected, being left amidst cobwebs and dust. So they erected a temple for the statue and named it Shinzo-in.

Around the temple were planted five pine trees, which soon grew big and became the guiding mark for fishing boats returning to the shore. One day a boat going from Edo to Gyotoku met a storm off Kasai shore, but the boatman saw a light in the stormy darkness and guiding his craft toward the light, managed to reach the shore. He saw that the light which had guided him was a pine tree. Looking closely at the light, the boatman saw that it was an eye of a dragon. As it had saved him, he bowed to it. The dragon then disappeared, dropping a sword. This sword was presented to the *Fudo* in Shinzo-in Temple.

In the Eiroku era (1558-1570), a great thunderstorm visited Kasai felling trees, breaking boats and tossing houses. Then from the direction of Shinzo-in came a loud groaning noise. The furious thunderstorm suddenly ended. As the villagers entered the temple they found blood covering the whole inside and a bloodstained sword on the floor. They learned that *Fudo* had killed the thunder with the sword.

They named it *Ikazuchi-Fudo* or Thunder *Fudo*. They became happy as the thunder was killed and no more thunderstorms would visit the village.

RABBIT IN THE MOON

A LONE RABBIT lives in the moon, and it is always pounding *mochi* in a wooden mortar, Japanese children say. They will tell you that in the full moon the rabbit is clearly visible.

Although it is not known how the idea of a rabbit in the moon originated, this belief was started by the common Japanese expression *mochitsuki* (the long-expected full moon). This name for the moon, of course, came from the eager impatience with which the people wait for the appearance of the full moon. *Mochitsuki* also means the pounding of *mochi* or rice-cakes. Thus in the people's and particularly children's minds, the full moon and *mochi*-pounding came to be associated together. Both are what are most desirable to them — one to view and the other to eat.

Somehow, it is also said that to the eyes of the people and children the dark patches on the surface of the moon formed the outline of a rabbit. Children, fond of rabbits, were pleased to see a rabbit in the moon. Thus, it is believed by many, the rabbit in the moon pounding *mochi* came into existence.

There is also a belief that in the moon stands a giant *katsura* or Japanese Judas tree. The *katsura* of the moon has become a synonym for something we can see but cannot touch. The *katsura* tree in the moon is said to be more than 500 feet high, and many persons say that they see its shadow on the surface of the moon.

There is a man in the moon who is constantly trying to cut down this *katsura* tree, according to Chinese tradition. But he will never be able to cut it down. Once in China there was a man named Wu Kang, who was a great master of the occult art. But because he abused his power greatly, he was sent to the moon and given the task of cutting down the *katsura* tree as his punishment. He therefore daily takes up his big hatchet and swings it against the tree trunk. Small chips of wood fly as his hatchet strikes the tree, but the cuts are instantly covered up. Every time he faces the tree with his raised hatchet, he sees the smooth and undamaged trunk. Hence he keeps on cutting at the tree but makes no progress.

THUNDER

THE ROLLING thunder is made by *Kaminari-san* or *Raijin*. He lives up on the summer clouds, and is always naked, wearing only a loincloth made of tiger skin. He has horns on his head and tusks in his wide mouth. On his back, he carries about a dozen round, flat drums, arranged in a circle, and holds drumsticks in his hands. When he beats his drums, the thunder rolls out through the sky and puts fear into the people on earth.

He comes down to this earth whenever he wishes to eat *o-heso* or human navels. He is very fond of them, and this fondness causes him to fall from the sky. Whenever children run around naked in summer, mothers say, 'Put on your clothes or *Kaminari-san* will come and take your *o-heso.*' Then little boys will hurry to cover themselves up. Many old persons still put their hands on their stomach whenever they hear the distant rolling of thunder.

Kaminari-san takes *o-heso*, but does not cause other damage. The damage that comes with thunder is done by *Raiju* (thunder-animal). It comes down with the thunder, and tears down trees and houses. On such trees or houses that are torn up by *Raiju* marks of its sharp claws are always seen, it is said. Nobody has seen the animal, but it is described to be somewhat similar in general form to a dog, and is covered with gray hair. But its tail is like that of a fox, and its claws are long and sharp. It is a lazy animal and is always found asleep while the weather is fair. But as soon as it hears the rolling of thunder, it opens its eyes and becomes suddenly active. It follows the thunder to the earth, and causes damage to humans, trees, houses and crops.

To protect temples from destruction by thunder and storm, statues of *Raijin* and *Fujin* are sometimes placed at the temple gates. *Fujin* is the god of wind, and it can be easily identified by the large bag of wind it carries over his shoulder.

In its general use, the term *kaminari* covers the whole phenomenon of thunder and lightning. Thus, in the Japanese language, *kaminari* rolls and also flashes.

Japanese farmers have always believed that *inazuma* or lightning brings them good rice harvests. This belief is based upon the tradition that *inazuma* is the husband of the rice plant, and that as lightning flashes over the rice-field, the rice plant conceives and bears grain. Thus without *inazuma* there will be no rice harvest.

Another word for lightning is *ina-bikari* which means rice flash. Thus both words tell the relation between lightning and rice crops. Lightning usually occurs when the rice plant is growing and ripening, as science may explain today. But the ancient farmers fully recognized this phenomenon.

In this belief, however, lightning is definitely entirely separate from thunder. There must be lightning without thunder to make the rice bear grain.

Thus, in Sagami (now Kanagawa Prefecture) it has been said that only when there is distant thunder and only flashes of lightning without thunderclaps is a good rice harvest assured. When such flashes appear over their rice fields, they rejoice.

Because of this happy prediction by lightning, the people have used various forms of lightning as designs for various purposes. There are many family crests which consist of forms of lightning flashes. On fabrics, lacquerware and other things designs of lightning have been widely used.

A kind of nail which is used to hang pictures on the *tokonoma* or alcove in the main room of the Japanese house is called *inazuma* nail, as it is bent to form a design said to represent the lightning flash.

Raiden-sama or god of thunderbolts is worshiped as a god of mercy. Throughout the farming regions stone tablets are still seen bearing the inscription of *Raiden-gami.*

These stone tablets are worshiped by the villagers as the guardian of their happiness. Particularly when farmers lack water and have to pray for rain, they make offerings to *Raiden-sama.*

However, in the mountain regions of Gunma and Tochigi where thunderbolts come very often during the summer and cause damage to forests, farms and villages, the stone tablets are believed to be charms for preventing thunderbolts.

But as rain usually comes with thunder and lightning, many farming areas welcome *Kaminari-san,* who as the god of mercy brings the needed rain. So in many districts, when a thunderbolt hits a ricefield, the farmers surround the spot with freshly-cut bamboo, and place *shimenawa* or cut white paper on the branches to mark it as a holy place.

Huge trees charred by thunderbolts are also regarded as sacred and often marked with *shimenawa.* In many regions there are big pine trees named *Raiden-matsu* or thunder pine, but such pines have never been hit by thunderbolts. Generally they are so named in thanks for some unusual phenomenon that has brought happiness to the district.

Thus, while thunderbolts are extremely dreaded by the people, there is also a strong conviction among rural folks in the traditional belief that they are to be worshiped as the bringer of happiness.

TSUYU

TSUYU or rainy season that generally lasts about one month from the middle of June is the most disagreeable season in Japan. Drizzling rain continues day after day, and dampness penetrates everything. The total rainfall does not amount to much, but it is the continued dampness that makes the season so unhealthy and unpleasant.

Thick molds have to be brushed off one's shoes every morning. Matches will not light. Cigarettes and tobacco become musty. Books are mildewed. *Tatami* and all clothing become damp. Rain, dampness and the lack of sunshine make people irritable and inactive. They become easy prey to all kinds of illness. Outdoor workers suffer particularly, as they can earn no wages for so long.

To fight the unhealthy effect of the season, the people have formed the habit of taking very hot baths. A hot bath will stimulate blood circulation and also the functioning of all internal organs which are dulled by the prolonged damp weather. The people's habit of taking a very hot bath is to protect their health during the *tsuyu* season.

Often too, many people burn incense over a charcoal fire to reduce the dampness in the house. *Okera* or a little plant of the chrysanthemum species is dried and burned in charcoal braziers. The burning of incense has some effect in dispelling the dampness in small houses. But it is the presence of live charcoals in the room to burn incense that dries the air of the room.

The season comes just when the wheat and barley are being harvested, and in years when rainfall is particularly great, these crops suffer. But again it is welcomed by farmers because it gives their paddyfields sufficient water for planting rice. When the rainfall in the season is slight, many districts have difficulty in planting rice. Hence there are also some good sides to this unpleasant season.

TYPHOON FORECASTING

IT IS JUST about the time when rice plants are blossoming or about to form their grain that typhoons visit Japan. When big typhoons hit the country squarely in their northeastern course, considerable damage is done to rice crops. The terrible storms carrying heavy rain not only directly injure rice plants by their brutal force, but also make them worthless by the damage caused by flooding that comes with the heavy rainfall.

To the farmers, therefore, typhoons are the most dreaded enemy. Yet they are helpless to combat the great force of nature. For ages, however, they have studied the natural phenomena that preceded the coming of typhoons, in the hope of learning beforehand of the enemy's arrival so that they might be ready for the coming destruction. Out of such observations, though not based on science, the generations of farmers found that there are certain natural happenings that always take place just before the coming of typhoons. Such discoveries made the farmers form their own system of forecasting typhoons.

The most common of such beliefs is that when birds build their nests or bees make their combs on lower branches of trees than in usual years, it is a certain sign that in the autumn of that year there will come big typhoons. It is also said that when ants and other insects come indoors in greater numbers than in normal years, a big typhoon is sure to come. These traditions are based on the theory that birds, bees, ants and other insects know somehow by their instinctive sensitivity that typhoons are about to come, and in order to save themselves and their eggs from destruction by flooding they build their nests or combs higher from the ground than usual and lower from the force of the wind.

Furthermore, various trees and plants are believed to know the coming of typhoons. When orange trees bear fruit to the very tip of their branches there will be no typhoon that year, but farmers are warned to be on guard when orange trees do not have fruit on the end of their branches. This is due to the belief that to protect their fruit from destruction by the strong wind, orange trees do not have fruit on the tender ends of branches when they sense the coming of typhoons.

When millet or maize (corn) have their strong roots rising up from the ground, that is a sign of coming typhoons. Against the ferocity of the wind and also the force of floods, those plants brace themselves up with stronger roots firmly implanted in the soil. It is also believed that when the vines of sweet potatoes stand up instead of crawling on the soil, that is another sign of typhoons.

Along seashore districts, it is believed that when turtles lay eggs on higher sand dunes than usual, it is a forecast of big typhoons. Turtles try to save their eggs from the force of typhoons and big waves.

There is a kind of reed called *kazegusa* or wind grass, and when its long leaves knot it is believed that there will be severe typhoons that year. The knots make the leaves strong to resist the force of the storm. Sometimes there are more than one knot on one leaf, and two or three knots mean there will come two or three typhoons.

If the leaves of *kozo* or paper mulberry tree roll up, there will surely be a big storm in the harvesting season, it is believed in some districts of the country.

YAKUBI

SEPTEMBER 1 or the 210th day, and September 11 or the 220th day, counting from *risshun* (beginning of spring) by the lunar calendar, are *yakubi* or evil days. The weather on those two days controls the rice crop of the year, so the people have learned from long experience. The farmer's fortune rests on the rice harvest, his main crop, and town dwellers, too, are concerned about the crop as a poor harvest means higher prices.

Just at the season when the rice begins to ripen, typhoons come from the southern region. There is seldom a year that does not have several typhoons which damage crops and destroy houses and roads.

Thus the month of September is a critical one for the people. Through long observation they have come to know that typhoons occur most frequently on the 210th and 220th days. So farmers as well as city people always pray for good weather on those two days. When the weather condition is favorable the whole nation rejoices.

When typhoons come later in the month the damage to the crop is comparatively small, though considerable harm might be caused to houses, forests and roads.

Chapter 11
Plants and Flowers

ASUNARO FLOWER

THE *ASUNARO* of the pine family growing in many mountain regions is much used as building material and also for making furniture, but in many old tales, its flower is mentioned as having a mystic power.

There once lived a poor couple and the husband became so depressed with their life of poverty that one day he left the house and his wife to go wandering. After his departure, a stranger came and said to the wife that her husband had asked him to take her away with him. So she went with the stranger.

When the husband returned home some days later, he found that his wife had gone and so he went in search of her. Three years passed and he met a white-haired old man who asked him what he was doing. He told the whole story of his search for his missing wife.

The old man then told him his wife had been stolen by a robber and was in a mountain hut with him. The robber had a great mansion, the old man explained, and at the gate there would be a long iron bar. 'Take up the bar and strike the ground with it three times, and the gate will open,' he instructed the husband.

So he went to the mansion in the forest, and finding the bar did as he was told. The gate opened, and his wife whom he had not seen for three years appeared.

They were both glad to see each other again. She brought out food for him but just then she heard the steps of her abductor returning, and giving her husband the sword of the robber, pushed him into a big empty jar. The robber entered the room and became angry when he saw two flowers blossoming on the *asunaro* in the room. The *asunaro* bears a flower when one male is present. Seeing two flowers, the robber knew that there was another man in the room beside him.

The wife lied that the other flower was for the boy to be soon born. Thus satisfied, the robber began to drink *sake*. When he became quite drunk, the husband came out of the jar and killed him.

The man and wife returned happily home. They became wealthy as they went again to the mountain mansion and carried away all the treasures the robber had hoarded on a thousand horses.

BAMBOO

TAKENOKO or bamboo sprout is a Japanese spring delicacy. It is used as a vegetable, and particularly *takenoko-meshi* or rice cooked with sliced *takenoko, shoyu* and other seasoning is welcomed as a sign of the season. Kyoto suburbs are especially famous for excellent table bamboo sprouts.

Bamboo is used in so many ways that a list of what is made of bamboo is really surprising. There are many kinds of bamboo, ranging in size from tiny slender ones to those over five or six inches across, some brownish in color and some spotted. Some are solid, but most kinds are hollow.

Its use is naturally different according to size and kind. Big ones are mostly used in making dippers, buckets, water pipes, eave troughs and bowls. For flag poles, step ladders, fences, gates and poles for hanging washing, those one to two inches in diameter are used. Those about one inch across are made into broom handles, various kinds of furniture, boxes, coat hangers and other articles. There are bamboo flutes and walking canes. Writing and painting brushes have bamboo handles. Slender bamboo makes fine fishing poles.

But it is split bamboo that has the widest range of utility. It is woven into matting, various kinds of baskets and handbags, or made into garden rakes. It is woven into bands that hold bath-tubs and other wooden tubs. In building Japanese houses, split bamboo is used for the base of mud walls. Bamboo chopsticks and nails are still used.

Bamboo is made into pulp for paper manufacture, and carbon filaments for electric bulbs are made of bamboo fiber.

The roots of bamboo are very strong and flexible, and are thus used as whips and walking sticks, and made into various ornamental articles.

The sheaths that the bamboo sheds as it grows are also valuable. They sometimes measure about eight inches wide and a foot long, and are extensively used for wrapping foodstuffs, as they are waterproof and strong. Split sheaths are woven to make sandals and other wares.

When bamboos blossom, it is a sign of a bad crop or some unlucky development, so it is traditionally said. It is also believed that bamboos have blossoms only when they are old, and after bearing seeds, they die.

In Japan there are more than 20 varieties of bamboo, but some blossom only rarely, while there are others that never have flowers. The seeds are edible and often have been eaten in rural districts when crops have failed.

Thus bamboo blossoms have come to be connected with bad harvests and unlucky years, but there seems to be no ground for this belief.

In tropical regions all bamboos blossom and bear seeds, but nothing certain is known as to the cause or circumstances that make them bloom in Japan. The colder climate is, however, said to be one cause of bamboos not regularly flowering in this country.

The traditional saying that they blossom only when they become old and after bearing seeds die, is also unfounded. Young bamboos are sometimes seen blossoming together with old ones, so the age of the plants has nothing to do with it.

It is because of its rare blossoming that various meanings have come to be attached to this phenomenon.

According to the study of botanists, the kinds called *madake*, *Hakone-dake*, *kanchiku*, *suzudake* and others are found to bloom occasionally, but *medake*, *hachiku*, *moso* and *yadake* very rarely bear flowers. *Shikakudake* and some others are not known to have flowers in this country.

BAMBOO LEAVES

BAMBOO is so widely used in Japan that it has become deeply imbedded in the people's life. Not only is it an indispensable material for building houses and making various utensils, but the bamboo and its leaves have also come to possess special meanings.

At the *Tanabata* festival of July 7, the people still hang strips of paper on which wishes are written on bamboo branches. A bamboo standing on the north of a tomb means good luck, it is widely believed. Even in such modern cemeteries as the Tama Public Cemetery, Tokyo, there are many bamboos.

The custom of tying wishing paper on the branches of trees and bamboos within shrine or temple compounds is still followed. Such wishes are made generally for love, marriage, success or recovery from illness.

In the old days, there was a custom in many parts of the country of writing one's name and age on the leaf of the *take* (bamboo) or *sasa* (grass bamboo) for good luck. In Edo days, the people used to bring their bamboo leaves with their names and ages written on them to a temple in Yanaka, to have a prayer said over them by the priest. Taking the leaves home, they put them over the ailing portions of their body, and then wrapping up the leaves in paper, buried them in the ground. For seven days they had to water the spot, and then it was believed they would be absolutely cured of their sickness or pains.

Many regions have tales of young people in love going to a bamboo hedge to tie their prayer paper for successful marriage.

The ancient people used to wrap up various foodstuffs in the leaves of *take* or *sasa. Chimaki*, a sweet which is still eaten on the May 5 Boys' Festival is wrapped up in bamboo leaves.

BIRO-O LEAVES

THE *BIRO-O* is a kind of palm tree that grows in the Okinawa Islands, Kyushu, Shikoku and Wakayama, and thus is quite unknown to dwellers in the northern or colder regions of the country.

In ancient days, the large soft *biro-o* leaves were regarded sacred and had wide significant uses. In Okinawa and other southern islands, the leaves are still considered as sacred symbols of *kami* or god.

Old records show that annually the leaves were presented to the Court from the lords of Kyushu and Shikoku for use at various festive occasions and also for ornamental purposes.

It is written that the maidens who undertook the rice-planting rite in the sacred ricefields of Ise Shrine wore big round hats woven of these leaves. In the 11th century nobles and Court officials used to decorate their carriages and horses with them. *Biro-o* leaf fans were widely used by aristocrats. When a Korean envoy came to Japan in 777, Emperor Konin presented *biro-o* leaves to him.

When Emperor Taisho was still Crown Prince, he visited Kagoshima where the prefectural officials presented him with *biro-o* hats and fans, following ancient custom.

In the old days the Okinawans used the leaves to make sails and also dippers for drawing water by folding them. They were used as mats for honored guests or visitors both in Okinawa and at Ise Shrine. The nuts and young leaves also used to be eaten by many southern residents.

Today the leaves have very little significance for most people. Also there are not as many trees as in the past, most of them being found in shrine compounds.

BIWA

BIWA, Japanese loquat (Eriobotrya japonica), is a delicious fruit that appears in early summer, but the people are afraid to plant any *biwa* tree in the garden, because of the belief that it brings sickness and bad luck.

Biwa was already a favorite fruit of the Japanese people in the Tokugawa period. It is recorded that even some Chinese species of the plant were imported and transplanted in the eighth century. Particularly among feudal lords and other wealthy families, it was a much valued delicacy. But it was further improved by the efforts of many scientists and horticulturists. Yoshio Tanaka in particular developed the delicious juicy kind as seen today.

A certain kind of wine was produced from *biwa*, but what has made it so popular among the common people from the past is *biwa* tea, drunk as a medicine. The leaves of the *biwa* trees are dried after the wool on their back is rubbed off and then put in a pot of water and brewed. The drink thus made is taken particularly in the summer season. It is believed that *biwa-yu* is good in relieving the effects of heat or protecting against sunstroke. It is good for stomach disorders that often come with summer heat. One who feels under the weather in the hot season is advised to take *biwa* tea.

Biwa leaves were thus believed to have medicinal properties. Yet there is another traditional belief that the *biwa* tree will bring sickness or invite evil fortune. Never plant a *biwa* tree in your garden, it is commonly said. If one plants it near the house, sickness will come or the fortune of the family will decline, it is believed.

The plant contains some poison, it is again said. Rain water or dew falling from the leaves and branches of the *biwa* tree will destroy even the toughest weed. Nothing grows under the shade of a *biwa* tree, the people say.

BLACK LILY

YURI, OR LILIES, grow wild all over Japan. The most common varieties are *teppo-yuri*, a large white lily, *yama-yuri* (mountain lily), *oni-yuri* (tiger lily), and *hime-yuri* (lady lily).

Teppo-yuri blossoms are in demand for Easter decoration, and they are cultivated for exporting bulbs to America and other countries. In Saitama and other places there are large lily bulb farms. Lily bulbs are also eaten as a vegetable and sold at greengrocers.

Yama-yuri and *oni-yuri* (tiger lily) have large yellowish flowers with dark purplish spots. They are found on hills. *Hime-yuri* are small and star-shaped. Kanagawa Prefecture has made *yuri* its official flower.

Yuri blossoms are mentioned in ancient literature, and in the *Kojiki*, the oldest record of the country, it is written that when Emperor Jinmu visited a maiden named Isukeyori-hime, he saw many lily blossoms blooming on the bank of a river nearby, and so he named the river *Sai-gawa*, as the lily was then called *sai*.

There are many local legends about *yuri*. Particularly of *hime-yuri* it is said in many districts that a lady in sorrow shed tears and from the spot where her tears fell *hime-yuri* grew.

A rare variety which is commonly called *kuro-yuri*, or black lily, is found on Mt. Hakusan, Mt. Tateyama and other high peaks. This lily is deep purple, almost black, and botanically famous as a rare variety.

This black lily has also a sad tradition. A local lord of Hokuriku district named Takezawa Kumashiro loved a young and beautiful girl named Sayuri. But he heard a rumor that Sayuri was really in love with another man. In a fit of wrath, he killed Sayuri and her lover, and also punished 16 of their families. The spirit of Sayuri who was killed by the jealous man was reincarnated as the black lily.

BONSAI

BONSAI is a product of the peculiar trend of the Japanese people to love nature and also to be fascinated by anything minute in size. Their love of nature made them wish to plant trees in pots so that their beauty can be appreciated within their rooms or gardens.

The present art of making *bonsai* is said to have started in the 13th century. In these 700 years, nature lovers of the country perfected an art of keeping a 100-year-old tree to the height of one or two feet, and making it look like a giant tree.

Looking at a pot planted with a few slender trees, about six inches high, one would see a great forest of huge trees before him. *Bonsai* is, in short, the art of reproducing natural plants and scenes in small potted areas.

The size of *bonsai* varies, ranging from the very tiny ones of one or two inches in height to those of five or six feet. The value of a *bonsai*, however, is not judged by its size, but by the naturalness it presents.

In appreciating *bonsai*, first attention should be given to the trunk, its form and appearance; the second thought to branches and their shapes; and the third to the rootage that gives the plant its solid foundation and makes it look gigantic and powerful.

The cultivation of *bonsai* is a delicate and painstaking task. Many of them are raised from seedlings. Then, finding a desirable branch, the cultivator ties earth or moss around a proper spot, and when roots come out there with con-stant watering, it is cut off there and planted in a pot.

The preparation of soil is very important, and each type of tree requires a different soil. Then, the potted plant has to be transplanted often to arrest its rapid growth and keep it in a desired form. Branches and roots have to be pruned every year. The watering of the plant must be done with utmost care, while needed nourishment has to be given at proper times.

There are *bonsai* trees that are growing on the top or side of rugged rocks in the pot. Such plants represent trees perched on mountain precipices or overhanging from cliffs. Seedlings for such *bonsai* are often collected from actual mountain cliffs at great risk. For making this type of *bonsai*, the selection of rocks becomes very important, as the shape and color of rocks control the effect of the whole picture.

Out of this *bonsai* with rocks has also developed *bonkei* (tray-gardens) which are made with various kinds of sands and stones to depict some natural scenes. No plants are used in *bonkei*.

CHRYSANTHEMUM

THE CHRYSANTHEMUM *(kiku)* is the noblest of all flowers. It came from China where it originated more than a thousand years ago, but it was the Japanese who developed the *kiku* to gorgeous blossoms as seen today. There are more than 5,000 varieties of *kiku*, with different blossoming seasons, but those flowering in autumn have been cultivated most.

The 16-petalled chrysanthemum is used as the crest of the Imperial Family of Japan, and the *kiku* is often called the national flower of the country. But the chrysanthemum was formally adopted as the Imperial crest only since the beginning of the Meiji era.

It is recorded that during the reign of Emperor Gotoba (1185-1198) the *kiku* flower design was used on Imperial carts and costumes and in the latter half of the 12th century, on the buntings in the courtyard also.

The flower was, however, a novelty for the aristocrats who cultivated the plant and composed poems on its beauty. They came to be admired by the common people only in the Edo period or since the beginning of the 17th century. Thus it was in the Edo era alone that the common people came to write poems on the *kiku.*

In the meantime the Imperial Court continued to use the *kiku* blossom on various costumes and utensils as a decorative design or a mark of the Court. The *kiku* design was even placed on paper used for official documents.

The two-yen postal stamp issued in commemoration of the Peace Treaty bears a chrysanthemum as its design.

An ancient Chinese tale made it sacred and gave it the virtue of long life. When Emperor Mu of the Chou dynasty went to India to obtain the secret of Buddhism, he took a young man named Tzu Tung among his retainers. The youth was the Emperor's favorite, but during the trip he committed the grave crime of kicking the Emperor's pillow with his foot. For this unpardonable crime, he was ordered to live at Li-hsien, a remote mountain region. When he had to part with the party, however, the Emperor took pity upon him, and told him to repeat a certain Buddhist formula daily for his salvation.

Living in the secluded mountain of Li-hsien, Tzu Tung faithfully repeated the passage every day. One morning he wrote the sacred words on a chrysanthemum leaf as he stood by a stream. The morning dew that collected on the lettered leaf fell into the water, and then a sudden change took place. The water became a sacred medicine to prolong life. Before the young man appeared a paradise of singing birds and fragrant blossoms, and angels came to wait upon him.

With joy he drank the water of the stream, and lived for 800 years. All people living along the lower flow of the stream prospered and lived almost indefinitely.

Chrysanthemums cultivated in Japan may be divided into two categories, the first having several large and gorgeous flowers, and the second with hundreds of small blossoms. The latter type is trained to form various shapes. This led to the making of *kiku-ningyo* or chrysanthemum dolls as early as the beginning of the 19th century. Plants are trained to form a doll representing the desired person, and blossoms of different colors are used for a gorgeous costume. The cultivators of this kind of chrysanthemum displayed in their gardens such creations made into forms of famous historical or dramatic characters. Later it developed into public shows to be visited on payment of small fees. During Edo days such shows were held at many locations, but later that at Dangozaka, Hongo, became the only one in Tokyo. This also disappeared about 40 years ago.

GIBOSHI

GIBOSHI is a flower that grows wild in mountain regions in summer. It is a cluster of light purple flowers on long stems and is also planted in gardens by many flower lovers. This plant of the lily species is so named because the shape of the leaf resembles the ornamental pointed metal balls placed on the rail posts of bridges, which are called *giboshi* (literally, modelled after jewel balls.)

In the old days, the young leaves of the plant were eaten. The people still believe that the flower stands for calm composure. In connection with the blossoms, a traditional tale of China, where the flower is called the jade hairpin flower, is recalled.

In the district of Chihchou, China, there once lived a musician named Chang who was particularly known for his skill in playing the flute. One summer evening, he was playing it as he enjoyed the cool breeze and the bright moon.

Suddenly before him a heavenly maiden appeared, who asked him to play a tune especially for the princess of the moon. Gladly complying with her request, he played his favorite tune. When the music ended, the heavenly maiden thanked him and was about to go away.

But Chang stopped her, and said that the evening was the most memorable in his life and he wished to have something by which to remember the joy of playing for the princess of the moon. Then the maiden pulled a jade ornament out of her hair and offered it to him.

But in receiving the beautiful token, Chang dropped it on the ground, and from that spot bloomed an unknown flower. Ever since, the flower came to be called the jade hairpin flower in China. The story was brought to Japan and is still remembered.

The Chinese legend and the delicate light purple *giboshi* blossoms have made the plant and its flowers still admired by lovers of wild plants.

GOURDS

THREE KINDS of gourds are commonly raised in Japan for different purposes. They are *hechima* (Luffa cylindrica), *yugao* (Lagenaria vulgaris), and *hyotan* (Lagenaria vulgaris Var. gourda).

Hechima is the most widely cultivated of the three, not only by farmers but also by city dwellers in their gardens. The gourd grows to about two feet long and a foot around. The ripe gourd is dried and the strong fiber that is closely woven inside is taken out. This fiber is used in Japanese households for scrubbing dishes, pans and tubs. It is also used for stuffing purposes. *Hechima* is exported a great deal.

When *hechima* gourds are picked, the vine is cut off at about a foot from the ground, and the cut end is put into a bottle, wherein the *hechima* water is collected. *Hechima-no-mizu* or *hechima* water has been used by Japanese from olden days as toilet water for their hands and faces. It is also used as a medicine to expectorate obstructive sputa.

Yugao is better known by its product, *kanpyo*. *Yugao* gourds come in all shapes and sizes, some round and some long, often reaching over three feet around. The outer skin is hard, and by hollowing it out the gourds are made into waste baskets, fruit baskets and receptacles for various things. But it is the edible *kanpyo* made by slicing the *yugao* inside into thin and narrow strips and drying them that has made the *yugao* cultivation important. *Kanpyo* is cooked in many ways, and is particularly indispensable in making *norimaki-sushi*, vinegared rice rolled in *nori*.

Hyotan, the third gourd, is also often planted in gardens. This gourd has a peculiar shape, being divided into two parts by a narrow neck in the middle. In the old days, *hyotan* hollowed out were used for carrying *sake* and other liquids. The *hyotan* gourd comes in all sizes, from one inch or less in length to over two feet. Small ones are used for ornamental purposes or as toys. *Hyotan* of good shape are very hard to find, and they are still highly valued.

HAGI BLOSSOMS

OF ALL AUTUMN blossoms the Japanese people love, the most outstanding is *hagi* or bush clover. The Japanese variety of this plant seems to be different from those of the same species found in other countries. It is a bush plant, growing to a height of about 10 feet, having slender branches growing in a cluster from one root.

In autumn it bears tiny purplish pink or white blossoms. As the people have been fond of tiny things, the small *hagi* blossoms on the slender stems have been admired since very early days.

Manyoshu, the oldest collection of poems compiled in 770, contains many poems on plants, but among them those on *hagi* are most numerous with 138 poems, while second position is held by the *ume,* Japanese apricot with 113, and the third by pines with 71. The large number of poems on *ume* is attributed to the fact that it was then just introduced from China and was in much favor with the aristocrats. In view of that fact, the popularity of *hagi* must have been very wide.

Hagi blossoms are best appreciated flowering on hillsides or mountains, but are also planted in many gardens.

In many poems, *hagi* is mentioned in connection with deer which like to eat the leaves. Such poems also prove that in the old days, deer were found roaming over the fields and valleys quite near human habitation. *Hagi* leaves make good fodder for animals.

The slender stems are cut after the blossoms are over and used in many ways such as making garden fences or various other wares. Many nature lovers of the past used to make chopsticks of *hagi* and used them at various autumn functions.

There are many districts or towns called *Hagi* or *Hagiwara* (*hagi* field), named for the plant that must have grown abundantly in those places in the past.

HAMAYU

ON THE WARM shores of Kyushu, Shikoku, Kii and Boso (Chiba Prefecture) there bloom in July large white flowers called *hamayu.* The name *hamayu* or *hama-momen* (shore cotton) comes from the fact that the slender petals of the flowers hang down like clusters of white cotton threads.

It is a gorgeous plant with a thick growth of long pointed leaves. It is also called *hama-omoto* or shore rhodea, as it resembles the *omoto* in its general appearance. The white flowers, appearing on top of the long stem, rise above the leaves to almost a meter high.

The white *hamayu* blossom has been admired by the people since very early days, as proved by the poems praising its beauty in the *Manyoshu,* the oldest anthology of Japanese poems written in the fourth to eighth centuries. The old records mention that at the great banquets of the nobles, pheasant legs were wrapped in *hamayu* leaves.

Thus the long leaves were regarded as not only beautiful but also significant of good luck. There was an old traditional belief that when one wrote the name of one's love on a *hamayu* leaf and slept with the leaf under his or her pillow, the named person would surely appear in a dream during the night.

Love letters were also written on *hamayu* leaves and it was believed that such letters would certainly bring favorable replies.

In many places it was said that if the receiver of a *hamayu*-leaf love letter failed to send a reply, some ill luck would be in store for that person. So it had to be speedily answered.

The plant does not prosper in the colder regions, and the Boso shore is believed to be the northern limit of its growth in this country.

HO-O TREE

HO-O OR *HO-O-NO-KI* is a Japanese tree belonging to the magnolia species and found in mountains and fields. This tree is noted for its fragrance, its large egg-shaped leaves growing about one foot long and bearing large white blossoms that come out in early summer.

The leaves that grow in clusters like a parasol at each branch end were used in the old days to wrap various foodstuffs. Even today in such mountain regions as Hida, they are used in this manner.

Ho-o flowers are one of the largest blossoms seen in the country. The bark of the tree was formerly used as a medicine.

The tree which grows to a height of 30 or 40 feet yields a valuable wood which is still used for making various utensils. Formerly it was used to make woodcut blocks for printing books or pictures because the wood is easy to cut. It was also used to make sheaths for swords as it is strong and light.

One item which is still made of *ho-o* wood are the cleats of a certain kind of tall *geta* or clogs.

The *ho-o* wood is also used to make cutting boards for dress-makers, because of its fine texture.

The tree had so many valuable uses that it used to be a sign of wealth to have them in one's compound. The sight of *ho-o* trees in the mountains, with their big leaves that are whitish on the underside and their large fragrant blossoms is not only magnificent but beautiful.

Yet city dwellers only know things made of *ho-o* and seldom have the opportunity to see the tree in its grandeur.

HOZUKI

AS THE SUMMER season begins, in the shops of green-grocers appear *hozuki* branches which have red berries hidden within the yellowish red calyx that develops into bags. *Hozuki* is also cultivated at home as the people admire its beautiful red fruits. It is sold at shops, however, for girls to play with.

Hozuki belongs to the eggplant species, and is scientifically known as Physalis francheti Var. Bunyardii. It bears white blossoms in early summer, and the calyx grows into a bag as the berry inside ripens. When the calyx bag is opened there is a perfectly round red berry, just like a ripe cherry, inside. The people have always admired the bright red *hozuki.*

Hozuki has been a toy of Japanese girls since very early days. Girls' fondness of *hozuki* as a plaything is mentioned in the *Makura-no-Soshi* which relates the court life of the 11th century, and also in the *Eiga Monogatari* which pictures life of the 12th to 14th centuries.

Girls collect the ripe *hozuki* from nearby farms, if they live in the country, or buy them at stores, in cities. Taking the red berry out of the calyx bag, a girl will bore a hole at the place where it was attached to the stem, and slowly squeeze the seeds out of the hole. She then has a hollow round soft ball with a tiny hole. She puts it into her mouth, and as she squeezes it against her teeth and lips, it makes a faint but pleasing sound. It is the joy of making the sound that has made *hozuki* so popular with the girls of Japan. All over the country, for generations and generations, girls and even middle-aged women have loved to play with the tiny sound-making bags in their mouths, whenever the season of *hozuki* comes. In olden days girls did not have much of a variety of things to play with, and so *hozuki* was particularly popular. Since then the habit has been kept up unabated.

There are also *umi-hozuki* or sea *hozuki*, used in the same way. They are egg bags of *naganishi* or *akanishi* (long or red whelks). The egg bags of *naganishi* are flat and round, while those of *akanishi* come in a long slender shape, somewhat curved. These whelk egg bags are also sold at toy shops and other places. A tiny cut is made at one end of the bag, and after the inside is squeezed out, the bag is used as *hozuki* to make a pleasant sound. Whelks lay their egg bags on rocks under the sea. They are gathered and preserved in salt for sale. Sometimes they are dyed red to make them look attractive.

Hozuki made of rubber appeared on the market, but it never gained popularity because of the rubber taste, and particularly because it took away all the joy of the delicate work of making tiny holes and squeezing the seeds out. *Hozuki* is just as popular now as it was 10 centuries ago.

KAKI

KAKI OR persimmon is the most representative of Japanese fruits. The tree is seen in many other countries, but Japan produces the best *kaki* in the world.

The ripe red *kaki* adds color to farming villages in autumn, as almost all rural houses have a few of these trees. The name, *kaki*, is a shortened form of '*akaki*' or red fruit tree. Since the people are so fond of the fruit, it is mentioned in many old tales. They also came to have various sentiments about the tree and fruit.

Kaki has been connected in the mind of the people with the spirit of the dead, although grounds for this idea are not clear. In cremating the dead, *kaki* wood was formerly used in many districts in preference to the wood of other trees. Offerings to the dead, particularly at the *O-bon* service, are often placed on *kaki* leaves. Furthermore, many still believe that offerings to the spirit of any unknown dead must be made on *kaki* leaves.

In Nagano districts, it is said that ghosts and other apparitions always appear under the branches of the *kaki*. Ghosts like the trees, it is believed.

On the other hand *hoshigaki* or dried *kaki* fruit is believed to be a charm for good luck, long life and prosperity. *Hoshigaki* is still used at New Year celebrations and on other happy occasions.

The wood of the *kaki* is used to make boxes, furniture and other utensils while the astringent juice obtained from the fruit is applied to fishing lines, fishing nets, paper and various wares to make them strong and waterproof.

Many new and better kinds of *kaki* are being developed but the small, hard *kaki* that ripen on trees around country houses are still loved by children and old-fashioned persons who cannot forget their young days.

KIRI TREES

MANY JAPANESE farmers still plant saplings of *kiri* or Paulownia tomentosa around their houses when girls are born to them. *Kiri* is a fast-growing plant, and by the time the girls reach the age of marriage, it is big enough to be cut and made into *tansu* or chests of drawers to take as part of the trousseau.

Formerly when a daughter was going to marry, the father would cut down one or two *kiri* trees and take them to a cabinet maker to have her *tansu* made. But now it is more customary to sell the *kiri* for lumber and buy a ready-made *tansu.*

The name *kiri* came from *kiru* (to cut) as it was believed that the tree would grow better and quicker when it was cut down often. The tree, which grows to over 30 feet high, blossoms in April or May. The flower is small, purplish in color, and very fragrant. *Kiri* blossoms and leaves have long been used for family crests and other ornamental designs.

Kiri wood is good for making *tansu* and other boxes, because it is very light in weight, and keeps out moisture. Many gift packages are placed in *kiri* boxes. The better kinds of *geta* or clogs are of *kiri* wood, and those with even and close grains are particularly valued.

Charcoal made from *kiri* wood is also very important, as it is used in making gunpowder and fireworks.

Because of the wide use of *kiri* wood, the growing of *kiri* trees is a profitable business, as they can be cut down every 20 years or so.

KYOCHIKUTO

THE BIG RED flowers of *kyochikuto* (sweet oleander) are welcomed as a symbol of summer by many flower lovers of Japan. This plant grows to a height of four meters. The leaves are thick and long and shaped like bamboo leaves.

This plant was introduced from China in the Kyoho era, 1716-1736, but it gained popularity immediately and soon came to be planted in gardens.

Poets and writers have praised the majestic beauty of the flowers. Originally the flower came from India, and in China and many Western countries it was highly admired from very early days.

There is a little-known legendary tale about the flower.

Shirotae-hime, daughter of the god of Earth had a beautifully fair complexion. Many young men came to win her but she rejected them all. Her father selected the god of plants as the most suitable mate for her and Shirotae-hime was also willing to marry him. But the god of plants would not have her, saying she was too fair and looked dead.

His refusal saddened her, and her health began to fail. Her father became alarmed and sought the god of heaven for help and advice. Hearing the story, the god of heaven gave the father a branch of *kyochikuto*.

When the father brought it to Shirotae-hime, she took the flowers and crushed them in her hand. She applied the red juice she obtained from the blossoms to her face which took on a healthy flush. So she was happily married to the god of plants.

Some say that the story came from China, but it has served to make the plant famous and its red or pink flowers a favorite of the people.

Kyochikuto blossoms are mostly red, but there are also pink and white ones.

MATATABI

'NEKO-NI MATATABI' (*matatabi* to the cat) is a common saying used to indicate anything good and tempting, because cats are very fond of it.

Matatabi is the green okra-like fruit of a vine plant that grows wild in the mountains. In June the plant bears white blossoms like *ume* flowers and the broad egg-shaped leaves turn whitish. When the fruits ripen in summer, they are gathered, dried and sold at drug stores.

It is believed to be the best medicine for curing cats of illness and all cat lovers keep it ready for emergencies. Not only cats but also tigers and other animals of the feline family are said to be very fond of it.

In the old days, *matatabi* was thought to be a good cure for such human ailments as lumbago, paralysis and rheumatism. So it was widely in demand.

Today, however, it is seldom used as medicine. But in many rural districts it is still eaten. Particularly in the Echigo district on the Japan Sea, the people are very fond of pickled *matatabi*. Generally it is pickled in salt and loved by *sake* drinkers. Often green *matatabi* is pickled in *ume-zu* (apricot vinegar).

Many of the Echigo people make their own *matatabi* pickles but they can also be bought in jars or bottles.

It is not known whether the pickled *matatabi* has any medicinal value, but some say that there must be something beneficial as it cures sick cats and formerly was used as medicine.

Lovers of pickled *matatabi* say, on the other hand, that they are very tempting things with a taste all their own.

MORNING GLORY

THE JAPANESE are probably the only people in the world who cultivate *asagao* or morning glory (Ipomaea purpurea) as an ornamental plant to enjoy its blossoms. The plant was originally brought from China in the first part of the ninth century, but at first it was planted for its seeds, which were used as medicine.

It is not known who first attempted to cultivate the plant to make its flowers bigger and more beautiful. But it is recorded that in the second half of the 17th century, in the Tokugawa period, the cultivation of *asagao* had already become quite a vogue among flower lovers of the country. The original plant had small blue or white blossoms, but by special breeding and care, they succeeded in not only enlarging the size of the flowers, but also producing purple, red and indigo blossoms. The shapes of the leaves were also changed.

In those days the cultivation of *asagao* became in fact so common, particularly in Edo, that it came to be called the commoner's flower. Day laborers, artisans and many other persons who could not indulge in the aristocratic pleasure of raising dwarf trees or chrysanthemums, eagerly became *asagao* cultivators. It was probably due to the easiness of its cultivation.

In the Tokugawa days, *asagao-awase* or shows to compare flowers were held every summer morning. Each cultivator took the best blossoms he produced to the gathering and compared them with those brought by others. This *asagao-awase* later developed in the Meiji days into *asagao* exhibitions.

Asagao blooms at dawn before the sun rises, and consequently *asagao* lovers have to rise early in order to appreciate the blossoms.

The *hokku* written by Chiyo of Kaga is still famous. 'Asagao ni tsurube torarete moraimizu' (Asagao taking hold of the well-bucket, I ask the neighbor for a bucketful of water). On going to the well to draw water, the poetess finds that an *asagao* vine has entwined itself to the bucket and beautiful blossoms are blooming. Having no mind to disturb the flowers, she goes to a neighbor to beg for water.

MURASAKI-GUSA

THE PROVINCE of Musashi or the present Tokyo metropolitan area was famous for *murasaki-gusa*, little wild plants which were formerly used for obtaining a purple dye. The *murasaki-gusa* of Musashi, however, has now almost disappeared, and it is very rarely found growing wild. Greatly lamenting its disappearance from Musashi, the Emperor has had several plants specially brought and planted within the Palace.

It is the roots of the *murasaki-gusa* which make a purple dye. It has been said that where *Murasaki-gusa* grows, the soil for several feet around becomes purple in color. Although this is of course a mere exaggeration, it is nevertheless true that a very bright purple dye is obtained from its roots.

Purple is considered the noblest color in Japan, and the color has always been used by the Imperial Court and those of very high rank. It is not known how long this purple dye has been used in this country, but it seems to be quite old. In the book called *Engi-Shiki* written in the 10th century, it is mentioned that 3,000 pounds of *murasaki* dye were presented to the Court from the province of Musashi. This proves that at that time the province was already famous for its purple dye, and produced quite a large quantity to be used in dyeing fabrics for the aristocrats.

Until the introduction of chemical dyes, *murasaki* roots had been used for obtaining the purple dye which was in popular demand by the people.

It is now only occasionally found in the mountains of Takao and Kobotoke in the extreme western end of the Tokyo metropolitan area. It is said, however, that in the old days, the plants grew abundantly and wild throughout the vast area.

NANTEN

NANTEN bears red or white berries in clusters on its slender stems. This plant grows wild in the southern sections of the country but is also planted in gardens all over the country, as it is said to be a lucky plant.

Engelbert Kaempfer, a Dutch physician who came to Japan in 1690, introduced this plant to the Western world.

The plant is said to be able to resist fire, and thus is planted near houses. It is to the branch of this tree that children tie their *teru-teru-bozu* or fair-weather paper dolls in prayer for a fine day.

Nanten berries, particularly the white kind, are said to possess medicinal properties, and in the old days they were used to cure asthma and coughs, and also to drive out the evil effect of alcoholic drinks.

It is furthermore believed that *nanten* wood has the power to protect the health of children. Many kinds of little toys made of *nanten* wood were made as charms for children. *Nanten* chopsticks were also made for little folks.

The wood is used in decorating some parts of the Japanese house, as it is believed to possess the power to turn misfortune into good luck. It seldom grows into a big tree but *tokobashira* or the decorative pillar in the guest room is mentioned sometimes as being made of *nanten.*

It is also believed that if a *nanten* tree planted by the side of the house grows taller than the eaves, it is a sign of prosperity for the family.

White *nanten* flowers that blossom in summer are not beautiful, but the berry-bearing branches are used for flower arrangements.

NEW YEAR FLOWER

AMONG potted plants displayed during the New Year season, the most prominent is *fukuju-so*, a kind of adonis. The golden yellow buds rising out of the soil are believed to invite happiness.

The plant grows wild all over the country from Hokkaido to the southern tip of Kyushu. There are many varieties; there is one that has pinkish yellow blossoms, which is found in the Chichibu district of Saitama.

Fukuju-so has been regarded as the New Year flower since very early days. In a book published in the Enpo era (1673-1682) it is mentioned that *fukuju-so* placed on the *tokonoma* at New Year's is noble.

As it is the symbol of happiness and traditionally used as a New Year decoration, it is also given various other names such as *ganjitsu-so* (New Year's Day plant), *choju-so* (long life plant), or *fukujin-so* (blessed men's plant).

There is a famous Ainu legend about the *fukuju-so*. Once there was a beautiful goddess named Kunou. Her father picked the god of the earth mole as her husband as he was brave and strong. But the goddess refused to marry him. On the day set for their wedding she ran away. The father god went to search for her and found her hiding amid the tall grasses in the field. Catching her, he angrily scolded her and turned her into a plant for disobeying him. This plant was the *fukuju-so*, which is still called *kunou* by the Ainus.

This is quite similar to the Greek story of Adonis who was killed and from the spot where his blood dropped there blossomed a plant.

The *fukuju-so* is beautiful, but the people particularly admire the plant as its bright yellow buds come out from the earth in the coldest season of the year. Also probably because flowers are rare in winter, the *fukuju-so* must have come to be highly regarded.

NIKKO'S TREES

THE AVENUES of giant cryptomeria trees, extending almost 20 miles and leading to Nikko Shrine, are world-famous. Seldom is such a magnificent avenue of huge trees that are more than 300 years old seen in any part of the world. The inspiration to plant these trees came from a single person.

Yet the man who planted these trees in Nikko has been quite forgotten. Even at the time when he proposed their planting he was ridiculed. He was Masatsuna Matsudaira, who was ordered by the Tokugawa Shogun to undertake the colossal task of rebuilding Nikko Shrine erected in honor of the first Shogun Iyeyasu which was destroyed by fire in 1638.

His immortality lies not in rebuilding the shrine, but in planting these trees. All the feudal lords donated lanterns and other ornaments to the shrine, but Masatsuna had quite a different idea. He undertook to plant *sugi* (cryptomeria) trees on the three roads leading to the shrine, even though others laughed at his seemingly ridiculous plan.

It is not clearly known how many trees were originally planted, but in 1925 there were 17,914 trees standing. A proposal was made to cut down the giant *sugi* trees during the last war in order to build wooden ships, but fortunately the plan did not materialize.

Sugi or Cryptomeria japonica has been highly valued since earliest times. Its wood is used for building and other purposes, while its bark has been used for roofing houses. There are two kinds, red and white, according to the color of the wood. The red kind is more valuable as it lasts longer than the white kind. Fans, chopsticks, boxes, chests, tubs, boats and other household utensils are also made of *sugi.*

OAKS FROM MOUNT VERNON

THE BIG OAK trees that stand just back of Futaba Girls' School, near Yotsuya-mitsuke, Tokyo, are said to have grown from acorns brought from George Washington's home, at Mount Vernon, near Washington, D.C., 70 years ago.

These trees have an interesting story that goes back to the visit of General Ulysses Grant to Japan in 1879, according Takeshi Kimura. When General Grant came to Tokyo, he had many intimate talks with Emperor Meiji. At the meetings there were two interpreters, an American by the name of Young and Kiyonari Yoshida. These two not only interpreted the conversation, but also took down what passed between the Emperor and the American ex-president.

The two versions of those talks were found very interesting, and a promise was made to submit one the copy to General Grant upon completion. So in 1882, Shogo Nagasaki was dispatched with the copy to Washington.

He was very cordially welcomed by General Grant who was very happy to receive the record of his talks with the Emperor. While in Washington, Nagasaki was told by General Grant that he should visit the home of George Washington, if he had not seen it before. The general provided him with a guide to take him to Mount Vernon.

Nagasaki and the guide went out to the garden after visiting the house where George Washington had lived. On the ground, acorns from oak trees were scattered about. Pointing to them the guide suggested to Nagasaki that he should take some and plant them in Japan. Pleased with the suggestion, Nagasaki gathered a handful and put them in his pocket.

After his return, he planted the acorns in the garden of his house. They soon sprouted and grew strong and big.

PERSIMMONS

KAKI OR persimmons are the finest Japanese fruit, many say. Long before modern improved kinds were produced, *kaki* trees were planted by farmers and others around their houses. In autumn, the ripened fruit still brightens the countryside. They also appear in many Japanese legends and customs.

First of all, the *kaki* fruit is considered a lucky charm. Dried *kaki* are therefore used in the New Year celebration and on other happy occasions. The *'naruka-naranuka'* (bear fruits or not) rite of the New Year season is performed on *kaki* trees. Children climb the trees and make slight cuts on them with knives or beat them with sticks, saying *'Naruka-naranuka.'* It is believed that then the trees will answer and bear good fruit in the autumn.

On the other hand, many bad things are told of the *kaki.* The trees break easily and children have been told to be careful when they climb them to pick the fruit. It used to be said that if one fell from a *kaki* tree, he would become a fool, or that he would never be cured of the injury received in the fall.

The wood is used to make fine furniture and boxes, but is never used in *irori* or fire-places, because it was used at crematories. Thus, it was thought that to burn the wood of the *kaki* in the house was to invite death. In Shinano and other districts it has been believed that ghosts and goblins lived under these trees. All were advised not to go near them in the dark. Food offered to the dead during the *O-bon* festival is still placed on *kaki* leaves in many districts. Thus, in the mind of the people, the *kaki* was formerly associated with death or the spirit of the dead.

The *kaki*, furthermore, has been regarded as a medicine. To mention some such uses, its blossoms were baked black and used as a cure for diarrhea. The last leaf left on the *kaki* tree in autumn was said to be good for curing coughs. The juice obtained by brewing dried persimmons was also good for curing coughs.

When one was sick from drink, he was given a few *kaki* to eat, and he would immediately feel better. When the unripe green *kaki* was crushed, it became a cure for apoplexy.

A few leaves were put in water for several days, and then the water became a cure for children's dysentery, and also an excellent drink for lowering blood pressure.

Kaki leaves are often eaten, and particularly when fried in oil, they are believed to be good for one's health.

Ancient people found it a valuable plant, as even without scientific knowledge, they knew by experience that the leaves and fruit contain much vitamin C and other elements valuable to maintain good health.

PINE TREES

MATSU or pine trees are regarded the noblest trees in Japan. The people have admired and even worshiped these trees from very early days. The scenic beauty of the country is greatly enhanced by them.

The pine stands for strength, firmness and security. Its branches spreading in all directions with their evergreen needles represent a united and peaceful family.

As the *matsu* was held in high esteem the highest official rank in feudal days was the pine rank, and the best room in a palace called the pine room. *Matsu-no-kotoba* (words of pine trees) was an expression meaning poems. *Matsunone* (pine roots) was synonymous with everlasting good fortune. *Matsuba* (pine needles) was used to express one's sincerity and sentiments in presenting gifts to others. *Sennin* (hermits) were also said to have lived on pine needles.

The use of pine branches as the main New Year's decoration indicates the popular belief in pines as the symbol of long life and happiness.

There are many kinds of pine in the country but the most common are the black and red pines which are found only in Japan. Black pines are also called male pines as their needles are long and thick and red pines are known as female pines as their needles are slender and short. Black pines are found near seashores rather than in mountain areas.

It is these black and red pines standing so nobly everywhere that made the people attach so much significance and importance to them. So this attitude toward pine trees is entirely Japanese.

In poems, paintings and decorative designs, the *matsu* is still widely used.

POMEGRANATES

THE POMEGRANATE is a beautiful fruit. It is beautiful as it hangs from the tree, and it surpasses all other fruits in beauty in appearance on the table. When it is green and unripe, it is ugly, but when it ripens and shows its gems of garnet through the cracks of the outer shell, it becomes beautiful. There is nothing in other fruits that comes close to the beauty of small garnet-like gems packed close together in a pomegranate. The garnet gems are transparent and have a luster that glistens in the morning sun. In Japan children eat the fruit when ripe, but it is not particularly good to eat. The color and the transparency are inviting. There is a certain fascination in taking out gem after gem from the closely packed fruit, each of different shape, and there are no two of the same shape.

Not only are pomegranates sold in autumn at fruit stores of Japan, but they are also considered as a holy fruit. *Kishibojin* (Hariti) is regarded in Japan as the guardian of children. Temples erected to *Kishibojin* are always visited by women who have many children or others who have none, because they believe that the goddess will bless children and also give children to those who have none. *Kishibojin* was originally a devil-woman who had 500 children, but she devoured other children. She was converted by Buddha to the faith and became the guardian of children. *Kishibojin* has even become a synonym for a woman having many children.

This goddess *Kishibojin*, it is believed, holds a pomegranate in her hand. This belief has been circulated in Japan since quite an early date. Statues of *Kishibojin* are usually made with this fruit in her hand. It is said that *Kishibojin* holds a pomegranate in her hand because the fruit contains 500 treasures — children. The goddess is believed to love the pomegranate tree as each fruit of the tree holds so many treasures.

Because of this belief that *Kishibojin*, the goddess of children, is so fond of the fruit and holds it always in her hand and also because of the fact that the fruit contains so many tiny gems, the pomegranate is believed to possess the virtue of giving children to barren women. This belief is current in many parts of the country. Also it is believed that, if children eat pomegranate fruits, they will be free from evil spirits. All this is because of the virtue of *Kishibojin* who loves the fruit.

In China also, the pomegranate has always been considered as a sign of many children, and at the Chinese New Year, they use pomegranates in the belief that it will bring many offspring.

It is related among stories of ancient Chinese emperors that, at a certain emperor's marriage, the mother of the bride presented her with two pomegranates. The emperor did not understand their meaning and asked a noted scholar who replied that as the pomegranate fruits contained so many little fruits, it showed that the mother of the empress wanted her to have many children. That greatly pleased the emperor and he gave gifts to the scholar who explained the meaning of the fruit.

It may be proper to hold that the Japanese belief in the meaning of the pomegranate has come from China, although there is no concrete proof. There is no other fruit in Japan which contains so many little gems inside, and the fact must have greatly impressed the people. The beauty and the color also increased the interest of the people and children in the fruit. Children love to play with the fruit, picking out the tiny gems of garnet. It is a good thing to play with, as with the fruit comes the blessing of *Kishibojin*, who watches over all children and the happiness of their mothers.

RICE PLANTING

ANCIENT tradition has it that the Sun Goddess Amaterasu-omikami gave rice seeds to Ninigi-no-mikoto and taught him how to grow rice. Thereupon descending to Takachiho Mountain in Kyushu, Ninigi-no-mikoto introduced rice cultivation to the country.

This tradition is expressed in the

taue-matsuri or rice-planting festival of Kirishima Shrine, Kagoshima, which is held on March 8. Young men of the village dress in ancient costumes as old men and old women plant rice as they chant the ritual song. They represent the farmers, and the rite is to report to Ninigi-no-mikoto that all the farmers are cultivating rice as the heavenly deity had originally taught them.

The music and dance of rice planting then follow. Farmers throughout the province bring offerings to Ninigi-no-mikoto to express their gratitude for teaching them rice cultivation and bringing good harvests.

The Yahikoyama Shrine, at Soeda, Fukuoka Prefecture, has its *taue-matsuri* on March 15. Here the rite is somewhat different. Eight young girls, dressed in rice-planting costumes, dance forming a circle to music by village musicians.

The rice-planting festival, particularly in appreciation of the goodness of Ninigi-no-mikoto in bringing rice as food to the people, is held at many places in Kyushu, because it is believed that the heavenly ancestors of the Japanese first came to Takachiho Mountain in Kyushu.

Taue (paddy-field planting), meaning rice transplanting, is still done with much ceremony. Upon it rests the whole livelihood of the people who eat rice as their principal food.

Rice seeds are first put in specially prepared beds, about a month before *taue*. When they grow to six to eight inches in height, they are transplanted to paddy-fields. In some cases, seeds are directly sowed in paddy-fields, but such is very rare.

The entire farming community makes *taue* quite an occasion. Many districts still have the custom of young girls dressed in bright costumes starting the work of rice transplanting, singing

taue-uta or rice-planting songs. Those *taue-uta* have in many cases been handed down for generations. Again, in some places, Shinto priests are called to offer praers for a good harvest, before undertaking the planting.

Formerly the *taue* for the paddy-fields specially reserved for the upkeep of shrines was very solemnly observed with colorful ceremonies, songs and dances.

Taue is generally done during June and July, the exact time differing according to districts. It is to be done when the temperature of the paddy-field water reaches a proper degree. Fields have to be plowed and given fertilizers before planting.

The planting itself is no easy work. Each planter takes up in his right hand five or six strands of young rice plants, and puts them securely in the muddy soil under water in straight lines at proper intervals.

Farmers and families feel relieved when the planting of their paddy-fields is over, as this signifies the ending of the important start of rice farming upon which their year's fortune rests. That does not yet imply, however, the end of their labor and worry. There are some years when the harvest is threatened by a long dry spell. Then during August there is the unpleasant and arduous task of removing weeds from paddy-fields. The summer sun heats up the paddy-field water, and farmers have to work in the hot water, under the glaring summer sun, bending low, and walking through the knee-deep mud, to remove the weeds between the rows of growing rice plants. Of course, mechanical weed pullers have been invented, but most farmers still follow the customary old way of removing the fast-growing weeds with their hands.

When that is over, autumn storms often damage the crop, tearing away blossoming branches or burying the plants under water.

Nevertheless, farmers go through all these toilsome duties and worries in the hope of reaping a good harvest. They know that the joy of harvesting good crops more than repays all the hard work and worries they go through during the five months.

Japanese farmers make much of the planting of rice. That is quite natural, firstly because rice is their main crop and the food of the people, and secondly, because they still traditionally believe that it is *kami* or god who gives them a good harvest. They thus hold rice-planting ceremonies, differing according to localities, when they plant rice, in prayer for a good crop.

Taue or rice-planting was originally believed to be the occasion of the union of *Hi-no-kami* (sun deity) and *Mizu-no-kami* (water deity), and the birth of *Ta-no-kami* (farm deity). Thus in ancient days, a little girl dressed gaily as a bride was the symbol of the occasion.

Rice planting is the most important work of Japanese farmers. The whole family takes part in the work which is also welcomed with joy. But the most important branches of the work have been undertaken by the women.

The actual planting is done by women, formerly brightly dressed, who sing their rice-planting songs as they work. Another important task of the day is the preparation of the meals which are eaten by all by the side of their paddy-fields.

In the old days, much meaning was attached to the several meals taken on the day. Care was given in not only selecting the food and cooking it, but even in gathering the kindling. All the food had to be entirely eaten up and anything left untouched was not taken home, but had to be thrown into the fields.

The meals eaten at the fields on planting day were considered sacred. In the village of Funao, Chiba, a story is told of a girl committing suicide because she unthinkingly desecrated the food.

She was told to bring the cooked food to the fields on planting day. The food was in a box which she placed in a big basket on her back. She was taking care of a little baby, and so she put the baby on top of the box of food in the basket.

When she reached the field the elders saw the baby sitting on top of the food. This was an unpardonable thing to do. She was ordered to hurry home and cook the food afresh. The girl felt sad and jumped into a pond with the baby.

Many features of the rice-planting festival have come from the old system of the local shrine or temple having the so-called *shinden* or sacred rice-fields for its support. It is the sacred duty of the villagers to undertake the planting, caring and harvesting of the sacred rice-fields of the community shrine. They make the occasion not only a religious service, but also an event for enjoyment. The ceremonial planting is usually followed by a community dance.

Many local districts have their peculiar customs in observing the rice-planting festival. As one of the most extraordinary, the festival at the *shinden* of the Wakamiya Hachiman Shrine of Kochi City, Shikoku, is to be mentioned. The festival lasts three days in the middle of May, during which the women are the absolute rulers of the community, and men have to stay quietly at home.

Several hundred men and women take part in the ceremonial planting of rice at the *shinden* of the Hachiman Shrine on the first day. But when the planting is over, the fun starts. Each woman takes up a wooden bucket, and fills it with the mud from the paddy-fields. They then throw the mud at any man they meet on the fields or street.

No man is spared, whatever his position might be, socially or officially. For three days, the 'reign of terror' lasts, and only when midnight of the third day comes, do the men feel at ease again.

The rice planting held for the rice-field of Doniwa Shrine, at Togane City, in Chiba Prefecture is called *Doronko-matsuri* or muddy festival.

The shrine has a small rice-field where the rice planting has been under-taken since early days by farmers of three villages in the area. Each year a person to take charge of the planting is selected by drawing lots from among the farmers.

Formerly each household had to send one man and one woman for the plant-ing, but now about 30 women and some men undertake the work.

The planting starts in the morning of the day selected in late May. When the work is almost finished, the *saotome* or women planters have a recess. Sitting along the field, they drink the holy *sake* of the shrine. Then they change their gay costumes to plainer ones and go back to the rice-fields to finish the planting.

Soon the women begin to push and jostle one another. Then they grab each other and wrestle. Some are thrown down in the muddy field. The free wrestling, with laughter and shouts, continues almost half an hour. When it ends, the women are covered all over with mud but laughing happily.

When all is over, each woman planter takes home one rice plant. But on the way home, if they meet any men they wipe the mud off their bodies and throw it at them. Mothers who have weak children often make the women smear some mud on such children, so that they will grow up strong.

The mud-covered women wash off the mud in a river nearby. At home they clean themselves and put on dry clothes. They then go to the house of the one who is in charge of the rite where all the villagers have already gathered.

There all of the villagers have a feast and dance and sing all through the night.

SABOTEN

THE CULTIVATION of *saboten* or cac-tus is quite a fad among plant and flower lovers of Japan. Not only flower shops and plant dealers have them for sale, but also many department stores in big cities display quite a wide range of the plant.

It was about 200 years ago that *saboten* was first introduced into Japan by foreign traders. The leafless plant, with gorgeous flowers, at once at-tracted the attention of the people. Par-ticularly in the latter part of the Tokugawa period, cultivators of *sabo-ten* became quite numerous, and it is recorded that in 1867, a year before the Meiji Restoration, a *saboten* show was held at Choshoji Temple, Iriya, Edo, where 48 potted cacti were displayed.

In the Edo days, *saboten* was regard-ed as a charm against big fires. It may have come from the fact that cacti are hard to burn.

It has been said that the *saboten* fad recurs every 20 years. On the other hand, some say that the year when *saboten* cultivation is popular indicates the beginning of a coming depression.

Cactus is named *saboten*, but it is not known how this name originated. One story says that it came from *shabon* (soap). Dutch seamen coming to Japan were seen scrubbing their clothes with pieces of cacti to make them clean. So the Japanese thought that it was a kind of soap and named it *saboten*. The truth of this story is not proved, however.

Cacti, as is well-known, originated in

Mexico. Then they were taken to Europe after the discovery of America. To Europeans they must have been quite a rare species of plant. They were brought to Japan by Dutch or Portuguese traders.

SAKURA

SAKURA, the national flower of Japan, is a type of cherry blossom not seen in any other country. In older days it was regarded as symbolic of the spirit of the people. The word sakura came from 'saku-urara' (blossoms brightly), and thus the beauty and brightness of the flower were appreciated from the very beginning.

Having come to be considered as the foremost flower of the country, sakura came to be referred to as 'hana' (flower). But there was a time when 'hana' stood for ume (apricot) blossoms, as they were loved above all other flowers soon after their introduction from China.

It is not clearly known when sakura came to replace ume, but it seems that the aristocracy first came to admire sakura in the Heian period (794-1192). The Manyoshu, the oldest collection of poems which contains poems written between 315 and 759, contains no poem on sakura, but in this collection, ume has 113 poems. But the Kokinshu compiled in 905 has many famous sakura poems.

Many authorities thus assert that it was in the latter part of the eighth century that the beauty of sakura came to be recognized by aristocratic flower lovers.

Yoshinoyama, a mountain region in the present Nara Prefecture, was the first district to become famous for sakura blossoms. It is recorded that Emperor Jito (690-697) made several trips to Yoshino to view its beautiful blossoms, and also brought sakura trees from Yoshino and planted them in the Palace grounds.

There is a legend which concerns the sakura trees in Yoshinoyama. Ennoozunu, a seventh-century Buddhist priest, who is commonly called Ennogyoja, went to the Yoshino mountain at the age of 32 for austere training, eating no cooked food. On the mountainside he planted sakura trees and consecrated them to Zao-Gongen, an incarnation of Buddha. He taught his disciples and people to love the trees and not to injure them if they wanted to enjoy an enlightened future life. He planted sakura trees to attract the people to the mountain, and taught them the wisdom of Buddha and human kindness through their respect and care for the blossoming trees.

As the years went on, he added more trees to the mountain, and finally the whole valley came to be covered with sakura blossoms in spring. Thus Yoshinoyama became the greatest and most famous place to view sakura blossoms.

In the era of Hogen (1156-1159), Yoshinoyama sakura trees were planted at Arashiyama, Kyoto, to enable the people of Kyoto to enjoy the blossoms without going to Yoshino. Arashiyama is still one of the most famous sakura-viewing spots of the country.

The first sakura-viewing party mentioned in history was one held by Emperor Saga in 812, when nobles and high officials were invited to view the blossoms in the Palace. The great sakura party held by Toyotomi Hideyoshi at the Daigoji Temple, Fushimi, in 1598, is said to have been the most magnificent party of its kind observed in the country.

But the love of sakura blossoms and particularly visits to Yoshinoyama were confined to people of the upper class until the Tokugawa era which began in the 17th century.

In the meantime, as aristocrats came to show much interest in *sakura* blossoms, there were found or developed many new species of the plant with different types of flowers.

The Tokugawa authorities planted *sakura* trees at Ueno, Mukojima, Asukayama and Arakawa in Edo. The blossoming of *sakura* at these places popularized *sakura* among the common people. Particularly around the Genroku era (1688-1704) when the Edo culture became highly developed and luxurious pleasure-loving habits became common, 'hanami' or *sakura*-viewing parties became the greatest recreation of the people.

Dressed in their finest costumes, the Edo people of all classes went to view *sakura* and enjoy a day's outing with food, drink, music and dancing.

Hanami becoming so popular, *sakura*-viewing scenes were adopted in *Kabuki* plays, and also *hanami* customs became topics of 'rakugo' or comic stories. *Hanami* and *sakura* flowers were even introduced into children's tales.

Thus it was in the latter Edo years that *sakura* became really the flower of the people. *Samurai* or fighting men regarded the blossoms as the symbol of their spirit. *Sakura* blossoms are scattered away by the spring breeze after a few days of glory, and it was thought they stood for the spirit of the *samurai* who was expected to die willingly whenever the time came.

There are many varieties of *sakura*, but the king of them all is the *yama-zakura* or mountain *sakura*. There are two kinds, one growing in the southern and central regions and called just *yama-zakura*, and the other in the northern area and called *o-yama-zakura* or big *yama-zakura*.

Many kinds of the so-called *sato-zakura* or town *sakura* have developed from *yama-zakura*.

As the most magnificent of *sakura* blossoms, *Oshima-zakura* or *sakura* of Oshima Island, south of Tokyo Bay, must be mentioned.

Oshima Island is a volcanic island, rising out of the sea. So at first there were no plants, but gradually seeds blown by wind from the Izu and Boshu peninsulas drifted to the island of volcanic lava and ashes and took root. The seeds of *yama-zakura* must have come to the island in the same way. In the ensuing many thousands of years, the seeds grew into big trees. *Sakura* stumps said to be more than 1,000 years old still remain.

On the island, *yama-zakura* seeds grew better than their parent trees on the main island, probably due to climatic and soil conditions. Trees have grown to an enormous size, with huge roots rising above the ground and stretching out in all directions, and in spring bear much larger blossoms and fruits than those seen on any *sakura* trees in other parts of the country.

SAKURA OF TOKYO

THERE ARE in Japan some 300 varieties of *sakura*, the flowering cherry. In Tokyo, however, *sakura* trees are mostly of the species called *Somei-yoshino*. This kind has also become very widely planted all over the country because of its gorgeous blossoms. *Somei-yoshino* cherries are wonderful, and are particularly suited for planting in cities, because of their rapid growth.

The origin of Tokyo's famous *Somei-yoshino* variety is not clearly known. According to Dr. Tomitaro Makino, eminent botanist, the *Somei-yoshino* is a unique variety of *sakura*, distinctly different from other varieties. It is certain, however, that it was first planted in Tokyo, and was not known anywhere else when it was introduced to Tokyo.

It was in about 1872 that the *Somei-yoshino sakura* was first brought to Tokyo. At that time, the Imperial Museum (now called the National Museum and located at Ueno) was at the site where the Imperial Hotel now stands. It was proposed to plant some *sakura* trees around the museum. When young *sakura* trees were brought there, the one in charge of their planting asked the gardeners where the trees came from. They replied that they were from Somei, a suburb of Tokyo, famous for raising garden trees.

Seeing that the trees planted around the museum were a variety of *Yoshino-zakura*, the botanist in charge called them *Somei-yoshino*. The new variety was not known even to scientists up to that time.

This new variety of *sakura* has now become national in popularity, giving gladness to the people all over the country every spring, but its origin is still unknown.

SAKURA-SO

SAKURA-SO is a little wild plant which has long been admired by the Japanese for its delicate tiny blossoms. It is a Japanese species of primrose of which there are almost 300 different varieties, with new ones being added almost every year.

It was at first admired as it grew wild on swampy land. For example, since Tokugawa days, the Toda district on the Sumida River, not far from the center of the capital, has been extremely famed for *sakura-so*. The people still make visits there to view the wide stretch of the little pink blossoms, though the flowering area is no longer so vast as it used to be.

Sakura-so is so named because the flowers resemble the cherry blossoms

in shape and color. However, *sakura-so* comes in many shades of pink, while some are white or purplish. It is a perennial that grows to a height of about six inches, and flowers appear in clusters. It blooms for nearly two months from the middle of April to the first to June.

It was almost 300 years ago that the people started to plant them in pots and admire the blossoms at home. Since then many flower lovers have begun cultivating and developing new varieties.

Potted *sakura-so* is one of the most popular flowers kept in Japanese households, because they are so inexpensive. Many districts hold annual *sakura-so* exhibitions, at which cultivators rival to show new and better varieties.

Foreign flower lovers have also begun to show interest in *sakura-so*, and the seeds are now exported.

SALT TREE

NURUDE (sumac), a kind of lacquer tree, is commonly called *shio-no-ki* or salt tree in many parts of the country. It grows wild on mountains and hills, often reaching a height of 20 feet. It bears small white flowers in clusters in summer and in autumn has round flat berries.

Village children loved to gather the berries if they found them in their walks through mountain areas. Often they put them in their mouths to enjoy the salty taste.

It is because the berries taste salty that the plant came to be called the salt tree. They were said to be used in place of salt in some mountain regions, in cooking and pickling vegetables.

The kernel of the berry was also used as a medicine in the old days. But today the *nurude* trees have no practical value. Yet as the leaves turn reddish yellow in autumn, the plant gives a welcome color to the mountainsides.

Nurude has another strange feature which is now almost forgotten. Little insects called *nurude-no-mimifushi* put their larvae on the leaves and branches of the plant. The irregular-shaped small bags containing the larvae or gallnuts were formerly used to obtain the base for making black ink, and also the teeth-blacking which was used by Japanese women in feudal days.

These bags of insect larvae are still seen on the *nurude* but are no longer noticed by the people who now have no use for them. Nor are the salty berries gathered now, though playful children like to see if the berries are really salty as they are told by the older folks.

Only the beautifully colored leaves that brighten the countryside remind the people of the existence of *nurude* trees everywhere in many hilly or mountainous regions.

SEEDLESS ORANGE

IN THE province of Kii, there was once a young man named Kichigoro. One day while he was talking with his friends, they told him that he must visit Edo or else he would not know the world. They particularly spoke of the gay life at Yoshiwara where there were beautiful women worth 1,000 pieces of gold a look.

Kichigoro wanted to go to Edo, and having managed to obtain 3,000 gold pieces, he hurried to Yoshiwara. There he asked to see a woman who was worth 1,000 gold pieces just to look at.

Soon a beautiful woman was brought before him for his 1,000 gold coins. When he gazed at her beautiful face and graceful figure, he was satisfied and glad that he had come. He wanted to see her again and paid another 1,000

pieces. But with the third look all his money was gone and he could do nothing but return home.

As he was sorrowfully leaving the the Yoshiwara quarters, a man came running after him, saying that the woman wanted to see him again. Kichigoro said he had no more money, but the man told him that money was no question. She just wanted to see him.

So he went and the woman told him that she had never met such a good honest man before and wanted to become his wife. He appreciated her kind words but said that he must first return home and talk with relatives before taking her as his wife. Finally they pledged themselves for future marriage. She then proposed to return his 3,000 gold pieces but he would not take the money, promising to return to Edo in 50 days. He only borrowed a few coins for his travel expenses.

When he returned home and told his relatives that he was going to marry the Yoshiwara woman, they all opposed him saying that she was only tricking him to get his money. But he insisted upon going back to Edo and marrying her. When he reached Yoshiwara after much delay, he found her already dead.

He was told that she had impatiently waited for him but died seven days before in despair. When he visited her tomb, her ghost appeared and told him that though she had died before his return she would not reproach him, and to make him enjoy a comfortable life, she gave him seven seeds that would grow seedless oranges.

With the seven seeds he returned home to Kii and planted them. Out of those seeds grew orange trees that bore seedless oranges. Thus Kii (present Wakayama) became famous for seedless oranges.

SHO-CHIKU-BAI

SHO-CHIKU-BAI or pine-bamboo-apricot is the traditional symbol of happiness which is used as a design on costumes and furniture. These plants in pots or vases are also necessary ornaments on all happy occasions.

The idea was originally brought from China, but there this combination of three plants had an entirely different meaning. It is recorded that in China, a painting depicting a pine, bamboo and apricot was once placed in a hut where several literary men used to gather. They called the three plants 'the three friends in winter.' The winter season was dreary, but the sight of pine, bamboo and apricot revealed to them the beauty of nature and comforted them, and so they considered the plants as their friends in winter.

In the Fujiwara period in the ninth to 12th centuries, pine trees were regarded the symbol of happiness and prosperity, while *tsuru-kame* (crane and tortoise) were models of long life. The two symbols came to be combined and soon the pine, crane and tortoise were lumped together as a symbol of happiness and long life. In the Ashikaga period (14th-16th centuries), the bamboo was added to these happy signs. Then during the Genroku period at the end of the 17th century, the apricot was used together with the crane, tortoise, pine and bamboo. The costumes of men and women came to be decorated with these gorgeous designs. Later, the use of the crane and tortoise came to be separated from the pine, bamboo and apricot. Thus the crane and tortoise came to stand for long life once again and the design of pine-bamboo-apricot came to signify happiness.

There is a *samisen* ballad called *sho-chiku-bai*, which was composed by Mihashi Koto in the middle of the Tokugawa era. The music is also adapted for the *koto* or Japanese harp. It is still played on various happy occasions. It sings of the beauty of nature, beginning with the spring scene of pine and apricot, and ending with the autumn scene of bamboo.

SHOGUN'S BONSAI

TWO OF THE *bonsai*, dwarf potted trees, owned by Tokugawa Iyemitsu who was the third Tokugawa Shogun from 1623 to 1651, are still preserved at the Tokyo Horticulture School, Matsubara-cho, Setagaya. One is *goyo-no-matsu* (five-leaf pine) and the other *kuromatsu* (black pine). They are relatively large for *bonsai*, being almost six feet tall. But thanks to the good fortune of having been under the constant care of *bonsai* lovers all through the past 300 years, they are still in good condition.

Bonsai is the unique art of presenting in pots of plants the grand beauty of nature. It has a long history, appearing in picture scrolls of the 13th century. But the name *bonsai* is more recent, being a little over a hundred years old.

The essence of the art of *bonsai* is to produce natural scenes in miniature. Three or four trees in a pot may look like huge trees standing in a vast field though only a few inches tall, or a single little tree becomes a giant tree of the mountain, with moss-covered trunk and raised roots.

As the plant is confined in the small space of a pot, painstaking attention is required to keep it alive. The branches and roots have to be properly pruned, and the soil has to be changed often. Watering is important, and proper fertilizers must be added.

Iyemitsu's pine trees have lived so long in fine condition, simply because they have been treasured by *bonsai* lovers who realized their great value, and they have been given proper care despite various difficulties.

Before these two *bonsai* were acquired by the Horticulture School in 1909, they were owned by Mr. Kizo Oyamada, and since then they have been cared for by Mr. Yasutaro Ichikawa of the school.

SHUKAIDO

SHUKAIDO, a kind of begonia, is one of the autumn flowers that is much admired by the people. It is a small perennial plant with large distorted egg-shaped leaves. The light pink blossom has four petals, two of them smaller than the others. It is called *shukaido* (autumn aronia) because the flower resembles the aronia. It grows well in moist places.

This plant was brought from China in the Kan-ei era (1624-1643) and immediately it came to be planted in many Japanese gardens. It is seldom found growing wild.

Chinese stories related to this flower were also introduced. In China the *shukaido* is often called the heart-breaking blossom. According to a tale, a young woman loved a man but her love was not returned. So she lamented and as her tears fell on the ground, a flower sprang up. It came to be called the heart-breaking flower and still grows in moist earth.

The blossom is also associated in China with Yang Kuei, consort of a Tang emperor and a great beauty of the eighth century. Emperor Hsuan lost his empress in 736 and was very sad. His officials advised him to marry again, but no woman attracted him.

Finally he met Yang Kuei, a famous beauty and accomplished dancer and musician. She was brought to the palace as a maid, but became the emperor's consort in 745 and was accorded the dignity and respect due an empress.

But in 755 a rebellion occurred in the country, and the emperor was obliged to flee to safety. As confusion and difficulty fell upon the people because of the rebellion, there arose a strong voice that the emperor was so infatuated with the beautiful Yang Kuei that he had neglected the administration and brought about the lamentable condition. Thus anger rose against her and she was killed when she was 38 years old.

It is said that just before she met her death she shed tears of sorrow that caused the heart-breaking flower to grow from the moistened soil.

The story of Yang Kuei has been made into the *Noh* play *Yoki-hi*, in which the emperor meets the spirit of Yang Kuei.

SUGI

OF ALL TREES growing in Japan, the *sugi*, called Japanese cedar or cryptomeria, is the most valuable. This tree grows tall, often reaching a height of more than 50 meters, and is characterized by its straightness and short branches. The avenue of great *sugi* trees at Nikko is world-famous. There are many huge *sugi* forests in many parts of the country.

Sugi is inseparable from the life of the people. In Japanese dwellings, pillars, boards and ceilings are made of this wood. The fine straight grains of this wood have been highly valued. In making unpainted boxes, screen doors and other things it is regarded as the best material. In the old days, they even built boats with *sugi*. Ornamental boxes used in packing cakes and other things as gifts are usually of *sugi*. There are also *sugi* chopsticks.

Since it grows straight, it is also most valuable as flag poles, telegraph poles and other kinds of poles.

This wood has a faint fragrance, so in the old days *sugi* boards were used in cooking. The meat of fowl or fish was placed on these boards and broiled. This type of cooking, similar to Western plank steaks, was called *sugi-yaki* or *sugi* broiling.

Because of its wide use mountains and hills are planted with *sugi*. It is the main tree used in afforestation in Japan.

Sugi cultivation has developed so highly that there are even specialists who gather the seeds. In autumn they go to the mountains in search of trees of good quality. Climbing up such selected trees, and passing ropes to other neighboring trees, they hang by the ropes to cut slender seed-bearing branches with their sickles.

The good seeds thus collected are sold. Some are now even exported.

SUI-BAN

WHITE, pink, yellow or purple blossoms of *suiren* (Nymphaea) blooming in garden ponds are welcome in the warm weather. They look fresh and cool with the round leaves and flowers floating on the water. *Suiren* is also put in large earthenware basins in the garden. *Hime-suiren*, a small-sized variety, is often put into basins and kept indoors.

To grow *suiren* in such a basin, it is planted with shallow soil at the bottom and water is poured in. But more often the plant is placed in a small earthenware pot and then put into a basin filled with water. The latter is preferred for indoor use, as the water can be kept clean.

The basin filled with water and with some flowering or other small plants is generally called *sui-ban* or water basin. In the summer season, they take the place of potted plants.

For *sui-ban*, other plants beside *suiren* can be used, such as *sagiso* which has tiny white blossoms which look like flying white heron; *chawan-basu*, a small variety of lotus; *omodaka* which has tall stalks of white flowers and graceful shield-shaped leaves; and *hitsuji-gusa*, a small variety of *suiren* with white blossoms.

Many non-flowering plants are also placed in *sui-ban*. Among such are *igusa*, the large variety of which is used for weaving *tatami* mats; *kuwai*, an edible root and many others. All these plants have lovely green leaves growing from the water. Properly raised and arranged, they make refreshing ornaments in rooms during the summer season.

SUMIRE

SUMIRE or violets appear to have been more loved by the Japanese in ancient days than at present. The flower has been popular because it is found wild all over the country. There are more than 100 varieties in the country, many more than in other countries.

The *Manyoshu*, a collection of ancient poems of the fourth to eighth centuries, has many poems on the *sumire*, some of which tell of the joy of going to fields and mountains to view and gather *sumire*.

The fragrance and lovely shape of the blossom have appealed to the people, and particularly women. With the development of big cities and towns, urban folks did not have much opportunity to enjoy wild *sumire*. Thus its popularity seems to have declined in the Tokugawa days, but in the early Meiji years the violet regained its popularity, and came to be sung of in poems and songs. It came to be associated with love and love affairs.

Since olden days, children have loved to gather these flowers and even play with them. Two boys or girls take a violet each, holding it by its stem and hook each other's flower. Then they pull to see which flower will be pulled off the stem first. From this little game, which is still played by rural children, *sumire* is often called *sumotori-gusa* or wrestling plant.

TETSUDO-SO

TETSUDO-SO (railway grass) is an insignificant plant that grows almost all over Japan, except in the high mountain regions. The people notice it in summer as it has small white blossoms, like tiny chrysanthemums on its slender branches, even though they may not know its name.

When they learn the name, they wonder why such a useless weed is named thus. But the plant has other names besides *tetsudo-so*. It is sometimes called *Meiji-so* (Meiji grass) or *Goishin-so* (Restoration grass). These names are all related to the beginning of the Meiji era and judging by it, the plant was one of the many new things that came with the new era or civilization of Japan.

The proper name of the plant is *Himemukashi-yomogi* (Eigeron Canadensis) and it came to Japan from America in the early years of Meiji as its name indicates. It is now believed by scientists that the seeds of the plant must have come with cargo reaching here from Canada or the United States.

The seeds quickly took root in the soil of Japan and multiplied. They were first found growing along railway lines, and thus came to be popularly called *tetsudo-so*. The first railway line was opened between Tokyo and Yokohama

in May 1872, and as the lines were extended to all parts of the country, it found its way to various districts. Now it can be seen not only along railway lines, but also on hills and plains.

Although the plant itself is of no use, it is botanically notable that within such a short period, it found its way to all parts of the country.

TWIN BAMBOOS

AT MIZUNAMI on the Chuo railway line, not far from Nagoya, there is a rare variety of bamboo called *sosei-yadake* or twin arrow bamboo, which is now protected as a valuable botanical specimen.

It is a slender kind of bamboo and was formerly used to make arrows. The significance of this variety lies in the fact that it always grows in pairs. Two slender bamboos rise from the ground about two inches apart; thus the origin of the name, twin bamboo.

A story is told about this bamboo in connection with Minamoto Yorimasa, a great warrior and archery expert of the 12th century. Emperor Konoe suffered nightly because of the weird sound made by the *nue*, a fabulous night bird. Yorimasa shot the evil bird with his arrow relieving the emperor from fear and sleeplessness. This tale made Yorimasa very famous.

It is said that the arrow Yorimasa used in shooting the evil bird was made of the *sosei-yadake* of Mizunami.

Mizunami is not the only place where this variety of bamboo grows. They are also found around the Azoga-ike pond at Nakatsu in Iyo province, Shikoku. This district also claims that Yorimasa's arrow was made from bamboo from Azoga-ike.

Iyo is far from Kyoto where the traditional incident took place, and it is unlikely that Yorimasa's arrow was made from Iyo bamboo, Mizunami people say. But the people of Iyo insist upon their claim.

Yorimasa's mother lived in Iyo, and in prayer that Yorimasa would become skillful in archery, she sent him several thousands of arrow bamboos from Azoga-ike every year, they say. Furthermore, the mother went daily to the pond to pray for Yorimasa.

One day, a strange cloud arose from Azoga-ike and as it stretched out in a narrow band, it drifted toward Kyoto. This was the very day on which Yorimasa killed the *nue* at the Imperial Palace.

There is also a story that the mother died on the evening when Yorimasa killed the *nue*.

UME BLOSSOMS

THE BLOSSOMS of *ume* (Japanese apricot) are welcomed as the first flower of spring. Their scent and pure whiteness make them one of the most admired plants of the country. Although *sakura* (flowering cherry) and *kiku* (chrysanthemum) may be more popular today and are regarded as the symbols of the nation, in ancient days *ume* was the first flower. In the *Manyoshu*, the ancient collection of poems, there are 113 poems on the *ume*.

Even today, *ume* are valued garden trees, and are also made into *bonsai* or potted dwarf plants. *Sho-chiku-bai* (pine-bamboo-apricot) are the symbols of happiness, so are often used as the theme for paintings. These three plants are also arranged in vases or planted in one pot.

The plant and blossom are now generally called *ume* but formerly the name was pronounced *'mume.'* Its botanical name is Prunus Mume, and Japanese and English dictionaries published by James Hepburn in 1868 write the name 'M'me.'

It is closely related to the daily life of the people. Besides the flowers, the fruit is indispensable as a daily food. It is pickled and called *ume-boshi*. On New Year's Day, the people take their first cup of tea with *ume-boshi*. *Ume-shu* or an alcoholic drink made with the fruit, tasting like cherry brandy, is very popular.

Large *ume* gardens were originally planted for the fruit which was used in making a kind of vinegar required in ancient dyeing processes. It is believed that one *ume-boshi* a day will keep the body in sound health, as its strong acid aids digestion and kills bacteria.

There are white, pink and red blossoms. Some have large fruits, while others bear only tiny ones. The shapes of the leaves are also different according to varieties. The white blossom, however, is regarded as the standard, although *kobai* or red *ume* is also very beautiful and popular.

Ume blossoms are valued for their noble fragrance, and as they come in the coldest season of the year, they bring a touch of beauty to the dreary winter scenery.

Ume is the symbol of beauty and virtue of women. It is one of the most popular names given to girls. Traditionally, women are thought to be pure and noble as the *ume* blossoms, and able to stand dignified and erect despite all adversities and difficulties of life.

To enjoy the blossoms, *ume* trees are planted in gardens and pots. Many large *ume* gardens are found in various parts of the country, and at blossom time people make special trips to view the fragrant blossoms. Particularly in the evening, from quite a distance, one can tell that a *ume* garden is near. *Ume*-viewing parties were very popular up to the end of the Meiji era.

Cherry-viewing parties are merry,

but *ume* parties are quiet and dignified. Probably that is the reason why the younger people have no interest in visiting *ume* gardens.

The trunks and branches of old *ume* trees are rugged and twisted, with cracked bark that is covered with moss. They make good garden trees. The *ume* wood was formerly much used in making boxes and furniture. For *toko-bashira* or the pillars of the guest-room alcove, the aged *ume* wood is still very highly valued.

There is a *Noh* play called *Ume-gae* (apricot branch). A Buddhist priest visits the town of Sumiyoshi, and at a house where he stops, he sees many splendid old dancing costumes. When he asks the story behind the costumes, he is told that they were left by a dancer named Fuji who was killed by a rival dancer. Impressed by the story, the priest recites Buddhist prayers for the spirit of the deceased dancer. Thereupon the spirit of the dancer's wife appears as a dancer, and dances the classic dance of Saibara before the priest as bush warblers sing on the branches of *ume* trees in the garden.

WILLOW

THE *YANAGI* (willow) has always been loved by the Japanese people, and its graceful slender branches that wave so delicately even in the slightest breeze appeal to their poetic tastes. *Yanagi* has been sung of by poets of all times, and it is quite inseparable from rivers and streams. The plant loves marshy places, and in Japanese pictures willows are always painted by the side of rivers or canals. The grace of the branches, the freshness of its young leaves, and the slenderness of the whole appearance have so greatly impressed the people that the *yanagi* is thoroughly woven into the literature of the country.

'Willow-like waist' or 'willow-like figure' is a common expression to describe a graceful, slender woman. 'Willow-eyebrow' means a gracefully arched eyebrow. Anything slender and graceful has always been compared to willow branches that wave so gracefully in the breeze, as well as anything that withstands the severest of storms. Being graceful and slender, *yanagi* is considered feminine, and in literature it is always used as an adjective for feminine things.

But the *yanagi* is also a lucky or felicitous tree. In olden days it is recorded that on New Year's Day the Emperor would exclaim: 'Under the *yuzu* (citron) tree?' to which the Empress replied *'Medetashi* (happy).' That was an ancient custom in the Imperial Court. But this strange expression was used only in the Court, and was never uttered by the common people. The people of Kyoto as well as many other districts formerly used another expression on the same occasion. When the master of the house sat down to the first family party of the New Year, he would ask: 'Under the willow tree?' to which the others replied *'Medetashi.'* Where the Imperial Court used *'Yuzu,'* the common people used the willow.

Yuzu was considered a noble tree fit only for noble persons, and the common people used no expression containing the name of this tree. So instead of *yuzu* they used *yanagi*, the common tree that they loved and considered lucky. It is said that the above-mentioned New Year expression was particularly used in Kyoto and its environs, but it is reported by the authorities that even in Edo it was used by many families.

It is probable that, from the ancient custom of using this happy expression on New Year's Day, chopsticks made of willow wood are still used during New

Year celebrations even today. During the several days of the New Year season, ordinary chopsticks are not used, but the people use *yanagi* chopsticks, which are burned after the season.

Yanagi is considered lucky and happy, because it buds easily. To bud *(me-ga-deru)* is synonymous with happiness *(medetashi)*, and thus *yanagi* is used as a symbol to indicate happiness and felicitation. Break off a branch of *yanagi* and stick it in a marshy place, and it will soon bud and grow. This vitality and adaptability are highly appreciated by the people.

Yanagi is, therefore, not only slender and graceful, but is also a lucky and happy omen. On that account, many people plant *yanagi* trees around their residences hoping that the family will multiply and grow as easily and prosperously as the willow tree.

We are also in the habit of associating *yanagi*, the willow, with rain. *Yanagi-ni-ame* (willow in rain) is a favorite expression used not only in our literature and common language, but is also a favorite subject of Japanese artists. The people love to watch the long swaying branches of willow tossed by rain and wind. They signify tenderness, weakness and also sorrow.

Willow trees grow on river-banks or on other marshy lands, and line the shores of many rivers, moats and canals. They are thus also associated with rivers or flows of water.

It is natural for willows to love rain, because they could not survive without much water in the soil.

But there is one particular kind of willow that is believed by the Japanese to be fond of rain more than other varieties. This variety is called *tei*, but also named *gyo-ryu* (honorable willow). The latter name came from China. It is said that Yang Kuei, the famous beauty

of the Tang dynasty, who was the favorite of the emperor, was very fond of this variety of willow, and as she planted many trees in her garden, the people called them *gyo-ryu* (honorable willow).

There is another explanation to this name. This story says that, as this kind of willow was especially fond of the river-bank, where many of these trees were found, fishermen were able to hook many catches. From this belief the tree was called *gyo-ryu* (fish willow).

But one outstanding feature of this peculiar willow is that it predicts rainfall. Just before a rain, the leaves of this willow tree rise towards the sky as if they were raising their hands to welcome the coming rain. Some people say that the tree is praying for rain when it raises its leaves sky-ward. It seems that the tree is really joyful when it realizes the coming of rain and stretches out its leaves to welcome raindrops. Because of its power of thus predicting rainfall, the tree is also called 'the sage of trees.'

YABU-KANZO

THE ORANGE-YELLOW blossoms of *yabu-kanzo* or yellow day lily brighten country roadsides and hills. In spring, the young leaves of the plant are eaten in rural districts as a vegetable. The blossom is often eaten, too, some people putting it in *sukiyaki*, but its color is more attractive than its taste.

The root of the plant was also used as a medicine or a sweetening substance formerly.

If a woman carries this blossom with her, she will give birth to a boy, it is traditionally believe, and in China women were said to have been particularly fond of the blossom.

In the old days, the plant was also called *wasure-gasa* or forgetting plant.

The *Manyoshu*, a collection of ancient poems, has a poem mentioning it. It was believed that when one had this plant he would forget any unhappy or unpleasant memories.

There is a story about the *wasuregusa* concerning two brothers who lost their parents. The brothers were never happy after the death of their parents and spent every day in sorrow and dejection. As his sadness continued day after day, the eldest brother wished to end his sorrow which was ruining him mentally and physically. So he planted the *wasure-gusa* on his parents' tomb.

The younger brother, on the other hand, desired to cherish their memory and planted around the tomb some *shion*, a kind of aster, which was known as a remembering plant.

One day, the devil guarding the tombs appeared and saying that he was impressed by the filial devotion of the younger brother, taught him the secret art of prophecy as a reward. The younger brother made a notable advancement with his new insight and became famous.

YAMATO-NADESHIKO

NADESHIKO or fringed pinks are listed among the seven flowers of autumn and have been regarded as a symbol of modest beauty since the days of the *Manyoshu*.

The *nadeshiko* has five light purplish pink petals, which are deeply fringed and look modest though very pretty. *Yamato-nadeshiko* is still used as a literary term for Japanese women.

It is found growing wild all over the country but to distinguish it from the Chinese variety of pinks that have also been introduced to the country, the Japanese species is often called *Yamato-nadeshiko* or *Kawara-nadeshiko* as it is found on river-banks.

A story is told about the origin of this pretty flower. Once there lived a brave warrior named Tokitsukasa at Shimada. On a mountain nearby there was a mysterious rock which was said to torment persons passing there at night. Determined to put an end to such a disturbing evil object, Tokitsukasa one night went up the mountain carrying his trusty bow and arrow.

Reaching the rock which was said to be bewitched, he shot his arrow at it. He was a good archer and his arrow went deep into the rock. That ended the bewitching power of the rock, but from the spot where his arrow hit it there blossomed a pretty flower. This flower was the *nadeshiko*, the story says.

This tale appears to have been based on the fact that the *nadeshiko* is also called *sekichiku* (stone bamboo).

It is sometimes also called *katamiso* (memento plant). How it came by that name is told in the following story.

There once lived a person in Yamato province who was very fond of the *nadeshiko* and used to grow them every year with tender care. But the man died, so his father kept on growing them thinking they were a keepsake his son had left him so that he would think of his son always.

YATATE-SUGI

IN THE OLD days, the border lines between provinces, towns or villages were marked by leaving two big trees uncut. Generally trees which were different from those around them or those that had heights or shapes that were easily recognized were selected. The *sugi* or cryptomeria were often selected as they grow to a large height.

The marking of a border line was a difficult task in the old days when there were no maps or surveying instruments. Often, the heads of two neighboring villages started on horse-back at a fixed time toward each other and the place they met was decided as the spot to draw the dividing line. Again to avoid disputes, a no-man's land was set up between two territories.

The provinces of Bungo and Hyuga, formerly Kyushu, had two border lines between them. On both sides of the dividing ridge of a mountain, lines were drawn a little below from the top. The marking trees, which came to be called the *Bungo* and *Hyuga* trees, were left standing at these lines.

About 100 years ago the *Bungo* tree died and when it was cut down, many arrowheads were found imbedded in the wood. In the early days, it was customary to shoot arrows into the border trees as a mark of respect to the spirit of the border.

There were, therefore, many *yatate-sugi* or arrow-hitting cryptomeria at many important borders. They are recorded to have existed at the Hakone barrier, Sasago pass between Musashi and Kai and other places.

These border trees which were so highly respected and protected by the people have mostly disappeared now, but in many remote mountain regions there still stand great big trees, tower-ing over the surrounding forests to mark the former dividing lines.

Generally the old border trees stood in pairs. Therefore there also developed in many places traditional stories that such trees grew from chopsticks planted by some ancient famous persons.

YUZU TREE

THE *YUZU* (true citron) is a holy tree. If ordinary persons plant it in their gardens, it is believed in Japan that the fortune of the family will decline, because they have planted a holy tree where it should not be. *Yuzu* came originally from China, and this im-ported tree was only planted in the gardens of noblemen. Therefore, for any common person to plant it was con-sidered an evil act certain to bring misfortune.

In the old days, on the morning of New Year's Day, the Emperor would in-quire, 'Under the *yuzu* tree?' to which the proper reply was, '*Medetashi* (hap-py).' These are strange expressions, but the old records state that such were the usual expressions used in the Court on New Year's Day. *Yuzu* is not only a no-ble and aristocratic tree, but is also con-sidered as happy and joyous, because it buds well and in plenty. Budding of trees was regarded as a sign of hap-piness. Of course, for plants to bud well and in plenty is a very happy and joyous thing.

It is said that, at some places, *yuzu* fruits are always employed when the *kami* of cereals are worshiped. The *yuzu* seeds are said to be always of the same size, and when they are planted they grow equally well, there being none that do not grow. Therefore, *yuzu* fruits are used in the worship of the *kami* of cereals, in the hope that cereals planted will grow together and equally strong, and there will be none that will not grow well.

Some old-fashioned people believe not only that the planting of *yuzu* in or-dinary gardens of common people will bring ill-luck, but that if a pestle be made of *yuzu* wood, it will turn into various other shapes. A *yuzu* wood pestle is believed to take various mysterious shapes, and there are many tales in which people are surprised by the strange shapes the pestle takes.

Once upon a time, there was an old man who used to go out every night to a hut erected on his farm, to guard it from the attack of wild beasts. But every night his wife came out to the hut and inquired if he had seen bears. Whenever he returned home, he scolded his wife for coming out and troubling him with such a foolish question, but the old woman replied that she never went out of the house at night. Then he told the wife that, if she came out again to the hut at night, he would shoot her. She agreed. The next night she again came to the hut and inquired if bears were seen, and the old man took up his gun and shot her. He later found that he had shot the pestle made of *yuzu* wood which he was using at home.

In some parts of Kii, it is believed that if the whole *yuzu* fruit is placed in a tub of *miso* (salted bean-paste), it will shout 'Yuu-zo (I will tell)' when any thief breaks into the tub of *miso* so that any thief may be scared off before entering. Again in some places, it is believed that when one has a boil, it should be picked with a *yuzu* prickle as the boil will then heal at once. The tree being holy, it is believed to have the power of driving away any poison or evil in the boil. Just as *tachibana* (Citrus Nobilis) is considered a holy tree in Japan, *yuzu* is a holy tree, and both trees came to Japan from foreign lands. This fact must have made them so noble and holy, having been at first enjoyed by aristocratic persons only.

Chapter 12
Popular Beliefs and Traditions

AMAGOI

WHEN DROUGHTS parch rice-fields, blight plants and flowers, and dry up wells and rivers, *amagoi* (rain prayers) are offered for a rainfall. There are many stories of such prayers bringing immediate results, and even today farmers invariably offer such prayers for rain whenever dry, sunny days continue without the blessing of rain.

These prayers for rain are offered to *Ryu-o* who is the god of rain and lives in the sea. When the prayer is heard, it is said, the god will rise from the sea and ascend to the sky, creating dense clouds from which rain will fall.

The name of *Ryu-o* is written Dragon King, and that of *Ryujin*, Dragon God; the god of rain is thus considered to be in the shape of a dragon. The rain god is believed to reside in the sea, but it also lives in lakes and large ponds. Not only are there many tales which relate incidents of dragons rising from lakes or deep pools of water, but in many parts of the country there are places named *Ryugasaki* (Dragon Point) or *Ryuga-fuchi* (Dragon Abyss).

Because *Ryu-o* dispenses rain, the prayer for rain has to be offered to him. It is probably because he lives in the depths of the sea that the prayer is usually accompanied by rocket-firing, ringing of bells, or singing of Buddhist sacred songs by the people.

The rising of the dragon from the sea

or from a lake is said to be very impressive. It is preceded by a strong gust of wind, and thick vapor or mist from the sea or lake surface. Suddenly the huge body of the dragon rises at terrific speed out of the water, causing the blackest cloud to rise from the water and spread wider and thicker as it goes higher. In the black cloud, the shining tail of the dragon is often seen by those who are fortunate enough to be present. Then the rainfall will come, blessing the earth and vegetation.

The custom of praying for rain whenever the rainfall is not sufficient to plant rice has been observed all over the country since very early days. Though the method of praying for rain differs according to time and district, it is written that in feudal days, it was held in a most elaborate manner, with gorgeous processions, singing and dancing.

Generally speaking, there are two great divisions in the method for praying for rain. One is to make offerings to appease *kami*, and the other is to threaten or punish the *kami*.

In the Hitachi district, whenever a drought comes and farmers want rain, they visit the Raijin Shrine at Mito to obtain sacred water. Coming from great distances, they kneel and pray before the shrine. Then, obtaining sacred water, they convey it away in a bamboo container. They must carry home the sacred water, without even once stopping on the way. If anyone carrying the sacred water stops, rain will fall at that spot and not on his farm. Those who come from distant places have comrades ready at several intervals to relay the bamboo holding the sacred water. Thus, the sacred water is carried from the shrine to their farms and emptied there. It is believed that the sacred water will invite the heavenly rain to fall on that spot.

The Togakushi Shrine at Togakushi, Shinano, is also famous for its power to bring rain. The fame of the shrine in this respect has reached such distant points recently that the shrine annually receives many telegrams from distant districts, asking for prayers for rain. Upon receipt of such telegraphic requests, the shrine holds prayers for rain for such districts. The Togakushi Shrine receives orders for the shipment of its sacred water to the drought districts. The sacred water of the shrine is shipped to such districts in caskets and barrels. Ordinarily, the people must go to the shrine and obtain sacred water, and taking it to their district, they place it on the *kamidana* of the head family of the village. In the daytime, the casket is taken round to all the farms of the village, and at night it is guarded by villagers. After seven days, the sacred water has to be returned to the shrine.

Merry and elaborate dancing parties are sometimes held for days and nights in praying for rain. This is called *amagoi-odori*. Amagoi dance is not so elaborate as it used to be in many districts. The custom is said to have developed from gathering together and loudly saying their prayers for rain.

At the village of Uchitani, Tokushima Prefecture, every farming household owns big drums and bells to be used on occasions of *amagoi-odori*. When the drought becomes severe and it is necessary to pray for rain, every household has to send at least one male to attend the dancing party. More than 700 men of the village assemble and are divided into seven groups of about 100 each.

The dancing continues for three days and two nights, during which time all the men participating cannot return home. But women are not allowed to take part, since they are considered unclean to participate in prayer. Even men have to purify themselves before joining the party. There are three shrines within the village, and the seven groups of dancers have to visit them in turn. Each of the seven groups has to visit the three shrines each day, and thus in three days, 63 visits to the three shrines take place.

The men in the dancing groups have to be dressed in *mino* (farmer's raincoat) and *waraji* (sandal). Each group is headed by a huge drum, and there is one small drum for each 10 people and one bell for every three persons.

Assembling before each shrine, they first stand at attention and after a short silent prayer, they loudly say 'Tenjuku Tenno Ryu-o, Ame-o-tamaware, Ryu-o (god of rain, give us rain, god of rain).' Then, forming themselves in circles, and beating their drums and bells, they dance around and sing. The beating of the drum is slow at first, but gradually it becomes faster and faster, and the dancers' steps also become faster and faster. While dancing, they sing various songs. After the conclusion of the dancing, they again pray silently before the shrine.

In the village of Kurina, Mie Prefecture, there was a unique form of dance until the early part of the Meiji era, but it is now discontinued. Here, both men and women took part in dancing at the beach of Shiratsuka, when *amagoi* took place. In the center were men with drums and bells, and around the musicians were drawn three concentric circles. In the innermost circle were men and women above 40 years of age, in the second were children, and in the outermost were those under 40 years of age. They sang and danced for several hours.

At various other places, *amagoi* dancing is still observed with eagerness and sincerity. While the people enjoy *amagoi* dancing, it is also a very serious matter for them. They regard it their big duty to participate in *amagoi* dancing.

Among various methods of praying for rain, in the drought season, one of the most common is called *hiburi* or waving fire at the sky.

Instead of obtaining the sacred water from various shrines for praying for rain, the sacred fire of the mountains is also brought down and used for praying for rain.

In the Yoshida district of Mikawa, when it becomes necessary to pray for rain, the farmers go up to the Akibasan mountain, Totomi, and after praying at the shrine at the mountaintop, obtain the sacred fire of the mountain from the priest. Then they bring down the fire to their respective villages, where pine torches are lighted with the sacred fire. Around the torch fire, they pray for rain.

South of the Ominesan mountain, Yamato, there is a small mountain named Inamura-dake. The farmers of the neighborhood go up the mountain to get the sacred fire at a time of drought, as they believe that, when the mountain fire is waved over the farms, rain will come. The procession of farmers to the mountain becomes quite lengthy if the drought continues, and they form a long line of torches coming down from the mountain with the sacred fire. The procession is accompanied by the beating of drums and bells.

In the village of Motoyama in Sanuki province, Shikoku, entire villages stop all work on the day when the rain-praying is to be held. They remain idle from early morning although the actual praying begins only in the evening. Towards evening, each carries a bundle of kindling wood to the center of the village, where a huge fire is started. The fire is continued throughout the night, and at the same time, they go to temples and shrines to pray for rain.

At Kokubu-mura, Okayama Prefecture, there is a unique method of praying for rain. While at other places, kindling wood or pine branches are generally used for making fire in praying for rain, rice-straw is used at this village. Children take bundles of straw to the side of the large village pond, where they light the straw and sing a song. But here the prayer custom has almost become children's play rather than an earnest prayer for rain.

In praying for rain in the drought season, various means of irritating the *kami* of mountains and rivers are also used. These are somewhat different from the custom of directly threatening or punishing *kami* in order to cause rainfall. Commonly the sacred streams, mountains and ponds of various deities are despoiled purposely by farmers desiring rainfall, in the belief that such acts would so irritate the *kami* that they would consent to cause rainfalls.

Farmers living in the lake district around Mt. Fuji regard these lakes as sacred, and never foul them by throwing in rubbish or waste. But when they wish to have rainfall in the drought season, they purposely take dried cattle bones to the lakes and throw them into the water. They believe that the fouling of the lake will so irritate the *kami* of the lake that he will cause rainfall so that such acts will not be continued.

Similar customs are observed at

many other rivers and lakes, and sometimes the *kami* of mountains are irritated in a similar manner. In the Ise district there is a popular belief that, when various rubbish and waste are taken to the mountaintops, rainfall is assured, because the mountain *kami* do not like such acts.

In the village of Tomita, Kii province, there is a strange custom in praying for rain. At the time of a great drought, the villagers employ persons who behead a cow or ox, and then carry the head to the shore of the Shogawa River. The people then swim across the rapids to the Ushiyadani Fall. The cattle head is tied by wisteria vines to the precipices. The presence of the cattle head on the precipices overlooking the waterfall irritates the *kami* of the river. The villagers believe that, as soon as the cattle head is hung there, rain will fall. But it is said that the custom is no longer observed, because one year the rain thus caused was so great that the people of the surrounding districts suffered greatly.

At the top of the Mizuishi mountain, at Akaimura, Iwashiro province, there is a huge stone named *Mizu-ishi* or water-stone. The stone is about 12 feet high and more than 50 feet in circumference. On the upper surface of the stone there is a small depressed spot, which is always filled with water. At a time of drought, the villagers take their dirty laundry to the mountain, and wash it in the pool of water, after which the rain is sure to come,

Rain prayers are often made to statues of Jizo (Ksitigrabha). When farmers in the Kyoto district desired rain, they used to go to the Enryakuji Temple and made the priest offer rain prayers. The prayers continued for one week, and in the middle of the week, the gathered farmers climbed Mt. Atagoyama. Coming to the statue of Jizo at

the mountaintop, they tied the statue up with straw ropes. The Jizo was promised release when rain came. Then bringing the sacred fire from the temple, they set fire to a huge pile of wood placed at the mountaintop.

In many parts of the country, farmers carried statues of Jizo and threw them into rivers or lakes, believing that Jizo would bring rain to save himself from drowning.

The village of Ninohe in Aomori had a very strange rain-praying custom. When farmers wanted rain, they carried bottles of *sake* or rice-wine to the Gongen Shrine of Orizune Mountain. While they offered *sake* to the shrine priest and drank themselves, they looked for a chance to carry the priest bodily outside and throw him into the pond nearby. When the priest came up after being thrown into the pond he was pushed back again, until he was completely exhausted. It was believed that Gongen-Sama being fond of the priest would bring rain to save his faithful servant from the cruel treatment.

In the Awa district of Chiba, the people lead water out of a river to make it very shallow and cause the fish to suffer. They believe that the dragon god who rules over all fish will come to save the fish by causing rainfall.

In some places, farmers build a platform over a river. They gather on it and pray for rain, and also hold rain-praying dances. In Kii province, farmers take a big crab to the mountaintop. Circling around it they dance for rain. Then they take the crab down to the seaside and place it on a rock. Rain is sure to come after this, they believe.

As one of strangest rain-praying customs may be mentioned the one followed in the Akita district. There women hold wrestling matches which are believed to bring rain without fail.

In Oita, they hold rain-praying theatrical performances, selecting plays related to rain or water. In some places they produce rain-praying masks. Masks relating to the dragon are kept in boxes all through the year, but when they pray for rain, such masks are taken out to bring rain.

BEWITCHING FOX

PROBABLY there is no other animal in Japan that has been so deeply woven into the traditional and superstitious beliefs of the people as the *kitsune* (fox).

First of all, it is known for the varied forms of mischief it plays on human beings, and its ability to assume the form of human beings, animals and plants is so thoroughly believed by the people that it became an important theme in Japanese folk tales, literature and even in drama.

It is even deified. *Kitsune* is the messenger of Inari-sama, the shrine dedicated to Uka-no-Mitama, *kami* of cereals. *Kitsune* of Inari-sama is believed to be always on the watch to see if farmers pay due offerings to the shrine, and to protect farms of those that are pious. Before the shrine of Inari are always seen stone statues of foxes, and to them are made various offerings. Farmers of today believe in the story of Inari and *kitsune*, and do not fail to pay their respects to the shrine and the fox. In rural districts, the festival of Inari-sama is the most important event of the year, as it is for a good harvest that the shrine is worshiped.

One story says that, in ancient times, there were innumerable foxes in the country which did no small damage to farms and harvests, and therefore to stop them from coming into the farms, the people selected a certain spot where they carried food for the foxes. Thus appeased and with lots of food ready at hand, the foxes ceased to molest farms. The spot became the shrine to which farmers made offerings of food so that their farms might not be damaged by foxes. This story may be true, and the people generally believe that *kitsune* is the sacred messenger of *Inari-sama*, the *kami* of cereals.

Foxes must have existed in the country in great numbers, as there are so many tales about them. Today, however, foxes are quite rare, and they are not seen on farms generally.

Kitsune assumes the form of a man, woman or child, by merely putting a few stray leaves onto its head, or covering its body with a few bits of straw. This is a very common belief held by the people of the country. There are many people living even today who will insist that they have been deceived by foxes which had assumed the form of human beings. Especially in the farming districts this belief is very strong. One returns home at night, walking through a lonely part of the country, and suddenly he sees a light, and finds a house. He enters it wondering who could be living there. He is treated to a good meal in the house. But next morning he finds himself sitting in a muddy pool by the road and eating rotten leaves. Such tales are abundant everywhere. Again *kitsune* takes the form of a beautiful woman and lures men to strange places and strange experiences. Men carrying home baskets of fish at night often find that when they reach home, they have carried in their hands baskets of stones instead of fish. Foxes have done the trick.

It is also believed that often people are possessed by foxes. It is said that when people are possessed by foxes they act strangely and insanely. In olden days such people possessed by foxes were given strange treatment. They were put in a closed room where pine needles and other leaves were burned, and by the excessive smoke, foxes were smoked out of the bodies of such people. Weak-minded people became the victims of foxes which took possession of their human bodies. There were even professionals who made it their business to drive foxes out of such fox-possessed people.

One of the strange fox tales goes as follows:

Once there lived a monk, who, on the way to a gathering of brother monks, found an aged fox asleep by the roadside. Taking up his conch shell trumpet, the monk blew hard at the ear of the fox, which was greatly surprised and ran away. A few days later, other monks saw a fox entering a pool and putting weeds upon its head. Instantly the fox turned out in the form of the first monk. The monks, who witnessed the strange act of the fox, knew that the fox was going to impersonate the first monk who surprised it while asleep. Therefore, when the monk came up soon after, they caught him and gave him a severe beating. They expected that the monk would assume the original shape of a fox, but the monk screamed and moaned, and did not change form. It was really the monk himself. The fox was revenged on the monk by making other monks believe that it was going to impersonate the first one.

A *samurai* named Sakagawa Hikozaemon went on a pheasant hunt, so one story goes. He carried his gun and was followed by several attendants. As he was walking through a dense forest in search of a bird, a stranger suddenly came out of a tall bush and bowing low asked Hikozaemon to include him among his attendants, adding that he even had the consent of the warrior's wife.

As Hikozaemon looked at the face of the stranger, he almost burst out laughing, as the face of the stranger was that of a fox, although he was dressed perfectly as an attendant. Motioning to his retainers not to laugh, he solemnly agreed to take in the stranger among his retainers.

He made the stranger follow him, and soon he handed his gun to him. He told him to go ahead and see if there were any birds around. The stranger disappeared into the forest. But when he came back, he reported that he had failed to see any birds.

Reaching a little resting place, Hikozaemon and his party rested a while and all drank tea. The stranger was also served tea, but he wanted water. So Hikozaemon ordered a big bowl of water for him. As the strange attendant lifted the bowl, he saw his reflection in the water — the face of a fox. Surprised to find that he had not completely disguised himself as a man, he ran away rapidly.

Next day, Hikozaemon went out pheasant hunting again. In the forest, a loud voice from a dense bush called out, 'Hikozaemon.' As the party stood in surprise, the voice said, 'It was funny yesterday.' Then nothing more was heard. No sight of the fox was seen.

Hikozaemon said he never thought a fox could be so comical as the one he had met the day before.

People also believe that foxes make wedding processions when they wed. The phosphorous lights often seen in forests or over the field are believed to be the lanterns of the wedding processions of foxes. It is also believed that, when foxes marry in the daytime, they always select a time when it rains while the sun is shining.

Foxes are said to cry much towards the year-end. It is because foxes desire to be counted among the 12 zodiacal signs, but because they cannot increase the signs to 13, they lament and cry as the year-end approaches.

BLIND GIRL

THE MYO-ONJI Temple in Edogawa Ward, Tokyo, has a small pond, which was much larger and very famous in the old days.

The story of the pond goes back to the 15th century. The village head there had no child and had long prayed for one. When he had almost lost hope, a girl baby was born. But she was blind, and the whole village who respected and loved the village head felt extremely sorry for him.

But the blind girl was beautiful and grew up strong. One year when the village had its annual festival, the girl was taken to the festival by her maid. As they were walking, the girl heard several ill-mannered urchins shout loudly, 'There comes the blind girl!'

She was so strongly affected by that utterance that after that she never went outdoors, afraid to show her blindness to others.

One day, a strange old woman came to the house and said that a family ancestor had committed many crimes of wantonly destroying life and as punishment the blind girl was born.

Learning of this curse, the father offered a 21-day prayer to the Myo-onji Temple, and on the day of the prayer's completion, the daughter's eyes saw light.

Thankful for the mercy of the Buddha of the temple, the father presented many *funa* or crucian carp to the temple pond. But soon the people found that the little fish given in thanks for the girl's gaining her eyesight became one-eyed. They believed that the fish had saved the girl by taking the blame for her ancestor's evil acts.

So the Myo-onji came to be visited and worshiped by all those who were blind or who were suffering from eye diseases.

BOAT LAUNCHING

MANY CUSTOMS connected with the launching of fishing boats and other wooden ships are still observed in many districts. Particularly to seacoast dwellers, boats have long played various important roles in their life. Even today such small wooden ships are still constructed by local builders, and the launching of a new ship is quite an event for the whole community.

Japanese fishermen do not generally welcome any women coming on board ship, as they believe that *Funa-dama* or the spirit of the boat is feminine and jealous of other women on board. But at the launching rite, usually the wife or daughter of the ship owner, or some other women must be present.

In the launching rite, the first step is to install *Funa-dama* in the ship. The spirit of the ship is generally represented by a woman's hair, dolls, coins and cereals which are placed in a small wooden box. The box is put into a hole made in the crossbar holding the mast, and covered securely with a tightly fitting lid. On small boats with no masts, the *Funa-dama* box is put in a division crossbar.

Sake is then offered to *Funa-dama*, and then a Shinto priest purifies the boat and offers a prayer for safety. Then the ship is drawn into the sea, and the crew sets sail or rows her away from the shore.

In many places, the ships are purposely rolled at the launching, and even capsized, in order to accustom them to raging waves and storms. In Kochi, the owner or captain of the ship is tossed into the sea, and in other places, sea water is poured over the ship and the crew.

Along Izu Peninsula, there was formerly a custom of dropping the daughter of the ship owner into the sea to bring good luck to the new ship. On the west coast of Shikoku, the new boat is taken near a rock projecting from the sea and purposely bumped against such a rock to initiate her to sea hazards.

BURGLARS' GUARDIAN

MANY SHRINES and temples are erected to *Nusubito-gami* or guardian deity of burglars. It was formerly said that, when any criminal went into such temples or shrines, he would never be caught, however serious his offense.

The people's belief in some deity that always guards their welfare and health has made them think that there must be some deity protecting burglars.

In the town of Ichihara, Chiba Prefecture, there stands a shrine called Tateishi-jinja, which was formerly worshiped by burglars and other criminals, as it was believed that the shrine protected them. When any burglar entered the compounds of the shrine, he was never found.

Sanpukuji Temple in Ohachiga village of Gifu Prefecture is another guardian of burglars. It was said when criminals entered the bamboo forests of the temple, they would never be caught.

Togakushi Shrine of Otomomura, Okayama Prefecture, was commonly called *Nusubito-gami* or burglars' shrine, and was popularly worshiped by many criminals.

In Edo, there was a thief named Jirokichi, nicknamed Nezumi-kozo (rat boy) because of his quick movement. The greatest burglar of the Tokugawa period, he is reported to have entered and robbed the houses of feudal lords and rich merchants, and distributed his spoils among the poor. He was so famous that his life was written into a *Kabuki* drama and also into many tales. Of course, many acts attributed to him by these stories are now said to be mere fiction. At any rate, he was finally caught, and put to death on August 19, 1832.

Nezumi-kozo's tomb stands in the compounds of Eko-in Temple in Honjo, Tokyo. Many pick-pockets, burglars, gamblers and others still burn incense at his tomb, praying for luck. His tombstone is chipped off by eager visitors, who carry the pieces away as a charm.

CHIKARA-ISHI

IN THE COMPOUNDS of many shrines of the country egg-shaped natural stones which are called *chikara-ishi* (strength stone) or stones for testing one's lifting power are seen. Mostly the stones are too heavy for ordinary persons to lift, but often there are smaller ones that can be heaved up by powerful men.

Many *chikara-ishi* have the names of historical or traditional persons who lifted them up engraved on them but such stones are very heavy, and cannot be used as power-testing stones.

Chikara-ishi often have small holes made in them so that persons trying to lift them up may get a good hold by placing their fingers in them. The stones are generally egg-shaped to make them easier for lifting.

Many tales of famous fighting men who not only lifted the heavy stones but also tossed them in the air are told in many places.

Some believe that if they sit on one, their physical strength will grow. Again fortunes are told by hoisting lighter stones. If a sick man manages to lift a *chikara-ishi*, it is a sign that he will soon recover.

Shrine *chikara-ishi* is thus merely for

testing one's strength, backed often by legendary tales, but there is another kind of *chikara-ishi*. In many rural districts little stones collected from rivers or seashores are called *chikara-ishi*. They are placed on the *tokonoma* (alcove in the main room of the house) or by the side of the pillow of a sleeping baby.

It is the custom in many districts soon after the birth of a baby in a household for the family members to go to the river or seashore and gather small stones. They are believed to possess the charm of protecting the baby from sickness and evil influences, and also bringing good fortune to the family. Thus they are called *chikara-ishi* or stones that give the baby strength to fight sickness and devils, and the family strength to build up its fortune.

CHILD-BEARING STONES

MANY STONES are not only believed to grow, but also to give birth to smaller stones.

The Kumano Shrine at Nakaimamura, Dewa province, is dedicated to a pebble which was picked up by one named Nakamura at the gorge of Nachi, Kii, when on a pilgrimage to worship at the Kumano Shrine, Kii, for the seventh time. As the pebble was enshrined there, it grew, and in 80 years reached such a size that a man could hardly encircle it with his two arms. Not only did this stone keep on growing, but it also gave birth to child stones, which in turn grew and gave birth to grandchildren stones.

The following story appears in a book titled *Unkonshi*:

'I treasure a strange stone: I do not know where it was produced. It was formerly kept by Mrs. Adachi of Chikushi, and I obtained it from her.

The shape of the stone is like a pigeon's egg: it has white and red marks on the smooth and hard surface. This stone gives birth to child stones from time to time. When it is about to give birth, the presence of the child-stone inside can be seen with the naked eye. When it gives birth to a child-stone, no scars are left on the mother stone. It keeps on giving birth to child-stones, but its original weight is never changed.'

In many parts of the country, there are various different tales about stones that gave birth to smaller stones. One named Tengu-Iwa at Omiya, Aizu, is sixty feet high and thirty feet wide, but a small stone is seen projected from this stone from time to time, which finally falls off.

The belief that stones give birth to child-stones has also originated the popular faith that some stones have the power to enable childless women to bear children. In different parts of the country there are still preserved stones that have the power to make barren women bear a child. In the compounds of the Hachiman Shrine, Kamakura, there is a stone called Masakoishi. It is commonly believed that, if a woman touches this stone with her hand, she will bear a child.

At the famous Goshiki Hot Springs, Yamagata Prefecture, there is a stone in a large bathtub, and it is said that if a woman embraces this stone in the bath, she will bear a child.

At many shrines and temples are kept small pebbles, and a woman desiring to have a child has to carry away one of the pebbles and keep it in her *obi*, and then she will have a child.

The story is different according to districts, but the belief that stones have the power to make barren women bear children is quite widely believed by the people.

CRAB CHARMS

DRIED CRAB SHELLS are often seen nailed over the doorway of Japanese houses. They are not ornaments, but charms to drive away evil spirits and disease.

The following story is narrated about the origin of this charm:

Once a number of crabs appeared on the shore of a village where the people had never before seen such strange creatures with many claws and walking sideways. Being so different from anything they had seen before, they thought that the creatures must be something supernatural. So they caught them, dried them, and placed them over their doorways so that nothing would touch them. When the evil spirit of the village came and saw the strange-looking thing over the door of every house, it was afraid because it had never seen anything like it. So the evil spirit kept away from the village. Thus the dried crab shell became a charm against evils.

Heike-gani is believed to be the incarnation of the spirit of Heike warriors who were defeated and drowned at Dan-no-Ura in the Inland Sea, by the Minamoto clan. On the back of the *Heike-gani* shell can be traced a rough outline of a human face. Heike crab shells are also used as charms against misfortunes and sickness.

CRAWLING THROUGH

VISITORS TO *Daibutsu*, the Big Buddha at Todaiji Temple, Nara, must have noticed that one of the big pillars of the building housing the statue has a small square hole at its base. Japanese visitors, particularly women, try to crawl through the hole, as it is said that one who succeeds will be blessed with happiness. In the case of women they are assured happiness and many good children.

For children and slender persons, it is quite easy to crawl through the hole, but large or fat persons have considerable difficulty in doing so. Many fail after long attempt at trying to squeeze their bodies into the small hole, and, of course, they are quite disappointed.

In other parts of the country there are many similar holes which visitors try to go through for good luck.

The Awashima Shrine at Midorikawa in Kagoshima Prefecture has a small stone *torii* or shrine gate. The opening between the upper bar and the two side pillars is about one foot square. Married women not only of the prefecture but also from distant areas come to the shrine and try to crawl through the *torii.*

They try to wriggle through the *torii* and if successful they are sure of having many good children.

There are many Awashima shrines throughout the country, and they are regarded as the guardian of women's health. Awashima Shrine is dedicated to *Sukunahikona* and believed to possess the power to cure women's illneses. Thus in many districts Awashima shrines are worshiped by women.

The Awashima Shrine at Kagoshima has become famous because of the small stone *torii* which gives good health and happiness to women who manage to pass through its small opening.

DAIDARABOTCHI

MANY REGIONS of the country have tales of great giants who are called by the strange name of *daidarabotchi* or *dairabotchi.* The Daita bridge at Daita in the Tokyo suburbs, is said to have

been first built by a *daidarabotchi.*
Onuma (big pond) on the Sagami plain,
Kanagawa, was made by a giant when
he attempted to carry Mt. Fuji on his
shoulders, it is said. As he stretched his
legs for this great effort, one of his feet
went deep into the soil and made this
pond.

On the Matsumoto plain, Shinano,
there is a so-called *daidarabotchi's* footprint. The depression there is 15 feet
long, 10 feet wide and two feet deep.
About a mile away there is another
footprint of the same size. So his stride
measures a mile.

The strange name of *daidarabotchi*
is believed to have developed from
Daitaro (big son), a name often given to
an unusually big and strong boy. In
Kyushu there is a tradition that a boy
named *Daita* who possessed tremendous physical strength was born between a *kami* (god) and a beautiful
maiden.

There are many tales of *daidarabotchi* carrying huge mountains and the
earth falling down from the mountains
he carried forming small mountains.

There is a story in connection with
the origin of the name of the town of
Taka in Harima (Hyogo). *Daidarabotchi*
found that the sky was so low everywhere that he had to crawl along, being
unable to stand up. But when he came
to this place, the sky was high, and he
could stand up. Joyfully he shouted
'*takai* (high),' and so the place came to
be called Taka.

In Okinawa, it is said that at the
beginning humans crawled along like
frogs, but finding it uncomfortable, the
heavenly giant stood on a firm rock, and
hoisted up the sky with his hands. His
footprints on the rock are still seen, it is
said.

West of Umaya, Hitachi, there is a
hill called Okushi, which is made by
shells the giant took out of the sea and

threw away after eating the meat. His
footprint is also left there.

DAILY LUCK

THE JAPANESE have many means by
which they know what luck is in store
for them every day. They differ locally,
but here are a few that are commonly
believed.

When one finds a knot formed in his
or her *obi* or cord for tying *kimono*, that
is a sign of good luck.

If the first person one meets in going
out of the house is a woman, the day
will be a happy one. If you meet a Buddhist monk first, it will be bad.

If you see a snake on the road,
something good will happen during the
day. If the snake crosses the road in
front of you right to left, unexpected
money will come in.

If you never eat pepper, you will
become a wealthy and respected
person.

If you beat your rice-bowl with your
chopsticks at the table, you will be a
poor man.

If you look at another person over the
bowl out of which you are eating, you
are sure to become ugly in looks.

If a funeral procession overtakes you
on the street, it is a bad luck sign.

If bird droppings fall on you, you will
be lucky.

When your ear itches, you will hear
some good news.

If you nose itches, a birth will take
place in some family you know.

When the cords on your *geta* or *zori*
break, you must expect some bad news
or misfortune.

If your mirror breaks, it is a bad sign,
particularly for women.

Sneeze once and it shows someone is
speaking well of you.

Sneeze twice and somebody is speaking ill of you. If you sneeze three times,

someone loves you. Sneeze four times, you have caught a cold.

DATSUE-BA

SANZU-NO-KAWA is the river the dead must cross to reach the other world, according to the Buddhist tradition. By the river stands *Datsue-ba* (clothes-taking old woman) who takes off the clothes of the dead passing there. She hangs the clothes on a tree branch, and by the way the branch hangs down with the weight of the clothing, a person's crimes are judged. It also teaches the shamefulness of going naked.

By the side of the Saidan-bashi bridge built across the Sozu River, at Atsuta, Aichi Prefecture, there stood a temple in which a large statue of *Datsue-ba* was enshrined.

There is a tale in connection with the building of this unique temple.

In the middle of the 16th century, a Buddhist priest named Sozu was accidentally drowned in the river, and the river came to be called Sozu-gawa.

At that time, there lived in the village a very greedy old woman. When she saw the drowned body of the priest, she robbed him of his clothes. The villagers were astonished at the wicked act of the old woman, and feared that her spirit might bring further evil on the villagers. So they agreed to do something to appease the spirit of the greedy old woman.

They decided to erect a big statue, almost two meters high of *Datsue-ba* by the side of the river into which Priest Sozu fell and was drowned, hoping that by the people's worship of the statue there, the spirit of the greedy old woman would be made to refrain from bringing evil influence on the villagers.

The story is still believed by the people of the neighborhood. The statue and temple however no longer exist, having been destroyed by an air raid in the last war.

DEMON'S GATE

WHEN ASKED about the superstition of *Kimon* or Demon's Gate, most Japanese would readily answer that it is absurd and they do not believe it. Yet when they are going to build a new house, they would not dare to ignore it. They would argue that, after all, there might be something in the *Kimon* superstition that was so long believed by their ancestors, or that it would be safer to follow it though they do not believe it.

Northeast is the direction from which demons come and bring misery and suffering to the people, and thus the northeast is called *Kimon* or Demon's Gate. All misfortunes and calamities are believed to come from this direction. In selecting sites for houses, in designing houses or making journeys, this direction is always avoided, even at the sacrifice of comfort and convenience. There should be no gate, no door, no window, or no other opening in this direction. Often when the believers in the superstition find that they must travel in the direction of the northeast, they first go to other directions, so that they will not follow the direction of the northeast.

This belief is quite old. When the city of Kyoto was being built, the Enryakuji Temple was erected on Mt. Hiei that lies to the northeast of the city, in order to stop the coming of demons from that direction, and thus to protect the city from all evils. The Kaneiji Temple at Ueno, Tokyo, was also erected to protect Edo from demons, by closing up the northeastern gate.

This belief originally came from China. According to the Chinese legend, there stands a huge mountain called Tososhan in the east, and upon the top of the mountain is a large peach tree, the branches of which extend 300 miles. On the branch extending to the northeast live demons. Thus demons always come from the direction of the northeast.

Then, the Chinese science of divination says that the northeast stands for the dividing line between day and night, between the positive and the negative. It marks the end of night, the negative and darkness, while it points to the beginning of day, the positive and brightness.

From these stories, it may be judged that, because the northeastern direction is negative, damp and sunless, it is avoided by the people. This explanation is generally given for the superstitious belief in *Kimon.* Thus, in building houses, for instance, any opening in the direction of the northeast is avoided, because it is damp and sunless.

Then, according to the original superstitions regarding directions, the northeast is bad for the fortune of the family, especially that of the eldest son; the southwest ruins the fortune of the mistress of the house, the northwest affects the fortune of the master of the house; and the southeast controls the fortune of the eldest daughter. Such are the directions from which misfortunes are to come to such members of the family.

The southwest is often called *Urakimon* or Demon's Back Gate, and it is believed that from this direction misfortunes come for the mistress of the house. The southwest is the positive, sunny and bright direction. It is believed, according to ancient ideas, that the woman of the house should be negative in disposition and conservative in ideas and action. Thus the positive and bright direction was regarded as an evil direc-

tion for her.

DIVORCE TREE

NEAR ITABASHI HILL, on the highway leading into Tokyo from the north, there once stood a huge *enoki* or Chinese nettle tree that was famous in Tokugawa days. The huge tree has died since, and now there remains only a dead stump. However, this stump is still worshiped by many Tokyo citizens who contemplate divorce.

In the early Edo period, Shinroku Ito came from Ise to Edo to start life anew as an oil merchant. He prospered, enjoying a very good business and a happy family life. But when he reached the age of 63 in 1733, he decided to give up his thriving business and spend the rest of his life in quiet meditation at the Sengen Shrine of Mt. Fuji.

With his mind made up, he left his home for Mt. Fuji, but his wife and children did not wish him to desert the family. They followed him, not willing to part with him. When they came to Itabashi, they rested in the shade of the huge *enoki* tree.

As Ito rose to continue his journey, he told his wife and children that they should go back as he would have nothing to do with them in the future. Sadly the wife and children left him and turned back to their house.

The story gained popularity and it came to be believed that the *enoki* tree was responsible for the separation of Ito and his family. Eventually happily wedded couples began to detour around the tree to avoid its spell. Those desiring divorce, however, ask the *enoki* tree to help them attain their wish.

DOSOJIN

ALONG COUNTRY roads there still stand natural stones or stone tablets.

They are generally called *dosojin*, but it is not clearly known what they represent or how they originated. The stones, however, are regarded as village guardians, but local traditions have been added to them as they came to be associated with various religious faiths.

Thus often *dosojin* are said to have the power to prevent illness, conclude a happy marriage, make children grow well and bring other benefits.

Dosojin may be divided into three types. The first, probably the oldest type, are just natural stones with no inscription. The second are natural stones with the inscription '*dosojin*' engraved. The third type have some affinity to religion and come as stone tablets with the engraved image of Buddha, *Jizo* (Ksitigarbha), *Fudo* (Acala), *Daikoku* (Mahakala) or others.

Among the tablets belonging to the last type are those with the forms of a man and a woman in relief. It is to be noticed that they are generally holding hands, or have one hand on the shoulder of the other.

Dosojin must have come from China, but it is not known when they were first erected in this country. Early ones, being just natural stones, bear no date of erection. However, among those having erection dates engraved, are found many that were set up in the 16th and 17th centuries.

It must be remembered, however, that the tablets were generally replaced with new ones when the original ones were lost or damaged. Thus, those with dates might have replaced earlier ones.

Villagers still worship these primitive stones standing along rural roads, believing in their traditional power to protect them and their villages.

DREAM-EATERS

ANYONE WHO suffers from nightmares is advised to put under his pillow a piece of paper on which is written the name or painted a picture of *baku* (dream-eater), as he will then have no more unpleasant or dreadful dreams causing him to sweat and tremble in his sleep, because *baku* will eat up his dreams and leave him unmolested.

Baku is an imaginary animal in the folklore tradition of the Japanese. It is a formidable animal, judging from its popular description as told by our ancestors. Old pictures of the animal show that, generally speaking, it resembles a bear, but it has a small pointed head, eyes like those of a rhinoceros, a nose shaped like that of an elephant but only one-half in length, legs like those of a tiger, and a tail like that of a cow. Its fur is piebald and very shiny.

It can be imagined from the above description how formidable and fierce-looking the animal is. Nothing is told about its teeth, but it most likely possesses a set of very strong teeth, as it is believed that there is nothing *baku* cannot eat. It eats rocks and heavy iron locks as easily as it feeds on fruits. Hence, however dreadful and unpleasant nightmares might be, they will be easily eaten by *baku*.

The traditional story of *baku* came from China, but its fondness for nightmares is not explained. Yet the belief that *baku* will gladly eat up any kind of dream is very strong in the country. Formerly, a pillow with a picture or the name of *baku* was popular among nightmare sufferers. It is now simplified to having a piece of paper with the name or picture of *baku* put under the pillow.

Yet there are some dreams that even

baku would not touch. When someone told of a foolish dream he had, his friends would say, 'Even *baku* wouldn't eat such a dream.'

Baku is an imaginary animal, but the description given above makes it similar to a tapir, an animal which is found in Malaya, India and South America. A tapir is a queer animal, too. It lives in dense jungles, and is shy and gentle, it is said. But it has a strange habit of sleeping in the daytime and prowling round through jungles at night to find food. It is described by scientists as having a heavy sparsely hairy body, the snout prolonged into a short mobile proboscis, a rudimentary tail, stout legs, and four front and three hind toes.

The tradition of *baku*, the dream-eater, may thus be traced to the night-prowling habits of the tapir. It can thus be understood how the imaginary animal was created to have many of the features of the jungle night-prowler. The original tapir, however, has no trait of being so formidable as the *baku* is made out to be.

DREAM PROPHECIES

DREAMS FORETELL one's fortune, many persons believe. Particularly, the first dream of the New Year is important, as it tells the fortune for the whole of the coming year. One has his first dream on the second night of the New Year, it is traditionally scheduled. But many persons do not have the luck of having good or any other kind of dreams on the second night. So, the first dream of the year, on whatever day it might come, is taken to tell one's fortune.

Of all *hatsu-yume* or first dreams, the happiest is that of *takara-bune* or ships loaded with treasures. Such a dream means prosperity and happiness for the whole year. Those of the rising sun are also very good.

The interpretations of dreams often differ according to districts, and many regions have their own particular dream traditions. Dreams of snakes are commonly regarded as very lucky, promising the dreamer money and wealth. When one dreams of being cut or wounded by swords or knives, it is a very happy sign, as it means the coming in of *kane* which stands for money as well as for metal.

Dreams of fear, danger or physical pain worry many persons, but in dream fortune-telling, they do not predict such horrid experiences for them. These awful dreams mean nothing ominous, though they leave their dreamers in fear and trembling even upon awakening.

If you dream and see yourself as a beautiful woman or a fine-looking man, that is a sign of bad luck.

If you drink *sake* on ships in your dreams, some good news will come from a distant place.

If you dream of continued rainfall, something is going to happen to make you worry.

If you receive a sword or knife cut in your dreams, money will come in unexpectedly.

If you dream of ice, a marriage arrangement for you will soon materialize.

If you dream of a sky bright with moonlight, you will rise in position and become famous.

If you dream of walking with a high and noble person, anxiety will fall upon you.

If you talk to a beggar in your dream, good fortune will come.

If you dream of sweeping the ground with a broom, you will have to spend money.

If a robber comes and steals things

from you, it means unexpected good luck.

But if a robber comes in and leaves without taking anything, it is bad.

If you dream of an earthquake, a change in your position or residence will come.

If you work on a farm, your family business will prosper.

If you go on a sea voyage, it is a good-luck sign.

If snow falls in your dream, the next day will be a happy one.

If you dream of the night advancing to dawn, a sick man will recover quickly.

EVIL DAYS

IN THE TOWNS of Okada and Senzu of Oshima Island, south of Tokyo Bay, January 24 and 25 have been called *Hiimi-sama* or evil days. On these days the people do no work, but close the wooden shutters early in the evening, stuff all holes and cracks in the wall so that no light goes out, put cattle and horses in small huts on distant hills and cover with straw mattings such beasts that cannot be moved. All try to make as little noise as possible, they never go out after dark and try to keep babies from crying.

For two days, no fishing is done and no boat is allowed to anchor in the bay. None is allowed to look at the sea. The only persons permitted to work on the days are telegram carriers and physicians called out to attend those seriously ill. If anyone comes to a house, despite all these taboos, he will be severely beaten, and the beaten person will have bad luck within three years, it is said.

In the house, the people offer 25 pieces of *mochi* or rice cakes to *Hiimi-sama* or the evil spirit. If mice carry away one of the *mochi*, it is a sign of bad luck. So the people stay awake all night and watch the *mochi* offerings.

Hiimi-sama is believed to come on a boat, carrying 25 lanterns. The *mochi* offered are carefully preserved, as it is believed that a sick man facing death will recover when he eats one, and a boat in a storm will be saved by tossing one into the sea.

Once on the island there was a bad official who tortured the people. Twenty-five public-minded young men rose in anger and killed the official. Fearing punishment, they hurriedly built a log boat by cutting down a huge tree of the Hajikama Shrine and went away, never to return.

The spirit of those 25 youths is said to be *Hiimi-sama.*

EVIL SNAKES

SNAKES ARE spirits or symbols of evil in many tales and traditions, and there are stories that tell about the killing of evil snakes for the safety and welfare of the people.

The famous old temple of Kuramadera, north of Kyoto, which is said to have been established by Priest Kantei in 770, tells one such snake tale. When Priest Ho-en, at the beginning of the 10th century was offering his prayer at the temple, two huge snakes appeared and tried to swallow him.

As he kept on praying and also lecturing to the snakes, the female snake listened to his words, and repenting, promised the priest that as the temple area lacked good water, it would see to it that a good spring would instantly gush out in the mountain. The promise was made good and a fine spring is still to be found there.

The temple still holds on June 20 every year a bamboo-cutting rite to tell the story of the evil snakes.

Four big bamboo, measuring about 36

centimeters around at the end, are brought out, two having roots, and the other two without. Four priests appear, paired into two sides. The priests carry long mountain swords and cut the rootless bamboo into three sections. As they cut, small chips fly. When the bamboo have been cut, the priests carry them, running into the temple.

Formerly the two pairs of priests represented the provinces of Omi and Tanba, and it was believed that if one pair succeeded in cutting the bamboo, the district represented by the winning pair would have a good harvest.

The bamboo with roots are not cut because they represent the female snake that listened to Priest Ho-en and gave the temple good water. After the rite they are planted again.

When the rite is over, the people who have been watching will rush to get the bamboo chips left on the ground, as it is believed that they have the power to drive away evil and sickness.

FARMERS' GUARDIAN

THE MOST popular deity in Japan is *Jizo-sama*. Not only is it regarded the guardian deity for children, but farmers also worship it as their divine protector. Thus *Jizo-sama* is given many different names, according to local traditions about *Jizo's* methods of helping farmers.

Migawari-Jizo or substitute *Jizo*, is worshiped in many localities, as it does the work for farmers who are sick or too poor to hire men.

Ashiarai-Jizo, foot-washing *Jizo*, is so named because the *Jizo* must wash its feet after doing the farmer's work in the paddy fields.

Mizuhiki-Jizo, water-drawing *Jizo*, brings water to paddy fields through canals it digs when the fields are in need of water.

Hanatori-Jizo, nose-leading *Jizo*, leads horses or cattle when farmers have no helping animals. At one place it is said that, while farmers were once planting rice, a wild horse appeared, running over the fields. The farmers could not stop the raging horse, but a little boy appeared and quieted it. Thus the farmers were able to finish their planting. The boy was *Jizo-sama*.

Amagoi-Jizo, rain-praying *Jizo*, are found all over the country. Farmers believe all that, by praying to *Jizo*, they can get rain whenever their farms go dry. The method of praying differs much according to localities. In some places, the head of the *Jizo* statue is taken into a river. More often water is poured over the *Jizo* statue. At other places the face of *Jizo* is splashed with mud. This means that unless the *Jizo-sama* brings rain, he cannot clean his own face of the mud.

Farmers firmly believe that *Jizo-sama* watches over their welfare and will do anything for them.

FISH STONE

IN NAGASAKI, KYUSHU, the strange story of a fish stone is told. Iseya, a rich man of Nagasaki, had a fine wall around his residence, formed with stones of various sizes and colors. A Chinese merchant who came to Nagasaki to trade passed by the wall and among the stones, he saw one bluish in color.

He entered the house and asked the master of the house to sell it to him. Iseya was surprised to hear such a request. He could not understand why the Chinese wanted that stone. He replied that if that stone was taken out, the whole wall would collapse. However he said that when the time to repair the wall should come he would keep that blue stone for the Chinese merchant.

The Chinese, however, said that he

wanted the stone at once and would pay 100 *ryo* (which was a big sum of money then). Iseya thought that the stone must be valuable if anyone would pay so much for it, and refused to sell it. Finally the Chinese offered 300 *ryo*, which was again rejected.

When the Chinese went away disappointed, Iseya had the blue stone taken out of the wall immediately and sent it to a gem polisher. Nothing was revealed by polishing the stone, and so Iseya had it broken into two.

As the stone broke, water gushed out and with it two little fish which soon died.

The next year, the Chinese merchant came again and when he was told what had happened to the blue stone, he shed tears of disappointment. He then told Iseya that the blue stone was a treasure stone called the fish stone. He said he wanted to polish the stone until the outside became thin and transparent, and then the little fish swimming inside could be seen.

Anyone who saw the fish would become happy and live long, he explained. So it was not only a valuable stone, but also a rare treasure. He wanted it so much that he had brought 3,000 *ryo* with him to get it, he said in tears.

FIVE ELEMENTS

THERE ARE many systems of telling fortunes in Japan, but the common one is based on the principle of positive and negative forces governing everything and the influence of *gogyo* or five elements.

According to the theory of *gogyo*, the five elements of wood, fire, earth, metal and water from the earth control human destiny. Each individual is under the influence of one of the five elements.

The five moving stars, wood star (Jupiter), fire star (Mars), earth star (Saturn), metal star (Venus), and water star (Mercury) influence human life as they pass over us.

That the combined force of the five stars and the five earthly elements govern the progress of all things on earth is a theory first set forth in China 3,000 years before the Christian era. From this developed the lunar calendar and such seasonal events as the spring and autumn equinoxes.

The character of a person is determined by the element that controls him, as each element has it own nature. His destiny is said to be influenced by the star that ruled the year of his birth. Furthermore, each month, each day and each hour is under the rule of its own star.

The nature of the five elements and their influence on human fate are determined by their interrelated positions. Wood produces fire; metal produces water; fire produces earth. Accordingly wood is stronger than water; metal than wood; water than fire.

Furthermore, zodiac signs came to be given to the year, month, day and hour. Even though the 12 animal signs are meaningless, 12 different meanings are given to the year, month, day and hour, as they rotate indefinitely.

The five elements and the 12 zodiac signs make a cycle of 60, and thus on his 61st year, one returns to his original birth year. It is generally through this combination that one's fortune is told.

From the belief that our destiny and everything in the world is controlled by the influence of the five stars and the five elements there have developed many customs and traditions of the people.

FUNADAMA

FISHERMEN and boat crews in Japan

are still very superstitious, and in prayer for a safe voyage and good fishing, they worship *funadama*, the deity guarding boat and crew. They make offerings to *funadama*, but as *funadama* is believed to be a woman, offerings generally consist of women's hair, little dolls, face powder and lip rouge. Of course rice and other cereals are widely offered, too. Some coins and pairs of dice are also presented.

The offerings to *funadama* are placed in a little hole cut in the beam holding the mast. After the offerings are placed in the hole which is about two inches square, it is again covered up with a piece of wood.

When there has been some bad luck, storms, a poor catch or the boat has carried the body of a drowned person, the boatmen wish to change their luck. Then they open up the plugged hole, and replace the buried offerings with fresh gifts.

Formerly fishermen and boat crews did not like to have women as passengers, because they feared that *funadama*, being female, might become jealous of other women on board, and thus bring bad luck.

The introduction of steam and motor boats has, of course, changed many of the old customs of Japanese boatmen. Yet they are very superstitious and are always keen in worshiping *funadama* or some other deity to ensure their safety. They know there are powers beyond their control, and hope to gain some superhuman help.

There were formerly many traditional rites and customs in connection with the belief in *funadama*, but today only the fishermen of Hachijo-jima and some other small islands preserve the ancient customs.

Funadama-sama is still very important to the people of Hachijo island. When a new fishing boat is to be constructed, a young girl of a happy family is selected to become *Funadama-sasagi* or the maid to serve the boat's soul. She is also regarded as the soul's incarnation. Formerly the girl selected was between 7 and 15 years of age, but now often much older girls are chosen.

In preparing for her role, the selected girl must first get together a new mirror, a comb, a pair of scissors, needles, a folding fan, a pair of white *tabi* (socks) and other things to make up the 12 accessories needed for her honored position. Then for seven days previous to the launching, she must go daily to the seashore and wash her hair with sea water, and keep her hair covered with a white cloth.

The master boat builder places a doll representing the soul of the boat in a hole made in the boat's cross bar. The doll's hair is made of the hair obtained from the *Funadama-sasagi*, and it is dressed in a piece of the cloth with which the dress to be worn by the girl at the launching ceremony is made.

At the launching ceremony, *Sasagi* and her attendant girl board the boat. Then the boat makes three turns rightward off the shore. When the boat returns to the shore, the offerings made to the *Funadama-sama* are taken off the boat, and the 12 accessories brought by *Sasagi's* family are given to the ship carpenter who built the boat.

Funadama-sasagi obtains a share of the hauls made by the boat she helped to launch, as she continues to be the boat's guardian.

Mike-neko or tortoise-shell male cats bring good luck to them, fishermen and boat crews still believe. They will offer any price for a male *mike-neko*. The origin of this belief is not known, but it is scientifically established that tortoise-shell male cats are rare and also have no reproductive power.

GONBEI

IN OLD FABLES, a farmer is often called *Gonbei*, and there is a commonly heard song that goes, '*Gonbeiga tane makya, karasuga hojikuru. Sando-ni, ichidowa owaneba narumai*' (When Gonbei plants seeds, crows dig them up. Once in three times they have to be chased away). Gonbei's planting of seeds was thus regarded as a useless or wasted effort.

The original Gonbei is said to have lived at Komaba in Meguro, Tokyo. This area in Tokugawa days was a vast uncultivated land with tall trees and was the *kariba* or hawking grounds of the shogun. None was allowed to enter the *kariba*. So crows and many other birds enjoyed safety there and kept on eating up the crops on the neighboring farms. But when the hawking season came they were prey to the hawks.

By the *kariba* lived a farmer named Gonbei who was very poor and always dressed in rags. He was lazy and very slow of motion. But he loved birds and used to feed those which gathered around his hut. He was happy when he saw them picking up the grain he scattered.

But bad crows also came. So once in a while he had to shout and chase them away. His constant fight with the crows became known to all his neighbors, and then throughout Edo. So originated the above-mentioned song. His scattering of grain for birds was made an example of wasted labor.

'*Maku*' means both 'to scatter' and 'to plant.' Originally Gonbei scattered grain for the birds, but the saying came to be interpreted to mean that planted seeds are picked up by crows. His act of feeding the birds was not wasted, but '*Gonbeiga tanemaku*' now means any wasted effort.

GOOD-LUCK RAKES

THE SO-CALLED downtown people of Tokyo eagerly purchase *kumade* or ornamented garden rakes at the *tori-no-ichi*, fowl fair, held at Otori shrines during November, for good luck in the coming year. The *kumade* come in all sizes, from tiny ones about one inch to the huge kinds measuring almost four feet across. Symbols of good fortune that decorate them include the ripe ears of rice, a treasure ship, the *uchide-no-kozuchi* or the mallet that shakes out anything desired, a sales book, fish and other charms standing for richness and abundance. The rakes will gather in good luck for the next year, it is believed.

Though they are expensive, all are willing to buy the largest their pockets can afford. Once you buy *kumade* you have to buy it every year to ensure your good fortune. Not only this, but the *kumade* you get must be larger every year.

The custom was started by the merchants of Edo, and eagerly adopted by the people of the Kanto area. At first *samurai* took no part in it. But wishing to have good luck, they gradually took interest in the *kumade* of the *tori-no-ichi*. Yet, afraid to buy the *kumade* themselves, they made others get them.

In Tokyo, the Otori Shrine's proper name is the *Washi* (eagle) shrine, but commonly it is called the *Otori* (big bird) Shrine.

Tori-no-ichi is held only on *tori-no-ichi* or Fowl Days in November. They come twice or three times during the month, according to the year. As the day comes every 12 days, some years have only two *tori-no-ichi*. The year following three *tori-no-ichi* markets is believed to be particularly prosperous. Traditionally it is said that in the winter after three *tori-no-ichi* occur there are more fires than usual, because prosperity makes the people careless.

HANNYA MASKS

THE MASK of *hannya* is fierce-looking, with two horns growing on its head, big glaring eyes, sunken and lined cheeks, and a big mouth with two long, tusk-like teeth sticking out at the ends.

This mask is often displayed at shrines, and is also used at festivals, because it is believed to possess the power to fight devils. This belief is astonishing because *hannya* (Prajina) stands for wisdom in the Buddhist tradition.

As to the origin of this fierce female mask, it is traditionally said that there was once a very jealous woman, and in his attempt to cure her of the evil, a Buddhist priest named *Hannya-bo* carved out such a mask to impress upon her how ugly she was at heart. This original *hannya* mask is said to be still kept by the Konparu School of *Noh*.

Thus the *hannya* mask at first represented the jealous nature of women that should be suppressed as much as possible. But later it came to mean all devilish women with fierce faces.

The *hannya* mask also seems to have some connection with the *hannya* sutra of Buddhism. In the *Noh* play named Aoi-no-ue, the vindictive ghost of a woman causes the suffering of many persons, and a priest prays for her salvation, chanting the *hannya-kyo* sutra, and then the evil spirit disappears.

Thus while the fierce-looking mask represents the spirit of jealousy or other evil sentiments, its fierce look is believed to be powerful enough to resist the influence of other evils.

Therefore, gradually the mask came to be used as a charm to expel evil with its awful appearance. Dancers with these masks often appear at shrine festivals in order to protect the community from devils and sickness. Even among the toy masks sold at shops, the *hannya* mask is always found, and despite its dreadful look, there are always ready purchasers.

HARA

HARA (abdomen or stomach) is more than an anatomical expression. Western people regard the head or breast the most important part, but the Japanese people think the abdominal region is the vital center of the human body and life. It is there that their mind or spirit is housed.

Because of this interpretation, *hara* stands for mind, courage, power, efficiency and other spiritual functions. The pit of the stomach which is called *tanden* is, therefore, the most vital spot in the entire body. It means the 'field of the elixir of life.' This idea is said to have originally come from China.

Thus, all were advised to concentrate their attention on this most important part of the body. By holding one's spirit and strength in the *tanden*, one would be able to maintain not only perfect health but also sound mental function, it was believed.

The importance of *tanden* was particularly taught in the training of *samurai*, feudal warriors.

This idea was emphasized by Hirata Atsutane, Kaibara Ekken, Priest Hakuin and other leaders of the country. Hirata Atsutane, a great teacher of the Tokugawa era, wrote: 'The *tanden* in the lower belly is the most august and important part of the body. Not only medical books but also various teachings and professional training have taught the necessity of storing and holding one's spirit and energy there.'

Thus, *tanden* as well as the belly came to stand for one's composure and training. People were taught to hold their belly always firm in order to be strong and dignified.

With the importance attached to *tanden*, there developed the so-called belly-breathing method. Instead of breathing by expanding and depressing the chest, breathing is done by expanding and depressing the belly. This type of breathing is still followed by many even today, as it is thought to be a good method of keeping one's internal organs in good condition.

Hara having such a strange meaning, there developed various expressions that are based on the above-mentioned abstract meaning.

Hara-no-aru-hito (man of stomach) is a very common expression, but it does not indicate a man possessing any special stomach. It means a man of courage, willpower or strength. *Hara-ga-okii* (big stomach) means broad-minded or understanding. *Hara-guroi* (black stomach) points out dishonest or untrustworthy persons, because anything evil is thought to be black. On the other hand, a person with *kireina-hara* (clean stomach) is an honest man, or a man of clear conscience. *Hara-ga-nai* (without stomach) is an expression to mean persons who have no courage or will.

Then, *hara-ga-wakaranai* (not able to understand stomach) is another strange expression. It is used as a term to show a person whose mind cannot be understood. In this case *hara* means intention or plan. *Hara-ga-dekiru* (stomach is made) and *hara-ga-dekite-inai* (stomach is not made) are terms to indicate persons who have definite views or principles and those who have not.

Of course there is no proof, but the custom of committing *harakiri* or killing oneself by cutting open his abdomen with a sword might have been started from this idea of one's mind or courage being located in that region. At any rate, *hara* is the most vital point of the human body according to this traditional idea, and so it might be natural to kill oneself by putting a sword to that spot.

HIMEJI CASTLE

HIMEJI CASTLE, not far from Kobe, was originally built by Akamatsu Sadanori in the 14th century, and is still known as one of the finest castles of the country. There is a legend concerning this castle commonly known as the White Heron Castle.

At the top of the castle tower there lived a woman named *Osakabehime* who did not allow anyone to climb up the *donjon* even in the daytime. Nobody knew who this mysterious woman was. One rainy evening when several *samurai* on guard were talking of the woman, Morita Zusho bravely proposed that he would go up to the top of the tower although all tried to stop him.

Carrying a lantern, he climbed up the stairway and reaching the top, pushed open a wooden door. Inside he saw a desk and a torch stand, in front of which sat a huge woman, white-faced and dressed in a rich *kimono* and a crimson skirt. She seemed to be about 34 years old. She loudly shouted, 'Who's there?'

Zusho calmly told her why he had come, as none was brave enough to climb up the tower. Hearing him, the woman smiled and said that to prove that he had come to her, she would give him something to show the others. Then she tossed him what seemed like a neckpiece torn from a warrior's armor.

Thanking her and carrying the neckplate, he descended the stairway.

But as he came to the third landing, his lantern went out. He went up again to the top and opened the door. The woman asked what he had come back for. When he explained, she gave him another lantern, but said that this was no place for humans and he should never come back.

Zusho's successful climb to the tower top became known to Matsudaira Yoshitoshi, lord of the castle, who called him and praised him highly for his courage. But when the lord looked at the neckplate that Zusho brought back from the tower, he was perplexed as it looked familiar. He ordered that all the old armor worn by his ancestors be examined. They found that one of them had its neckplate torn off.

HI-NO-KAMI

FIRE WAS HELD sacred in the old days, and *Hi-no-kami* or the god of fire was worshiped by the people. In northeastern districts *Hi-no-kami* is still believed to be in the *irori* or floor hearth which is also considered as a sacred place.

In those regions where the people live around the *irori* during the winter months there are many traditions and tales about *Hi-no-kami.*

Once a cattleman went into a vast forest where he met a mountain witch. Surprised and frightened, he ran wildly through the forest. He saw a little hut ahead, and hurriedly entered it to hide himself from the chasing witch.

But the witch followed him into the hut which happened to be her house. Trying not to be caught by the witch, he jumped up and hid himself above the great wooden beam over the *irori.* Fortunately the witch did not notice him and started to toast some *mochi* over the fire.

The smell of the toasting rice cake

tempted him, and drawing a piece of reed from the reed roof, he caught the *mochi* with it and ate it while the witch was looking the other way.

When she found the *mochi* gone, she said, 'It must be *Hi-no-kami* who ate the *mochi*, so it can't be helped.' Next she put on the fire a kettle of *amazake* or sweet drink made of fermented rice. When the *amazake* was properly warmed, the cattleman hiding on the beam drew another reed and putting one end into the kettle, sipped the *amazake* through it while the witch was not watching. Again she said, 'It must be *Hi-no-kami* and can't be helped.'

As everything she had prepared for herself was taken by *Hi-no-kami*, she went to bed. When she was asleep, the cattleman came down the beam and poured the boiling hot water from the kettle over the fire on her. As she was dead now, the cattleman ran out of the hut and escaped to his village, so an old story says.

HITODAMA

WHEN ONE dies, his soul leaves the body in a ball of glistening blue-white light, it is believed among the Japanese. Of course, it does not happen in all cases of death, but under certain circumstances, the soul takes this form.

Hitodama (human soul ball), as it is called, is eerie, particularly because of its bluish light and the way it slowly floats through the air, with a trailing tail. It appears mostly on dark drizzling nights, frightening and giving most people the creeps when it unexpectedly passes nearby. It does not fly high, but generally just hovers around rooftops or slowly floats through the fields and town.

Hitodama tells rural folks that one of their neighbors has died. It has always been associated with ghost stories or dramas. The belief in *hitodama* is of remote origin, as it is mentioned in *Manyoshu* poems and the early classics. Whenever a ghost is described in literature or painting, *hitodama* is necessary to add to its gruesomeness. Told from childhood of ghosts and *hitodama*, the people have thus become extremely afraid of the weird floating soul, though there is really no cause for dread if it is only the departing soul of a neighbor.

What then are the circumstances that make the soul take this form and float through the air? Nobody can explain. But judging from many stories of *hitodama*, it appears as though hatred, jealousy, strong attachment to some persons or goods and such make one's soul take the form of *hitodama*. There is a story that the *hitodama* of a man who had a stong grudge against another, frightened the latter to death. *Hitodama* also appears in love stories as the soul of disappointed men or women. Again, the *hitodama* of a certain person visited the house of his friend to express thanks for all the latter had done for him in his life time. Furthermore, strong attachment to money or goods makes the soul of the owner hover around the house in the form of *hitodama* to watch over his possessions.

Whatever science might say, *hitodama* is no illusion, and is actually seen quite often, particularly in rural districts. Scientists say that *hitodama* is only a bubble filled with sulphur-laden air. Whatever it might be, it is uncanny.

HITSUJI-NO-DAIFU

THE MINTING of Wado-kaiho, the first Japanese coin, in 708 was such a great event that Emperor Genmyo named the era 'Wado' (Japanese copper). The coin was made from copper mined in Chichibu, Musashi (present Saitama Prefecture). In the mining operation at Chichibu, Hitsuji-no-Daifu, a Korean mining expert who came there in 711 with 193 Korean workers, played a notable role. His services were appreciated and the district of Tago was given him. The Emperor also extended him much honor and favors.

About him are told many tales, most of which are so fanciful that later people have regarded him a legendary person. One of such tales is that he often visited the Emperor at Nara, going on his horse, but he covered the distance and back in one day.

One day, he saw a strange youth, walking fast, going back and forth over the same place. He asked the youth what he was doing. The young man replied that he was acting thus so as to attract someone's attention and obtain employment. Hitsuji-no-Daifu gave him work putting him to take care of his horse. Whenever the new man was with the horse, it traveled exceptionally fast, and the rider and the horse were never tired. Thus Hitsuji-no-Daifu was able to travel to Nara as fast as he did.

One day he saw the youth napping in the yard, half naked, and under his arms there were small wings. Playfully, Hitsuji-no-Daifu plucked a feather from his arm. Next day, his horse walked so slowly that he returned home late at night greatly tired. The following morning the youth disappeared.

Hitsuji-no-Daifu had seven daughters, all beautiful. One messenger of the Emperor fell in love with one of them and asked for her hand. But her father rejected the proposal. Thereupon the messenger became angry and reported to the Emperor that Hitsuji-no-Daifu was planning to revolt. So a troop was sent to capture him.

As the troop attacked his house, he sent away his daughters, and then he and his wife committed suicide. The daughters were soon caught, but as they refused to marry the captors, they were killed.

HOUSE GOD

IN THE northeastern district of the country various customs based on the ancient tradition of *ie-no-kami* or house god are still seen. Particularly in the rural regions of Iwate Prefecture, tales of *zashiki-warashi* (room child) are still heard.

Zashiki-warashi is believed to be in the form of a 5- or 6-year-old child, either a boy or a girl, with a ruddy face and short bobbed hair. It is invisible but sometimes one unexpectedly collides with it in the house.

As long as the *zashiki-warashi* stays in the house, the family will enjoy prosperity and happiness. When it disappears, the family fortune will decline, it is believed. Sometimes it leaves one house and goes to another, and thus their fortunes are suddenly reversed.

Generally the *zashiki-warashi* lives in the *kura* or storeroom of the house. So often it is called *kura-bokko* (warehouse child). It is also said that if one sees the *zashiki-warashi*, it is a sign that the family fortunes will soon decline. But sometimes its footprints are seen, particularly on grains spread out to dry.

Its existence in the house is revealed in many strange ways. When a member of the family sleeps in a back room, his pillow is removed or changed. Often in the daytime, the people suddenly hear a rustling sound, indicating that the *zashiki-warashi* is walking by. In the old days, the family spinning wheel was heard to be turning, even though nobody was near it.

That the family guardian in the shape of a little boy lived in the house was commonly believed even in Edo (Tokyo), and many other districts had similar tales. But Tohoku or the northeastern region may be one of the few places where such a belief is still preserved in many forms.

Zashiki-warashi in the northeastern district, and the house god in other regions, were believed to exist in the houses of the wealthy or other families that had a long, illustrious history, and thus among the common people there was a sense of jealousy against such families.

HUMAN PILLARS

THE YODO River that runs from Lake Biwa to Osaka used to flood the vast area along its course even in very olden days. As early as in the fourth century, Emperor Nintoku decided to build a strong embankment along the river to prevent flood damage to farms and villages.

To call the aid of *kami* in executing This gigantic engineering work, he offered human sacrifices. Two persons were selected to be buried alive in the foundation of the embankment so that their spirit would guard the people along the river. This is said to be the first mention of *hitobashira* or human pillars that came to be used often in constructing bridges and river embankments.

Later, the custom was adopted by military lords who believed that their castles or fortresses were stronger when live persons or animals were buried under their foundations. Hence tales of *hitobashira* have been told about many castles. In many cases, however, *hitobashira* stories are told by later people just to attach romance and historical interest to local castles. The stories of *hitobashira* used for the construction of the castles at Marugame, Matsue, Iwakidaira and Yoshida are very famous.

How did persons to be sacrificed come to be selected? In most cases they were volunteers, but cases of drawing lots are mentioned also. In a few instances, officials made up an imaginary person of uncommon appearance or dressed in a costume of unique design or materials. A person who was found to fit the description was selected to be sacrificed, it is said.

Mori Motonari (1497-1571), Lord of Chugoku, however, put a stop to this custom. He said that the strength of a castle depended on the harmony of men within it. Since then the *hitobashira* custom has not been followed in building castles.

HUNGER SPIRIT

IN MANY mountain regions which were formerly traversed by travelers on foot a story is told of *Hidaru-gami* or hunger spirit. This spirit is given different names according to the locality, such as *Dari-gami, Darihotoke, Dani* or *Darashi.*

As a traveler passes a lonely mountain place, He suddenly feels very hungry and faint and cannot proceed a step further. he is then caught by *Hidaru-gami*, it is said. On roads far from villages, many beggars and travelers died because of hunger and fatigue, and the spirit of such unfortunate persons rises as a traveler comes by, making him hungry.

Merchants and others who used to pass such lonely mountain places were prepared for the attack by the hunger spirit. When they took meals on the way, they put aside a few grains of cooked rice, and wrapping them up in a sheet of paper, carried them in their bosom. As soon as they began to feel hungry and knew that the hunger spirit was upon them, they would take out the rice grains and throw them on the road. The few grains would satisfy the hunger spirit and travelers were no longer molested. When they did not have rice to give to the hunger spirit, the advice given was that they should write the character for rice on the palm of the left hand with a finger and then lick the spot with the tongue. That was prescribed as a sure way to appease *Hidaru-gami.*

It is believed that in the old days, many travelers going on long journeys through uninhabited regions without carrying sufficient food, died on the way from hunger and fatigue. Stories of such miserable incidents are said to have started this belief in the existence of *Hidaru-gami* and its attack on travelers.

INUGAMI

IN THE WESTERN parts of the country, particularly in Kyushu, Shikoku and Chugoku, the belief in *inugami* or dog witch still exists. The dog possesses or bewitches a person, it is said, but contrary to other tales of animals that bewitch and harm human beings, the dog acts as a friend or servant to the family to which it attaches itself. Of course, the dog sometimes harms others in protecting the welfare and happiness of the family to which it belongs.

The dog is said to be very small, being of the size of a mouse. It is seen only by the members of the family, and remains invisible to all others. It is also said that the family which has the dog prospers rapidly, but at the same time also falls unexpectedly.

The dog attaches itself to both men and women, but more to women. Some families have several dogs. In some districts it is believed that when a girl reaches the age of 15, her mother's dog comes to her. Thus the dog is handed down through the female members of the family.

In some places there are said to be two kinds of *inugami*, one attaching itself to persons, and the other to animals.

The dog is highly respected by all members of the family as it understands their wishes, and acts for their interests without being seen by outsiders. Therefore, *inugami* is often worshiped and even enshrined as *yashiki-gami* or the god of the house.

IZUMISHIKIBU

IZUMISHIKIBU was a great poetess of the Heian period. Her diary *'Izumishikibu-nikki'* covering the period from April 1003 to January 1004 is particularly famous. But many strange legendary tales are told about her.

First she must have traveled all over the country as so many places have something to tell of her visit. More than 15 places are mentioned as the locality where she died, and many districts claim to be her birthplace. A commonly told story, furthermore, says that she was born of a deer, and again in some places, that a boar was her mother.

To the Fukusenji Temple at Izumi Village, not far from Nagasaki, Kyushu, a boar used to come from the mountain behind the temple. The priests petted it and gave it the tea leaves thrown out of the tea kettle. The animal became quite used to the priests who welcomed its daily visit.

One morning, the priests heard a baby crying behind the temple building. When they went out to investigate, they found the boar giving her breast to a human baby. They discussed what should be done with the baby nursed by the boar, but they came to no happy conclusion.

Just at that moment, a couple named Shioda came to the temple. They said they had been praying for a baby and the night before in their dreams they were told to come to the temple and receive the baby left behind the temple. So the priests decided to give the baby to the couple who named her Izumi-shikibu after the village. When she was 9 years old she was taken to Kyoto, and later served at the Court.

It is often said that as she was born of a deer or boar mother, her feet had only two toes each. To hide her clumsy feet, she always wore *tabi*. She was the first Japanese to wear *tabi* or Japanese socks, it is traditionally believed.

Tabi of course were worn before her time, but because of the tale that she was born of a deer or boar and had only two toes on her feet, she came to be named as the inventor of the bifurcated Japanese socks.

JEALOUS GODDESS

BENZAITEN or more commonly Benten, is one of the so-called Seven Gods of Fortune, and is very widely worshiped. She, Sarsavati, is a goddess of beauty, music and eloquence. Yet her worshipers are now mostly stock speculators, gamblers, shop-keepers and others, who desire to make more money. The fact that she stands for beauty, music and eloquence seems to have been almost entirely forgotten by the people.

On the other hand, Benzaiten is believed to be very jealous, becoming angry if happy couples pay visits to her shine.

When men and their wives, or boys and girls in love propose to visit Benten shrines, older folks advise them to appear before Benten separately, so that they will not incur her wrath and have their happy love or married life spoiled.

Generally, Benzaiten is represented in pictures and statues as a goddess in a thin green dress, carrying a *biwa* (Oriental lute), a sword and a jewel. On her head she wears a crown decorated with white snakes. She is always in a seated pose, with her legs crossed in front, and one knee raised.

White snakes on her crown might have started the belief that she is jealous. Again, it is not known how she came to be the guardian angel for speculators, shop-keepers and others who desire good business. Whatever might be the reason, it is true that all Benten shrines receive prayers for business and money.

There is another unexplained feature of Benten shrines. It is that all Benten shrines stand on islands or on the shores of the sea or lakes. The most famous Benten shrines in the country are those at Itsukushima, an island in the Inland Sea, at Chikubu Island on Biwa Lake, and at Enoshima, an island not far from Kamakura. Then in Tokyo, the Benten at Shinobazu Pond, Ueno Park, was formerly very famous. One view offered to explain this is that Benten's lute would sound well if she played it on an island or by the water.

In Kamakura, there is a Benten shrine which is commonly called Zeni-Arai-Benten. It is so named because the worshipers wash their coins in a pool of water at the shrine. It is believed that the coins or bank-notes washed in the shrine's water and charmed by it will multiply.

KAMA-ITACHI

MANY PEOPLE, particularly those of the northeastern areas, still believe in *kama-itachi*. Some tell about their own experiences with *kama-itachi*, while others have heard of it from grandparents.

Those working in fields or mountains, or even walking on country roads suddenly feel forceful slaps on their bare arms or legs, and find that sharp long cuts have been inflicted with blood flowing therefrom. The victims believe they have been attacked by *kama-itachi*.

It is unknown how the word *kama-itachi* originated. The combination of *kama* (sickle) and *itachi* (weasel) is meaningless. It is generally explained that, as the cuts look as if they were made by sharp knives or sickles, the people thought they must have been caused by some kind of sickle. A weasel is a common animal found all over the country, quick in action and mischievous. So the people made an imaginary creature by putting the two words together to indicate the cause of the accidental cut.

Nevertheless, as accidents still happen, scientists have directed their attention to its study, and they now say that when a person comes in the path of a whirlwind and his bare arms or legs touch the center of the vacuum, the mysterious cut is caused.

In the rural districts, the traditional belief in *kama-itachi* has not died even yet, despite such scientific explanation.

KAMI-KAKUSHI

TALES OF persons mysteriously disappearing are heard all over the country, and they are generally called *kami-kakushi* (hidden by *kami*). These missing persons are not believed to have died but to have been merely hidden by *kami*.

Children disappear most, but men and women are also said to have been spirited away. When anyone disappears, parents, neighbors and friends search the neighborhood. They beat drums and bells, calling the lost one's name. In many districts they beat *masu*, or wooden rice measures. But they never find the lost ones.

A child playing with others fails to come home. A woman who just stepped out of her door in the evening dusk is never seen again. Many grownups disappear in a similar manner. But strangely, it is said in most districts that the lost person is seen by someone once before completely disappearing. The lost person is seen by his parents or friends in the crowd at a festival or on a busy street for a moment, but then disappears, never to be seen again.

At one place, a daughter of a wealthy farmer was to go to her wedding ceremony. Dressed in the finest bridal costume, she was put on a horse, according to the local custom. The family went into the house for a moment to attend to some details of the preparations for the bridal procession. But when they came out, they saw only the horse, and no daughter. Their search was fruitless. But several months later, at a store of a neighboring village several persons were gossiping, and a woman entered to buy *sake*. When she left the shop with her purchase, the people realized that she was the missing bride, and rushed out of the door after her, but she was nowhere to be found.

KAMI-NA-ZUKI

THE JAPANESE have for long called the month of October *kami-na-zuki* or *kan-na-zuki* meaning the *kami*-less (godless) month. It has been traditionally believed that all *kami* of the country leave their respective shrines in October to attend a conference at the Izumo Taisha Shrine in Shimane Prefecture. At the Taisha Shrine there actually stands a large narrow building to house the visting *kami* during the conference.

The origin of this belief is not known. But the name came from *kamina* which means to make new *sake* with newly harvested rice. Thus it was called *kamina-tsuki*, or the month to make new *sake*. But somehow it was changed to mean the absence of *kami*.

All over the country rites are held to send the *kami* off to Izumo. In some localities, the sending-off rite is regarded as an occasion for selecting marriage partners. Young men and women worship at the shrine to have their future mates picked before the *kami* leaves for Izumo.

While all *kami* are given quite a send-off, no ceremony is held to welcome them back because the time of their return varies. Most of them come back in a month, but some stay away until February of the following year.

It is now explained that this belief in *kami's* departure from the shrines in October is related to the harvesting of rice. With the gathering of the crop, the duty of the *kami* of farms to protect rice plants from evil spirits and insects is completed. Thus their departure is marked with rites to show the farmers' appreciation of their service. This is said to have started the belief that all *kami* leave local shrines in October.

KANTAN DREAM

KANTAN - YUME - NO - MAKURA (dream pillow of Kantan) is a commonly used expression to indicate that human life is as empty as a dream. The expression comes from an old Chinese story, which was brought to Japan and adopted into a *Noh* play and many tales.

In the Tang period (seventh to 10th centuries), a scholar named Lu went to the town of Hantan (Kantan), and at the inn there he met a young man who was in tatters. The young man complained that he had failed in everything, and becoming weak and poor, had no hope for the future. As the youth looked very tired, Lu brought out a porcelain pillow and advised him to lie down and sleep.

Laying his head on the offered pillow the young man went to sleep immediately. In his sleep he noticed a small hole on one side of the pillow, and when he went into the hole, he found himself in a magnificent house. A beautiful girl was there and he married her. Becoming an official he rose rapidly in rank and power, but he was put into prison, though innocent, because of the slanderous schemes of his enemy. Several years after he was pardoned by the emperor, and given a vast territory to rule. He had five children and many grandchildren, and finally died at the ripe age of 80.

Then the young man awoke from his sleep and realizing that it was only a dream, felt disappointed. Then the scholar told him that life was just like the dream he had in his sleep.

When the Chinese tale was introduced to Japan, the dream the young man had as he slept with his head on the porcelain pillow became famous among the people. So the Kantan pillow-dream became a synonym for the emptiness of human life which is only a dream.

Formerly pillows were respected and handled with care; people were told not to throw, kick or step on them. When a dead person's body was not discovered as in a case of drowning, his pillow was buried in place of his body in some districts. In some places there was the custom of burying the pillow with the body.

KAPPA

WHEN A CHILD drowns in a lake or river, old-fashioned people still believe that he was dragged to the bottom of the water and killed by a *kappa*. *Kappa* is an imaginary animal, and though the belief in its existence and murderous intent is traditional, at present probably no city dweller believes it. But in rural regions the belief is still common among the older people.

In the popular literature of Japan, *kappa* is mentioned frequently since very early days. Then there are pictures of *kappa* drawn by old artists. Such pictures and descriptions give *kappa* a common type. Consequently, in the long traditional belief in the grotesque animal, it came to be made out in a definite form.

To give the common description of a *kappa*, it is first of all an amphibious animal, preferring muddy lakes and rivers. In its general shape it resembles a body of about 3 or 4 years of age. The face is pointed and is of a bluish dark color. It has thick hair, but on top of the head there is a dish-like depression which has no hair. This dish is very important, as it is for holding water when the *kappa* goes out of the water. When the water in the shallow dish on top of its head dries up, the *kappa* dies, it is said. Its back is covered with carapace. The hands and feet are webbed, and the nails are sharp and pointed as claws. It may thus be seen that the *kappa* is quite a grotesque animal.

It lives in muddy lakes and rivers, never being found in clear or rapidly flowing streams. It has a particular fondness for children. When it sees a child in the water nearby, it will rush to him and, gripping him firmly by its claw-like fingers, kill him finally. But even grownup persons often become victims of *kappa*, it is believed.

Little children have always been warned by their parents to look out for *kappa*, whenever they go to have a swim in rivers or lakes in summer. Thus the belief in *kappa* has been planted in the minds of children from very early days.

Though the *kappa* tradition is common almost all over the country, it is now known how such a grotesque animal came to be created in the people's mind. One explanation is that it is the *suppon* or mud-turtle that originally gave the idea for this illusionary existence.

Mud-turtles are found in most muddy rivers and lakes. When excited, they can become quite vicious. It is said that, when one has his finger snapped by a turtle, it will never let go. Many children must have lost their fingers or otherwise been hurt by trying to grasp turtles or while swimming in rivers and lakes. Thus, in order to create a sense of fear in the minds of children and make them be always on guard against turtles, the *kappa* was created.

In some parts of the country the mud-turtle is called *kappa*. This may be regarded as another proof that *suppon* is the origin of the *kappa* story.

According to stories about them, regions in Kyushu have more of them than other districts. In Kyushu rivers, they form many big groups, which sometimes stage wars to gain supremacy.

The *kappa* is said to be able to draw anyone into the water. Tales are told of children, men and even domestic animals being pulled into the water and killed by the *kappa*. But in some stories the *kappa* is made out to be quite humane.

Once in the vilage of Tomoe, Oita in Kyushu, a horse was pulled into the river by a *kappa*, according to one story. As the horse was caught, it jumped in alarm, but the sudden movement of the horse made the *kappa* lose its balance, and the water in its head dish spilled out. The *kappa* became helpless and was easily caught by the horse's owner.

The owner then made the *kappa* promise that it would never again molest people and animals of the village. The *kappa* meekly wrote a letter of apology, so the tale goes.

KITSUNE-TSUKI

PHILIPP FRANZ von Siebold, German physician and scientist who came to Nagasaki in 1823 and taught Western medical science to Japanese students, found in Japan several peculiar diseases that he had not seen before. One of such strange diseases is *kitsune-tsuki* or fox-possessed.

When one has this malady, he suddenly acts strangely and violently. Not understanding the cause or nature of the sickness, the people attributed it to a fox or other animal that is believed to possess the power to bewitch humans. Such was the origin of the name. But in some districts it is called *saru-tsuki* (monkey-possessed) or *tanuki-tsuki* (badger-possessed).

Usually the patient has a high fever and talks in a delirium. He loses all control over himself. Often he eats what he would never touch ordinarily. He throws things around or breaks them. Sometimes he goes outdoors at night, jumps into a river, or walks up a steep mountain.

Commonly when such a patient appears in a family, priests, monks or witches are called in to offer prayers to drive the fox out of his body. When prayers are given for a few days, the patient generally regains his normal condition just as suddenly as he became afflicted. When he recovers, he knows nothing about what he did during the state of bewitchment.

Kitsune-tsuki is found only in rural districts, and seldom in towns. Most patients are women who are physically and mentally weak and very sensitive.

The first mention in any record of *kitsune-tsuki* (fox-possessed) was made in 823, when a man suddenly declared, 'I am a fox.' Also it is said that once a man came home after drinking *sake* heavily, and said that he did not feel well. Then he suddenly rose and said, 'There goes a fox,' and began to act strangely. So he was called fox-possessed.

Besides foxes, dogs, snakes and other animals are said to have possessed humans and made them speak and act abnormally.

A man shouted as though in a delirium that a fox came from A's house, a story goes. It was learned that he had sold rape-seed oil at a very high price. When the overcharge was paid back to A, the fox left him and he became normal.

As the idea of fox possession came to be widely believed, many witches and fortune tellers profited by announcing sick or temporarily insane persons as fox-possessed.

It is recorded that Ashikaga Yoshimochi, a great military leader, was seriously ill in 1420 for more than three months. His attending physician, Takama, declared that the great general was possessed by a fox. By prayers the fox was driven out of his body and the palace. But later it was found that there was no fox possessing Yoshimochi. It was an invention by the physician and so he was heavily punished.

Usually a fox that possessed a person was driven out by prayers offered mostly by witches and priests, or by burning green pine needles in the room, as the fox did not like smoke.

Though the belief was widespread, even in the old days it was found out that there was no real fox possession.

KOBO DAISHI

KOBO DAISHI (774-835) is one of the greatest Buddhist scholars and priests of Japan. He studied in China from 801 to 806 and, upon returning home, he created the Shingon sect and erected the great temple at Koyasan, Wakayama Prefecture, with the support of the Imperial Court. He traveled extensively throughout the country, preaching the faith and comforting the people. Everywhere he was welcomed by Buddhists, and at many places his visit was marked by the building of a temple or other memorial.

At several places, he left his bamboo cane standing in the earth. It took root and grew upside-down. These *sakasadake* or upside-down bamboo of Kobo Daishi are nationally famous and regarded as a miracle, telling of his great spiritual power.

The one at Toyano-machi, Niigata Prefecture, is perhaps most famous. His cane which he put into the earth and forgot, grew into a big forest of upside-down bamboo in a lot behind the Seibo Temple.

One may say that all this is fiction. But when he visits the spot, he will actually see the bamboo plants growing upside-down with all branches extending downward. This discovery generally convinces all skeptics.

But botanically, there is no upside-down bamboo. It is only a trick played by an unusual kind of bamboo that has branches pointing downward. The growth of this special kind at the very place where Kobo visited must have started the story. The existence of the bamboo with drooping branches has always convinced the botanically ignorant public of the miracle.

The same kind of bamboo is also found at Shosenkyo, Yamanashi Prefecture, and other places, where similar stories of Kobo's cane are told.

LIVING ISLAND

IKI IS A small island in the Tsushima Strait, west of Kyushu, measuring only 13 kilometers by 8 kilometers. This island is traditionally believed to be alive and moving. *Iki* means 'alive' and thus the name of the island.

The island was alive and moving when it was created, it is said, and therefore eight strong pillars were driven in around the island. With strong ropes the island was tied to the pillars to secure it. The ancient name of the island was *Ame-no-hitotsu-bashira* or One Pillar of Heaven.

Those eight pillars, however, collapsed in time, and the parts now remain as huge pillar-like rocks, of which one named *Kose* is the largest.

As it kept on moving, the inhabitants often hoped that it would drift and move to reach the mainland of Kyushu.

A traditional tale of *Takeda-no-Bansho*, the god of the island, is still remembered. It is said that the god wished to move the island to the shore of Kurozaki on the mainland.

To move the island, the god planned to make 3,000 straw dolls, and turning them into working men, complete the moving in one night. But *Amanojaku*, a person known for his perverse character became mischievous upon hearing of the attempt of the god, and played a trick on him. Long before daybreak, *Amanojaku* imitated a cock's crow. Hearing the crowing that heralded the coming of the morning, the island god lost his magic charm.

Thus the task of moving the island was not completed, and his noble attempt failed. Disappointed, the island god threw the 3,000 straw dolls into the sea. There is a belief that those dolls

turned into *kappa* or legendary water imps, many tales of which are still told throughout the Kyushu region.

LIVING STONES

AN OLD MAN named Matsumoto Haruhiko of Mie followed Sugawara Michizane in his journey to Tsukushi, Kyushu, in 901, and on his return home, he picked up a pebble at the beach of Sode-ga-ura, Harima, and put it in his sleeve. When he returned home, he placed it in his garden. However, the stone soon started to grow to a considerable size. By the side of the stone that had grown from a mere pebble, a shrine was erected in honor of Sugawara Michizane.

The above story is only one of the numerous tales that are told about living or growing stones. In the above story, it appears that the growth of the stone was comparatively slow but the following tale tells about a stone that grew quite rapidly.

In the Shimoda district of Nagano Prefecture, there is an *iki-ishi* or living stone. Once a woman picked up a beautiful pebble on the shore of the Tenryu River, and put it in her sleeve. But as she continued on her journey, she felt her sleeve became heavier and heavier. She looked into her sleeve, and to her surprise, she saw that the little pebble had grown to a considerable size. Alarmed, she threw the stone away, but there it continued to grow to attain the present size.

A farmer of Shimoda, some 700 years ago, made a pilgrimage to the Kumano Shrine, Kii province, and on the journey home, a green pebble, about the size of a peach stone, became stuck in his sandal. He took it out and threw it away, but again it got stuck in his sandal. Thinking it very strange, he picked up the stone and put it in his pouch for holding his flint stone. He felt the pouch became heavier and heavier daily, and when he returned home and opened the pouch, it had grown so large that he had considerable difficulty in taking it out. Thus he erected a shrine and enshrined the stone. He kept on worshiping the stone and it continued to grow. By the time he had great-grandchildren, the stone had become three feet one inch high and four feet in circumference. Year after year it kept on growing.

There are hundreds of similar tales in the legends of the country, and it is believed that people believed in the growth of their sacred stones. This belief is said to have developed from their sense of respect for and worship of stones. Also, it is to be remembered that, in most cases, these legendary tales are connected with some strange or unexpected incidents which gave rise to the sacredness of such stones.

LOVE-LETTER CHARM

IN LATTER Tokugawa days, the visit of *kesobumi-uri* or love-letter peddlers at New Year and other seasonal occasions was welcomed by men and women. They sold love-letters, not to be mailed, but to be kept as charms by the purchasers. Love-letter peddlers were particularly popular around the Genroku era, 1688-1704.

According to ancient records, *kesobumi-uri* were dressed in bright red costumes and *eboshi*, pointed hats, or deep straw hats that hid their faces entirely. At first they came only at New Year's, but later, as their popularity grew, they came periodically once or twice a month.

Walking down the street, the love-letter peddler shouted 'Anyone want love-letters?' When he was called in, he took out a love-letter written in the most flowery language, and gave it

together with two or three cleaned rice grains. Men and women in love were willing to pay high prices for those charms.

It was believed that when one possessed such charms, not only would he or she be successful in love, but would also enjoy happiness and good forture.

The *kesobumi-uri*, in selling love-letters, said congratulatory words to the purchasers, and also made happy predictions on all family and business affairs. They thus had to be good talkers and possess wide knowledge. It was said that most of the love-letter peddlers were formerly shrine priests or some learned persons who had lost their positions and had to make their living.

LUCKY BIRD

HO-O, WHICH is called *zuicho* (lucky bird) or Chinese phoenix is used as a symbol of happiness or good fortune in sculpture and painting. It is also seen in brocades and embroidery. This gorgeous and strange creature is a mythological bird introduced to this country from China.

According to Chinese tradition, the *ho-o* makes its appearance only when peace and prosperity reign over the country. Thus it has become a sign of happiness and good luck.

It is believed to possess a head like a chicken's, a snake neck, swallow cheeks, and a back like a tortoise's. The whole body is bright with five colors and it stands six feet high. It lives in paulownia woods, eating bamboo seeds. All other birds respect it and follow it.

Such is the description of the *ho-o* in Chinese mythology. The Japanese have also accepted it as a lucky bird and so its design has been used on dresses and ornaments for happy occasions, or in prayer for good luck. The *ho-o* in metal adorns the roofs of many court and other buildings, as well as the *mikoshi* or portable shrines carried in processions in shrine festivals. Thus it is even regarded as sacred.

The Byodo-in at Uji near Kyoto, is also called Ho-o-do or Phoenix Hall, as the building was originally designed to represent the bird as it was about to descend to the ground. The building was erected by Fujiwara Yorimichi as his villa, but in 1052 it was turned into a monastery.

Facing the beautiful Uji River, the Ho-o-do is still one of the most outstanding masterpieces of Japanese architecture, symbolizing the tradition of the mystic bird.

Even in these modern times, the people still love to use the design of this bird on many things.

MAMAKO TALES

THERE ARE many stories about *mamako* or stepchildren but mostly they are about stepdaughters. The stepmother mistreats the *mamako*, but usually in the end the stepdaughter has a happy life. In many of these tales, the stepdaughter who is the elder is helped by her younger sister who is her own mother's favorite.

Once, a story goes, a mother had two daughters, the elder of which was her stepdaughter. One day she sent the two out to gather chestnuts, giving the elder a torn bag and the younger a perfect one. The elder's bag never got full, no matter how hard she worked. But a kind mountain-dweller gave her a good bag, and also a small treasure box. He gave the younger sister some roasted beans. On the way home, a devil appeared and threatened them, but the younger threw the beans at him and they managed to return home safe.

On a festival day, the elder was given a bamboo basket to fill the bathtub with water, while the younger, dressed in her fine clothes, went to the fair. A priest appeared and helped the elder to fill the tub. Then a neighboring girl invited her to go to the festival. She went, dressed in a fine costume she took out of the treasure box given by the mountain man. The rich man of the village saw her and asked her to be the wife of his son. So she was married and lived happily ever after.

In another story a stepmother became so angry with her stepdaughter that she cut off both her arms. As the daughter was good and beautiful she married the son of the village head, although she was now armless. In chagrin, the mother wrote a letter under a forged name to the man, denouncing his wife with many false accusations in an attempt to break up her happy married life. Because of the letter, the young wife was sent away by her husband's family. But after many years of suffering, she met her former husband again, and they were reunited to lead a happy life together.

MATAGI

AMONG THE hunters of the mountain regions of Aomori, Akita, Yamagata and Niigata Prefectures many old customs and traditions are still preserved. These hunters are still called *matagi*, a name which is said to have developed from forked trees *(matagi)* which they used as a rest to position their guns for aiming.

Until one is fully trained as a hunter, he is not allowed to join a group of *matagi*. A solemn rite at a mountain hunting hut was held when one became a disciple of *Yama-no-kami* or mountain god, who ruled over the mountain and wild life.

The hunters still have many taboos. When a baby is born in a hunter's house, he must not go hunting; if he does, he will never get game or will meet with an accident. If he lights his pipe with a fire at a house where there has been a recent childbirth, his hunting will be unsuccessful, it is said.

While a man is away hunting, no beans should be roasted at his house, as the cracking noise made by the beans will cause an avalanche.

When *matagi* leave their house to hunt, they should not sing or yawn. If one does, his headman will punish him by making him go naked and pushing him into the water.

Matagi have their own peculiar mountain language, which is quite difficult for others to understand. They never use it with outsiders, nor do they teach it to those other than their own group. Only when apprentices are accepted as full-fledged hunters is the mountain language taught to them.

The hunters use *okoze*, a small fish, as a charm because the mountain god is believed to be very fond of this fish. Many carry dried *okoze* on their hunting trips, but in some places other kinds of fish are also used as a charm. The *okoze* charm, they believe, will guide game to come toward them. Even when cows go astray, farmers often use *okoze* to find their cows.

MIGAWARI

A NEIGHBOR'S dog died suddenly. When sympathy was expressed for the loss of the dog, the old woman of the family said Shiro was a faithful dog and had died for Jiro, her 5-year-old grandson. Jiro, she explained, had been sick for some time, and because Shiro was particularly attached to the boy, it sacrificed its life to save him. Not only dogs, but also many other pets — cats,

canaries and horses — die in substitute for their masters or mistresses and save their lives, it is believed.

This idea, of course, is based on the loyalty of pets to their masters. There is a popular idea that a minor misfortune saves one from a graver one.

When people have some misfortune or lose some valuables, they are told not to be depressed by what has happened. They are told they should be thankful because their suffering or loss could have been much greater. The dog's death is sad, but it is more bearable than the boy's death. Hence the people think that the dog saved the boy's life. It is called *migawari* or acting as a substitute with one's life.

It is also said that the life of every human is predetermined. That is to say, none is able to live a day more than the number of years which is given him upon his birth. It is a consolation to many mothers to believe that, when their children die young, they have lived out their destined span of life and nothing could have prolonged their lives.

This belief that the day of one's death is decided upon his birth gave rise to another strange tradition of sacrificing one's years for prolonging the life of another. When one dies before his predetermined time, he can give the balance of his life to another. There are many old tales of persons ending their lives purposely and giving their remaining years to others whom they loved or respected.

MOUNTAIN GENIE

ALL MOUNTAINS were ruled by their spirits, who did not welcome intruders to their domains, it used to be believed. All over the country many customs and traditions about the divine rule of a mountain genie have developed.

The spirits had their own roads through their domains, and in many parts of the country, woodsmen or travelers avoided such paths. When woodsmen had to camp overnight they selected spots away from the roads of the mountain master. So they camped at such unpassable places as under cliffs and never along the tops of ridges.

Many tales tell about campers getting a rain of stones when they displeased the mountain spirit by entering its domain. Sometimes, at night, campers heard loud noises of huge trees being cut down all around them. They waited for daybreak in fear, but when morning came, they found that no tree had been cut near them. It was just a threat of the mountain spirit to warn woodsmen off the mountain, it was believed.

Once a *samurai* of Kanazawa entered a deep wooded mountain. On the other side of a stream he saw several persons sitting together and talking. He wanted to cross the stream and reach them, but the water, though not wide, was so deep that he could not cross it. He had a dog with him, and so he threw the dog to the other side, but instantly the dog was thrown back at him. The dog was dead as it hit the ground. The mountain spirit did not like his intrusion.

There is a story of a man trying to mine sulphur in Myoko Mountain who was killed by the mountain master. Nobody had tried to mine it before because it was believed to be the property of the mountain spirit. But one adventurous man went up with quite a large number of working men. At night, stones rained upon their camp, and all heard loud shouts of 'Don't take it away.' In the morning the man's head was twisted off and all the others fled in fear.

NIJUSANYA

THE HALF MOON rises on the evening of the 23rd day of the month by the lunar calendar and a rite called *Nijusanya* or 23rd evening is held. The month when this rite is held differs according to district, but generally it is held two to four times a year.

The rite is quite old but became popular during the Tokugawa era when tablets for *Nijusanya* were erected at many street corners.

Nijusanya, however, is a family rite, observed by only the female members of the family in some districts.

Originally it was a day when all were made to reflect on their conduct and stop their evil habits. Thus there developed in many places the custom of refraining from doing certain acts or from eating some foods.

It is commonly believed that a family which holds the rite will be free from sickness as the half moon is said to come with a bag of medicine. Fishermen think that it brings a good catch of fish.

There are also many traditional tales about *Nijusanya*. It is often said that on the evening, three half moons appear over the mountain top. The visit of a strange old man poorly dressed is told in many regions.

In one story a poorly dressed old man comes to the house where the rite is being held and asks to be allowed to enter and take part in the *Nijusanya* observation. Although he is an unknown stranger, the family kindly asks him to enter. Upon leaving the house, the stranger says that in thanks for the kind treatment, he would like to invite the family to visit him on *Nijusanya* evening the next year, giving his address.

When the members of the family go to the address of the strange visitor the next year, they find a magnificent mansion, although he came to their house in tatters. Invited inside they are given a hearty welcome and treated to an elaborate dinner.

O-BINZURU

BINZURU or Pindola Bharadvaja is the first of the 16 *rakan* (Arhan) or disciples of Buddha. It is hence natural that his statues stand at the entrance of many Buddhist temples in Japan. *O-Binzuru* is pictured as an old man with white hair and prominent eyebrows in paintings and old records. Yet in general, Japanese do not know what he looks like despite so many of his statues standing throughout the country.

It is because those statues have all been rubbed smooth and made featureless. On many of them, even ears and noses have been rubbed flat and the folds of his dress have disappeared.

Statues of *O-Binzuru* are mostly of wood, though some are of stone. At first, of course, the face, features and dress of *O-Binzuru* were clearly carved out in detail. They were then brightly lacquered in colors, in the case of wooden statues. However, as time went on, all the lacquer, colors and features were rubbed out smooth by human hands.

Originally, these statues were placed in temples, as he was a great disciple of Buddha. Later on, however, it somehow came to be believed by the people that the *O-Binzuru* statue had the power to cure illness. Under this belief, which quickly became common throughout the country, ailing Buddhist worshipers came and touched as well as rubbed the statue over the part corresponding to where they felt unwell.

As this belief became quickly popular, the statues soon became worn smooth. This is why all these statues one now sees in the country have come to look ugly without nose, eyes, ears or other features, apart from losing all lacquer and colors that originally made them so beautiful.

The unsightliness of the statues does not matter to those who believe in the power of *O-Binzuru*. Throughout the rural districts, old folks still believe in the ancient tradition, and whenever they feel unwell, they visit a nearby *O-Binzuru* and rub it with their hands — and they will tell you how their sickness was cured by the virtue of *O-Binzuru*.

O-IWA'S CURSE

YOTSUYA KAIDAN (The Ghost Story of Yotsuya) is one of the popular *Kabuki* plays, in which the ghost of O-Iwa brings curses on many persons. It is a thrilling story of murder and ghosts. O-Iwa, wife of a *samurai* named Tamiya Iemon, is poisoned by her husband who is having an illicit love affair with another woman. Becoming disfigured, she kills herself and her ghost torments Iemon to the end, causing many other deaths.

This play written by Tsuruya Nanboku and first produced in 1825, is based upon the life of Tamiya Iemon, and his wife O-Iwa. It is believed the curse of O-Iwa still exists. Whenever any theater is to produce this play, actors and theater managers must visit O-Iwa's tomb or the O-Iwa Inari Shrine and offer prayers to her; otherwise her curse will fall on all those connected with the production.

Recently an author writing of historic sites and traditions of Tokyo went to the O-Iwa shrine and took some photographs. Though an experienced photographer, he found that all his films came out blurred with strange streaks running across. Then he remembered O-Iwa's curse and on his second visit he made offerings and asked O-Iwa-san's sanction. His second shots came out clear.

Thus the O-Iwa Inari Shrine at Samon-cho, Yotsuya, and the Myogyo-ji Temple at Nishi Sugamo to where her tomb was removed from Samon-cho, are constantly visited by theatrical people as well as writers and others who wish to either produce the *Kabuki* play or write about O-Iwa-san.

It may sound unbelievable to many, but recently a publisher who intended to publish a book on *Kabuki* written by an eminent authority experienced many unexpected little mishaps, such as type mysteriously moving when the printing started or little errors made in binding. The printer and binder were perplexed, as they could not find how such mishaps occurred.

Finally all realized that a mention was made of *Yotsuya Kaidan* and O-Iwa-san in the book. So they visited the O-Iwa Shrine and made offerings and prayers to her.

ONDO STRAIT

THE ONDO STRAIT in Hiroshima Bay, Inland Sea, is famous for the rapid sea current that makes it impossible for small boats to pass through. Traditionally it is said that this strait was excavated by Taira-no-Kiyomori, the great head of the Taira family in the 12th century, and there still stands a monument to him.

But there is another tale about the origin of the strait. Itsukushima Shrine on Miyajima in the Inland Sea, which is famous as one of the most beautiful spots in the country, was worshiped by Kiyomori.

Once when he was visiting the shrine, he saw a very beautiful girl, whom neither the shrine priest nor others on the island knew. Kiyomori was much attracted to her and asked her to marry him.

The girl who was as beautiful as a goddess replied that she would marry him if he constructed a new shrine building in one day. As Kiyomori was determined to marry her, he immediately set himself to the task of constructing a magnificent new building.

As he applied his adze on timber, flying wood chips turned into thousands of carpenters who eagerly started to build the shrine. The sun began to set, and Kiyomori waved his fan to stop the sun from going down. The sun stayed still and permitted him to finish the great building in one day.

Kiyomori told the girl that now she must be his wife as the shrine was erected as promised, and waited for her in a boat. But the girl climbed up the great *torii* standing in the sea, and turning into a dragon, jumped into the sea. In surprise Kiyomori speeded his boat from the island, but the dragon followed him.

As he reached Ondo he glared at the sea and prayed to stop the dragon from catching him. The current started to move rapidly toward the pursuing dragon. It could not swim speedily against the strong current and Kiyomori managed to escape.

The current caused by Kiyomori still flows rapidly at Ondo.

ONE-EYED MONSTER

HITOTSUME-KOZO or one-eyed monster appears in many traditional tales of Japan. *Hitotsume-kozo* is always one-legged, usually has one eye in the center of the face but sometimes the eye is on one side as though it had lost the other one.

In many districts it is believed that *Hitosume-kozo* visits every house in January and December. Often it is worshiped as *yama-no-kami* or mountain god, and many mountainous districts have the tradition of *Hitotsume-kozo.*

It is generally believed that the guardian deity in descending from heaven to the local district stumbled over a rock, tree or bamboo, and as he fell down injured his eye on a projecting rock or tree branch and became one-eyed.

But there is another theory that in ancient days, those who performed the sacred service to the guardian deity wanted to look different from ordinary persons in order to keep up their dignity and purposely injured their eye.

The Gongen at Tadoyama, Ise, is one-eyed. It is said that the guardian deity was originally a big snake, and at the moment of a huge landslide, one of its eyes was blinded.

In one district of Chiba, farmers formerly did not plant *daikon* or Japanese radish, because their guardian deity was said to have stumbled over a *daikon* and his eye was pierced by a branch of a tea tree.

In Aomori district, *yama-no-kami* has one eye on one side, and also one leg on one side. The people of the neighborhood annually offer *waraji* or straw sandals to him.

In the mountain regions of Wakayama Prefecture, the people say that their *Hitosume-kozo* leaves a huge footprint, measuring over one foot in width, on the snow.

Among fish and snakes worshiped there are in many districts one-eyed ones. Such fish or snakes lost their eye under various circumstances, for which they are regarded as sacred.

ONI

ONI IS A Japanese word which is hard to define. Commonly it is translated as demon, devil, ogre or evil spirit. The word is said to have meant at first anything hidden or invisible that harms or even kills humans, and it was in such a sense that it was used in the *Kojiki* or ancient records.

Then Buddhism brought the idea that in *jigoku* or Hades there are *aka-oni* and *ao-oni* (red and blue devils) who torture those who are unfortunate enough to be sent to that region because of their regrettable conduct in this world. From this Buddhist idea, *oni* came to be presented as a hideous-looking monster with horns on its head and a large mouth showing sharp tusks. It is naked, dressed only in a tigerskin loincloth. It is also reputed to possess tremendous physical strength.

It also came to be believed that the spirit of the dead is turned into an *oni.* Thus there appeared many different types. But in a vague way it stood for anything that brought sickness, unhappiness and suffering.

'*Oni-wa-soto, fuku-wa-uchi*' (Out with devils, in with happiness) shouted by the people with the throwing of beans on the eve of *Setsubun* in February shows the general conception of *oni* as anything and everything that mars our happiness.

Thus anything undesirable came to be called *oni,* and even money-collectors are often called that. From such an idea of *oni* developed many sayings or colloquial expressions.

'*Oni-ga-warau*' (even the *oni* laughs), '*Oni-nimo-namida*' (even the *oni* sheds tears), — all indicate that the *oni* is inhuman or powerful.

It also appears in many fairy and folk tales, and though they vary in character and features, they all represent some inhuman beings that threaten or injure humans.

ONOKORO-JIMA

NUSHIMA is a little rocky island situated off Awaji-shima, in the Inland Sea. It is traditionally believed to be the first island created by the heavenly descendents Izanami and Izanagi and where they lived together.

The mythology of Japan tells that when the earth was not yet firmly formed, Izanami and Izanagi thrust down a heavenly spear into the sea brine to stir it, and the first drop that dripped from the spear became the first island which was called Onokoro-jima.

It is believed that Nushima is Onokoro-jima.

On the island is a 20-meter-high pointed rock which is said to represent the heavenly spear used to stir the sea and create the island, and is still regarded as the symbol of the island.

Onokoro-jinja on the island is the center of worship of the people. A shrine of the same name is also found on Awaji-shima, but this shrine is said to have been erected there for the convenience of those who do not or cannot visit Onokoro-jinja on Nushima.

Nushima is much older than Awaji-shima geologically, and is said to have been formed about 150,000 years ago or in the glacial age. Thus the creation of the Nushima tradition is now explained by some authorities to have been connected with the geological history of the island.

When the great glacier practically destroyed all living things on earth, Nushima shot out of the sea depths by the force of the great heat underneath. This fact gave birth to the mythological tale of the birth of Nushima, some say.

OSAN-NO-SUGI

IN THE national forest at Sakihama Village, Kochi Prefecture, Shikoku, there once stood a giant *sugi* or cryptomeria tree which was called *Osan-no-sugi* (childbirth cryptomeria) and worshiped for easy child delivery.

This great tree was blown down by a terrible typhoon that visited the area in 1895 and only a dead stump of about four meters high now remains.

Even today the villagers worship the dead stump of *Osan-no-sugi*, and mothers with babies carry tiny chips of the wood to safeguard their child birth. The stump is also worshiped for the healthy and happy growth of little children.

Behind this local belief a traditional story is told. During the days when the area was not yet much inhabited, a *samurai* and his wife happened to pass by the giant *sugi* tree on their journey over the mountain. When they came to the spot, the wife felt labor pains and could not walk any more.

As no help or house was available in the neighborhood she had to give birth to her baby under the shade of the tree. But while she was in labor there, a pack of wolves appeared and surrounded her. The old wife of the blacksmith of the village of Sakihama was also said to have been the leader of the wolves.

But fortunately the *samurai* was able to kill most of the hungry wolves and chase the others away. So his wife was able to give birth to her baby after all, by the lonely giant tree.

Thus is came to be believed that the old tree had the charm of helping mothers to have an easy delivery.

O-SHIRA-SAMA

IN MANY Tohoku or northeastern districts of the country, the people still worship *O-Shira-sama*. It is said to be the *kami* or deity of silkworms or sericulture, but in many places it is worshiped as the deity governing all farm work. Various different customs developed in worshiping *O-Shira-sama* according to district.

O-Shira-sama is said to have originated from a tradition about a beautiful maiden and a fine horse. The beautiful daughter of a wealthy family fell in love with a magnificent horse kept at the house. Learning of the affair, her father angrily killed the horse. In despair the girl died. Then the spirit of the maiden and the horse rose to heaven, and as they came down on the mulberry tree in the family garden they turned into silkworms.

O-Shira-sama, as it is still worshiped, is represented by a pair of crude dolls, made of short mulberry sticks, about 8 to 10 inches long, loosely wrapped up in cotton or silk cloths, the top ends of the sticks forming crude heads. One doll stands for the male and the other the female. In some places, the male is made from the mulberry tree from the east side of the house and the female of that from the west. Again in some places, the dolls are made of bamboo sticks.

Once a year, the *O-Shira-sama* are taken out of their box, and dressed in new dresses called *Osendaku.* Their faces are given a fresh whitening. *Osendaku* is believed to possess curing powers and when one has a pain in any part of the body, the sore spot is supposed to heal when rubbed with *Osendaku.* When a horse is sick, *Osendaku* is tied to its mane.

O-Shira-sama is also the guardian of children, and when a baby is born it is made *O-Shira-sama's* baby. Children also play with *O-Shira-sama* to tell their fortune. Holding *O-Shira-sama* in the hand, a child turns around a tree branch with a bent end, and the direction pointed by the end shows from where good luck will come.

OTAFUKU

TO CALL A Japanese woman *otafuku* is an insult, because the expression is now used to mean a homely or ugly woman. But it originally came from *otafuku-men* or *otafuku* mask, which has nothing ugly or unpleasant in its features. It is not known why this symbol of pleasantness, joyousness and good nature came to have such a meaning.

Otafuku masks have full, round cheeks that make the face wider at the bottom than at the top, and a small flat nose, the tip of which comes lower than the cheeks and forehead. So the face is concave. The eyes are narrow and curved, and the mouth small. The whole face is not beautiful, but it has something charming and delightful, full of joy and good nature. These features of the masks may be understood when one realizes that they are made after Ame-no-Uzume-no-Mikoto, according to the accepted tradition.

When the Sun Goddess, Amaterasu-Omikami, was displeased and hid herself behind the rock door of heaven, it was Ame-no-Uzume-no-Mikoto who danced and sang before the closed door, and caused the Sun Goddess to peep out. That gave an opportunity to bring her out and restore sunlight and happiness to the whole country.

The *otafuku* mask thus stands for all the good qualities of Uzume-no-Mikoto. However merely because it has a small flat nose and puffed cheeks, it seems the people have come to style ugly women as *otafuku.*

Yet, the mask itself is still used as a symbol of good fortune, happiness and joy. It is made in all sizes and sold at various shrines as well as toy shops throughout the country. There is no relation now between the happy mask and *otafuku* used as a term to insult women. *Otafuku* is also called *okame* in common use.

The term *otafuku* has become so popular that a kind of big round bean is called *otafuku-mame*, while parotitis is commonly named *otafuku-kaze* because it swells up the patient's cheeks.

There is a children's game called *fukuwarai* (happy laugh). On a sheet of paper the outline of an *otafuku* mask is drawn. Her eyes, eyebrows, nose and mouth are cut out from another sheet of paper and properly colored. While one is blindfolded, he is handed the eyes, eyebrows, nose and mouth separately. The game is to put them in their proper positions on the paper marked with the outline of the mask. Extremely simple though it may sound, the game is certain to make spectators laugh.

O-TAKE'S SINK

PEOPLE LOOKING for good housemaids visit the Shinko-in Temple at 4-chome, Iigura, Azabu, Minato-ku, Tokyo, as it is still believed that the spirit of O-Takesan enshrined there will find them maids.

In the early 17th century, a young maiden named O-Take came from Yamagata to become a maid at a family named Sakuma at Denma-cho, Nihonbashi, Edo. She was a perfect maid, rising early and going to bed late, being ever willing to work and never feeling tired. The well from which she daily drew buckets of water is still at Denma-cho, and visited by Tokyo residents who still love her. Furthermore, upon finishing one task, she would go to the Buddhist altar and worship there. It was also rumored among neighbors that everything she touched shone brightly, and even the wooden kitchen sink over which she worked daily gave off a bright light. She was loved by all, but

the family and neighbors often wondered who she was.

One day a Buddhist monk came to the house of Sakuma, and asked if there was a maid who came from Yamagata. Then the monk told a strange story. He said that when he went to Gongen Temple on Yudono Mountain in Yamagata, he found that the statue of Gongen (Avatar of Buddha) was missing from the temple. Upon his inquiry the priest of the temple explained that Gongensama had gone to Edo and become a maid for a family named Sakuma to save the people of Edo.

O-Take, hearing the talk of the visiting monk as she worked in the kitchen, suddenly turned into *Dai-Nichi-Nyorai* (Mahavairocanastahagata) and flew away through the roof opening.

The story of O-Take was widely told all over the city. Toyokuni painted her and many *Kabuki* plays were written about her. Keisho-in, mother of the fifth Tokugawa Shogun Tsunayoshi, became greatly interested in her story, and ordered that the kitchen sink at which she worked daily be presented to the Shinko-in Temple. It came to be popularly believed that a visit to the temple will bring a good maid to the family desiring help.

PRAYING FOR A BABY

THERE ARE many charms, rites and customs for praying for a baby, as the people have always thought that a married couple should have a baby or babies to keep up the family line. In the old days, many wives were divorced simply for being childless.

They consequently prayed for babies. Among the various different customs, there is one that used to be observed particularly in Sendai, Fukushima and other northeastern regions. This custom is comical and caused considerable laughter and merriment in families where it was held.

This was mostly observed on January 15 and 16, and several women, mostly old, took the leading roles. Generally, one dressed like a male physician, another as a midwife, and others as their assistants.

They secretly went to the house of a young childless couple. While the wife of the house was still ignorant of their arrival, they would rush into the house. One of them would catch hold of the wife by her waist. Of course, sometimes she would try to escape, and then there would be quite a merry chase in the house.

When she was finally caught, the old woman holding her would shout, 'Will you bear a baby or not?' She was held fast until she said, 'I will bear a baby.'

With her affirmative reply, they would produce a doll which they had brought, and go through the act of caring for a newborn baby. The doll baby was given a birth bath and dressed.

Then a feast celebrating the birth of the baby would follow, and the whole party including neighbors and friends had a joyful time. The young wife was then assured she would soon have a baby to the joy and satisfaction of all concerned.

PRAYING FOR MARRIAGE

THOSE DESIRING a good marriage make pilgrimages to Oyashiro (Great Shrine) at Izumo, and pray for the blessing that they may have happiness and fortune in marriage. The Great Shrine of Izumo was erected in honor of Okuni-nushi-no-mikoto, an illustrious figure in the early period of Japan.

It is indeed rather strange that such a personage is made the god of love and marriage. At any rate, according to the popular tale, Okuni-nushi-no-mikoto

was fortunate in love and marriage, and consequently the people believe that his spirit resting at the Great Shrine of Izumo is able to confer a similar blessing on all who come and pray there.

Okuni-nushi-no-mikoto was the youngest of many brothers who treated the little one rather mercilessly as he was willing and eager to please his elder brothers. In the province of Inaba, east of Izumo, there resided a beautiful maiden named Yasaka-hime. All the brothers tried to win her, and they decided to visit her house in person to see who could win the fair maiden. Okuni-nushi-no-mikoto was not counted by his brothers as an eligible youth for the hand of the lady, but he was ordered to accompany them as the carrier of their baggage. All the brothers were dressed in the finest that could be obtained, but the youngest was attired in rags and carried heavy baggage.

Upon arrival at the house of the maiden, each brother pleaded for the hand of the maiden, but each was in turn rejected. Okuni-nushi-no-mikoto stood in a corner, without saying a word, but the fair maiden took notice of him, and after refusing all his elder brothers, she proclaimed her wish to be the wife of Okuni-nushi-no-mikoto. The modesty, honesty and manliness of Okuni-nushi-no-mikoto touched the heart of the maiden.

This accounts for the reason people go even nowadays to Izumo to pray at the Great Shrine in the hope that they will be just as fortunate in love and marriage as the great *kami.*

Marriages are arranged by a *kami* (god), according to the ancient traditional Japanese belief. Thus formerly superstitious persons did not hold wedding ceremonies in the month of October which was called *kami-na-zuki,* *kami-*less month, or the month without a god to arrange a marriage. It was believed that in October all local deities went to attend a convention of *kami* at Izumo Shrine, in the province of Izumo, and thus all local shrines were left empty.

Annually, even at present, there are numerous pilgrims who trek to the shrine. They usually make special trips from all parts of the country to pray for a marriage arrangement for themselves, their children, their sisters, brothers and relatives. The deity of Izumo Shrine takes much joy in arranging marriages for such people, it is said, and therefore does not welcome the visits of married couples because, apart from not being able to do them any good, the deity might instead only make them feel jealous. Some superstitious persons even think that the deity of Izumo Shrine calls a convention of all local deities in October, for arranging marriages for the residents in their respective districts for the coming year.

It is now said that there is no foundation whatsoever for such a convention of the gods and consequently there is no *kami*-less October. Yet old folks still believe in it, because their ancestors did or because the idea is so romantic.

The custom of praying for marriage at shrines, however, originated quite early, and is still kept up in many rural districts. Visitors to many small local shrines will find, even today, tiny pieces of paper tied to the wooden grilles of shrine entrances or sometimes on the branches of trees around them. These small pieces of paper are the prayers for marriage. Men and women who wish to marry write out on the small pieces of paper their own names and whoever they desire to marry. They may write the names of others to whom they have never spoken before. Then, folding the paper into a narrow oblong strip, they tie it to tree branches by using only the

small or ring fingers of both hands. It is said that their prayers will then be heard and the shrine deity will arrange their marriage. This is another indication of their belief that marriage is arranged by a *kami*. The tying of the paper is believed to have come from the Japanese expression *en-musubi*, or marriage tying.

One may say that if a marriage is arranged by a *kami*, divorce must also be divinely settled. There is no such belief among the people generally, because divorce is regarded undesirable. In the Edo days, however, there stood a giant *enoki* or nettle tree in Itabashi which was called *en-kiri-enoki* or a divorce nettle tree. In those days, those who desired to be divorced from their husbands or wives, went to the tree and prayed, and then took home pieces of tree bark. Then the bark was boiled in water, and if the brew was secretly given to the husband or wife from whom one wished to be freed, the desire would be granted, it was then commonly believed. In the Edo days, the tree had quite a large number of daily visitors who peeled off its bark, according to old stories.

PRAYING FOR SNOW

FARMERS STILL welcome snowfall as they believe that snow is a sign of a good harvest. Actually, snow is good for farms, as it gives good moisture to the soil and kills insects and larvae.

Farmers therefore pray for snow and feel disappointed if it doesn't come.

On the other hand, in the Japan Sea coast regions and some northeastern districts, the snowfall is very heavy, covering farms, roads and mountains to a depth of more than 10 feet. In these regions the people suffer from the long sunless winter and inactivity. No outdoor work can be done, and streets and roads become impassable.

In many such villages and towns, all houses have wide eaves so that the people can walk under them, however deep the snow drifts. It is not seldom that houses are entirely buried under snow or the people walk into a second-story window from the snow-covered road. Moreover, the snow on the roof must be shoveled off almost daily, or else the house might collapse under the weight.

Children, however, are happy, playing on or in the snow. They dig holes in the snow and play in it as it is very warm. Tunnels are bored to cross the street to the other side.

In these snow districts, a traditional tale of *yuki-onna* or snow maid is circulated. It is believed that she spells misfortune if one meets her on the road. She generally appears at night, and might have originated in the strange-shaped objects formed by snow covering trees or rocks.

In some places she is believed to be an old woman who brings a curse upon children who are told not to go out after dark. Sometimes *yuki-onna* carries a baby; she asks anyone she meets to hold it for her. If he does, the baby becomes heavier and heavier and finally he dies from the weight and cold, it is said. The baby is a ball of snow.

There are many other strange tales about *yuki-onna* in those regions where snow covers the ground for more than three months every year.

RED TRADITIONS

RED IS THE color that is used in Japan on all happy occasions, as it is believed to be lucky. But in many districts there are many superstitious customs which still regard the color an evil omen or a sign of bad luck.

On all happy occasions *sekihan* or rice with red beans is cooked, and red-colored *mochi* or rice cakes are made. In celebrating the 60th and other old-age birthdays, the aged person is dressed in a red jacket and red cap. Red silk cloth was formerly used as a gift on happy occasions.

Red was also a charm against smallpox. When an epidemic of smallpox broke out, the people would hoist red flags. Smallpox patients were dressed in red clothes in the belief that the red color would cure them quickly. When prayers were offered for the cure of a smallpox patient or to prevent its spread, the Shinto priest used *gohei* or a sacred staff decorated with red paper, although usually white paper is used.

The idea of red as an evil omen or bad luck occurs in such beliefs as that if a man picks up a red pebble, his house will be burned up or he will be separated from his parents. Or if one dreams of a red horse, he will have a fire in his house.

In some parts of Japan when one broke the rules of the village or acted contrary to general custom, he was obliged to wear a red cap. Until the whole village was convinced that such a person had completely reformed the sentence of the red cap was not withdrawn. The punished person had to wear the red cap to all social and public gatherings.

The language still has such expressions as *aka-haji* (red disgrace) meaning disgrace in public; *sekihin* (red poverty), extreme poverty; *seki-men* (red face) shame-faced; *makkana-uso* (red lie), downright lie and others.

REED DIVINATION

IN THE EARLY periods of the country it is certain that there were practiced various forms of divination, and while many methods were brought over from China, some are believed to have originated in this country. To read fortunes by reading the cracks made in animal bones or turtle shells when heating them seems to have been most popular, but this method of divination is well-known.

Frequently it is mentioned that, in olden days, there was a method of divining by means of *ashi* (reed) leaves. The manner and method of such divination seem to be very vague, as ordinary history books do not mention it. Some mention its use, but do not explain the particulars. Even modern students of such subjects are not clear as to what part of the reed was used for this divination.

According, however, to a certain authority, the practice of divining by reeds was used until a late period, and for this purpose only the leaves were used. If this report is to be relied upon, it will explain the ancient custom which is similar to that of the later date. Or it may be considered that the later practice copied the older one.

At the beginning of the 18th century, a Japanese boat was carried by storm and current to a South Sea island. Out of the 11 on board the ship, only three returned finally and they came home 22 years after their departure. According to the report made by those returning, the island to which the boat drifted was not inhabited by any human being. But one day 22 years after the wreck, there came another Japanese boat drifting to the same island. On the second boat there were 18 men. The captain of the second boat said that, if they embarked upon the ocean, there might be one chance in 10,000 to return safely, and all decided to take the risk, as staying on the uninhabited island would be the same as death to them all. But to embark on such an adventurous and risky voyage, the day had to be carefully selected; otherwise, they would again

meet some storm or current and be swept away somewhere else again. The day of departure was therefore all important. Hence, in order to decide upon the date, all cleaned and purified themselves with water, and prayed most earnestly to the Ise Daimyojin, and then to the *kami* of Mishima, Akibasan, Izu, Hakone, and other places to accord them a safe voyage home. They then used reed leaves to decide upon the important day of departure. Thirty leaves were selected upon which were written the days of the month, from the first to the 30th. Placing the 30 leaves face down, they prayed and then solemnly rubbed them with the end of the purifying stick. Thereupon one of the 30 leaves rose with the stick. When it was examined, the date written on it was the ninth. Therefore the party left the island on the ninth morning, trusting to heaven, wind and tide to take them home to Nippon. On the eighth morning after the departure the ship reached Hachijojima, and they were all able to return home safely.

Judging from this tale, which is regarded as a true narration of the shipwrecked men, they seem to have employed divination by reed leaves. Further, they set themselves to the task of divining by purifying themselves and then praying to various *kami*. It is on this account that the authorities now believe that divination by reed leaves was in practice as late as the 18th century, and that the reed divination mentioned in the very early records of the country must have been of a similar kind. In fact some believe that the 18th-century practice was only a survival of the ancient custom.

The story of the shipwrecked men, at any rate, proves that divination by reed leaves has existed in Japan, although some doubts are attached to it by many authorities.

and should be respected.

SACRED EELS

IT SEEMS strange that the people of Japan who are so fond of eating *unagi* or eels, also think of them as sacred. Incidentally, however, eels have been worshiped in many rural districts as sacred deities.

The Mishima Shrine of Izu has for its messenger an eel, and the worshipers of the shrine pay homage to the eel. This is not the only such case in Japan. Many other localities have shrines dedicated to eels which are said to possess the virtues of protecting and giving fortune to those who believe in them.

In Wakayama Prefecture, there is a one-eyed eel enshrined. When the neighboring farmers offer prayers to the shrine, rain is certain to come. Thus, in dry seasons, the shrine has become a place of pilgrimage.

In many parts of the country, it is believed that a great and aged eel inhabits a river or pond in the neighborhood, ruling over all fish and plants in the water.

A widely circulated story says to the effect that when Gamo Hideyuki attempted to throw poison into the Tadami River in 1611, a Buddhist monk suddenly appeared. He preached the Buddhist doctrine of not taking any life, and succeeded in convincing Hideyuki of the evil of killing any living thing. It is said that the monk was a huge eel, the *nushi* (master) of the river. Upon learning that Hideyuki was thinking of poisoning the water and killing all the fish, the eel took the form of a monk, and appeared before Hideyuki.

The story of a big eel being the *nushi* of a river or lake is still very widely believed by rural folk. When they catch an exceptionally big eel, they are afraid to kill it, believing that it is the *nushi*

SACRED RICE

RICE IS SACRED to the Japanese people: it signifies not only harvests and food, but also the blessings of *kami* that has brought the food and the joy of eating it. It is holy and clean: it is the first offering to *kami*. One who handles rice carelessly or wastes it commits an unpardonable sin. Its holiness and sacredness have, therefore, the power to dispel evil spirits.

The custom of throwing unhulled rice around a room so that the baby will not cry at night is still observed even today among a large number of old-fashioned rural people. The holiness of rice drives away the evil spirit that haunts the baby and makes it cry at night. It is commonly believed that the evil spirit that haunts babies comes in the shape of tiny little men in armor. This little man in armor dreads rice, even though he is capable of entering any house unseen and frightening the most stout-hearted baby.

An ancient book of tales gives the following incident. Once, a long time ago, a certain person went to a house in a different part of the town with a baby. He did not know that an evil spirit resided in that house. Placing a light by the pillow of the baby, he slept nearby. There were also two or three other persons sleeping in the same room. At midnight the nurse maid was giving her breast to the baby when she noticed the door, of lacquered bamboo work, being slowly opened. When the door was opened about an inch or so, from the narrow opening entered 10 little men, about four inches in height, on horseback. They cantered toward the pillow of the baby. The nurse was frightened and afraid, but she mustered her courage and, taking up the dish of 'throwing rice' which was placed according to the traditional custom by the baby's pillow, threw the dish and rice at the tiny horsemen. As the rice struck them, they disappeared as if in a vapor. When examined, the dish was blood-stained.

From this account it is proved that the belief in the power of rice in dispelling evil spirits had been common since quite an ancient time. It is still believed by many, and the custom of throwing rice to ensure comfortable and sound sleep for the baby is practiced in many rural districts.

Beans are often used for the same purpose. The custom of throwing roasted beans on the eve of *Setsubun*, the last day of winter according to the lunar calendar, is well-known. At every house, roasted beans are scattered by the master, who shouts 'Devils without, fortune within.' It has the same meaning as throwing rice, and it possesses the power to drive out evil spirits and devils. At many temples the ceremony of *Setsubun* bean-throwing is held in a very elaborate manner. To obtain a few of such scattered beans is regarded as very fortunate, and many travel far to attend famous ceremonies of bean-throwing on the occasion of *Setsubun*.

In some quarters of the country, beans are used as a means of stopping a toothache. They believe that, so long as beans do not sprout, toothaches will not come. They therefore take a handful of beans to a nearby temple and bury them deep in the soil. As they are buried so deep, they will not sprout soon. Again, to completely prevent sprouting, some resort to the trick of burying roasted beans — then, of course, one will be immune from toothaches for life.

Also, in ancient tales, it is often mentioned that people buried roasted beans in sacred grounds such as temple or shrine compounds and prayed for recovery from smallpox. This is also from the belief that, while the beans do not bud, they can be in good health.

'Mame' (beans) also means 'healthy' or 'active,' and the above belief might have originated from this play on the word. Cooked beans are used on felicitous or other occasions, signifying that the eaters will be as active and healthy as *mame*.

Both rice and beans constitute the staple food of the people, who naturally think well of these two products of the soil. According to district, many other virtues are given to rice and beans, but in all cases they signify power, fortune, or health. It is no exaggeration to state that the health of the Japanese people is generally built on rice and beans which also guard the health and fortune of the people by preventing the approach of evil spirits and devils.

SALT TRADITIONS

SALT OR SEA water purifies us of evils and sickness, it has been long believed. Thus salt is still extensively used whenever purity and cleanliness are demanded. Salt is necessary for shrines for purification rites. The Grand Shrine of Ise makes its own salt even today for its rites, and also distributes it to other shrines that wish to use the Ise Shrine salt.

One returning from attending a funeral service must by cleansed by salt showered over him at the entrance. *Sumo* wrestlers scatter it on the wrestling arena for a clean match. Many restaurants and such still place at their entrances small piles of salt every day for good luck. Tubs of sea water are kept at house entrances in many seaside regions to wash hands or feet for purification.

In many parts of the country the

custom of obtaining buckets full of sea water or shore sand on New Year's Day and sprinkling it over the door is still followed. In south Kyushu children come to sell New Year salt on January 2.

Some old-fashioned people still believe that salt is sacred, and to waste it is to invite evil or punishment. In the old days, salt was not to be purchased at night, and in some districts it was believed that a family which did so would have difficulty in marrying off its daughters. When they needed salt at night, they had to borrow it from a neighbor.

The word 'shio' (salt) was never to be uttered at night. Whenever it was necessary to refer to it at night, it was called 'nami-no-hana' (flowers of waves), a pretty expression which is still used by some women.

Some people used to put salt in cooking rice, in the belief that the salt in the rice would purify them of evils. In Kagoshima, Kyushu, there was formerly a custom of placing a weak or undeveloped child under the care of the salt dealer, who was then called 'shiototo' or salt father. It was believed that under his care the child would become healthy and strong.

SANDO-ME

WHEN A Japanese family has occasion to receive two visitors in one day, they will say that a third person is sure to call during the same day. Or when they receive two gifts on the same day, they speculate as to what will be the third present to come during the day. It is because the people believe that what happens twice will take place a third time.

This also applies to misfortune, sickness or accidents. When a child is injured twice in succession in rough play or mischief, his mother will say, "Be careful now, you've had two accidents already, and the third may be really serious." *Sandome-no shojiki* (the third time is the real one), it is said, and the third happening is bound to bring the most important or serious result. It is the third game that will win you the big pot, the third illness that will threaten your life, the third dealing that will bring you a great fortune. On the third trial the people place the greatest hope, and also the third year will bring reward for past efforts. Yet, again the third may bring you calamity.

Then, there is another saying, *Hotoke-no kao-mo sando*, meaning even Buddha would not grant mercy for a third time. That is a warning against counting on others' patience or good nature too often.

For good or bad, the third marks an important turning-point.

Formerly it was said that a family's fortune was established for good if its prosperity continued for three generations. A man builds up his business or fortune with hard work and untiring efforts; his son manages to keep up family honor, spending what his father accumulated in leading a comfortable life, and the third generation comes to bankruptcy, it was said. So runs a saying *Sandaime-no kashiyafuda* (the third generation puts up a house-to-let sign).

Sneezing also tells one's fortune. The common belief is that if you sneeze once, somebody is speaking well of you; sneeze twice, and someone is speaking bad of you; sneeze three times, someone loves you; sneeze four times — you have caught a cold.

So even in sneezing, the third time brings the best fortune. Test this when you sneeze the next time, and see if it comes true.

SEKI-KANTO

ALMOST ALL over Japan, one sees stones two to three feet around, tapering at the top, standing at street corners, bridges or in front of house gates. They are generally called *seki-kanto*. They are charms for peace and prosperity and for preventing the entrance of devils and enemies.

It is the opinion of Mr. Kunio Yanagita, foremost authority on Japanese folklore, that these stones are *hakariishi* or weighing stones to judge one's fortune by trying to lift them up. When one has a problem or wishes to have his fortune told, he tries to lift one of the stones up. If he can lift it easily, it is a good sign, but even when he cannot, his feeling in the attempt will give a hint to his coming fortune.

The word *seki-kanto* is the Japanese pronunciation of Shih Kan-tang, the name of a great wrestler of China whom no one could overpower. In China, stone tablets bearing his name came to be erected for subjugating devils, suppressing calamities, and bringing good fortune and happiness.

Some of the stones in Japan bear the same inscriptions, and thus they are called *seki-kanto*. It is said, however, that the Japanese belief in the charm of such stones dates back very early, and that with the introduction of the tradition of Shih Kan-tang, the ancient charm stone came to be mixed up with the Chinese belief. This is proved by the fact that very old charm stones have no inscription, while comparatively new ones also have no writing on them. Thus the Chinese tradition was popular when it was first introduced to the country. Today, the people still call these stones *seki-kanto*, but generally they do not know that it stands for a Chinese wrestler.

In some districts, it is believed that when a *seki-kanto* falls down, rain will come. Consequently, when farmers desire rain, they pull down *seki-kanto* in prayer for rain.

SEKI-NO-OBASAN

IN MANY places in Edo, up to about a hundred years ago, there was a small stone image of an old woman, called generally *Seki-no-obasan* or old cough woman. The most famous of them was at the residence of Lord Inaba of Tsushima, at Tsushima, Tsukiji.

Parents of children suffering from a bad cough or whooping cough entered the residence, after obtaining permission from the gate-keeper, to pray at the image for the recovery of their children from the illness. The image was about two feet high, showing the woman in a sitting position.

Soon, however, another image, of an old man with a fierce expression, was placed by the old woman. The two were not on friendly terms, it was said, and when the two images were put close by, the anger of the old woman made the old man fall sideways. So they were placed a little apart.

The worshipers always brought roasted beans and brewed tea to offer to both images. To obtain quick results, the help of the two had to be asked. First, they went to the old woman and asked her to cure their children. Then they went to the old man and told him that, although they had asked the old woman to help their children, they had not much confidence in her power, and the help of the old man was necessary to effect a cure quickly. All believed that an appeal to both images brought a cure without fail.

In other parts of the country, there are also many images or stone tablets which were believed to possess the power to cure coughs, particularly of children.

SEKKU

WHEN TWO or more persons eat from the same pot or drink from the same cup, an invisible chain is created binding them together in unity, according to the ancient belief of the people. Cereals, fruits, vegetables, *sake* and even cooked food are offered to *kami-sama* or the guardian deity and then the offerings are partaken of by the members of the household, in order to maintain relation with the divine spirit.

In order to keep up harmonious relations with the guardian spirit, the act of eating or drinking together must be repeated occasionally. Thus *sekku* (festival) or holidays came to be fixed as days when spiritual unity with the divine spirit and neighbors was maintained by gathering together and eating out of the same pot, and drinking from the same cup.

The passing of the *sake* cup between the bride and the groom at the wedding service unites them in marriage and also in spirit. When a housewife cooks something special, she never fails to distribute, even small bits, to neighbors and friends. When the rite for celebrating the completion of a new house is held, small pieces of *mochi* or rice cakes are distributed among the gathered people.

This habit of distributing or sharing food on such happy occasions is not just for sharing joy, but also for cementing the people spiritually in unity.

Sekku originally meant food to be offered and shared but gradually it came to mean seasonal festivals or holidays when offerings were made to the guardian deity and shared by all. Various different kinds of foods, offered and partaken of on such *sekku* days, developed.

The expression 'eaten from the same pot' is still used by the people to indicate close and intimate friendship.

SEVEN GODS OF FORTUNE

THE SEVEN GODS of Fortune are among the most popular deities in Japan, and there are shrines dedicated to them all over the country. Even their picture is regarded as something that will bring good luck. On the night of January 2, for instance, the Japanese put under their pillows a picture of what is called the *Takara-bune* (treasure ship), consisting of the Seven Gods of Fortune and such lucky treasures as rice, gold coins, coral, etc. It is a kind of charm, and a lucky dream that one sees on the eve of January 2 is a sign of a good year.

There are different opinions as to the true origin of the Seven Gods of Fortune, but it is generally believed that the gods were first selected by Priest Tenkai, who was a great favorite with Tokugawa Iemitsu who became the third Tokugawa shogun in 1623.

"Man has two kinds of nobility, natural and human," Iemitsu once said to Priest Tenkai. "The former makes peers, while the latter consists of human virtues. But tell me, Reverend Priest, what are your views on the two kinds of nobility?"

"I am glad that you ask this question," said Priest Tenkai to the shogun. "Natural nobility consists of seven virtues, which are: 1. longevity, 2. fortune, 3. popularity, 4. candor, 5. amiability, 6. dignity, and 7. magnanimity."

The shogun was so pleased with the explanation of the seven virtues that he told the priest to select seven deities in representation of the seven virtues. Priest Tenkai called Kano, one of the best painters of the day, and had the seven deities painted by him.

They became the Seven Gods of Fortune. They are probably the most favorite charms of the Japanese. They are painted in pictures, and made into statues, ornaments and toys, singly or in a group.

BENTEN: *Benten* representing amiability, came from India, but coming over to Japan, she suddenly changed her character and virtues. In her new role, however, she became one of the most popular goddesses of the country.

She is the only goddess among the Seven Gods of Fortune.

Benten's full name is *Benzai-ten* (Sarasvati) and while she was in India, she was the famous goddess of fortune, knowledge and eloquence. But in Japan she became the goddess of music and feminine beauty.

She is represented always in the form of a beautiful woman, holding a *biwa*, a musical instrument, in her hand. Her name is synonymous with a beautiful woman. As the goddess of music, she has a large number of followers among professional musicians, men and women, and especially women musicians or *geisha*, because she stands for both music and beauty.

Being however, very feminine in character, she is also said to be very jealous. In former days, Court musicians who played *biwa* did not often marry, because it was firmly believed that when such musicians married, *Benten* would become very jealous, and take away their musical talents.

Around the statue of *Benten* is often seen coils of snakes, and these snakes are believed to stand for jealousy.

Even today, couples are advised not to visit *Benten* together, as their presence before the goddess will make her jealous, and they may be caused to separate before long. Hence, such people visit many of the famous *Benten* of the country separately when they approach the presence of the goddess, fearing that if seen together, the anger and jealousy of the beautiful goddess of music will bring obstacles in the path of their love.

BISHAMON: Dignity has the image of *Bishamon* in representation of another Indian deity called Vaisravana.

Bishamonten (Vaisravana) is the god of treasure, fortune, and happiness, but his appearance is greatly misleading. He wears a war helmet and armor and holds a threatening halberd in his hand. His look is martial and war-like, being thus attired in the costume of battles. Only the tower of treasure that he has in his other hand shows a glimpse of his nature and virtues.

But his helmet, armor and halberd are not meaningless. He needs them to perform his duties. He is one of the Four Guardians of Buddha, and it is his duty to protect Buddha and Buddhism. He needs his helmet, armor and halberd to fight all evils and devils that might threaten to endanger the virtues of Buddha. Therefore, his armor and war-like costume are merely for protection, and not for attack.

Besides being the guardian of Buddha, he bestows upon good people happiness and fortune, as represented by the tower of treasure that is held in his hand.

Bishamonten, as one of the Seven *Fuku-no-kami* of Japan, has a large following among the people, and his temples are alway crowded with worshipers who believe in the power of *Bishamon* to protect Buddha and give them happiness and treasures.

So many of the Buddhistic deities are presented in fierce and war-like appearance and costumes, making them often appear extremely grotesque and hideous. Nevertheless they are also venerated and worshiped by the people, because they know that the fierce appearance is only for the sake of fighting devils and evils that are enemies to the gospel of Buddha. The strength of these deities to fight is often regarded as proof of their virtues.

DAIKOKU: *Daikoku* represents fortune. With his broad smiling face, and wearing a flat black cap, *Daikoku* is a pleasing figure, and as the god of wealth, is worshiped by all who desire to become rich and wealthy.

As to his identity, however, there are two opinions. One says he is of Indian origin, and the other declares that he is of Japanese origin.

The Indian theory says that he is Mahakala who was formerly the god of death, but who later became the god of war and fortune. As many of the Indian or Buddhistic deities have been brought to Japan, *Daikoku* may also be one of such foreign settlers. But many of the people of Japan desire to think that *Daikoku*, their god of wealth, is native-born.

Okuni-Nushi-no-Mikoto, one of the greatest rulers of prehistoric Japan, is said to be the origin of *Daikoku*, the most popular *kami* of the country.

However, to the average Japanese, the origin is not of much concern, as they worship *Daikoku* as their god of fortune and wealth. He is generally represented sitting on two bulky straw-bags of rice, and holding in his hand a golden mallet. The rice-bags stand for the rice harvest from the field, and the golden mallet, *uchide-no-kozuchi*, represents monetary wealth. It is said that when one shakes the mallet, coins will flow out at any time, and in unlimited quantities.

Minute statues of *Daikoku* done in gold are often carried by many people as a talisman for wealth and prosperity.

As *Daikoku* wears a flat cap, such caps came to be known as *Daikoku-boshi* (Daikoku caps).

EBISU: *Ebisu* personifies candor. With his broad, smiling and pleasant face, holding a huge *tai* (sea-bream) under his left arm, and a long fishing pole in his right hand, Ebisu looks really contented and happy. He is the god of wealth and fortune, and is especially worshiped by tradesmen and shopkeepers.

The sight of his face makes one happy, and the large fish under his arm represents the success of efforts. Hence he stands for wealth and fortune. He wears a rather strange costume for a god of wealth or business. He wears the tall headgear of the ancient Court, and also official dress. The fishing pole and fishing seem out of place with so distinguished a costume, but by the right of birth, *Ebisu* is entitled to such official dress.

His real name is Kotoshiro-Nushi-no-Mikoto. As this name is too long, he is commonly called *Ebisu-sama.* He is the son of Okuni-Nushi-no-Mikoto, an illustrious ruler of prehistoric days. Kotoshiro-Nushi-no-Mikoto was also a wise and just ruler, and often acted for his father. But he was of a very happy and easygoing frame of mind.

Once when his services were required by his father and other people, he could not be found. It was finally discovered that he was spending his days leisurely at Miho-no-Seki, Izumo, indulging in his favorite sport of fishing. It is said that, on that account, statues of *Ebisu* have always been represented with a fishing pole and a big fish.

Nevertheless, he is the popular, smiling and contented god of wealth and fortune. Some hold that *Ebisu* is another foreign god, Indian or Tibetan.

FUKUROKUJU: Popularity is deified in *Fukurokuju* representing a Chinese hermit, who is said to have lived during the Sung dynasty.

He is always represented in the shape of a small old man with a prominently long and bald head, but *kukurokuju* is a *kami* of all trades. He stands for wealth, happiness and longevity, all that human beings wish and hope for. If one believes in *Fukurokuju*, and is in good grace with him, he has no need for other *kami*.

He is one of the Seven Gods of Fortune, but he almost does alone what the other six *kami* accomplish together. But, despite his many virtues, he is not so popular as *Daikoku* or *Ebisu*.

Fukurokuju is bald, and has long white whiskers. He usually is accompanied by a *tsuru* (crane), which is a symbol of long life. He must be wise, as he possesses a high and unusually long head, and also carries a book of sacred teachings tied to his staff. His long head may stand for 'long-headedness,' although such an expression is never used in Japan.

He does not have so happy and smiling a face as *Daikoku*, but his name is of a very happy sound and meaning. *Fuku* (happiness), *roku* (wealth) and *ju* (long life) explain his virtues. From his name, he may be judged as the most illustrious of all gods of fortune.

It appears though, that his extraordinarily long and narrow head makes him rather ridiculous and strange. If he were of a more joyful and pleasant appearance, he would naturally be the most popular of all *kami*. His long head has prevented him from becoming the most famous of all. 'Long-headedness' may make one wise, but not always happy.

He has, however, a venerable looking expression on his face, and with the sacred book tied to his staff, he looks wise and learned. But strangely, he is not reputed to be wise.

HOTEI: For magnanimity Priest Tenkai selected another Chinese hermit, who lived during the Leang dynasty. Included among the Seven Gods of Fortune, he is called *Hotei*.

As his name is generally used in describing stout people, or especially those with big potbellies, *Hotei* is always represented in the shape of a very fat person with a conspicuously big belly. His face is fat, full and smiling. He dresses in the costume of a Buddhist priest, and carries a huge cloth bag over his shoulder.

He is the god of fortune. He looks prosperous and happy. His fatness makes him appear contented and well-nourished.

His big cloth bag, however, makes him appear rather greedy, and is thus out of place with his priestly costume. But the bag is to hold all supplies necessary, not only for himself, but also for all his followers. The bag, really, holds fortunes for the believers in his virtues. It is a mystic bag which never ceases to give, despite continual demand.

The big belly being the main characteristic of this god of fortune, *Hotei* became an adjective for anything especially big or projecting. A certain kind of bamboo is called *Hotei-dake* (*Hotei*-bamboo), because its joints are big and projecting.

He is happy and therefore, while he dispenses fortune, he is also considered as the god of contentment and happiness.

JUROJIN: *Jurojin*, who represents longevity, is always mentioned at the beginning of the list of the Seven Gods of Fortune. He is said to be the South Pole star incarnate, but he is modeled after a Chinese hermit who lived in the Sung dynasty.

He is short of stature, but has a big head. He holds in his hand a long stick, to the top of which is tied a little book. It is traditionally believed that this book contains the life-span of every individual in this world.

Moreover, he is accompanied by a deer, which is black in color. According to ancient Chinese belief, a deer becomes blue when it reaches the age of 1,000 and then turns white when it passes the age of 1,500. Finally it becomes black after the age of 2,000. So a black deer is very rare, and if a man eats a piece of its meat, he will live 2,000 years. Thus, the black deer has been regarded as a symbol of long life. *Jurojin*, being the god of longevity, naturally is accompanied by a black deer.

The people have for long worshiped *Jurojin*, hoping for long life. Many also wished to have a look at his book, but that has not been accomplished by any person.

SHADOW OF DEATH

ONE'S SPAN of life is predestined, and nothing can change it. When a man's end nears, *Shini-gami* or the god of death beckons him to come, and he obeys and dies. Then his family and friends say that he died as his given life expired. *Shini-gami* has a book on which a date is written down for each person to die. It is his duty to see that the death dates entered in his book are faithfully followed. Daily and hourly, he looks at the book and calls each person at the proper moment to come.

Men die according to their predestined fate, and death is beyond human influence, it is believed. Then when the time of death approaches, one's shadow becomes faint. When people hear of the death of someone, often remarks such as "I thought he would not last long, because the last time I saw him his shadow was faint *(kage-ga-usui)*" are made.

The dead person has no shadow, it is said, and therefore it is believed that, as the end approaches, one's shadow becomes faint. But the people know, at least in recent times, that one's shadow will not be affected by the approach of death. Yet, they see some change in his attitude, expression or manner that tells the coming of the fated hour. This change is due to the beckoning of *Shini-gami*.

The change, of course, comes in different ways according to persons. Those who are known for their stinginess or narrow-mindedness, for instance, suddenly become generous and considerate. Then their friends are wont to say that the end is not far off. They see in the unexpected change in mind or attitude the beckoning hand of *Shini-gami*.

Then again, it is also said that in his last days or hours, a man returns to the goodness and nobleness with which he was born. Yet the common belief that the older people become the more greedy they are, seems to hold in many actual cases.

SHAMOJI CHARM

OVER THE entrance of many Japanese houses in rural districts throughout the country are nailed *shamoji* or flat wooden rice scoops. They bear various inscriptions, but some of them have become illegible with age. Generally speaking, they are replaced every two or three years.

These *shamoji* are charms to ensure the good health and growth of children. Thus, families with many children have several *shamoji* over their entrances, but again, in other cases, one is used for several children. Inscriptions vary according to districts. The simplest has only the name of a child and nothing else. Prayers for the health of children are the usual inscriptions, though texts might differ. A certain time-limit is sometimes specified in the inscription, asking, for instance, for the good health of a child until he is 15 years old.

It is unknown when or how this custom of writing a prayer for children's health on *shamoji* and nailing it over the entrance started. Yet it is one of the most widely used charms all over the country. The public faith in this charm is, similar to many other customs, believed to have been founded on the people's belief in the divine grace which is represented in the harvest of rice that enables them to sustain their life. *Shamoji*, of course, stands for rice, the daily food. *Kami*, who is so benign as to provide rice for their sustenance, will kindly look after the welfare of their children, particularly when they pray for it. That is believed to be the thought behind this custom.

Shamoji are also used as symbols of divine grace in another way. At Itsukushima Shrine in the Inland Sea, renowned as one of the three most beautiful spots in the country, *shamoji* are sold as sacred charms for happiness and prosperity. They are made in various sizes, and visitors purchase them not only for their homes, but also to mail to their friends.

It is a sign of good luck and fortune to unexpectedly receive an Itsukushima *shamoji* mailed from the shrine by a friend. When one who buys or receives a *shamoji* from the shrine has really exceptionally good fortune, he offers a new *shamoji*, generally bigger than the one he has, to the shrine as an indication of his appreciation. Many such *shamoji*, some of them almost 10 feet high, are offered in thanks and kept in the shrine building.

In the northeastern district a *shamoji* is called '*hera-tori*' or scoop holder. This was because only the housewife used the *shamoji* for dishing out rice, and nobody else was permitted to undertake the task.

In most farming districts women worked as hard as the men. The housewives were the administrators of goods and economic matters of the family. Their authority as the mistress of a household was never infringed upon by others.

In the farming regions of Tohoku in the northeastern region, the housewife is not only still called '*hera-tori*,' but she also enjoys a high position and authority. She has her designated seat by the *irori* or fire-place, which must never be taken by any other person. The cooking and serving of the food are entirely in her charge.

Only when she is unable for various reasons to perform her duties to a guest as mistress of the house is a daughter or servant allowed to serve meals to him.

Even when her son is married, the housewife does not easily transfer her authority to her daughter-in-law. It is only after the young woman has fully proved herself to be competent to act as the mistress of the household that the old housewife hands over her '*hera*' to her.

SHIRAHIGE SHRINE

SHIRAHIGE (white whiskers) Shrine at Yotsugi in Tokyo's Katsushika Ward, relates a traditional tale of swans and a mysterious white-whiskered old man.

In the winter of 1779, Tokugawa Ieharu, the 10th Tokugawa shogun, went crane hunting with hawks to the Katsushika region. But the hunting party had no luck that day. Disappointed, they were about to go home.

Then over the swamp they saw many swans and Ieharu gave the order to release his hawks after them. But as the hawks neared the swans, a strange white-whiskered old man appeared and chased them away.

This angered Ieharu and he ordered that the old man be caught. But none could come near the old man who seemed to be able to walk quickly over the swamp.

Then Fukushima Hachizaemon, the official in charge of hawk hunting, realized the nature of the strange old man. He told the shogun that the swamp area was under the protection of *Shirahige-sama* or white-whiskered deity, and the swans should not be molested.

But the shogun would not listen to such explanations and angrily said that unless the swans were caught, Hachizaemon and all the hawkers would be beheaded.

Thereupon, Hachizaemon prayed to *Shirahige-sama* to permit him to catch some swans, promising that he would offer a large *ema* (votive picture tablet) in appreciation of the deity's goodness. His prayer was heard and his hawkers were able to catch the birds and thus save their lives. The shogun was also satisfied.

A large tablet with a painting of hawks chasing swans, bearing the signature of Hachizaemon and his 11 hawkers, was shortly presented to the shrine. This *ema* made the shrine quite famous.

At Mukojima on the other side of the Sumida River there is another shrine named Shirahige Jinja which is quite famous, but there are no traditional tales associated with it.

SHOJO

HEAVY DRINKERS are often called *shojo* (orang-utang), but *shojo* in this case is not the animal one sees at the zoo. *Shojo* as the model of heavy drinkers is a mythic animal of Chinese

tradition and is generally represented in pictures and dolls as a red-faced stubby man with a mass of hair on his head.

It is described as an animal with a body like that of a dog, but with a manlike face. It is said to be very clever and talks human language. It is, of course, fond of alcoholic drinks.

Since its face is red, *shojo-hi (shojo* scarlet) stands for bright scarlet. Bright red woolen clothes were also called *shojo.*

To catch the *shojo,* the Chinese tradition says, one must take many huge tubs of alcoholic drinks, drinking bowls, dippers, and wooden shoes to a dense mountain forest. Leaving those things, the hunters hide some distance away. The *shojo* appear, but as they are clever they know instantly that humans are playing some trick to catch them.

So, they sit around those articles, and utter angry and abusive words against humans. But the smell of the alcoholic drinks becomes too inviting for them. First they dip their fingers in the tubs and taste the liquor. Then taking up bowls and dippers they begin to drink. The whole group soon becomes quite drunk.

Fully satisfied, they want to go home and put on the wooden shoes. As they are drunk and the shoes are clumsy, they tumble and cannot easily get up. Waiting for that moment, the men in hiding come out and tie up the *shojo.*

This animal is also the subject of the famous *Noh* play, 'Shojo.' The play was based on a Chinese tradition.

There once lived in China a man who was respected by the whole neighborhood for his tender care of his parents. He ran a wine shop and did a very prosperous business. One day a person of strange appearance, as small as a boy, came to his shop. He was the *shojo* who lived under the sea.

This strange and grotesque visitor

knew all about the wineshop keeper, and while he was drinking wine there, he praised him highly for taking such good care of his old parents.

On leaving the shop, the visitor left an earthenware jug, filled with wine, as a token of his respect for the filial shopkeeper.

The shopkeeper tasted the wine in the jug. It was a very fine wine. He sold the wine but strangely he found that the jug was always full, no matter how many dipperfuls he might take out of the jug. So the good man prospered and became very wealthy.

In the *Noh* play, other tales and pictures, the *shojo* has thus come to stand for the spirit of *sake* or wine. Heavy drinkers are still called *shojo*, while many red things are also called by that name.

SHOKI-SAN

SHOKI-SAN is pictured as a mighty man of vigor and courage. His face is red and half-covered with stiff whiskers: he is tall and well-built. His eyes are especially piercing and large. He dresses in solemn clothes of black, and wears a black cap. In his hand he carries an unsheathed sword. Under one foot, he crushes a little devil.

He looks terrible, and is really so, but he was born of a dream.

Shoki is an imaginary person of China, where he is highly admired for his courage and physical power. The story of *Shoki*, which is the Japanese pronunciation for Chung Kuei, originated at the beginning of the Tang dynasty, or early seventh century.

The Tang emperor dreamed one night that a mouse had stolen his favorite jade flute, but suddenly a warrior dressed in a black costume appeared and, turning into a devil, caught the mouse and regained the lost flute

for the emperor. Appreciating what he had done, the emperor asked the warrior his name, and he replied that he was Chung Kuei from Chungnan. He told the emperor that he had failed the civil service examination, and disappointed, he had struck his head against the stone steps of the examination hall, and died. The emperor, hearing of his sad fate, expressed sorrow for him. Learning that the emperor was so good as to feel sorry for him, he resolved to catch and kill all devils who harmed the people of the land, to show his appreciation of the emperor's kind thought.

Then the emperor woke up from his dream. Immediately the emperor called Wu Tao-tsu, a noted painter, to his side, and gave him a minute description of Chung Kuei who had appeared in his dream. He wanted a picture of the strange warrior made before his memory became faint.

The picture Wu painted according to the description given by the emperor has become the standard figure of Chung Kuei followed for all these centuries, not only in China, but also in Japan.

Thus *Shoki-san* came to be the driver out of devils, and the protector of the people from evil influences.

On the Boys' Festival of May 5, the portrait of *Shoki* or an image of him is put in the place of honor, in the hope that the boys for whom the festival is held will become strong enough to fight devils as *Shoki* does. Also, it is believed that the presence of *Shoki* at the festival will keep all devils and evils away from the boys.

There is no beauty or tenderness in *Shoki*. He is rather ugly and vicious. 'A face like *Shoki*' means a strong face, but it also conveys a meaning that the face is not beautiful.

His statue often represents him crushing little devils under his feet. It makes him appear rather merciless, but *Shoki* will have nothing do with little devils. Devils are pictured so small to emphasize the strength and courage of *Shoki-san.* In his hands, the biggest of devils are handled like babies.

SHOULDER-CHIPPED JIZO

AT THE KIUNJI Temple, Tozaki-machi in Bunkyo-ku, Tokyo, there is still a stone Jizo statue with a chip broken off its shoulder. There is a legendary tale concerning this statue.

The temple area used to be thickly wooded, and foxes and badgers lived there and often did mischief.

In a village nearby was a *tofu* (bean curd) shop operated by one Kichibei. At night when he counted his sales in the money box, he sometimes found a leaf. He realized that it was always on the day when a boy priest came to buy *tofu* that he found a leaf in the money box.

So when the priest came to buy *tofu* the next time, Kichibei and his assistant Otoji followed him. When they came to the gate of the Kiunji Temple, the priest disappeared. They thought it must be a fox that was taking the shape of a priest and coming to buy *tofu* with leaves.

When the boy priest came again, Kichibei raised his big *tofu*-cutting knife and struck at the boy's shoulder. The boy mysteriously disappeared, leaving the *tofu* basket and a stone chip covered with blood. Kichibei also found drops of blood trailing from the shop.

Kichibei and Otoji followed the drops of blood and came to the Kiunji Temple. There they saw blood exuding from the shoulder of the stone Jizo statue there.

They knew then that it was the Jizo who had come to buy *tofu* but they could never understand why the stone statue wanted to eat *tofu.*

The mystery is still unsolved. The Jizo statue with a chip off its shoulder has become famous, as the story came to be widely told all over the neighborhood.

The temple was burned during the Pacific war but the famous statue still stands there.

SNAKE WORSHIP

SNAKES APPEAR in many legends and folk tales of Japan, and while there are snakes that bring curses and death on humans in such stories, snakes are also worshiped as benevolent deities. Shrines dedicated to them still exist and are worshiped.

Many deities are believed to take the shape of a snake. There is a belief that the snake is the spirit of the dead. It is the deity of the water which it rules, and often floods are believed to be caused by it. In many stories, snakes are the guardians of treasures to protect them from robbery or destruction. Some snakes are the forerunners of the deities on their journeys. Again in many tales, they are the masters of ponds and rivers, and the protector of fish.

Fishermen of the seaside villages of Izumo province worship sea serpents caught on the beach as the messenger of the sea god. The people of the Takada district in Niigata used to judge the weather by snakes they caught in the mountain on the 'mi' or snake day of April.

Snakes also take the form of men or women and often marry humans in many popular folktales. The snake-women's love for their children in their marriage with human-husbands, even at their own sacrifice, is told in many stories.

Whatever virtue or power might be attributed to these creatures, they are worshiped for their mysterious power.

Furthermore, it is customary in many regions to offer toy snakes made by twisting straws to local shrines on their festivals.

White snakes are regarded the most sacred kind. To find one, or even to have a glimpse of one has been regarded as a good-luck sign. The white snake is beautiful, as it is shining white with ruby-like eyes. They are found particularly in the mountains of the San-in district and Shikoku. Of couse they are occasionally seen in other parts.

The white snakes of the Iwakuni district, Yamaguchi Prefecture, are especially famous. Designated as a natural treasure, they are protected by law.

SQUINT EYES

SQUINT EYES were the sign of evil, many believed, as they were punishments for wrongs committed in this or a previous life. But squint eyes are also regarded as a mark that the person was especially loved by some deity. Some traditional deities have squint eyes. Hence, while some squints mean evil, others stand for good fortune.

There are many tales about men or women with squint eyes. Most of such tales say they were cursed for their own evil conduct.

Yazaemon, village chief and priest of Ogiroku in the mountains of Echigo province, went hunting one summer day and, entering a dense forest, lost his way. As he walked about, he came upon Makibata-yama, a sacred mountain where no humans were allowed because of the medicinal plants growing there.

As he walked along this strange sacred mountain, he saw a beautiful woman working at a weaving loom. She noticed him, and told him that he had come to a place which no human should enter, and that if he entered he would never be allowed to go back to his village. "But you are fortunate because I saw you," she said.

"As you have seen me, I will go with you to the village to be ever enshrined as the guardian deity of the villagers," she continued.

Then she ordered him to carry her on his back down the mountain to the village. "But you must not look back at me on the way," he was told.

So he carried her on his back and started toward the village. Becoming curious, he turned his head slightly to the right to look at her despite her command.

Instantly, his eyes became squinted. Since then, every male member of his family has had cross-eyes. The mysterious maiden saved his life, but punished him and all his male descendants for disobeying her and looking back at her face.

STONES TO MOUNTAIN TOPS

IN MANY rural regions, the traditional custom remains of taking sand and stones to the top of a mountain. On the other hand, if one takes sand or stones from a mountaintop, it is said that the mountain will become angry and punish the offender.

At the foot of Mt. Fuji there was formerly a spot called Sunaburui (sand shaking), where all climbers took off their *waraji* or straw sandals and shook the sand out.

It was also formerly believed that sand that came down from Mt. Fuji in the daytime, returned to the top at night.

All this came from the mountain's pride in its height, and the fear that sand and stones taken away by climbers might lower its top.

Kofuji (Little Fuji) of Owari is a

mountain of very good shape which is the pride of the local people. This mountain once matched in height Mt. Hongu, a neighboring mountain, but later it was found that Kofuji was slightly lower. Therefore, at the annual festival of the mountain held on June 1, the villagers went up to its top carrying stones and earth, in the hope that the mountain would become higher and defeat Mt. Hongu.

An attempt was once made to see if Mt. Hakusan was higher than Mt. Fuji. A bamboo pipe was laid from its top to that of Mt. Fuji, and water was poured into the pipe. The water flowed toward Mt. Hakusan. Thus all those watching the test on this mountain took off their *waraji* and piled them under the pipe until it became level. Thus all climbers to Mt. Hakusan used to leave their *waraji* at the top to make it higher.

In many districts, it is believed that, when one takes stones and earth to a mountain top, he will be blessed with good fortune. But if he takes stones from the top, he will be bitterly punished by the spirit of the mountain.

STONE WORSHIP

AMONG the most popular objects of worship by the Japanese people are stones. Legends about stone worship are numerous, and there still stand many shrines erected for stones, which are usually of natural shape. Stones are symbols of *kami* or divine beings.

Some of such worshiped stones have legendary tales, but most have no history or background and are merely worshiped as stones. Some of the stones were found on seashores or mountains where no stones were seen before, and the people who found them thought that some divine power had brought them. They thus regard them as symbols of *kami* and worship them.

The island of Iki, in the Korean Strait and many localities of Izu Peninsula have particularly numerous stone shrines. On the island of Iki are shrines for the gods of fire, mountains, water, rivers, sea and farms, but all of them have natural round stones as objects of worship.

There is also a belief that stones are alive and grow. A story goes that a Nagano woman picked up a beautiful pebble on the bank of the Tenryu River, and put it in her sleeve. As she continued on her journey, she felt her sleeve becoming heavier and heavier, and to her surprise the pebble had grown to a considerable size. Many districts have such tales of growing stones.

Another belief is that stones have the power of enabling childless women to bear babies. At many shrines small pebbles are kept and a woman desiring a child worships at such shrines and carries away one of the pebbles, keeping it in her *obi* or sash.

People in many districts have the custom of carrying pebbles and stones to shrines as offerings on festival days, as it is believed that stones are divine. Often huge rocks are carried up to high mountain tops by many worshipers to show their faith.

According to Prof. Shinobu Orikuchi, such stones are regarded as symbols of the *kami*. A stone is suddenly found at a spot where there was none, and the incident is strange. But the stone might have always existed under the soil, and when a rainstorm washed the soil over it, the stone was suddenly revealed to the human eye. Whatever the real cause of the appearance of the stone, the people regarded it as a symbol of the *kami*, as only superhuman *kami* could perform such a miracle of bringing out a stone overnight.

Little stones enshrined for popular

worship are found in many parts of the country. But they are particularly numerous on the island of Iki and also in many localities of the Izu Peninsula. In these cases, either a single stone or several stones are housed within the shrines. They seldom measure more than one foot in height, most of them being five to seven inches tall. The shapes of the stones are of course varied. Some are round, some are a shapeless mass, while others are narrow or oblong.

There are districts called Ishigami or stone-*kami* in various localities. This name also indicates that at such places, stones had been worshiped. At the seashore, strange-looking stones that were washed ashore have been worshiped as divine. There are many shrines erected for such stones brought from distant places.

While most of the worshiped stones are small, there are also cases where the stones are large, and are generally of various shapes, for instance, of swords, sticks or jewels.

There are also many tales of stones that grew bigger and heavier. A little pebble a traveler found on the road and picked up because of its beauty, grew heavy into which he placed it, and by the time he reached home it weighed many pounds. There are many similar stories still told all over the country.

There are stories of stones that gave birth to many little baby stones. The Ikeda Shrine of Tojo Village in Shinano (present Nagano Prefecture) possessed some divine stones, which were believed to have the ability of multiplying every year.

The divine stones were wrapped up in many layers of strong paper, and every year the wrappings were opened to ascertain the number of baby stones produced during the past year. The villagers used to tell the fortune of the village and individual families by the number of newborn stones.

There was a record made of baby stones annually found in the wrappings. In 1655 there were 60 baby stones, but in 1706, or 50 years later, there were 292.

On the mountain at the back of the shrine, there also stands an *oyaishi* (parent stone), measuring six feet across. It is believed to be the mother of the sacred baby stones.

STRAW HORSES

IN MANY rural districts, old-fashioned people still make little crude horses by twisting pieces of straw and offer them to shrines as a symbol of their prayers. Children also make such straw horses to play with.

Horses have been regarded in many localities as symbols of happiness, marriage or love, and many customs have developed from such beliefs.

In the district of Saihaku in Tottori Prefecture, young unmarried men and women rise early on the morning of December 15 and go to the Hoshoji Temple at about 2 or 3 a.m., carrying their straw horses. Reaching there, they throw up their horses into the branches of the sacred tree in the temple's compounds.

As it is believed that the higher one's straw horse is tossed up among the tree branches, the better luck he or she will have in love and marriage, all make their utmost efforts in throwing their horses, creating quite an excited atmosphere.

At Hanamaki, Iwate Prefecture, only girls use straw horses for luck in love. When a woman loves a man and is not certain whether her love is returned, she makes a little straw horse, and takes it at midnight to the Kannon Temple. But in doing so, she should not be seen by any person, nor should her horse offering be known to anyone.

When her prayer is answered, she goes to the temple and brings back her straw horse. After decorating it with strips of variously colored cloth, she again takes it to the temple, without being seen by anyone, to show her thanks to Kannon.

In the Miharu district of Fukushima, which is famous for horses carved out of wood called *Miharu-goma* or Miharu horses, young wives who wish to have babies pray to these horses for the blessing of child-bearing.

TAKASAGO

AT WEDDING ceremonies and banquets an ornamental tray with an old man and his aged wife sweeping the ground with a rake and a broom in front of big pine trees is seen. This is a symbol of longevity and a happy married life. The use of these figures or paintings of such a couple on all happy occasions became particularly popular in the latter half of the Tokugawa period. Some regard it absolutely necessary at wedding ceremonies.

Province of the figures originated in the legend of Takasago. A poem in *Kokinshu*, compiled in 905, points out the beauty and grandeur of pines on the Takasago shore. This poem may have inspired Zeami, great *Noh* master of the 15th century, to compose a play called *Aioi*, meaning growing together.

In the play a Shinto priest, Tomanari of Higo (Kyushu), came to the shore of Takasago in Harima province (present Hyogo Prefecture), and there he saw an aged man and his old wife sweeping the sandy shore under the big pine trees.

He asked them why they were sweeping, and he learned that they were the spirits of the two pine trees which grew so closely together as to appear as a single tree. The red or female pine leaned close to the black or male pine, that rose high.

The *Noh* play made the Takasago pine trees famous. Up to 1931, the Aioino-matsu, or pines that grow together, were in the compounds of the Takasago Shrine in Takasago-machi, Hyogo Prefecture. The ancient black and red pines stood with their branches entwined together. They were widely worshiped as a symbol of long life and wedded bliss. Unfortunately, however, the red pine died in 1931.

TATARI

TATARI ORIGINALLY meant the appearance or revelation of a divine spirit, but has come to mean a curse or punishment for disobeying or slighting a divine wish, of failing to observe taboos. Furthermore, it is commonly believed that a *tatari* punishment comes when one shows disrespect to shrines, temples, divine statues, sacred trees and other places or things which are to be honored or respected.

There are many old tales in which persons were cursed by *tatari* because they killed animals, snakes or fish. Burying treasures or swords have also brought punishment to persons who owned them or those who caused their burial.

Tatari differs according to the nature of the evil or disrespectful acts. They come as sickness or slight injuries, but many are made blind, dumb, crippled or insane as punishment. The curse often continues for many generations and families come to loss and ruin.

It is the divine spirit which usually brings a *tatari* upon evildoers. But some *tatari* are brought about by the spirit of human beings. It is believed the spirit of a wronged person brings punishment on the evil person. A curse by a human spirit is the same as divine punishment.

Many unexpected deaths, sicknesses or a sudden decline in fortune are attributed to *tatari* for some evil conduct committed by one's ancestors.

The idea of *tatari* has been reinforced by the Buddhist principle of *inga*, or cause and effect. Buddhism teaches that any evil thought or act in this life will bring a bad future life and that a person enjoying a happy and comfortable life today has done some good in a past life.

TATARI-ISHI

WHILE STONES are worshiped and enshrined in many places, there are also stones which are believed to bring ill-luck, illness or death to the people. Such stones are called *tatari-ishi* or cursing stones.

In the midst of a farm at Minami-otari-mura, Shinano province, there stood two stones about three feet apart. It had long been believed that if anyone touched the stones, there would be a disastrous fire. Thus, for ages, the people of the neighborhood did not even dare touch the stones with their hands. About 100 years ago, however, a stranger came and, finding the stones great obstacles in cultivating the farm, dug one out and threw it away. Instantly his house was completely consumed by a mysterious fire. Since then the fear of such stones was revived in the minds of the people who were afraid even to approach the remaining stone.

In a stream of Shirakawa-yama mountain, Yamashiro province, there stands a huge stone which looks like a sleeping cow. Once a man attempted to break the stone with a chisel, but instantly vomited blood and died.

Also in a mountain stream near the Seta bridge, Omi, there stands a stone in the middle of the stream. In the Tokugawa days, once when the surrounding district had a great drought and farmers suffered from a lack of water, they attempted to remove the stone in order to increase the volume of flowing water. More than 50 workmen were brought together, and they started to break up the stone. Instantly there came a serious earthquake and thunder. Also the water level rapidly rose, and the workmen as well as their boats were immediately carried away and destroyed. The number of workmen killed is reported to have been more than 30. Even today, when the river water rises, the people of the neighborhood believe that someone has insulted the stone and incurred its anger.

On the bank of the Kamisue River, Yamato, there stands a stone named *Hanaji-ishi* or nose-bleeding stone. It is believed that, if persons who do not know it is the *Hanaji-ishi* throw pebbles at it, their noses will instantly bleed. But when people who know all about the stone throw anything at it, it never causes such a curse. It seems that the stone is proud of its reputation, and while the people recognize its power, it does no evil. To others who do not appreciate its power, it brings punishment.

TAXLESS PARADISE

A TAXLESS paradise has been the dream of many peoples, past and present. There are legends of such paradises long believed in by the inhabitants of many southeastern islands south of Okinawa.

Particularly the people of Hateruma Island, about 20 miles southwest of Ishigaki Island and quite near Formosa, believed that there was such a paradise island, beyond the waves to the south, and thus called it *Minami Hateruma* or

South Hateruma.

In the old days, when farmers of Hateruma suffered under heavy taxes, there was a farmer named Yaku Akamari in the village of Yaku. He thought of saving himself, his family and neighbors from the hard life made unbearable by high levies and went out to find a better place to live. In his boat he went all over the sea in search of a suitable island.

Finally he found the island he had been looking for, and returned to his village with bright hopes for the future. Gathering his family, relatives and friends one moonless night, he decided to leave Hateruma Island for the promised paradise.

Just as the boat was to leave, one woman remembered that she had forgotten to bring a cooking pan from her house, and asked to be allowed to go back for it. But before she returned with her pan, dawn began to break and all were afraid that they might be seen by others. So without waiting for her return, they pushed the boat into the sea.

There still remains a spot on the island shore named *Nabe-kari* (pan scraping) to mark the place where the woman scraped the sands with her pan in despair when she found that the boat had left without her.

It is not known how those persons fared in the taxless paradise, but among various small islands in the Okinawa group and southern islands similar stories are told of brave men finding new islands of wealth and happiness. Such tales may be due to the hard life the inhabitants of such small islands had to lead.

TEKONA OF MAMA

MAMA-NO-TEKONA is a maiden who is said to have lived more than 15 cen-turies ago, but her memory is still vivid among the people of Chiba Prefecture, who worship even today at the Tekona Shrine, located not far from Konodai.

Tradition makes Tekona to be a sweet and beautiful maiden of 18 years. Every young man of the neighborhood fell in love with her. It is said that any young man who saw her once could not help thinking her the most exquisite of girls and falling in love with her, though she was always dressed in plain clothes.

As so many men declared love to her and wanted to marry her, she was much troubled. Finally she said, "Alas. This life is not long. Why should I live and cause misery to so many persons." So saying, Tekona jumped into the sea and gave her life to the waves, so that she might go to heaven a holy virgin and peace might come to all young men of the neighborhood.

Thus after her death, she was deified, and a shrine was erected by her grave. Not only did the people come there to pray for her, but also many poets sang of her life and sacrifice in words of high esteem. Yamabeno Akahito, a *Manyoshu* poet, yearned after her in the following words:

"Oh, maid of Tekona, in thy days of great age, men put on their best belts, built their cottages and came for thy hand. Thy eternal resting place is here, they say; but nought I see save the bowering yew trees and a great pine striking out its branches. But thy name, thy story shall never go out man's memory."

The poet sang true, as she is still remembered after 15 centuries, and her tomb and shrine are visited by men and women. It is still believed that women visiting the shrine will enjoy a happy married life and their children will be free from smallpox.

TENGU

THE *TENGU* is the most widely feared of traditional superhuman monsters. It is known to abduct young women, kidnap little children and do other mischief but at the same time, much power in punishing the bad and helping the good is attributed to it.

In common traditional belief, literature and pictures, the *tengu* is generally classified into two types, dai-*tengu* (big *tengu*), and *sho-tengu* (small *tengu*). The *tengu* is a semi-human, semi-bird monster. It has big wings and is able to fly freely at a terrific speed. It has long and sharp claws on its hands and feet. The face of the big *tengu* is red and has a very prominent nose. It is dressed in a costume similar to that worn by *yamabushi* or mountain priests, carrying a *kongo* stick and a sword. Usually it also holds a big fan made of feathers. The small *tengu* has a pointed bill like a bird, but its nose is not so high as that of the big *tengu*.

All *tengu* live in high wooded mountains, far from villages. Occasionally they descend to the plains and inflict harm upon innocent villagers. The people have so long been in fear of *tengu* that many parents still mention its name to make children behave. In many mountain regions, children still fear *tengu*, and believe that it will attack and carry them away, if they go out alone or do something bad.

The origin of the traditional *tengu* is very vague. It is now generally believed that it is a creation from three different things, the features of which are combined to make *tengu*.

The first of these three elements is the spirit of the mountain, which rules the mountain and of which the people were in great fear in the past, as they believed that lightning, thunder, storms and many things that happen in great mountains were the doings of the spirit of the mountain. The spirit of the mountain forms the basic characteristics of *tengu*, also giving it its bird-like features.

The second are *yamabushi* or Buddhist priests who underwent austere training in the mountains. They lived in great mountains far from human influence to train their minds and bodies. Some of them are reputed to have not only gained high Buddhistic knowledge, but also superhuman power.

Foreigners, probably Caucasians, are the third element that formed *tengu*. In the ancient *Konjaku-Monogatari* it is written that *tengu* came from *Tenjiku* (India) and went to the Omi lake (Lake Biwako). The red-faced, tall Caucasian, with his high nose, must have greatly surprised the people, if he did come to the country at that time. They feared the stranger, and seeing him so different from themselves, regarded him as superhuman. This stranger gave *tengu* the red face and high nose.

It is also said to be originally a satiric figure representing a proud and boastful person, and is still commonly used in that sense. In the picture scroll named *Tengu-zoshi* first printed in the Enbun era (1356-1361), many high leaders and priests who were known for their proud attitude are satirically represented as *tengu* with a long nose.

Yasha (Yaksha) mentioned in Buddhist sutras as a she-demon of supernatural power also came to be called *tengu*. Thus the original meaning of being boastful and the Buddhist Yasha came to be mixed to produce the popular idea of *tengu*.

Strangely it was the upper class of people who adopted Buddhism who first believed in the story of *tengu*.

In *Azuma-kagami*, it is mentioned that during the Kamakura period

(1185-1333), a *tengu* appeared in Kyoto and caused a big commotion among the residents. As the people became afraid of this creature, some priests utilized it for their interests. They staged a show with a *tengu* figure, and called it *Tengumatsuri* or demon festival. They showed tricks before the gathered people, and made them offer coins to *tengu*.

As the idea of the *tengu* spread, powerful mountain men with exceptional physical strength came to be regarded as such. They would come down to villages and their demands for *sake* were eagerly met by those in dread of their power.

TOJI

TOJI (winter solstice) comes usually on December 22, and old traditions of the day are still kept up by the Japanese. *Toji* marks the day when the ecliptic longitude reaches 270 degrees, or the sun reaches the farthest point from the northern hemisphere.

It is therefore a joyous occasion, as from this day the sun comes nearer again. Particularly in ancient days, a great celebration was held by the Imperial Court. The earliest mention of the day's Court celebration is that held by Emperor Shomu in 725. It may thus be gathered from this that the movements of the sun were known to Japanese scientists since quite remote times.

The day brings joy to farmers in particular, as the sun becomes again warmer and makes plants grow. Throughout the country *Toji* is celebrated as a joyous day.

Thus *Toji* is often called *Ichiyoraifuku* or return of spring and happiness.

It was formerly believed in many rural districts that on this day a holy traveler would visit every village to bring blessings to all, just as Santa Claus does to Western children. In the Aichi-Gifu district it has been believed that Kobodaishi (774-835), a famous Buddhist priest, visits every village on *Toji*.

It is said in many parts of the country that *Toji-no-kami* or *Toji* deity does not like dogs, and so it goes away when the day of the dog comes. *Toji-no-kami*, furthermore, is a big eater, so when his stay until the dog day is long, he eats up all the food in the village and villagers face a shortage of food.

Toji, however, is a joyful occasion as it promises the return of the warm spring, and many old-fashioned families still hold various rites on the day to ensure happiness and prosperity. Special meals are prepared and cold *sake* is drunk.

It has also been the custom of the people to eat pumpkins on *Toji* in the belief that *Toji* pumpkins will make them healthy. This seems to have developed from the custom of offering various farm products to the deity of *Toji*.

There are various traditional customs observed on the day. Commonly the people take *yuzu-yu* or citron baths. The *yuzu* is sliced and put in the bathtub. It is believed that it will ensure good health and protect people from catching colds.

Particularly in rural districts, it has been believed that no work should be done on the day and it is better to remain indoors. Offerings are made to the ancestors, and servants and workers are not only given a holiday, but also treated to good meals and drinks.

In some places, it is said that no marriage ceremony should take place within 10 days before or after *Toji*. This comes from the idea that the period of *Toji* should be spent quietly without any change.

Farmers also used to predict the

following year's crops by divination made on the day.

Kusushi-no-kami or the god of medicine also used to be worshiped by physicians and medicine shopkeepers on *Toji.* However, this worship has almost died out.

TSURU-KAME

TSURU (CRANE) and *kame* (turtle) are symbols of long life and happiness. They appear in Japanese literature, and are used in art and decorations as designs. It is commonly said that the *tsuru* lives 1,000 years and the *kame* 10,000 years, and thus they have become symbols of longevity. This traditional belief is said to have originally come from China.

Tsuru and *kame* not only stand for long life, but also for happiness and good luck, as it is believed that happiness comes with long life. Furthermore, the term '*tsuru-kame*' has also come to be used as a charm to prevent or suppress any threatening or imaginary bad luck. When one speaks of ill fortune falling on another, he will hurriedly say '*tsuru-kame,*' in the hope that no similar evil will come to him.

There is a *Noh* play called '*Tsuru-kame,*' which is regarded as the most felicitous piece to be given on all happy occasions. Thus it is always performed during the New Year season. In the play the emperor makes the crane and turtle dance happily.

It is not known how the ancient Chinese came to select turtles as the symbol of long life, but the fact that many thousands of years ago they found turtles the longest-living creatures on Earth is surprising as today scientists have found turtles which are 300 to 500 years old. The *kame* does not live 10,000 years, as the common saying goes, but lives longer than anything

else.

Yet turtles are not the longest-living things, as there are trees which are said to be more than 15,000 years old. Among animals, birds and fish however, turtles live the longest.

Compared with turtles, cranes have a short life, living for only about 100 years. Furthermore, there are other birds that outlive the *tsuru.* Yet since the old days, it has been regarded as the noblest bird that brings good luck. Its meat was highly valued in the old days.

The tradition that makes *tsuru* and *kame* the symbols of longevity and happiness is not altogether unfounded.

TURNED TO STONE

HIGH MOUNTAINS were formerly regarded sacred by the Japanese. So women, who were thought to be unclean, were not permitted to climb such holy mountains. Even today there are mountains still taboo to women.

But even in the old days there were brave women who attempted to make the prohibited climb. Such women were mostly Buddhist nuns or Shinto *miko* (handmaiden). But their attempts always failed.

On many high sacred mountains of the country there are stones which are believed to be these women climbers, petrified as punishment for defiling the holy regions.

Many of the mountains have Buddhist temples at the top and thus their holiness is connected with the Buddhist faith.

Kinpoku Mountain of Sado was sacred to Shinkoji Temple, and women were banned from it. But once a *miko* tried to climb it despite the rule, declaring that being a Shinto shrine servant, she was not unclean. But as she went up, a storm arose with thunder and lightning and she was lost.

Some men climbing up the mountain later found a big stone which was not seen before, its top twisted in the shape of a woman's hairdo. They believed that the *miko* had been turned into that stone and named it *Miko-iwa* or *Miko* stone.

Of Horohazan Mountain in Ugo, it is related that once a woman named Moriko went up the mountain to visit the Gongen Temple on its top, but on her way she was punished and turned to stone. There is a stone named the Moriko stone.

Thus on many high mountains there are stones called *Miko-ishi* or *Uba-ishi*, marking the spot where these adventurous women were petrified.

UDONGE

IT IS SAID in Japan that when *udonge* flowers blossom, it is a sign that some exceptional good luck will come.

Udonge appears on the leaves of plants, and also on ceilings, pillars and other woodwork of Japanese houses. Several slender thread-like stalks, about half an inch long, come out with a little white ball on each top. Such are *udonge* flowers, and as they are pretty, they were at first called *gin-no-hana* or silver blossoms. As it is believed that they bring good luck, their appearance in any part of the house is still highly welcomed by the people.

It so happens, however, that although they look like pretty little flowers, they are not blossoms. They are in actuality eggs of *kusa-kagero*, an insect resembling a tiny dragonfly. Nevertheless the people have long regarded them as signs of good luck. Even today many persons do not realize they are insect eggs.

It is not known how the insect eggs came to be called *udonge*, which orig-

inally derived from udumbara, a traditional plant of Himalaya, India. It is said that the udumbara blossoms only once in 3,000 years to mark the time when Buddha appears in this world. udumbara is a happy sign, if it blossoms.

The Japanese have never seen udumbara, and somehow they must have thought that the slender eggs which looked like blossoms that sometimes appeared in unexpected places in the house might be the traditional rare flowers of India. Hence they gave the insect eggs the name of *udonge*.

VOICE OF THE DEAD

A LITTLE BOY of a neighboring farmer died. After funeral rites were solemnly observed in the traditional Buddhist manner, and his remains were buried by the side of his forefathers in the family burial grounds, his mother went to visit an *ichiko* or medium, living in a village nearby, in order to have *kuchiyose* or spiritual communications with her lost child.

"Think of it, he is just as impertinent as he was before he died," the mother said when she came to report the result of her visit to the *ichiko*. "Of course, I know he was speaking because the voice was just like his, but he said that he would not have died if I had taken better care of him. Then, in the end he told me to take good care of grandmother, as though I am not taking good care of her." The mother, however, did not seem to be particularly concerned about the accusation made by the dead child that he had died because she did not take good care of him. The boy had become ill, but the mother did not pay any attention to his complaint. It was only when the boy's condition became serious that she called in a doctor. But then it was too late.

However, with great eagerness, she

narrated how eagerly the *ichiko* prayed, and in a trance he spoke for her boy. This woman visits the medium whenever any death occurs in her family or among relatives. It is her joy to listen to the voices that come from the mouth of the *ichiko*. By the voices she learns what the dead persons desire, and what they know of complicated family affairs. Upon the information given by the voices of the dead, she relies to form her opinions and decide her actions. She may not believe the words of living persons, but she has absolute confidence in the words spoken by the dead through the mouth of the medium.

She is not at all exceptional, but rather,one of the innumerable old-fashioned rural folks who still have a strong belief in the traditions of the spirit of the dead entering the body of the *ichiko* and speaking through his mouth. *Kuchiyose* is found important in settling many family affairs and disputes.

Ichiko is quite an ancient institution in the country, and mention is made of it in the *Makura-no-Soshi, Eiga Monogatari* and other ancient records. In olden days, *ichiko* carried skulls in their bosoms, and the skulls had the power to invite the spirit of the dead, it was believed. Also a bow was used to arouse the dead and make him or her speak out. *Ichiko* brought out a bow, and by pulling the string and suddenly releasing it to make a sharp noise, he called the spirit of the dead.

However, recently no such ancient processes are gone through. Generally, the *ichiko* gives fervent prayers, which are sometimes Buddhist in nature or of Shinto in substance. The words of the prayers are quite unintelligible, but he becomes so fervent in praying that his hands, head or even his whole body begin to shake violently as the prayer

progresses. Finally he falls into a trance, and then the spirit of the dead comes to him, and through his mouth the dead speaks. The medium says that he does not remember anything he has done or said during his trance.

Professional *ichiko* are generally men of quite advanced age, but often they are women, quite young in some cases. Throughout rural districts they do quite a prosperous business with their trance speaking.

WEATHER GODS

THE AINU people in Hokkaido believed that rain, snow, wind and temperature were controlled by their respective *kami*. So whenever there was too much rain, too heavy a snowfall or too strong a wind, they appealed to each *kami* to stop its fury.

When the rain continues, wetting kindling wood and raising the water level, an Ainu family makes a boy born on a fine day go outside naked with a bamboo basket. Then they loudly shout. "If you want to pour down rain, keep on pouring until the basket is full. But if you cannot fill the basket, stop pouring rain at once."

When it snows heavily, an old woman born on a fine day goes outdoors holding a large lighted torch and says, "If you want to snow, snow enough to extinguish this torch. If you cannot, stop snowing!"

When it blows very hard, the Ainus put a sickle on the roof top and shout, "If you rage so furiously, you will touch this sickle and cut your waist bone."

The Ainus believe that such threats will make the *kami* obey their wish and stop their furious actions.

But when the weather is dry and they want rain, they catch a river shellfish and, prying the shell open by inserting a stick, they place it by the river side. Then pouring a little water on the shell they say, "Does the water taste good? If you want to return to the water, bring down rain and call for river water."

When the sea remains calm, it is time for all fishermen to engage themselves busily fishing. Often, however, the work tires them and they wish to rest. At such times the fishermen catch a bullhead and bury it in the shore sands. "If you wish to return to the sea, call the sea to come up or else you will die," they threaten. A storm is sure to arise and the fishermen can then have a few days of rest.

But when this trick is discovered by their employer, the men are buried in the sand in place of the bullhead, it is said.

WEAVING GODDESS

ALL OVER the country there still stand shrines to Hataori Gozen or loom-weaving lady, the goddess of weaving. In the old days it was the duty and task of women to weave clothing for their entire families, and they worshiped the loom-weaving lady. The goddess and her shrines are given different names according to districts.

At Otohime-Jinja in Noto, it is said that Otohime first came to Noto to make clothing for all *kami* of the country. When her task was finished, she threw her weaving loom in the ocean. The loom grew into an island off Togino-ura and is now named Origu-jima (weaving loom island).

On April 21 every year the women of the district hold an annual festival for Otohime and bring millet glue to the shrine, as it was Otohime who taught the art of putting millet glue on the thread for weaving.

At Nasu, Tochigi, there is a shrine called Ayaori-Jinja (twill silk-weaving shrine) by Lake Ayaori. In the early days, the village head invited Ayaori Daimyojin (twill weaving goddess) to teach his daughter the art of weaving. Some 300 years ago, a big landslide occurred and filled the lake. But there is a tradition that the *nushi* or master of the lake transformed himself into a beautiful woman and went to the capital. There she married and wove beautiful cloth. When her husband looked into her room where he was napping, she was in the form of a big spider. Surprised, the spider ran away, but the husband went after her, and caught her at the lake.

The weaving goddess of Fukushima is called Kotohime Gongen. She traveled all over the country teaching how to weave until the age of 70. Finally she killed herself by jumping into Oshimizu Lake. The shrine for her stands near Iizaka Hotspring. There run two clear streams in front of the shrine. The village women present to the shrine the seams of the cloth they have woven in appreciation of her teaching.

YAKUDOSHI

EVERY JAPANESE, man or woman, has in his life certain ages which are critical or unlucky, and unless every precaution is taken, some unpleasant calamity, misfortune or even death will come in such years. Those critical years are called *yakudoshi*, and though since ancient days the unlucky ages for men and women have changed, it is generally thought now that 25, 42 and 60 are the *yakudoshi* for men, and 19 and 33 are those for women. These are the so-called Japanese ages; in the West they would be one year less.

Of all the *yakudoshi*, 42 is the most critical for men and 33 for women. People of these ages are advised to be careful of their health and conduct. In

454

particular, they should refrain from trying any new venture or going on a long journey. Some unexpected misfortune or death will come to them, if they are careless in those years.

While the above-mentioned ages are regarded as *hon-yaku* or really critical ages, the years immediately preceding and following them are called *mae-yaku* (previous *yaku*) and *ato-yaku* (later *yaku*). That is to say, even in the years before or after the *hon-yaku* there is some threat of calamity.

The idea of *yakudoshi* originally developed from the fact that those ages mark the times when men and women undergo particular mental and physical changes, and when many of them will experience notable changes in their social position. For instance, in the case of men, 25 would be the time when they reach manhood, and so the time is very important and critical. Then at 42, they would reach their height of development, and at 60 their decline begins. For women, 19 is the age when they attain womanhood, and at 33 they are at their full bloom.

In the old days, many persons refrained from starting a new business or building a new house or going on a journey in their *yakudoshi*. Of course they may travel or start various activities, if they wish, but it is safer to exercise caution. *Yakudoshi* warns the people that they are at a critical stage, and has saved many persons from experiencing unlucky failures.

YAKU-OTOSHI

THE JAPANESE have *yakudoshi* or ages of calamity. At such ages, they are destined to meet sickness, death, business failure, loss of property and other unwelcome happenings. *Yaku* or calamity comes to males at the ages of 25, 42 and 60, and to females at 19 and 33.

All are told to be very careful about their health and daily conduct when they approach their calamity ages, so that whatever might befall them will be lighter and easier to bear.

When one in any *yaku* age is laid down with sickness for two or three weeks and recovers, the whole family rejoices that his calamity year has ended with such a slight illness and holds a celebration of *yaku-otoshi* (calamity dropping). Losses of little amounts of money, insignificant injuries, and such minor ill fortunes are welcomed as *yaku-otoshi*, when they happen to men or women of *yaku* ages.

This belief of having calamities at fixed ages is not groundless. These ages are important stages in the life of both men and women, physically and mentally.

The belief is thus to warn them of their danger years so that they may be careful.

In the old days, *yaku*-age persons used to throw away some of their clothing or other articles in the distant fields or mountains in the belief that they might carry away their calamities.

YAMABIKO (ECHO)

IN THE MOUNTAINS echoes sometimes resound so distinctly as to surprise climbers. In the old days, the people thought that these echoes were uttered by *yama-otoko* or the mountain man who was believed to be a wild devil, in imitation of the human voice or other sounds. In some districts echoes were believed to be the voice of monsters used by *yama-no-kami* or mountain god.

A hunter had to spend a night on a snow-covered mountain, according to a story told in the Izumo district. To start a fire to warm himself he broke off a tree branch. It snapped off and then from a distant forest came the same snapping sound, only much louder. He cried out in surprise and his exclamation was repeated from the mountain across the valley. He could not stand it any longer and hurried down the mountain to the village.

In Awa, Shikoku, it was believed that *yama-otoko* imitated the human voice. When a woodcutter was warming himself in a mountain hut at night, a huge one-eyed monster entered and sat by the fire. The woodman became afraid, whereupon the monster said 'You are afraid.' When he thought of killing it, the monster seemed to read his thoughts, and said, 'You want to kill me.'

Then a branch of a tree the woodman was bending to feed the fire flipped back and hit the monster in the face. 'The human mind is hard to understand,' the monster said and fled the hut.

Thus it was believed that the mountain monster was able not only to imitate a human voice, but also to fathom a man's unuttered thoughts. When something happened which he could not foresee, such as the branch hitting him, it fled as it could not tell what the man would do next.

YAMA-NO-KAMI

THE *YAMA-NO-KAMI*, or guardian deity of the mountain, is still worshiped by hunters, lumbermen and charcoal makers, who are afraid of the deity's anger which comes as a sudden storm or furious wind.

Yama-no-kami is a female deity, although in some districts it is a male deity. It is probably from the fact that the deity is female and often shows her furious temper or anger that her housewives are often called *Yama-no-kami.*

Formerly, lumbermen used to offer *sake* to *Yama-no-kami* before starting to cut down mountain trees, to ask the deity not to become angry for cutting down her trees.

Not only is *Yama-no-kami* a female, but it was believed that she gave birth annually to 12 children. Thus, in many districts, the help of *Yama-no-kami* was asked when any woman was going to have a child.

It was also said that *Yama-no-kami* disliked the number 12. When lumbermen had to sleep in a mountain hut, it was believed that if they numbered 12, some calamity would occur.

Being also considered the deity of childbirth, women offered baby clothes at shrines erected to her. *Yama-no-kami* is reported to be fond of *okoze*, a tiny sea fish and the fish is also offered to her.

Yama-no-kami's messengers are wolves in most districts, but sometimes snakes and monkeys are regarded as her messengers. Worshipers of *Yama-no-kami* do not dare to harm these animals.

It is widely believed that *Yama-no-kami* comes down from the mountain to the fields in spring, and becomes *Ta-no-kami*, or deity of the rice-fields. *Ta-no-kami* returns to the mountain on October 10, after seeing to a good rice harvest.

Chapter 13
Recreation and Entertainment

ARCHERY

ARCHERY is still practiced by many Japanese, and there are professional master archers who maintain archery schools. The present type of Japanese archery is, however, not practiced for hunting game, but is studied as training for physical and mental discipline.

Bows and arrows were first used for hunting, and later became weapons of war in all countries. However, in the 17th century or the beginning of the Tokugawa period, they lost their value as arms in Japan with the introduction of firearms. Warriors practiced archery, but it gradually became a ceremonial affair.

When *samurai* disappeared with the Meiji Restoration, archery was entirely forgotten. It was in the middle of Meiji just before the beginning of the 20th century that *kyudo* or archery suddenly became popular again.

Those engaged in the daily practice of archery are those who aim at maintaining health, and particularly developing the power of concentration. Of course, the art of archery is to hit a target with an arrow. But to hit the mark, they are taught to stand erect with proper posture, and handle the bow and arrows so as to concentrate their mind, forgetting all other matters. The arrow is released when the man, the bow and the arrow become one, and it hits the bull's eye.

The so-called master archers are skillful, but will have no success if they try to hit a rabbit or a bird. They study archery only for mental and physical training.

Yumi or Japanese bows were first made of the wood of *azusa* (catalpa), *haze* (wax tree) or other tough trees. Later, strips of bamboo came to be placed on the two sides of such wooden bows. It is often wrapped with threads, vines and tree bark. *Yumi* used by nobles and great *samurai* were beautifully lacquered and decorated with designs painted in gold, and are still treasured as art objects.

AYATSURI

AYATSURI (marionette) plays now shown in Japan are mostly of the European type which were introduced about 60 years ago. But *ayatsuri* shows first appeared in the country in the Kanbun era, 1661-1673, in Kyoto and Osaka, probably imitating the Chinese type of marionette.

Ayatsuri is quite different from Bunraku puppet shows which appeared about a century later, and in which dolls are manipulated by hand. *Ayatsuri* dolls are controlled by strings, and as they are small, the show was commonly called *Nankin ayatsuri*, meaning small doll plays.

In the Genroku period, 1688-1704, as the shows became popular, *ayatsuri* theaters appeared in Kyoto, Edo and other cities. Good plays were written for *ayatsuri*, and many expert manipulators developed.

Some of the *ayatsuri* plays were grotesque. In one play, a warrior was killed by his enemy and cut into small pieces. Crows carried away the pieces. But the dead man's brother arriving there, prayed for the return of the warrior. Suddenly pieces of the dead man fell on the ground and joined to form a whole body, and then he revived. The hunting of tigers and other wild beasts was also a popular theme for *ayatsuri*.

Because of its popularity, toy *ayatsuri* dolls were sold for children.

Ayatsuri was popular until the middle of the Meiji era. With the introduction of the Western marionette technique, a new school, mostly giving comic plays, was started by Matsune Suekichi, who held his shows at Hanayashiki in Asakusa and other places. It was at the beginning of the Taisho era, about 1912, that *ayatsuri* shows about Momotaro and other folk tales became popular among children.

Thus, while the original Japanese *ayatsuri* has declined, the Western-type marionette is now popular.

AYU FISHING

THE *AYU* FISHING season usually opens on June 1. *Ayu* is a kind of trout peculiar to Japan, and is regarded as the best-tasting fish in the country. It is also called the 'fragrant fish,' because it has a particularly fragrant taste.

Ayu eggs hatch in clear streams in autumn, and the little fish go down the river to the sea. In the sea the fish grow on animal plankton. In March it approaches the shore, and in May swims up the river. As it enters the river, its diet changes to diatom or rock mosses, and the shape of its teeth also changes in order to eat the moss.

Ayu prefer clear running streams and those living in the streams where diatom is abundantly found taste the best. The female *ayu* lay eggs on rocks in September and then go down the river. Most of them die soon after laying the eggs, and so the fish is often called *nengyo* or year-fish.

Not only does *ayu* taste good, but it is also valued because it is a lucky fish. There is a tradition as old as the nation about the fish. When Jinmu, the first Emperor of the country, was still engaged in the task of pacifying the country, there was a strong tribe named Ukashi in Yamato. Desiring to know whether he would be able to defeat the powerful Ukashi, the Emperor resorted to divination. He filled an earthenware jar with wine and put it into the river, saying that if he was to pacify the country, let the fish of the river become drunk and float to the surface. As he watched, an innumerable number of *ayu*, large and small, floated up to the surface, drunk. Soon he had all the country under his rule.

This tradition has made *ayu* a lucky fish. The Banner of Banzai which is still used at the enthronement ceremony of the Emperor, has a design of a wine jar and floating *ayu*. The commemorative postal stamp issued to honor the celebration of the 2,600th anniversary of the founding of the nation held in 1940 had as its design this Banner of Banzai.

BON-ODORI

IN URBAN districts, *bon-odori* is becoming a kind of summer recreation but in rural regions it is still held according to old customs and traditions.

It is connected with the Buddhist *Bon* festival of July 15 but originally it was a purely Japanese custom. With the introduction of Buddhism, it became a part of religious rites.

The old meaning of *bon-odori* is still retained in Miyagi, Tochigi, Ibaraki and other districts where it is called *honen-odori* or good-harvest dance, performed as a prayer for a good harvest.

Commonly *bon-odori* is held during the two weeks in the middle of July, but in some places it is danced early in July or even in August and September. Although generally it is held in the evening and often continues throughout the night, some districts hold it in the daytime.

The tendency of men and women, young and old, to dance together is spreading but in some places only men participate, or dancers are limited to women. At Hachinohe, Aomori, it is believed that young girls dancing will please the spirit of the dead. Only unmarried women dance in many villages.

Roughly speaking, there are two types of *bon-odori.* One is to dance in a circle, and the other is to dance in a long line like a procession. In many rural districts, the dancers visit the houses where someone has died in the past year and dance in the gardens of such families. Sometimes they visit temples and shrines and hold their dancing there.

Bon-odori is danced both outdoors and indoors, but the outdoor type is more generally seen.

Each village or district has its own style of dance, music and traditional customs. In the case of outdoor dancing, a raised platform is erected in the center on which the dance leader and musicians stand. The leader may be a man or woman, but enjoys the respect or even admiration of all.

In districts where old customs are strictly followed the dance program is not only definitely fixed, but also very solemnly carried out. The dance and music have not changed for generations in such cases.

CHA-NO-YU

CHA-NO-YU is generally called the tea ceremony, but that name is misleading as it is not a ceremony. In his 'Book of Tea,' Kakuzo Okakura uses 'Teaism' and 'the cult of tea.' Teaism may represent the original significance of *cha-no-yu* that was related to the Zen sect of Buddhism. However, *cha-no-yu* as it has been generally practiced by the people has no particular philosophical meaning.

The habit of drinking tea came from China, and then in the 16th century, Rikyu started *cha-no-yu* in the form as it is still followed in principle.

In the days of Rikyu the country was in a turbulent condition, and fighting men and local leaders had a very difficult time. *Cha-no-yu* was eagerly adopted by such persons for relieving their mind of all worries, and giving them complete rest and tranquil thoughts.

The guests invited to *cha-no-yu* walk from the main house of the host to the tea room through *roji* or a garden path. This short walk is the dividing line, and as they step on the cleaned path, they leave every worry, and attain tranquillity.

In the tea room everybody is equal, as no official ranks or social positions are recognized there. Sitting within the room of 10 feet square, as that is the orthodox size, all become just fellow humans brought together in close contact. The host, who might be a rich and powerful leader outside the room, becomes humble, and waits on the guests who might be younger and much lower in social or business rank. Equality and peace prevail at *cha-no-yu.*

No talk on business or political affairs is permitted in the tea room. Hence they speak of the beauty of nature, arts, tea utensils and other common human topics. But etiquette and propriety are strictly observed.

The host takes pain in selecting his guests so that the gathering will be congenial and pleasant.

There are extremely complicated rules in preparing and serving the tea. But those rules were made after long study and experience to minimize the work and to do it efficiently. The bowl is placed at a spot in anticipation of the next movement. It is wiped in the minimum and most effective way. But as every little movement is calculated and has a special meaning, it becomes not so difficult when one grasps its significance.

But the most important in *cha-no-yu* is not the preparation of the tea and its drinking. The congenial atmosphere of harmony, and restful talks with intimate friends is what *cha-no-yu* aims at.

CHIKARA-MOCHI

WEIGHT-LIFTING is now a sport, but in the old days, it was performed as a show to amuse the people. It is recorded that in 1672, a show was opened at Edo to exhibit a 4-year-old boy lifting a big stone mortar. There were many similar shows by boys.

What made this show of *chikara-mochi* (strong person) become particularly popular was the appearance of an *onna-chikara-mochi* (strong woman) at a show opened at Kokokuji Temple, Edo, in 1764. Following this, many strong women appeared to surprise the public with their extraordinary strength. Yanagawa Tomoyo, a strong woman from Osaka, who appeared in Edo in May 1776, is reported to have lifted a big wooden cart on which were piled five big rice bales.

Some of these women were big, and Yokotaki who appeared in Asakusa in 1806 was advertised as being seven feet five inches tall. It is said she tied a writing brush to a big rice bale, and lifting the bale, she wrote some words on a piece of paper. In the Bunsei period, 1818-1830, *chikara-mochi* shows reached the height of their popularity.

One *chikara-mochi*, a strong Osaka man, held a show at Ryogoku, Edo. He lifted a big temple bell reputed to weigh 120 *kan* (about 450 kg). Kinzo, an amateur weight lifter, who visited the show, thought that the bell did not weigh so much. Rising, he shouted that the temple bell did not weigh 120 *kan.*

The show manager replied that if anybody doubted its weight, he should come forward and lift it and that if he managed to lift it, he could take it home. Kinzo went on stage, and easily lifting the bell, walked out with it. Outside, he said that if the bell weighed more than 90 *kan* (338 kg), he could never have carried it.

Chikara-mochi shows continued to be popular until the first years of Meiji. Since then they seemed to have been pushed aside by new attractions introduced from foreign countries.

CHINDON-YA

CHINDON-YA, who disappeared during the war, have come back to the great joy of children and many grownups. They are welcome because they add brightness to the life of the people.

First of all, *chindon-ya* is a one-man orchestra, as the name indicates. *Chin* stands for the ring of a bell, and *don* represents the sound of a drum. Then, usually he is very gaily dressed, almost womanlike, in all colors and frills. Of course, there are many women *chindon-ya* too. He plays his *shamisen*, drums, bells and many other musical instruments, some of which he manages to operate with his feet. He plays, and sometimes sings, too, to draw people. When he has a sufficient crowd around him at a street corner, he stops his music and makes his announcements. Some tell funny stories to amuse the gathered people.

The new bill at the town theater or cinema house is announced, or he tells the people of some special sales at certain stores. Again, he advises the people to try certain patent medicines or toilet preparations. When he finishes his announcements, he starts his music and walks off to another corner.

The *chindon-ya* is thus an advertising man, who is hired to go around and make announcements. *Chindon-ya* first appeared in the middle of the Meiji period, and at once became very popular. He is an improvement over the *tozai-ya* who worked in the Tokugawa period. *Tozai-ya* were not so gaily costumed as *chindon-ya*, nor played any music. To gather people he merely beat his *hyoshigi* or wooden clappers. He made announcements for theaters, shops and others. He came to be called *tozai-ya* (east and west man), because he always started his announcement with '*Tozai, tozai*,' an expression which meant 'I ask the attention of all people, from the east and the west.'

The custom of saying '*Tozai, tozai*' at the beginning of public statements is still observed at theaters and others. This is why the *chindon-ya* who succeeded the old *tozai-ya* still announces himself to the gathered public by saying '*Tozai*,' though modern children do not know what it means.

A head *chindon-ya* trains others, and takes orders from advertisers. It takes many years' training to make a good *chindon-ya*.

COCK FIGHT

COCK FIGHTS appear to have been held in Japan since very early days, but at first they were mostly held at shrines to amuse the deities, and also as a means of divination or fortune-telling. They were also held at the Imperial Court as a game or amusement.

It is recorded that by the 14th century, cock fights called *tori-awase* (bird fight) became very popular. In the Tokugawa period beginning in the early 17th century, they were held for gambling purposes and called *keai* (kicking game) or *tokei* (cock fight).

It is not clearly known what kinds of cocks were used in the early days, but as the game became popular, cocks were greatly improved, particularly by the introduction of a fighting species from Siam. Thus fighting cocks are now commonly called *shamo*. Siamese cocks have been further improved by cock breeders of the country.

The *shamo* today is a big bird, weighing about 10 lbs. and standing more than two feet high, with a short but strong neck and powerful legs. It has a short cockscomb and tail with little feathers on the head, neck and shoulders. The cockspurs are long and sharp.

Cock fighting is now prohibited by law, but there are still many breeders and fights are occasionally held, being particularly popular in Chiba and the Kawachi district of Osaka.

For cocks, the pedigree is very important, even more so than for racing horses. But the *shamo* breed lays only a few eggs, and also more hens are born than cocks. Thus good cocks are very rare.

The *shamo* also has a peculiar trait. When it loses in a fight, it becomes downhearted and depressed and cannot even attract a hen. Once he loses a fight, he becomes useless.

Thus it has become customary for fighting cock breeders or owners to eat the defeated cock immediately after a fight, inviting their friends. The meat is very good, many preferring it to ordinary chicken. The rearing and training of fighting cocks are done with utmost care by the breeders.

CORMORANT FISHING

UGAI OR cormorant fishing starts at Nagaragawa in Gifu on May 11. This unique method of catching *ayu* (a kind of trout) by using cormorants is very old and in ancient days it was a common practice in many districts. The *ugai* at Nagaragawa has been particularly famous as the Imperial Court and military rulers protected it. Today the old *ugai* is preserved only at Nagaragawa and a few other places.

At Nagaragawa, those who handle the birds are still dressed in old costumes and the ancient way is faithfully preserved.

The cormorants used for *ugai* are caught during the winter on the rocks of the sea coasts at Ibaraki or Owari. It takes about two weeks to train them. A ring is put on the bird's long neck to prevent it from swallowing the fish it catches. When a few have been caught, the cormorant is made to give them up.

Ugai is done only on a moonless night, or before the moon rises and after it sets. Torch fire is used to lure the fish. The *usho* or chief cormorant handler and his assistants take their birds on a small boat. At the proper spot, the kindling in an iron basket hanging from the bow of the boat is lighted.

The *usho* handles 12 birds at a time, maneuvering each with a rope, and his assistants take care of about five birds

each. The bird dives in and catches *ayu*, and when the neck is swollen with fish, it is hoisted into the boat to release the fish.

The cormorant is a big bird, almost two feet high and black in color. It has a very peculiar characteristic. Each group has a leader whom all others follow. Then after the leader, they have a definite order in which they jump into the river or come back to the boat. There is always loud squawking and flapping of wings whenever this order is violated.

Ugai has also been made into a *Noh* play, in which the ghost of an aged cormorant handler who died in the river at Isawa in Yamanashi, appears and the preaching of Priest Nichiren saves his soul. It has also been made into a *Kabuki* play.

DANCING CAT

IN EDO there was once a dancing cat which was featured in a show and gained public applause. It appeared on stage and danced to *shamisen* music, being able to do several different dances.

It was a showman named Tomizo who trained the cat. Tomizo's training method was unique. Over a charcoal fire, he placed a copper plate, and just above it he suspended his cat with ropes from the ceiling. He lowered the cat just enough to make its paws touch the hot plate. But care was taken not to make the plate so hot as to scorch his paws; just hot enough to make the cat uncomfortable.

As the cat's paws touched the hot plate, he would lift one paw, and as it put that paw down, lift the other. Sometimes it lifted both front paws and alternated them with his two hind paws.

At first Tomizo played his *shamisen* to follow the cat's movements. But with training the cat gradually learned to move its paws to follow the *shamisen* music.

Tomizo then made up several different tunes. The cat learned to dance differently to each tune. In the meantime, the cat got the habit of dancing whenever it heard *shamisen* music.

There was another show at Asakusa in which mice were used. An actress named O-Ito appeared on the stage dressed richly as an ancient lady. She was tied to a cherry tree and with her toe drew the outline of a mouse.

As she drew, several lively mice appeared and gnawed off the rope that bound her to the tree. Then the mice jumped on her body, crawled all over her head and snuggled into her bosom.

It is not known how she trained her mice.

DARUMA-SAN

THE *OKIAGARI-KOBOSHI* (tumbling doll) is one of the oldest and most common toys and also a charm for good luck. It is a doll made with a weighted and rounded bottom so that it will always come back to its upright position whether it be put down sideways or upside down. Because it comes up and never stays down, it is regarded as a charm for good luck.

The doll comes in different shapes, sizes and materials, and various districts have their special types. Mostly, however, it is made in a stubby papier-mâché or clay form, and this type is named *daruma* after the famous Chinese Buddhist priest Dharma of the sixth century. He is reputed to be the founder of the Zen sect of Buddhism. Tradition has it that he sat in meditation for many years on a piece of rock on an uninhabited mountain. This long torturous austerity caused him to lose his legs, and he remained legless the rest of

his life. So he came to be represented by a stubby statue, legless, in sitting posture, with a loose coat covering his head, shoulders, body and all, showing only his face.

The *daruma* form is just the thing for *okiagari-koboshi.* Thus the *daruma* doll is made an *okiagari-koboshi* by weighting its bottom and rounding the edges of its base.

The *daruma* is usually painted red all over, except the face. The face is round and has two big round eyes. Its shape and expression are grotesque. It is made in all sizes from those less than half an inch high to those of three or four feet tall. As it is regarded as a goodluck charm, many persons have large collections of them, picked up from various parts of the country and made in different sizes and shapes and of various materials.

In many parts of the country there is observed a custom of buying *daruma* dolls on New Year's Day for ensuring good fortune for the year. The *daruma* market held on New Year's Day at Haijima, near Hachioji, west of Tokyo, has been famous for hundreds of years, and the people of the neighborhood as well as from distant villages come to the market every New Year's Day and buy *daruma* dolls.

There are also *daruma* dolls that have no eyes painted. The people purchase the eyeless *daruma* doll for the express purpose of bringing good luck to them. When something particularly good happens, the purchaser paints one eye on the doll as a token of his appreciation of the *daruma-san's* kindness. When another lucky event happens, the doll is given its other eye. That is to say, if the *daruma-san* fails to bring good fortune to the purchaser, it has to remain eyeless.

Me (eye) in Japanese also means bud or sprout. *Me-gaderu* (to bud, or to have eyes) means to be lucky or prosperous. So the eyes of the *daruma* stand for good luck. To be eyeless is not good luck for the *daruma-san* or its purchaser.

DOG CHASE

FORMERLY there was a sport called *inu-oi* or dog chase, which was particularly enjoyed by *samurai* or military men. It became especially popular in the Kamakura period (1192-1333). Dog fights which were held in many parts of the country became extremely common among Kamakura warriors. It is said that Hojo Takatoki held dog fights 12 times every month, bringing the animals from all parts of the country.

The popularity of dog fights might have also brought about the sport of *inu-oi*. Dog chases, however, were quite different from dog fights, as they were contests to show the participants' ability in shooting at running dogs.

The first dog chase is recorded to have been held at Kamakura in 1222. A large enclosed area, surrounded by bamboo fences, was laid out and 20 dogs were set free. Then four warriors entered on horseback, armed with bows and arrows.

The aim was to shoot at the running dogs with arrows. But the arrows used were not ordinary ones with sharp arrowheads, but had pads at the ends of the shafts so that they would not hurt the dogs.

As it was a game of skill, no point was given for hitting the dog's body. Only hits made on the head or any of the four legs were counted.

It was quite an exciting game, not only for the participants, but also for the spectators. The *inu-oi* was generally held in a large horse-riding area, and thus the sport required not only good riding but also skillful archery.

Dog fights were kept up all through the Tokugawa days, but somehow the dog chase lost its popularity among the *samurai* class.

DOG FIGHTS

DOG FIGHTS are still held from time to time among lovers of this game, although it is prohibited by law. Up to the Pacific war, they were publicly held twice a year, spring and autumn, in Tosa, Shikoku, under prefectural license. Tosa is famous for its dog fights, which started there more than a century ago.

The native Tosa dog was a particularly good fighter. It was small in build, with ears standing up and tail curled up. Tradition has it that, in the first year of Kaei (1848), one Otaka Sakamusu of Tosa brought from Nagasaki a dog which was said to be the fiercest fighting dog of the port town. It was crossed with the native Tosa dog.

With the spread of this new species, the game of having two dogs fight rapidly became popular in the district. Although such fights were strictly prohibited even during the Tokugawa period, they were held secretly in mountain valleys or remote places. It goes without saying that the dog fight was, and still is, being used as a means of gambling.

In 1893, an organized movement was started by lovers of fighting dogs in Tosa to obtain a license for holding dog fights. They appealed to Taisuke Itagaki, the famous Meiji statesman and one of the organizers of the Jiyuto (Liberal Party). The movement succeeded and dog fights came to be held under the jurisdiction of Kochi Prefecture, the prefectural assembly passing a resolution for licensing such fights.

Tosa fighting dogs are still very highly valued, and good fighters command very high market prices.

DOLLS

AT FIRST DOLLS were not toys in Japan. It is only a little over 200 years since Japanese children had their first dolls to play with.

The early dolls were symbols of *kami* (gods) or human beings. *Ningyo* was a charm to protect one from sickness, disaster or evil spirits. Dolls in this sense still remain. In rural districts, at doors or the entrance to a village, crude dolls made of twisted straw, which are charms against insects that destroy crops, sickness or fire, are often seen. The huge dolls seen on gorgeous floats used at shrine festivals are also remnants of the ancient dolls.

Later, such dolls came to be made better and more artistically, and so they gradually developed into becoming symbolic ornaments. Yet they were still not things to play with.

The real development of Japanese dolls was not seen until about the middle of the 17th century. In the first part of the Tokugawa period, not only did the technique of doll-making advance rapidly, but there also appeared dolls made as toys for children.

For instance, *hadaka-ningyo* or naked dolls appeared. These were made of wood or clay, with movable or fixed heads, arms and legs. They were sold in their naked forms, and children made clothes for them. This led to the wonderful art of making doll costumes. Fabrics were specially woven to make dolls' dresses, and dolls' fans, purses, footwear, hair ornaments and such were beautifully made in minute sizes. The *hina-matsuri* dolls became elaborate in this period.

In the Tokugawa period, various different types of dolls of artistic value were developed. The most unique was *karakuri-ningyo* or mechanical dolls. Dolls that walked, played the flute or *shamisen*, performed acrobatic acts, served tea or danced, were made. Their movements were controlled by springs or the force of gravity, through the use of materials of different weights.

EBI-JORO

EBI-JORO (lobster lady) or a doll made from a lobster's eye may now be remembered by old folks only, as it is no longer seen. But since the early Tokugawa period, 17th century, this doll had been fondly made and loved by women and children up to the first part of Meiji. Whenever large lobsters were found, they made *ebi-joro.*

Ise-ebi or large Japanese lobsters have projecting eyes almost as large as the tip of the little finger. The eyes are shaped like *soramame* or broad beans, and have dark brown marks on the top, which look like parted hair. To make the doll, the eye is pulled out and put on a small stick, and then a dress made by folding paper or cloth is wrapped around the stick.

The doll was particularly popular among people living in sea-coast districts where lobsters are caught in abundance. But the habit of making *ebi-joro* spread even to women and children of cities.

The *ebi* is regarded as a symbol of old age, the Japanese characters for *ebi* meaning 'the aged of the sea.' Thus *ebi* has been used on various happy occasions, not only on the table but also as ornaments. Lobsters used in New Year decorations were formerly preserved often as a charm for curing sickness and preventing evil fortune.

Sukuna-hikona-no-kami enshrined in Awashima shrines as the guardian deity of women is said to have been so small in stature as to slip through a person's fingers. Thus there was a custom of presenting the deity with small dolls made of folding paper. In the Wakayama district women used to present *ebi-joro* to the deity on the festival day of Awashima Shrine, as the district is famous for lobsters.

FLOWERS-IN-WATER

SUICHU-KA or flowers-in-water have recently attracted the attention of foreign visitors. They are quite old in origin, but are still a favorite with children. Tiny pressed pieces open up into beautiful blossoms when placed in water.

These flowers are made of the pith of *yamabuki* (yellow rose) or *tara* (Aralia elate). After shapes of flowers are cut out of the pith, they are properly dyed, and then pressed into small pieces. Many flowers have leaves and stems.

Originally these flowers were made for grown-ups and were called *shuchu-ka* or flowers-in-*sake*. It started in the middle of the 17th century as an amusing trick to be performed at drinking parties. Into the cups of *sake*, they put flowers-in-*sake*, and watched them turn into blossoms. They drank from the cups in which the tiny blossoms were floating.

Flowers-in-*sake* became so popular that they even became subjects on which *hokku* or short poems were composed.

While at first they were used by upper-class men at their parties, in the Genroku period (1680-1704), *shuchu-ka* became so much in demand even among the common people that many little shops dealing exclusively in them were opened. All tried to make prettier and smaller blossoms.

Toward the end of the Tokugawa period, flowers-in-*sake* lost their hold on drinkers, but they came to be loved by children and known as *suichu-ka.*

FUKUSUKE

FUKUSUKE (man of good fortune) is a doll representing a stubby man with an enormously big head, dressed in a formal feudal costume, and sitting down with a fan in his hand. *Fukusuke* dolls and pictures are placed in many households to bring prosperity and happiness.

Fukusuke are said to have originated in Kyoto almost 200 years ago, but they became immediately popular all over the country.

In the latter half of the 18th century, there lived in Kyoto a very rich merchant named Daimonjiya. He was highly respected and popular in the city, as he was not only a big and rich merchant, but also was very charitable and always willing to give rice and money to the suffering poor. Many who were assisted by his generous help worshiped him.

Daimonjiya was very short in stature, had a very big head, and walked in a funny rolling way. But he always had a smile on his face, and was pleasant to all people.

Many Kyoto people desired to become as rich and generous as he was. Those who respected him highly or had received his aid made little dolls representing him, and placed them in their homes, in thanks for his benevolence or in prayer that they would also some day become rich and able to help others.

Those dolls of Daimonjiya became popular not only in Kyoto, but also in other regions, and finally came to be used as a charm to bring good luck and make one generous in helping others in need.

GAGAKU

GAGAKU, which is generally called Court music, is unique in the world of music. It is unique because it has been preserved under the patronage and protection of the Imperial Court, unchanged for 13 centuries, and is therefore the oldest music in the world. A far more important fact is that in *Gagaku* is preserved not only the ancient music of Japan, but also that of China, Korea, Siberia, India and Central Asia. Thus it may be said that *Gagaku* represents the ancient music of the entire Asiatic continent, and even some traits of earlier European music.

Gagaku owes its origin to Prince Shotoku who encouraged the introduction of foreign music to Japan in the seventh century, and brought over many Chinese and Korean musicians. *Gagaku* music pieces are of many foreign origins. For instance 'Ryo-o,' 'Taiheiraku' and 'Etenraku' came from China; 'Nasori' and 'Hohin' from Korea; 'Garyobin' from India; 'Bairo' from Annam; 'Genjoraku' from Tibet; 'Konju' from Central Asia; and 'Shinmaka' from Siberia.

Then there are purely Japanese pieces composed by great Japanese musicians for *Gagaku* on traditional motifs. 'Kumemai' and 'Azuma-asobi' are representative of purely Japanese *Gagaku* pieces.

Musical instruments used today in *Gagaku* are just as old as the music. As wind instruments there are three kinds of *fue* or flute, *hichiriki* or nine-holed clarinet-like instrument, and *sho* which has 17 bamboo tubes placed upright in a circle. String instruments consist of *wagon* or Japanese lute with six strings, *koto* with 13 strings, and *biwa* with four strings. There are several kinds of drums, and the most important of them is *kakko* which is beaten with two sticks. The *kakko* which is beaten to keep time leads the other instruments.

Over the long period of 13 centuries, *Gagaku* has been reverently preserved to enrich the artistic sentiment and culture of the people. Until quite recently the general public was not given any opportunity to hear the music.

GAMES AND SPORTS

JAPANESE GAMES and sports have all originated with festivals. Since very early days, the people have held sports or games at festivals to amuse the *kami* and also to amuse themselves. They have been quite earnest in taking part in these festival games, as they firmly believed that the outcome of the contests was decided by the wish of the *kami* or gods.

Games that were performed at festivals included many kinds. Most common were wrestling matches, horse races, tug-of-war, archery contests, ball games and others. These games were eagerly looked forward to by all persons, as festivals were not only solemn services, but also occasions for recreation.

In ancient days, games also became a means of telling fortunes or making predictions for the future, as games ended in the way *kami* wished, they believed. It is recorded that at old festivals, 10 horses were raced, each horse being named for each month of the year, excepting January and February. The order in which the 10 horses finished the race foretold the weather for each month. In those early races, the horses had no riders, since it was *kami* who guided them.

Formerly in January, an archery contest used to be held. The arrow was meant to drive away all evils, and it was regarded the duty of each young man to take part in the archery contest at least once in his life. Young archers represented their respective districts, and the results predicted which districts would be more fortunate during the year than others.

All participants in these games played earnestly and with all their skill and strength, knowing that *kami* would guide them to victory. At the same time, they highly enjoyed these sports, whether they won or lost.

GEISHA AND GEIKO

THE *GEISHA* is a product of Edo civilization. In fact it was Yoshiwara that gave the *geisha* to Japan. The first mention of the word *geisha* was made in 1761. Before that time there was no class of women corresponding to *geisha*. During the Edo period the name *geisha* was not used outside Edo; in Kansai districts even today women known as *geisha* in Tokyo are called *geiko* there.

The origin of *geisha* tells the development of Yoshiwara. At first, the women of this famous quarter were highly accomplished, having been well trained as musicians, dancers and singers. Many wrote excellent poems. Thus they entertained visitors with their various talents. It was in 1751 that there appeared at Yoshiwara, *odori-ko* or dancers, who specialized in entertaining visitors with dances. They formed a distinct class by themselves and were different from ordinary Yoshiwara women, even in costume and manner of hair-dressing. Then *geiko* who were musicians and singers made their appearance in 1754. These two new types, the *odori-ko* and *geiko*, added to Yoshiwara entertainments.

Then, in 1761 another type who came to be known as *geisha* appeared to play popular songs and music, while *geiko* did more formal or orthodox music and dances. These three types of entertainers — *odori-ko*, *geiko* and *geisha* — had their clearly marked fields of entertainment. *Geisha*, however, became rapidly more popular than the other two, who soon disappeared. *Geisha* thus became the sole entertainers at Yoshiwara. In 1804, there were 163 *geisha*, but in 1865 the number increased to 341. They maintained the distinction that they were different from the so-called Yoshiwara women, and on that account continued to occupy a special social position.

Geisha soon came to appear at various other places in Edo, but those at Fukagawa, Yanagibashi, Yoshicho, Kyobashi, Horiecho and others were called Edo *geisha*, because Yoshiwara was not included then in Edo proper.

GEISHA IN PARIS

THREE *GEISHA* OF Edo appeared in Paris in March 1867, embarking from Yokohama on a British ship and going around the Cape of Good Hope. The *geisha* who first went abroad were Osumi, Okane and Osa from Yanagibashi, Edo. They were sent by the Tokugawa Bakufu to offer entertainment at the Japanese exhibits at the Paris International Exposition.

In the fair grounds was erected a tiny Japanese house, with a six-mat room, a small unfloored room, and a garden. Several life-size dolls dressed in various kimonos were displayed. In the room, the *geisha* served tea and offered *sake* to visitors.

French visitors were particularly interested in their kimono, and the girls had a hard time protecting their clothes from being pulled and handled by both men and women.

These girls neither danced nor sang, but were the first *geisha* from Japan who appeared before foreign people.

When they returned home after the Paris Fair, they became very famous and the French cosmetics and other things they brought from France were the envy of all *geisha* and other women of the capital.

In 1900 or 33 years later, eight Tokyo *geisha* went to Paris on the occasion of another Paris Exposition. This time, the women were from Karasumori (Shinbashi). They were Wakataro (25), Sumiko (18), Sumiryu (18), Katsuta (19), Kisen (17), Tasuke (27), Chocho (16), and Ito (28). With maids and cooks, the party numbered 15 in all.

These women danced and sang at the fair, showing for the first time what accomplishments *geisha* possessed to the Western people. After the fair, some of the party went to Denmark, Russia, Hungary and Germany, where they had varied successes with their dancing and singing.

It was also at the 1900 Paris Exposition that *Shinpa drama* was shown for the first time in Europe by the troupe led by Otojiro Kawakami and Sadayakko, who went to France from the United States where they performed Japanese dramas for American audiences.

GHOST STORIES

THE JAPANESE are fond of hearing ghost stories, though many are afraid to walk dark streets at night after listening to weird *obake* tales. Particularly in summer, ghost stories are popular, as they make the audience shiver with fear and forget the heat. When such tales are told in dark gardens on summer evenings, the effect is great.

That accounts for why, since Tokugawa days, *obake* plays have been put on *Kabuki* stages, and story-tellers billed tales of ghosts in summer, to satisfy those who love to feel the sense of fear creeping over them.

There are different kinds of *obake*, but those that mostly appear in Japanese dramas and tales are apparitions of love or hate. The deceased woman comes back to see her loved one from whom she was separated by death. The dead mother reappears often to give her breast to the baby she left in this world. The *samurai* ghost tells his son who was his betrayer. Though such *obake* may come in uncanny appearances, there is nothing dreadful about them.

However, the ghosts that appear with feelings of hate or revenge are generally the kind that is particularly grim in appearance. The people believed that a wronged person would get revenge by appearing as a ghost and haunting the perpetrator of the misdeed. 'I will haunt you' has thus become a threatening expression.

These ghosts are made out to be most dreadful. When little children do not obey or commit mischief, their mothers will say 'Obake will come,' and then the children behave. Thus, in their childhood, the people are given a strong impression that *obake* is something to be afraid of. To back this, in dramas, stories and pictures, ghosts have been made so ghastly in appearance.

Obake appearing in Japanese tales have a haggard look, a pale face and long hair falling over the face and shoulders, and are dressed in a white costume. Some appear in armor or Court costumes. Their hands are raised to the breast, with fingers limply pointing downward.

The most notable feature of all is that they have no legs, the lower body tapering to a narrow waving end. The leglessness is believed to be the first

469

characteristic of *obake*. When one is surprised by the sudden appearance of an apparition-like figure at night, he is advised to look and see whether it has legs or not. If it has legs, it is no ghost.

Nevertheless there are, of course, many exceptions. In the famous tale of *Botan-doro*, the two ghost girls appear in beautiful costumes, wearing *geta* or wooden clogs, and walking with a clattering sound. But most *obake* have no legs.

Again, in pictures, *obake* appear very often under the branches of weeping willow trees, as such backgrounds help to make them eerie. Then also, greenish floating balls of fire are seen burning around them. Such fires are called ghost-fire or death-fire, as *obake* are dead persons.

In Edo or Tokugawa days and early Meiji years, those fond of *obake* tales used to hold *obake* story-telling evenings in summer. They gathered to tell or hear ghost stories, and to make them most realistic, the room was lighted with a few small candles, and little tricks were used to scare the audience. A sudden wind blows out the lights; something wet and cold passes over one's face or neck; a weird sound is heard somewhere; a woman's voice is heard somewhere; a woman's sobbing is heard. They made quite a study of such tricks.

Some of such tricks were formerly used at *yose* or Japanese variety halls when they had ghost tales on their programs. But as such practices went too far, and many persons were really scared, they are no longer in use.

It may be because of such ghost tales and plays that the people are still afraid of ghosts. But, as in the case of other dreadful things, they love to hear *obake* stories because they fear them. Then again, the fear of ghost haunting may have served as a moral lesson to many ignorant persons and kept them from committing crimes and wrongs.

There are many stories that are heard in rural districts telling of persons dying from fear of haunting ghosts that came to avenge wrongs done to them.

HAGOITA

AS NEW YEAR'S approaches, *hagoita* or Japanese battledores are displayed in all their glory in shops. Particularly women, young and old, crave for these *hagoita*. These beautiful battledores are, however, not to be used for playing the game of *hane* or Japanese battledore and shuttlecock. It is the plainer ones that are used for this purpose.

The game of *hane* is quite old, having already been very popular in the Muromachi period, 1392-1573. It is played with a shuttlecock made by putting four or five little feathers in a hole bored in a soapberry nut, and an oblong-shaped battledore, made of paulownia, cryptomeria or other light wood.

The early *hagoita* was very simple, but the nobles of Kyoto gradually made them elaborate with paintings of persons, flowers, fish and other objects. Those were called *Dairi-hagoita* or Court battledores.

Later on, Edo citizens with wealth and culture added so many artistic touches and such elegance to them that they became unsuitable in actually playing the game. They became big in size also, often more than three feet long, and too heavy for girls to play with. Thus they became merely ornamental articles.

As *Kabuki* dramas were popular, there appeared in Edo *hagoita* bearing the likenesses of famous actors in their great roles, made with *oshie* or gorgeous silk and brocade pieces pasted together to represent persons and their costumes. Master artists specializing in making such *hagoita* came to be highly respected.

The decorative *hagoita* are now displayed at home during the season. They have thus come to be called *sagicho-hagoita*, or battledores for the festival of January 15.

HANAMI

THE JAPANESE have traveled to the mountains to view cherry blossoms since very early days, and existing records tell that such picnics were quite popular more than 15 centuries ago. At first they were only for aristocrats, and it was not until about 300 years ago that *hanami*, or cherry blossom-viewing parties, became a popular recreation of the general public.

It is recorded that Empress Jito (690-697) went to the Yoshino mountains to view *sakura* blossoms several times during her reign. At that time, Yoshino had the most famous cherry blossoms.

When the Heian Palace was built in Kyoto in 794, a large garden was laid out and many cherry trees were planted. In 812 Emperor Saga held the first *hanami* party. The famous cherry trees of Arashiyama, Kyoto, were also planted then. Thus Kyoto residents were able to enjoy *sakura* without going to Yoshino.

Toyotomi Hideyoshi was fond of *sakura*, and he took his military officers and poets often to Yoshino. The so-called *Daigo-no-hanami* held by Hideyoshi on March 5, 1598, at the Daigoji Temple, Fushimi, is still famous. The party enjoyed *sakura* blossoms and wrote poems the whole day.

When the Edo Bakufu was established in 1603, *sakura* trees were planted at many places, and there were 33 districts famous for cherry blossoms, among which Ueno, Mukojima, Asukayama, and Arakawa were the most famous. In the Genroku period, 1688-1704, *hanami* became most elaborate, with women going in specially made gorgeous *hanami* dresses, and parties were held in grand style.

There are 247 varieties of *sakura*, or flowering cherry, in Japan, but the most common are *Yama-zakura*, *Yoshino*, *Someiyoshino* and *Sato-zakura*. *Yama-zakura* are found in mountain regions, with white or pink blossoms and leaves coming out together with the flower buds. A great number of Yoshino trees were planted at Koganei, a suburb of Tokyo.

Someiyoshino is a new variety of Yoshino developed at Somei, Tokyo, in the early Meiji years, and most of the *sakura* trees in the Tokyo area are of this variety. This kind grows rapidly, but its life is short, lasting only about 50 years. *Sato-zakura* flowers have multipetals, white, pink or yellow. Some blossoms of this kind have more than 300 petals in one flower. *Higan-zakura* blossoms early, with small flowers. It is mostly found in western regions, grows very big, and often reaches more than a 1,000 years of age. *Shidare-zakura* or drooping cherry, has slender branches drooping downward, and is a variety of *Higan-zakura*.

HAWKING

TAKAGARI or hawking has been a Japanese sport since the very beginning of the nation, and even today it is kept up by some sportsmen, though very few. As early as in the fourth century, Emperor Nintoku held a big hawking party on the Mozuno plain. By the 10th century, particularly in the reign of Emperor Ichijo, the sport reached a very highly developed stage, and special breeds of hawks were produced and trained.

At first the sport was mostly for Court nobles, but in the Kamakura period or 13th century, warriors who rose in power took up the sport, while its popularity among Court nobles declined.

During the Tokugawa period that started in the beginning of the 17th century, hawking became a noble sport fit for *samurai.* Tokugawa shoguns, feudal lords and many *samurai* kept hawks trained by special retainers. Whenever hawks belonging to the Tokugawas went out, the common people had to salute them and make way for them, as if the shogun were there in person. Anyone who accidentally killed a hawk kept by the shogun was punished by death.

The popularity of hawking developed a new trade of catching small live birds to feed them. These bird-catchers were called *tori-sashi,* and used long slender bamboo poles, on the top of which was put bird lime. Skilled bird-catchers caught flying birds by throwing their poles after them. The technique of catching birds by this method is still followed by children all over the country.

With the Meiji Restoration, the sport of hawking went out of fashion, as *samurai* lost their position. Some who were used to this sport could not give it up, and have preserved the technique, but we no longer have specially bred and highly trained hawks as our forefathers had.

HOZUKI

AS THE SUMMER season begins, in the shops of greengrocers appear *hozuki* branches which have red berries hidden within the yellowish red calyx that develops into bags. *Hozuki* is also cultivated at home as the people admire its beautiful red fruit. It is sold at shops, however, for girls to play with.

Hozuki belongs to the egg-plant species, and is scientifically known as Physalis francheti Var. Bunyardii. It bears white blossoms in early summer, and the calyx grows into a bag as the berry inside ripens. When the calyx bag is opened there is a perfectly round red berry, just like a ripe cherry inside. The people have always admired the bright red *hozuki.*

Hozuki has been a toy of Japanese girls since very early days. Girls' fondness of *hozuki* as a plaything is mentioned in the *Makura-no-Soshi* which relates to the Court life of the 11th century, and also in the *Eiga Monogatari* which pictures the life of the 12th to 14th century.

Girls collect the ripe *hozuki* from nearby farms, if they live in the country, or buy them at stores, in cities. Taking the red berry out of the calyx bag, a girl will bore a hole at the place where it was attached to the stem, and slowly squeeze the seeds out of the hole. She then has a hollow round soft ball with a tiny hole. She puts it into her mouth, and as she squeezes it against her teeth and lips, it makes a faint but pleasing sound. It is the joy of making this sound that has made *hozuki* so popular with the girls of Japan. All over the country for generations and generations, girls and even middle-aged women have loved to put the tiny sound-making bags in their mouths, whenever the season of *hozuki* comes. In olden days, girls did not have much variety of things to play with, and so *hozuki* was particularly popular. Since then the habit has been maintained undiminished.

There are also *umi-hozuki* or sea *hozuki,* used in the same way. They are egg bags of *naganishi* or *akanishi* (long or red whelks). The egg bags of *naganishi* are flat and round, while those of *akanishi* come in a long slender shape, somewhat curved. These whelk egg bags are also sold at toy shops and other places. A tiny cut is made at one end of the bag, and after the inside is squeezed out, the bag is used as *hozuki* to make a pleasant sound. Whelks lay their egg bags on rocks under the sea. They are gathered and preserved in salt for sale. Sometimes they are dyed red to make them look attractive.

Hozuki made of rubber appeared on the market, but it never gained popularity because of the rubber taste, and particularly because it took away all the joy of the delicate work of making tiny holes and squeezing the seeds out. *Hozuki* is just as popular now as it was ten centuries ago.

INU–HARIKO

HEALTHY AS PUPPIES is a common expression used in Japan in referring to the good health of children, because puppies grow rapidly and are always active. Dogs being the symbol of good health, toy dogs have been presented to new-born babies since ancient days, as a charm to ensure their healthy growth. At the same time, it is commonly believed that bitches giving birth to many puppies at one time suffer no pain in delivery. Thus they came to be regarded as charms for mothers to make their delivery easy and painless, and also to make them bear many healthy children.

Dogs were considered in early days to possess the power to expel evils, and thus there was a custom of writing the character for *inu* on the forehead of babies, so that they would be protected from evil influence.

It is recorded that the Empress Komyo (eighth century) made the Hokke Temple of Nara issue toy dogs of clay as a charm for pregnant women to have smooth child delivery. In the old days these charm dogs were made in pairs, a dog and a bitch. Mostly of clay or wood, they were made in a sitting position, the one facing the left being the dog and the other facing the right the bitch. Sometimes these toy dogs were made as small boxes, in two parts, upper and lower, and hollow inside, to be used as boxes for holding face powder and other toilet goods. A pair of these box-like toy dogs was always included among articles to be taken by a bride to her new house and were called *inu-bako* or dog-boxes.

It is from those *inu-bako* of the old days, that the modern *inu-hariko* or toy dogs made of papier-mâché has developed. The old *inu-bako* is no longer seen, and it is the new *inu-hariko* that is now presented to a new-born baby. Particularly on the day when the newly born baby is taken for the first time to the local shrine, his health and growth are ensured by the purchase or presentation of *inu-hariko*. These toy dogs are made in all sizes, running from very tiny ones of less than an inch up to those almost a foot high. Though the *inu-bako* had the dog sitting down, the *inu-hariko* has the dog standing up.

Inu-hariko developed from the little boxes made in the shape of dogs which were formerly used by women for holding face powder, paper, eyebrow brushes or other handy things. They were generally made in pairs — male and female. When a woman gave birth to her baby, the baby's first clothing was wrapped around the dog box before putting it on the baby, in prayer that the new-born baby would take after the dog and grow healthy.

When the *omiyamairi* custom developed in the Tokugawa period, the popularity of dog boxes brought about *inu-hariko*. *Inu-hariko* is now also placed on the shelves of *Hinamatsuri* or

Dolls' Festival of March 3, but they are used in place of the old dog-shaped boxes formerly used by girls which are not seen today.

JANKENPON

JUST AS Americans flip a coin to decide anything, the Japanese play *jankenpon*. It is one of many variations of *ken*, the game of forfeits that is believed to have come originally from China. In playing *jankenpon*, at a given signal one shoots out his hand with the fist closed, or with the hand open flat, or with the index and middle fingers pointing out and the other fingers closed. The closed fist stands for a stone, the flat open hand means paper, and the two fingers outstretched symbolize scissors. The stone wins over the scissors because the latter cannot cut stone. The scissors win over the paper, as they can cut the latter. The stone loses to the paper that can wrap it up.

Jankenpon is usually played by two persons, but several people can participate at one time. When it is played by more than three, elimination is done by removing the losers. To save time when many people participate, the signs are limited to two, for instance the stone and paper. This method is usually followed by children when they are selecting teams.

Jankenpon is played to decide anything, and children play it just for fun. It serves the same purpose as the Western coin-flipping, but it may be more interesting as it requires some skill and mental calculation.

Another and more complicated game of forfeits is called *tohachiken* or *kitsuneken*. It is only played by grown-ups because of its intricate nature and the training required to play it smoothly. The signs in this game are a man, a fox and a gun. The man is represented by holding both hands open on the knees or downward with the palms forward. The fox is shown by holding both hands open and upward with the palms forward, picturing the fox's ears. The gun is represented by the closed fist pushed forward. Only two can play this game. *Tohachiken* is generally played at drinking parties, and a cup of *sake* is the forfeit, the loser being required to drink it. However, sometimes other forfeits are demanded, or some strange stunts have to be performed by the loser.

The man loses to the fox that has the power to bewitch him. The fox loses to the gun that can kill it. The man wins over the gun which he can use. Usually in playing this game, three successive wins are required to make a decision. Thus sometimes it takes quite a long time for the players to come to a decision. It is played at a surprisingly quick tempo, and thus those who are not acquainted with the game cannot follow it.

Geisha are good *tohachiken* players, as they are asked by their patrons to play at parties. But when the game is played at drinking parties, the *geisha* do not lose anything, because the *sake* to be drunk as forfeits will be paid for by their patrons whoever might be the loser. Incidentally, they like this game because it forces their patrons to drink and that is good business.

JAPANESE POLO

DAKYU or Japanese polo was a favorite pastime of the aristocratic people, and was played until the Meiji era. It first came from China in about the sixth century, and immediately became popular in Court circles.

Dakyu is played on horseback by five men on each side. At first it was played by seven persons. The *dakyu* racket is of slender bamboo, three feet six inches long, and to the end is attached a split bamboo which is bent to form a frame, four by two and a half inches. Silk netting covers the frame. The ball, which is about one and a half inches in diameter, is made with a pebble at the core, around which straw and threads are wound and then covered with many layers of thick paper.

The court is 180 by 60 feet fenced in. At one end of the court stands the goal board, with a one-foot-six-inch hole in the center and about seven feet above the ground. Eighteen feet from the board there is a railing which the players cannot pass over.

The game is to throw five balls into the goal hole. The balls can be picked up, carried and thrown only by the racket. It requires delicate skill to keep the ball on the racket while riding fast and avoiding opponents. The players, each side in single file, enter the court from the opposite end. Reaching their positions, each player puts his ball in the racket and holds it breast-high across the chest, horizontally. At the starting signal, the players rush to the goal rail and try to throw their balls in the goal-hole. If any ball does not go in, another ball is thrown into play.

The game is divided into two periods. The first period is for each side to put in five balls. There are red balls for one side and white ones for the other. As soon as one side throws in five balls, the second period commences. Then a striped ball is thrown into the court. The side that succeeds in getting the striped ball in the goal-hole first wins. When one side receives the striped ball, and tries to win, the other makes efforts to prevent the striped ball from getting in, while it tries to complete throwing in their five balls. The game becomes lively as chances become even and each tries to prevent the scoring of

the striped ball by the other.

JUDO

JUDO DEVELOPED from the old art of *yawara* or *yawara-tori*, which was created 300 years ago as a military technique for hand-to-hand fights on the battlefield.

Originators of *yawara* are believed to have adopted much of the Chinese art of fist fighting which was introduced by a Chinese expert in the middle of the 17th century, and added to it the technique of Japanese *sumo* or wrestling. To fight with hands instead of with the forceful blows of swords is said to have been the aim of the new arts. Compared to the force of swords, it came to be called *yawara* or gentle.

It is said to be around 1663 that the new *yawara* school of *kitoryu* was established. Soon various different schools were organized, and experts were eagerly sought by feudal lords, while *yawara* schools were opened in big towns to teach the art to *samurai*.

Of course, with the abolition of the *samurai* class and feudal system with the Meiji Restoration, *yawara* lost its significance as a military technique. Yet those *yawara* schools remained in the early years of Meiji.

Jigoro Kano, the famous educator, established a new school of *judo* and opened the Kodokan in Koishikawa, Tokyo, in 1882. He made a signal change in the old *yawara*, and made it physical training for self-defense. But he attached greater importance to the spiritual training that is to be gained through *judo*.

As *yawara* was originally a military art, it had tricks to kill or disable the opponent. These tricks were all abolished in the new *judo*. It became a sort of sport and not a fighting method. In the Kodokan under Mr. Kano, strict discipline was maintained between the teachers and pupils, and the pupil's character was regarded more important than technical skill. In giving *dan* or rank of excellence, the pupil's character and discipline were fully considered. Young students were not given any rank, however proficient they might be in the actual *judo* technique.

The Kodokan has now become more popular and democratic, but the original spirit of Mr. Kano still rules.

KABUKI

KABUKI of Japan is a unique stage art, rich in color and tradition. It is a strange composite of dance, music and acting, retaining the ancient arts and culture of not only Japan, but also of China and many southern regions. With its remote origin in the primitive form of dance performed before shrines, its prevailing element is rhythm.

Kabuki made its debut at the beginning of the 17th century. Its originator is commonly said to be a woman named Okuni. The Okuni troupe of girls traveled all over the country with its show consisting of dancing, singing and simple dialogue acts, girls taking men's parts. *Onna-kabuki* or Girls' *Kabuki* prospered rapidly, but in 1707 it was prohibited by law on the ground that it had an undesirable influence upon public morals. Hence, only such shows as given by male actors were allowed to be given for public entertainment.

Kabuki thus developed has never had actresses, and all female roles are still played by male actors. This has become one of the unique characteristics of *Kabuki*. Women played on stage by *onnagata* (male actors taking female roles) are more feminine than women themselves. *Onnagata* are specially trained for taking the role of women. In Edo days, *onnagata* dressed and lived

as women in their private life. They felt ashamed when they had to refer to their wives, as they were supposed to be females, it is reported.

Many techniques of *ningyo-joruri* or puppet shows, which came before *Kabuki*, were eagerly adopted by *Kabuki* producers and actors. Puppet show plays were adopted on the *Kabuki* stage. Many exaggerated gestures, facial makeup and other pantomime features of *Kabuki* came from *ningyo-joruri*.

Main themes of *Kabuki* plays are loyalty, love, intrigue, sacrifice, revenge and class conflict. In sentiment they are all feudalistic. They are full of sad scenes of tear-shedding, death, murder and separation. Yet there are also comical scenes that produce hearty laughter.

Music plays a two-fold role in *Kabuki*. One is to lead the actors on the stage rhythmically in their movements and postures; the other is to tell the story of the play and explain the thoughts and sentiments of the characters. Several different schools of chorus are used, according to the plays and scenes presented.

Shamisen, a three-stringed instrument, is the main musical instrument, but there are also flutes and different kinds of drums. The narrators and musicians appear on a raised platform at the back, or the right of the stage.

Kabuki first gained the support of the common people, particularly the wealthy merchant and artisan classes, while the *samurai* and noble classes despised it as a low form of amusement in the early period. Later, however, many of the upper classes came gradually to be interested in *Kabuki*.

Kabuki is being much modernized with new plays, but the main features and traditions of the past 300 years are nevertheless carefully preserved.

KADO

KADO (FLOWER ART) which is now more generally known as *ikebana*, is 14 centuries old.

The art of arranging flowers began with the introduction of Buddhism in the sixth century. In offering flowers to Buddha, the Japanese desired to arrange them as artistically as possible. From this custom of offering flowers to Buddha developed an artistic type of flower arrangement in the Heian period (794-1185), which was called *rikka*, meaning to set up flowers. The *rikka* arrangement which became particularly popular among aristocrats was formal and stiff. This style reached perfection in the Muromachi period (1392-1573).

Then in the 15th century, Ikenobo Senkei of Kyoto started a new school called Seika or Nageire (thrown-in). This was a notable improvement. A basic rule of arrangement commonly known as *ten-chi-jin* (heaven-earth-man) or that of having the highest point of the flower arrangement representing heaven, the lowest point for the Earth, and a point between for man, was followed. The first book on *kado* was published in 1470.

The new school of Seika was also combined with the ancient *rikka* style, and this was called *Heika* (vase flower) which became popular among military men.

Up to that time, generally speaking, all flower arrangement styles were formal and stiff. But in the Momoyama period (late 16th century), a new trend was introduced by tea masters, who arranged their bowers in a much simpler and natural way. This tendency caused a signal change in the people's attitude to flower arrangements.

In the Meiwa-An-ei eras (1764-1781) *kado* reached its peak in development, with numerous different schools springing up. In *samurai* and aristocratic circles, the stiff and gorgeous style of Ikenobo was appreciated, while the common people loved Heika or a more natural style. But all tried to produce harmony as taught by Buddha and Confucius, in their arrangement of flowers.

In the Meiji era the *moribana* style was introduced. This is easier to arrange and can be used in Western-style rooms. The postwar period gave rise to another new style which is abstract.

KAGETORI

KAGETORI (shadow stealer) was formerly believed in many regions to be an invisible monster who stole a person's shadow. It was said that one who lost his shadow would soon die. Only living things had shadows, and when one approached his death, his shadow became faint, it was believed.

When photography was first introduced to the country, the people were afraid to pose before a camera, as they believed it took their shadows, thus shortening their lives.

Near Ashikaga City in Tochigi Prefecture, there is a temple called Kagetori Gongen, which is said to have been erected 180 years ago. The image enshrined there is a small wooden statue of a girl dressed in the ancient Court costume of *junihitoe* (12-layer *kimono*). In one hand she carries a wooden dipper, and in the other a wooden bowl. The *gongen* is worshiped particularly by women.

As to the origin of this temple, it is related that in the household of Yobe Kotaro, the head of Imabe village, there was once a maid-servant who had a 7-year old girl. One day while the maid went to the farm to take the midday meal to the workers there, the little girl opened the cage of a pet bird kept by the master and made it fly away. The master became so angry that he beat the girl to death.

When the maid returned from the farm and learned what had happened, she became so ashamed of what her child did that she jumped into a river nearby and killed herself.

The maid's spirit inhabited the water and floated wooden dippers and bowls on the river surface. When someone was tempted to catch a floating dipper or bowl, she would pull that person into the water by catching hold of his shadow.

An eminent Buddhist priest heard her story, and prayed for her salvation. She became *Gongen* or the incarnation of Buddha and stopped her evil act of *kagetori*. Since then she has been worshiped by women.

KAIAWASE

HAMAGURI, a kind of clam, is used for wedding feasts and also on various happy occasions. It has always been regarded as the best of all shellfish. The shell, too, has been widely used since ancient days. Since it is hard, it has been used to hold medicine and incense.

Because of the particular nature of *hamaguri* shells that only the original pair and none other will fit together, they came to be used as toys. *Kaiawase* (shell matching) became a popular game among Court ladies, as mentioned in Tsurezure-gusa written by Kenko Hoshi (1283-1350). As the game was played at that time, 360 half-shells were divided between two groups of players. Each side played out one shell and when a player found a shell that matched his, he gained that shell.

Later, the shells were laquered or beautifully painted. Then came *uta-kai* (poem shell). One half of a poem was written inside a shell, and the other half

on its matching half. The people played to find the matching half. The game of *kai-awase* was played by the upper-class women up to the end of the Tokugawa period.

There is an old tale of a woman who was born out of a *hamaguri* shell and became a famous weaver of fine cloths, and her husband who became a rich respected man.

It was in the Kyoho era (1716-1736) that the custom of having *hamaguri* soup at wedding banquets started. The reason given for this is that even when a thousand *hamaguri* shells are gathered, there is only one that fits the selected half.

KAKUNORI

KAKUNORI or trick riding by lumberjacks at the lumber-storing pools or canals at Fukagawa, Tokyo, has attracted much attention recently as it has been decided that this unique entertainment is to be preserved as a folk art.

Small canals in that area have been used for storing lumber since the very beginning of Edo's rise as a big capital. Huge logs, cut and uncut, are brought to the canals by lumber wholesalers, and lumber handlers work all day on floating lumber, either to sort them out or to move them. Thus, they acquired acrobatic skill in jumping or running on the logs and moving long square pieces lengthwise by turning them with their feet.

At festivals and on other occasions, they proudly displayed their acrobatics by racing on the logs and standing on high ladders erected on floating lumber.

Their feats were noticed by showmen who saw the chance to make money by showing *kakunori* in localities where they were not known. The first *kakunori* show was held in a small pool made at Dotonbori, Osaka, in 1747. Even in Edo itself, those living far from the Fukagawa area had no chance to see it. Thus, in 1820, at the festival of Juniso, near Shinjuku, a show was opened. Later it was held not only at Nanba-shinchi, Osaka, but also at Eko-in, Honjo, in Edo.

The skill and tradition of *kakunori* have been preserved by young men working at lumber pools in Fukagawa. It is strictly an Edo tradition which is now only known in Tokyo. It has thus been declared worthy of being preserved and protected.

KAMI-SHIBAI

THE BEATING of wooden clappers is a call for little children to gathe. at the street corner, heralding the start of *kami-shibai* or a paper show. Children in Tokyo and other sections of the country, particularly those of the poorer residential quarters, wait daily for the coming of the *kami-shibai* man.

As children gather, the *kami-shibai-ya* sets up his wooden frame on the saddle of his bicycle. He then opens a box containing little pieces of candy. Eager children give their pocket money to buy the candies. Those who have made a purchase are privileged to take front places before the frame.

When sufficient sales are made, the man starts his show. A series of brightly colored pictures illustrating a story that he recites to the children is slid into the frame. Stories told are mostly adventures or mystery tales. After the recital, he packs up and goes away with a promise to be back the next day with a new story.

This sales method, adopted particularly to interest children, became popular about 25 years ago, and during the war, it was extensively utilized for militaristic and patriotic propaganda. Today the police keep a watchful eye on the kind of stories and pictures so that no undesirable influence should be brought on little children. There are headquarters for the *kami-shibai* men, which supply them with stories and pictures, as well as candies to sell.

Children love *kami-shibai* because it tells absorbing stories and candy is sold, but mothers mostly do not approve of it because children ask daily for money for the *kami-shibai* man. *Kami-shibai* is a development from *kage-e* (shadow picture) which was popular in the Tokugawa days. Behind a large sheet of paper or a paper screen, shapes cut out from thick cardboard were held with the light projected from behind so that shadows appeared to represent various objects. These shadows were sometimes made to move. This used to be quite an entertainment at home in the old days.

KAMO-RYO

DURING the winter months, the Imperial Court holds *kamo-ryo* or duck hunts at special duck reserves to entertain the diplomatic corps and other personages. The duck hunting method used is unique and has become quite famous among foreigners. But this *kamo-ryo* is not old, as it is said to have originated in the early Meiji years.

In the old days, ducks were caught by trained hawks or shot with arrows. It was Lord Date of Uwajima, Shikoku, who first used this novel method of catching ducks, it is said.

Kamo-ryo was adopted by the Imperial Court as a new recreation, and several duck reserves came to be established to hold the duck hunts. Up to the Pacific war, *kamo-ryo* was even held at the Hama Palace in Shiba, Tokyo, but today it generally takes place at the duck reserves at Koshigaya in Saitama Prefecture, Niihama in Chiba, and other places.

At such game resorts, several small canals are made on the shore of the lake, and tall slender bamboos are planted on the banks. The hunters hide, armed with triangular nets on long poles, behind the bamboo fence or earth banks.

Decoy ducks are led into the canals by scattering feed. The ducks on the lake follow the decoys into the narrow canals. Watchers peeping through tiny eye holes made for the purpose wait for the ducks to come into the canals. At the proper moment, the watchers make the ducks fly up, and as the birds fly over their heads, the hunters catch them in their nets.

Sometimes a duck is not caught and tries to fly away to join the flock on the lake. Then a hawker who is stationed by the canal, releases his hawk to catch the escaping duck. If the duck reaches the flock and gives alarm, the whole flock might fly away. So to prevent its departure, the escaping duck is always caught by a hawk.

Thus hawkers play an important role in duck hunting.

After successfully netting many ducks, the hunters enjoy eating them.

The meat is sliced and cooked on individual, shallow, thick iron plates over a charcoal fire. It is said to be the best way to eat duck meat, and suggests the origin of the present *sukiyaki.*

While the *kamo-ryo* of the Imperial Household is famous, it is never enjoyed by the common people, as only privileged ones are invited to the function.

KANKAN DANCE

THE *KANKAN* dance craze gripped the people of Edo more than a hundred years ago. Men and women of all ages and even children danced it every evening in tea houses and on the street. Of course, this *kankan* dance is not related to the modern cancan that originated in France.

It was at the Araki Theater, in Horie, Osaka, that dancers from Nagasaki dressed in Chinese costumes presented a snake dance and the *kankan* dance, in April 1820. In the snake dance, 15 dancers waved and twisted a 15-foot snake made of cotton. But it was the *kankan* dance that gained wild applause.

To a weird tune played on Chinese musical instruments, dancers went through crazy movements, turning their heads, hands and legs in the most fantastic ways. They sang a song called *Kankanno,* because it started with those words. Nobody understood the words because it was not in Japanese. Some said it was a Chinese song, but others insisted it was a Dutch song with very immoral meanings.

The *kankan* dance was so popular at Osaka that the dancers soon went to Nagoya where they made another big hit. When the dancing troupe went to Edo, they took the capital by storm. Quickly the dance spread to all classes of people, and the *Kankanno* song was heard everywhere. In many busy quarters, the street was almost impassable as it was filled with mad dancers. It was danced at tea houses, restaurants and homes every day.

Finally in February 1822, or less than two years after the first *kankan* dance show was given at Osaka, the Bakufu authorities had to issue a law prohibiting it. Yet its popularilty was hard to suppress, and the people danced it secretly. The song is mentioned in many stories and literature of the late Edo days and early Meiji years.

KAZA-GURUMA

THE *KAZA-GURUMA* or wind wheel is a simple toy that still delights little children. It is a popular toy sold on festival days in many rural districts. It is said to have originated as a toy given to children in celebrating the New Year as early as the 10th century.

In those days, when they were mainly used in the New Year season, *kaza-guruma* were more elaborately made than those seen today. They are now made of paper or celluloid.

A piece of paper is cut round about five or six inches in diameter and then cut from the center in a curved line into five strips. Each point is bent back to the center to form a flower-like shape. The flower is fixed on a slender bamboo cane by a peg that goes through its center. The hole is made slightly larger than the peg and the flower revolves when the wind strikes it.

When a child holding it runs, the wheel turns. If there is a good wind, it revolves even when the holder remains still.

When it was more elaborate in construction, not only was the flower wheel itself made like blossoms, but several wheels were attached on one bamboo cane. As many as 10 wheels are said to have been put on one stick. But such elaborate *kaza-guruma* are no longer seen.

Kaza-guruma peddlers appear, to the delight of children, in the warmer seasons. They usually display their wind wheels by sticking them in a tightly bound bundle of straw, about one foot across and three feet high. Numerous pretty little wheels turning at the same time in the bundle of straw is a pretty sight that brings children from far away.

KEMARI

KEMARI or *shukiku* is the ancient Japanese football that has been one of the few sports enjoyed by Japanese aristocrats for more than 10 centuries. It originally came from China but, being played by only a few Court nobles, it was often feared the game would die out. However, it is still played today, with increasing interest shown by a wide circle of people.

Four, six or eight persons play at *kemari.* A ball made of deerskin is kicked up from one person to the next who has to kick it up again before it falls to the ground. The game lasts about 20 minutes. The court is about 40 feet square.

Thus *kemari* is a dignified and slow-motion game. There is no excitement, no rush, no running. The players still dress in ancient Court costumes, although they are now much simplified. They wear black lacquered Court shoes.

Becoming particularly popular among Court nobles during the Heian period in the ninth century, *kemari* become a Court function. It was kept up through the feudal days. In 1881 Emperor Meiji, who was very fond of the game, wished to have it encouraged and preserved, as there were signs of its losing popularity with modern changes. Hence the Kemari Preservation Society was formed in Kyoto.

The society still holds five games a year, one in January, on May 7, July 7, November 3, and in December.

Public interest in *kemari* is recently increasing with many wishing to join the society and learn the ancient game. But financially the preservation of the game is very difficult, as the cost of the deerskin balls and costume is rising.

KITE FLYING

IN MOST PARTS of the country, kite flying is enjoyed by children in the New Year season. Some districts, however, fly kites in May or have special seasons for it.

Kite flying as a pastime for children and grown-ups seems to have existed since early days. People were known to have flown huge kites. Even today, in some places kites as large as 30 to 50 feet long are being flown every year. A hundred or more persons are required to hold and fly such big kites.

There is a story that once a robber attempted to fly his accomplice on a kite to the roof of the Nagoya Castle tower and steal the gold scales of the huge dolphin adorning the roof-top. It is also told that, when Minamoto Tametomo was exiled to Oshima Island some 800 years ago, he tried to return his boy to the mainland by tying him to a kite. These tales may not be true, but they may serve to prove that huge kites were very commonly flown in the old days.

Japanese kites come in many shapes — round, square, oblong or in a bird-like form. The so-called box kite is, however, a recent introduction. Japanese kites have generally long stabilizing tails of paper or straw ropes. These tails are what made the people call kites *tako* (octopus) in the Kanto district and *ika* (cuttle-fish) in Kansai, as they greatly resemble an octopus or cuttle-fish.

In some parts of the country, boys have kite fights. They try to pull down other kites by clever manipulation of their own. Sometimes they attach little knife blades or pieces of glass on their kite strings. Various crudely made whistles are also attached to the lines, which make loud whistling noises as the wind blows strongly.

KOKESHI DOLLS

KOKESHI, simple charming wooden dolls, have now become famous. They are produced in quite a large quantity and sold all over the country. They were first made by wood turners of the mountain regions of the northeastern provinces of Iwate, Miyagi, Yamagata and Fukushima.

The wood turners made wooden bowls, trays and other household wares for generations. Some 150 years ago they began to produce crude dolls of *mizuki* or other white wood for the amusement of children, probably their own.

The master turners with skill and an artistic sense put their own ideas into their *kokeshi*, and thus each district and each artist came to produce its or his own characteristic type of doll.

Kokeshi made by such masters of the past years are treasured by modern collectors, and in many old families of the region, *kokeshi* more than 100 years old are still kept. Today, of course, cheaper ones are turned out by factories to meet increased demand.

The *kokeshi* has a round head and a cylindrical body, but is without hands or legs. The eyes, eyebrows, nose and mouth are painted on and the body is decorated mostly with floral or other bright designs. At first the colors used were only black and red, but recently various other colors have come to be used.

Small *kokeshi* are usually made from one piece of wood, but in the larger ones the head and the body are made separately and joined together. Some heads are so made as to turn around, often with a screeching noise. The shape of the head differs according to district and maker, some perfectly round, some egg-shaped and others pointed. The body is generally cylindrical, but in some it is made narrower or broader in the middle.

The most important part of the *kokeshi* is the face, and the value of the doll is mostly decided by the way the face is painted. Also it is the face that clearly marks the locality where it was made and often the maker. According to district and maker, the shape of the eyes, nose and mouth are different. Old traditions are kept up in the face.

Thus there are many types of *kokeshi*, some elaborate and some very crude. Among the well-known types, there are the *Tsuchiyu* of Fukushima, *Yajiro* of Miyagi, *Togatta* of Miyagi, *Zao-takayu* of Yamagata, *Sakunami* of Miyagi, *Narugo* of Miyagi, *Nanbu* of Iwate and others.

KYOKUBA

JAPAN HAS had its own circus for nearly 500 years. It is called *kyokuba* or trick horse, as trick horse-riding was at first its main attraction. *Kyokuba* started in the middle of the Muromachi period (1394-1573), and from its very beginning consisted of fancy horse-riding, acrobatic acts, comic plays and performances by monkeys and dogs. Harada Hyoe is said to have been the one who perfected this type of *kyokuba* show.

In the Tokugawa period, beginning in 1603, it became extremely popular all over the country. *Kyokuba* troupes entirely made up of women performers rivaling male troupes also appeared. Female *kyokuba* had wide followers, and one of their features was dramatic plays enacted by women on horseback.

The first Western circus came to Japan in 1864, four years before the Meiji Restoration that opened the country to foreign intercourse. The coming of the Western circus greatly stimu-lated the development of Japanese *kyokuba* which was quick to adopt many foreign features. Then a French circus came in 1874, followed by an Italian troupe in 1886 and a British one in 1892.

These Western circuses with performing elephants showed that *kyokuba* troupes also had to have such animals. It should be mentioned that it was these foreign circuses which came in the early Meiji years that introduced band music to the people. Bands made up of a few musicians became the symbol of *kyokuba* troupes.

Kyokuba troupes are mostly now called circuses, and many young people think that they are entirely Western, forgetting that Japan has had its own *kyokuba* for many centuries.

MANZAI

SINGERS KNOWN as *manzai* dressed in an ancient costume and wearing *eboshi* — a tall hat — come to all houses during the New Year season. They sing happy songs, while beating on their *tsuzumi* (drums).

This custom is said to have started more than a thousand years ago, when artists from China danced and sang in the Imperial Court to express their New Year greetings. The costumes of those ancient days are still kept up. But of course the music and words have changed.

At first there were two kinds of *manzai*. To show their New Year's sentiments, many people went to the houses of relatives and friends, and there sang happy songs and danced. This kind of *manzai* represented the voluntary expression of New Year greetings in songs and dances.

Then a professional group developed which went around singing and dancing in front of each gate, and received a few coins in return. People are eager to give them money, being pleased to be wished a prosperous New Year.

Today only the latter kind of *manzai* remains. *Manzai* men come from rural districts to earn some money during the New Year season when there is no farm work to be done.

There are many different *manzai* songs, differing according to districts. One that is most commonly sung in the Tokyo area is said to have been written by Mujuhoshi, a Zen priest of the Kamakura period. The song may be translated as follow: 'Cranes have a life of a thousand years: tortoises have the joy of ten thousand years. May your life prosper and continue longer than that of cranes, tortoises, pines and bamboo.' However the words may differ, all *manzai* songs pray for long life and prosperity.

As the entertainers mostly come from the Mikawa and Owari districts, they are commonly known as *Mikawa-manzai* or *Owari-manzai*. Sometimes whole villages in these areas go to other towns and cities in the New Year to sing and perform for the benefit of others.

The *manzai* dance and music developed from ancient Court music and dance, which were used on happy occasions. Adopted as the common people's entertainment, *manzai* has been very popular all through the Tokugawa and Meiji periods.

Kakubei-jishi is another New Year entertainment which developed from the *shishi-mai* (lion dance) of *Kabuki*. It is said to have first started in Echigo province on the Japan Sea coast. Some hundreds of years ago, the farm crop, it is told, was so bad that all the people suffered. Then one man named Kakubei thought of training children for acrobatic performances and plays in other districts to earn some money.

Thus the entertainment came to be called *Kakubei-jishi* (*Kakubei* lion dance).

Generally boys of 10 to 12 years old are trained. On their heads they wear the head of a lion made of paper and decoratd with feathers.

MATSUTAKE-GARI

MATSUTAKE (pine mushroom) is a table delicacy which Japanese look forward to in autumn. It is the best and most highly valued of all edible fungi, and its appearance particularly excites the people because the season lasts only about one month.

As its name implies, *matsutake* grows in red pine forests, where the top soil is of granite sand. Kyoto and many other Kansai districts are famous for *matsutake* but it is seldom found in Kanto regions.

All must eat *matsutake* to taste the joy of autumn. It is cooked in various ways. Soups with *matsutake* are very good. *Dobin-mushi* (cooked in an earthenware pot) is the most famous of *matsutake* soups. The soup is cooked in an individual earthenware pot and served steaming hot. *Matsutake* is also fried in oil or butter. It is broiled over a charcoal fire and eaten with citrus juice and also cooked with vegetables or used in *sukiyaki*.

Matsutake-gari or mushroom gathering is a delightful outing enjoyed in regions where *matsutake* grows. After making arrangements with the owner of a *matsutake*-growing pine forest, a party goes out for a day of outdoor enjoyment, carrying all cooking utensils and various foodstuffs, not forgetting rice and bottles of *sake*.

Arriving at the forest, they hunt for *matsutake* amidst the red pines, and when they have enough they prepare and cook them. The merry drinking and feasting then starts. After spending many hours in the forest, they return home, carrying baskets of *matsutake* they have gathered.

There are many other fungi eaten besides *matsutake*, and among the most common are *nameko*, *shimeji* and *hatsutake*, all of which appear in autumn.

There is another kind called *shiitake* which is consumed in a much larger quantity than *matsutake*. This variety is dried and preserved, so it can be used all year around. It is cultivated in many mountain districts. On logs of oak, beech or chestnut trees, shallow cuts are made and *shiitake* spores are placed in them. The logs are kept in the shade and properly watered. Then in spring and autumn, the fungi appear. It has a very good taste and is used in various dishes to improve the flavor of food.

MAWARI-DORO

MAWARI-DORO, or revolving lanterns, are regaining their popularity, and many, both children and grown-ups, are making them to add to their joy on summer evenings.

Mawari-doro were quite popular in the late Tokugawa period and Meiji years, and many persons strived to make better and bigger ones than their neighbors.

The *mawari-doro* is a lantern showing a moving picture when a candle is lighted within. There is much pleasure in designing and making one's own *mawari-doro*.

The lantern consists of two frames. The inner frame is cylindrical, made of split bamboo or wire. A picture of running persons, dogs, horses and such is cut from black or colored paper. This is then put on the cylindrical frame. The upper end of the inner frame has several blades, slanting like propellers running from the center outward. The bottom is open, and the frame is suspended loosely from the center of the outer frame.

The outer frame, which is larger than the inner, is generally square in shape, and covered with thin paper or silk. At the bottom is a place for a candle. When the candle is lighted, the inner frame slowly revolves, casting the shadow of the moving pictures on the outer frame of paper.

Placed in a dark garden or in a room, the *mawari-doro* gives a very pleasing picture. The outer frame is generally made square, and as a figure reaches a corner it becomes larger, as the distance from the source of light increases. Thus the figure not only moves, but also becomes bigger. The outer frame is often made in an octagonal shape.

Formerly a wick in an oil pan was used to heat the air to revolve the inner frame, but an electric bulb is now more often used.

MIBU-KYOGEN

MIBU-KYOGEN or pantomime plays of Mibu-dera Temple, Kyoto, which is performed for 20 days from April 21 to May 10 on a stage in the compounds of the temple, is unique in meaning and technique.

Mibu-dera is an old temple, having been established in 761. Enkaku, the priest there, conceived the idea of holding these plays in 1300, to propagate Buddhist teachings. For the past six and a half centuries, the plays have been kept up, and although the original significance of the pantomimes is greatly lost, *Mibu-kyogen* is still a unique attraction of Kyoto that draws Buddhist followers and others to the temple during the 20 days.

There are said to be 27 different plays still preserved. The pantomime is given with the music of drums and flutes. The original plays are said to have been very simple. With the influence of *Noh* dramas, they have been much improved but still all *Mibu* pantomimes are very simple in form and performed by actors who mostly wear masks.

The plays tell stories in which devils and evil are driven away by the mercy of Buddha. The costumes worn by the actors are donated by faithful worshipers.

In one of the plays, named *Bofuri* (stick waving), many lay believers also join in. This is a play signifying the beating of devils with sticks.

In the play named *Horokuwari* (breaking of an earthenware parching pan) a *horoku* is used which is donated to the temple. The pan is placed at the edge of the stage, and in the course of the play it is purposely knocked off by one of the actors. As it falls, it breaks up into small pieces. This is a moment of joy for all the worshipers as it signifies the removal and defeat of all that is bad.

Mibu-kyogen is performed wordlessly; it has many features that make it comical and enjoyable even to little children. Thus it remains popular even today.

MONKEY TRAINERS

PERFORMING monkeys carried on the shoulders of *saru-mawashi* or monkey trainers quickly attract many children who follow them around to see the monkeys do their tricks. Generally the monkeys dance, and also act in imitation of dramatic characters.

These performing monkeys are quite old in origin, having become particularly popular since about a thousand years ago. They are said to have been first brought from China. Shih Huang Ti of the Chin dynasty, after conquering six territories in 221 B.C., wished to build a great fort and palace. Innumerable coolies were hired to carry huge stone blocks and trees from various distant districts. To amuse and encourage these hard-working coolies, a large number of monkeys were collected and tied to the carts drawn by the coolies. Monkeys acted playfully on the carts and put the coolies in a cheerful mood, making them forget their fatigue and hard work. Thus the palace construction made good progress.

In Japan there is a similar story. Emperor Kanmu moved the palace from Yamato to Heian or Kyoto in 794. In the construction of the new palace, monkeys were used to cheer the workers. Monkeys wearing *eboshi* or Court officials' caps and waving *gohei* — sacred stick with cut paper — danced around the laborers. Since that time *saru-mawashi* has been officially recognized as a profession.

Monkeys are said to be good friends of horses from time immemorial. Feudal lords used to place pictures of monkeys over the entrance of their stables. Later *saru-mawashi* were called in to bring their monkeys to the stable, and make them exhibit amusing tricks for the horses.

As *saru-mawashi* were thus allowed to go inside the *samurai's* residences, military spies disguised as *saru-mawashi* were often used to spy upon the activities of rival lords.

NANIWA-BUSHI

NANIWA-BUSHI is the most popular item on radio broadcasts of Japan, although some say it is a low and undesirable entertainment. It is a mixture of *kodan* (story-telling) and singing with *shamisen* accompaniment. It is said to have developed from *saimon*, religious chanting. It is so popular that it is sung by delivery boys on bicycles, farmers tilling their land, apprentices in factories, and even maids cooking dinner.

Popular *kodan* stories of revenge and chivalry are adapted for *naniwa-bushi.* Naturally, lovers of *kodan* are generally fond of listening to *naniwa-bushi.*

It appeared in the first quarter of the 18th century, but before attaining special popularity it ceased to be heard. It was early in the Meiji era or about 80 years ago that it was suddenly revived, and since then has steadily gained popularity.

At first it was called *chobokure* in Kanto or the Tokyo area, and *ukare-bushi* in Kansai or the Kyoto-Osaka district. It was named *naniwa-bushi* only after its Meiji revival.

As *chobokure* reciters increased in Tokyo, the Tokyo governor recommended to them that they should form a union or association. They hence formed an association and decided to adopt the name of *naniwa-bushi.*

Strange to say, the name adopted in Tokyo is based on Naniwa, the old name of Osaka.

Even modern popular songs of the Western style which are rapidly gaining favor with the younger people have not lessened the popularity of *naniwa-bushi.*

NET CASTING

JAPAN BEING surrounded by the sea and the people being a great fish-eating race, fishing has become an important industry. Thus excellent fishing methods have been developed. But at the same time, fishing has also been enjoyed as a sport by many who are not professionally engaged in fishing.

To-ami or net casting is one type of fishing for sport that is unique. This way of fishing was also practiced in China, but in Japan it developed into a delicate sport.

The net used in *to-ami* is round in shape, and ranges in size from small ones of about four meters across to the large type measuring almost 15 meters across. A long and strong rope is attached to the center of the net and lead sinkers are attached around the edge of the net.

The net is cast from the seashore or river bank, or from boats. For shore casting small nets are used, and large ones for boat casting.

To-ami requires considerable skill and experience, as the net must be cast into the water so that it will spread out in a perfect circle to catch all the fish in the area.

The art of *to-ami* developed particularly in the Tokugawa era when many *samurai* or warriors took it up as a sport. Since then it has become a favorite sport of many who love fishing.

To cast the net, generally one holds the rope in his left hand, stretches half the net over his bent and extended left elbow, and catches the remaining half in his right hand. Swinging the upper part of his body, he tosses the net out over the water. If he is a good *to-ami* caster, the net spreads out in a perfect circle as it drops into the water. The sinkers at the edge close up the net as they go down, and the caster pulls up the rope and net, with all the fish in the area inside.

At the Isuzu River in Ise, a *to-ami* festival is still held at night every year, in which both boat and shore casters participate. It is a gay occasion with more than 100 boats with lanterns joining in the fete, and even has many women participants.

NIWAKA

NIWAKA are the mimic or comic talks and acts that formed a popular entertainment through the Tokugawa and Meiji periods. They are said to have been started by Niwaya Kasoji of Osaka during the Kyoho era (1716-1736), and named after him.

He started them for entertainment purposes at drinking parties. At first he told jokes and funny stories with comic gestures. As his mode of entertainment was received with applause, he elaborated on it. As *niwaka* became more popular, many persons took it up as a profession. There soon sprang up several master *niwaka* artists. *niwaka* was soon introduced to Yoshiwara, Edo, where it was called Yoshiwara *niwaka*.

With the increasing demand and popularity, *niwaka* artists developed from party entertainers to public performers. They performed their acts at theaters, with music, dialogue and comic plays. At first they appeared on the stage without makeup and wearing ordinary clothes, but later on they began to paint their faces and wear theatrical costumes as their acts became dramatic.

All through the Meiji years, *niwaka* continued to enjoy popular support, and was performed not only at theaters in towns, but also at rural festivals.

The end of *niwaka* came suddenly and unexpectedly. There might have been other causes, but some authorities say the main reason was the appearance of two new comic actors, Soganoya Goro and Soganoya Juro. In 1904 they gave their first performance of *kigeki* or comic plays at the Naniwaza in Osaka. The success of these new comedians ended the *niwaka* that had been so popular for two and a half centuries, probably because the public became tired of the old *niwaka* plays and wanted something new to amuse them.

OIRI-BUKURO

THE THEATRICAL people of Japan have a unique system of giving bonuses or profit dividends to actors, musicians and all other employees. This custom is even followed by cinema houses and other amusement halls.

In Edo days, *kabuki* theater operators used to give actors and employees *soba* or buckwheat noodles after each performance which drew a capacity attendance, to share the joy and profit of a full house. It was named *oiri-soba* or full-house noodles.

Then, for convenience, big theaters started to give cash instead of noodles to all connected with performances that brought full attendance. The cash is put in a small envelope which sometimes is brightly decorated with the theater's name. This was the origin of *oiri-bukuro*.

Each envelope holds the same amount of money, but leading actors and other important persons are generally given several envelopes while lower ones get only one each.

The amount in the envelope naturally changed with the times, but as it originally represented the sum to pay for two portions of *soba*, the amount has been in keeping with its current price.

The issue of *oiri-bukuro* is even now an occasion of joy for all connected with the theater, and many of them still love to display or keep these envelopes at home, without taking out the cash. Only when a special need for money arises, are all the envelopes opened.

O-KAGURA

O-KAGURA or sacred music and dance, is indispensable to shrine festivals. *O-kagura* is said to be as old as the country. Its origin is commonly believed to be the dance and song given by Ameno-Uzume-no-Mikoto to urge Amaterasu-Omikami to reappear from the cave in which she was hiding.

At shrines o-kagura is held to invite and entertain the kami. On the other hand, from many features of o-kagura, it may be also said that o-kagura was a performance of kami for the happiness of the people.

At any rate, o-kagura came to be firmly established in the middle of the Heian period (794-1192), as Court music. The musical instruments used are flutes, drums, lutes and gongs.

There are today two types of o-kagura, kagura-mai and sato-kagura (village kagura). The former is the original song and dance held to amuse the kami, and the latter to amuse the people coming to shrine festivals.

Sato-gakura developed in various localities and has different styles and traditions. It was particularly very popular in Edo days. While kagura-mai is performed by shrine musicians and dancers, sato-kagura is given by professionals who travel from one festival to another to give their performances.

With the music of flutes and drums, sato-kagura gives tales from Kojiki and other ancient records. Various kami, snakes, oni (devils), foxes and other animals appear on the stage. Some plays are comical and played by actors wearing masks of hyottoko and okame, a comic man and woman.

The outstanding feature of sato-kagura is that the actors who wear masks never speak. Their plays are interesting as they are always pantomimes. Nowadays there is an explainer who outlines the story of the play, as modern people have become unable to understand the mute plays of the old days.

OKAME AND HYOTTOKO

OKAME is the symbol of a homely looking but good woman, and hyottoko stands for a funny-faced man or a man who acts comically. These two have been main figures in folk farces offered at shrine festivals or given by children for amusement, from ancient days. Masks are used to indicate these characters, but of all the okame and hyottoko masks, there have never been any so elaborate as those for Noh or Court dancers.

The mask of okame shows a young woman with narrow eyes, a small upturned nose, a small mouth, and bulging full cheeks. The face is furthermore known to stand for good luck and womanly virtues. Popularly it is said that the mask of okame is patterned after Ameno-Uzume-no-Mikoto, who danced before the heavenly cave when Sun Goddess Amaterasu-Omikami shut herself in behind a rock door in displeasure, and the loud laughter Ameno-Uzume-no-Mikoto caused among all present lured the Sun Goddess to come out again.

Okame is often called otafuku, meaning a puffed-up face.

The hyottoko mask represents a man with one eye smaller than the other, and a pouting mouth. It is not known how this face has come to be selected as the symbol of a funny man. Not only funny-looking men, but also comical acts are sometimes called by this name.

To call a man hyottoko or a woman okame is insulting, but both terms are generally used in a good-natured sense.

OLDEST TOY

SOMIN-SHORAI is the oldest toy in Japan, originating in the mythological age, and is still seen in the country today. Of course, being so crude and primitive in construction, it is not much welcomed by present-day children as a toy. It is now used more as a charm against sickness or misfortune than as a toy.

Somin-Shorai is a simple spindle-shaped wooden piece with eight faces. On each of its eight faces is written *Somin-Shorai* in Chinese characters. There is a mythological story about its origin.

Susano-o-no-Mikoto once traveled to the Nankai region. Fatigued and hungry, he went to the house of Kyotan-sho who was wealthy but greedy. Kyotan refused to shelter him. So he went to the house of Somin-Shorai, Kyotan's younger brother. Somin, being kind-hearted though poor, welcomed Susano-o-no-Mikoto and offered him a meal and a bed. In expressing thanks for the kindness, Susano-o taught Somin to make a ring of reed leaves and use it as a charm against diseases. Soon there raged an epidemic throughout the district and many died. But all the members of Somin's family were saved, because they put the reed leaf ring at their door as Susano-o had taught them.

This led to the popular custom of making little octagon-shaped spindle-like wooden pieces, with the name of *Somin-Shosai* written on every face, and having them kept in houses to dispel epidemics and evil spirits. It was believed that epidemics or evils would not enter when they saw the name. In those early days, children had no playthings, and as they saw the *Somin-Shorai* wooden pieces in their houses, they played with them and made them their first toy.

Thus originated the first toy of Japanese children. It never lost its popularity through 20 or more centuries, and is still made in many parts of the country. The Yokado Temple at Kamikawa-

mura, Chisagata-gun, Nagano Prefecture, still sells *Somin-Shorai* on New Year's Day. The occasion is the greatest annual event, and people throng to the temple from distant villages to buy the wooden charm. Villagers make the wooden charms in their spare time, and it is said that their sales provide a livelihood for the entire village.

The Susaki Shrine at Nagoya also sells *Somin-Shorai* on Setsubun, or New Year's Eve by the lunar calendar. Then in many parts of Ise Province, *Somin-Shorai* is also sold as a charm.

As to the identity of the original *Somin-Shorai* who sheltered and fed Susano-o-no-Mikoto, nothing is known. At any rate, it is generally believed that he was not a Japanese. Neither is it known, however, whether he was a Chinese, Korean, Ainu or a native of Ryukyu.

ORIGAMI

ORIGAMI or paper-folding is a pastime popular among Japanese children, particularly girls. Various paper models of a crane, boat, flower, desk, box, tray, war helmet and others are made by folding colored paper, generally four to six inches square. It requires considerable skill to make the more complicated models as the objects have to be made just by folding the paper, without the use of scissors. *Origami* is so popular among children that in kindergartens, it is almost always adopted as a means of amusing and training the little ones.

Sometimes one loves to show his skill in *origami* by making things out of tiny pieces of paper, measuring not more than one inch square. Then again, two pieces of paper of different colors are used so that the colored side is on the outside.

Children take joy not only in making

various things in this way, but also in displaying them. *Orizuru* or folded crane is the most common of *origami*, and often many of them are strung on pieces of thread and hung from the ceiling to amuse babies.

Origami as children's play is mentioned in many records written as early as the Heian era (794-1192). It became highly developed in the Muromachi period (1394-1574) and tremendously popular in the Tokugawa and Meiji periods. During the Meiji era, little children were taught *origami* at school. Many new games and toys for children have appeared since then, but the popularity of *origami* has not diminished at all. On the contrary, its techniques have greatly advanced in recent years.

It is recorded that in Edo days there were already more than 70 ways of folding square sheets of paper. The most common objects were cranes, frogs, boats, crabs, windmills, lilies, irises, lotus flowers and such, forms which are still popularly made today.

In the old days, plain square paper was used as *origami*, but during the Meiji years *chiyogami* or paper with figured designs in colors, and also special *origami* paper in different colors came to be sold at toy shops.

The *tsuru* or crane is the most widely made *origami* object, it being a symbol of long life and happiness. Many paper cranes are strung together to make a long line. This is called *senbazuru* or a thousand cranes.

New and complicated forms, such as *shishi-mai* (lion dance), peacocks and others have been devised by clever folders. Experts are said to be able to make several thousand different forms.

Orizuru or folded cranes are used as offerings to shrines and temples. At many rural shrines and temples, many paper cranes of various colors strung on long threads are seen hanging down from the ceiling. These paper cranes have been made by children and old women of the village and offered with their prayers to shrines or temples, which they believe guard and protect their good fortune. The origin of this custom is not clearly known, but it is suggested that at first they were offered for decorative purposes, and later came to be connected with prayers.

Kirigami or paper cutting is another art. Various pictures or designs are made by cutting paper with scissors. The paper is folded many times and cut in different ways. When it is opened up, beautiful designs or pictures representing flowers, faces, animals and other things are produced. The joy in this pastime is that, until the cut paper is opened up, it is not known what the artist has made. There are professional entertainers who have developed marvelous skill in cutting out intricate designs and forms in less than a minute.

PEACOCK TEA-HOUSES

KUJAKU-JAYA or peacock tea-houses first appeared in Asakusa and Ryogoku, the two popular amusement centers of Edo in the Kansei period, 1789-1801. At those places, peacocks were kept in big cages, around which were placed comfortable benches. As the visitors sat and watched them, tea was served. The charge was small, so that *kujaku-jaya* instantly became famous.

Shows given at amusement places were noisy and exciting, but at the *kujaku-jaya* all was quiet and restful. Hence people came to rest after an exciting show. Soon similar tea-houses were opened at Shimoteramachi, Osaka, and Suehiro-cho, Nagoya.

As they became popular, *kujaku-jaya* were enlarged and various other birds and animals were shown besides peacocks.

Thus in the Bunka-Bunsei period, 1804-1831, some of them were called *kacho-jaya* or bird-flower tea-houses.

They were so popular even as to surpass other shows. Particularly on rainy days, other forms of amusement were closed as there were practically no visitors, but *kujaku-jaya* were kept busy despite unpleasant weather.

Realizing the public interest in birds and animals, many showmen started shows of queer or strange birds and animals, but they did not succeed as the public soon tired of grotesque- or unpleasant-looking birds and animals, most of which were fakes.

The *kujaku-jaya* as well as bird and animal tea-houses which prospered may be said to be the forerunners of modern zoological gardens.

QUIZ SHOWS

QUIZ SHOWS are now popular radio as programs, having been introduced from America. But quiz games have been a very interesting amusement indulged in by the Japanese since very early days. In Edo days there were even professional quiz men who drew crowds and also money.

The earliest record of *nazo-toki* or quiz answering as public entertainment is that on March 11, 1770, when the Yushima Shrine, Edo, held a festival. A man named Yatobozu sat on the ground, beating his *mokugyo* (wooden drum), and asked the assembled people to ask him any question or puzzle. He promised to answer them instantly, but requested that they throw him some money. He was able to give an answer instantly and very amusingly. He thus did quite a good business.

In the Asakusa amusement quarters, a special hut was erected in 1814 by a blind man named Junzo. He charged the

people a small amount of money to come into his hut. Around him, he piled bales of rice and charcoal, which he offered to any person who asked him a question he could not answer. His answers were so amusing that they were compiled into booklets and sold. He went to Osaka to answer riddles.

Another improvement was made in 1838 by Senka, famous singer of *ukare-bushi*, a kind of popular song. He first appeared at the Waradana Variety House, Ushigome, Edo. His trick was to sing his answer to any question. As he was a good singer and his answer in song was amusing, he became very popular.

But later, these entertainers disappeared as public interest waned.

RAKUYAKI

IN MANY cities and summer resorts there are *rakuyaki* shops where one can enjoy painting his own designs or have his own writing reproduced on plates, ash trays, vases, cups and other pieces of pottery.

The painted pieces are glazed and baked in the shop kiln in a few hours. A visit to the *rakuyaki* shop is always pleasant and amusing as you come away with something to be cherished for many years.

Rakuyaki is often a feature at garden or other social parties that always amuses guests of all ages.

The so-called *rakuyaki* pottery-making has become particularly popular since the Meiji years, but it is said to have originally developed from private pottery kilns kept in Tokugawa days by feudal lords and tea masters for making tea-bowls of their own designs.

Rakuyaki or *raku* pottery originally meant pieces made by the famous Raku family of potters. Early in the 16th century a Korean named Ameyo became naturalized and married a Japanese woman. Their son who was later called Sokei went to Korea to study the art of pottery making. As the tea ceremony was at its height of development then, upon his return from Korea he made black or red tea-bowls, which at once became very famous. In 1576 he presented a black bowl to Oda Nobunaga, who was so pleased with the bowl that he gave Sokei a gold seal with the character for *raku* (enjoyment). Sokei, thus honored, adopted Raku as his family name, and his pottery was called *rakuyaki* (Raku pottery). For generations the Raku family produced excellent bowls and other utensils for the tea ceremony, which are still highly treasured by tea masters.

Pottery painting for amusement is named after these old famous Raku pieces, and one may hope to make just as good pieces as the Raku family did.

SANBASO

WHEN A NEW *Kabuki* theater is opened or at the beginning of a special performance, a lively *sanbaso* dance is performed by an actor made up as an old man in a black costume and carrying a folding fan and tiny bells to ensure success and good luck. Formerly the *Kabuki* program started with *sanbaso* every morning.

The Japanese do not say *'odoru* (dance) *sanbaso.'* They say *'fumu* (stamp) *sanbaso!'* The phrase is derived from *hanbei*, stamping done by *yama-no-kami* or god of the mountain, when he came to the village at New Year, and in autumn, according to tradition. *Yama-no-kami* stood at the door of each house, and stamped his feet firmly on the ground to oust evil spirits.

To ensure good harvests, *Yama-no-kami* also stood in rice fields and stamped his feet.

In some districts, a young man was selected to act for *yama-no-kami.* He went to some uninhabited spot on a high mountain and stayed there in a wooden box so that he would not be molested by wild beasts. When he was ready to act as *yama-no-kami,* he came out of the box, put on a wide and deep straw hat and straw raincoat, so that his identity would not be known. Coming down to the village, he stood at every door, and stamped his feet on the ground to drive away evil spirits and bad luck.

The *hanbei* by *yama-no-kami* eventually developed into the stamping dance of *sanbaso.* In many districts *sanbaso* is still performed during shrine festivals. For the *Kabuki* performance, it came to possess a special importance since Tokugawa days.

SARU-MAWASHI

CHILDREN welcome the coming of *saru-mawashi* (monkey leader) with a trained monkey on his shoulder, as they like to watch various trick performances given by the monkey. *Saru-mawashi* means the monkey leader, but it also refers to the monkey's performance.

Wild monkeys are found in many parts of the country, and they have been tamed and made pets since early days. Particularly they have been kept as companions for horses, as it is believed there exists a natural bond of intimacy between them. Nobles and warriors of feudal days who kept horses used to place pictures of monkeys over the stable entrance. Then, *saru-mawashi* were called from time to time to perform before the horses to amuse them.

Performing monkeys were also used to cheer and encourage workers. It is recorded that when Emperor Kanmu built his new capital in Kyoto in 974, a large number of workers were employed to construct the palace buildings. To hurry the construction and to urge all workers to exert their best efforts, monkeys were brought to the site. The funny dances of the monkeys made the workers forget their fatigue and enabled them to do better and more work. Officially recognized as a profession since that time, the popularity of *saru-mawashi* increased with the honor accorded it.

Saru-mawashi is mentioned in many ancient literary works and dramas, and in all cases some happy significance is attached to monkeys or their performances. Monkeys bring good luck, it is commonly believed, and so *saru-mawashi* appear during the New Year season and at many festivities.

SHAKUHACHI

THE *SHAKUHACHI* is a bamboo flute, originally introduced from China. At first it was a musical instrument for Buddhist services. It is about one foot and eight inches long, and thus is called *shakuhachi* (one foot and eight).

A bamboo about one inch in thickness is cut at the root to make one *shakuhachi*. The inside joints are knocked out, and four holes are made in front and one at the back. A reed is inserted at the front top and the flute is held upright for playing.

These instruments were first brought to Japan in the seventh century. One that came from Tang in the eighth century is still preserved at the Shoso-in, Nara. Prince Shotoku performed on it but in those early days it was not generally played.

It was in the Kamakura period or the 13th century that the *shakuhachi* was reintroduced. Priest Kakushin who went to China to study Buddhism learned to play it from a Chinese expert. Coming back to Japan, he used it at his Buddhist services.

At the Kokokuji, Yura, Wakayama which was established by Priest Kakushin, *shakuhachi* music is offered at the memorial service held for its founder on October 13 every year.

Kakushin taught the *shakuhachi* to his disciple Kyochiku. When he went on his mendicant trips, Kyochiku played his *shakuhachi*. His statue at the Tofukuji, Kyoto, represents him with this instrument in his hands.

Thus it came to be associated with the Rinzai sect of Zen Buddhism. It is only since the middle of the Edo period or about 150 years ago that the *shakuhachi* came to be gradually used as a musical instrument to be played in common households. Particularly it came to be used to accompany the *koto*, a harp-like instrument.

Many laymen learned to play it and priests of the Fukke sect of Buddhism continued to carry the instrument on their begging trips. *Shakuhachi*-playing priests wearing deep straw hats that cover the whole head and face are still to be seen on the streets.

SHAMISEN

SHAMISEN or *samisen* is the representative musical instrument of Japan. It is used to accompany all kinds of singing, and *Kabuki* and *ningyo-shibai* (Japanese puppet shows) would never have developed as they did without it.

Yet *shamisen* is a foreign instrument introduced to Japan in the Eiroku era (1558-1570). The origin of *shamisen* is unknown, though generally it is believed to be an instrument of Siam or some other southern region. But to Japan it came from the Ryukyus. It was a *biwa* (lute) player named Nakashoji who took interest in the new instrument when it first came to Sakai.

The instrument, which was called *jahisen* (snake-skin string) in the Ryukyus because its sound box was covered with snake-skin, was a three-stringed instrument played with a bow. But Nakashoji played it with a plectrum as he did his *biwa*, and also made some changes. As it was impossible to obtain snake-skins for the instrument, he covered it with cat-skin.

Thus, it became a Japanese instrument called *shamisen* or *samisen* (three-stringed). It became very popular at once, and served to promote *ningyo-joruri* (puppet recitation) that appeared in the Keicho era (1596-1615). *Ningyo-joruri* was a dramatic show made by manipulating puppets following the recitation of a story, accompanied by *shamisen* music.

Ningyo-joruri, as it gained popularity and developed, greatly influenced *Kabuki*, the stage drama of the country.

Since then, *shamisen* has been not only indispensable for both *ningyo-joruri* and *Kabuki* plays, but also is used in accompanying all schools of Japanese singing.

Shamisen is made in three different styles, called *futo* (thick), *naka* (medium) and *hoso* (narrow), classified by the thickness of the stem over which the three strings are strung. The heavier ones give a deeper tone than the lighter ones.

SHIOHI-GARI

FOR PEOPLE residing in seaside regions, *shiohi-gari* is an event for which they await most impatiently as spring approaches. *Shiohi-gari* means 'low-tide gathering,' and is a seashore picnic to gather shellfish. The spring low tide that comes in the latter part of March and early in April offers an unusual opportunity for common people to gather shellfish easily. The great ebb-tide reveals a vast stretch of sandy sea bottom, and thus places where many shellfish live that are usually under water are exposed. Those shellfish would never be caught if there were no spring ebb-tide.

The spring picnic of *shiohi-gari* has been very popular with the people since very early days, though it is not known when it really started. Some say that the custom is as old as the people. Yet it can be said that during the Tokugawa period it came to be featured as a national event. In the old days when sea bathing was not popular among the people, it was the only occasion when the citizens of towns and cities became acquainted with the sea and seashores.

On the spring low-ebb day, if the weather is clear, the people throng to nearby seashores. Tucking up their clothes high above the knee, they run over the wet sandy beach which is usually under water. Walking into shallow water, they dig into the sand with rakes and small shovels to gather up various shellfish. For children and particularly women it is a great occasion because it gives them the novel experience of gathering shells. Various fish are also caught in little pools of water that are left as the tide rolls out. Crabs and octopuses are found in some places also, under rocks that are left above the water-level. Oysters are found on rocks and in sand.

Shells which are mostly gathered at *shiohi-gari* are *hamaguri* (clam), *asari* (tepes) and *shijimi* (corbicula). *Mate* (*Solen gouldi*) is found on some shores, and the gathering of this shellfish is most interesting. On the sand are found tiny holes which indicate that *mate* are underneath. When some sea-water is poured into the holes, the shellfish, thinking that the tide has returned, then come up from the holes. They are caught as they emerge from the holes. *Mate* live inside a flat and long shell. It is eaten as a delicacy but is not so common as *hamaguri* or *shijimi.*

Scenes of *shiohi-gari* have been depicted by many artists in the past, and particularly by *ukiyoe* artists, because it is one of the very few outdoor picnics that have been popular with the people.

Sometimes tragedy accompanies the enjoyment of shell gathering. Often, some people, particularly unattended children, are so engrossed in shell gathering that before they realize it, the tide has returned and they are marooned on rocks or patches of sand. Moreover, when a strong wind blows on the day, many boats in which the people go out for their shell gathering are liable to meet with disaster.

Shiohi-gari is the most picturesque and enjoyable spring picnic of Japan, which is favored with long shore-lines and abundant shellfish at all beaches.

SHISHI-MAI

SHISHI-MAI or lion dance is one of Japan's representative dances. It is danced on *Kabuki* stages, and also at local shrine temples. There are many kinds, some being very elaborate and artistic, while others are very crude and primitive.

The *shishi-mai* dancer places his head within a big lion head, often with flowing mane, and covers his body with a loose baggy cloth to make him look like an animal.

Although it is called *shishi-mai* or lion dance, it did not originally represent a lion. *Shishi* is an old word referring to all kinds of wild beats. It is to be noted that some *shishi* masks have horns. In many districts *shishi-mai* is called *shika-odori* or deer dance. The dance originally represented wild

animals, and as their symbol, the deer was selected for gracefulness.

Gradually, however, the animal mask used in the dance came to look more and more like a lion, an animal which was known to the early Japanese only in tradition and pictures.

However, the *shika* or deer has always been the representative animal and regarded as *kami*'s steed, or even as the deity in its worldly form. This tradition is still kept up at Kasuga Shrine, Nara, and many other old shrines, where deer are kept as holy symbols or sacred animals.

Such shrine deer were included in festival processions as the symbol of *kami.* Also, eager persons came to impersonate sacred deer in such processions, wearing deer masks. Human impersonation of deer at festivals appealed to the public and dancers came to dress and act more dramatically to please and amuse the public. It was thus that *shishi-mai* originated.

Another kind of *shishi-mai* also became popular. This new dance has no connection with shrines, but the performer goes around from door to door to cast charms against evils and diseases, and receives offerings. This new *shishi-mai* is danced by a single person, and the lion head has rooster's feathers or twisted paper strips instead of hair. The dance itself is much simpler.

The coming of the *shishi-mai* is always welcomed by children and those who believe in its powers.

SHOGI

THE GAME OF chess was introduced into Japan quite recently, but there are many expert chess players. It is because Japan has had its own *shogi,* a variation of chess, that the newly introduced Western game has been very easy to learn.

Shogi has been very popular in the country since the Kamakura period about 700 years ago, it is recorded. Some claim the game came from China very early, but as *shogi* differs so much from Chinese chess, others attribute its origin to India.

Chess, which is said to have originated in Persia, spread to various countries in the East and West, and underwent changes as it was played by different peoples. After its introduction to Japan as *shogi*, it also underwent great change. The present *shogi* is quite unlike the game played in the Kamakura days.

Nevertheless, *shogi* is quite similar to chess with pieces moving in similar ways, because they both developed from the same game. But one outstanding difference is that in *shogi*, when one takes the opponent's pieces, they can be used as his own. The captured pieces can be placed at any position. This makes the game more complicated, as one has to calculate in what way he or the opponent can use the pieces exchanged.

When an expert plays with one not so good at the game, he removes some of his pieces before starting, so the chance of winning will be made as equal as possible. Ranks are decided by the number and kinds of pieces to be taken away to balance the difference in ability.

Shogi has always been a game of the commoner from its early days, especially among farmers, artisans, fishermen and such people. It is also played by office workers and factory men in their spare hours. Even little children play it, and sometimes children of less than 10 years of age show a marked expert ability at the game.

The national *shogi* champion formerly held his title for life. But recently the rules have been changed and the champion in order to retain his title has to play against a challenger selected by tournament games among high-ranking men every year.

SHO-NO-FUE

SHO OR *SHO-NO-FUE* is a unique instrument used in *Gagaku* and shrine music. It was brought originally from China more than 13 centuries ago. It was used in China and Korea in ancient days, but it is now seen only in Japan. It is a wind instrument, but differs much from others in construction and manner of playing.

It is made of 17 slender bamboo pieces of five different lengths, arranged upright in a circle. *Sawari* or a metal reed is attached to the lower end of each bamboo, except for two. The bamboo, with holes in their lower ends, are set in a round lacquered base which has an opening. The instrument is held in the palms of the two hands, and fingers are used to stop the holes. The player puts his mouth to the opening in the base, and blows or inhales, as the reeds are made to sound either way.

Sho music is often likened to the singing of the *ho-o* or phoenix, though people have never actually heard this bird sing.

In *Gagaku* or shrine music *sho* do not give any melody. Generally five or six bamboo are sounded together and a harmony of notes is sounded. The melody is supplied by the *shichiriki* or nine-hole flute.

The making of *sho* is extremely difficult. First of all, bamboo of proper thickness and quality must be obtained. Only well-seasoned bamboo that has been dried many years can be used. In the old days, the bamboo from thatched roofs was often used, as they were seasoned and smoked by fire over many years. Many good *sho* instruments have bamboo a hundred or even 200 years old.

The reeds are also very important, and old instruments have Chinese reeds. Their quality governs the tone of the instruments. To give proper tone, the reeds must not be too dry or too moist. The player therefore keeps a small charcoal brazier by his side, and warms the base of his instrument whenever necessary so that the reeds will be in good condition.

STEP-LADDER FISHING

KYATATSU-ZURI, step-ladder fishing, is a unique method of fishing first invented by Edo anglers, and still popular among Tokyo fishermen.

During the month of May along the shallow sea of Tokyo Bay, fishermen are seen perched on high *kyatatsu*, more than 10 feet above the sea, trying to fish *kisu* (Sillago sihama), a little fish growing to five or six inches. There are two kinds of *kisu*, white and blue, and it is *ao-gisu*, the blue kind, that is generally fished for in Tokyo Bay.

This method of fishing is used because the *kisu* is very sensitive and timid. The slightest sound or movement in or above the sea startles and scares them away. It is, therefore, quite impossible to fish from boats as the movements of boats or the noise of waves beating against the sides will send them away. Fishermen cannot wade in, as that is the surest way to chase all the *kisu* away.

Fishermen erect the step-ladders beforehand and take boats to the ladders before dawn. They sit on the ladder-tops and have to remain there until their boats come again to take them home. They must make no noise and as little movement as possible.

The fish live near the bottom of the shallow sea, and as they are extremely timid, it requires considerable skill and experience to hook them. The difficulty, of course, makes *kisu* fishing so interesting, but it is also quite a physical trial.

As they are perched so high above the water, the fishermen must carry bamboo fish baskets with long net handles into which they put their catch and keep them alive under water. They have to also take thermos bottles and something to eat to be comfortable on the ladder-tops.

STORY TELLERS

KODAN or story-telling is one of the most popular items on radio programs, and also at numerous *yose* or variety halls. *Kodanshi* or professional story-tellers are in much demand all over the country telling their stories at halls and private gatherings.

The first *kodanshi* appeared in the compounds of Kannon Temple, Asakusa, Edo, and as he became instantly popular, many imitated him. Most of the tales are about feudal battles and historical figures told in an interesting and amusing manner. Of course, interesting details added to give color to the stories are not true in many cases. Recently modern stories, which however generally follow the traditional types, have also appeared.

The real pioneer in this profession was Ginnan-Osho (Gingko Tree Priest) whose real name is not known. He appeared every day under the gingko tree on the grounds of Kannon Temple, Asakusa, and there he told various historical tales while his listeners tossed him many coins.

However, before he became really famous, he was chased out of the temple grounds by a better story-teller. The newcomer was Shidoken who is generally considered as being the originator of the *kodan*.

Shidoken was a son of a Kyoto farmer who, at the age of 12, entered a Buddhist temple. He soon became disgusted with temple life. When he was 20 he ran away to Edo, where he found himself without any means of earning his daily rice. One day he went to the Asakusa Kannon Temple, and saw Ginnan-Osho telling his tales. Shidoken thought it was an easy business that could be started without capital. Immediately he sat down under a pine tree nearby and began to tell his stories. He added humorous remarks to his tales. A larger crowd gathered around him than in front of Ginnan-Osho, and the latter had to leave. His audience became so large that it was necessary to build a simple platform on which he sat to tell his stories.

Until the age of 83, Shidoken continued his story-telling, becoming one of the famous figures of Edo. He died in 1765, but he had developed a new profession which is still followed by many today.

SUGOROKU

SUGOROKU is still a favorite game among Japanese children. Of course, it is now modernized and is seemingly quite different from the game that was popular in the Edo or Meiji days.

It can be played by two or more persons. On a large piece of paper, about two by three feet, there are printed in various colors small pictures arranged in order, starting at one corner and going around to end at the center. These pictures give incidents of a story or a journey, but often they are independent. The players roll dice and move their markers ahead for as many sections as the dice indicates. One who reaches the goal first wins. But there are hazards at many points, where one must remain stationary or is ordered to go back several sections. This makes the game interesting.

Sugoroku developed from *ban-sugoroku* or board *sugoroku*, introduced from Korea. This was a game like checkers. The board had squares drawn on its surface, and two players moved their black and white pieces as they shook the dice.

In the 12th century, Buddhist priests adopted this game to teach students. They made a game called *Jodo-sugoroku* (Pure Land *sugoroku*). On a piece of paper they drew many squares and on them they wrote down important points in their doctrine. Students were made to play it so that these points could be memorized by them. Another kind of *sugoroku* appeared with official ranks and titles, to make people remember them. But these did not become popular.

During the Genroku era (1688-1704) *sugoroku* with pictures were made and became popular. The most common kind was *dochu-sugoroku* or travel *sugoroku* depicting places along the Tokaido highway. They were soon followed by *sugoroku* representing the life of warriors, actors, *sumo* wrestlers and others. Various tales were also used.

Tokaido dochu-sugoroku was popular until the Meiji days. Modern *sugoroku* depict adventures on motor cars and planes in keeping with the times.

SUMO

SUMO OR Japanese wrestling is the oldest sport of Japan. It seems to have started very early in the nation's history, but *sumo* matches were at first held at the Court or shrines as offerings to *kami* for a good harvest and the people's welfare. Even today on such occasions as shrine festivals, *sumo* matches are held by local people for the amusement of the shrine *kami*. Strict rites unchanged since the old days are still observed by *sumo* wrestlers.

But it was in the eighth century that it was established as a national sport. Emperor Shomu held the first national tournament in 728. *Sumaibito*, as the wrestlers were called at that time, were selected from all parts of the country. The tournament was held at the south garden of the Imperial Palace.

After several stages of elimination, 34 were finally selected. The Emperor appeared to watch them fight for the championship. There was no fixed ring for wrestling then, but two '*tachiawase*' or watchers stood on both sides of the wrestlers to oversee the match.

This *sumo* tournament came to be annually held by the Court on July 7, and the day was named *Sumo-sechie* or *sumo* fete and became a great Court event. Thus wrestling was greatly encouraged by the Court and many strong wrestlers appeared. But this annual fete was discontinued after 1174.

Later in the Kamakura period (13th-14th centuries), wrestling was taken up by warriors. Matches held at the Hachiman Shrine in Kamakura on its festival day became nationally famous. In the 16th century when Oda Nobunaga and Toyotomi Hideyoshi ruled the country, the techniques of the game were developed and the wrestling ring established.

It was, however, in the Tokugawa era that professional wrestlers appeared and feudal lords became interested in the sport, competing with each other to keep strong wrestlers under their patronage.

Since early days, *sumo* matches have also been held at shrines and temples on their festiveal days. When new temples or shrines were to be erected

or when old ones had to be repaired, *kanjin-sumo* or collection wrestling matches came to be held since the 15th century to collect donations from the public. The Eko-in Temple in Ryogoku, Tokyo, which has been long connected with *sumo* tournaments, was erected for those who were killed in the big fire of 1657. *Kanjin-sumo* was held at the Eko-in to solicit public offerings for the temple.

SUZUMI-BUNE

SUZUMI-BUNE or 'cooling boats' were the most luxurious method Edo residents utilized to cool themselves in summer. Sitting on richly decorated boats and surrounded by beautiful women and many servants, they enjoyed cool breezes as their boats slowly glided down the Sumida River, while they drank *sake* and ate delicious foods.

Of course, at that time, the river was beautiful and the water was clear. The 'cooling boats' were specially constructed and were generally called *yakata-bune* or roofed boats. Some of them were quite big, reaching a length of more than 50 or 60 feet.

It is said that this custom of cooling off on river boats started in the Keicho era, 1596-1614. In a certain year of that era, the summer was exceptionally hot, and thus it is believed the people thought of enjoying the cool river breezes on little boats.

At first *suzumi-bune* were used by rich merchants, but soon, as they became popular, many feudal lords and great *samurai* followed the new fashion. It is recorded that some of the *samurai* who held such boat parties, displayed their family banners and spears on the boats to maintain their dignity.

Before long, *suzumi-bune* developed into a social function, and large parties came to be held on the boats floating on the Sumida River. This was one main factor that made the boats bigger and bigger. Not only did many wealthy families have their own boats, but there also developed *funayado* or boat-houses, which hired out boats.

As families as well as *geisha* came to be invited to these boating parties, the women trained themselves in graceful boat conduct. Firstly it was quite a task for women dressed in *kimono* to step gracefully from the landing onto a boat that had a low roof. Then they had to acquaint themselves with the narrow space on the boat where they had to serve their husbands or masters.

TAIKO

THE SOUND of *taiko* or drums was at first regarded sacred. Thus they came to be used to dispel evil and devils. The idea of the *taiko* being sacred is still retained in many local customs in holding shrine festivals.

At the *Hanamatsuri* (flower festival) of Hisawa, Aichi Prefecture, the shrine drum is still treated as a sacred object and not merely as a musical instrument. There the drum is called *Taikomyojin* or drum deity.

Drums have been beaten since very early days not only to drive away evil influences, but also birds, insects and animals harmful to crops. In praying for rain, drum beating has also been considered essential.

The famous *Noh* play named *Tori-oi-bune* (bird-chasing boat) tells of a servant who, sitting in a boat, beat a drum the whole day to chase away evil birds. On the battleground it was used to scare off the enemy.

The Japanese *taiko* was first made by cutting a length of big bamboo and covering both ends with leather. Then a wood block was hollowed out to make the cylinder for the *taiko*. Thus the drum became larger and various types appeared — flat, long and huge. Monkey leather was said to be the best for drums at first, but now horse hide is mostly used.

Being regarded sacred, the *taiko* has been used at shrines and shrine festivals, even becoming their symbol, while bells stand for Buddhist temples.

Nichiren-sect Buddhists use the *uchiwa-daiko* or round, flat fan drums, made of a single piece of leather.

Developing as a musical instrument for shrine music, the *taiko* came to be an important instrument in Japanese music. Particular *taiko* for different kinds of music appeared.

Drums were at first called '*tsuzumi*,' but later this term came to indicate a certain type of *tsuzumi*, which is still widely used. A peculiar characteristic of the present *tsuzumi* is that by tightening the strings that hold the leather covering at both ends, the tone can be changed. *Kakko* and other drums used in *Gagaku* or Court music also have this string-tuning system.

TAIKO-MOCHI

TAIKO-MOCHI (drum man) was a professional jester and entertainer, very popular in the late Tokugawa period and through the Meiji era, but now almost extinct.

It is believed that *taiko-mochi* made their first appearance in the Kanbun era (1661-1673) at the Yoshiwara gay quarters of Edo. It was their task to make gay parties more pleasant and agreeable to visitors. They thus had to be wits and be well-versed not only in music and songs, but also in *Kabuki* plays which were often topics at such parties.

It is not clearly known how they came to be called *taiko-mochi*, but it is generally said that the name came from the drummer in Buddhist chanting who was the leader and made the loudest noise.

Taiko-mochi as a profession was established around the Horeki era (1751-1764), and thus took almost a century to become perfected.

Samurai and rich merchants who frequented the gay parties were their patrons. With the gradual expansion of their field of activity, they became invited to parties held at restaurants and other places outside the Yoshiwara quarters.

However, it was not easy to become a good *taiko-mochi*, because of the required qualifications.

Taiko-mochi no longer exists as a profession, but the term is now widely used to imply flatterers.

TAKE-UMA

TAKE-UMA (bamboo horse) are Japanese stilts commonly used by children. Two bamboo poles about five feet long are attached to narrow wooden boards at convenient heights. Boys and even girls stand on the boards, holding the upper ends of the poles in both hands. They walk and run, and even do tricks on them.

But originally *take-uma* were quite different. The old *take-uma* are mentioned as early as in the 12th century. To a bamboo pole, about two or three feet long, were attached ropes as reins, and a small wooden wheel was placed at the other end. The child put *take-uma* between his legs, holding the reins. They walked or ran, and imagined that they were riding horses. It was really a bamboo horse, and so it was called *take-uma.*

As they became popular, they began to be made more elaborately. In the Kan-ei era, 1624-1644, wealthy children's *take-uma* came to have a horse's head, made of cloth or papier-mâché at the pole's top. The horse head had a flowing mane of silk or cotton yarn. Some also had two wheels at the lower end, instead of one as in the earlier type.

Thus improved, *take-uma* were very popular all through the Tokugawa period. Particularly *samurai* families encouraged children to play with *take-uma* in the belief that it would teach children the martial spirit. It is recorded that when the toy was at its height of popularity, both boys and girls rode *take-uma* until they were almost 20 years old.

The present type of *take-uma*, varying considerably from the former ones, is believed to have developed from Chinese stilts. The first Chinese stilts introduced to Japan in the seventh century were made of a single pole with a cross-bar about a foot from the lower end. Holding the pole and standing on the bar, one jumped around. Later came Chinese stilts that were tied to the legs. Chinese stilt dancers appeared in shows in the 17th century.

TEMARI

TEMARI or hand-balls are still popular with Japanese girls. Formerly they were not monopolized by girls alone, as both boys and girls played with the balls.

At first the balls were tossed from one hand to another. After the 13th century, when balls made of cotton and cotton yarn appeared, they began bouncing the balls on the ground. Up to the 17th century all played it outdoors, standing up. But since about that time, girls of the better classes began to play it indoors. Thus they acquired the habit of bouncing the balls on the floor, in a kneeling position. It was thus generally played outdoors in rural districts, and indoors in cities.

During Edo days, *temari* became beautiful, being covered with colored silk threads that formed various bright designs. Furthermore, various different ways of playing with *temari* developed.

Girls still sing *temari-uta* or ball playing songs while bouncing the balls. *Temari-uta* differ according to district, but generally they are very simple, being mainly made up by children, and some are quite meaningless. A typical Tokyo *temari-uta* goes:

'To *Inari-san* on the side lane, I offered one *sen* and quickly worshiping, hurried to *Osen's* teahouse; as I sat down a cup of tea was brought; looked side-ways at the tea, mud-cakes or rice-cakes; there I won one count.'

Generally when one keeps on bouncing the ball until the end of a song, the player wins a point. Many old *temari-uta* are still sung by little girls.

Rubber balls were introduced in the early Meiji years. Of course they are light and bounce better than the old cotton balls. But old-fashioned cotton balls, decorated with silk in colorful designs, are still in demand as they are beautiful.

TOP SPINNING

KOMA-MAWASHI or top spinning is still popular at variety shows and private parties. This form of entertainment is said to have been started by a boy named Hatsutaro of Hakata in Kyushu, who opened in 1700 a show of trick top-spinning in a small hut erected by the Kamo River in Kyoto.

He became instantly famous, and there soon appeared imitators. It was at first known as Hakata *koma-mawashi*. His show so popularized top spinning among boys that in 1701 the government issued an order prohibiting top spinning on the street. It was never

heeded, and the same order had to be reissued in 1710 and 1729.

Professional *koma-mawashi* became so skillful that they needed perfectly balanced tops, and top-making developed to a high level.

Professional performers put tops on long threads stretched across the stage, make them ride sword blades, or spin over their arms, sleeves and shoulders. They spun tops with long slender cords, or again by a simple twist of the hand, and set tops spinning for many hours. They developed new and more difficult tricks, and also introduced short plays to go along with top spinning to draw people.

Tops used are of all sizes, ranging from tiny ones to large tops measuring one, two or even three feet in diameter.

Matsui Gensui, a medicine peddler who adopted top spinning as an attraction to gather crowds at Asakusa, Edo, was the greatest top-spinning genius. On November 13, 1826, when the Shogun visited Asakusa Temple, Gensui was selected to entertain the august person with his top-spinning. The name of Matsui Gensui was held by successive top-spinning masters.

Matsui Gensui XIII, and Matsui Kakujiro were invited to visit the United States to make a tour of that country. They went in 1866 and returned home in 1869 or the second year of Meiji, after a successful trip throughout the United States. Thus Japanese top-spinning came to be known in foreign countries.

TOSEN-KYO

TOSEN-KYO (fan-throwing game) used to be a very popular game among children and women until the end of the 19th century, but today it is only remembered by old people. This game, played with a folding fan, is full of refinement and artistic beauty, and it may be said to be most typical of the people's sentiment, particularly in the Tokugawa period.

The game is played with a *sensu* or folding fan, and a target made in the form of a gingko leaf, set on a little round weight. The target is placed on a box about six inches tall. The goal is to throw the opened fan from a distance of several feet at the target. Each player throws in turn, and the one who brings down the target wins. There is a more complicated way of playing the game, in which different numbers of points are given according to the manner in which the fan and the target fall on the floor.

The game appears simple, but even at a few feet one will find it quite difficult to hit the target. As it can be played in a room, it became a particular favorite with women and children in the old days.

This game of *tosen-kyo* is believed to have been thought up first by one Kisen in the An-ei era (1772-1781), and it soon became popular among the aristocracy. Particularly since the Bunka era (1804-1818), it was played by almost all classes of people. First it was played by women and children, but men also joined in play. With its popularity it began to be used for gambling purposes, and it was once prohibited.

But as an innocent indoor game it continued to be played by women and children until the Meiji era.

TSUNAHIKI

TSUNAHIKI or tug of war is now mostly played as a game or contest. But it was originally a sacred rite performed at shrines, to foretell the year's crop or to pray for a good harvest.

It is still performed in many rural districts for the original purpose and not as a mere athletic contest. In the northeastern provinces it is still held in January as a rite of divination. The district represented by the winning side will have good crops, it is believed in many areas.

In the southern Kyushu region, the ancient *tsunahiki* is still widely held on the evening of the full moon in July or August. It is quite an elaborate and sacred affair. Weeks before the people start to make a new rope with freshly harvested straw.

The rope is made with a long vine as its core; sometimes two ropes, male and female, are made and joined together by passing the male rope through the loop of the female rope. The rope at the thickest point is one to two feet around. When the rope is finished, a boy of 15 is made to sit down in the middle of the coiled rope and bow to the moon.

Two villages, one against the other and called the east side and the west side, hold a *tsunahiki*. Wives take the side of the village from where they came. Thus often there are quarrels between husbands and wives. Children, women and men join in pulling the rope.

The outcome of a *tsunahiki* is said to determine the crop, but generally the winning side is previously decided, so that good crops and happiness will be predicted.

In some districts *tsunahiki* is held in January as a part of the New Year celebration, and again some districts hold it at the May 5 boys' festival. Besides praying for a good harvest, sometimes it is held in appreciation of good crops, or to drive away insects or chase devils away. Often the *tsunahiki* rope is carried through the town, to add further gaiety to the occasion.

TURNING DRUMS

FURITSUZUMI or turning drums are one of the earliest toys of the country and also one of the most charming and beautiful. They are mentioned in *Eiga-monogatari*, a historical tale covering the ninth to 11th centuries. The toy developed from musical drums and is believed to have been introduced from China.

Furitsuzumi, or *furifuri-taiko* as it is called in the Kyoto-Osaka area, is a small, flat and round miniature drum, generally about two inches across, with a wooden handle attached. It is about half an inch thick. From each side of the flat frame hangs a short string, at the end of which is attached a bean.

Placing the handle between the two palms, the drum is revolved by rubbing the hands. The beans strike the drum and produce a soft musical sound.

In the old days, this turning drum used to be the most popular toy for little children, and even today it is sold in rural districts.

Up to the beginning of the 19th century, *furitsuzumi* used to be made of cut bamboo pieces. By cutting a big bamboo sideways, round frames were obtained, and the drums were made by covering them with paper, usually yellow in color.

But later the drum came to be made with paper frames and in Edo days red paper was used for the cover. Also the drums began to be more gaily decorated. A *tomoe* design looking like a big curving comma was painted in the center, and dragons decorated the side.

Their charm lies in the adoption of a drum for a toy, and the ingenious way of turning the handle to make the suspended beans beat the drum and produce the music.

That is why it is still used by little children and remembered tenderly by all grown-ups.

UMA-NO-ASHI

UMA-NO-ASHI (horse's leg) is the popular term for *uma-yaku* or those acting as horses on the *Kabuki* stage. Generally, however, this term is applied to a sham actor. This may have started because the audience never sees the face of an *uma-no-ashi*.

Nevertheless, the role of being the horse's legs is very difficult, and only with hard training of many years can one become a good *uma-no-ashi*.

On the *Kabuki* stage horses appear in many plays, including such famous ones as *Kirihitoha, Shiobara Tasuke, Ichinotani* and others. But no real animal comes on the stage. The *Kabuki* horse has a papier-mâché head and a cloth-covered body built on a wooden frame.

This head and body are carried by two men, the front-leg man and the back-leg man. The man in front puts his head into the horse's head, and he and the back-leg man carry the wooden-frame body on their shoulders and backs. The legs of the two men are clothed in tightfitting cloth trousers.

The front-leg man can see through small openings under the horse's head and moves his head as required. The back-leg man can see only the stage floor, but he must step in accordance with the movement of the front legs. The back-leg man moves the tail.

Carrying another actor upon their shoulders and backs, the *uma-no-ashi* must move as naturally as real horses while following the progress of the play, and so their role is not as easy as it looks.

An actor who is not on good terms with the *uma-no-ashi* is sometimes at the mercy of the *uma-no-ashi* as the 'leg' men do not always follow his commands, thus spoiling the act.

UNDER-ICE FISHING

AT HACHIROGATA, Akita, fish are caught in winter by running nets under the ice that covers the water. Though this fishing method at Hachirogata is famous, it was originally copied from the under-ice fishing done at Lake, Suwa, Nagano Prefecture.

At Suwako, however, this type of fishing is no longer followed as intensive fishing in the early Meiji years has almost exhausted the fish in the lake.

It is recorded that a merchant of Akita named Takakuwa Koshiro visited Lake Suwa in 1794, and studied the unique under-ice fishing there, making many sketches. Returning to Hachirogata, he carried out the first under-ice fishing there. The old method brought by Takakuwa is still followed by Hachirogata fishermen.

For this type of fishing, a large hole is first made in the ice, and at a short distance to the right and left of the hole, small holes are cut out. Rows of many holes at proper intervals are made in an oval curve and reach another big hole on the opposite end.

After the holes are made, one end of a long dragnet is dropped into the first big hole. The current carries it toward the first small hole in one direction. The net is caught by a hook thrust into the first small hole and pulled up. Then the net end is passed into that hole to be carried by the current to the second hole. There the net is again caught and pulled. In this manner the net is drawn under all the small holes in one direction to the opposite big hole.

The other end of the net is passed in a similar manner in the other direction to reach the big end hole. The long net lies under the curved line of the holes. Then the two ends of the net now in the end hole are pulled by several men and women. They pull the net with short ropes which are tied around their waist, walking slowly backward.

A net full of many kinds of fish is finally pulled out from the end hole. It is said that fish are easily caught in this way, because in the cold water they are not very active.

UTA-GARUTA

UTA-GARUTA (poem card) parties are held throughout January in Japanese homes. This game was formerly played only in aristocratic circles, but in the Meiji era it became the foremost social function at which young men and women were given the rare opportunity of meeting and enjoying long evenings together.

It is also called *hyakunin-isshu* (one poem each by one hundred poets), as it is these poems which are written on the cards. This collection of poems was made by Fujiwara Sadaie, a 13th-century poet, by selecting the best poems of 100 outstanding poets.

On one set of 100 cards are written the first half of the poems and on the second set are the last parts of the poems. The game is to find the second card as the reader reads the first half. The second set of cards is divided among those present who lay them down in front of themselves. As the reader, who does not participate in the game, reads from the first set of cards, the players look for the corresponding cards in their lot first, but if it is not there they look for it among the others.

If one should pick up a card in another's lot, he wins a point and gives one of his cards to that person. The person who gets rid of all his cards first wins the game. Sometimes the game is played by groups.

Karuta playing requires considerable skill and memory work. Annually a national championship game is held.

Children have their own *iroha-garuta* (alphabet cards) which consist of two sets, one bearing popular sayings, and another set with pictures illustrating the sayings. As the card is read, the children pick up the corresponding picture card.

There are also *hana-garuta* (flower cards) which have pictures of flowers and natural phenomena of the 12 months of the year.

All these Japanese cards developed from the Western playing cards first brought by the Portuguese, but they have been changed and incorporated with the game of *kai-awase* (shell-matching) which was played by the ancient people. Cards became popular from the beginning of the 16th century.

WAKASAGI FISHING

WAKASAGI fishing is a delightful winter sport in Japan. The fish is similar to *ayu* (a kind of smelt) but smaller, being only about three inches long.

The manner in which it is fished is unique. Fishermen go out on the frozen lakes and with hatchets, break the thick ice to make holes about two feet across. Long lines with several hooks on each are lowered into the holes. When lucky, they feel a slight pull on their lines as soon as they lower them. Four or five *wakasagi* are hooked to the lines.

While most of the fish in the lake are hibernating under the ice, the *wakasagi* is active despite the freezing temperature. Thus even when the lake is covered with ice, *wakasagi* can be caught.

Wakasagi fishers make themselves as comfortable as possible on the ice. They bring portable chairs and erect canvas wind shields to protect themselves from the biting cold wind. But the joy of catching many *wakasagi*

from under the ice makes them forget the cold, and lucky ones catch hundreds in one day.

Usually the fish go down the rivers to the sea after laying eggs. But some *wakasagi* stay in fresh water all the time.

Often the *wakasagi* of one lake are taken to another lake to improve their growth.

It is also caught in the sea by nets. Fishing in this case is done mostly by professional fishermen, and generally only on moonless nights or before the moon rises or after the moon sets. In winter, however, net fishing is done in the daytime.

However, it is in the winter fishing on the frozen lake that *wakasagi* fishing becomes an enjoyable sport. It is said that *wakasagi* tastes best when the freshly caught ones are slightly broiled over a charcoal fire. But they are also eaten fried in oil.

WRESTLING SHOW

IN THE Tokugawa days when professional wrestling became popular, many wrestling shows appeared that presented odd or comical matches for the amusement of the public.

These farcical wrestling shows made their appearance in Edo in about 1745, but they were said to have been popular in Osaka much earlier. The most common shows of this type were given by women wrestlers and blind men.

Women wrestlers attracted much attention because of the novelty of seeing women wrestling half-naked. Some women wrestlers were quite big and strong, but many were also popular because of their beauty. Wrestling by blind men also provoked much amusement, as two sightless men groping for an opponent in the ring was quite a comical sight.

Matches between a woman and a blind man were staged in many places. But when such a show was opened at Asakusa Temple, the Bakufu authorities closed it on the ground that the matches had immoral features. Several blind men appeared in the ring against one woman wrestler and went through various comic acts.

Besides these, other strange wrestling matches were staged. A match between a woman and a sheep was held at Ryogoku and Shiba Shimmei Shrine, Edo, in the Kansei period, 1789-1801. In 1822 at Nagoya a woman wrestled with a bear.

At Osaka and Edo, the matches between women and blind men continued to be very popular, with many shows running for several months.

At first women wrestlers had their hair done up in the usual women's styles, which were known as *shimada* and *marumage*. But in Osaka, from 1848, women wrestlers styled their hair similarly to male wrestlers.

After the Meiji Restoration, wrestling matches between men and women were prohibited by a law issued on March 19, 1872.

YOKOZUNA

YOKOZUNA is the highest rank in *sumo* — Japanese wrestling. It differs however, from the championship title in Western sports. A *yokozuna* retains his title until he retires, regardless of his tournament results. If there is none worthy of the honor, there is no *yokozuna*. There can be more than one *yokozuna* at a time.

The first *yokozuna* in history was Akashi Shiganosuke of the Kan-ei era, 1624-1644.

Yokozuna is so named because he wears as the emblem of his rank a *yokozuna* (horizontal rope) around his body when he makes formal appearances. The heavy rope is made of twisted hemp, and generally weighs about 60 pounds. It is decorated with cut paper.

The tradition of *yokozuna* is said to have come from the ancient *'Musubi-no-kami-no-o'* (tied *kami*'s rope which was used in offering prayers to *kami*). It is recorded that Empress Jingu (170-269) tied *'musubi-no-kami-no-o'* over her clothes to pray for health and the success of her Korean expedition.

The same rope came to be used by ancient wrestlers at matches held for shrines. Originally, *sumo* matches were sacred and were performed at shrine festivals to entertain *kami*. At these shrine matches, wrestlers wore the hemp cord decorated with cut paper.

A *yokozuna* still wears his rope only when he makes a formal or ceremonial appearance, and never on any other occasion.

The Yoshida family of Kumamoto still has the traditional authority to confer the honor of *yokozuna* on wrestlers. The Sumo Association recommends one to the Yoshida family, and then the formal announcement of giving the *yokozuna* rank to that wrestler is made.

YOSE

YOSE or Japanese-type houses are becoming fewer, but are still very popular among both old and young people. The *yose* are a product of Edo, and were the sole popular amusement houses in Edo and the early Meiji years.

Yose are said to have been started by Seizaemon Akamatsu at Asakusa in the Genroku era (1688-1704) for storytellers who became quite popular at that time. *Yose* implies 'to gather people' and the first was named *yose-seki* or gathering place.

Yose houses were originally constructed with a raised platform about 15 to 20 feet square, before which the people sat on *tatami*. Story-telling, singing, dancing, music, acrobatic acts, juggling and other forms of amusement made up the *yose* program.

Under the retrenchment reform of Tenpo started by Lord Mizuno in 1838, the number of *yose* was reduced to 15 in the whole of Edo. However, when he was removed from his post about 10 years later, the number suddenly rose to more than 300, proving how eager the Edo people were to have *yose* amusements.

The introduction of motion pictures drew the public away from *yose*. Moreover, all Tokyo *yose* houses, excepting Suehiro at Ningyo-cho only, were destroyed by bombing and fire during the Pacific war. Today there are about 30 in the metropolis. Suzumoto at Ueno is the oldest and largest now, having been first opened in 1876, and rebuilt after the Pacific war into a steel-concrete structure, with a total seating capacity of 362. The first floor of the house is made in Western-style with seats, but the second floor is covered with *tatami*, and must leave their shoes and *geta* at the entrance.

At all other *yose* except one, the people still have to take off their footwear and sit down on *tatami*. It is said that *yose*-goers do not feel at home unless they sit down on *tatami*.

They can rent *futon* or cushions. Ashtrays are provided, and women selling sweets and soft drinks walk through the seated audience. In many other ways, the *yose* still retains Edo traditions.

YOTSUTAKE

YOTSUTAKE (four bamboos) are Japanese castanets, though they are seldom used now. Four flat bamboo pieces generally about one by two inches long are used. One piece is tied by a string to the thumb, and another to the middle finger. By bringing the thumbs and the fingers of both hands together, the bamboo pieces click and produce a sharp sound. *Yotsutake* are used to mark time in dancing and singing.

These castanets are believed to have developed from the Chinese music board. They became popular first in the Okinawa islands where they are still widely used by girls in singing and dancing. Then they were introduced to Kyushu. It is said *yotsutake* came to be used in this country early in the 17th century. One record says that they were first brought to Edo from Nagasaki in 1652. They immediately became popular in Edo and began to be used together with *shamisen* and other musical instruments. Strolling singers in particular used *yotsutake*, in addition to music by *shamisen* players.

Yotsutake were heard on the streets and other places until the early years of Meiji, but they are seldom used today. Modern people only know of them as mentioned in Edo tales and literature.

In Okinawa, girls must have *yotsutake* when they sing or dance even today. But in Edo the bamboo clappers were never used in the same way as in Okinawa.

Western castanets are now used. The people seem to have forgotten their own *yotsutake*.

Chapter 14
Religious Rites

AIZENMYO-O

CUPID, the Roman god of love, is represented as a little boy carrying a bow and arrow. Venus is also shown in delicate, slender and endearing forms. But the Japanese god of love is shown in quite a different form. In fact, from its appearance, one would never think of it as relating to love.

Aizenmyo-o, the god of love, is usually represented by a statue painted red all over, with three faces and three pairs of arms. He came from India where he is known as Raga. Originally he is to fight avarice, to speedily destroy evil thoughts of the people, and thus to make them attain enlightenment.

Three faces and three pairs of arms appear rather coquettish on the god of love. But with three pairs of eyes, ears and hands, one may see better, select more wisely, and know better. It is probably for such reasons that Aizenmyo-o has three faces and three pairs of arms.

But the whole statue being red all over appears rather hideous, and it has no features of sweetness or loveliness. It is indeed strange that such a statue is selected to represent the god of love. But love comes from the most unexpected quarters, and Aizenmyo-o may thus be right after all.

This god of love came with Buddha from India, and at first he was only worshiped by families which believed in Buddhism. It was much later that Aizenmyo-o came to be generally regarded as the god of love. One may often see Aizenmyo-o placed in Buddhist temples where however, he appears quite out of place, especially as the people rarely associate love in connection with Buddhist temples.

AMACHA

IT IS MAINLY because of *amacha* or sweet tea that children look forward to April 8, when Buddha's birthday is celebrated at Buddhist temples throughout the country. Though *amacha* was popularly used daily in ancient days, of late it is on Buddha's birthday that children come to first learn its taste and then annually look forward to April 8.

The birthday of Buddha is celebrated at all temples, but the main feature of the celebration is *kanbutsu* or the rite of pouring *amacha* over Buddha statues. On that day, a temporary temple decorated with blossoms, called *hana-mido* or flower temple, is erected in the compounds of each temple. Within *hana-mido* is placed the *Tanjo-butsu* or the statue of Buddha at his birth.

It is traditionally said that, upon his birth, Buddha stood erect, walked a few steps and then loudly shouted, 'I am my own Lord throughout heaven and earth.' The *Tanjo-butsu* is sculptured according to this traditional tale. Baby

Buddha stands erect with one hand raised toward heaven and the other toward the earth, and is about to make his birth declaration.

In front of the statue are placed tubs of *amacha* or sweet tea, and worshipers coming there pour the tea over the head of the statue with a small dipper. The temple also gives the tea to worshipers who take it home to be partaken of by their family members. The drinking of the tea given by temples on Buddha's birthday will not only stimulate their religious faith, but will also ensure good health, it is believed.

The sweet tea is made of the leaves of *amacha* (Hydrangea hortensis), a bush abundantly found in mountainous regions. The leaves are steamed and then dried, after which they are put in hot water to make the sweet tea. The leaves as well as the sweet juice obtained by brewing the leaves were extensively used for sweetening purposes in ancient days, before the introduction of sugar. After the coming of sugar, however, it was forgotten except on Buddha's birthday.

The *kanbutsu-e* or the ceremony of bathing Buddha's statue on April 8 was first performed at the Genkoji Temple, Yamato Province, in the 14th year of Empress Regnant Suiko, 606. With the rapid spread of the Indian faith among the people, it is natural that the observation of Buddha's birthday as a religious event of the year has become popular throughout the country.

At first, however, it is recorded that either a perfume water or the sweet tea was used in bathing Buddha's statue on April 8. But sometime later, the use of perfumes apparently was abandoned due to the overwhelming popularity of the sweet tea. It is probably due to its sweet taste that *amacha* has thus become the main feature of the birthday celebration and worship of Buddha.

ASHURA

ASHURA is the king of Ashura (Asura), the land of punishment, where all those who died fostering angry thoughts or enmity against others, descend. It is not, therefore, a beautiful or comfortable place. It is one of many places which all people avoid going to after death, and they are not fond of Ashura who rules over this unpleasant territory.

Ashura is fittingly described as the king of Ashura. He is a large person, and naturally possesses a big appetite, but is always hungry and cannot even stand erect because of his empty stomach. It is a miserable condition for any big man to always go hungry, and fate has made Ashura unable to have a full stomach. And probably on account of his being always hungry, he is angry at everything, and his anger leads him to quarrels and fights.

He knows no happiness or any contentment. Spurred by his hunger and anger, he picks quarrels with everything and everyone.

It is natural then that he is hated and dreaded by all people of heaven as well as those of this mortal world.

He is the king of hunger, anger and quarrels, and stands for meanness, cruelty, misery and wickedness. His name has became an adjective to describe conditions of wars and battlefields, desperate craving for necessities, and the wicked meanness of heartless people.

No one loves him, as he loves none; everyone hates him as he is angry at everyone else. He is hungry, and is therefore mad at his hunger. He picks quarrels as he cannot be friendly with anyone.

But with his own miserable conditions, he teaches the mass of people what sort of life awaits them in the land of Ashura if they go there after death. One must refrain from being angry at other people, if he does not want to be as Ashura and taste his misery.

BOILING-WATER RITE

THE ANCIENT custom of having a huge iron kettle with boiling water at a shrine festival is still kept up at many shrines, but its original significance is almost forgotten.

In the old days, the kettle of boiling water was very important, and in many shrines there still remains in the shrine building a special unfloored space where the kettle was placed. But today, the kettle is brought out and placed in the shrine garden temporarily at festival time.

The boiling water represented the power or wish of the *kami*, it was originally believed. The rite of boiling water was solemnly performed. The priest cut a branch of bamboo or some other tree, and dipped it into the boiling water. With the branch he scattered the drops of hot water over the worshipers who gathered around him. The dipping and scattering of the hot water were repeated many times, until all the fine clothes of the worshipers were dampened with the hot drops.

It was a service at which the people were told to listen to the words of *kami*, and at the same time, it was a form of purification.

Later, this rite came to possess a feature of fortune-telling. The people would tell their fortunes by the sound of the boiling water which differed in tone and pitch according to the weather and fire temperature. There also developed a belief that, if one was pure of heart, one would never be scorched even by putting one's hand into the boiling water of the shrine kettle.

It was from this belief that boiling water was sometimes later used to test the innocence or guilt of crime suspects.

BONFIRES

BONFIRES are built in shrine or temple compounds on festival days. Originally they were meant to invite and welcome *kami* or the divine spirit, but later they became a special feature to brighten the festival and entertain visitors. In many districts people still tell their fortunes by festival bonfires and their smoke. They watch the direction in which the flame and smoke sway or how high they rise, telling their fortunes by locally set rules. In the old days bonfires were particularly numerous in shrine gardens on festival evenings as there was no other lighting method.

At some shrines or temples, enormously big bonfires with piles of wood reaching 20 or more feet high are burned on festival days. Or huge torchlike wood-piles, standing 40 or 50 feet high are burned. Festivals where there are huge bonfires are commonly called *hi-matsuri* or fire festivals. The *hi-matsuri* at Yoshida on the slope of Mt. Fuji or at Togakushi, Nagano Prefecture, are particularly picturesque and impressive as the towering flames rise bright and high against the dark forests surrounding the shrines.

The custom of burning bonfires at shrines on *Toji* or day of winter solstice which comes in the latter part of December is still observed in many parts of the country. This is to urge the early coming of spring.

Bonfires are also used by the people when they pray for rain whenever a long drought continues. Carrying wood to the top of a high mountain nearby, they set them on fire while they pray for rain.

BUDDHIST ROSARIES

JUZU OR *ZUZU*, Buddhist rosaries, have 108 beads, symbolizing the 108 worldly sins. One moves each bead in prayer to be saved from committing the particular evil it stands for. Thus the original and proper use of *juzu* is to touch or move each bead with the prayer of *Namu-amidabutsu* (May the soul rest in peace).

For common use, however, there are also shorter *juzu*, with only 54, 27 or even 14 beads. Many persons do not follow the original custom of turning or touching *juzu* beads, and only hold *juzu* over joined hands, palm to palm, raised in front in prayer. For this the shorter ones are more convenient, and the long ones are sometimes wound twice over the joined hands.

When the service of *hyakuman-ben* (1 million prayers) is held at temples, a hugh *juzu* measuring 50 or 60 feet, with beads as big as four or five inches in diameter, is sometimes used. Those gathered for the service sit in a circle in a big temple room, or around a Buddha statue. The big *juzu* is placed on their laps, and with each chant of *Namu-amidabutsu*, everyone moves the bead on his or her lap to the next person. This service sometimes continues all night.

It is also recorded that the Chion-in Temple of Kyoto used a giant *juzu* with 1,080 or 10 times the number in an ordinary *juzu*, in holding a million-prayer service.

Juzu beads are generally made of iron, copper and gold alloy, crystal, coral, amber, glass, various kinds of hard and fragrant wood, and many other materials. Kyoto is the center of *juzu* manufacture, and many are very elaborately made and are quite expensive.

DAIKOKU-SAN

THE WORSHIP of *Daikoku-san*, so popular among the Japanese, is a mixture of Buddhist and Shinto traditions.

Daikokuten (Mahakala) is an Indian deity who was originally the god of war, but came to be regarded as the guardian deity protecting Buddha and his teaching. Mahakala is also commonly worshiped by Indians as their kitchen god and stands for happiness and prosperity.

Priest Saicho, who went to China to study Buddhism in 804, gave a prayer to Daikokuten or Mahakala at Hieizan, Kyoto, upon his return, it is recorded. Thus the Indian deity of happiness and prosperity and the guardian of Buddhism was introduced to the Japanese.

But the image of this Indian deity soon came to be merged with Okuninushi-no-Mikoto, the ruler of the Izumo district in mythological days, in whose honor the shrine of Izumo still stands. This happened from the fact that both Daikokuten and Okuninushi are worshiped as gods of happiness and prosperity, and commonly both are represented as smiling old men.

Daikoku-san is included in the seven gods of good fortune as the god of happiness and prosperity. He is usually represented as a smiling old man, sitting on rice bales and carrying a small mallet in his right hand and a bag in the left.

There is also quite a large group of persons who worship Daikoku as the savior of humans. Thus Daikoku worship is often regarded as one of the popular religions. It is believed that by worshiping Daikoku they will be saved from evil and crime, and will have good fortune and happiness.

According to the worship of Daikoku, the mallet in Daikoku's hand represents the happiness of workers, and the bag contains wisdom and patience. Daikoku teaches all workers the joy of working, and also to be always smiling and patient.

This simple faith in *Daikoku-san* appeals to many persons, particularly the working class, who form groups for worship in many districts.

DAINICHI–NYORAI

DAINICHI-NYORAI (Mahavariocana) is compared to the great shining sun, because he is reputed to bless the world as the sun warms every corner of the earth. His other name is Birushana, but he is more commonly known as Dainichi-nyorai, because Dainichi implies 'great sun' and so typically illustrates his virtues and blessings given to all living beings.

When Buddhism was introduced to Japan it was well received by the Court, and has thus become the national religion of the country. Shintoism was before that time the religion of the people. But there occurred no rivalry between the two, and the native cult went hand in hand with the Indian faith.

This was because the people believed that Dainichi-nyorai and Amaterasu-Omi-kami were the same, one being the incarnation of the other. Both were symbolized by the great shining sun, and both were known to bestow their blessings to all people under them as the sun shines on everything. Thus Buddhism and Shintoism became one and the same teaching to the people. The two faiths were connected, and further brought together by this belief.

It was during this period that Dainichi-nyorai became so widely known throughout the country. If there were no Dainichi-nyorai, the people of Japan might not have welcomed Buddhism so warmly as they did, and the followers of Shintoism might have strongly opposed the preaching of the foreign faith as a strange cult of 'foreign devils.'

Dainichi-nyorai thus has done much in propagating the Buddhist faith in Japan, and in that sense his blessings are as universal and far-reaching as the rays of the great sun.

DANCING RELIGION

ODORU-SHUKYO or dancing religion has now become very popular among some classes of the people, but this new postwar 'faith' has no connection whatever with Buddhism or any other recognized religion.

However, Japanese Buddhism has had dancing sects since the end of the 16th century. It is recorded that in the era of Keicho, some Buddhist priests and others wearing Buddhist costumes gathered together and, beating bells and drums, they danced while loudly singing Buddhist songs.

It was called *Odori-nenbutsu* and first started in Kyoto. It appealed to the people and at the beginning of the 18th century, it spread not only to Edo, but also to many rural districts. Through the Tokugawa days and Meiji era, it was eagerly kept up by Buddhist enthusiasts throughout the country.

Generally speaking, Buddhist services are gloomy and solemn, but *Odori-nenbutsu* or *Nenbutsu-ko*, as it is sometimes called, is cheerful, active and enjoyable to the people. Though it started in Kyoto, it later became so popular with rural people that it finally became a sort of social function, particularly for elderly folks of rural villages.

In most rural districts, *Nenbutsu-ko* are held either at Buddhist temples or at the houses of believers. From time to time they gather together to enjoy an evening of dancing with the chanting of songs and beating of drums and bells. They then engage in gossiping over cups of tea and some frugal refreshments.

Older people who have no occasion to indulge in amusement find the *Odori-nenbutsu* a great treat, while also appreciating its religious significance. However, it may be said that the religious side of the affair is now almost forgotten by all.

EBISU-SAMA

EBISU, one of the *Shichifukujin* or seven gods of good fortune, is widely worshiped as the god of wealth, but there is another *Ebisu-sama* who is also popularly worshiped in many local districts. This *Ebisu*, of course, has no connection whatever with the *Ebisu* of *Shichifukujin*. It seems to derive from an older idea than the seven gods of good fortune.

In some districts in the central part of the country, *tano-kami* or god of the farm was called *Ebisu*. Ancient hunters of Iwate in the northeastern region called monkeys *Ebisu*. In many seashore districts, stones fished out from the sea were also worshiped as *Ebisu*.

Thus in the old days, various things the local people worshiped seem to have been called by the name of *Ebisu*.

In Kagoshima, Kyushu, there was a custom of boat owners and young men jumping into the sea blindfolded at the beginning of the fishing season and coming up with stones from the sea bottom. They worshiped these stones as symbols of *Ebisu-sama*.

In some places, when women divers enter into the sea, or fishermen start to drop their fishing lines, they shout 'Ebisu,' in prayer for good catches.

Such customs prove that they believe *Ebisu-sama* to be a deity who brings them good luck in fishing.

Anything they fished out of the sea, or any drifting article they found on the sea was also regarded as a symbol of their *Ebisu-sama*.

Thus it is presumed that the belief in this type of *Ebisu* originated among fishermen and people of seaside districts. But this belief was gradually followed by the inland people, who came to consider *Ebisu-sama* as the guardian deity of their trade or work.

ENKIRI-DERA

TOKEIJI TEMPLE at Kita-Kamakura is generally known as Enkiri-dera or divorce temple, because in the old days any wife could obtain a divorce merely by going to the temple.

The nunnery is said to have been originally erected by Mino-no-tsubone, aunt of Minamoto Yoritomo who established the Kamakura military regime in 1192. But it was Kakuzan-zenni, wife of Hojo Tokimune, who made it a refuge for wives suffering under the tyranny of husbands.

Soon after the death of Tokimune in 1284, his widow became a nun and took the name of Kakuzan-zenni. She saw many wives having to live an unhappy life, unable to be separated from their cruel husbands. She thus proposed to the *Bakufu* a system of suffering wives obtaining divorce by entering the nunnery for three years. Her wish was not granted immediately. When her son Sadatoki became regent, her appeal was sent to the Imperial Court, and Emperor Go-Uda approved her plan.

Suddenly Tokeiji became famous and important. It was guarded by Court officials, and even called Matsugaoka Palace.

If a wife wanted to escape from the bondage of marriage, the only thing she had to do was to run into the nunnery compounds, which no authority could enter. It was commonly said that, when she threw one of her wooden clogs within the temple gate, none could touch her.

Wives entering the nunnery had to lead a Buddhist life for three years, and were not allowed to step outside the gate. But if a compromise was reached with their former husbands, they were permitted to leave. Of course after three years, they were free to marry again. Later the period was reduced to two years.

It is recorded that annually 70 to 80 wives entered the nunnery.

Many noble women entered the nunnery, and among the head nuns there were a daughter of Emperor Godaigo and a daughter of Toyotomi Hideyori.

ENMA-DAIO

'IF YOU TELL a lie, *Enma-sama* will come and pull out your tongue,' children were formerly told by their mothers. To many Japanese children, Enma is still a dreadful monster as it has been commonly said that Enma is the master of Hades or the judge of the after-world.

Enma or *Enma-Daio* (Great King Enma) as he is more commonly called, is originally the Yamaraja of Indian mythology. He is said to be the first human who died, and is the guide in the after-life who leads the spirit of the dead to paradise to meet old relatives and friends.

But in Japan, Enma is regarded as one who travels all over the world urging all humans to die. He is also the judge who decides the destiny of the dead, whether they go to heaven or Hades. He is at the same time the keeper of those who are sent to Hades, and it is his task to torture all prisoners as punishment.

January 16 and July 16, by the lunar calendar, are the only days in the whole year when Enma rests from his duty. Thus, the people thought that on those days the spirits of the dead would return to their former homes. From this idea also originated the old system of giving servants and apprentices holidays on those two days.

Thus, Enma is regarded as a fearful being, but on the other hand there are many Enma statues which are worshiped by the people. Enma is generally represented as a figure possessing a fierce-looking face, glaring eyes and open mouth. Yet this fierce-looking statue is worshiped for mercy and help.

EYE-OPENING SERVICE

WHEN A Buddhist picture or sculpture is completed, a *kaigen-kugyo* or eye-opening service is held. It is a rite to install soul into the statue or picture.

The eyes are already painted in the picture, or carved in the statue, but the eye-opening service is required to make it worthy of worship. At the service, a painting brush is passed over the Buddha's eyes in a symbolic act of painting them. It is not definitely known how this custom originated. Eyes are regarded as the 'windows of the soul,' and by opening them, the soul is activated to reach others, it is said.

When the famous Daibutsu or Great Buddha of Todaiji, Nara, was completed 12 centuries ago, an elaborate *kaigen* mass was held with the attendance of thousands of priests and the general public. It is also recorded that numerous colored threads were attached to the eye-opening brush, and worshipers took hold of these threads to become one with Buddha.

The eye-opening service is also observed as a popular custom. Papier-mâché *daruma* or stubby legless dolls that stand upright, in whatever position they are put down, are sold. The dolls come in all sizes, and are made after the famous Indian priest Dharma who is reputed to have lost his legs after sitting on a stone for many years in meditation. The *daruma* dolls are symbols of good luck, and are fondly kept in many homes. They are also toys for children.

Some *daruma* dolls have no eyes painted in. They are purchased in the hope of some good fortune. When the desired fortune comes, the owner paints one eye in and with another bit of good luck the second eye is painted. In this way the *daruma's* eyes are finally opened.

FAMILY SHRINES

EVERY MORNING, many Japanese, particularly old folks, bow before *kamidana* or family shrines and clap their hands together in prayer for good luck and divine protection. On the first and 15th days of each month, *sake* and fresh branches of *sakaki* (Euryaochnacea) are offered.

Kamidana literally means a sacred shelf. It was called also *kamibako*, sacred box, in the old days. Thus it was originally a shelf or box where the sacred tablet of the Grand Shrine of Ise and other local shrines were kept. This custom of every household having its *kamidana* is believed to have originated with the nationwide distribution of the Ise Shrine tablets. But sacred tablets issued by other shrines also came to be placed together.

In most houses, *kamidana* is still only a plain wooden shelf placed high in one corner of a room, so that the tablet will not be soiled or handled by children. But in many old houses, especially in rural districts, magnificent *kamidana*, often measuring six feet high, five feet wide, and three feet deep are found.

Such *kamidana* are made in the style of shrine architecture, but there are several distinctly different types.

It is most interesting to note that many households have both *kamidana* and *butsudan* (Buddhist altars), sometimes even in the same room. In the mind of the common Japanese, the worship of the shrine or local deities does not interfere with their faith in Buddha.

This old custom of Japan seems to remain despite the people's loss of faith in many ancient traditions, as is proved by the continued sales of *kamidana* shrines at department stores and other shops.

At first a temporary shrine was made at home for special worship or ceremonies. *Kamidana* developed after Buddhism brought *butsudan* or family altars into the home.

As the family shrine is dedicated to various different *kami*, different names are used according to the deities enshrined. For instance there are *Taijingu-dana*, *Yebisu-dana*, *Kojin-dana*, *Toshitoku-dana*, and others. The *Taijingu-dana* is the *kamidana* having the tablet of the Grand Shrine of Ise.

To the *kamidana* the family not only presents *omiki* and *sakaki*, but also rice, fruits and other offerings. The *kamidana* is lighted at night. Formerly the light for the *kamidana* had to be made with flint and stone, as other fires and lighting were considered unclean. But recently, with the advent of matches, the *kamidana* lights are generally lighted with matches. Again, with the popular use of electricity, the custom of giving light to the *kamidana* has mostly been discarded.

It is customary to worship at the family shrine particularly on New Year's Day and the first day of every month for the purpose of praying for happiness and prosperity during the year or the month.

Kamidana are placed high near the

ceiling, as they are sacred and should not be touched by children or spoiled by dirt. Nothing is allowed to be placed above them. This accounts for the reason why, in two-storied houses of the common people, there developed a custom of placing on the ceiling above the *kamidana* a piece of paper marked with the character *'kumo'* or clouds, to indicate that above the clouds there is nothing. This was done to ease the minds of the people of the house who have to go upstairs, walk or sleep above the *kamidana.*

Furthermore, when a death occurs in the house, a piece of white paper is placed in front of the *kamidana,* as anything dead is impure and the fact and news of the death must be kept from the *kami.*

FISHERMEN'S EBISU

FISHERMEN worship *Ebisu,* one of the seven gods of fortune as their guardian deity. *Ebisu* is represented as a fat smiling man carrying a big fish and a pole. It is customary with many fishermen to offer their first catch of the year to *Ebisu-sama.* When they launch new boats or at the beginning of the fishing season they pray to *Ebisu.*

But in many districts, the fishermen's *Ebisu* is not the same *Ebisu* of the seven gods of fortune, but a deity to bring them a good catch or a deity that rose from the sea. In some places whales or sharks are called *Ebisu.* Some fishermen call even foreigners *Ebisu.* In such cases *Ebisu* seems to mean something strange or something that came out of the sea.

In worshiping *Ebisu,* the fishing villages of Kyushu and other parts have a strange custom. A boy of about 10 who has both parents alive is selected. He is blindfolded and made to dive into the sea. Reaching the sea bottom, he must locate a small stone and bring it

up. A young man, also blindfolded, receives the stone and carries it to an *Ebisu* shrine.

There the stone is worshiped as *Ebisu-sama.* The stone which is already placed in the shrine is pushed into a corner to give the fresh stone the central position.

When a poor fish catch continues, a fresh stone must be obtained. So the shrine has many old stones which, however, are never thrown out or treated carelessly.

As *Ebisu* is believed to possess the power to bring good catches of fish, floats tied to the nets are called Ebisu in many fishing villages.

FIVE HUNDRED RAKAN

IF YOU WISH to see a face that looks exactly like yours, you will find it among the statues of *Gohyaku-rakan* or the 500 *rakan,* it is said. *Rakan* (Arhanarhat) is the title given to enlightened Buddhist priests, and 500 of them gathered at Rajagiha to hold the first conference to compile the teachings of Sakyamuni after his death. Thus the *Gohyaku-rakan* have become famous, and their statues are placed at many temples.

As the statues are made to represent the 500 different *rakan,* each has a distinctly different facial expression. If anyone examines them closely, he may find a face that he desires to see. In Tokyo, the *Gohyaku-rakan* of Rakanji located at Shimo-Meguro are famous. This temple was erected in 1699 originally at Honjo by Kei-sho-in, mother of the fifth Tokugawa shogun, Tsunayoshi. The statues were made by Genkei, a Buddhist sculptor of Kyoto who later became a priest. In Tokyo, however, only about 380 statues are left. Also, there are often pictures or statues showing a group of 16 *rakan* who pledged to live permanently in this world and save humanity. They are mostly found in mountainous regions.

The 1,000 statues of Sanjusangen-do in Kyoto, are world-famous. However, they represent the *Senju Kannon* (Saharabhuja-Saharanetra-Avalokitesvara) or *Kannon* with 1,000 arms, and there are said to be no two exactly alike in facial expression. Each statue has 1,000 arms, and in each palm is an eye. The 1,000 arms, palms and eyes represent the boundless blessings of *Kannon.*

FUDO

THERE IS NO statue that is so fierce-looking and grotesque as the Fudo statue. Its features are not only awe-inspiring, but full of anger. But the virtue of Fudo lies in its grotesque countenance. Its duty is to subdue and conquer devils. From what we hear about devils, we realize that only one that has such a fierce expression and such anger as Fudo could be able to conquer them.

Fudo is often represented with two of his assistants, one on each side. Fudo (Acala) is the incarnation of Dainichi-nyorai (Mahavairocana).

Fudo is often represented as having the power to withstand fire and water, and its statues and pictures show it standing over burning flames. Not only does it represent righteousness, but it also represents physical strength.

At many temples to Fudo, the ceremony of *mizu-gori* (water-purification) is performed. Pious people pray there, pouring buckets and buckets of water over their heads. It is usually done in the coldest period of winter, as it requires more strength and determination to perform the rite on a cold night.

Again in many compounds of Fudo temples there are waterfalls, and peo-

ple sit under the falls for hours, praying for the purification of mind and body.

Formerly Fudo fought only devils and its worship was to cleanse the minds of people, but recently it has become possessed of many other virtues. Some Fudo are said to enable one to win at gambling and in stock-deals.

Fudo is one of the most popular deities believed by the people to bring luck and fortune.

GAN-KAKE

THE CUSTOM of *gan-kake* or prayer offering, for curing sickness, bringing good harvests, leading a happier life, or having good luck is quite old. But at first in Japan, such prayers were mostly a community affair, and individual prayers were few.

When a person became sick, the whole village joined in prayer for his recovery, each family sending one representative to perform *gan-kake*. Many fishing villages had the custom of all residents going to the seashore and picking up small stones. Carrying the stones in their hands, they proceeded to their shrine to pray.

The rain prayer or prayer for driving away insects, still held in many farming districts, retains the ancient community-prayer custom.

Often the whole village stayed at their shrine overnight to offer prayers. Even when individual prayers became more common, the custom of staying at the shrine was kept up.

Nissan (daily visit), *ohyakudo* (100 visits) or *mizu-gori* (water ablution prayer) also developed, to be held by groups or individuals. Prayers were also offered by going naked to the shrine or fasting. Such methods of prayer offering are still kept up by many.

In the old days, when the people offered their prayers, they used to present to the shrines or temples their hair, bottomless wooden dippers, stones with holes, seashells, food bowls and other things. Such offerings are now replaced by foodstuffs or money.

When their prayers were answered, they went to the shrines or temples to express their thanks, taking various offerings. In some districts it was customary for a man and wife to go together, or the head of the family went with his son. When the prayer offered concerned a horse, that horse had to be taken to the shrine to show its appreciation.

There was also a custom of asking the priest of the shrine, the monk of the temple, or professional supplicants to offer prayers in place of the persons desiring to make prayers.

GATE GUARDS

AT THE ENTRANCES of many Shinto shrines and Buddhist temples there are statues of huge gate guards. These wood sculptures are housed in gate buildings which are often magnificent and towering structures.

The guard gate of a Shinto shrine is called *Zuishin-mon. Zuishin* were the ancient Court guards who were detailed to guard the Emperor, princes and high officials. So the guard figures at the shrine are made after those ancient officials and dressed in Court costume, carrying swords, bows and arrow-holders. They always come in pairs, one standing at each side of the entranceway, to protect the shrine from evil and wrong-doers.

These shrine guards are commonly called *yadai-jin* (arrow minister) and *sa-daijin* (left minister), but the titles have no meaning, though they are popularly used. The arrow minister might have been so called as an honorific term for

an armed guard in Court costume, but to call the other guard 'left minister' is incomprehensible, because the *sa-daijin* or left minister was the second highest official in the Court and would never have taken up guard duty.

The guard gate at a Buddhist temple is called *Nio-mon* or Deva gate, because of the statues of two Deva kings. These guards are fierce-looking, massive men with glaring eyes. The one on the right has his mouth closed, but the left one's mouth is open. The figures with open and closed mouths are said to stand for *'a-un'* (inspiration and expiration) that also signify the beginning and end, or the positive and negative.

According to Buddhist tradition, Deva stands for the power of wisdom that protects Buddha. But the *Ni-o* or Deva statues standing at the gate of a Buddhist temple look so strong and fierce that they protect the temple and its worshipers through their physical strength and not by wisdom.

That the guard figures were regarded important may be judged by the effort put into having finely sculptured ones made and housing them in imposingly constructed and beautifully decorated gate buildings.

GOHEI

GOHEI or *nusa* originally meant offerings to *kami*, and representing offerings, they came to be used in praying to *kami*. Later, *Gohei* were also used in purifying persons and other things, and it is in this latter sense that they are now generally used. *Gohei* are commonly strips of white paper tied to a wooden stick or bamboo.

At first, the offering to *kami* consisted mostly of flax yarns. *Fusa* (flax) is said to have been changed to *nusa*. Flax yarns later were generally replaced by woven fabrics, but as time went on, the things offered to *kami* changed gradually. There came to be used not only flax and silk fabrics, but also clothing, paper, jewels, arms, coins and other things.

For convenience and also because white stood for purity, white paper became the common offering to *kami*. Strips of white paper were tied to a stick or bamboo and offered to *kami* or shrines. Often the paper was dyed in five different colors. This is the origin of the present day *gohei*.

Then there were used *shohei* (small *gohei*). Paper, rice and sometimes silk fabrics were cut into minute particles, and these were offered to *kami*. These *shohei* were mostly used for spreading over the road when one was travelling in order to ensure safety and comfort on journeys. It is said that, as ordinary *gohei* were inconvenient to carry on journeys, the cut paper, rice and silk were carried on trips, and offered to *kami*.

Today, these early uses of *gohei* and *shohei* have mostly disappeared, and *gohei* are now used by Shinto priests in purifying visitors and other things. It signifies that, by making offerings to *kami*, prayers are offered to make visitors or other things pure and clean.

Gohei represent a development of praying for purification by making offerings to *kami*.

GOMA RITE

AT MANY Buddhist temples of the Shingon and Tendai sects the rite of *goma* burning is held. This consists of burning prayer sticks at the temples. *Goma* (*homa*) is the fire rite to burn all roots of carnal desire.

The rite differs according to sect and temple, but generally speaking a person desiring to offer a special prayer for his health and welfare goes to a temple holding the *goma* rite, and pays a certain fee for the service. A flat wooden stick, 1 cm wide and 30 cm long, made of cedar or *nurunoki* (sumac), is given him. On the stick he writes his name and the outline of his prayer.

But at temples where many persons offer *goma* prayers, they have prayer sticks already printed with such common prayers as *Shinganjoju* (realization of wish) or *Mubyosokusai* (perfect health). Then one only has to write his name on the stick.

The chief priest of the temple burns the prayer sticks offered by visitors in the temple building with a prayer. Many big temples have separate halls for the *goma* rite, called *goma-do*. Often the priest waits until a proper number of prayer sticks are collected to start the burning.

But at big temples to where many persons come daily to offer *goma* prayers, the burning is held several times a day according to fixed schedules. Thus those offering the prayer may choose their time of going to the temples so that their prayer sticks will be burned in their presence.

The inside and outside of many *goma-do* are black from the dense smoke rising from the daily burning of prayer sticks. To watch the red flames consuming their own prayer sticks in the hall dark with the heavy smoke, is to the believers an experience that gives them the satifying assurance that their prayers will be answered and their souls purified of all evil thoughts.

GOOD-LUCK COINS

VISITING temples or shrines, the Japanese offer coins before saying their prayers. The coins are offered as a charm to bring good luck, and in many cases they constitute a major portion of the revenue of shrines and temples.

Such offerings, however, are comparatively modern. In the old days visitors offered handfuls of rice, wrapped up in paper. This custom represented the farmer's thanks for a good crop and also prayer for another. But as coins are regarded as a good-luck charm and more convenient, they gradually replaced the rice offering.

Good-luck coins are also scattered at shrine festivals among the assembled people, or tossed to neighbors who gather to join in the celebration of a new house. The house builder wishes good luck for his new dwelling, and also desires his friends and neighbors to share his happiness.

Coins have been often used in fortune-telling. At Lake Towada in the northeast section of Japan the custom of dropping a coin into the lake and judging one's fortune by the way in which it reaches the bottom is still observed.

During the Muromachi period (1394-1574) a special type of coin came to be used in praying for good luck. Such coins were called picture coins as they bore a picture of a monkey leading a horse by the bridle on its head. The combination of monkey and horse has long been considered a lucky sign.

The picture coins were considered more important and valuable than coins circulated in trade, as they were primarily used as an offering to the deity, to tell fortunes or as a charm for good fortune.

Nothing certain is known as to how such special coins of good luck originated. One opinion is that the special coins were made when one mint was first officially opened, in celebration of the event. Another is that officials of the mint coined them as a side business.

HACHIMAN

ALTHOUGH he no longer retains his militant character, Hachiman has long been the god of war. During periods of war and feudal times, Hachiman was the *kami* to whom all warriors offered their prayers. Especially did Minamoto Yoritomo, who established the Kamakura *Bakufu*, make Hachiman his guardian deity, and built the splendid Hachiman Shrine at Kamakura which still stands to the present day.

The origin of the Hachiman Shrine is mystic. At first it was erected for a foreign deity, the nature of which, however, is unknown. Fishermen on the southern coast of the country, one day in remote times, found on the shore a certain object which was washed ashore from a distant foreign land. Realizing that the object had come across the ocean, braving storms and waves, they thought it miraculous that it had safely reached the shore. So they worshiped it as a talisman for a safe voyage. This is said to be the origin of the Hachiman Shrine.

Thus, Hachiman shrines became popular among fishermen all along the coast. Early Hachiman shrines were, therefore, established near the sea, and those in inland areas are of comparatively later periods.

The original deity for whom the shrine was erected is not clearly known. But as the shrine became so popular, the people became desirous of having something definite to worship.

Antoku Tenno, the child Emperor whose early death so touched the hearts of the people, came to be regarded as the deity which is enshrined in Hachiman shrines.

The Hachiman shrine is dedicated to Emperor Ojin (270-310). At the time of his reign there were still vast territories which were not under Imperial rule, and Emperor Ojin with his wise and brave campaign enlarged the territory under his control. It is said that 21 provinces were added during his reign. So the Emperor naturally became the representative character of battles and war. His spirit was enthroned in the Hachiman shrine as the god of war.

At every Hachiman-sama there is a side-deity. Takenouchi-no-Sukune is always the guest of Hachiman-sama. He is a fit person to be a companion to the Emperor. He served under Empress Jingu (170-269) and directed the war against Korea. He is respected as an exemplary loyal servant of the sovereign.

It is usually believed that Takenouchi-no-Sukune lived for 270 years or more. He is therefore regarded as a symbol of long life. But many authorities state that there were in fact many Takenouchi-no-Sukunes, who were all loyal servants to the Court. So all the ages of the several persons were added together to represent the most famous of all who served under Empress Jingu. But it is more romantic to believe that he lived for nearly 300 years, as is generally believed by the people.

HANAYOME MATSURI

APRIL IS THE time when brides in Chiba Prefecture who were married during the past year hold a *hanayome matsuri* (brides' festival) by visiting their local shrines. The day differs according to district, but this fete is quite old, having originated in the early 16th century.

It is believed that if women who married in the past year visit their shrines on a fixed day in April, they will be assured of family happiness and easy child delivery.

Hanayome (brides) must visit the shrines in their wedding costumes, and so the occasion becomes a gorgeous fete with the gathering of richly dressed women, and the many who come to view them. At most shrines, many stalls are opened on the day, selling souvenirs and also farm implements and household goods to interest the visitors.

The bride visiting the shrine is given a cup of *sake* by the priest and then they walk around the shrine building, to ensure good health and happiness. Many unmarried girls also come to the shrine to look at the beautifully dressed brides, and are often heard expressing words of envy or admiration.

Husbands often accompany their wives in making the shrine visit, but generally they are jeered at by the public who come to look at the brides and not at their husbands. At some shrines sacred music and dances are held in honor of the occasion.

It is said that *hanayome matsuri* came to be held in April because it is just when the farming community has leisure time and the weather is good for outings. So it has developed into an outdoor fete enjoyed by all.

The *obi matsuri* or sash fete held at Shimada City on the Tokaido Line is another type of *hanayome matsuri*, but there brides do not go to the shrine personally. Instead, the ceremonial *obi* worn by the brides at the wedding ceremony is carried to the shrine and displayed to all.

HAND CLAPPING

AS PIOUS persons approach shrines, they softly clap their hands before they bow or pray. The hand clapping is a custom at all places of worship and during all rites.

The hand clapping is done to concentrate one's attention, and also to arouse the spirit of the shrine and draw its attention to the prayer to be offered. When shrines are crowded as on the occasion of a festival, the hand clapping done by so many people becomes noisy and unpleasant. In such cases the hand clapping loses its original significance.

When one goes to a quiet place of worship, for instance, situated at the top of a mountain or in a dense forest far from human habitation, his hand clapping before the sacred structure resounds though the quiet air with holy echoes. It vibrates through the mountain and forest, and awakens not only the spirit of worship, but also birds and animals nearby.

Kashiwade, as the hand clapping is called, is one of the solemn customs of the people, although it is more or less done today through habit rather than from knowledge of its meaning. But the people never forget to clap their hands as they come before a shrine or attend Shinto rites. *Kashiwade* originally came from *kashiwa* which meant feast or ceremony, and at first indicated the hand clapping by all attending such functions for the expression of felicitation.

The name *kashiwade* is said also to have derived from the idea that the human hand resembles in shape the leaf of *kashiwa* (Mongolian oak). It is also said that it means offering, as formerly Court ladies who attended to the serving of food were called *Kashiwade-no-tsukasa*. At the Grand Shrine of Ise, the official who took charge of the offerings to the Shrine was called *kashiwade-no-osa*. Thus the latter meaning might be the origin of the term *kashiwade*.

As to the number of clappings, there are also various different records. In one of the ancient records it is said that the hand clapping was done 32 times, and again there are stories that it was made four times only. Today it is generally done twice, although it is in no way wrong to clap the hands more than twice.

Also under the eaves of many such buildings of worship, there are suspended large bells with long, flowing tassels. The bell is rung by shaking the tassel. Some bells have a silvery tinkling sound, but many sound harsh and dull. The ringing of the bell is also done for the purpose of awakening the spirit of the shrine.

HARVEST PRAYER

FARMING folks still retain many old customs and have various rites in January to pray for good crops during the year. In many northern districts, they have a rite of planting rice on January 15. This is very widely known. Farmers go through the act of planting rice in their yards on this day, believing that the rite will assure them good crops.

In various districts the so-called *tori-oi* or bird chasing is performed on January 14 or 15. It is a rite to chase away birds that eat up their crops. Children particularly love it. They go into woods around their farms, beating sticks and loudly shouting and singing *tori-oi* songs.

'Shijukara-to iu toriwa hitotsu nikui tori-dayo. Atama watte, shiotsukete, kago-ni irete karagatte. Toi shima ni otteyare, hoi, hoi' (The birds called tits are hateful birds. Break their heads, salt them, put them in baskets, tie them up. Send them away to faraway islands, away, away) sing children of Miyagi.

The song differs according to district, but the meaning is practically the same.

Farmers with fruit orchards have a similar rite to make their trees bear abundantly during the year. This is also performed mostly on January 14 or 15.

Children go around the orchards with hatchets, making shallow cuts on the trees and shouting, *'Naruka, naranuka, naranunara kiruzo'* (Will you bear fruit or not? If you do not, we will cut you down).

In some districts, they sing songs in which trees promise to bear fruit. *'Naranunara kiruzo, naraneba kiruzo. Nari-masu, nari-masu, zettai nari-masu.'* (We will cut you down if you do not bear fruit. No fruits and we will cut you down. We will bear fruit, we will, we will absolutely, we will bear fruit). This is sung in many districts.

The *tori-oi* and *naranuka* songs are still popularly sung by children in many localities, because they love the songs, though they no longer have any faith in the songs or the act of chasing birds and cutting orchard trees.

HARVESTING RITES

RICE HARVESTING is marked with feasts of joy and rites of thanksgiving. Farmers first thank the *kami* or god of the mountain, the *kami* of the farm, or the community deity for protecting their rice from destruction by insects, disease and typhoons. It is firmly believed by them that without divine protection, no good crop can be obtained. Consequently, their first thought upon seeing the ripe grains of rice in actually harvesting the crop, is to offer thanks to the *kami.*

A good harvest is something to rejoice about, and consequently feasts are held to share the good fortune with family and neighbors. In appreciation to the gods, the villagers make offerings to the shrine and hold entertainments to amuse the divine beings. Most of the autumn festivals have originated from the thanksgiving rites for the rice harvest.

The farmer places the first ripe rice grains on the family shrine, and offering *sake*, he thanks the guardian *kami* and ancestors for the good crop. Sometimes a handful of the new grain is taken to the family cemetery to inform the ancestors of the good luck. In some places, the first grain is placed on the pot-hanger over _the *irori* or open Japanese fireplace, in appreciation of the crop, and in the hope that good luck will also be extended to the entire family.

Offerings are also made to *kakashi* or scarecrows and farming implements, in thanks for their service in bringing the good crop. At the household celebration, *mochi* or rice cakes are usually made from the newly harvested rice and after being presented to the *kami*, are partaken of by the whole family, and distributed among the neighbors. Then men-folk indulge in drinking *sake*, while the women and children are happy with the *mochi* and other good things to eat.

HATSU-MAIRI

VISITS TO Shinto shrines are important in the life of the Japanese people, and not only do they make periodic visits to their *ujigami* or district shrines, but they also make special trips to pay their respects to distant shrines. Of all such visits to shrines, however, the most important is *hatsu-mairi* or first visit made on New Year's Day.

New Year's Day symbolizes the beginning of the nation, and thus, on the first day of the year, the people are particularly reminded of the worship of Amaterasu-omikami.

On New Year's Day, they make special visits to shrines, and they especially love to make a trip to the Grand Shrine of Ise. Trains leaving various parts of the country late on

New Year's Eve are usually bound for the Grand Shrine of Ise, arriving early in the morning of New Year's Day.

Local shrines are also visited on New Year's Day and, for instance, in Tokyo many persons visit the Meiji Shrine. Local *ujigami* shrines have swarms of visitors as soon as the 108 bells are sounded to usher in the New Year.

At many local shrines, special charms to protect the happiness of worshipers are issued in the New Year season. It is the aim of the *hatsu-mairi* to pray for a bright and happy year. The beginning of the year is quite significant to the Japanese people who believe that the year begins on New Year's Day and ends on New Year's Eve, and that each year is a separate unit.

This belief regarding the beginning of the year, and the association with the origin of the nation, are the factors that made *hatsu-mairi* popular and significant in the country.

HI-NO-KAMI

THE JAPANESE have a *hi-no-kami* or god of fire, but they do not worship fire itself as other peoples have done. The god of fire they worship is the deity who controls fire, and thus is generally regarded as the guardian of the family cooking or floor hearth. Thus *hi-no-kami* not only controls the kitchen fire, but also the welfare of the whole family.

In many districts, the newly harvested rice is offered to the kitchen hearth. *Hi-no-kami* is also worshiped to bring divine protection to babies and children.

In Okinawa, three stones, about the size of human knuckles, are worshiped as *hi-no-kami*. At first, a kettle was placed on three stones when cooking food, and these stones became the symbol of the *hi-no-kami*. These stones are now placed on the family shelf and wor-

shiped as the guardian of the kitchen. A bride entering her new house must first worship the *hi-no-kami* stones.

Fire itself has been regarded sacred, and at many shrine festivals bonfires are lit to guide the deities to the earth. Huge towering bonfires are burned at many festivals, and the great bonfires at Yoshida at the foot of Mt. Fuji, and at Togakushi, Nagano, are still very famous.

Formerly at shrines and in many great families, a fire was kept burning continuously for generations to prove the unbroken lineage of the family.

On the other hand, there was a belief that when fire was kept burning for a long period, it became unclean. Thus whenever a sacred fire was required, the people extinguished their fires and lit new ones, or brought sacred fire from their shrines.

The *hi-no-kami* worshiped by the people is not concerned with such sacred fires. Shrines for *hi-no-kami* are, therefore, erected for the protection of the district from fire destruction. The Atago Shrine, standing northwest of Kyoto, is erected to *hi-no-kami* to protect the city from fire. The shrine also issues charms to prevent fire damage.

INARI-SAN

JAPAN IS A land of shrines, which are not only extremely numerous, but also play a big role in the people's life. Inari shrines are, however, the most popular and numerous. Everywhere, in rural villages and in big cities, there stand many Inari shrines, conspicuous with the bright vermilion color in which their buildings and *torii* are painted. Inari was originally the guardian shrine of farmers, as it is dedicated to Uga-no-mitama-no-kami, or god of cereals and farm products. But city dwellers too are all worshipers of Inari. They hold such respect for Inari that they never call it simply Inari, but always say *O-Inari-san*, with double honorifics.

Of the many Inari shrines, some are of elaborate architecture and grand in scale, such as the famous Inari Shrine at Fushimi, Kyoto. Then again, there are tiny insignificant ones which form the majority of them. Such small shrines of only a few feet square are erected in all villages, towns and cities. Many persons, both rural and urban, have their own Inari shrines in their gardens.

All Inari shrines are painted in vermilion, and the *torii* erected before them are of the same bright color. The color makes the shrines very picturesque, particularly in contrast to surrounding green forests or gardens. *Torii* are mostly donated by the worshipers, and as in the case of Fushimi Shrine, Kyoto, some shrines have hundreds of such vermilion *torii* that form long tunnels leading to the shrines.

Another striking feature of Inari shrines is that a *kitsune* or fox sculptured in stone or wood is always placed in front of them. It is currently believed that the *kitsune* is the messenger of the shrine. There are some rural people who traditionally believe that Inari shrines are erected for the fox because of the presence of foxes in front of the shrines.

In olden times there was a custom of placing various foods at a certain place outside a village, so that various wild animals would be kept away from the village. According to some authorities, the erection of stone or wooden foxes at Inari shrines came from the mixture of the belief in the Inari shrine and this ancient custom.

To Inari shrines the people still bring various foods as offerings. Particularly *aburage* or fried *tofu* is believed to be the favorite food of foxes of Inari shrines. Cooked rice, *aburage*, fish,

meats and other foodstuffs are offered. Because of the reputed fondness of foxes for *aburage*, a kind of *sushi* wrapped up in *aburage* is commonly called *O-Inari-san*.

The Hatsu-uma (first horse day) festival at Inari shrines is celebrated early in February. This is the most popular and widely held festival of the country, and in rural districts it is still regarded as a community holiday. In the old days, it was a nationally observed holiday. The first recorded mention of Hatsu-uma was of one held on February 9, 708.

Children particularly enjoy the festival. They beat drums at Inari shrines, which are decorated with tall banners. All through feudal days, it was observed not only by farmers, but also by *samurai* and the merchant class. Feudal lords used to make offerings to Inari shrines.

It was originally however a farmers' spring festival, as it was the day to welcome Ta-no-kami (deity of farms) back to farms. Ta-no-kami goes back to the mountain after the autumn harvest, and returns to the field as spring comes. Furthermore, at first it was a day when farm horses were given a holiday.

It was thus at first not a festival of Inari shrines only, but it appears that the festival also came to be held at Inari shrines which are dedicated to the god of cereals. The Hatsu-uma festival was also a market day in rural districts, as various goods for household use were offered for sale at temporary shops opened at Inari shrines.

INGA-OHO

INGA-OHO (a reward in accordance to deed) is one of the most commonly used sayings of the country. It came from the Buddhist idea of *inga* meaning cause and effect. It is believed the present life is the result of the deeds we committed in our former life, and our future life depends equally on what we do in this world.

The term *inga*, however, is now also used in a different sense. It often stands for karma or fate. This idea sometimes leads to the fatalistic thought that our life is determined by fate and no effort can change it. This conception makes one hopeless and reckless.

Inga also includes the idea of misfortune or unluckiness. *Inga-na-ko* or a child of *inga* means a child born of sin. A person who constantly complains and worries without proper cause is often called *inga-na-hito* or a man of *inga*.

The fatalistic pessimism often seen among Japanese is due to the concept of *inga*. Thus, the people say *'shikata-ganai'* (cannot be helped) whenever they meet with misfortune, loss or hardship.

This fatalistic idea is believed to have been much encouraged by the frequent natural disasters which the people have suffered from the very beginning of history. Floods, typhoons, thunderbolts, volcanic eruptions, earthquakes and such cause mass destruction and much loss of life almost every year. The people have been helpless in preventing or stopping natural calamities. They accept them as their fate, or as something they have to bear with stoic surrender.

ISHI-AGE

ROADSIDE statues of Buddha and other deities often have pebbles and small stones piled high upon their heads, shoulders, hands or other parts. Sometimes *torii* (gates to Shinto shrines) also have small stones piled upon their beams, and lanterns erected in temples and shrines likewise are covered with little stones.

Visitors to temples and shrines believe that the stones they offer and pile upon Buddha statues, *torii* or lanterns will bring them good luck, preserve their health, and make them happy. Particularly in the case of tall *torii*, it requires skill and luck to toss small stones upon their beams. If one succeeds in placing a stone upon a beam, he will be assured of good luck. Stones are piled also upon statues of Buddha and other deities, as the people believe that stones are sacred and symbols of their respect.

This custom of offering stones and pebbles is called *ishi-age*, and from this custom developed festivals called *ishi-age-matsuri*.

One such fete is that of Kuwana, Ise province, which is held for three days, July 10 to 12, every year, when the people of the neighborhood draw 40 highly decorated carts, and with music and singing, proceed to the shores of the Machiya River. There they pick up clean, beautiful little pebbles, and pile the carts high with them. With music and singing, they make a procession of the loaded carts to the shrine, to which the pebbles are given as their annual offering.

This custom is observed at various places. Then there are also festivals of carrying stones up to the tops of steep mountains. Along the Kiso River stands a mountain which is generally called the Owari-Fuji. On June 1 every year, the people of the villages along the base of the mountain carry huge stones, 200 to 300 pounds each, to the top of the mountain, in order to worship the spirit of the mountain.

This task requires enormous labor, and several hundred young people, both women and men, join in pulling such stones up the steep side of the mountain. They sing to encourage themselves in their arduous task. The stone-pulling procession starts in the evening, and it takes all night for them to reach the top. This custom comes from the belief that the stone is the symbol of the spirit of mountains, and thus the offering of stones to mountains is observed in many different places throughout the country.

JIZO

STONE STATUES of Jizo (Ksitigarbha) are seen all over the country. Some are housed in beautiful temples, some are in little huts, and others are standing by the country roadside. It is one of the most popular statues that has become a characteristic of country life.

Jizo is the Bosatsu (Bodhisattva) who was entrusted with the task of saving the people after the death of Buddha until such a time when the second Buddha would appear. He thus came to hold an important position in Buddhism, and coming to Japan he has been popularized by having become the protector of the people.

There are commonly said to be six Jizo which represent the six characters of the original Jizo. They are *Enmei* (long life), *Hosho* (treasure place), *Hoshu* (treasure hand), *Jichi* (land possession), *Hoin* (treasure seal), and *Kengoi* (strong determination). In many places these six Jizo are placed together.

Further, there is a common belief that Jizo is the protector of children, and there is also a Jizo who is especially named *Ko-sodate-Jizo* (children raising Jizo). It is said that when children die, they go to the banks of the Sanzu River, but as they play there, devils come to disturb them. Then Jizo arrives to protect these children.

Many people go to this Jizo and take a talisman home, in the hope that they may be able to raise their children properly.

Jizo is thought to be a mild, gentle and kind Bosatsu. *Jizo-gao* (Jizo-face) implies a gentle, smiling face, while *Jizo-mayu* (Jizo eyebrow) stands for long, slender eye-brows in the shape of the young moon.

Fortune-Telling Jizo: When one loses some valuables, or wishes to know the meaning of a dream he had the night before, or desires to locate a missing person, or wants to find a remedy for his illness, it is customary in some districts to consult Jizo.

Jizo is believed to be able to give ready answers to all such questions. But, as to obtaining the Jizo's answers to such questions, methods differ according to district.

In the Tajima district, the fortune-telling ability of Jizo is firmly believed in by the people, and whenever they wish to have Jizo's words on such problems, old women and wives of the village gather at a house.

They form a circle in a room, and in the center of the circle is placed a little child carrying *gohei*. Then, all begin to shout 'Namu-jizo-bosatsu otsukiyare Jizo-san' (Jizo, become inspired 'Jizo-san') and the chanting is continued until the little child in the center falls into a state of sleep. They then believe that the spirit of Jizo has entered the child, and they ask various questions, as the answers given by the child are believed to be the words of Jizo.

In various rural districts, it is still believed that lost articles, missing men and means of curing illness can be learned by this method.

From this custom of making a circle around a little child and chanting in order to have the spirit of Jizo enter the child, there has developed a game for children which is almost universally played in the country.

Little children form a circle around a child in the center, and while chanting and singing, they ask all sorts of questions of the child in the center who is called Jizo. In some cases, the children dance in a circle while singing. It is only a playful game for little children, but it has developed from the more serious custom of regarding Jizo as a good fortune-teller.

Hikeshi-Jizo: Probably because fires are quite frequent in the country, there are many Jizo which are believed to have the power to extinguish fire. These Jizo are worshiped in various districts by rural people who believe that this god will save them at a time of fire.

At Matsushima, Miyagi Prefecture, there once stood a Buddhist temple, the chief statue of which was a Jizo about three feet high. An old couple living in the village worshiped this Jizo in all sincerity. One day, a fire broke out in the village, and fanned by a strong wind, it spread rapidly, burning down the houses. The old couple, at the start of the fire, first thought to save the Jizo statue in the temple. Running to the temple, they found that the house next to the temple was already on fire. But with a superhuman effort they managed to save the temple from burning down, and thus saved the statue. Satisfied and happy, they returned to their house, and found their own home on fire. They were too late to do anything to save the house. Just at that moment a little boy came running out of the crowd, and entering their house, he began to take out all valuable household articles. They wondered who that little boy might be, but there was no way of ascertaining his identity. As day dawned, the fire was finally brought under control. The old couple rejoiced that, although almost all the houses of the village had been burned down, their household goods and valuables had been saved because of the aid given by the unknown boy. They went to the Jizo temple to express their thanks, but to their utter surprise, they found that both feet of the Jizo statue had been burned.

The belief that Jizo will come to save people at a time of fire is widely believed in by the people. In this connection, it is very strange that some Jizo are thought to have the power to fly through the air for when they are going to save people from fire.

Near the Murakami-dera Temple, in a suburb of Kyoto, there stands a Jizo statue of wood, about seven feet high. The people of the surrounding districts believe that once when there was a fire nearby, the Jizo statue flew through the air in order to be instantly at the site.

There are many other deities in Japan who are believed to possess the power to fly through the air, and among them are several Jizo.

Mawari-Jizo: There are many statues which are called *Mawari-Jizo* or traveling Jizo. They are so called because those statues are taken around to different villages. The villagers make elaborate ceremonies in welcoming the coming of the Jizo statues to their respective districts. There is nothing strange about these traveling Jizo and their worship by the people of different villages, although in some cases the Jizo stay only about one month at their proper temples, traveling around for the rest of the year.

There are also other kinds of Jizo which are believed to walk out of their temples of their own accord, causing much trouble to priests and worshipers.

In Matsuzaki-mura, Rikuchu province, there is a Jizo called *Asobi Jizo* or going-out Jizo. The Jizo is always absent, there being only the foundation stone under a huge tree on which it may stand. It is believed that sometimes the

Jizo stands on its proper place, but the next day, it disappears somewhere. Usually about once in three years, the Jizo returns to its proper place. Of course, the statue must be carried around by some people, but it is commonly believed that it goes away on its own.

The village of Harase, Iwashiro province, built a Jizo temple, but the Jizo statue soon disappeared, and from then disease became frequent among the young people of the village. They believed that the absence of the statue was the cause of the bad luck, and started to search for it. Finally it was located in the Ryusenji Temple nearby. But strangely, nobody of the temple had ever seen it before, and it was not known how it was brought there.

In the Seiho-in Temple, in Saga City, Kyushu, there is a Jizo statue which is protected by strong steel netting, as it has an evil habit of going out to buy *sake*. Once, at a *sake* shop in the city, there one night appeared a richly dressed priest coming for a bottle of *sake*. Then at the end of the year, bills were brought to the Seiho-in Temple from three different *sake* shops in the city, for a large quantity of *sake* sold to the priest of the temple.

The priest of the temple never went out to buy *sake*, but he paid these bills, thinking that if he refused to pay, evil reports would be circulated about him. One day, the priest went near the Jizo statue, and found it smelling of *sake*. Thus it was revealed that the Jizo statue went out to get *sake* from *sake* shops, giving the name of the priest. To prevent the Jizo from going out again for *sake*, strong steel netting is now placed over the statue.

Migawari-Jizo: In many different places throughout the country, there are Jizo statues called *Migawari-Jizo* or Jizo taking the place of people. It is

commonly believed that, if a man worships Jizo, Jizo will take his place when he is in some great difficulty or in danger of losing his life. There are numerous stories telling how Jizo statues were killed or attacked in place of their worshipers. Jizo statues having such traditional tales have many worshipers because the people believe that such Jizo would save them in emergencies.

At the Ryochiji Temple at Yako-cho, Tsurumi, in Yokohama there is an old blackened statue of Jizo, called *Migawari-Jizo*. This Jizo is widely worshiped as it has the power to save the lives of worshipers by taking their place in difficulties. The origin of this faith in the *Migawari-Jizo* at this Yokohama temple is believed to be as follows. Once at Tsurumi, there lived an old man named Magobei. He had a son 12 years old, but his wife died, and the old man lived together with his little son. Magobei was a packhorse driver, and he and his son used to go out daily with their horse, in order to earn their daily food. His neighbors, however, persuaded Magobei to take a second wife. Thus he married again, but the new wife hated the little son, and used to maltreat him daily.

One winter's night, the new wife was waiting for the return of Magobei and while waiting, she started to cook the horse's meal in a huge kettle. The little son happened to come near the kettle and peeped into it. The wife then suddenly pushed the boy from behind and caused him to tumble into the boiling kettle. The son died without even uttering a cry.

She took out the body of the boy from the boiling kettle, and placing it aside, covered it with matting. Then Magobei returned home, but to her great surprise, she saw the boy entering the house together with his father. Astonished, she lifted the matting that covered the boy's body, and there was the statue of Jizo which the boy used to worship day and night.

The Jizo had noticed that the wife had evil intentions regarding the boy, and taking the form of the boy, he appeared by the side of the kettle to be thrown into it by the wife.

Thus the people of the neighborhood came to worship the Jizo statue which was at first only worshiped by the boy, and later it was enshrined in the Ryochiji Temple.

Shibarare-Jizo: The stone statue of Jizo of the Nanzo-in Temple, Katsushika Ward, Tokyo, has coarse straw ropes tied around its body. It is commonly called *Shibarare-Jizo* or tied Jizo.

When a person has had any valuables stolen, he goes to the Jizo and ties him up with straw ropes, reporting the loss and promising his release upon finding the culprit. The statue is almost always tied with thick layers of ropes, as many thieves reported are not caught.

The tradition goes back to the early part of the 18th century, when the statue was in Honjo district, from where it was removed about 25 years ago to the present site. The story goes that a dress-goods peddler rested in the shade of a tree by the Jizo statue one hot summer afternoon. As he rested he dozed, and when he woke up, his bundle of goods was gone. Quickly he reported his loss to the *Bugyo-sho* or the magistrate's office.

Hearing the complaint, Lord Echizen, the magistrate, instantly ordered the arrest of the Jizo statue. Tied tightly, the stone statue was carried on a cart from Honjo to the *Bugyo-sho* at Yurakucho. The neighbors, seeing the arrest of the Jizo, followed the cart with interest. But when they entered the compounds of the *Bugyo-sho*, following the Jizo on the cart, the gate was suddenly closed, and they found themselves held for entering the *bugyo's* office without any reason.

Lord Echizen sentenced them to bring a piece of dress goods each as punishment for their illegal entry into his office compounds. Sadly they went home, and brought some to the *Bugyo-sho*. Among the pieces brought by them, Lord Echizen found one belonging to the peddler's bundle. In this manner the culprit was found, and the Jizo was released from suspicion and untied, and taken back to its site.

Speaking Jizo: There are statues of Jizo which are said to talk. One such statue believed to be able to speak stands by the Torio Pass, in Chikuzen province, Kyushu. At present the road through the mountain has been much improved, but formerly it was only a narrow winding-way up the mountainside. The district being uninhabited, robbers often appeared and attacked lone travelers.

One day, many years ago, a robber was hiding behind the Jizo statue standing at the height of the pass, waiting for the coming of some travelers. A *samurai* came along, slowly climbing up the mountain road, and as he passed by the Jizo statue, the robber suddenly appeared from behind the statue, and killed him. The robber stole all the money and valuables from the body of the *samurai*.

The robber then looked around and saw no one, except the stone Jizo statue. Facing the statue, the robber said: 'Jizo-san, please do not speak of what happened here to anyone.'

But to the utter surprise of the robber, the Jizo statue readily replied: 'I will not speak, but take care that you do not.' Taken aback, the robber rose, and in anger struck a heavy blow with his sword on the head of the Jizo statue.

One side of the Jizo's face was cut off by the sword.

Ten long years passed, and one day there came a young *samurai* before the Jizo statue on the top of the Torio Pass. He was the son of the *samurai* who was killed at the spot 10 years before. He sat down behind the Jizo and pondered upon his future which seemed to be void, as the murderer of his father had not yet been found.

Then, another traveler happened to pass by. Coming to the Jizo he stopped, and looking at the face of the statue, he muttered: 'Time really passes quickly. It is already 10 years since I killed that *samurai* at this spot.'

The young *samurai* who sat behind the Jizo heard this, rose, and saying that he had finally found the man who killed his father, he drew his sword and attacked the traveler. Thus he was able to avenge the death of his father.

Ta-ue Jizo: Throughout Japan there are quite a number of Jizo statues which are called *Ta-ue Jizo* or rice-planting Jizo, and worshiped by farmers for aiding their rice-planting.

These *Ta-ue Jizo* all have traditional tales telling the virtues of giving aid to farmers at the rice-planting season.

Once by the Grand Shrine of Izumo lived a poor farming couple who had a wooden statue of Jizo in their house and daily worshiped it. However, the old woman died, and the old man then lived alone. Soon the old man also became ill. Just then the village chief demanded that each household should send a man to plant rice on his farms. Anyone who failed to do so would be severely punished. But the old man could not go himself because he was sick, and had nobody else to go in his place. He knew he would be punished, and daily prayed to the statue of Jizo for mercy. When the day for rice-planting on the village chief's farms arrived, the name of all household heads were called. When the old man was called, a boy about 17 years old had come forward saying that he had come for the old man. During the strenuous work of rice-planting, the boy worked so well and hard that the village chief gave him a wine-cup as a prize when the work was finished. The boy put the cup on his head and went away. On the following day the village chief went to the house of the old man to praise the work of the boy, but to his surprise the old man knew nothing about the boy. The old man realized then that the boy had been sent through the mercy of his Jizo statue, and he went to the Jizo statue to express thanks. To his surprise, he found that there was a cup on the Jizo's head, and his feet were covered with paddy mud.

In the village of Tatsukon, Rikuzen province, there stands a Jizo shrine, called *Dorokake* (mud-covered) *Jizo*. Once when the villagers were short of help at of rice-planting time, there suddenly appeared a little boy who worked with them. In the evening the boy disappeared, and when the villagers looked around they found that the Jizo statue was covered with mud. Thus it came to be known as the *Dorokake Jizo*.

In the district of Yae, Izumo province, there was a tenant farmer who worshiped Jizo. One summer, he could not get enough water in his rice-fields, and as he attempted to draw water from the river nearby he was beaten up by other farmers. One morning there appeared a strange priest on his farm, who drew water into his fields. Other farmers seeing the priest became angry, and shot an arrow at him. The priest disappeared, but when the tenant farmer worshiped his Jizo, he found that the Jizo's feet were covered with mud, and an arrow had pierced the back of the stone Jizo.

These tales about *Ta-ue Jizo* are found all over the country. Because of this belief that Jizo helps farmers at rice-planting time, the *Ta-ue Jizo* is extensively worshiped by farmers.

Toge-nuki Jizo: *Toge-nuki Jizo* or the splinter-removing Ksitigarbha at Koganji Temple, Sugamo, is still popular among Tokyo residents, and whenever people have splinters or thorns they go there to pray that the foreign matter be removed quickly. The Jizo was originally located in the Shitaya district, but it was moved to the present site about 60 years ago.

The wife of a *samurai* named Tamura, who lived in Koishikawa, was very ill. Her husband prayed to Jizo for her recovery. Jizo appeared to him in a dream and told him to make Jizo pictures and float them on a river. Awakening the next morning, he was surprised to find by his pillow a strangely shaped block of wood on the surface of which was carved a faint picture of Jizo. He immersed the wooden block in red seal ink and printed 10,000 impressions of Jizo. When he took the sheets and threw them into the Sumida River, as directed in his dream, his wife was completely cured.

The *samurai* thought that such a sacred block of wood with the picture of Jizo should not be kept as private property, and so donated it to Koganji Temple. This is said to have happened in the Keicho era (1596-1615).

In the fifth year of Shotoku (1715), a maid employed in the household of Lord Mori accidentally swallowed a broken needle she was holding between her teeth. The needle stuck in her throat and could not be taken out. A print of Jizo was quickly obtained and she was made to swallow it floating in water in a tea-cup. Instantly she threw up the needle.

This story added further strength to the belief that the Jizo has miraculous powers of removing thorns and splinters. All through the Tokugawa and Meiji days, the tradition has been popularly maintained. Many modern persons still believe it.

KAGAMI

FOREIGN visitors to the country always wonder what is inside the Shinto shrines. None other than the priests of the shrines are allowed to enter the inner room of the Shinto shrine, and even the Japanese public has not seen the inside of shrines.

The *Shintai (kami's* body) in Shinto shrines is usually a mirror, although in some exceptional cases swords or other objects are also enshrined. Moreover, in the case of Shinto shrines dedicated to the memory of former Emperors, great warriors and others, there are statues or relics of such personages.

The *kagami* or mirror is sacred in Shinto, as it was Amaterasu-omikami who gave a mirror to Ninigi-no-mikoto when the latter was ordered to come down and rule the land of Yamato, and advised the heavenly ruler of the country by saying: 'Regard this mirror as myself.'

Thus in the Shinto faith, the mirror is considered as the symbol of Amaterasu-omikami. Because of this belief the mirror has come to be treated as a sacred object even in common households. It is enshrined in Shinto shrines as the *Shintai.*

Purity and cleanliness are the first requirements of a mirror as it is regarded as one's soul. Clouded mirrors are like souls clouded with evil thoughts. It is because of this belief in the mirror that the art of making mirrors has developed. Mirrors have always been considered not only as sacred, but also as objects of art.

Because of the high respect the people have for mirrors, they never put them down on the floor. In ancient times it was thought to be a serious crime for anyone to step over a mirror.

The presence of a mirror in a Shinto shrine means that the spirit of Amaterasu-omikami is there. It teaches the people to keep their souls as pure and clean as the shining mirror.

The *kagami* is furthermore the protector of women's virtue. Old-fashioned women still are very careful not to break their *kagami*, as a broken mirror will bring them bad luck.

Magnificent mirrors of bronze and other metals with gorgeous designs on their backs were made by master artisans in the old days. Until the introduction of glass mirrors, metal mirrors were commonly used in the country. As they tarnished quickly, mirror cleaners used to go around from house to house.

The people do not generally use metal mirrors any more in their daily life. But many old families still keep metal mirrors, not only as relics but also as *mitama-shiro* (symbol of ancestors' spirit). Metal mirrors used as *mitama-shiro* are generally small, mostly being one to three inches in diameter. These mirrors are preserved in memory of the ancestors, and are displayed and worshiped at their memorial services. This custom is still followed in aristocratic families.

When a person in the family was dying or had just died, a small round metal mirror was brought near his face, so that his spirit would enter into the mirror. The mirror was then wrapped up in a silk cloth and placed in a box, upon which the name of the person was written.

KAGAMI-MOCHI

AMONG IMPORTANT offerings made to Shinto shrines is *kagami-mochi*. *Mochi*, which is a rice-dumpling or cake, is commonly used on happy and felicitous occasions in ⁻Japan. *Kagamimochi* or mirror-*mochi* consists of two pieces of round *mochi*, one smaller than the other, with the smaller one being placed on top of the larger one.

Kagami-mochi is offered to *kami*, and in ordinary households, it is customary to offer small *kagami-mochi* to the family *kamidana* at the beginning of every month. The use of *kagami-mochi* at the New Year celebration is universal. Every house places one set of *kagami-mochi* on the *tokonoma* of the main room, and also small sets are often placed in every room of the house.

The use of *kagami-mochi* in the New Year celebration signifies that it will bring in a happier and brighter year. This meaning tells the origin of *kagami-mochi*. Like many other Shinto customs, it originated in the incident of Amaterasu-omikami hiding in the Amano-iwato. When the Sun Goddess had hidden in the cave and the world became dark, a mirror was taken out and all prayed to the mirror which symbolized the Sun Goddess, that she would reveal herself again to the world. The prayer was successful, and the world was made bright and happy by her reappearance. *Kagami-mochi* is made in the shape of a mirror, and represents the mirror used at the time when the Sun Goddess hid.

Thus, the offering of *kagami-mochi* signifies a prayer for a brighter and better life. At the New Year celebration, it is the symbol of the hope of the people that the new year will be brighter and happier than the last.

KAGURA

DENOTING Shinto music and dancing, *kagura* is presented at Shinto festivals and Court functions. The purpose of performing *kagura* is to amuse *kami*. The origin of *kagura* was the dancing and singing performed by Ameno-uzume-no-mikoto when Amaterasu-omikami had hidden in the cave of Amano-iwato. It is recorded that her dancing and singing were so comical that all the *kami* who witnessed it laughed merrily.

In the days of Emperor Jinmu, first Emperor of Japan, it is recorded that *kagura* was offered for the spirit of Uma-shimade-no-mikoto. It is not known today, however, what sort of music and dancing was performed at that time. Nevertheless, *kagura* has since that time become an important feature of Court and Shinto ceremonies. The original *kagura* became much influenced by the introduction of Chinese music and musical instruments, but the ancient music and dancing are still preserved in the present *kagura*.

Kagura has also been performed, since very early days, at local shrines and it is performed at the time of festivals. While the *kagura* of the ancient classical standard is offered to shrines at their festivals and other special occasions, there have also developed what is known as *sato-kagura* or village *kagura*.

Sato-kagura is performed by villagers at the time of the festivals of their *ujigami* shrines. *Sato-kagura* is comical and very crude, as it is done by farmers and other common folk. Whereas the *kagura* of the classics has become very solemn and sacred, *sato-kagura* is quite enjoyable, being full of comic songs and gestures. There are also professional performers of *sato-kagura* who are hired at various shrine festivals. But the real feature of *sato-kagura* lies in its being performed by amateurs.

KAKURE-KIRISHITAN

IN NORTHERN Kyushu and particularly in Nagasaki Prefecture, there are Christians who are called *Kakure-Kirishitan* or hiding Christians. They do not belong to any established Christian sect or church, but follow peculiar rites of their own. They are called *Kakure-Kirishitan* because they keep their faith secret, and wish to make it appear they are not Christians. They are said to number about 50,000 now.

These Christians form local units called *cho*, with the *kanbogata* as the father. All babies are baptized by the *kanbogata* who holds all rites and services. They have books written in a code. They have no church or special place of worship, but generally gather at the house of the *kanbogata*.

In order not to outwardly appear to be Christians, they all attend community festivals, and go to Buddhist temples and Shinto shrines. In the case of a funeral, they first hold a Shinto or Buddhist service similar to their neighbors', after which they follow it with a Christian service. In the old days, *Kakure-Kirishitans* seldom married with people of other faiths.

This custom of hiding their Christian faith developed in Japan's early Christian days when those believing in the foreign faith were persecuted. Particularly after the famous Shimabara Rebellion (1637-1638) in which Christians participated, those who were found to be Christians were massacred. These pressures, however, did not discourage Japanese Christians who were firmly determined to adhere to their faith. Nevertheless, in order to save themselves from massacre, they conducted themselves as though they were not Christians, while holding their services secretly.

KAKURE-NENBUTSU

A SECRET BUDDHIST sect commonly called *Kakure-nenbutsu* (hidden prayer) had many followers in many northeastern provinces during the Tokugawa period and early Meiji days. Even today there are still some followers of the sect though they no longer try to make their faith a secret.

It is not clearly known how this strange sect developed, but it belonged to the Jodo-Shinshu sect that was started by Shinran. Believers of this sect tried their best to keep their faith a secret, not revealing their faith even to their own parents or intimate friends. The believers were known only to each other. Furthermore they held their services in secret so that other people would not know of them.

Thus they used to gather in an unoccupied hut of a farmer, or a *dozo* (storehouse) of a merchant. They held their meetings late at night, and often on an evening of a heavy rain, snow or storm when nobody else would be outdoors. Then they posted watchmen to see that no stranger came near the meeting place. Men and women and sometimes even children gathered for the service.

The room where the meeting was held was lighted with candles. They chanted 'Namu-Amidabutsu' (Save us, merciful Buddha) as they walked around the room. With the chanting, they often went into a trance.

When the persecution of Christians commenced in the middle of the 17th century, the religious faith of all the people came to be watched and questioned by the authorities. Though no

order was issued against any Buddhist sect, the *Kakure-Nenbutsu* was regarded as a heretical faith, and whenever any leader of the secret sect was found, he was punished by death.

The execution in 1754 of Yamazaki Mokuzaemon and several others for believing in the faith is recorded.

Kakure-Nenbutsu followers are said to have numbered over 40,000. Even after the Meiji Restoration, the Honganji Temple at Kyoto dispatched in 1878 an order to the heretics of Mizusawa district, Iwate, to send a representative to Kyoto and explain their faith. Ohashi Ryosuke who was sent to Kyoto never expected that he would return alive, but he was able to satisfy the Honganji officials, and returned home.

KAMI-NASHI-ZUKI

THE MONTH of October is called *kami-nashi-zuki* or *kami*-less month, and in old days the people did not hold wedding ceremonies during this month, because they believed that without the presence of *kami*, a wedding could not be performed.

The origin of this belief is not known. However, the name came from *kamina* which means to make new *sake* with newly harvested rice. Thus it was called *kamina-zuki*, or the month to make new *sake*. But somehow it changed to mean the absence of *kami*.

It is commonly believed that in the month of October all the *kami* of the land leave their shrines and assemble and confer from October 17 to 26 at the Izumo Shrine. Thus, while the rest of the country call October the *kami-nashi-zuki*, it is named *kami-ari-zuki* or *kami*-present-month at Izumo. It is also said that October is *kami-nashi-zuki* because goddess Izanami-no-mikoto died in this month.

The people of the country have observed the custom of visiting the Izumo Shrine during October, because then they can worship all the *kami* in the country.

In the compounds of the Izumo Shrine, there are two rows of long buildings on both sides of the main shrine building for accommodating these visiting *kami* from other parts of the country in October. Moreover, at a place some five miles southeast of the Izumo Shrine, there is a shrine named Mankusen Jinja or Nineteen Thousand Shrine. It is traditionally said that the 19,000 *kami* who came to Izumo started out from that shrine for their respective home shrines on October 26, when the people of the neighborhood visit this shrine to pay homage to the departing *kami*.

All over the country rites are held to send the *kami* off to Izumo. In some localities, the sending-off rite is regarded as an occasion for selecting marriage partners. Young men and women worship at the shrine to have their future mates picked before the *kami* leave for Izumo.

While all *kami* are given quite a send-off, no ceremony is held to welcome them back because the time of their return varies. Most of them come back in one month, but some stay away until February of the following year.

It is now explained that this belief in *kami*'s departure from the shrine in October is related to the harvesting of rice. With the gathering of the crop, the duty of the *kami* of farms to protect rice plants from evil spirits and insects is completed. Thus their departure is marked with rites to show the farmers' appreciation for their service. This is said to have started the belief that all *kami* leave local shrines in October.

KAMI-NO-TSUKAI

MANY SHRINES have *kami-no-tsukai* or *kami*'s messengers. They are generally birds, animals, insects or fish that are particularly related to the *kami* enshrined at those shrines. These are highly respected as the messengers of *kami*, and in many cases they are worshiped by the people.

There are traditional tales of how those animals or birds became the messengers of *kami*, but every shrine has its own story. The most famous *kami-no-tsukai* among shrines of the country are pigeons for Hachiman Shrines; crows for Ise, Kumano, Itsukushima, Hiyoshi and other Shrines; black kites for Atago Shrine; herons for Suwa and other shrines; chicken for Mishima Shrine of Izu; pheasants for Kita Shrine; deer for Kasuga, Kashima, Itsukushima and Funabashi shrines; monkeys for Hiyoshi and Kasuga shrines; rats for Daikoku Shrine; foxes for Inari, Suwa and Oyama shrines; boars for the Atago Shrine; bees for the Futara Shrine; turtles for Matsuo and Hikamiyama shrines; carp for Tsukuda-jima, Namikawa, Sumiyoshi and Shin-mei shrines.

These messengers of *kami* have often become so popular and regarded as the object of worship of the people, that many ignorant persons even believe that those animals or birds are the deities enshrined in those shrines. The case of the Inari Shrine is a representative one. There are many people who still believe that the Inari Shrine is dedicated to the fox, and thus offer *age-dofu* (fried *tofu*) to foxes at those Inari shrines.

Those messengers of *kami* are regarded sacred, and their movements or acts are supposedly said to foretell the fortunes of the believers. Any unusual movement of such messengers is believed to predict some extraordinary development or calamity. At most of those shrines, the messengers of *kami* or other images are kept in their compounds.

KAMI-SAMA

THE JAPANESE people worship *kami-sama*, not one but hundreds. *Kami* worship has been so deeply rooted in the people's thoughts and habits that without knowing their *kami-sama*, it would be difficult to understand many ideas and customs of the people. Often the Japanese conception of *kami* is misunderstood by Western peoples who are apt to interpret it as something similar to their own idea of God.

Kami originally meant 'invisible,' and later came to be used as a term for indicating the invisible spirit or force that controls natural phenomena, human life and happiness. Then to *kami* was ascribed the power to bring happiness, protect the good, and punish the wrong.

Thus in primitive days, the sun, the moon, thunder and lightning, high mountains, big trees, animals, fish, birds and many other things came to be regarded as *kami* or manifestations of *kami*. The people still see something divine in living things and inanimate matter, as evidenced by the custom of observing a service for broken needles, still followed by housewives and girls, and many other customs.

There are hundreds of *kami*, and they can be roughly divided into two groups. One is for worship by the family or community, and the other for individual worship. Many *kami* are believed to have the power to bring good fortune to the family or community. The spirits of ancestors guard the fortune of the family, the old people thought, and so ancestral spirits are to them *kami* to worship, and one who serves the interest of a locality becomes a community *kami*.

Individually worshiped *kami* are such that cure sickness, protect people from evils, bring children, cause happiness and look after health.

As they worship *kami*, they erect shrines as dwellings for the invisible spirit, and community shrines are the center of village life. For such shrines, they hold annual or seasonal festivals, for expressing their thanks, offering prayers and amusing the enshrined *kami*. Such festivals are a social function of the people, as all have to participate in it. From such festivals also developed the modern market, as on the day of the festival, the people of the district and neighboring areas brought various wares and products for exchange or sale.

Then at the festival, various games, music, dance and other forms of amusement are offered to amuse the *kami-sama*. All Japanese sports, wrestling, horse racing, tug-of-war, archery and such all developed from games offered at shrine festivals.

Of course, it is the joy of the people to perform such entertainments and games at the festival, and also the attending villagers and neighbors enjoy them. But primarily, the music, dance and games are offered to please and entertain the *kami*. So all performances are solemn and serious in their execution.

Shrine music and dance are the foundation upon which Japanese music and dance have developed, while shrine buildings and ornaments played a big role in the history of Japanese architecture.

The original attitude of the people toward *kami-sama* and shrines has changed much over these many centuries, and modern people may be said to be merely following traditional forms and customs, without understanding their significance. Yet shrines and shrine festivals are still great community factors that bind local people together in community spirit, and keep the ancient attitude to nature still alive.

To Western observers, shrine festivals of Japan may appear as events for amusement of the people to enable them to have a few days of recreation, to be beautifully dressed, to watch various shows and entertainments, to eat specially prepared food, to drink *sake*, and to mix joyfully with all neighbors and friends.

But it is to be remembered that the people do not forget to make a solemn visit to their shrine on the festive day, to make offerings and say their prayers. The program of the festival brings joy to the participants, and amuses visitors, but yet is carried out with the original meaning of pleasing and entertaining the *kami*. That is to say, the idea of the festival is still seen in many of its details. The *kami-sama* comes first, not the public.

Foreign visitors often ask for what a local shrine stands, but very often it is impossible to obtain a satisfying answer. It is because the villagers and believers in the shrine do not know what the shrine they worship stands for. To them it does not matter who or what their *kami-sama* is; they have faith in its benevolence.

The shrine building is always closed and none, except the priest, is allowed to enter it. Foreigners sometimes wonder what is inside the shrine. They do not need to peep in, as there is nothing inside. A shrine is a house for the invisible. Of course, some shrines have mirrors or other relics in their buildings, but most of them are simply empty.

The invisible *kami* travels through its domain in a *mikoshi* or palanquin on the festival day, to make an inspection tour.

Kami-sama has been worshiped by individuals, the family and the community, and there was no *kami* that had national significance. The Imperial Family worships the Ise Shrine, dedicated to the mythological ancestor, but this shrine was not worshiped by the general public until the Tokugawa period, up to which time the public was not allowed to approach it. In old days, the Imperial Family paid much attention to the worship of the mythological ancestor and the Ise Shrine, but this was motivated by its policy of maintaining the authority and dignity of Imperial rule. Yet the Imperial Family kept the Ise Shrine only for worship by Imperial Family members and officials.

Now the Ise Shrine is regarded as the greatest Shinto shrine of the country, but it has nothing to do with the general *kami* worship of the people.

Shinto, based on the way of *kami*, with the Ise Shrine as the main shrine, developed also from nature and ancestor worship. Thus it may be called one type of *kami* worship, with the idea that the mythological ancestor of the Imperial Family is the guiding spirit of the country.

So Shinto and the popular *kami* worship may be of the same origin, but are quite different.

Thus *kami* worship is individual and local, but not national.

KANNON-SAMA

KANZEON (Avalokitescara), commonly called Kannon-sama, is the most popularly worshiped Buddhist saint in Japan. Statues representing him are seen all over the country. The oldest Kannon statue in Japan is the Guze Kannon of the Yumedono, Horyuji,

Nara, founded in 607 by Prince Shotoku.

There are 36 kinds of Kannon and their statues have different features, such as having nine or 11 faces, 1,000 hands, a horse's head, holding a lotus flower and so on.

Kannon stands for mercy, so the facial expression is tender and loving. Thus it looks feminine and generally is believed to be a female saint, though it is male.

Many Japanese think that the saint stands for a mother's love. Consequently, mothers pray to Kannon for the health and happiness of their children or take them to visit Kannon temples. In the old days, fond mothers, particularly those who lost their children, used to make long pilgrimages to various Kannon temples to pray for the happiness or salvation of their children.

The merciful Kannon is also believed to bring wealth and good fortune to worshipers whose number has increased among merchants and artisans.

Kannon worship spread particularly during the Muromachi period (15th-16th centuries) and gradually gained influence among the common people.

As such people still worship Kannon-sama, it may even be said that they worship Kannon as a merciful saint without knowing what Buddhism teaches.

Juichimen-Kannon (eleven-faced Kannon) has actually 12 faces. Around the main face are added 11 smaller faces of different expressions. This statue sometimes has two hands, but again, in many, there are four hands.

Senju-Kannon (thousand-hands Kannon) really has only 40 hands. Each hand has an eye on it and also holds some object. The eye is the symbol of Kannon implying 'sovereign who beholds.'

One of the strangest Kannon-sama is *Bato-Kannon* (horse-headed Kannon). It differs from other Kannon, and has a fearful countenance. It has the head of a horse, of either white or blue color. It is said that Kannon is shown with a horse-head as she thinks of the deliverance of men as the horse does about eating and drinking. According to another version, however, the goddess does away with evils and terror as effectively as the horse eats up food and water. The blue head of the horse stands for the power of destruction, and the white one represents the purity of Kannon. This Kannon is often seated on a buffalo, and also carries an axe in her hand.

KAZA-MATSURI

THE PEOPLE of Japan have suffered much from heavy rainstorms ever since the beginning of time. Believing that they were caused by some divine power, people came to offer prayers to the rainstorms so that they would be spared from the fury of such phenomena.

There are also shrines and temples dedicated to the deity of wind and rain, which are generally called *fujin-do* or *kazakami-do*. At such places, prayers are offered from June, the beginning of the so-called typhoon season, to September. At some places they are called *kaze-no-miya* or wind shrines.

In many parts of the country *kaza-matsuri* or wind festivals are still held to protect crops from damage caused by storms. This festival is observed in various ways. At some places sickles are placed on housetops, threatening to cut the deity of wind and rain into pieces if it visits the region. The villagers also go up to the tops of nearby mountains and start big bonfires.

The Suwa-myojin Shrine, at Suwa, Nagano Prefecture, is one of the oldest shrines of the country and is said to have been dedicated to Takeminakata-no-mikoto, son of Okuninushi, the mythological ruler of Izumo, who fled to Suwa and never returned. But according to accounts in the *Nihon-shoki*, the Suwa-myojin was erected to the deity of wind and rain.

It is recorded that one named Kasenojafuri used to pray in the Suwa-myojin for 100 days continuously against storms visiting the district, and that if he failed to go on with the prayer for that duration, a devastating storm would certainly arise, or when he started his prayer during a storm, it would never stop if he neglected his prayers.

KIRISHITAN-MURA

THE PERSECUTION of Christians was started by Toyotomi Hideyoshi in 1587. Foreign missionaries were driven out of the country and Japanese believers were killed. But there were a number of determined Christians who followed their faith, hiding in remote mountain regions, particularly in northeastern areas, and giving up their social rank, position, wealth and even families.

Many of those ardent Christians found shelter in mining camps in the mountains. These camps were far from towns beyond the reach of the law and officials. Criminals hiding in such camps could never be caught. Many Christians, in running away from officials, entered such camps which were willing to aid any who asked for help. It was through the mining camps that the propagation of Christianity continued despite the strict official prohibition.

Thus there came to be formed districts which are still called *Kirishitan-mura* or Christian villages where all the inhabitants are Christians.

In the northern province of Iwate, for instance, on the slope of the Kitakami mountain range near the border between Iwate and Miyagi prefectures, there is a little village named Okago, where there is no Buddhist temple but instead there is a tall Christian church which is the village landmark.

The district was opened up several centuries ago by sand-iron miners. Escaping Christians from the southern regions found shelter and friends among the miners who were rough and ignorant and even lawless and evil. But out of their kindness in hiding the Christians, the *Kirishitan-mura* is still preserved.

KOJIN-SAMA

THE POPULARITY of *Kojin-sama* is proved by the fact that he guards one of the most important things of our daily life, that is necessary for all classes of people. None are able to live without the blessing of *Kojin-sama* in Japan as he is the god of the kitchen.

His duties are to see that the supplies of the kitchen are always ample, that things cooked there are always of good taste, that the kitchen fire always burns well, and that there will be no fire accidents in the kitchen. Therefore, when a family worships *Kojin-sama*, and is in his good graces, the family will always be happy.

It is believed that *Kojin-sama* lives in the kitchen hearth, and therefore in Japanese houses, the hearth is always considered sacred.

Kojin-sama was originally, however, not the god of the kitchen. While the guardian of the kitchen has a noble function, he formerly had much nobler duties to perform while in India.

At first *Kojin-sama* punished bad people and protected the Three Treasures, viz. Buddha, Buddhist teachings and priests. So he was one of the most important personages while in India, as his duties were of such noble and distinguished character.

It is not known how he came to be the god of the kitchen after reaching Japan. But any god who is able to punish bad people and protect the Three Treasures, may be able to protect the kitchen and keep the family in a happy and contented condition. Moreover, there may possibly be some people who consider the kitchen equally as important as Buddha, Buddhist teachings and priests.

KOMAINU

KOMAINU (wolf dog) is a stone or metal figure representing an animal that looks like a dog or a lion, placed in front of a shrine to guard its sanctity from devils and evil. They always come in pairs, one standing on each side of the entrance-way. Sometimes they are both lions while others represent dogs. Or again the one on the left is a lion and that on the right a dog.

Komainu came from China, but some say it was from Korea as *koma* means Korea. In China they were placed at the gates of government offices or at cemeteries. But the Chinese *komainu* is a strange animal looking like one-horned cattle, black in color. Its hide is said to have been very tough, and was used for making war helmets.

This strange animal became a symbolic guard for protecting palaces and tombs. But the lion, which was considered the strongest wild animal by Indians, was introduced to China and lion figures made of stone also came to be placed at the gates of palaces, temples and cemeteries.

When Chinese customs were brought into Japan, the *komainu* and lions became mixed. It does not matter to the Japanese whether they place one or the other at shrine entrances, as both are regarded as effective guards.

There is, however, another legendary tale that goes back to mythological days about the origin of the *komainu.* Hosuseri-no-mikoto greatly admired the virtue and character of Hikohohodemi-no-mikoto, and pledged that not only he but also his sons and future generations would guard the palace gate of Hikohohodemi, becoming his 'dog-man.' He meant that all his family and future descendents would always remember the great Mikoto's virtue, faithful as dogs are to their masters. So some say the origin of *komainu* is traced to this tale.

KO MEETINGS

KO ARE social institutions that play a big role, particularly in rural districts. They originally started as religious meetings, but today their social features are more emphasized than the religious.

Ko developed from *ko-e* or classes for student Buddhist priests, which started in the eighth century. *Ko* became a general term later for any class or meeting of persons gathered for the same object. Thus local gatherings, at first by a few neighbors or villagers who met regularly for religious purposes, came to be called *ko.* Well-known are Iseko, Daishi-ko, Fuji-ko, Kannon-ko, Konpira-ko, Koshin-ko, and many others.

Although *ko* were first related to Buddhism, there are *ko* for shrine and other worship. Many *ko* are formed for making pilgrimages to temples, shrines or mountains, as in the case of Ise-ko and Fuji-ko. Members of such *ko* pay monthly dues to cover the cost of their annual pilgrimages.

There are *ko* formed by women alone, and *ko* composed of old men only. Persons engaged in the same profession often form their own *ko*. Carpenters have their *ko*, while in many mining areas, miners have one of their own.

Besides annual pilgrimages, *ko* members usually meet monthly or seasonally. Some religious talks or services are held, following which the meetings become social affairs, with tea, sweets, *sake* and many good things to eat, which are brought by attending members. Particularly for rural women, such *ko* meetings are the only hours for their recreation and release from daily toil.

While there are large-sized *ko* with thousands in their membership, most local *ko* are small, formed by immediate neighbors or relatives. These small *ko* are the ones which have so much social influence in the local community.

KOMUSO

MEN ARE often seen on the streets of Japan playing *shakuhachi*, a long bamboo flute, wearing a deep straw hat that completely covers their heads, and dressed in a monk-like costume, stopping at every door begging for alms. They are called *komuso*.

Komuso was originally the name given to the priests of the Fuke school of Zen Buddhism. They wore *tengai*, the deep sunshade, because they were not allowed to show their faces when they went out of their temples.

During Edo days, *ronin* or masterless *samurai* and fugitives hid themselves in Fuke temples, where no outsiders, official or private, were permitted to enter. For safety's sake, some of the said class of *samurai* dressed themselves up in the *komuso* costume whenever they went out. It is also recorded that many military spies went about as *komuso* in order to keep their identity unknown.

The *komuso* thus frequently makes an appearance in various feudal tales. Traditionally the *komuso* wears the deep *tengai*, carries a *shakuhachi* in his hand, has another *shakuhachi* wrapped up in a cloth bag tucked in his belt at the back, and has a pair of black lacquered *geta* or wooden clogs on his feet.

With the Meiji Restoration, however, the Fuke sect was dissolved, and *komuso* disappeared. Nevertheless, the habit of wearing such costumes, playing *shakuhachi* and going around for alms is still kept up by beggars, as oldfashioned folks are still willing to give alms and food to those attired in the style of *komuso*.

KONPIRA

KONPIRA-SAMA has a strange history. He is a famous *kami* of ships and voyages, and every shipowner, sailor, merchant sending goods by ship and shipbuilder carries a talisman of *Konpira* so that the ship or voyage may be safe. Models and pictures of ships are presented to Konpira shrines. The shrine at Takamatsu, Sanuki province, on the island of Shikoku, is especially famous and receives pilgrims from all parts of the country.

But this *kami* of ships and navigation was originally the *kami* of a mountain in India. He was the *kami* of the Lingchiu Mountain, according to the Chinese version of the legend. He is usually pictured in a priest's costume, wearing a close-fitting cloth cap, and holding in his hand a feather fan.

Though he took up an entirely new role in Japan, *Konpira-sama* became immensely popular here among shipowners, sailors and merchants. Not only is there the big shrine at Sanuki, but there are erected many smaller ones all over the country. The *kami* of ships and navigation is so much in the minds of the people that *Konpira* finally became an adjective for ships and voyages. In ancient literature and songs, *Konpira* is frequently mentioned with ships and voyages, although the expression does not possess any special meaning. It is only attached to *fune* (ship) to make it more literary or poetic.

As it is the guardian of ships and navigation, many of the *Konpira-sama* have large collections of pictures and models of ancient ships.

KOYASU-SAMA

A CRUDE statue representing a woman with her hair hanging down the back and holding a baby in her arms is called *Koyasu-sama* (deity for easy childbirth), and worshiped for easy birth and abundant milk in Chiba, Ibaraki and many other localities.

Such *Koyasu-sama* are generally placed in a simple stone house by the roadside, but there are also others which are erected in more elaborately made structures and are called *Koyasu-jinja* or *Koyasu* shrines.

The worship of *Koyasu-sama* or *Koyasu-gami* seems to be very old. The *Koyasu* Shrine at Hachioji, Tokyo, is said to have been erected in 731 in prayer for easy delivery by Empress Komyo.

Koyasu shrines are reported to be dedicated to *Konohana-sakuya-hime*, a mythological deity who gave birth to three sons while her delivery hut was on fire.

Koyasu-Kannon and Koyasu-jizo are also worshiped throughout the country, particularly in western districts. Kannon is the Buddhist goddess of mercy, and Jizo is the Buddhist guardian of children. Both these Buddhist statues are worshiped by pregnant mothers for the easy delivery of their babies.

The ancient *Koyasu-sama* worship came to be mixed with Buddhism as the new religion spread among the people. Christians under persecution in Tokugawa days worshiped Christ in the statue of Kannon. Likewise *Koyasu-sama* came to be worshiped in the shape of Kannon or Jizo.

In the old days mothers formed groups to worship *Koyasu-sama* in many rural districts, and their worship gave rise to many traditional customs.

At Gonohe in Aomori, there was formerly a custom of mothers offering bags of rice to *Koyasu-sama* in prayer for easy child delivery. The bags were called milk bags. Mothers who did not have enough milk for their babies went to *Koyasu-sama* and borrowed the bags already presented there. They took the rice, cooked and ate it. If such mothers as a result got more milk, they thanked *Koyasu-sama* by offering new bags of rice.

KUMA-MATSURI

THE *KUMA-MATSURI* (bear festival) of the Ainus is very famous. As a bear is killed for the festival, it is often regarded as a rite of sacrificing a bear for their god, but actually it is a rite for sending back the spirit of god to heaven.

The Ainus believe in many gods which live in heaven. When a god descends to Earth, it comes in a covering, they say. The mountain god that gives the Ainu the bounty of the mountain, comes in the covering of a bear. He stays as a guest of the Ainus, bringing them gifts of food.

At the *Kuma-matsuri*, a bear is killed to release its spirit from the covering. The Ainus place the skull bone in an honored place, offering it drinks and many good things to eat. It is a rite to send the spirit of the god that came in the shape of a bear with bountiful gifts, back to heaven with their thanks and many presents.

When the god is freed of its bear covering and returns to heaven, the Ainus believe it shares with other gods what presents were offered on its departure from Earth. Also they think the god will tell how kind and appreciative the Ainus were of the gifts bestowed on them.

Upon hearing of the experience of the god with the Ainus, other gods will become willing to visit Earth with gifts to bless the kind people.

Thus by holding the *Kuma-matsuri* and sending back the spirit of the god to heaven, the Ainus look forward to the coming of more gods with blessings and gifts.

KUMANO SHRINE

SUSANO-O-NO-MIKOTO, the son of Izanagi, whose brave act, as is known to every child in Japan, of destroying the eight-headed dragon which brought sorrow to the people of Izumo, is the god of the sea. He was a spirited, active and adventurous young man. He once displeased his father by his reckless conduct.

However, the Kumano Shrine in which Susano-o-no-mikoto is enshrined is considered not only the guardian of the sea and navigation, but also as the protector of agriculture and sericulture. For a *kami* of such physical strength and adventurous temperament to be made the god of sericulture and agriculture is indeed seemingly strange. But there is a traditional story that gives him this added honor.

While Susano-o-no-mikoto was in disgrace, he traveled in rags. He was hungry, and his features were unkempt and dirty. On the road he met Ogetsu-hime-no-mikoto and, not having eaten for many days, he asked for some food.

Thereupon the friend produced food from her eyes, mouth, ears and nose. This greatly angered Susano-o-no-mikoto who thought that his friend was insulting him on account of his poor appearance. He finally drew his sword and killed his friend.

The body fell to the ground, but suddenly from the head appeared silk cocoons, from both eyes flowed wheat, from the ears came millet and from the nose streamed beans.

At that time these were new foodstuffs, and cocoons were rare. Consequently Susano-o-no-mikoto, who was responsible for the production of these cocoons and seeds from the body of Ogitsu-hime-no-mikoto, came to be regarded as the god of sericulture and agriculture.

Factually, however, it was Kami-musubino-oya-gami who collected these new seeds and made them prosper in the land of Japan.

LOTUS THRONE

HASU or Japanese lotus (Nelumbo macifera) is cultivated throughout Japan. In parks, lakes and private gardens it is planted for its gorgeous red or white blossoms that bloom in summer. Farmers cultivate it for obtaining *renkon*, the long edible roots. Though it is for either viewing its flowers or eating its roots, *hasu* is primarily associated with Buddhism and particularly paradise in the mind of the Japanese people.

'To sit on the throne of *hasu*' means rebirth in paradise after death, and is the goal of the Buddhist faith. Ardent Buddhist believers pray day and night for their future glory of sitting on the lotus throne, as all Buddhist saints are represented in their statues.

In the Edo period, a group of clever priests of the Nichiren sect made big fortunes by taking advantage of this popular religious ambition of sitting on the lotus throne. They approached wealthy old folks and inciting their religious ardor, promised them a real lotus throne upon death.

When an applicant was secured, they held an elaborate Buddhist ceremony in their temple. In the middle of the temple a seat was made in the center of a huge *hasu* flower, made of paper and wood. On the seat the applicant was placed, while many priests and his relatives and friends loudly prayed for his salvation as gongs and drums were beaten incessantly.

At the height of the prayers and loud music, the petals of the artificial *hasu* rose smoothly and finally enclosed the applicant entirely in their fold. The noise and prayer were kept on for some time, and then the lotus flower was reopened, to show the applicant peacefully dead on his glorious lotus throne.

It is not necessary to explain that, held in the fold of thick lotus petals, he was killed by one of the priests who hid himself under the artificial blossom. But the applicant himself died on the throne of *hasu* as he so eagerly desired, and his family was contented as he had realized his wish. The priests were satisfied with the large donation made by the applicant and his family.

To view the *hasu* blossoms, it has been customary to form an early-rising party, because it opens before dawn every summer morning and closes as the sun rises high. It has been traditionally said that *hasu* blossoms open with a popping sound, but recently scientists have proved by various tests that no such sound is made.

Formerly *hasu* leaves and blossoms were believed to possess curative power, and dried leaves or flowers were used in curing boils or toothache. The seeds are of course edible and greatly enjoyed by children.

The roots of *hasu* are long, sometimes reaching more than four feet. They come in three to four sections, and are two to four inches in diameter. There run small holes within the root along its length. When broken, very fine silk-like threads are seen running through the holes.

There is the story of the 'Mandala,' a picture of Buddha woven of *renkon* threads. Chujo-Hime, daughter of Minister Fujiwara Toyonari, entered the Taima Temple of Yamato in 763, when her father was forced to resign due to malicious false charges made against him by his enemies. Becoming a nun, she resolved to weave a Mandala with the *hasu* threads. It was a most delicate and difficult task to collect those fine threads out of lotus roots, to make them into yarn and then to weave them into the Mandala picturing Buddha. But she accomplished it in 12 years and died in 775 at the age of 29.

MARIA-KANNON

IN THE LITERATURE of the 17th and 18th centuries, and especially those connected with the persecuted Christians, there is often mention made of Maria-Kannon. Even today, the people of Nagasaki and its vicinity are familiar with the expression, and there are many statues of Maria-Kannon preserved there.

It is a strange combination, Maria and Kannon. Maria is, of course, the Virgin Mary, the mother of Christ; Kannon is the Buddhist Goddess of Mercy. For these two to be brought together is rather an unusual thing. But the so-called Maria-Kannon statue appears to be only that of Kannon, and bears no likeness to the Virgin Mary in its features.

The early Christians were ordered to forsake their religion, and throw away all crosses, pictures and statues of Maria. Many were persecuted for not obeying the order, but there were some who meekly obeyed the order. These, however, did not forsake the religion entirely, and worshiped Maria in some way or other that would not attract the attention of the officials. Some, it is reported, found that on the breast of a certain Kannon statue imported from China there was a swastika. It was a happy revelation to these Christians, who thought that the swastika stood for the cross, and worshiped the Kannon as a disguised image of Maria. So to the statue was given the name of Maria-Kannon.

Another story says that these persecuted Christians designed such statues in order not to be caught by the watchful eyes of the authorities. This story, however, sounds incredible, as all such statues in existence are of Chinese origin and of very poor and cheap quality at that.

Kannon being the Goddess of Mercy, her alliance with Maria is not impossible. But a statue of Maria-Kannon sounds outrageously strange.

MARISHITEN

MARISHITEN is one of the popularly worshiped Buddhist deities. There are many temples dedicated to it. It was particularly worshiped by military men in feudal days, as the deity of victory.

Many foreign deities introduced into Japan changed in character as they came to be worshiped by the Japanese. Marishiten may be said to be one of the most notable of such cases.

Originally Marishiten or Marici was a female deity depicted in the form of an angel. She stood for light or brightness. She was always before the sun and possessed supernatural powers. She could not be caught, could not be burnt and could not be drowned. When one believed in her, he would be safe from all calamities, it was said. In China Marishiten was regarded as the mother of the Great Bear Star.

But coming to Japan, Marishiten became a male deity of victory. Nobody can explain how its sex and character changed so markedly. But change it did and warriors worshiped it by erecting temples in its honor which are still popularly visited by many.

Following the warriors, those engaged in theatrical and entertainment activities came to worship Marishiten. Gradually all those who wished for victory and success went to Marishiten temples to pray.

Thus the female Marishiten became a male deity of victory, but the statues of Marishiten in many temples generally have a mild-looking countenance that is almost feminine, and are dressed in a flowing costume that may also suggest a woman.

Marishiten (Marici) is the war-god under Taishakuten (Sakradevanam Indra) who rules over Four Worlds and Thirty-three Heavens. It was the duty of Marishiten to constantly inspect the Four Worlds, to protect Buddha's followers, and to destroy all enemies of the merciful faith. He is the war-god because he had to fight all sorts of devils and evils in the discharge of his task of protecting Buddha's followers and punishing their enemies.

Marishiten is a strong protector of the faithful, because he is always on tours of inspection through the Four Worlds, and knows whatever is happening in every corner of the worlds. Any good act one performs will be noticed by him, but again, any evil done will be also known to him however small and trifling.

Temples of Marishiten are found in many parts of the country, and they are popular places of worship. Now he has not only lost his distinction as being the war-god, but also he has extended his blessing to all people, regardless of religion. Formerly he protected only followers of Buddha, but now anyone, even those not believing in Buddha, will go to his temple and pray for protection. This popularity proves that he is giving his blessing to all who need his protection, despite religious differences.

MIKO

SHRINES have young girl attendants called *miko* or children of *kami*, generally dressed in white kimono and red skirts. It is because in ancient days little children were regarded as the symbol of *kami* or deities. They were respected and even worshiped as the young had the best and longest future, and thus were the hope of the world. Furthermore children are pure, untainted by human evils and cravings. Being as sacred as *kami*, they have been selected to serve shrines and perform important roles at festivals.

The fact that Ninigi-no-mikoto who was sent by the Sun Goddess to rule the country was a newborn baby, as recorded in the *Kojiki* or ancient records, is also said to have influenced the people to regard children as the symbol of *kami*.

At many shrine festivals, richly dressed little children who are also called *miko* are still to be seen. On the huge decorated floats drawn through the street on the festival day, as at the Gion Festival of Kyoto and many other famous festivals of the country, ride beautifully dressed *miko*. They are the symbol of the shrine *kami*, and the parents of such children feel highly honored.

Likewise, the idea that little children represent purity of soul and an untainted mind has been manifested in many customs of the country.

Thus at first the *miko* was a servant of the *kami*, but gradually there developed another kind of *miko* who considers herself as the interpreter of the wishes of the *kami* or as a communicator with the dead.

All over the rural districts of the country, there are still many *miko* of the latter type who are skillfully performing their parts in such a manner that many believers do just as they command in the belief that it is the *kami*'s wish or the advice of the dead.

When people are sick the *miko* is called for driving out the devil by prayers. Her ability to cure illness is believed by a large number of rural people. Anyone desiring to hear from a dead person, may be able to do so with the help of a *miko* who puts herself in a trance and then speaks the words of the dead person.

She is also consulted on many matters. The building of houses, journeys, a change of business, and marriages are all decided after consultation with *miko*.

But this *miko* who performs these superstitious ceremonies for rural believers is not a young virgin. She is generally an old and dried-up person. She is often ugly and vicious, but to those who believe in her, her word is most sacred.

The practice of *miko* is illegal, but it is hard to kill the superstitions of rural people, among whom there is still quite a demand for the service of *miko*.

Although this kind of *miko* might have originally developed from the *miko* who serve the Shinto shrines, the medium *miko* has no relation with Shintoism or shrines.

MIKUJI

MANY SHRINES of the country give *mikuji* (sometimes called *omikuji*) or written oracles to worshipers at their request. Sometimes small payments are demanded for giving *mikuji*.

Visitors to such shrines who have faith in the power of the *kami* to guide and protect their lives desire to know the wishes of the *kami* regarding their present and future. Particularly when such visitors are troubled or unable to decide on some important questions, they wish to be guided by the *kami*'s wish. In order to ascertain the future in store for them or the wish of the *kami* regarding any particular matter, they ask for *omikuji* at the shrine office.

There are several different methods in giving *mikuji*. But the most common method is to draw a stick bearing a number, out of a large wooden or bamboo case of *mikuji* sticks. According to the number given on the stick, the priest will hand over a sheet of paper on which the *kami*'s message is given. Generally there are 100 sticks in the box, and each stick represents a different fortune.

The writing on the oracle paper, of course, differs according to shrine, but usually it tells whether the drawer is in good or bad luck, whether he should go on with the intended business or start on a proposed journey. Also it tells which direction is bad and which is good. It says whether a missing article or person will be found or not, and also foretells where he will meet an unexpected person.

Believers in the powers of the *kami* have faith in the message given by the oracle, and they decide their future actions according to its message. Many believers make special visits to shrines in order to obtain *mikuji* and thus learn the wish of the *kami*.

When a happy and prosperous future is predicted by *omikuji*, it is good and well, but the box also contains just as many unhappy and unfortunate messages. Such will greatly depress the drawers, especially as they believe the truth of the message given.

But there is a happy custom at many such temples and shrines. It is called *sute-mikuji* (thrown-away oracles). When one draws his fortune from the *omikuji* box, and finds it an unlucky one, not only is he depressed, but he is not satisfied. Then he wishes to return such an unlucky message, and thus ties the *omikuji* (the paper bearing the message) on a tree or the fence around the temple. At temples, trees and fences have many such white papers bearing sacred messages tied to branches or put into holes or cracks. The person who has tied his *omikuji*, selects one from the many that are already tied there and takes it.

The meaning of *omikuji* changes according to the sex and age of the drawer, and consequently one that is unlucky for a youth of 20 may be a lucky one for an old man of 50. Hence the exchanging of *omikuji* is done whenever the first draw is found unsatisfactory.

MIROKU-BOSATSU

MIROKU-BOSATSU is included among the *Jusan-bosatsu* (Thirteenth Buddha), but he is the rearguard of Buddhism and has not yet appeared on this Earth.

When Buddha died, many of his disciples were appointed to take his place in saving humanity. But Miroku was given the last position in the line. According to the general belief, he is to descend on this world 5,670,000,000 years after the departure of Buddha from the mortal world.

Now, that is many, many generations

after us, and it is so far away that we are not even sure of human existence in so remote a time. But many people worship Miroku-Bosatsu and ask his blessing to be given 5,670,000,000 years later. They make the wish because they believe that their soul transmigrates and has rebirth through the six stages of existence. In their belief there is no end to transmigration of their soul, and so it is necessary that the welfare of their soul hundreds and thousands of million years later be thought of.

Miroku-Bosatsu (Maritreya) is, however, known to be full of mercy and blessing, and he will protect and save our soul when the time arrives for him to take up the task of the savior.

Our trust in Miroku, however, is not wholly fruitless in the near future, as it is also said that he is taking an interest in us even before his descent to this world.

If one does not wish to have his soul reborn in the shape of animals, devils or insects many millions of years later, he should be a believer in the virtues of Miroku and ask him to save his soul from such degradation.

MITOSHI-NO-KAMI

FARMERS nowadays are neglecting their guardian deity. It is probably on this account that droughts, floods and insects are causing them much trouble, and bringing them smaller harvests. Their new knowledge has led them astray from their important guardian *kami.*

The protector of farmers' interests is Mitoshi-no-kami, who is to be honored with many offerings and worshiped with sincere prayers by all farmers of the country. The virtues of Mitoshi-no-kami can be judged by the following incident:

When O-tokonushi-no-kami was in control of a vast stretch of rice fields, he once fed his farmers with extremely poor food. This fact angered Mitoshi-no-kami who always had the interests of farmers at heart, and in order to punish O-tokonushi-no-kami for such insults to farmers, he called out *inago* (rice locusts) to the farms of O-tokonushi-no-kami. Innumerable *inago* gathered at the farms and ate up all the ears of rice in a field in one night.

Observing his fields of rice after destruction, O-tokonushi-no-kami realized that he had displeased Mitoshi-no-kami and that, unless he regained the favor of the protector of farmers, he would be unable to harvest any rice. Consequently, he went to Mitoshi-no-kami and pleaded for pardon and mercy. Thereupon, the *inago* left his fields as suddenly as they came.

The above is just one incident handed down from the earliest period of the history of Japan. The farmers of today are forgetting that they should always offer their best to Mitoshi-no-kami who guards over the fields of farmers every day and every night, and sees that the harvest of the faithful is never molested.

MIZU-GORI

THE CUSTOM of purifying oneself of evil thought and sickness by pouring water over one's body, or jumping into the sea or a river is quite ancient. Water purification has thus become an important Shinto shrine rite. In many parts of the country the custom of a person in charge of a shrine festival purifying himself by going into a river or the sea is still observed. At first for water purification, they mostly went to the sea.

Later, water purification also came to be regarded as being effective in avoiding calamities and inviting good fortune. When someone was seriously ill, all the family members and relatives took *mizu-gori* or water purification for his recovery. *Mizu-gori* became particularly popular at the beginning of the 18th century in the Tokugawa era. Some even observed it for luck in gambling or as a sign of repentance.

Those visiting Oyama Mountain (Kanagawa Prefecture) used to purify themselves by entering the Sumida River at Asakusa or Ryogoku. Members of *Fuji-ko* (groups to worship Mt. Fuji) also jumped into a river before climbing the mountain, shouting 'Zange, zange' (repent).

In praying to Buddhist or Shinto deities at home, many people poured water over their heads and bodies at the well at home, believing that by purifying themselves of evil thoughts, their prayers would be answered. Many Buddhist priests, too, in the course of their austere training, used to sit for hours or even days under waterfalls in the mountains. Many temples still have small waterfalls in their compounds under which priests and laymen sit hours for their enlightenment.

It is also commonly believed that those who are insane or mentally unbalanced will benefit by undergoing the waterfall treatment. During the coldest season of *kan*, many persons still perform the rite of *kanmairi*, or cold-season pilgrimage. Dressed in the scantiest clothes, they visit their shrines at night, and pour cold water over their heads and bodies.

MONJU-BOSATSU

THE *KAMI* of wisdom and intellect is Monju-Bosatsu (Manjusri) who is more commonly known merely as Monju. A proverb says, '*Sannin yoreba Monju no chie*' (three heads will produce the wisdom of Monju) meaning that three heads will produce more wisdom than one head, not that the wisdom of Monju is only three times that of an ordinary man.

Monju is thus the standard of wisdom, and the highest stage of intellect. It appears, however, that while the people of the country have been in the habit of building shrines and temples to almost everything, they have forgotten to erect many temples in honor of the *kami* of wisdom. Some may say that the people desire good luck, happiness and wealth, if they are to be judged by the number of shrines and temples built for other deities.

In India, Manjusri was held in a higher position than many other Bosatsu, and when it comes to wisdom he was not approached by any other. His wisdom, however, is apparently not so much esteemed in Japan, although everyone is aware that he is the *kami* of wisdom and intellect.

Tenjin-sama, which is erected in honor of Sugawara Michizane, is a far more popular shrine for the people. Tenjin is worshiped as the *kami* of learning and wisdom.

Maybe it is a case of thinking more of a native *kami* than of a foreign deity. Yet, there exist numerous foreign gods and goddesses who are extremely popular with the people. It may thus be said that, despite his great wisdom and intellect, Monju has been somewhat unfortunate in Japan in not being able to win the hearts of the people.

MT. FUJI

MOUNTAINS are sacred to the Japanese, but above all Mt. Fuji is the most sacred mountain of the country. The worship of Mt. Fuji is reported to have started from the very beginnings of the country, and the *Manyoshu* contains many poems that give proof to the worship of the mountain by the people.

The sacredness of the mountain has naturally brought about the custom of making a pilgrimage to the mountain, and while it is not known clearly when such pilgrimages to Mt. Fuji actually commenced, it is believed that many people climbed the mountain to worship its spirit from a very early period. In a document written in June 1500, it is mentioned that there was an endless chain of people climbing the mountain, and it is thus certain that the climbing of Mt. Fuji was already then quite popular among the people. The worship of Mt. Fuji subsequently developed into a sort of religious faith, and the Fuji-ko, organization of Mt. Fuji worshipers, was formed.

Even today, a greater portion of the thousands of people who climb the mountain every day in summer belong to this organization. To these people, the climbing of Mt. Fuji is not a sport or pleasure, but a religious pilgrimage. They are dressed in a costume of white, signifying the purity of their heart, although the white garment is usually dirty with long use and with the impression of numerous red seals of the mountain. They carry *kongozue*, long wooden sticks for supporting their body and conscience. They make the annual pilgrimage to the mountain to pray for their health, happiness and prosperity.

Modern mountain climbing has become very popular in the country, and spiked shoes and other Western mountain-climbing equipment are largely used by young climbers. But on Mt. Fuji, still, the white-costumed Fuji-ko climbers are numerous. It is these people who are keeping up the tradition of the pilgrimage to Mt. Fuji. Among the younger mountain climbers who love to wear spiked shoes and carry pickels, Mt. Fuji is not so popular because the mountain does not give them a chance to try their rock or rope-climbing techniques.

Mt. Fuji stands by itself in the minds of the people, and climbing that mountain cannot be classed together with the climb up the Japan Alps or numerous other mountains which are becoming so popular.

The worship of Mt. Fuji is said to have originated from the very beginnings of the country, but the present form of the Fuji-ko or organization of Mt. Fuji worshipers came into existence in the first part of the 16th century. In the Tokugawa period it began to grow significantly.

According to a popular tale, the origin of Fuji-ko is attributed to one named Kakugyo. In 1532, Sokan Hasegawa Hisamitsu of Nagasaki felt greatly distressed because of the disturbances prevailing in the country and the suffering of the people.

He realized that the saving of the nation and people could only be accomplished by praying to *kami*. He was unable, however, to fully carry out his plan due to his weak health. In 1541, a son was born to him, and the child was named Takematsu. As he grew up, he vowed to carry out his father's plan. He traveled through many parts of the country and prayed at various temples and shrines. He later came to be known as Kakugyo. He believed that Mt. Fuji was 'the beginning of heaven and Earth, pillar of the nation, and foundation of national administration.' Thus he formed the Fuji-ko to propagate his belief and gather together the worshipers of Mt. Fuji. In 1646, this founder of the Fuji-ko died in a cave on a slope of Mt. Fuji.

From then, the Fuji-ko movement became exceedingly popular, and not only the descendents and followers of Kakugyo carried on the work started by its founder, but also there appeared numerous other groups of Mt. Fuji worshipers. During the Tokugawa period it was popularly said that there were 808 organizations of Mt. Fuji pilgrims.

As the worship of Mt. Fuji became further popular with the development of so many groups of Mt. Fuji pilgrims, there came to be erected miniature Mt. Fujis in Edo and other parts of the country, to afford an opportunity of worshiping the mountain to those who could not go to the mountain. The first such miniature Mt. Fuji was built in Shitaya, Edo, in 1827. With the erection of such miniature Mt. Fujis in various districts, the women and aged were given an opportunity to worship the mountain. Mt Fuji being sacred, women were at first denied the privilege of climbing it, and it was in 1872 that women were permitted to climb it.

After the Meiji Restoration, the Fuji-ko underwent some changes, and many of them were made into the Fuso-kyokai and became a purely Shinto sect. But on the other hand, the worship of Mt. Fuji did not change, and there appeared more groups of Fuji-ko although some of them now bear various different names.

Each Fuji-ko has a *komoto* (leader), *sendatsu* (guides), and the members are called *koju*. Besides conducting the annual pilgrimage to Mt. Fuji, the Fuji-ko followers worship Sengen-Daibosatsu, *kami* or spirit of Mt. Fuji, for guidance in their daily conduct as well as business matters.

Fuji is sacred as well as the symbol of the destiny of the people's thought and conduct.

The delight of the Mt. Fuji climbers lies in the view of the rising sun from the top of the mountain. As they see the bright red sun rising from the east, above the clouds and mountains, they feel the glory and future prosperity of the nation. Mt. Fuji is the foundation of

the national administration, pillar of the country, and beginning of heaven and Earth, the founder of the Fuji-ko declared.

In worshiping the sacredness of the mountain, men and women, as well as little children, climb the mountain every summer. The hardship of climbing the mountain is nothing but joy, as every step over the volcanic ashes is an answer to their prayer for their good fortune and the nation's welfare.

NEMURI-NAGASHI

DURING the week of *Tanabata* or star festival of July 7, old rites that have no connection with the legend of the Weaver meeting Altair once a year in the evening are held in many localities. From ancient days, a service of worshiping ancestors was observed on the full-moon day of July, and thus this month has become the time for various local rites.

In Aomori a rite called *nemuri-nagashi* (shaking off sleepiness), which is believed to drive out drowsiness and make all alert and active, is held.

First the people make *nebuta-toro* or 'sleepy lanterns,' which come mostly in the shape of folding fans or dolls. Elaborate big lanterns are made while children make small simple ones. They have lighted candles inside and are carried around or drawn on wheels through the streets for several days before July 7.

On the evening of July 7, all *nebuta-toro* are taken to rivers and left to float away. It is believed that the lanterns will carry away drowsiness to the sea.

As to the origin of this rite, there is a tale of Sakano-ue-no Tamuramaro, who was sent by Emperor Kanmu in 804 to subjugate the northern districts. The local chief at Tsugaru stopped the advance of the forces under Tamuramaro.

Tamuramaro then resorted to a novel strategy to defeat the opposition.

He made many large dolls, in which armed fighters hid. With gay music and dancing, they carried them toward the enemy. Attracted by the music, the enemy soldiers came out from hiding to watch. When they came near the dolls, the men inside sprang out and caught them. The captives were thrown into the river.

In some places logs or branches of *nemu* (silk tree) or *ibota* (wax tree) are thrown into the river to drive away sleepiness on July 7. It is also traditionally believed in many places that if women wash their hair on that day, it will be thoroughly cleaned of all dirt.

NETARO-KOJIN

AT ASA, Yamaguchi Prefecture, stands Netaro-Kojin, a shrine dedicated to Netaro (sleepy boy), who was famous for his laziness and sleepiness.

He was from a rich and good family, but because of his habit of sleeping long hours and all the time, he was called Netaro by the villagers. It is said that once he slept continuously for three years and three months. As he did not work because of his laziness and sleepiness, he exhausted his stock of food and had to go hungry.

Netaro was no fool, though children laughed at him and the villagers despised him. By the village there was a vast stretch of dry wasteland, where nothing could be cultivated. While nobody had any inkling about it, Netaro thought in his lazy brain that the great wasteland should be utilized. He conceived a plan of drawing water to the dry land from a river nearby and making the waste stretch productive. Eagerly he undertook his first work.

His scheme, carried out without telling anybody, soon succeeded and not only did he become very wealthy but the whole village also benefited. He died at the age of 210, a happy and respected man, it is said. So the villagers erected a shrine for him.

The story of Netaro became famous, and in a travel account written in 1821, he and the shrine in his honor are mentioned.

Within the shrine there is a wooden statue of Netaro, which represents a smiling, happy-faced man. Not only is the shrine worshiped by the villagers but they also started an annual custom of offering to the shrine straw monkeys in prayer for a good crop.

Some may say that the Netaro story is fiction, but the people of Asa still point to the lot called *Netaro-yashiki* (residence) and say that it was there that the house of Netaro stood. The village also sells *Netaro-mochi* (rice cake) named after him, of which the villagers are very proud.

NEW YEAR

TO THE PEOPLE of Japan, New Year is not merely the beginning of a year; it has much greater significance than the heading of a new calendar. To them the New Year brings new life, new hope and a chance to start fresh again. With the last reverberation of the 108th stroke of the temple bell at midnight, all the evils of the past year are dispelled, and the listeners acquire a fresh hold on life with all its happiness. Whatever may have been the fortune, good or ill, of the past year, the New Year opens with only the brightness of hope and joy.

As the people believe that happiness and good fortune come with the New Year, there developed a former custom of observing an extra or special New Year, when they were particularly suffering from epidemics, famine or economic depression, in hope of turning the evil fortune to happiness. On such extra New Years, they put New Year decorations on their house, and ate New Year *mochi*, so that with them joy would come.

Such special New Years are recorded to have been held in June 1778; May 1781; October 1827; August 1858; November 1880 (13th year of Meiji), and other times. Of course such extra New Years were unofficial, and also often only locally observed.

Very definitely does the Japanese year start on January 1 and end on December 31. Also New Year's Day quite distinctly separates the year that has passed and the year to follow. Each year is an independent unit, always starting on January 1, and not at any other time. It is inconceivable that the period from February 1, say, to the following January 31 could be considered a year; nay — they are parts of two separate years. It is from this conception of a year that the Japanese way of counting ages has arisen. To people of other countries it is bewildering to be told in all sincerity that a Japanese baby born on December 31 is two years old on the very next day, merely because it is New Year's Day. The explanation is that he has lived in two separate years, having been born in the one and continuing to live in the next.

Inasmuch as the New Year marks the beginning of a fresh lap on life's journey, it is naturally considered important that a proper start be made. Consequently, as the year-end draws near, the people find themselves with various matters to attend to. Debts must be paid and accounts settled by the close of the year for, should any unsettled accounts be carried over into another year, one's reputation would be impaired. Such a custom can, and often does, cause considerable worry to a per-

son who is heavily in debt for somehow or other, by hook or by crook, he must wipe his slate clean before the last stroke of the temple bell on December 31st!

Not only one's business, but one's home, must be put in readiness for the New Year and very important is the custom of *susuharai*, or year-end house cleaning. As in the case of debts, the dust and dirt of the old year must not be carried over into the new, for only into a clean place can the good fortune of the New Year come. Even the wardrobe of the family should be renovated and if possible new clothes made for each member of the family, for it is only seemly that the New Year should be welcomed in fresh, clean garments.

New Year, then, because of its significance, has to be celebrated both seriously and joyously. In times past, this celebration was considered so important that half of January was given over to festivity, but gradually the period of celebration has become shortened. Even so, there are several days at the beginning of the new year when no business is transacted, and, in fact, a festive spirit is abroad in the land throughout the whole first month.

The spirit of seriousness shown in the observance of the New Year comes from the conviction that the year, if started correctly, will bring success and fortune. It would never do to set an unpleasant pattern for the whole year by allowing quarrels to arise, or angry words to cause tears. And so, during the season of celebration one hears only expressions of joy and happiness, while merry people, young and old, make friendly calls or amuse themselves with games or other pastimes.

The Japanese name for New Year's is *Osho-gatsu*, meaning the just-right, or standard, month. As a government keeps in its capital the standards of weights and measures, so Japan keeps January as a standard for the rest of the year. All of this leads to the making of New Year resolutions and the determination to achieve prosperity and happiness in the coming months.

With the year ending at midnight on December 31, all the events of the preceding year are definitely relegated to the past, and the *bonen-kai* or year-forgetting parties of the Japanese are not inappropriate.

The very greetings of the season suggest that even friendship has come to a time for renewal. People meet one another, saying, 'New Year congratulations! Thank you for your kindness to me throughout last year! Please bestow upon me your kindness during the present year.'

What a pleasant, peaceful sight it is to see a village street where the New Year decorations have been set out in front of every house! It is the time when Japanese beautify a space outside of their house and garden. At each gate stands a pair of *kado-matsu*, or gate-pines, which are an arrangement of dark green pine and emerald-colored bamboo with, perhaps, a sprig of sweet-scented plum blossom. And over each doorway is a drape of yellow straw, hanging down in knots and tails, and caught together at the center of the lintel with a bunch of oranges, seaweed and green leaves. Very early the street is dotted with people setting out in their new clothes to exchange greetings with their friends.

The *kado-matsu*, never seen at any other time, is indispensable on this occasion. In its simplest form it is merely small branches of pine nailed on the door-posts; but the grander the house, the bigger and more elaborate is the arrangement which is set out at the gate. The pine, bamboo and plum combined in this decoration are called by their Chinese names, *sho-chiku-bai;* and as they are symbols of congratulation they are often used in designs by weavers and artists. The pine is not only strong and rugged; it also keeps its youthful verdure throughout its long, long life. The bamboo, straight and enduring, bends before the wind but does not break. The plum, pure and sweet, blooms bravely in its season even though snow lies on the ground. The *kado-matsu* is thus set in front of every house, with the hope that the new year will bring vigor and long life, and strength or steadfastness and virtue.

On January 7th the *kado-matsu* is removed and burned, and a sprig of pine is left in its place. The *kado-matsu* seems to have had its origin in the use of branches of the *sakaki* (Cleyera ochanacea) evergreen, placed before the entrance to a house or shrine as a symbol of purification or as a talisman against evil. The use of the pine at the gate became customary in the feudal ages, possibly because it is more easily obtained than the *sakaki.*

It is the caller who comes inside the gate who sees above the front door the *shime-nawa* or screen of long straws, sweet with the scent of the field, dangling from the thick horizontal rope of twisted straw. Quite often, however, this decoration takes the shape of a huge, twisted knot, from which protrudes a fringe of straws. The *shime-nawa* had its origin, supposedly, in the taboo of the South Seas, where it is still the symbol of sacred ownership — a fringe of straw encircling a tree — the straw skirt of a young woman. There is a tradition that, when the Sun Goddess was finally coaxed out of the cave wherein she had hidden, her subjects stretched a *shime-nawa* across the entrance to keep her from re-entering the cave and so bringing darkness upon the world again. In

Japan today, when hung in front of shrines, it indicates a holy place, sacred to the gods, where pollution may not enter; when seen above a house entrance at New Year's, it reminds us that the house is clean and that evil sprits are 'taboo.' Sometimes tiny replicas of this decoration are to be found in each room of the house.

Japanese, with their delight in puns, have added to the *shime-nawa* such felicitous decorations as *daidai* (the bitter orange), which also means 'generation after generation'; *konbu* (a kind of seaweed), with a slight variation in the pronunciation suggesting a wish for joy and happiness; the lobster, to bring long life, because its name is written with the Chinese ideographs meaning 'the aged of the sea'; also white-backed *urajiro* fern fronds for purity, and *yuzuri-ha* leaves for humility.

Another indispensable New Year object is the *kagami-mochi*. It is a pair of large cakes of *mochi*, made of rice steamed and pounded. They are placed one upon the other, the upper one being smaller than the lower. The use of *kagami-mochi* on festive occasions is quite old, it being recorded that it was already in use in the Engi era (901-923).

Mochi has been made since earliest times, and offered to deities and shrines. It is eaten on all festive occasions. New Year being the greatest annual event, *mochi* is not only eaten by all the people, but also each household places *kagami-mochi* in the best room.

Since ancient days, not only were *kagami-mochi* offered to deities and shrines on festive days, but were also placed in front of things the people valued highly to invite good luck. *Samurai* placed *kagami-mochi* in front of their boxes of armor; women before their mirrors, and merchants in their counting rooms. It is from women's *kagami-mochi* being placed before their *kagami*, or mirrors, that the name is said to have developed.

The ancient custom of displaying *kagami-mochi* on festive occasions is now preserved only in the New Year season.

This *kagami-mochi* is placed on two sheets of pure white paper and set on a little stand of whitewood in the *tokonoma* (alcove) of the parlor. Four *yuzuri-ha* leaves are laid around it, pointing in the four directions. It is further bedecked, not only with a red-and-white cord, but also with two ears of white corn, two dried persimmons, roasted chestnuts and dried sardines. On January 11 the *kagami-mochi* should be broken and eaten. Good sharp knives have never been used to cut this symbol of good fortune, and even today it is customarily broken with one's hands.

In the *tokonoma* alcove of the house the master likes to hang a special picture, a peaceful scene, perhaps in which are included some of the congratulatory emblems.

There is a Japanese saying: 'Even the devils smile on New Year's Day,' and whether this be the reason or not, one seldom observes even a scowl during this season. Even the arrogant, threatening creditor of the previous day offers a cheerful, smiling greeting for his erstwhile victim, his *'Omedeto!'* the New Year greetings exchanged by one and all.

Festivities begin early in the morning of the first day with formal calls, the master of the house making a round of his friends. Sometimes he merely bows at the entrance, leaves his card and departs; but the caller who goes inside is served with spiced *sake* and various delicacies. Should one's friends live at too great a distance for making a call, a post card serves instead. In former years, the first three days were the master's calling days, while the mistress stayed at home to entertain. After that, the mistress took her turn at calling. Nowadays, conditions are such that even this custom is in danger of dying out.

Japanese say, 'If the first caller of the year is a prosperous friend, the ensuing months will bring success and happiness; but alas for the year ushered in by the call of a beggar or a person of ill repute!'

Utagaruta, or poem cards, is the most popular indoor New Year game, and its popularity has not waned these 300 years. There are numerous varieties of card games in the world, but *utagaruta* is unique.

Fujiwara Teika, a great poet who died in 1242 at the age of 80, picked out the 100 best poets, and selected one poem from each. This collection of poems is called *Hyakunin-Isshu,* or 'One Hundred Persons, One Poem.'

Each of the hundred poems is divided into two parts, and the first half is written on one set of cards, and the latter half on the other. The cards bearing the latter part of the poems are distributed among the players. A reader then reads off the first parts, one by one. The game is to pick up the card bearing the second half. Expert players are able to pick up the second half as soon as the reader reads the first syllable of the poem.

The one finishing his cards first wins, and when someone picks up a card in another's pile, he gives one of his cards to the opponent who failed to find the card in his portion.

It is quite an exciting game, but requires lengthy practice to attain proficiency.

The game was played all through the Tokugawa period, and has not lost any of its popularity despite the introduction of modern games. In the old days, the *Utagaruta* party represented the

only occasion when young men and women were allowed to be together.

In recent years, championship games for determining the best players of districts and in the country have been held.

There are two outdoor sports closely associated with the beginning of the year — *hane-tsuki* for girls and occasionally boys, and *tako-age* for men and boys. The first might be called the Oriental variety of the Western battledore-and-shuttlecock. It is a charming sight to observe gaily dressed girls, with long sleeves flying, batting the elfin shuttlecocks high up into the air and catching them again on their ornate battledores. Sometimes it is agreed that, as a penalty for missing a strike, the player receives a daub of India ink on his or her face. At the end of the day the losers' faces present a strange sight; but even so, there is a smile behind the black steaks.

Meanwhile, men and boys have been flying their kites or *tako.* There is great rivary amongst communities and villages in making the largest kites that are capable of flying. Boys often play also at downing each other's kites by maneuvering to cross the kite-strings, so as either to cut or entangle the rival's string.

Inasmuch as New Year activities center around the feasting, and since there is almost no cooking done during the first few days, the women of the household spend several days ahead in preparation, thus justifying the use of the somewhat vulgar expression, of *kui-shogatsu* or an eating New Year.

In country places, where people still draw water from a well with an 'old oaken bucket,' there is quite a ceremonious drawing of the first water of the year. This *waka-mizu* or young water, has been the theme of many a poem in days gone by; and due to water's importance for the human body, this drawing of the first water is in the nature of a token of appreciation.

To be quite proper, the family should rise at dawn, wash in young water, dress in new garments, and sit down in the best room of the house. Here they all exchange New Year greetings and drink tiny cups of *fuku-cha*, the tea of good fortune. This may be seaweed tea, or ordinary green tea served with a pickled apricot in each cup. From ancient times tea and pickled apricot have been thought to guard against sickness.

Next comes the serving of *toso*, a special rice-wine for the occasion, which contains various medical herbs and spices, such as pepper, ginger, cinnamon, red beans, rhubard and bellflower root. A little silk bag filled with these ingredients and dropped into the cold wine will give it disease-dispelling properties. It is not unreasonable to claim that this spiced wine stimulates the digestion and quickens the circulation of the blood. In Japan, the drinking of this wine has become more a solemn rite than a mere ceremony; first the master, then the children and lastly the servants drink the *toso*.

Following this comes the eating of *zoni*, the soup peculiar to this time of year. The foundation may be either a clear soup or bean-mash soup; but the ingredients should include toasted squares of rice-*mochi*, bits of chicken meat, and perhaps vegetables and some greens. This is the national dish of New Year, and it is as much a necessity for the poor as for the rich, being partaken of by people of all classes.

The *mochi*, made of rice steamed and pounded, allows preservation for a lengthy period without spoiling and may be used in various ways. Having *mochi* on hand saves the trouble of boiling rice each day. Also, *mochi*, it is said, provides warmth for the body.

Any food which many be prepared beforehand is made ready and served during the first seven days. The bigger one's purse, the greater the amount and variety of delicacies which grace the occasion. One seasonal dish greatly in demand is *kazu-no-ko* or herring roe; the very name of which means innumerable offspring, and therefore the serving of it suggests a wish for prosperity and a large family. Also beans and dried sardines, especially when served together, are said to give the eater good health and vigor. The feasting used to last for seven days, and in more ancient times for half the month or more.

Numerous interesting customs have developed concerning the New Year. As for example, the house must not be swept out on the first day, lest all the good fortune be also swept out; hence the broom enjoys a well-earned rest. However, on the second day, there is quite a ceremony of doing things for the first time. A tradesman likes to make a show of sending out his first consignment of goods, piled high on gaudily decorated carts or wagons, drawn by a very gaily bedecked horse or ox; or decorated trucks are dispatched as well as received with appropriate ceremony. People, particularly students, do their first reading, albeit rather perfunctorily. Women make a few stitches, just enough to let the needle know that idleness will be frowned upon in the coming year. Private teachers of the various arts and crafts — music, dancing, tea ceremony, etc. — like to hold the first meeting of the year on January 2.

The night of the second is important, too, for it is then that one dreams his first dream of the year, a dream which reveals one's fate for the year. In order to lure a lucky dream, one may purchase for this purpose a good-luck paper from some hawker, whose voice may be heard toward evening, crying out, 'Otakara!' The *otakara* or honorable treasure, is a paper on which is written in Japanese *kana* letters a poem which reads the same either forwards or backwards. It is 'Na-ga-ki-yo-no to-no ne-bu-ri-no mi-na-me-za-me, na-mi-no-ri fu-ne-no o-to-no yo-ki-ka-na'; it means, 'In the sleep of the long night I hear, half asleep, the sound of a ship coming in, riding over the waves — oh, what a pleasant dream!' The ship of this poem is the *takara-bune* or treasure ship, on which come riding the Seven Gods of Wealth and Happiness, each bringing his own particular treasures.

During the New Year season, the people pay visits to various shrines to pray for good fortune during the year. At many shrines, special charms are issued to ensure the visitors good luck.

The Tsurugaoka Hachiman Shrine of Kamakura is famous for the *hama-ya* which it issues in the New Year season. It is an arrow with white feathers. The name *hama-ya* is believed to mean 'an arrow to defeat devils.' Hundreds of thousands of people visit the shrine during the first days of the year to obtain *hama-ya.*

In Edo days, children played with *hama-yumi* at the New Year. *Hama* denotes a target made of straw rope and *yumi* stands for a bow. Archery used to be a boy's game at New Year in olden days, and was very popular until the end of the Tokugawa period.

On the other hand, in earlier days, archery was one of the main fighting weapons of warriors. Warriors thus held the rite of opening the archery grounds at New Year's. It is recorded that on January 2, 1185, Kamakura Bakufu held the first New Year archery rite.

All through the Edo period, the formal opening of archery grounds was held in January, though the date dif-

fered from time to time.

It is said to be from this that the *hama-ya* signified merely 'an arrow and target' and no other meaning was attached. Somehow, however, the name came to be written out in Chinese characters meaning 'devil-defeating arrow.'

Whatever its origin, a large crowd of visitors visit the shrine to obtain *hama-ya* for the year's good luck.

NIO-SAN

IN FRONT of various temples and shrines there stands a magnificent gate, with huge vermilion pillars and a heavy curved roof. *Nio-mon* is typical of Japanese temples and shrines.

The gate has a wing on either side, and within the wing is seen a huge statue of a vicious-looking individual. Generally one statue is painted red, and the other green.

These statues are *Nio-san* (Vajrapani, or Two Deva Kings), and the gate is called *Nio-mon* (Two Deva Gate) as it houses two Deva Kings. The statues are placed before temples and shrines in order that these huge, powerful and fierce-looking kings may guard the sacred enclosure.

The Deva Kings are known to possess immense physical strength, and thus they are called *Kongo-rikishi* in Japan. This name implies that they are strong men of super-power. One of the two statues represents positive strength, and the other negative power. They are painted in different colors to designate the difference, and also for the sake of a color scheme.

Again there are some gates, also before temples and shrines, that house statues of much different character. Such statues are dressed in old Court costumes, and are milder and more peaceful in their expression. They are

Sadaijin (the Left Minister) and *Udaijin* (the Right Minister). *Sadaijin* is also called *Ya-daijin* (Arrow Minister) because he holds a bow and some arrows. In ancient times *Sadaijin* and *Udaijin* were the guardians of the Imperial Court, and on that account their statues came to be used at the gates of shrines for protecting and guiding spirits.

NORITO

THE PRAYERS offered to Shinto shrines are called *norito*. But *norito* are somewhat different from prayers of other religions, as they not only beseech the blessings of *kami*, but their essential part consists of offering thanks and praising *kami's* virtues.

The origin of *norito* is quite ancient, and it is believed that when Amaterasu-omikami had hidden in the cave of Ama-no-iwato, Ameno-koyane-no-mikoto offered *norito*, praising the virtues of the Sun Goddess. It is believed that from this incident, the custom of offering *norito* to *kami* has developed.

At all festivals and ceremonies of Shinto, *norito* are invariably offered by the priest. Then again, even at private worship at shrines, *norito* are offered.

For festivals, ceremonies, and other ordinary Shinto functions, there are the formal *norito* already written, and these are read by the priests on such occasions. The language of those formal *norito* is quite ancient, but there have appeared many occasions when new *norito* are offered, and the language used in such new *norito* is comparatively modern, although attempts have been made to retain and preserve the ancient style of *norito*.

In ancient times, the descendents of Ameno-koyane-no-mikoto had been given the duty of reading *norito* on all Shinto functions held at the Imperial Court, because of the belief that *norito* was first given by their ancestor.

Norito has very close relations with the daily life of the common people, as when the land is to be purified for building houses, the priest is asked to offer *norito*, and when children are taken to shrines on the *shichi-go-san* festival, *norito* are offered to ensure their health and thanks for the past blessings of *kami* upon them. Thus, on many ordinary occasions, the public offer the *norito* to *kami*.

O-CHIGOSAN

AT SHRINE festivals one often sees gaily dressed *o-chigosan* or sacred children, who make the festival procession bright and colorful. But originally they were not merely attractions.

Formerly there was a belief that *kami* or deity of the shrine appeared in the shape of a child, and so the festival *o-chigosan* was the symbol of *kami*.

Thus in early days, children who were to play the part of *o-chigosan* were very carefully selected. Only children who had living parents were chosen. For seven days they had to live esthetically, eating only specially prepared foods.

On the festive day, they were gaily dressed and had their faces painted, an old account relates. Then they were put on horses. Just before the start of the festival procession, the priest came to them and whispered into their ears a sacred prayer. Then the *o-chigosan* fell asleep. That was the signal for the procession to start. The *o-chigosan* sat on horses asleep all through the procession. When the procession was over the priest again came to the sleeping children and whispered a prayer into their ears, whereupon they woke up.

Such was the original *o-chigosan*. But later this idea changed. *O-chigosan* became only children to serve *kami*. Since then their task was to place offerings to the *kami* and do other little services. Often they were also made to dance for the gods.

Some large shrines have their regular *o-chigosan*, but generally they appear only on the annual festival day. Even today many parents consider it a great honor to have their children selected. They are still very gaily dressed, of course at their parents' expense.

In the festival procession *o-chigosan* still occupy an honored position.

O-FUDA

ON THE WALLS, doors, pillars, and ceilings of many temples are pasted pieces of paper bearing the names of visitors. They are called *o-fuda*, and generally are four by eight inches big, though there are also some much larger ones.

The custom of placing these *o-fuda* on temples is almost 10 centuries old. Emperor Kazan, 10th century, became tired of the worldly life, and retiring, became a Buddhist priest. He started on a pilgrimage of 33 Kannon temples in the western part of the country. When he reached the Kegon Temple, Kokkyuzan, Mino province, the last of the 33 temples, he placed a board there inscribed with words announcing the completion of his pilgrimage. This is said to be the origin of *o-fuda* pasting. It was soon followed by other pilgrims and in the Tokugawa days, it became particularly popular.

The custom is also called *senjamairi* (a thousand temple pilgrim). One named Tengen Kohei made a vow to visit a thousand temples and put his *o-fuda* on all of them. From this came the term *senjamairi* and *senja-fuda* (thousand-temple card). At first only commoners followed the custom, but soon several

feudal lords adopted it and placed wooden boards instead of paper pieces.

With the vogue of the custom, *o-fuda* came to be made elaborately in colors and fancy designs. Color print makers made these *o-fuda* at the order of pilgrims. As these placing *o-fuda* became numerous, they vied to place them at higher or better places to display their *o-fuda* to better advantage. Attached to lengthy poles, they were placed on ceilings of temples.

O-fuda pilgrims, it is recorded, met in Edo on April 5, 1807, and exchanged their *o-fuda*. This is the beginning of the hobby of collecting *o-fuda*. Today there are many *o-fuda* collectors and old ones are traded at fancy prices.

O-HARAI

THE CEREMONY of *o-harai* held at the end of June and December is one of the most important Shinto as well as Court functions. It represents the basic idea of purification. The ceremony is performed to remove all evils of the past.

Its origin dates back to the time of Izanagi-no-mikoto who purified himself when he returned from the underground world. Since the earliest time, it has become an important Court ceremony.

The ceremony of *o-harai* was formerly observed by the people, but later the custom of observing it on fixed days was discontinued. In the fourth year of Meiji or in 1871, it was revived. Thus at the end of June and December, many shrines throughout the country observe this ceremony of purifying the people of all past evils and diseases.

While the *o-harai* observed at the Imperial Court is held according to the ancient customs, the manner in which it is held at various shrines differ, and there are several different styles of the service. One of the most common services is called *ama-harai* or flax purification. In this service a large loop made of flax is used, as flax is considered as the symbol of purity and offered to *kami*. After sacred music and the reading of *norito*, the priest as well as the general public attending the ceremony pass through the flax loop. It is believed that, as one steps through the loop, all his bad luck, evil thoughts, diseases, and impure thoughts will leave him.

The ceremony to be held at the end of June is becoming somewhat unpopular and it is observed only by very few shrines, but that at the end of December is extremely popular, and there are large attendances of people at various shrines throughout the country, who go in their desire of ridding themselves of their ill luck and diseases in the coming New Year.

OMAMORI

THERE ARE not many temples and shrines that do not issue *omamori* (talismans), and the few which do not may be considered as the most insignificant, and not boasting of many believers. The more popular the temple or shrine, the more widely it is known for its *omamori*.

From the Great Shrine of Ise, down to Kannon, Fudo, Inari, and other popular places of worship, all have their *omamori* which are known to protect the possessors.

Omamori are usually small pieces of white paper on which the name of the temple or shrine as well as some special words of blessings are printed. However, there are also some very valuable *omamori* made in gold and silver.

Omamori may be roughly divided into two classes: one for placing in houses, and the other for carrying on one's per-

son. Those under the first category are larger, some of them being almost 10 inches wide and two feet long. For carrying the latter kind, they are smaller, being about half an inch wide and one inch long, or even smaller.

There are no time-limits on the charms, but the people mostly replace the old ones with new charms every year.

Visitors to famous temples or shrines often bring back many of their charms to distribute among friends. Around Tokyo, *omamori* issued by the Asakusa Kannon, the Suitengu (Nihonbashi), or the Narita Temple, Chiba Prefecture, are most popular.

Children are frequently made to carry little bags made specially for carrying *omamori*, so that they may not meet with accidents, may not be run over by motor cars, or may not lose their way home. In the children's *omamori-bukuro* (talisman bag), an *omamori* of Kishibojin, the Goddess of Children, is most popular.

People always carry the *omamori* of the deity in which they specially believe. Special *omamori* are required, however, for special occasions. For instance, those who go on a sea voyage carry the *omamori* of Suitengu, the God of the Sea so that they may not be shipwrecked, or may not have a stormy passage. Soldiers carry talismans of Hachiman or other gods of war, so that they may be brave and victorious.

Many tales of the special virtues of such *omamori* saving the lives of the people are believed. Many soldiers may be hit by bullets in battles, but the *omamori* carried in their inner pockets are said to stop the bullets and save their lives. Many are thankful for a calm voyage on account of the Suitengu *omamori* they carry, while other talismans save many houses from destruction by fire which at times burn every house but their own.

Formerly, in the feudal period, children invariably used to carry their *omamori* on their *obi*. Little bags of silk or cotton cloth were made for carrying *omamori*, and those bags were tied to children's *obi*. This custom of children carrying *omamori-bukuro* has died out in cities, but in rural districts it is still extensively observed. Then, many grown-up people still have faith in their *omamori*, which are carried either in their pockets or in their pocket-books or bags.

The sale of *omamori* is one of the greatest revenue sources of many temples and shrines which sell hundreds of them every day.

O-MIKI

AT SHINTO shrines, *sake* is offered to the *kami*, which is commonly called *o-miki*. The prefix of "o" meaning "august" is used on many nouns of the Japanese language, but in case of *o-miki*, it is superfluous, as *miki* already signifies honorable *sake*. However, it has become common to call the *sake* offered to the *kami* as *o-miki*.

Sake is a most important offering to the *kami*, not only at various ceremonies at Shinto shrines, but also as an offering at the family Shinto shrines.

At the ceremony of the Daijosai held for the enthronement of a new emperor, specially brewed *sake* is offered to Imperial Ancestors. *Sake* and rice represent the material inheritance of the Imperial Family from the ancestors. The public offer *sake* to *kami* as thanks for blessings.

Sake has been regarded as a medicine since the earliest times. The makers of *sake* were highly respected and honored in former days. As the offering of the first crop of rice to the Imperial Ancestor became a traditional rite since the beginning of Japan, the offering of *sake* brewed from newly-harvested rice had also become a significant rite of the Imperial Family. It is said that this custom of offering newly-brewed *sake* to the *kami* originated when Ataka-ashitsuhime-no-mikoto, consort of Ninigi-no-mikoto, brewed *sake* from newly-harvested rice in celebration of the Niiname-sai or new rice rite.

It is from this rite of offering the newly-brewed *sake* by the Emperor to the Imperial Ancestors, that the custom of offering *sake* to Shinto shrines by worshipers has developed.

The *sake* offered to the *kami* is regarded as sacred. In private households, the family drinks the sake offered to *kami* with thanks and respect. When several people purchase a bottle of *sake*, they offer a portion first to the *kami*, and then drink the rest.

O-MIZU-TORI

AT NIGATSUDO Temple, in the compounds of Todaiji Temple, Nara, one of the oldest, quaintest and most solemn rites of the country is held beginning at midnight, February 12. It is called *O-mizu-tori* or water drawing and is more than 12 centuries old.

The origin goes back to Priest Jitchu who erected the temple in 752 and held in February of that year a service for the 12-faced Kannon enshrined there. Hence the temple came to be called Nigatsudo (February temple). It is furthermore said that Jitchu asked for the blessing of Daimyojin Shrine at Unose, Wakasa province, on the coast of the Japan Sea and water came from Wakasa to Nigatsudo by an underground channel.

Thus it came to be believed that on the day the rite is held at Nigatsudo, water flows from Wakasa to the well at the Nigatsudo Temple, which remains dry all through the year. At Unose, Wakasa, a rite of sending water to Nara is also held.

The *O-mizu-tori* rite begins at midnight in solemn darkness. Formerly the priests of the temple who participated in the rite lived in the temple for two weeks, cut off from the outside world. The water drawing rite starts at 2 a.m. on February 13. The priests enter Nigatsudo, walking around its corridors, carrying large torches and chanting sutras. Except for the torches there is no light in the whole compound. It is believed that sparks from the torches will not set fire to anything.

Then water is drawn from the hitherto dry well, which has a roof over it, while ancient music is played. The water is called fragrant water and believed to have power to expel sickness.

An old record says that once an attempt was made to find out whether water actually flowed from Wakasa to Nara, and some chemicals were thrown into the river at Wakasa. The same chemicals were said to have been discovered in the water drawn at Nigatsudo on the early morning of February 13.

PICTORIAL SUTRA

AS BUDDHISM was introduced to Japan through China, Buddhist sutras used in the country are all in the ancient Chinese language. Priests who make a special study of the sutras are able to understand them. But the common people, however educated and intelligent they might be, cannot understand a word of it, though they listen in solemn silence.

Thus from the very beginning, priests have explained the teaching of Buddha in their own words. Yet the chanting of sutras has become such an important part of the Buddhist service that many worshipers have learned to read and repeat them, without understanding the meaning.

Many priests have tried hard to make worshipers repeat the sutras daily. This has always been a very difficult task. One of the most ingenious methods adopted by some priests is to represent the sounds in pictures. Thus when one pronounces the name of the object represented by the picture, he utters the first word of the sutra.

Many such sutras in picture are still preserved. The Daiji Temple at Morioka City has an excellent specimen of this type. It is a woodblock print made during the Edo period.

This specimen gives the text of Hannyakyo (Prajna-paramitasutra). The picture of a *kama* (rice cooking pot) placed upside down is to be read '*maka*,' for instance. Then comes a picture of a *hannya* (demon) mask to be read '*hannya*,' followed by a picture of the human belly which is '*hara*,' a picture of *mi* (winnow) and a picture of a rice field to be pronounced '*ta*.' Thus the sutra reads '*maka-hannya-hara-mi-ta*.'

PILGRIMAGES

DEVOUT Buddhists — men and women — particularly of rural districts patiently make monthly savings out of their scanty pocket money for years, so as to be able some day to attain their life ambition of going on *henro* or pilgrimages. According to sects, the number of temples they are supposed to visit on their pilgrimage differs. The Shin sect designates the visiting of 24 temples in various regions, and the Jodo sect 25. Worshipers of Kannon, Goddess of Mercy, are required to visit 33 temples, and Kanto and other districts have their own 33 Kannon temples selected for this purpose.

Nevertheless, the most famous of all is the *Shikoku-henro*. Eighty-eight temples in Shikoku are visited on this pilgrimage. All the temples are related to Kobo-daishi or Kukai, a great Buddhist priest of the ninth century, who was born in Shikoku. The custom of *henro* has lost its popularity, and the younger people have no ambition to make such a journey. The *Shikoku-henro*, however, is still made by devout men and women from all parts of the country.

The 88 temples of Shikoku are scattered all over the island. The entire route is about 750 miles long, and usually requires 40 to 50 days when made on foot.

Originally those desiring to cure themselves or others of illness, or to seek religious salvation constituted the majority of pilgrims. But there is another group who make the trip only for the enjoyment of many days of a carefree life. In old-fashioned families, wives and daughters particularly, seldom have occasion to see the world or enjoy themselves. These women form a party and go on *Shikoku-henro*. For nearly two months they are away from their homes and household drudgery.

The traveling is not easy, but there is a certain freedom and joy of travel. Pilgrims from all parts of the country meet on the road or at inns and become friends.

The pilgrims go mostly in groups, those of neighboring districts getting together for the common object. Quite a number, however, go singly.

To most of them the pilgrimage is the last and greatest enjoyment in this world, for the realization of which they have long sacrificed to save up enough money.

In the old days, the pilgrims used to wear wide flat hats made of reeds, as they had to walk every day in the sun. Individual pilgrims observed the custom of writing *Doko-ninin* (two on the trip) on their hats signifying that he is not traveling alone, as Buddha is always with him. With this belief, they never felt lonesome and discouraged on the long journey, nor were they afraid to walk through densely forested mountains at night.

Along the road *henro* pilgrims are still given food and alms by the people of villages they pass through. To give alms to pilgrims is a prayer for one's salvation, it is believed.

PRAYING STONES

JIZO OR Ksitigarbha-Bodhisattva is probably the most widely worshiped deity in Japan. Stone Jizo statues are found everywhere, particularly in rural villages and at country crossroads. Jizo is the Buddhist guardian of children.

Those stone Jizo statues are symbolic of the rural life of the country. Most of them are very crudely made and are in an extremely dilapidated condition, frequently due to exposure and mischievous children who play around them. Many are minus noses, have their ears chipped off, and some have their hands broken off.

Little stones or pebbles are seen piled upon the heads, shoulders or bases of those Jizo statues. Furthermore, little stones are sometimes piled up around them, covering them up to their knees. Some of such stones might have been mischievously placed by playful children, but they originally stand for the parents' eager prayer for the salvation of their children who were taken away from them by death.

A mother who lost her child will stop at the Jizo statue as she goes to the village, and murmuring a Buddhist prayer for salvation, she picks up a stone and adds it to the pile on the statue's head or shoulder. By placing the stone, she feels assured that the Jizo-sama will answer her prayer and watch after her lost child.

In some districts there is an ancient custom of placing a bamboo basket on a pole by the side of the statue, for receiving the praying stones. Then again, some people set up a wooden tablet bearing the Buddhist name of the dead child by a roadside, and hang a bamboo basket on it, in the hope that passers-by will place stones into the basket for the sake of their lost child.

When the Jizo statue is in a temple or tiny hut, as is frequent in farming districts, the praying stones are piled on the steps or window sills.

Round stone wheels, six inches to one foot in diameter and two to six inches in thickness, are sometimes placed on upright poles standing by the Jizo statue. The wheels are so placed that they can be easily turned by hand. The stone wheels take the place of the praying stones. They are made by the families of the richer class for their lost children. The members of the families, whenever they pass by the statue, turn the wheels as they say their prayers. Strangers passing along the road will also turn the wheels.

The custom of placing stones on Jizo statues is one of the most primitive religious customs of the people, and represents the people's love of children and also their sympathy for others' sufferings.

RAKAN

IN THE CITY of Kawagoe, Saitama Prefecture, there is a very old and famous temple called Kita-in, which is known particularly for its numerous historical and art objects of the Tokugawa period.

This temple is also well-known for the statues of Gohyaku-rakan or the 500 disciples of Buddha. Gohyaku-rakan is found in many old temples, and as each statue looks different, it has been always said that one will find among them a face that anyone is wishing to see. Thus many people wishing to have a look at the face of a lost child, a mother who died long ago or a sweetheart, visit Gohyaku-rakan.

But at the Kita-in Temple in Kawagoe, a very strange custom is observed in visiting the old Gohyaku-rakan which were made in 1782.

When one desires to see the face of anyone, dead or alive, he must visit the temple at midnight, preferably when it is moonless. Then, proceeding to the Rakan statues, he must feel the head of a statue with the palm of his hand. He must go from one statue to another, and as he goes on, he will suddenly reach one that feels warm to his palm. This will be the statue he is in search of and which he must mark with a strip of paper around its neck.

The next morning the visitor usually goes to the temple early and with anticipation. He hurries to the Rakan around the neck of which he tied the paper the previous night. The face of that Rakan is said to be that of the dear one he has for so long wished to see.

REINCARNATION

THE OLDER Japanese still believe in the reincarnation of the soul and think that, if they are not good at heart, their soul will reincarnate in the form of some hideous animal or insect in the future world. Likewise their present condition is due to what they did in their former life.

Children are often scolded by their elders with the warning that, unless they behave themselves, they will become beasts in their next life. Then again, when the people observe a lucky person appearing to be exceptionally favored with good fortune, they say, "He must have done something good in his past life."

An elderly women is so fond of a cat that she purchases fish for it even though she cannot afford it for herself. Her devotion to the cat is the talk of neighbors, who frequently make the comment that they must have been man and wife in their former life.

The belief that what we have done in our former life decides our present fortune, and what we do in this world will rule what kind of life we will have in an extremely future life, is originally based on the principle of reincarnation taught by Buddhism. *Sanze* (three worlds) signifies *Zense* (former world), *Gense* (present world), and *Gose* (future world). The soul lives through the three worlds, but not necessarily in the same form. Those in the human form today might, in the former world, have been animals, birds, fish or plants. Various animals, birds and fish are supposed to have been given human form in the present life because of the good they have done in their life.

The souls of men and women of bad heart or those having committed evil acts will, it is believed, be punished in the next world and be reincarnated in the form of some ugly beasts, animals of burden or insignificant insects.

This theory of reincarnation has greatly ruled the minds of the Japanese people in the past. The present younger generation do not, of course, believe in it, but the older folks, particularly those in rural districts, are still governed by this belief. From this belief in reincarnation developed *Sanze-so* or three-world fortune telling. This method of fortune telling is based on the cycle of cause and effect in the three worlds — the past, the present and the future. The fortune of one's birthday, and the relative nature of persons and things are told.

ROKKON-SHOJO

MANY OF THOSE climbing Mt. Fuji and other high mountains still chant *'Rokkon-shojo'* (six roots purification) as they struggle up the steep paths. High mountains were sacred to the people, and those of evil mind were not allowed to climb them, as it was believed that the presence of any evil person would anger the mountain spirit and bring storms and bad luck.

'Rokkon-shojo' originated in Buddhist teaching, which taught that the four human sufferings of birth, sickss, old age and death are caused by the *rokkon* (six roots) of eyes, ears, nose, tongue, body and mind. That is to say, the human senses, body and mind are the sources of evil, and when those roots are pure, there will be no human suffering.

Thus the chant of *'Rokkon-shojo'* developed as a prayer to be freed of evil influences that bring all sorts of suffering, by keeping the senses, body and mind pure. Pilgrims to sacred mountains shouted the chant as they climbed. Particularly when one's legs become weary in the difficult climb, shouting the chant gives one courage and seems to strengthen wobbly knees. So even though the original meaning of *'Rokkon-shojo'* is not known, the chant is still welcome to many mountain climbers.

In winter, too, this Buddhist chant is shouted by those observing the rite of *kan-mairi* or pilgrimage to shrines or temples at night for 30 consecutive days in the coldest season. Such pilgrims are dressed in the thinnest costume, and as they run in the cold night, they shout 'Rokkon-shojo' to fortify themselves against the bitter cold. *Kan-mairi* is still believed to bring divine guidance for one's advancement in his work or business.

SACRED FAN

THE TOSHODAIJI at Nara is one of the oldest and most famous Buddhist temples of Japan, having been erected in 759 by Chien Chen, a famous Chinese priest, and its main statue, Rushanabutsu is a world famous Buddhist sculpture. This old temple issues a charm called *hosen* or sacred fan.

It is a small heart-shaped fan, about 10 cm. across with a slender handle 26 cm. long running through it. On its face are written Sanskrit characters. This sacred fan has been highly treasured as a charm or a toy since the old days. It is believed that a person or family possessing it will not suffer lightning damage or fire destruction. Women will have easy child delivery. The sick will soon recover health, and children will grow healthy. When it is planted in the paddy field, there will be no insect damage and the crop will be good.

The following legend is told as to the origin of this remarkable oracle. One summer, *Daihi-bosatsu* or Sho-kannon was sitting in the meditation room of the temple. Mosquitoes and horseflies swarmed into the room. The insects covered *Daihi-bosatsu's* face, neck and hands and stung him, but he did not try to chase them away.

Seeing this, his disciples came with fans and started to shoo the stinging insects away from him, but he stopped them, saying, "I am conducting austerities of giving alms, so do not interfere."

Because of this incident, it became customary for the temple priests, disciples and worshipers to make fans

and offer them in honor of *Daihi-bosatsu.* The small fans with the long handle came to be made and offered to worshipers as a charm.

Fans are used by the people for various purposes besides fanning a cool breeze on hot days. They often have a solemn and sacred meaning, but the *hosen* of Toshodaiji is a rare case where they are given a religious significance and used as an oracle.

SACRED HORSE

MANY SHRINES keep a sacred white horse. It is most tenderly cared for, and the people worship and make offerings to the horse. The color of the sacred horse is invariably pure white.

In some places, however, instead of a white horse, there is kept a wooden horse, painted white and properly decorated. Even the sacred wooden horse is housed in a separate building, with an opening through which the people may worship and look at it.

The sacred horse, wooden or otherwise, is there to hear the confessions of the people. It represents a relic of the ancient and important Shinto ritual of purification *(harai)*. Purification, held to clean people of evil thoughts and deeds, was originally for the benefit of those who committed crimes, although in later periods it became a preventive measure to guard people against committing evils.

At these early ceremonies of purification it was necessary for such people to confess their crimes or evil thoughts. To hear such confessions there was always present a horse, because it was believed that with its two long ears, the horse could hear well. The horse was thus present as a witness of the confession, and he was a valuable assistant to the *kami* as well as to those who officiated at the ceremony.

However, to keep a live white horse in a shrine became troublesome and expensive, and in its stead came the wooden horse. It may seem strange that a wooden horse should act as a witness of confessions, but the horse itself must be happy even though confined to so narrow a space all the time, because it is worshiped by all people and hears all the confessions of secrets.

These sacred horses are donated by the shrine worshipers and given the most respectful attention, by being placed in specially built stalls. They are favorites of the neighboring people and particularly children who come daily to feed them. Often little dishes of soya beans are put on sale by the stalls, so that visitors to the shrines may purchase them and feed the sacred horses.

On the occasion of the shrine festival, *jinme* plays a very big role as the horse for the deity, in whose honor the festival is held. It is groomed beautifully, and then given a beautiful saddle, lacquered, inlaid and adorned with gold ornaments. It is led by purple silk ropes held in the hand of its attendant. Proudly it marches in the festival procession.

The common people who could not afford to present live horses to the shrine but still wished to show their concern in the *kami's* need finally found a way of presenting wooden horses or paintings of horses. Many old shrines have valuable collections of what is known as *ema* or painted pictures of horses, many of them done by master artists of the period.

Ema are generally painted on a five-cornered wooden board, each side measuring about one foot. Occasionally there are some which measure much larger or smaller than the usual size.

The presentation of *ema* to shrines became so popular as to even give rise to a special style of *ema* painting. Originally all *ema* were of course paint-ings of horses, but later paintings of other subjects as well were presented to the shrines. Whatever the subject, however, they are all called *ema.* The original meaning of *ema* became lost, and to the common people *ema* merely signified the presentation of pictures to a shrine.

In the Meiji days, some people began collecting *ema,* and in so doing, were able to include in their collections some masterpieces of art. This was done while the shrine authorities failed to realize the value of their numerous old *ema,* but they have become wiser and it is impossible now to make any shrine give up its fine *ema* paintings.

In many parts of the country there are *batei-seki* (horse hoof stones) showing the mark of horse hoofs. In many places, it is said that the horse hoof stone marked the place where the heavenly *kami* descended on his horse. Some of these stones are also believed to show the spots where some great heroes of the past stood on their horses. There is also a shrine named *Komagata-jinja* (horse-mark shrine), said to have been erected to mark the hoof impression left by a deity's horse.

SACRED TREES

IN MANY PARTS of the country, and particularly in mountain regions, there still stand huge trees. They are not to be felled, and many persons visit them and bring home their leaves or little branches for good luck. These sacred trees are believed to be related to the primitive idea that *kami* descends from heaven to a tall tree. There, however, appear to have been occasions when woodcutters discovered some trees distinctly different from others and, regarding them as sacred, left them untouched.

The species of trees regarded as

Kami-no-ki differ according to districts, and this fact may support the last mentioned origin of those divine trees. In some districts, a tree with big branches spread in two opposite directions is selected, while in others trees divided into three trunks are chosen. In some places, trees that have all their branches leaning to one direction are selected.

At any rate, in most cases, such sacred trees are visible from a distance, as they have grown tall and all surrounding trees have been cut down in the past.

Tall trees are also connected with many shrines, and on festivals big trees are often cut and placed in the shrine compounds to mark the occasion.

Some shrines have a *miya-bashira* or shrine pillar in their construction. This pillar differs from other pillars used in building the structures, and is regarded as sacred. The Suwa Shrine of Nagano holds a special festival every sixth year to install a new *miya-bashira*. Big trees are selected from a high mountain, brought to the shrine, and used as pillars at the four corners of the shrine structure.

Even without such associations, big trees have always been regarded sacred by rural folks who see in them something noble and strong.

SAISEN-BAKO

IN FRONT OF Buddhist temples and Shinto shrines is placed a *saisen-bako* or a huge wooden box for receiving offerings of money. Worshipers toss money into the box, in hopes that their prayers will be answered.

On festival days when huge crowds gather at shrines and temples the money tossed by the worshipers not only drop into the *saisen-bako*, but also fall onto the steps of the building. In former days when copper, nickel and silver coins were generally used, showers of hard coins fell on persons praying in front.

However, this habit of offering money to shrines and temples is comparatively new. In the old days it was considered impolite to offer money to Buddha or Shinto deities.

Originally, rice and hemp or silk fabrics were offered to shrines periodically and on special occasions by the worshipers. No one then thought of offering money.

It seems to have been from around the 16th century that the offering of money started. It is recorded that when a box for receiving coins was first placed at the Tsurugaoka Hachiman Shirne, Kamakura in the Tenmon period (1532-1554), a strong protest arose as it was considered insulting to offer money to the shrine. Nevertheless, the people must have been charmed by the new custom of tossing coins into the box, as it rapidly became popular.

In early days, when rice was offered to shrines it was wrapped up in a sheet of paper, with its corners twisted together to hold the grains. It was called *o-hineri* or twisting. Later, when coins came to be offered, it was considered proper to place coins in paper and make *o-hineri*. However, this practice has gone out of fashion except among the rural people.

SAKAKI

SAKAKI — the sacred tree of Shinto — is not only offered to *kami* and shrines, but is itself worshiped at times as the symbol of *kami*.

When offered to *kami* and shrines, *sakaki* is generally decorated with strips of white paper to indicate what it is offering. At various Shinto services, branches of *sakaki*, with or without *hei* (white paper strips), are offered to the shrines by those attending the functions.

The use of *sakaki* as the sacred tree is quite ancient, and the character to indicate the name of the plant is composed of one character meaning tree and another meaning *kami*. In other words, *sakaki* implies *kami's* tree.

According to the *Kojiki*, when Amaterasu-omikami had hidden in the rock cave of Ama-no-iwato, a huge *sakaki* tree decorated with jewels, mirrors and other things, was offered. Thus it seems that, since that prehistoric period, *sakaki* has been always used as the offering to *kami*, and as a sacred tree.

Being regarded so sacred and being always used as the offering to *kami*, the *sakaki* is also regarded as the symbol of *kami* or sacred objects. Consequently, there developed a custom of worshiping *sakaki*.

A pair of *sakaki* are often planted in front of a shrine. It is offered in little white porcelain vases on the *kami-dana*, but is most widely used as *tama-gushi* or holy offering. White paper cut in narrow strips are tied to little branches of the *sakaki*. Formerly white cotton threads were tied to the branches.

At Shinto services, the worshiper takes one *tama-gushi* and offers it to the deity, with a prayer for divine protection. *Tama-gushi* is always offered at festivals, weddings, funerals and other Shinto services.

There is an ancient *kagura* or sacred music, named *kagura-uta*, in which praise is given to the *sakaki* for bringing growth and prosperity.

The *sakaki* is a plant belonging to the Camellia species, and its scientific name is Cleyera japonica. Found only in Japan, China, India, Mexico and the West Indies, it is an evergreen tree growing to the height of 10 to 40 feet. In Japan, it grows very rapidly. Its leaves

are small, narrow and pointed. In spring, it bears small yellowish white blossoms which are extremely fragrant. It bears small berries which turn yellowish brown in autumn. *Sakaki* wood is hard and beautiful, and is used in making various small articles.

Being the sacred tree, it is largely planted in shrine compounds and also in gardens. It is traditionally believed in Japan that *sakaki* is the first plant that grew out of the chaos during the creation of the universe.

SAKE-NO-KAMI

SAKE IS THE national drink of Japan, and it has been famous since the earliest period of the country. It has been always used in ceremonies of the highest importance. Strange to say, however, the guardian *kami* of *sake* is not generally known among the people.

Even habitual *sake* drinkers unable to pass a day without several cups of the beverage and heavy drinkers who do away with tubfuls of *sake* at one sitting fail to pay homage to the *kami* of *sake*. While holding *sake* dearer than anything else, including their own very life, they fail to recognize the virtues of the *kami* that guides, protects and superintends the making and storing of *sake*.

The Japanese Bacchus is Toyo-ukano-me-no-mikoto who is more commonly known as Sakadono-kami (*kami* of *sake* storehouse) on account of his duty. But there is no known shrine erected in his honor. He is quite unknown to the people.

On the other hand, there is the Oyamazumi Shrine which is commonly believed to be the shrine erected for the Bacchus. The shrine was originally established for Oyamazumi-no-kami, as its name implies. But this *kami* is also called Sakatono-kami. The first part of his name is commonly written with the character meaning *sake*, although originally it had no such meaning. On account of this first character used for the name, this *kami* came to be regarded as the Bacchus of Japan.

It is difficult to state whether this *kami* is pleased with the mistake or not. It is obvious, however, that Toyoukanome-no-mikoto must feel displeased at the neglect he has been put to by the worshipers of *sake* and its flavors.

SEISHI-BOSATSU

ALTHOUGH Seishi-Bosatsu is counted among the *Sanzon* (Three Holy Ones of Buddhism), he is not commonly known even among the followers of Buddhism. Amida, Kannon, and Seishi-Bosatsu are the "Three Holy Ones of Buddhism." Amida and Kannon are more than famous, and temples, lofty and gorgeous, that have been erected in their honor, prove their popularity as well as holiness and virtues. By their side, however, Seishi-Bosatsu appears insignificant as there are only very few temples for this great Holy One.

Amida and Kannon are merciful, and their love is extended to all. But Seishi-Bosatsu is not a *hotoke* of mercy. He is that of wisdom and power. His force and strength are said to have no rival, and his power is infinite and limitless. Again, his wisdom is so lofty and extensive that the whole world is made bright by it.

But his wisdom, it appears, is not welcomed by the mass of the people of Japan as willingly as the mercies of Amida and Kannon. Consequently, of the Three Holy Ones, he is left to be the most slighted in this country. His wisdom shines upon the whole world, but the light is not appreciated.

From this fact it may be surmised that the people desire more of love and mercy than wisdom and power. Men are unable to possess such limitless force and infinite wisdom as Seishi-Bosatsu, and mercy and love, that are given for the asking, are naturally more sought after.

Seishi-Bosatsu is, however, unfortunate because his wisdom and power are not recognized by the majority of people who have almost forgotton that he is one of the "Three Holy Ones of Buddhism."

SENBON-NOBORI

ALONG THE road to a shrine, one may occasionally find tiny paper flags on sticks four or five inches long in the ground, at intervals of a few steps. Sometimes there are hundreds and thousands of such small flags along the lane. Each flag bears the name of the deity of the shrine, and the name and age of the persons who made and placed them.

These tiny flags are called *Senbon-nobori* or a thousand flags. One who has a special prayer to make to a deity makes these small flags and places them along the route to the place of worship. *Senbon-nobori* supports one in his prayer and make it come true.

At many popular places of worship, the routes are literally lined with these small flags on both sides. Most of the writing on them is already unreadable, as they have been exposed to rain and weather, while freshly placed ones stand out conspicuously in the sunlight.

The people always use *nobori* or long flags at shrine festivals. Generally the names of the shrine are written boldly in black on those big banners. *Nobori* originally indicated the site of shrines or the places where festivals were held.

In the old days, large standing trees were worshiped. Also trees which had been cut were set up to indicate the site where the *kami* was supposed to descend from heaven. Large-sized trees or tall poles have thus come to be used as sacred marks.

Later, banners came to be attached to such poles. Festival banners and small flags placed on the way to the shrines are symbols of worship and prayer.

SHIME-NAWA

LENGTHY straw ropes with narrow strips of white paper hanging down at intervals are seen in front of Shinto shrines and other places. These straw ropes are called *shime* or *shime-nawa*. They serve as the mark to indicate the boundary of sacred places and unholy areas. Being sacred, Shinto shrines always have *shime-nawa* at their entrance. But it is not only shrines that have those ropes, and even before family shrines, or other places they are used to indicate that places so marked are sacred.

The origin of *shime-nawa* is as ancient as the history of Japan. *Shime-nawa* were first used, according to the legend of the nation, at the time when Amaterasu-omikami hid herself in a rock cave. Tajikarao-no-mikoto drew Amaterasu-omikami out from the rock cave, and placed a rope of straw there to mark that the cave was unholy. It is said that, since that time, *shime-nawa* have always been used to symbolize sacredness.

In the early literature of the nation, the rope used at the rock cave of Amaterasu-omikami was called *shime-kuri-nawa*. *Shime-nawa* that came to be used later is believed to be a contraction of the original name of *Shirikume-nawa*, denoting a rope made by twisting rice-straw.

There are various different styles of *shime-nawa*, some being thick and short, while others are thin and long. But all have narrow strips of white paper placed at intervals all along the length of the rope. Moreover, in making *shime-nawa*, it has to be twisted leftward.

The use of *shime-nawa* at Shinto shrines is another indication that purity is the first essence of Shinto. Shinto shrines are sacred and they are so marked with *shime-nawa* that evils and foul thoughts should not enter.

For the New Year decorations, *shime-nawa* is also necessary, because it is believed that good fortune and happiness will only come to houses that are clean and pure. It is to indicate that the houses are clean and pure that *shime-nawa* is placed in front of all houses during the New Year season. Furthermore, traditional belief says that *shime-nawa* will drive out evil spirits.

Also, when ground is to be broken for building houses, *shime-nawa* are placed on the lot after the purification ceremony held by Shinto priests, for the purpose of indicating that the land has been purified and it should be so marked to prevent the coming of evils.

Shime-nawa are also used at various other occasions, and although in some cases such uses might not be directly connected with Shinto rites, they are always used to signify purity or cleanliness.

SHRINES

JAPAN IS A LAND of shrines. Everywhere one goes, one may find shrines, large or small, not only those publicly worshiped, but also private ones erected in individual gardens, or even on the roofs of office buildings. The total number of *jinja* or shrines is not known, but those publicly worshiped number between 100,000 and

200,000.

These *jinja* are dedicated to mythological deities, legendary persons, ancestors, illustrious men and plants. They all have traditions and backgrounds, and new ones are being added even today.

There are family shrines worshiped by one family and its relations. These often develop into community or district shrines.

The Meiji government issued rules governing all shrines, and classified them into six categories: Government shrines, national shrines, prefectural shrines, district shrines, village shrines and shrines without special standing. They were given monetary aid by the Imperial Family, the government, prefectural governments and local bodies, according to their standings.

In 1938, there were 116 government shrines, 89 national shrines, 1,090 prefectural shrines, 3,616 district shrines, 44,823 village shrines, and 60,496 shrines without standing, making a total of 110,238, according to an official report.

But this shrine system was abolished in 1946, whereby the shrines lost all official help. Many became thus placed in an extremely crucial position, but the majority of them have gained public support.

With newer ones being built every year, shrines still maintain their position as local community centers.

SUITENGU

SUITENGU SHRINE at Kakigara-cho, Nihonbashi, is one of the most popular shrines of Tokyo. For a century and a half, the shrine has been eagerly worshiped by the residents of the capital. The charm tablet it issues is often seen in many Tokyo taxis, for not only does it ensure safe childbirth, but it also prevents accidents, particularly marine disasters. Seamen and fishermen always carry the Suitengu charm.

Suitengu was erected in 1816 at the present site, which was the residence of Lord Arima, as a branch of the Suitengu Shrine of Kurume, Kyushu.

The original Suitengu of Kurume is said to have been erected in memory of Emperor Antoku, and Kenreimon-in, his mother, by Iseko, her lady-in-waiting. Emperor Antoku died in the Sea of Danno-ura in 1185, when he was seven years old, upon the defeat of the Heike family which supported him. Upon his death, Kenreimon-in became a Buddhist nun and lived in Kyoto, dying in 1213. Then Iseko constructed the Suitengu Shrine in memory of the boy emperor and his mother.

Thus the shrine became the guardian deity for childbirth and safety at sea. But there is another story that the Suitengu Shrine was originally erected for the spirit of the Chikugo River that flows nearby.

The Kyushu Suitengu must evidently have become very popular, considering the fact that a branch came to be erected in Edo. The Edo residents gladly came to worship the shrine bringing many offerings, and the sales of its charms became a colossal source of income for the Arima family.

The popularity of Suitengu has not waned in the least to this very day as seen from the large numbers of worshipers visiting the shrine on the fifth day of every month.

SUMIYOSHI SHRINE

DEALERS in fish and other sea products worship the Sumiyoshi Shrine. The three gods of Sumiyoshi are considered the guardians of dealers in fish and other marine products. The three gods who are worshiped at the Sumiyoshi Shrine are the three brothers, Sokozutsuno-ono-kami, Nakazutsuno-ono-kami and Uwazutsuno-ono-kami.

These three brothers, however, are in actuality the gods of the sea, and fish, sea-weeds, shellfish and other sea products are said to be the offspring of the three brothers.

Thus dealers in fish are actually the enemies of the three *kami*, as they are destroying and selling what these *kami* are producing.

At first, people selling fish and other products of the sea regretted that they were daily killing so many things of the sea, and therefore went to the Sumiyoshi Shrine to offer apologies for their cruel deeds and to solicit the pardon of the three *kami*. This custom continued for a while, but the sentiment of the dealers towards the temple has gradually changed, and such people came to regard the three *kami* as their guardian deities.

The three *kami* being the gods of the sea and fathers of all things in it may feel somewhat strange when fish dealers come to make them offerings. Being probably extremely magnanimous, the three gods pardon the fish dealers and become their guardian angels, accepting the faithful pilgrimage and offerings made to them.

SUN WORSHIPERS

MANY JAPANESE are still sun worshipers. Particularly old folks, both in cities and rural areas, are seen worshiping the sun every morning. Rising early, they step outside, and facing the eastern sky, they clap their hands and bow towards the sun. To these people the sun rules their lives. The sun gives them food, and so they must be thankful to it. When children waste food, mothers tell them that they will anger the sun and be punished.

Although many of the traditional customs and beliefs of the people originated in China, sun worship was not brought over from China. Neither did the original inhabitants of these islands worship the sun.

As to who the original inhabitants of the islands were before the coming of the Tunguse and Ainu from the north, and the Malay, Mon, Khmer and other tribes from the south, nobody really knows. But anthropologists concur in their opinions that aboriginal inhabitants must have already been in existence prior to the coming of those foreign peoples. It is now generally believed that the southern races who came to Japan brought agriculture and particularly rice cultivation to this country. There southern peoples were sun worshipers, and in teaching the cultivation of land, they also taught the inhabitants of these islands the greatness of the sun.

As rice cultivation brought new and good food, sun worship was implanted in the minds of the people. The mythology of the Sun Goddess developed from this sun worship.

SUWA SHRINE

OKUNINUSHI-NO-MIKOTO is said to have been worshiped as Daikoku, one of the most popular *kami* of the people. His son, Takeminakata-no-kami, however, is not so famous as his father. He is enshrined at the 'Suwa Shrine,' the main shrine being at Suwa, in Shinano province.

Takeminakata-no-kami was given a certain district to rule under his illustrious father, but being of a reckless and wild nature, he failed to obey orders from his father. It is said that Okuninushi-no-mikoto once demanded of him to surrender his district to the central control.

For some reason or other, the young man was not very favorably impressed with this order, and thus igonored it time and again. Finally his father despatched an official to make his son conform to his wish.

At the sight of the messenger, the young man became exceedingly infuriated, and first attempted to wrestle with the official, hoping that, by forcing the messenger to defeat, he would make him leave without further discussing the matter of his father's order. However, as is frequently the case in regard to one's expectations, the outcome of the wrestling match was unfavorable to the young man who made a very poor showing against the powerful official.

The youth then took to his heels and ran away, shouting that he would never surrender his district to his father or anybody else. The official chased him all over the country. Whenever he was caught up, the young man opened discussion and then again ran away. Thus the two—the pursuer and pursued—travelled all over the main parts of the country.

It was finally at Suwa in the province of Shinano that the young man was brought to his knees, and was forced to declare his willingness to obey the command of his father. So he stayed at Suwa, and has been enshrined there as the Suwa-no-kami in the shrine of Suwa.

TA-NO-KAMI

AS RICE IS harvested, farmers hold rites for *ta-no-kami* (god of the ricefields) to express thanks for good crops made possible by divine protection. The occasion is also significant as it was formerly believed that *ta-no-kami* left the rice-fields and returned to the mountain upon the completion of harvesting.

In some places it is believed that *yama-no-kami* or mountain god came down to the fields in spring and became the *ta-no-kami.*

The thanksgiving rites for *ta-no-kami* differ according to districts. In many regions the newly harvested rice plants are piled up in the shape of cones as an offering to the god. In many villages children used to make thick bundles of rice straw and beat the ground with them, as an expression of their thanks to the deity. Thanks are given to scarecrows and farming implements also at many places.

Ta-no-kami is generally believed to be a female, although *yama-no-kami* is regarded as either a male or female deity. Stone statues of *ta-no-kami* used to be erected in many rural regions.

There was a very common belief that *ta-no-kami* was blind because it remained so long under the ground. It was also dirty with mud. Thus there developed a custom of making an imaginary act of giving the *ta-no-kami* a bath as a thanksgiving rite.

The farmer goes to his rice-field and pretends he is carrying the *ta-no-kami* on his back. When the deity is cleaned of the field mud, dinner is offered to him.

Also it is said that frogs follow *ta-no-kami* with offerings when the deity is taken to the farmer's house for bathing and banqueting, as frogs are always with the deity in the field mud.

Some districts believe that *yama-no-kami* and *ta-no-kami* are man and wife. Where *yama-no-kami* is considered a female, it is said that she gives birth to 12 children every year. The deity's help is asked whenever a woman is going to have a child.

TE-ARAI

AT THE ENTRANCE of a Shinto

shrine, there invariably stands a large basin of water. Sometimes it is an elaborate and artistic basin made of stone or metal, placed under the high roof supported by lacquered pillars. Then again, it is often a simple and small wooden or stone basin.

It is customary for all people entering the shrine compounds to wash their hands, and rinse their mouths at the basin. There are small wooden or metal dippers placed at those basins, for use by visitors.

This custom of washing and rinsing at the entrance of a shrine is based upon the belief that the shrine compounds are sacred and things soiled or evil may not enter. Persons with sickness or evil thoughts are not permitted to approach the shrine. Thus, to purify one's soul and body, the custom of washing hands and rinsing mouths has developed.

Purification is the first essence of Shinto, and the method of purifying body and soul by means of water originated in prehistoric days. When Izanagi-no-mikoto returned from the nether world, he went to the sea at a place called Odo and washed off all the evil and dirt of the nether world with sea water.

This is the origin of *misogi* or purification.

The cult of Shinto has taught cleanliness, and no person who is not clean of body and mind can approach the presence of the sacred *kami*. The compound of any shrine is considered sacred, so that no disease, crime, filth, or evil thoughts can enter.

Bodily cleanliness was just as much emphasized as cleanliness of mind. The ceremony of purification is one of the most important of the Shinto rituals.

Even in paying a casual visit to a shrine, one must clean himself of evils, crimes, diseases, and the grime of the

world. In order to make oneself presentable in the presence of the sacred *kami*, he washes his hands and cleans his mouth at the basin of clear, overflowing water.

The act of washing hands and cleaning mouths give the psychological realization that they are about to approach the presence of the holy and sacred, and that they are unclean in body and soul.

Scientifically speaking, washing of hands and rinsing of mouths will not make one clean. But the faith that such a practice will purify his soul and body is in itself effective in making him think that he has been purified.

In ancient days, pregnant women were considered impure and were thus not permitted to approach Shinto shrines or participate in any Shinto service.

TENJIN-SAN

TENJIN-SAN is dedicated to Sugawara Michizane, a great scholar and royalist of the ninth century. To the shrine are offered many *fude* (writing brushes) by the people with the prayer that they become more skilled in the writing of Japanese and Chinese characters. Michizane is known as a most skilled calligrapher, but it is said that, when young, he was a poor writer, and by diligence and practice he attained a skill that surpassed all.

The compound of a Tenjin Shrine is always planted with numerous *ume* (Japanese apricot) trees, as the pure, noble, and fragrant flowers of the tree well characterize the spirit of Michizane. He was fond of *ume* flowers from childhood, and it was for a poem on the flower written when he was 11 years old that he was first recognized by the emperor. When he was finally exiled, after a most brilliant career at

Court, he wrote the following famous poem:

Kochi fukaba nioi okoseyo ume-no hana Aruji nashitote haru na wasureso

(When the east wind blows, send your fragrance, Flower of *Ume*. Never forget spring even though your master is gone.)

Thus the Tenjin Shrine and *ume* flowers became inseparable, and in many places the best *ume* blossoms are seen at the shrine.

To children of the country, Michizane is the model of learning, calligraphy, and loyalty, and they pay their homage to the spirit that will guide them to develop their characters and accomplishments.

THREE MONKEYS

BY THE VILLAGE road, and more often at the dividing line between two villages there stands a *koshin-zuka* or a *koshin* stone tablet. *Koshin* is one of the most common deities worshiped by rural folks. As it usually stands on a village road, it is regarded as the guardian of the road or the protector of travellers. But originally it was the guardian deity for all the local people. Though *koshin* is so common, it is not clearly known what it stands for.

Nevertheless the *koshin-zuka* with the engraving of three monkeys has left a deep impression on the minds of all the people. These monkeys have even become world-famous. Said to have come from China, the three monkeys, covering the eyes, ears and mouth with their hands respectively, symbolize the old teaching: "See no evil, hear no evil, say no evil."

It is generally said that it was the Buddhist priest Dengyo (767-822) who first engraved the three wise monkeys on the *koshin* tablet, as he placed great value on the old teaching. If this be so,

the three monkeys are a later addition to the original *koshin* tablet which was already an object of public worship.

The *koshin* festival comes on the day of *koshin* or the Day of the Monkey. It seems that the unknown deity was named after the date of the festival. One tradition has it that, on the eve of *koshin* (monkeys) day which comes every 60 days, an insect living in a human being leaves the body while he is asleep, and goes to heaven to report on his conduct. So no one should sleep that night. In the old days, the festival was quite an important community function with all the village people gathering around the *koshin* tablet on the Day of the Monkey and having a merry time, drinking and eating from early evening to dawn. *Koshin* day comes every 60 days, but actually the festival was not held so often because of unfavorable weather conditions.

Later however, the affair came to be held indoors at the houses of principal residents. It was called *koshin-machi* or "waiting for *koshin*." This is mentioned in *Eiga-monogatari*, a story of Court life from the ninth to the 11th centuries.

Koshin-machi is still kept up in many rural districts, but its original meaning is almost lost, it being held recently only as a local gathering for recreation and drinking.

On the other hand, the three monkeys, which were at first engraved on the *koshin* tablet to teach the people how to keep away from evil, have become dear to all people of the country and even to many foreigners. Besides their wise teaching, they are loved because they look so comical and lovable.

TOKANYA

IN MANY RURAL districts, and particularly in the eastern half of the country, October 10 is still celebrated by farmers as *tokanya* (10th evening). It is one of the harvest rites observed by farmers, and an occasion to express their thanks to *ta-no-kami* or farm deity who leaves the field and returns to the mountain on the day.

It is also a day when thanks are expressed to scarecrows which are regarded as the representatives of *ta-no-kami.* Thus in many regions scarecrows are taken from the fields to the yard of their farmer's house. Offerings are made to them with thanks. In some places *daikon* or Japanese radishes are offered. Thus the rite is called *daikon-matsuri.*

One outstanding feature of *tokanya* is the making and eating of many kinds of sweets and food to be enjoyed by the whole family.

In many districts children have their own play on the day. They make thick straw ropes, and go around the house and farms, beating them on the ground. The ropes are often called *wara-deppo* or straw guns. It was originally a charm to drive away earth moles, which sometimes do considerable harm to crops.

So *tokanya* is a joyful occasion for all children, not only because they love the rope beating, though they no longer give any thought to moles, but also there are many good things to eat on the day.

As children beat the ground with their straw guns, they sing the *tokanya* song. It differs according to districts, but it always sings of good things they eat on the day.

"*Tokanya.* What a good day! Buckwheat in the morning, dumplings at lunch, a good meal in the evening. Beat on!" runs one song.

"Straw gun of *tokanya.* Eat *mochi* and beat the ground" goes another.

UBUGAMI

RURAL FOLKS still worship *Ubugami* (God of Birth) when a woman in the household is about to deliver a child, as they believe that *Ubugami* is the only deity who protects the mother and her baby. It is commonly believed that all other deities will not come at such times, as birth-giving is considered unclean.

It is not clearly known what kind of god it is, but in some districts *Ubugami* is believed to be Yama-no-kami or mountain god because Yama-no-kami is a woman and gives birth to children.

There are various customs to bring *Ubugami* when the deity's help is needed. When a woman feels labor pains and enters the delivery room, her husband quickly saddles his horse, and starts off to bring the god. He will not try to lead the horse, but let the animal go as it pleases. When the horse suddenly stops and shivers, it is a sign that *Ubugami* has come and sat on the horse's back. So the man leads the horse back to the house. All are then happy as *Ubugami* is with them and the child delivery will be easy.

Before the first meal after delivery is given to the mother and the baby, it is offered to *Ubugami.* In some districts a small stone symbolizing the deity is placed on the table with the first meal.

Ubugami, however, is not worshiped at any other time. It comes when other deities shun the impurity of child delivery.

VISUALIZATION OF THOUGHT

TO DEVELOP the ability to visualize thought has been one of the principal trainings of Buddhist monks. The ultimate aim of this training is to become able to visualize clearly in one's mind the form of Buddha or the scenes of *Gokuraku* (paradise).

This power cannot be attained all at once. The progress is slow and gradual, the students first becoming able to visualize only intimate objects such as the faces of persons and natural scenes. It is said that when one sees clearly in his mind a running stream, he has made a notable progress.

The Zen sect of Buddhism particularly emphasizes this training. Zen means thought, and the sect is named after *kanzen* or thought visualization. Sitting in meditation, Zen monks try to cultivate their power of seeing things in their mind.

As ancient monks saw various objects, the great priests of past days, Buddha or paradise clearly in their minds, they reproduced such pictures in painting or sculpture. The reproduction of their visions became their custom, and many paintings and sculptures of Buddhistic subjects, executed by ancient priests showing their visualized thought, are preserved.

Thus Buddhist monks became painters and sculptors, besides being religious men. Gifted priests produced great works of art, but as they were the reproductions of their visionary thoughts, they are naturally idealistic and impressionistic. These works became the essence of Buddhist art, and furthermore implanted in the general Japanese arts and literature the peculiar, unrealistic but highly impressionistic quality.

To the present day, the Japanese thought as well as arts and literature are under the influence of the practice of visualizing thought.

WAKA-MIYA

THERE ARE many shrines in the coun-try which are called *Waka-miya* (young shrines). Generally they are secondary or side shrines attached to and under the rule of main shrines and built on the same grounds.

Originally, however, *Waka-miya* had a sinister meaning as it was erected to prevent the curse of a human soul from bringing evil effects on others. Particularly when a peron met an untimely or violent death, it was feared that the soul might be angry and bring a curse upon others.

In such cases, priests or maidens in the shrine service caused the erection of a shrine for such a soul, so that it could be appeased and its curse prevented. They urged the people to respect such shrines if they wished to be happy and free from evil curses. It was, furthermore, thought that if rites for such *Waka-miya* were neglected, the curse would descend on the people.

So the soul for which *Waka-miya* was erected was not a deity, but an angry or disappointed human. Thus *Waka-miya* naturally did not have the same standing as ordinary shrines for deities. Some authorities now explain that it was the professional desire for activity of shrine priests or maidens that originally made them erect *Waka-miya* and keep them under their control. This can be seen in the custom still remaining in Aizu and other districts of calling mediums *waka-sama*.

Among shrines called *Waka-miya*, the most common are those connected with Hachiman and Kasuga shrines. Many are branch shrines, but there are others which have separate deities

WARAI-BOTOKE

IN THE COMPOUNDS of various large Buddhist temples, there stand special buildings erected for the purpose of storing Buddhist scriptures. Such storehouses are often built in antique and dignified architecture, and were formerly extremely important, as scriptures were difficult to obtain and also exceedingly costly. Such storehouses were necessary in olden days as the scriptures were printed on large wood-plates, and one Sutra often consisted of hundreds and thousands of volumes. These storehouses are called *hozo* or *kyozo*.

In these *hozo* buildings there is placed a statue which is generally called *Warai-Botoke* (Laughing Buddha). It is the guardian of the sacred scriptures.

While he is in so sacred a service of guarding the Sutra, his name is rather too common. *Warai-Botoke* sounds joyous and happy, and one would more readily associate the name with a Buddha of some lesser duties than one to whom the guardianship of the sacred Sutra is entrusted.

Warai-Botoke is so named, however, because the statue has a very pleasant smiling face. The smiling face is rather out of place among the century-old volumes of Sutras stored in the ancient and gloomy *hozo* building.

It is said that *Warai-Botoke* was Fu-Tai-Shih of Liang who built the first Sutra storehouse in China. In honor of his service in building such a structure for the preservation and protection of the sacred scriptures, he was made the guardian of all such storehouses. Should this be true, Fu-Tai-Shih must apparently have had a smiling countenance and an extremely happy and pleasant disposition.

YAKUSHI

YAKUSHI-SAN boasts of the largest number of prayers offered. Every day, rain, shine, or storm, the temple of Yakushi has pious believers who kneel on its front steps and engage in silent prayer. Toward dusk, one may often observe persons praying in an audible tone, but silent prayers are just as eloquent and appealing to Yakushi-sama as the most loudly uttered ones.

Yakushi-sama (Bhechad jaguru) came from the land east of Sumeru and has the virtue of curing diseases of the people and bestowing fortune and happiness upon them.

People with illness or those of delicate health worship Yakushi as their protector. However, the majority of those coming to seek the blessing of Yakushi-sama are friends, wives, husbands, children or parents of those who are sick in bed. Such people make regular visits every day to ask Yakushi-sama to cure the illness of those near to their hearts. In rain, or in storm, and often in the dark midnight, such prayers are offered at the temple.

But Yakushi-sama also looks after those in good health, and gives them happiness and fortune.

There are several kinds of Yakushi in Japan, and while all of them cure diseases and make people happy and contented, each has its own special characteristic. The believers in one Yakushi often dislike the others, thinking that the others are not so good as the one they worship and have confidence in.

Whatever be its kind, Yakushi always has a great number of worshipers, who come to pray for blessing on behalf of sick people.

Chapter 15
Social Customs

ADOPTED CHILDREN

THE SYSTEM of *yoshi* or adopted children has existed in Japan since ancient days. It arose from ancestor worship and developed under the family system during the feudal age. It is the foremost duty of the Japanese family to worship the spirit of the ancestors and take care of their tombs. This important responsibility is performed by the head of the family generation after generation.

Families that have no children, therefore, have to adopt children to make them their heirs to undertake the family duty. That is how the *yoshi* system originated.

In addition, in feudal days Court and military positions and ranks were hereditary. The male heir of a family always succeeded to the position held by his father and also to the family property. It is to the interest of the family, thus, to have a succeeding heir to retain the position and the property. In the case of farmers and merchants, the heirs inherited the farmland or business. Of course, the family head is responsible for the livelihood and welfare of the entire family.

All couples that had no son adopted children to perpetuate the family name, position and wealth. When the family had only a daughter, the adopted son married her. But one who is adopted by a family that has no daughter has his wife selected by his adoptive parents. In such a case, there is no blood relation between the older and the new generations, but the family lineage was considered to have been continued without interruption, and the worship of the ancestors was not neglected.

Children are also adopted even when the families have sons and daughters of their own. In most cases, they are adopted to marry their daughters whom the parents do not wish to give away to other families. It was traditionally believed that once girls were married and entered other families they were no longer family members but became outsiders. Parents who are fond of their daughters could not bear to have them taken away, so they adopted desirable young men to be husbands of their daughters.

The adopted son gained great benefits by entering the new family, as he inherited the prestige, wealth and position of the adoptive parents. Yet it is generally said that the life of the *yoshi* is a miserable one. His wife is the daughter of the family, while he is from another. In such a case his wife often holds all the power in the family. Family servants, too, pay more respect to the family daughter than to her husband. The *yoshi* then is often henpecked. There is a saying that if a young man possesses as much as a cupful of rice bran in his name, he should not become a *yoshi*. Yet he inherits the name and wealth of the adoptive family when he becomes its head.

The position of the *yoshi* changed with the Meiji Restoration upon the abolition of hereditary positions and particularly with the new Constitution and the revised Civil Law that abolished the family system. Yet, many families still adopt sons, as it is difficult to alter traditional family sentiments that have been implanted so long in the people's consciousness. Of course, the adoption of war orphans by charitable families is from a different motive.

AMANOJAKU

PERSONS WHO delight in opposing anything others say or propose, or do things in unusual ways purposely are called *amanojaku*. Sometimes the name is also applied to those who love to irritate or annoy others. This expression for cross-grained people is said to have been used since very early days, and to have derived from Amano-sagume, the name of a mythological woman.

But it is not clearly known how the name of the woman mentioned in the mythological tales came to have such a meaning. Some authorities try to explain that the name of Amano-sagume was mixed with some Buddhist traditions to acquire the prevailing meaning.

Amano-sagume was a maid to Amano-wakahiko, according to the Kojiki or ancient records. The following incident mentioned in the same book might have made the people think that she was a cross-grained person.

One day Amano-sagume saw the Sacred Pheasant, messenger from heaven, coming, and watching the bird, she told Amano-wakahiko, her master, "That bird sings badly. It should be shot to death."

It is difficult to know what she really meant. But many say that by making that statement she clearly proved herself a cross-grained person. The pheasant was beautiful and loved by all, as it was a messenger from heaven. Yet knowing that, she said the bird's singing was bad and demanded its instant killing.

So her name is still used to let the people know how *amanojaku* she was.

APPRENTICE SYSTEM

THE FEUDAL system of apprenticeship has contributed much to the development of Japanese culture, arts, crafts and even trade. The system, though largely abolished, is still found in many professions and trades. The master-pupil sentiment constituting the essence of the apprentice system is still found in the thought and habits of the people.

In the old days, to undergo training in any profession, craftmanship or trade, one had to serve as an apprentice to a good master. Apprentices to scholars, physicians or fencing masters were called *deshi*, while those to tradesmen or craftsmen were named *detchi* in Kansai and *kozo* in Edo.

The apprentice period differed according to the kinds of work and other circumstances, but generally boys became *deshi* and *detchi* at the age of about ten years, though sometimes much younger. The apprentice stage ended when they mastered the art and technique, or when they reached the age of maturity. Often there were apprentice agreements fixing the period to five, seven, 10 or more years.

Deshi or *detchi* were accepted as members of the masters' families. They were given food and clothing, and they performed all the household work which was asked of them, besides learning the profession or trade. But they received no pay. There were, of course, good masters and hard ones, but all

586

masters strove their utmost to make good scholars, workmen or businessmen out of their apprentices, because it was to their benefit also to have good assistants or workers under them. Good masters also gave their apprentices moral training.

When boys had finished their apprenticeship and attained such skill as to make them independent workers, the masters helped to set them up in their own business, permitting in most cases to use their own trade names. Masters also found wives for them. Masters always looked upon their former apprentices as their young friends and never as competitors. The former apprentices, on the other hand, always paid homage and respect to their former masters.

In case a master did not have a succeeding son to carry on his work, one of the apprentices was selected to be the successor.

In the field of painting, literature, fencing, arts and medicine, this system also ruled. It is through the apprentice system that the arts and techniques of the country have been handed down from generation to generation. It was different from the training which modern apprentices receive at factories, where there are no intimate relations between the teacher and the student.

AZANA

IN READING Japanese history, foreigners are often surprised to learn that two or three names which, they think represent different persons, stand for one and the same person.

Rai Sanyo, the great historian and scholar of Edo days, was for instance, also called Rai Yuzuru, Rai Shisei, and Rai Kyutaro.

This custom of a person having more than one name came from China. Educated Chinese disliked to use or be called by their formal names. They adopted other names for common use. For instance, Sun Yat-sen, the great revolutionary leader of China, always called himself Sun Wen, never using Sun Yat-sen.

This habit of using *azana* (other name) was adopted by the early Japanese who studied Chinese literature. Thus educated persons in days gone by had their *azana*, in the Chinese fashion.

Furthermore, besides this *azana*, writers, painters, artists, actors, wrestlers and artisans have professional names which have no connection with their family and other names in the old days. Boys had childhood names which they dropped upon attaining manhood. It is because of this custom of a person having more than one name that considerable confusion and even misunderstanding is caused in reading historical tales of the country. The difficulty mainly arises from the fact that persons become better known by their *azana* or professional names rather than their legal names.

Young people now often confuse *azana* with *adana* (nickname), but *adana* is purely and simply a nickname, and has no connection with *azana*.

BRIDE TRAINING

FORMERLY wives were very often divorced for not conforming to the traditional customs of the husband's family. So young brides were severely trained to learn the traditional ways of their parents-in-law.

Oshima Island, famous for its volcano Miharayama and camellias had its own wedding customs, as did many other districts. The courting was done in the first place by the girls. When a girl loved a young man, she gave him a *tasuki* (band for tucking up sleeves), beautifully made with good material and decorated with tassels. If he accepted it and used it in his daily work, it was a sign that her love was answered. Young men without sweethearts wore straw ropes as *tasuki.*

To make a pledge of marriage, the girl is taken to the house of the man by her parents and introduced to his family. But on this occasion, the girl wears her everyday dress and does not sit in the room where dinner is served, but helps in the kitchen.

After this, the man is allowed to visit the girl's house, and may even stay overnight. But the girl must come every morning to the house of her promised-husband. There she does all the household duty as well as work on the farm. Thus the period of her training starts.

The training period ranges generally from three to six months, but if it continues much longer, neighbors begin whispering that something might be wrong.

The wedding ceremony is held when the girl is accepted by the man's parents as fully mastering the ways and customs of the family. But the ceremony itself is simple, the bride not even dressing in a special costume. Lately however, modern ways are gradually being introduced.

Another strange custom in Oshima is that when the wedding ceremony is held, the parents of the young man move to a separate house. The coming of the bride and the moving away of the old parents take place on the same day.

CHRISTENING

NAZUKE or christening of the newborn baby was formerly a very important affair, as it was thought that be-

fore it was given a name, its existence was not recognized.

The *nazuke* ceremony, however, was not generally held until the evening of the seventh day after birth. In many districts it was done on the 10th, 11th or 14th day. Such a long delay despite the urgency of giving the baby a name was due to the idea that the mother and also the father were subject to seven days of *imi* (taboo) or abstinence from social or public appearance because of the childbirth.

A tendency appeared to hasten the christening, coming to be observed on the fifth or even on the third day after birth in many districts. But generally it is on the seventh day that the baby is given its name.

During the unnamed period, the baby was believed to be at the mercy of evil influences. In Kyushu it was believed that if a thunderstorm arose before the baby was named, it would become dumb. In some Kanto regions, it was said the baby's head would break if it thundered. So often the baby was given a *kari-no-na* or temporary name to protect it until it was properly named.

Furthermore, the mere act of giving the newborn baby a name was not sufficient. A party had to be held to announce its name to relatives and friends, and until this party was given the existence of the baby was not socially recognized. Even today quite an elaborate party for announcing the baby's name is still held in many rural districts.

The father is the person to select the name for the newborn baby, but often it is believed that if the grandfather is alive and gives it a name, the baby will be assured of good fortune. A person other than the father or grandfather is often selected as a *nazuke-oya* or christening father.

This is done generally when previously born children are weak or have died young or when the baby was born in the father's *yaku-doshi* or evil years, or when there is doubt as to the healthy growth of the baby.

In selecting the name for the baby, there are names or characters hereditarily used by families, or those commonly adopted locally. Often by the names the people's native districts can be told. Many regions believe that when babies are named after animals they will grow healthy and strong.

The name announcing party has different customs according to districts. In some places, a small pebble upon which the baby's name is written is placed on the table for the baby, and this stone is taken to the local shrine.

DAIKOKU

THE WIVES OF Buddhist priests are still called *daikoku-san*. They are not generally addressed as *oku-san*, the common term used to address married women. This is because formerly Buddhist priests were not allowed to marry, and so wives they might have in secret could not be publicly recognized as *oku-san*.

The term Daikoku came from Mahakala, or Indian god of plentiful food. Introduced to Japan, it was named Daikoku and became the god of good luck and also of the kitchen. Images of Daikoku are placed in family kitchens to ensure the plentiful supply of food. Thus kitchens came to be called Daikoku. The term was applied to the wives of Buddhist priests to mean they are the women of the kitchen.

Buddhist priests did not marry at first, and many temples even prohibited the entrance of women to their compounds. This was due to the thought that women are unholy or are temptations to priests. It was Shinran Shonin

(1174-1262), founder of the Shin sect of Buddhism, who formally married a daughter of the noble family of Kujo, and then made the priests of his sect also marry so as to bring the priesthood closer in contact with the general community. Today Buddhist priests are not prohibited to marry, but those of the Zen sect still persist in not marrying. There is no longer any need of differentiating the wives of Buddhist priests from general *oku-san*, but the old custom is still preserved, and they are called Daikoku.

In Japan, Daikoku is generally represented as a fat smiling god, wearing a flat cap, holding a big bag over his left shoulder, carrying an *uchide-no-kozuchi* (a magic mallet that produces anything desired) in his right hand, and standing on a pair of straw rice bags with mice on them. Mice are said to be the messengers of Daikoku and therefore in the old days, the people liked to have mice around their houses. Where there are mice there is food, and so the presence of mice, they thought, was well provided. Also the presence of mice saved the house from fire, it was thought. They would know of a coming fire and leave the house beforehand.

DANNA

DANNA, danna-san or *danna-sama* is an extremely commonly used Japanese word. The wife calls her husband *danna-sama*. Servants address their masters *danna-san*. Shopkeepers greet their prospective buyers *danna*. Beggars approach men on the street, saying *danna-sama*.

The word is originally a Buddhist term. It has been corrupted from the Sanskrit word *dannapati*. The original Sanskrit means Buddhist followers who give alms and show kindness to other Buddhist priests. At first the corrupt *danna* was also used in the original Sanskrit meaning. Thus Japanese Buddhist priests came to call their followers who gave them alms and other assistance their *danna*. Gradually in all ancient towns and villages of the country, the leading or rich families became the *danna* of Buddhist priests and temples in their districts. To those families, the temples became their *danna-dera* (*danna* temples). This expression, however, also came to mean the temples where families had their cemeteries.

With the popular use of the term *danna* the common villagers followed the example set by priests and called the heads of those leading families *danna*. In this way, gradually losing its original meaning, the term became a simple honorific title to be used when referring to the wealthy or old families in towns and villages.

Becoming a word to express respect or importance, *danna* has come to an extremely wide field of use. Firstly, the members and servants of the family which was the *danna* of the village temple learned to call the family head as *danna*. Then, this use for indicating the head of the family gave the term the new meaning to signify the family provider. Originally the term was used for both males and females, when it means the givers of alms to priests, but as it came to indicate the head of the family, naturally, it was commonly used for men only, because of the custom in Japan of the male being the head of the family. It is in this sense that the term is now generally used.

Thus, shop-keepers came to greet men entering their stores as *danna*, and beggars address passers-by as *danna*. On the other hand, the old use of the word to show respect is still preserved. Lower class people often call those of higher social rank or position as *danna*,

though there is no direct relation between them.

Except in ordinary households, the term is most widely used now in restaurants, the so-called tea-houses, *geisha* circles and such, because all those businesses entirely depend on the generous "providing" of their patrons. Women are often said to be *danna-mochi* (having a *danna*), and that means such women have their patrons. There is a saying that to find joy in being called *danna* spells one's ruin.

The recent democratizing process, however, is rapidly narrowing the field where the ancient term *danna* is generally used. It is so also with the term *sensei* that means teacher or master which was very extensively used for men in public career or persons of knowledge and importance.

ETIQUETTE

THE JAPANESE people have guided their social and individual conduct according to the rules of the Ogasawara school of etiquette for well-nigh four centuries. The rules laid down by this school have become the standard by which the people's manner and culture are judged.

The Ogasawara family was a noble and ancient one, started by Sadazumi, the sixth son of Emperor Seiwa who reigned from 858 to 876. The family was known for their skill in archery and horsemanship. At the same time they were also a recognized authority on etiquette. The family, therefore, served as advisers on ceremonies and etiquette to many leaders, including Minamoto Yoritomo and Tokugawa Ieyasu.

It was, however, Ogasawara Takatoki, 1519-1583, who compiled a book on etiquette which was published in 1632. This Ogasawara Book on Etiquette became the standard of ceremonies and conduct for the people.

This book is extremely exhaustive and complete. It gives guidance on holding and attending ceremonies, and dressing for them. It also gives directions on every minor detail of daily human conduct. For instance, it teaches how to sit down, how to open sliding doors, how to eat, how to offer a present, as well as how to use trays and fans.

Another important point is that, due to the then prevailing feudal system, it gives three different forms of etiquette for one act, one toward a person in a higher social position, one to an equal, and one to a person in a lower rank.

Though Ogasawara rules appear dignified and complicated, those for daily conduct are based on the simple idea of respecting the personality and comfort of the other. The fundamental essence of etiquette is cleanliness, quietness and leisure.

Of course, various rules of the Ogasawara school are no longer observed today as they do not fit in with the changed social conditions. But if the present-day Japanese followed the basic rules of the Ogasawara etiquette, the country would no doubt be a far more pleasant place to live in.

EXTRA NEW YEAR

THE CONVICTION of the Japanese people that New Year brings them happiness and good fortune has been so strong that during Tokugawa days, there developed a unique custom of holding an extra or special New Year fete, whenever they suffered from epidemics, famine, economic depression or social unrest, and hoped that a new turn of good fortune would come.

Of course, such an extra New Year was not formal, but when the people determined to observe it to ward off ill luck and suffering, they faithfully went through the customary New Year rites. First they erected *kado-matsu* or gate pine, made New Year *mochi* (rice cake), and drank *toso* or New Year drink, and greeted each other with a bright "Happy New Year."

The first such special New Year is recorded to have been held on June 1, 1778, when a serious epidemic threatened the life of many Edo people. It was also held in May 1781; October 1827, and August 1858.

It was even held in the 13th year of Meiji or 1880.

This was a year of calamity. People in many districts underwent serious suffering. There was a big fire in Niigata that destroyed more than 5,000 houses. A big typhoon struck the Tokyo region and caused the death of more than 2,000 persons and a fire at Osaka sent more than 3,000 houses up in flames. A serious economic depression and social unrest ensued.

To regain their confidence and restore a happy and comfortable livelihood, the people proposed to hold another New Year celebration, which they firmly believed, would bring peace, happiness and good fortune.

Such New Year celebrations were commonly called *yakuyoke-shogatsu* or evil warding-off new year.

FAMILY NAMES

THERE WERE no family names at first in Japan. However, from the necessity of distinguishing different persons, Nakatomi (chamberlain), Imbe (ritualist), and Mononobe (guards), which were posts of Court officials, and the eight ranks of Mabito, Ason, Sukune, Imiki, Michinoshi, Omi, Muraji and Inagi which were adopted by Emperor Tenmu in 684, came to be gradually used as family names. Local officials and leaders were called by the names of their localities. Early geographical family names included Soga, Ashikaga, Hojo, Chiba, Takeda, Ito, Utsunomiya and others.

During feudal ages, however, only Court officals and the *samurai* class possessed family names; common folks not being allowed to have them. Only a few village heads and others were specially granted the privilege of having family names in recognition of their meritorious services.

With the abolition of feudalism by the Meiji Restoration, all were ordered to have family names. Families which were more or less connected with some noble or *samurai* families, took the opportunity to adopt their names. To many it was a big problem, and in most cases, priests and village heads had to find names for rural families. Cases where the entire families of one village were given one and the same name are not rare. Many families had nicknames or names by which they were commonly called. Such were readily adopted as family names. A family who had a big tree in the garden was called Oki (big tree) and adopted it as its proper name.

Among newly selected family names were many which described the locations or conditions of their houses, as Ogawa (little river), Yamashita (under the mountain), Kobayashi (little forest), Yamada (mountain farm), Nishiyama (west hill), Kawakami (above the river), Fukagawa (deep river) and several others.

FEMALE SUICIDES

SUICIDES have been quite numerous in Japan, as to end one's life is considered the best and shortest way to escape from difficulties or to terminate misery. The most common method of suicide has been *minage* which means throwing oneself into the water.

Minage is still selected by those wishing to die as the best and simplest method. In the old days, particularly during the Tokugawa era or between the 17th century and the middle of the 19th century, the people felt more kindly toward female suicides than to the male.

Whenever a fisherman or a boatman found a woman's body in the river, he would do everything to revive her. But if it was a man he would pass it by, giving it no further thought. This was quite customary among all boatmen and fishermen in Edo days.

The reason behind this custom is that women are timid and small minded, and therefore, even though they do not have good reasons for dying, they end their life by jumping into a convenient river. Such women should be saved if at all possible, as they might realize when they were revived that there was no cause to die.

In the case of men, it was different. If a man had decided to kill himself, there must be good enough reasons or circumstances that made it impossible for him to live. So it was better to let him die as he wished.

A man and a woman often commit *shinju* or love suicide. Many couples also jump into the water. If a couple was saved, the woman was always better treated than the man.

At first there was no set rule for punishing those who attempted *shinju*. In the Kyoho era, 1716-1736, the eighth Tokugawa shogun Yoshimune laid down a law punishing *shinju* attempts. When a man and a woman attempted *shinju* and the man survived while the woman died, he was held responsible for her death and punished as a murderer. But when the woman survived she was only made a *hinin* or outcast, but she could regain her civil rights by paying some money.

house.

FINDING AN ADDRESS

MANY FOREIGNERS wonder why it is difficult for them to find an address in Japan. It is equally as difficult for the Japanese. Firstly, it is because Japanese streets have no name, excepting a few that were named recently. Land lots on both sides of a street have their names. But it frequently happens that a lot is named differently from one just across the narrow street.

Then, there is no order in numbering the lots, starting from any corner and going in any direction. Furthermore, the numbers seldom run in sequence. Even when one finds Lot No. 1, he may have to go several blocks to find Lot No. 2, which he is looking for.

This irregularity is due to the fact that lot numbers were given in the order of application or registration. In various regions land lots were first given, and then streets were constructed to run through them. Each registered lot, moreover, is given one number, however big or small.

When several houses or shops where built on a single large lot with the same number, another confusion appeared. Under one lot number, there are hundreds of different houses, scattered over a wide area.

In Tokyo, numerous old residences of feudal lords occupied vast areas. Such lots are divided into hundreds of small building lots, but they all have one original lot number. In particular, No. 3 Yaraicho, Shinjuku, or No. Nishikatamachi, Hongo, are very famous for having hundreds of residences under one lot number.

In old towns and cities, to find an address is an extremely cumbersome task. One is obliged to ask policemen or some shopkeeper to guide him to the

FORTUNE STEALING

FUKU-NUSUBI, or fortune-stealing, is one of the strangest, yet common, customs observed in various parts of Japan. The idea that by an act of theft one will be able to gain good fortune sounds strange. While, according to districts, articles to be stolen in order to have good fortune differ, it is believed that it has originated in a custom of stealing statues of gods of good fortune. To secure a statue of a god of good fortune by stealing it, is regarded by some to assure good fortune. Originally articles to be stolen were mostly statues of gods of good fortune. Later various other articles which stand for good fortune became equally popular.

At the year-end market, 'Toshi-no-ichi,' held at Asakusa Kannon temple, this custom was formerly observed. Among the rows of little stalls selling various articles to be used for the New Year celebration, there are those offering little statues of Daikoku (Mahakala), God of Wealth. It was believed by the people of Edo that if one stole one Daikoku statue from those stalls at 'Toshi-no-ichi' he would have good fortune. It is said that many people purposely visited the 'Toshi-no-ichi' in order to steal such Daikoku statues. Of course they ran the risk of being caught, and if they were caught they would become common thieves, but if not they would be happy because their good fortune was assured. Then again, if one stole the statues of both Daikoku and Ebisu, his fortune would be greater.

In the province of Hoki, it is believed that if one steals a stone statue of *kami* from other villages, good fortune would come, with single persons getting their mates, farmers having a good harvest,

593

and fishermen having big hauls.

At the *daruma* markets held in various districts of Kanto in the New Year season, it is also believed that the stealing of *daruma* statues from stalls without being caught will assure a man's good fortune.

In Formosa, there was formerly a custom for girls to steal flowers for good luck. Among the people of Manchu and Mongolia, there were formerly similar customs of stealing articles for good fortune, it is reported.

In the Kyoto district it is still said that if one succeeds in stealing a Fushimi doll at the festival of Fushimi Inari shrine, one will have good fortune. Particularly *geisha* of the Kyoto district still believe in this custom, and they attempt to steal dolls at the festival. But successful stealing is quite difficult, and those who steal with success are said to be few.

FUTAGO

WHEN TWINS WERE BORN, mothers formerly felt ashamed, because it was believed only beasts gave birth to more than one child at one time. Formerly it was thought that twins would not live happily, so on that account the mothers treated them with special consideration. They were mostly given happy names in the hope that they would lead a joyful life. They were treated as one child, dressed in exactly the same dress, in color, design and material.

It was believed that when one of the twins died, the other would die soon.

Though mothers felt ashamed of having twins, the children themselves were very kindly treated. But the mothers did not wish to have more sets of twins. In some districts, when twins were born, the father went up on the roof or put his head out of the window, and loudly shouted, "Twins are born." This loud public announcement of the twins' birth was believed to stop the birth of another set.

As to the cause of the birth of twins, there are many locally believed theories, but all of them are without any foundation. In one district it is believed that a woman had twins because she slept on the seam of two mattings. A woman had twins because she was friendly with another who had twins, and ate food out of the same bowl. In many places association with mothers of twins was avoided as much as possible.

Superstitious beliefs concerning twins have not died out altogether, but in modern Japanese families, *"futago"* are more often welcomed than thought shameful.

GENPUKU

GENPUKU was the ancient rite for marking the growth of a boy to manhood. No fixed age was set, but generally it was held when a boy became about 15 years of age, though often it was held for boys of 10 or 11.

The rite originally consisted of placing a ceremonial hat upon the boy's head, but later it was simplified to that of cutting or shaving a bit of *mayegami* or forelocks, as the front hair was cut to wear the hat.

The person who performed this ceremony was called *Genpuku-oya* or *Genpuku*-father and much respected.

The boy then adopted his manhood name, discarding the childhood name by which he was called up to that time.

For girls there was the *mayu-harai* or eyebrow-shaving rite to mark their attainment of womanhood. This rite for girls was not as elaborate as boy's *Genpuku*, for in feudal days boys were regarded more important than girls.

The woman who performed this rite of shaving the eyebrows was called *kenuki-oya* or hair-pulling mother, as the hair was either shaved off or just pulled out.

Besides these ceremonies to mark the growth of children to manhood or womanhood, there were also little observances that served to make them realize their growth.

Children's *kimonos* have tucks along the shoulders and around the waist, and these tucks are let out from time to time to widen and lengthen the *kimono* to fit the growing body. But when they reach manhood or womanhood, they wear tuckless kimonos. Girls who wore soft sashes around their waist graduate to wide *obi* and do up their hair. These are also marks of their womanhood.

GIFTS

THE JAPANESE people take much joy in presenting gifts to friends and others on any conceivable occasion. In this respect they probably have no equal in the world. Of course it is customary everywhere to give presents on birthdays, marriage anniversaries, weddings, Christmas or New Year. But it is not on such special formal days or occasions of celebrations alone that the Japanese people give presents. It is an unwritten law among the people to give presents to relatives, friends and neighbors on the building of their new houses, removal to new addresses, appointments to new posts, departures on long trips, and all other conceivable occasions.

In making social calls, it is absolutely necessary to take some *omiyage* or gifts. Of course when men call on others on business there is no consideration for *omiyage*. But when a family or women folks make any social call on others, it is a violation of etiquette not to take something as presents. On such occasions, of course, *omiyage* can be almost anything, from toys or sweets for children, to vegetables or fish. However trifling, such *omiyage* has to be carried when any visit is made.

Yet it is also prescribed by the unwritten social code that one must always make a proper return for any *omiyage*. No gift should be left unreturned and that causes quite some anxiety and trouble for the people. When a visitor brings *omiyage* when calling, the return is often made immediately by wrapping up something in the *furoshiki* in which the gift was brought and given back to the caller.

There is a rule that the return must be of about the same value as the gift as far as possible. There are, however, some exceptions to this rule. School teachers, priests and physicians are exempt from this rule. Teachers are not required to return the presents from their students or their parents. Priests can receive gifts from their followers without giving anything in return. Physicians too are privileged to receive anything from their patients without any thought of returning the courtesy.

When one receives a gift from another who is lower in position socially or otherwise, it is usually necessary to return something which is more valuable than the original present.

Gift-giving has thus become almost second nature to the people, and sometimes the custom is followed to extremes. Often quite valuable gifts are given to almost unknown persons, without any reason at all. It may appear foolish, but such persons feel satisfaction in giving presents.

In big modern cities, where one does not know who his next neighbor is, the old custom is not observed so strictly, but in rural districts, *omiyage* giving and receiving are quite an important social and neighborly duty. Anyone who does not fully observe the custom will be instantly stamped as unsocial or even an outcast. The customs may be foolish and extravagant, and is sometimes criticized, but at the same time, it reveals the neighborly and friendly sentiment that lies in the heart of every Japanese toward others.

But originally this gift-presenting habit was not a mere social custom. It had a considerably deeper meaning. It represented the spirit of mutual help and particularly of sharing food with all.

Even today, whenever a housewife prepares some special cakes or food, she usually distributes small portions to her neighbors. In some rural districts there remains a custom of offering some food to the shrine and carrying away what another has brought there. At festivals and parties, the people often bring their own food and exchange them with what other folks have brought.

In the old days, on the chrysanthemum festival on September 9 the worshipers of Kannon Temple, Asakusa, brought branches of *kiku* or chrysanthemum and exchanged them with *kiku* blossoms brought by others.

To share food with others was one of the most important principles of the early Japanese. The habit of willingly offering food to others may have lost its original significance, but the spirit is now retained in the custom of offering special foods and bringing presents to friends, neighbors and others.

GIFT CERTIFICATES

THE JAPANESE are fond of giving gifts to friends and acquaintances, and sometimes become almost reckless in doing so. But they think it is not polite to give money as presents. To express

thanks for kindness or acts of good-will, they always send something as gifts. When money is sent, as is often done nowadays, it is given in addition to some goods offered as formal presents.

It is this habit of regarding money gifts as something to be avoided under polite etiquette that has popularized the use of *shohin-kitte* or gift certificates. These are sold at all department stores and other big shops. The bearer of *shohin-kitte* can buy merchandise to the amount marked on it. As it is given as a gift, it is printed on good fancy paper and then put in a paulownia wood box.

Shohin-kitte simplifies the task of giving presents, as there is no need of selecting suitable articles, and the receiver can buy anything he or she desires. The amount ranges from ¥1,000 to almost any figure, and certificates for tens of thousand of yen are very common.

The system is extremely profitable to shops that issue it. The amount is paid in advance and sometimes it is months or even years before the purchase is made with the *shohin-kitte*.

The system originated with Nimben, a famous *katsuobushi* (dried bonito) shop in Nihonbashi in old Edo about 150 years ago. At first Ninben's *shohin-kitte* was a thin silver plate with the proper wording engraved. *Katsuobushi* is always presented on marriages or other happy occasions as gifts, and to make it fit the occasion, the original certificates were elaborate. But as the idea grew in popularity, the certificate came to be printed on paper.

This gift system was soon copied by other big Edo stores dealing in *sake*, oil, tea, fish, tobacco, sweets, *sushi* and other goods.

The modern popularity of *shohin-kitte* dates from about 40 years ago, when big department stores appeared in the country. Besides *shohin-kitte* issued by individual stores, there are those jointly sold by several merchants dealing in the same line of goods, and are good at all participating stores. Various stores in one district also sometimes get together and issue a common *shohin-kitte*.

GIRI

GIRI IS STILL a factor in guiding the people's thought and daily conduct. To violate *giri* is the worst thing one can do and many make him a social outcast.

Giri is a unique factor that governs the daily thought and conduct of the Japanese people, but it is something very difficult to explain, as there are no foreign words to convey its meaning. Even the Japanese themselves find it hard to define.

Giri is often expressed as the sense of duty and honor, but that explanation is inadequate.

In the common concept *giri* means the observation of community customs, developed from the old idea of sharing food, happiness and sorrow. *Giri* demands the full recognition of community or cooperative life.

Giri demands that all should give a helping hand to others in farming, building houses, holding wedding feasts, funeral services and other affairs or work that requires help. They must help others even putting aside their own work.

Those who fail to offer such services are said to lack *giri*, and are regarded as disturbers of the community life. Such are unwelcome persons, and are often ostracized by the villagers.

In some districts, *giri* is often carried to extremes and causes various unpleasant incidents.

Thus it often happens that personal sentiments and feelings such as love or friendship are in conflict with the rules and customs of *giri*. There have been many tragedies because a person was torn between *giri* and *ninjo* (human feeling). *Giri* asks a daughter to marry a man selected by her parents, though her heart is for another. If she does as *giri* directs, she would be a good and dutiful daughter although she would be unhappy. However, if she goes to the man she loves, her family and community would regard her as an undesirable person. Often unable to decide, a girl in such a situation commits suicide.

Then again, even if one fails to perform his required service to another family at the time of a funeral or marriage, he has also violated *giri*. Failure to join any community activity or service is generally considered as a notable case of *giri* violation.

The hold of the feudal idea of *giri* is gradually becoming weak. But among old folks and especially in rural districts, *giri* is still the guiding spirit of their daily life.

Giri-gatai, or to be strict in the observation of *giri*, is the highest praise to be given to any person. But for being so, one has often to make bitter sacrifices.

GIRLS' NAMES

JAPANESE GIRLS are commonly named after flowers, plants, and natural objects. Hana (flower), Matsu (pine), Take (bamboo), Ume (Japanese apricot), Kiku (chrysanthemum), Yuki (snow), Midori (green), Haru (spring), Natsu (summer), Aki (autumn), Fuyu (winter) and others are representative girls' names.

Then there are names symbolizing womanly virtues, like Kiyo or Sei (purity), Yoshi (good), and Yasu (comfort).

Since olden days, aristocratic families have loved to give more elaborate names to their girls.

Today, there are many girls' names that end in 'ko' (child). This is a habit that became popular in the early part of the Meiji era. Now it is said that in cities girls with names not having *ko* are fewer in number than those with *ko*-names. This habit of suffixing *ko* is becoming less popular, probably because the *ko* termination has become too common.

Different localities have special names for girls, and sometimes by their names their native places are indicated. In some places girls are given names which sound like boys' names. For instance, Kesao is a very common name for girls in the Tohoku district. Then, often parents who hoped to have a boy and were disappointed in having a girl, have consoled themselves by giving her a boyish name.

The most common name now for girls under 30 years of age is probably Kazuko, the character for which is the same as the last character in Showa, the present era.

GORYO-SAN

OSAKA HAS BEEN a great commercial center ever since the 15th century. Particularly during the Tokugawa reign, the city was the greatest trading center of the country. Osaka merchants came to stand for clever and active traders.

Wholesalers of each kind of merchandise gathered together in a fixed section of the city. Their residences were their shops and warehouses at the same time. In those feudal days, the Imperial Palace and the residences of great lords were clearly divided into official and private quarters. The same distinction was made in the life of the great Osaka wholesalers.

The wholesaler looked after the business and his wife the household af-fairs, including the feeding and clothing of numerous employees who lived with the family. The wholesaler's wife came to be called *goryo-san* or house head.

During the Tokugawa and Meiji years, the *goryo-san* never had anything to do with the business, but she exerted great power in the household. It was said that the success of the business depended on her wise housekeeping and care of employees. Thus the *goryo-san* was highly respected not only in the household but also by the community.

Things have changed greatly in recent years, but in the wholesale quarters of Osaka, the *goryo-san's* position is unchanged. It has even become much more important than in the past. That is to say, while in the old days, the *goryo-san* never interfered in business matters, many *goryo-san* now take an active part in the business.

HAIR-CUTTING

UNTIL THE Meiji era, all Japanese, both men and women, kept their hair long, attaching great importance to it. In those days, both men's and women's hair was elaborately done up.

When one committed some wrong or hurt the feeling of others, he often cut off his long hair as a proof of repentance. Or the wronged person demanded the one who caused his suffering to cut of his hair. Wives accused of infidelity had their hair shorn as punishment. Also warriors going to battlefields left strands of their hair as a memento if they should die.

Thus the people feared cutting their hair as much as they did losing their lives. Many women offered their hair to temples and shrines when important prayers were made. Ropes made of human hair were offered to temples to be used for the construction of new buildings.

In the Tokugawa days, there were many cases of women having their hair cut off by unknown persons. Such an act was done purposely or in sheer mischief. There are even recorded cases of women finding upon waking up in the morning that their hair had been cut off while they were asleep.

In the old days, widows cut their hair short to show their intention of never marrying again. It was a sign their womanhood was gone. This custom of widows cutting their hair short was followed by old-fashioned women until the end of the Meiji era.

For men to cut off their long hair under the new order of the Meiji government was indeed a great change that caused them much sorrow. But there was a common saying then that when a head with short hair was slapped it gave the sound of *bunmeikaika* (civilization and enlightenment).

HARAKIRI

SEPPUKU or *harakiri* — literally, the cutting of the stomach — is suicide by disembowelment, an ancient practice among the former *samurai* or the warrior class of Japan.

This method of committing suicide seems to have been in use in Japan from ancient times. The first mention of *seppuku* is to be found in the *Hogen Monogatari* or the Tales of Hogen, which mentions that Minamoto Tametomo (1139-1190) died by *seppuku.*

In the Kamakura period, 1192-1333, the practice was limited to the *samurai* or warriors. The reason for its limitation to a certain class is believed due to the pain and the difficulties involved in this method of committing suicide. Warriors came to prefer this method of taking their own lives since it testified to their courage and willpower.

In the Tokugawa period, *seppuku* assumed an entirely different nature. Under the regulations of the Tokugawa Shogunate, *seppuku* was the heaviest punishment that could be imposed upon a *samurai* guilty of a grave crime. On the other hand, by passing a sentence of *seppuku* on any criminal *samurai,* the feudal lord felt that he was allowing the guilty man a chance of maintaining his honor and dignity by killing himself in contrast to the common criminals who were beheaded for a similar offense.

With the fall of the Tokugawa Shogunate, the *seppuku* system came to an end. Today, there are no Japanese who commit suicide according to this ancient custom, since it is too difficult and too painful. In the first place, tremendous will power is needed to perform the prescribed ritual involved in this method, namely describing two inter-crossing diagonal cuts and a sharp final thrust into the body organs. In the second place, it is seldom possible to inflict a deep enough cut to make the blow fatal.

In the Tokugawa period, a short sword was stabbed into the stomach at the left side after due ritual. Then it was drawn across to the right side. However, only a superficial cut was made and a trusted retainer, known as the *kaishaku* or helper, officially appointed for the task — raised a sword and cut off the dying man's head to end his agony.

In time, *seppuku* became a mere formality and the guilty *samurai* usually died, not by the actual process of disembowelment but by the ensuing striking off of his head.

In older days, a man committing *seppuku* pulled out his sword after cutting his bowels and applied it to the right side of the neck to sever the carotid artery. In this case, death was caused by the cutting of the artery and not the abdomen.

Scenes of *seppuku*, highly dramatized in Kabuki plays and fiction of the Edo period, have made it world-famous. Some of the accounts of this method of committing suicide are not short of gruesome, with some men reported as sticking their fists into the abdominal opening so formed and pulling out the bowels.

But those who committed *seppuku* in the orthodox fashion were very rare. The suicide of General Maresuke Nogi, however, is an outstanding exception. In the tradition of the *samurai*, General Nogi, upon the death of Emperor Meiji in 1912, decided that he, as a retainer, should follow his master to the grave.

Not only did he perform the required diagonal cut, but thrust his sword into the jugular vein. The feat must have required great courage, calmness of mind and singular will power.

It is interesting to note that his wife followed her husband's example in a separate room, where she died almost simultaneously as her husband by putting a sword through her throat in the manner prescribed for the women of the *samurai* class.

HIYOKUZUKA

UNDER THE feudal social structure, men and women who were deeply in love often found it impossible to be formally married. In despair they committed suicide together 'to be married in the other world,' as the common expression went. The bodies of these love-suicides were generally buried together by their parents or friends so that at least after death they would be together. Such tombs are called *hiyokuzuka*, and are found in various parts of the country.

Hiyoku is an imaginary bird that originated in Chinese tradition. It is found in the mountains of southern regions, according to the Chinese tale. The bird is unique in having only one eye and one wing. Hence it cannot fly, and is helpless by itslef. Only when a *hiyoku* finds its mate and becomes one, the bird can see, fly, and be happy. Thus *hiyoku* is regarded as a love-bird. The feathers of the bird are said to be blue and red. In this way *hiyoku* has become a symbol of lovers who are able to find happiness and life only when they are united in love as one.

Of numerous *hiyokuzuka* still remaining, the most famous is that at the Toshoji Temple, Meguro, Tokyo for Gonpachi and Komurasaki. The story of Gonpachi and Komurasaki is one of the most popular love stories of Edo, and has been made into drama and song. Gonpachi Shirai was a *samurai*, but had to run away upon accidentally killing his comrade. While he was hiding, he saved a young girl. Later Gonpachi who became one of the Edo *kyokaku* (chevalier) found that Komurasaki, a famous woman of Yoshiwara was indeed the girl he saved. They fell in love. But Gonpachi was finally caught and ordered to be beheaded.

Hearing of his execution, Komurasaki hurried to the spot and killed herself by the side of his body. The priest of the Toshoji Temple took sympathy and buried them together in the temple compounds. He marked the tomb with a stone tablet inscribed *hiyokuzuku*. There also stands another tablet bearing the following inscription, as translated by Lord Redesdale:

"In the old days of Genroku she pined for the beauty of her lover, who was fair to look upon as the flowers; now beneath the moss of this old tombstone all has perished of her save her name. Amid the changes of a flitful world, this tomb is decaying under the dew and rain; gradually crumbling beneath its own dust; its outline alone remains. Stranger, bestow an alm to preserve this stone; and we, sparing neither pain nor labor, will second you with all our hearts. Erecting it again, let us preserve it from decay for future generations, and let us write the following verse upon it: 'These two birds, beautiful as the cherry-blossoms, perished before their time like flowers blown down by the wind before they have borne seed.' "

HOTEL BILLS

OLD-FASHIONED Japanese hotels still follow the old custom of not charging for rooms and presenting guests only bills for meals. They serve tea and cakes to guests, but there is no charge for them. When the guest leaves the hotel, he pays the bill for meals and tips for the maids, but he is also expected to give the hotel keeper *chadai* or payment for tea.

Chadai is a voluntary present to the hotel man and so there is no fixed sum. Receiving the gift from the guest, the hotel keeper observes the etiquette of returning it in the form of a towel or some local product.

Sometimes it becomes a puzzling problem to decide the amount of *chadai* which is generally regulated by the class and service of the hotel, and the satisfaction and pocket book of the guest. Before the war, a ¥10,000 *chadai* for staying one night at a hotel, while the regular hotel charge was only ¥10, was not at all rare.

Chadai originated in roadside rest houses. The rest houses offered tea to all travellers but asked no payment. So travellers left some money to pay for the tea and the privilege of resting there.

In the old days there was a special type of hotel called *kichinyado*, or wood-cost hotel, where the only charge made was for the wood used by travellers in cooking their meals.

In primitive times, travellers brought their own food, and innkeepers charged them for the wood used in cooking their meals. So *kichin* or the charge for wood was the only payment asked by innkeepers, and rooms or sleeping quarters were free.

As travelling became more common, inns developed to provide travellers with meals, but even then charges were made only for meals and not for rooms. Thus the primitive type of inns where travellers brought their own food came to be called *kichinyado*.

Hatago is another old term for hotels. It originally meant small woven baskets in which travellers carried their cooked food.

The custom of charging only for meals and never for rooms is still observed at many Japanese-style hotels. The hotel service is graded according to the kind of meals the guests desire, and the best rooms are given to those ordering the highest class of meals.

On the other hand, there are hotels in Japan which charge only for rooms and never serve meals. Such are found at many hotspring and other resorts in rural areas. There the guests cook their own meals over charcoal braziers. This style of inn is preferred by many country folks who wish to enjoy long stays at such resorts without much expense. In such inns, peddlers come daily to sell various food-stuffs to the guests.

IMPERIAL POETRY PARTY

ONE OF THE important New Year functions is the Imperial Poetry Party although it is generally held late in January. It is the occasion to announce the poems composed by the emperor,

Empress, princes and princesses, and also those submitted by common persons on a theme specially given by the Emperor in celebration of the New Year.

The Poetry Party is held according to solemn and ancient customs, and has served in preserving the people's traditional interest in poem composition. This interest has been exceedingly keen since very early days. Particularly in the Imperial Court, poetry has ever been regarded as a high cultural accomplishment. The custom to hold occasional poetry parties at which invited guests composed poems on given subjects and exchanged opinions on them started very early. The Emperor also held such parties, while rural poetry lovers had their own.

The custom of the Imperial New Year Poetry Party is said to have been started by Emperor Murakami, 946-967, the 62nd Emperor. He gave a New Year poetry theme and asked all his subjects to submit their poems. Since then the custom has been observed by the Court, while local feudal lords and others also came to have similar parties of their own.

But it is since 1869 when the Imperial Poetry Bureau was organized in the Imperial Household Department with the formation of the new Meiji government that the people came to show greater and wider interest in composing New Year poems and submitting them to the Court.

Emperor Meiji who was himself a great poet encouraged people of all classes to send their poems on the New Year theme. Thus yearly, thousands of unknown poets, men, women and children, have come to submit their compositions on the subject given by the Emperor for the New Year celebration.

INFORMATION STONES

FOR INFORMATION on lost children or missing persons, and also to announce articles or children found or any unidentified dead, there were established in the Bunka-Bunsei period (1804-1830) *shirube-ishi* or information stones in various parts of Edo. By the stone a wooden board was placed on which sheets of paper giving such information were posted.

Today in Tokyo there remain only three relics of such stones at the Yushima Tenjin Shrine, near the Nio Gate of Asakusa Kannon, and the other at 1-chome, Gofukucho, Nihonbashi. Of course there is nothing left of the wooden boards that stood by those stones.

As *shirube-ishi* served to bring separated persons together, the Edo people thought that it must also possess the power to unite those in love. Consequently, youthful lovers who could not be united in marriage began to pray to those information stones.

At the Yushima Tenjin Shrine, in particular, they developed a custom among men and women in love, to write the names of the other party who would not respond to their affection on pieces of paper and tie them to the branches of trees near the stone. They firmly believed that the stone would respond to their prayer and lead them to successful marriage.

On the annual festival day of the shrine on May 24 the custom has been very popularly followed.

INKYO

INKYO IS A unique family and social institution in Japan. It means one who has voluntarily abdicated from the headship of a family. His wife is also called *inkyo*. The new Constitution, of course, abolished the system legally, but the *inkyo* still has much influence not only in individual families, but also among relatives and neighbors.

To old-fashioned Japanese, it has been their ultimate ambition to become *raku-inkyo* or comfortable *inkyo*. The life of an *inkyo* is supposed to be most pleasant and easy. Having cast aside the duty and responsibility of looking after the welfare of the entire family, upon becoming an *inkyo* one is freed of all worldly worries. The family property is transferred to the succeeding head, but even under the old Constitution he was allowed to have his own wealth.

Thus the *inkyo* has nothing else to do but to enjoy the fruits of his long hardworking years, to indulge in whatever hobby he might have or to devote himself to the care of his dear grandchildren. He has lost all authority over the family or its members, but that does not make him lose their respect. His opinion is sought on all subjects, because his lengthy experience in life has given him much wisdom. Thus, sometimes, an *inkyo* becomes the actual ruler of the family, when his son proves to be not good in directing the family affairs. History mentions many ex-emperors wielding greater power than the reigning emperors. It has been often the same in private families.

The *inkyo* system is quite old. Under the military rule that started in the Kamakura period (13th to 14th century) it was firmly established. Feudal lords and *samurai* were ordered to become *inkyo* by the shogun or lords, as punishment for some wrong they committed. In such cases, their sons succeeded to the posts vacated by their fathers.

The system of retirement of the parents upon the marriage of their oldest son and living in a separate house started very early in the days when the country was not so densely populated and there were still lands for development. When the eldest son became of age and took a wife, the old parents left the house and farm to the young couple. They built a new house and cultivated their own farm. When there were other children, the old couple took care of them.

When the second son married, the old parents left and again built a new house. Thus, under this system, the old folks died at the house of the youngest son.

There was also another system. When the eldest son married, he left with his wife to build their own house and farm. The second son also left in due time, and so on. Thus, again it was the youngest son who inherited the house and farm of the old parents.

Even in a much later period, this system of the youngest son inheriting the family property was observed in many districts.

During the feudal period when military and official positions became mostly hereditary, the father retired to give his son position and rank in the family. The retired parents generally built their own houses and lived separately from the younger couples.

The custom of old or retired couples living in separate houses from the younger people was followed as far as possible. In cases when this was impossible because of various reasons, the old and young couples had separate kitchens and cooking utensils.

This custom is still seen in many rural districts, particularly in the Izu Islands.

INVITATION

JAPANESE invitations often puzzle foreigners who are not used to the customs of the people. Of course, in case of formal invitations sent by printed cards, letters or telephone messages, giving specific dates and times there is no confusion whatever.

But the Japanese are in the habit of saying to all friends and acquaintances — "Drop in at any time whenever you are in the neighborhood," or "come any Sunday, as we will be always home."

Such invitations become quite a problem for foreigners. In most cases, such invitations do not mean anything at all. Those words are spoken for the sake of courtesy. If any foreigner thinks that he is really invited and goes to visit his Japanese friends, he will be greatly disappointed and embarrassed, as the host is not expecting him.

Of course, in some cases, even these vaguely given invitations are really meant, but it is extremely difficult, particularly for foreigners, to distinguish real invitations from 'courtesy' invitations.

Foreigners must also be prepared to receive calls from Japanese friends at any time, day or night. They will furthermore find that their visitors, particularly women, will not enter the house, but keep on talking at the entrance, with the door open. This is particularly unbearable in winter.

Old-fashioned people do not enter the house when they come on some errand or unexpected calls, because if they enter the house, it becomes a social call. Once a guest enters the house, tea and cakes must be served, and meals have to appear if it is mealtime. It has thus been regarded good etiquette not to enter the house, when one is calling unexpectedly or on mere errands.

KANDO

KANDO (disowning) was a system developed in the Tokugawa period for parents to punish disobedient or unruly children who disgraced the family. It meant that the parents had no more responsibility over them because they were disowned and unrecognized by the family.

To disown a child legally, parents had to apply to the bugyosho or magistrate's office to have the name of such a child taken out of the official register.

The kando system was also applied to students, disciples or apprentices when their teachers or masters found them unworthy of further care or guidance.

There were also numerous cases of unofficial kando. In such cases wild or disobedient children were not formally disowned, but were merely kicked out of their homes without allowance or help and left to fend for themselves. In most such cases, disowned children were pardoned when they showed repentance or after the lapse of a certain period.

There are many tales of persons being pardoned by very simple acts. When a fire broke out near the house of his parents, a son who had been disowned rushed there and worked hard to put out the fire. He was pardoned for thinking of his parents and coming to their help at a time of need.

This story became so famous that it is said that many disowned sons daily hoped that a fire would start near their paternal residences. Most disowned children were taken care of in secret by persons who were friends or acquaintances of their parents.

This official system of kando had its bad side. It resulted in increasing the number of criminals and lawless persons. Not used to making their living honestly, the disowned resorted to unlawful acts. So the Bakufu authorities had to issue a warning to the public that they should give more consideration in disowning their children.

Cases of unofficial *kando* still remain, although the meaning has changed much.

KOSEKI

KOSEKI or the Japanese system of registry is unique, as the record of birth, marriage, divorce, death and even criminal acts of each person is accurately kept. Theoretically speaking, there is no Japanese who is not registered. To be a *museki-mono* or non-registered person is the greatest disgrace. If the fingerprint of each is also kept, the system will become perfect.

No birth, marriage, divorce or death is officially recognized until such facts are duly entered in the official register. A copy of the official entry is issued on demand, and serves for identification.

The registry is made for each household and when one establishes his own household on marriage or other reasons, a separate entry is made.

Koseki, of course, developed from the family system, and helped the maintenance of the system. It is particularly noteworthy that the system of keeping the record of all inhabitants of the country started in 646 under the so-called Taika Reform, or more than 13 centuries ago. At the Horyuji Temple, Nara, is still preserved the register of Harube village, dated 702.

Even earlier than the Taika era there was a certain register of inhabitants for recruiting people for labor. At first one houshold was made a unit, and 50 households formed a village. Later, the enforcement of the system was much slackened. For the convenience of maintaining public peace and order, *goningumi* (five family unit), and *junin-gumi* (10 family unit) were formed. Buddhist temples also kept records of all families whose religious matters and tombs were under their supervision.

It was in the fourth year of Meiji or 1871 that the *kosekiho* or registration law was promulgated. Since then all are registered with municipal, town or village offices.

LAUGH AT ME

IF I FAIL TO REPAY this loan, you may laugh at me in public, an Edo resident wrote in his I.O.U. note, it is said. The note was accepted by the moneylender in good faith, and the loan was made, as this offer had more weight than any other security.

The Japanese have always believed that to be laughed at by others is the greatest disgrace, and have gone to extreme means to save themselves from such ignominy. To be despised or sneered at by others was the worst one could expect from neighbors and friends.

An artisan of Edo went to a moneylender for help, but he could not offer any security which the moneymonger demanded. So he proposed to pledge one sleeve. That is to say, he would not pass one arm through the sleeve, but would go around with the loose sleeve flapping until the loan was repaid.

This offer was readily accepted by the money-lender. As soon as he got the desired amount, the artisan pulled in his arm and went about at home and on the street, with one sleeve loose.

The people looked at him in surprise and laughed. That was the punishment he was receiving for keeping his arm out of the sleeve. But until his debt was repaid, he could not wear his *kimono* properly.

The story goes that finally the man obtained enough money to pay back the loan. Only when he placed the money before the money-lender did he put his arm in the sleeve.

Old-fashioned parents still tell their children "act so that you will not be laughed at." The people are still afraid of being laughed at. This has come from their desire to keep their dignity and community standing.

MEN'S NAMES

BOYS OF NOBLE and *samurai* families were first given childhood names, and upon their attainment of manhood they were given manhood names. Manhood names of aristocratic families were dignified in sound and meaning, but boyhood names were simple, with the termination of *maru* in many cases.

Many families have certain Chinese characters which are always used in the names of their male members, like Yoritomo, Yoriie, Sanetomo and Tametomo in the Minamoto family. Common families, however, have always given their children much simpler names. Very often the first-born son is called Ichiro or Taro (first son), the second Jiro (second son), the third Saburo (third son), the fourth Shiro (fourth son), the fifth Goro (fifth son) and so forth. Names for boys ending in 'O,' 'Ro' and 'Kichi' are exceedingly numerous, and they all mean manhood.

Boys are often given a part or parts of the names of their fathers or ancestors. Particularly in business circles, there is a custom of the son adopting the father's name upon succeeding to the business, so that the hereditary business can be kept on under the same name.

There are names composed of numerals, Isoroku (56), Ichizo (13), Yasohachi (88), Goroku (56), Jushichi (17) and so on. These numerals generally indicate the year or month of their birth, or the father's age when the boys were born, or their combinations.

Some are given extremely funny or grotesque names, some fathers taking pride in giving such names. Koshiro (tiger, lion, boar) or Totsuo (convex concave) are representative of such strange names.

MIMAI

SHOCHU-MIMAI or summer season inquiry is still observed by the Japanese. It is customary etiquette to visit relatives and friends and inquire how they are faring in the hot season. Of course, as in the case of other social calls, it is necessary to take some presents on such visits. To people far away, letters are sent, sometimes accompanied by presents, to inquire after their health in the season.

Similar courtesy must also be extended to all friends during the cold winter season. Furthermore, on various other occasions, inquiries such as *byoki-mimai* (sick inquiry), *kaji-mimai* (fire inquiry), *osan-mimai* (birth inquiry), *shin-chiku-mimai* (inquiry when a new house is built), *kichu-mimai* (mourning period inquiry) are commonly made. That is to say, when any relative or friend, or a member of his family is sick, a visit has to be made. When one has a fire in the house or in the neighborhood, friends must call and inquire. When someone one knows builds a new house, a call has to be made. During the mourning period for any friend, a visit has to be made to inquire after the health of all the members of the family.

Furthermore, when the head of a family is away on a journey, his friends will call to make *rusu-mimai* (absence inquiry) to inquire how the family is while he is away.

All these *mimai* visits are made with presents. Of course, the receivers of *mimai* gifts must return the presents.

MON

THE PEOPLE of Japan have a very deeply rooted attachment to their *mon* or family crest. It stands for the honor and history of the family, and in many cases it is due to the great achievements of their ancestors that they were allowed to use their crests. Thus, it is quite natural for all families to be proud of them and endeavor to keep them from being dishonored.

Furthermore, whenever the people form some organization, they are not satisfied until they have a design and adopt it as the *mon* for their organized bodies. Thus, every city of the country has its *mon*, as do the clubs, associations and business offices or shops.

Many big business firms are so proud of their *mon* that they put them not only on their letterheads and products, but also on tea kettles, tea cups, silverware, automobiles, furniture and everything else. To them the marks are not mere trademarks, but symbols of their history, fame and standing.

The peculiar *mon* system of Japan originated in the warring period, some 700 years ago. Warriors used various marks on their banners, tents, buntings and other things in battlefields for identification. This custom soon was extended to the warriors' dresses. The *samurai* class was thus the first to adopt *mon* as the symbol for each family. Dresses of the *samurai* thus came to bear the family *mon*, both for men and women. The custom was soon followed by the Court circles as well as the commoner.

The designs of *mon* are mostly floral from the very beginning, and this fact is often pointed out as an indication to show how the people are fond of plants and flowers. Of course, butterflies, cranes and other animals are often used as *mon* designs. Then there are also geometrical designs. These designs are mostly placed within borders of circles, squares, octagons or other shapes.

Branches and descendents of one family all use the same *mon*, and sometimes in such cases, different branches or descendents have different borders to their *mon*. Thus even today, *mon* serve to tell the relationship between families. However distant the families might be, the same *mon* tells that they have been related in early dates. That is to say, the family *mon* tells its history.

In feudal days, particularly, great respect was paid to the *mon*. Feudal lords often permitted their retainers to use their *mon* in recognition of special services. Dresses and utensils bearing the *mon* of the feudal lord were articles that demanded respect on all occasions. The family that was permitted to use the *mon* of its feudal lord was envied by all others.

A family without any *mon* is still treated as an outcast, and the people must have their *mon* even for their offices or organizations. It is because they still think that the family's honor is represented by the *mon*. The family system may change, but it may be quite difficult to make the people go without their family *mon*.

MOTHERS-IN-LAW

JAPANESE wives in olden times had no trouble with their mothers-in-law because they did not live with them. The Japanese family in those days consisted of the wife, husband, her parents and the children, as picturesquely described in *Genji-Monogatari*. In other words, the husband lived in his wife's house. In those early days, when a man married a girl, he went to the wife's house every night, until he was accepted by the family and allowed to live with them. So, there was no mother-in-law trouble and Japanese wives were very happy.

A remant of this custom is still left in the practice maintained in many rural districts for a wife returning to her parents' house to give birth to children.

It was toward the end of the 14th century that the wife's position underwent a significant change as the feudal system developed. The male lineage became important, and the wife was taken into the home of her husband to keep up the family line. Thus marriage came to be arranged by the heads of families for family interest. The wife's position became secondary. Mothers-in-law ruled the household and wives were treated almost as servants.

In the process of this change, the custom of erecting a separate house for aged parents started. It was regarded unlucky for two generations to eat out of the same cooking pan. Separate cooking places were made in one family. Even today, at Toshijima, one of the seven islands of Izu, the ancient custom of the old parents and the young couple having separate cooking facilities in one house is observed.

Thus in Japan, wives' troubles with mothers-in-law are of comparatively recent origin.

MUJIN

THE JAPANESE have a system of mutual financing and saving called *mujin*. A *mujin* was at first formed by a group of neighbors or friends. Each month, one puts up a certain amount for a period generally from 10 to 30 months. As they gather to pay the monthly sum, they draw lots and the winner of the lucky number obtains the privilege of receiving in advance the total amount that he agreed to save in

the fixed period. If someone else is in particular need of the money, he many buy that privilege from the winner upon paying a premium. The winner, however, has to keep on paying his monthly due until the end. When the monthly payments are completed, they start all over again. Thus it came to be named *mujin* or endless.

Mujin became particularly popular in Tokugawa days among petty merchants, artisans and farmers. Today, however, private *mujin* groups are prohibited and *mujin* companies organized under banking and other laws operate the system in a modernized way.

Mujin was called *tanomoji* (mutual aid) in earlier days. It is believed to have started in the Kamakura period, 700 years ago. At first a quantity of rice was saved in many cases. The term *mujin* first appeared in the Muromachi period (1392-1573).

Tanomoshi or *mujin* developed from a much earlier mutual aid system. Under this, each resident, rich and poor alike, contributed every year or periodically a fixed amount of money or rice to the mutual aid fund. When anyone had no money to buy food or to pay extra expenses or tax, he obtained the necessary amount from the fund. It was thus always the poor members of the community who benefited from the system, while the rich received no return whatever though they paid their dues regularly. This is the original community chest of Japan.

MURA-HACHIBU

NEWSPAPERS from time to time have reported a few cases of *mura-hachibu* (village ostracism), a feudal system of punishment. It was orginally adopted with the good intention of making all villagers cooperate in community welfare and happiness. However, as in the case of all laws, it was sometimes abused. *Mura-hachibu*, as it still exists in some rural districts, is of course detestable, as social conditions and individual status have now changed considerably from feudal days.

In olden times, for maintaining order and peace in a community, each village possessed its own rules of conduct and systems of punishment. Such systems, of course, differed according to districts. But commonly speaking, those who committed murder, incendiarism or other serious crimes were driven out of the village. For other criminal acts, they were ordered to live in a secluded corner of the village. Those who committed such offenses as not participating in the village festival, not attending village meetings, not cooperating in common village activities, or not observing proper etiquette or moral codes, were made *hachibu* or ostracized persons.

Hachibu were completely excluded from the social contact and activities of the villagers. Nobody even spoke to them. In some places *hachibu* were made to wear red sashes or a black *tabi* (sock) on one foot and a white one on the other, so that they could easily be identified.

However, there was also a system for them to regain their rights and privileges. When they fully repented of their misconduct and apologized, they were pardoned. Sometimes fines had to be paid or somebody else had to guarantee for their good conduct. But one who was once a *hachibu* was often obliged to take the lowest seat at village meetings and parties.

MUSEKIMONO

THERE IS NO greater infamy for the Japanese people than being a *musekimono* or a man without re-

gistered domicile, because such a man can never enter a school nor obtain employment. It means that his name is not in the census register, and therefore he does not legally exist.

The system of *koseki* or census registration is highly developed in Japan, and all Japanese are registered at the city, town or village office. Births, marriages, divorces, deaths or changes of residence are not recognized until entered in the register. If one is given a court sentence for any crime, the fact is also entered. Hence none in Japan can hide his former crimes, if punished legally.

The system of *koseki* is 13 centuries old, as it was first proclaimed in January, 646. At first it was ordered that about 50 households should be formed into a *sato* or village, and one person be appointed its head. It was his duty to keep the record of all the households and their members in his village. Thus the *koseki* system started. At some time, the duty of keeping the household records was taken up by Buddhist or Shinto priests, as temples and shrines became the center of religious and social local activity.

It was, however, at the beginning of the Meiji era that the system was formally and thoroughly enforced, with the issue of the 'koseki-ho' or the law of census registration. Each village, town or city has a register of all the people residing within its jurisdiction, and those who are not registered become *musekimono*.

The original record of a family and its members is kept at the office of the locality where the family makes its permanent domicile or *honseki*. When the family or any of its members moves to another place, the removal is to be entered not only in the original register, but also with the office of the new locality. The second residence is called *kiryu-chi* or temporary residence.

A copy of the register is issued upon request. This copy is required for identification. Applications to enter schools, or for employment must always be accompanied by the copies of the census register. *Han* or seal is also registered with the local office, and the certificate of the seal also serves as a means of identification.

One look at the register will tell the whole history of a family, its members and its related families.

NAMING BABIES

THE JAPANESE baby is christened on the seventh day of life when its birth is celebrated with feasting. The naming of the baby is quite a task for the parents because it is believed that the name will govern its entire life. *Na-wa-tai-o-arawasu* (the name reveals the body), goes an old saying. To make the baby healthy, happy, prosperous and intelligent, the parents must think out a name that will give it all those qualifications. Such names are mostly formed by putting together two or more Chinese characters with good meaning, and they thus sometimes become extremely difficult to read or write, to the utter misery of the children.

The task of naming babies is beyond the common people's ability, and so village priests, teachers and such are asked to name newborn babies. There are even professionals who specialize in selecting names.

Nevertheless giving difficult names is quite a modern trend. Formerly common people were given simple names. For instance, sons were mostly named by number, so to speak. The first son was called Taro or Ichiro (first son), followed by Jiro (second), Saburo (third), Shiro (fourth), Goro (fifth),

Rokuro (sixth), Shichiro (seventh), Hachiro (eighth), Kuro (ninth) and Juro (tenth). The 11th boy was not welcome to many parents and was often named Yoichi (surplus one). A lad named Koichiro means the son of Ichiro, Kojiro, the son of Jiro, and so on, signifying the son.

Girls' names were also very simple, being mostly taken after flowers, plants and such common things, as Hana (flowers), Haru (spring), Kiku (chrysanthemum), Take (bamboo), Ume (apricot), Matsu (pine), Yuki (snow), Natsu (summer), Aki (autumn) and others. The addition of *ko* at the end of a girl's name became popular after the beginning of the Meiji era. Daughters of nobles and war lords always had *ko* at the end of their names, and this custom was adopted by commoners with the abolition of feudalism.

Old families, both nobles and military, used particular characters in the names of their sons, so that by their given names their families could be told. For instance, Tokugawa men had "ie" in their names, as shown by Ieyasu, Ietsuna, Ienari, Iemochi, Ieyoshi, Ietsugu and Iesato. The Minamoto family used 'yoshi' or 'tomo', as Sanetomo, Tametomo, Yoritomo, Yoshiie, Yoshitsune, Yoshinaka and Yoshimitsu. The Hojo family used 'toki' as Tokiyori, Yasutoki, Yoshitoki, Tokimasa and Takatoki.

In the old days, the eldest sons of farmers and merchants took the names of their fathers, so that the business could be carried on in the same name. But this custom has almost died out because of the legal difficulty in changing names.

Some rural districts have special names which are given to their sons and daughters. In some villages, many boys and girls have the same names.

NEW YEAR CARDS

NEW YEAR greeting cards the Japanese people send out to relatives, friends, associates and others reach an enormous quantity, many individuals sending thousands of such cards every year. This custom, however, is quite modern, dating back to some 80 years ago.

The New Year call or greeting was formerly called *nenshi* or year-beginning, but in recent years it has come to be known as *nenga* (year felicitation) which was formerly a term for expressing felicitation on the attainment of certain ages such as 40, 50, 60, 70 or 80.

The rite of *nenshi* was at first a family affair. On New Year's Day, the heads of branch families used to go to the house of the main family early in the morning to open the house gate or door to express felicitation on the happy occasion. Later the main family head returned their calls. The visitors were treated to *sake* and food, according to the ancient idea of sharing food and happiness. This custom is still observed in Shikoku and other rural areas. Later, this custom came to be followed also by pupils and workers who went to the homes of their teachers or employers.

Thus the New Year visit became popularized and people began to visit all their neighbors, friends and relatives to express New Year greetings. The New Year call became an important duty for all.

When the postal service developed in the Meiji era, the people adopted the easier method of sending their greeting by postcards. This custom started around 1880 and soon became very popular. As the New Year cards suddenly increased, the postal authorities adopted a special system for handling them in 1900. That is, New Year cards posted in the latter part of December were delivered to the addressees on the morning of New Year's Day.

NOSHI AND MIZUHIKI

THE PEOPLE of Japan are very fond of giving presents to friends on various occasions. They perfected the art of presenting gifts. Every little gift has to be properly selected, packed, boxed and decorated. In the early days, it was vegetables that were regarded as the most proper things to offer to others. The *noshi* that came to be attached to all gifts is the remnant of the ancient custom of presenting fish to *kami*, shrines, or friends. Made of the sliced meat of abalone *(awabi)*, which is dried and stretched out long, this *noshi* was originally presented as a gift in place of fish, to manifest the sender's respect. Gradually it came to be a symbol for gifts and used to be placed on anything to be presented as gifts as a mark of respect and good will. Later it was simplified and attained its present form, which merely consists of an extremely tiny piece of dried abalone meat, stretched as thin as paper, wrapped up in red and white paper, cut square and folded to form a long pentagon, wider at the top and narrower at the bottom.

All gifts must bear this mark of *noshi* in order to show the respect of the sender to the addressed. When proper *noshi* is not available, people often write *noshi* on the wrapping paper. Use of *noshi* is quite ancient, as it is mentioned in the *Ise-Monogatari* (ninth century).

Besides the *noshi*, gifts must be also tied with *mizuhiki*, a strand of three or five paper strings. It comes in all lengths, from about five inches to more than eight feet for tying presents of all sizes. It is always made in two colors, each color taking one-half of its length. Thus it is red-white, gold-silver, red-gold, black-white, or blue-white. The origin of *mizuhiki* is very old, though no definite date can be given. Those of red-white, gold-silver and red-gold are used on gifts presented on happy occasions, while those made in black-white or blue-white are for death, funeral or memorial services.

There are fixed rules in tying the *mizuhiki*. The red-white *mizuhiki*, which is most common, must be tied so that the white end comes to the left; the gold-silver *mizuhiki* with the silver half to the left, and the red-gold one with the gold end to the left. But the black-white *mizuhiki* or the blue-white, which is used at funerals and such occasions, must be tied so that the black or blue half comes to the right.

The *noshi* and *mizuhiki* make all presents very decorative and beautiful. Those which are used to decorate wedding presents are often every elaborate and expensive. They are both quite necessary to express the friendly sentiment of the gift-givers. It is thought impolite or vulgar to offer anything without *noshi* and *mizuhiki*.

NUE-LIKE PERSONS

PERSONS WHO are always changing their ideas or plans, or whose attitude is difficult to guess are called *nue*-like persons.

Nue is an imaginary creature. Originally it is said to be an evil bird that brings bad fortune to the people. It is about the size of a pigeon, and lives in high mountains. Its feathers are yellow and red. The upper bill is black and the lower yellow. Its legs are yellow and red. It sleeps in the daytime, and becomes active at night. Its voice is said to be like to a baby crying.

Later, however, there appeared another *nue* which assumed the form of a fierce evil animal, harming humans. It became particularly famous in 1153, when it tormented Emperor Konoe. Fortunately Minamoto Yorimasa, a great warrior in attendance to the Emperor, shot it with his arrow one night, and released the Emperor from further torture. By this brave act, he became renowned as the bravest warrior of the time, but it also made the *nue* famous.

According to the story told about Yorimasa's killing of the evil animal, *nue* had a head like that of a monkey, a tiger's body and a tail similar to a snake's.

The story of Yorimasa shooting the *nue* has been made into a *Noh* play, and also a *Kabuki* drama.

Because of its elusive nature, and also because it may be either a bird or an animal, the name has been used to indicate anything that cannot be definitely defined or is changeable.

O-CHUGEN PRESENTS

DEPARTMENT STORES and other shops start special *o-chugen* sales in early July as the people still observe the old tradition of giving presents on *o-chugen*, July 15.

Originally there were three seasonal beginnings which were occasions for felicitations: *jogen* (first seasonal beginning) on January 15, *chugen* (middle seasonal beginning) on July 15, and *gogen* (last seasonal beginning) on October 15. On all three occasions presents were exchanged and *omedeto* (happiness to you) was expressed to friends and neighbors. Nowadays those of January and July are observed, whereas that of October 15 is entirely forgotten.

It is because of this gift exchanging custom on *o-chugen* that salaried men and employees are given a summer bonus, which in turn enriches store-keepers.

In the old days generally foodstuff, particularly fish, were exchanged, but of late, except in some rural districts, *o-chugen* presents have taken the form of various household goods, dress goods and such. Merchants, too, bring *o-chugen* presents to their patrons. The custom is also followed by banks and business firms.

O-chugen is old in origin, having come from China, but with the introduction of Buddhism, it came to be often confused with *o-bon* or Ullanbanr, a service for the salvation of the dead, held on July 14 and 15. The earliest *o-bon* rites are said to have been held in the 14th year of Emperor Suiko, or 606.

As both *o-chugen* and *o-bon* are held in the middle of July, some of their features came to be mixed. But in many rural districts fish still constitutes the main *o-chugen* present, proving that it has no connection with Buddhism which prohibits the eating of fish or meats.

While originally *o-chugen* was an occasion for wishing happiness, that important significance is almost lost now, and the younger people think of it as merely an occasion to receive bonuses and exchange presents.

O-OTSURI

THE JAPANESE people are fond of giving presents and many gift giving customs have developed. Presents received on various occasions must be returned. Those who do not observe the usual present giving and receiving custom are often called unsociable.

In connection with the receipt of presents, there is a habit of giving *o-otsuri* (reward) as a sign of acknowledg-

ing and appreciating the gifts. *O-otsuri* usually consists of one or two sheets of white Japanese paper or a box of matches. In rural districts a handful of rice or beans wrapped up in paper is also given.

In handing back the *furoshiki* (wrapping cloth), tray, basket , or lacquered box in which the present has been brought, the *o-otsuri* is generally placed in such a wrapper or container.

The custom of giving a box of matches as *o-otsuri* is quite new. Formerly *tsukegi* or slender woodchips with sulphur dipped ends which were used to start a fire were used as *o-otsuri*, because *iwo* (sulphur) was similar in sound to *iwau* (to felicitate). When matches became common they replaced the old *tsukegi.*

In rural districts rice and beans are often used, as they are always in the house. The habit of offering to shrines or temples rice or coins wrapped up in paper has been followed since early days. The rice or beans used as *o-otsuri* has the same meaning as *ohineri* or offerings presented to shrines or temples.

But the returning of the *furoshiki* or basket with *o-otsuri* does not end the obligation of the gift receiver, as the present must be properly returned with fitting gifts as soon as possible.

Gift offering and receiving have developed into quite a systematized social custom must be strictly observed by all who wish to be in good standing with relatives, neighbors and acquaintances.

ORDER OF SEATING

IN THE Japanese room, the seat-of-honor is in front of the *tokonoma* or alcove, and the principal guest sits there with his back toward it. The second guest sits at his left, and the third on the other side of the room, facing the principal guest. The host sits at the lower end of the room, diagonally from the first guest. When the room is large and many guests are present, it is impossible for the host to talk to his principal guest who sits so far away from him.

When two persons stand side by side, one who is lower in rank or seniority must be at the right of the other. The left side is the place of honor in Japan. When a man and his wife sit side by side, the wife always takes the seat at the right of her husband, because the place of honor must be given to the head of the family.

This seating custom came from the ancient Imperial Court etiquette. The Emperor always faces the south, which is the direction to be honored. Most of the Japanese palaces and shrines face south, though there are a few exceptions. Then in a room or building, the crown prince sits at the emperor's left, and the Empress at his right, when the three are side by side on formal occasions. This is because in Japan the crown prince, the heir to the throne, is higher in rank than the empress. The crown prince is called *Togu* or eastern prince, because he sits on the left or east of the Emperor.

The introduction of Western manners has made the problem of seating guests very confusing. But now generally the Western way is adopted at foreign type functions, and the Japanese way in Japanese rooms or houses.

O-SEIBO

AS THE YEAR-END approaches everybody is giving and receiving *o-seibo*, which has now come to mean year-end presents. Originally it meant only the end of the year. Some even use the term for *o-bon* or summer gifts.

At first *o-seibo* were simple presents given by one household to another. it never stood for gifts to individuals. *O-seibo* was presented to the parental household by the children's family, to the main family by the branch household, to the landowner by the tenant, to the patron by the shopkeeper, or to the master artisan by the parents of his apprentice. It was used for expressing appreciation for past favors and kindness.

Things brought as *o-seibo* were formerly fresh fish, dried or salted fish, dried noodles, rice flour and such common foodstuff. Of course these who received *o-seibo* were obliged to make a gift in return, sometimes with money. Often return presents were more costly than the original presents, as the receivers were generally richer than the givers.

The custom of giving *o-seibo* often differs from one area to another, and in some regions family heads and employers give *o-seibo* to their employees and others who worked for them during the year. In such cases, there are no return presents.

The original meaning of *o-seibo* has almost been lost, and it has become customary to exchange presents at the year-end not only among households, but also among individuals. Presents themselves have tended to become more showy and expensive.

The introduction of Christmas has furthermore widened the scope of the year-end gift exchange. Often one has to give both Christmas presents and *o-seibo* to the same person. Then again, when New Year comes, the people again give *o-toshidama* or New Year presents.

O-TOSHIDAMA

O-TOSHIDAMA (year's gem) are little

gifts presented in the New Year season. Generally in these days, it is given to children who come to make New Year calls, or is brought by merchants who wish for business in the new year. The presents are generally simple things, toys or candies for children or *tenugui* (Japanese towels) brought by merchants.

But originally *O-toshidama* had a deeper meaning. It started with the idea of dividing the good fortune by *kami* or gods. Thus formerly the *mochi* presented to *kami* on New Year's Day was cut up and distributed to extend *kami's* grace to all.

The habit of giving pieces of *mochi* to children on New Year's Day was followed very widely.

In the mountain villages of Mikawa province, there was formerly a strange custom of presenting little stones to the local shrine on its festival day. Each visitor to the shrine was given one of the stones to ensure his good luck and health. These stones are called *toshidama*, as they guarded the holders for the whole year and had the same significance as the *toshidama* given on New Year's Day.

From these ideas and customs has developed the present *O-toshidama*-giving habit. *O-toshidama* makes the New Year happier and pleasanter for many little children, who welcome visitors and love to accompany their parents in making New Year calls.

OYABUN-KOBUN

THE FEUDALISTIC institution of *oyabun-kobun* (boss and henchmen) still exists among some groups of people, though in a much changed form.

The custom of some parents treating children of other families as if they were their own is said to have developed almost 10 centuries ago. It came from the system of the main family and branch families in the military and aristocratic classes. The second or third son established his own separate family, but as he lacked prestige and economic power, he depended on the main family for aid. So his children were looked after by the main family and in return, they gave whatever help they could.

Thus it became customary for the master of the main family to give names to the children of the branch family, and bring them to his house for proper bringing up. A relation of foster father and stepchildren developed. This was the beginning of the *oyabun-kobun* relationship which was based on family and personal sentiments as well as economic considerations. This relationship continued for generations.

In the Tokugawa period beginning in the 17th century, the *oyabun-kobun* system extended to commoners, particularly the artisan class. The master worker took into his house children or young men and trained them treating them as his proteges. They obeyed their master absolutely, regarding him as their master-father even after they became independent, while the master always took a fatherly interest in their work and life.

Today the *oyabun-kobun* system is seen only among construction workers, street stall vendors, gamblers and such. *Kobun* or henchmen are looked after by their *oyabun* or bosses whose word is law. All henchmen under one boss become *kyodaibun* or brothers who are bound together by solemn pledges.

One is accepted as a henchman of the boss with the solemn ritual of receiving a cup of *sake* from him. Then he exchanges cups with all the henchmen to be initiated into the *kyodaibun* (brotherhood). Between the boss and henchmen, and among brother henchmen, absolute trust is pledged. At the word of the boss, *kobun* are willing to offer even their lives.

RESPECTING THE AGED

THE JAPANESE people respect aged persons, and in the past have had various ways of expressing this sentiment. Even today various districts have Keiro-kai, associations for respecting the aged, and annually they invite old people to parties for recreation.

As early as the Nara period, seventh to eighth century, the Court had a system of giving special favors to nobles and officials above the age of 80. Those reaching the age of 90 were given one attendant each, those above 92 two attendants, and those above 105 attendants. Farmers and common people attaining the age of 76 were given the rank of good citizens.

The system of awarding *hatozue* (pigeon cane) to aged nobles and officials also started in the Nara period. Fujiwara Toshinari received the pigeon cane in 1203 when he attained the age of 90. He was the first to have this honor under the formally adopted system, which was kept up by the Imperial Court until the Pacific war.

Occasionally the Court held parties specially to honor people above 70. Such honors were also extended to the common people. It is recorded that Lord Kamei of Imba invited farmers and commoners above the age of 60 to a party at Shikano every year. Many young maidens were in attendance and looked after the comfort of these old people, who were given gifts and food. Entertainments were held for them, and they felt very highly honored.

Recent Keiro-kai gatherings are not so picturesque as those ancient affairs. But each district invites its old men and women and honors them with words of appreciation and various gifts.

SEAL

SIGNATURES are not used in Japan as a means of identification. Only in the remote ancient days it was used by the Emperor and Court officials for signifying their approval on official documents. Today, seals are the legal method of identification, and the signature is given no official recognition, except in some special cases.

Ancient people followed a tendency of writing only a portion of their names in a very decorative manner. From this habit came *kakihan* or the written seal. A character or a combination of several characters or their parts were made into a sort of design, and it was affixed to documents or writings. Pictorial designs were sometimes also used. In making up such *kakihan*, they took pains to make them inimitable. *Kakihan* became the fashion between the ninth and 10th centuries, particularly among Court officials, local governors and military lords.

The use of seals is believed to have come from China. Emperor Mombu issued an order in 704 to all provinces to make and use provincial seals on all official documents. This is the first mention of the official use of seals in Japan.

Seals are mostly of crystal, metal, stone or wood, with the engraving of the family or personal name, and pictorial designs in some cases. There are expert seal engravers and many people take pride in using seals made by master artists.

It was, however, only since the beginning of the Meiji era that seals came to be generally used. The bureaucratic administration demanded the presentation of written documents from the public on all matters. Such documents had to bear the seals of the writers.

Suddenly, therefore, all family heads were required to have their own seals.

There are now two kinds of seales in use, *jitsuin* or registered seals, and *mitome* or unofficial seals. One must have an official seal and have it registered with the city, town or village office, which issues the seal certificate on demand at any time. All official and legal documents must be accompanied by the certificate of the seals used on them.

The registered seal system is extremely convenient in identifying an individual, because the one who uses it is the person who is designated in the accompanying seal certificate. That may be one advantage over the use of the signature, because in case of unknown persons, their signatures do not mean anything. Seals and their certificates may be stolen, of course, but the thief can be punished when found.

The Japanese cannot live a single day without their *mitome* or unofficial seals. Every family has several *mitome*, which are simple inexpensive seals, bearing their name. It must be impressed on the receipt of a registered letter, on the monthly pay envelope. *Mitome* is used in drawing deposits from banks or post offices. It is necessary in cashing checks or postal money orders. In fact it is used where the signature is used in other countries.

The legal and common use of seals makes the signature almost worthless. Checks are worthless unless they bear the seals which the depositors registered with their banks. The name of the check issuer is often rubber-stamped or printed, as it is the seal that counts and not the signature.

The system of registering seals has also made the public notary system of a very limited service.

Following the examples of Chinese seals, seals were made at first in Japan also of jade, gold, silver or copper. Later crystal, ivory, horn, coral and agate came to be used as materials for making seals. Today metal seals are very rare, and generally they are of crystal, ivory, horn or wood. Rubber seals have come into use of late, but they do not last long. The engraving of seals is an independent art and occupation. Modern people do not appreciate the art of seal engraving, and are contented with mass-produced seals. But well-designed and engraved seals appeal to the sense of beauty just like paintings. Materials are also very important in making good seals, and a trained person can tell the material of a seal by looking at its impression on paper.

The cinnabar pad is used in stamping seals. Its bright red color is attractive. In common or commercial use of seals, black, purple or other cheap pads are used.

SEIMEIGAKU

THERE IS IN Japan a unique profession of telling fortune by one's names, curing illness, or saving one from financial ruin by changing his name, or guaranteeing newly-born babies their future wealth and prosperity by giving them lucky names. This is called *seimeigaku* or science of names. There are now quite a number of those engaged in this profession and many of whom make quite a big business of it.

This science is said to have been brought from China about 12 centuries ago by the Buddhist priest, Kobo Daishi, who went to China to study Buddhism, but the present *seimeigaku* is entirely Japanese. It may have been based upon the original Chinese science, but in its application, *seimeigaku* is distinctly Japanese. Further, many of those engaged in this profession have their own independent systems.

The basic principle of *seimeigaku* is to judge one's fortune by the number of strokes and dots contained in the Chinese characters of his name. There are lucky and unlucky numbers. The strokes for the entire name must be lucky, while the total for the family name or the given names should also be lucky.

The idea of *seimeigaku* lies in the belief that a good name creates a good conscience. Those who believe in the science will tell how one sick and weak was made strong and healthy by changing his name to a lucky one, while another was given a sudden favorable change in business as soon as he adopted a new name. Instances are also cited where persons who met unexpected death because of accidents or those who were murdered without cause bore unlucky names. On the other hand, successful men all have lucky names, it is said.

Thus mothers desiring to have their children become successful and prosperous will go to such professionals to have lucky names selected for them. Then others go and ask them to give them new names so that their business will prosper, their married life be happier or their health will improve.

Chinese characters consist of strokes and dots are thus very convenient to make mathematical calculation and speculations. The system adopted varies according to professionals, but according to the most common one, the numbers are divided into five groups. First Class Lucky, Second Class Lucky, Third Class Lucky, Middle Lucky and Unlucky.

First Class Lucky:—1, 3, 5, 6, 12, 13, 15, 16, 21, 23, 25, 29, 31, 39, 40, 41.

Second Class Lucky:—7, 8, 17, 18, 24, 33, 45, 52, 57, 67.

Third Class Lucky:—32, 35, 37, 47, 49, 51, 58, 61, 63, 71, 73, 75, 77, 78, 79, 81.

Middle Class Lucky:—27, 30, 38, 53, 55, 59, 65, 68, 69.

Unlucky:—9, 10, 19, 20, 26, 34, 36, 42, 43, 44, 46, 50, 54, 64, 66, 70, 74, 76.

Thus most of the odd numbers are lucky, and 13 and 23 are included in the First Class Lucky numbers.

When a man's name agrees in its total number of strokes and dots with one of the First Class Lucky numbers, his career is that of greatest felicity. His highest ambition will be realized. His enterprise receives no check. He can push anywhere with equal success. Especially one endowed with intelligence and ability will be astonished with a marvelous success in all he does. So many go to the *seimeigaku* professionals and change their names to those of the First Class Lucky numbers.

SENBETSU

WHEN A Japanese goes on a journey or moves to another locality, his friends and relatives give him *senbetsu* or parting gifts. The present may be something to be used on the journey, foodstuffs, or other things. Of late, for the convenience of both parties, cash is often given.

In the old days when one was going from Edo to Kyoto or Ise, or coming from various districts to the capital, he was given *senbetsu* by his friends. But as travel has become so common, *senbetsu* is no longer given on such short trips, but if anyone goes abroad or goes aways permanently or for any length of time, the custom is observed.

Of course, it is very pleasant to receive gifts, but the trouble is that the receivers of *senbetsu* must bring *o-miyage* or souvenirs of their travels to those who have given them the parting gifts. Many of those going abroad carry lists of *senbetsu* donors so that they may pick up appropriate *o-miyage*. The purchase of these *o-miyage* becomes quite a burden, financial and otherwise, to travellers.

The term *senbetsu* came from China, and originally meant the offering of parting words or presents toward the head of the horse on which the traveller was to start on his journey. In other words, when the intending traveller sat on his horse to start on his trip, his friends stood before the horse and made the offerings toward the horse's head.

The habit of sending poems expressing the sentiment of parting also came from China and is still observed by many Japanese.

This deep-rooted custom of expressing parting sentiments is one reason why the Japanese gather in such large numbers at railway stations or ship docks when their friends or relatives leave on journeys.

SENSEI

S*ENSEI* IS THE most commonly used honorific in the Japanese language, but it is also much abused. It originally meant older or senior in age, and was used in addressing the father, elder brothers and other persons who were older than the speaker. Then as the people paid high respect to persons of advanced ages, and realized that knowledge comes with age, the term was used to indicate respect or admiration.

Since the older people taught the younger, *sensei* also came to be used as a term meaning teacher. The common use of the word in this sense has also developed *deshi* (younger brother or son) to mean pupil.

Sensei in the meaning of teacher became very common in Tokugawa days. Soon it was extended to physicians, as at that time most physicians were also scholars and teachers.

It was, however, in the Meiji era that *sensei* began to be very much abused, probably due to the new social structure that so suddenly replaced the former feudal system. All educated persons, lawyers, officials, politicians and many others were called *sensei*, besides teachers and physicians who formerly monopolized the honor of being so addressed. Writers and artists are also called by the honorific or *sensei*. It has been generally regarded that those who are addressed by others as *sensei* are persons worthy of respect. It became a sort of cultural or social honorific to distinguish such persons from the commoner.

This new use of the term gradually developed a desire among the common people to be called *sensei* and thus enjoy public respect or social advantage. As nobody else called them *sensei*, many of them went and still go to the extreme of making their wives, children and servants call them *sensei*. Such persons have the self-satisfaction that at least in their homes they are honored as *sensei*. On the other hand, taking advantage of this vain desire people are sometimes called *sensei* to flatter them though they are not worthy of the honor.

The almost crazy desire of some people for the honor of *sensei* has created a common saying "I am not such a big fool as to be called *sensei.*"

As the term became widely used, it took on another meaning not of respect, but with a touch of slander. *Ano-sensei*, for instance, means colloquially only "that fellow."

SEVEN FOES

JAPANESE boys and girls leave their

homes for school in the morning, loudly shouting *Ittemairimasu* or "I am going"; and return home in the afternoon with a cheery *Tadaima* or "I have just come back." These peculiar greetings are also made by all the members of the family whenever they go out or return home. These expressions are the remnants of an old custom of feudal days, but they no longer have the solemn significance they originally had.

A man has seven enemies the moment be steps out of his house, an old saying went. In those days of constant battles and rivalry among clan lords and individuals, there was no knowing what enemies one might have. Many a man left the house happy and contented in the morning, but never returned. All the people and particularly *samurai* and their families were, therefore, warned of dangers that might befall anyone out of the house.

These conditions developed the habit of making solemn greetings when one was leaving his house. It might be the last time when he would see his family alive. So whenever one was going out, he first went to his parents and bowing, said, *Ittemairimasu.* Then his wife, children and servants would gather at the entrance of the house, and say, *Itteirasshai* or "Be on your way," which greeting was also a prayer that he would have *kami's* or a god's protection for another day.

When he returned safely home, he would say *Tadaima* or "I have just returned," while the whole family would welcome him at the entrance with *Okaerinasai* or "You have returned," implying joy and thanks for his safe return.

These expressions were the prayers of the people for the safety of their dear ones, which they believed would protect them while they were out of their houses. Such original meanings are, of course, almost entirely lost now, but the custom of making these remarks on one's departure or return is still kept by the people.

The custom has so long been in practice that many wives still feel unhappy the whole day, if they failed to say *itteirasshai* to their husbands in the morning.

SHIMANAGASHI

SHIMANAGASHI or exile to islands, was one form of punishment given to criminals in Tokugawa days. It had a very early origin, as it is recorded that in 434 a woman was sentenced to *ruzai* or exile.

This punishment was meted out all through various periods and, even great and famous were thus banished. The case of Shunkan, a priest, is famous. Dissatisfied with the rule of Taira Kiyomori, Shunkan, Fujiwara Narichika and Fujiwara Naritsune schemed to remove him. They were caught, and in 1177 all three were exiled to Kikaigashima, a small uninhabited island. In one year, pardon was granted to Fujiwara Narichika and Fujiwara Naritsune. When officials came to the island to take away the pardoned two, Shunkan alone was left behind to die in despair and ill health.

Under Edo rule, *shimanagashi* was the heaviest punishment and second only to death. The family members of a *samurai* sentenced to death were also all exiled. In the early days, criminals were exiled not only to remote islands but also distant districts. But in the Edo period they were mostly sent to islands.

Criminals sentenced to *shimanagashi* in Edo were sent to the Seven Islands of Izu in the Pacific. Those from Kyoto, Osaka, Shikoku and Chugoku districts were sent to Satsuma, Goto, Oki, Iki, and Amakusa.

These exiles were allowed to take their families, clothing and other properties at first but, in Edo days they were not allowed to take anything with them.

The exiles rented land from the island head, and cultivated various foodstuffs or helped the fishermen. Thus some were able to make a comfortable living, even marrying the island girls. On the other hand, there were others who went through hardship and privation, and finally died in sickness and despair, unattended.

SUTRA COPYING

MANY JAPANESE, both men and women, still follow the old custom of copying Buddhist sutras. Daily they devote many hours in solemnly copying Buddhist texts for months and years. Originally, of course, it was done from religious devotion. It was also believed that sutra copying sows a seed of goodness in the soul. But now more often it is done to forget worries, noises and troubles of the worldly life. While they are copying they live in another world of quietude and peace.

Whatever might be the motive, the copier sits down solemnly before his desk, and copies each character slowly and with much care. Nobody is allowed to interrupt him.

The copying is done mostly on black paper in gold or silver, but now plain white paper and *sumi* or black writing ink are commonly used. Among old copies there are some done in blood. Any sutra may be selected for copying but lengthy texts take many years to complete.

The copies are donated to temples in prayer for the souls of ancestors, parents and friends. The donation of sutra copies to temples was at first a common practice done for Buddhist propagation.

Though it is mostly old men and women who have retired from active busy life who take up the copying of Buddhist sutras, there are often young men and women who find peace and comfort in this custom also.

The oldest copy of Buddhist sutras that is still preserved was made by Priest Horin in 687, but it is also recorded that Emperor Temmu ordered the copying of a sutra in 673. In those early days Court nobles, priests and common Buddhist believers followed this custom of copying sutras and presenting them to temples.

This custom resulted in encouraging the development of the technique of printing in Japan. Empress Kogen had one million copies of sutras printed in 770, and distributed them among Horyuji and nine other temples. Over ten thousand of them, encased in small wooden containers, are still preserved at Horyuji. These are the oldest specimens of printing in the world.

TE-UCHI

THE OLD CUSTOM of *te-uchi* or hand-clapping is still observed by old-fashioned businessmen to signify the conclusion of business deals. When two parties come to an agreement, one will say *'Oteo kashite kudasai'* (Give me your hands), and then the two clap their hands together, generally repeating the motion three times. The contract is then concluded.

Transactions to which both parties have given *te-uchi* are just as binding as written agreements with stamps, seals, signatures and witnesses.

Hand-clapping has always symbolized the joyous sentiment of the people. it has come to possess many different meanings, but the original character of representing joy is always retained.

Hand-clapping at shrines is probably the oldest. It conveys the revered sentiment of the worshiper. Some explain that hands are clapped to draw the attention of the *kami* or gods.

At joyous gatherings the people have clapped their hands to express their sentiment since the earliest times. This custom may have been the origin of the *te-uchi*, at business transactions.

In feudal days, hand-clapping was used to indicate the settlement of disputes or fights. When they were amicably settled, the parties concerned sat together and held the *te-uchi* rite. After clapping hands, they held drinking parties in celebration of the settlement. This custom was observed in particular by gamblers and gangsters.

Te-uchi is still carried out by many businessmen and others to denote they will keep their verbal promises, although no written contracts are made.

THUMB MARKS

THE JAPANESE used fingerprints as a means of identification several centuries before Western people recognized the theory that there are no fingerprints identically the same, and began to adopt the fingerprint system for finding criminals.

Tsumein (nail seal), or *boin* (thumb seal) as fingerprints are called in Japan, was first widely used by the lower class people, who did not have *han* (seal) nor *kakihan* (written seal) for their identification. In other words, the nobles, warriors, big merchants and artisans and such persons had their seals, but common farmers, fishermen, merchants and workmen did not. Nor did such persons have *kakihan* that was used only by nobles and military lords since the Kamakura period, 15th century. *Kakihan* which is also called *kao* (flowery) is made by turning a part or

parts of the Chinese characters forming one's name into a floral design. The custom of using *kakihan* is still observed by high government officials and others.

Thus, the common people who did not possess any means of identifying themselves came to use their thumb mark. In writing contracts, agreements, notes for debts and other documents, they put their thumb marks under their names. Generally, it was the right thumb that was impressed on the paper after putting some writing ink on it or pressing it against a seal-ink pad.

Then, particularly in obtaining confessions from criminals, their thumb marks were used to certify that the statements written were true. Thus, in Japan, too, finger prints were very closely related to criminal investigation during the Tokugawa period, while in western countries the use of finger prints for the same purpose started only about 50 years ago.

This custom of *boin* is said to have originally come from the older *keppan* (blood seal). In the warring period of Muromachi from the 14th to 16th century, *keppan* used to mark warriors' documents of allegiance or pledge.

With a small knife the ring finger of the left hand was pricked just below the nail, and the blood coming from the cut was dabbed on the tip of the ring finger of the right hand. Then the finger was pressed on the document under its writer's name to show his sincerity.

Greater importance was given to *keppan* than to seals of other kinds in those days. So documents sealed with *keppan* were regarded something unusual.

Some Japanese palmists say that the fortune of a person can be told by his finger marks.

Finger marks consist of whirls, loops and arches. It is generally said by the

Japanese that those who have whirls on all or most of the fingers are luckier than others who have only arches or loops. Loops generally do not predict as good a fortune as whirls do, many say. Of course, the interpretation of finger marks differs according to palmists.

The lines — whirls, loops and arches — differ in clearness and depth, and also come close together or are wide apart. These distinctions tell different characters. Deep whirl lines, with clear spaces between, for instance, show that the person has a strong imagination, while those with close and fine whirl lines are practical and active, making them good businessmen.

Loops that taper gradually to a faint line, not disappearing suddenly, are particularly good for women, as they represent loving tender sentiments, some palmists say.

Of course, there are so many combinations of finger marks, all fingers having different marks, that only those who have studied them patiently can correctly read them. But generally the people do not realize what kinds of finger marks they have. So it is always interesting to see how many whirls, loops or arches on has one his ten fingers.

Palmists who believe in finger mark fortune-telling say that finger marks are decided by the mother's condition, the atmosphere of the family and the general social situation while the child was in the mother's body.

TOKUSEI

TOKUSEI was a benevolent regulation, adopted often by the Kamakura, Ashikaga and Tokugawa authorities for lightening the burden of the poor, such as the cancellation of past taxes and debts, both private and public. The first tokusei was given by Emperor Tenmu in July 686 in consideration of the farmers, and cancelled all debts more than seven months old. Mostly tokusei cancelled past taxes to benefit the poor. However, this caused much confusion and difficulty, particularly to the rich who lost what money they had loaned to others, and properties accepted as securities.

One order issued in 1297 prohibited the pledging or pawning of property owned by samurai families and caused the surrender to former owners of valuables already pledged for loans.

Once to an inn at Awadaguchi, Kyoto, came a samurai carrying a pair of beautiful swords. Just then the innkeeper learned that a tokusei order would be soon issued, and he schemed to gain possession of those fine swords. So he asked the samurai to rent them to him for a few days so that he could admire them. The samurai readily consented. A few days after, the tokusei was issued.

When it became time for him to depart, the samurai asked for his two swords. But the innkeeper said that because of the tokusei the swords were now his. The samurai agreed that his swords went to the innkeeper by the provisions of the tokusei, but that, if so, the inn became his property as he was renting it. So he asked the innkeeper to leave the inn at once. The innkeeper took the matter up with the local official. Upon hearing both sides, the official verdict said that just as the swords became the innkeeper's property, the inn became the samurai's.

TOSHIKOSHI

FORMERLY the Japanese held toshikoshi, or year-passing rites to mark the end of the year. In the old days, they did not go to sleep at all on the first night of the year. In many districts they stayed all night at local shrines to wait for the New Year.

Of course all preparations for celebrating New Year's Day had to be completed on the last day of the year, but in the old days everything had to be done before dark. Then a *toshikoshi* meal was served.

One of the outstanding features of ancient *toshikoshi* rites was burning a big fire in the *irori* or open hearth on New Year's Eve. Large logs were collected for the *toshikoshi* fire which was kept burning for three days.

Many also took their New Year's Day meal during the evening of December 31, following the old belief that a new day starts in the evening.

Even today there are many people who do not sleep at all on New Year's Eve. Many will not go to bed until they hear the ringing at midnight of the 108 temple bells which are sounded to expel the 108 evil thoughts which Buddhism tells that all humans possess.

Visiting of local shrines at midnight is also a remnant of the ancient custom of not sleeping on the last night of the year.

In the Tokyo area there prevails a custom of eating *soba* or buckwheat noodles on New Year's Eve, called *toshikoshi-soba* or year-passing noodles.

UBUGE

NEW-BORN Japanese babies had their *ubuge* or downy hair on the head shaved off on the third or seventh day after birth in the old days. The custom is still followed in some rural districts. The shaving day differs according to regions. In some places it is not shaved but cut off with scissors.

Many families used to keep the *ubuge* of babies. In Iwate and other districts it was placed in bags or boxes and buried in the compound of the local shrines which looked after the welfare of the babies.

The custom of leaving a small spot unshaved on the back of the head was seen on Iki Island. It was believed there that if the baby were dropped into water or fire by accident, *Aragami-sama* would come and pull him out by the few hairs left on the back of the head.

The people attributed some mystic power to hair. In praying to *kami* or Buddha, women often cut off their long hair and offered them to shrines and temples. Many old temples or shrines still boast huge piles of such hair offered by devotees.

At the ceremony of *mune-age* or setting up of the framework of a house, human hair is still attached to a bow and arrow hoisted on top of the structure as a charm to expel evil spirits.

When a new fishing boat is built, a handful of women's hair is placed in a hole made in the main beam, as a symbol of *funa-dama* or spirit of the boat.

Hair dressing styles have special significance for Japanese women, and different styles developed for different ages and social status. Formerly young maidens and married women were differentiated by their hairdos, and widows had their own way of doing their hair. During mourning period, women often fixed their hair in special mourning fashion.

Old hair fashions have disappeared from cities and towns, but are still to be seen in many country districts.

UNWELCOME GUEST

IT IS EXTREMELY irritating for any family to have an unwelcome guest who is over-staying his hospitality and does not show any sign of making his departure. Particularly in Japan, where the people visit others at any time of the day and night, often the whole family is kept from having their dinner because a visitor will not leave. Yet they are too polite to tell him to go. What can be done in such cases? The Japanese have a superstitious method of driving out such unwelcome guests, and it is believed to be very effective.

Take up a broom, and set it upside down against the wall or door, with its handle on the floor. This is said to have a charm in sending the unwelcome visitor away at once. The fact that it is still done in many families may be proof of its effectiveness. Furthermore, in some districts, after setting up the broom upside down, a *shamoji* or wooden ricescoop, is brought from the kitchen and the standing broom is fanned with it three times. This is said to increase the effectiveness of the charm.

Another method is to put *mogusa* or moxa on the underside of the *geta* (Japanese clogs) or the soles of the shoes, which the guest has left at the entrance, and set the moxa on fire. This is certain to send him away at once. It is believed that when the moxa is lighted on the soles of the shoes or *geta* the soles of the guest's feet itch, and he cannot feel happy until he puts on his *geta* or shoes and leaves the house. This must be done without letting the visitor know what is happening to his shoes or *geta.*

WOMEN'S EVENING

THE EVENING of May 4 is still remembered in many rural districts as woman's evening, when women are permitted to be proud and act naughty. In the old days, women had to be humble and obey whatever men told them to do, but on this evening alone the position was reversed. It was also the day when the men gave *sake* to women who had been thankful for the drink given by women.

May 4 was an important day in bygone times, in preparation for the coming rice planting. At first it was the women who undertook the task of planting rice, as maids to *Yamano-kami,* god of the mountain who came down to the plain to supervise the planting. To serve the *kami,* women had to be pure and sincere. Thus they secluded themselves on the night before to free themselves from the outside evil and ate only clean food.

Of course, this ancient importance of women in rice planting gradually declined as men also joined in the task as farms became larger. Yet this ancient tradition of a woman's service to the deity in planting the rice and their divine role in supplying the family with food remains in this fete of May 4.

On the evening women are still treated as persons of more importance than men, and they enjoy the privilege of ordering men about relishing the power and authority that are denied them on other days of the year.

The meaning of the day is now almost entirely forgotten. It now remains mostly as an occasion for holding a family feast and enjoying good food and drink, in many rural districts.

YAKIMOCHI

YAKIMOCHI (toasted *mochi*) is a commonly used term signifying jealously or particularly jealous wives.

Jealousy has been regarded as the worst vice of women since feudal days, and young girls are taught not to become jealous wives after marriage. The ancient custom of wearing *tsunokakushi* (horn hider) or a band of cloth over the bride's hair at the wedding ceremony is still observed. It is traditionally said that jealous women have horns of jealousy on their heads, and the band is to hide them. Of course there are no such horns, but the custom is just to warn the brides against becoming jealous wives.

The strange expression of *yakimochi* is said to have developed from a New Year game that has been played by young women in northeastern regions.

Mochi or pounded rice-cake is much eaten in the cold season by the rural folk, not only for meals but also in between. Particularly on long cold evenings, they love to put several pieces of *mochi* over the fire and eat them toasted.

Young girls often tell fortunes by *mochi* toasting. They put two pieces of *mochi* side by side, and name them for an imaginary girl and boy. Then they watch the pieces puff up. When the *mochi* named for a boy produces a big bubble that leans toward the *mochi* named for a girl and finally become attached together, they think it is a sign that the boy will propose. Sometimes the girl is predicted to make the first move in love.

Sometimes they have real persons in mind when playing this game, and have quite a happy time in seeing how the love affair between the two will develop.

It is from this play of rural girls that *yakimochi* came to mean jealousy.

YATAI-MISE

YATAI-MISE or little stalls on wheels are opened nightly along many busy streets of the big cities, offering cheap but good-smelling food. To many workers such little shops offer the pleasure of having a few drinks and enjoying palatable food after their hard work of the day.

Yatai originally meant a miniature house on wheels with a roof, and was used to indicate festival floats. Such *yatai* are still displayed at festivals all over the country.

Yatai-mise is said to have first appeared in Edo in 1785, when a serious famine caused a shortage of food, and, the people were eager to buy anything cheap and available to eat. Ever since, *yatai-mise* has become specially popular whenever food grows scarce due to various causes.

In 1886 or the year following the famine of Tenmei, a huge fire in Edo destroyed the major portion of the capital. On the devastated streets, there suddenly appeared rows of *yatai-mise* offering various kinds of prepared food.

Yatai-mise so strongly appealed to the popular demand for cheap foodstuffs that during the Kansei era, 1789-1801, they came to appear nightly along the main streets of Edo. Particularly Ryogoku, the busy district on the Sumida River, became famous for *yatai-mise* and their cheap food.

Thus *yatai-mise* became even a feature of the Edo life, and was introduced to other parts of the country. But later their number declined as the supply of food became abundant, and the people could buy what they desired at proper shops.

Then a great revival of *yatai-mise* took place in Tokyo after the great earthquake of September 1, 1923. Along the burned-out streets of the city suddenly appeared *yatai-mise* selling various cheap foodstuffs, which were eagerly purchased by the people.

Then after the Pacific war, *yatai-mise* again became popular as the food supply became short. The food situation has greatly improved now, but *yatai-mise* are still nightly opened on many streets of the city, though the kinds of food offered have changed and have become much better.

626

YONIGE

WHEN A Japanese family finds itself in heavy debt with no prospect of paying it, or any of its members commit some acts that have disgraced it, it packs up all belongings and secretly leaves the house at night to some unknown place. This is to escape from the shame of losing their dignity or "face" among their neighbors.

The wrong they have committed need not necessarily be a criminal act or a misdeed punishable by law, but anything that may make them lose public respect or incur public disdain may be the cause for this extraordinary conduct. It is called *yonige* or night escape.

The custom was particularly prevalent at the year-end when it was formerly customary to settle all debts of the year. An unpaid debt was regarded as an unpardonable sin. Then, also for anything that might make them the laughing stock of the community or for becoming the object of hatred by the neighbors, many persons made their *yonige*.

This old custom developed from their sensitive idea of maintaining public respect or "face." They could not bear the disdaining eyes of the neighbors upon them. Thus, to escape from public condemnation the family would rather leave the locality dear to them and go somewhere else, where they would be strangers. Thus it is no easy matter to commit *yonige*.

On the other hand, the people's strong attachment to their native place has also developed the unique punishment of banishment to distant places. For certain crimes, the offenders were ordered to leave their places of birth and domicile for certain period. In Tokugawa days, this punishment was very extensively used. Offenders were sent to the Seven Islands of Izu which lie south of the Kanto area.

Under the Edo law, crimes of gambling, killing persons by accident, wronging women and such were punished by the sentence of *ento* (distant island), which consisted of whipping and then banishment to one of the seven Izu islands. The period of banishment was six months to life. Arriving at these islands, the punished leased land from the island chief and maintained their living by cultivating the farm. The life of these banished persons became the theme of many tales and fiction.

In other parts of the country, too, the sentence of banishment was given to certain criminals. They were mostly sent to distant islands, from which it was difficult to return unnoticed, but in some cases the offender was sent to some distant district of the main island.

The punishment of banishment may be called the *yonige* enforced by law. It was just as difficult as voluntary *yonige*.

Chapter 16
Historical Tales and Relics

EDO CASTLE

IT IS OFTEN erroneously said that Edo Castle was first built by Ota Mochisuke (commonly known as Dokan), but Edo Castle existed more than 270 years before Dokan's time. The mistake appears to have been made because Dokan, who also had his castle at Edo, was very famous, while the original builder of the castle at Edo was generally unknown.

Taira Shigetsugu who lived in the Edo district in the 10th century adopted the family name of Edo and became one of the leading families in the district. In 1185, Edo Taro Shigenaga was appointed by Minamoto Yoritomo as the governor of the whole Musashi area in which Edo was located. Soon Edo Taro built his Edo Castle. Nothing is known of his castle, but it must have been only a crude one built of earth and timber.

It was in 1457 that Ota Dokan erected a castle in Edo as an official under the Uesugi family, and his castle too was small and insignificant. After his death in 1485, Edo Castle came under the direct rule of the Uesugi family until 1505. Then the Hojo clan of Odawara had it from 1524 to 1590. All this while the castle was repeatedly reconstructed.

At the end of the 16th century, the Edo area was only sparsely populated. The castle was in such pitiful condition that when Tokugawa Ieyasu came eastward to look for a site for his headquarters in 1590, his first choice was Kawaguchi on the Arakawa (Sumida) river. But that place was found unsatisfactory, so he finally selected Edo.

Ieyasu found the castle at Edo so poor that he had to construct his own castle to meet his requirements. Ieyasu's plan was gigantic from the beginning, and the construction of the new castle which started in 1606 was not completed until 1640. This castle is preserved in many outward appearances in the present Imperial Palace.

Thus it must be said the builder of the first Edo Castle was Edo Taro, and the planner of the great Edo Castle was Tokugawa Ieyasu.

ENOSHIMA

ENOSHIMA, a little island off Katase, Kanagawa, is a famous sightseeing spot. Its Benten Shrine is still visited by many believers in its merciful benevolence. But present visitors are often unaware of the history of the island.

Once there was a time when no one was allowed to live on the island and fishermen on the mainland went there only to fish. Later it developed as a fishermen's island as it was not fit for farming. Enoshima Shrine was erected by fishermen as a shrine for their guardian deity in very early days.

It remained as an insignificant little island until 1182 when Minamoto Yoritomo, founder of the Kamakura military rule, consecrated a statue of Benten in a cave of the island to pray for his successful pacification of the northern regions. Successive Kamakura generals, Yoriie and Sanetomo, also paid homage to Benten. The worship by such great leaders naturally made the public regard Enoshima Benten as the deity granting them happiness and luck.

Furthermore, great Buddhist temples were established on the island, the most important of which was the Iwamoto-in with its many massive and beautiful structures. Thus all through the Tokugawa era, Enoshima was a mecca for Benten worshipers as well as Buddhist followers.

But by the Meiji era, the great Buddhist temples had disappeared, and on the spot where the great Iwamoto-in stood there now stands a hotel named Iwamoto-ro where many documents and relics of the former temple are still preserved.

The island also played quite a role in Meiji civilization. Prof. E. S Morse, whose finding of shell mounds at Omori in Tokyo is well-known, erected a little hut on the shore of Enoshima in 1877 and lived there some months to conduct his study.

There is now a botanical garden on the island top, and this was first laid by Samuel Cockling, a British merchant, in 1874 or the seventh year of Meiji. He built hot houses to raise various tropical plants there. Later the original botanical garden disappeared, but in 1949, the city of Fujisawa reopened the old garden, and now it is again full of tropical plants.

FIRST DUEL

JAPANESE *samurai* or warriors took pride in their fighting ability and possessed a high sense of honor, but they seldom fought duels as gallant men of Europe did. The first duel in Japan is said to have taken place in the 12th century.

Minamoto Atsuru, father of Watanabe Tsuna who traditionally slaughtered the *oni* or devil at Rashomon and was immortalized in plays and films, and Taira Yoshifumi are two great warriors famed for bravery and fighting skill.

One day a talkative servant of Atsuru spread a story that his master had a very poor opinion of Yoshifumi's attainments. When this tale reached Yoshifumi, he was greatly enraged at the slander cast at him by Atsuru, and dipatched a proposal that they should fight a duel and settle the matter.

The challenge was accepted and at the appointed time the two warriors appeared at the designated spot with several hundred of their retainers. The two groups of fighting men stood face to face, ready to fight. But Yoshifumi declared that it was a duel affecting only two men, and it was wrong to sacrifice the lives of many.

So the two ordered their men to keep away and not to interfere. The duelists were on horseback and they were to shoot three arrows each at each other. The first and second arrows did not touch either of them, but the third arrows hit each other's hip. The two were equally matched in skill and were satisfied with the result.

This first duel in Japan effected a change in battlefield fighting and established a new etiquette.

Since then when two opposing leaders or prominent *samurai* met on a battlefield, they announced their names and fought a duel, spurning any help from others and depending only on their own skill.

FIRST TEA GARDEN

TEA WAS brought to Japan first by Priest Eisai in 1191, and the site where the tea seeds he brought home from China were planted is still preserved at the Kozanji Temple at Togano-o on the bank of the Kiyotaki River, in the western part of Kyoto. Togano-o and the surrounding hills are famous for their beautiful autumn leaves.

Eisai was a great Zen priest who visited China twice to study Buddhism, in 1168 and 1186. It was when he returned home from his last visit that he brought the tea leaves and seeds. As Buddhist priests of China were in the habit of drinking tea, Eisai also learned to love the drink, which was particularly found effective to keep him awake from drowsiness, and also to keep his health sound. He introduced tea drinking first to Buddhist priests and the habit rapidly became popular among all classes of the people.

The tea seeds he brought home were given to Priest Kyo-e-shonin, who planted them on the hill of Togano-o. There the first tea leaves in the country were obtained. As the tea drinking habit spread, tea plants came to be cultivated soon at Daigo and Uji. Other districts soon followed as demand rose.

The original tea garden planted by Kyo-e-shonin disappeared, though it is not known when. But recently a tea garden was laid out at the spot which is believed to be the original site.

The Kozanji Temple, though not so famous as many great temples of Kyoto, has many valuable specimens of ancient art and literature. Among those may be mentioned several caricature sketches of animals drawn by Priest Kakuya (1053-1140), who is commonly known as Toba-sojo, and is honored as the first Japanese caricaturist.

Many tea lovers however, regret that the public has forgotten that it was at Kozanji that the first tea trees were planted in Japan, though they know Japan is a great tea drinking and tea producing country.

FUCHU

FUCHU IS NOW known to Tokyo residents as the site of the horse racing course where the Japanese Derby is annually held. But even those who live in Fuchu and the surrounding residential areas which have developed in recent years do not remember that Fuchu was once the administrative and cultural center of the whole of Musashi including the present Tokyo.

The system of *Kuni-no-tsukasa* or provincial governor was established by Emperor Nintoku in 374 and the *Kuni-no-tsukasa* for Musashi was stationed at Fuchu to administer the district and also look after the religious rites and cultural life of the people. Thus Fuchu became a city of many officials sent from Kyoto.

The Jindaiji Temple, located about three kilometers from Fuchu Station, is believed to have been erected in 733, and its spacious wooded compounds still tell of some of its former grandeur.

Then when Kokubun-ji or the provincial Buddhist temple was erected in most of the principal provinces of the country in 741, the Musashi Kokubun-ji was built at Fuchu, larger and more splendid than most such temples. Some of the foundation stones are still there, and roof tiles and other relics are unearthed even today.

In constructing such great temples, Korean and Chinese artisans were brought to the Fuchu area in quite large numbers. It is said that their descendents contributed greatly to the development of Musashi culture.

The authority of *Kuni-no-tsukasa*, however, began to decline round about the 10th century, when military leaders rose in various regions, and the Musashi district was also enveloped in disorder. But the *Kuni-no-tsukasa* at Fuchu continued to hold his influence on matters concerning religious rites and particularly temples and shrines.

But as an administrative center, Fuchu has since become a mere shadow and its former grandeur now can only be imagined from the old temple and ancient relics. But influences of the old culture, particularly of Korean civilization that was brought there more than 1,000 years ago, are still seen in shrine festivals and other local customs.

FURISODE-KAJI

THE GREATEST fire Edo ever had is one commonly called *furisode-kaji* (long-sleeve kimono fire). This fire that raged for two days on January 18 and 19, 1657, burned up a major portion of the city, including Edo Castle, mansions of 500 feudal lords, and 770 *samurai*, and an inestimable number of small houses, and caused the death of 107,046 persons.

The great conflagration was caused by a *furisode* that had already caused the deaths of three young girls.

Okiku, a daughter of an Asakusa merchant named Omasuya Juemon, saw a fine-looking young man when she went to view the *sakura* blossoms at Ueno. Later, she became lovesick and finally died on January 16, 1655. Her funeral was held at the Honmyoji Temple in Maruyama, Hongo, and a beautiful purple *furisode* which she wore on that cherry viewing was spread over her coffin.

Ohana, a daughter of a Hongo merchant, Mariya Kichibei saw the beautiful purple *furisode* at a second-hand shop, and asked her parents to buy it for her. Soon, however, she became ill and died on January 16, 1656. The parents of Okiku who visited Honmyoji on the anniversary of their daughter's death were surprised to meet another funeral at the temple, and the coffin covered with the same purple *furisode* as their Okiku had had.

Otatsu, a daughter of a pawnshop keeper of Nakabashi named Iseya Gohei took a fancy to the purple *furisode* brought to the shop and made it hers, but she, too, became ill and died on January 16, 1657. Her funeral was also held at Honmyoji.

The parents of Okiku and Ohana visited the temple for the anniversary of their daughters' death, and again saw the same purple *furisode* on the coffin.

The parents of the three unfortunate daughters who died on the same day on three successive years began to talk and realized that the *furisode* must have cast a curse on the girls. They decided to burn it up so that it would not cause the death of any more girls. But as the *furisode* was being cast into a fire in the temple compound, a gust of wind came and carried the burning kimono away to cause the huge fire.

HACHIJO CATTLE

HACHIJO-JIMA is a small island only 60 kilometers around situated 315 kilometers southwest of Tokyo, being the southern end of the so-called chain of Seven Izu Islands. This island is now famous for its dairy products, but while it always had many cattle and no horses, the islanders never drank milk nor ate beef until recently.

From ancient days, almost every

household on the island kept some cattle, but only for carrying loads. The island is mountainous, and to transport anything from one part to another, the people had to depend on cattle.

They are mostly kept in enclosures in the village, but there are also grazing cattle, which are called mountain cattle. Formerly the cattle in pastures were regarded as the common property of the people, and the money obtained by selling the grazing cattle was used to build stone walls to prevent the mountain cattle from coming down and damaging farms.

The villagers never killed their cattle in the old days, and when they became old and useless, they drove them to the mountain to fend for themselves. Some feeble old cattle were taken to the seashore, and tied to poles there so that after the grass under their feet was eaten up, they would die of starvation.

The villagers faithfully observed the custom of not killing cattle and not eating beef, but the island has several records of rare cases of beef eating. The earliest record is dated 1445 when a severe famine gripped the island, due to storms and diseases. Being unable to obtain sufficient food, some resorted to eating beef in desperation, despite the traditional taboo.

As late as the second year of Meiji or 1869, 10 persons who secretly killed cattle and ate the meat were caught and sentenced to banishment to Kojima, a small island nearby, it is recorded.

But since the beginning of the Meiji era, the old taboo has been gradually disregarded, as the dairy industry has proved to be profitable.

HIEDA-NO-ARE

THE NAME OF Hieda-no-are may be known only to students of the ancient history of Japan, but the *Kojiki* as told by her from memory is accepted as the oldest historical record of the country.

It was long disputed whether this person was a man or a woman, but now it is recognized by historians that Hieda-no-are was a woman. More remarkable is the fact that she was only 28 years old when she was given this important task. She is also reported to be a descendant of Ameno-uzumeno-mikoto who danced before the Amano-Iwato, the cave into which Amaterasu-omikami hid, and urged the sun goddess to come out again.

In 682 Emperor Tenmu ordered the compilation of the record of past important affairs of the country. Hieda-no-are, who was an official of *Kataribe* (reciter's office) of the Court, was commanded to tell Ono-Yasumaro from memory all ancient matters from the beginning of the mythological age.

In the early letter-less period, all races appear to have possessed good memory, as past affairs and legends were handed down from mouth to mouth for generations. The Ainus memorized all their long tales of the past up to quite recent times.

The *Kojiki* dictated by Hieda-no-are covers the nation's history from the mythological beginning to 682 in the reign of Emperor Suiko. That it contains not only stories of mythological court, government matters and such, but also accounts of Court life, poems and other features prove in one aspect that the original teller was a woman.

In the preface written by Ono-Yasumaro it is clearly mentioned that Hieda-no-are was a remarkably bright person possessing good memory. It is regrettable that nothing more is known about her. When the *Kojiki* was completed in 712, one record says she was 65 years old.

The oldest existing text of the *Kojiki* copied in 1266 is preserved at the Shunpukuji Temple, Nagoya.

HIMIKO

IN THE PREHISTORIC period, Japanese women seem to have played many important roles. Numerous tales of women chieftains or local rulers are mentioned in ancient records. Many districts were controlled by powerful groups led by women.

Among such women chieftains of the early days, Himiko of Kyushu appears to have been one of the most powerful. Her name was known as far away as China in the Han dynasty, almost 200 years before the Christian era.

Himiko was not the head of one group or tribe, but ruled over several groups which were united together by her influence. She was not the direct ruler of one group, but stood above many groups under different heads.

She lived in luxury, surrounded by 1,000 women-in-waiting. Her place of residence was guarded by many armed strongmen. She secluded herself within her house, never meeting visitors from outside. Even men under her rule seldom had an opportunity to see her.

Her brother acted as her deputy or secretary and was her only means of contact with other people. It was he who brought food to her daily. Though she never made direct dealings with the tribal chiefs under her rule, she commanded the respect and admiration of all the people within her domain and also even those of remote districts to whom her fame and power were known.

She has been thus recognized as one of the most powerful local chieftains in the Kyushu area, and her name still remains in many legends of that part of the country.

It was common in those early prehistoric days for women to be the heads of families, and the family name and fortune were handed down to the elder daughters. The family line was kept up by maternal descendents. Himiko of Kyushu is the most representative of the Japanese women of those early days.

Many ideas and customs still observed today can be traced to the ancient idea of the women being the head of the family, and the mother being responsible for the welfare of all descendents of the line.

HIRADO

ALTHOUGH Hirado played a big role in Japan's history as the first trading port, its name is now forgotten by many. The island of Hirado, named after its main city, lies off the western end of northern Kyushu, just north of Sasebo. It is a small island, being only 32 kilometers long and eight kilometers wide.

Japan sent ambassadors and students to China from the time Ono-no Imoko went in 607. Most of the Japanese ambassadors and students embarked from Hirado to China, which proves that the port was already recognized as an important shipping center.

Hirado thus became the center of trading with China. It also became famous as the headquarters of many pirates.

Coming down to the modern age, it is remembered that in 1550 Francis Xavier came to Hirado and stayed there two months. A Portuguese ship first used the port in 1549, followed by Dutch and British ships. For 93 years until 1641 when the Tokugawa Bakufu issued an order closing the country to foreigners, Hirado was the only port where Western ships entered and foreign trade was conducted.

Thus Hirado still possesses many

relics of interest to students of Japan's foreign trade during the last half of the 16th and the first half of the 17th century.

Remains of the breakwater laid down by the Dutch in 1616 are still to be seen. Stone walls erected by the Dutch traders, a well dug by the Dutch and relics of the office of the British East India Co. also are still preserved.

William Adams died at Hirado in 1620 at the age of 56 at the house of Kida Yajiro. A monument still stands erected in his honor.

Lord Matsuura Takanobu erected a Catholic temple in 1564 at Hirado.

KAMAKURA DAIBUTSU

THE DAIBUTSU (Great Buddha) of Kamakura is now world famous, but its history is not clear and there are various different opinions even about the year of its erection.

Priest Joko started to construct a Buddhist image in 1238 at Kamakura for the benefit of the people of the eastern district. It was completed in 1243 or five years later, it is recorded in *Azuma-kagami.* But this statue is now believed to have been of wood. Some say that the head was of wood and the body of metal. However this image was soon removed or destroyed.

The casting of the present image is recorded to have been started at Fukazawa (Kamakura) on August 17, 1252. But there is no record as to the date when it was finished. It is believed to have taken several years.

The Kamakura Daibutsu is a fine specimen of work, but nothing is known of the person who made the original model. Only from its style it is believed to have been designed by some Buddhist statue maker of Kamakura.

The one who undertook the casting of the image is reported to be either Ono Goroemon or Tanji Fusatomo. Many authorities now say that in casting the big image, Ono, Tanji and other great image casters worked together.

The image is of bronze but with a very small content of copper. The Hojo Government supplied most of the required funds to make it. It was once planned to send a trading ship to China to obtain funds for the Daibutsu construction.

The statue represents Mida or Buddha, but the Azuma-kagami and many other records mention it as representing Shaka (Sakya).

The image has met several calamities in the past. In 1495, the building which housed it was destroyed by a huge storm and tidal wave. Since then the image has stood without any covering.

In the past it was once under the supervision of the Gokurakuji Temple; then it came under Kenchoji Temple and later under Komyoji, all of Kamakura.

KANDA MYOJIN

THE KANDA MYOJIN is one of the oldest and greatest shrines in Tokyo. Since Edo days, its festival has been regarded as one of the two main festivals of the metropolis, the other being that of the Sanno Shrine.

The Kanda Myojin is said to have been first erected in the eighth century by settlers who came from the province of Izumo and dedicated it to Okuninushi-no-Mikoto, the prehistoric ruler of that province.

But there is another traditional tale about the shrine's origin. The shrine is said to be dedicated to Taira-no Masakado, the famous rebel general of the 10th century.

Masakado revolted against the ruling government and set up his own regime at Shimoosa province. He is reputed to have been a very skillful general and gathered a considerable following. But finally he was defeated by the government forces despatched against him.

He was caught, taken to Kyoto, and beheaded in 940. His head was placed on a branch of a big tree in that city. But the eyes opened and the mouth angrily shouted, "Let me have another battle and I will win." At night, the head was visible in the darkness.

The head wanted to return to the eastern district. One night it flew from the tree and landed in a paddy field in Musashi where it shone brightly. The people of the neighborhood were astonished at the sight, and also feared that Masakado with his strong sense of revenge might do some mischief to the district.

So they erected a shrine to appease him. That is the origin of the Kanda Myojin, the story says. Some still believe that Masakado is enshrined in the shrine, even forgetting that Okuninushi-no-Mikoto was the original deity to whom the shrine was dedicated.

According to the traditional tale, the people have been worshiping the memory of a rebel. But as in the case of many shrines, it does not matter to the present worshipers whom their shrines stand for, as it is sufficient for them to know that local shrines are guarding them.

KANEGAFUCHI

THE DEEP POOL at the confluence of the Sumida River and the Ayase River, on the other side of Minamisenju, Tokyo, is commonly called Kanegafuchi (bell pool), because it is said that a big temple bell is buried under the water there.

The identity of the mysterious bell is not clearly known, as there are several different stories. One says that at the time of the big flood in 1720, the bell tower of the Chosoji Temple was destroyed and its bell was carried away by the river. Another story goes back a hundred years and relates that in 1620 Lord Chiba of Sumida moved the Fumon-in Temple he erected to Kameido on the Sumida River, but while the big temple bell was being transported to the new site, it fell into the river. It is also said that the bell originally belonged to the Hogenji Temple.

But whichever story is true, it was firmly believed by the Edo people that a big temple bell was buried at the spot, and they came to call the place Kanegafuchi.

Tokugawa Yoshimura who reigned as the eighth Tokugawa shogun from 1716 to 1746, once happened to be at Kanegafuchi on a hunting trip. He heard the story of the bell and became so interested that he ordered a search for the bell.

An attendant told him that the bell could not be drawn up with an ordinary rope as there must be a dragon monster in the water which would prevent the moving of the bell. He suggested that only a rope made of human hair could pull the bell out of the water.

The making of a heavy rope with human hair was then instantly ordered. Several hundred women had to cut off their long hair and offer it to the shogun to make the required rope.

The rope was finished and a man called Ryutaro was selected to dive into the river and attach the hair rope to the loop at the top of the buried bell. He succeeded in finding the bell and tying the rope to it. As many men pulled the rope, the bell was raised to the water surface, but the rope broke and the bell fell back on the river bottom, where it still remains, it is said.

KANSUKE JIZO

THE SYSTEM of *sankin kotai* (alternate year residence in Edo) was started by the fourth Tokugawa shogun Ietsuna to keep control over the feudal lords. All *daimyo* or lords had to live in Edo every other year, while their wives and children had to be in Edo all the time. So all the *daimyo* traveled to Edo and back to their home provinces every other year. The processions were gorgeous, as all tried to display their power and magnificent retinues, who carried fine arms. While the lords traveled in *kago* or palanquins, all *samurai* walked.

Lord Matsudaira of Echigo was proud of his great *yari* or spear which he had always carried before him in his procession to and from Edo. The metal part was over four feet long, and the shaft nine feet long. The whole thing weighed 10 *kan* or about 83 pounds. As this *yari* had to be carried upright all through the journey, only a very strong person could perform the duty.

Kansuke, a young man of 27, who stood six feet, was selected as the carrier of this famous heavy *yari*. Though he was strong, the task was hard on him. When he reached the age of 50, he asked to be relieved of the duty. But his request was not heard, because no one capable of carrying the spear could be found.

Two more years passed. Kansuke found it no longer possible to carry the heavy spear on the long journey. When he reached Edo, he was exhausted. He thought that if he had quit, another person would be suffering in the same way.

Reaching the Edo residence of his lord, he rested the spear against a tree in the compound. Then suddenly he drew out his sword and attacked the spear cutting the shaft in two. For his

mad act, he was punished to die, and he committed *seppuku* on September 3, 1701.

His associates and friends took pity on his fate and made a statue of Jizo for him. It was erected within Seishoji Temple, Shiba.

The stone Jizo still stands at Seishoji, Atago-cho, Shiba, and is widely known as Kansuke Jizo. Many visitors come to visit it even today.

KIRISHITAN-DORO

IN THE COMPOUND of the Taisei-in Temple, Gyonin-zaka, Meguro, Tokyo, there stand three thick stone slabs, close together, the center one being about four feet high and the two others about three feet and all about one foot wide. The tops of the slabs are wider, shaped in a semicircle. Two of them have flat stones on top as a roof but the third one seems to have lost the roof stone. Lower in front, all have oblong cut-outs within which are placed tall robed statues, carved out of the stone.

These slabs of stone, said to be over 300 years old, are called *Kirishitan-doro* or Christian lanterns. They are believed to have been brought to the temple from some residences of feudal lords in the neighboring districts. Those lords were interested in Christianity, if not actual believers. Furthermore, this district is known as the area where many Christians hid under persecution.

Almost 100 *Kirishitan-doro* have been found all over the country to date. Many look like garden lanterns with a place for a light but all have priest-like figures carved in front. One feature that makes *Krishitan-doro* differ from garden lanterns, however, is the fact that whereas the latter stand on base stones, the *Kirishitan-doro* are set right into the ground.

Similar relics of the early Christians

of Japan are the tea bowls found with the mark of the holy cross in white over a dark glaze. From this it seems that many tea masters were Christians.

Early foreign Christian missionaries were greatly impressed with the tea ceremony and there are records of their being invited to it by Japanese of both the military and common classes.

The Japanese loved their gardens and tea bowls for which they did not hesitate to spend huge amounts of money and used them to express their faith in the new religion.

KIRISHITAN-YASHIKI

AT MYOGADANI, Koishikawa, Tokyo, there is a slope which is still commonly called *Kirishitan-zaka* (Christian hill), as in Edo days there stood a *Kirishitan-yashiki* (Christian house) for detaining Christians.

The place was the residence of Inoue Chikugo-no-kami, who was appointed *shumon-bugyo* or religious administrator, and as Christians arrested were kept there, it came to be called *Kirishitan-yashiki*.

It stood from 1646 to 1792, but was abolished when there were no more Christians in Edo. But for about 150 years, it was a prison for Christians, and many of them were put to death in the compound.

A monument was erected to mark the spot where the prison stood, and it came to be known as *Asazuma-sakura-no hi* (monument to Asazuma's cherry tree). On the monument was engraved the history of *Kirishitan-yashiki* including the fact that Asazuma, a woman of the gay quarter, was imprisoned there, and put to death for being a Christian.

On the day of her execution, she saw a cherry tree in the garden, out of her prison window. She expressed a desire that her execution be postponed so that she could see the blossoming of the cherry tree once more before she died. Her wish was granted and her execution was put off. When spring came and the cherry blossomed, she was executed under the blooming *sakura*.

Thus the cherry came to be called by Edo citizens *"Asazuma-zakura."*

KORAKUEN

KORAKUEN is one of the finest gardens in Tokyo, but with a stadium, cycling course and skating rink erected right by it, the famous garden has been overshadowed and forgotten by many people.

Korakuen is a relic of Edo culture and is more than 300 years old.

The garden, located near Suidobashi Station and open to the public for a small charge, was laid at the former Edo mansion of Tokugawa Mitsukuni, Lord of Mito. Shu Shun Sui, a Chinese scholar (1600-1682) who came to Japan as a refugee and was patronized by Mitsukuni, is said to have designed the garden.

In laying out the garden, the landscape of Arashiyama, Kyoto, was taken as the model, while various features of famous Chinese scenes were also introduced. The lake in the garden is reported to have been specially designed by the third Tokugawa shogun Iemitsu. There is an island in the lake and the stone bridge named Full-Moon Bridge is famous. The bridge is in a semicircular shape, and its reflection in the water below completes the circle.

Formerly there was a tea house, commonly called Glass Teahouse, as glass was used in the windows. The tea house was quite a novel attraction during the Tokugawa era when glass was very rare. The original tea house was destroyed by the 1923 earthquake. Now a small new tea house has been built.

There are still some *ume* or apricot trees, which were quite famous in the old days. It is said that seeds from the trees in Korakuen were taken to Mito and planted there.

Korakuen is fairly well-preserved, as until quite recently it was not opened to the public, and even after the Meiji era, when the army built an arsenal by the garden, only those with special permits from the army authorities were allowed to visit the garden.

NEZUMI-KOZO

NEZUMI-KOZO (Rat Boy) is traditionally believed to be the greatest robber of Edo days. He is even called *"gizoku"* (righteous or benevolent robber), as it is believed that he robbed the rich to give to the poor.

His tomb is in the compounds of the Eko-in Temple in Ryogoku and there are still constant visitors to the stone that marks his resting place. Many break off his tombstone and carry the chips as charms for good luck. Particularly gamblers and women of the gay quarters are prominent among those visiting the tomb.

Jirokichi who was given the pet name of *Nezumi-kozo* or Rat Boy was not really such a big thief nor did he rob to give money to the poor. Born in the Kansei era (1789-1801), he was first apprenticed to a cabinet maker, but as he led a wild life, his father disowned him.

Left to his own means, he took to stealing. Generally he selected the residences of great *daimyos* or feudal lords, as he found the magnificent mansions with large numbers of servants and many visitors easier to enter and a likelier place to find money to steal.

When he was finally arrested he confessed that he had robbed 90 times from 71 *samurai* residences. He was sen-

tenced to death. Put on a saddleless horse he was led through Edo before his execution on August 18, 1832.

Thus Jirokichi was a common robber, duly punished, but he became famous at once when his life was made into a *Kabuki* drama by playwright Mokuami. Ichikawa Dansho played his part in this and as it was a huge success, he erected a tomb for Jirokichi at the Eko-in Temple in 1876.

This act of the actor, done in thanks for the play's success, and also probably to advertise himself, further made *Nezumi-kozo* famous. Many persons came to visit the tomb, believing that a prayer offered there would bring them money. Thus gamblers, speculators and also thieves and pickpockets worshiped at the tomb.

OBAKUSAN

OBAKUSAN Manpukuji near Uji, Kyoto, is not as well-known as many other famous Buddhist temples in the country. But this temple is unique and worthy of more attention. It is the main temple of the Rinzai Zen sect, established by Priest Ingen, a famous Chinese priest, in 1661. It is named after the Manpukiji Temple at Obakusan, Fukien Province, China, which was the leading Zen temple of China.

In planning the temple, Ingen tried to make it after the style of Chinese temple architecture. Thus it became distinctly different from temples erected in the country by Japanese priests. As the 13 successive priests who headed the temple after Ingen were all Chinese, this tradition was faithfully followed. The 14th priest Ryuto was the first Japanese priest to head the temple.

Standing in the big densely wooded area and surrounded by high earthen walls covered with white clay in a region famous for tea cultivation, the Manpukuji represents a unique sight. Priest Ingen's original scheme was grand, and it took more than 30 years to complete most of its buildings.

Inside the great gate, there are a pond, several temple buildings, a bell tower, a drum tower and other structures. Its many corridors and masonry are distinctly Chinese. The whole atmosphere of the temple is Chinese. Even in China today there does not exist a temple which is so thoroughly Chinese in architecture.

There is a special hall erected in honor of Priest Ingen, the founder. There is also what is commonly called the Tea Hall in which is kept the statue of Kao-Iwai, a famous Chinese who developed the art of tea brewing, to tell that tea cultivation in Japan started there.

Among various historically and artistically important treasures of the temple, there are preserved wood blocks made by Tetsugan in the Kanbun era (1661-1673) for printing the Issaikyo or the complete collection of Buddhist scriptures.

O-DAIBA

O-DAIBA ARE the little flat islands off the shore of Shinagawa, Tokyo, which are uninhabited and of no practical value today, but they are interesting relics that tell about the nation's turbulent period 100 years ago.

The arrival of Commodore Perry's Black Ships at Uraga in 1853 gripped the whole nation in terror of foreign invasion, and the Tokugawa Bakufu authorities thought it imperative to adopt defensive steps against any possible attack.

Deciding upon a plan of erecting 11 *O-daiba* or fortress islands along the shore of Edo, and mounting thereupon 250 cannons to fire at foreign invaders, the whole energy of the government was concentrated in the immediate execution of the program.

The earth from the heights at Gotenyama and Sengaku-ji area was carried by 2,000 boats to the designated spots in the sea, and 2,000 masons were gathered to build defense walls around the islands. The work was carried out in such dispatch that in the first eight months three fortresses were completed.

But in March 1854, or a year after, the Kanagawa Treaty was signed between Japan and the United States, and as friendly relations were established, there was no more need to expect an American attack. Therefore the work was suspended, after erecting six *O-daiba* and placing 32 guns there.

Since then the six *O-daiba* have been left neglected, uninhabited and useless. But because of their historical value, the government decided in 1926 to preserve the No. 3 and No. 6 *O-daiba* as historic relics, as on those islands the stone walls, some buildings, gates and gun mounts are still left. These two are the farthest from the shore of all the six *O-daiba* erected.

The remaining *O-daiba* are doomed to be destroyed. The first one has already been absorbed in the reclaimed area and an electric generating plant now stands there. No. 2 is also to be demolished to widen the ship passage. Nos. 4 and 5 are also to be removed.

OLDEST BELL

MANY BUDDHIST temples of Japan have large bells. Some of them are famous for their artistic forms and designs, while others are known for their musical tone.

The oldest temple bell in Japan, said to be almost 12 centuries old, is preserved at the Kannonji Temple in Dazaifu, Kyushu. It is also recognized as one of the finest specimens of temple bells.

Dazaifu was established in the seventh century as the administrative and military center for the Kyushu area, and at one time there stood many magnificent buildings, some remains of which are still seen.

The temple is said to have been proposed by Emperor Tenchi (661-671) in memory of Empress Saimyo, his mother. The construction of the temple was started in 745, but it took 80 years to complete, it is recorded.

The Kannonji was a great temple with various buildings and a fine, tall belfry. The buildings were repeatedly destroyed by fire and other calamities, and now very little remains to show its former magnificence.

But in the bell tower there, which is now a poor structure, the bell which was made when the temple was erected is still there. It is said that a Korean artisan was commanded to cast the bell, though nothing certain is known.

The bell is 1.25 meters high, six centimeters thick, and weighs 862 kilograms. There are some temple bells which are larger in the country but not as old as the one at Kannonji Temple. Furthermore, in its artistic execution and tone, it is recognized as one of the best among the numerous temple bells preserved in the country.

ONMITSU

ONMITSU or spies are mentioned in historical records and tales of the Tokugawa period, but they differ much from ordinary spies or detectives. *Onmitsu* were not engaged in such work as a profession, but only commissioned to carry out a specific investigation.

It is said that Tokugawa Iemitsu who reigned as the third Tokugawa shogun, 1623-1651, first used an *onmitsu.* A *samurai* named Mizuno who was supervising the palace garden was commissioned personally by Iemitsu to go to Kagoshima to obtain information as to the military equipment and other conditions at the Kyushu town.

Upon his return and submission of his report, he was honorably treated, but never again sent on a similar mission. After him there were many *onmitsu* sent by the shogun to various districts. But in all cases they were dispatched on specified missions and nobody else knew of them.

Of course, various feudal lords had similar systems and tried to learn secretly about their neighboring or hostile lords.

But the Tokugawa *onmitsu* had a very hard task because they were not trained for such work and their commissions came suddenly and secretly. They were not even allowed to return after starting on their journeys. Assuming disguises most suitable for their characters and accomplishments, they disappeared mysteriously. Some became monks, musicians, actors, fortune tellers, beggars, peddlers and artisans.

When they successfully fulfilled their missions they gained a life of honor and leisure with high pay. They were never given offices that demanded daily attention. But if they failed, they never returned home.

The fact that they became *onmitsu* on special missions by the personal selection of the shogun was never revealed to others. It was a matter only between the shogun and the *onmitsu.*

ONO-NO-KOMACHI

ONO-NO-KOMACHI, poetess of the ninth century, is one of the most outstanding female characters in

Japanese literature. She is also known as a model of womanly beauty. Her poems are known to lovers of poetry and are included in such famous anthologies as the *Kokinshu, Gosenshu* and *Shin-Kokinshu*.

She served in the court of Emperors Ninmyo and Buntoku, but not much is known about her. She is said to have been a daughter of a high official of Dewa. According to some authorities she was said to be a grandchild of Ono Takamura, a great scholar who was sent to China as an ambassador in 838.

Throughout the country there are various traditions about her. Many different places claim themselves as her birthplace, and her relics are reported from numerous districts. From such relics and tales, it even appears as though there might have been many different Ono-no-Komachi. Probably her fame and beauty caused such stories in many different localities.

Yukobori, Fukushima Prefecture, is one of the places where Ono-no-Komachi is said to have been born. It is famous for peony blossoms which the local people believe were first planted by her.

Onogawa hot spring, not far from Yonezawa in Yamagata Prefecture, is proud of the tradition that she bathed in the spa and regained her health.

According to a story told at Onogawa, when Ono-no-Komachi was 17 years old, she started on a journey to look for her father who had become a Buddhist monk. When she came to Onogawa she became ill. One night she had a dream in which Yakushi-Nyorai appeared and said that if she went to a hot spring by the Azuma River, she would find her father and she herself would be cured.

So she went to the hot spring, where she not only regained her health but also found her lost father. Thus Onogawa Spa is still called *Ama-no-yu* or Lady's Bath.

OYAMAZUMI SHRINE

OYAMAZUMI Shrine is a little shrine located on Omishima, a small island about 45 kilometers in circumference in the Inland Sea. It is not generally known, but this little island has played an important role in the country's history ever since the time of Emperor Jinmu. At the shrine are still preserved the greatest collection of ancient armors, swords, mirrors and other relics, even though the collection has now been reduced by frequent fires to one-third of what there used to be.

In particular the ancient armors and mirrors at the shrine make up the best collection in the world. More than 80 percent of old armors and mirrors which are designated as national treasures are found here.

Omishima, though small in size, has been an important point for navigation in the Inland Sea, from the days of the first Emperor, and all through the latter warring periods. It was said that one who controlled Omishima ruled the Inland Sea.

Oyamazumi, son of Izanagi and Izanami, mythological deities who created the country, has been regarded as the guardian of the sea and worshiped by all navigators and particularly captains of fighting vessels from ancient times down to Tokugawa days. Whenever they won sea battles, they presented their swords, armors and other arms to the shrine. Thus the armors and swords still preserved at the shrine are relics of actual fighting.

Oyamazumi Shrine is said to have been first erected by Ochino-mikoto, a descendant of the deity, when he became the lord of Iyo province in Shikoku.

RAIN IN PRISON

WHEN IT RAINS continuously day after day, as often happens in Japan, it is very unpleasant and makes one very irritable. There was a Japanese emperor, who, becoming angry at the continued rain, put rain in prison.

It was Emperor Shirakawa who reigned from 1072 to 1086. He was a great emperor, noted for his scholarly attainment and skill as an archer. He was a firm believer in Buddhism and took the Buddhist name of Yukatsu. He built temples and erected many Buddha statues.

Though he abdicated in 1086, he remained a great power behind the succeeding three emperors, Horikawa, Toba and Sutoku, guiding state affairs and creating the so-called cloister rule, which was practiced by many ex-emperors in later periods.

He once decided to present to the Hoshoji Temple one copy of the Daizokyo, the complete collection of Buddhist sutras, laws and treaties written in gold letters. But he could not carry out this wish as he intended because it rained many days, day after day. He hated the rain that prevented him from holding his planned rite to carry out his devout wish and wished to punish it.

So he put rain water in a vessel and placed it in a prison, which he named *'Ukingoku'* (rain prohibition prison).

Despite his wisdom and power he could not control rain. But there were other things besides rain which he found beyond his power. A remark uttered by him is still remembered. He said, "What are hard to control are the flow of the Kamo River, dice and *yamahoshi* (powerful militant monks)."

Though he was unable to control rain or the Kamo River water, dice and monks, he was a great emperor and in 1929 a rite was held to observe the 800th anniversary of his death. He is still remembered as the only person who put rain in prison.

RAKANJI

THE RAKANJI at Shimo-meguro, Tokyo is famous for its 380 statues representing Rakan or Buddha disciples. The temple originally stood at Honjo, the present Koto Ward. There is an interesting story about those statues.

Kyubei, a son of a Buddhist statue maker of Kyoto, was an unruly young man who spent his days drinking and following a gay life. He left Kyoto and went to Osaka in a wild desire to enjoy life in his own way. But in 1670 he met Priest Tetsugan there who so strongly influenced him that Kyubei became his disciple and took the name of Genkei, when he was 23 years old.

Desiring to gain salvation through pilgrimages, he went to Kyushu. When he visited the Rakanji at Yabakei, he was so impressed by the group of Rakan statues, carved out of the natural rock, that he determined to make some.

With this determination he returned to Edo, and erecting a small hut in the compounds of the Jumyoji Temple at Asakusa, he commenced his task of carving. His neighbors were surprised at the great skill, hitherto unrevealed with which he made his first statues. Many came to offer him help to make more statues, bringing him money and rice. By 1692, he had finished 10.

His supporters increased, among whom were many feudal lords and rich merchants such as Asano Takumino-kami, Echigoya (present Mitsukoshi) and others.

By the time he was 48, he had carved

536 Rakan statues, and in 1699 he erected the Rakanji at Itsutsume, Honjo to house and display them. He died in 1710 at the age of 63.

After his death, the temple declined in fortune, and many of the Rakan statues were sold by thoughtless priests who came to take charge of the temple.

Later, it was moved to the present site with all the remaining statues, but there are only 380 of them now.

SAKURA SOGORO

THE STORY OF Sakura Sogoro is still widely told. He is known as a *gijin* (public-spirited righteous man) who sacrificed his own life for the welfare of the whole village. A shrine erected in his honor, standing where he was executed, southeast of Narita in Chiba Prefecture, is still worshiped not only by the local people but also by many from distant regions. *Kabuki* plays describing his life are very popular, while story tellers relate his fight against the tyrannic rule by Lord Hotta.

In such tales and plays, he is called Sakura Sogoro, but his actual name was Kiuchi Sogo, a farmer and village head of Sakura.

In 1642 Hotta Masamori was made the lord of Sakura, and immediately levied taxes on the people under his rule. His tyrannic rule caused much suffering among the people, and Sakura Sogoro appealed to the lord for kinder treatment.

Because he criticized the officials who oppressed the people, he was persecuted. Under difficulties, he bravely continued his work of saving the villagers. Many times, he and his associates were called by the officials and were reprimanded.

As the earnest and repeated appeal

to the local officials brought no result, Sogoro went to Edo, and personally approached Lord Hotta who was living in the capital. His righteousness and efforts finally won, and many of the tyrannic laws were abolished.

Thus, Sogoro succeeded in his brave fight for the villagers, but he was punished by death, for making a direct appeal to Lord Hotta, which was unpardonable for a mere farmer to attempt. Thus he was put to death.

But the brave act of Sogoro came to be highly praised all over the country, and 200 years after his death, a *Kabuki* play describing his fight was staged at an Edo theater in 1851. Two years later another play appeared, and again in 1884 Kawatake Shinshichi wrote a *Kabuki* play on Sogoro.

SENKE FAMILY

IN MANY COUNTRIES there are old families which can trace their histories back several generations, but they have seldom lived in the same locality or followed the same occupation or profession. But in Japan there is a rare family which is not only one of the oldest families in the world, but has always inhabited the same spot and followed the same profession for 81 generations.

This is the Senke family of Izumo, Shimane Prefecture, whose head has been the chief priest of the Izumo Grand Shrine, the oldest shrine in Japan, dedicated to *Okuninushi-no-mikoto*, who surrendered his area to Emperor Jinmu when he came to rule the country. It is traditionally said that the place to where he retired was made the Izumo Shrine in his honor. The Senke family became the priest to look after the shrine in the mythological age, and its descendants have occupied the post ever since — until the present.

While there are no records of the

earlier periods, an existing document mentions that in 1432 Senke Takamune was appointed governor of Izumo district and concurrently priest of Izumo Shrine. Senke Takamune was the 56th of the family line and as priest of the shrine. Thus the family appears to have occupied the post for almost 2,000 years.

At Izumo there is another old family named Kitajima and it is recorded that this family also served the shrine. Thus this family may be just as old as the Senke family.

Throughout the country there are several families which have long been priests to various shrines for generations. It seems that the honorable post of shrine priest has been regarded as a hereditary position, so the status of shrines was not disturbed by various political and civil changes, as shrines and shrine worship stood outside of such worldly affairs.

But the Senke and Kitajima families are exceptional cases and rarely seen elsewhere.

SHIP CARPENTER

EMPEROR OJIN had a big ship, 30 meters long, built at Izu in 935. It was fast and strong but in a little more than 20 years the ship began to decay and the Emperor asked his ministers to what use the ship's timbers could be put.

It was then suggested that the old timbers be used as fuel to boil sea water to make salt. Five hundred big buckets of salt were made and the Emperor distributed it among the different provinces. The people receiving the salt were so thankful that they made 500 ships and presented them to the Emperor.

While the ships were in a harbor, a ship came from Korea. The Korean ship caught on fire and most of the 500 ships were destroyed. The Court complained to the Korean court, which was alarmed to hear of the accident and dispatched a group of expert ship carpenters to help build new ships.

It was the descendents of those carpenters who later took part in constructing the great temples of Nara.

Among the carpenters who came from Korea was one expert who hacked at a thin plane placed on a stone all day, but never hit the stone. The Emperor, who was watching him, was amazed at his skill and asked if he ever hit the stone and damaged his hack. The man boasted that he had never done so. His tone angered the Emperor.

The Emperor brought two young Court ladies and made them dance naked in front of the carpenter. Attracted by the sight of the dancers, his hand slipped and he hit the stone.

The Emperor accused him of making an empty boast and sentenced him to death. But a fellow carpenter composed a poem lamenting the fate of his *suminawa* (inking string to mark a straight line) which would become masterless when the sentenced man was killed. This poem softened the anger of the Emperor, and the carpenter's life was saved.

SHIRAHIGE SHRINE

IN TOKYO and its surrounding areas there are many shrines named *Shirahige Jinja* (white beard shrines). It is estimated that such shrines number more than 130 in this district. Those most famous are by the Sumida River, at Hanno and also at Kasai.

These Shirahige shrines are said to have been originally erected by Koreans who settled in the province of Musashi which covers the present Tokyo metropolis and its surrounding plain areas. It is not clearly known when the first Korean settlement opened in this district but it is recorded that in the reigns of Emperor Tenmu (673-686), Emperor Jito (687-697) and Emperor Gensho (715-724) quite a large number of Korean settlers came. Particularly in the reign of Emperor Gensho one record says that 1,799 Koreans came to Musashi.

These Koreans were Buddhist priests, physicians, metal workers, leather workers, temple architects, painters and other artisans. Thus they contributed greatly to the development of the area, particularly in cultural and technical fields. The Shirahige shrines still standing are eloquent monuments to the early Korean influence on the civilization of the district.

The early Koreans erected shrines for their king Fukutoku and as the statues or pictures of the king showed a person with white hair and a beard, the shrines came to be commonly called *Shirahige* or white beard shrines. As time went on, the Korean shrines became community shrines worshiped by all residents.

When Emperor Shomu ordered the erection of temples in all the provinces in 741, Kokubunji (provincial temple) for Musashi province was built with the help of many Korean carpenters and other artisans. That further increased the number of Korean settlers in Musashi. The Musashi Kokubunji still has its foundation stones at Kokubunji, as the place came to be called after the temple.

Seiten-in, a Buddhist temple of the Shingon sect at Korai, Tokyo was erected by Korean settlers in 720 for Korean king Jakuko. Korai (Kaoli) is an ancient kingdom of Korea. The place was named Korai as a large Korean settlement was formed there as early as the seventh century.

SOBEI'S STONE

A HUGE LUMP of stone, apparently weighing almost 200 kilograms, stands by the street at Nishi-oizumi-machi, Nerima Ward, Tokyo. On its face are engraved the Chinese characters for Bato-Kannon or horse-headed goddess of mercy, and on the other side, it says that the stone was placed in September in the 11th year of Tenpo (1840) by Kato Sobei.

The people now pass by the stone without giving any notice to it, but in Edo days, Sobei's stone as it was called, was quite famous because of the story behind it.

Sobei was a farmer living at the spot where the stone still exists. He was quite widely known because of his great physical strength. While he cultivated his farms, he also used to take his vegetables on the back of his horse and visit various households of *samurai* and other classes in the residential quarters of the capital.

One day he went with his vegetables to the house of a *samurai* family in Ushigome, as was his custom. The master of the house who happened to be in the garden saw him, and knowing that Sobei was proud of his great weight-lifting power, pointed to a great stone in the garden and asked Sobei if he could lift it.

Sobei smiled, and then the master said that if he could, the stone would be given him as a reward. Setting his legs wide apart Sobei put his hands under the stone and slowly lifted it above his shoulders.

The master marveled at Sobei and gave him some money as well as the stone as he promised. Joyfully Sobei put the stone on the back of his horse and started home, well pleased with the good fortune of gaining the stone and money.

As he neared home his old horse suddenly crumpled down under the weight of the huge stone and died. It was more than eight miles from Ushigome to Nerima and the stone proved too heavy for the old horse.

Sobei was sad because he killed the old horse. Burying the horse at the spot, he placed the stone over it, engraving the letters for Bato-Kannon in prayer for its soul.

TEMPLE OF DOLLS

THE HOKYOJI Temple at Horikawa, Kyoto, is commonly called the Temple of Dolls, because there is a wonderful collection of exquisite old dolls. Buddhist temples and dolls are never associated together. However certain circumstances brought them together here.

This ancient temple was first erected in 1368 by a nun named Keigan-zenni, in her wish to rebuild a defunct temple. The nun was an Imperial princess, but entering the service of Buddha, she took the name of Keigan-zenni. As she was its founder it had always been a nun who has acted as the presiding priest here.

As the Imperial Court was among the first to embrace the new religion there were many Imperial princesses and other noble ladies who became nuns. Also there have been many temples headed by nuns. So the case of the Hokyoji having a nun as the principal priest is no exception.

Following the example set by Keigan-zenni, Imperial princesses succeeded to the headship of the temple up to the Meiji Restoration. In the Meiji era, daughters of the families of peers took the position. While the peers are now abolished, the temple still has a nun at its head.

As Imperial princesses headed the temple, it became customary for the Imperial Court to present dolls to each of them, and the custom was kept up by the peers.

Thus, naturally a collection of a large number of artistically made dolls grew. The dolls were formerly never shown to the public although the collection was well known.

As the number of people wishing to see the magnificent dolls became larger some of the outstanding ones have been placed in glass show-cases for public view. Thus a new attraction has been added to the old city of Kyoto.

TENJIN-SAMA

THE BLOSSOMS of *ume* (Japanese apricot) are often associated with Tenjin-sama or Tenmangu, the shrine dedicated to Sugawara Michizane, great statesman and scholar of the ninth century because he was very fond of the flower.

Michizane was right minister under Emperor Daigo and highly respected by the whole country, particularly for his scholarly talents, poems and calligraphy. But through slander by Left Minister Fujiwara Tokihira, he lost his position and was exiled to Dazaifu in Kyushu. After three years' stay at Dazaifu, he died in 903.

Soon after his death, however, the Emperor realized his mistake, and accorded him the honor of his former rank. The Tenmangu was erected at Dazaifu in 905 in his honor. The Kitano Shrine was also erected in his honor at Kyoto. Soon Tenjin shrines came to be built in many parts of the country, as Michizane's talents and sad end deeply impressed the people.

Tenjin-sama is still worshiped by the people, particularly by those who wish to become good scholars or calligraphers. Writing brushes and specimens of calligraphy are often presented to Tenjin-sama by them.

Michizane loved the *ume* blossoms, and the trees are planted in many Tenjin shrine compounds. In the minds of old folks, *ume* blossoms are thus associated with Michizane and they offer the flower in his memory.

In the old days, the blossoms were regarded as the most noble and beautiful flower of the country. When they said "the flower," it naturally meant *ume*. It was much later that *sakura* blossoms came to be given more regard than the *ume*. *Sakura* may be gorgeous, but *ume* are noble and fragrant, a fitting symbol of the noble character like Michizane.

TOYOKAWA INARI

WITHIN THE compounds of the Myogonji, a Zen temple at Toyokawa, Aichi Prefecture, there stands a shrine named Inari, which has become more famous than the main temple, and is commonly called Toyokawa Inari. This is one of the most famous Inari shrines of the country, although the Inari Shrine at Fushimi, Kyoto is older, having been erected in 711.

There is a story about the Toyokawa Inari. When priest Kangon was returning home by boat from China where he stayed many years, he saw a vision of Dagini, an Indian goddess riding on a fox. He was so impressed by the vision that immediately upon his return, he carved out the statue of Dagini in wood himself. This statue was handed down to his disciples.

Priest Gieki who was in charge of the statue came to Mikawa province (present Aichi) and erected the Myogonji Temple in 1441. He also built a shrine in the compound to house the statue of Dagini made by Priest Kangon.

The Dagini statue immediately became the object of popular worship, the people believing that the Indian goddess would bring good luck and happiness. As Dagini was shown riding on a fox, the statue came to be called Inari, particularly because of the great popularity of the Fushimi Inari Shrine. Subsequently it came to be generally believed that Dagini was the fox who came to Japan from India through China.

It was however due to Tanuma Okitsugu, who later became a high official of the Tokugawa shogunate, that the Toyokawa Inari came to be nationally worshiped. Tanuma worshiped the Toyokawa Inari, and had also a small shrine built in his residence to worship it. The rapid advance of Tanuma to power surprised all, and as it became known that he worshiped Toyokawa Inari, many thought that his good luck was brought by the god.

Other *samurai* and common people wishing advancement or wealth came to worship Toyokawa Inari, too.

VINE BRIDGE

THE ONLY VINE bridge now existing in the country, and preserved under government protection as a cultural relic, is at Iyazan, Tokushima Prefecture, Shikoku, at the upper source of the Iya River in the highest mountain range of Shikoku.

There were formerly many bridges in the country, which were constructed only with vines. There were nine 80 years ago. But most of them have been replaced by wood or concrete bridges.

The bridge at Iyazan is entirely woven of strong mountain vines and measures 66 meters long, 1.2 meters wide, and sways 25 meters above the stream below.

It is traditionally said that the early

inhabitants of the region saw monkeys crossing the valley by hanging to vines and swinging to the other side. They realized the possibility of using vines for building a bridge over the valley.

As the region is high in the mountains, far from the populated plains, many ancient customs are still preserved. There is a story that some remnants of the Heike clan who were defeated by the Minamotos in 1185 at Yashima escaped and hid themselves in this mountain region. There are still families there who proudly show documental proof that they are descended from those Heike warriors.

The dwelling house architecture is unique, with the bathtub and toilet in separate outside structures. Of course, changes have been made in the life of the people in the region recently with improved transportation facilities.

According to a government report made in the late Meiji period, *tatami* was used only in temples and the house of the village head and all other houses had only straw-mats on the wooden floor.

ZENKOJI

THE ZENKOJI Temple in Nagano City is one of the oldest, being founded in 664, and most famous Buddhist temple, and its Amida statue is said to be the oldest in the country. It was in 552 that the Korean king presented the Japanese Court with Buddhist statues, but a strong movement against the new religion broke out and one of the statues was thrown into the Horie canal at Naniwa (Osaka).

Fifty years later, Honda Zenko happened to walk by the canal and heard someone call his name. Looking around, he found a golden Buddhist statue in the canal. He picked it up and brought it to the Zakoji Temple at Ina, Shinano. The statue was subsequently moved to many different places, but finally in 1599 it was installed at Zenkoji.

Annually a great number of pilgrims come to the temple from all parts of the country. The expression *'Ushini hikarete Zenkoji mairi'* (Led by an ox, go and worship at Zenkoji) became popular. It is generally used when one has to do something or go somewhere, unwillingly or reluctantly with another.

The origin of this expression is traced to a strange incident. Once there lived near the temple an evil-minded old woman. One day when she was spreading a piece of cloth to dry, an ox came along, and catching the cloth on its horns ran away.

Seeing her cloth carried away, she gave chase. But dusk fell and she lost sight of the beast. She found herself standing in front of Zenkoji Temple. In the gathering dark she saw the light of Buddha. Repenting, she turned a Buddhist and became a good woman. Thus she was led to Buddha and her salvation by an ox.

Chapter 17
Miscellaneous

AESOP'S FABLES

AESOP'S FABLES was the first Western literature introduced to the Japanese people. It also may be said to be the first Western book translated into the Japanese language. Of course, before the appearance of Aesop's Fables, Christian books were translated and published in Japan.

The first edition of Aesop's Fables in Romaji appeared in 1593, or two years after the appearance of the first Christian book, Sanctos Nogosagveono, in 1591.

The first Aesop edition bore the title of 'Esopono Fabvals, Latinuo vaxite Nippon no cuchito nasu mono nari' (Aesop's Fables, rendered into the language of Japan, according to the Latin version).

The fables were immediately loved by the people, and as the demand for the book increased, several more editions had to be printed. Soon after, of course, Aesop's Fables in Japanese characters was published.

But with the persecution of Christians, the fables lost their popularity, because the people feared that if they were seen with the book of foreign tales, they might be regarded as Christians and consequently persecuted.

However, these interesting tales had already gone into such wide circulation that many people did not realize that they were foreign stories. Many of the tales were told by rural folks as though they were their own.

Thus, during the Tokugawa period the books had practically disappeared, but the stories themselves were remembered by many.

It was in the early part of the Meiji era that the popularity of the fables rapidly revived. Since then they have been read and loved by all Japanese children.

AKITSUSHIMA

JAPAN IS sometimes called Akitsushima. Akitsu is the ancient term of dragonfly which is often used as the country's symbol. There is a story told in the *Kojiki*, the oldest records of the country, about the origin of this symbol.

When Emperor Yuryaku, 456-479, went on a hunting trip in Yamato Province, a horsefly came and stung his elbow. Then from somewhere appeared a dragonfly, and catching the mischievous horsefly, killed it. Seeing the unexpected act of the dragonfly, the Emperor was much pleased, and said, "The insect thinks of me, and I will name the country Akitsu."

While the *Kojiki* story is interesting, it is also recorded that Emperor Koan built his palace at Akitsumura, Yamato in 391 B.C., and called it Akitsujima-miya or Palace of Akitsu. The name of the palace came to stand for the province of Yamato, and later the whole country.

Again some say that in the old language, *"aki"* means the rice plant, and so Akitsushima means the land of abundant rice. In the *Manyoshu* the Emperor is called *Akitsu-mikami* or Lord of Brightness. So Akitsushima means the country of the Emperor.

However, it is generally believed that *'akitsu'* stands for dragonfly, and the country has been called the land of the dragonfly. There are also some persons who believe that the country has been called Akitsushima because the shape of the land, with is numerous islands, resembles a dragonfly. But this opinion is not convincing.

Seirei, the Chinese characters for dragonfly, has also been used to signify Japan quite often, particulary in old literature and writings. Military men loved to use the term *Seirei* or *Akitsu* because the dragonfly is a courageous fighting insect.

BIWAKO-SOSUI

KYOTO IS famous as the ancient capital of arts and culture, rich in old customs and traditions. However, it is often forgotten that this old and beautiful city played a big role in the modern industrialization of the country.

Japan has now a gigantic hydraulic electric generating industry. But the first hydroelectric plant was built in Kyoto, and the first electric tram car line was operated in this city.

These pioneering industrial achievements of Kyoto were made possible by the Biwako-Sosui or water channel from Lake Biwa, bringing water from the lake to the city through the six-mile tunnel dug under Higashiyama and Osakayama mountain ranges. The great engineering feat was the dream of a young engineer, Sakuro Tanabe, who presented the plan as his university graduation thesis, and his dream came

true.

The *sosui* which was completed in 1894 has not only brought water from the lake to the city and produced electric power, but also opened a new transportation system. Boats carrying passengers and goods float down through the tunnel from Lake Biwa, and as they reach Keage, Kyoto, near Miyako Hotel in about one hour and a half, they are put on steel trucks on rails and pulled down by steel ropes on an incline to the River Kamo, as the water from the lake is carried from there through pipes to the generating station and water reservoirs. Boats are also pulled up on the incline from the river to enter the tunnel to reach Biwako.

The electric power produced by the water from Biwako revolutionized Kyoto industries by giving them a new supply of cheap power. Thus the young engineer's dream put the old capital of arts and refinement prominently on the pages of the modern industrial development of the country.

BOAT DWELLERS

THERE ARE about 2,500 families or 6,000 persons living on little boats in the canals, rivers and water fronts in Tokyo. These boats of the Japanese type are small, generally being 30 to 50 tons, and built for carrying various kinds of goods. The boat man, his wife and children live in a tiny room of two or three mats at the bottom of the boat's stern. They are generally called "water residents" to whom many sides of land life are unknown.

The boats never stay at fixed localities but constantly move from one place to another. So school-age children must live in at their special schools, and come home for the weekend. For the little pre-school children staying behind with their parents on the boat, the tiny dark room, and the boat deck, when there is no cargo, are the only places they can play around in. They often fall into the water, and it is said that every child has several falls, some meeting with disaster. The mother, therefore, has to tie a rope to a toddling baby.

Drinking water has to be brought from the land, but peddlers come around on little boats to sell food and daily necessities.

Used to the small dark room on the boat, children become bewildered when they first come to a large bright open house on land. Going to a house on land, a child hurriedly enters a closet as he feels more at home in small dark place, so it is said.

Formerly most boat children never went to school, but thanks to the efforts of metropolitan authorities, they now have their own schools.

BUSHI AND SAMURAI

THE JAPANESE word *samurai* is now familiar to many people abroad. Originally military men were called *bushi*, the term coming from China. But in recent years *samurai* has been more commonly used to represent Japanese feudal warriors than *bushi*.

Samurai developed from *saburai* which, however, did not at first mean military men. The verb *saburo* means 'to serve or wait upon.' In ancient days, therefore, Court officials who waited upon the Emperor were called *saburai-bito* or service men. Girl attendants in Court were known as *saburuko*.

Then *bushi* who were given the duty of guarding the Emperor's person came to be called *saburai*. Since about the 14th century officials serving princes, Court ministers and other high rank persons also came to be called *saburai*, and their offices were known as *saburai-dokoro*. Furthermore, in the households of military men, those of high ranks were called *saburai*. Thus the original meaning of waiting upon the master was still retained in the meaning of *saburai*.

In those days *saburai* actually meant higher class of *bushi* or warriors; so strictly speaking, there was quite a difference between *bushi* and *saburai*.

Then *saburai* became *samurai*, because the latter is easier of pronounce. Now *samurai* generally means all warriors of feudal days, although it should not be applied to those of earlier times.

DEVIL'S MACHINE

THE FIRST daguerreotype camera was brought to Japan in 1840, only a year after its invention by L.J.M. Daguerre. It came to Nagasaki, but Uwano Toshinojo, a merchant who was also a Dutch language student, obtained and presented it to Lord Shimazu Narioki of Kagoshima on July 1 of the following year.

As the secret of the camera became known, the people called it *hitome maho no kikai* (one-eyed devil's trick machine), and believed that the machine sucked out the soul of the object to get the impression of its picture. Therefore, no one was willing to be photographed by the machine and lose his soul.

Lord Narioki wished to try the camera, but there was no willing subject to pose for it. When one retainer was ordered to pose for the camera, he could not refuse the command, but not wishing to lose his soul, he committed suicide. He left a letter in which he said that if the soul of one Japanese was lost to the devil, he could not face his ancestors.

That did not stop Narioki. He called

his son, Nariakira, to pose before the camera. The young man bravely faced the devil's machine, and the first daguerreotype photograph was taken in Japan.

Not only did Nariakira, however, not lose his soul to the devil, but he also became a great pioneer in modernizing the country, erecting the first cotton mill, casting modern guns, making gunpowder, and proposing to the Bakufu the construction of iron-clad warships. He died in 1858 at the age of 50.

Yet the public's hatred of the devil's machine continued and even in the early Meiji years, old-fashioned persons never posed before cameras, believing that photographing them would shorten their lives.

EDO FIREMEN

EDO WAS famous for its fires, but it was really the firemen who made Edo fires so well-known. Their bravery and chivalrous spirit that brought them into fights with *samurai* strongly appealed to the popular sentiment of the *Edokko* who regarded them as their heroes.

In 1658, soon after the establishment of the Tokugawa Government at Edo, a system of fire-fighting was set up, with fire corps maintained by feudal lords and Tokugawa retainers. However, the big fire of 1717 caused such vast damage to the capital that a need of establishing a better fire-fighting system was recognized. Thus in November, 1718, *machibikeshi* or civilian fire-fighting companies came to be formed. At first there were 45 companies, but later the number was increased to 48, named after each characters of the Japanese *kana* alphabet.

With the formation of *machibikeshi*, there were erected *hinomi-yagura*, fire watchtowers at their headquarters or other places. Men stood constantly on the top of the tower to watch for fires, and it is said that those on duty slept at the headquarters with their heads on one long wooden log. When a fire was detected, a man would strike one end of the log-pillow with a hammer to wake them up. When the watchman discovered a fire, he would ring a huge bell. One ring meant a distant fire, two strokes for one in the neighborhood, three for one in a close-by district, and continued ringing for a fire in the immediate vicinity. A man also used to go out to announce the location of a fire, by clapping *hyoshigi* or wood clappers and shouting where the fire started.

Fire-fighting equipment used then was crude, mainly being hand-pumps, ladders and picks. The usual method was to pull down half-burning houses to stop the spread of the fire. Firemen stood on the roof of a house where they intended to stop the fire, and often fell and were killed.

At the ringing of the fire bell, many people laid aside their work or jumped out of their beds to rush to the place of the fire to watch the destruction. They ran even to distant fires and were disappointed when the fires were already extinguished when they reached the spot.

Of course, many of the people went to offer their help to relatives and friends in the fire area. So they always had their fire-fighting costumes ready at hand. To rush to a fire and join in the fire-fighting was the desire of many *Edokko*.

So much confusion was caused at every fire, with firemen fighting the flames and a huge crowd of willing helpers and fire watchers milling about. Officials therefore adopted some excellent measures to maintain order and prevent crime at the locality of a fire. Firemen and officials stood around the burning area to stop the curious from entering the fire area. Only those who proved their connection with the families in the burning district were permitted to enter.

This strict measure was taken to stop the theft of goods carried out of the burning houses. Persons caught stealing at a fire were given the severe punishment of death.

To prevent confusion, all persons carrying out their goods were not allowed to use carts. They had to take their valuables either by hand or on their backs.

As so many families lost their houses in big fires, Edo authorities maintained establishments to care for those burned out in several parts of the city, each big enough to handle about 200 persons, where they were given food, clothing and other necessities.

EDO WATERWORKS

IT WAS A matter of pride with *Edokko* or Edo residents, that, upon their birth, they were given *ubuyu* (birth-bath) with Kanda Josui (waterworks) water. Edo was the first city in the country to have a waterworks, and *Edokko* were proud that their *ubuyu* was not of well water, but of water supplied by the Kanda waterworks.

Tokugawa Ieyasu came to Edo in 1600. However, ten years earlier, in July, 1590, he had conceived the idea of laying waterworks in Edo where he decided to make his headquarters. He ordered Tadayuki Okubo to plan and design the waterworks. This waterwork system ran from Inokashira pond, through Nakano and Shinjuku to Kanda. Thus it came to be called Kanda Josui.

Kanda Josui was the pride of all *Edokko*, and soon required expansion. Fourth Shogun Ietsuna started a new water system in 1653 and completed it in 1655. The water was drawn from Tama River at Hamura near Hachioji, and was supplied to Yotsuya, Kojimachi, Mita, Kyobashi and Fukagawa areas. This was called the Tamagawa water system, extending about 50 miles in length.

In 1670, cherry trees were planted along the waterway. Some of those trees are still standing near Koganei.

Another water system, drawing its water from Sone Lake in Saitama, was made. This was called the Kameari Josui.

Edo's water system was soon followed by Mito, Kagoshima, Sendai and Takamatsu. But Edo had the first waterworks, and for these three and a half centuries, the residents of Edo and Tokyo have enjoyed the benefit of the far-reaching scheme laid down by Ieyasu Tokugawa.

ENCYCLOPEDIA

JAPAN HAD her first encyclopedia in 1712. *Wakan-sansai-zue* or illustrated encyclopedia of heaven, earth and men had one hundred and five chapters, and was published in 81 volumes. The astonishing fact is that this great work was written by a single man, Terajima Ryoan, an Edo physician. It took him 20 years to complete the volume. They were published in Osaka.

He followed the style of the famous Chinese encyclopedia in writing his Japanese one. As was customary at that period, he wrote the entire book in the Chinese language.

As its title indicates, the book is illustrated, and almost every item in the 81 volumes is accompanied by one or more illustrations. Thus, it is made very easy for the readers to grasp the explanations given.

Items covered in the work include all matters concerning heaven, earth and men. It starts with the description and explanation of the movements of the sun and stars. Natural phenomena are explained. History, geography, religion, human thought, ancient customs, philosophy, animals, plants, farm products, minerals, manufacturing, industries, architecture, clothing, household utensils, and almost all conceivable things that the people generally come in contact with or think about are fully explained.

The book was long the source of information and knowledge of the Japanese. The fact that it was reprinted twice in the Meiji era, proves the worthiness of the book.

Of course, today, *Wakan-sansai-zue* is out-of-date, but it still gives much valuable information that is not found in modern books and encyclopedias.

GINZA

THE GINZA is the most famous street in Tokyo known as a busy and colorful shopping center, but 300 years ago the district was famous for duck hunting. It was originally a vast swamp land, and particularly the area from Hibiya to Tsukiji was noted as duck hunting grounds. Until 1603 when Tokugawa Ieyasu ordered the reclamation of the area, his *samurai* and others went there with bows and arrows to hunt ducks.

The reclamation work was given to several feudal lords, and lots thus made were named after them. So we had Owari-cho, Izumo-cho, Yamashiro-cho, Kaga-cho and other streets until 10 years ago. Kobiki-cho was named after *kobiki* (timber sawers) who were employed in building Edo Castle, as they camped there.

The name Ginza originated in 1612 when Ginza or the official silver mint was opened there. The modern history of Ginza started with the construction

in 1873 of two-storied brick houses and brick sidewalks on both sides of the street from Shinbashi Bridge to Kyobashi Bridge. This was the first street in Japan with brick houses and pavement.

Yuraku-cho was named after Oda Yuraku-sai, a famous tea ceremony master, who had a vast mansion with a beautiful garden. Upon his death in 1621, his garden was made a public park, but no trace of the magnificent garden is now left.

Tsukiji (reclaimed land) was so named as the land there was reclaimed after the big fire of 1658.

HANASHI-ZUKA

HONPOJI TEMPLE at San-chome, Kotobuki-cho, Asakusa, Tokyo is a small temple, but has two unique features.

The first is Hanashi-zuka or tomb of stories erected within its tiny compounds. The other is its fence, standing more than seven feet high, each stone block bearing the inscription of the name of one prominent story-teller. Both features are quite new, having been added to the temple during and after the Pacific war.

During the war, military authorities attempted to control the thoughts of the people, and as one of such measures, they prohibited professional storytellers from narrating any love or effeminate stories as they would weaken the fighting spirit of the people, they argued.

Thus, out of numerous texts used by *hanashika* and *kodanshi*, they banned 53 stories. Professional story-tellers were saddened and felt particularly sorry for those stories which they had loved to tell and which were a means of earning their livelihood.

At the suggestion proposed by

Mumeian Nomura, story-tellers got together to erect a tomb for the banned stories in the compound of the Honpoji in 1941. Erecting the tomb and burying the texts they gathered annually to offer their prayers to the "dead" stories in appreciation of their value to them in the past.

Of course, with the ending of the war, the ban on these stories was lifted. But story-tellers still visit the Hanashi-zuka and hold annual prayers for the unfortunate stories.

Bombing caused considerable damage to the temple, though the small main building was left intact. So about 200 story-tellers proposed to put it in a presentable state. Each contributed a stone block to build a fence around the temple. The new fence erected is more than seven feet high and almost 30 feet long. Each block bears the name of the contributor. Standing before it one is able to read the names of all the prominent story-tellers of the country.

HINOMARU

HINOMARU or Rising Sun was officially made the national flag of Japan in the fifth year of Meiji or 1872. Until that time the country had no national emblem, although the Imperial Court, aristocratic families and others had their family crests or marks since very early days.

It was Shimazu Nariakira, Lord of Satsuma, who first designed the flag, originally to mark ships owned by the clan. The building of big sea-going ships was prohibited by the Tokugawa government under its policy of seclusion. But as foreign ships began to reach Japan in the 19th century, Nariakira desired to build ships and engage in foreign trade, and thus appealed to the *Bakufu* for permission to construct big ships. The permit was finally granted in 1848.

In submitting his plan for the building of 12 large sailing ships and three steam-propelled ships, he also asked for permission to use the Rising Sun flag as a mark for his ships.

The *Bakufu* authorities were impressed by the grand design of the Rising Sun flag, and hesitated to grant his request, as they thought that such a good flag should not be monopolized by Satsuma boats alone. They thought of using the flag on all Japanese ships. The negotiations continued long, but finally on July 11, 1854, Nariakira won, and the Rising Sun became the Satsuma flag.

Several months later, on February 13, 1855, the 'Shohei Maru' of Satsuma voyaged to Edo Bay and anchored off Shinagawa, flying the Rising Sun. Thus, the flag was introduced to Edo people for the first time.

After the Restoration, it became necessary to adopt a national flag, and Nariakira's Rising Sun became the national flag of the country.

HINOMOTO

IN WRITING TO THE court of the Sui Dynasty of China, Emperor Suiko, 592-628, used the title, "the Emperor of the Land where the sun rises." Then, Emperor Kotoku, 645-654, formally adopted Nihon as the name of the country. Nihon means the source of the sun and is a shorter term to express 'the land where the sun rises' used by Emperor Suiko. Since then the country has been called Nihon.

But when one thinks of it, it is irrational for anyone to think that the sun rises from the spot where he stands. Wherever one may be, the sun rises from the east, far away from where he is. Therefore the people who called this country 'the land of the rising sun' must have been on the coast of the Asiatic continent.

It thus seems that the name of Nihon (Jihpen in Chinese) was first given by the Chinese to the islands to the east, from where they saw the sun rising. It is from the same Jihpen that the name Japan has developed.

But there is another theory as to the origin of Nihon. To primitive people, the discovery of fire was a great event, and its use marked the beginning of human civilization. At first it was difficult and troublesome to start a fire, and so the duty of keeping a fire fell on the tribe chief. The fire even represented his power and authority.

It was the same in old Japan, and the Imperial Family as the head of the people kept a constant fire, from which the people obtained fire for cooking, lighting and heating. Thus the Imperial Family was called Hinomoto, or the source of fire, which name was then gradually used to indicate the region under the rule of the Imperial Family.

When Chinese characters were adopted to write out Japanese words, a mistake was made in transcribing Hinomoto. Instead of making it 'the source of fire,' it was made 'the source of the sun,' as 'hi' means both the sun and fire.

This theory sounds reasonable. At any rate, Nihon, the land of the rising sun, is a name given to the country by the Chinese. Hinomoto seems to be the name the people at first called the country.

HOUR BELL

IN A SMALL park at Kodenma-cho, Nihonbashi, stands a concrete tower with an old bronze bell. This is the original bell which announced the correct time to Edo residents in Tokugawa days.

It was Tokugawa Hidetada, reigning as the second Shogun from 1605 to 1622, who inaugurated the system of announcing the correct hour to the public. A bell was erected within the palace at first, and the hours were struck 12 times a day, as a day was then divided into 12 'hours.' But the palace bell was heard only by those within the palace and families of great *daimyos* who had their residences around the palace moats.

Soon it was realized that the hour bell should be located at a place where it would benefit the general public. Thus a bell tower was erected at Sanchome, Hongoku-cho, Nihonbashi. This tower was burned down by a fire in 1710, and the next year the bell had to be recast.

The hour bell was so welcomed by the people that the system was soon adopted at seven more places in Edo. But all these places were Buddhist temples where temple bells were sounded hourly. A bell at Hongoku-cho was the only one that was specially cast to announce the time.

This bell tower was located near the Kodenma-cho prison. It is recorded that, whenever a prisoner sentenced to death was to be executed, those in charge of the bell delayed the time to strike the bell so that the sentenced man could enjoy a few more minutes of life.

With the Meiji Restoration, the hour bell system was stopped, and the Kodenma-cho bell tower was also pulled down. For many years, nothing was known of the ancient hour bell. But in 1930 the bell was found, and to preserve it, a concrete tower was erected at the former approximate site. But the bell is no longer sounded hourly.

IEMOTO

IEMOTO (headmaster) is a unique institution of Japan. Every school of Japanese singing, dancing, tea ceremony, flower arrangement, and many other arts has its *iemoto*, who rules and controls the teaching and public shows of the school's art.

This system is believed to have developed from the ancient custom followed by Court and aristocratic artists since the seventh century of the Nara Period. Court musicians, dancers, *kemari* (football) experts and many other artists were highly honored. Their positions were hereditary. Each branch or school of such arts had a designated family to serve the court in its respective field of attainment.

When one of these families had no able son to succeed to the post, someone with talent was adopted into the family to be the head of the family and also of the school. This system was primarily for the family's self-preservation, artistically and economically.

Subsequently, private artists followed this system of each branch or school having its head, *iemoto*.

Iemoto is the highest authority in each field. He issues certificates of proficiency to his pupils. No pupil is allowed to become a teacher until he receives the permission of the *iemoto*. Many *iemoto* have graded ranks of certificates. When pupils under permitted instructors attain proficiency, the teacher must request the *iemoto* to issue certificates to his pupils. The *iemoto* is the only authority who can officially recognize the attainment or standing of the students of the art.

Iemoto has absolute power over all pupils, whether taught directly by him or indirectly by others. Of course, sometimes one revolts against the *iemoto* and opens his own school. This has happened many times in the past.

KAKITSUBATA STAMP

THE ¥500 postal stamp is unique, as its design is taken from the famous lacquer box made by Korin, which is preserved at the National Museum as one of the most exquisite masterpieces of lacquer. Never before has a lacquer work design been adopted for a postage stamp, even in Japan which is famous for her lacquer ware.

The design is believed to have been selected because it represents a typical art of the country. On Korin's *suzuribako* (inkstone box) the *kakitsubata* or iris blossoming at the Muryoji Temple at Yatsuhashi in Mikawa province is shown, and thus the box has been generally called Yatsuhashi Suzuribako. The iris of this temple has been famous for many centuries and mentioned in many literary works. Korin reproduced this iris on the lacquer box.

The famous *suzuribako* is a delicate work of lacquer and inlay. The iris is of inlaid abalone shells, the wooden bridge of lead plates, the wood piles in the pond made of silver plates, and the leaves and stalks of the iris plants are of gold dust lacquer.

The box is about 350 years old. Korin, who was born in Kyoto in 1658, first became interested in designs of dress fabrics as his father dealt in drygoods. He studied at the Kano school of painting and rose to be one of the greatest painters of lacquer work style of painting which subsequently influenced many later artists. In recognition of his talent, he was given the title of Hokkyo, the highest honor given to priests, artists and poets.

659

KAWARABAN

KAWARABAN is the forerunner of newspapers in Japan. It was a means by which any big happening was reported to the people very quickly. *Kawaraban* (roof-tile print) is so named because it was printed on a roof tile. This method of printing was adopted because it was the quickest and easiest. It is not so good as a woodblock print but can be made more quickly.

Kawaraban is said to have first appeared giving the news of the fall of Osaka Castle in 1615 which ended the fight between the Toyotomi clan and the Tokugawas, and established the rule of the Tokugawa Shogunate.

Following this, *kawaraban* news became very popular, and all big events were reported in this manner. Of course, popular songs and interesting pictures were also printed in the same manner and sold.

To make *kawaraban*, an article or picture was drawn on a thin sheet of paper, and the paper pasted on the tile, with the written side next to the tile. The written parts were left in relief by chiselling off the rest. After the chiselling, ink was applied to the engraved face of the tile, and paper placed against it to gain an impression. Thus even without skill or experience, *kawaraban* was easily made.

When the 47 *ronin* of Ako attacked the residence of Lord Kira in Honjo, Edo on December 14, 1702, to avenge the death of their master, *kawaraban* reports of the big news appeared on the same day, it is said. There were eager buyers all over Edo, and *kawaraban* makers made great profits.

All through the Tokugawa days, *kawaraban* was the only and most efficient means of giving the latest news to the public. Since newspapers were first published in the Meiji era, big news has been reported by extras. These extras are still carried by shouting men and sold all over the city, in the same way that *kawaraban* used to be sold in the old days.

KIMIGAYO

KIMIGAYO was officially adopted as the national anthem in 1890, but the song is one of the oldest in the country and has been sung for more than 1,100 years. As the song was very popular in those early days, it is included in the *Kokinshu*, a collection of ancient poems compiled in 905.

As written in the *Kokinshu*, it runs: *Wagakimi wa chiyo ni mashimase, sazare ishi no iwaho to narite koke no musumade.* (May your life last a thousand years, till pebbles grow to rocks and gather mosses.) Of course *kimi* in the poem meant anybody for whom it was sung. At banquets and gatherings the song was sung by all present.

Soon, however, the opening part of the song was changed to *Kimigayo wa chiyo ni yachiyo ni* (May your life last a thousand, eight thousand years).

The ancient Japanese believed that stones and pebbles grew, and this belief is still found in many folk tales.

It is not known how it was sung in ancient days. It was in 1880 or the 13th year of Meiji that Hiromori Hayashi, Court musician, wrote music for *Kimigayo*, adopting an ancient *Gagaku* tune. Franz Eckert, a German musician who was teaching Western music in Tokyo, was greatly impressed by the *Kimigayo* music composed by Mr. Hayashi and wrote the harmony for it.

It was in 1890, 10 years later, that *Kimigayo* was officially adopted as the national anthem. Thus *kimi* which originally meant anybody came to be interpreted to mean the Emperor. Since

1893 it has been taught to all school children, and sung on all national holidays and other occasions of celebration.

KINDNESS TO DOGS

IT WAS THE fifth Tokugawa shogun, Tsunayoshi, who issued in 1687 a law commanding all people to be kind to animals. Actually, however, the order was intended for dogs only. Tsunayoshi wanted all dogs to be treated kindly because he was born in 1646, a year of *inu* or dog. The law commanded the people to be kind to canines, punished those who mistreated or were unkind to them, and provided for housing and care of stray dogs.

Under the law, many persons were sentenced to death or sent to remote islands for killing or beating dogs. Stray dogs were gathered and kept in dog pounds which were established at Okubo, Nakano, and other places. In 1694 the dogs kept at the Okubo pound numbered more than 100,000.

To meet the huge expenditure required to keep up the dog pounds, a dog tax was started in 1696, and each *cho* or district in the capital had to give annually five *to* or about four bushels of rice for the maintenance of dogs in the pound. It was recorded that 330 *koku* or about 1,650 bushels of rice were required daily to feed them.

It was a golden time for all dogs. The *Bakufu* appointed numerous attendants and physicians to look after the health and welfare of the animals. But the law was a burden to the people, because even when something a boy threw accidentally hit a dog, the whole family was punished severely.

When Shogun Tsunayoshi died in January 1709, the law was rescinded and the people were happy again. With the cancellation of the law, 12,659 persons who were either in prison or under investigation for violating the law were all set free.

KOBAN

THE JAPANESE still associate the police force with *koban* or police boxes, and they regretted it very much when the Occupation authorities closed many a *koban*, encouraging the American patrol system.

The system of having a box-like hut at a street corner is more than 300 years old. It started in Edo in 1628 when the Tokugawa government under Shogun Iemitsu adopted this system to prevent crimes. *Tsujigiri* (street-corner murder) of innocent persons by young *samurai* who wanted to test their fighting skill became particularly numerous, and the Tokugawa authorities adopted this system to prevent such crimes. Thus the *tsujiban* or a corner guard was established at important street corners throughout the city.

But this *tsujiban* was solely for prevention of crimes by *samurai*, and had nothing to do with common lawbreakers. The policing of the common people of the city was under the *machibugyo* or civil administrator who had his men all over the city for police duty.

There were three kinds of *tsujiban*, one operated by the *Bakufu*, the second by *daimyo* or feudal lords, and the third jointly by *daimyo* and Tokugawa retainers. It is recorded that once there were 898 *tsujiban* in Edo.

When the modern police system was adopted in the Meiji era, the old *tsujiban* system was continued with policemen stationed at each corner to look after the safety and protection of people. The people have thus become used to having a *koban* just around the corner, to which they can rush in case of emergency. A record of all the residents within its area is kept at the *koban*.

Many people are glad that the *koban* system is again being revived to a large extent, although they recognize the efficiency of the new patrol system.

KOJIKI

KOJIKI or beggars of Edo did not merely beg for money or food. Nor did most of them look unhappy. They were quite ingenious. They did not merely sit down on the street and beg, but thought of various means by which to make the public give them money.

Two beggars would go around together, for instance, and selecting a shop or a house, start to wrestle in front of it. When the match was over, the winner would go into the shop and ask for a reward for winning. If money was given, they would leave after thanking the donor. But if the demand was refused, the loser would lie down on the ground in front of the house, until money was given.

Some carried snakes made of twisted paper or cloth. As women did not like snakes, they waved the dreadful thing before their faces to scare them. They left only when they were given some money. Others went around carrying brooms, and offered to sweep the street in front of a house. Even when they were given money, they did not sweep, but stayed there at the entrance until they were paid more.

Some beggars were called 'sand writers.' They carried bags of sand. On the street in front of a shop they wrote the word *shobai* (business) with the sand, and then asked for money. If no money was forthcoming, they would add the word *fuhanjo* (not prosperous) in sand. Business folks were superstitious and did not like to have such signs in front of their shops, and so they

eventually paid the beggars.

Others were quite dramatic, and dressed themselves as *samurai*, carrying toy swords. Going around to a house, they would say: 'Happily I have avenged the death of my master. Please reward me for my heroic act.' It was from such dramatic-minded *kōjiki* that beggars started singing songs or playing on musical instruments.

Edo beggars were more picturesque and humorous than present-day beggars who merely sit down on the sidewalk and wait for coins to fall into their laps.

MARUNOUCHI

THE STORY of the development of Marunouchi reads like a romance. Today Marunouchi is the business center of not only Tokyo but also of Japan. The land value in Marunouchi is reported to be the highest in the city, while only a few years ago Ginza had the honor of being the highest-priced district in the whole city.

Marunouchi today looks like the business center of any large foreign city. Fifty years ago, the district was nothing but a vast weed-covered vacant lot. Even 30 years ago there were only a few scattered houses in the entire district.

A crude map that was made 480 years ago shows that the district now called Marunouchi was nothing but a swampy field, including a little village called Sakurada-mura. By its side was another, Hibiya-mura.

When the Edo castle was erected by Iyeyasu Tokugawa in 1606, residences of *daimyo* or feudal lords were built around the castle, and the district now called Marunouchi was also covered with *daimyo* residences. Those *daimyo* residential quarters were given different names, but all the names had *maru* as a suffix, and thus even in the Edo days the term Marunouchi was used to indicate the entire *daimyo* residential district.

Until the time of the Meiji Restoration in 1868, Marunouchi continued to be the district of *daimyo* residences. With the Restoration, the Marunouchi district became government property, and at first there were built army barracks with a part made into a drilling ground.

In 1890, when the first session of the Imperial Diet was held, the Yamagata Cabinet had its budget drastically reduced by the opposition party. In order to obtain funds required for various purposes, the Cabinet decided to dispose of the Marunouchi land. The government ordered the Mitsui, Mitsubishi, Okura, Shibusawa, and other wealthy families to bid for the land. But none of those rich men made a bid for the land. Finally Finance Minister Matsukata urged Yataro Iwasaki (later made baron) to buy the land, and after much prolonged negotiation, the land was sold to Mr. Iwasaki at ¥1,500,000.

The so-called Marunouchi district is the region surrounded by a line starting at Hibiya crossing, and running along the moat to Otemachi, and turning to the Gofukubashi, and then along the outer moat to Sukiyabashi and back to Hibiya.

When Mr. Iwasaki purchased that lot, he was much ridiculed and was called a fool for paying so much for the worthless land. Then, for many, many years, Marunouchi was known as the Mitsubishi-no-hara or the waste-land of Mitsubishi.

The present development of Marunouchi can be said to be entirely due to the foresight of Heigoro Soda of the Mitsubishi firm. When the Iwasaki family purchased the land, Mr. Soda

remembered that Lord Westminster became extremely wealthy because of his possession of lands in the central section of London. He realized that Marunouchi was situated in the center of the city, near the Imperial Palace, and saw a visionary future for the district.

Mr. Soda's first step to improve the value of the Marunouchi land was to build a wide paved street from Babasakimon to Kajibashi, passing through a part of the lot. He then decided that buildings to be erected on both sides of the newly-made wide street must be of stone or brick.

The first Western-style building erected in Marunouchi was the Tokyo Prefecture Office built in 1893. Then the Mitsubishi buildings Nos. 1 to 3 were built on the new street, between 1894 and 1895. In 1898 the Tokyo Chamber of Commerce erected its new building at the corner of Babasakimon. At that time, buildings in Marunouchi consisted of the Mitsubishi bank (west of the present building), Meiji Life Insurance Company (present site) and the Nippon Yusen Kaisha (west of the Municipal Office). It was with the opening of the Tokyo Chamber of Commerce building in 1898 that Marunouchi became a business center.

The vast remaining portion of the Marunouchi district was, however, still unoccupied, and it was after the construction of the Tokyo Station building in December 1914 that the district began to make real progress. As Tokyo Station became the central station in the nation's rail transportation system, various buildings were erected in the district one after the other. Then appeared the Marunouchi Building, commonly called Marubil, and also the Kaijo Building.

Soon those new buildings were followed by the Mitsubishi Main

Building, Bankers' Club, and Industry Club. The Mitsubishi Bank building was completed in 1921, followed by the Yurakukan and Tokyo Kaikan. The Nippon Yusen Building, Industrial Bank Building, Eiraku Building, and others soon followed.

As a matter of fact, though, it was the great earthquake of September 1, 1923, that made the Marunouchi district the business center of the capital. The earthquake did not cause much destruction to the buildings in Marunouchi which were mostly reinforced concrete or stone buildings. Moreover, there were no fires in the district. As other business districts in Ginza, Nihonbashi, Kyobashi, and Kanda were all destroyed by fire, business firms established their temporary quarters in Marunouchi. This development is the factor that caused the subsequent rapid development of the district.

MASTERS OF INVISIBILITY

AS RIVALRY and suspicion among military leaders became intense in the feudal days, the art of spying suddenly developed. Spies were sent to the territories of neighboring or hostile lords to obtain information as to their plans and intentions. These expert spies finally succeeded in attaining *ninjutsu* or the art of invisibility.

Legends and popular tales describing the campaigns of military lords usually exaggerated the art of invisibility, and made these experts almost superhuman magicians able to become invisible at will. All this is, however, mere fiction.

Nevertheless *ninjutsu* experts did really exist. They attained their art only after several years of hard and difficult training. First they learned to walk and run faster than ordinary persons, and trained themselves to go without eating or sleeping for several days. This ability of quick physical movement and endurance was the first step. Then, as the second step, they learned to walk softly and noiselessly anywhere, to climb up perpendicular walls, jump over high fences, open and shut doors without making any noise, see things in semi-darkness and to have a specially keen sense of hearing.

A *ninjutsu* expert dressed himself in a tight black costume, covering his entire head and face except for openings for the eyes. He selected a moonless night, and scaled the outer wall or fence of the place he intended to enter. Opening a convenient door noiselessly, he entered the house. If he met anyone in the corridor, he flattened himself against the wall or jumped up and held his body in mid-air above the person, by grabbing the side posts. He went wherever he pleased and listened to the talk of the members of the household, or carried away anything that would be valuable in learning the affairs of the family.

NIHONBASHI

UP TO THE middle of Meiji or about 50 years ago, Nihonbashi was the business and shopping center of Tokyo. Its fame has now become overshadowed by Ginza and Marunouchi, but most old folks still possess a deep attachment to the Nihonbashi district.

Nihonbashi Bridge was first constructed in 1603; before that date, there was no bridge. The first bridge was 233 feet long and 28 feet wide, the river then being much wider than at present. The water was clear and tall pine-trees lined both banks. It is recorded that when the third Tokugawa shogun Iemitsu was a boy, he used to swim there in the summer.

The construction of the bridge gave new significance to the district, and probably because of its name, it became the center of Edo as well as the whole country.

Then in 1604, a year after the bridge was constructed, the Tokugawa government adopted the system of measuring distance by *ri* (about 2½ miles). *Ri* had been in use before, but it differed according to localities, and a standard *ri* was fixed to stop confusion. Nihonbashi was made the point from which the distance to all places throughout the country was to be measured. At the bridge a stone was erected to mark the center of the country. *Ichirizuka* or milestones were placed along all important roads throughout the country, indicating the distance from Nihonbashi. This proved to be a great help to travelers.

Nihonbashi having thus become the center and business quarters of Edo, all public notices were put on the board there. Furthermore, various criminals were displayed there for public view and humiliation. All journeys started from the bridge.

Although the bridge has lost all this honor and glory, there are still numerous big firms and wholesalers in the district.

NISHIJIN

NISHIJIN IS A district in the city of Kyoto, but it stands for the Japanese art of elaborate weaving. Silk brocades and other artistically woven fabrics made at Nishijin are representative of delicate handicrafts of the Japanese.

The northwestern district of Kyoto came to be called Nishijin or West Camp, because during the Onin War (1467-1477) the west camp of fighting forces was established there. The war devastated most of the city, and Kyoto weavers, who lost their houses to fire in the war, moved after the war to the

place where the West Camp was set up. Thus Nishijin became the center of the Kyoto weaving industry which had already come to be nationally famous.

Kyoto had many master weavers, but the introduction of the Chinese art of weaving which was first brought by Chinese weavers who came to Sakai during the Tensho era (1573-1591), prompted Kyoto weavers not only to adopt Chinese techniques but also to develop their own designs and methods.

Thus they came to produce gold brocades, damasks, satins, and many other silk fabrics of rich colors and intricate designs. The coming of Dutch fabrics also inspired them, and in the Keicho era (1596-1615), Nishijin weavers produced velvets after the Dutch style and also figured satins.

Subsequently, the Tokugawa government helped the development of the weaving art of Nishijin by ordering that all costumes of the Imperial Court and nobles must be of the fabrics woven at Nishijin.

Nishijin brocades are beyond the reach of common Japanese women because of their high price, but are still widely used in making *Noh* and dramatic costumes. They are also widely used for making ornamental *obi*.

NOON-GUN

TOKYO RESIDENTS of the Meiji era had quite an attachment to '*don*' as they called the noon-gun. The gun was fired daily at noon, and the people not only set their clocks and watches by it, but it also reminded them that it was time to eat lunch. Furthermore, it also told them the direction and velocity of wind and the next day's weather, because the '*don*' sounded differently according to the wind and weather.

The first use of a clock in Japan is said to have been in 671 during the reign of Emperor Tenchi. From then the hour was announced by the beating of drums and bells. In Edo, too, the hour was first told by the beating of drums, but later temple bells became more widely used for this purpose. The time was then announced every two hours, according to the old way of dividing the day into twelve 'hours.'

The noon-gun of Tokyo was started in 1875. On September 9 of that year the Shogo-sho or Noon Office was established within the Imperial Palace. The correct time was announced to that office from the Meteorological Observatory at 11:30 a.m., and 30 minutes later a gun was fired to indicate noon.

At first this noon-gun firing was done by the army department, but later it decided to discontinue it for reasons of expense. Thus the Tokyo City Office came to undertake the daily 'don' firing.

Soon, however, an electric siren replaced it. Tokyo residents regretted the passing of the noon-gun, to which they had become so attached.

In Meiji days Tokyo was an extremely quiet city, and the shot resunded all through city, as old residents still remember.

OLDEST PRINTING

THE OLDEST specimens of the art of printing are preserved in Japan. These printings were made 675 years before Johannes Gutenberg made his first type press in 1445.

When a civil war was successfully suppressed in 764, Empress Koken wished to express her joy and thanks by presenting sutras to Buddhist temples. She ordered the printing of 1 million copies of four different kinds of sutras, and placed them in miniature wooden pagodas. One hundred thousand of these printed sutras were presented each to the Horyuji Temple,

Nara, and nine other big temples in 770.

In the succeeding 12 long centuries, most of the sutras were lost, but at the Horyuji Temple, more than 100,000 or more than 10 percent of the original million are still preserved. The sutras are believed to have been printed on copper or wooden blocks, while some people offer a theory that they were printed by movable type.

At the British Museum, London, one sutra from the Horyuji Temple is described as being the oldest printing specimen in the world.

In the field of printing, Asia played an important role. It was China that first made paper in 105 by using tree bark, hemp, and rags. Japan has been making excellent paper since 610, having learnted the technique from China. It was the introduction of paper invented by the Chinese that opened the way for the later development of the art of printing.

The first movable type in the world was made in China during the Sung period, between 1041 and 1048. This early type was of hardened clay, and consequently did not come into general use. But in 1403 Korea produced cast copper printing type, almost half a century before Gutenberg's type.

The introduction of modern printing presses and type to Japan was made in 1590 by Allessandro Valegnani, Italian missionary, who brought a printing press, type and type-making artists. This press was used to print the early Christian literature in Japan.

PAPER MONEY

THE FIRST paper money appeared in Japan in the Genna era (1615-1624). Up to that time only coins were circulated. At that time there was a silver coin called *chogin* which was long in shape. For convenience sake, the people cut this coin into small pieces and used them. The Edo government finally prohibited this practice. Later, when small change was needed, some merchants of Yamada, Ise began to issue pieces of paper upon which were written out various amounts in ink. This practice was soon followed by merchants of Osaka and Sakai.

Feudal lords also issued clan notes and did not stop their use despite the repeated order of the *Bakufu* prohibiting their circulation. In Tokugawa days all notes were made of Japanese paper, printed in black or black and red on woodblocks.

The Meiji government at first issued four kinds of paper money, *Dajokansatsu* (Cabinet notes), *Minbusho Kinsatsu* (Civil Ministry gold notes), *Okurasho Dakanshoken* (Treasury Department convertible notes) and *Kaitakushi Dakanshoken* (Development Commission convertible notes). They were all copperplate notes, but as numerous counterfeits appeared, the government had notes printed in Germany. In 1871 the money unit was changed from *ryo* to *yen.*

Modern banks appeared in 1862, and all Kokuritsu or national banks issued their own notes, which were at first printed in America. Hence the country became suddenly flooded with paper money. The government issued its own notes, but they were not welcomed by the people who came to use them only at a discount. Finally the government recovered these unpopular notes at a discount of ¥1.80 of the notes for ¥1 in silver.

The Bank of Japan, founded in October 1882, issued its first ten-yen notes in 1885.

Since January 1, 1901, only Bank of Japan notes have been circulated, all other banks being deprived of the privilege of issuing paper money.

RENDAI

BAD AND NARROW roads in Japan may be said to have been partly due to the strategic policy of the Tokugawa government which thought it advisable to keep roads at important strategic points narrow and in bad condition, so that any possible attack on Edo, the capital, would be difficult.

Thus, the Hakone mountain path, for instance, was kept narrow, steep, and winding, with broken stone steps, as it was the main thoroughfare to Edo, from the central and western regions. Despite many complaints, no improvements were made on the path. The old Hakone path still exists showing how hard it was for travellers.

Bridge construction was also controlled for strategic considerations. Many local lords were punished for building bridges without permission. Wide rivers crossing principal thoroughfares had no bridges, and travellers had to ford them or cross by boat.

Shallow rivers were waded by all, but for great feudal lords and their families, a unique way of crossing rivers developed. This was the *rendai.* Under a narrow wooden board, two to three feet wide and four to six feet long, were placed two long poles lengthwise. The people sat on the board, and two men carried the poles on their shoulders, one at each end. Thus they waded through rivers.

Elaborate *rendai,* laquered, with roofs, railings, and curtains were made for lords and rich folks. Such were carried by many persons, as they were quite heavy.

Poor people crossed rivers on the backs of naked carriers. But when river waters rose high, the crossing on *rendai* was impossible, and travellers were obliged to remain at inns until the water subsided sufficiently for waders and carriers.

SAMURAI'S TRAINING

THE BOY'S FESTIVAL of May 5 reminds the people of *samurai* or fighting men, whose deeds of bravery, courage and loyalty are told brilliantly in history and tradition.

For many centuries *samurai* ruled the country, and as fighting was their principal duty, they were required to be skillful in the art of war. Swords were the principal weapon then, and they even worshiped swords as the symbol of their duty and spirit.

But to gain masterly skill in using swords for attack and defense, they had to go through most strenous training. The physical handling of swords alone did not make a master swordsman. Not only in battles which were a man-to-man affair, but even in their daily life, *samurai* needed to be constantly prepared for a hostile attack.

Thus they had to develop their five senses, and learn to concentrate the mind. To this end, many *samurai* studied the Zen doctrine of Buddhism, because Zen meditation gave them calmness and composure of mind, and increased their power of vision.

To illustrate the training of *samurai*, there is told a very famous story about Tsukahara Bokuden, master swordsman of the 16th century. He was living in a mountain hut in seclusion after his retirement. One day, a young man came to him and asked for fencing lessons. The old master asked the young man only to wash dishes and sweep the garden, but never spoke to him about swords or fencing.

That continued for several months, and finally the young man became disgusted, and took the courage to ask for fencing lessons. The master then said that if he was so eager, he should try to hit him, giving him a stout wooden sword. At the same time, Bokuden would also hit the pupil whenever possible.

The young man thanked him and started to leave the room, but Bokuden's wooden sword came down sharply on his head. Then, at every turn the young man was hit by the master, while he was washing dishes, sweeping the garden, or sleeping at night.

On the other hand, the pupil could find no opportunity to hit the master. One day, he saw the master cooking something in a pan, holding the wooden lid in one hand and chopsticks in the other. As both his hands were engaged, the young man thought it was a good chance to hit Bokuden. He thereupon softly sneaked behind the master's back, making sure that his approach would not be noticed, and then raised his sword to strike, but the wooden lid held by Bokuden's hand stopped it.

The training was of course physical, but without spiritual strength and a trained mind none could become a master in the use of swords.

SEA-GYPSIES

GIRLS DIVING for pearls in the Bay of Shima, Ise, have become world-famous. Before the Pacific war, many Japanese divers were active in pearl collecting in the southern regions. Furthermore, Japan has also produced many famous swimmers who established new records at international swimming events. Moreover, the Japanese are known as daring fishermen, going on small boats on deep-sea fishing trips lasting many weeks in all sorts of weather. There seems to be something that binds the life of the people with the sea.

Of course, the geographical circumstances of having the sea all around have naturally made the people skillful in fishing, swimming, and diving. This is a great factor, but there is also presented a very interesting historical background for this characteristic of the people.

In ancient days, there was in the tropical Pacific area a tribe that was commonly called 'sea-gypsies.' This tribe was reputed for its particular ability to dive into the sea and catch fish with long spears. The people of the tribe did not fish with lines or nets, but always dived into the deep sea to catch them. Making their livelihood by diving and catching fish, the tribe migrated to various islands and seas which were favorable for their life. Thus they came to be given the name of 'sea-gypsies.' Some of the tribe gradually came northward along the China coast, through the Philippines to the Marianas, while others went eastward to other islands in the Pacific. Finally those going northward reached Japan. It is generally surmised by those who believe in this theory of the northern advance of the tribe, that they must have come to the coasts of Japan just about the same time when the Malayan and other southern races came to the country.

Sea-gypsies coming to Japan lived mostly on the southern sea coasts, and then gradually spread inland. It is impossible to estimate how large this tribe was or how it prospered in the country, or how much its blood is now preserved in the present-day Japanese. Nor is this theory of the northern migration of the sea-gypsies yet fully established by historians and anthropologists.

Yet, many authorities are now inclined to believe the theory. Certainly the Japanese are a great fish-eating race, and they are good swimmers and divers if the chance is given. Along the sea coast, the practice of spearing fish underwater is still observed. These facts support the theory of the sea-gypsies coming to Japan.

It is said that the name of 'sea-gypsies' was first given by the Chinese, but it is not certain whether it indicated one specific tribe, or whether it was a general term to cover those southern tribes who lived by diving into the sea and catching fish.

At any event, there seems to be a certain connection between the Japanese people and the so-called 'sea-gypsies.' If the foregoing theory is established, many traits and manners of the Japanese people can be better explained. This may be a problem that may interest many and that will demand further studies so that a conclusion can be reached.

SHOTOKU TAISHI

EVERY APRIL the Japanese are reminded of Shotoku Taishi and his memorable work in propagating Buddhism, encouraging arts and culture, and formulating the administrative system. The Horyuji Temple at Nara, where a great ceremony is annually held on April 11, the anniversary of his death, stands as a symbol of his great accomplishments. At many other places throughout the country the day is specially observed to remember and pay respect to him.

He died in 621 at the age of 49, but during the short period of 30 years while he was the prince regent of Empress Suiko, the prince brought to the country inspiring and lasting influences of culture that laid the foundation of the latter civilization of the country.

To mention some of his outstanding achievements, he popularized Buddhism and introduced the arts, literature and culture of Korea and China, but his greatness is revealed in his efforts to adopt such foreign cultures to supplement but not to replace the original national character of Japan.

He drafted the first constitution of Japan consisting of 17 articles, and thus laid the foundation for national administration. He gave the people a new calendar to guide their daily life. He opened formal diplomatic relations with China, dispatching envoys and students to that country. Nor did he forget the need for developing commerce and industry, and built roads and ships to trade with Korean and Chinese ports.

When Emperor Yomei became ill, the emperor called his sister (later Empress Suiko) and Prince Shotoku, his son, to his bedside, and asked them to erect a Buddhist temple and make a statue of *Yakushi* (Bhechadjagura), in prayer for his recovery. Emperor Yomei, however, died shortly before the temple was erected. Empress Suiko and Prince Regent Shotoku carried out the wish of the late Emperor Yomei. Thus the Horyuji Temple was built in 607, and the *Yakushi* statue was installed there.

Today, the Horyuji still stands as a repository of ancient Japanese arts, many Buddhist statues and mural paintings there being regarded as great art masterpieces. It is believed to be the virtue of Prince Shotoku that has guarded the temple buildings and many treasures for more than 13 centuries.

SNAKE BRIDGE

THE AYASE RIVER that marks the border of Tokyo and Saitama Prefecture used to flood often in autumn even in Tokugawa days.

The Tokugawa authorities hence built an embankment on the Edo side to protect the farms and farmers on that side from the flooding of the river. One autumn soon afterwards, the river water rose and flooded the farms on the Saitama side. Shimpachi, village head of Hachiman, appealed to the Edo authorities to break the Edo-side embankment so that the farms of his and neighboring villages could be saved from destruction. The authorities did not listen to his earnest plea.

Determined to save his village and others from flood damage, Shimpachi secretly broke the embankment and caused the water to subside on his side. But while the farms were saved, his deed was discovered. Caught by Tokugawa officials, one of his eyes was gouged out, and then he was killed. His body was thrown into the river.

Learning the sad fate of her son, his mother, swearing that she would turn into a snake and take revenge on the Tokugawa authorities, jumped into the river.

A huge one-eyed snake was said to be seen in the river by the villagers from then.

Shogun Yoshimune once passed the village during a hawking trip, and hearing the story of Shimpachi felt sorry for him. He gave the village a sum of money to have a bridge built at the spot where Shimpachi broke the embankment, for the salvation of his soul.

Thus the bridge was built, and came to be commonly called *Hebi-bashi* or Snake Bridge. It still stands not far from Ayase Station.

TAKARA-KUJI

TAKARA-KUJI or lottery was first held in Japan to obtain funds for temples and shrines. Lotteries are said to have been held as early as the Kan-ei period, 1624-1643, but became popular in the middle of the 18th century.

The Ninnaji Temple of Yamato asked the permission of the Tokugawa *Bakufu* in 1730 to sell *tomikuji* to raise money required for rebuilding its temple. When the Gokokuji Temple of Edo started to sell tickets for the Ninnaji lottery, it was so successful that the sale was continued for three years. As lotteries appealed to the public, many temples and shrines started to hold them with official permission.

The lotteries of the Kan-oji of Yanaka, Ryusenji of Meguro, and Tenjin Shrine of Yushima were called the three lotteries of Edo.

Soon similar lotteries were held by many temples in Osaka and Kyoto. In those days, the whole amount realized by the sale of tickets was divided as prizes, and the winners were asked to donate some portion of their prize to temples or shrines.

As lotteries became popular, there also appeared *kagetomi-kuji* or shadow lotteries. Private persons issued tickets and sold them in connection with the legitimate temple lotteries. Holders of tickets with numbers corresponding to those of winning temple lotteries received prizes.

In view of such evil effects of lottery issues, the *Bakufu* prohibited them in 1842 when it carried out strict administrative reforms. Thus the popular *tomi-kuji* only lasted for about 100 years.

TAKUHON

TAKUHON is an ink rubbing from engraved stone or metal carving. For several centuries the Chinese and Japanese people have had the custom of visiting monuments, where writing or etching is engraved, and obtaining prints of these. The *takuhon* is highly valued by the owner, and often displayed in the place of honor in a room.

The process of making *takuhon* is said to have developed in China as early as the Tang (seventh to ninth century) period. Generally speaking, there are two types of *takuhon*. One is called the wet print, and the other the dry print. To make a dry print, soft thick paper is placed over the engraved face and a soft-wax ink stick is passed over it, applied with some pressure. In this case the engraved parts remain white, while the rest of the paper comes out black. This method is easy and quick, but fails to reproduce the finest details of the engravings.

The wet method is superior but more complicated. A specially made paper which has been slightly dampened is placed over the engraved face, and the paper is lightly tapped with a soft brush or pad. This causes the paper to follow the indentations of the engraving. Then a ball of cotton soaked in oil ink is passed over the surface. The engraved parts come out white. Specially-made paper and ink must be used for *takuhon*.

The Chinese method was to apply ink directly to the engraving and then to put a white paper against it. However, the image obtained was reversed.

Many anglers in Japan make practical use of the *takuhon* method by making prints of their catch.

TOBA SOJO

KAKUYU was a great Buddhist priest of the 12th century, but after becoming the head of the Enryakuji Temple of the Tendai sect, he retired to Toba. Thus he came to be known as Toba Sojo. He was also an artist and loved to draw pictures. During his retired life at Toba (he died in 1140 when he was 88 years old), he drew many delightful pictures caricaturing the life and conditions of the people at that time.

These pictures of his became famous and they were called *Toba-e* or pictures by Priest Toba Sojo. His caricatures were so famous that all caricatures came to be called *Toba-e*. Thus it may be said that Priest Kakuyu was the first and most famous caricature artist of Japan.

Once he drew a picture in which rice bales were shown being blown about by the wind, with many persons trying to hold them down. Ex-Emperor Shirakawa saw this picture, and learning that it was drawn by Toba Sojo, the retired Emperor called for him and asked the meaning of the picture.

'Recently many persons have been violating the rules regarding rice submitted as tax,' he explained. 'Many bales offered do not contain rice at all, but are filled with bran and being light, they are blown about by gusts of wind. The people of the temple to which the bales were brought are trying to hold them down so such violations would not be known.'

The ex-Emperor was so impressed by his explanation that an order was immediately issued to enforce the rules regarding the rice bales to be presented as tax. Thus no more rice bales were blown about by a gust of wind.

WOOD BLOCK PRINTING

JAPANESE wood block printing has become famous the world over. While wood block printing started in Japan about 12 centuries ago, the art of *mokuhan* or wood block printing developed in the last 200 years. The earliest specimens of *mokuhan* printing are said to be of sutras ordered by Empress Koken in 764 and completed in 770 for distribution to various temples of the country. In China, Buddhist sutras were printed on *mokuhan* as early as 593.

In both countries *mokuhan* was at first used mainly for printing sutras and Buddhist pictures. In 1346 the first Japanese book printed on *mokuhan* was issued at Sakai. One of the copies is now preserved at the National Museum, Tokyo. With this innovation many books such as *Genji-Monogatari*, *Ise-Monogatari* and other literature followed. In the Tokugawa period, *mokuhan* printing greatly improved, with the issue of many popular books.

It was in the latter part of the 17th century that *nishiki-e* or wood block picture prints appeared. At first, however, they were of a single color. What was called *Edo-e* or Edo prints had colors added by hand, but they were generally very crude.

It was Harunobu Suzuki who first produced multicolored *ukiyo-e* in 1764. He consulted Kinroku, master wood block engraver, on his idea of reproducing many colors in prints, who hit upon a process. He started to make a separate block for each color, putting exact edge marks on all blocks. Thus one sheet of paper could be placed on each block in the exact position. In this way he produced *ukiyo-e* printed in four or five different colors. With this success, *ukiyo-e* suddenly made tremendous progress, with numerous masterpieces produced since the beginning of the 19th century.

The name of Tokujiro Kimura cannot be overlooked in the history of *mokuhan* printing. In 1884, paintings of birds and flowers by Katei Taki were made into wood blocks by Kimura. His work showed considerable improvement over past pieces. The publication of this volume so impressed Kakuzo Okakura and other art lovers that they started the publication of *Kokka*—an art magazine—five years later.

YODOBASHI

THE YODOBASHI district of Tokyo

was named after a small bridge which was formerly known as Sugatamizu-no-hashi or disappearing bride, but later given its present name.

A *samurai* named Suzuki Kuro of Kii province gave up his rank and settled as a farmer in the Nakano district, Edo, more than 500 years ago. He prospered and became a big landowner. But he was a miser and buried his money deep in various parts of his vast holdings.

Whenever he made his workers carry money bags to bury, he killed them at a small bridge and threw the bodies into the stream on his way home to keep the burial spot secret. The number of such workmen killed is said to have reached 10.

Suzuki had a beautiful daughter named Tsuyuno. She fell in love with a young man named Takata Kojiro, and the father agreed to their marriage. But, on the evening when they were to be formally married, a thunderstorm arose unexpectedly and Tsuyono mysteriously disappeared. Many of the neighbors said that during the storm a huge snake raced from the Suzuki mansion and dived under the bridge. When the storm ended, the bride was nowhere to be seen. It was said that she was carried away by the snake.

Thus the bridge came to be known as Sugatamizu-no-bashi. Since then, newly married brides of the neighborhood have never walked on the bridge as they might also be pulled into the river.

Tokugawa Shogun Iemitsu heard the story as he happened to be in the neighborhood on a hawking trip, and said that such an unpleasant name should be changed. He renamed the bridge Yodobashi after the famous Yodo River of Osaka.

Yet the local people did not forget the unpleasant story of the bridge, and many brides avoided it. In 1919 Keikichi Asada, a great landowner of Nakano, held a gigantic Buddhist service to purify the bridge and remove the traditional curse, inviting more than a thousand prominent officials and citizens of the district.

INDEX

A

Abalone 42, 135, 611
Abayo 306
Abdomen 403
Absence inquiry 606
Abstention 308
Abu 130
Aburage 178, 273, 279, 528
Acala 230, 344, 520
Acid spring 292
Acorns 174, 363
Actor 7, 95 102, 198, 505
Actress 95, 103
Acupuncture 58
Adachi-hime 158, 168
Adams, William 635
Adana 587
Address 301, 593
Adonis 193, 362
Adopted children 585
Adoption 585
Advertising 461
Aesop's Fables 651
Agar-agar 279
Aged person 616
Age fete 90, 100, 103
Ageless woman 158
Aho-dori 109
Ai 21
Ainu 96, 145, 169, 188, 194, 241, 362, 453, 546
Aioi 446
Aioi-no-matsu 446
Aitaijini 300
Aizen-myo-o 511
Aizu 131, 139, 216
Ajuhime 206
Aka-gaeru 147
Akagi Mountain 176

Akagi Myojin 176
Akaki 358
Akakura 292
Akane 8
Akanishi 358, 472
Akashi, Kanichi 55
Akashi, Shiganosuke 508
Akegarasu Samanosuke 204
Aki 652
Akiba, Taisuke 24
Akita 140, 216, 260, 277
Akitsu 651
Akitsushima 651
Ako Ronin 660
Akoyagai 42
Albatross 109
Alcove 72, 83
All-night praying 324
Aloe 31
Alphabet card 507
Altair 105, 229
Altars 325
Alum spring 292
Amacha 62, 511
Ama-gaeru 147
Amagasa 26
Amagi Mountain 281
Amagoi 383
Amagoi Jizo 399
Amagoi-odori 384
Amami-Oshima 223
Amanogawa 105
Amano-hashidate 191
Ama-no-iwato 97
Amanojaku 586
Amanori 235, 265
Ama-no-sagume 586
Ama-no-wakahiko 586
Ama-no-yachimata 134
Amaterasu-omikami 49, 97, 181, 365, 424, 489, 515, 536, 633
Amazake 405
Ame 99, 104, 231, 289
Ameno-koyane-no-mikoto 563
Ameno-uzume-no-mikoto 424, 489, 633
Ameyo 492

684

426, 587
Marriage arrangement   321, 330, 343
Marriage ceremony (see wedding
   ceremony)
Marriage go-between   321
Marriage prayer   426
Marriage presents   183
Marriage song   196
Martyrs   167
Maru   606
Maru ships   301
Maruko   128
Marunouchi   662
Masakado   196
Mascots   114
Masks   33, 170, 192, 403, 424
Masons   273
Massage   55
Masseurs   59
Masters of invisibility   664
Masu (wooden rice measure)   411
Matagi   417
Matatabi   359
Matcha   275
Matches   287, 290, 347
Mate   495
Maternal system   329
Matoi   34
Mats   43, 80, 272, 287, 295, 351
Matsu   364
Matsuba   364
Matsudaira Ietada   204
Matsudaira Masatsuna   362
Matsudaira Yoshitoshi   405
Matsugasaki   209
Matsui Gensui   503
Matsumoto, Lord of   178
Matsumoto Sakon   175
Matsumushi   148
Matsu-no-kotoba   364
Matsu-no-ne   364
Matsura Sayohime   205
Matsuri   17, 32, 54, 97, 114, 524
Matsutake-gari   484
Matsutake-meshi   253
Matsuyama   36
Matsu-zumi   4

Mattings   350
Mattress   42
Mawari-doro   32, 485
Mawari-Jizo   531
Mayudama   35
Mayu-harai   594
Meal   245, 280, 294
Measles   60
Measures   295
Meats   138, 164, 239, 247, 255, 265,
   268, 278, 281, 308, 316
Mechanical dolls   465
Medake   350
Medical tea   62
Medicine   56, 58, 60, 63, 110, 136, 187,
   237, 245, 254, 262, 266, 268, 273, 283,
   342, 352, 354, 357, 359, 364
Medicine God   451
Medicine peddlers   63
Mediums   167, 452
Meetings   544
Meiji, Emperor   363, 602
Meiji Shrine   527
Meiji-so   376
Melancholia   156
Melon Maid   226
Melons   175, 226, 280, 302
Melon-seed face   302
Memorial tablets   319
Men (face)   287
Menrui   253
Men's names   606
Merchants   101, 301
Mercy God   346
Mercy Goddess (See Kannon)
Meriyasu   35
Mermaid   233
Meshi   259
Metals   295, 331, 335
Metric system   295
Mi   331
Miai   322
Mibojin   322
Mibu-kyogen   485
Mice   234, 462, 589
Midwife   311
Migawari   418